Bharat's

MEDICAL PROFESSION & CONSUMER PROTECTION

INVITATION TO AUTHORS

We invite Judges, Lawyers, Law Teachers and other legal experts to write books for us. We firmly believe that authors form strong pillars of our organisation. We offer very attractive terms to handsomely compensate them for the time and money spent and for the efforts contributed by them.

We also invite all those, who have manuscripts ready and are looking for favourable opportunities for publishing them, to please get in touch with us.

We appreciate and value quality in content and the presentation of the text of the books we produce. On our part, we assure them of quality production.

Bharat's

MEDICAL PROFESSION & CONSUMER PROTECTION

By

Dr. Niraj Kumar

BHARAT LAW HOUSE PVT. LTD.
New Delhi
2012

First Edition 2012

PRICE ₹ 1095

ISBN: 978-81-7733-789-1

Printed in India

WITH THE BLESSINGS OF "MATA VAISHNO DEVI"

Published by D.C. Puliani for Bharat Law House Pvt. Ltd., T-1/95, Mangolpuri Industrial Area, Phase-I, New Delhi-110 083.
Printed at Shanti Enterprises, New Delhi
(Phones 2791 0001-03)

Bharat?

Bharat is a 'trade-name' for a group of concerns, popularly known as Bharat Law House and Bharat Law House Pvt. Ltd.

Bharat is one of the most reputed publishers of law books with an experience of over five decades. We possess a very diverse range of publications covering not only the area of taxation — direct and indirect — but also company law, capital market, finance, industrial law, foreign exchange, commercial, civil and criminal laws.

Bharat's new and most ambitious venture of publishing the Budget Publications has received an unprecedented success. They establish new heights of accuracy, authenticity and excellence. The students publications for CA, CS, CWA, CFA, MBA, graduate and post-graduate studies have carved out a niche for themselves. As such, we adequately serve the needs of students and the professionals.

Bharat works hard to make things easy for you. We want our passion for excellence to translate in your satisfaction. Ours is a professionally qualified team-work with strong in-house capabilities. Our strength lies in the patronage of legal luminaries in every field. We strive for accuracy, authenticity and sincerity. No wonder our publications adorn the bookshelves of the discerning, judicious and the learned readers.

Bharat invites you to be a member of its family; share your thoughts and expertise with the readers and 'live forever'.

Om Asatoma Satgamaya
Tamasoma Jyotirgamaya
Mrityorma Amritam Gamaya

Let Us Lead From Untruth To Truth
From Darkness To Light
From Mortality To Immortality.

(1-3-28, *Brihadaranyaka Upanishad*)

Gayatri Mantra

Om Bhur, Bhuvah, Suvah
Tat Savitur Verenayam
Bhargo Devasya Dhimahi
Dhiyo Yo Naa Prachodayat

(*Yajurveda* 36-3)

Om, Who is Dearer than Our Breath
Is Self Subsistent.
All Knowledge and All Bless.
We Meditate upon That Adorable Effulgence of the Respledent Vivifier of the Marcrocosm, Savita,
May He Illumine Our Intellects Unto The Right Path.

समर्पण

ऊँ

शिरडी के साईं बाबा
के पावन, पवित्र चरणों में

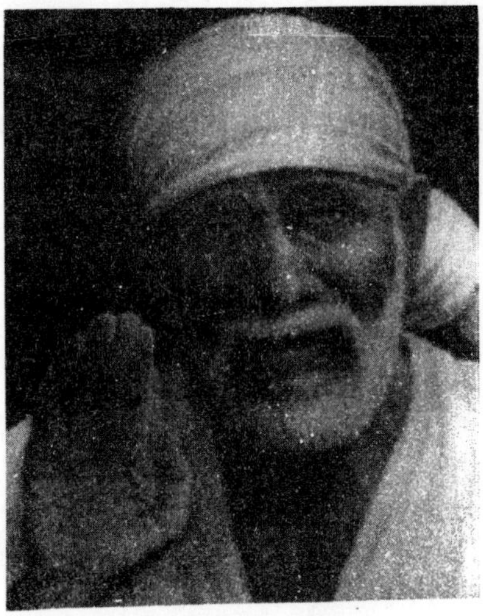

जिनकी प्रेरणा एवं आर्शिवाद के बिना,
लेखक का यह
प्रयास असम्भव था
उन्ही को आभार सहित
सादर एवं सविनय
यह प्रस्तुति समर्पित है।

(डॉ0 नीरज कुमार सी–4/8, रिवर बैंक कालोनी, लखनऊ–226018)

PREFACE

Medicine is of all the arts the most noble; but, owing to the ignorance of those who practice it, and of those who, inconsiderately, form a judgment of them, it is at present far behind all the other arts. Their mistake appears to me to arise principally from this, that in the cities there is no punishment connected with the practice of medicine (and with it alone) except disgrace, and that does not hurt those who are familiar with it. Such persons are the figures which are introduced in tragedies, for as they have the shape, and dress, and personal appearance of an actor, but are not actors, so also physicians are many in title but very few in reality. Whoever is to acquire a competent knowledge of medicine, ought to be possessed of the following advantages: a natural disposition; instruction; a favourable position for the study; early tuition; love of labour; leisure. First of all, a natural talent is required; for, when Nature leads the way to what is most excellent, instruction in the art takes place, which the student must try to appropriate to himself by reflection, becoming an early pupil in a place well adapted for instruction. He must also bring to the task a love of labour and perseverance, so that the instruction taking root may bring forth proper and abundant fruits. Instruction in medicine is like the culture of the productions of the earth. For our natural disposition, is, as it were, the soil; the tenets of our teacher are, as it were, the seed; instruction in youth is like the planting of the seed in the ground at the proper season; the place where the instruction is communicated is like the food imparted to vegetables by the atmosphere; diligent study is like the cultivation of the fields; and it is time which imparts strength to all things and brings them to maturity. Having brought all these requisites to the study of medicine, and having acquired a true knowledge of it, we shall thus, in travelling through the cities, be esteemed physicians not only in name but in reality. But inexperience is a bad treasure, and a bad fund to those who possess it, whether in opinion or reality, being devoid of self-reliance and contentedness, and the nurse both of timidity and audacity. For timidity betrays a want of powers, and audacity a lack of skill. They are, indeed, two things, knowledge and opinion, of which the one makes its possessor really to know, the other to be ignorant. Those things which are sacred, are to be imparted only to sacred persons; and it is not lawful to impart them to the profane until they have been initiated into the mysteries of the science.

HIPPOCRATES, the celebrated Greek physician, was a contemporary of the historian Herodotus. He was born in the island of Cos between 470 and 460 B.C., and belonged to the family that claimed descent from the mythical AEsculapius, son of Apollo. There was already a long medical tradition in Greece before his day, and this he is supposed to have inherited chiefly through his predecessor Herodicus; and he enlarged his education by extensive travel. He is said, though the evidence is unsatisfactory, to have taken part in the efforts to check the great plague which devastated Athens at the beginning of the Peloponnesian war. He died at Larissa between 380 and 360 B.C. The works attributed to Hippocrates are the earliest extant Greek medical writings, but very many of them are certainly not his. Some five or six, however, are generally granted to be genuine, and among these is the famous

"Oath". This interesting document shows that in his time physicians were already organized into a corporation or guild, with regulations for the training of disciples, and with an esprit de corps and a professional ideal which, with slight exceptions, can hardly yet be regarded as out of date. One saying occurring in the words of Hippocrates has achieved universal currency, though few who quote it today are aware that it originally referred to the art of the physician. It is the first of his "Aphorisms": "Life is short and the Art long; the occasion fleeting; experience fallacious, and judgment difficult. The physician must not only be prepared to do what is right himself, but also to make the patient, the attendants, and externals cooperate."

Medical Professionals today are experiencing frustration as changes in the health-care delivery systems in virtually all industrialised countries threaten the very nature and values of medical professionalism. Medicine's commitment to the patient is being challenged by external forces of change within our societies.

The medical profession everywhere is embedded in diverse cultures and national traditions, but its members share the role of healer, which has roots extending back to Hippocrates. Indeed, the medical profession must contend with complicated political, legal and market forces.

The practice of medicine in the modern era is beset with unprecedented challenges in virtually all cultures and societies. These challenges centre on increasing disparities among the legitimate needs of patients, the available resources to meet those needs, the increasing dependence on market forces to transform health-care systems, and the temptation for physicians to forsake their traditional commitment to the primacy of patients' interests. To maintain the fidelity of medicine's social contract during this turbulent time, we believe that physicians must reaffirm their active dedication to the principles of professionalism, which entails not only their personal commitment to the welfare of their patients but also collective efforts to improve the health-care system for the welfare of society.

Medical Professionals must ensure that patients are completely and honestly informed before the patient has consented to treatment and after treatment has occurred. This expectation does not mean that patients should be involved in every minute decision about medical care; rather, they must be empowered to decide on the course of therapy. Medical Professionals should also acknowledge that, in health care, medical errors that injure patients do sometimes occur. Whenever patients are injured as a consequence of medical care, patients should be informed promptly because failure to do so seriously compromises patients' and societal trust. Reporting and analysing medical mistakes provides the basis for appropriate prevention and improvement strategies and for appropriate compensation to injured parties.

13-1-2012

New Delhi
kumarniraj1000@rediffmail.com
Mobile: 0-94157 87095

Dr. NIRAJ KUMAR

ACKNOWLEDGMENTS

I am indebted to a large number of people — medical, law and management — from whom I have drawn material as well as inspiration in presenting this volume before you.

With due acknowledgment to all my friends and well-wishers, whose countdown may be a Herculean task to present here, have been a constant source of inspiration and encouragement. I express my sincere thanks to all of them albeit keeping them anonymous.

I am deeply grateful to the authors and publishers and web sites of the various works from which consciously and unconsciously material has been drawn to prepare the present book. Every attempt has been made to acknowledge the debt as and where required.

No work could ever emerge without the interest and cooperation of the individuals who typed and retyped the untidy handwritten manuscript. I express my sincere thanks to my computer feeder Shri Ravi Sachan for providing timely computer facilities and publishers who took all the pains to present it before you in this form.

Thanks are due to S/Sri S.P. Shukla, Nandit Srivastava, Rajan Misra and Rajesh Shukla, all advocates of High Court of Judicature, Allahabad, Lucknow Bench for their valuable suggestions and providing their all possible support whenever required.

Thanks are also due to Sri Ashok Kumar Srivastava, Ll.M., Shri G.D. Shukla, Ll.M. and many others for logistical support.

The work stretched from almost year to year; placing upon me the need to have help from many of my friends in the profession and outside. Let me record that unique had been their zeal in this regard. I cannot but express my thanks to Dr. S.K. Agarwal, Former Vice Chancellor of Chatrapatti Sahuji Maharaj Medical University, Lucknow (formely King George Medical College, Lucknow), Dr. C.G. Agarwal and Dr. Ashok Chandra both former Dean of Medicine, Chatrapatti Sahuji Maharaj Medical University, Lucknow (formely King George Medical College, Lucknow), my Advocates S/Shri S. P. Shukla, Nandit Srivastava, and Rajesh Shukla, all advocates of High Court of Judicature at Lucknow Bench. Time and again, I had occasions to discuss the topics with friend, philosopher and guide like Dr. V.D. Gupta, who had been the Vice Chancellor of two U.P. State Universities. I must acknowledge that their suggestions have helped in shaping of some of the paragraphs in the pages that follow.

My special thanks are due to my publishers M/s Bharat Law House Pvt. Ltd., New Delhi and their Directors Ravi Puliani, Ashok Puliani and Mahesh Puliani for they have done a great deal to bring intellectual respectability to the entire discipline of consumer protection law. They risked heavy financial resources in a bet on the viability of this discipline. My sincere thanks are due to the editorial team, who worked day and night to make it presentable, comprehensive and interesting.

Finally, I recognise that my efforts have been stimulated by the positive sets of values for education held by my parents and extended family, specially, my late father Prof. Gyan Chandra Gupta. Forty three years ago, when I was at my tender age and needed him most, he left me weeping, which actually inspired me to do something new and creative.

I have made all possible efforts to cover major area. It is hoped that my efforts will bear fruits. If the present book fulfils some of the unending needs of the readers, my efforts will be amply rewarded. Suggestions and opinions will be highly appreciated and duly acknowledged.

I would like to assure that a healthy criticism of the work will give me positive motivation not only to refine the present work but also to place before its readers some thing more new and never touched upon topics.

Dr. NIRAJ KUMAR

Contents at a glance

Detailed Contents

CHAPTER 3

Medical Professional's Negligence

CHAPTER 4

Criminal Liability for Medical Negligence

CHAPTER 5

Categories of Cases on Medical Negligence

CHAPTER 6

Categories of Cases in which Medical Negligence Not Considered

CHAPTER 7

Law and Doctor's Negligence

CHAPTER 8

Euthanasia and Doctor

CHAPTER 9

Various Indian Legal Systems *vis-a-vis* Medical Negligence

CHAPTER 10

Some General Clarifications on Medical Negligence

CHAPTER 11

How Doctors to Avoid Litigation

CHAPTER 12

The Consumer Protection Act, 1986 with Short Comments

Chapter I

Preliminary

CHAPTER II

Consumer Protection Councils

CHAPTER III

Consumer Disputes Redressal Agencies

CHAPTER 13

Consumer's Checklist & Tips

CHAPTER 14

Other Laws Showing Spirit of Consumerism

CHAPTER 15

Consumer Sovereignty in India

CHAPTER 16

Consumerism and Consumer

CHAPTER 17

Consumer Protection & Guidance

CHAPTER 18

CHAPTER 19

EPILOGUE

Table of Cases

CHAPTER 1
Co-Relationship of Doctor and Patient

SYNOPSIS

1. Introduction

Since the earlier times the co-relationship of patient and doctor was based on trust and confidence. The rapid growth of super specialty corporate hospital has totally changed the co-relationship of patient and doctor based on trust and confidence. The personal link of doctor and patient relationship is not seen anymore. The big medical institutions have become impersonal and profit oriented. The consumers are fully aware of their rights and seek good service.

The medical professionals are not above the law; they are accountable like any other citizen if there is any negligence or deficiency in service on their part.

Since the ancient times certain duties and responsibilities have been imposed on medical practitioners as exemplified by Charak's Oath (1000-BC) and Hippocratic Oath (466-BC).

Charak's Oath (1000-BC)

According to this the teacher instructed the disciples in the presence of the sacred fire, Brahmans and Physicians thus:

> "Thou shall be free from envy, not cause another's death, and pray for the welfare of all creatures. Day and night thou shall not desert, nor commit adultery, be modest in thy attire and appearance, not to be drunkard or sinful while entering a patient's house be accompanied by a person known to the patient."

Hippocratic Oath (460-BC)

I swear by Apollo the physician, by Aesculapius, Hygiea and panacea, and I take to witness all the gods, all the goddesses, to keep according to my ability and my judgment the following oath:

"To consider dear to me as my parents him who taught me this art, to live in common with him and if necessary to share my goods with him, to took upon his children as my own brother to teach them this art if they so desire without fee or written promise, to import to my sons and the sons of the master who taught me and the disciples who have enrolled themselves and have agreed to the rules of the profession, but to these alone, the precepts and the instruction. I will prescribe regimen for the good of my patients according to my ability and my judgment and never do harm anyone. To please no one will prescribe a deadly drug, nor give advice which may cause his death. Nor I will give a woman a peccary to procure abortion. But I will preserve the purity of my life and my art. I will not cut for stone, even for patients in whom the diseases are manifest; I will leave this operation to be performed by practitioners (specialist in this art). I every house where I come I will enter only for the good of any patients, keeping myself far from all international ill doing and all seduction, and especially from the pleasure of love with women or with men, by they free or slaves. All that may come to my knowledge in the exercise of my profession or outside my profession or in daily commerce with men, which ought not to be spread abroad, I will keep secret and will never reveal. If I keep this oath faithfully, may I enjoy my life and practice my art, respected by all men and in all times, but if I swerve from it or violate it may the reverse be my lot."

To understand the co-relationship of doctor and patient, it is necessary to know about the duties and obligations of doctor, contract of doctor and patient and medical negligence.

2. Prerequisites of medical practice

A duly qualified medical doctor has a right to seek to practice medicine, surgery and dentistry by registering himself with the Medical council of the state of which he is a resident by following the procedure as prescribed under the Medical Act of the state.

The State Medical Council in empowered to warn, refused to register and remove the name of the medical doctor who has been awarded sentence by any court of law for non-bailable offence or found to be guilty of infamous conduct in any professional respect. The State Medical Council can also reenter the name of the doctor in the register. The Medical Council of India formulated the Indian Medical Council Regulations, 2002. The provisions regarding offences and professional misconduct which may be brought before the appropriate Medical Council (State/Medical Council of India) have been stated in the Regulation, 2002. The appropriate Medical Councils have the power to award such punishment as deemed necessary. But no action against a doctor can be taken without giving them an opportunity of personal or through an advocate.

3. Duties of doctors

The duties of doctors are enlisted in national and international code of medical ethics and various declarations. On the basis of various Codes of Ethics and Declarations the duties of doctors are given as under:

(A) Duties of Patient
(B) Duties to public
(C) Duties towards professional ethics
(D) Duties towards law enforces
(E) Duties to each — other

(A) Duties of patient

Duties to patient are:

(*a*) *Standard Care:* Standard care means application of the principles of standard care which an average person takes while doing similar job in a similar situation. "The test is the standard of the ordinary skilled man exercising and professing to have that special skill, it is well established law that it is sufficient if he exercises the ordinary skill, it is well-established law that it is sufficient if he exercises the ordinary skill of an ordinary competent man exercising that particular art." (*Bolam* v *Frien Hospital Management Committee* MC NAIR J (1957) 1WLR 582 at Page 586)

A doctor can be held guilty of medical negligence only when he falls short of the standard of reasonable care.

Hospital/Nursing Home must comply with all applicable laws and must be registered whenever required.

The junior doctors and paramedical staff must be competent and experienced to do the job and they have prescribed qualification.

(*b*) *Duty to provide information to patient and their attendant:* It is the duty of doctor and hospital to provide all necessary informations to patient and their attendant regarding treatment, alternative modalities of treatment, investigations, procedure, surgery, duration of treatment, gravity of patient condition and expenses.

(*c*) *Consent of patient/attendant for treatment:* Section 13 of Indian Contract Act, 1872 defines the term 'consent' according to which, when two or more persons agree upon the same thing in the same sense they are said to consent.

Sections 88 and 90 of the Indian Penal Code, 1860 provides that for the purpose of clinical examination, diagnosis and treatment consent can be given by the person who is conscious, mentally sound and is of and above twelve years of age section 11 of the Indian Contract Act, 1872 provides that only those persons who are of and above 18 years of age are competent to enter into a contract. Since co-relationship of doctor and patient amounts to a contract therefore, it is advisable that a written consent should be obtained from parent/guardian of a patient who is below 18 years.

Indian Medical (Professional Conduct, Etiquette and Ethics) Regulations, 2002 *vide* Regulation No. 7.16 states that before performing an operation the Physician should obtain in writing the consent from the husband or wife, parent or guardian in the case of minor, or the patient himself as the case may be. In an operation which may result in sterility the consent of both husband and wife is needed.

(*d*) *The consent is not valid:* When the consent is given under fear, fraud or misrepresentation of facts or by a person who is mentally unsound, not fully conscious, intoxicated or who is ignorant of the implications of the consent or who is under 18 years of age is invalid.

Kinds of Consent

The consent may be implied, express, informed or proxy.

(1) Implied Consent: This is the most common consent in general practice and hospital practice. When a patient comes to a doctor for treatment of illness there is an implied consent of patient. The consent is implied when a person hold out his arm for an injection.

(2) Express Consent: Express consent may be oral or written. Oral consent is obtained from minor examinations or therapeutic procedures. Express written consent is required for all major diagnostic procedures, general anesthesia, for surgical operations, intimate examinations, examinations for determining age, potency and virginity and in medico-legal cases.

(3) Informed Consent: The concept of informed consent has come to the fore in recent years and many actions have been brought by patients who alleged that they did not understand the nature of the medical procedure to which they have given consent. All information about disease must be explained in comprehensible non-medical terms, preferable in local languages. Informed consent must be obtained for:

(*i*) diagnosis

(*ii*) nature of involved

(*iii*) risk involved

(*iv*) prospectus of success

(*v*) prognosis if the procedure is not performed, and

(*vi*) alternative methods of treatment.

The Physicians duty to disclosure is subject to the expectations,—

(*a*) If the patient prefers not to be informed, and

(*b*) If the doctor believes in the exercise of coming to sound medical judgment, then the patient is so disturbed or anxious that the information provided would be processed rationally or it would probably cause significant physiological harm. This is known as therapeutic privilege. In such a case it is advisable that the doctor should concern the patient's family Physicians. Revelation of risk is always a compromise between reasonable information and the danger of frightening off the patient from beneficial treatment. The three important components of such fun center are in formation, voluntariness and capacity.

(4) Proxy Consent: Such type of consent is to be obtained by parent for child, close relative for mentally unsound patient.

In an emergency, when their parents or guardians are not available, consent is taken from the person in charge of the child, e.g. a school teacher can give consent for treatment a child who become sick during a take to make of it from hometown, or the consent of the head master of a residential school.

Where consent may not be required

It may not be necessary to obtain consent where lifesaving procedures are to be undertaken. Such as:

(1) Where a court may order for Psychiatric examination or treatment.

(2) New admissions to prisons.

(3) Members of armed force.

(4) Handler's of food and dairymen.

(5) In an accident case.

(6) In a major surgery or post-surgery in which additional emergency procedure is required.

(B) Duties of public

Our doctor is bound to provide health education on public health issues, medical help on occurrence of natural calamities like flood, fire, earthquake and drought, train accidents.

(C) Duties towards professional ethics

A doctor must not:

(*i*) Associate with unregistered medical practitioner,

(*ii*) Refuse professional service on grounds of religion, race, party, politics, social and status and nationality,

(*iii*) Issue for the certificate debts and bills,

(*iv*) Write secret formulations, and

(*v*) Keep the information of patient as secret.

(D) Duties towards law enforces

It is the duty of a doctor:

(*i*) To call a magistrate for recording of dying declaration,

(*ii*) To inform the police all cases of poisoning, burns injury, illegal abortion, suicide, manslaughter, bride burning.

(*iii*) To inform authorities about death occurring during any medical procedure or operation.

(*E*) *Duties to each — other*

When a patient is referred by a doctor to another doctor it is his duty to provide a statement of case to that doctor. The second doctor should communicate his opinion to the first doctor.

Our doctor must observe the principals' enunciated in 'Declaration of Geneva' approved by World Medical Association.

Doctors difference of opinion should not be divulged in public.

4. Duties of patient/attendant

A patient has following duties; and

(1) He must cooperate with the doctor for any investigation to diagnose the disease,

(2) He must disclose all relevant information for proper diagnoses,

(3) He must follow all the directions of doctor as regards drugs, food, rest and exercise, etc.

5. Nature of contract between doctor and patient

The doctor and patient contract is almost implied nature. An implied contract is one inferred from conduct of parties and arises where no person renders services under circumstances indicating that he expects to be paid thereof, and the other person knowing such circumstances, avails himself of benefit of those services, but where a written informed consent is obtained it is an express contact. A doctor-patient implied contract and is established when continuous treatment is given by a doctor with reasonable care and skill without disclosing the secrets of the patient.

Implied contract is not established when —

- The doctor renders first aid in an emergency,
- The doctor performs an examination for Life Insurance purpose,
- The doctor performs a medical examination for the purpose of employment.
- The doctor makes an examination for law suit purposes at the request of an attorney.

The contract of doctor and patient requires that doctor must treat a patient with the reasonable care and skill and treatment must continue. The doctor must not divulge secrets about the patient except under certain circumstances e.g. where required by law.

Reasonable care of doctor means doctor must use clean and proper instruments for the treatment purpose. He should give full directions to his patients as regards administration of drugs. Reasonable means that because of the office, the doctor undertakes the average degree of skill possessed by professional brethren of the same standing as himself.

A professional secret is one which a doctor comes to learn in confidence from his patients, on examination, investigations or which is noticed in the ordinary privacies of domestic life. A doctor is under a moral and legal obligation not to divulge any such seated except under certain circumstances such as:

- A witness in a court of law,
- Informing patents/spouses of AIDS patients and those found infected with which HIV.
- Informing public health authorities of food poisoning from public places.
- Informing law enforces about medico-legal cases, etc.

CHAPTER 2

Provisions of the Consumer Protection Act, 1986 Relevant to Medical Profession

SYNOPSIS

1. General introduction

India is still a developing country and its biggest problem is that perennial shortages taking place in the various types of consumer goods. The pressure of the population is very high. A large part of population is below the poverty line. Majority of the population is illiterate and ill informed and has limited power. They are not in a position to meet the basic necessities of life. A number of non-essential, traders by means of unfair practices and deceptive methods, composition in the market is often reduced to composition in advertising, as companies is spend more and more money on exaggerated, misleading and deceptive advertising claims, rather than developing functional features, making the distribution system more efficient or reducing the price.

In the free market, it is said that consumer is the King. He communicates his decision or wish through price. In reality, consumer is not King. And the most, he is a Prince without a privy purse. He pays more and earns a much less in the real terms. He is the one who is often cheated fleeced even given shoddy and adulterated goods. Shot weights and measures, deceptive packing, misleading advertising, hoarding, profiteering and countless frauds committed by trade on the poor and innocent consumers clearly indicate gross exportation of the consumer by industry, trade and by organized labor.

Thus, it becomes necessary to protect the consumers from the exploitation and to save them from adulterated and sub-standard goods and deficiency in services and to safeguard their interest.

In India, consumer justice is a part of social and economic justice as enunciated in the Constitution. Following the Constitutional mandate a number of legislation's have been enacted in the field of consumer protection relating to the standardization, grading, packing and branding, prevention of food adulteration, short weight and measures, hoarding, profiteering, etc. But all these are the scattered pieces of legislations. The legislation's under these legislations are costly and troublesome to the small consumer. The compact of these legislations in protecting the consumer has been relatively small.

The well organized sectors of manufacturers, traders and service providers, armed with knowledge of the market and manipulative skills, often attempt to exploit the consumers, in spite the provisions in different laws protecting their interests. Moreover, various factors including increase in the population resulted in enormous pendency and delay in disposal of cases in civil courts. Consumer can not be asked to wait for years for settlement of even a small claim.

The Parliament, therefore, passed a very important legislation, viz, the Consumer Protection Act, 1986 to provide better protection to the interest of the consumers. The aims and objects of the Act as given in the Preamble, *inter alia* are the better protection of the interests of the consumers and for settlement of consumer disputes. It provides for a speedy and inexpensive settlement of disputes within a limited time frame, as against civil actions which are costly and would take years in coming to a settlement. Provisions of the Act are in addition to and not in derogation of any other law for the time being in force and are compensatory in nature.

The Act envisages a three-tier quasi-judicial machinery, i.e., District Consumer Disputes Redressal Forum at District level, State Consumer Disputes Redressal Commission at State level and National Consumer Disputes Redressal Commission at the National level.

The Act was amended by the Consumer Protection (Amendment) Act, 2002, w.e.f. 15-3-2003.

Chark's Oath (1000 BC) and Hippocratic Oath (460 BC) illustrates the duties and responsibilities of the person who adopt the noble profession of medicine. However, the events, which have been taking place in recent times, have raised doubts in the minds of members of society on the sincerity and commitment of those in the profession to adhere to the Hippocratic Oath (460 BC). In fact, medical negligence is a matter of major concern all over the world. The standards of the medical profession are deteriorating, pursuits of money rather than the pursuit of excellence appears to be the most important motive force in patient care.

The Consumer Protection Act, 1986 aims at simplification of procedures for seeking redressal of grievances of patients and their relatives. The process can be initiated without any cost or without any court fee.

Now they shall deal selectively the provisions of the Act which are relevant to the medical profession.

2. Definitions

2.1 Complainant [*Section 2*(*1*)(*b*)]

To initiate an action under the Consumer Protection Act what is required a complaint from the complainant. A complaint can be made by any one of the following:

(*a*) A consumer, or

(*b*) Any voluntary consumer association registered under the Companies Act, 1956, or under any other law for the time being in force, or

(*c*) The Central Government or any State Government, or

(*d*) One or more consumers, where there are numerous consumers having the same interest, or

(*e*) In case of death of a consumer, his legal heir or the preventative, who or which makes a complaint.

The above provisions indicate that it is not necessary that the complaint be made only by the aggrieved consumer himself. It can be made by any organized Consumer Association even if the consumer is not a member of such association. The Central Government or any State government can make complaint under the Act.

2.2 Complaint [*Section 2*(*1*)(*c*)]

"Complaint" means any allegation in writing made by complainant in regard to one or more of the following:

(*i*) An unfair trade practice or a restrictive trade practice has been adopted by any trader or service provider,

(*ii*) The goods bought by him or agreed to be bought by him suffer from one or more defect,

(*iii*) The services hired or availed of or agreed to be hired or availed of by him suffer from deficiency (negligence) in any respect,

(*iv*) A trader or service provider, as the case may be, has charged for the goods or for the service is mentioned in the complaint, a price in excess of the price —

(*a*) Fixed by or under any law for the time being in force,

(*b*) Displayed on the goods or any package containing such goods, (*c*) Displayed on the price list exhibited by him by or under any law for the time being in force;

(*d*) Agreed between the parties,

(*v*) Goods which will be hazardous to life and safety when used are being offered for sale into the public,

(*a*) In contravention of any standards relating to safety of such goods as required to be complied with, by or under any law for the time being in force,

(*b*) If the trader could have known with due diligence that the goods so offered are unsafe to the public,

(*vi*) Services which are hazardous unlikely to be hazardous to life and the safety of the public when used, are being offered by the service provider which such person could have known with due diligence to be injurious to life and safety,

with a view to obtaining any relief provided by or under this Act.

2.3 Consumer [*Section 2(1)(d)*]

The definition of the term 'consumer' is given in clause (*d*) of section 2(1) of the Act. According to which 'consumer' means any person who —

(*i*) Buys any goods for a consideration which has been paid or promised or partly paid and partly promised, or under any system of deferred payment and includes any user of such goods other than the person who buys such goods for consideration paid or promised or partly paid or partly promised, or under any system of deferred payment when such use is made with the approval of such person, but does not include a person who obtains such goods for resale or any commercial purpose, or

(*ii*) Hires or avails of any service for a consideration which has been paid or promised or partly paid and partly promised, or under any system of the deferred payment and includes any beneficiary of such services other than the person who hires or avails of the services for consideration paid or promised or partly paid and partly promised or under any system of deferred payments, when such services are availed of with the approval of the first-mentioned person but does not include a person who avails of such services for any commercial purpose.

[1]*Explanation.*—For the purposes of this clause, "commercial purpose" does not include use by a consumer of goods bought and used by him and services availed by him exclusively for the purposes of earning his livelihood by means of self employment.

Thus, the definition of the term 'consumer' given under clause (*d*) of section 2(1) of the Act is comprehensive one so as to cover not only consumer of goods but also consumer services. The definition is wide enough to include in

---

1 Substituted by Act 50 of 1993, Section 2 (w.e.f. 18-6-1993).

'consumer' not only the person who buys any goods for consideration but also any user of such goods with the approval of the buyer. Similarly, it covers any person who hires or avails of any services for consideration and also include any beneficiary of such services, other than the actual buyer or hirer, is a consumer for the purpose of the Act and is competent to make a complaint before the Consumer Disputes Redressal Forum under the Act. The Act aims to protect the economic interest of a consumer as understood in commercials senses as a purchaser of 'goods' and 'services' under the Act is that such goods are supplied at a price to cover the costs which consequently result in profit or income to the seller of goods or provider of service.

Consideration: According to the definition of 'consumer' given in the Consumer Protection Act, the buying of goods or hiring of services must be for consideration. The payment of consideration must be under any of the three circumstances —

(*i*) has been paid or promised to be paid, or

(*ii*) partly paid and partly promised to be paid, or

(*iii*) may have not been paid under any system of deferred payment.

Thus, it is not necessary that considerations should be paid at once. May be paid at once or may be partly paid and partly promised or may have to be paid under some deferred system of payment.

The term 'consideration' has not been defined in the Act. It is not clear whether consideration should be in terms of money on it can be otherwise also. Under the Sale of Goods Act, the reconsideration for the sale of goods must be money only called the 'price'.

The consideration with reference to medical profession means free/payment. These may have been fully paid in cash or by cheque or undertaking that given that it will be paid, which is accepted by the doctor/hospital. The fees may have given partly with undertaking that the remaining bill will be paid subsequently. The payment may be done by the patient himself, or by someone else for the patient.

The user of the services of free hospital does not fall in the category of consumer. A person who receives a medical treatment in a government hospital or charitable hospital free of cost is not the consumer under the Act. Payment by way of registration charges or a nominal charge for administrative expenses will not constitute consideration and patients getting treatment in such hospitals are not consumers.

2.4 Deficiency [*Section 2*(*1*)(*g*)]

The term 'deficiency' has been defined in section 2(1)(*g*) of the Act. 'Deficiency' means, any fault, imperfection, shortcoming or inadequacy in the quality, nature and manner of performance which is required to be maintained by or under any law for the time being in force or has been undertaken to be performed by a person in pursuance of a contract or otherwise in relation to any service.

Thus, the complainant under the Consumer Protection Act can be made in respect of only those services which suffer from any deficiency. The definition of 'deficiency' given above is wide enough to include any fault, imperfection, shortcoming or inadequacy in the quality, nature and manner of performance in relation to any service.

Thus, deficiency in service may occur due to violation of any standards as to quality, nature and manner of performance laid down in any of the existing laws. Some cases of negligency in rendering the services may also fall within the ambit of the Act. The negligence by a doctor rendering medical services for consideration is deficiency.

In *Indian Medical Association* v *V.P. Shantha* AIR 1996 SC 550. The Supreme Court has held that determination about deficiency in service for the purpose of section 2(1)(*g*) of the Act is to be made by applying the same test as is applied in action for damages for medical negligence. Deficiency in medical services has thus been equated with the medical negligence.

2.5 Person [*Section 2(1)(m)*]

The term 'Person' has been defined in clause (*m*) of section 2(1) of the Act. Person includes —

(*i*) a firm with registered or not,

(*ii*) a Hindu undivided family,

(*iii*) a Co-operative Society, and

(*iv*) every other association of persons whether registered under Societies Registration Act, 1860 (2 of 1860) or not.

That definition is an exclusive and not exhaustive. The 'association of persons' means an association in which two or more persons join in common purpose or common action. Thus the definition of 'person' extends to companies, firms, cooperative societies, joint families, any other association of persons.

In the case of *Rambal Engg. Products* (*P*) *Ltd.* v *Patel Roadways Ltd.* (*1994*) 1 CPR 559 (T.N.) the State Commission under section 2(1)(*m*) of Consumer Protection Act, 1986, defines ' person' in an inclusive way. But is not exhaustive and therefore, we have to find out the definition of 'person' under General Clauses Act, 1897. Section 3(42) of this Act defines 'person' shall include any company or association or body of individuals, whether incorporated or not.

2.6 Service [*Section 2(1)(o)*]

According to clause (*o*) of section 2(1) of Consumer Protection Act, 1986, 'service' means—

(*i*) Service of many description which is made available to potential users, and

(*ii*) Includes, but only limited to, the provisions of facilities in connection with banking, financing, insurance, transport, processing, supply of electrical or other energy, board or lodging or both, housing construction, entertainment, amusement or the purveying of news or other information, (*iii*) But does not include the rendering of any service free of charge or under a contract of personal service.

It is evident from definition of term 'service' that it can be a split into three parts. The main part itself is very wide. The expression 'any description' widens the ambit of definition and extends it to any service. It applies to any service made available to potential users. The word 'any' and 'potential' are significant. Both are of wide amplitude. The use of the word 'any' in the aforesaid definition of the data service indicates that it has been used in wider sense extending from one to all. The word 'potential' is again very wide. It means service which is not only extended to actual users but those who are capable of using it are covered in the definition.

The Landmark Judgment

In the case of *Indian Medical Association* v *V.P. Shantha III* (1995) CPJ 1 SC, the question for consideration before the Supreme Court was in what circumstances, a medical practitioner can be regarded as rendering 'service' under section 2(1)(*o*) of the Consumer Protection Act and whether the service rendered at the hospital/nursing home can be regarded as a service under section 2(1)(*o*) of the Act. The Supreme Court come to the following conclusions:

(*a*) Service rendered to a patient by a medical practitioner (except where the doctor rendered service free of charge to every patient or under a contract of personal service) by way of consultation, diagnoses and treatment, both medical and surgical, would fall within the ambit of 'service' as defined in section 2(1)(*o*) of the Act.

(*b*) The fact that medical practitioner belong to the medical profession are and are subject to the disciplinary control of the Medical Council of India/or State Medical Councils constituted under the provision of Indian Medical Council Act would not exclude the service attended by them from the ambit of the Act.

(*c*) A 'contract of personal service' has to be distinguished from a 'contract for personal service'. In the absence of a relationship of master and servant between the patient and the medical practitioner, the service rendered by a medical practitioner to the patient can not be regarded as services rendered under a 'contract of personal service'. Such service is service rendered under a 'contract for personnel service' and is not covered by exclusionary clause of the definition of 'service' contained in section 2(1)(*o*) of the Act.

(*d*) The expression 'contract of personal service' in section 2(1)(*o*) of the Act cannot be confined to contracts for employment of domestic servants only and the said expression would include the employment of a medical officer for a purpose of rendering medical service to the employer. The service rendered by a medical officer to his employer under the contract of employment would be outside the purview of service as defined in section 2(1)(*o*) of the Act.

(*e*) Service rendered free of charge by a medical practitioner attached to a hospital/nursing home or a medical officer employed in a hospital/ nursing home where such services are rendered free of charge to everybody, would not service as defined in section 2(1)(*o*) of the Act. The payment of a token amount for registration purpose only at the hospital/nursing home would not alter the position.

(*f*) Service rendered at a non-government hospital/nursing home where no charge whatsoever is made from any person availing the service and all patients (rich or poor) are given free service is outside the purview of the expression 'service' as defined in section 2(1)(*o*) of the Act. The payment of a token amount for registration purpose only at the hospital/nursing home would not alter the position.

(*g*) Services rendered at a non-government hospital/nursing home where charges are required to be paid by the person availing such services was within the purview of the expression 'service' as defined in section 2(1)(*o*) of the Act.

(*h*) Services rendered at a non-government hospital/nursing home where charges are required to be paid by the person who are in a position to pay are rendered service free of charge would fall within the ambit of the expression 'service' as defined in section 2(1)(*o*) of the Act irrespective of the fact that the services rendered free of charge to person who are not in a position to pay for such service. Free service would also be 'service' and the recipient a consumer under the Act.

(*i*) Services rendered at a non-government hospital/health centre/dispensary where no charges whatsoever is made from any person availing the service and all patients (rich and poor) are given free service — is outside the purview of the expression 'service' as defined in section 2(1)(*o*) of the Act. The payment of a token amount for registration purpose only at the hospital/nursing home would not alter the position.

(*j*) Services rendered at a non-government hospital/health centre/dispensary where services are rendered on payment of charges and also rendered free of charge to other persons availing such services would fall within the ambit of the expression 'service' as defined in section 2(1)(*o*) of the Act irrespective of the fact that the 'service' is rendered free of charge to persons who do not pay for such service. Free service would also be 'service' and the recipient a 'consumer' under the Act.

(*k*) Service rendered by a medical practitioner or hospital/nursing home can not be regarded as 'service' rendered free of charge, if the person availing the service has taken insurance policy for medical care where under the charges for consultation, diagnosis and medical treatment are borne by the insurance company and such services would fall within the ambit of 'service' as defined in section 2(1)(*o*) of the Act.

(*l*) Similarly, where, as a part of the condition of service, the employer bears that expenses of medical treatment of an employee and his family members dependent upon him, the services rendered to such an employee and his family member by a medical practitioner or a hospital/ nursing home would not be free of charge and would constitute 'service' under section 2(1)(*o*) of the Act.

3. Patient is consumer

From the definition of 'consumer' and 'service' given respectively in section 2(1)(*d*) and section 2(1)(*o*) of Consumer Protection Act, 1986 and Supreme Court decision given in the case of *Indian Medical Association* v *V.P. Shantha* (1995) III CPR 412 (SC) it is clear that services rendered to a patient by a medical professional and service within the meaning of Consumer Protection Act, 1986, the persons who hire or avails of such services are, therefore, 'consumers'. But where the doctor/hospital renders service free of charge to every patient or under a contract of personal service, a patient availing of such free of charge service will not be a consumer. The user of the services of a free hospital has been held not to fall in the category of consumer.

A railway employee treated at a free railway hospital was held to be not a consumer of railway medical services. *S. Tharani* v *Southern Railway* (1999) III CPR 336 (TN) where a complainant's son received free medical treatment from a hospital run by the employer company. The son died of fever while in hospital and under treatment. Father was not consumer under this Act and could not raise the matter.

A person who receives medical treatment in a government hospital or charitable hospital free of cost is not the consumer under the Act. Where the patient pays for pathological tests and the investigations in a government hospital but the treatment and a surgery is done free of cost, such patient is not a consumer. [*Rabinarain Sahoo* v *Dr. B. Jayaram Patra* 2004 (1) CPJ 31 NC DRC]

A person entitled to the benefit of the Central Government Health Service has been held to be not a consumer and, therefore, Consumer Forums have no jurisdiction over the matter. [*Union of India* v *A.P. Mathur* (1997) III CPJ 424 Del]

Where apart from token free one connected towards several connected and incidental objects, it was held that services could not be said to be free and, therefore the patient had the status of a consumer. [*Amblaapa V Sriman D.* v *Veerendra Heggade* (1999) III CPR 72 Kar]

4. Contract for personal services

The relationship between a medical practitioner and the patient is of trust and confidence. In the absence of a relationship of master and servant between the patient and the medical practitioner, the services rendered by a medical practitioner to the patient can not be regarded as service rendered under the 'contract of personal service'. Such service is a service rendered under a 'contract for personal services' and is not covered by exclusionary clause of the definition of 'service' contained in section 2(1)(*o*) of the Act.

The expression 'contract for personal services' in section 2(1)(*o*) of the Act cannot be confined to contracts for employment of domestic servants only and the said expression would not include the employment of a medical officer for the purpose of the rendering medical service to the employer. The service rendered by a medical officer to his employer under the contract of employment would be outside the purview of service as defined in section 2(1)(*o*) of the Act.

5. Free charge treatment at government and non-government hospitals

The medical service rendered free of charge in a government and non-government hospital/nursing homes does not fall within the ambit of section 2(1)(*o*) of the Act. The free services rendered by the municipalities in the form of facilities like sanitation, roads, street lights, etc. are also outside the ambit of the Act. These services are managed by the municipalities or other government agencies out of taxes paid by the citizens, these taxes does not constitute consideration for the services rendered by the state to citizens.

The Supreme Court held that "doctors and hospitals who rendered service without any charge of whatsoever to every person availing the service would not fall within the ambit of 'service' under section 2(1)(*o*) of the Act. The payment of taken amount for registration purposes only would not alter the position in respect of such doctors and hospitals" [*Indian Medical Association* v *V.P. Santha* (1995) III CPR 412 (SC)].

Following the Supreme Court judgment, the Karnataka State Commission in *Anthony Dass A* v *Ex Engineer, Earth Movers Division, BEM, KGP* (1997) III CPJ) has held that where the employees and the families were given free treatment in a medical center run by the employer except that a sum of 17.50 was deducted towards EMA from their salaries as a statutory deduction, it amounted to only a token payment and not as a consideration for the treatment. It, therefore, held that payment of such contribution could not be classified as 'consideration' for availing services and such services would not fall within the ambit of 'service' under section 2(1)(*o*) of the Act.

6. Patient paying pathological test charges

In *Rabinarayan Sahoo* v *Dr. B. Jayram Patra* [(2004) I CPJ 3 NCDRC], the National Commission held that the patients paying for pathological tests but not paying any charge for the treatment/operation in a government hospital are not consumers, since no fee was paid for operation as it was a government hospital, not any fees for operation is charged from any other patient in the hospital. Payment of charges for tests prior to operation for which no negligence or deficiency of service was attributed, cannot be extended to a later event (operation) which is done without any fee. This cannot be clubbed together while claiming that consideration was paid for operation.

7. Treatment of paying and non-paying patient

There are in most government hospitals, separate paying wards where patients seek admission as contrasted with the general ward where of one patient is treated. Can we say that a patient, in a paying ward in a government hospital is a 'consumer' within the meaning of the Consumer Protection Act, but not an ordinary patient admitted to a general ward.

The National Commission in *Consumer Unity and Trust Society* v *State of Rajasthan* [(1991) 1 CPR 241 (NCDRC)] observed that in regard to 'paying wards', the payments are specifically related to special room/beds for which the separate charge is made, the medical facilities available in a government hospital are common to all patients inclusive of those in the paying wards, without discrimination.

However, the Supreme Court in *Indian Medical Association* v *V.P. Shantha* (1995) III CPR 412 (SC) at 430 has held that the service rendered at a government or non-government hospital/health centre/dispensary/nursing home where charges are required to be paid by persons who are in a position to pay and persons who cannot afford are rendered service free of charge would fall within the ambit of the expression 'service' as defined in section 2(1)(*o*) of the Act irrespective of the fact that the service is rendered free of charge to persons who are not in a position to pay for such service.

Following this Supreme Court Judgment, the Karnataka State Commission in *Rohani Pritam Kabadi* v *Dr. R.T. Kulkarni* (1996) III CPJ 441, has held that in a situation where part of the service is free of charge and part of it is charged for, such medical service will fall in the category of 'service' within its definition under section 2(1)(*o*) of the Act and persons availing of such service will be "consumers" within the meaning of the Act.

8. Treatment under CGHS scheme

Some schemes of health and medical facilities have been instituted by the Union Government, a few State Governments and autonomous bodies. In such schemes the members making a regular contribution are entitled to free medical facilities in government hospitals. The Central Government Health Scheme (CGHS) is of this category. A government employee, making the regular contribution to the CGHS is entitled to medical facilities available in an appropriate government hospital to which his case may be deferred by the nearest dispensary to which he may normally report of ordinary ailments.

In *Consumer Unity and Trust Society* v *State of Rajasthan* (1991) I CPR 241 (NCDRC), the National Commission held that the contribution to the CGHS should be taken to be in lieu of free treatment in the diverse dispensaries as well as the free provision of the medicines from these dispensaries, where cases are referred by the dispensaries to a government hospital, the facilities are provided by a welfare state free of charge, same as to 'out patients and others admitted to the hospitals. The payment of token amount under CGHS scheme has been held to be no consideration for the purpose of definition of 'consumer' under the Consumer Protection Act and the forum has no jurisdiction to entertain cases relating to deficiency in service as far as CGHS is concerned.

9. Consumer disputes redressal agencies

To provide simple, speedy and inexpensive redressal of consumer grievances, the Act envisages a three-tier quasi-judicial machinery at the district, state and national level. (Section 9)

The hierarchy of three redressal forums, as Act provided is given below —

(*a*) District Forums

(*b*) State Commissions

(*c*) National Commissions

9.1 District Forum composition

Each district of state shall have a Consumer Disputes Redressal Forum known as the 'District Forum'. Each District Forum is to be established by the state government by notification to be published it in Official Gazette. The State government may establish more than one district forum in a district if it deems necessary in view the requirement of that district.

Under section 10 of the Act the District Forum is to be composed of—

(*i*) One President who is, or has been, or is qualified to be a District Judge,

(*ii*) Two other members complete the quorum one of whom has to be a woman, having the qualifications:

- (*a*) To be not less than 35 years of age,
- (*b*) Possess a bachelor's degree from a recognized university,
- (*c*) Be a person of ability, integrity and a standing and have adequate knowledge or experience of at least 10 years in dealing with problems relating to the economics, law, commerce, accountancy, industry, public affairs or administration.

9.1.1 Jurisdiction of District Forum

According to section 11 of Consumer Protection Act, 1986, the District Forum shall have jurisdiction to entertain complaints where the value of the goods or services and the compensation, if any, claimed does not exceed rupees twenty lacs. A complaint shall be instituted in a District Forum within the local limits of whose jurisdiction,

(*a*) The opposite party or each of the opposite parties, where there are more than one, at the time of institution of the complaint, actually and voluntarily resides or carries on business or has a branch office, or personally works for gain, or

(*b*) Any of the opposite parties, where there are more than one, at the time of institution of the complaint, actually and voluntarily resides, or carries on business or has a branch office, or personally work for gain, as the case may be, acquiesce, in such institution, or

(*c*) The cause of action, wholly or in part arises.

9.1.2 Who can make the complaint

Section 12 of the Consumer Protection Act, 1986 provides that a complaint may be filed with District Forum by —

(*i*) The consumer to whom such service is provided or is agreed to be provided,

(*ii*) Any recognized consumer association, whether the consumer to whom the service is provided or is agreed to be provided is a member of such association or not,

(*iii*) The central or the state government,

(*iv*) One or more consumers, where there are numerous consumers having the same interest, with the permission of the District Forum, on behalf of, or for the benefit of, all consumers so interested,

(*v*) In case of death of a consumer, his legal heir or representation.

(2) Every complaint shall be accompanied with such amount of fee and payable in such manner as may be prescribed.

(3) On receipt of a complaint the District Forum may, by order, allow the complaint to be proceeded with or rejected, provided that a complaint shall not be rejected unless an opportunity of being heard has been given to the complainant, and the admissibility of the complaint shall ordinarily be decided.

9.1.3 Civil court's power to District Forum [*Section 13*(*4*)]

Section 13(4) of the Consumer Protection Act, 1986, provides that the District Forum is also vested with the following powers as are vested in a Civil Court under the Code of Civil Procedure, 1908, while trying a civil suit —

(*i*) The summoning and enforcing attendance of any defendant or witness and examining the witness on oath,

(*ii*) The discovery and production of any document or other material object producible as evidence,

(*iii*) The reception of evidence on affidavits,

(*iv*) The requisitioning of the report of the concerned analysis or test from the appropriate laboratory or from any other relevant source,

(*v*) Issuing any commission for the examination of any witness,

(*vi*) Any other matter which may be prescribed (by the rules).

9.1.4 Remedies to the consumers

Section 14 of the Consumer Protection Act, 1986 enumerates the relief that can be granted to a complainant by any goods sold or delivered or any service provided.

9.1.5 Procedure on receipt of complaint [*Section 13*(*2*)]

Section 13(2) of the Consumer Protection Act, 1986 provides that the District Forum shall on admission of a complaint —

(*i*) Refer a copy of admitted complaint within 21 days from the date of its admission to the opposite party directing him to give his version of the case within a period of 30 days or such extended period not exceeding 15 days as may be granted by the District Forum,

(*ii*) Where the opposite party, on receipt of a copy of the complaint, denies or disputes the allegations contained in the complaint, or omits or fails to take any action to represent his case within the time given by the District Forum, the District Forum shall proceed to settle the consumer dispute,

(*a*) On the basis of service brought to its notice by the complainant and the opposite party, where the opposite party denies or disputes the allegations contained in the complaint, or

(*b*) *Ex parte* on the basis of evidence brought to its notice by the complainant where the opposite party omits or fails to take be decided within 21 days from the date on which the complaint was received.

9.1.6 Contents of the complaint

A complaint must contain the following particulars —

(*i*) Name, address and description of the complainant,

(*ii*) Name, address and description of the party or parties, as the case may be, so far as they can be ascertained.

(*iii*) The facts relating to complaint and when and where it arose.

(*iv*) Documents in support of the allegations contained in the complaint.

(*v*) The relief which the complainant claims.

The complainant or his authorized agent can present the complaint in person before appropriate Consumer Redressal Forum/Commission. The complaint may also be sent by post to such forum/commission. The complaint should be signed by the complainant or his authorized agent. The complainant can be filled even from clauses which arose after the effective date of operation of the Act irrespective of whether the Consumer Redressal Forums were constituted at the time or not.

The complaint may relate to any action to represent his case within the time given by the Forum.

Where the complainant fails to appear on the date of hearing before the District Forum, the forum may either dismiss the complaint for default or decide it on merits.

District Forum: The provisions of this section are also applicable to the State Commission under section 18 and to the National Commission under section 22 of the Consumer Protection Act. The Forum/Commission may grant only such relieves as are enumerated in section 14(1) of the Act and not beyond that. According to the Act, section 14(1) if, after the proceeding, conducted under section 13, the District Forum is satisfied that the goods complained against suffer from any of the defects specified in the complaint or that any of the allegations contained in complaint about the services are provided, it may grant relief by directing the opposite party to do one or more of the following things, namely:

(*i*) To replace the goods with new goods of similar description which shall be free,

(*ii*) To replace the complainant the price, or as the case may be, the charges paid by the complainant;

(*iii*) To pay such amount as may be awarded by it as compensation to the consumer for any loss or injury suffered by the consumer due to negligence of the opposite party,

(*iv*) To remove the defects in goods or deficiencies, in the services in question,

(*v*) To discontinue the unfair trade practice or the restrictive trade practice or not to repeat them,

(*vi*) Not to offer the hazardous goods for sale,

(*vii*) To withdraw the hazardous goods from being offered for sale,

(*a*) To cease manufacture of hazardous goods and to desist from offering services which are hazardous in nature,

(*b*) To pay such sum as may be determined by it, if it is of the opinion that loss or injury has been suffered by a large number of consumers who are not identifiable conveniently,

(*c*) To issue corrective advertisement to neutralize the effect of misleading advertisement of the cost of the opposite party responsible for issuing such misleading advertisement,

(*viii*) To provide for adequate costs to parties.

The Amendment Act, 2002 has inserted clauses (*h*) [a, b, c] in section 14(1) of the Act.

9.1.7 Appeal against the order of distant forum (*Section 15*)

Section 15 of the Act provides that any person aggrieved by an order made by the District Forum may appeal against such order to the State Commission within a period of 30 days from the date of the order. The State Commission may entertain an appeal after 30 days, if it is satisfied that there was sufficient cause for not filing it within that period. No appeal by a person, who is required to pay any amount in terms of an order of the District Forum, shall be entertained by the State Commission unless the appellant has deposited 50% of the amount or ₹25,000 whichever is less. No stamp duty or court fee payable. The appeal shall be decided, as far as possible, within ninety days from the first date of hearing.

The expression 'date of order' should be construed as date of knowledge of the order, i.e. when copies of the order are received by the party. [*Hindustan Paper Corporation Ltd.* v *Dhir Copy House* 1992 (2) CPR 753].

9.2 State Commissions

9.2.1 State Commission composition

According to section 9(*b*) every state shall have a Consumer Disputes Redressal Commission to be known as the 'State Commission'. The commission is to be established by the State Government by the notification to be published in the Official Gazette. The office of the State Commission shall be located at the Capital of the State.

Under section 16 of the Act every State Commission is to be composed of—

(*i*) A person who is or has been judge of a High Court, appointed by the State Government, who shall be its president,

(*ii*) Not less than two, and not more than such number of members as may be prescribed (under the rules), one of whom shall be a woman with qualifications and experience (as for the District Forum), provided that not more than fifty per cent of the members shall be from amongst persons having a judicial background.

9.2.2 Jurisdiction of the State Commission (Section 17)

The State Commission has been vested with three types of jurisdiction, namely (*i*) Original Jurisdiction, (*ii*) appellate jurisdiction, and (*iii*) revisional jurisdiction.

(*i*) Section 17 of the Act provides that the State Commission has jurisdiction to entertain —

(*a*) Complaints where the value of goods or services and compensation claimed exceeds rupees twenty lakhs and does not exceed rupees one crore.

(*b*) Appeals against the orders of any District Forum within the state,

(*c*) Revision petitions against orders of the District Forum,

(*ii*) A complaint shall be instituted in a State Commission within the limits of whose jurisdiction —

(*a*) The opposite party or each of the opposite parties, where there are more than one at the time of the institution of the complaint, actually and voluntarily resides or carries on business or has a branch office or personally works for gain, or

(*b*) Any of the opposite parties, where there are more than one, at the time of the institution of the complaint, actually and voluntarily resides, or carries on business or has a branch office or personally works for gain provided that in such case either the permission of the State Commission is given, or the opposite parties who do not reside or carry on business or have a branch office, or personally works for gain, as the case may be, acquiesce, in such institutions, or

(*c*) The cause of action wholly or in part, arises.

9.2.3 Procedure to be followed by a State Commission

Procedure of the State Commission for entertaining original complaints is the same as for District Forum. (Sections 12, 13 and 14 of the Act)

9.2.4 Appeal against the order of the State Commission to National Commission

Section 19 of the Act provides that any person aggrieved by an order to State Commission may appeal against such order to National Commission may entertain an appeal after 30 days if it is satisfied that there was sufficient cause for not filing it within that period.

No appeal by a person, who is required to pay any amount in terms of an order of State Commission, shall be entertained by the National Commission unless the appellant has deposited 50% of the amount or ₹35,000 whichever is less.

9.3 National commissions

9.3.1 National Commission composition

The Consumer Protection Act provides for the establishment of the National Commission by the Central Government by notification [*Section* 9(*c*)]. The National Commission is the apex body at the centre to settle the consumer disputes under the Act.

Under section 20(1), the National Commission shall consist of—

(*a*) A person who is or has been a judge of the Supreme Court, to be appointed by the Central Government who shall be its president. (No appointment under this clause shall be made except after the consultation with the Chief Justice of India.)

(*b*) Not less than four, and not more than such number of members, as may be prescribed (under the rules), one of whom shall be woman (with qualifications and experience as for the District Forum/State Commission), provided that not more than fifty per cent of the members shall be from amongst persons having a judicial background.

9.3.2 Jurisdiction of National Commission

The jurisdiction of the National Commission may be classified into three categories namely —

(*i*) Original jurisdiction,

(*ii*) Appellate jurisdiction, and

(*iii*) Revisional jurisdiction

Section 21 provides that the National Commission shall have jurisdiction to entertain —

(*i*) Complaints where the value of goods or services and compensation, if any, claimed exceeds rupees one crore, and

(*ii*) Appeal against the orders of any State Commission,

(*iii*) To entertain revision petitions against orders of the State Commission.

The jurisdiction, Powers and authority of the National Commission may be exercised by Benches thereof which may be constituted by the President with one or more members as the President may deem fit.

9.3.3 Procedure to be followed by National Commission

Rule 14 of the Consumer Protection Rules, 1987 framed by the Central Government lays down the procedure to be followed by the National Commission. The said procedure has been summarized as follows:

(1) A complaint containing the following particulars shall be presented by the complainant in person or by his agent to the National Commission or be sent by registered post addressed to the National Commission.

(*a*) The name, description and the address of the complainant,

(*b*) The name, address and description of the party or parties, as the case may be, so far as they can be ascertained.

(*c*) The facts relating to complaint and when and where it arose.

(*d*) Documents in support of the allegations contained in the complaint

(*e*) The relief which the complainant claims.

(2) The National Commission shall, in disposal of any complaint before it, as far as possible, follow the procedure and conditions including the provisions governing adjournments as laid down in sections 12 and 13 in relation to complaint received by the District Forum.

(3) On the date of hearing or any other date to which hearing could be adjourned, it shall be obligatory on the parties or their agents to appear before the National Commission.

(4) Where the complainant or his agent fails to appear before the National Commission on such days, the National Commission may in its desertion either dismiss the complaint for default or decide it on merits.

(5) Where the opposite party or its agent fails to appear on the date of hearing, the National Commission may decide the complainant *ex-parte*.

(6) The National Commission may, on such terms as its deems fit and at any stage of the proceedings, adjourn the hearing of complaint but the complaint shall be decided, as far as possible, within a period of three months from the date of notice received by opposite party where complain does not require analysis or testing of commodities and within five months if it requires analysis or testing of commodities. In the event of complaint being disposed of after the specific period. The National Commission shall record in writing, the reasons for the delay in such disposal. [*Added by the Consumer Protection* (*Amendment*) *Rules, 2004*]

(7) If after the proceedings, the National Commission is satisfied with allegations contained in the complaint, it shall issue orders to the opposite party or parties, as the case may be, directing him or them to take one or more of the things as mentioned in sub-section (1) of section 14.

(8) The National Commission shall also have the power to direct that any order preferred under section 23 or where the order of the National Commission has been affirmed by the Supreme Court under that section, be published in the Official Gazette or through any other media and no legal proceedings shall lie against the National Commission or any media for such publication.

A complaint filed under section 22 of the Consumer Protection Act requires the National Commission to decide the matter in accordance with the evidence, documents and respective case of the parties including the submission made before it and not by referring the matter to an Arbitrator for giving an award. [*Skypak Couriers Ltd.* v *Tata Chemicals Ltd.* (2000) II CPJ 6 (SC)]

9.3.4 Appeal against order of the National Commission (*Section 23*)

Section 23 of the Act provides that any person aggrieved by an order made by National Commission, may appeal against such order to the Supreme Court within 30 days from the date of order.

The Supreme Court may entertain an appeal after 30 days if it is satisfied that there was sufficient cause for not filing it within that period.

10. Limitation period (Section 24A)

Section 24A of the Act provides that the District Forum, the State Commission or the National Commission shall not admit a complaint unless it is filed within two years from the date on which the cause of action has arisen.

In case there are sufficient grounds for not filing the complaint within such period, delay may be condoned at the discretion of the consumer at the direction of the consumer Forum/Commission.

11. Dismissal of frivolous and vexatious complaints (Section 26)

Section 26 of the Act provides that the District Forum, the State Commission or the National Commission, may dismiss a complaint, if the complaint is found to be frivolous or vexatious. The Forum/commission must record its reasons in writing for such dismissal. The Forum/commission may also pass the order that the complainant shall pay to the opposite party such cost, not exceeding ten thousand rupees, as may be specified in the order.

12. Penalties

Where a person against whom a complaint is made or the complainant fails or omits to comply with any order made by the District Forum, the State Commission or the National Commission, as the case may be, such person or complainant shall be punishable with imprisonment for a term which shall not be less than one month but which may extend to 3 years, or with fine which shall not be less than 2,000 rupees but which may extend to 10,000 rupees or with both.

The District Forum or the State Commission or the National Commission as the case may be, shall have the power of a judicial magistrate of the first class for the trial of offences under this Act, and on such conferment of powers, the District Forum or the State Commission or the National Commission, as the case may be, on whom the powers so conferred, shall be deemed to be a Judicial Magistrate of the first class for the purpose of the Code of Criminal Procedure, 1973.

All offences under this Act may be tried summarily by the District Forum or State Commission or National Commission.

CHAPTER 3
Medical Professional's Negligence

SYNOPSIS

1. What is profession?

Profession is an occupation requiring intellectual skill and manual skill, while an occupation is substantially the production or sale or arrangement for the production or sale of commodities.

Rupert M. Jackson and Joh. L. Powell laid down following characteristics, viz.,

(*i*) The nature of the work which is skilled and specialized and is substantial part is mental rather than manual.

(*ii*) Commitment to moral principles which goes beyond the general duty of honesty and a wider duty to community which may transcend the duty to a particular client or patient.

(*iii*) Professional association which regulates admission and seeks to uphold the standards of the profession through professional codes on matters of deducts and ethics, and

(*iv*) High status in the community.

Mainly, following occupations have profession status —

(*a*) Solicitors

(*b*) Barristers

(*c*) Medical practitioners

(*d*) Engineers

(*e*) Architects, and

(*f*) Surveyors

2. Professional liability

The professional man owes a duty to exercise reasonable care to his client. Medical practitioners may be liable on the ground of failure to exercise reasonable skill and care. The Medical practitioners are not immune from a claim for damages of their negligence. They can be sued in tort and contract for not performing their duty with reasonable care. The person who suffers due to negligence of medical practitioner has a right to seek redress under Consumer Protection Act, 1986.

3. Meaning of negligence

Negligence is the breach of a duty caused by the omission to do something which a reasonable man, guided by those considerations which ordinarily regulate the conduct of human affairs would do, or doing something which a prudent and reasonable man would not do. (*Black's Law Dictionary, 6th Edn*)

According to Winfield, "negligence as a tort is the breach of a legal duty to take care which results in damage, undesired by the defendant to the plaintiff."

The definition involves three constituents of negligence:

(1) A legal duty of exercise due care on the part of the party complained of towards the party complaining the former's conduct within the scope of the duty,

(2) Breach of the said duty, and

(3) Consequently damage.

The idea of negligence and duty are strictly correlative. Negligence means either subjectively a careless state of mind, or objectively careless conduct. Negligence is not an absolute term, but is relative one, it is rather a comparative term. No absolute standard can be fixed and no mathematically exact formula can be laid down by which negligence or lack of its can be infallibly measured in a given case. To determine whether an act would not be negligent, it is relevant to determine if any reasonable man would foresee that the act would cause damage or not.

In medical profession it may be stated that every person who enters into the profession undertakes to bring to the exercise of it, a reasonable degree of care and skill. It is true that a Doctor or a surgeon does not undertake that he will positively cure a patient nor does he undertake to sue the highest possible degree of skill, as there may be persons more learned and skilled than himself, but he definitely undertakes to use a reasonable and competent degree of skill.

In *Bolam* v *Friern Hospital Management Committee* (1957) 2 All ER 118. Nair J summed up the law as under:

> "The test is the standard of an ordinary skill man exercising and professing to have that special skill. A man need not possess the highest expert skill, it is well established law that it is sufficient if he exercises the ordinary skill of an ordinary competent man exercising that particular art. In the case of a medical man, negligence means failure to act in accordance

with the standards of reasonably competent medical men at the time. There may be one or more perfectly proper standards, and if he conforms with one of these proper standards, then he is not negligent."

3.1 Gross negligence

The international failure to perform a manifest duty in reckless disregard of the consequence. Gross negligence rests on the assumption that one knew results of his acts, but was recklessly or wantonly indifferent to results.

3.2 Negligence per se

Conduct which may be declared and treated as negligence without any argument or proof. It is a violation of a statute or violation of valid municipal ordinance. As a general rule, the violation of a public duty, enjoined by law for the protection of person or property, so constitutes.

In (*Dr.*) *L.D. Bajaj* (*Fauji doctors*) v *Hari Chand* AIR 1996 SC 2111 where a cancer patient was treated by a doctor who was not qualified to treat that disease (he was not even an MBBS), it was held that this amounted to negligence *per se*. A compensation of ₹80,000 was awarded.

3.3 Contributory negligence

Where complainant's negligence contributes to the damage, the damages may be reduced to such an extent as the Forum/Commissions thinks just and equitable having regard to the complainant share in the responsibility for damage. Thus complainant and the opposite party both are involved for damage for contributory negligence.

However, it is the duty of doctor to give clear and unambiguous instructions, and to explain in intelligible terms what is required of the patient and to give him any necessary warning. If the patient fails to follow these instructions and this is a cause of his injuries then it will be possible to argue that the patient/attendant had been contributory negligent.

When the defence is raised in a clinical negligence claim, the defendant doctor will have to establish that the claimant's conduct contributed to the damage and that he has failed to take reasonable care his won safety. The claimant need not owe any duty to the defendant doctor.

When a complaint is filed against a doctor for negligence, the defendant doctor must plead that there was contributory negligence on the part of complainant or his attendant, of it is not pleaded it is not open to the court to find that the complainant had been contributory negligent.

In *Master Ashok Kumar* v *Agadi Nursing Home* (1995) III CPJ 142, the contributory negligence of the minor boy in tampering with the plaster and giving movement to the fractured elbow without waiting for the full period for the removal of plaster, was held to be cause of deformity and the complaint was dismissed.

In *Md. Aslam* v *Ideal Nursing Home* (1997) III CPJ 81 (NCDRC), wife of the complainant underwent hysterectomy (removal of uterus). During the post-operative period, despite repeated caution to take only liquid and semi-solid diet, she continued to consume ice-cream, roti, meat, dal, puri and fried eggs. This led to burst abdomen for which she had to undergone an emergency operation to close her abdomen, but she died next day. The State Commission dismissed the case on the ground that the patient was not following the advice repeatedly given to her (a case of contributory negligence).

In *Mohd. Azeemuddin* v *Dr. M. Nagabhushanam* (2003 (5) CLD 653), a case of choleyslectomy, the patient developed complications, she was advised for post-surgical follow up and corrective and treatment and ultimately died. The opposite party-doctor was held not negligent.

3.4 Criminal negligence

Negligence of such a character, or occurring under such circumstances as to be punishable as a crime by a statute, or such a flagrant and reckless disregard of the life and safety of others, or willful indifference to the injury liable to follow, as to convert an act, otherwise lawful, into a crime against the state when it results in personal injury or death. Here the negligence is so great as to go beyond matter of mere composition. Doctor may be prosecuted for such negligence in criminal court for injury to or the death of his patient. Such negligence is culpable homicide under section 304A of Indian Penal Code.

Some instances of criminal negligence are:

(*i*) Transfusing wrong blood,

(*ii*) Applying too tight plaster which may cause gangrene or paralysis,

(*iii*) Unqualified person conducting operation,

(*iv*) Performing an act which is prohibited or punishable by law,

(*v*) Leaving instrument or sponges inside the part of body operated upon.

In *Shanta* v *State of A.P.* (1997) III CPJ 481, the Andhra Pradesh High Court, while granting compensation against a Government hospital for negligence of leaving a mop in the work for violating fundamental right of right to life under Article 21 of the Constitution observed that the petitioner shall be free to take action in tort for the damages under the private law against the hospital and others and also to make complaint for any criminal act of the hospital, if so advised.

4. Meaning of medical negligence

Medical negligence is defined as lack of reasonable care and skill or willful negligence on the part of his doctor in respect to acceptance of a patient, taking history, examination, diagnosis, investigation, treatment, etc. resulting in injury or damage to the patient. A medical practitioner owes him certain duties, namely, a duty of care in deciding whether to undertake the case, a duty of care in deciding what treatment to give and duty of care in his administration of that treatment. A breach of any such duties will support an action for negligence by the patient. The practitioner must bring to his task a reasonable degree of skill and knowledge, and must exercise a reasonable degree of care. A delegation of responsibility to another may amount to negligence in certain circumstances. A consultant could be negligent where he delegates the responsibility to his junior with the knowledge that his junior was incapable of performing of his duties properly. The law requires that the practitioner must bring to his task reasonable degree of skill and knowledge and must exercise a reasonable degree of care. The law does not support the very highest not a very low degree of care and competence judge in the light of the particular circumstances of each case." (*Halsbury's Laws of England,* 3rd edn, vol 26, P.17)

In *Vinitha Ashok* v *Lakshmi Hospital* 2001 (8) SCC 731, the Supreme Court has observed:

> "... in a large majority of cases, it has been demonstrated that a doctor will be liable for negligence in respect of diagnosis and treatment inspite of a body of professional opinion approving his conduct where it has not been established to the court's satisfaction that such opinion relied on is reasonable or responsible. If it can be demonstrated that the professional opinion is capable of notwithstanding the logical analysis, the court would be entitled to hold that the body of opinion is not reasonable or responsible."

The Supreme Court of India in a landmark decision *Indian Medical Association* v *V.P. Santha* AIR 1996 SC 550 observed as under:

> "The duties which a doctor owes to his patient are clear. A person who holds himself out ready to give medical advice and treatment impliedly undertakes that he is possessed of skill and knowledge for the purpose. Such a person when consulted by a patient owes him certain duties, viz, a duty of care in deciding whether to undertake the case, a duty of care in including what treatment to give or a duty of care in the administration of that treatment. A breach of any of those duties gives a right of action for negligence to the patient. The practitioner must bring to his task a reasonable degree of skill and knowledge and must exercise a reasonable degree of care. Neither the very highest nor a very low degree of care and competence judged in the light of particular circumstance judged in the light of particular circumstances of each case is what the law requires. The doctor, no doubt, has a discretion in choosing treatment which he proposes to give to the patient, and such discretion is relatively ampler in case of emergency."

In the above case, the doctor reduced the fracture without anesthesia to the patient, who died. This was held to be negligence and carelessness, the elementary precaution being giving of anesthesia.

In recent times, the Supreme Court in the case of *Jacob Mathew* (*Dr*) v *State of Punjab* III CPJ 3 (SC) has sought to answer the question as to whether it has granted an impetus to the medical professionals when it comes to medical negligence. The judgment of the apex court is marked as the landmark judgment in the field of medical negligence. The Supreme Court held that a simple lack of care, an error of judgment or an accident is not proof of negligence on the part of the medical professional. Mere error in judgment does not amount to medical negligence. The Supreme Court laid down the principles on which the liability of a medical professional is determined generally and in the field of criminal law in particular.

5. Deficiency in medical services and medical negligence

According to definition given in section 2(1)(*g*) of Consumer Protection Act, 1986 deficiency means any fault, imperfection, shortcoming or inadequacy in the quality, nature and manner of performance which is required to be maintained by or under any law for the time being in force or has been undertaken to be performed by a person in pursuance of a contract or otherwise in relation to any service.

The apex court of country held in *Indian Medical Association* v *V.P. Shantha* (1995) III CPR 412 (SC) that, "a determination about deficiency in service under section 2(1)(*g*)" of the Consumer Protection Act is to be made by applying the same test as is applied in an action for damages for negligence.

Thus deficiency in medical service is equated with medical negligence.

However, in many cases where there is no negligence in treatment but only deficiency in service is there. Non-handling over of medical records, loss of pathological samples, excessive or wrong billing, undue delay in conducting, investigations are some of the cases which would come within the purview of deficiency of service and would certainly not be negligence.

6. Error of judgment and negligence

Prescribing a particular line of treatment by a qualified doctor by itself may not be an act of negligence. However, if the doctor prescribes a medicine or administers a treatment, which by all standards should not have been given, then such a situation does amount to an act of negligence.

The basic distinction is that negligence is not merely an error of judgment, it is more deep-rooted. However, to think that an error of judgment would never be culpable, may also be erroneous because if the error is not an ordinary error of judgment because of a grave nature and reflective of grass negligence on the part of medical practitioner concerned, such an error will be held to be gross enough to make the doctor liable.

To establish liability on that basis it must be shown:

(*i*) That there is a usual and normal practice,

(*ii*) That the doctor has not adopted it,

(*iii*) That the course adopted is none which no professional man of ordinary skill would had he been acting with ordinary care.

Liability of third person: There may be circumstances in which it is foreseeable that a patient could be potential hazard to third person where a doctor would be held to owe a duty of care. If a patient's medical condition or the side effects of a drug that the doctor has prescribed render certain conduct (such as driving a motor vehicle) hazardous, the doctor will be under a duty to warn the patient. If he fails to do so and as a result the patient causes an accident injuring other would owe a duty of care, both to the patient and the other parties.

7. Emergency cases and medical negligence

In the case of *Parmanand Katara* v *Union of India* (1989) ACJ 1000, SC), the Supreme Court observed:

(*i*) There is no provision in the Indian Penal Code, Criminal Procedure Code, Motor Vehicles Act, etc, which prevent doctors from promptly attending serious injured persons and accident cases before the arrival of police.

(*ii*) The treatment of the patient would not wait for the arrival of the police or completing legal formalities.

(*iii*) All government hospitals, Medical institutions should be asked to provide immediate medical aid to all the cases-medico-legal or not.

Article 21 lays down that no person shall be deprived of his life or personal liberty except according to procedure established by law. Thus the right to health and health care is protected under Article 21 of the Constitution of India as right to life. It extends to receiving proper and complete medical attention from medical practitioner. It is axiomatic that one who causes loss or injury to another by accident, negligence or design is required to compensate the loss of injury.

Article 21 of the Constitution casts the obligation on the state of preserve life. A doctor at the Government Hospital positioned to meet this state obligation is, therefore, duty bound to extend medical assistance for preserving life. Every doctor whether at a Government Hospital or otherwise has the professional obligation to extend his services for protecting life.

In *Mrs. Shanta* v *State of Andhra Pradesh* (1997) III CPJ 481 (AP HC), the petitioner was admitted in the Government Maternity Hospital, Afzalganj, and was subjected to Caesarean Operation. The abdomen was closed leaving foreign body mop in the womb which caused many complications. She was to go for another operation for removal of foreign mop by private Nursing Home. The Andhra Pradesh High Court on the fact of the case came to the conclusion that second and third respondents who were the servants of the first respondent (Govt. of Andhra Pradesh) has been negligent and had violated the petitioner's right under Article 21 of the Constitution of India.

In *Paschim Banga Khet Mazdoor Samity* v *State of West Bengal* AIR 1996 SC 2426, Hakim Seikh, a member of Paschim Banga Khet Mazdoor Samity, fell off a train and suffered serious head injuries and brain hemorrhage. He was taken to N.R.S. Medical College Hospital, but was refused admission as there was no vacant bed. He was taken to other state hospitals, who also refused admission on grounds of 'no vacant bed', no facility of neuro-surgeon. Ultimately, he was admitted in a private hospital, where he recovered after incurring heavy expenditure on his treatment.

The question considered by the Supreme Court was whether the non-availability of facilities (bed/neuron-surgeon) had guaranteed under Article 21 of the Constitution.

The Supreme Court held:

"The Constitution envisages the establishment not a welfare state of the federal level as well as the state level. In a welfare state the primary duty of the Government to secure the welfare of the people. Providing adequate medical facilities for the people is an essential part of the obligations undertaken by the government in a welfare state. The government discharges this obligation by running hospitals and health centers which provide medical care to the persons seeking to avail those facilities. Article 21 imposes an obligation on the State of safeguard the right to life of every person. Prevention of human life is thus of paramount importance. The government hospitals run by State and the medical officers employed therein are duty bound to extend medical assistance for preserving human life. Failure on the part of the government hospital to provide timely medical treatment to a person in need of such treatment results in violation of his right to life guaranteed under Article 21."

In this case, Hakim Seikh was denied medical treatment at various government hospitals and the state could not avoid its responsibility, which was the breach of the right to life guaranteed by Article 21 of the Constitution. ₹25,000 awarded as a compensation.

CHAPTER 4

Criminal Liability for Medical Negligence

SYNOPSIS

1. Introduction

Doctors are liable under the prevailing laws such as Civil Penal Code, Indian Penal Code, Law of Contract, Sale of Goods Act, Law of Torts and other specific legislation. Under section 304A of Indian Penal Code (IPC), the doctor who commits criminal liability is punishable with imprisonment for a term which may extend upto two years, or with a fine, or both. Civil liability arises in case of medical service rendered on payment of fee under sections 73 and 74 of the Indian Contract Act. Under the Law of Torts (a wrong that is independent of contract) civil liability is applicable to doctors of all categories, that is whether they provide their services for a fee on a charity without doctors committing professional misconduct and it can direct the removal of the name of any person enrolled on a the state medical register on the grounds of the professional conduct.

Every profession has its guidelines and needs a scrutiny. Every professional body should ideally scrutinize whether their members are following the principles and practices as laid down by their ethics. Medical profession is governed by code of medical ethics and etiquettes laid down by Medical Council of India. Although they are for internal self regulation of profession, it is an obligation on the part of the professionals to fulfill certain rights, exemptions on the parties. But there has been fast spreading misconduct amongst the medical professionals. The unethical practice has gone to a level where the basic purpose of medical profession that it is service to humanity fails. Few unethical practices like the sharing, or cut practice, particularly prescribing a company's medicine, selling of body parts, etc. for personal monitory gains are openly discussed among them but they never come up to the surface due to lack of concrete proof. To err is human nature but mistakes of medical professional which may result in death of a person or permanent impairment can be particularly costly but the law does not aim to punish doctors for all their mistakes, but only those which are committed out of negligence. Mistakes occur but which occurs from carelessness and negligence cannot be left off.

Unfortunately Medical Council of India and other associations have not been efficient, the only alternative is Consumer Protection Act, 1986.

In *Dr. Suresh Gupta* v *Govt. of NCT of Delhi* 2004 (2) CPC 422, the Supreme Court has held that standard of negligence required to be proved should be so high as can be described as "gross negligence" or "recklessness" and not merely necessary care, attention and skill.

2. Meaning of criminal negligence

Where the doctor not only made a wrong diagnosis and treatment, but also made a gross ignorance, gross carelessness or gross neglect for the life and safety of the patient that a criminal charge is brought against him. For such gross ignorance, gross carelessness or gross neglect the doctor may be prosecuted in a criminal court under section 304A of Indian Penal Code. High degree of negligence is required to be proved. There must be direct nexus between the death or any other serious injury of the patient and negligent act of the doctor. A doctor is not criminally liable for the patient's death unless his negligence or incompetence showed such disregard for life and safety as to amount to a criminal against the state. Section 304A of IPC reads as "causing death by negligence — whoever causes the death of any person by doing any rash or negligent act not accounting to culpable homicide shall be imprisoned with imprisonment of either description for a term which may extend to two years or with fine or both.

The jurisprudential concept of negligence differs in civil and criminal law. Negligence which is neither gross nor a high degree may provide a ground for action in civil law but can not form the basis of prosecution in criminal law.

We have noticed that in the case of doctors being subjected to criminal prosecution are on the rise, such prosecutions are filed by private complainants or by the police on an FIR lodged and cognizance taken. The criminal process once initiated, subjects the medical professional to serious embarrassment and harassment. He has to seek bail to escape arrest, which may or may not be granted to him. At the end he may be exonerated by acquittal or in his reputation cannot be compensated by any standard.

The judgment given by the Honourable Supreme Court of India consisting three judges bench in *Jacob Mathews* v *State of Punjab* (2005) III CPJ 9 (SC) ruled by doctor should not be held criminally responsible unless there is a *prima facie* evidence before the court in the form of a credible opinion from another competent doctor, preferably a government doctor in the same form of medicine, supporting the charges of rash and negligent act. It is a laudable judgment in the light of criminal procedures filed against them in trivial cases under sections 307 and 304A, IPC where the *prima facie*, there seems to be no neglect in these medical treatments.

The distinction between civil and criminal negligence was clearly laid down by Lord Hewart in the case of *R* v *Bateman* (1925) 94 L JKB 791. Throughout the civilized world the public has became more compensation minded. The burden of proof in action for negligence rests with the plaintiff, it follows thereafter that the medical practice is for the patient party to establish his claim and not for the medical practitioner to prove that he acted with due skill and care. In few cases the court will accept that the nature of the occurrence complained of is that as to relief the plaintiff from establishing that there was negligence and to place on the defendant the burden of proving that have a sense of negligence. In such cases the legal maxim *res Ipsa loquitur* applies.

In *R.* v *Adomako* (1993) 4 All ER 935 (CA), the following tests were laid down for bringing home a charge of criminal negligence in medical accidents,

(*i*) Indifferent to an obvious risk of injury to death,

(*ii*) Actual foresight of the risk coupled with the determination nevertheless to run it,

(*iii*) An appreciation of the risk coupled with an intention to avoid it, but the attempted avoidance involved such a high degree of negligence as the jury considered justify conviction, and

(*iv*) Inattention or failure to advert to a serious risk which goes beyond "mere inadvertence" in respect of an obvious and important matter which the defendant's duty demanded, he should address.

In *Haripada Saha* v *State of Tripura* 2002 ACJ 1877, the eye of the patient was operated. The patient's eye was damaged due to infection. Doctor defended that infection was developed after the discharge of the patient from hospital. According to expert committee report the infection was developed during the course of operation because of contamination in operation theater. Negligence of doctor was headed established.

In *Jan Sangharsh Morcha* v *State of Gujarat* 2001 (1) AJR 397 (Guj), the allegation was the death of the patient occurred due to transfusion of wrong group of blood in a gynaecological problem. Apart from an award of compensation of ₹50,000 the case was not of the purview of section 304A of the Penal Code.

3. Criminality in medical negligence

Criminality in medical negligence is actionable in tort as well as culpable under the penal law of the land. In tort, the official elemental is damage but in criminal evidence in medical profession the damage is not essential element, the essential element is gross ignorance, gross carelessness or the gross neglect for the life and safety of the patient. Medical practitioner who committed criminal negligence is punishable with the imprisonment or with a fine or both.

In the law of crimes, there is a series of offenses, based on negligence, in which loss or injury is not material and it is enough if the act is likely to cause injury or endanger life.

Kedar Nath v *State* AIR 1965 All 233, section 357 of the Code of Criminal Procedure, 1973 provides for award of compensation, out of fine if imposed as sentence or part of sentences, or otherwise, in addition to the sentence, imposed in case a doctor be held criminally liable for any offense. Medical negligence being both a tort as well as a crime, the condition that compensation for a criminal liability can be awarded only in such cases where a compensation can be recovered by civil process gets fulfilled in cases involving criminal negligence.

4. Criminal liability of doctor

Criminal liability would extend to a doctor as to any other accused for violation of law. In *MC Mehta* v *Union of India* AIR 1987 SC 1086, the Supreme Court of India aggraded the criminal liability and is made subject to *mens-rea*, meaning that the act itself does not make a man guilty unless his intention was not so. Thus the intention and the act must concur to constitute of crime. No act is *per se* criminal, unless coupled with an antecedent intent and the consequent result thereof.

> "Balance is a powerful weapon. When used appropriately and according to morally defensible criteria, it has an indispensable role in human affairs. It's inappropriate use, however, distorts tolerant and constructive relationship between people, some of the life misfortunes are accidents for which nobody is morally responsible, others are wrongs for which responsibility is diffuse, yet others are instances of culpable conduct and constitute grounds for compensation and at times for punishment. Distinguishing between these categories requires careful, morally sensitive and scientifically informed analysis."
>
> ***"Errors, Medicine and the Law"***
> ***By Alan Mary and Alexander Mc call Smith.***

The Supreme Court judgment in *Jacob Matthews* v *State of Punjab* (2005) III CPJ 9 (SC) is marked as the landmark judgment in the field of medical negligence. The Supreme Court held that extreme 'care' and caution should be exercised while initiating criminal proceedings against a medical practitioner. It has framed obligatory guidelines under which a medical practitioner could be held criminally liable on account of his professional negligence or deficiency of service. The Supreme Court laid down the principles on which the liability of a medical professional is determined generally and in the field of criminal law in particular. The relevant criminal principles culled out from the case are as follows:

(*i*) The jurisprudential concept of negligence difference in the civil and criminal law. What may be negligence in civil law may not necessarily be negligence in criminal law. For negligence to amount an offense, the element of *mens rea* must be shown to exist. For an act to amount to criminal negligence, the degree of negligence should be much higher, therefore, gross or of a very higher degree. The negligence which is neither gross nor a higher degree they provide a ground for action in civil law but cannot from the basis for prosecution.

(*ii*) The word gross has not been used in section 304A of IPC, yet it is sector did that in criminal law negligence or recklessness, to be so held, must be of such a high degree as to be 'gross'. The expression 'rash or negligent act' as occurring in the section 304A of the IPC has to be read as qualified by the word 'grossly'.

(*iii*) To prosecute a medical professional for negligence under criminal law it must be shown that the accused did something or failed to do something which in the given facts and circumstances no medical profession in his ordinary senses and produce would have done or failed to do. The hazard taken by the accused doctors should be of such a nature that the injury resulted was most likely imminent.

(*iv*) *Res ipsa loquitur* in only a rule of evidence and operates in the domain of civil law specially in the cases of torts and help us in determining the onus of proof in actions relating to negligence. It can not be pressed in service for determining *per se* the liability for negligence within the domain of criminal law. *Res ipsa loquitur* has, if at all, a limited application in trail on a charge of criminal negligence.

The apex court in deciding this case had established three necessary guidelines so as to determine whether the medical practitioner is criminally liable or not. These guidelines are as mentioned under:

(*i*) A complaint against a doctor is not to be entertained unless the allegation against him is supported by a credible opinion given by another doctor. If the doctor feels that negligence on the part of medical practitioner has resulted to the loss of well being of the plaintiff, then the complaint and may be registered.

(*ii*) The investigating officer before proceeding against the accused ought to be get a medical opinion from a competent doctor, preferably in the government services, qualified in that field of medical sciences who can give an impartial opinion.

(*iii*) The arrest of accused should be withheld unless it is believed by the investigating officer unless he believes that it is necessary to arrest the accused so as to further the investigation of the case. It may further be withheld unless it is believed that the accused doctor will not make himself available to face the prosecution unless he is arrested.

In another landmark judgment in the case of *Suresh Gupta* v *Govt. of NCT of Delhi* 2004 (3) CLJ 312, the Apex Court has held that standard of negligence required to be proved should be so high as can be described as "gross negligence" or "recklessness" and not merely lack of necessary care, attention and skill. The court observed:

"To convict, therefore, a doctor, the prosecution has to come out with a case of high degree of negligence on the part of the doctor. Mere lack of proper care and, prosecution and attention or in advertence might create civil liability but not a criminal one. The courts have, therefore, always insisted in the case of alleged criminal offense against a doctor causing death of his patient during treatment, that the act complained against the doctor must show the negligence or rashness of such a higher degree as to indicate a mental state which can be described as totally apathetic towards the patient, such gross negligence is punishable."

In this case, the patient was a young man with no history of any heart ailment. The operation was to be performed for nasal deformity which was no complicated or serious. Medical opinions produced by prosecution showing the cause of death to be "not introducing a cuffed endo-tracheal tube of proper size as to prevent aspiration of blood from the wound in the respiratory passage." The court held that this act attributed to the doctor, even if accepted to be true, can be described as negligent act as there was lack of due care and prosecution. For this act of negligence he may be liable in tort but his carelessness or want of due attention and skill cannot be described to be reckless or grossly negligent as to make him criminally liable. Therefore, the criminal proceedings against doctor were quashed.

5. Reasonable foreseeability test

Whether the defendant owes a duty to the plaintiff or not depends on reasonable foreseeability of the injury to the plaintiff. If at that time of the act or omission the defendant could reasonably foresee injury to the plaintiff he owes a duty to prevent that injury and failure to do that makes him liable.

Jurists have distinguished on the basis of the reasonable foreseeability test between directness and remoteness of consequence, and if remoteness of consequences could be foreseen or pre-recognised, the doer would be held responsible even of the remote consequences of his act.

The test of reasonable foreseeability was established by the decision of the Privy Council in *Tankship (UK) Ltd.* v *Morts Dock and Engineering Co.* (1961) 1 All ER 404 (PC). The facts of the case were the following. While an oil-burning vessel, the Wagon Mount, chartered by the appellants, was taking in oil in Sydney Port, a large quantity of oil was through the carelessness of their servants allowed to spill into the harbor. The escaped oil was carried by wind and tied beneath a Wharf about 600 feet away, owned by the respondents, ship-repairers, whose employees had been using for their work electric and oxy-acetylene welding equipment. Soon after the oil had spread itself on the water, the Wagon Mount left the harbour, but the oil remained. Two days and a few hours elapsed when it caught fire from molten metal falling on some cotton waste or rag on the piece of debris floating on the oil underneath the Warf. The resulting conflagration caused serious damage to the respondent's property, the wharf and the equipment therein. The Australian Courts found as a fact that the damage was not foreseeable as the appellants did not know and could not be reasonably expected to have known, that furnace oil could catch fire when spread over water, but held that the appellants were still liable for the damage by fire as it was the direct result of their negligence.

In appeal the privy council held that the defendants were not liable. The judgment of Viscount Simonds on behalf of the Board laid down two propositions:

(*i*) The only test applicable was foreseeability of the damage complained of, which in this case was that damage caused by fire.

(*ii*) Though the contact and of the oil with the property of the respondents caused damage, by interfering with the use of their ship-ways, and this damage was foreseeable, this fact was irrelevant and would not make the defendants liable for unforeseeable damage, viz, the damage by the fire.

Reasonable foreseeability further considered: The expression 'reasonable foresight' in the context of existence of a duty of care will bear a different meaning from that expression indicated as a test for remoteness of damage. Then again neither the extent of the damage nor the method of its caution needed to the foreseeable. The House of Lords has given the word foreseeable a meaning which is totally different from the word probable or likely. In *C. Czarniknow Ltd.* v *Koufos* (1969) 1 AC 350 at 385, it was observed "that the defendant will be liable for any type of damage which is reasonably foreseeable as liable to happen even the most unusual case, unless the risk is so small that a reasonable man would in the whole circumstances feel justified in neglecting it."

Negligence is often used in the sense of careless conducted without reference to any duty to take care. In case of any duty to take care, the standard of care is frequently that of a reasonable man, though some is not always necessary, since failure to take care and negligence are sometimes used as synonymous, regardless of whether or not there is duty to take care.

The result of a careless act of the doctor may often be termed as accident, because the word 'accident', as construed in judicial decisions is an unlooked for mishap or untoward event not expected or designed but that which is something fortuitous and unexpected, yet the liability even for a careless act becomes criminal if carelessness and *mens rea* coincide.

6. Maxims

(*a*) *Mental element in negligence*

Mental element is an essential element in most of the forms of criminal negligence under criminal law, mere act of a person is not enough to create his liability. Guilty mind or *mens rea* is also required. A man, therefore, is not ordinarily punishable for something which he never meant, or the consequences of which he could not foresee.

The word intention or mental element is used in the sense of a design to produce damage complained of. It implies an antecedent knowledge of the injurious consequence and desire to produce it. When a person commits negligence with a mental condition of this kind, his liability is clear and does not need any discussion. The question whether the consequence is direct or remote does not arise, as a consequence which is intended is not remote in law.

Mental element or *mens rea* is essentially a culpable mental state, but if the result of a careless act amounts to an offense, there is no difficulty in presuming a culpable mental state, because as the Supreme Court has held in *Nath Lal* v *State of M.P.* AIR 1966 SC 43, that it is sound rule of construction adopted in England and adopted in India to construe a statutory provision creating an offence in conformity with a common law rather than against it unless the statue expressly by necessary implication has excluded *mens rea,* and it can be excluded only where it is absolutely clear that implementation of the object of the statute would otherwise be defeated, and when *mens rea* is in-built in the concept of negligence leading to an act amounting to an offence, and, as held by the High Court of Andhra Pradesh in case of *N. Panduranga Rao* v *State of A.P.* 1975 (II) A.P., any contravention of law would be punishable even if it is not done knowingly or intentionally and if the conservation is proved, the punishment follows.

(*b*) *Res ipsa loquitur*

In certain cases, mere fact of the injury or accident is *prima facie* evidence of negligence. It is usual to refer to such cases by a Latin phrase, *Res ipsa loquitur*, the thing itself speaks '*Res ipsa loquitur*' means thing speak for themselves. The leading illustration is *Scoot* v *London Dock Co.* (1865) 3H and C 566, where the plaintiff, a custom officer, went into the defendant's docks on business and in passing from one door way to another, six bags of sugar which were hung by a chain fell on him. It was held that on these facts negligence of the defendants servant would be inferred. The rules applicable to such cases was stated thus, "where the thing is shown to be under the management of the defendant on his servants, and the accident in such as in the ordinary course of things does not happen if those who have the management use proper care, it affords reasonable evidence, in the absence of explanation by the defendant, that the accident arose from the want of care."

In India, the rule has been applied in several cases.

In *State of Punjab* v *Modern Cultivators* AIR 1965 SC 17, the Supreme Court held that the Punjab State Government is liable in damages for negligence in the maintenance of an irrigation canal under its management resulting in a breach of canal and subsequent flooding of the plaintiff's land. It was for the Punjab State Government to show how the breach occurred and this was not done.

The medical negligence, if a negligent act is done by a doctor he is to be held liable for the deed. In such cases the damage is caused to be patient is so obvious that no proof as to the negligent act of the doctor is required. While discharging this burden, the plaintiff needs to satisfy the court of the truth in his allegations, after which the onus shifts to the defendant to prove his innocence. For the application of the maxim of *res ipsa loquitur*, the following the principles of the utmost importance:

(*i*) Common norms suggesting that the injury in itself cannot happen without negligence,

(*ii*) The cause of the incident must be unknown or unascertainable.

The maxim *res ipsa loquitur* applies not only to a case where the thing that inflicted the damage was under the same sole management and the control of the defendant but also where it is under the sole management and control of someone for whom he is responsible for whom he has a right of control. The thing need not to be in exclusive control provided that evidence shows outside influence of a remote possibility.

The principal of *res ipsa loquitur* only shifts the onus of proof, in that a *prima facie* case is assumed to be made out, throwing on the defendant the task of providing that he was not negligent, that does not mean that he must prove how and why the accident happened, it is sufficient if he satisfies the court that he personally was not negligent. Even if the defendant gave no rebutting evidence but a reasonable explanation equally consistent with the presence as well as with the absence of negligence the presumptions or inferences based on *res ipsa loquitur* cannot further be sustained.

The maxim does not apply when the facts are sufficiently known. But this does not necessarily mean that negligence is not proved for the facts found may by themselves give rise to an inference of negligence.

The offences concerned with medical rashness or/and negligence are only few where *mens rea* is implied if negligence is proved whereas others concerned with this profession are those where there is no element of negligence but are committed with the full deliberation to which the principal of *res ipsa loquitur* can have no application.

(*c*) *Negligence per se*

Negligence *per se* means where a person is guilty of negligence no further proof is needed. Negligence *per se* is defined in Black Law Dictionary as – conduct, whether of action or omission, which may be declared and treated as negligence without any argument or proof as to the particular surrounding circumstances either because it is in violation of a statute or valid municipal ordinance, or because it is so properly opposed to the dictates of common prudence that it can be said without hesitation or doubt that no careful person would have been guilty of it. As a general rule, the violations of a public duty, enjoined by law for the protection of person or property, so constitutes.

The Supreme Court of India has applied the principal of Negligence *per se* in a case of *Poonam Verma* v *Ashwini Patel* AIR 1996 SC 2111, where respondent, *Ashwini Patel*, a homeopath doctor registered as medical practitioner and entitled to practice in Homeopathy only, treated the patients suffering from viral fever and then typhoid with allopathic medicines, and the patient died within two weeks. The doctor was held to be negligent and liable to compensate the wife of the deceased for the death of her husband on the ground that the doctor who was entitled to practice in homeopathy only, was under the statutory duty not to enter the field of any other system of medicine and since he trespassed into prohibited field and prescribed the allopathic medicine to the patient causing the death, his conduct amounted to Negligence *per se* actionable in civil law.

In *(Dr) L D Bajaj (Fauji Doctor) (Cancer Hospital)* v *Hari Chand* (2003) I CPR 328 (Pun) where a cancer patient was treated by a doctor was not qualified to treat that disease (being not MBBS), it was held that this amounted to Negligence *Per Se*. A compensation of ₹80,000 was awarded.

(d) Actio personalis moriter cum persona

The maxim *actio personalis moriter cum persona* means that personal right of action dies with the person. They destroys the right of action. The complainant filed a complaint against a doctor for medical blunder but the doctor died during the pendency of the proceedings, the maxim *actio personalis moritur cum persona* applied and destroyed right of action.

In a case *G. Jayaprakash* v *State of Andhra Pradesh* AIR 1977 AP 20, the Supreme Court held "The death of the doctor extinguished his liability for damages and the suit against him stood abated. The maxim "*actio personalis moritur cum persona*" applied to the case."

In *Melepuratch Sankunni Ezhuthassan* v *Thekittel Gopalankully Nair* (1986) 1 SCC 118, during the pendency of appeal filed by plaintiff in case of defamation suit the defendant had died, the Supreme Court held that his legal representatives could not be brought on record as the cause of action stood extinguished.

In *Winfield Law of Tort* book at page 740, 8th Edition, the following passage occurs: "In case of lawful surgical operation in general negatives the liability. But in case where actionable negligence is committed by the doctor which amounts to a personal wrong done by him, he may be liable for damages. But his death extinguishes his liability in tort and the right to sue also gets extinguished."

7. Medical negligence under IPC

Offences due to medical negligence under the Indian Penal Code are as follows:

(*i*) Section 304A — causing death by medical negligence by medical practitioner.

(*ii*) Section 336 — act endangering the life of personal safety of others.

(*iii*) Section 337 — causing hurt by act endangering life or personal safety of others.

(*iv*) Section 338 — causing grievous hurt by act endangering life or safety of others.

(*v*) Sections 269 and 270 — a negligent act of medical practitioner for infection of disease endangers to life.

(*vi*) Section 287 — negligent conduct with respect to medical machinery and equipment.

The other offenses where medical negligence is not involved but submitted with deliberation are:

(*i*) Section 312 — causing miscarriage.

(*ii*) Section 313 — causing miscarriage without woman's consent.

(*iii*) Section 314 — deaths caused by act done with intent to cause miscarriage if act done without woman's consent.

(*iv*) Section 315 — act done with intent to prevent child being born alive or to cause it to die after birth.

(*v*) Section 316 — causing death of quick unborn child by act amounting to culpable homicide.

(*vi*) Section 318 — concealment of birth by secret disposal of dead body.

These are offenses where the defence of good faith and *bona fides*, otherwise a valid defence for the doctor, will be of no avail.

8. Defence of good faith

The concept of good faith in relation to criminal activity has been couched in negative terms whereas in relation to civil liability has a positive phraseology. In criminal liability 'good faith' refers to due care and attention which must be considered with reference to general circumstances, the capacity, skill and intelligence of the medical practitioner. While an honest blunderer may act in good faith in relation to civil liability, he can never be said to act in good faith in relation to criminal liability for being negligent. In civil liability the concept of the good faith lays stress only on one aspect, that is of honesty, but in relation to criminal liability the concept places emphasis on two aspects, namely, belief, due care and attention.

The concept of good faith has its own impact on other defenses available to doctor raising a plea of any general exception under the Penal Code.

Section 80 of the Indian Penal Code states nothing is an offence which is done by the accident or misfortune and without criminal intention or knowledge in the doing of a lawful act in lawful manner by lawful means and with proper care and caution.

Section 81 of the Indian Penal Code states that nothing is an offence merely by reason of its being done with the knowledge that hit is likely to cause harm, if it be done without any criminal intention to cause harm, and in good faith, for the purpose of preventing or avoiding other harm to person or property, and it is a question of fact in such a case whether the harm to be prevented or avoided was of such a nature and so imminent as to justify or excuse the risk of doing the act with due knowledge that it was likely to cause harm.

Sections 88, 89 and 93 have a direct bearing on the medical profession.

Section 88 is not intended to cause death, is an offense, by reason of any harm which it may cause, or being intended by the doer to cause, or be known by the doer to be likely to cause, to any person whose benefit it is done in good faith, and who has given consent, whether express or implied to suffer that harm, or to take risk of that harm.

Section 89 states that nothing which is done in good faith for the benefit of a person under twelve years of age, or of unsound mind, by or by consent, either express or implied, of the guardian or other person having careful charge of that, is an offense by reason of any harm which it may cause, or be intended by the doer to cause or is known by the doer to be likely to cause to that person.

It must be noted that section 91 of the Indian Penal Code excludes from the purview of the exceptions carved out under sections 88 and 89 such acts which are and otherwise offenses independently of the harm which may be caused or be intended to be caused, or be known likely to cause to the person giving consent or whose behalf the consent as contemplated under sections 88 and 89 as has been given.

Thus causing miscarriage, unless caused in good faith for the purpose of saving the life of woman, or unless protected under the Medical Termination of Pregnancy Act, 1971, is an offense independently of any harm which it may cause or to be intended to cause to the woman. Therefore, it is not an offense "by reason of such harm" and the consent of the woman or her guardian to the causing of such miscarriage does not justify the act.

Section 92 of the Indian Penal Code states that nothing is an offense by reason of any harm which it may cause to a person for whose benefit it is done in good faith, even without the person consent, if the circumstances are such that it is impossible for that person to signify consent, or if that person is incapable of giving his consent and has no guardian or other in lawful charge of him from whom it is possible to obtain consent in time for the thing to be done with benefit.

Section 93 of the Indian Penal Code states that no communication in good faith, is an offence by reason of any harm to the person to whom it is made, if it is made for the benefit of the person.

The element of good faith is an essential ingredient almost all the above referred expectations and therefore, to escape the criminal liability, the burden to prove good faith shall always rest on the doctor himself for the reason that:

(*i*) the definition of the good faith had been couched in negative phraseology, therefore, the doctor will be required to prove the positive of it,

(*ii*) section 105 of the Evidence Act, 1872 has specifically place the burden of proving the particular exception on the person who plead to avoid criminal liability on the basis of that exception.

9. Compensation under RTI and IP.C

Compensation for loss or injury caused to the consumer is the most common relief provided under Consumer Protection Act, 1986. The term 'compensation' is used to indicate that constitute or is regarded an equivalent or recompense for loss of privation under section 14(1)(*d*) of the Consumer Protection Act, the opposite party may be directed to pay such amount of compensation to the consumer for any injury suffered by the consumer due to the negligence of the opposite party. The claim must be substantially by sufficient evidence and the composition has to be addressed not arbitrarily but on the basis of well accepted legal principals.

The principles of law permits that the damages can be recovered only for the direct consequences and not for the indirect or remote consequences of a wrongful act.

The Supreme Court in *Charan Singh* v *Healing Touch Hospital* (2000) 7 SCC 668 has observed as follows:

> "While quantifying damages, Consumer Forums are required to make an attempt to serve the ends of justice so that compensation is awarded, in an established case, which not only serves the purpose of recompensing the individual, but which also at the same time, aims to bring about a qualitative change in the attitude of service provider. Indeed, calculation of damages depends on the facts and circumstances of each case. No hard and fast rule can be laid down for universal application. While awarding compensation, a consumer forum has to take account all the relevant factors and assess compensation on the basis of accepted legal principals, on moderation."

The National Commission has jurisdiction, without pecuniary limitations, to award proper compensation, even less than the one claimed in a given case, depending upon the established fact and circumstances of the particular case and the evidence led by the parties.

The District Forums and the State Commission on the other hand, have pecuniary jurisdictional limitations for granting compensation beyond their jurisdictional limits.

Compensation under criminal liability of Medical Professionals

A doctor who is criminally liable may also be liable for compensation to the aggrieved person.

Section 357 of the Code of Criminal Procedure, 1973 provides also for award of compensation, out of fine if imposed as sentence or part of sentence, or otherwise, in addition to the sentence, imposed in case a doctor to held criminally liable for any offence. Medical negligence being both a tort as well as a crime, the condition that compensation for criminal liability can be awarded only in such cases where compensation can be recovered by civil process gets fulfilled in cases involving criminal negligence.

Sub-section (1) of section 357 deals with a situation when a court imposes a fine or a sentence of which fine also forms a part. Imposition of fine is a statutory requirement. If no fine is imposed, sub-section (1) of section 357 has no application.

Sub-section (3) of section 357 deals with a situation where the fine does not form part of the sentence imposed by the court and in such case, the court when passing a judgment can order the accused persons to pay by way of compensation such amount as may be specified in the order to the person who has suffered a lose or injury by reason of the act or which the accused has been convicted and sentenced.

Sub-section (5) of section 357 deals with a situation when the court fixes the compensation in any subsequent civil suit relating to the same matter and while awarding such compensation, the civil court is required to take into account any sum paid or recovered under the section.

In a case, where a homoeopath doctor conducted abortion and caused the death of the woman. He was convicted under section 304 of IPC and sentenced to four years rigorous imprisonment and to a fine of ₹5,000. The Supreme Court in appeal reduced the sentence of imprisonment to two months and enhanced to fine to ₹1 lakh. *Dr. Jacob George* v *State of Kerala* (1994) 3 SCC 430.

CHAPTER 5
Categories of Cases on Medical Negligence

SYNOPSIS

1. Abortion

The compounder of a Primary Health Center conducted abortion of 27 years old wife of complainant. He conducted abortion without taking proper precaution and administering injection without there being any prescription. The wife of complainant died. Held that compounder was not qualified to perform the operation and responsible for death. He rendered deficient medical service and ₹1 lakh awarded as compensation. [*Kalu Ram* v *Kana Ram, Compounder* 2006 II CPJ 243]

Where incomplete abortion was performed, resulting remnants left in uterus. Held that principles of *res ipsa loquitur* would apply and ₹2.5 lakh awarded as compensation. [*Shakila Sathanandam* v *Dr. S.S. Kodmani* 2005 III CPJ 121]

2. Adverse inference

It was responsibility of the hospital to have ensured the presence of dóctor, their employee at the relevant time before the commission. An adverse inference had to be drawn against hospital for having failed to do so. [*Sushma Sharma* v *Bombay Hospital* 2007 II CPJ 9]

Non-supply of relevant by hospital regarding treatment of pain. Adverse inference could possibly be drawn with regard to deficiency in Service in service. [*S.R. Shivprakash* v *Wockhardt Hospital Limited* 2006 II CPJ 123]

3. Amputation

Hip replacement operation of complainant performed result no sensation below left knee due to development of gangrene. Her left leg from above knee amputated. Thereafter two more operations performed on her. Order of the State Commission directing reimbursement of ₹1,11,000 and damages of ₹1,50,000 with interest @ 12% held justified. [*Ghanta Mohan Lakshmi* v *Dr. C.V. Ratnam* 2003 IV CPJ 12 (NC)]

Surgery done on finger without ensuring that the patient's blood sugar level is in permissible limit, finger had to be amputating due to development of gangrene later on. Doctor contended that said surgery was never done and only prescribes medicine for genital infection but it was not based on evidence. It was held that there was deficiency in service. [*P.K. Ghosh* v *Pradyut Rakshit* 2006 II CPJ 247]

Where doctor negligently administered 'Novallgin', infection resulting in amputation of the right leg. Compensation of ₹1,25,000 awarded. [*Gursewak Singh* v *Dr. Jaskaran Singh* 1996 III CPJ 300]

Where injection administered to complainant at wrong side Thumb, index finger and middle finger amputated due to development of gangrene. The injection given by the doctor was proved. The doctor was negligent. Order of District Forum directing payment of ₹65,363 by way of compensation to the complainant upheld. [*Dr. Gian Chand Aggarwal* v *Darshana Devi* 2002 I CPJ 351]

4. Anaesthesia

Anaesthesia administered it to a child by the Anaesthetist at 10:00 AM and 10:30 AM and child was pulse less. Operation notes silent about the names of the doctors. It is the hospital, which would be accountable for whatever happens in the hospital. Hospital directed to pay compensation of ₹3 lakh with the 18% interest. [*Meenakshi Mission Hospital and Research Center* v *Samuraj* 2005 I CPJ 33]

Anaesthesia administered by eye surgeon resulting death of patient, Held that any long practice without authority will not legalize his practice. A sum of ₹2.5 lakh awarded as compensation. [*Vinod Prasad Nautiyal* v *Savitri Uniyal* 2005 III CPJ 126]

Where Cerebrospinal Fluid test conducted without administering Anaesthesia. Held that hospital and doctors were negligent in performing LP. [*Nirmal Kumar Jain* v *Indraprastha Appollo Hospitals* 2007 IV CPJ 274]

Anaesthesia administered without taking due care and without conducting the necessary pre-operative and pre-anaesthetic tests. There was no emergency. As a result of negligence, the child is in vegetative state and will remain so for the rest of his life. Respondents held jointly and severally liable to pay compensation of ₹3 lakh to complainants. [*Karan Veer Singh* v *Garg Nursing Home* 2007 I CLT 319 (MP)]

Anaesthesia administered for performing hernia operation without conducting pre-operative tests. Few crepts and rhonchi developed within ten minutes after restarting surgery and patient died during operation. Medical negligence established. The patient was not properly prepared for Anaesthesia. [*Bhanupal* v *Dr. Prakash Padode* 2000 II CPJ 384]

Their family planning operation performed without calling the anaesthetist who was called subsequently. The patient died during the course of operation. This would show negligence of the concerned doctor. Order of the District Forum awarding compensation of ₹4 lakh upheld. Order of the District Forum regarding payment @ 18% interest set aside. [*Dr. A. Athilakshmi* v *A. Ravi* 2007 new I CPJ 177]

Where deceased aged 21 years brought to the hospital for a simple procedure called encirclement of the cervix by making sutures at the mouth of uterus to retain pregnancy and prevent miscarriage. She died in the same hospital within 24 hours of the procedure. The doctors who have performed postmortem have clearly stated that the cause of death was due to the result spinal Anaesthesia. The treating doctors have failed to explain the cause of death stating that even today they could not determine the same and the state that it would be an act of God. Finding of the State Commission of medical negligence on the part of appellant-OP upheld compensation of ₹3 lakh awarded in case enhanced to ₹6 lakh. The complainant held entitled to costs fixed at ₹50,000. [*Sathy M. Pillot* v *S. Sharma* 2007 IV CPJ 131]

Where the husband of complainant had some injury and deformity on his right arm for which he was operated upon by doctor. He died during the operation. The complainants alleged that amount of drug used for Anaesthesia was more than maximum and death was direct result of such use of drugs. The proper monitoring of the patient was not done.

The State Commission held that Physician-cardiologist negligent both for acts of omission and commission. The State Commission awarded ₹3,60,000 as compensation, ₹40,000 for loss of estate and ₹15,000 for medical and other expenses. [*Aruna Ben D. Kothari* v *Navdeep Clinic* 1996 III CPJ 605 (Guj)]

5. Ayurvedic doctor/RMP

Where daughter of complainant aged about 4½ years was taken to an Ayurvedic doctor whose qualification was DAM and DMS in the Ayurvedic System for treatment of Jaundice. He got her urine test and prescribed some allopathic and Ayurvedic drugs, but no improvement occurred and she was shifted to medical college, but ultimately expired.

The State Commission held that he was not competent to prescribe allopathic medicines. Doctor was held negligent and the compensation of ₹25,000 awarded by District Forum was enhanced to ₹40,000 [*Dr. S.N. Namboodiri* v *Haneefa* 1998 I CPJ 389 (Ker.)]

6. Ayurvedic Doctor

Where complainant had abdominal pain and had consulted a registered medical practitioner in Ayurveda. Doctor administered injection containing four medicines namely Fortwin, Calmpose, Anafortan and Morphen IV in his right arm. Following this, he developed severe pain in fingers and ultimately his three fingers in right hand had to be amputated in CMC Ludhiyana, due to development of gangrene.

The State Commission awarded in total ₹70,007.50 against medicine and hospital charges ₹5,800 as taxi bills and ₹50,000 for physical handicap. State Commission held that he was not competent to administer injection containing allopathic medicine. [*Khairati Lal* v *Kewal Krishan* 1998 I CPJ 181 (Punj)]

7. AIDS

Where the complainant was operated for connection of atrial septal defect and mitral stenosis. During surgery, patient BP came down below the danger level and it became necessary to give four units of blood. The first three units were tested for HIV infection, but the fourth unit had to be given despite not being tested for HIV due to urgency of the patient's condition. The blood in the fourth unit was later on found to be HIV positive, due to which the patient became infected with AIDS virus, and later on her husband was and her small child born after the operation was infected with AIDS.

On the issue of the maintainability of the complaint it was held that as the hospital is a charitable hospital run by the Christian Mission Aid as no consideration was paid the complainant is not a consumer.

On compassionate grounds, the hospital offered to provide free treatment to wife, her husband and child and also offered employment to her husband. [*Sunita Vasant Heganawar* v *Miraj Medical Centre* 1994 II CPJ 544]

Where blood bank collected the blood from donor and gave a donor card stating that "HIV I and II negative". On the basis of the said report, the said unit of blood was transfused by the hospital to a boy and the boy was discharged from hospital. As there was no improvement, the boy was again taken to the hospital. Blood of both parents of patient tested and the report was "HIV (I and II) negative". The blood of donor was found HIV positive on subsequent tests. From this fact, it is clear that the child got the virus transmitted through transfusing one unit of blood.

The State Commission held that blood bank was deficient in service and a compensation of ₹1 lakh with cost ₹5,000 (*J. Gopal* v *Nagarjuna Blood Bank* 2003 II CPJ 434 (AP)]

Where the fact that the appellant was HIV positive disclosed by the hospital, the appellant claimed for damages. Applying the provisions of sections 269 and

270 of IPC it was held that appellant was not entitled to damages. According to sections 269 and 270 of IPC, if a person suffering from dreadful disease "AIDS" knowingly marries a woman and thereby transmits infection to that woman he would be guilty of offence. [*Dr. Tokugha Yepthomi* v *Apollo Hospital Enterprises Limited* 1999 I CPJ 11]

Where blood of HIV positive donor transfused into the body of complainant without testing the blood. Resultantly, complainant contacted with HIV infection. Complainant and his wife could not lead a normal marriage life. Medical negligence established. Opposite party directed to pay compensation of ₹2 lacs with 10% interest p.a. to complainant. [*S. Murlidhar* v *Basappa Memorial Hospital* 2005 I CPJ 237]

In the facts of the case, it was open to the hospital or the doctor concerned to reveal such information to person related to the girl whom appellant intended to marry. She had a right to know about the HIV positive status of the appellant. Court further declaring in general as to what the rights and obligations arise in such context as to right to privacy and confidentiality. Observation made by the Court held to be uncalled for. [*Mr. 'X'* v *Hospital 'Z'* 2003 I CPZ 14]

Blood supplied by the second opposite party for transfusion had HIV antibodies, which resulted in contacting HIV infection, which after gestation period became full-blown AIDS and patient succumbed to her terminal illness. Second opposite party had failed to carry out the test required to ensure that the blood was not infected. Rules 66(A) of the Drugs and Cosmetics rules clearly stipulates a mandatory condition of conducting HIV antibody test before certifying the purity of blood which was not complied with. Held that this is a clear-cut case of medical negligence. A consolidated sum of ₹4 lacs as compensation with 6% interest from the date of filing complaint awarded to be paid jointly and severally by the respondents. [*M. Chinnaiyan* v *Sri Gokulam Hospital* 2007 III CPJ 228]

8. Blood transfusion

Finding of the State Commission that there has been serious deficiency and negligence on the part of the PGI and its attending Doctors/staff for transferring wrong blood group to the patient which caused death of the wife of complainant No. 1 upheld by National Commission. [*PGI, Chandigarh* v *Jaspal Singh* 2000 III CPJ 32 (NC)]

Where multi-organ failure and death occurred due to transfusion of wrong blood group to patient, Error and negligence on the part of Pathological department of hospital established. Hospital as well as doctor held liable. ₹6 lac awarded as compensation. [*Ramswaroop Singh and others* v *S. Diwan* 2005 III CPJ (Chhat.)]

Where contaminated blood transfused to 17 years old complainant resulting in attack of Hepatitis, Hospital could not produce satisfactory explanation, Held that there is a clear medical negligence on the part of opposite party. Direction issued to pay cost of medical treatment already incurred and cost of further medical treatment. [*Shefali Bhargava* v *Indraprastha Apollo Hospital* 2003 I CPJ 216]

Where Petitioner's wife was admitted in S.M.S. Hospital Jaipur for the operation of removal of gallstone. She was operated upon for removal of gallstone. The medical staff working under the operating surgeon was advised giving blood transfusion of blood group O+ to the wife of the practitioner. A wrong blood group B+ in place of O+ transfused. The practitioner's wife lost her eyesight and died after few hours. The cause of death as shown in the death certificate is cardio respiratory arrest. The final enquiry submitted established that the death occurred due to transfusion of wrong group of blood to the patient. Thus, the death of patient was because of the negligence and carelessness in performance of their duties by the doctors and the servants of the hospital *i.e.* state of Rajasthan.

The State of Rajasthan is directed to pay ₹3,04,000 to the petitioner as a compensation for the loss of his wife. [*R.P. Sharma* v *State of Rajasthan* AIR 2002 Raj 104]

9. Blood transfusion — Caesarean delivery case

The deceased was admitted Nursing home with labour pains and delivered her second baby. There was profuse bleeding after the delivery. When the blood group was tested it was found to be 'A negative' and when 'A negative' blood was not available 'A positive' blood was given to the patient with dopamine drip. One of the reason for acute renal failure is transfusion of matchless blood. From the record it was not found whether this aspect was kept in mind when 'A positive' blood was given instead of 'A negative'.

There was lack of diligence on the part of respondent. Doctors should have anticipated blood requirement in such case and kept blood of required group ready failure of which amounted to negligence. Compensation of ₹3,00,000 with interest @ 12% p.a. and cost ₹2,000 awarded. [*Katra Satyanarayana* v *Lakshmi Nursing Home* 2003 II CPJ. 262]

10. Blood transfusion — Failure to cross match

Where blood brought from blood bank transfused to patient without cross checked. Blood Transfusion was discontinued after 50 ml of blood transfusion when the patient developed chills and other two complications. Patient when showed reactions soon sifted to super specialty hospital and got treatment and subsequently died after 5 days due to cardiac arrest. The complainant has not been able to prove through expert evidence or any other evidence that there was mismatched blood transfusion and that it caused of his wife.

Therefore the order of the District Forum is modified to the extent of finding deficiency in service is not cross matching of the blood before transfusion by the appellant and direct to appellant to pay ₹20,000 instead of awarding ₹88,000 for the negligence amounting to deficiency in service. [*Medical Superintendent, Geetha Maternity and Nursing Home* v *Shaik Mahboob Saheb* 2003 (6) CLD 736 (AP SCDRC)]

11. Blood transfusion — Infected

Where the complainant's wife suffered because of the transfusion of blood containing hepatitis virus subsequently the complainant himself was infected, a compensation of ₹20,000 was allowed. [*Haresh Kumar* v *Sunil Blood Bank* 1992 I CPJ 645]

Where the patient was suffering from the stage renal disease and ultimately died four years after the treatment complained of and there was no evidence to link the blood transfusion with any of the resultant complications, the order of the State Commission for payment of compensation of two lac rupees for deficiency in service because of the alleged wrong group blood transfusion was struck down by the National Commission. [*Calcutta Medical Research Institute* v *Bimalesh Chatterjee* 1999 I CPR 3 NC]

12. Blood pressure

The patient died due to cardio-respiratory failure while being operated upon for fixation of broken bone of the right arm. The allegation in the complaint filed by the legal representatives of the deceased was that the cause of death was excessive use of drugs at the time of Anaesthesia. Admittedly, no postmortem was done and for this adverse was drawn against the doctors. Medical records showed that at the time of cardiac examination of the patient before the operation, his blood pressure was reading 150/100 mm Hg and associated ST.T. changes in Anterolateral leads in the ECG. Thus, the blood pressure was on the high side. All doctors were held jointly liable to pay ₹4,15,000 as compensation. [*Arunaben D. Kothari* v *Navdeep Clinic* 1996 II CPR 20]

13. Blood Group Report

Report given by practitioner that blood group of a complainant was AB+ whereas it was AB-. Whether harm came to the patient or not would not be a criteria. It is failure on the part of the petitioner to take due care to return correct finding. Direction to pay a compensation of ₹25,000 along with the cost of ₹2,000 by District Forum as affirmed by State Commission requires no interference. [*Chandigarh Clinical Laboratory* v *Jagjeet Kaur* 2007 IV CPJ 157]

14. Breast Cancer

The breast of patient was removed on the basis of wrong medical report. However, there was no cancer in the subsequent report. It was held that doctor should not have persisted for operation on the first and primary report only. He should have got conformity report from some pathologist also. There was medical negligence on the part of doctor. Awarded compensation of ₹63,500 State Commission justified it — no excessive. [*Uttaranchal Forest Hospital* v *Raisan* 2004 I CPJ 257]

15. Burden of proof

Onus to prove medical negligence lies on the complainant. [*Baban Rao Yadav* v *Lion Tarachand Bappa Hospital* 2003 I CPJ 36]

Burden of proof of medical negligence is very heavy on the complainant. [*Nita Singla* v *Dr. Karnail Singh* 1998 II CLT 118]

Burden of proving that the doctors were negligent rests with the complainant. [*Indira Kartha* v *Dr. Mathew Samuel Kalariekal* 2002 I CPR 171]

Allegation that the doctor has been negligent in treating the patient and on account of his fault; some injury has been caused to the aggrieved person. Burden to prove this fact is on the complainant. [*Manohar Lal* v *Dr. Ajai Kumar Jain* 1999 II CLT 226]

Where a patient was suffering from a blood clot, Treating doctor never consulted the Neuro Physician or a Neurologist and ultimately patient died the case of due care and caution of good faith in treating patient. Held that there was negligence in treating the patient her ailment was allowed to aggravate, possibility of surgical intervention to remove the blood clot from brain was not explored which ultimately led to death. A sum of ₹3.Lakh in all with cost of ₹15,000 awarded to be paid by the hospital. [*T. Rama Rao* v *Vijay Hospital,* 2008 I CLT 582 (NC): 2008 I CPJ 170]

Where wife of complainant operated upon hysterectomy and ultimately wife died. The case sheet not given to the complainant by appellant doctor despite several requests. They were only filed during the course of arguments, which motivated the State Commission to take adverse note to their conduct. These records were written at one stretch, long after the events have occurred, not as, and when events took place. No test conducted before surgery. Held that the complainant has successfully discharged the initial burden that the doctor was negligent and as a result of said negligence, the patient died. The doctor concerned has not discharged the burden to prove that there was no negligence in her treatment. [*D. Rama Rajyam* v *P.K. Vasudeva Rao* 2007 III CPJ 295]

16. Cancer — Breast Cancer

The breast of patient was removed on the basis of wrong medical report. However, there was no cancer in the subsequent report. It was held that doctor should not have persisted for operation on the first and primary report only. He should have got conformity report from some pathologist also. There was medical negligence on the part of hospital. Complainant awarded compensation of ₹63,500 State Commission justified it. [*Uttaranchal Forest Hospital* v *Raisan* 2004 I CPJ 257]

17. Cancer — Advertisement

An advertisement was published promising cure of any type of disease with guarantee. Complainant suffering from throat cancer approached for treatment. However, same not cured by respondent as guaranteed. Held that respondent was not qualified enough to cure patient like complainant. Complainant entitled to compensation. [*L.D. Bajaj* (*Dr.*) v *Hari Chand* 2003 III CPJ 49]

18. Cancer — Wrong report

Where review of slides by other doctors showing that complainant was not suffering from cancer. Medical negligence held and order awarding compensation on ₹1 lac affirmed. [*Dayanand Medical College and Hospital, Ludhiyana. Through its President/Secretary* v *Jugal Kishore Syal* 2003 III CPR 450]

19. Caesarean operation

Where the deceased was admitted nursing home with labour pains and delivered her second baby. There was profuse bleeding after the delivery, when the blood grouping was tested it was found to be 'A' negative and when 'A' negative blood was not available 'A' positive blood was given to the patient with dopamine drip. One of the reason for acute renal failure is transfusion of matchless blood.

There was lack of diligence on the part of respondent. Compensation of ₹3,00,000 with interest @ 12% p.a. and cost ₹2,000 awarded. [*Katra Satyanarayana* v *Lakshmi Nursing Home* 2003 II CPJ 262]

Where pair of scissors left in abdomen during caesarean operation. Compensation of ₹2,000 awarded by state Commission enhanced to ₹10,000. [*Sau Madurai* v *Dr. Rajendra* 1996 III CPC 328]

Where Caesarean Operation was performed without necessary arrangement and tests. Due to excessive bleeding blood transfusion required. However, required blood group was not available. Required blood group arranged too late. District Forum held opposite party doctors were guilty of medical negligence. Direction for award of compensation of ₹99,000 upheld. [*Urmila Upadhyay* v *A.K. Pandey* 2003 I CPC 328]

Where complainant was operated upon for caesarean operation. Thereafter she complained of pain and irritation in the lower abdominal region. From the report of the X-ray, ultrasound and CT scanning established that the foreign body stood lodged in the system of complainant. The foreign object was removed in the very hospital where she was operated. Doctor had a duty to act with a reasonable degree, care and skill which element is missing in this case. State Commission awarding compensation of ₹1 lakh. [*Dr. Satya Atri* v *Smt. Shashi Sharma* 2003 (1) CPJ 612]

20. Caesarean operation — Sterilization operation

Where sterilization operation performed without consent, medical negligence held and ₹75,000 awarded as compensation. [*Dr. Janki S. Kumar* v *Mrs. Sarafunnisa* 2000 I CPJ 66]

21. Caesarean operation — Sponge not removed

Where sponge left in the abdomen and not removed after caesarean operation. The foreign item was removed by another operation. Held medical negligence and awarded ₹1 lakh compensation. [*Harvinder Kaur* v *Sushma Chawla* 2001 III CPJ 143]

22. Caesarean operation — Excessive bleeding

The patient died while delivering her baby in a caesarean operation due to excessive bleeding. It was observed that in spite of the fact that the patient was under the regular care of the doctor, the relatives were not informed about the emergency. Nor was any blood arranged to meet any contingency. The doctor failed to be present for cross-examination. There was a postmortem report regarding excessive abdominal bleeding. Held that there was medical negligence in taking due care and advance precaution. Compensation of ₹2,35,000 was granted. [*Devendra Kantilal Nayak* v *Kalyaniben Dhruv* 1996 II CPR 36]

23. Caesarean operation — Foreign matter left

The complainant operated upon for caesarian operation some foreign matter left inside the operated area. That being a negligence in itself a compensation of ₹2.lakh awarded. [*Rohini Pritam Kabadi* v *R.T. Kulkarni* (*Dr.*) (1996) III CPJ 441 Kant]

24. Cataract operation

Where a cataract operation was performed without conducting the pre-and post-operational test resulted in complete retinal detachment, which caused loss of vision of complainant permanently. Held medical negligence and compensation awarded. [*Dr. Vivek Sahay* v *Ajai Prasad* 2003 I CPC 332]

25. Cataract operation — Vision test

Enquiry by a committee of three eminent doctors, Report stated that out of 52 cases operated in the New Operation Theater, 14 patient developed infection in operated eye. Held that there was deficiency in service on the part of the hospital and the staff is not maintaining the autoclave's equipments and other materials, which were used before and after the operation. Opposite Parties No. 5, 6 and 7 held jointly and severally liable to pay compensation. A lump sum amount of ₹5 lakh would be appropriate compensation in this case. [*Sarwati Ali Khan* v *Prof. (Dr.) R. Gogi* 2007 III CPJ 179]

26. Cataract operation — Loss of vision

Where doctor was failed to diagnose the problem correctly as endophthalmitis which is a complication of the surgery performed by him and due to his failure to prognosis the disease the complainant paid heavy price and lost total vision in her operated eye. District Forum rightly awarded compensation of ₹50,000. [*Dr. A. Siabada Gaud* v *L. Thomas* 2002 I CPJ 199 (AP)]

Complainant's contract operation was performed by the appellant doctor. Complainant paid ₹9,000 for the operation to the doctor. However, the vision lost after the operation. [*Ashpal Singh Kohli* v *Sher Singh* 2002 I CPJ 73 (Del)]

27. Cataract operation — Complete loss of vision

Where doctor him-self admitting that it was not a case of operation, but he conducted the operation at the asking of the complainant. Deficiency in service held and awarded compensation of ₹50,000 affirmed. [*Dr. S.B. Jain* v *Smt. Munni Devi* 1998 II CPJ 239]

28. Cardiology

Acute Anterolateral wall myocardial infection with diabetes mellitus. High-risk patient with very high blood sugar on insulin even while shifting to opposite party hospital. No test for urine acetone done to ascertain Ketoacidosis, which was the case with the patient, and Ketoacidosis could be reversed only with insulin, which was not done, between 7 p.m. When the patient admitted at 8

A.M., the day insulin first administered. Death of the patient at 10 A.M. the same day. Negligence held ₹5 lakh awarded as compensation. [*Bombay Hospital and Medical Research Centre* v *Krishnabehari M. Agarwal* 2004 CLT 468 (Del SCDRC)]

29. Cardiology — Angioplasty

Where angioplasty performed successfully on patient on account of cardiac arrest patient died after three days. Post-operation treatment equally important as the operation itself, doctor, and nursing staff to be alert to meet post-operative complications. Deceased having giddiness falling down in bathroom, was restless and had nausea. Such indications ought to have made the doctors and staff alter at least from ECG examination, which was not done on a pretext that the deceased was sleeping. Deficiency in post-operative care occurred. ₹2 lakh awarded as compensation with interest @ of 6% and ₹10,000 as a costs. [*Sheela Hirba Naik Gaunekar* v *Apollo Hospitals Ltd* 2005 III CPJ 56]

Patient not put on cardio-pulmonary bypass machine in time following cardiac arrest. Opposite party took 30 minutes to put patient on machine but by that inordinate delay blood supply to brain stopped and death due to dead brain. Negligence held. ₹2 lakh awarded as compensation. [*SC Mathur* v *All India Institute of Medical Sciences* 2006 III CPJ 414 (Del)]

30. Cardiology — Staircase climbing exercise

Patient asked to undergo a test to strain his chest by climbing five or six times patient got exhausted, fell down and died due to acute myocardial infarction, staircase exercise not in tune with present day requirement and treadmill test is safer. Opposite party supposed to update his knowledge and not to lag behind other ordinary assiduous and intelligent members of the profession in the knowledge of new advances, discoveries and development in this field. He was supposed to prefer treadmill test to staircase exercise. Negligence held ₹3 lakh awarded as compensation with interest 9% p.a. [*Mohan Laxman Maninakatch* v *Dr. Anil E. Kegal* 2006 III CPJ 427]

31. Compensation — Anaesthesia

Comparison of duties of the Anesthetist relating to monitoring as also the medical record showing that Anesthetist was completely negligent no record of recording of blood pressure during the surgery or any recording of the E.C.G. Surgery could have been delayed in order to ensure that the B.P. is normal at the time of surgery. Award of total compensation of ₹4,15,000 upheld. [*Rashmi Vora* v *Arunaben D. Kothari* 2005 IV CPJ 164 (NC)]

Responding not conducting the necessary pre-operative and pre-anesthetic tests. Performing operation when there was no emergency, not taking due care in administrating the Anesthesia as a result of the negligence, the child is in a vegetative state and will remain so for the rest of his life. Respondents held jointly and severally liable to pay compensation of ₹3 lakh to complainants. [*Karan Veer Singh* v *Garg Nursing Home* 2007 I CLT 319 (MP)]

32. Compensation — Dandruff

The patient suffering from dandruff went to the appellant clinic to get treatment after coming across the advertisement given by appellant. Paid ₹7,000 for said purpose. Treatment resulted in falling of hair making him bald. These are such unfair trade practices, which need to cure with heavy hand. [*The Baby Care* v *Ashok Kumar Solanki* 2005 I CPJ 402 (Del)]

33. Compensation — Blood transfusion

Blood of HIV positive donor transfused into the body of complainant without testing the blood, resultantly, complainant contracted with HIV positive, Medical negligence. Complainant and his wife could not lead a normal life. Opposite party directed to pay compensation of ₹2 lakh with interest @ 10% p.a. to complainant. [*S. Murlidhar* v *Basappa Memorial Hospital* 2005 I CPJ 237]

Transfusion of wrong blood group multi organ failure, Patient died Error and negligence on the part of the pathological department of Hospital. Hospital as well as doctor held liable. ₹6 lakh awarded as compensation. [*Ramswaroop Singh* v *Dr. S. Diwan* 2005 III CPJ 108. (Chhat)]

34. Compensation — Blood Bank

HIV Virus transmitted through transfusing blood collected from donor certified by blood bank under donor card, amount to deficiency in service. Blood bank directed to pay compensation. [*Gopal* v *Nagarjuna Blood Bank Ltd.* 2003 II CPJ 434 (AP)]

35. Compensation — Death of wife — Medical negligence alleged

Without prejudice to the respective contentions to the parties, and without in any way laying the claim of negligence on the shoulders of opposite Party No. 2, the opposite party to pay ₹4 lakh to the minor children of the deceased. [*Akhil Bhartiya Grahak Panchayat* v *Sevaayan Nursing Home* 2001 III CPR 39]

36. Compensation — Deficiency in service

Deficiency in service is not referring the patient (deceased) specifically or advising him to contract the cardiologist and giving him treatment for gastric trouble even after looking at the ECG, which revealed 'Mild Ischemia'. OP required paying compensation. It is just and reasonable to award a compensation of ₹5 lakh to the complainant. [*Indrani Bhattacharjee* v *Farakka Super Thermal Power Project* 2007 III CPJ 354]

37. Compensation — Diabetic patient

Leaving an old diabetic and heart patient without monitoring the blood sugar level under their skilled observation itself is deficiency in service on the part of the OPs. Order of District Forum directing compensation of ₹50,000 along with interest @ 12% p.a. affirmed. [*Guru Teg Bahadur Sahib (Charitable) Hospital* v *Dr. N.K. Nayyar* 2002 I CPJ 395]

38. Compensation — Administration of anti-malarial injection by Ayurvedic practitioner

Medical practitioner on Ayurvedic side holding some certificate of "Vaidya Visharad" Whether authorized to administer medicine by way of injection not clear. Patient suffering from fever, given injection of some Ayurvedic anti-malarial preparation the details as to the compensation of which O.P. failing to furnish injection-causing abscess to the patient. Negligence held. However, no evidence on record to show the negligence of O.P. directed and proximate cause of death of patient. Compensation reduced from ₹1 lakh to ₹20,000. [*Ramesh Mahajan* v *Yashoda Bai Sawale* 2005 III CPR 89]

39. Compensation — Quantum — Enhancement

Death of patient caused by medical negligence proved on record Deceased aged 31 earning ₹4,061 P.M at the time of death leaving behind window, minor child and parents. Compensation of ₹50,000 as awarded by sate commission enhanced to ₹5 Lakh having regard to the provisions of the motor vehicle Act and other relevant provision of general law in considering. How much harassment and loss would have been caused to complainants on account of negligence of O.P. [*Hemina Hitesh Kotak* v *Dr. Ashok Nathwani* 2004 II CPJ II]

40. Consent

Consent of patient not obtained before preparing her for MTP. Consent for husband alone no consent at all. [*Navya S* v *Manipal Northside Hospital* 2006 II CPJ 48 (Karn)]

41. Consent cesarean operation — Sterilization operation

Person who should give consent must be aware of the risk-involved operation performed without consent ₹75,000 awarded as compensation. [*Janki S Kumar* v *Sarafunnisa* 2000 I CPJ 66 (Ker)]

42. Consent —When not necessary

Deceased seriously injured in an accident brought by passers by. Consent to surgery implicit and doctor refusing to conduct emergency surgery for want of consent to prove the refusal of patients to undergo to surgery both at initial stage and after he was informed the consequences of not undergoing surgery. [*Kumar Mukharjee* v *Ruby General Hospital* 2005 II CPJ 35]

43. Consent — Surgery

Contention that the complainant gave his written consent to undertake the risk involved in the surgery of his wife. Held that the consent cannot be taking to be a valid defense where the complainant is able to show that there was negligence and carelessness on the part of the opposite parties at the time of surgery. [*Devendra Kumar Sharma* v *Post Graduate Institute of Medical Education and Research* 2002 I CPJ 211]

44. Consent — Amputation of leg

There is no separate specific consent for amputation of the leg. However, it is clear from the affidavit of the operating surgeon that when the complainant's wife was told about this and she swooned and hence she was taken to a separate room for treatment. She has not filed any affidavit to deny this. After performing the arteriography when it was found that this limb had became non-viable and gangrene has set in the surgeon attending on him has no choice but to perform amputation to save the life of the patient by that time it had became an emergency procedure. [*B.N. Gurudev* v *N. Ramanna* 2008 I CPJ 84]

45. Consent — Surgical procedure

When the consent form refers to diagnostic and operative laparoscopy and Laparotomy if needed, it refers to a consent for a definite laparoscopy with a contingent Laparotomy if needed. It does not amount to consent for OH BSO Surgery removing the uterus and ovaries/fallopian tubes. [*Samira Kohli* v *Prabha Manchanda* 2008 I CPR 237]

46. Complaint — Maintainability

Complaint filed by husband of the victim — not only the victim but also the beneficiary entitled to file complaint. Husband whom all though acting for his wife, talked with opposite party doctor, paid the charges, being the beneficiary, complaint filed by him maintainable. [*Dr. P.B. Lal* v *Suresh Chandra Roy* 2006 III CPJ 452]

Compliant by brother of deceased consumer alleging medical negligence while the widow and son of the deceased still surviving — complaint not maintainable since brother not be treated as legal heir overriding the widow and son who are not coming to file the complaint. [*Parimal Kumar Acharya* v *Dr. Tapan Kumar Chakroborty* 2005 I CPR 474 (WB)]

Objection on ground that complainant approached motor Accidents Claim Tribunal and in receipt of compensation under the Motor Vehicles Act — unsustainable. The two causes of action were different to be deciding by different Forum having limited jurisdictions. [*Pravat Kumar Mukherjee* v *Ruby General Hospital* 2005 II CPJ 35]

47. Complaint — Maintainability — Legal representative

Complainant widow of deceased consumer remarries subsequently to filing of complaint. She is being no legal representative of her deceased husband, complaint not maintainable. [*Shantha Gowda* v *Kempegowda Institute of Medical Sciences* 2005 I CPR 493 (Karn)]

48. Complaint — Misjoinder of parties

Patient, a student all consideration for whose treatment paid by his patents. Patients are also consumers and complainant not bad for Misjoinder. [*Sundeep Agarwal* v *Modern Medical Institute* 2005 II CPJ 601]

49. Complaint — Two complaints

One complaint by husband of the deceased and other by minor children through their guardian, children of the diseased are also eligible for compensation. As they are minors and as they were staying with their guardian, hence, they have filed a separate complaint and State Commission has rightly awarded compensation to them. [*D. Rama Rajyam* v *P.K. Vasudeva Rao* 2007 III CPJ 295]

50. Consumer

Complainant paid advance of ₹1,100. Entries in the admission register to that effect. Complainant is a consumer. [*Namita Nursing Home* v *Smt Anita* 1999 II CPR 528]

Services availed on payment of fees of a non governmental hospital (Medical Research Center) whose patients are diagnosed and treated for cancer. Complainant is a consumer. [*Jai Prakash Saini* v *Director, Rajiv Gandhi Cancer Institute and Research Centre* 2003 I CPJ 305]

51. Consumer — Beneficiary of services

Beneficiary service is included in the definition of consumer. When a young child is taken to a hospital by his parents and the doctor treats the child, the patients would come within the definition of consumer, having hired the services and the young child would be a consumer under the inclusive definition being a beneficiary of such services. [*Spring Meadows Hospital* v *Harjot Ahaluwalia* 1998 I CPJ 655]

52. Consumer — Donation

Contention that no amount charged after operation, Amount paid for donation in reality was charge for operation. Complainant had to be consumer. [*Bhajahari Chail* v *Dr. Debasis Banerjee* 2002 II CPJ 21]

53. Consumer — Medical service

Medical services rendered by hospital not free to all patients. Each patient be a paying patient or not become a consumer. [*Amblappa* v *Sri Ram D. Veerendra Heggade* 1999 III CPR 72]

54. Consumer — Patents of patient — Misjoinder of parties

Patient a student consideration for whose treatment paid by his parents. Parents also consumers and complaint not bad for Misjoinder. [*Sandeep Agarwal* v *Modern Medical Institute* 2005 II CPJ 601]

55. Consumer — Recipient of services of government hospital

Services rendered on payment of charges to some and free of charged to others. Fall within the ambit of the expression 'service' as defined in section 2(1)(*o*) of the Consumer Protection Act would be 'service' and the recipient a consumer under the Consumer Protection Act. [*Ramswaroop Singh* v *Dr. S. Diwan* 2005 III CPJ 108]

56. Consumer — Free service

Services rendered by a government hospital to some on payment of charges and to others free of charge is also a service as defined in section 2(1)(*o*) of Consumer Protection Act, 1986 and a person availing of services of that hospital is consumer under section 2(1)(*d*) of the Act. [*Pavittar Singh* v *State of Punjab* 2006 III CPJ 287]

Medical treatment given in a hospital run by Port Trust of its employees or their family members availing of such services is consumer under the Act. [*G. Kondala Rao* v *Board of Trustees* 2006 III CPJ 97]

57. Consumer — Treatment in charitable hospital

A poor patient getting treatment in a charitable institution free of charge and a consumer means of the Consumer Protection Act, 1986. [*Dhanmani Devi* v *Dr. Sudha Kumari* 2006 III CPR 94]

58. Consumer — availing of service for consideration

Central Government Health Scheme (CGHS) in consideration of service rendered to the government till the age of Superannuation, if right is conferred upon an employee to get pension as well as other benefits including medical treatment prescribed by various rules or the schemes framed by government, it can be held that it is free service. Consideration can be in cash or kind and such employees would be a consumer has defined in section 2(1)(*d*) of the Consumer Protection Act. Services rendered by the government employee before retirement would be consideration for providing medical facilities for him or his family members. [*Jagdish Kumar Bajpai* v *Union of India* 2006 I CPR 157]

59. Drug reaction

Child of 2½ years taken to opposite parties only for micro stitches on minor injury administered Ketamine stated to be the safest Anaesthesia agents, never gained consciousness and died within 3 days. Merely because a drug is safest, it does not mean that it can be administered on each and every patient. Medical literature states that the drug reacts differently of different patients, therefore, it has to be administered with great care and caution, particularly with regard to an infant child. While administering Anaesthesia, care to be taken to decide the quantum of the dose, nature of the drug in relation to type of patient, his age and his allergic or idiosyncratic reaction. Where the adverse reaction cannot be predicted or prevented as to the case of Ketamine, extra care to be taken to decide the quantity in view of the age of patient, physical built, metabolism and capacity excrete Entire drug not excreted through urine and remained in the body of the child. Negligence held ₹2 lakh awarded as compensation. [*Madhu Sudan* v *Dr. Suresh Gupta* 2006 II CPJ 348]

60. Contributory negligence

A 13 years old boy riding cycle on the national highway should not be regarding as a person incapable of exercising a reasonable judgment or understanding the traffic rules and carrying to the degree of care and caution expected of all a user of road. [*G. Padmanabdhan Nair* v *G.M. Kerala State Road Transport Corporation* 1989 ACJ 873 (Ker HC)]

Complainant not going to medical college or consulting a Neuro Surgeon despite serious position of injury having explained to him, Compensation of ₹24,700 has awarded by District Forum reduced to ₹10,000 with ₹500 towards costs. [*Manager, Martine Medical Centre* v *E.V. Thomas* 1999 I CPR 466]

MRI Scan — In-spite of her having told opposite parties to staff that patient had taken breakfast she was taking for MRI. The opposite party started conducting MRI, may be for monetary reasons. Death occurred due to asphyxia because of certain food particles having been choking in the windpipe. As contributory negligence of the complainant is there token compensation, ₹25,000 awarded. [*Mukesh Jain* v *LK Anand* 2007 III CLT 456 (NC)]

61. Costs — Imposition of

Allegations of negligence on the part of the opposite parties, complainant failed to produce evidence to support his allegations. Complaint dismissed. Complainant directed to pay costs of litigation of ₹5,000 to the opposite parties. [*Paramjeet Kaur* v *Doaba Hospital, Jalandhar City* 1998 II CPJ 265]

62. Costs — Imposition of caesarean operation — Death

Opposite party MBBS doctor well qualified and eligible for conducting caesarean operation. No expert evidences. No postmortem, complaint dismissed with costs of ₹2,000. [*Surinder Kumar* (*Laddi*) v *Dr. Santosh Menon* 2000 III CPJ 517]

63. Costs — Imposition of — Frivolous complaint

Costs of ₹5,000 imposed for filing frivolous and vexatious complaint. [*Amar Singh* v *Frances Newton Hospital Ferozepore* 2001 I CPJ 8 (Pb)]

64. Costs — Imposition of — Loss of vision

Allegedly, due to Argon Laser performed by opposite parties on complainant eye. After Argon Laser, the complainant never went to opposite parties at all. He went to all places except the opposite parties. No expert evidence produced. Complainant failed to make out any case of medical negligence against opposite parties, Made False and uncorroborated statements in the complaint. Complaint dismissed with costs of ₹5,000 (to be pay to each of the opposite parties). [*Shataben Mulibhai Patel* v *Beach Candy Hospital and Research Centre* 2005 I CPJ 10]

65. Costs — Imposition of — Vexatious complaint

Due care and caution was not observing by the complainant in filing complaint. Even the non production of record of AIIMS, glaring, inconsistency in between the stand taken by the complainant and the production of selectively torn document on record. Complaint held not filed a requisite care and caution and was filed to harass respondent doctor, with preconceived and misconceived notions. Filing of such complaints and persisting in it by filing an appeal would just amount to abuse of the process of Consumer Fora. Appeal dismissed with cost of ₹25,000 in favour of the respondent doctor. [*S. Saleemuddin* v *Dr. Sunil Malhotra* 2006 III CPJ 396]

66. Costs — Imposition of — Laboratory operation — Abortion operation

Resulting in 'gut loop cut' developing into septicemia and ultimately death of patient, Petitioner attempted to disown any responsibility despite the ultrasound test and MTP operation. All through proceedings, he did not appear to have any remorse feeling for the patient and her family who had passed through trauma result her death. The petitioner for his attempts to escape liability deserves to be several penalized. Revision petitioner liable to be dismiss with costs of ₹20,000. Order of the State Commission directing the practitioner to pay compensation of ₹4,50,000 upheld. [*Ramesh Jain* v *Jagroop Singh* 2008 I CPJ 233]

67. Constitution of India — Article 21 — Right to life

Government hospitals run by the state and the medical officer employed therein are bound to extend medical assistance for preserving human life. Failure on the part of the government hospital to provide timely medical treatment to a person in need of such treatment results in violation of his right to life guaranteed under article 21 of the Constitution of India. Adequate compensation can be awarded by Court for such a violation. [*Paschim Banga Khet Mazdoor Samity* v *State of West Bengal* AIR 1996 2426 SC]

68. Cystostomy — Trocar Cystostomy

Wrongly perform by private doctor. Operation report of government hospital to that affect. Doctor held negligent in performing Trocar Cystostomy. Compensation of ₹25,000 awarded by District Forum No interference. [*Dr. P.N. Gupta* v *Mr. Indrajeet Singh Sidhu* 2005 III CLT 22]

69. Criminal liability of doctor — Nasal deformity operation — Death

Due to "not introducing of cuffed-endo-tracheal tube of proper size as to prevent aspiration of blood from the wound in the respiratory passage". Lack of due care and precaution. Not so reckless or grossly negligent as to make the doctor criminally liable. Doctor may be liable in Tort. [*Suresh Gupta* v *Govt. of NCT of Delhi* 2004 III CLT 312]

70. Criminal liability of doctor — Standard of proof

Mere lack of necessary care, attention and skill is not sufficient. There should be "gross negligence" or "recklessness". [*Suresh Gupta* v *Govt. of NCT of Delhi* 2004 III CLT 312]

71. Criminal Negligence — Abortion

Opposite parties have not any qualification in allopathy to conduct operation, one of the opposite parties put her hand in the abdomen of patient and took out a newly born child. Saying that the placenta has not come out she again put her hand took out the placenta immediately. Whereafter both mother and child died. Cause of death of mother due to excessive uterine bleeding and inverted uterus due to mismanagement of third stage labour. Both accused opposite parties convicted by criminal Court. Negligence held ₹1 lakh awarded as compensation. [*Dr. Ram Sushil Tripathi* v *Ghanshyam Khanik* 2006 II CPJ 218]

72. Criminal negligence — Eye surgeon

Prosecution under section 336/338, IPC, Limitation Child patient suffering injury in left eye operated and subsequently operation was done for cornea grafting in future. Second operation done on right eye instead of the affected left eye. Patient becoming inactive due to diffuse injury to brain that occurred during the course of second surgery as per opinion of senior neuro surgeon. Father of the child went from one medical institute to another but in vain. Complaint filed after prescribed period of limitation of three years saved by section 473 Cr PC where under cognizance of offence can be taking even after expiry of limitation period. Delay condoned. [*Dr. Mukesh Khare* v *State of U.P.* 2006 III RCR (Criminal) 397 (All)]

73. Diagnosis — Wrong report

Patients Blood tested by opposite party, Diagnostic center to be Australian Antigen (HBs Ag) positive. Another hospital giving report for the same test to the affect that Hepatitis B Antigen found negative. Person who put signature on the report of the diagnostic center not qualified in the science to give such report. Negligence held. Plea that wrong reported having no nexus with treatment given by the hospital. Compensation of ₹25,000 as awarded by District Forum, not being commensurate with the damage or injury caused, and reduced to ₹10,000. [*Chaudhary Diagnostic and Research Centre* v *Mahaveer Prasad Gupta* 2005 III CPJ 768]

74. Diagnosis — Wrong

Pregnant woman treated for pulmonary tuberculosis. Patient was not all suffering from tuberculosis evidenced by medical certificate issued by medical officer of government hospital. Administration of strong drugs and injections for T.B. due to wrong diagnosis deficiency in service ₹50,000 awarded as compensation. [*Kalyani General Hospital* v *Bhuveneshwari* 2005 IV CPJ 29 (TN)]

75. Diagnostic center — Blood test — Contradictory report

Two tests conducted after collecting blood samples of complainant in the same diagnosis center. On first test complainants blood reported as of group 'O' Rh negative, therefore she had to undergo antibody test and take injection Antid 350 (Vinoblin) one each before and after delivery. When blood group tested in government hospital same having found 'O' Rh positive. The complainant getting the blood again tested in the opposite parties diagnostic centre, where it was found 'O' Rh Positive. There may be error in regarding the group of a person without doing any negligence on the part of the doctor, but when the same diagnosis center gives, another reporter contradictory to its previous report negligence on the part of center established through complainant suffered no damage ₹10,000 awarded as compensation. [*R.C. Purohit* v *Usha Devada* 2006 I CPJ 489]

76. Diabetes

Patients suffering from heart problems shifted to appellant hospital for better management. Also suffering from diabetes mellitus, Allegation that knowing fully well known that the patient is in known case of diabetes mellitus, yet between 7:00 PM on the 8-11-1993 to 8:00 PM on 9-11-1993 insulin was not administered to control the diabetes which resulted in complication and death of the patient. Medical literature and affidavit of doctor to the effect that insulin should have been give to control diabetes. One does not require a better evidence for establishing medical negligence. Order of the State Commission awarding compensation of 4.50 lakh along with interest at the rate of 12% upheld. Appeal dismissed with cost of ₹10,000. [*Bombay Hospital and Medical Research Centre* v *Krishnabehari M. Aggarwal* 2003 IV CPJ 61 (NC)]

77. Diabetes — Diabetic patient

Leaving an old diabetic and heart patient without monitoring the blood sugar level under their skilled observation itself is deficiency in service on the part of the opposite parties. Order of District Forum directing compensation of ₹50,000 along with interest @ 12% per annum affirmed. [*Guru Teg Bahadur Sahib* (*Charitable*) *Hospital* v *Dr. N.K. Nayyar* 2002 I CPJ 395]

78. Diabetes — Diabetic patient — Eye surgeon — Post-operational treatment — Loss of vision

Complainant suffers from diabetes for 40 years. Incumbent upon the surgeon and the hospital to monitor the blood glucose on a continuing basis, Blood sugar levels of the patient not recorded either prior to the operation or during operation even until fifteen days after the operation. Sugar merely relied on the statement of patient that his blood sugar is under control. Post surgical fungal endophthalmitis occurring two to three weeks after the surgery is a clear possibility. Important for ophthalmologist to be aware of this and treated it carefully. Opposite party failed to treat the complainant when the complainant informed him of hazy and blurred vision. Postoperative required care was not taking deficiency in service. Opposite party was directed to pay ₹2 lakh to complainant. [*H.S. Sharma* v *Indraprashta Apollo Hospital* 2007 II CLT 26 (NC)]

79. Drug Reaction — Diabetic Patient

Ayurvedic tablets prescribed — Consumption leading to severe stomach pain. Capsule found to contain 1681 PPM. Lead against permissible lead of 20 PPM, in drug prescription and administration of hazardous drug amounts to a deficiency in service. Compensation awarded. [*K.M. Balakrishana and Premnath* v *Padma Ayurveda Vaidyasala and Research Centre* 2003 III CPJ 645 (TN)]

80. Drug Reaction — resulting in loss of eyesight

Compensation of ₹2 lakh awarded. [*Devi Rani* v *Prakash Rao* 2002 III CPJ 123]

81. Drug Reaction — Intra Venous Pyelogram (IVP) Test

Administration of full dose without preceded by a test dose. Death of patient due to anaphylactic shock (drug reaction) Patient weather allergic to the drug or not, not recorded by Radiologist before administering the drug. Negligence held ₹1.5 lakh awarded as compensation and ₹2,000 towards costs. [*Vidya @ Uma* v *Vivekanand General Hospital* 2006 III CPJ 388 (Karn)]

82. Drug Reaction — Test dose — Asthma patient allergic to Penicillin

Opposite party administering test dose of penicillin despite objection of patient and his wife. Sudden collapse and death due to anaphylactic shock. In case of anaphylaxis, immediate injection of adrenalin to be given. Opposite parties not stating that administered adrenalin immediately or had it ready. Basic precautions intended in medical texts not observed, when patients had already complained of allergy to penicillin. Negligence held ₹2 lakh awarded as compensation. [*Cherian* v *Fatima Mary* 2006 I CPJ 147]

83. Drug Reaction — Administration of overdoes

Child aged 9 years suffering from fever given four Reziz 500mg tablets, a sulfadoxine drug for two days after two weeks patient developing skin rash and eye problems and opposite party prescribing two more Reziz tablets, Death of child due to Stevens Johnson syndrome. Manufacturers of the drug recommended single dose of Reziz tablet age wise: for 4-8 years one tablet, and for 9-14 years two tablets and warned to discontinue the administration of same on appearance of a skin rash. Overdoes administration of the drug against warning of its manufacturers even after noticing the side effects, Held in negligence and deficiency in service. ₹2.6 lakh awarded as compensation. [*Lella Veerajaneyulu* v *Dr. V.C. Bendale* 2006 I CPR 453 (Mah)]

84. Drug Reaction — Drug overdose — Death of three months old child

Over medication of antibiotic drug like gentamycin on an infant without considering its age, nature of drug, its does and duration, resulting in renal failure and ultimate death as confirmed by other hospitals including AIIMS where the child treated subsequently. Negligence held. ₹50,000 awarded as compensation. [*Dr. M.M. Bagai* v *Nihal Singh* 2006 III CPJ 48 (Del)]

85. Drug Reaction — Dry eye syndrome

Opposite party, doctor diagnosing Malaria prescribing "Amalar" in the first instance. Amalar is a drug for treatment of cases of Malaria, which are resistant to chloroquine, no clinical finding that complainant resistant to chloroquine. On administration of Amalar tablets complainant developing dry eye syndrome. Lost of vision of both her eyes, duty of doctor to warn about reaction of drug and give proper instructions. Negligence held. Compensation of ₹2 lakh awarded. [*Devi Rani* v *N. Prakash Rao* 2002 III CPJ 123 (AP)]

86. Drug Reaction — Permanent disability

Complainant a minor girl of 7 years suffering from cold and fever given an injection resulting in paralysis of her lower limb thus they become disabled for life. Patient hale and healthy before taking the treatment of cold and fever, have no case of polio paralysis or anything that sort nor had any disablement in the past. Opposite party administering injection without ascertaining whether the child had any reaction to medicine, not explaining what inject able medicine administered, what is the reason of the paralysis and in what part of the body of the patient? Burden on him to rule out the possibility of faulty administration or administration of reachable medicine. Doctrine of *res ipsa loquitor* applies. Child specialist also opines that child sustained non-polio paralysis attack as against submission of opposite party that possibility of polio paralysis might not be ruled out. Negligence held ₹1,50,000 awarded as compensation upheld by state commission. [*Dr. G.D. Jiladia* v *Minor Dharmistha Chhotubhai Goswami* 2003 II CPJ 381]

87. Due care — 'Due care' by doctors is by now settled

Since the treating doctor, who treated deceased doctor, did not have the qualification to handle such a case, a case of medical negligence stands established. Deceased aged 45 years himself was a surgeon of repute. Even if his income taken as ₹1 lakh per month and contribution towards running household about ₹40,000 per month compensation of ₹12 lakh awarded by the State Commission not on high side. [*Karuna Hospital* v *Kochurani Jose* 2007 I CLT 363 (NC)]

88. Due care and caution — Heart Problem — Staircase exercise test — Stress test — Death of patient while undergoing the test

Held to be a case of deficiency in rendering medical services by not opting to take due care and caution in submitting the deceased to a stress test which would be acceptable to a large body of medical professionals. Compensation of ₹3 lakh with interest @ 9% per annum awarded. [*Mohan Laxman Mavinakatte* v *Dr. Anil E. Kagal* 2006 III CPJ 427]

89. Donation — Government Hospital

Token amount given as a donation does not amount to payment of consideration. Complainant is not a consumer. [*Narendra Singh Rastogi* v *Shaskiya Gyan Panch Trust* 2002 II CPJ (MP)]

90. Donation — Operation — ₹18,000 deposited

Contention that it was in the form of a donation whether the complainant is consumer? Held yes. That is nothing but a method of taking the fee in different form. [*Kumud Garg* v *Raja Bhatiya* 2004 I CPJ 369]

91. Donation — Operation

Contention that no amount charged after operation, Amount paid for donation in reality was charge for operation. Complainant held to be consumer. [*Bhajahari Chail* v *Dr. Debasis Banerjee* 2002 II CPJ 21]

92. Discharge card — Refusal of issue

Opposite party number, three refused to issue the discharge card of the patient immediately after the death of the patient. Deficiency in service on the part of the opposite parties. Compensation generated. [*Vijayamma* v *Apollo Diagnostic Centre* 2002 I CPJ 230]

93. Discharge summary — Evidentiary value

Complainant after undergoing choleystectomy on 13-8-1991 at the hospital of opposite party, developing severe jaundice, referred to their hospital at Madras for expert treatment and after getting treatment at Madras referred to Apollo Hospital at Hyderabad where he was again operated for same complaint. Discharge certificate issued by Apollo Hospital shows that complication like jaundice due to defective earlier operation performed on 13-8-1991. Negligence held as discharge certificate itself enough to held negligence. [*Gangapam Ramlinga Reddy* v *Apollo Hospital* 2003 I CLD 494 (AP)]

94. Delivery of child

Deceased due to bleeding after delivery and was semi-conscious state due to profuse bleeding after delivery. Admitting the deceased for delivery by these opposite parties, when there was no arrangement available for blood transfusion, held wholly unwarranted. This by itself constitutes not only negligence but deficiency in service too. [*Sai Mahima Hospital* v *Anil Rana* 2007 I CLT 449 (HP)]

95. Delivery of child — Caesarean operation

Mother suffers from brain damage. Necessary precautions, obvious therapy, effective and careful treatment not extended to her. Opposite parties held liable to pay total compensation of ₹9 lakh. (3 lakh each). [*Neeta Singh* v *Dr. K.K. Kakkar* 2005 I CPJ 154 (UP)]

Pair of scissors left in abdomen, operation. Compensation of ₹2,000 awarded by the State Commission enhanced to ₹10,000. [*Sau Madhuri* v *Dr. Rajendra* 1996 III CPJ 75]

96. Delivery of child — *Res ipsa loquitur*

Patient had to spend 108 days in the hospital for a normal delivery with forceps and episiotomy. She had to be taken to the operation theater six times and had to undergo untold suffering. It leads to one veritable conclusion this is a case of *res ipsa loquitur*. It is clear that medical practitioner has not brought to her task a reasonable degree of skill and knowledge and has not exercised a reasonable degree of care, Held that there has been a gross negligence on the part of the opposite parties. Apart from grant of final bill of ₹186849.90 rose by opposite party hospital damages and for mental agony a sum of ₹10 lakh granted. [*S. Tamil Selvi* v *Dr. Sooriya Kola* 2009 II CPJ 216]

97. Delivery of child — *Res ipsa loquitor* — Government Hospital

Sterilization operation subsequently complication arose. Second operation due to the negligence of respondent No. 2 a mop (towel) was leftover inside her peritoneal cavity. Formation of pus. Development of peritonitis resulted in death. Doctrine of *res ipsa loquitur* clearly applies. Absence of any valid explanation by the respondents Held that deceased died due to negligence of respondent nos. 2 and 3. [*Achutrao Haribhau Khodwa* v *State of Maharashtra* AIR 1996 SC 2377]

98. Delivery of child — Normal delivery

Death of wife of respondent no. 1 during normal delivery, the patient who was only 23 years old had bleeding at 5 P.M. heavy bleeding from vagina. The treating doctor sent requisition for blood only at 7 P.M. and specialist came at 8 P.M. when the condition of patient had become critical. Finding the State Commission holding medical negligence against the appellant and award of compensation of ₹1,03,000 with interest @ 12% upheld. [*Kalyani Nursing Home* v *P. Chandra Mouli* 2007 IV CPJ 341]

99. Delivery of child — Delay in surgery — Death of complainant wife

Since there was no anesthetist present opposite parties tried for normal delivery even after they realized that in all probability caesarean section was the only alternative left, and, therefore, delayed the surgery had to be performed without his presence and subsequently when Amniotic fluid. Embolism manifested there was no specialist to administer oxygen or perform suction from the lung. Though there was deficiency in service in not contracting Anesthetist earlier, the opposite parties cannot be hold responsible for her death that was an accident. ₹50,000 awarded to complainant for negligence of opposite parties. [*Dr. M. Radhakrishna Murthy* v *Parakulam Elishma Babu* 2002 III CPJ 193 (AP)]

100. Denture — Defect

Opposite party directed to refund the cost of denture. Compensation awarded. [*Dr. K.C. Nasa* v *Sahib Chandra Sharma* 2003 III CPJ 622]

101. Dehydration — Medical treatment

Patient suffering from acute and severe dehydration, not given the least medical services, unduly detained. Patient was lead to reach the point of "no return". Glaring example of rendering deficient service by a medical man,. Compensation of ₹2 lakh awarded. [*Birdhi Chand Meena* v *Dr. Prabhakar Sethi* 2003 I CPC 45 (Raj)]

102. Dandruff — Advertisement — Wrong treatment

Appellant went to the appellant clinic to get treatment after coming across the advertisement given by appellant. ₹7,000 paid for said purpose. Treatment resulted in falling of hair making him bald. These are such unfair trade practices, which need to be curbing with heavy hand no interference with the order awarding compensation of ₹50,000. [*The Body Care* v *Ashok Kumar Solanki* 2005 I CPJ 402 (Del)]

103. Delegation of responsibility

A consultant could be negligent where he delegates the responsibility to his junior with the knowledge that the junior was incapable of performing of his duties properly. [*Spring Meadows Hospital* v *Harjot Ahluwallia* 1998 I CPJ 655]

104. Drugs and Cosmetics Rules Rule 66(A) — Blood transfusion

Blood supplied by the second opposite party to the first opposite party for transfusion had HIV antibodies, which resulted in contracting HIV infection, which after gestation period became full- blown AIDS and patient succumbed to her terminal illness. Second opposite party had failed to carry out the test required to ensure that the blood was not infected. Rule 66(A) of the Drugs and Cosmetics Rules clearly stipulates a mandatory condition of conducting HIV antibody test before certifying the purity of blood, which would, not complied with. Held that this is a clear-cut case of negligence. A consolidated sum of ₹4 lakh as compensation with 6% interest from the date of filing complaint awarded to be pay jointly and severally by the respondents. [*M. Chinnaiyan* v *Sri Gokulam Hospital* 2007 III CLT 177 (NC)]

105. Drug manufacture

The complainant purchased one ampule of Deriphyllin injection to be given intravenously to his mother. While preparing for the injection the doctor saw some black pieces in the ampoule, he sealed the ampoule and gave certificate that there was foreign material in the ampoule and as such, it was unfit for human consumption. Compensation of ₹500 in addition to cost of ampule ₹1.62 lakhs was awarded to be paid by the manufactures M/s German Remedies Ltd. The complain against chemist was dismissed on the ground that as he had merely sold the ampoule. [*Chaman Singh Faujdar* v *German Gemedies Ltd.* 1992 II CPJ 915]

106. Drug manufacture — Ophthalmologist

The complainant, an ophthalmic surgeon, while performing cataract surgery, used a drug "Irrisol" which is a balance salt solution to prevent cornea from becoming dry, during eye surgery. It was alleged that four of his patients became blind on account of impurities, such as detergent contained in Irrisol. State Commission held that the drug 'Irrisol' was purchased neither for using in the course of contract operation and not for buying and selling nor for financial business and hence it cannot be said that the drug was purchased for commercial purpose. The commission also held that pharmaceutical company not only does business, but also renders service to the medical profession and public when it manufactures and sells the drugs. Therefore, manufacture and sale of defective, impure or spurious drug would amount to deficiency in service compensation of ₹15 lakh awarded. [*Jagdip Mohanlal Kakadia* v *Ophthalmic and Drugs India* 1997 III CPR (Guj)]

107. Drug and equipment manufacturer/Chemist

Defective medicine (eye drops), laboratory reports, Two different reports of two different laboratories. No expert analysis of the drug and no specimen sent for independent laboratory for examination by District Forum and State Commission liable to set aside. One of the complainants not pressing complaint and another not available. National Commission awarding ₹20,000 to complainants on compassionate grounds with consent of parties. [*Ophthalmic and Drugs India* v *Dr. Jagdip Mohanlal Kakadia* 2003 III CPJ 21 (NC)]

The complainant doctor had purchased an ultra sound scanner for his nursing home. The machine was found to be defective and State Commission had ordered to refund its price amounting to ₹3,85,000. The National Commission upheld the order of the State Commission. [*Kody Elcot Ltd.* v *Dr. C.P. Gupta* 1996 I CPJ 7 (NC)]

108. Medical equipment

Purchase of Mobile Intensive Care Unit Vehicle by a doctor. Delay in supply. Required to pay increased excise duty and increased price. Held due deficiency in service. Awarded refund of ₹1,07,000 for such increase and compensation of ₹25,000 for interest, ₹50,000 for loss of business and ₹30,000 for mental agony. [*Dr. Ajay H. Katharia* v *Car Mart Pvt. Ltd.* 2000 III CPJ 502 (Mah)]

109. Epilepsy

Boy aged 13 years, admitted to hospital for the treatment of epilepsy and died within 48 hours of his admission of septicemia. Principles of *res ipsa loquitur* held applicable. [*Dr. Janka K. Nathan* v *Murlidhar Eknath Masane* 2002 II CPR 138]

110. Epilepsy — Medical treatment

Patient not treated by Neurologist and modern facility for tests and first choice drug for disease not available. Patient not referred to a place where the entire essential for the treatment of disease available, Cardiac arrest resulting in death of patient. Case of deficiency in service. Compensation of ₹1 lakh awarded. [*Channaveerashetty* v *Dr. Vijay Kumar* 2005 II CPR 450]

111. Erb's palsy

Due to birth injury, same could have avoided if proper care taken. Deficiency in service. [*Baby Ramya* v *Dr. Aruna Reddy* 1996 I CPR 244 (AP)]

112. Employees State Insurance Act, 1948, Section 75(1), (2) and (3) — Jurisdiction

Medical negligence ESI hospital Damages claim for Consumer Fora. Bar of jurisdiction. The Consumer Forum has jurisdiction to adjudicate upon the case of the appellant. The jurisdiction of the consumer Forum is not ousted by virtue of sub-section (1) or (2) or (3) of section 75 of ESI Act. [*Kishori Lal* v *ESI Corporation* 2007 II CPJ 25]

113. Employees State Insurance Act, 1948 — Section 75(3) — Jurisdiction — Surgery

Medical negligence, Claim for compensation and medical expenses, Held that main claim for compensation as made by the respondents does not fall in any of the categories enumerated in section 75 of the Employees State Insurance Act, 1948. Therefore, jurisdiction of the District Forum to entertain and decide the complaints is not ousted under section 75(3) of the 1948 Act. [*Employees State Insurance Corporation* (*Medical Hospital*) v *Sri Siddaramaiah* 2006 IV CPJ 10]

114. ESI Hospital — Amenability to Consumer Protection Act, ESI hospitals not rendering services free of cost amenable to jurisdiction of Consumer Protection Act

Under section 3 of Employees State Insurance Act, 1948, a corporation was set up and the Act applies to all factories whether belonging to government or not. Under section 38, all employees in the factories or establishments to which the Act applies shall be insured. Sections 39 and 42 contemplate contribution by both the employer and employee. In view of this, the ESI hospitals do not render service free of cost. Hence, they are amenable to the jurisdiction under Consumer Protection Act. [*M. Ramesh Reddy* v *State of Andhra Pradesh* 2003 I CLD 81]

115. Excessive bleeding

Delivery of child — Death after 18 hours. Delay of five hours in calling for Anesthetist for requiring surgical treatment. Condition of patient deteriorated. Anesthetist found the patient not fit for general/spinal Anaesthesia for surgical operation. Case of medical negligence. Taking ₹15,000 as normal income of deceased (housewife) and by applying multiplier of 15, compensation of ₹1,19,500 awarded. [*Hemant Bahadur Singh Parihar* v *Dr. Maya Pathak* 2000 I CPR 191]

Medical treatment. Patient remains unattended by doctor for 12 hours. Condition deteriorated. Failure on the part of the doctor and hospital in administration of treatment. Negligence. Compensation awarded. [*Ujjain Charitable Trust Hospital* v *Ramesh Chandra* 2003 III CPJ 181 (MP)]

Delivery of child — Death of mother. Allegation that death occurred due to delay caused in referring the patient to Medical College hospital. No definite evidence to that effect doctor cannot be held liable for negligence. However, hospital not disclosing the true cause of death. Amounts to negligence on the part of the hospital. Total compensation of ₹1,37,750 awarded. [*Leela Bai* v *Sebastian* 2002 II CPJ 363]

116. Eye operation

Deformity in left eye 6 years old child operation. Superior rectus muscle was cut resulting in injuries to the cornea and eyeball. Operation carried out in a negligent manner. Compensation of ₹50,000 awarded. [*Jaswinder Singh* v *Dr. J.S. Saini* 2000 II CPJ 262]

Right eye operated upon without getting the B scan done. permanent loss of vision. Doctor acted in a rash and negligent manner. Compensation of ₹1 lakh awarded. [*Souindra Mohan Ghosh* v *Dr. D.* v *Pahwa* 2002 II CPJ 243]

Stitches found loose after operation. Re-stitching. Loss of vision. Negligence. Order awarding compensation upheld. [*Dr. J.P. Goel* v *Smt. Pushpa Verma* 2002 I CPJ 28]

117. Eye operation — Cataract — Vision lost

Enquiry of a committee of three eminent doctors. Report stated that out of 52 cases operated in the new operation theater, 14 patient developed infection in the operated eye. Held that there was deficiency in service on the part of the hospital and the staff in not maintaining the autoclaves, equipments and other materials, which were used before and after the operation. Opposite party 5, 6 and 7 held jointly and severally liable to pay compensation. A lump sum amount of ₹5 lakh would be appropriate compensation in this case. [*Sarwat Ali Khan* v *Prof. (Dr.) R. Gogi* 2007 III CPJ 179]

118. Eye surgery

Post-operation treatment:.- loss of vision. Complainant suffers from diabetes for 40 years. Incumbent upon the surgeon and the hospital to monitor the blood glucose on a continuing basis. Blood sugar levels of the patient not recorded either prior to the operation or during operation even until 15 days after the operation. Surgeon merely relied on the statement of patient that his blood sugar is under control. Post-surgical fungal endophthalmitis occurring 2 to 3 weeks after the surgery is a clear possibility, Important for ophthalmologists to be aware of this and treat it carefully. Opposite party failed to treat complainant when the complainant informed him of hazy and blurred vision. Post-operative required care was not taken deficiency in service. Opposite party was directed to pay ₹2 lakh to complainant. [*H.S. Sharma* v *Indraprashta Apollo Hospital* 2007 II CPJ 27]

Loss of eyesight RKD operation performed whereas "advance glaucoma filtering surgery" was required to perform first. Relevant record also not produced before the State Commission. Appellant doctor rightly held negligent and deficiency in service. [*P.S. Hardia* v *Kedarnath Sethia* 2004 III CPJ 90]

119. Expert evidence

Affidavit of two experts doctors verbatim productions and there is no variations including coma, full stop. It gives room for arriving at a conclusion that these might have been drafted by the lawyer or by some interested person and the doctors might have blindly appended their signatures without any application of their mind. They lost much of their evidentiary value. Findings of a State Commission holding medical negligence, based on the treatment recorded of CMC hospital duly supplemented by the affidavit of doctor of an expert in the field upheld. Appellant a young man of 24 years who was earning ₹10,000 per month lost his one leg due to medical negligence. As per certificate given by civil surgeon the complainant is handicapped to the extent of 80% compensation of ₹2,75,619 enhanced to ₹5 lakh. [*Bassi Hospital Pvt. Ltd.* v *Pankaj Gupta* 2007 IV CPJ 239]

Contract operation, Loss of eyesight. Proof of negligence. Uncontroversial evidence. Under section 13 of the Consumer Protection Act, if in the written version the matter is contested, parties to prove the case by evidence. Complainant filled affidavit by way of evidence but opposite parties, neither filed any affidavit nor cross-examined the deponents. Evidence brought by the complainant remained uncontroversial. Negligence held. ₹1,25,000 awarded as compensation along with ₹1,000 towards cost. [*Dr. Ponnusamy* v *Ramkrishanan* 2006 IV CPJ 213]

120. ENT surgeon

Tonsillectomy. Improper administration of Anaesthesia. Cardiac arrest following brain damage due to shortage of oxygen supply to brain at the time of operation. Patients suffering cerebral hypoxia resulting in loss of a speech and eyesight and inability to move both upper and lower limbs. State commission finding that complainant not established on the bases of the expert evidence that mishap occurred due to improper application of Anaesthesia and negligence in performance of surgery. Unsustainable Anaesthesia not impleaded as a party. Commission should have directed parties to implicate him as a party to the case or at least taken the steps to summon or record his evidence, he being a key person. No medical record of what happened during the operation produced which is in the exclusive domain of opposite parties. Surgeon the most responsible person cannot run away putting the responsibility on others like anesthetist or other medical staff. *Prima facie* case made out against opposite parties and it was for them to rebut the same, which they could not. Principles of *res ipsa loquitur* applies. Negligence held with joint and several liability of the opposite party, surgeon and Anaesthetist. Compensation of ₹5 lakh awarded with interest at the rate of 7% per annum and cost of ₹5,000. [*Raje Mathew* v *Radhakrishan* 2004 CJC 553]

121. ENT surgery

Cosmetic surgery. Corrective surgery for mending inbuilt defect of nose and permanent scar on lip. Emission of foul smell from nose as gauze pack left inside nose cavity. Smell not subsiding despite second operation by opposite parties when under treatment of another doctor who removed the gauze pack smell stopped. Complainant a young college girl kept away from college and hostel due to foul smell and she had to stay away from friends, teachers and warden for no fault of her. Negligence held. ₹1 lakh awarded as compensation. [*Rekha* v *B. Sadashiva Murthy* 2006 II CPJ 285]

Septoplasty, Post-operative complications due to leaving behind ribbon gauze in the nasal cavity as evident from C.T. Scanning. Patient not undergone any other surgery, Negligence held. Compensation of ₹1 lakh with interest @ 6% p.a. from date of complaint as awarded by State Commission upheld. [*Dr. Ravishankar* v *Jery K. Thomas* 2006 II CPJ 138]

122. Fracture — Leg operation

Leg operation. Leg put under plaster. On removal of plaster, it was found that the portion where the operation was conducted, an abscess had developed. On examination, it was found that some foreign substance left inside the leg. Emergency operation done. Prolonged hospitalisation. Complaints case supported by the statement of independent witness, a professor of orthopedics. Same corroborated by material on record. State commission rightly held that the doctor was negligent in the treatment and proper care and ordinary skill expected of a doctor had not been taken while treating the complainant. Award of compensation of ₹2 lakhs upheld. [*P.P. Ismail* v *K.K. Radha* 1998 I CPJ 16 (NC)]

123. Fracture — Neck

Fracture neck — Surgery — Guide wire left in the body of patient while performing operation. Corrective surgery performed. Patient also suffered severe pain in the lower abdomen and right thigh. Even passed blood in urine. Suffered mental and physical agony. District Forum rightly awarded a compensation of ₹50,000 with cost of litigation of ₹5,000. [*Dr. Anil Nadir* v *Dr. Rakesh Dullu* 2004 I CLT 70 (Del)]

Fracture neck. Total hip replacement was performed to salvage complications of femoral neck fracture. Four major defects in the first operation. Compensation of ₹1,25,000 with interest @ 12% p.a. awarded. [*R.P. Dahiya, Advocate* v *Dr. Pradeep Aggarwal* 2000 III CPJ 175]

124. Fracture — Simple

Simple fracture:-Two surgical interventions deteriorated the condition of patient, resulted in part disability. Order granting compensation upheld. [*Avadh Hospital and Heart Center* v *Mugdha Paul* 2001 II CPJ 186]

125. Fracture — Improper alignment of bones

Medical Advice and Communication. Fracture of hand. Plastered. Improper alignment of bones. Opposite party failed to ensure that instructions given in writing and patient's relatives have been made to understand the importance of repeated X-Ray. Compensation awarded. [*Laxmi* v *Dr. S.K.G.* 2001 II CPJ 335 (MP)]

126. Fracture — Operated upon without x-ray and blood report

Patient suffering from fracture injury resulting in accumulation of puss. Operated upon without x-ray and blood report, including preliminary investigation regarding health of the patient before performing of such operation. If operation is conducted without necessary pathological tests, it amounts to deficiency in service. Order of District Forum directing appellant doctor to pay ₹1 lakh by way of compensation upheld. [*Dr. Dwivedi Pannag Bhushan* v *Balram Kumar Singh* 2003 IV CPJ 735 (Jkh)]

127. Fracture — Hair line

Hairline fracture Developed into displaced fracture due top wrong handling in the opposite parties hospital. Opposite party performed a Hemi-arthrolasty on a young patient of 42 years a bank employee without considering open reduction and internal fixation and against established medical practices. Post-operative infection was not properly attended to and the Hemi-athroplasty was not properly conducted with the result that prosthesis was loosened within a period of two months, held to be a case of negligence and deficiency in service rendered by opposite party. Opposite party directed to pay a sum of ₹5,50,000 to the complainant, which reduced ₹2.50 lakh for initial claim and ₹3. lakh for future operation. [*S. Ramanujam* v *Dr. C.P. Sree Kumar* 2007 I CLT 155 (NC)]

128. Foreign substance left inside

Mob — Delivery of child — *Res ipsa loquitur*. Government Hospital. Sterilization operation subsequently. Complications arose. Second operation due to negligence of respondent no. 2 a mop (towel) was leftover inside her peritoneal cavity. Formation of pus. Development of peritonitis. Resulting in death. Doctrine of *res ipsa loquitur* clearly applies. Absence of any valid explanation by the respondents. Held deceased died due to negligence of respondent no. 2 and 3. [*Achutras Haribhu Khodwa* v *State of Maharashtra* AIR 1996 SC 2377]

Operation for fracture of leg. Leg put under plaster. On removal of the plaster, it was fond that the portion where the operation was conduct, an abscess had developed. On examination, it was fond that some foreign substance left inside the leg. Emergency operation done prolonged hospitalization. Complainant's case supported by the statement of independent witness, a professor of orthopedics. Same corroborated by material on record. State commission rightly held that the doctor was negligent in the treatment and proper care and ordinary skill expected of a doctor had not been taken while treating the complainant. Award of compensation of ₹2 lakhs upheld. [*P.P Ismail* v *K.K. Radha* 1998 I CPJ 16 (NC)]

Sporty Caesarean operation — sponge not removed. Leading to another operation. Medical negligence. Compensation of rupees one lakh awarded. [*Harvinder Kaur* v *Sushma Chawla* 2001 III CPJ 143]

Sponge — Operation. Sponge left inside the body. Opposite party *per se* negligent. [*Meena Vyas* v *City Nursing Home and Hospital, Ludhiana* 2001 II CPJ 172]

Operation — Mopping gauze piece left inside while closing operated area. Medical negligence compensation granted. [*Beti Bai Saxena* v *Dr. S.L. Mukharjee* 2001 III CPJ 251 (MP)]

Caesarean operation. Respondent complaining of pain and irritation in the lower abdominal region. It was fond that a foreign body stood lodged in the system of complainant. Fact established from the report of X-ray, ultra-sound and CT Scanning. The foreign object was removed in the very hospital where she was operated. Doctor had a duty to act with reasonable degree, care and skill which element is missing in this case. State commission awarding compensation of ₹1 lakh. No interference. [*Dr. Satya Atria* v *Shashi Sharma* 2003 I CPJ 612]

Surgery. Leaving of cotton gauze behind by the doctor. Clear case of medical negligence on the part of the appellant doctor. [*Ravi Shankar* v *Jery Thomas* 2006 II CPJ 138]

Surgery for the collection of cleft clip (Harelip), post-operative treatment. Cotton gauze pack inserted in nose cavity by doctor at the time of surgery, not removed from the nose cavity. It resulted in foul smell from nose. Complainant suffered a lot on that account. Doctor guilty of deficiency in service. Negligent for not informing the complainant that gauze pack should be removed within a day. Respondent opposite party directed to pay ₹1 lakh as compensation along with ₹10,000 as costs. [*Kumari Rekha* v *Prof. B. Sadashiva Murthy* 2006 II CPJ 285]

129. Family planning operation

Death of patient during operation Operation performed without calling the Anaesthetist who was called subsequently. This would show negligence of the concerned doctor. Order of District Forum awarding a compensation of ₹4 lakh upheld. Order regarding payment of interest @ 18% by the District forum set aside. [*Dr. Athilakshmi* v *A. Ravi* 2007 I CPJ 177]

130. Fees

The hospital charged ₹200 as medico legal charges. The State Commission held that these charges were wrong, as it had no relation with the treatment and directed refund of amount. [*Champa Ben Babulal* v *C.H. Shah Medical Centre. Appeal No. 82 of 1992, decided on 10-7-1992* (*Guj SC DRC*) (*unreported*)]

Collection of professional fee twice the same day. Fibroid Uterus Laparoscopic Myomectomy. Professional fee payable to gynecologist who performed the surgery and another fee termed professional charges to be pay to other gynecologists who assisted operating surgeon. Deficiency in service. Plea that the doctor who performed operation only a visiting consultant and not a doctor attached to the hospital not taken in written statement not be considered. Professional fee and professional charges being one and the same thing, amount collected in the name of professional charges to be refunded. [*C.R. Jose* v *Mother Hospital (P) Ltd.* 2005 CTJ 1168 (Ker SCDRC)]

131. Free of charge service

Family planning programme Tubectomy operation Free of charge, under family planning programme of State government. Operation unsuccessful Complainant gave birth to female child. Complainant is not a consumer. [*Pushpabai* v *S. Joseph* 2000 II CPJ 566 (MP)]

Government hospital. Such consumer who has not paid any consideration cannot answer the description of the term 'consumer' as referred to in sub-clause (*d*) of clause (1) of section 2 of the Consumer Protection Act, 1986. [*B. Sailor* v *Superintendent, Omani Hospital* 2003 IV CPJ (AP)]

Railway Headquarter Hospital. By pass operation Railway employee treated in Railway, headquarter hospital free of charge, died due to deficiency in service alleged by LRs Neither the complainants nor the deceased was consumer. Complaint not maintainable. [*S. Tharani* v *Southern Railway Headquarters Hospital* 2000 I CLT 304 (TN)]

132. Gastroenterology

Explorative Laparotomy. Suspected teratoma. Surgery to remove big lamp from abdomen along with one of the ovaries. Leaving surgical mop in abdominal cavity and resultant complications necessitating second surgery. Negligence held. Compensation ₹3.5 lakh awarded. [*Dr. K. Ravindra Nath* v *Vitta Veera Surya Prakasam* 2006 IV CPJ 105]

133. Good faith

Burden of proof. Adverse inference. Compensation withholding or the non-production of the Neuro physician. It would show that a Neuro Physician or a Neurologist did not attend to the patient. Non-production will draw adverse inference. Had the medical record and the witness been produced, they would have gone against the case of the respondent. The case is of the due care and caution of good faith in treating patient. Held that there was negligence in treating the patient her ailment was allowed to aggravate, possibility of surgical intervention to remove the blood clot from the brain was not explored which ultimately led to death. A sum of ₹3, lakh in all the cost of ₹15,000 awarded to be pay by the hospital respondent number 2. [*T. Rama Rao* v *Vijay Hospital* 2008 I CPJ 170]

134. Government hospital

Doctor of government hospital. Compensation. Government hospital alone is liable because the doctors are their employees. They do not have direct contact with the consumer nor do they receive consideration from the consumer case wise for treatment. [*Som Nath* v *Union of India* 2007 III CLT 447 (NC)]

135. Hernia

Operation and treatment. Death. Negligence proved. Deceased aged 50 years. In active business. Total compensation of ₹3,85,000 awarded. [*Fakruddin Abbas Barmal* v *Dr. B. Dasgupta* 1998 III CPJ 677]

Death during operation. Pre-operative test not done. Anaesthetist saw the patient only four hours prior to administering the Anaesthesia. Very fact that few crepts and rhonchi developed within ten minutes after starting of the surgery establishes that the patient was not properly prepared for Anaesthesia. Negligence Compensation of ₹1,75,000 awarded. [*Bhanupal* v *Dr. Prakash Padode* 2000 III 356 (MP)]

136. Hepatitis-B

Allegedly developed during blood transfusion. Reports of two doctors to that effect. However, reports not correct in view of the medical literature. Patient might be suffering from Hepatitis-B before coming to the hospital. [*Jagat Narayan Chaube* v *Dr. Achal Sepaha* 2004 I CPJ 435]

137. HIV Virus

Blood transfusion — blood bank. Incorrect donor card issued. HIV virus transmitted through transfusing blood collected from donor certified by blood bank under donor card. Amounts to deficiency in service. Blood bank directed to pay compensation. [*Gopal* v *Nagarjuna Blood Bank* 2003 II CPJ 434 (AP)]

Blood transfusion. Blood supplied by the second opposite party to the first opposite party for transfusion had HIV antibodies, which resulted in contacting HIV infection, which after gestation became full-blown AIDS and patient succumbed to her terminal illness. Second opposite party had failed to carry out the test required to ensure that the blood was not infected. Rule 66(A) of the Drugs and Cosmetics Rules clearly stipulates a mandatory condition of conducting HIV antibody test before certifying the purity of the blood which was not complied with. Held that this is a clear-cut case of negligence. A consolidated sum of ₹4 lakh as compensation with 6% interest from the date of filing complaint awarded to be pay jointly and severally by the respondents. [*M. Chinnaiyan* v *Sri Gokulam Hospital* 2007 III CPJ 228]

138. Hearing impairment

Medicine. Excessive dosage. Resulting in hearing impairment. Respondent doctor held responsible for his following acts of negligence.

(*I*) prescribing Micatin 500 mg twice a day for 10 days when the patient had already taken this injection for 4 days prior to this,

(*ii*) Not modulating the does based on the well-established parameters.

(*iii*) Not doing the audiogram before the treatment, during the treatment or after the treatment. Directed to pay ₹4 lakh (for cochlear implant surgery) with interest @ 12% compensation of ₹2 lakh for mental agony and harassment also awarded. [*Mohd. Ishaq* v *Dr. Martin D' Souza* 2003 I CPJ (NC)]

139. Heart disease

Patient suffering from heart problem shifted to appellant hospital for better management. Also suffering diabetes Mellitus. Allegations that knowing fully well that the patient is a known case of diabetes Mellitus yet between 7 P.M. on 8-11-1993 to 8 P.M. on 9-11-1993 Insulin was not administered to control the diabetes, which resulted in complication and death of the patient. Medical literature and affidavit of doctor to the effect that insulin should have given to control diabetes. One does not require to better evidence for establishing medical negligence. Order of the State Commission awarding compensation of ₹4.50 lakhs along with interest @ 12% upheld. Appeal dismissed with costs of ₹10,000 [*Bombay Hospital and Medical Research Center* v *Krishnabehari M. Aggarwal* 2003 IV CPJ 61 (NC)]

Angioplasty — Post-operative treatment. Deficiency in service. Compensation of ₹2 lakhs with interest @ 6% p.a. awarded. [*Sheela Hirba Naik Gaunekar* v *Apollo Hospitals Ltd.* 2005 III CPJ 56 (NC)]

Deficiency in service in not referring the patient (deceased) specifically or advising him to contact the cardiologist and given him treatment for gastric trouble even after looking at the ECG which revealed 'Mild Opposite party required to pay compensation. It is just and reasonable to award a compensation of ₹5 lakh to the complainant. [*Indrani Bhattacharjee* v *Farakka Super Thermal Power Project* 2007 III CPJ 354]

Bypass heart surgery. Patient was not subjected to the required tests before surgery, which resulted in complication after 4 years of operation. Doctor gave wrong report. Limited deficiency in service. A lump sum of ₹50,000 would meet the end of justice. [*Somnath* v *Union of India* 2007 III CLT 447 (NC)]

140. Heart Problem

Stress test, Staircase exercise test. Death of patient while undergoing the test. Held to be a case of deficiency in rendering medical service by not opting to take due care and caution in submitting the deceased to a 'stress test' which would be acceptable to a large body of medical professionals. Compensation of ₹3 lakhs with interest @ 9% p.a. awarded. [*Mohan Laxman Mavinakatti* v *Dr. Anil E. Kangal* 2006 III CPJ 427]

141. Hysterectomy operation

Death of wife of complainant. Case sheet not given to the complainant by appellant doctor despite several requests. They were only filed during the course of arguments, which motivated the State Commission to take adverse note of their conduct. These records were written alone stretch, long after the events have occurred, not as, and when events took place. No tests conducted before surgery. Held that the complainant has successfully discharged the initial burden that the doctor was negligent and a result of said negligence the patient died. The doctor concerned has not discharged the burden to prove that there was no negligence in her treatment. [*D. Rama Rajyam* v *P.K. Vasudeva Rao* 2007 III CPJ 295]

Total abdominal hysterectomy/oophorectomy would have been sufficient. Total abdominal hysterectomy was not at all necessary, Negligent cutting of rectum. Erroneous cutting of ileum. Gross medical mistakes. Compensation awarded. [*Varadhas S. Nair* v *Dr. Remani Rajan* 2005 III CPJ 36 (NC)]

Medical negligence. Total abdominal Hysterectomy. Where the stomach of the patient was kept open for more than half an hour on the operation table to get the stapler gum from the residence of the doctor, held that it amounts to gross negligence and deficiency in service. [*Varadhas S. Nair* v *Dr. Remani Rajan* 2005 III CPJ 36 (NC)]

142. Homeopathy Practitioner

Indulging in Allopathy. Amounts to deficiency in service. [*Dr. A.M. Mulla* v *Mashakab Ismailsab Nonawada* 1999 II CPR 353 (Kant)]

Medical negligence. Death of patient. Since, the law under which the respondent no. 1 was registered as Medical Practitioner required him to practice in Homeopathy only. He was under a statutory duty not to enter the field of any other system of medicine, as he was not qualified in other system. He having practiced in Allopathy, without being qualified in that system was guilty of negligence *per se*. [*Poonam Verma* v *Ashwin Patel* 1996 II CPJ 1]

143. Hip Replacement

Negligence. After operation, no sensation below left knee. Gangrene developed. Amputation of left leg from above knee. Two more operations performed on her. Held that the left leg was affected by gangrene due to thrombosis or obstruction to the supply of blood through blood vessel, which could not have occurred overnight. First opposite party has not taken proper care or diligence to arrest it. Reimbursement of ₹1,11,000 and damages of ₹1,50,000 with interest @ 12% directed. [*Ghanta Mohan Lakshmi* v *Dr. CVS Ratnam* 2002 II CPJ 144 (AP)]

Negligence. After operation no sensation below left knee. Gangrene developed. Amputation of left leg from above knee. Two more operations performed on her. Order of the State Commission directing reimbursement of ₹1,11,000 and damages of ₹1,50,000 with interest @ 12% held justified. No interference. [*Mohan Lakshmi* v *Dr. CVS Ratnam* 2003 IV CPJ 12 (NC)]

144. Hospital

Deficiency in service. Patient shifted to AC room, after surgery, as it was mid summer, where the AC was not working though he was charged for AC accommodation. Getting bad sore and suffering from same, as his moment had to be restricted and consequent delay in post-operation recovery. Allegation uncontroversial. Deficiency in service. Compensation of ₹30,000 awarded for inconvenience. [*Kethiri Sai Reddy* v *Apollo Hospitals* 2004 III CPJ 412]

Government hospital. Tort — Vicarious liability. Patient lying in the corridor of hospital bleeding through mouth, nostrils and ears unattended by hospital staff and ultimate death. *Res ipsa loquitur* applies. State vicariously liable to pay compensation to deponents of deceased. Fact that government hospitals treat patients freely does not disentitle complainants to get compensation for loss due to negligent act of authorities. Compensation of ₹3 lakhs awarded. [*C. Rangnathan* v *Govt. of T.N.* AIR 2005 Mad 171]

Liability. Administration of Anaesthesia by two Anaesthetists at 10:00 AM and 10:30 AM. In case of surgery of secondary cleft lip connection. Within half an hour of Anaesthesia patient becoming pulse less and death. Neither operation notes nor progress record naming the person who administered Anaesthesia. What the two Anaesthetist were doing in the operation theater and where was the necessity of the two being there not clarified, one of whom, who allegedly had administered Anaesthesia, not even examined. Thus the patient was administered Anaesthesia by two Anaesthetist. Negligence held. Since all operation notes/ progress record silent about the names of doctors and no name of Anaesthetist mentioned anywhere, the hospital would be accountable. ₹3 lakh awarded as compensation. [*Meenakshi Mission Hospital and Research Centre* v *Samuraj* 2005 I CPJ 33]

Emergency care. Denial of treatment. Treatment of deceased injured in an accident started due to emergency. Discontinuance thereof due to failure of persons who brought the injured to deposit an amount. Expert opinion that discontinuance of treatment amounting to denial of treatment hastened death. Held, gross negligence and deficiency in service of hospital. Recovery of fee can wait, but not the death nor treatment for trying to save life. Deceased a young B.Tech Engineering IInd year student ₹10 lakh awarded as compensation. [*Pravat Kumar Mukherjee* v *Ruby General Hospital* 2005 II CPJ 35]

Wrong administration of IV Fluid counter puncturing of blood vessels, leading to extra vasation. Instead of piercing vein opposite parties staff nurse pricked artery in close proximity to the vain. Blood started gushing up the tube resulting in Oedema. Thumb and index fingers amputated leading to 35% disability affecting the complainant's prospects of working of his livelihood. Negligence held ₹1 lakh awarded as compensation. [*A. Kumar* v *Hindu Mission Hospital* 2006 I CPJ 343 (TN)]

145. Injection

Doctor administering Novalgin injection negligently. Resulting in amputation of right leg. Patient was totally ignored. Compensation of ₹1,25,000 awarded. [*Gurusewak Singh* v *Dr. Jaskaran Singh* 1996 III CPJ 300]

Administering of injection led to complications. Failure of doctor to repute the prescription of medicine. Fact that complainants name is not mentioned in the prescription slip does not weaken complainant's case. Distinct from awarded ₹10,000 as compensation. No interference. (1997- I CPR 169).

Administering of injection. Doctor administered injection in the artery instead of vein. Development of gangrene on the fingers. Three fingers had to partly amputated. Compensation of ₹5,000 awarded apart from cost of medicine and travelling expenses. [*Khairati Lal* v *Dr. Kewal Krishan* 1998 I CPJ 181 (Pb)]

Administered at wrong side. Gangrene developed. Amputation of thumb, index finger and middle finger. Fact that injection was given by the opposite party proved. Opposite party negligent in performing his duty towards complainant. Order of District Forum and directing payment of ₹65,363 by way of damages to the complainant upheld. [*Dr. Gian Chandra Aggarwal* v *Darshana Devi* 2002 I CPJ 351]

Administered intravenously instead of intramuscularly. Death. Order of State Commission awarding a total compensation of ₹6 lakh. ₹2 lakh to the complainant widow of the deceased ₹1 lakh to each of the three children and ₹50,000 each of the parents and cost of ₹50,000. Held to be just and equitable in the fact and circumstances of the case. Complainant held entitled to interest @ 12% on the compensation amount from the date of filing the complaint. [*Dr. Sham Lal* v *Saroj Rani* 2003 I CPJ 47 (NC)]

Administering of injection. Laches and negligence causing death of minor child. Opposite parties not qualified to run dispensary. Order awarding compensation upheld. [*Dr. Baleshwar Prasad* v *Firtu Das Mahant* 2003 II CPJ 457 (J&K)]

Administering of injection. Night sister administered wrong injection. Patient suffering from total muscular Paralysis, Cyanosis and Bradycardia died. Doctor and Hospital vicariously was liable. Directed to pay sum of ₹two lakh as compensation with interest @ 12% p.a. [*P. Sudhakar* v *Gowri Gopal Hospital* 2004 I CPJ 329 (AP)]

Administering of injection on the wrong part of the body. Resulting in permanent disability (above 40%) ₹4 lakhs awarded as compensation. [*Ankush Nithoba Dhokale* v *Dr. Anand Dinkar Bhosale* 2004 IV CPJ 316 (Madras)]

Administering of injection. Gangrene in left hand. Held that respondent had remedies available both under criminal and under civil laws. Therefore, the relief in the shape of compensation of ₹25,000 granted by the District Forum has nothing to do with the pendency of criminal appeal. [*Dr. Ramdhuni Sahu* v *Dulari Bai* 2005 III CPJ 35]

146. Impleadment of doctor

Non-impleadment of doctor. Effect. Evidence to the effect that patient died because of lack of proper care and due to negligence on the part of treating doctor/hospital. Non-impleading a particular doctor will not absolve the hospital of their responsibilities. Distinction between 'contract of service' and 'contract for service' also cannot absolve the hospital. [*Savita Garg* v *Director, National Health Institute* 2004 IV CPJ 40]

Vicarious liability of hospital. Unless the doctor is made, a party vicarious liability cannot be fastened to the hospital. [*D.H. Kumari* v *Director, Nizam's Institute of Medical Services* 2003 IV CPJ 441]

Vicarious liability. Necessary party. Impleadment of doctor. Irrespective of the way a particular doctor is impleaded or not, if there is negligence on his part the hospital has to be held to have vicarious responsibility. [*Sushma Sharma* v *Bombay Hospital* 2007 II CPJ 9]

147. Impleadment of insurance company

Insurance company may not be a necessary party but it is certainly a proper party. Application of doctor for impleadment of insurance company allowed. [*Dr. C.C Choubal* v *Pankaj Srivastava* 2003 IV CPJ III (NC)]

No right is given to the insurance company to be impleaded as a party to an action against the doctor/tortfeasor. [*Gurudutt Uro Hospital Lithotripsy Centre* v *Nusrut* 2001 III CLT 516 (MP)]

Under Consumer Protection Act or Rules framed thereunder no right is given to insurance company to be impleaded as a party to an action against doctor/ tortfeasor. Therefore, the application to implead insurance company as the party on the ground that it is in the interest of the complainant or it will give finally to the litigation between the doctor and the insurance company in the case the insurance company denies to indemnify the insured doctor under contract of indemnity, cannot be accepted. [*Ram Dhan* v *Noida Medicare Centre Ltd.* 2003 I CPJ 636]

Case of medical negligence filed against a doctor. Insurance company concerned may not be necessary party. However, it is certainly a proper party. [*Deep Nursing Home* v *Kiran Minhas* 2005 I CPC 206 (Chd.)]

148. Indian Medical Council Act, 1956

Indian Medical Council Act, 1956, section 15(2). Medical negligence. Opposite party acted in contravention of section 5(2) of the Indian Medical Council Act, 1956. This act is punishable under section 15(3) of the Act. [*Avtar Singh Bhatora* v *Dr. Swaran Parkash Garg* 2001 I CPJ 197 (Pb)]

149. ICU

Post-operative treatment. Allegation that patient's death was caused by medical negligence, as he was not immediately kept in ICU after the operation. Same not proved. A conscious decision was taken to keep the patient in her cabin having regard to the stable condition of her at that time. Decision was taken after taking into consideration various factors. Finding of the State Commission found that there was no lack of care and attention on the part of the doctors and the nurses in treating the patient. Upheld. [*S.K. Iyengar* v *Bombay Hospital and Medical Research Centre* 2001 I CPJ 23 (NC)]

150. ICCU

The patient had been put on oxygen and was otherwise being monitored in ICCU, yet there were two serious lapses. One of the nurse not noticing that the oxygen tube had come out and the other of delay of about two hours in incubating the patient. There was a further lapse on the part of the nurse to ensure that oxygen tube remained in place. The patient was restless and his condition was deteriorating very fast. The lack of extra care and vigilance contributed to the acceleration of the end. Held that the hospital liable to pay a compensation of ₹2 lakh to the complainant. [*Bhajan Lal Gupta* v *Mool Chand Khairati Ram Hospital* 2001 I CPJ 31 (NC)]

151. IUCD

Removal of. Sufferings undergone by the complainant were at least partly owing to the negligence and deficiency in service on the part of the doctor during removal of IUCD. Compensation of ₹35,000 with interest at the rate of 10% per annum awarded. [*J.S. Paul* v *Dr. (Mrs.) A Burkataki* 2004 IV CPJ 743]

152. Jaundice

Main deficiency in service that petitioner is not properly treating the complainant for obstructive jaundice after the surgery. Instead of taking immediate steps to drain the fluid collection, the petitioner delayed to correct the problem and did not take protective steps to do the necessary surgery. Held that there is deficiency in service and negligence on the part of the petitioners due to which the respondent had to suffer which was not at all necessary in the present case. Order of the Fora below directing the practitioner to pay ₹3,20,000 jointly and severally along with costs of ₹10,000 upheld. [*M. Alyappan* v *Lakshmi* 2008 I CPJ 50]

153. Jurisdiction

Territorial jurisdiction. Complainant going many a time from Firozabad to Delhi for treatment by opposite party doctor. Doctor not alleged to have come to Firozabad for treatment. District Forum at Firozabad has no jurisdiction to entertain complaint as no part of cause of action arisen within its jurisdiction. [*Dr. A.H. Rizvi* v *Ku Divya Mittal* 2001 III CPJ 223 (UP)]

State commission. Pecuniary jurisdiction. Complainant claiming ₹15 lakh as compensation. State commission competent to obtain the claim, and in determining the question of pecuniary jurisdiction, costs and interest part as prayed for not be taken into account. [*Meena Vyas* v *City Nursing Home and Hospital* 2002 CPJ 1537 (Pb)]

It is not a mandatory or obligatory on the part of the complainant to ask for a specific relief and the Consumer Forums are not debarred from granting relief not prayed for by the complainant in the complaint. [*KM Balakrishana @ Prem Nath* v *Padma Ayurveda Vaidyasala and Research Center* 2003 III CPJ 645 (TN)]

Sterilization operation. Conception. No bar in claiming damages on account of tort of medical negligence in not carrying out sterilization operation with due care. Jurisdiction of Consumer Fora not ousted. [*Pavittar Singh* v *State of Punjab* 2006 III CPJ 287]

Surgery. Medical negligence. Claim for compensation and medical expenses. Held that main claim for compensation as made by the respondents does not fall in any of the categories enumerated in section 75 of the Employees State Insurance Act, 1948. Therefore, jurisdiction of the District Forum to entertain and decide the complainants is not outside under section 75(3) of the Act, 1948. [*Employees State Insurance Corp. (Medical Hospital)* v *Sri Siddaramaiah* 2006 IV CPJ 10]

Medical negligence. ESI hospital. Damages. Claim for. Consumer Fora. Bar of jurisdiction. The Consumer Forum has jurisdiction to adjudicate upon the case of the appellant. The jurisdiction of the consumer Forum is not ousted by virtue of sub-section (1) or (2) or (3) of section 75 of the ESI Act. [*Kishori Lal* v *ESI Corporation* 2007 II CPJ 25]

154. Kidney transplantation

Allegation that transplantation of the kidneys of complainant was necessitated on account of wrong diagnoses/wrong treatment given by the opponent doctor. Complainant failed to obtain expert opinion with regard to the medicines prescribed by the opponent doctor having reacted on kidneys of complainant. Alleged medical negligence not proved. Complainant liable to be dismissed. [*Prasannakamar Digamberdas* v *Dr. Hardasbhai G. Patel* 2005 I CPJ 453]

Kidney transplantation done successfully and patient was well for 7 days. Death of patient after 7 days. It is high-risk operation. Acute rejection typically occurs 5 to 7 days of post-transplant. No negligence in the surgery of kidney transplantation and post-operative care. No sufficient grounds for deficiency in service and negligence are proved against opposite party. [*P.B. Rao* v *D.S. Sunder* 2006 II CPJ 223]

155. Kidney damaged

Complainant was suffering from pain in the left side of his abdomen. RG stone clinic and Urological Research Center operated on him for removal of the stone and discharged him the next day. His condition did not improved and he was having problems with his left kidney. The complainant got himself admitted to the medical colleges Rohtak and he was told that his left kidney had stopped functioning totally. He filed a complaint with the State Commission against R.G. Stone Clinic and Urological Research Center for giving wrong information that everything was normal. A State Commission awarded ₹20,000 as compensation and ₹5,000 as costs. The National Commission enhanced the compensation from ₹25,000 to ₹1,29,000 along with interest at the rate of 6% per annum from the date of filing the complaint until the date of payment along with ₹5,000 as costs. [*RG Stone Clinic and Urological Research Centre* v *Kali Ram Rana* 2008 II CPJ 226 (NC)]

156. Laparotomy operation

Abortion: Operation was resulting in 'gut loop cut' developing into septicemia and ultimately death of patient. Petitioner attempted to disown any responsibility despite the ultrasound test and MTP operation. All through proceeding, she did not appear to have any remorse feeling for the patient and her family who had passed through trauma result her death. The petitioner for his attempts to escape liability deserves to be severely penalized. Revision petition liable to be dismissed with the cost of ₹20,000 order of the State Commission directing to practitioner to pay compensation of ₹4,50,000 upheld. [*Ramesh Jain* v *Jagroop Singh* 2008 I CPJ 233 (NC)]

Gastroenterologist performed explorative Laparotomy in a suspected case of Teratoma to remove the bog lump from the abdomen along with one of the ovaries and left a surgical mop in the abdominal cavity. Resulted in complications which necessitated a second surgery by a surgical oncologist. Findings of the State Commission about deficiency in service upheld. A sum of ₹3.5 lakhs awarded as compensation towards medical expenditures, mental agony trauma faced by the complainant. [*Dr. K. Ravindra Nath* v *Vitta Veera Surya Prakasam* 2008 IV CPJ 105]

Consent surgical procedure. Whether consent form refers to diagnostic and operative laparoscopy and Laparotomy if needed it does not amount to consent for OH BSO surgery removing the uterus and ovaries/fallopian tubes. [*Samira Kohli* v *Prabha Manchanda* 2008 I CPJ 56]

157. Laproscopic operation

Stone in gall bladder. Laparoscopic operation performed. Common bile duct was cut whereas only cystic duct was required to be cut. *Per se* amounts to negligent act. Compensation of ₹1 lakh awarded. [*Gurmit Mahal* v *Chauhan Nursing Home* 1998 II CLT 399]

Consent surgical procedure. When the consent form refers to diagnostic and operative laparoscopy and 'laparotomy if needed', it refers to consent for a definite laparoscopy with a contingent laparotomy if needed. It does not amount to consent for OH BSO surgery removing the uterus and ovaries/fallopian tubes. [*Samira Kohli* v *Prabha Manchanda* 2008 I CPJ 56]

158. Lithium therapy

Prescription. Neither history of patient recorded nor relevant tests advised prior to starting lithium therapy. Heavy dosage of lithium administered. Serum lithium level not properly monitored for 6 months. Cerebellar degeneration due to lithium toxicity. Permanent disability. Compensation awarded. [*Sundeep Agarwal* v *Modern Medical Inst.* 2005 II CLT 368]

159. Lung cancer

Decortications surgery. Historical report not taken. Case of negligence. ₹2,25,000 awarded as compensation. [*S.V.S. Panchori* v *Dr. Kaushal Pandey* 1999 I CPJ 332 (Bom)]

160. Liability of hospital

Anaesthesia., Administering of Child was administered Anaesthesia by two anaesthetists at 10:00 a.m. and 10:30 a.m. Child was pulseless. Operation notes silent about the name of the doctors. It is hospital which would be accountable for whatever happens in the hospital. No interference with the order directing hospital to pay compensation of ₹3 lakhs with interest @ 18% p.a. [*Meenakshi Mission hospital and Research Centre* v *Samuraj* 2005 I CPJ 33 (NC)]

If the pharmacy had supplied the medicine other than the prescribed one, it was the burden of duty of the doctor on duty to have ensured that that the medicine being administered to the patient was the one prescribed and if any alternative was being given the same was proper and safe alternative. Lapse on the part of the hospital staff. Hospital cannot escape liability compensation awarded. [*Deepak Gokaran* v *Chairman Mohant Gurumukh Singh Charitable Hospital Trust* 2003 I CPJ 518]

Injection. Administration of. Night sister administered wrong injection. Patient suffered total muscular paralysis, cynosis and Brady cardia. Died. Doctor and hospital vicariously liable. Directed to pay sum of ₹2 lakhs as compensation. [*P. Sudhakar* v *Gowri Gopal Hospital* 2004 I CPJ 329]

Medical negligence. A patient who approaches the hospital does not know the doctors. She approaches that hospital because of reputation of the hospital. Here the primary responsibility of the hospital authorities is to see that there is no negligence on the part of his officers. Non-providing of a doctor or anaesthetist or an assistant is essentially lapse on the part of the hospital authorities. [*Leela Bai* v *Sebastion* 2002 II CPJ 363]

Death due to 'septicaemia shock'. Attending doctors did not care to know actual problem with patient. Deficiency in service. Non-production of enquiry report. Adverse inference to be drawn. Hospital held vicariously liable. Compensation of ₹2,50,000 awarded. [*Gopal Vashisth* v *State of Uttaranchal* 2005 I CPJ 630]

161. Legal representative

Bringing record: Permissible where there is a breach of legal duty which the doctor has *vis-a-vis* his parent. [*K.N. Joshi (Deceased) through LRs* v *Dr. Neelam Kaul* 1999 I CPC 49 (Del)]

Death of patient. Complain filed by legal representative. Held maintainable. [*P.V.S. Kunhikrishnan Nambiar* v *Speechitra Terunal Institute for Medical Science and Technology* 2001 III CPJ 86 (Ker)]

162. Limitation period

Time barred complaint. Complaint filed after more than three years of the alleged treatment taken by complainant from the opposite party. Complaint hopelessly barred by time. Liable to be dismissed. [*Survarna* v *Rohit Bhatt* 1996 II CLT 403 (NC)]

Surgery done on 10-1-1994, on 16-11-1994 the complainant was told that his eye cannot be cured, Period of limitation start from that day. Complaint filed on 16-5-1996 not barred by time. [*V. Pahwa* v *Surindra Mohan Ghose* 2004 IV CPJ 1 (NC)]

Surgery of glaucoma done in 1990 Treatment continuing in various hospitals till it was found in 1997 that patient lost complete eye sight. Complaint filed within two years, Thereafter, not barred by limitation. [*Dr. P.B. Lal* v *Suresh Chandra Roy* 2006 III CPJ 452]

Abortion and Tubectomy Complainant becoming pregnant agreed to advice of doctor in medical college not to go for abortion and to have birth of the child. Clear indication that she was aware of a growing pregnancy despite abortion and Tubectomy, yet waited for birth of child and filing complaint after the prescribed period without an application for Condonation of delay. Complaint barred by time. [*Dhanmani Devi* v *Dr. Sudha Kumari* 2006 III CPR 94 (Bih)]

Impleading doctor after a period of limitation Impermissible unless sufficient reason shown. Non-impleading of doctor does not absolve the hospital or doctor of liability for medical negligence if complainant can prove the same because of facts and records of the case. [*K. Venkateshwarlu* v *Managing Director Nagarjunu Hospital* 2006 I CPJ 47]

Plea that complaint being filed more than two years after treatment of complainant by opposite party barred by limitation. Said plea not raised before District Forum, but since the question of limitation goes to the root of the matter, opposite party to be allowed to raise the plea provided the complainant being given sufficient opportunity to resist the question of limitation. Matter remanded. [*Dr. S. Samickannu* v *Dr. Vijayasankar* 2006 II CPR 173 (TN)]

Sufficient cause Condonation of delay. Complainant receiving treatment from opposite parties between 6-10-1993 and 29-10-1993 and complaint filed on 17-2-1997 nearly 3½ years after treatment. Plea for Condonation on ground that he was not keeping well, not supported by documentary evidence, but it is in the averments in the complaint that during the period he had visited his native place in far away Kerala showing that his mobility not affected by alleged sickness. No sufficient ground made out in the explanation given for such inordinate delay. Complaint dismissed. [*P. Gopinathan* v *Dr. Anand Somaya* 2004 II CPR 381 (Mah)]

Condonation of delay containing cause of action, Plastering of fractured hand by opposite party unqualified person. Patient taken to other doctors without complaint, yet damaged hand becoming permanent. Complaint filed after 4 years since complainant last seen by opposite party without application for Condonation of delay, barred by time, though cause of action, a continuing one. Taking lenient view Supreme Court allowed complaint and awarded compensation. [*Md. Suleman Ansari* (*DMS*) v *Shankar Bhandari* 2005 III CPJ I (SC)]

163. Medical negligence

A mistake by a medical practitioner which is not no reasonably competent and a careful practitioner would have committed is a negligent one. [*A.S. Mittal* v *State of UP* AIR 1989 SC 1570]

Death of patient, Since, the law under which Respondent no. 1 was registered a Medical practitioner required him to practice in HOMOEOPATHY ONLY, he was under statutory duty not to enter the field of any other system of medicine, as he was not qualified in the other system. He having practiced in Allopathy, without being qualified in that system, was guilty of negligence *per se*. [*Poonam Verma* v *Ashwin Patel* 1996 II CPJ 1]

Death of patient due to shock resulting from reduction of the fracture attempted by the appellant doctor without taking the elementary caution of giving anesthetic to patient, Concurrent findings of the Trial Court and the High Court that the appellant doctor was guilty of negligence and wrongful acts towards the patient and was liable for damages no interference. [*Laxman Balakrishan Joshi* v

Trimbak Bapu Godbole AIR 1969 SC 128]

Hysterectomy Operation. Total abdominal hysterectomy where the stomach of the patient was kept open for more than half an hour on the operation table to get the stapler gum from the residence of the doctor held that it amounts to gross negligence and deficiency in service. [*Varadhas S. Nair* v *Dr. Remani Rajan* 2005 II CPJ 36]

In order to decide whether negligence is established in any particular case, the alleged act or omission or course of doctor, complained of, must be judged not by ideal standards nor in the abstracts but against the backgrounds of the circumstances in which the treatment in question was given. [*Deepak Gokaran* v *Chairman, Mahant Gurmukh Charitable Hospital Trust* 2003 I CPJ 518]

In order to prove medical negligence Fora can take up the case of apparent negligence or negligence act proved by expert opinion. Burden of proving the negligent act or wrong diagnosing was not the complainant. [*Manjit Walia* v *Dr. Upinder Singh Ghai* 2001 I CPR 660 (Pb)]

Medical practitioner is not an insurer and so cannot be blamed every time if something goes wrong. In medicine, in particular, things can go wrong in the treatment of a patient even with the very best available care. [*Indira Kartha* v *Dr. Mathew Samuel Kalarickal* 2002 II CLT 314 (NC)]

Not be treated as an ordinary negligence. Medical negligence must be patently looked to be so and strict proof is warranted for such negligence. For *ipse dixit* allegations against a doctor before consumer, Forum is not justifiable to hold doctors responsible for medical negligence and to award the compensation. [*Afroza* v *Dr. Saleema Bano* 2004 III CPJ 765 (J&K)]

True test for establishing negligence on the part of a doctor is as to whether he has been proved to be guilty of such failure as no doctor of ordinary skill would be guilty of acting reasonable care. [*Ghisa Ram* v *Dr. P.K. Bansal* 2003 IV CPJ 299 (Del)]

Where there is more than one option available, exercise of one option by a doctor cannot be said to be a case of medical negligence. [*Manju Garg* v *Goel Hospital* 2005 IV CPJ 62 (NC)]

Whether medical negligence are established in any particular case the alleged act or omission or cause of conduct complained of, must be judged neither by ideal standards nor in the abstract but against the background of the circumstances in which the treatment in question was given. [*J.S. Paul* v *Dr. (MRs) A. Barkataki* 2004 IV CPJ 743 (Megh)]

164. Medical practitioner

Allegation that death caused by surgical procedure resorted to by petitioners who were holding qualification in practicing in medicines known as GCIM and not having specialization in surgical procedure not a case of extreme emergency. There was enough time to reach the patient to an appropriate centre for such a surgical procedure. Award of compensation of ₹2,01,000 upheld. [*K. Mahabala Bhat* v *K. Krishna* 2002 II CPJ 127 (NC)]

Doctor not qualified and authorized to practice in Allopathic system of medicines, prescribing Allopathic drugs resulting in aggravation of pain medical negligence. Compensation awarded. [*Avtar Singh Bhatora* v *Dr. Swaran Prakash Garg.* 2001 I CPJ 197 (Pb)]

Doctors treating patient were not qualified in allopathy could not identify the disease early resulting in severe complications, case of deficiency in service. [*Ch. Padma* v *Sudha Nursing Home* 2002 I CPJ 53 (AP)]

Homeopathic doctor could advice ultrasound test in order to arrive at right diagnosis. Fact that he could prescribe the use of only homeopathic medicines is fully known to the complainant, administering medicine. No negligence *per se.* [*Naresh Kumar* v *Vaid Ram Phal* 1998 II CLT 191 (Hry)]

Homeopathic doctor not legally qualified to practice in allopathy. After administering, Homeopathic medicines treated the deceased in allopathy by administering glucose saline and other injections. Held to be negligence *per se.* [*Shive Kumar Gautam* v *Amina B.* 1991 I CPR 592 (MP)]

Death of patient Medical negligence, since the law under which the respondent no. 1 was registered a medical practitioner required him to practice in homeopathy only, he was under a statutory duty not to enter the field of any other system. He, having practiced in allopathy, without being qualified in that system, was guilty of negligence *per se.* [*Poonam Verma* v *Ashwin Patel* 1996 II CPJ 1]

165. Medical record

No negligence found on part of doctor in respect of intestinal operation. However, he could found partially negligent in not producing any papers pertaining to the day-to-day treatment and hospital record regarding admission of patient, examination and treatment given to maintain transparency in the treatment record. Compensation of ₹10,000 awarded by District Forum upheld. [*Dr. Pradeep Kayal* v *Balchand* 2004 III CPJ 144 (MP)]

Adverse inference. Non-supply of relevant documents by hospital regarding treatment of patient. Adverse inference could possibly be drawn with regard to deficiency in service. [*SR. Shivaprakash* v *Wockhardt Hospital Limited* 2006 II CPJ 123 (NC)]

Death of 19 years old girl after administration of the Saline drip can causal treat given by the appellant on phone when the patient developed fits. Conduct of the appellant in not attending the patient at first call. Findings of the State Commission that the cause of death is septicemia ,which arose during the treatment of the appellant has not maintained record of treatment and has not explained as to why the condition of patient deteriorated so rapidly after administration of the drip. Compensation of ₹2,15,000 awarded by the State Commission just and reasonable. [*Dr. A. Jayaseelan* v *Anadian* 2007 II CPJ 101]

Treatment records non-production of the treating doctor and Nursing Home refused to gave any treatment records either to the complainant or even to the District Forum, held that needle of suspicion about medical negligence can pointed towards the treating doctor and the nursing home in such a case. [*Dr. Balagopal* v *K.V. Radhakrishna Menon* 2007 II CPJ 244 (NC)]

Blood group report, report given by petitioner that blood group of complainant was AB+ whereas it was AB- whether harm came to the patient or not would not be criteria. It is failure on the part of the petitioner to take due care to return correct finding. Direction to pay compensation of ₹25,000 along with the cost of ₹2,000 by District Forum as affirmed. State Commission requires no interference. [*Chandigarh Clinical Laboratory* v *Jagjeet Kaur* 2007 IV CPJ (NC)]

Blood test, wrong report. Compensation. Nor adverse consequences refund to fee directed. Compensation of ₹5,000 each awarded by District Forum reduced to ₹2,000 each. [*Purohit Charitable Laboratory* v *Vijay Kumar* 2001 III CPJ 239 (Raj)]

Ultrasound of abdomen report showing multiple shadows of the stones, 18 days of clinical tests Operation. No stone found, deficiency on the part of respondents in conveying the report. Refund of amount charged for the examination together with costs of ₹1,000 directed. [*Darshan Kaur* v *Dr. J.S. Sodhi* 1999 I CPJ 557 (UT)]

Bypass heart surgery. Patient was not subjected to the required tests before surgery, which resulted in complication after 4 years of operation. Doctor gave a wrong report limited deficiency in service. A lump sum compensation of ₹50,000 would meet the need of justice. [*Som Nath* v *Union of India* 2007 III CLT 447 (NC)]

Wrong report. Resulting in removal of breast. No cancer as per subsequent report. Doctor should not have persisted for operation on the first and primary report only. He should have got confirmatory report from pathologist also. Medical negligence. Compensation of ₹63,500 not excessive. [*Uttaranchal Forest Hospital Trust* v *Raisan* 2004 I CPJ 257 (Uttr.)]

Wrong report. Cancer operation. Review of slides by other doctors showing that complainant was not suffering from cancer. Medical negligence order awarding compensation of ₹1 lakh affirmed. [*Dayanand Medical College and Hospital, Ldh, through its president/secretary* v *Jugal Kishore Syal* 2000 III CPR 450 (Pb)]

Wrong report. Compensation. Due to incorrect report, the complainant has lived for one day with an idea that he is suffering from dangerous disease. Complainant has spent ₹2,500. An additional compensation of ₹5,000 for one-day agony will be justified and reasonable. [*Diagnostic Clinical Laboratory* v *Bhagwan Singh* 2004 II CPJ 587 (Uttr.)]

HIV Test. As per report dated 3-12-2002, the petitioner was found to be HIV positive through the screening test, which was done from HIV Niwa Kit of Cadila. The petitioner was advise o co-relate the result by Western Blot Technique. In report dated 10-12-2003 the basis for reaching the conclusion in regard to petitioner being HIV negative has not been disclosed. Order of the State Commission allowing the appeal of respondent and dismissing the complaint of petitioner alleging deficiency in service upheld. [*Susheel Kumar* v *Virendra Mahala* 2007 III CPJ 395]

166. Medical tests

Ultrasonography test. Wrong done. Resultantly, twin babies in womb could not be detected and the complainant was prevented from taking extra care, Amounts to deficiency in service. Compensation awarded. [*Krishna Mont Tiwari* v *Dr. Gauri Bandyopadhyay* 2003 I CPJ 286 (WB)]

Requisite tests not conducted on the day of taking sample. Laboratory attached to hospital is 24 hours laboratory. Explanation given by opposite party that microbiology department of hospital ceases to work after 5:00 PM and been offered in order to get themselves wriggle out of the legal consequences of not conducting the necessary and requisite test on the day of taking sample. If such circumstances, none conducting of tests on the day of taking the samples amounts to deficiency in service. Compensation of ₹2,000 awarded. [*Shahul Hameed* v *Apollo Hospital Enterprises* 2002 II CPJ 189 (TN)]

Rheumatoid Arthritis, Imuran tablets 50 mg prescribing without holding any prior test resulting in hair loss and bone marrow suspension. Gross negligence, Award of compensation of ₹25,000 held justified. [*B.K. Ghosh* v *Dr. Prof. P. Maulick* 2005 I CPJ 737 (WB)]

MRI Scan. In spite of her having told opposite parties to staff, that patient had taken breakfast. She was taken for MRI. The opposite party still started conducting MRI, maybe for monetary reasons. Death occurred due to asphyxia because of certain food particles having been choking in the windpipe. As contributory negligence of the complainant is there token compensation, ₹25,000 awarded. [*Mukesh Jain* v *LK Anand* 2007 III CLT 456 (NC)]

167. Medicines

Compensation- Insect found in a sealed bottle of B. protein. However, District Forum erred in holding that because of the consuming B. protein earlier by complainant his health deteriorated on the supposition that earlier bottles contained insects. Complainant entitled to a reasonable compensation. Order of District Forum awarding compensation of ₹20,000 and costs ₹500 modified. Complainant held entitled to compensation of ₹7,500 with costs of ₹500. [*Manager, British Biologicals* v *PL Prasad* 1996 I CLT 284 (AP)]

Diabetic patient Treatment by opposite party. Ayurvedic tablets prescribed. Consumption leading to severe stomach pain. Capsule found to contain 1681 ppm. Lead against permissible lead of 20 ppm in drug. Prescription and administration of hazardous drug. Amounts to deficiency in service. Compensation awarded. [*K.M. Balkrishnan @ Premnath* v *Padma Ayurveda Vaidyasala and Research Center* 2003 III CPJ 645 (TN)]

Excessive dosage. Resulting in hearing impairment. Respondent doctor held responsible for his following acts of negligence. (1) Prescribing Amikacin for four days prior to this, (2) not modulating the dosage based on the well established parameters, (3) not doing the audiogram before the treatment, during the treatment. Directed to pay ₹4 lakh (for Cochlear implant surgery) with interest @ 12% compensation of ₹2 lakh for mental agony and harassment also awarded. [*Mohd. Ishaq* v *Dr. Martin D'souza* 2003 I CPJ 116 (NC)]

168. Medical treatment

Allegation that death caused by surgical procedure resorted to by petitioner who were holding qualification in practicing in medicines known as GCIM and not having specialization in surgical procedure. Not a case of extreme emergency. There was enough time to reach the patient to an appropriate centre for such a surgical procedure. Award of compensation of ₹2,01,000 upheld. [*K. Mahabala Bhat* v *K. Krishna* 2002 II CPJ 127 (NC)]

Child of few days examined by doctor. Gardinal tablet prescribed to be consumed by infant for a period of one month without conducting further tests. Condition of child deteriorated. Doctor should have taken care that patient was simply an infant. Doctor held negligent in rending professional service to the child. Order directing payment of compensation of ₹25,000 by the said doctor confirmed. [*Dr. Shyam Sunder Tantia* v *Deepika* 2002 I CPJ 411 (Raj)]

Excessive bleeding Patient remains unattended by doctor for 12 hours. Condition deteriorated failure on the part of the doctor and hospital in administration of treatment. Negligence. Compensation awarded. [*Ujjain Charitable Trust Hospital* v *Ramesh Chandra* 2003 III CPJ 181 (MP)]

Fracture of Tibial plethora with an open wound. Plaster of Paris applied. Gangrene developed Amputation of leg, Permanent disability. Complainant established negligence on the part of opposite party doctor by overwhelming evidence most of which is uncontroversial and untrammeled. Total compensation of ₹1,75,000 awarded with interest @ 12% p.a. [*Dulipudi Srinivas* v *Dr. Prasad Yogaling Eswara Rao* 2003 IV CPJ 326 (AP)]

Patient in serious condition was left unattended without the services of specialist for over three hours, which was critical in the life of patient. Hospital held negligent. [*Bombay Hospital and Medical Research Centre* v *Krishnabshari M. Aggarwal* 2003 IV CPJ 61 (NC)]

Patient suffering from acute and severe dehydration not given the least medical service, unduly denied. Patient was led to reach the point of "no return". Glaring example of rendering deficient services by a medical man. Compensation of ₹2 lakh awarded. [*Birdhi Chand Meena* v *Dr. Prabhakar Sethi* 2003 I CPJ 45 (Raj)]

Opposite Party No. 1 — doctor treating petitioner. Abruptly went out of town without referring the patient for any test, or advising the patient to be admitted as inpatient or referring to any other hospital with better facilities. Condition of patient deteriorated. Shifted to another nursing home where he was left unattended by opposite party no. 2 doctor, deficiency in service on the part of both the doctors directed to pay compensation of ₹2 lakh. Burden to be shared at the ratio of 3:1 by the doctors. [*Varanasi Subrahmanyam* v *Dr. G. Ravi Kumar* 2004 I CPJ 125 (AP)]

Lithium therapy. Prescription. Neither history of patient record. Nor relevant tests advised prior to starting Lithium therapy. Heavy dosage of Lithium administered. Serum Lithium level not properly monitored for 6 months. Cerebellate degeneration due to Lithium toxicity. Permanent disability. Compensation awarded. [*Sandeep Agarwal* v *Modern Medicine Inst.* 2005 II CPR 268 (Chitt.)]

Epilepsy: Patient not treated by Neurologist. Modern facility for tests and first choice drug for disease not available. Patient not referred to a place where all the essentials for the treatment of disease available, Cardiac arrest resulting in death of patient. Case of deficiency in service. Compensation of ₹1 lakh awarded. [*Channaveerashetty* v *Dr. Vijaya Kumar* 2005 II CPR 450 (Karn)]

Accident victim. Emergency treatment by doctors discontinued because of failure on the part of the persons who brought him to the hospital to deposit ₹15,000. Resulting in death. Doctors on duty failed to do what a prudent and reasonable doctor is expected to do. Deficiency in service on their part. Compensation awarded. [*Pravat Kumar Mukherjee* v *Ruby General Hospital* 2005 II CLT 196 (NC)]

Patient admitted in the opposite party hospital for the complaint for fever. Patient was having Epistaxis for which he was given nasal packing placed anteriorly. The ENT specialist saw the patient only at 3:40 P.M. even though he was having repeated attacks of Epistaxis throughout the day. Clearly establish negligence of the respondent in treating the patient. Doctor who treated the patient was competent to give allopathy treatment that he gave, as he was a qualified to give unani medicines. Diseased was aged only 23 years and completed M.A. and B.Ed. Compensation of ₹7,50,000 awarded. [*P.N. Thakur* v *Hans Charitable Hospital* 2007 III CPJ 340]

169. Medical ethics

Rule of confidentiality. Exception appellant who is about to marry tested HIV positive and his marriage called off as the hospital authorities informed his HIV status to the relatives to the girl whom he intended to marry. Such disclosure does not affect the appellant's right in any way. It is open to the hospital or doctor to reveal the information to the relatives of the girl as she got a right to know the HIV status of the person to whom she intended to marry. [*Mr. 'X'* v *Hospital 'Z'* 2003 I CPJ 14]

170. Medical literature

Evidentiary value. Judge's preference of the opinion expressed in the books relied on behalf of the complainant over the opinion given in the books citied by on behalf of opposite party. It would not be sufficient to establish negligence to opposite parties. [*Bishwa Nath Das* v *Bijoy Sinha Roy* 2007 III CPJ 223]

171. Mental retardness

Res ipsa Loquitor. Case of post-term pregnancy. Treated as a normal case despite of the fact that there was no labour pain even after twelve hours of the pitocin drip administration, pitocin drip was replaced after two days. Mind labour pain developed after two hours. Another induct method namely artificial rupture of membrane was done and appellant number 2 delivered a child. Within sixteen hours after discharge from the hospital, the child had to be rushed back to the hospital with high fever, convulsion and breathing difficulties. No proper ante natal fetal monitoring. Respondent No. 2 could have easily averted the result of a child with Hypoxic Ischemic Encephalopathy if only she acted diligently with enough care and caution this is expected in the present case. She has totally failed to take into account all warnings signals and failed to take step to immediately conducted a cesarean delivery to avert birth asphyxia. Presence of the pediatrician also not insisted at the time of delivery to ensure the baby progress from anoxic insult and to prevent on set of septicemia. It has resulted in life long mental retardation of child, epilepsy and physical disability necessitating custodial care. Case of *res ipsa loquitur*. Respondents directed to pay compensation of ₹4.5 lakhs with interest @ 10% p.a. [*Baby Geetha* v *All India Institute of Medical Sciences* 2006 III CPJ 8 (NC)]

172. Mismatching of blood

Due to negligence of attending doctors. Resulting in death of patient. ₹2 lakhs awarded as compensation. [*Jaspal Singh* v *The Post Graduate Institute of Medical Education and Research* (*PGI*) *Chandigarh* 2000 II CPJ 439]

173. MRI Scan

In spite of her having told opposite parties staff that patient had taken breakfast when she was taken for MRI. The opposite party started conducting MRI, maybe for monetary reasons. Death occurred due to asphyxia because of certain food particles having been choked in the windpipe. As contributory negligence of the complainant is there token compensation, ₹25,000 awarded. [*Mukesh Jain* v *KL Anand* 2007 III CLT 456 (NC)]

174. Medical advice

Compensation. At the time of treatment, availability of Immunohistochemistry test was well known. It was recommended by senior consultant pathologist of the respondent hospital on 9-4-1987. Treating doctors of the same hospital disregarded this advice and continued to treat the patient on the basis of their own assumptions. Subsequently, when their line of treatment did not give any relief to patient the very same doctor referred the same specimen for immunohistochenistry test to the specialty Ranbaxy Ltd. Report submitted on 6-10-1997 disregarded by doctors of the respondent hospital by inventing their own logic which is not comprehensible. Opposite party held to be negligent in treating the patient for Hodgkin 's disease despite the fact that she was suffering from non-Hodgkin's disease. Compensation of ₹7,62,000 allowed against respondents. [*Nand Kishore Verma* v *Batra Hospital and Medical Centre* 2007 II CPJ 336]

Fracture of hand. Plastered. Improper alignment of bones. Opposite party failed to ensure that instructions given in writing and patient's relatives have been made to understand the importance of repeated X-Ray. Compensation awarded. [*Laxmi* v *Dr. S.K.G.* 2001 II CPJ 335 (MP)]

175. Negligence/*Res ipsa loquitur*

Res Ipsa loquitur. Applicability of doctrine — operation for hernia under general Anaesthesia — Anesthetist leaving operation theater immediately after extubation, at least with implied consent of surgeon. Patient not gaining consciousness and death occurring within 10 minutes. What was condition of patient at the time of extubation, what happened after surgery and extubation, why patient not shifted to ward, why anaesthetist left before shifting patient to ward, who monitored to him during this period and what steps taken for prevention are all questions remaining unanswered. Res Ipsa Loquitur applies. Both surgeon and anesthetist liable for deficiency in service. ₹4 lakh awarded as compensation. [*Dr. Yogendra A. Pandya* v *Harshaben E. Patel* 2004 I CPR 308 (Guj)]

Applicability of maxim. MTP. Incomplete abortion resulting in dysfunctional uterine bleeding (DUB). Remnants left in uterus causing bleeding and other consequential physical and mental suffering as per scan report. Evacuation of uterus for incomplete abortion. Maxim *res ipsa loquitur* applies. Failure of opposite parties to exercise necessary expertise and skill as a result of which incomplete abortion had come about. A clear case of negligence and deficiency in service. ₹2.5 lakh awarded as compensation. [*Shakila Sathanandam* v *Dr. S.S. Kodmani* 2005 III CPJ 12 TN)]

Scope and applicability. *Res Ipsa loquitur* only a rule of evidence operating in the field of civil law especially in cases of torts in determining onus of proof in actions relating to negligence. Said doctrine cannot be pressed into service for determining *per se* the liability for negligence with in the dominion of criminal law. It has, if at all, a limited application in trial on a charge of criminal negligence. [*Jacob Mathew* (*Dr*) v *State of Punjab* 2005 III CPR 70 (SC)]

Applicability of the maxim: - Performance of three operations, one for cataract and two for glaucoma & Loss of sight. Opposite party not producing records of pre-operative ,and the post-operative findings and other investigation reports. No expert can give an opinion whether treatment/operation correct or not. Opposite party not explaining what was the condition of respective eyes before every operation, what was indication of each operation, what operation he performed, what was the result of each operation and why in spite of that the complainant lost his vision. Doctrine of Res Ipsa loquitur applies and opposite party to be held liable for medical negligence and deficiency in service, ₹1.85 lakh awarded as compensation. [*Dr. Shyam Kumar* v *Rameshbhai Harmanbhai Kachhiya* 2006 I CPJ 16 (NC)]

Applicability. Surgery for removal of mesenteric cyst. Diseased pregnant women. Removal of functional kidney while removing cyst. Death of patient and foetus despite dialysis and kidney transplantation. Opposite party, an experienced general surgeon is expected to know the location of the cyst and location of kidney. Even after commencement of surgery undertaken by him, he failed to differentiate between a cyst and kidney. Principle of *res ipsa loquitur* clearly attracted. Negligence held ₹6.2 lakh awarded as compensation and ₹20,000 towards costs. [*Consumer Education and Research Society* v *Dr. Prakash R. Modi* 2006 I CPJ 537 (Guj)]

Applicability: Kidney transplantation. Patient pregnant woman. While removing mesenteric cyst, functional kidney removed resulting in death of patient as well as foetus. Doctrine applies. Negligence held ₹6.2 lakh awarded as compensation. [*Consumer Education and Research Society* v *Dr. Prakash R. Modi* 2006 I CPJ 537(Guj)]

Obstetrics/Gynecology to held of experts available in the hospital casualty officer• on duty, subordinate of opposite party, Head of the Department of Medicine and Nephrology, referring patient to a private clinic run by opposite party, where no dialyses available at relevant time. The day when patient shifted to the clinic being Sunday the Pharmacy from which opposite party intended to purchase dialysis machine not open and patient remained uncared for a whole day and died the next day. Negligence held ₹1 lakh awarded as compensation. [*S.S. Prasad* v *Sunitra Devi* 2006 IV CPJ 210 (Jhar)]

176. Neurology

Application of traction: - Pain in neck and arm Patients suffering unbearable pain while on traction, getting relief after treatment in Neurology Hospital and cause of problem of patient stated to be non-organic in origin recommending conservative treatment. Opposite party not adducting any evidence particularly. District Forum relying on medical reports filed by the complainant held the opposite party deficient in service ₹40,000 awarded towards cost of treatment ₹10,000 as compensation and ₹2,000 as costs by the District Forum upheld. [*Dr. Paras K Paka* v *Anant Vithal Tarkasband* 2004 III CPJ 82 (Mah)]

Epilepsy. Opposite party an ENT surgeon not knowing what drugs to be given to epileptic patient and what tests to be done. EEG test necessary but could not be done. Valproic acid and sodium valproate, the first choice of drugs for patient's disease as per authoritative text books neither suggested nor available. Patient not shifted to a place where all essentials for treatment of the case available. Condition of patient worsening day by day within 5 days and despite specialist supervision, cardiac arrest resulting in death of patient. Negligence held ₹1 lakh awarded as compensation. [*Channaveerashetty* v *Dr. Vijaya Kumar* 2005 II CPR 450 (Karn)]

177. Operation

Urinary blockage: Complainant aged 23 years. Penis became dead and lost organ. Complainant has been rendered impotent. Passing of urine through an artificial hole. Compensation of ₹8 lakh awarded. [*C. Shiv Kumar* v *Dr. John Arthur* 1998 III CPJ 436 (TN)]

Patient of potential risk essential steps, which should be taken in any major surgery not taken. Resulting in death of patient on the operation table itself. Failure to take normal care and diligence. Negligence and deficiency in service proved. [*Rashmi R. Fadnavis* v *Mumbai Grahak Panchayat* 1998 III CPJ 21 (NC)]

Fracture of leg: -Leg put under plaster. On removal of plaster, it was found that the portion where the operation was conducted, an abscess had developed. On examination, it was found that some foreign substance left inside the leg. Emergency operation done. Prolonged hospitalisation. Complainant's case supported by the statement of independent witness, a professor of orthopaedics. Same corroborated by material on record. State commission rightly held that the doctor was negligent in the treatment and proper care and ordinary skill expected of a doctor had not been taken while treating the patient. Award of compensation of ₹2 lakh upheld. [*P.P. Ismail* v *K.K. Radha* 1998 I CPJ 16 (NC)]

Complications. Resulting in performing of second operation. Resulting in performing of second operation. Doctor not possessing adequate knowledge of all aspects. Negligence. Total compensation of ₹1,00,000 awarded. [*Aphraim Jayanand Rathod* v *Dr. Shatish Shah* 1996 I CPJ 243 (Guj)]

Hernia operation. Death during operation. Pre-operative test not done. Anaesthetist saw the patient only four hours prior to administrating the Anaesthesia. Very fact that few crepts and rhonchi developed within ten minutes after starting of the surgery establishes that the patient was not properly prepared for Anaesthesia. Negligence. Compensation of ₹1,75,000 awarded. [*Bhanupal* v *Dr. Prakash Padode* 2000 III CPR 336 (MP)]

Mopping gauze piece left inside while closing operated area. Medical negligence compensation granted. [*Beti Bai Saxena* v *Dr. S.L. Mukharjee* 2001 III CPJ 251 (MP)]

Sponge left inside the body. Opposite party *per se* negligent. [*Meena Vyas* v *City Nursing home and hospital Ludhiyana* 2001 II CPJ 172 (Pb)]

Sponge not removed. Leading to another operation. Medical negligence. Compensation of ₹1 lakh awarded. [*Harvinder Kaur* v *Sushma Chawla* 2001 III CPJ 143 (Pb)]

Skull of patient was cut and removed for clipping the aneurysm with clipper but the same had to be abandoned due to the unavailability of the drill procedure. This clearly amounts to carelessness and negligence on the part of the opposite parties. In adequate arrangements regarding the drill machine had been made. The operation could be finished on that day itself. Necessity to operate the patient for the second time could be avoided. Consolidated sum of ₹2 lakh awarded as compensation. [*Devendra Kumar Sharma* v *Post Graduate Institute of Medical Education and Research* 2002 I CPJ 211 (Chandi)]

Hip replacement. Negligence. After operation, no sensation below left knee due to development of gangrene. Amputation of left leg from above knee. Two more operations performed on her. Order of the State Commission directing reimbursement of ₹1,11,000 and damage of ₹1,50,000 with interest @ 12% held justified. No interference. [*Ghanta Mohan Lakshmi* v *Dr. C.V.S. Ratnam* 2003 IV CPJ 12 (NC)]

DHS operation. Surgery. Not properly performed. Post-operative treatment. Not satisfactory. Complainant producing sufficient evidence to prove negligence and deficiency in service. Opposite party failed to show that operation was done in accordance with procedure following the accepted method. Case of medical negligence. [*Devadass* v *N. Arumugam* 2005 III CPJ 10 (TN)]

Complainant aged about 43 years was having problem of Dysfunctional Uterine Bleeding (DUB). Consent given for total abdominal Hysterectomy alone but operation performed known as Bilateral Salpingo Ooporectomy. Held that avulsion of vein was encountered when the respondent transgressed the authority and consent given by the patient for TAH but operation performed known as Bilateral Salpingo Ooperectomy (removal of both ovaries and fallopian tubes) without the knowledge of consent of the patient. Opposite party 1 and 2 held jointly and severally liable to pay a sum of ₹5 lakh to the complainant. [*Saroj Chandhoke* v *Ganga Ram Hospital* 2007 III CPJ 189 (NC)]

178. Ophthalmology

Retinal Detachment. Intra-ocular lens (IOL) implantation. Surgery carried out without getting B-Scan report, a necessary pre-requisite to ascertain the status of eye. Negligence held ₹one lakh awarded as compensation. [*Dr. V. Pahwa* v *Surendra Mohan Ghose* 2004 IV CPJ 1 (NC)]

Radia Keradiathermy (Keratotomy) (RKD operation). Loss of eye-sight. Patient suffering from Glaucoma. When a person suffers from glaucoma. RKD is contra-indicated. Performance of RKD ignoring contra-indications without operating for glaucoma. Negligence held. ₹4 lakh awarded as compensation. [*Dr. P.S. Hardia* v *Kedarnath Sethia* 2004 III CPJ 90 (NC)]

Radia Kerototomy. False and misleading advertisement. Attracted by newspaper advertisement of opposite parties that they had attained perfection in the art of refractive surgery for removal of spectacles/contact lenses in case of myopia, complainant getting both his operated by opposite parties. Eyesight becoming weakened post-operation forcing complainant to wear glasses of higher power than those she was wearing earlier. Unfair trade practice, as also deficiency in service. ₹50,000 awarded as compensation. [*S. Khanna* v *Dr. Nitin Verma* 2005 III CPR 543 (Del)]

Breach of duty. Patient feeling pain and burning in one of his eyes found to have some foreign element in the eye and also pus. Opposite party, an MBBS degree holder, not being an eye specialist duty bound to consult an eye specialist before giving any treatment and for becoming, an eye specialist a degree of MS in ophthalmology is must. A specialist in a particular branch is one from whom, in a case of contract, more skill can be expected than from a general practitioner. Without consulting such a specialist, opposite party administering certain medicines only to further deteriorate condition of patient ultimately resulting loss of vision. Negligence held ₹10,000 awarded as compensation. [*Bhiwani General and Eye Hospital* v *Ramesh Chandra Sharma* 2005 IV CPJ 310 (Raj)]

Removal of foreign body struck in eyeball. Hospital having no X-ray and CT scan though C.T. scan essential to locate foreign body in the eye. X ray taken not giving clear idea whether foreign body was in walls of eyeball or within it. Still operation done and foreign body remaining in eye thereafter. Negligence held. ₹1 lakh awarded as compensation. [*D. Philip* v *Narayana Nelralaya* 2005 IV CPJ 351 (Karn)]

Cataract operation. Loss of eyesight. Proof of negligence. Under section 13 of Consumer Protection Act, if in the written version the matter is contested, parties to prove the case by evidence. Complainant filed affidavit by way of evidence but opposite parties, neither filed any affidavit nor cross-examined the deponents. Evidence brought by complainant remained uncontroverted. Negligence held. ₹1,25,000 awarded as compensation along with ₹1,000 towards cost. [*Dr. Ponnuswamy* v *Ramakrishnan* 2006 IV CPJ 213 (NC)]

179. Orthopaedics

Fracture collarbone and ribs. Patient suffering unbearable pair after being bandaged by opposite party. Bone fragments being widely separated their union impossible without internal fixation. Minor surgery done by another orthopedic surgeon, bones set properly which was not done by opposite party. Negligence held ₹10,000 awarded as compensation. [*Queen NRI Hospital* v *B. Ramakrishna Rao* 2004 II CPJ 521 (AP)]

Fracture left Tibial plethora with an open wound. Plaster of Paris applied. Gangrene set in with swelling over left thigh. Tenderness over left knee, loss of sensation and multiple blisters, resulting in amputation of leg. Application of P.O.P. on open would oppose to all medical practices. Negligence held. Total compensation of ₹1,75,000 awarded [*Dulipudi Srinivas* v *Dr. Prasad Yogelingeswara Rao* 2004 CTJ 310 (AP)]

Fracture right humerus shaft. Case being diagnosed as spiral fracture plastered X-ray showing bone not set at right position. Surgery for internal fixation inserting screws and wires. Second operation for removal of wires and screws as party felt that these cause of infection. Simple fracture becoming a comminuted one causing radial nerve palsy rendering the hand paralytic with 64% disability. A spiral fracture unlikely to be converted into a full-fledged comminuted fracture. Negligence held. ₹3 lakh awarded as compensation. [*Avadh Hospital and Heart center* v *Mugdha Paul* 2005 CTJ 1130 (NC)]

Comminuted fracture of upper third of left humerus. Surgery for bone reduction and internal fixation. Non-union of bone necessitating second surgery in another hospital. Patient sensitive to Betadine, but opposite party applied Betadine without sensitivity test and put on steroids not caring for the consequences. Expert opinion that opposite party had not applied the proper and well established line of treatment during surgery of complainant patient. Negligence held. ₹68,000 awarded as compensation. [*Randhir Garg* v *Inscol Teritary Care Hospital* 2005 I CPJ 505 (Chdg.)]

Comminuted fracture in left hipbone. Surgery and plate fixation with nailing. Nails in plates going loose turning the angle resulting in "coxa-vara" and head of the screw opened in skin of the wound in left trochanteric region. Negligence while operating and fixation of bone. ₹60,000 awarded as compensation. [*Suresh Chandra Sharma* v *Dr. Sharad Nayak* 2005 I CPR 289 (MP)]

Fracture hand. Plastering by opposite party unskilled person not authorised to give treatment, that too without X-ray. Patient taken to other doctors without any complaint against opposite party and damage hand becoming permanent. Complaint filed after a lapse of 4 years without accompanying application for condonation of delay. Barred by limitation though the cause of action, a continuing one, especially when the patient had been taken to other doctors. Still opposite party not being qualified to practice medicine, taking a lenient view the Supreme Court awarded lump sum ₹80,000 as compensation reducing sum of ₹1,75,000 awarded by the State Commission and upheld by National Commission. [*Md. Suleman Ansari* (*DMS*) v *Shankar Bhandari* 2005 III CPJ I (SC)]

Surgery for correcting deformity of arm. Administration of Anaesthesia at 9 a.m. and death of patient at 9.40 a.m. due to cardiac arrest. What happened in between and why cardiac arrest occurred is not explained. Contradictory statements of orthopaedic surgeon, assistant surgeon, cardiologist, anaesthetist and assistant anaesthetist as to exact time of cardiac arrest. Anaesthetist not even knowing any other agent used for general Anaesthesia except used by her. Recording of blood pressure, E.C.G. and heart beat not properly monitored. Surgery performed not one of life saving nor an emergency one. B.P. of patient very high and could have been delayed to ensure normal B.P. at the time of surgery. Negligence held. Award of total compensation of ₹4,15,000 upheld. [*Rashmi Vora* v *Arunaben D. Kothari* 2005 IV CPJ 164 (NC)]

Fracture leg — wrong and repeated plastering — development of gangrene and ultimate amputation of leg. No X-ray taken after plaster of paris applied to ascertain whether fractured portion rightly set. Had the opposite party taken X-ray he could have ascertained whether plaster of paris rightly applied. Gangrene developed alleged to be due to tight plastering, supported by expert opinion. Negligence held. ₹10 lakh awarded as compensation with costs ₹5,000 [*Devendra Singh* v *Bokaro General Hospital* 2005 III CPJ 764 (Jhar)]

Spinal tumour — performance of operation on minor without obtaining consent of complainant father. Patient complaining of back pain. Complainant not informed that his son was suffering from cancer. Opposite party not handing over medical report to complainant despite request for producing the record maintained in his hospital. Though opposite party an orthopedic surgeon cannot be said to be incompetent to carry out operation of spine, no reason assigned for not involving a neurosurgeon in the operation. Victim operated upon on complaint of backache rendered paralytic after surgery resulting in his untimely death. Opposite party failed to perform his duty towards the patient under code of medical ethics. Negligence and deficiency in service held. ₹2.5 lakh awarded as compensation with interest @ 9% p.a. from date of complaint. [*Rajendra Kumar Goswami* v *Dr. Arun Madharia* 2006 I CPJ 337 (Chhattis)]

180. Physician/General Practitioner

Negligent treatment. Complainant falling from a scooter suffering minor injuries. Nurse while cleaning wounds with saline, carelessly breaking the ampule and broken glass pieces being embedded in complainants face and neck. Doctor applying certain solution, which according to complainant was spirit instead of saline, which should have been used for cleaning wounds, causing blisters on face. Complainant not allergic of savlon. Plea of blisters caused by allergy untenable. While it may be possible to say categorically that, it was spirit and not savlon it is admitted that the complainant developed blisters in areas not affected during her fall from the scooter after application of liquid. Three foreign bodies removed from her upper lip and face also. Negligence held. ₹30,000 awarded as compensation. [*CDR Hospitals* v *Mrs. Nirmala Manaseh* 2004 I CPJ 70 (NC)]

False discharge certificate. Opposite party declaring live baby brought by its parents as dead and writing in the discharge certificate "brought dead". While infant's father suggested taking it to the village for burial and his brother even went for the coffin for the "dead" believing the doctor's declaration of death, the mother for a second opinion believing her baby was still alive took it to another hospital where it was in fact found quite alive. Negligence of the highest degree on the part of the doctor. ₹1.2 lakh awarded as compensation. [*Dr. M.L. Deb* v *Rose Mary Lyngdoh* 2004 III CPJ 744 (Meghalaya)]

Non-examination of patient. Patient having pain in penis and inflated stomach remaining unattended for 13 hours of hospitalization. Condition of the patient becoming critical and despite being repeatedly informed, except prescribing some medicines on phone opposite party choosing not to physically examine the patient and ultimately death of patient on account of actual pancreatitis. Non-examination of patient physically by opposite party itself suggestive of the fact that he was negligent and deficient in rendering medical service to the patient admitted in his unit of the hospital. ₹10.00 lakh awarded as compensation for which the hospital and the doctors jointly and severally liable. [*Krishna Sharma* v *Raj Hospital* 2005 III CPJ 314 (Jhar)]

Prescription of treatment over telephone. Patient having pain in stomach and vomiting remaining unattended by opposite party and treatment given by junior doctor on instructions of opposite party senior in whose unit patient admitted. Given over phone without physically examining the patient. Death of patient due to acute pancreatitis. Had opposite party, doctor been vigilant during the hospitalization of patient life of the patient could have been saved. Gross negligence and laches. ₹10.00 lakh awarded as compensation. [*Krishna Sharma* v *Raj Hospital* 2005 III CPJ 314 (Jhar)]

Administration of injection on telephonic instruction. Serenace injection given in case of anxiety and administered to psychiatric patients with cardiac disease. Patient having no such anxiety or agitation. Prescribing such an injection over phone without personal examination of patient. Negligence held. ₹3 lakh awarded as compensation with interest @ 6% p.a. [*V. Pradeep* v *Ramakrishna Nursing Home* 2006 II CPJ 332 (Karn)]

181. Psychiatry

Lithium therapy. Cerebral degeneration. Treatment for depression. Opposite party, doctor not recording history of patient while writing prescription, not advising relevant tests prior starting lithium therapy not issuing advice and warning either on prescription or otherwise and not properly monitoring serum lithium level for a long period of 6 months, whereas it should have been done at least intervals of 2-3 months. Without taking the precautions administration of heavy dosage of lithium in combination with carbamazepine leading to lithium toxicity resulting in cerebral degeneration of a bright young medical student rendering him 100% handicapped. Gross negligence ₹5 lakh compensation awarded. [*Sandeep Agarwal* v *Modern Medical Inst.* 2005 II CPJ 601 (Chitt.)]

182. Pregnancy

Death due to 'septicaemia shock'. Attending doctors did not care to know actual problem with patient. Deficiency in service. Non-production of enquiry report. Adverse inference to be drawn. Hospital held vicariously liable. Compensation of ₹2,25,000 awarded. [*Gopal Vashisth* v *State of Uttaranchal* 2005 I CPJ 630]

183. Piles

Surgery. Removal of sphincter muscle. Loss of control over rectum, sensing organs. Passing of stool without any notice. Failure on the part of opposite party to held the complainant in not relieving her suffering after operation. Complainant was forced to approach other doctors at different places. Opposite party held deficient in her operation and treatment. Physical suffering and medical agony. ₹1 lakh awarded as compensation. [*Sunandabai y. Patil* v *Dr. B.L. Patil* 2005 II CPR 70 (Karn)]

184. Quackery

Very fact that unqualified person attempted to render services of a doctor on charging fees will amount to quackery. [*Nachhattar Singh Tohra* v *Malkeet Singh* 2001 II CPJ 233]

185. Radiologist

C.T. Scan. Patient having a malignant lesion. It is only prudent on the part of the attending physician to have a careful look at the medical history of the patient before prescribing a treatment on the basis of the scan report. Relying totally on the impression of Radiologist in such cases is not correct, particularly when the medical history does not create a suspicion of malignancy. State commission rightly concluded that no negligence in service could be attributed to the Radiologist who did the scan in question. [*Rahul Sinha* v *Dr. Ashok Mitra* 1995 III CPJ 162 (NC)]

Digital subtraction angiography (DSA). Assurance of cent per cent safety. Complainant suffering from diabetes and hypertension for several years, having developed pain in both lower limbs getting himself admitted in a hospital to under go angiography. In investigation by cardiologist, endocrinologist and nephrologist, early stage of nephropathy was found. In view of kidney, status of the patient said doctors explained that angiography using a contrast dye medium carried significant risk of acute renal failure and advised alternative investigation by Magnetic Resonance (MRI), patient referred to hospital of opposite party. As MRI, angiogram will not reveal peripheral vascular disease opposite party suggested, DSA using a special dye stated to be 100% safe to kidneys and not affecting kidney functions in any way. After undergoing DSA, condition of complainant worsened ultimately resulting in kidney failure. Negligence held. ₹1.5 lakh awarded as compensation. [*Shanthappa* v *Dr. Naveen Chandra Raj* 2006 II CPJ 316 (Karn)]

Erroneous report. Ultrasound test of abdomen. Report stating that gall bladder contained multiple echogenic shadows of stones. No stone found on surgery. Negligence held. Plea of disappearance of stones within short span of time, unacceptable. Sum charged for examination to be refunded with costs. [*Darshan Kaur* v *Dr. J.S. Sodhi* 1999 I CPR 522 (Chd)]

186. Reimbursement

Hip replacement operation. After operation no sensation below left knee due to development of gangrene. Amputation of left leg from above knee. Two more operation performed on her. Order of the State Commission directing reimbursement of ₹1,11,000 and damage of ₹1,50,000 with interest @ 12% held justified. No interference. [*Ghanta Mohan Lakshmi* v *Dr. C.V.S. Ratnam* 2003 IV CPJ 12 (NC)]

187. Rheumatoid-Arthritis

Imuran tablets 50 mg. prescribed without holding any prior test. Resulting in hair loss and bone marrow suppression. Gross negligence. ₹25,000 awarded as compensation. Held justified. [*B.K. Ghose* v *Dr. Prof. P.. Maulick* 2005 I CPJ 737 (WB)]

188. *Res ipsa loquitur*

Abortion. Incomplete abortion performed. Remnants left in uterus. Bleeding and pain. Evacuation of contents. Held that principles of *Res Ipsa loquitur* would apply. A sum of ₹2.5 lakh awarded as compensation. [*Shakila Sathanandam* v *Dr. S.S. Kodmani* 2005 III CPJ 121]

Applicability. Boy aged 13 years. Admitted to hospital for treatment of epilepsy. Died within 48 hours of his admission of septicemia. Principles of *Res Ipsa Loquitur* held applicable. [*Dr. Janak K. Nathan* v *Murlidhar Eknath Masane* 2002 II CPR 138 (NC)]

Applicability. Kidney transplantation. Patient's pregnant woman. While removing mesenteric cyst, functional kidney removed resulting in death of patient as well as foetus. *Res Ipsa Loquitur* applies. Negligence held. ₹6.2 lakh awarded as compensation. [*Consumer Education and Research Society* v *Dr. Prakash R. Moli* 2006 I CPJ 537 (Guj)]

Medical negligence. Burden of proof. Petitioner surgeon gave Anaesthesia himself. He has not shown how the complication of 'Anoxic Encephalopathy' arose. Whether immediate action was taken to avoid the complication and the petitioner does not show whether timely treatment has been imparted to the patient to avoid Anoxic Encephalopathy. Findings of the State Commission that there is deficiency in service and negligence by petitioner upheld. Doctrine of *Res Ipsa Loquitur* applies in the present case. [*G. Vivekananda Verma* v *Chinta Bhramaramba* 2006 III CPJ 104 (NC)]

Patient had to spend 108 days in the hospital for a normal delivery with forceps and episiotomy. She had to be taken to the operation theater six times and had to undergo untold suffering. It leads to one veritable conclusion that this is a case of *Res Ipsa Loquitier*. It is clear that medical practitioner has not brought to her task a reasonable degree of skill and knowledge and has not exercised a reasonable degree of care. Held that there has been a gross negligence on the part of the opposite parties. Apart from grant of final bill of ₹1,86,849.90 raised by opposite party hospital damages and for mental agony, a sum of ₹10 lakh granted. [*S. Tamil Selvi* v *Dr. Sooriya Kola* 2009 II CPJ 216]

189. Right of privacy

AIDS —Claim for Damages. Hospital disclosing the fact that appellant was HIV positive. Appellant seeking damages. If a person suffering from dreadful disease "AIDS" knowingly marries of woman and thereby transmits infection to that woman he would be guilty of offence indicated in sections 269 and 270, IPC. [*Dr. Tokugha Yepthomi* v *Apollo Hospital Enterprises Limited,* 1999 I CPJ 11]

AIDS — Personal medical information. Appellant HIV positive. In the facts of the case, it was open to the hospital or the doctor concerned to reveal such information to person related to the girl whom appellant intended to marry. She had a right to know about the HIV positive status of the appellant. Court further declaring in general as to what the right and obligations arise in such context as to right to privacy and confidentiality. Said observation made by Court held to be uncalled for. [*Mr. 'X'* v *Hospital 'Z'* 2003 I CPJ 14 (SC)]

190. Right to life

Government hospitals run by the state and the medical officer employed therein are bound to extend medical assistance for preserving human life. Failure on the part of the government hospital to provide timely medical treatment to a person in need of such treatment results in violation of his right to life guaranteed under Article 21 of the Constitution of India. Court can award adequate compensation for such a violation. [*Paschim Banga Khet Mazdoor Samity* v *State of West Bengal* AIR 1996 SC 2426]

191. Right to sue

Death of complainant during pendency of complainant. Personal action dies with the death of the claimant. Claim for unliquidated damages for tortuous liability. Right to sue does not survive after the death of complainant. [*Janak Kumari* v *Dr. Balwinder Kaur Nagpal* 2003 II CPJ 28 (NC)]

192. Stone in gall bladder

Laproscopic operation performed. Common bile duct was cut whereas only cystic duct was required to be cut. *Per se* amounts to negligent act.

Compensation of ₹1 lakh awarded. [*Gurmit Mahal* v *Chauhan Nursing Home* 1998 II CPR 405]

Surgery. Common Bile duct also cut down Digestion stopped causing jaundice. Medical negligence. Compensation of ₹1 lakh awarded. [*Mumtaj Ansari* v *Zubeda* 2005 I CPJ 673 (Uttr.)]

193. Stitches

Eye operation. Stitches found loose after operation. Re-stitching. Loss of vision. Negligence. Order awarding compensation upheld. [*Dr. J.P. Goel* v *Smt. Pushpa Verma* 2002 I CPJ 28]

Post-operative care — Negligence. Removal of stitches at earlier stage. Wound got burst due to severe bouts of Courts of cough. Death of patient. Order awarding compensation upheld. [*Smjash Hospital Pvt.* v *Prassanna Kumar Ojha* 2003 II CPJ 150 (NC)]

194. Sterilization operation

State government family planning programme. Complete sterilisation operation not performed. Claim for damages allowed State Vicariously liable. [*State of Haryana* v *Santra* 2000 I CPJ 53 (SC)]

National Family Welfare Programme. Operation failed. Operation done free of charge and voluntaries paid incentive money. Held that complainants are not consumer. [*Shashikala* v *Command Hospital Air Force* 2003 III CPJ 84 (Kar)]

Performed without consent ₹75,000 awarded as compensation. [*Dr. Janki S. Kumar* v *Mrs. Sarafunnisa* 2000 I CPJ 66 (Ker)]

195. Septicemia

Laprotomy operation. Abortion operation. Resulting in 'gut loop cut' developing into septicemia and ultimately death of patient. Petitioner attempted to disown any responsibility despite the ultrasound test and MTP operation. All through proceedings, he did not appear to have any remorse feeling for the patient and her family who had passed through trauma and resulting her death. The petitioner for his attempts to escape liability deserves to be severely penalized. Revision petitioner liable to be dismissed with costs of ₹20,000. Order of the State Commission directing the practitioner to pay compensation of ₹4,50,000 upheld. [*Ramesh Jain* v *Jagroop Singh* 2008 I CPJ 233]

Liability of hospital. Pregnancy. Death due to 'septicaemia shock'. Attending doctors did not care to know actual problem with patient. Deficiency in service. Non-production of enquiry report. Adverse inference to be drawn. Hospital held vicariously liable. Compensation of ₹2,50,000 awarded. [*Gopal Vashisth* v *State of Uttaranchal* 2005 I CPJ 630 (Uttr.)]

Res Ipsa Loquitur. Boy aged 13 years. Admitted to hospital for treatment of epilepsy. Died within 48 hours of his admission of septicemia. Principles of *Res Ipsa Loquitur* held applicable. [*Dr. Janak Nathan* v *Murlidhar Eknath Mosrane* 2002 II CPR 138 (NC)]

196. Service

Hiring for consideration. Services rendered by railway hospital to railway employees or their family members for nominal charges as part of service condition of the employee. Service not free but for consideration, since hospital run and subsidized by the employer Union of India and the employees are consumers within the meaning of Consumer Protection Act, 1986. [*Laxman Thamappa Kotgiri* v *G.M. Central Railway* 2006 III CPJ 6]

Service rendered at AIIMS. Under law, medical practitioners working either in private, public or in governmental hospital were and are liable for negligence in discharge of their duties, the remedy being to approach civil Court, and the Consumer Protection Act does not create any new right, liability or obligation, but only providing for an additional Forum. Services rendered at AIIMS not free of cost as the institution, apart form registration fee, recovers various amounts such as hospital charges, diagnostic charges etc from patient. Services rendered at institution covered by the provisions of the Act despite the fact that it is established for educational and research purposes. It is not covered by the exclusion clause, namely, "service does not include the rendering of service free of cost". Hence, complaint against AIIMS maintainable. [*Sailesh Munjal* v *All India Institute of Medical Sciences* 2004 III CPJ 93 (NC)]

Hiring for consideration. Blindness after eye operation. Opposite parties well qualified medical professionals duly authorised by competent authorities to perform eye operations besides treating eye troubles according to Ayurvedic system of treatment. Treatment at government hospital and prescription slips issued there from not giving any indication that the patients consulted any doctor before reaching the hospital and their eyes ever operated upon by such private doctors. No evidence to prove that the complainants hired services of opposite parties for consideration and opposite parties rendered deficient service. District Forum erroneously allowed the complainants and awarded compensation. Order of the Forum set aside. [*Bhunesh Kumar Bhatnagar* v *Dhopa Devi* 2005 II CPJ 268 (Raj)]

Free medical service under service contract. Medical treatment given in hospital run by Port trust to its employees is 'service' within the meaning of Consumer Protection Act, 1986, and an employee or any of his family members availing of such service is a consumer under the act. [*G. Kondala Rao* v *Board of Trustees* 2006 III CPJ 97]

Definition under Consumer Protection Act, 1986. Service rendered by doctors and hospitals without any charge whatsoever to any person not 'service' as defined under section 2(1)(*o*) of the Act. Payment of a token amount for registration purpose only would not alter the position. [*Mahaveer Prasad* v *State of Rajasthan* 2006 II CPJ 402 (Raj)]

Free service. Service rendered by hospital to some on payment of charges and to other free of charge is also 'service' as defined in section 2(1)(*o*) of the Consumer Protection Act and a person availing of service of that hospital is consumer under section 2(1)(*d*) of the Act. [*Pavittar Singh* v *State of Punjab* 2006 III CPJ 287 (HC)]

Central Government Health Scheme (CGHS). Where as a part of the conditions of service, the employer bears the expenses of medical treatment of an employee and his family members dependents upon him, the service rendered to the such employee and his family members dependent on him, the services rendered to such employee and his family members by the medical practitioner or hospital or Nursing home would not be free of charge and would constitute service within the meaning of section 2(1) (*o*) of the Consumer Protection Act, 1986. Employees in service and pensioners are treated at par with regard to medical facilities, which are to be provided by the Central Government employee before retirement would be consideration for providing medical facilities for him or his family members. [*Jagdish Kumar Bajpai* v *Union of India* 2006 I CPR 157 (NC)]

197. Surgery

For increasing height. Fixing for ring fixation. Left leg remain shorter. Burden of proof not discharged by opposite parties by filing affidavit. Negligence/deficiency in service. Compensation awarded. [*Nadia* v *Proprietor, Fatima Hospital* 2001 III CPJ 572 (Ker)]

Patient of potential risk. Essential steps, which should be taken in any major surgery not taken. Resulting in death of patient on the operation table itself. Failure to take normal care and diligence. Negligence and deficiency in service proved. [*Rashmi R. Fadnavis* v *Mumbai Grahak Panchayat* 1998 III CPJ 21 (NC)]

Wrong fixing of clip. Defected within 6.7 months. Complications. Complainant also negligent inasmuch as he did not resort to surgical exploration for removal of clip. Complainant held entitled to a compensation of ₹1 lakh only. [*Dr. R.V.S. Rao* v *Dr. Y.R. Krishna* 2003 I CPJ 210 (MP)]

Sponge left inside the body. It found at the time of second operation. Deficiency in service on the part of opposite parties. Complainant entitled to the amount spend for medicines and for pathology charges. However, compensation ₹1 lakh awarded by District Forum reduced to ₹50,000. [*Aruna Mani Misra* v *Bhagwati* 2003 I CPJ 69 (U.P.)]

Fracture in the neck of left femur. Guide wire left in the body of patient while performing operation. Corrective surgery performed. Patient also suffered sever pain in the lower abdomen and right thigh. Even passed blood in urine. Suffered mental and physical agony. District Forum rightly awarded a compensation of ₹50,000 with cost of litigation of ₹5,000 [*Dr. Anil Nadir* v *Dr. Rakesh Dullu* 2003 III CPJ 40 (Del)]

Anaesthetist — operation for hernia under general Anaesthesia. Anaesthetist leaving operation theatre thereunder immediately after extubation, at least with implied consent of surgeon. Patient not gaining consciousness and death occurring within 10 minutes. What was condition of patient at the time of extubation, what happened after surgery and extubation, why patient not shifted to ward, why anaesthetist left before shifting patient to ward, who monitored to him during this period and what steps taken for prevention are all questions remaining unanswered. Both the surgeon and anaesthetist equally liable for negligence and deficiency in service. Maxim Res Ipsa Loquitur applies. ₹4 lakh awarded as compensation. [*Dr. Yogendra A. Pandya* v *Harshaben E. Patel* 2004 I CPR 308 (Guj)]

Intestinal tuberculosis. Intestine developing septicemia and removal of infected portion. No lapse or negligence in the exploratory procedure. Use of analgesia instead of Anaesthesia for operation also not deficiency in service as analgesia found more suitable for seriously ill patients. Due care and precaution taken by opposite party while performing operation and death of patient not having any direct nexus with the surgery. However, he could be found partially negligent in not producing any papers pertaining to the day-to-day treatment and hospital record regarding admission of patient, examination and treatment record. Compensation of ₹10,000 awarded by District Forum upheld. [*Dr. Pradeep Kayal* v *Balchand* 2004 III CPJ 144 (MP)]

Secondary cleft lip connection. Administration of Anaesthesia by two anaesthetists at 10:00 AM and 10:30 AM in case of surgery of secondary cleft lip connection. Within half an hour of Anaesthesia patient becoming pulseless and death. Neither operation notes nor progress record naming the person who administered Anaesthesia. What the two anaesthetists were doing in the operation theater and where was the necessity of the two being there not clarified, one of whom, who allegedly had administered Anaesthesia, not even examined. Thus the patient was administered Anaesthesia by two anaesthetists. Negligence held. Since all operation notes/progress records silent about the names of doctors and no name of anaesthetics mentioned anywhere, the hospital would be accountable. ₹3 lakh awarded as compensation. [*Meenakshi Mission Hospital and Research Centre* v *Samuraj* 2005 I CPJ 33 (NC)]

Gallbladder. Profuse bleeding after operation. Hospital not having ICU and ventilator still undertook major operation though such emergency operation was not warranted. Instead of shifting patient to a higher hospital, second operation to control bleeding unsuccessful as the point of bleeding could not be traced. Pre-operative assessment for abnormal bleeding tendency not done. Patient shifted to another hospital where she died. Negligence held. ₹2 lakh awarded as compensation. [*A. Xavier* v *Cantonment Polyclinic* 2005 I CPJ 229 (Karn)]

Cholecystectomy — Removal of gallbladder stones. Along with operation of gall bladder common bile duct also cut down. Development of bismuth level-3 stopping process of digestion of food causing jaundice. Plea that cutting of CBD a well known complication in gallbladder operation and there are 30% cases of this type-unsustainable. Patient not informed about the recognized complications of the surgery and no evidence to show that mandatory duty performed by opposite party before operation informed the patient that the leakage of bile or occurrence of jaundice due to inadvertent injury to the bile duct is a complication of gallbladder surgery. When the doctor knows the cutting of bile duct and jaundice as possible effect of operation, he should have taken precautions that this might not occur. Negligence held. ₹1 lakh awarded as compensation. [*Mumtaj Ansari* v *Zubeda* 2005 I CPJ 673 (Uttranchal)]

Delay in conducting operation for removal of gallbladder stones delayed as the machine for conducting operation hired from outside not arriving on date fixed for operation. Patient 63 years of age, operated the next day and reporting back after 3 days with breathing problem. Kept in ICCU and death occurring after 3 days. Held negligence and also unfair trade practice. But considering the age of the disease and the fact that she was breathing trouble on re-admission, compensation of ₹1.5 lakh as awarded by District Forum reduced to ₹1.25 lakh. [*CDR Medical Centre* v *Kailash Nath Srivastava* 2005 III CPJ 34 (Del)]

Injury in index finger — surgery done without blood sugar level being brought down to permissible limits. Development of diabetic gangrene resulting in amputation of finger. Failure to take precautionary measures before surgery. Negligence held. [*Dr. P.K. Ghose* v *Pradhyut Rakshit* 2006 II CPJ 247]

Explorative laprotomy. Suspected teratoma. Surgery to removing big lump from abdomen along with one of the ovaries. Leaving surgical mop in abdominal cavity and resultant complications necessitating second surgery. Negligence held. Compensation ₹3.5 lakh awarded. [*Dr. K. Ravindra Nath* v *Vitta Veera Surya Prakasam.* 2006 IV CPJ 105 (NC)]

198. Teeth extraction

Syringe put in the mouth without setting the needle properly. Needle slipped into the throat and then in the stomach — operation — complainant remained in hospital for 25 days. Doctor did not exercise the care expected of him. Deficiency in service. Compensation of ₹3,00,000 awarded by District Forum reduced to ₹1,00,000. [*Amblappa* v *Sriram D. Veerendra Heggade* 1999 III CPR 72 (Kar)]

199. Territorial jurisdiction

Case of medical negligence — complainant came to know about the alleged default/imperfection on the part of the opponent doctor while she had been at her parental home at 'R' — however, every part of cause of action occurred at 'S'. Held that Forum at 'S' will have jurisdiction to entertain the complaint. [*Dr. Prafulbhai V. Shiroya* v *Rekhaben Prakash Bhai Joshi* 2003 IV CPJ 492 (Guj)]

200. Thalassaemia

Medical Test. Wrong Report. Pre-natal diagnostic analysis report. Allegation that the opposite party no. 2 was negligent in not separating the contaminated mother's tissue and the doctor was not vigilant before analysis the sample that resulted in erroneous foetus diagnosis report. Complainants going ahead with pregnancy and second child also suffering from thalassaemia. Requiring continuous treatment of blood transfusion and medicine. That error, fault or imperfection has resulted in onerous duties on the parents. Difficult to compensate in terms of money. AIIMS directed to give medicines without any charges after getting the patient periodically examined by the consultant on the subject. Blood transfusion also to be done without any charges. [*Sailesh Munjal* v *All India Institute of Medical Sciences* 2004 III CPJ 93 (NC)]

201. Torts

Nasal deformity. Operation. Death. Due to "not introducing of cuffed-endotracheal tube of proper size as to prevent aspiration of blood from the wound in the respiratory passage". Lack of due care and precaution. Not to reckless or grossly negligent as to make the doctor criminally liable. Doctor may be liable in Tort. [*Suresh Gupta* v *Govt. of NCT of Delhi* 2004 III CLT 312 (SC)]

Medical negligence. In a case where the doctors act carelessly and in a manner, which is not expected of a medical practitioner, then in such a case on action in torts would be maintainable. [*Bhajan Lal Gupta* v *Mool Chand Khairati Ram Hospital* 2001 I CPJ 31 (NC)]

Medical negligence. Suit for damages. Plaintiff undergoing laproscopic sterilization in a medical camp. While performing the surgery infection and septicemia set in due to unhygienic conditions in the camp, resulting in five subsequent operations and T.O. mass covered in the pelvic region due to infection suffered when undergone laproscopic sterilization. In a camp where, hundreds of patient comes from laproscopic, infection only normal possibility, but the doctor should exercise reasonable degree of care while performing the surgery. Trial judge non-suiting plaintiff on the ground that she failed to prove beyond all reasonable doubts that the surgeon was negligent in performing the surgery. Finding of trial judge erroneous, the suit being for damages and what is required is preponderance of probabilities i.e. whether the defendant doctor exercised reasonable degree of care unlike fool proof evidence required in criminal case. Notwithstanding the defendant being an expert in the filed of performing laproscopic operations, a certain degree of negligence on his part not to be ruled out. Medical negligence held, and suit decreed awarding a compendious compensation of ₹2 lakh. [*Sou Shevanta* v *State of Karnataka* 2004 IV TAC 977 (Karn HC)]

Damages. Vicarious liability of state for negligence of doctor found negligent on account of dilatory attitude in attending the patient as found in inquiry conducted into the matter by Deputy Director, Medical and health services. State Government vicariously liable for negligence of its doctors for damages. Compensation of ₹6.62 lakh awarded. [*Sobhag Mal Jain* v *State of Rajasthan* AIR 2006 Raj 66]

202. Tubectomy operation

By recognised government surgeon. Free of cost. Woman on whom the said operation is performed becomes entitled for benefits such as green card issued in her favour, which in turn entitled her to other benefits. That being the position, the compliant alleging deficiency in service on the part of the surgeon. Would certainly fail. [*Premlata Dhokonia* v *Dr. Dheeraj Garha* 2002 III CPJ 224 (NC)]

Free of charge. Under family planning programme of State government. Operation unsuccessful. Complainant gave birth to female child. Complainant is not a consumer. [*Pushpabai* v *S. Joseph* 2002 II CPJ 566 (MP)]

203. Unfair trade practice

Sale of medicine after expiry date. Amounts to unfair trade practice under section 2(1)(*nnn*) and 2(1)(*r*) of Consumer Protection Act. Explanation that salesman had unauthorizedly sold said defective medicines after the expiry date and opposite party medical store not be held liable for having sold defective goods, no deficiency. Compensation of ₹1,000 for mental agony awarded. [*Saroj Vyas* v *Sethi Medical Store* 2004 CPJ 546 (Raj)]

False and misleading advertisement. Attracted by newspaper advertisement of opposite parties that they had attained perfection in the art of refractive surgery for removal of spectacles/contact lenses in case of myopia, complainant getting both her eyes operated by opposite parties. Eye sight becoming weakened post-operation forcing complainant to wear glasses of higher power than those she was wearing earlier. Unfair trade practice, as also deficiency in service. ₹50,000 awarded as compensation. [*S. Khanna* v *Dr. Nitin Verma* 2005 III CPR 543 (Del)]

Surgery under package seal. Collection of anything more than the amount fixed under the deal. Amounts of unfair trade practice. [*Geetha* v *Wockhardt Hospital and Heart Institute* 2006 III CPJ 207 (Karn)]

Advertisement. Wrong treatment. Dandruff complainant went to the appellant. Paid ₹7,000 for said purpose. Treatment resulted in falling of hair making him bald. These are such unfair trade practices, which need to be curbed with heavy hand. No interference with the order awarding compensation of ₹50,000. [*Body Care* v *Ashok Kumar Solanki* 2005 I CPJ 402 (Del)]

Medical negligence case. Delay in operation due to late arrival of machine. Resulting in death of deceased. Appellant held guilty of unfair trade practice and gross negligence. However, the compensation reduced from ₹1.5 lakh to ₹1.25 lakh. [*CDR Medical Centre* v *Kailash Nath Srivastava* 2005 III CPJ 34 (Del)]

204. Urinary problem

Complainant having difficulty in passing urine. Catheterization done. No relief. Catheter removed. Profuse bleeding. Condition worsened. On account of negligence of the doctor in process of catheterization rant caused in the wall of the bladder making a hole to the rectum inside. Complainant throughout his life had to live with a bag attached to his back where the refuse of the body will accumulate. Compensation of ₹20,000 awarded by District Forum as upheld by State Commission enhanced to ₹1,20,000 with interest @ 12% p.a. [*D.D. Trikha* v *Devinder Mohant* 2002 II CPJ 116 (NC)]

205. Urinary blockage

Operation. Compliant aged 23 years. Penis became dead and lost organ. Complainant has been rendered impotent. Passing of urine through an artificial hole. Compensation of ₹8 lakh awarded. [*C. Shiv Kumar* v *Dr. John Arthur* 1998 III CPJ 436 (TN)]

206. Ultrasound

Abdomen. Report showing multiple shadows of the stones. 18 days of clinical tests. Operation. No stone found. Deficiency on the part of respondents in conveying the report. Refund of amount charged for the examination together with costs of ₹1,000 directed. [*Darshan Kaur* v *Dr. J.S. Sodhi* 1999 I CPJ 557 (UT)]

Medical Ethics. General practice being followed by the doctor in the hospital in referring the patients to centers outside for ultrasound etc. on the ground that they were to get some commission. Such a practice, if followed, has to be condemned on moral as well as ethical grounds. [*Harbhajan Singh* v *Daya Nand Medical College and Hospital, Ludhiana* 1994 I CPR 518 (Pun)]

207. Ultrasonography

Ultrasonography test. Wrongly done. Resultantly, twin babies in womb could not be detected and the complainant was prevented from taking extra care. Amounts to deficiency in service. Compensation awarded. [*Krishna Mont Tiwari* v *Dr. Gauri Bandyopadhyay* 2003 I CPJ 286 (WB)]

208. Unqualified doctor

Delivery of child. Patient died in the course of delivery of dead child. Doctor only an A.N.M. Not qualified doctor. compensation of ₹2,00,000 awarded. [*Dilbagh Hussain* v *Harjindar Kaur* 2000 III CPJ 17 (Pb)]

Very fact that unqualified person attempted to render services of a doctor on charging fees will amount to quackery. [*Nachhattar Singh Tohra* v *Malkeet Singh* 2001 II CPJ 233]

Patient admitted in the opposite party hospital for the complaint for fever. Patient was having Epistaxis for which he was given nasal packing placed anteriorly. The ENT specialist saw the patient only at 3:40 P.M. even though he was summoned at 11.20 a.m. No efforts made to clear the blocked airways till 8.55 p.m. though he was having repeated attacks of Epistaxis throughout the day. Clearly establish negligence of the respondent in treating the patient. Doctor who treated the patient was competent to give allopathy treatment, which he gave, as he was a qualified doctor to give unani medicines. Deceased was aged only 23 years and completed M.A. and B.Ed. Compensation of ₹7,50,000 awarded. [*P.N. Thakur* v *Hans Charitable Hospital* 2007 III CPJ 340]

Administration of allopathic medicines. Patient suffering from gastroenteritis given dextrose drip and other injections by homeopathy practitioner. Deterioration of condition and death. Deficiency in service. Production of an internship certificate from District Hospital during pendency of proceedings before District Forum to establish entitlement of opposite party to administer of allopathic treatment, of no consequence as the said certificate was issued after the case was filed. Award of compensation of ₹32,000 by the State Commission upheld. [*Dr. Shiv Kumar Gautam* v *Alima B.* 2006 IV CPJ 182 (NC)]

Medical negligence. Death of patient. Since, the law under which the respondent no. 1 was registered as Medical Practitioner required him to practice in Homeopathy only. He was under a statutory duty not to enter the field of any other system of medicine, as he was not qualified in other system. He having practice in Allopathy, without being qualified in that system was guilty of negligence. *Per Se*. [*Poonam Verma* v *Ashwin Patel* 1996 II CPJ 1]

209. Vicarious liability

Running of hospital, where the members of the general public can come for treatment, cannot be regarded as being an activity having a sovereign character. This being so, the state would be vicariously liable for the damages which may become payable on account of negligence of its doctors or other employees. [*Achutrao Haribhau Khodwa* v *State of Maharashtra* AIR 1996 SC 2377]

Paediatrics — Burn injuries. Both legs of child burnt by keeping extremely hot water bags during operation. Negligence held. Vicariously liability of hospital. Anaesthetist also made liable. Compensation of ₹5 lakh awarded. [*Master P.M. Ashwin* v *Manipal Hospital, Bangalore* 1997 I CPJ 238 (Karn)]

Obstetrics/gynecology. Sponge left behind scrub nurse held responsible. Negligence held. Vicarious liability of hospital. Compensation of ₹98,000 awarded against the hospital and insurance company with whom the hospital was insured. [*Aleyamma Varghese* v *Dewan Bahadur Dr. V Varghese* 1997 III CPJ 165 (Kar)]

Hospital. Nursing staff. Left foot drop following injection. Negligence held vicarious liability of hospital. Compensation of ₹1,05,000 awarded against hospital with cost of ₹1,000 [*A.M. Mathew* v *Director, Karuna Hospital* 1998 I CPJ 476 (Ker)]

Sterilization. Operation under family planning scheme. Failure. Subsequent conception, negligence held. Vicariously liability of state. Complainant entitled to claim full damages from State Government ₹54,000 decreed by lower Courts representing amount of expenses to bring up the child up to the age of puberty upheld by Supreme Court. [*State of Haryana* v *Santra* 2000 I CPJ 53 (SC)]

Sterilization. Vasectomy at Government hospital. Failure. Vicarious liability of state. Petitioners husband undergoing Vasectomy operation in government hospital. Petitioner subsequently becoming pregnant, giving birth to an unwanted child. Her relation within laws strained and even husband started doubting her character. On her persuasion husband's semen examined and report indicated 60% Spermatozoa present revealing that operation not successful. For mental agony and torture, insult and humiliation due to negligence of doctor who conducted vasectomy ₹1,25,000 granted as compensation and ₹50,000 to the child, to be given by State Government on basis of vicarious liability for negligence of its servant, the doctor in exercise of writ jurisdiction under Article 226, Constitution of India. [*Shakuntala Sharma* v *State of U.P.* 2001 ACJ 620 (All)(DB)]

Obstetrics/gynecology. Delivery case in Government Hospital. Negligence. Tort. Vicarious liability of State. Excessive bleeding after giving birth to a child and emergency surgery required could not be performed in time due to non availability of doctor or anesthetist resulting in death of patient. State vicarious liability for compensation awarded by the Court. Compensation of ₹1,37,750 awarded. [*Leela Bai* v *Sebastian* 2002 II CPJ 363 (Ker)(DB)]

Negligence. Tort. Compensation for medical negligence of doctor in conducting surgery leaving a foreign object inside the body of patient. Plea of hospital disowning liability on the ground that the doctor was an independent consultant and an employee of the hospital. Unsustainable. Patient admitted in the hospital after collecting fees and it was hospital that arranged the services of the doctor. hospital, therefore, vicariously liable for negligence of doctor despite absence of master and servant relationship between the hospital and the doctor. [*Aparna Dutta* v *Apolo Hospitals Enterprises Ltd.* 2002 ACJ 954 (Mad HC)]

Negligence. Complainant, a minor, given paracetamol injection by the nurse on left buttock as advised by the doctor. Left leg of the patient paralysed immediately. Sciatic nerve of the minor damaged. District Forum holding nurse negligent awarded ₹1,00,000 as compensation and costs against the doctor, which was upheld by the State Commission. Though injection given by the nurse, doctor vicariously liable as the injection administered on his advice and supervision, and nurse need not be made a party to the proceedings. National commission dismissed revision against order of lower fora. [*Dr. K.G. Krishnan* v *Praveen Kumar* (*Minor*) 2003 II CPJ 125 (NC)]

Sterilization. Failure — Tort. Operation performed in government hospital. Vicarious liability of State. Subsequent unwanted pregnancies. Complainant entitled to damages for alleged unwanted pregnancies complaining medical negligence on the part of the doctors working in the hospital and the State is vicariously liable for such damages. Damages cannot be claimed under writ remedy. Petitioner to approach civil Court or consumer Forum, as the case may be for claiming damages compensation. [*Rukmani* v *State of Tamilnadu* AIR 2003 Mad 352]

Sterilization. Failure — Tort. Vicarious liability of State. Petitioner, a poor and illiterate lady already having four children undergoing tubectomy operation in Government hospital family planning programme of Government, conceiving subsequently giving birth to a fifth (unwanted) child due to negligence of doctors in performing the operation. Failure of parties to avail of full opportunity to prevent birth of unwanted child by terminating pregnancy. Court awarded token compensation of ₹10,000. State liable to pay compensation for negligence of its doctors. [*Shobha* v *Government, NCT of Delhi* AIR 2003 Del 399]

Vicarious liability of State. Right to life. Constitutional Tort. Compensation. Death of the wife of army personnel due to negligence of doctors in military hospital who claimed themselves as specialist officers. Standard of due care expected from such doctors same as that of any other doctor or surgeon. Both the government and the negligent doctors cannot escape tortuous liability. Court competent to award compensation by way of public remedy in its writ jurisdiction for deprivations of the constitutional right of deceased to life under article 21. Awarded ₹3,00,000 as compensation to be paid by Union of India, which is vicariously liable for Tort committed by its employees, which may be recovered from the delinquents. This amount may be adjusted against any damages or compensation that may be awarded by a competent civil Court. In case petitioners fail to get a decree in their favour from civil Court, said amount paid not to be recovered from them. [*A.V. Janaki Amma* v *Union of India* 2004 VII CLD 662 (AP)]

Necessary party. Impendent of doctor. Irrespective of the way, a particular doctor is impleaded or not, if there is negligence on his part the hospital had to be held to have vicarious responsibility. [*Shushma Sharma* v *Bombay Hospital* 2007 II CPJ 9]

Hospital would be vicariously liable for the negligence on the part of their employees and not having sufficient staff to deal with emergencies. [*St. Gregarious Mission Hospital* v *Roji George* 2008 I CPJ 68]

210. Ventilator

Ventilator. Not functioning. Compensation. Deceased admitted in hospital as a case of accident. X-rays and tests were carried out. Fracture of mid shaft of right femur detected. Deceased shifted to private hospital. Respondent No. 1 where surgery done with proved fatal. Ventilator was not functioning. Deficiency in service. Respondent no. 1 hospital and the doctor liable to compensate the complainant. Respondents directed to reimburse the complainants a sum of ₹4,00,000 which they have spent for medical expenses, including hotel expenses etc. [*Geetu Sapra* v *Dr. BL Kapoor Memorial Hospital* 2006 III CPJ 1]

211. Video conferencing

Medical negligence case. Consumer Protection Act, 1986 empowers Consumer Forum and commission to follow the procedures which will give the speedy remedy e.g. evidence by way of affidavit under section 13(4)(III) — issue of commission for examination of any witness under section 13(4)(*v*). Cross examination of doctor or expert. By way of video conferences or telephone conference. However, at the initial stage the cost of these conferences will be born by the persons who claims such conferences. [*Dr. J.J. Merchant* v *Shrinath Chaturvedi* 2003 I CLJ 127 (SC)]

212. Wrong operation

DHS operation. Surgery. Not properly performed. Post-operative treatment. Not satisfactory. Complainant producing sufficient evidence to prove negligence and deficiency in service. Opposite party failed to show that operation was done in accordance with procedure following the accepted method. Case of medical negligence. [*Devadass* v *N. Arumugam* 2005 III CPJ 10 (TN)]

Hernia operation. Death during operation. Pre-operative test not done. Anaesthetist saw the patient only four hours prior to administering the Anaesthesia. Very fact that few crepts and rhonchi developed within ten minutes after starting of the surgery establishes that the patient was not properly prepared for Anaesthesia. Negligence. Compensation of ₹1,75,000 awarded. [*Smt. Bhanupal* v *Dr. Prakash Padode* 2000 III CPR 356 (MP)]

Patient of potential risk. Essential steps, which should be taken in any major surgery not taken. Resulting in death of patient on the operation table itself. Failure to take normal care and diligence. Negligence and deficiency in service proved. [*Rashmi R. Fadnavis* v *Mumbai Grahak Panchayat* 1998 III CPJ 21 (NC)]

No pre-operative precautionary measures taken. Absence of any documents showing expenses incurred. Compensation of ₹1 lakh awarded. [*Kedarnath Sethia* v *P.S. Hardia* 2000 III CPR 438 (MP)]

Hip replacement. Negligence. After operation no sensation below left knee. Gangrene developed. Amputation of left leg from above knee. Two more operations performed on her. Held that the left leg was affected by gangrene due to thrombosis or obstruction to the supply of blood through blood vessel, which could not have occurred overnight. First opposite party has not taken proper care or diligence to arrest it. Reimbursement of ₹1,11,000 and damages of ₹1,50,000 with interest @ 12 % directed. [*Ghanta Mohan Lakshmi* v *Dr. CVS Ratnam* 2002 II CPJ 144 (AP)]

213. Wrong diagnosis

Wrong report. Blood of patients tested by opposite party. Diagnostic center to be Australian Antigen (HBs Ag) positive. Another hospital giving report for the same test to the affect that Hepatitis B Anitgen found negative. Person who put signature on the report of the diagnostic center not qualified in the science to give such report. Negligence held. Plea that wrong report having no nexus with treatment given, no defence given. Treatment received by patient was from the report given by the hospital. Compensation of ₹25,000 as awarded by District Forum, not being commensurate with the damage or injury caused, and reduced to ₹10,000. [*Chaudhary Diagnostic and Research Centre* v *Mahaveer Prasad Gupta* 2005 III CPJ 768 (Raj)]

Pregnant woman treated for pulmonary tuberculosis. Patients not all suffering from tuberculosis evidenced by medical certificate issued by medical officer of government hospital. Administration of strong drugs and injections for T.B. due to wrong diagnosis. Deficiency in service ₹50,000 awarded as compensation. [*Kalyani General Hospital* v *Bhuveneshwari* 2005 IV CPJ 29 (TN)]

Blood test. Contradictory reports. Two tests conducted after collecting blood samples of complainant in the same diagnosis center. On first test complainants blood reported as of group 'O' Rh negative, therefore she had to undergo antibody test and take injection Antid 350 (Vinoblin) one each before and after delivery. When blood group tested in government hospital same having found 'O' Rh positive, complainant getting the blood again tested in O.P.'s Diagnostic Centre where it was found 'O' Rh. possitive. There may be error in regarding the group of a person without doing any negligence on the part of the doctor, but when the same diagnosis center gives, another reporter contradictory to its previous report negligence on the part of center established through complainant suffered no damage ₹10,000 awarded as compensation. [*R.C. Purohit* v *Usha Devada* 2006 I CPJ 489 (Raj)]

214. Wrong treatment

Dandruff. Advertisement. Complainant went to the appellant clinic to get treatment after coming across the advertisement given by appellant. Paid ₹7,000 for said purpose. Treatment resulted in falling of hair making him bald. These are such unfair trade practices, which need to be curbed with heavy hand. No interference with the order awarding compensation of ₹50,000. [*Body Care* v *Ashok Kumar Solanki* 2005 I CPJ 402 (Del)]

False and misleading advertisement. Attracted by newspaper advertisement of opposite parties that they had attained perfection in the art of refractive surgery for removal of spectacles/contact lenses in case of myopia, complainant getting both her eyes operated by opposite parties. Eyesight becoming weakened post operation forcing complainant to wear glasses of higher power than those she was wearing earlier. Unfair trade practice, as also deficiency in service. ₹50,000 awarded as compensation. [*S. Khanna* v *Dr. Nitin Verma* 2005 III CPR 543 (Del)]

Pain in finger. Treatment. Anaesthesia given. Gangrene developed. No direct evidence of negligence. Doctrine of "*Res Ipsa Loquitur*" comes into play. In light of admitted fact of treatment by opposite parties and deformity resulted and its reasoned explained by PW2, the burden of proof shifted from the complainant to the opposite parties. Hospital not producing relevant documents. Adverse inference is to be drawn against the hospital. Award of compensation of ₹10,000 is on the higher side. Same reduced to ₹5,000 [*Dr. Gangadharan* v *K.A. Abdul Salam* 2003 IV CPJ 633 (Ker)]

Rheumatoid Arthritis. Imuran tablets 50 mg prescribed without holding any prior test. Resulting in hair loss and bone marrow suspension. Gross negligence. Award of compensation of ₹25,000 held justified. [*B.K. Ghosh* v *Dr. Prof. P. Maulick* 2005 I CPJ 737 (WB)]

215. Writ

Right to life under Article 21 of Constitution. Sterilization failure. Vasectomy at Government hospital. Vicarious liability of state. Right to life includes right to live with dignity. Violation of writ. Petitioner's husband undergoing Vasectomy operation in government hospital. Petitioner subsequently becoming pregnant, giving birth to an unwanted child. Her relations with in-laws strained and even husband started doubting her character. On her persuasion husband's semen examined and report indicated 60% Spermatozoa present revealing that operation not successful. For mental agony and torture, insult and humiliation due to negligence of doctor who conducted vasectomy ₹1,25,000 granted as compensation and ₹50,000 to the child, to be given by State Government on basis of vicarious liability for negligence of its servant, the doctor in exercise of writ jurisdiction under Article 226, Constitution of India. [*Shakuntala Sharma* v *State of U.P.* 2001 ACJ 620 (All) (DB)]

Tort — Medical negligence in a hospital of Government undertaking. Patient operated for hysterectomy been transfused blood of her brother doner. Doner's blood not screened for HIV. Patient becoming HIV positive. Later her husband's blood on test found to be HIV negative, but that of the doner positive. Invoking, the doctrine of Constitutional Tort, Compensation of ₹1,00,000 awarded to be paid by the hospital management towards medical expenses of the victim by way of public remedy, independent of any damages or compensation that may be awarded by the civil Court for alleged tortuous liability. [*M. Vijaya* v *Chairman and Managing Director, Singareni Collieries Co. Ltd.* 2002 ACJ 32 (AP)]

Sterilization failure. Liability of State. Jurisdiction of writ Court to award compensation. Petitioner, a poor and illiterate lady already having four children undergoing Tubectomy operation in Government hospital family planning programme of Government, conceiving subsequently giving birth to a fifth unwanted child. Court has jurisdiction to hold the State liable for the negligence of its doctors in the performance of operation. [*Shobha* v *Government, NCT of Delhi* AIR 2003 Del 399]

Right to life — Tort — Death due to negligence of doctors in military hospital. Writ petition claiming compensation. Plea of sovereign immunity. Defence of sovereign immunity. Defence of sovereign immunity being inapplicable and alien to the concept of guarantee of fundamental rights, there had to be no question of such a defence being available in the constitutional remedy of awarding compensation against the government of the principle of vicarious liability for tortuous acts of its servants. [*A.V. Janaki Amma* v *Union of India* 2004 VII CLD 662 (AP)]

CHAPTER 6

Categories of Cases in which Medical Negligence Not Considered

SYNOPSIS

1. Adverse inference

Delivery of child. Allegation that though a male child was delivered, yet a female child was handed over. Complainant not agreeing for conducting DNA test. Presumption to be raised against complainant. No deficiency in service. Complaint liable to be dismissed with the cost. [*Manish Agarwal* v *Kamla Nehru Memorial Hospital* 2001 I CPJ 42 (UP)]

Prescription of two dates was torn on its corner and there are certain indications indicating selective tearing cf the prescription. Documents from AIIMS had neither been produced, nor otherwise proved. It would certainly lead to draw adverse inference against the complainant to the effect that in case those documents would have been produced they would have gone against the case of complainants. [*S. Saleemuddin* v *Dr. Sunil Mehrotra* 2006 III CPJ 396 (NC)]

2. AIDS

Damages – claim for – Hospital disclosing the fact that appellant was HIV (+) Appellant seeking damages. If a person suffering from dreadful disease "AIDS" knowingly marries of woman and thereby transmits infection to that woman, he would be guilty of offence indicated in sections 269 and 270, IPC. Appellant not entitled to damages. [*Dr. Tokugha Yepthomi* v *Apollo Hospital Enterprises Limited* 1999 I CPJ 11 (SC)]

HIV Test. As per report dated 3-12-2002 the petitioner was found to be HIV positive through the screening test which was done from HIV Niwa Kit of Cadila. The petitioner was advised to co-relate the result by Western Blot Technique. In report dated 10-12-2003 the basis for reaching the conclusion in regard to petitioner being HIV negative has not been disclosed. Order of the State Commission allowing the appeal of respondent and dismissing the complaint of petitioner alleging deficiency in service upheld. [*Susheel Kumar* v *Virendra Mahala* 2007 III CPJ 395]

3. Allergy

Case of the complainant that the Doctor knew that wife of the complainant was allergic to penicillin and yet the doctor administered Ampicillin and oral Cosavil, cephalosporin resulting in the patient Steven Jones Syndrome and ultimate death. Stand of the doctor that on many occasions he administered ampicillin to the wife of the complainant and she did not develop any adverse reaction and was never allergic to that. Doctors examined by the complainant stated that the treatment given to the patient was proper in the circumstances. No negligence. Concurrent finding of fact. No interference. [*Kashiram Bhimrao Kambale* v *Uday A. Paul* 2001 III CPR 117 (NC)]

Allergical reaction. Medicine. Wrong prescription. Expert evidence. Absence of. Held that even if there had been some reaction or allergy, unless there is some negligence or deficiency in service of the doctor, he cannot be said to be negligent. No negligence. [*Mohd. Istiqar* v *Dr. Rajesh Gupta* 2005 II CLT 216 (Uttr.)]

4. Amputation

Hand Medical treatment. Medical negligence. Allegation of. Attempt to suicide by consuming oleander poisonous seeds. Gangrene developed. Amputation of right hand in order to save life of complainant. Complainant not abducting any expert evidence to prove that treatment and practice adopted by the doctor is not accordance with the established procedure. No negligence. [*S. Veerasamy* v *Dr. Murugaiyan* 2005 I CPJ 665 (Pondichery)]

Leg. Diabetic patient. Injury on toe. Went to doctor only after a period of 15 days. Amputation of leg. Medical negligence alleged. No expert evidence produced. Neither examined himself nor any member of his family. Not a case of medical negligence but a result of complainant being a chronic diabetic. District Forum wrongly allowed the complaint. [*CSR Memorial Hospital* v *M. Ramaswamy* 2004 III CPJ 62 (TN)]

Leg Consent Treatment record showed that high risk consent was given by father and uncle of patient for about knee amputation is falsified. Doctors of hospital not only passed the Bolam's test but got excellent marks. Appeal liable to be dismissed. [*Purman Chandriah* v *Balanagar Hospitals Pvt. Ltd.* 2008 I CPJ 138 (NC)]

Leg Fracture, Medical treatment. Operation, Gangrene developed. Amputation of leg. Plea that another line of treatment should have been adopted. Held that both the lines of treatment were in order and the doctor cannot be faulted, if he adopted one of them. [*Mam Chand* v *G.S. Mangat of Mangat Hospital* 2004 I CPJ 79 (NC)]

Leg. Medical treatment. Negligence. Allegation that tight plaster of paris caused infection which resulted in loss of sensation and ultimately amputation of leg. Stand of the O.P. that complainant left the clinic after first aid and the leg was not plastered by him. Held that the broken of proof lies on the complainant which he failed to discharge. Complaint liable to be dismissed. [*Soni Kumari* (*Minor*) v *Dr. Nagendra Narain Bhagat* 2003 I CPJ 196 (Bihar)]

Leg. Injury. Suffered in accident. Amputation of leg. Same was not on account of negligent act on the part of doctor but on account of injuries suffered. No negligence on the part of the doctor either in the matter of providing treatment or in the matter of alleged delay in referring the patient to C.M.C. Ludhiana. Complainant liable to be dismissed. [*Lekh Raj* v *Bharat Nursing Home, Hoshiarpur* 1998 II CPJ 335 (Pun)]

Leg Diabetic Patient. Had unhealing wound in the left second toe. Developed gangrene. Amputation of left leg below the knee. Went into coma. Died. Negligence alleged. Doctor adequately explained the proper course of treatment he adopted. No fault in the initial treatment adopted by the doctor. No negligence, complaint rightly dismissed. [*Rajkuwarbai* v *Dr. R.R. Dhoot Medical Practitioner* 1999 III CPR 2 (Mah)]

Medical treatment. Professional judgment. Allegation that gangrene not managed in time by not amputing the arm, patient suffering from complicated ailments. Could not be saved in spite of best efforts of doctors. Decision not to carry out surgery/amputation based on doctor's professional judgment and knowledge. No deficiency in service. Complaint liable to be dismissed. [*Rekha Gupta* v *Bombay Hospital Trust* 2003 II CPJ 160 (NC)]

5. Anaesthesia

Administering of. Anaesthetist followed accepted medical procedure having less than 1% of risk. Complainant fell in that 1% of spinal anaesthesia and suffered infrequent complication. Anaesthetist not guilty of any negligence. [*Charan Singh* v *Healing Touch Hospital* 2003 III CPJ 62 (NC)]

Improper application of. Death of patient. Negligence alleged as patient become unconscious till death after surgery due to failure in proper administration of anaesthesia. What the anaesthetist was supposed to do which he did not do or he did what he was not supposed to do, not shown by complainant. No negligence. [*K. Sadanandan* v *Lisie Hospital* 2006 I CPJ 24 (NC)]

6. Ayurvedic doctor

Practice of modern allopathic system of medicine. An Ayurvedic doctor holding BAMS degree entitled to practice modern scientific system of medicine. Science integrated course of ayurvedic medical education comprises various topics under modern medicine and when such persons put in considerable years of practice covering such topics also they are entitled to prescribe allopathic drugs also. [*Manpreet Kaur* v *Dr. Veena Ghumber* 2005 I CPJ 63 (Pun)]

7. Back pain

Operation. Allegation of negligence. Patient was having a tendency to have bulges and fibrosis as a result of which he suffered discomfort and pain. Pain caused in back of the complainant cannot be attributed due to negligence in the performance of operation. No negligence. [*Nuruddin Kutubuddin Baloti* v *Dr. L. N. Vora* 1995 I CPJ 459 (Mah)]

8. Blood cancer

Patient's negligence. Patient was advised to come after two weeks and required BMT operation. Patient brought for treatment after six months. Serious condition. Patient died despite treatment according to standard practice. Patient could not be saved due to delay on his part in getting treatment. No deficiency in service. [*Pasumarthy Narayana* v *M/s Apollo Hospital Enterprises Ltd.* 2004 IV CPJ 19]

9. Blood pressure

Hysterectomy Operation. Deceased having high blood pressure and lower level of HB. Medical literature showed that the surgical procedure could be done on a patient with diastolic blood pressure of not more than 110 mm Hg and haemoglobin concentration of even 6g. dl. Before start of procedure the BP of the deceased was 180/100. Procedure performed was not elective as the deceased was having severe bleeding. Both the OPs are highly qualified and acted in according with the practice accepted as proper by the medical literature. Cannot be held guilty of negligence. [*Biswanath Das* v *Bijoy Sinha Roy* 2007 IV CPJ 223 (NC)]

10. Blood transfusion

Absence of any evidence to link the blood transfusion with any of the resultant complications in the case. Appellant or its doctors cannot be held guilty of any negligence/deficiency in service. [*Calcutta Medical Research Institute* v *Bimlesh Chatterjee* 1999 I CPJ 13 (NC)]

Allegation that blood purchased from the blood bank contained virus of vital Hepatitis and because of that the wife of complainant got that deceased. Onus of proving the fact lies on the complainant. No sufficient evidence to establish that the wife of the complainant caught the deceased through blood transfusion. [*T. Harendran Nair* v *Dr. P. Ashokan* 1995 I CPJ 220 (Ker)]

Open Heart Surgery. Allegation the death was caused due to severe blood transfusion reaction. Opposite party exercised reasonable amount of care. No medical negligence. [*Gopi Ram Goyal* v *National Heart Institute* 2001 II CPC 262 (NC)]

Allegation that death occurred due to transfusion of contaminated blood. Absence of evidence showing that blood was improperly stored from time of procurement till time of administration. No expert evidence produced. No medical negligence. [*P. Kallianikutty Amma* v *Unity Health Services (P) Ltd,* 2005 IV CPJ 84 (NC)]

Mother of the complainant suffering from systemic Lupus Erythematosus needed blood transfusion. Blood transfusion on 4-6-1996. It was allegedly blackish and was not saline washed. Allegation that high dose of cortisone being prescribed by doctor. Death after 4 months of the transfusion of blood. Compatibility report in regard to both the units were obtained procured from National Heart Institute, the date of expiry was 26-6-1996. Medical literature produced showed that prescribing of higher dose of cortisone by doctor was in the interest of the patient. Alleged deficiency in service not proved. [*Gurjit Chowdhury* v *Apollo Hospital* 2007 III CPJ 142 (NC)]

11. Bone grafting

Death of senior surgeon who was actually consulted and who took the decision to operate in the manner he did. Whether any relief can be granted to the complainant. Held No. [*Balbir Singh Makol* v *Chairman, M/s S.G.R. Hospital* 2001 I CPJ 45 (NC)]

12. Bolam's test

Surgery. Amputation of leg. Consent. Treatment record showed that high risk consent was given by father and uncle for about nee amputation. Contention of the complainant that no informed consent was given for knee amputation is falsified. Doctors of hospital not only passed the Bolam's test but got excellent marks. Appeal liable to be dismissed. [*Purnam Chandiriah* v *Balanagar Hospitals Pvt. Ltd.* 2008 I CPJ 138 (NC)]

13. Brain tumor

Eye treatment. Nothing to show that treatment given by the respondent doctor had caused tumor in the brain and loss of vision. The complainant has not filed any expert medical evidence or medical test to prove the alleged negligence by respondent. Revision petition liable to be dismissed. [*Agarulakshmi Rajyam* v *K. Sudhakar Rao* (*Dr.*) 2007 II CPJ 240 (NC)]

14. Burden of proof

Allegations of medical negligence. Complainant to discharge the burden of proof. Failed to do so. Dismissed complaint. Upheld. [*Sanket Raju Shinde* v *S.T. Watve* 2004 IV CPJ 526 (Mah)]

Medical treatment negligence allegation that tight plaster of paris caused infection which resulted in loss of sensation and ultimately amputation of leg. Stand of OP that complainant left the clinic after first aid and the leg was not plastered by him. Held that burden of proof lies on the complainant which he failed to discharge, complaint liable to be dismissed. [*Soni Kumari* (*Minor*) v *Dr. Nagendra Narain Bhagat* 2003 I CPJ 196 (Bihar)]

Wife of complainant undergoing TCRE. Bleeding. Death. Allegation neither supported by any medical literature nor by an expert evidence. Burden of proof was on the complainant which he failed to discharge. Complaint dismissed. [*Abdulla Modiwala* v *G.D. Birla Memorial Health Centre* 2000 II CPJ 502 (MP)]

Congenital cardiac anomaly. Open heart surgery. Patient advised to be brought back for balloon dilatation to relieve the obstruction in the remaining residual under developed arch of the Aorta. Patient developed pain. However, he was not brought back to the hospital as advised. Held that the doctors performed their duties with proper care and attention. Complainant failed to discharge the burden of proof with regard to negligence. Complaint liable to be dismissed. [*Prafulla Kumar Das* v *Apollo Hospital* 2002 II CPJ 106 (NC)]

Repeated advice for 'Bone Marrow Aspiration test' was unheeded. This is clearly a case of negligence on the part of the complainant himself who repeatedly refused or did not heed the advice of the doctors to get the bone marrow aspiration test done which is the test to finally determine that the patient is suffering from leukemia. He has not been able to show as to what the respondent should have done which he did not do or he did what he should not have done. The onus of proof in this regard lay with the complainant to prove his case of medical negligence which he completely failed. Appeal liable to be dismissed. [*P.N. Sudhakar Gupta* v *Anugraha Vittal Nursing Home* 2008 I CPJ 57]

15. Cancer

Blood Cancer Patient's Negligence, Patient was advised to come after two weeks and required BMT operation. Patient brought for treatment after six months in serious condition. Patient died despite treatment according to standard practice. Patient could not be saved due to delay on his part in getting treatment. No deficiency in service. [*Pasumarthy Narayana* v *M/s Apollo Hospital Enterprises Ltd.* 2004 IV CPJ 19 (NC)]

Error in judgment. Removal of prostrate as symptoms of prostrate cancer found during surgery. Allegation that biopsy was not carried out before surgery. Held that there was no ground for doctors to get biopsy before surgery in as much as there was no indication of cancer recorded. Error in judgment does not amount to medical negligence. [*Dr. R.C. Sharma* v *Jage Ram* 2003 I CPJ 248 (NC)]

Medical Treatment. Allegations that OPs rendered deficient services to the deceased in not taking due care and caution in regard to the presence of cancerous cells in the gallbladder while removing the Gall stones. No positive evidence to the effect that the appellant knew or could have known after exercise of the knowledge, learning and experience of a medical professional that the deceased was or could have been suffering from Cancer in Gallbladder or other related areas and that he did not take due care and caution in ascertaining those relevant facts, before conducting the operation. No deficiency in service. [*Behal Hospital and Medical Research Centre* v *Sahi Ram* 2003 I CPJ 14 (Raj)]

Medical treatment. Cancer at advanced stage. Administering of combination of chemotherapy and radiotherapy. Doctor following accepted procedure. No negligence. Complaint liable to be dismissed. [*S.K. Sharma* v *Dr. Praful B. Desai* 2003 II CPJ 90 (NC)]

16. Cataract operation

Implantation of Intra Ocular Lens. Loss of vision. Not enough to state that after eight months of the IInd operation Intra Ocular Lens Implantation had to be removed, thus providing negligence of the doctor. This could at best be a ground but not a proof of negligence. Complainant not producing any evidence to contradict the evidence of the doctor. No negligence on the part of the doctor. [*Rohni Devi* v *H.S. Chaudavat* 2001 III CPR 172 (NC)]

Complainant vision was raised to 6/8 (with the use of glasses) after operation. Eyesight of right eye improved, underwent laser treatment at AIIMS whereas it was not permissible at least for the period of 6 months after the contract operation. No negligence on the part of opposite party in performing the operation in implementation of the Intra Ocular lens. [*Yoginder Beri* v *Grover Eye and ENT Hospital* 2001 III CPJ 106 (UT Chd)]

Allegation of negligence in post-operative care. Doctors have taken all necessary care. No lapse on the part of the doctor in performing cataract operation because after operation gain of vision was proper and it is due to some infection that the case turned into the case of Endophthalmitis. Doctor and hospital staff acted with due care and diligence and has taken all necessary precautions for treatment and also in post-operative care. No negligence. [*Hari Prasad Chukai* v *Mannulal Jagannath Trust Hospital* 2003 IV CPJ 17 (MP)]

Patient was having corneal opacity. He was explained before hand, the complications which may occur. His care is a case of known complications. No expert medical opinion produced to prove that there has been any negligence on the part of appellant doctor, compliant dismissed. [*Marbal City Hospital and Research Centre* v *V.S.R. Soni* 2004 II CPJ 102 (MP)]

Right eye. Alleged loss of sight. After operation the complainant petitioner suffering from Uveitis. It has not been proved that Uveitis has been caused due to surgical trauma. Complainant admitted that he had voluntarily abandoned the service of the opposite party respondent doctor and had approached several hospital and doctors for treatment from different doctors of her own choice. As per the words of opposite party she did not need to his advice at the post-operational stage. Concurrent findings of fact. Petitioner failed to prove that there was any deficiency in pre operative or post-operative care on the part of the respondent. [*Munni Devi* v *Dr. R.P. Tandon* 2006 IV CPJ 259 (NC)]

17. Coma

Child went into coma after operation. Allegation that no proper nursing care given for recovery from coma. No evidence of any negligence or recklessness or departure from accepted and established rule of treatment. No negligence established. [*Study Circle Society* v *Choithram Hospital and Research Centre,* 2000 II CPJ 436 (MP)]

18. Caesarean operation

Death of patient. No specific allegation regarding negligence on the part of the attending physician. Service of the renowned Gynecologist and other expert doctors requisitioned. Patient taken to Calcutta for better treatment. No expert witness produced to substantiate the allegation. No negligence. [*Prasanta Kumar Chakraborty* v *Dr. Johar Debnath* 2000 III CPJ 91 (WB)]

Death. Opposite party MBBS doctor. Well qualified and eligible for conducting caesarean operation. No expert evidence. No postmortem, complaint dismissed with costs of ₹2,000. [*Surinder Kumar* (*Laddi*) v *Dr. Santosh Menon* 2000 III CPJ 517 (Pun)]

Allegation that during the operation carried out at the time of delivery, the respondents were negligent which resulted in making a hole in the bladder leading to U.V.F. and Manouria and mental trauma of living with a catheter for sometime. Complainant failed to prove cause connection between the delivery and the U.V. Fistula finally located later on. Medical literature and expert opinion not supporting the case of complainant. Complaint rightly dismissed by State Commission. [*Beena Garg* v *Kailash Nursing Home* 2002 III CPJ 99 (NC)]

Necessary pre-operational tests allegedly not conducted. When foetus developed distress there was no alternative left except emergency caesarean. Though blood urea level, serum creatinine levels increased day-by-day but below the range for recommending dialysis. In such circumstances, failure to send patient for dialysis. Does not amount to negligence. [*M. Srinivas* v *Dr. (Smt.) Rama Thulasi* 2003 I CPJ 449 (AP)]

Medical negligence alleged. Restitching of torn stitches. Allegedly resulting in indigestion and vomiting. Held that gastro problem was one of the causes which contribute to weakness of patient. Mother and baby not suffering any complication. No positive against doctor. complaint wrongly allowed. Liable to be dismissed. [*Dr. Sheila Das* v *Serajuddin* 2005 III CPJ 323 (Jhar)]

Discharged on the 9th post-operative day without any complications, contention that after some days she got abdomen pain and she got surgical procedure from another hospital and sponge like object removed. Doctor who operated neither his affidavit produced nor has been cross examined. Foreign body which was removed in operation not sent for further test for malignancy. Case decided on the statement of Junior/Assistant doctor who was also not cross-examined. Held that in view of the findings that the alleged swab has neither been produced/preserved nor has it been proved that this was indeed a swab, unable to agree with the findings of the state commission which has been considered evidence on record. There is no negligence or deficiency in service on the part of the petitioner. District Forum rightly dismissed the complaint. [*Dr. Shushma Chawla* v *Harvinder Kaur* 2007 II CLT 523 (NC)]

19. Compensation

Child delivered prematurely died. District Forum awarding compensation of ₹25,000. Same not based on any evidence. Impugned order liable to be set aside. [*Prem Nath Hospital, Gurgaon* v *Poonam Mangala* 1998 II CPJ 205 (Hry)]

Hip replacement operation. Had the first operation been successful even then the complainant would have incurred expenses on the purchase of the material/articles for hip replacement. Complainant not entitled to reimbursement of said amount. [*R.P. Dahiya, Advocate* v *Dr. Pradeep Aggarwal* 2000 III CPJ 175 (Hry.)]

20. Complaint

Bona fide Complainant working as a nurse in a hospital in Tamil Nadu choosing to go to opposite parties for undergoing sterilization operation in 1991 and leaving the Gulf countries. Becoming pregnant in 1993 and sent back to

India being pregnant in 1994. Without thinking of or taking steps to terminate pregnancy going to the opposite parties, obtaining a certificate that they performed the sterilization operation and filing complaint against them in 1995. Claim of complainant not bona-fide. [*Padma N. Rao* v *Asha Bai* 2004 II CPJ 365 (TN)]

Abuse of process of consumer fora. Non-production of relevant document and glaring inconsistency in between stand taken by complainant and production of selectively torn documents indicating that the complaint filed with pre-conceived and misconceived notions amounting to abuse of process of fora. Complaint dismissed with costs of ₹25,000 in favour of opposite party doctor. [*Saleemuddin* v *Dr. Sunil Malhotra* 2006 III CPJ 396]

21. Consent

Amputation of leg, Treatment record showed that high risk consent was given by father and uncle of patient for about knee amputation contention of the complainant that no informed consent was given for knee amputation is falsified. Doctors of hospital not only passed the Bolam's test but got excellent marks. Appeal liable to be dismissed. [*Purnam Chandriah* v *Balanagar Hospitals Pvt. Ltd.* 2008 I CPJ 138 (NC)]

Stone in Gallbladder. Operation for. Change in mode of operation. Surgeon providing justification for converting from the Laparoscopic method into the conventional open surgery procedure. Prior consent from the husband of the petitioner taken for such change in the procedure of operation in case of necessity. No negligence or deficiency in service. [*Dhanwati Kumar* v *Dr. S.K. Jhunjhunwala* 2004 II CPJ 162 (WB)]

Surgery. Contention that complainant gave his written consent to undertake the risk involved in surgery of his wife. Held that the consent cannot be taken to be a valid defence where the complainant is able to show that there was negligence and carelessness on the part of the opposite parties at the time of surgery. [*Devendra Kumar Sharma* v *Post Graduate Institute of Medical Education and Research* 2002 I CPJ 211 (UT Chd)]

Surgery. Non-obtaining of consent. Gives rise to cause of action for seeking remedy. Even if medical negligence/deficiency in service not established. [*Punjabi Nursing Home* v *Kailash Marodia* 2003 III CPJ 194 (MP)]

Surgical procedure. The appellant who was neither a minor nor mentally challenged was only temporarily unconscious undergoing only a diagnostic procedure by way of laparoscopy. The respondent ought to have waited till the appellant regained consciousness, discussed the result of laparoscopic examination and then taken her consent for the removal of her uterus and ovaries. In the absence of an emergency and the matter was still at the stage of diagnosis, the question of taking her mother's consent for radical surgery did not arise. Such consent by the mother cannot be treated as valid or real consent. Further a consent for hysterectomy is not a consent for bilateral salpingooopherectomy. [*Samira Kohli* v *Prabha Manchanda* 2008 I CPJ 56]

Authenticity of consent form, when signature of the woman obtained in prescribed format, no endorsement as to consent written on the form, but written portion interpolated subsequently to accommodate the space available above the signature, giving rise to *bona fide* and legitimate doubt about authenticity and genuineness of consent. [*Dr. S.K. Kulkarni* v *Khandoba Mairal Kodalkar*]

22. Consumer

Donation-Government Hospital. Token amount given as donation. Does not amount to payment of consideration. Complainant is not a consumer. [*Narendra Singh Rastogi* v *Shaskiya Gyara Punch Trust* 2002 II CPJ (MP)]

Medical negligence, no fee charged for operation. Though ₹100 and ₹25 charged for room rent and for glucose, respectively, however, person under treatment has to pay incidental expenses complainant is not consumer. [*T. Khatoon* v *Government of UP* 2001 II CPJ 354 (UP)]

Tubectomy operation. Fee of charge. Under family planning programme of state government. Operation unsuccessful. Complainant gave birth to a female child. Complainant is not consumer. [*Pushpabai* v *S. Joseph* 2002 II CPJ 566]

Sterilisation operation. Under National Family Welfare programme. Failed. Operation done free of cost and voluntaries paid incentive money. Held that complainants are not consumer. [*Shashikala* v *Command Hospital* (*AIR Force*) 2003 III CPJ 84 (Kar)]

Token amount. Delivery of child. Alleged deficiency in service in not taking proper pre-and post-operative precautions. Government hospital. Payment of token amount of ₹2 for registration purpose does not alter the position of doctors and hospital. Complainant is not consumer. [*Dr. Smt. N.R. Yadav* v *Smt. Manorama Tomarkar* 2001 II CPJ 402 (MP)]

Legal representative. Brother of deceased consumer. Not a consumer within the meaning of Consumer Protection Act while widow and son of the deceased still alive. Brother cannot maintain complaint under the Act, he not being the legal heir of deceased whose widow and son not coming to file the complaint. [*Parimal Kumar Acharya* v *Dr. Tapan Kumar Chakroborty* 2005 I CPR 474 (WB)]

Hiring services for consideration, complainant alleging payment of fee to opposite party doctors, but no receipt proved nor any reason given for why receipts could not be obtained. Statement of opposite parties that patients father, officer-in-charge of the local police station at the relevant time, taking advantage of his official position got doctor's services of treating the patient free of charge not controverter. If complainant not a consumer and the complaint not maintainable. [*Dr. Dwijadas Som* v *Krishna Hazara* 2005 III CPR 570 (WB)]

23. Costs

Imposition of. Surgical operation. For urinary bladder. Non-removal of the stones from the kidney. Both the organs are vital human organs and can never be operated simultaneously because their position and functions in the body. Allegations of deficiency in service not substantiated. Compliant rightly dismissed with costs. [*Sewa Ram* v *Dr. Vitul K. Gupta* 1999 II CPR 68 (Pb.)]

Imposition of suppression of material facts. Allegations of deficiency in service against doctor. Complainants did not set out true and complete facts before the learned Forum. Complaint right dismissed with cost. [*Chandulal Gokuldas Patel* v *Dr. Harshad* v *Kaamdar* 2003 IV 521 (Guj)]

Imposition of. Complaint seeking recovery of ₹55,90,000 alleging medical negligence. Complainant totally failed to make out any case against opposite parties. It appears that the motive of the complainant is only to indulge in speculative litigation taking undue advantage of the fact that no court fee is payable for institution of a case under the Consumer Protection Act. Complaint liable to be dismissed. Complainant to pay costs of ₹10,000 to each of the parties. [*Brij Mohan Kher* v *Dr. N.H. Banka* 1995 I CPJ 99 (NC)]

Imposition of. Frivolous complaint. Cost of ₹5,000 Imposed for filing frivolous and vexatious complaint. [*Amar Singh* v *Frances Newton Hospital, Ferozepore* 2001 I CPJ 8 (Pb)]

24. Cardiology

Angioplasty preponement of surgery. Reasons for preponement or postponement of procedure based on availability of Operation Theater. Priority had to be given to other critical patients scheduled earlier for similar procedure. No evidence adduced by complainant for procedure from 9 a.m. to 7.45 p.m. on 12-7-2002 adversely affected the condition of patient. No negligence. [*Prabha Shanker* v *Narayana Hrudayala* 2006 IV CPJ 182 (Karn)]

Post-operative treatment. Coronary Artery Bypass Graft Surgery. Death of patient after two days of successful surgery due to sudden extubation of endrotracheal tube (E.T. Tube) resulting in cardiac arrest. Deceased a diabetes mellitus patient science 15 years. Patient and relatives were explained that operation scheduled to be performed an extremely high risk operation. Displacement of E.T. Tube due to sudden violent coughing which is not unknown to medical profession and not due to failure of opposite parties to provide proper post-operative care. No negligence. [*SR. Shivaprakash* v *Wockhardt Hospital Ltd* 2006 II CPJ 123 (NC)]

Coronary bypass surgery. Hepatitis B infection. Allegation that infection might have come during blood transfusion or due to use of improper sterilized medical equipment or linen. Almost all the blood required for transfusion freshly taken from relatives and friends of complainant and only one unit from hospital blood bank having no Hepatitis infection as proved by hospital records. Fresh and disposable cardiac catheters and equipment and hospital linen shown to be properly sterilized. Complainant had earlier undergone angiography in another hospital and also a tooth extraction somewhere else before being admitted in opposite party hospital. Hepatitis B infection reveals itself upto 100 days after infection, but in complainant case it revealed after 5 months. There are various possibilities from where infection would have come and during period in question and thereafter no other case of Hepatitis B infection reported by any other patient from the opposite party hospital. No negligence. [*Supriya Gupta* v *Trustees of Breach Candy Hospital and Research Centre* 2005 IV CPJ 26 (NC)]

25. Delivery of child

Allegation that though a male child was delivered, yet a female child was handed over. Complainant not agreeing for conducting DNA test. Presumption to be raised against complainant. No deficiency in service. Complaint liable to be dismissed with the cost. [*Manish Agarwal* v *Kamla Nehru Memorial Hospital* 2001 I CPJ 42 (UP)]

Delivery of child by Dai at home. Mother profusely bleeding when brought to hospital. Necessary steps taken. Attendants asked to arrange blood. They shifted the patient to other hospital. Certificate issued by Gram Panchayat Sarpanch showing that the death of the patient was due to heart failure. No medical negligence. Frivolous complaint. Dismissed upheld. [*Manpreet Kaur* v *Dr. Mrs. Veena Ghumber* 2005 I CPJ 63 (Pun)]

Child delivered prematurely. Died. District Forum awarding compensation of ₹25,000. Same not based on any evidence. Impugned order liable to be set aside. [*Prem Nath Hospital, Gurgaon* v *Poona Mangala* 1998 II CPJ 205 (Hry)]

Caesarean Operation. Death of patient. No specific allegation regarding negligence on the part of the attending physician. Services of the renowned Gynecologist and other expert doctors requisitioned. Patient taken to Calcutta for better treatment. No expert witness produced to substantiate the allegation. No negligence. [*Prasanta Kumar Chakraborty* v *Dr. Johar Debnath* 2000 III CPJ 91 (WB)]

Death of deceased due to Post Partum Hemorrhage suffered by deceased as a result of prolonged labour which she had to suffer for want of timely consent for caesarean section which was given after 8 hours. Unrebutted evidence of respondent doctor supported by other surgeons and medical literature. Petitioner did not file any affidavit of any expert nor he chose to cross-examine neither of the doctor. Order of the Fora below dismissing complaint of the petitioner upheld. [*Raj Kumar Vishve* v *Vandana Gupta* 2007 III CPJ 89]

26. Dialysis

Medical treatment. Paramedical staff of the hospital knew that patient for dialysis fistula. Allegation regarding bursting fistula or occurrence of bleeding not proved. No medical negligence. [*Jagat Narayan Chaube* v *Dr. Achal Sepaha* 2004 I CPJ 435 (MP)]

27. DNA test

Delivery of child. Allegation that though a male child was delivered, yet a female child was handed over. Complainant not agreeing for conducting DNA test. Presumption to be raised against complainant. No deficiency in service. Complaint liable to be dismissed with the cost. [*Manish Agarwal* v *Kamla Nehru Memorial Hospital* 2001 I CPJ 42 (UP)]

28. Diabetes

Diabetic patient. Injury on toe. Went of doctor only after a period of 15 days. Amputation of leg, medical negligence alleged. No expert evidence produced.

Neither examined himself nor any member of his family. Not a case of medical negligence but a result of complainant being a chronic diabetic. District Forum wrongly allowed the complainant. [*CSR Memorial Hospital* v *M. Ramaswamy* 2004 III CPJ 62 (TN)]

Diabetology. Improper diabetic management. Allegations of. No super specialty like others in diabetology. Physician being an M.D. had ample qualification to deal with the complainant diabetes. [*Dr. S. Gurunathan* v *Vijaya Health Centre* 2002 III CPJ 211 (NC)]

Diabetic patient. Medical treatment. Deceased was not only patient of diabetes but she was a patient of chronic obstructive pulmonary disease, asthamatic bronchitis, hypertension and obesity. It may be that combination of all these disease to be caused for death of patient. It cannot be attributed to only Nivaguine injection or treatment of diabetes. Appellant doctor has properly diagnosed and treated the patient. No medical negligence. [*New India Assurance Co. Ltd.* v *Jai Kumar* 2004 IV CPJ 719 (MP)]

29. Diagnosis

Diagnostic centre. Wrong ultrasound report. Complainant suffering from stomach pain. Advised by opposite parties to have ultrasound of her stomach and the report found perfect with no defect. Pain not subsiding, complainant taking ultrasound from another centre which showed a cyst in her stomach and some removed by surgery. Allegation of deficiency in service against opposite party for giving wrong diagnostic report. Cystic solid mass develops monthly in ovary and then finishes. Concerned surgeon operated complainant only for financial gains. No deficiency in service on the part of opposite parties. [*Hemlata* v *Dr. Vipin Premi* 2004 IV CPJ (Uttaranchal)]

30. Drug reaction

Allegedly due to prescription of Sulfa medicine without resorting to necessary tests. Prescription chit not produced. Allegation not proved. Complaint rightly dismissed. [*KVS Narayan* v *Dr. P. Gopinathan* 2001 III CPJ 498 (Ker)]

Allegation that doctor prescribed over dose of Sizopin tablets beyond the limits and he has not done W.B.C. count test before prescribing these medicines, therefore the reaction of the Sizopin tablet developed as AGRANULOCYTOSIS which was potentially life threatening event. Complainant had not produced the opinion of any expert doctor to show that the treatment given by the doctor was not as per medical ethics and principles. Held that the doctor has exercised and applied his knowledge with full care and precautions. Not guilty of medical negligence. [*Vaqar Mohammad Khan* v *Dr. S.K. Tandon* 2002 II CPJ 169 (MP)]

Loss of sight. Complainant treated for fever. Eruption of boils in her body and subsequent loss of vision of one of the eyes alleged to be due to drug reaction not proved nor any expert evidence produced by complainant. Expert from the side of opposite parties opined that drug prescribed by opposite parties safe and likely to cause loss of vision. No negligence on the part of opposite party. [*Phool Bai Gupta* v *Dr. R. Bhattacharya* 2005 III CPJ 399 (Chhattisgarh)]

Low blood pressure and asthma. Death of patient. Administration of Imferon injection without giving test dose alleged. No poisoning in viscera detected in autopsy. Defence of opposite parties that only test does given corroborated by M.L.C. report. Final report in criminal case also ruling out any anaphylactic reaction or death due to Imferon injection. No deficiency in service or negligence. [*S.K. Sethi* v *Dr. Rakesh Malhotra* 2006 IV CPJ 222 (NC)]

Loss of eye sight. Treatment for toxaplasmosis. Complainant a pregnant woman. Administration of Revomycin Forte. Revomycin Forte, the only prescribed drug during pregnancy for toxoplasmosis. If complainant felt some reaction, she should have stopped taking the drug and immediately contacted opposite parties. Instead, she went for treatment to another hospital in another village on the way to which the hospital of opposite parties situated, but had not visited said hospital for treatment of alleged reaction of drug. No deficiency in service. [*Indumati* v *Dr. Shyamala A. Masurkar* 2006 IV CPJ 138 (Karn)]

31. Due care

Perusal of injury statement showed that all three fingers were badly crushed. There was no alternative for the doctor except to cut the same as the same could not have been saved. Respondent no. 1 after examining the injury with due care and caution to the best of his judgment came to the conclusion that dobridement of bones was required. After explaining to complainant, he cut three fingers in order to save the right hand of his son and also to save his life. No negligence proved against respondent no. 1. Respondent no. 2 was also not negligent as he gave only first aid to the son of the complainant and referred him to the government hospital complaint liable to be dismissed. [*Gurumukh Singh* v *Rajiv Gupta* 2004 III CLT 496 (UT)]

Delivery of child. Premature birth of baby. Death due to *Hirschsprung's* disease. Mother of the deceased child had four miscarriages before this conception. Report of Dr. Jana which is placed on records of no consequence as he is neither a paediatrician nor a paediatrics surgeon. He was also not available for cross-examination. Both the doctors possessed skill and knowledge to handle the case. They exercised the duty of care in undertaking the case, duty of care in deciding what treatment to give and duty of care in the administration of the treatment. They have brought to their task a reasonable degree of skill and knowledge and have exercised a reasonable degree of care. No negligence on the part of the opposite parties. Complaint dismissed. [*Mandira Saha* v *Dr. Ujjal Chatterjee* 2006 II CPJ 159]

32. Dentistry

Orthodontic treatment. While extracting tooth of complainant, opposite party alleged to have negligently and carelessly dropped spirit in the eye of the complainant, due to which she had to wear spectacles, opposite party a competent and an accomplished orthodontist not shown to have adopted procedures contrary to the established procedures in the field of orthodontics by any expert evidence from that field. When there is no oral or documentary evidence on record to substantiate allegation of medical negligence it would be impossible to hold opposite party guilt of medical negligence. [*Babandeep Kaur* v *Dr. (Brig) S.C. Anand* 2004 III CPJ 577 (Chdg)]

33. Error of judgment

Operation gross negligence on the part of the doctor. He cannot take the refuse of the principle or error of judgment. [*Smt. Gurmit Mahal* v *Chauhan Nursing Home* 1998 III CPR 405 (Pb)]

Wrong treatment. Absence of medical evidence. Even if it is assumed that the Doctors had erred in their judgment, it can not be held straightway that there was medical negligence or deficiency in service. [*Subhashis Dhar* v *Smt. Sanjukta Sen Gupta* 1999 III CPJ 29]

Error of judgment in diagnosis. Allegation that wrong diagnosis recorded in the Histopathalogy Report resulted in available sufferings and ultimate death of patient. Even if the ailment would have been detected 45 days earlier, position would have been no different. Error of judgment not contributed to the suffering of patient. No negligence/deficiency in service. [*M.P. Balamani* v *Medical Administrator, Ravi Kirloskar Memorial Hospital and Research Centre* 2001 II CPJ 483 (Kar)]

It cannot be straightaway held that there was medical negligence or deficiency in service. Onus to prove medical negligence lies on the complainant. [*Baban Rao Yadav* v *Lion Tarachand Bappa Hospital* 2003 I CPJ 36 (Mah)]

Held that it could be negligence if it is an error which would not have been made by a reasonably competent professional man acting with ordinary care. [*Saroj Chandhoke* v *Ganga Ram Hospital* 2007 III CPJ 189]

34. ENT surgery

Plastic Surgery. Removal of nasal deformity. Cause of death stated to be introducing a cuffed endotracheal tube of proper size to prevent aspiration of blood from the wound in the respiratory passage. Same, even if accepted as true, only negligent act for lack of due care and precaution, cannot be described as gross negligent so as to make the doctor criminally liable. Section 304A, IPC not attracted. [*Dr. Suresh Gupta* v *Govt. of NCT of Delhi* AIR 2004 SC 4091]

Post-operative care. Chronic Suppurative Otitis Medica (CSOM). Loss of hearing of the ear diagnosed as labyrinthine damage alleged to be due to negligence in post-operative care. Expert opinion that it was a clear case of pre-operative profound sensori-neural loss of right ear and not caused due to operation. No negligence. [*Raj Kumar Khilwani* v *Dr. Pankaj Gupta* 2006 II CPJ 242 (MP)]

Ear operation. MRM. Partial paralysis of face muscles with facial palsy/disfigurement, defect in eye and ear due to damage to veins leading to eye caused during alleged. Complainant patient of right Chronic Suppurative Otitis Media (CSOM) allicoantral type (unsafe) operated earlier in 1992 with the 7th nerve (facial nerve) paresis (weakness) and left CSOM (safe). Since type of disease of left ear safe and that of right ear unsafe, feeling that if right ear not operated immediately it would lead to fatal complications of brain abscess or meningitis, *modified radical mastectomy* (MRM) of right ear done. Patient already having facial weakness and asymmetry at the time of registration of OPD. No expert evidence to show the face disfigurement due to operation conducted by opposite parties in 2002, and also while operating right ear some veins leading to eye damaged and for this reason right eye remained open while in sleep leading to permanent facial disfigurement. No negligence. [*Gulab Singh* v *PGI* 2005 IV CPJ 479 (Chandigarh)]

35. Expert witness

Non-consideration of. Conclusion of consumer fora that hospital and operating surgeon negligent without considering the evidence of experts as well as extracts of medical tests and also when expert who gave evidence on affidavits not cross-examined despite opportunities given to complainant. State commission's decision set aside and complaint dismissed. [*Baburao Satappa Irrannanavar* v *KLE Society's Hospital and Research Centre* 2006 IV CPJ 71 (NC)]

36. Expert evidence

Laparoscopic Surgery to be an expert of laparoscopic surgery, one need not be a surgeon, but if one research and otherwise study of subject, one is capable to teach the student, he would be classified as an expert witness. [*Smt. Gurmit Mahal* v *Chauhan Nursing Home* 1998 CPR 405 (Pb)]

Not produced to support the allegations of medical negligence. Disputed questions of facts. Complaint rightly dismissed. [*Makhan Singh* v *Dr. Prem Singh* 2001 III CLT 199 (Pb)]

Pace maker. Implantation of. Complainant failed to establish that the body of the deceased was not accepting the implantation of the pace maker, still it was implanted and the same was the cause of death of deceased. Complainant's affidavit not corroborated by any expert evidence. Medical negligence/deficiency in service not established. [*Rajesh Kumar* v *Tagore Heart Care and Research Centre* 2001 III CLT 618 (Pb)]

Medical treatment. Doctor cannot be responsible for failure in their treatment unless a positive evidence including expert evidence is brought on record. [*Nagarmal Modi Sewa Sadan* v *Anita* Devi 2002 III CPR 163]

Eye operation. Medical test. Surgery carried out by appellant doctor without obtaining a report of B. Scan, which was a pre-requisite for knowing the exact status before carrying out the surgery. Admission of laps on the part of doctor. No other expert evidence is required. [*V. Pahwa* v *Surindra Mohan Ghose* 2004 IV CPJ 1 (NC)].

Child suffering from cerebral malaria. Doctor advising respondent to take the child to a bigger hospital. However, doctor treating the child on humanitarian ground giving him life saving injections. Child died due to process of disease and complications. Allegation that petitioner did not give a proper dosage as he did not take the weight of the child, making no sense. Expert evidence to the effect that petitioner gave proper treatment. No medical negligence. [*Dr. Prasad* v *Lal Janmenjoy Nath Shahdeo, Revision petition no.* 515 of 2004 (NC)]

Eye operation. Allegation that 75% of vision lost due to wrong operation of the left eye. Complainant not produced expert evidence. Medical negligence not proved. [*Inderjeet Singh* v *Dr. Jagdeep Singh* 2004 III CPJ 20 (HC)]

Wrong diagnosis. Kidney transplantation. Allegation that transplantation of kidneys of the complainant was necessitated on account of wrong diagnosis/wrong treatment given by the opponent doctor. Complainant failed to obtain expert opinion with regard to the medicines prescribed by the opponent doctor having reacted on the kidneys of the complainant. Alleged medical negligence not proved. Complaint liable to be dismissed. [*Prasanna Kumar Digambardas* v *Dr. Hardasbhai G. Patel* 2005 I CPJ 453 (Guj)]

Three experts given their evidence on affidavit. Not cross-examined by the complainant or his Advocate despite opportunities being given. Sincere efforts made by the hospital authorities and the doctor concerned to perform the procedure and post-operative care. Held that the consumer Fora not correct in holding the operating surgeon/hospital negligent. [*Baburao Satappa Irrannanavor* v *KLE Society's Hospital and Research Centre* 2006 IV CPJ 71 (NC)]

Anaesthesia. Deceased allegedly not administered proper dose of anaesthesia. Work up during surgery. Again given over dose of anaesthesia resulted in respiratory arrest for four minutes during operation. She was removed to second respondent hospital where she finally died. Not brought on record that the doctor was not competed or did not possess the skill, resulting in unfortunate end or did not do what ought to have been done or did what should not have been done. No infirmity in the order of State Commission dismissing the complainant. [*B. Anthony Raj v St. Thomas Hospital* 2006 II CPJ 20]

Both the appellant experienced and qualified surgeons capable of undertaking the treatment in question. Merely because some complications developed which led to the death of the patient by itself, is not sufficient to jump upon any conclusion regarding negligence on the part of the appellants. In absence of any expert evidence it was not possible to hold them guilty of medical negligence. [*Dr. Sanjay Sharma* v *Ana Singh* 2007 I CLT 177 (MP)]

Delivery of child. Death of complainant's wife after delivery. Post mortem showed death due to cardio-respiratory failure, due to haemorrhage and shock due to post-mortem haemorrhage due to Disseminated Intravascular coagulapthy. No medical expert's opinion or any medical literature has been shown to prove that this haemorrhage was caused by any act of medical negligence on the part of the respondent. It has not been shown that doctor who attended to any delivery was not qualified to handle the case. No medical expert opinion has been led by the appellant to show whether the treatment given by her was improper and for that anything was wrong in the administration of treatment. No reason to interfere in the well reasoned order passed by the State Commission dismissing the complaint. [*Naseem Mohammed Bashir Ansari* v *Dhange Hospital* 2007 II CPJ 259 20 (NC)]

Eye operation, after the operation and transplantation of lens of eye sight was not restored to the complainant. However, no expert evidence to come to the finding that operation conducted by the appellant was negligent which resulted into the loss of eye sight of the complainant. No medical negligence. [*Dr. Akhil Kumar Jain* v *Lallan Prasad* 2004 II CPJ 504]

Angioplasty. Death of husband of the complainant during the procedure of Angioplasty. Opposite party a qualified, experienced cardiologist with enough experience in procedure of angioplasty. Opposite party has explained the pros and cons of angioplasty and carried out procedure after due written, explained concern. No expert examined by complainant though a family friend and a qualified and experienced cardiology who was physically present during the procedure of Angioplasty. From available records evaluation of evidence, literature and citations, the complainant has failed to prove her case. [*Gulnaz Sharifkhan Malik* v *Dr. Prakashvir Parikh* 2007 I CLT 633 (Guj)]

37. Free of charge service

Military Hospital. Deceased wife of the petitioner got treatment in the Military hospital. Service rendered free of charge. It would not mean service within the meaning of section 2(*o*) of the Consumer Protection Act, 1986. Complaint rightly dismissed. [*Brig A.S. Sibia* v *Union of India* 2003 I CLT 10 (NC)]

Government hospital. Allegation that was negligence in attending the patient. Hospital in question, a government undertaking, not meant for treating major illness. No consideration charge. Held that there is no deficiency in service. Complaint liable to be dismissed. [*Vinod Kumar Srivastava* v *Hindustan Aeronautics Ltd.* 2003 I CPJ 246 (UP)]

Donation Government Hospital. Token amount given as consideration. Complaint is not consumer. [*Nurendra Singh Rastogi* v *Shaskiya Gyara Punch Trust* 2002 II CPJ 3 (MP)]

Medical negligence. No fee charged for operation. Though ₹100 and ₹25 charged for room rent and for glucose respectively, however, person under treatment has to pay incidental expenses. Complainant is not consumer. [*T. Khatoon* v *Government of Uttar Pradesh* 2001 II CPJ 354 (UP)]

38. Fracture

Leg. Multiple injuries on leg. Allegation of faulty and negligent treatment. Nothing to show that the fractured bones had taken more time than is usually taken. No deficiency in service. [*Ashok Kumar Singh* v *Mohan Thakur* 2000 II CPJ 220 (Bihar)]

Titanium plates for refixing the fractured bones of the legs. Cracked. Allegation that same broken down due to inferior quality. District Forum holding that plate broken due to pressure put by patient in absence of union bone. Laboratory reports showing that plates were of standard quality. Complainant failed to prove his allegations. District Forum rightly dismissed the complaint. [*Pritpal Singh* v *M/s Arya Muni and Co.* 2001 II CPJ 1290 (Pb)]

Due to wrong exercise on the part of the nurse no allegation of faulty operation on the part of the opposite party doctor. Doctor held not liable for negligence. [*Tapas Das Gupta* v *Dr. Kalyan Mukherjee* 2002 II CPJ 73 (WB)]

Multiple fracture femur left thigh bone. Plea of the complainants that insertion of K. nail in the left femur of complainant No.2 who is aged 12 years was not suitable and was not suitable and was against the established principle of medical service and should have been treated with flexible intramedullary nailing i.e. the rush rod repelled. Held that even in boys of age 12 to 13 years, the treatment with rigid intramedullary rod fixation in the most convenient method which gives good results. If the complainant no.2 had suffered due to negligence of doctors who had subsequently treated him in Bihar and U.P., then opposite party in not liable to be blamed. There is no expert evidence on file to prove that the present condition of complainant no. 2 is due to negligence on the part of opposite party. Onus to prove negligence of opposite party was on the complainants which they have miserably failed to prove. Complaint liable to be dismissed. [*Jai Shanker Prasad* v *Dr. D.R. Bhupinder Singh* 2006 III CLT 502 (UT)]

Thigh-plate fixed. Expert doctor advising removal of plate. Operation. Allegation that the thigh bone which has earlier joined have again been broken and five screws were still fixed in the bone. Contention that appellant performed operation defectively to extract money. Operated again by another doctor. Fresh plate with screw fitted. District Forum returned the finding of negligence on the part of the appellant. Finding not based on any expert evidence. District Forum wrongly relied on the prescription and report of another doctor in which it was not mentioned that earlier operation performed by appellant was wrong or such type of operation should not have been performed. Finding of the District Forum not sustainable. Impugned order set aside. [*Dr. Uday Shankar Bhagat* v *Santosh Kumar Sah* 2003 IV CPJ 665 (Bihar)]

Medical treatment operation Gangrene developed. Amputation of leg. Plea that another line of treatment should have been adopted. Held that both the lines of treatment were in order and the doctor can not be faulted, if he adopted one of them. [*Mam Chand* v *G.S. Mangat of Mangat Hospital* 2004 I CPJ 79 (NC)]

Arm. Medical Negligence. Close reduction procedure carried out by the doctor who was qualified to do so. Reports of different doctors in favour of opposite party doctor. Absence of expert opinion in favour of the complainant. Complaint liable to be dismissed. [*Smt. Manju Garg* v *Goel Hospital* 2005 IV CPJ 62 (NC)]

Leg. Implantation of screw. Nothing on record to establish that fracture was not well united. Complainant disregarded the advice and never came up to said hospital. Subsequently, took treatment at another hospital. Amputation below knee after an year. Complaint alleging medical negligence on the part of doctor of first hospital. Rightly rejected by the State Commission. [*H.V. Venkatasubhaiath* v *Dr. Hanumanthaish* 2005 CPJ 77 (NC)]

39. Frivolous complaint

Cost Complaint seeking recovery of ₹55,90,000 alleging medical negligence. Complainant totally failed to make out any case against opposite parties. It appears that the motive of the complainant is only to indulge in speculative litigation taking undue advantage of the fact that no court fee is payable for institution of a case under the Consumer Protection Act. Complaint liable to be dismissed. Complainant to pay costs of ₹10,000 to each of the parties. [*Brij Mohan Kher* v *Dr. N.H. Banka* 1995 I CPJ 99 (NC)]

Delivery of child by Dai at home. Mother profusely bleeding when brought to hospital. Necessary steps taken. Attendants asked to arrange blood. They shifted the patient to other hospital. Certificate issued by Gram Panchayat Sarpanch showing that the death of the patient was due to heart failure. No medical negligence. Frivolous complaint. Dismissed upheld. [*Manpreet Kaur* v *Dr. Mrs. Veena Ghumber* 2005 I CPJ 63 (Pun)]

40. Gastroenterology

Wrong diagnosis and treatment alleged. Patient admitted with swelling of abdomen and legs, diminished urine output and profused discharge from fistula tracks, diagnosed as a case of fistulous crohn's disease, earlier undergone as emergency laparotomy for intestinal obstruction elsewhere. On examination he was found extremely sick with distended abdomen and discharging multiple tracks and vomiting, I.V. fluid, antibiotic and I.V. albumin administered condition deteriorating and critical because of hypotension, feculent urine and jaundice. Surgeon was called but he found the patient unfit for operation. Multi organ failure and other associated problems common in such critical case, and eventual death due to cardio-respiratory failure. No negligence. [*Soma Ghose* v *Director, Peerless Hospital and B.K. Roy Research Centre* 2004 I CPR 709 (WB)]

Acute alcoholic pancreatitis. Patient in a precarious condition when admitted given all care and treatment and simultaneously steps taken to prevent and check other correlated eventualities likely to arise due to physical state of the patient including renal failure, liver malfunction, etc, despite necessary drugs being administered blood urea having risen grossly above normal rate, dialysis advised and shifted to another hospital for dialysis. Condition of patient deteriorating and death course of treatment adopted by opposite party, broadly in line with that suggested by expert. No negligence. [*S.V. Nongrum* v *Woodland Nursing Home* 2004 III CPJ 664 (Meghalaya)]

Peptic ulcer. Non-performance of surgery. Patient, a chronic alcoholic and smoker with elevated serum bilirubin, suffering from ulcer since long and at the relevant time having bleeding peptic ulcer with metabolic encephalopathy, and not following regular diet habits. Endoscopy done once but not repeated as insertion of tube might cause complication of bleeding. Condition of patient being critical adopting conservative method of treatment by giving medicines, surgery not done on the date fixed for same. No negligence. [*L. Sunil Reddy* v *Rohini Hospital* 2005 II CPJ 58 (NC)]

41. Government hospital

Appellant a doctor in government hospital. Treatment and operation of the deceased boy done in Government District Hospital where no fee was charged for any such treatment. Complainant alleged that the fees was charged by the appellants at their residence. No documentary evidence of payment of any such amount to the appellants could be adduced by the respondent. Even assuming that some such amount as paid by the respondent to the appellant doctors then it cannot be treated as a consideration for the service rendered at Government District hospital providing free treatment to all without any exception. Amount if any received by the appellants would be deemed to be illegal gratification. Cannot be treated as consideration as envisaged under Consumer Protection Act. Dispute raised by respondent did not constitute a consumer dispute. Remedy of respondent lay else where and not under the provisions of Consumer Protection Act. [*Dr. Sanjay Sharma* v *Ana Singh* 2007 I CLT 177 (MP)]

42. Hospital

Vicarious liability unless the doctors or staff against whom negligence alleged impleaded as parties to the complaint so that they may get an opportunity to defend themselves, hospital not be held vicariously liable. Allegation of delay in commencement of dialysis. No doctor or staff impleaded. Hospital not liable as the allegations not one relating to the primary duties of the hospital. [*S.V. Nongrum* v *Woodland Nursing Home* 2004 III CPJ 664 (Meghalaya)]

Impleadment of doctors as necessary party. Liability of negligence of doctor. Non-joinder of treating doctor as party to complaint. No ground for hospital to escape liability. Once all allegation made that patient admitted in a particular hospital and evidence produced to satisfy that he died because of negligence on the part of treating doctor/hospital. Summary dismissal of complaint by National Commission for not impleading doctor as a necessary party unsustainable. [*Savet Garg* v *Director, National Heart Institute* AIR 2004 SC 5088]

Non-admission of patient. Where the number of beds available in the hospital less than the number of patients referred to it, a patient is hospitalized only when a necessity is so felt by attending doctors and vacancy available. Mere non-admission of a patient as an impatient when there is no vacant bed, no negligence or deficiency in service. [*Sukumari Sahu* v *Tata Memorial Hospital* 2006 III CPJ 293 (NC)]

Medical services. Patient who had a fall taken to another hospital for scanning as suggested by opposite party, hospital. Delay in scanning since required fee not paid, to get patient scanned privately from outside as there were many patients waiting for scanning in the opposite party, hospital to avoid delay. No deficiency in service. [*KV Anita* v *National Institute of Medical Health and Neuro Sciences* 2006 1 CPR 24 (Karn)]

Deficiency in service. Failure to provide film of scan. Camera attached to scanning machine unexpectedly not functioning. As film not available, doctor who took the scan found nothing, the features from the monitor and preparing a report. Said report not stated to be not acceptable to the doctors consulted by complainant nor they entertained any doubt about the impressions noted from the monitor. Failure to provide film not be said to have put complainant in a disadvantageous position or affected proper diagnosis of her ailment. Failure to camera to function cannot be attributable to any carelessness or negligence of opposite party. [*Krishna Hospital* v *P. Shanti* 2006 I CPJ 114 (TN)]

43. Hospital records

Failure of supply copies of the hospital record pertaining to the surgical operation performed on the complainant. Does not constitute "negligence" unless there was a legal duty cast on the hospital to furnish such documents to a patient. Complainant was only given the discharge card, slip and a case sheet where in the particulars of diagnosis and administered to him had been mentioned. [*Poona Medical Foundation Ruby Hall Clinic* v *M.L. Tiikare* 1995 I CPJ 232 (NC)]

Non-supply of copies. Complainant failed to prove that he was legally entitled to have copies of document. No negligence. [*V. Chandrasekar* v *Malar Hospitals Ltd.* 2001 I CPJ 137 (TN)]

44. Homeopathy practitioner

Homeopathy practitioner could advice ultrasound test in order to arrive at right diagnosis. Fact that he could prescribe the use of only homeopathic medicines, was fully known to the complainant. Administering medicine. No negligence. [*Naresh Kumar* v *Vaid Ram Phal* 1998 II CLT 191 (Hry)]

45. Hip replacement

Had the first operation been successful even then the complainant would have incurred expenses on the purchase of the material/articles for hip replacement. Complainant not entitled to reimbursement for said amount. [*R.P. Dahiya Advocate* v *Dr. Pardeep Aggarwal* 2000 III CPJ 175 (Hry.)]

46. Hepatitis-B

Allegation that blood transfused was contaminated with hepatitis-B virus and as a result of transfusion of such blood complainant was affected with hepatitis B virus. Alleged tampering of report of blood bank. Complainant has not been able to show that the record of the blood bank has in any way been manipulated. Reliance on the report of doctor. Doctor stating that he prepared said report only on the basis of information furnished by the complainant and it was not prepared on the basis of any serological and pathological tests reports and at that stage his opinion that the complainant had hepatitis B infection was only provision and not confirmative. A person can be positive of HBs Ag tests without any blood transfusion complaint failed to prove his case. Directed to pay ₹5,000 to respondents as costs for making unfounded allegations. [*A. Narain Rao* v *Dr. G. Rama Krishna Reddy* 1994 I CPJ 54 (NC)]

Allegedly developed during blood transfusion. Reports of two doctors to that effect. However, reports not correct in view of the medical literature. Patient might be suffering from Hepatitis-B before coming to the hospital. [*Jagat Narayan Chaube* v *Dr. Achal Sepaha* 2004 I CPJ 435 (MP)]

47. Hysterectomy operation

Patient's negligence procedure for carrying out an excision of lump in breast and surgery for abdominal hysterectomy after obtaining consent from the patient. Surgery carried out based on reports of the family doctor of complainant that she has been advised by her Gynaecologist to go for Hysterectomy. In such a situation no negligence can be fastened on the appellant. [*Vanashi Padmanabhan* v *Lakshmi Rajan* 2007 II 463 (NC)]

Consent, consent for carrying out an excision of lump in breast and abdominal hysterectomy was obtained from the patient. It does not lie in the mouth of the complainant to now state that she was shocked on being told that uterus was removed. Surgeon had carried out surgery based on the reports of his family doctor that she had been advised by her gynaecologist to go for hysterectomy. Complainant was carrier of the letter and contents would be known to her. Her not making doctor a party to the complaint speaks more about the complainant. In such situation no negligence can be fastened on the appellant. Moreover general physician view could not be given the creditworthiness of being an expert opinion. He nowhere stated that the line of treatment surgery done by the appellant was in any way not as per medical advice and not warranted. [*Ravindra Padmanabhan* (*Dr.*) *through LRs* v *Lakshmi Rajan* 2007 II CLT 21 (NC)]

Deceased having high blood pressure and lower level of HB. Medical literature showed that the surgical procedure could be done on a patient with diastolic blood pressure of not more than 110 mmHg and haemoglobin concentration of even 6g dl. Before start of procedure the BP of the deceased was 180/100. Procedure performed was not elective as the deceased was having severe bleeding. Both the opposite parties are highly qualified. Opposite parties acted in accordance with the procedure accepted as proper by the medical literature. Cannot be held guilty of negligence. [*Biswanath Das* v *Bijoy Sinha Roy* 2007 IV CPJ 223 (NC)]

48. Injection

Administering of. Allegation that due to wrong administering of injection complainant's son died. Absence of expert evidence. Fact that the drug has any side effect or likely to cause certain adverse effects in certain circumstances, not established. No medical negligence. [*R. Shanmuganathan* v *V. Sankaranarayanan* 2005 III CPJ 87 (TN)]

Sudden pain in right knee. Corticosteroids injection administered. Leg developed pus. Injection a prescribed one and one of the methods applied by doctors. Further no evidence produced. Complaint rightly dismissed. [*Laxmi Narain* v *Eshita Nursing Home and Amish X-ray* 2001 III CPJ 394 (UP)]

Allegations of wrong administering of intravenous injection not supported by evidence. District Forum wrongly allowed the complaint. Impugned order set aside. [*Jot Maternity and Children Hospital* v *Sanjogitta* 2003 III CPJ 136 (Pb)]

Administering of death allegedly due to reaction held that any injection reaction acts as a poison in the body and all changes as are specific to poisoning are seen in viscera. In case of any reaction, changes would occur in larynx and trachea. No poisoning detected in the viscera. Autopsy report does not indicate any change in larynx or trachea of the deceased. Stand taken by opposite party that only a test dose of injection Imferon was given to the deceased supported by MLC. Held that reaction due to test dose could not have caused death of the deceased. Opposite party cannot be held deficient in service in treating a deceased. Complainant failed to prove the case of medical negligence on the part of the opposite party. [*S.K. Sethi* v *Dr. Rakesh Malhotra* 2006 IV CPJ 222 (NC)]

Xylocanine administered by doctor 'K' when the patient was already under general anaesthesia in the operation theater. There is nothing before the Fora to show that whatsoever was done by doctor 'k' was as per accepted medical practice or followed by large body of doctors. In the absence of which above medical negligence on account of failure to take due care is writ large as within minutes of administering the injection the heart of the patient arrested and the patient had become brain dead. [*St. Gregarious Mission Hospital* v *Roji George* 2008 I CPJ 68 (NC)]

49. Injury

Suffered in accident. Amputation of leg. Same was not on account of negligent act on the part of the doctor but on account of injuries suffered. No negligence on the doctor either in the matter of providing, treatment or in the matter of alleged delay in referring the patient to CM Ludhiana. Complaint liable to be dismissed. [*Lekh Raj* v *Bharat Nursing Home, Hoshiarur* 1998 II CPJ 335 (Punjab)]

Death of woman alleged to be due torture and assault by husband and in laws. Postmortem report of opposite party showing cause of death as poisoning. Allegation of negligence in not sending injury reports to police station not the duty of the doctor but of the staff concerned government hospital. No negligence. [*Ajit Kumar Singh* v *Balmiki Choubey* 2005 I CPJ 569 (Jhar.)]

50. Impleadment of doctor

Whether non-impleading of the doctor absolves the hospital or doctor of medical negligence, even if the complaint can be proved on the basis of the facts and records of the case? Held No. [*K. Venkateshwarlu* v *Managing Director, Nagarjunu Hospital* 2006 I CPJ 47 (NC)]

Error of judgment. Complainant's wife who suffered from a rare disease 'Toxic Epider amal Necrolysis' (TEN) remained under treatment of opposite party and ultimately died. Claim in complaint Rupees seven crores seventy-six lakhs seventy-three thousand and five hundred of compensation by complainant who himself is a doctor for deficiency in service rendered by doctor and hospital. Doctor who first diagnosed the disease suffered by the wife of the complainant not made party in the case. No record produced by the complainant what of treatment was given by him to his wife from 1 April, 1998 to 7th May, 1998 despite her condition was deteriorating day-by-day. Complaint directed against solely on disagreement in the pattern of treatment rendered by the doctor 'M' and others after the death of his wife. From medical literature quoted no specified treatment for TEN, only supportive treatment is provided. Held that error of judgment in the process of diagnosis does not amount to deficiency in service as the disease, TEN is a rare one occurring 1 to 1.3 million per year. A lot of difference of opinion among the doctors worldwide. In such a case, with regard to diagnosis of disease, it varies from doctor to doctor worldwide. For want of exact diagnosis, the doctor cannot be held liable. Matter also taken up by the complainant with West Bengal Medical Council and finding of council challenged by him before High Court in writ petition which was dismissed. Allegation of deficiency in service against opposite party nos. 1, 2, 3, 5 and 6 without substance complaint dismissed. [*Kunal Sahu* v *Sukumar Mukharjee* 2006 III CPJ 142 (NC)]

51. Impleadment of nurse

Fracture. Due to wrong exercise on the part of the nurse. Said nurse has been made a party to the proceedings nor the name and description of the Nurse has been given in the complaint. No allegations of faulty operation against the opposite party, doctor. Doctor held not liable for negligence. [*Tapan Das Gupta* v *Dr. Kalyan Mukharjee* 2002 II CPJ 73 (WB)]

52. I.C.U.

Post-operative treatment. Allegation that patient's death was caused by medical negligence as he was not immediately kept in ICU after the operation. Same not proved. A conscious decision was taken to keep the patient in her cabin having regard to the stable condition of her at that time. Decision was taken after taking into consideration various factors. Finding of the state commission found that there was no lack of care and attention on the part of the doctor and the nurse in treating the patient. Upheld. [*S.K. Iyengar* v *Bombay Hospital and Medical Research Centre* 2001 I CPJ 23 (NC)]

53. Intraocular lens

Intraocular lens. Implantation of. Cataract operation. Complainant's vision was raised to 6/18 (with the use of glasses) after operation. Eye sight of right eye improved. Underwent laser treatment at AIIMS whereas it was not permissible at least for the period of 3 months after the cataract operation. No negligence on the part of opposite party in performing the operation in implementation of the intraocular lens. [*Yoginder Beri* v *Grover Eye and ENT Hospital* 2001 III CPJ 16 (U.T. Chd.)]

54. Kidney transplantation

Allegation that transplantation of the kidneys of complainant was necessitated on account of wrong diagnosis/wrong treatment given by the opponent doctor. Complainant failed to obtain expert opinion with regard to the medicines prescribed by the opponent doctor having reacted on kidneys of complainant. Alleged medical negligence not proved. Complainant liable to be dismissed. [*Prasannakamar Digamberdas* v *Dr. Hardasbhai G. Patel* 2005 I CPJ 453 (Guj)]

Kidney transplantation done successfully and patient was well for several days. Death of patient after 7 days. It is high risk operation. Acute rejection typically occurs 5 to 7 days of post-transplant. No negligence in the surgery of kidney transplantation and post-operative care. No sufficient grounds for deficiency in service and negligence are proved against opposite party. [*P.B. Rao* v *D.S. Sunder* 2006 II CPJ 223]

55. Laser treatment

Cataract Operation. Complainant vision was raised to 6/8 (with the use of glasses) after operation. Eyesight of right eye improved. Underwent laser treatment at AIIMS where as it was not permissible at least for the period of 3 months after the contact operation. No negligence on the part of opposite party in performing the operation in implementation of the Intra Ocular lens. [*Yoginder Beri* v *Grover Eye and ENT Hospital* 2001 III CPJ 166 (UT Chd)]

56. Legal representatives

Maintainability of complaint. Allegation of medical negligence. On the date of filing of complaint, the complainant's wife was legal representative who can succeed in law to the estate of the deceased husband. Subsequently, she remarried. She cannot maintain a complaint as she is no longer the legal representative of her deceased husband consequent of remarriage. [*Shantha V.S. Gowda* v *Kempegowda Institute of Medical Sciences* 2005 I CPJ 792 (Karn)]

Allegations of medical negligence against doctor. Death of doctor. Held that the death of the doctor extinguishes his liability in tort and right to sue also gets extinguished against his legal representative. [*Dr. (Mrs.) Ranjana Bhardwaj* v *Rekha Rani* 2003 III CPJ 697 (Chd.)]

57. Liability of hospital

Background/history of the patient does not absolve the hospital from its professional obligations. [*Jaspal Singh* v *the Post Graduate Institute of Medical Education and Research (PGI), Chandigarh* 2000 II CPJ 439 (UT Chd.)]

Impleadment of doctor it was imperative for the complainant to impleaded doctors guilty of medical negligence to hold the hospital vicariously liable same not done. Hospital cannot be held vicariously liable. [*Basant Seth* v *Regency Hospital Ltd.* 2002 III CPJ 407 (NC)]

Unless the doctor is made a party vicarious liability cannot be fastened to the hospital. [*D.H. Kumari* v *Director, Nizam's Institute of Medical Services* 2003 IV CPJ 441 (AP)]

58. Medical ethics

As long as a doctor acts in a manner which is acceptable to the medical profession and the court finds that he has attended on the patient with due care, skill and diligence and if the patient still does not survive or suffers permanent ailment it would be difficult to hold the doctor to be guilty of negligence. [*Smt. Vinitha Ashok* v *Lakshmi Hospital* 2002 I CPJ 4 (SC)]

Medical opinion may differ with regard to the course of action to be taken by a doctor treating a patient, but as long as a doctor acts in a manner which is acceptable to the medical profession, and the court finds that he has attended on the patient with the due care skill and diligence and if the patient still does not survive or suffers a permanent ailment, it would be difficult to hold the doctor to be guilty of negligence. [*Achutrao Haribhau Khodwa* v *State of Maharashtra* AIR 1996 SC 2377]

Rule of confidentiality. Exception. Appellant who is about to marry tested HIV positive and his marriage called off as the hospital authorities informed his HIV status to the relatives to the girl whom he intended to marry. Such disclosure does not effect the appellant's right in any way. It is open to the hospital or doctor to reveal the information to the relatives of the girl as she got a right to know the HIV status of the person to whom she intended to marry. [*Mr. 'X'* v *Hospital 'Z'* 2003 I CPJ 14 (SC)]

59. Maintainability of complaint

Bypass operation. Railway employee treated in Railway headquarter hospital free of charge. Died. Deficiency in service alleged by LRS. Neither the complainants nor the deceased was consumer. Complaint not maintainable. [*S. Tharani* v *Southern Railway Headquarters Hospital* 2000 I CLT 304 (TN)]

Complainant alleging deficiency in service on the part of doctor. Treatment in Government hospital without any fees/consideration. Complaint held not maintainable. [*B.C. Joshi* v *Dr. Sandeep Kumar* 2002 II CPJ 125 (Del.)]

Complaint filed by uncle of the patient. Contention that complainant is maintaining the patient. No record to show that patient is minor. Unless he is minor the complainant cannot file the complaint on his behalf. [*Dr. R.S. Sharma* v *Gulam Zilani* 2002 III CPJ 272 (UP)]

Allegation of medical negligence. On the date of filing of complaint, the complainant's wife was legal representative who can succeed in law to the estate of the deceased husband. Subsequently, she remarried. She cannot maintain a complaint as she is no longer the legal representative of her deceased husband consequent of remarriage. [*Shantha V.S. Gowda* v *Kempegowda Institute of Medical Sciences* 2005 I CPJ 792 (Kar)]

60. Medical advice

Medical treatment. Negligence alleged. There was casual talk on phone and ultimately the complainant's wife was taken to doctor's consulting room only for the purpose of advice. She was never admitted in the hospital. Thereafter there was no meeting with the doctor except telephonic contracts. No responsibility can be pinned on the opposite party. Complaint dismissed. [*Digvijaysinh A Zola* v *Dr. Narendra T. Vani* 1995 I CPJ 186 (Guj)]

Congenital cardiac anomaly. Open heart surgery. Patient advised to be brought back for balloon dilation to relieve the obstruction in the remaining residual underdeveloped arch of the Aorta. Patient developed pain. However, he was not brought back to the hospital as advised held that the doctors performed their duties with proper care and attention. Complainant failed to discharge the burden of proof with regard to negligence. Complaint liable to be dismissed. [*Prafulla Kumar Das* v *Apollo Hospital* 2002 II CPJ 106 (NC)]

Medical tests. Prescription of. MRI and CT Scan prescribed by opposite parties. However, patient did not follow medical advice and went to another place for further treatment. Subsequently complications resulting in death of patient. Opposite party cannot be held liable. [*Pyarelal Gupta* v *S.K. Jiwanmal* 2004 III CLT 132 (Chh)]

Blood Cancer. Patient was advised to come after two weeks and required BMT operation. Patient brought for treatment after six months. Serious condition. Patient died despite treatment according to standard practice. Patient could not be saved due to delay on his part in getting treatment. No deficiency in service. [*Pasumarthy Narayana* v *M/s Apollo Hospital Enterprises Ltd.* 2004 IV CPJ 19 (NC)]

Cataract operation. Right eye. Alleged loss of sight. After operation the complainant petitioner started suffering from Uveitis. It has not been proved that Uveitis has been caused due to surgical trauma. Complainant admitted that he had Voluntarily abandoned the service of the opposite party respondent doctor and had approached several hospital and doctors for treatment from different doctors of her own choice. As per the words of opposite party she did not need to his advice at the post operational stage. Concurrent findings of fact. Petitioner failed to prove that there was any deficiency in pre-operative or post-operative care on the part of the respondent. [*Munni Devi* v *Dr. R.P. Tondon* 2006 IV CPJ 259 (NC)]

Hysterectomy. Medical negligence. Consent for carrying out an exercise of lump in breast and abdominal hysterectomy was obtained from the patient. It does not lie in the mouth of the complainant to now state that she was shocked on being told that uterus was removed. Surgeon had carried out surgery based on the reports of his family doctor that she had been advised by her gynaecologist to go for hysterectomy. Complainant was carrier of the letter and contents would be known to her not making doctor a party to the complaint speaks more about the complainant. In such situation no negligence can be fastened on the appellant. Moreover general physician view could not be given the creditworthiness of being an expert opinion. He nowhere stated that the line of treatment surgery done by the appellant was in any way not as per medical advice and not warranted. [*Ravindra Padmanabhan* (*Dr.*) *through LRs* v *Lakshmi Rajan* 2007 II CPJ 21 (NC)]

Repeated advice for 'Bone Marrow Aspiration test' was unheeded. This is clearly a case of negligence on the part of the complainant himself who repeatedly refused or did not heed the advice of the doctors to get the bone marrow aspiration test done which is the test to finally determine that the patient is suffering from leukemia. He has not been able to show as to what the respondent should have done which he did not do or he did what he should not have done. The onus of proof in this regard lay with the complainant to prove his case of medical negligence which he completely failed. Appeal liable to be dismissed. [*P.N. Sudhakar Gupta* v *Anugraha Vittal Nursing Home* 2008 I CPJ 57]

61. Medical negligence

Fora can take up the case of apparent negligence or negligent act proved by expert opinion. *Ipse dixit* of the complainant in such like matters cannot be accepted. [*Satwant Kaur* v *Dr. Kanwaljit Kaur* 1998 I CPJ 298 (Pb)]

One of the test of the medical negligence is that something which is required under medical practice to be done was not done or what was done was contradicted. [*Bhajan Lal Gupta* v *Mool Chand Khairati Ram Hospital* 2000 I CPJ 31 (NC)]

There must be direct connection between injury suffered and the treatment given. Merely because something went wrong with the patient, negligence cannot be assumed. [*P. Venkata Lakshmi* v *Dr. Y.S.* 2001 III CPJ 402 (A.P.)]

Allegation that the doctor was not on the bed side of the father of the complainant when he expired. Cannot be expected that the doctor would always remain by the side of the patient. Doctor left the nursing home after leaving some instructions to nurses on duty. No negligence. [*Kamlesh Gupta* v *Dr. Abhijit Roy Chowdhary* 2000 III CPR 498 (W.B.)]

Mishap duping operation cannot be said to be deficiency or negligence in medical service. Negligence has to be established and cannot be presumed. [*Vaqar Mohammad Khan* v *Dr. S.K. Tandon* 2002 II CPJ 169 (MP)]

Respondents were possessed of skill and knowledge to deal with the nature of complaints with the deceased reported to respondents. Deceased received due negligence. Care and attention. No medical negligence. [*Rajinder Singh Nandal* v *Anmol Hospital* 2002 III CPJ 324]

Complainant failed to prove any negligence on the part of hospital or to show that the Hospital or the treating doctors fall short of the standard skills of any doctor or they failed to do what they should have done or *vice-versa*. Complaint liable to be dismissed. [*Dr. S. Gurunathan* (*Dead*) v *Vijaya Health Centre* 2002 III CPJ 211 (NC)]

Deficiency in service. Has to be established. Same cannot be presumed. [*R.P. Sharma* v *Honda Nursing Home* 2003 IV CPJ 585 (Del.)]

Though the doctor attended the patient with due care, skill and diligence, yet the patient died. Whether the doctor can be held guilty of negligence. Held no. [*Savitri Singh* v *Ranbir Prasad Singh* 2004 I CPJ 25 (Bihar)]

Two choices available. Exercise of one, which is the best, in the judgment of the doctor and nothing else is available to contradict this. Whether in such circumstances the doctor can be held negligent. Held no. [*Charan Singh* v *Healing Touch Hospital* 2003 III CPJ 62 (NC)]

62. Medical report

Allegation that findings incorporated in the reports of pathologists were wrong. Complaint not taking any steps to get the slides re-examined despite the offer for re-examination of slides by another pathologist mere assertion by complainant. Not sufficient to give finding of negligence. [*Consumer Protection Council* v *Dr. M. Sundaram* 1997 II CPJ 540 (NC)]

Wrong report. Test report showing TSH count for below the normal range. Blood test by another laboratory showing the TSH count on the higher side of normal range. Practically no material to show that the petitioner had suffered any injury because of the first report. Consulting Physician did not rely upon the first report. No treatment had been stated on the basis of the first report. Forum justified in not allowing any claim for compensation. [*Madhyamgram Consumer Welfare Society* v *Dr. Kalyan Kumar Chatterjee* 2002 II CPJ 381 (WB)]

Wrong report of pathology lab. Alleged causing abortion. Held that the complainant was already diagnosed as a case of "missed abortion". No negligence on the part of pathology lab. District Forum wrongly held pathology lab negligent and directed payment of compensation. Impugned order liable to be set aside. [*Rajni Shukla* v *Rajendra Kumar Agarwal* 2003 I CPJ 551 (MP)]

Allegation that due to faulty report of the opposite party complainant's left lung was removed unnecessarily. Opposite party had not given any final diagnosis in the matter. Surgeon was responsible for taking hasty decision in operating the left lung of the petitioner. Allegations against opposite party not conclusively substantiated. Complaint liable to be dismissed. [*Leena Bhattacharjee* v *Nightingale Diagnostic Centre and Eye Care Research Centre (P) Ltd.* 2003 IV CPJ 311 (WB)]

Removal of uterus. Allegation that the wrong report of the respondent led the appellants to rush to hospital where the uterus of appellant was removed whereas the report of Histopathological examination showed that there was no carcinoma of uterus. Report of Histopathology after removal of uterus not proved by leading credible evidence. Mere difference in opinion cannot be said to be a ground for fastening liability on respondent. [*Santosh Kaur Sodhi* v *Vijay Mujoo* 2003 II CPJ 344 (UT Chd.)]

Wrong treatment. Mis-pregnancy. Allegation that wrong urine report led to wrong treatment leading to miscarriage and evacuations. In order to prove that the report was wrong, fresh sample of urine could have been taken immediately thereafter and urine report might have sought other pathology centre(s) without there being any comparison, it would be difficult to say that there was negligence in examining the urine and the report was wrong. Petition dismissed. [*Rajni Shukla* v *Rajendra Kumar Agarwal* 2005 IV CPJ 2 (NC)]

63. Medical treatment

Alleged deterioration in the health of child (irreparable mental handicap) after discharge from hospital. Discrepancy in statement of complainant and his witness. No appropriate precautions taken after discharge by complainant his wife. Opposite parties held not liable false and frivolous complaint filed. Same liable to be dismissed. [*Lalluram Meena* v *Dr. S. Mathur* 2001 III CPJ 2000 (Raj)]

Allegations of improper treatment resulting in cardiac arrest and death of patient. No medical expert evidence to show that the treatment prescribed by the doctor was contrary to the established norms of treatment of heart attack. No negligence. Complaint liable to be dismissed. [*Surjit Kaur* v *Dr. Deepak Kaur* 2003 I CPJ 622 (UT Chd)]

Child suffering from cerebral malaria. Doctor advising respondent to take the child to a bigger hospital. However, doctor treating the child on humanitarian ground giving him life saving injections. Child died due to process of disease and complications. Allegation that petitioner did not give a proper dosage as he did not take the weight of the child, making no sense. Expert evidence to the effect that petitioner gave proper treatment. No medical negligence. [*Dr. Ganesh Prasad* v *Lal Janmenjoy Nath Shahdeo, Revision petition no.* 515 of 2004 (NC)]

Consumer has right to be informed of possible after effects of line of treatment or operation adopted by doctor. Mandatory for doctor to warn patients about recognized complications. [*Mumtaj Ansari* v *Zubeda* 2005 I CPJ 673 (Uttr.)]

Amputation. Hand. Medical negligence. Allegation of. Attempt to suicide by consuming yellow oleander poisonous seeds. Gangrene developed. Amputation of right hand in order to save life of complainant. Complainant not abducting any expert evidence to prove that treatment and practice adopted by the doctor is not in accordance with the established procedure. No negligence. [*S. Veerasamy* v *Dr. Murugaiyan* 2005 I CPJ 665 (Pondichery)]

Error of judgment. Complainant's wife who suffered from a rare disease 'Toxic Epideramal Necrolysis' (TEN) remained under treatment of opposite party and ultimately died. Claim in complaint Rupees seven crore seventy-six lakhs seventy-three thousand and five hundred of compensation by complainant who himself is a doctor for deficiency in service rendered by doctor and hospital. Doctor who first diagnosed the disease suffered by the wife of the complainant not made party in the case. No record produced by the complainant what of treatment was given by him to his wife from 1 April 1998 to 7th May, 1998 despite her condition was deteriorating day-by-day. Complaint directed against solely on disagreement in the pattern of treatment rendered by the doctor 'M' and others after the death of his wife. From medical literature quoted no specified treatment for TEN, only supportive treatment is provided. Held that error of judgment in the process of diagnosis does not amount to deficiency in service as the disease, TEN is a rare one occurring 1 to 1.3 million per year. A lot of difference of opinion among the doctors worldwide. In such a case, with regard to diagnosis of disease, it varies from doctor to doctor worldwide. For want of exact diagnosis, the doctor cannot be held liable. Matter also taken up by the complainant with West Bengal Medical Council and finding of council challenged by him before High Court in writ petition which was dismissed. Allegation of deficiency in service against opposite party nos. 1, 2, 3, 5 and 6 without substance, complaint dismissed. [*Kunal Sahu* v *Sukumar Mukharjee* 2006 III CPJ 142 (NC)]

Eye treatment surgery was done in 1992 and complainant came with complaint of irritation and redness in 1995. Sutures were removed and medicines given nothing shown that they were not the proper medicines or line of treatment. Neither any expert evidence nor any medical literature filed by the complainant to counter the material brought on record. The complainant not able to show that the opposite party was not competent in taking up his case. Complainant completely failed to prove any case of medical negligence against the opposite party. [*Vasant Mehta* v *Dr. Kullin J. Kothari* 2007 II CLT 620 (NC)]

64. Medicines

Administering of. Homeopathic doctor, could advice ultrasound test in order to arrive at right diagnosis. Fact that he could prescribe the use of only homeopathic medicines, was fully known to the complainant. Administering medicine. No negligence. [*Naresh Kumar* v *Vaid Ram Phal* 1998 II CLT 191 (Hry)]

Strip of capsules only a capsule found in strip whereas price charged for 10 capsules. Chemist offered to replace the strip. At the most the only relief that can be granted to the complainant would be to direct the chemist to pay the price of the capsule. No further compensation on that account is payable. [*Chander Mohan Kaura* v *M/s Mercle* (*India*) *Limited, Bombay* 1998 II CLT 77 (Pb)]

Drug reaction. Allegedly due to prescription of Sulpha medicine without resorting to necessary tests. Prescription chit not produced. Allegation not proved. Complaint rightly dismissed. [*KVS Narayan* v *Dr. P. Gopinathan* 2001 III CPJ 498 (Ker)]

Expiry dated medicine. No receipt for the alleged purchase of medicine submitted. District Forum wrongly allowed the claim on the basis of the presumption. Impugned order liable to be set aside. [*Chhedi Lal Piyarey Lal* v *Daya Bux Singh* 2001 III CPJ 261 (UP)]

Non-submission of specimen of the drug to the independent laboratories. This aspect should not have been overlooked by the State Commission. Complainant doctor not pressing his complaint. Complaint dismissed. [*Ophthalmics and Drugs India* v *Dr. Jagdeep Mohanlal Kokadia* 2003 III CPJ 21 (NC)]

Administering of. Allegation that because of administration of drug genlamyein child because deaf. Medicine opinion to the effect that dose was prescribed within permissible limits. No negligence. [*Sidharth Balta* v *Dr. Maj Gen M.L. Magotra* 2003 IV CPJ 182 (J&K)]

Defective ear drop. Causing damaged to ear. Aggravation of pain. Led to operation. Manufacturer directed to pay compensation. However, defects of medicine not known to medical stores. Medical store held not liable. [*Jamna Devi* v *FDC Ltd.* 2003 III CPJ 509 (Raj.)]

Use of prescribed medicine. Allegation that due to negligence on the part of the doctor both eyes damaged and there was loss of loss of eye sight. Medicine has been used by the patient in low doses for a very few week. No expert evidence to show that use of prescribed medicine has affected his eye sight. No negligence or deficiency in service. [*Ajay Kumar* v *Dr. Davendra Nath* 2004 II CPJ 482 (Bihar)]

Wrong prescription. Allergical reaction. Expert evidence. Absence of. Held that even if there had been some reaction or allergy, unless there is some negligence or deficiency in service of the doctor, he cannot be said to be negligent. No negligence. [*Mohd. Istiqar* v *Dr. Rajesh Gupta* 2005 II CLT 216 (Uttr.)]

Prescription. Opposite party prescribing allopathic medicine to complainant. Not deficient in service as the State Government has recognized the BAMS Degree Holders in integrated course being eligible to practice and prescribe Allopathic medicine. [*Ankush Vithoba Dhokale* v *Dr. Anand Dinkar Bhosale* 2005 I CLT 55 (Mah)]

65. MRI scan

MRI and CT Scan prescribed by opposite parties. However, patient did not follow medical advice and went to another place for further treatment. Subsequently complications resulting in death of patient. Opposite party cannot be held liable. [*Pyarelal Gupta* v *S.K. Jiwanmal* 2004 III CLT 132 (Chh)]

66. Nephrology

Kidney transplantation-Secondary infection, consequent ailments and ultimate death complainant not pin pointing as to where the negligence or fault of opposite parties as alleged lies and has not examined any medical expert to substantiate plea of negligence of opposite parties or that they failed to prescribe the right medicines or diagnose the disease correctly or the procedure or the method they followed was wrong. Kidney being a vital organ while transplanting it extremely high dose of immunosuppressive drug to be administered with specific object of preventing rejection of foreign body and this is why the patient having being transplanted kidney carries high risk of secondary infection and once such infection occurs chances of survival are extremely vulnerable. Merely because the patient did not survive and succumbed to her ailment, the opposite parties doctors do not become automatically negligent in the absence of proof to the hilt as to where the opposite parties failed. [*Topan Banarjee* v *Dr. Jayan Basu* 2005 III CPJ 631 (WB)]

Kidney transplantation. Post-operative care. Patient remained well for several days after successful transplant and only one day prior to discharge the developed acute tubular necrosis (ATN) which was interpreted on doppler and on isotope scans as showing deceased blood flow to the kidney on re exploration of operated site kidney appeared extremely normal. When some bleeding seen same controlled and on arterial thrombosis and graft rupture seen. Acute rejection typically occurs 5 to 7 days of post transplant but it can occur at any time after this. kidney salvaged and opposite parties continuously tried their best to save the life of the patient. Death of patient. No negligence in the surgery or post-operative care. [*P.B. Rao* v *D.S. Sundar* 2006 II CPJ 223 (NC)]

Nephrolithotomy removal of kidney. Patient diagnosed as a case of pyelonephritis (renal stone) advised lithotripsy. Despite repeated lithotripsy thrice stone could not be crushed it being hard and large and so patient advised to undergo Nephrolithotomy (removal of stone by renal incision). During the surgery as there was severe haemorrhage which is known complication, Nephroiectomy (removal of kidney) performed and one of the kidneys removed to save the life of patient with the consent of patient's husband. All this showing that the doctor had taken reasonable care in treating/operating the patient. No negligence. [*Reeta Ajanta Sahu* v *Dr. Y.R. Krishna* 2006 II CPJ (Chhattisgarh)]

67. Neurology

Wrong diagnosis and treatment. Complainant having pain in leg operated twice by opposite party but condition continued to deteriorate and there was severe pain in spinal cord as a result of which he was not able to sit and walk. When a third surgery advised patient got discharged and got admitted to another hospital where the third operation performed whereafter he got relief. Patient developed another disease, namely pain in vertebral disc and leg due to deficiency in service on the part of the opposite party. Alleged. Details of diagnosis and line of treatment adopted by opposite party given. Complainant not showing the new disease due to lack of care, attention or caution on the part of the opposite party. Complaint dismissed. [*Jugbir Singh* v *Dr. Manoj Sharma* 2004 II CPR 558 (Del)]

Wrong diagnosis and treatment. Complainant having progressive numbness in limbs. After several tests, opposite party diagnosing the problem as viral disease, i.e. Guillain Barre Syndrome (GBS). Opposite party later advising the complainant to undergo MRI test and after seeing the MRI report (cervical spine) noticing significant compression of spinal cord by C-6 vertebra, immediately referring, complainant to neurosurgeon who advised surgery for cervical spondylotic myclopathy (CSM). Allegation that in view of wrong diagnosis done earlier patient as well as his family members suffered physically, mentally and financially cannot be accepted. Symptoms which prompted the doctor to diagnose the decease as GBS cannot be said to be irrelevant and as such diagnosis based on the symptoms cannot be said to be unwarranted. History recorded in case sheet. Clearly pointing out that CSM could not be noticed earlier. No deficiency in service. [*Kethiri Sai Reddy* v *Apollo Hospital* 2004 III CPJ 412 (AP)]

Comprehensive myclopathy. Before surgery patient capable of walking but after operation of spinal cord organs below waist up to feet becoming senseless. Allegation that MRI test should have been necessarily done before opening spinal cord which was negligently not done rendering patient disabled for the whole of his life. Spine of patient under absolute pressure as seen from myclogram plus CT Test calling for immediate operation without wasting time for MRI test. Since there was complete blockage of spinal cord, only course open was to operate and professional ethics motivated opposite parties to perform the operation. No intentional negligence. [*Surendra Nath Singh* v *Dr. SC Tandon* 2005 IV CPJ 587 (Uttaran)]

Spinal injury operation performed by orthopedic surgeon instead of neuro surgeon as alleged to have been promised. Deterioration of condition of patient post-operation alleged due to professional malpractice and negligence of opposite parties. Since disease was of spinal cord patient required orthopedic surgery and if the doctor, an expert in orthopedic surgery performed by operation he cannot be said to be an unqualified person to do so. If the treating surgeon feels neurological examination not necessary, that is no professional malpractice or medical negligence. MRI report of patient much earlier to the operation showing that she was suffering from cauda equina syndrome which can be treated by both orthopedic and neuro surgeons. Patient already having advanced degenerative lumbar spine with paralytic condition got operated to save her from further damage, hence it is wrong to say that her condition deteriorated because of the operation. [*Virendra Singh* v *National Institute of Medical Sciences* 2006 I CPR 152 (Raj)]

68. Needle biopsy

Allegations of mishandling. Not supported by any evidence. Nothing to show that here is any negligence in the procedure adopted by the opposite party. [*Mrs. O Aisha Bi* v *Prof. J. R. Danial* 2003 III CPJ 178 (NC)]

69. New plea

Prostrate operation. Allegation that incontinence with which the complainant suffering was for the reason that his sphineter muscle was cut during the TUR operation by the respondents. Plea taken for the first time in the rejoinder filed by the complainant. Complainant did not produce any reliable evidence/expert evidence is support of the case. Charges of negligence not proved. Compliant liable to be dismissed. [*Tarachand Jain* v *Sri Ganga Ram Hospital* 1999 III CPJ 53 (NC)]

70. Oncology

Acute Mycloid Leukemia. Patient given two phase of chemotherapy treatment and advised to come after 15 days for Bone Marrow Transplantation (BMT) but he was brought only after six months with serious relapse of cancer. Death of patient. No negligence. Allegation that opposite party failed to explain that treatment would be complete only after BMT unsustainable where the discharge certificate contained all details the authenticity of which not challenged. [*Pasumarthy Narayana* v *Apollo Hospital Enterprises Ltd.* 2004 IV CPJ 19 (NC)]

Auxillary tumour. Biopsy. Extraction of 9 cm diameter piece for the purpose of. Allegation that since the entire lump removed, what was carried out was not biopsy but a surgery which remained in complete resulting in death of patient. Unsustainable. As per medical literature normally the piece taken out in the size of 2 x 2 x 1 cm or a piece as large as possible and hence it cannot be concluded that 9 cm diameter piece would not fall in the definition of a piece extracted for biopsy in the absence of expert evidence to the contrary. No negligence. [*Saleemuddin* v *Dr. Sunil Malhotra* 2006 III CPJ 348 (NC)]

Mastectomy, Painless tumor on breast malignancy test. Fine Needle Aspiration Cytology (FNAC) showing features (*i*) high cellularity and cellular overcrowding, (*ii*) cellular atypia and (*iii*) fragments of myxoid stroma not found. Leading to diagnosis of malignancy necessitating mastectomy for removal of breast. Operated lump on histopathological examination or management of ailment not be ruled out. Mannography and FNAC combined, the best diagnostic method for correct pre-operative diagnosis of mammoral lesions as per medical literature. Surgery done in the best interest of patient. No expert evidence to the contrary adduced. No negligence. [*Hinaben Nikunjbhai Bhavsar* v *M.P. Shah Cancer Hospital and the Gujrat Cancer and Research Institute* 2006 I CPJ 502 (Guj)]

71. Ophthalmology

Redness of eye. Case diagnosed as cornial infection or cornial ulcer for which both application and oral medicinal treatment given, despite loss of vision. Even the doctors consulted subsequently given the same treatment and found the treatment given by opposite party as correct and proper. No negligence. [*Karimbhai Desai* v *Dr. Mahendra J. Thakkar* 2004 I CPJ 543 (Guj.)]

Surgery and transplantation of lens. Loss of eye sight alleged due to negligent use of knife. It actually knife was used in the eye, it would have damaged entire eye ball and resulted in excessive hemorrhage. Simply because eye sight deteriorated after operation and transplantation of lens no valid reason to conclude that opposite party was negligent in the absence of any expert evidence to that effect. [*Dr. Akhil Kumar Jain* v *Lallan Prasad* 2004 II CPJ 504 (Bihar)]

Macular hemorrhage — Laser therapy. After FFA test Argon Laser successfully done. Allegation of loss of vision. Evidence. Certificate by a doctor later consulted by patient to the effect that due to Laser therapy. Permanent searing developed and vision greatly reduced to finger counting close to face. Said certificate not filed along with complaint nor any such entry in the OPD card nor any affidavit of said doctor filed. Subject of complaint has to allege which action of opposite parties not as per accepted medical practice and what was done should not have been done or what was not done should have done supported by expert evidence or medical literature which has not been done. No negligence. [*K.S. Bhatiya* v *Jeevan Hospital* 2004 CTJ 175 (NC)]

Vitrectomy. Post-operative recurrent vitreous hemorrhage with retinal detachment after one month of surgery. Vitreous hemorrhage associated with retinal detachment in operated eye, a phenomenon not uncommon in proliferative Retinopathy for which vitrectomy and endolaser procedure accepted procedure as done by opposite party. Opposite party noting the recurrent nature of disease referring patient to a higher centre. No negligence. [*Tapas Basu* v *Dr. Sandeep Mitra* 2005 CTJ 1282 (WB)]

Cataract operation. Deficiency in post-operative care. Infection of operated eye. Post-operative Endophthalmitis, one of the most serious known complications of cataract surgery usually occurring after flawless surgery frequently leading to permanent visual loss, removal of infected eye so as to prevent infection to the other eye. Not a case of negligence in post-operative care. [*Hari Prasad Chunkai* v *Mannulal Jagannath Trust Hospital* 2005 I CPJ 783 (MP)]

Iridocyclites. Administration of injections Gentacin and Decadron in sub corneal portion. No improvement and vision diminishing. Allegation the gentacin and decadron should not have been administered not corroborated by medical expert evidence or medical literature. Prescription of said injections a proper treatment as per medical literature. No negligence. [*R.S. Sisodia* v *Dr. R. David* 2005 I CPR 65 (MP)]

Epithora. Watering and pain in both eyes subsisting after surgery. Allegation of wrongly operating left eye and even after operating, both eyes problem continuing. Patient a case of bilateral ephithora with dermatitis and lid infection in right eye and partial blockage in naso-lacrimal duct in left eye and full blockage in right eye. In view of lesser disease and absence and absence of infection with consequent better prognosis left eye operated first and then after disappearance or control of infection, right eye operated. Two expert bodies, one a committee constituted on a complaint lodged with hospital authorities and the other a Board of doctors constituted at the request of SHO on the basis of FIR filed with the police simultaneously finding the procedure adopted as correct and in the interest of the patient. No negligence. [*Gheesa Ram Soini* v *Dr. A.S. Malhotra* 2005 I CPR 504 (Raj)]

Cataract operation. Loss of vision in right eye. Correctional operation undergone and vision regained. Another operation for retinal detachment also done and infection in eye subsequently. Patient referred to high tech hospital where his right eye ball removed. No record from the higher centre produced to show that removal of eye ball due to surgeries conducted in opposite party hospital. No negligence on the part of opposite party while conducting operation as also thereafter. [*M.A. Ganesh Rao* v *Dr. T.M.A. Poi Rotary Hospital* 2006 II CPJ 96 (Karn.)]

Glaucoma surgery. Loss of sight. Second operation in a higher hospital, still no improvement, and the surgeons therein regretted to complainant that in the disease with which patient was suffering nothing more could have been done to restore eye sight and the operation was done in desperation and they have not alleged any negligence on the part of opposite party, when he performed the first operation. No evidence to show that opposite party, a qualified ophthalmologist, performed with carelessness and he did adopt the practice prescribed under the medical norms to treat such patient. No case of negligence. [*Dr. P.B. Lal* v *Suresh Chandra Roy* 2006 III CPJ 452 (Bihar)]

Cataract operation. Cornea damage and loss of vision. Medical council of India, after obtaining expert opinion from two renowned institutions, coming to the conclusion that standard treatment protocol followed and operation procedures carried out. No negligence. [*Farangi Lal Mutneja* v *Sri Guru Harkishan Sahib Eye Hospital* 2006 IV CPJ 96 (Chdg.)]

Cataract operation Loss of eye sight development of redness and swelling post-operation diagnosed by opposite party as a case of uveitis and steroid injection advised. Patient not turning up after first injection, but turning to other hospitals and doctors of her choice quite often. Patient careless in adhering to advicę of opposite party to take injection in time and not appearing for timely check up and abandoning opposite parties treatment. No negligence. [*Munni Devi* v *Dr. R.P. Tondon* 2006 IV CPJ 259 (NC)]

72. Obstetrics/Gynaecology

MTP. Death due to meningitis with cerebral vein thrombosis and infarct and oedema of brain alleged to be consequent to incomplete D and C. Evidence of two medical experts concurrently showing MTP not the cause of meningitis that ultimately resulted in death and suggesting that the patient was already incubating meningitis at the time when MTP performed. No negligence. [*Salvodor Francis Borges* v *Dr. Arun Bhobe* 2004 IV CPJ 794 (Goa)]

Lower segment caesarean section (LSCS) Birth of twins. Pregnancy induced hypertension prior to surgery and disseminated intravascular coagulation (DIC) defects due to amniotic fluid embolism. Death due to amniotic fluid embolism. Death due to cardio respiratory arrest. PIH with DIC resulting cardio-respiratory arrest, a sudden complication which may arise at any time during delivery. Bleeding from mouth and nose cannot be due to negligence in surgery of LSCS. DIC means massive hemorrhage and coagulation failure which may prove fatal. Complaint liable to be dismissed. [*Syed Mohammad Owais Quadri* v *Dr. Neena Desai* 2004 CTJ 598 (AP)]

Caesarean operation. Death of patient due to jaundice after delivery. Patient not disclosing any symptoms suggestive of jaundice and there was no clinical manifestation of jaundice till operation done except painful urination. Based on clinical examination and history of patient doctor excluding all other causes and finding that painful urination due to lower urinary tract infection (UTI) for which prompt treatment given to reduce acidity in urine and blood pressure. Doctor having noticed no progress in labour and development of foetal stress and also foetal heart sounds below normal and irregular, based on clinical evidence deciding that urgent caesarean called for. No deficiency in service or negligence. [*M. Srinivas* v *Dr. Smt. Rama Thulasi* 2005 I CPJ 64 (NC)]

Hysterectomy. Continued bleeding for nearly two years. Another doctor diagnosing some thread left on the vault of vagina and granulation of tissues. Thread removed and granulation cauterized. Hysterectomy performed by opposite party as per prescribed standard method wherein catgut, an absorbable suture used, ruling out possibility of leaving any thread. Patient had earlier undergone TT operation and the thread found and removed by the second doctor probably be the reminiscence of said operation in which as per then prevailing practice thread used for tying the fallopian tube. No negligence. [*Indirawati Shukla* v *Dr. Asha Gupta* 2005 I CPR 704 (M.P.)]

Hysterectomy. Ultrasonography revealing uterus bulky with bilateral T.O. masses and Pelvic Inflammatory Disease (PID) patient developing pain and leakage of urine from vagina after 4½ months of removal of infected uterus. Case detected as small vesico vaginal fistula (VVF) with simple right ovarian cyst, which was repaired by another surgery. Again after 6 months due to similar complaint VVF repaired and cystoscopy surgery done. VVF is pressure necrosis caused due to protected or neglected labour or prolonged pressure on interior vaginal wall and may also be due to intercourse, but not attributable to hysterectomy. No negligence. [*Prem Bai* v *Dr. Satinder Saluja* 2005 II CPR 216 (MP)]

D and C operation. Patient carrying dead foetus in womb for quite some time. Laminaria Tent procedure adopted. Tent removal and evacuation done during which patient going to shock cyanosis and cardiac arrest due to sudden and massive pulmonary embolism. When revived as she started oozing blood from all punctures, emergency hysterectomy done to prevent further bleeding form uterus. Despite all corrective measures and treatment death on account of pulmonary embolism. Profuse bleeding alleged to have been caused due to negligence of opposite party not stated nor any expert opinion produced in favour of complainant despite opportunity. No negligence proved. [*K. Sadanandan* v *Lisie Hospital* 2006 I CPJ 24 (NC)]

73. Operation

Prostate operation. Allegation that incontinence with which the complainant suffering was for the reason that his sphineter muscle was cut during the TUR operation by the respondents. Plea taken for the first time in the rejoinder filed by the complainant. Complainant did not produce any reliable evidence/expert evidence in support of the case. Charges of negligence not proved. Complaint liable to be dismissed. [*Tara Chand Jain* v *Sri Ganga Ram Hospital* 1999 III CPJ 53 (NC)]

Post-operative care. Patient has to be careful to abide by the instructions of the doctor. Complainant did not take post-operative measures. Merely because the complainant had to be re-operated, it cannot be said that the earlier operation was not properly and carefully done. [*R. Ponnappan* v *V.S. Mohan* 2004 I CPJ 518 (TN)]

Medical negligence. Mishap during operation cannot be said to be deficiency or negligence in medical service. Negligence has to be established and cannot be presumed. [*Vaqar Mohammad Khan* v *Dr. S.K. Tandon* 2002 II CPJ 169 (MP)]

Merely because the operation was not successful that does not mean that the surgeon was negligent and careless. [*Ashok Nandi* v *Dr. Ajit Saha* 2003 IV CPJ 95 (WB)]

Fracture. Gangrene developed. Amputation of leg. Plea that another line of treatment should have been adopted. Held that both the lines of treatment were in order and the doctor cannot be faulted, if he adopted one of them. [*Mam Chand* v *G.S. Mangat of Mangat Hospital* 2004 I CPJ 79 (NC)]

74. Oxygen

Non-supply of. Medical negligence. Concurrent finding of the fact on the point of non-supply of the oxygen to the deceased. The patient was on ventilator in the ICU when the oxygen exhausted. Both the lower Fora have held this is to be a clear case of medical negligence. No illegality or lack of jurisdiction shown to call for any interference under section 2(*b*) of the Act. [*Arun Raj* (*DR*) v *N. Ramanathan* 2007 III CPJ 75]

75. Orthopedics

Fracture in shaft femur plastering of fractured leg causing infection resulting in amputation alleged. Evidence on record showing that opposite party gave only first aid and treated patient in single day, and nothing to show that patient remained admitted in the clinic for the period alleged and opposite party plastered her leg which caused infection. Complainant failed to prove negligence on the part of opposite party. Complaint dismissed. [*Soni Kumar* v *Dr. Nagendra Narain Bhagat* 2004 I CPJ 471 (Bihar)]

Injured elbow. X ray showing dislocation of bone, plaster of paris applied. Complainant not turning up the next day as advised. Re-operation in another hospital due to excessive pain. If at all there was any lack of care, it was only on the part of complainant. No negligence or deficiency in service on the part of the doctor. [*Dr. R. Ponnappan* (*Dentist*) v *V. Mohan* 2004 I CPJ 518 (TN)]

Fragmentation of bone in elbow. Surgery for removal of. One of the fragmented bones not removed it being lodged in soft tissue removal of which not advisable as it was lodged near median nerve, attempting to removal might affect nervous system leading to restriction in movement of the arm. Pain and swelling even after reduction alleged to be due to negligence and deficiency in service of the surgeon. Discharge summary stating that excision of head of radius right done with removal of comminuted bone under with removal of comminuted bone under G.A. and T.Q. control, butterfly fragment left alone, a fragment had got displaced into arterial compartment entrapped in the soft tissue near the median nerve, hence it was not removed. X ray not produced by complainant trying to suppress certain relevant materials from the purview of the Forum. No expert evidence produced to show any flaw in the operation and treatment or to prove accepted and standard of practice not followed by the surgeon. No negligence or deficiency in service. [*K. Srikumar* v *K. Muthalal* 2005 II CPJ 15 (TN)]

Fracture knee. Surgery for implantation of screws done and fracture well united. Patient diabetic, asked to control same before operation, asked to come after 15 days of operation but not turning up. Amputation of a portion below knee after one year in another hospital. No negligence. [*H.V. Venkatasubhaiah* v *Dr. Hanumanthaiah* 2005 CPJ 77 (NC)]

Fracture lower right femur. Open reduction and internal fixation with 95 DCS-bone grafting without removing bone pieces. Pus formation alleged due to negligence of opposite parties in not removing bone pieces. Expert opinion that loose fragments for normal bone during fracture fixation should not be removed as most of the tracture fragments from part of the articular surface of distal femur and removal of same would result in loss of joint surface and shortening of limbs. No negligence. [*S. Manjunathan* v *Dr. Sri Ram* 2006 I CPJ 231 (Karn)]

Comminuted fracture of leg, bones set through process of image intensifier and external fixator laid around affected part of leg. Patient on his own getting himself discharged as against medical advice to remain in hospital for continuous dressing and supervision development of gangrene and amputation of leg. No negligence. [*Mohd. Abrar* v *Dr. Ashok Desai* 2006 II CPJ 8 (MP)]

76. Pathology

Wrong report Blood of complainant alleged to be tested positive to hepatitis B by opposite party, but declared by another doctor that he was not suffering from said disease but from gas trouble. Over writing in the pathological report not bearing signature of the doctor. No negligence. [*Rakesh Ranjan Sinha* v *Dr. S.K. Das* 2004 II CPJ 497 (Bih.)]

Wrong diagnosis. Patient suffering from obstructed umbilical hernia undergone surgery, Surgeon suspecting cancer sending specimen of intra-abdominal mass with multiple lymph nodules for biopsy. Investigation report after 3 months declaring the case of calcified caseous necrotic nodules for biopsy. Investigation report after 3 months declaring the case as calcified caseous necrotic nodules (cancer). Death of patient. Fair chance of developing cancer within the time span of 3 months. No negligence. [*G.P. Gupta* v *Mehrotra Pathology* 2006 II CPJ 40 (UP)]

77. Paediatrics

Hischsprung's disease. Death of new born baby after 7 days of birth. Mother has several miscarriages earlier. Prematurely born baby not passing stools even 24 hours after birth and visible persistent complications on its health compounded day after day. Condition of the body deteriorating, operative decompression done as an energy. Diagnosis and treatment of the neonate done correctly by paediatrician and paediatric surgeon. No negligence. [*Mandira Saha* v *Dr. Ujjal Chatterjee* 2006 II CPJ 159 (NC)]

Wrong treatment alleged. Loss of eye sight. Allegation that patient 1½ year old child lost vision on account of reaction of some medicine administered by opposite party for fever. No positive evidence in support of allegation. Patient suffered from Grade III deficiency of nutrition and pus was oozing out from ear, having ulcer in the cornea of both eyes on account of vitamin A deficiency as per certificate issued to investigating officer the hospital where child treated later. No negligence. [*Mongalsinh Ratan Singh Gohil* v *Dr. Kanubhai Himatbhai Joshi* 2006 I CPJ 50 (Guj)]

Administration of over dose drug Patient a 4½ old child suffering from cerebral malaria given one ml of E-mal injection. Death of child shortly thereafter alleged to be due to overdose of drug. E-mal injection most acceptable for a child of more than 4 years of age and a dose of 40 to 100 mg of the drug on the first day of treatment very safe. Patient could be given 80 mg/kg dose maximum, but opposite party gave 75 mg/kg which is within the range 1000 mg/kg very much well within the prescribed dosage. No death reported with this drug in the specified dose, death of patient due to process of disease and its complication. No negligence. [*Dr. Ganesh Prasad* v *Lal Janamajoy Shahdeo* 2006 I CPJ 117(NC)]

78. Pace maker

Implantation of. Complainant failed to establish that the body of the deceased was not accepting the implantation of the pace maker, still it was implanted and the same was the cause of death of deceased. Complainant's affidavit not corroborated by any expert evidence. Medical negligence/deficiency in service not established. [*Rajesh Kumar* v *Tagore Heart Care and Research Centre* 2001 III CLT 618 (Pb)]

Implantation of. No infection at any time while the complainant was in the hospital. Complainant discharged from the hospital in a very satisfactory condition. Pace maker implanted continued working regularly. No deficiency in service. [*Commander Sohan Singh Sandhu* (*Retired*) v *Dr. H.K. Bali Cardiology Department, PGI* 1999 I CPJ 392 (UT Chd.)]

79. Patient's negligence

Self medication. Extra dose of steroids taken without regular advice from the doctor and without contacting him for three months. Self medication by the complainant cannot be considered as deficiency in the service on the part of the doctor. [*Hans Raj* v *Dr. S.K. Chugh* 2000 I CPR 310 (UT Chd)]

Removal of drainage pipe against medical advice. Prescribed treatment not followed up by patient. Negligence on the part of the opposite party not proved. Complaint dismissed. [*Balwinder Kumar* v *Arya Hospital* 2001 II CPR 394 (UT Chd.)]

Medical tests. Prescription of. MRI and CT Scan prescribed by opposite parties. However, patient did not follow medical advice and went to another place for further treatment. Subsequently complications resulting in death of patient. Opposite party cannot be held liable. [*Pyarelal Gupta* v *S.K. Jiwanmal* 2004 III CLT 132 (Chh)]

80. Pregnancy

Ultra sound. Not suggested at the primary stage of pregnancy. No deficiency in service. [*Geeta Devi alias Geeta Rani* v *Dr. Karki Garg* 1999 II CPJ 593 (Pb.)]

Medical Termination. Allegation that medical termination of pregnancy of deceased was the cause of meningitis that ultimately resulted in her death. Evidence of two medical experts to the contrary. No evidence to suggest any negligence or lack of due care on the part of opposite party. Compliant dismissed. [*Salvador Francis Borges* v *Dr. Arun Bhobe* 2004 IV CPJ 794 (Goa)]

81. Post-mortem

Complainant's son died due to surgery of head. Medical negligence alleged. No post mortem report on record. Absence of expert evidence. Allegations of medical negligence not established. Compliant liable to be dismissed. [*Namita Nursing Home* v *Smt Anita* 1999 II CPR 528 (Pb.)]

Where the cause of death is established, there is no reason for carrying out any autopsy. [*Smt. Manju Garg* v *Goel Hospital* 2005 IV CPJ 62 (NC)]

82. Prostate operation

Allegation that incontinence with which the complainant suffering was for the reason that his sphincter was cut during the TUR operation by the respondents. Plea taken for the first time in the rejoinder filed by the complainant. Complainant did not produce any reliable evidence/expert evidence is support of the case. Charges of negligence not proved. Complaint liable to be dismissed. [*Tarachand Jain* v *Sri Ganga Ram Hospital* 1999 III CPJ 53 (NC)]

83. Post-operative care

Child went into coma after operation. Allegation that no proper nursing care given for recovery from coma. No evidence of any negligence or recklessness or departure from accepted and established rule of treatment. No negligence established. [*Study Circle Society* v *Choithram Hospital and Research Centre* 2000 II CPJ 436 (MP)]

Fracture of femur neck operation. Allegation that there was no proper post-operative care which resulted in death of the patient. Papers filed by the petitioner show that regular treatment was given to the patient but she did not survive. Allegation totally baseless. Petitioner not entitled to any relief. [*Partha Sarathi Sen Gupta* v *Dr. S. Basu* 2003 IV CPJ 419 (WB)]

Carelessness on the part of the complainant after the first surgery. Second surgery by same doctor. Allegations of negligence. Not substantiated. Neurological problem. Cannot be set right by surgery. Suffering of complainant not linked to any act of the omission or commotion on the part of the doctor. Compliant liable to be dismissed. [*S. Amanullah* v *Dr. Mohandas* 2005 III CPJ 530 (TN)]

84. Pre-operative treatment

Eye operation, following the surgical operation, the left eye of the complainant got damaged and there was profuse bleeding. Appellant doctor stopped the operation, closed the eye of the complainant by pad and referred her to another hospital for better treatment. Before fixing the date for operation, the complainant was examined thrice and several routine pre-operative investigations were suggested. Appellant doctor did not fall short of the standard of a reasonably skilled man when this type of incident may occur in one out of 1000 cases. District Forum not justified in finding the appellant guilty of negligence in the matter of performing operation. Impugned order set aside. Complaint dismissed. [*Dr. I Ahmed* v *Sumitra Biswas* 2002 II CPJ 275 (WB)]

Cataract operation, right eye alleged loss of sight after operation the complainant petitioner suffering from Uveitis. It has not been proved that Uveitis has been caused due to surgical trauma. Complainant admitted that he had Voluntarily abandoned the service of the opposite party respondent doctor and had approached several hospital and doctors for treatment for different doctors of her own choice. As per the words of opposite party she did not need to his advice at the post-operational stage. Concurrent findings of fact, Petitioner failed to prove that there was any deficiency in pre-operative or post-operative care on the part of the respondent. [*Munni Devi* v *Dr. R.P. Tondon* 2006 III CLT 609 (NC)]

85. Practice and procedure

Impleadment of parties. Necessity of. Improper application of anesthesia and negligence in performance of surgery. Anesthetist not impleaded as a party. Commission should have directed parties to implicate him as part to the case or at least taken steps to summon or record his evidence, he being a key person. [*Reji Mathew* v *Dr. Radha Krishnan* 2004 CTJ 553 (NC)]

State Commission. Baby born with sphyxia, an indication of inadequate oxygen supply. Dismissal of complaint by state commission for failure to show negligence on the part of opposite parties while liberal references to medical literature put forward by opposite parties, no reference at all the medical literature procedure by complainant made by commission on the points in issue. Matter remanded to the state commission for hearing a fresh taking into consideration the literature procedure by complainant in support of the complaint. [*P. Venkata Lakshmi* v *Dr. Savitha Devi* 2004 II CPJ 14 (NC)]

Abatement of proceedings. Death of opposite party doctor pending complaint. Proceeding against the doctor stand abated by applying the maxim *action personalis moriture cum persona*. [*Gurudas Morajkar* v *Dr. (Mrs.) Seema Kharangate* 2004 II CPJ 154 (Goa)]

District Forum. Non-consideration of affidavit for non-appearance for cross-examination despite being summoned for cross-examination with reference to the affidavit, and decision on the basis of evidence of complainant ignoring said affidavit. Forum competent to do so. [*Chandigarh Administration* v *Ram Singh* 2005 I CPJ 62 (UT Chd.)]

Complainant approaching opposite party for performance of D and C of his pregnant wife. After administration of certain medicines, name of which not disclosed by opposite party, condition of patient deteriorating. Patient operated upon by another doctor who took out a dead child from her womb. Dismissal of complaint by District Forum on ground that consideration for hiring services and proved and the name of the medicines not disclosed by complainant. Unjustified. Before coming to a final conclusion Forum should have called for relevant records like patient's register, admission register, prescription register, bed head ticket, etc from the possession of opposite parties matter remanded to the Forum for further injury by calling the records. [*Krishna Kumar* v *Dr. Subhash Bansal* 2005 I CPJ 487 (Raj)]

While written version was filed by the appellant but he did not file any affidavit by way of evidence nor did he bring on record any case paper 'investigation' report and 'operation' notes. Despite several opportunities and notices appellant did not present himself for cross-examination. Complaint duly supported by affidavit by way of evidence and his cross examination remain unrebutted. Based on material on record, the state commission has held the appellant guilty of medical negligence. No fault can be found in this conclusion. [*Jayantlal Patel* v *Mukesh Parikh* 2007 IV CPJ 87 (NC)]

86. Physician/General practitioners

Wrong diagnosis and treatment. Snake bite. Non-administration of antivenom drugs. Doctor entertaining a doubt as to whether patient a case of snake bite. No systematic signs of envenomation noted. Delay in taking patient to hospital. Death of patient. No negligence on the part of the doctor for not administering antivenom drugs. [*Dr. Bijaya Lal Biswal* v *Purushottam Ponda* 2004 I CPJ 110 (Ori)]

Wrong diagnosis and wrong prescription of medicines. If there is a chance of wrong diagnosis but if it is not *mala fide* but *bona fide*, doctor not be held liable for something wrong occurring to the patient. Patient's liver and spleen having being found enlarged, a symptom of malaria, opposite party, prescribed Lariago D.S. which the patient has taken only for four days. Loss of eye sight. Said medicine used by patient in low doses for a very few days cannot affect eyes, and there is no expert evidence to the effect that the medicine caused damage to the eyes. No negligence. [*Vadlamudi Nageshwara Rao* v *Dr. Koneru Gangadhara Rao* 2004 II CPJ 639 (AP)]

Diabetic patient. Carelessness of complainant himself. Complainant, a chronic diabetic patient tripped by a stone forming a cyst on his left big toe not going to the doctor periodically against medical advice despite he being diabetic and having treatment from opposite party doctor since long for diabetes and other ailments. Development of cellulites and gangrene resulting in amputation of leg patient's body not responding to treatment administration of primaquin having no effect of kidneys. No negligence. [*Vadlamudi Nageshwara Rao* v *Dr. Koneru Gangadhara Rao* 2004 II CPJ 639 (AP)]

Wrong treatment. Drug reaction. Complainant treated for fever. Eruption of boils in her body and subsequent loss of vision of one of the eyes alleged to be due to drug reaction not proved nor any expert evidence produced by complainant. Expert from the side of opposite parties opined that drug prescribed by opposite parties safe and likely to cause loss of vision. No negligence on the part of opposite parties safe and not likely to cause loss of vision. No negligence on the part of opposite parties. [*Phool Bai Gupta* v *Dr. R. Bhattacharya* 2005 III CPJ 399 (Chh)]

Wrong treatment. Burden of proof. Complainant feeling pain in back of his body given injection in the vein of left arm. Nails of fingers of the hand turning bluish and ultimate amputation of three fingers of the hand resulting in 20% disability. No evidence to show as to what drug administered having any adverse effect on the body of complainant. In the absence of proof to establish amputation of fingers as the direct result of injection administered, no negligence be attributed to opposite party. [*Umed Singh Berwal* v *Sripal* 2005 IV CPJ 377 (Har)]

Wrong diagnosis ailment of patient diagnosed as 'Typhoid' on the basis of 'widal test' which showed positive. Advice of opposite party to have C.T. scan not carried out immediately due to lack of funds. Another doctor diagnosed the disease as 'brain tumor' and patient operated. Death due to right temporal brain abscess with meningitis. No deficiency in diagnosis. [*Yashwant Kisan Dahale* v *Dr. Vishwas Soni* 2006 II CPJ 500 (Mah.)]

Wrong treatment loose motion and vomiting, gangrene set in after IV injection and subsequent amputation of hand. No evidence to show the cause that led to development of gangrene while patient under treatment of opposite party. No negligence. [*Swati Prakash Patel* (*Ms*) v *Dr. Kiran Rajaram Vanarase* 2006 II CPR 370 (Mah.)]

Qualification. Opposite party holding M.B.B.S. degree, though duly signed by chancellor, not carrying seal of the office of chancellor. Registration certificate issued by the registrar of 'Travancore-Cochin Council' permitting opposite party to practice in modern medicine also on record. Veracity of the certificate cannot be doubted. Opposite party cannot be held incompetent to practice modern medicine. No deficiency in service. [*Sukumaran* v *Dr. Joy K. Cheriyan* 2006 III CPJ 312 (NC)]

87. Radiologist

C.T. Scan. Patient having a malignant lesion it is only prudent on the part of the attending physician to have a careful look at the medical history of the patient before prescribing a treatment on the basis of the scan report. Relying totally on the impression of Radiologist in such cases is not correct, particularly when the medical history does not create a suspicion of malignancy. State commission rightly concluded that no negligence in service can be attributed to the Radiologist who did the scan in question. [*Rahul Sinha* v *Dr. Ashok Mitra* 1995 III CPJ 162 (NC)]

Wrong diagnosis Metastatic disease. Difference between reports of two centers. Ultrasound or CT scan provides only a presumptive diagnosis and not be said to be final as for positive diagnosis of metastatic disease best method biopsy of the affected part of body. Report of the radiologist or sinologist only an opinion passed on impression recorded by the machine. If the report not to he satisfaction of the treating doctor, report tests to be done and it is the duty of the attending doctor not to rely entirely on reports. [*Sarana Diagnostic Research Centre* v *Shashi Kapoor* 2006 IV CPJ 158 (Raj.)]

88. Reimbursement

Hip replacement operation. Had the first operation been successful even then the complainant would have incurred expenses on the purchase of the material/articles for hip replacement. Complainant not entitled to reimbursement of said amount. [*R.P. Dahiya, Advocate* v *Dr. Pradeep Aggarwal* 2000 III CPJ 175 (Hry.)]

89. Spinal anaesthesia

Administering of Anesthetist followed accepted medical procedure having less than 1% of risk. Complainant fell in that 1% of spinal Anaesthesia and suffered infrequent complication, Anaesthetist not guilty of any negligence. [*Charan Singh* v *Healing Touch Hospital* 2003 III CPJ 62 (NC)]

90. Skin disease

Cause of death as per post mortem to be 'Viral Hepatitis with Hepatic Encephalopathy'. The patient continued in his treatment for dermatolololoical problem. That has no bearing on the death of the patient. The treatment given by doctors has no relevance to the death of the patient. There is no negligence or deficiency in service by opposite parties. [*Santosh Gupta* v *G.G. Dhir* 2007 III CPJ 322 (NC)]

91. Self medication

Extra dose of steroids taken without regular advice from the doctor and without contacting him for three months. Self medication by the complainant cannot be considered as deficiency in the service on the part of the doctor. [*Hans Raj* v *Dr. S.K. Chugh* 2000 I CPR 310 (UT Chd)]

92. Septic elbow

Treatment. Condition of the patient did not improved. Refund of fee claimed alongwith compensation. Complainant not producing any contrary report or opinion of any other orthopaedic specialist. Medical negligence not established. [*Ramphal* v *Vijay Gupta* 1998 II CPJ 216 (Hry.)]

93. Snake bite

Medical treatment. No delay on the part of the doctor in attending the deceased. Doctor had doubt as to whether the deceased was bitten by a snake. Had he been sure about the deceased having been bitten by a poisonous snake, and he would not have taken the steps as suggested by the medical theory, then he would have been held liable for act of negligence. Not a case of medical negligence. [*Dr. Bijaya Lal Biswal* v *Purushottam Ponda* 2004 I CPJ 110 (Ori)]

94. Surgery

Change of procedure. Gall Bladder stone. Laparoscopic Cholecystectomy started but finding the gall bladder swollen, inflamed and adhesion present, shifting to conventional procedure of open cholecystectomy after intimating husband of patient that the former procedure would not be possible. A decision to be taken a the spur of the moment to be taken by the surgeon on the spot. No negligence. [*Smt. Dhanwati Kumar* v *Dr. S.K. Jhunjhunwala* 2004 II CPJ 162 (WB)]

Gall bladder. Advanced laparoscopy. Swelling in pancreas after operation alleged due to negligent performance of surgery. Though complainants stating that they got treatment of pancreas from opposite parties, no authoritative opinion of any medical expert produced to show that alleged swelling of pancreas has been the result of any deficiency or defect in operation performed by opposite parties. Complaint failed to prove negligence. [*Dr. K.M. Bhandari* v *Mrs. Tara Mathur* 2004 II CPJ 99 (Raj)]

Chronic Cholecystitis with Cholecystolithiasis Laparoscopic Surgery for removal of gall stones patient again suffering pain in abdomen after months. CT scan report showing stone in gall bladder larger in size that found prior to surgery. Open surgery done in another hospital and stone removed. Opposite party performed surgery in accordance with the established procedure. From mere fact that complainant had to undergo a second surgery for removal of stones it can be inferred that due to act of opposite party in performing operation the stones formed in gall bladder. Formation of stones depends upon physical condition of patient. No expert evidence to show that even if first instance open surgery would have been the best treatment for removing the stone without any injury to liver. No negligence. [*Selvamani* v *Dr. K.P. Singh* 2004 IV 660 (Chd-UT)]

Appendectomy. Development of septicemia and death. Medical board constituted the State Government in connection with criminal case registered concluding that there was no negligence on the part of the opposite parties and expert opinion sought by commission to the same effect. Septicemia a known complication following operation in appendicitis. No negligence. [*Preeti Daksh* v *St. Thomas Hospital* 2005 CTJ 1233 (NC)]

Gall bladder stone. Vitals and other parameters found within normal limits but all of the sudden patient developing dysponea and consequent death. Allegation that opposite parties committed gross negligence in operating the patient without getting fresh ultrasound and TMT reports before surgery. Untenable. Ultrasound done earlier showed gall bladder stone which could be removed only by operation. There is no law or rule to show that TMT test to be concluded before performing any operation. Heart of patient found properly working and ECG report also perfect without any abnormality. Opposite parties not be said to have committed any negligence in not doing fresh ultrasound or TMT. [*Sanjay Haster* v *Subham Surgical Center and Nursing Home* 2005 II CPJ 287 (Uttaran)]

Bullet shot injuries. Death of injured. Delay in detecting perforation in stomach and other viscera alleged to have proved fatal to patient. Gun shot injury on chest region and abdomen not showing any clinical sign of injury X-ray of chest and erect abdomen and ultrasound scan not showing any evidence of abdominal injury. Patient continuously monitored by highly qualified doctors/specialists and patient not showing signs of abdominal injuries for 72 hours and the moment he did so, abdominal X-ray taken immediately, ultrasound scan done and after reviewing all investigation reports and clinical findings delayed perforation suspected he was promptly operated by conducting suturing to close the perforation. No other means of detecting abdominal injury by use of other tests and laparoscopy now in use not a known investigation at relevant time. No. negligence. [*B.S. Krishna Kumar* v *Manipal Hospital* 2005 IV CPJ 558 (Karn)]

Failure to perform patient having bleeding peptic ulcer with metabolic encephalopathy. Blood transfusion and I.V. fluids given but condition deteriorating resulting in death negligence alleged that opposite parties failed to carryout necessary operation for stopping and controlling bleeding. Deceased suffering from ulcer since long, not following regular health habits, a chronic alcoholic and smoker with raised endoscopy his condition found to be so critical that he had been operated he would have died on the operation liable itself. No negligence. [*Narasimha Reddy* (*deceased*) v *Managing Director, Rohini Hospital* 2006 I CPJ 144]

Crushed fingers no alternative for doctor except to cut the same as it could not have been saved. Distal phalanx of right index and middle fingers and distal phalanx of right ring finger up to the level of distal 1/3 middle phalanx finger had to be cut. Fingers cut after obtaining consent of the father of patient complainant not coming forward with any evidence to show that the fingers of his son could have been saved without cutting. No negligence. [*Gurumukh Singh* v *Dr. Rajiv Gupta* 2006 III CPJ 337 Chd. (UT)]

Acute appendicitis Cardio respiratory arrest and death allegation that administration of overdose anesthesia followed by IV Calmpose injection for appendectomy led to stoppage of oxygen supply to brain causing death. No expert evidence or medical literature brought on record to prove as to what done in operation theatre which was not as per standard medical practice or it was this specific act of commission or omission resulting in failure of oxygen supply to brain. Nothing record to show that the doctor was not competent or did not posses skill resulting in death of patient or did not do what ought to have been done or did what ought to have been done. No negligence. [*B. Anthony Raj* v *St. Thomas Hospital* 2006 II CPJ 80 (NC)]

Batholines Abscess and septic shock. Based on medical literature brought on record with regard to the disease as also several inquiry reports, post mortem reports, no specific act of medical negligence has been shown much less proved by the complainant. Not the case of complainant that the opposite party no. 2 was not qualified to handle the case nor for that matter the treatment given was wrong and nor that matter, that was not administered properly. Complainant held to have completely failed to prove the case. [*CVVSSR Prasad* v *Vasudha Nursing Home* 2007 IV CPJ 58]

By pass heart surgery. Necessity of multiple vessel heart surgery not denied in the case. Being a doctor himself, appellant complainant was competent to make proper choices of hospitals and doctor before undergoing surgery. It is not a case of complainant that the surgery was negligently performed or any complication arose during the performance of surgery or administration of anesthesia. It is the case of complainant that surgery was not successful. Not disputed that the treating surgeon had told the patient that it is a high risk surgery and that the consent was given by the complainant himself. The complainant himself prosecuted his case before the State Commission which indicates that he was healthy enough to undertake the strenuous task. Judgment of the State Commission dismissing the complaint upheld. [*SC Lahri* v *Pawan Kumar* 2008 I CPJ 372 (NC)]

Amputation of leg. Consent. Treatment record showed that high risk consent was given by father and uncle of the patient for about knee amputation. Contention of the complainant that no informed consent was given for knee amputation is falsified. Doctors of hospital not only passed the Bolem's test but got excellent marks. Appeal liable to be dismissed. [*Parnam Chandrish* v *Balanagar Hospitals Pvt. Ltd.* 2008 I CLT 397 (NC)]

Cancer. Recurrence after 9 years. As seen from the report of the hostopatholgica test done with 10 days after the first operation, the entire cancerous tumour was removed in the first instance itself. Recurrence are not uncommon. Do not see any case of negligence on the part of the opposite parties who have taken adequate and timely care of the complainant as per the medical practice. [*Kamla Gupta* v *Shardendu Bali* 2008 I CPJ 368 (NC)]

Medical negligence. Whether abdominal surgery conducted by surgeon on the child who was suffering from acute abdominal pain and fever for several days after conducting certain tests including x ray which were indicative of sub-acute intestinal obstruction which left a sear on the abdomen can be construed as a case of medical negligence?. Held no. [*Baby Preeti Goel* (*Minor*) v *Batra Hospital and Medical Research Centre* 2007 III CPJ 123]

95. Sterilization operation

Failure of. Operation not 100% safe in case of female sterilization. No negligence can be attributed to doctor if due care and caution has been taken. [*Sayed Amtad Husain Naqvi* v *Laklianpur Hospital, through Dr. VSK Aggarwal* 2001 II CPJ 130 (UP)]

Free of charge. Opposite party no. 5 as a doctor in the Referral Hospital where service is rendered free of charge to all the patients. It is not the case of the complainant that she paid any amount to doctor for performing sterilization on her. Complainants is not a consumer. [*Smt. Babita Jha* v *State of Bihar* 2002 III CPR (Bihar)]

National family welfare programme. Operation failed. Operation done free of charge/cost and voluntaries paid incentive money. Held that complainants are not consumer. [*Shashikala* v *Command Hospital, Air Force* 2003 III CPJ 34 (Kar.)]

Failure. Birth of female child against wishes. Opposite party an expert doctor of high reputation registered for doing sterilization operations on behalf a government and her nursing home, also approved by CMO office for sterilization. To prove negligence some expert evidence should have been produced by the complainant to show the procedure adopted by opposite party not correct procedure which was not done. Risk of failure inherent in female sterilization and no doctor can guarantee cent per cent success. Negligence cannot be presumed and unless complainant specifically proves negligence on the face of the record, no negligence be attributed to opposite party. [*Balbir Singh* v *Dr. Savita Luthra* 2005 III CPJ 317 (Uttaranchal)]

Failure. Reconception after more than 4½ years of tubectomy, sterilization done at the request of complainant as per modified pomeroy method considered the best method of sterilization procedure. Tubectomy operation cannot be treated as 100% fool proof and possibility of reconception after successful operation not be completely ruled out. No expert opinion procedure to show the pregnancy after operation by opposite party. No negligence or deficiency in service. [*Dr. Mrs. B. Dubey, Dubey Nursing Home* v *Mrs. Bhagvati Sharma* 2005 II CPJ 487 (Chh)]

Failure. Bandhyakaran under National Family Welfare Scheme. Subsequent pregnancy and of child. Under government scheme. Females operated by qualified doctor posted in government hospitals free of cost and paid an amount also as incentive, hence no hiring of services under Consumer Protection Act, 1986. As per reputed medical tests, risk of failure inherent in any form of female sterilization and so the doctor cannot be held guilty of negligence merely because procedure adopted by him failed. No allegation that the doctor who performed the operation lacking skill and knowledge to perform the operation nor that he did not adopt the technique prevalent at that time during the operation and also no expert opinion to show that he performed the operation negligently and was deficient in service. Complaint rightly dismissed by District Forum. [*Sushma Devi* v *Balgobind Biswas* 2005 II CPJ 344 (Bihar)]

Failure. Birth of unwanted child after successful performance of tubectomy method of sterilization so far as known to medical science which are most popular and prevalent not 100% safe and secure. Despite successful performance of surgery without any negligence on the part of surgeon, sterilized woman can become pregnant due to natural causes. Once the woman misses menstrual cycle, it is expected of the couple to visit the doctor and seek medical advice. Mere failure of sterilization cannot be attributed to negligence of operating surgeon. [*State of M.P.* v *Parvati Bai* 2006 III CPJ 459 (MP)]

96. Tubectomy operation

Wife of complainant admitted in medical centre for delivery of child. Doctor advised caesarean operation as the baby in the womb found dead. Allegation that the complainant agreed for caesarean operation but not for tubectomy operation and the doctor conduct tubectomy operation also which resulted in great trouble to his wife. Subsequently, she died in another hospital. Material on record not showing that the tubectomy operation was done without his consent. Cause of her death was "Irreversible septic shock" (Periferal circulatory failure) No material to hold that the death the deceased was in any way connected with the operation. No negligence or deficiency in service. [*S.B. Venkatappa* v *Dr. Kasthuri S. Shattikeri* 1995 II CPR 80 (Kar)]

Deficiency in service alleged on account of failed operation of tubectomy on appellant. If an operation fails it cannot all the times be attributed to the negligence. If the felt so much aggrieved they would certainly have issued notice to the respondent immediately after pregnancy came to their knowledge. No explanation why they did not do so and waited for the birth of the child. Competence of the respondent to perform tubectomy operation not question. State commission rightly dismissed the complaint. [*Smt. Premlata Dhokania* v *Dr. Dheeraj Garha* 2002 III CPJ 224 (NC)]

Failure alleged. No expert evidence produced. No interference in order of the State Commission whereby the order of the District Forum awarding compensation set aside. [*Shikha* v *Dr. Ashok Jindal* 2003 I CPJ 239 (NC)]

Failure alleged. There are several reasons for failure of Tubectomy operation for which the doctors cannot be blamed. Doctor acted with due diligence and care and later on also did not attempt to perform medical termination of pregnancy because it could have endangered the life of the appellant. No negligence. [*Hardeep Kaur* v *Dr.* (*Smt.*) *Satinder Saluja* 2004 I CLT 102 (MP)]

97. Tracheotomy

Medical treatment. Line of treatment. Administration of Sintrom. Allegation that patient died on account of increase in dosage of sintrom from 2.00 mg to 2.5 mg resulting in all subsequent problems of bleeding, low urination, low B.P. and subsequent Tracheotomy, suction and death of the deceased. That Tracheotomy was done on the deceased without informing the complainant. No literature, documentary evidence brought. No expert evidence led in support of the line of treatment especially the administration/dosage of Sintrom to patient. No negligence. [*Mrs. Kiran Bala Rout* v *CMC and Hospital* 2002 II CPJ 131 (NC)]

98. Teeth extraction

Complainant got his tooth extracted from respondent doctor. Allegation that there was continuous bleeding from the wound. Subsequently, his condition found to be serious. Admitted to ICU. Damages claimed stating that all this trouble was due to negligent act of the respondents inasmuch as while extracting tooth they did not check his blood pressure and also did not give any consideration to his heart problem of which the complainant said he appraised them. State Commission examined the evidence both oral and documentary and came to the conclusion that there was no negligence on the part of the respondent. No ground to take different view. [*S. Major A Gopinath* v *Dr. James* 2001 I CPR 143 (NC)]

99. Torts

Medical negligence. Sterilization failure. Pregnancy and birth of unwanted child. Claim for damages. Maintainability. Cause of action for claiming compensation in cases of failed sterilization surgery arises on account of negligence of the operating surgeon and not on account of child birth. Failure due to natural causes would not provide any ground for claim. It is for the woman who has conceived the child to go or not to go for MTP. Having gathered the knowledge of conception despite having undergone sterilization surgery if the couple opts for bearing the child, it ceases to be an unwanted child. Claim for compensation for maintenance and upbringing of such a child cannot be maintained unless there was negligence on the part of the surgeon or the surgery assured cent per cent exclusion of pregnancy after surgery. [*State of Punjab* v *Shiv Ram* AIR 2005 SC 3280]

100. Ulcer

Bleeding peptic ulcer with metabolic encephalopathy. Patient in critical condition, would have died on the operation table in case of operation. State commission rightly set aside the order of the District Forum allowing complainant. [*L. Sunil Reddy* v *Rohini Hospital* 2005 I CPJ 657 (NC)]

Medical treatment. Patient was brought too late to the hospital was continuously monitored. Seen by a qualified surgeon. Surgeon did not undertake to perform surgery as in his opinion, the condition of the patient was too critical and he would not withstand surgery. Inspite of best efforts, he could not be saved. No deficiency in service. [*Rohini Hospital* v *Sunil Reddy* 2004 I CPJ 299 (AP)]

101. Urology

Surgery. Urinary tract. Stoppage of urine due to stricture urethra. Minor operation after cystoseapy test. After operation patient again approaching the surgeon with continued pain in urethra, who referred patient to government hospital doctor who in turn referred to a higher hospital where after undergoing two operations getting relief. Conduct a patient in again going to opposite party acted in good faith with no lack of care and caution on his part in rendering professional services to the complainant-patient. No negligence. [*Dr. Mukesh Mishra* v *Ram Swaroop* 2004 III CPJ 158 (Raj)]

Multiple stone in kidney and uterus. Surgery for removal. Subsequent bleeding from drain and urine diagnosed showing development of acute disseminated intravascular coagulation (DIC), a rare complication after major surgery happening to one out of 1000 patients, worsening death with few days. No negligence. Allegation that condition of the patient not improving after the surgery being successful due to blood transfusion subsequent to surgery not supported by any expert opinion, as it is known procedure. [*Saiyad Insaf Hussain* v *Dr. Azam Nawaz* 2004 III CPR 316 (MP)]

Kidney stones. Percutaneous-nephro-lithotripsy done twice and stones removed from both kidneys. Patient suffering hemiplegia alleged to be due to non-supply of blood after 24 hours of the second surgery. Allegation that opposite party conducting surgery not suggesting blood transfusion not substantiated as blood kept ready so as to transfuse when needed. Immediately after surgery blood transfusion done. Evidence showing that patient suffered the disease due to hypertension. No evidence to show said disease a consequence of non-supply of blood. No negligence. [*Narain Harjani* v *Medical Relief Society of South India* 2005 II CPR 37 (Karn)]

Staghorn calculus. Adoption of traditional surgery for removing the stone instead of two other more sophisticated methods. All the three methods considered as correct procedures. Complainant alleged to have undergone five surgeries. Subsequent surgeries relating to post-operative care. No negligence. [*Sultana Ram* v *Dr. B.K. Chawla* 2006 III CPJ 199 (NC)]

Bladder stone Supra-public cystolithotomy, Post-operative complications and death of patient. Any operation may be associated with both preventable and not preventable complications merely because some complications developed leading to death of patient by itself not sufficient to come to the conclusion that the operating surgeon was negligent Qualified and experienced surgeons fully competent to undertake the surgery in question. In the absence of any expert evidence to the contrary they cannot be indicated and held guilty of professional negligence. [*Dr. Sanjay Sharma* v *Ana Singh* 2006 IV CPJ 45 (MP)]

102. Vaccination

Allegation that DTP administered to the child was defective. None of the other children who had also been vaccinated out of the same batch of the vaccination had suffered any complication of the present kind. No negligence. [*Tapan Kumar Nayak* v *State of Orissa* 1997 II CPJ 14 (NC)]

103. Vexatious complaint

Costs. Imposition of. Due care and caution was not observed by the complainants in filing complaint. Even the non-production of record of AIIMS, glaring, inconsistency in between the stand taken by the complainant and the production of selectively torn document on record. Complaint held not filed a requisite care and caution and was filed to harass respondent doctor, with preconceived and misconceived notions. Filing of such complaints and persisting in it by filing an appeal would just amount to abuse of the process of consumer fora. Appeal dismissed with cost of ₹25,000 in favour of the respondent doctor. [*S. Saleemuddin* v *Dr. Sunil Malhotra* 2006 III CPJ 396]

104. Wrong diagnosis

Allegation that wrong pathological report given. Pathological examination done in nature for report. No treatment advised. No negligence. Complaint liable to be dismissed. [*Raj Kumar* v *Dr. Ajay Gupta* 2001 I CPJ 495 (UP)]

Allegation of. Physicians could not be said to be negligent as they had the report from a Histopathylogist cytologist that Malignant cells are not detected. No expert evidence to prove to the contrary. Allegation of wrong diagnosis not proved. [*Rani Devi* v *Dr. S.R. Agarwal* 2002 III CPJ 136 (NC)]

Allegation of. Nothing on record to prove that the attending doctors were negligent in his diagnosis or treatment and that the alleged medical complication was caused by medication prescribed by the doctors. Complaint liable to be dismissed. [*Sukhchain Singh* v *Chandigarh Administration through Secretary, Health* 2003 I CPJ 262 (Chd.)]

Allegations of. Deceased was not only patient of diabetes but she was a patient of chronic obstructive pulmonary disease, asthamatic bronchitis, hypertension and obesity. It may be that combination of all these diseases to be caused for death of patient. It cannot be attributed to only Nivaguine injection or treatment of diabetes. Appellant doctor has properly diagnosed and treated the patient. No medical negligence. [*New India Assurance Co. Ltd.* v *Jai Kumar* 2004 IV CPJ 719 (MP)]

Kidney transplantation. Allegation that transplantation of kidneys of the complainant was necessitated on account of wrong diagnosis/wrong treatment given by the opponent doctor. Complainant failed to obtain expert opinion with regard to the medicines prescribed by the opponent doctor having reacted on the kidneys of the complainant. Alleged medical negligence not proved Complaint liable to be dismissed. [*Prasanna Kumar Diagambardas* v *Dr. Hardasbhai G. Patel* 2005 I CPJ 453 (Guj)]

105. Wrong treatment

Allegation of. Complainant has to prove: (*i*) that there was a breach of duty on the part of doctor, and (*ii*) that the breach of duty was the real cause of the damage complained of and such damage was reasonably foreseeable. Seen in this light no case of negligence made out against the appellants. [*Dr. Devendra Madan* v *Shakuntala Devi* 2003 I CPJ 57 (NC)]

Allegations of. Patient has been treated by the opposite party on the correct line of treatment. No medical negligence on his part while he examined the patient and prescribed the medicines. Complainant failed to produce any evidence in support of their complaint. Complaint liable to be dismissed. [*Dinesh Kaushal* v *Dr. K.K. Khurana* 2002 I CPJ 414 (Chd.)]

Contention the opposite party followed wrong line of treatment and continued with the same line of treatment. Finding of the state commission that the line of treatment by opposite party was nor there was any act of negligence or deficiency in service. Affirmed. [*Dinesh Kaushal* v *Dr. K.K Khurana* 2002 III CPJ 297 (NC)]

Medical report. Mis-pregnancy. Allegation that wrong urine report led to wrong treatment leading to miscarriage and evacuation. In order to prove that the report was wrong. Fresh sample of urine could have been taken immediately thereafter urine report might have sought from other pathology centers. Without there being any comparison, it would be difficult to say that there was negligence in examining the urine and the report was wrong. Petition dismissed. [*Rajni Shukla* v *Rajendra Kumar Agarwal* 2005 IV CPJ 2 (NC)]

106. X-Ray

Chest X-ray. Nowhere plea taken by the appellant that the deceased was having any lung problem or for that matter he had mentioned this at the time of pre-surgical stage and it was not entered into by the concerned doctor. Not taking the chest X-ray in a minor operation of patient less than 40 years. Cannot amount to be a case of medical negligence. [*Mini* v *G. Mohan* 2008 I CPJ 201]

CHAPTER 7

Law and Doctor's Negligence

SYNOPSIS

1. Introduction

The importance and utility of consumerism has been felt considerably due to changed role of state from merely a welfare state to that of a service state. This is because there was a systematic demand that the state and its repositories must serve the people and generate confidence to secure creditability among the consumers. This otherwise with all persuasive terms, mean nothing more than realizing better values against the prices paid for it in this regard, the Consumer Protection Act, 1986 is a sound force designed to aid and protect the consumer by existing legal moral and economic pressure on the defaulters against inadequate or deficient services. The Act while describing the meaning of 'services' also included service of any description which is made available to a potential user but does not include rendering of service free of charge or under a contract of personal service. [Section 2(1)(*o*) of Consumer Protection Act, 1986]

After the Consumer Protection Act, 1986, came into effect, a number of patients have filed cases against doctors, related to medical negligence. With the awareness in society and the people in general gathering consciousness about their rights, measures for damages in tort, civil suits and criminal proceedings are on the augment. Not only civil suits are filed. The accessibility of a medium for grievance redressal under the Consumer Protection Act, 1986 (CPA), having jurisdiction to hear complaints against doctors has given rise to a large number of complaints against doctors alleging commission of offences punishable under section 304A or sections 336, 337 and 338 of the Indian Penal Code, 1860, alleging rashness or negligence on the part of the doctors resulting, in loss of life or injury of varying degree to the patient. This has given rise to a situation of great distrust and fear among the medical profession and an ensuring protection from unnecessary and arbitrary complaints is the need of the hour. The liability of the doctors must be clearly demarcated so that they can perform their benevolent duties without any fear of legal sword. At the same time, justice must be done to the victims of medical negligence and a punitive sting must be adopted in deserving cases.

2. Rules of medical practice

The Medical Council of India has published "Regulations relating to the professional conduct, Etiquette and Ethics for registered medical practitioners (*Indian Medical Council professional conduct. Etiquette and Ethics Regulations 2002. Gazette of India, dated 6-4-2002 Part III Section-4*). This replaces an earlier version published as far back as 1970.

This new code of ethics has rules for medical practice organized into eight chapters. The first chapter contains the duties of the doctors in general-how to maintain good medical practice and medical records, display registration numbers, use generic drugs, ensure quality assurance, expose unethical conduct and rules regarding payment for services.

The second chapter covers physician's duties to their patients, obligations to the sick, incapacity to practice, secrecy of patient information, explaining the prognosis, patient neglect and rules for obstetric care.

The third chapter provides guidance during consultation including avoiding, unnecessary consultations, observing punctuality, informing the patient, treatment after consultation and charges.

The fourth chapter deals with the responsibilities of doctors towards each other.

The fifth chapter covers the duties of doctors to the public and the paramedical professions.

The sixth chapter covers unethical acts including advertising soliciting patient's rebates and commission using secret remedies, human right violations and euthanasia.

The seventh chapter deals with misconduct and violations of the code and ethics.

The last eighth chapter covers punishment and disciplinary action.

The code has covered the entire range of medical ethics and, if followed, will restore the dignity and honour of our once noble profession.

3. Controversy on medical service

There has been considerable debate as to whether medical service is within the scope of 'services' as provided under the Act. The nucleus of the problem emanates from the negligence of duty by the doctor which is being caused by the omission to do something which a reasonable man ordinarily would perform or doing of something which a prudent and reasonable man would not do. In respect of medical service, it may be stated that, every person who enters into the medical profession undertakes to exercise a reasonable degree of care and skill, whereas a surgeon does not undertake that he will perform a cure, nor does he undertake to use the highest possible degree of skill but a doctor when consulted by a patient owes him certain duties namely a duty of care in deciding whether to undertake the case, a duty of care in deciding what treatment to give or a duty of care in administration of that treatment. They may be helpless victims of mistaken identity, for example, a patient suffered an attack of epilepsy before surgery and was apparently unable to speak, when the doctor asked if he was, in fact, the person named on his regulation identity bracelet or similar document like bed head ticket, the patient gestured in the affirmative and the surgeon undertook an operation. But later it was detected to be a case of mistaken identity, since the patient having the similar name was admitted to the hospital for simple circumcision and not for testicular removal. A breach of any of those duties gives a right of action for negligence to the patient.

But such a clarification leads to a controversy to the extent that where the medical service is hired. The ambit and the scope of the Consumer Protection Act, 1986, gets automatically attracted since the purpose of the law is served, but where the medical services are free and voluntary, the Act becomes mute. But the decision *Cosmopolitan Hospitals* v *Vasantha* (1992) CPJ 302 (NC), the National Commission has paved the way for awarding compensation to the complainants for the negligence of doctors. On the one hand, the National Commission provided to the patients or their family members by including them within the definition of consumers, but on the other hand the Court caused furore to the doctor by fixing accountability in the medical profession. By virtue of this landmark judgment the rights of a consumer to seek redressal before the Consumer Court for any negligence or deficiency in the service rendered by medical professionals or hospitals for a fee was recognized and such medical service became consumer service.

A new controversy also began for decision whether a patient availing medical facility in a government run hospital or where such services are free of any fees or are voluntarily rendered could be redressed through the Act. The National Commission held that such patients are not consumers and therefore not entitled to any relief. (*Consumer Unity and Trust Society* v *State of Rajasthan* (1992) CPJ 259) The haunted controversy was on legal aspect of contract of service, as to whether the service rendered by medical practitioners to a patient was under a contract or was under a personal service. Since the patient was provided with free medical treatment in a government hospital or in a charitable hospital. The services of the consumer will not be a consumer service.

4. Relief against medical service

The Medical treatment rendered to a patient by the doctor is clearly a service falling within the ambit of the Act. It is not a contract of personal service but a contract of professional service. It was decided in *M.A. Azeez* v *Nagaru Rajanna unreported judgment delivered on dated 5-4-1990 in FA 3790 (NC)* that a legal representative of a deceased person is entitled to claim compensation for his death on the ground of alleged negligence on the part of a medical practitioner. In *Mappooyan* v *Premavatha* (1991 CPC 78) it was held that the medical treatment given by the private medical practitioner for consideration is a service within the ambit of the Act and responsibility can be fixed on the doctor for his negligence in the matter of treatment. In another case, contrastingly, a patient was admitted into a nursing home for delivery by caesarian operation. Post-operation Complication developed for which there was a claim for compensation and the Court held that since such service of the doctor is personal service and not on professional service, it can not be within consumer service. (*Y. Meenakshi* v *Dr. H. Nandesh* (1991) II CPJ 533 (Kant) whereas, if patient dies while undergoing treatment in a private hospital on payment of hospital charges, then such deficiency of service would fell within consumer service (*V.P. Nair* v *Cosmopolitan Hospital* (1991) II CPJ 444 (Ker). A doctor, no doubt has the discretion in choosing treatment which it proposes to give to the patient and such discretion is relatively under in cases of emergency. If a doctor makes unnecessary delay to pay immediate attention and to operate a patient brought to him in a critical condition, not subjecting him to the intensive care unit of the hospital, by virtue of which the patient dies, it would amount to doctor's negligence for which he is responsible to pay compensation. (*D.P. Bhandari* v *Sri Ganga Ram Hospital* (1991) II CPJ 409) such an observation of the Court also extends to doctors working in state government hospitals. In *S.K. Sukur Abdul* v *State of Orissa* (1991) II CPJ 202, the complainant's wife was admitted into the gynaecology and obstetrics Department of S.C.B. Medical College hospital for treatment. The doctor advised for an immediate blood transfusion. The complainant thereafter approached the blood bank learnt that they supply the blood only by way of exchange of blood or donation. In the process, a bottle of blood together with the cross matching slip was delivered to the doctor for effecting blood transfusion while the transfusion was being given to the patient she developed abnormal reactions and consequently died. The Court held that compensation claim is maintainable for negligence for the doctor. Similarly in *Dr. C.S. Subramanian* v *Kumar Swami* (LLR (1994) 1 Mad 533), it was held that the medical practitioners or doctors of hospital undertaking and providing para-medical services of any category can be held responsible under the Act.

Occasionally, for medical negligence, instead of Doctors the nursing homes are considered responsible. But if the award of the compensation is based on tender evidence which is really in the nature of mere conjecture, such award becomes unsustainable. In *Orissa Nursing Home* v *Anuradha Sahu* [*unreported judgment delivered on dated 4-8-1994 in F.A.312/1992* (*NC*)]. The National Commission decided on the facts that the complainant was pregnant and as soon as the experienced pain resembling labour pains, she was shifted to Orissa Nursing Home, where she was injected with wrong medicine (Syntocinon) in order to induce labour. Failing upon such treatment, she was operated upon for taking out the child who could not emerge and who could not be pulled out by the use of surgical instruments. Such attempt to pull out the child also failed and therefore the child was pushed back to the uterus and the vaginal area was stitched up and she was not shifted to S.C.B. Medical College and hospital for further treatment. In the process was the child died. After eventual recovery she complained about the deficiency of medical service against the Nursing home. It was held that proper explanation as to the cause of shifting of the patient was not made out in order to establish negligence on the part of the doctor or to that extent the Nursing Home and therefore no compensation could be granted.

Towards the end of 1995, in a historic judgment, the Supreme Court made doctors accountable for any act of medical negligence and ruled out that they could be sued for compensation under the Act. The Court made it clear that doctors and hospitals that rendered service without any change whatsoever or the payment of a token amount for registration purposes only may not be sued for compensation. It was decided that where the charges were required to be paid by everybody for availing medical service, and where the doctors and hospitals do provide free service to some patients belonging to the poor class but the bulk of the service is rendered on payment basis would be covered under the Act. (*The ruling was given while disposing a batch of appeals including one by them Indian Medical Association* v *Per Agarwal, Hindustan Times dated 15-11-1995*).

Among the reliefs that could be granted for deficiency in service are:

(*i*) return of charges paid by the complainant,

(*ii*) payment of such amount as may be awarded as compensation to the consumer for any loss or injury suffered by the consumer due to negligence of opposite party, and

(*iii*) removal of defects or deficiencies in the service in question. Medical practitioners do not enjoy immunity and they could be sued in contract or tort on the ground that they had failed to exercise reasonable skill and care.

Thus a patient with multiple sclerosis has bad sores not receiving adequate medical service it might be a disability of the patient but not terminally illness, but if it is otherwise the doctor cannot escape legal trials on the ground of euthanasia. For example, a patient might have a painful form of rheumatoid arthritis and might request a doctor to ampute his/her legs and in such case doctors are required to treat the patient so as to provide case to the sufferings and not otherwise.

5. Medical negligence

Negligence can be described as failure to take due care as a result of which injury ensues. Negligence excludes wrongful intention since they are mutually exclusive. Carelessness is not culpable or a ground for legal liability except in those cases in which the law has imposed the duty of carefulness. The medical profession is one such section of society on which such a duty has been imposed in the strictest sense. It is not sufficient that the medical professional is expected to have the requisite degree of skill and knowledge. The question in every case would be whether the medical practitioner in fact attained the degree of due care established by law. Medical negligence is a sub-species of this tort which falls within the larger species of profession negligence. Medical negligence, like other forms of negligence, is a criminal offence for which a doctor even be imprisoned. Medical malpractice, however, is not merely the negligence on the part of the care given, is a conscious decision of the care given to offer and/or force a product, procedure or investigation upon a patient for monetary gain either personally or for the institution.

There are three essential components of negligence:

(1) The existence of a duty to take care, which is owed by the doctor to the complainant,

(2) The failure to attain that standard of care, prescribed by the law, thereby committing the breach of such duty,

(3) Damage, which is both causally connected with such breach and recognized by the law, has been suffered by the complainant.

This is the ordinary legal meaning of negligence. But for the professionals such as medical practitioners, an additional perspective is added through a test known as Bolam test which is the accepted test in India. In the case of *Bolam* v *Friern Hospital Management Committee* (1992) 109 AIR 625, the Queen's bench Division of the British Court held that a doctor is not guilty of negligence if he has acted in accordance with a practice accepted as proper by responsible body of medical men skilled in particular art.

As set out in the judgment of the Supreme Court in the case of *Jacob Mathew* v *State of Punjab* AIR 2005 SC 3180, the standard of care, when assessing the practice as adopted is judged is the light of knowledge available at the time (of the incident) and not at the date of trial.

When the charges of negligence arises out of the failure to use some particular equipment. The charge would fail if the equipment was not generally available at that point of time on which it is suggested as should have been used. In this decision, the Supreme Court also observed that for inferring negligence on the part of a professional, including a doctor, additional consideration applies. A simple lack of care, an error of judgment or an accident, is not proof of negligence on the part of medical professional so long as a doctor follows a practice acceptable to the medical profession of that day, he cannot be held liable for negligence merely because a better alternative course or method of treatment was also available or simply because a more skilled doctor would not have chosen to follow or resort to that practice or procedure which the accused followed.

6. Professional negligence

Profession involves the idea of an occupation requiring purely intellectual skills or of manual skills controlled by the intellectual skills of the operator, as distinguished from an occupation which is substantially production or sale of commodities. The line of demarcation may vary from time to time. According to Rupert M Jackson and John L. Powell observed in *Indian Medical Association* v *V.P. Shanta* AIR 1996 SC 550, that occupations which are regarded as professions have four characteristics, they are:

(1) the nature of the work which is skilled and specialized and substantial is mental than manual,

(2) to commitment to moral principles which go beyond the general duty of honesty and wider duty to community which may transcend the duty to a particular client or patient,

(3) professional association which regulate administration and seeks to uphold the standards of the profession through professional codes on matters of conduct and ethics, and

(4) high status of community.

Medical profession is one of the oldest professions of the world and is the most humanitarian one inherent in the concept of any profession is a code of conduct. Containing the basic ethics that underline the moral values that govern professional practice and is aimed at upholding its dignity. Medical ethics underpins the value at the heart of the practitioner client relationship. Medical negligence and malpractices by doctors were the grey areas in health care where legal issue operated.

7. Civil law and negligence

Negligence is a breach of a legal duty to care. It means carelessness in a matter in which the law mandates carefulness. A breach of this duty gives a patient the right to initiate action against negligence. Persons who offer medical advice and treatment implicit state that they have the skill and knowledge to do so, that they have skill to decide whether to take a case, to decide the treatment, and to administer that treatment. This is known as an "implied undertaking" on the part of medical profession.

In the case of *State of Haryana* v *Smt. Santa* AIR 2000 SC 3335, the Supreme Court held that every doctor "has a duty to act with a reasonable degree of care and skill".

Doctor in India may be held liable for their services individually and vicariously unless they come within exceptions specified in the case of *Indian*

Medical Association v *V.P. Santha* AIR 1996 SC 550. Doctors are not liable for their services individually or vicariously if they do not charge fees. Thus free treatment at a non-government hospital, government hospital, health centre, dispensary or nursing home would not be considered a service as defined in section 2(1)(*o*) of the Consumer Protection Act, 1968.

However, no human being is a perfect and even the most renowned specialist could make a mistake in detecting or diagnosing the true nature of decease. A doctor can be held liable for negligence only of one can prove that she/he is guilty of a failure that no doctor with ordinary skills would be guilty of if acting with reasonable care. (*Observations of Lord President Clyde in Hunter* v *Hanley* (1955) SLT 213. *In: Nathan HL. Medical Negligence, London: Butterworths, 1957*: In a key decision on this matter in the case of *Dr. Laxman Balkrishna Joshi* v *Dr Trimbak Bapu Godbole* AIR 1969 SC 128, the Supreme Court held that if a doctor has adopted a practice that is considered 'proper' by a reasonable body of medical professionals who are skilled in that particular filed he or she will not be negligent only because something went wrong.

Doctors must exercise an ordinary degree of skill. (*Smt J. S. Paul* v *Dr* (*Mrs.*) *A Barkataki* (2004) 11 CLD 37) However, they cannot give a warranty of the perfection of their skill or a guarantee of cure. If the doctor has adopted the right course of treatment, if he/she is skilled and has worked with a method and manner best suited to the patient, he/she can not be blamed for negligence if the patient is not totally cured. [*Dr Prem Luthra* v *Iftekhar* (2004) 11 CLD 37 (SCDRC-Uttaranchal]

Certain conditions must be satisfied before liability can be considered. The person who is accused must have committed an act of omission or commission, this act must have been in breach of the person's duty and this must have caused harm to the injured person. The complainant must prove the allegation against the doctor by citing the best evidence available in the medical science and by presenting expert opinion. [*Dr. Janak Kantimatho Nathan* v *Murlidhar Eknath Masane* 2002 II CPR 138]

In some situations the complainant can invoke the principle of *res ipsa loquitur* or "the thing speaks for itself". In certain commission applied this principle in (*Dr Janak Kantimathi Nathan* v *Murlidhar Eknath Masne.*)

The principle of *res ipsa loquitur* comes into operation only when there is proof that the occurrence was unexpected, that the accident could not have happened without negligence and lapses on the part of the doctor and that the circumstances conclusively show that the doctor and not any other person was negligent.

8. Criminal negligence

Section 304A of the Indian Penal Code of 1860 states that whoever causes the death of a person by a rash or negligent act not amounting to culpable homicide shall be punished with imprisonment for a term of two years or with a fine or with both.

Similarly, section 336 of the Penal Code provides that it is an offence to endanger the human life or personal safety of others through a rash or negligent act. The punishment is three months imprisonment or fine of ₹250 or both.

Sections 337 and 338 of the Indian Penal Code makes it an offence to cause simple hurt or grievous hurt through rash or negligent act. The punishment can be upto six months of imprisonment or fine upto ₹500 or both for simple hurt and sections 337 and 338 of the Indian Penal Code makes it an offence to cause simple hurt or grievous hurt through rash or negligent act. The punishment can be upto six months of imprisonment or fine upto ₹500 or both for simple hurt and punishment upto two years or fine upto ₹1,000 or both for causing grievous hurt.

Criminal negligence applies to medical practitioners when he shows gross negligence in the treatment of patient leading to serve injury or death. The doctor should not be held criminally responsible for the patient's death unless his negligence or incompetence shows such disregard for the life and safety of the patient as to amount to a crime. The most important criterion is the degree of negligence required to prosecute medical practitioner under the charge of criminal negligence which should be gross one or of very high degree.

In *State of Haryana* v *Smt. Santa* (2000) 5 SCC 182: AIR 2000 SC 3335, the Supreme Court has pointed out that liability in Civil Law is based upon the amount of damages incurred, in criminal law, the amount and degree of negligence is a factor in determining liability. However, certain elements must be established to determine criminal liability in any particular case, the motive of the offence, the magnitude of the offence, and the character of the offender.

In *Poonam Verma* v *Ashwin Patel* (1996) 4 SCC 332, the Supreme Court distinguished between negligence, rashness and recklessness.

A negligent person is one who inadvertently commit an act of omission and violates a positive duty. A person who is rash knows the consequences but foolishly thinks that they will not occur as a result of her/his act. A reckless person knows the consequences but does not care whether or not they result from her/his act. Any conduct falling short of recklessness and deliberate wrong doing should not be the subject of criminal liability.

Thus a doctor cannot be held criminally responsible for a patient's death unless it is shown that she/he was negligent or incompetent with such disregard for the life and safety of his patient that it amounted to a crime against the state. [*House of Lords decision in R* v *Adomako* (1994) 3 All ER 79]

The Supreme Court judgment in *Jacob Mathew* v *State of Punjab* (*Criminal Appeal No. 144-145 of 2004 decided by Supreme Court on August* 5, 2005: (2005) 6 SCC 1) have given following guidelines for prosecuting medical professionals against the charge of criminal negligence.

(1) A private complaint may not be entertained unless the complainant has produce *prima facie* evidence before the Court in the form of a credible opinion given by another competent doctor to support the charge of rashness or negligence on the part of accused doctors.

(2) The investigating officer should, before proceeding against the doctor accused by rash or negligent act or omission, obtain an independent and competent medical opinion, preferably from a doctor in government service qualified in that branch of medical practice who can normally be expected to give an impartial and unbiased opinion.

(3) Unless the arrest is necessary for furthering the investigation or for collecting evidence unless the investigation officer feels satisfied that the doctor proceeded against, would not make himself available to face the prosecution unless arrested, the arrest may be withheld.

The essence of Supreme Court judgment is that 'intention' and 'lack of proper care and caution, are important ingredients before which a criminal action can be launched against a medical practitioner under Criminal Law.

Sections 80 and 88 of the Indian Penal Code contain defences for doctors accused of criminal liability. Under section 80 (accident in doing a lawful act) nothing is an offence that is done by accident or misfortune and without any criminal intention or knowledge in the doing of a lawful act in a lawful manner by lawful means and with proper care and caution.

According to section 88, a person cannot be accused of an offence if she/he performs an act in good faith for the other's benefit, does not intended to cause harm even if there is a risk and the patient has explicitly or implicitly given consent.

9. Some Supreme Court Rulings

Before the case of *Jacob Mathew* v *State of Punjab* AIR 2005 SC 3180, the Supreme Court of India delivered two different opinions on doctor's liability. In *Mohanan* v *Prabha G. Nair* (2004) CPJ 32 SC, it ruled that a doctor's negligence could be ascertained only by scanning the material and expert evidence might be presented during a trial. In *Dr Suresh Gupta* v *Govt. of NCT of Delhi* (2004) 6 Scale 432, the standard of negligence that had to be proved to fix a doctor's or surgeon's criminal liability was set at "gross negligence" or "recklessness".

In *Suresh Gupta's* case the Supreme Court distinguished between an error of Judgment and culpable negligence. It was held that criminal prosecution to their guilt would do great disservice to the community. A doctor cannot be tried for culpable or criminal negligence in all cases of medical mishaps or misfortunes.

A doctor may be liable in a civil case for negligence but mere carelessness or want of due attention and skill cannot be described as so reckless or grossly negligent as to make her/him criminally liable. The Court held that this distinction was necessary so that the hazards of medical professionals being exposed to civil liability may not unreasonably extend to criminal liability and expose them to the risk of imprisonment for alleged criminal negligence.

Hence, the complaint against the doctor must show negligence or rashness such a degree as to indicate a mental state that can be described as totally apathetic towards the patient. Such gross negligence alone is punishable.

On September 9, 2004, justices Arijit Pasayat and C.K. Thakkar referred the question of medical negligence to a larger Bench of the Supreme Court. They observed that words such as "gross", "reckless", "competence" and "indifference" did not occur anywhere in the definition of "negligence" under section 304A of the Indian Penal Code and hence they could not agree with judgment delivered in the case of *Dr. Suresh Gupta*.

The issue was decided in the Supreme Court in the case of *Jacob Mathew* v *State of Punjab*. The Court directed the Central Government to frame guidelines and they would prevail.

A private complaint of rashness or negligence against a doctor may not be entertained without *prima facie* evidence in the form of a credible opinion of another competent doctor supporting the change. In addition, the investigating officer should give an independent opinion, preferably of a government doctor. Finally, a doctor may be arrested only if the investigation officer believes that she/he would not be available for prosecution unless arrested.

10. Doctors and Consumer Courts

Medical negligence gives rise to a civil and criminal liability. We have already mentioned that as regards civil wrongs, an aggrieved person can claim compensation either through a civil suit or a complaint lodges with Consumer Forum. Since the enactment of Consumer Protection Act, 1986 there has been a significant rise in medical negligence cases behind field. In one sense, the passing of this law has given a boost of consumers for approaching Courts in respect of negligence.

For quite sometime after the passing of the Consumer Protection Act, furious debate was ranging whether it at all applies to doctors, hospitals and nursing homes and if so under what situations. The Supreme Court finally set at rest this controversy in the case of *Indian Medical Association* v *V.P. Shantha* AIR 1996 SC 550. The Court held that proceedings under the Consumer Protection Act are summary proceedings for speedy redressal and the remedies are in addition to private law remedy. The issue was whether patients are consumers under the Consumer Protection Act and could they claim damages for injury caused by the negligence of the doctor, hospital and nursing home.

Apart from submitting that patients could not be classified as consumers under the Consumer Protection Act, the Medical Association argued the following points that are briefly reproduced:

(*a*) Deficiency in service, as defined under the Act, means any fault, imperfection, shortcoming or inadequacy in the quality, nature and manner of performance which is required to be maintained under any law or has been undertaken to be performed by a person in pursuance of a contract or otherwise in respect of any service (*Bolam* v *Friern Hospital Management Committee* (1957) 1 WLR 582). Thus deficiency is ascertained on the basis of certain norms and relating to quality, nature and manner of performance and since medical services cannot be judged on the basis of any fixed norms, therefore practitioners are not covered under the definition of service.

(*b*) Such person can fairly and justly decide on medical malpractice cases who are themselves qualified in medical fields as they will be able to appreciate the complex issues involved in such cases. It was submitted that as the members of the Forum are not qualified to deal with medical malpractice claims medical practitioners should be exempted from the ambit of the Act.

(*c*) Medical malpractice claims involve complex issues that will require detailed examination of evidence, deposition of experts and witnesses. This is contrary to the purpose of summary proceedings involving trial by affidavits, which is to provide speedy results. Hence consumer Forum should not adjudicate medical malpractice cases.

(*d*) If the medical practitioners are brought within the purview of the Act, the consequences would be a huge increasing in medical expenditure on account of insurance charges as well as tremendous increase in defensive medicine, that medical practitioners may refuse to attend to medical emergencies and there will be no safeguards against frivolous and vexatious complaints and consequent blackmail.

The Supreme Court, however, rejected all these arguments and drew the following conclusions:

(*i*) Services rendered to patient by a medical practitioner (expert where the service is free of charge to every patient or under a contract of personal service) by way of consultation, diagnosis and treatment, both medical and surgical would fall within the ambit of services as defined in section 2(1)(*o*).

(*ii*) The fact that medical practitioners belong to the medical profession and are subject to the disciplinary control of the medical council of India and/or state medical councils would not exclude the services rendered by them from the ambit of the Act.

(*iii*) Services rendered by a medical officer to his employer under the contract of employment is not 'service' under section 2(1) (*o*) for purposes of the Act.

(*iv*) Services rendered at private or a Government hospitals, nursing homes, health centres and dispensaries for a fee are 'services' under the Act while services rendered free of charge are exempted. Payment of token amount for purposes of registration will not after the nature of services provided for free services rendered at government or a private hospital, nursing homes, health centres and dispensaries where services are rendered on payment of charges to those who can afford and free to those who cannot are also 'services' for the purposes of the Act. Hence in such cases the person who are rendered free services are beneficiaries under section 2(1)(*d*) thereby 'consumer' under the Act.

(*v*) Services rendered free of charge by a medical practitioner attached to a hospital/nursing home or where he is employed in a hospital/nursing home that provides free medical facilities, are not 'services' under the Act.

(*vi*) Where an insurance company pays, under the insurance policy, for consultation, diagnosis and medical treatment of the insurer then such an insurer is a consumer under section 29(1)(*d*) and services rendered either by the hospital or the medical practitioner is a service under section 2(1)(*o*). Similarly, where an employer bears the expenses of medical treatment of its employee, the employee is a consumer under the Act.

The remedy under Consumer Protection Act is in addition to civil remedy and it can not be denied to a consumer merely on the ground that either the facts are too complicated or the complainant's claim is unreasonable.

11. Burden of proof and chances of error

The burden of proof of negligence, carelessness, or insufficiency generally lies with the complainant. The law requires a higher standard of evidence than otherwise to support an allegation of negligence against a doctor. In cases of medical negligence, the patient must establish her/his claim against the doctor.

In *Calcutta Medical Research Institute* v *Bimalesh Chatterjee* (1999) I CPJ 13 (NC), it was held that the onus of proving negligence and the resultant deficiency in service was clearly on the complainant.

In *Kanhaiya Kumar Singh* v *Park Medicare and Research Centre* (1999) III CPJ 9 (NC), it was held that negligence has to be established and cannot be presumed.

Even after adopting all medical procedures as prescribed, a qualified doctor may commit an error. The National Consumer Disputes Redressal Commission and the Supreme Court have held, in several decisions, that a doctor is not liable for negligence or medical deficiency if some wrong is caused in her/his treatment or in diagnosis or she/he has acted in accordance with the practice accepted as proper by a reasonable body of medical professionals skilled in that particular art, though the result may be wrong. In various kinds of medical and surgical treatment, the likelihood of an accident leading to death cannot be ruled out. It is implied that a patient willingly takes such a risk as a part of the doctor-patient relationship and the attendant mutual trust.

12. Difficult task of judiciary

Referral of judgment of Supreme Court (*Dr. Suresh Gupta* v *Govt. of NCT of Delhi*) to the bench further confirms the divided opinion of judiciary and complexity of legal words used in cases of negligence. The much-debated judgment of the Supreme Court is now referred to a larger Bench for reconsideration. A Bench of Mr. Arijit Pasayat and Mr. C. K. Thakkar observed that the words "gross negligence" or "reckless act" did not fall within the definition of section 304A, IPC, defining death due to an act of negligence or the culpable homicide not amounting to murder.

Between civil and criminal liability of a doctor, causing death of his patient the Court has a difficult task of weighing the degree of carelessness and negligence alleged on the part of the doctor, for conviction of a doctor for alleged criminal offence, the standard should be proof of recklessness and deliberate wrong doing with a higher degree of morally blameworthy conduct. (*Dr. Suresh Gupta* case).

13. Applicability of sections 304 and 304A of IPC

The legal position is almost firmly established that where a patient dies due to the negligent medical treatment of the doctor, the doctor can be made liable in civil law for paying compensation and damages in 'Tort' and at the same time, if the degree of negligence is so gross and his act was reckless as to endanger the life of the patient, he would also be made criminally liable for offence under section 304A of IPC. (*Dr Suresh Gupta* case).

Incidence are reported in which cases are registered against the doctor under section 304, IPC as doctors are murderers and even not granted bail ("High Court Rejects Doctor's bail application" published Sunday Times of India, dated 15-8-2004).

14. Defence taken by hospitals

When too many hurdles are raised against a sector, it evolves new ways and means to defend itself strategically. The following methods are strengthened now which were not given importance before 1995.

14.1 Doctrine of estoppel

The Doctrine of Estoppel, hitherto applicable to civil laws turned out to be helpful to the medical sector. Estoppel means if an individual acts or deposes before an institution/judicial Forum about a particular fact, he cannot go against the same in a later date. In short, by obtaining informed consent from the patient properly the hospitals/medical professionals set a proper ground before a Court or Forum.

14.2 Application of Bolam Test

The British Court during 1954 by its order in *Bolam* v *Fried Hospital Management* (1957) 1 WLR 582) has decided that a medical professional would be absolved of any allegation of any negligence, if he practiced a sufficient care to select a procedure which is normally followed in that course of time and in that place. It also set three criteria for the safety of the medical professional:

(*i*) He must posses adequate skill in that area of medical practice.

(*ii*) He exercises reasonable care while performing his skill.

(*iii*) Mere negligence will not make out a case for compensation against him but that negligence should have a direct nexus with the injury caused to the complainant. If the injury does not have a direct link towards negligence, no award of compensation exists. The Supreme Court adopted the principles enunciated in the Bolam Test fully and followed us all their historical judgments in *Dr Laxman Balakrishnan Joshi* v *D.*

Trimbak Bapu Godbok AIR 1969 SC 128; *A S Mittal* v *State of Uttar Pradesh* AIR 1989 SC 550; *Indian Medical Association of India* v *V.P. Shantha* AIR 1996 SC 550; *Spring Meadows Hospital* v *Harijit Ahluwalia* AIR 1998 SC 1801 and lastly in *Kunal Saha* v *Dr. Sugumar Mukherji* 2006 II CPR 14 (NC).

Following the orders of the Supreme Court, all consumer for a followed the principles and saved the medical fraternity from awarding compensation. [*Jacob Mathew* v *State of Punjab* AIR 2005 SC 3180]

In this case, the Supreme Court saved medical professionals from being harassed by the State through its prosecution authorities. This is how it involved. A patient died because of cancer. The relatives of the patient, highly influential in politics brought criminal proceedings against the doctor who was working in CMC Ludhiana. The bail petition filled before the District Sessions Court and High Court were dismissed, thus paving way for his imminent arrest, while he filed a revision petition before the Supreme Court, it quashed the FIR and laid down principles to be followed while dealing with such cases against medical professionals by the state. It laid down that:

(*i*) The prosecution must be convicted that there is a criminal negligence on the part of the doctor.

(*ii*) It distinguished between the negligence of tort and criminal negligence.

(*iii*) The prosecution may proceed further if a case is made out, only after obtaining a medical report from a doctor who has specialized in that branch of specialization, preferably working in government hospital.

15. Latest trend

The case decided in *Dr. Kunal Saha* v *Sukumar Mukherjee* 2006 III CPJ 142 (NC) became a milestone judgment towards the jubilation of the medical fraternity. In this case, a claim of ₹77,76,73,500 was made by a complainant who himself is a medical professional. He took treatment of his wife both in AMRI Hospital, Calcutta and Breach Candy Hospital, Mumbai. She died of Toxic Epidermal Necrolysis (TEN). The Verdict dismissed claims on the following grounds:

(*i*) There is contributory negligence on the part of complainant himself.

(*ii*) The patient was brought to Mumbai from Calcutta against medical advice.

(*iii*) The Medical professional gave their best treatment available in India in this particular time and place.

(*iv*) The award of this nature if granted, may cause a rise in professional insurance by the hospitals and directly the premium paid to the insurance company may pass on the poor patient as in existence in the U.S.

16. Law of Torts: Recourse to claim compensation

As the Law of Torts comes under Civil Law, the Code of Civil Procedure, 1908 becomes applicable. A tort means 'wrong'. It is a violation of the general duty which every member of the society is obliged so as not to do any harm without lawful jurisdiction or excuse. If by the act of an individual, an injury is caused to a third person, the affected person is entitled to claim compensation from the doer. Under the torts, only the petitioner has to prove the case against the respondent. However, if the damage and injury is quite apparent to the core, the principle of *res ipsa loquitur* is applied and the defendant has to prove that he is not guilty.

Under civil laws, at a point where the Consumer Protection Act ends, the law of torts takes over and protects the interest of Patient. This applies even if the medical professionals provide free 'services' as defined in the Consumer Protection Act, patient can take recourse to the law relating to negligence under the law of torts and successfully claim compensation. The onus is on the patient to prove that the doctor was negligent and that the injury was a consequence of the doctor's negligence. Such cases of negligence may include:

(*i*) transfusion of blood of incorrect blood groups,

(*ii*) leaving, mob in the patient's abdomen after opening

(*iii*) unsuccessful sterilisation resulting in the birth of child,

(*iv*) removal of organs without taking consent,

(*v*) operating on a patient without giving anaesthesia, administrating wrong medicine resulting in injury.

17. The Doctrine of *Res Ipsa Loquitur*

"*Res Ipsa Loquitur*" means "thing speak for themselves". If a negligent act is done by a doctor he is to be held vicariously liable for the deed. In such cases the damage caused to the patient is so obvious that no proof as to the negligent act of the doctor is required. While discharging this burden, the plaintiff needs to satisfy the Court of the truth in these allegations, after which the onus shifts to the defendant to prove his innocence. For the applicability of the maxim of *Res Ipsa Loquitor*. The following three principles are utmost important:

(*a*) The opposite party must have been in control of things,

(*b*) Common norms suggesting that the injury in itself cannot happen without negligence.

(*c*) The cause of incident must be known or unascertainable.

Some common examples as to when this principle is invoked are in cases where a wrong patient is treated or where operation has been done on a wrong part of the body.

18. Defence provided to the doctors

The doctors may plead the following defences when they were subjected to an allegation of medical negligence:

(*a*) Where the doctor is confident that he had not been negligent in fulfilling his duty, he may simply deny the allegation.

(*b*) Where the patient has been negligent in following the orders of the doctor, for example if the doctor had asked the patient to come in for frequent check ups and the patient did not comply with the orders resulting in the damage of his health the doctor cannot be held liable in such a case.

(*c*) Where the duty of the patient was delegated to a third party. In such a case the responsibility is on the person to whom the duty was delegated was incapable, then the blame shall lie with the doctor. He shall be liable for the duty of his staff if they are incapable (*Spring Meadows* v *Harjot Ahluwalia*).

(*d*) Where the question is whether there was an act of negligence or not. There is always an assumption of risk in treatment. Once a person consents to treatment voluntarily he cannot ask for legal action. This is best explained by the maxim "*volute non fit injuria*". However if some where during the procedure negligent act had been done then he can ask for action.

(*e*) Where the complication is well known in the use of drug. Sometimes certain drugs have some well known complications. If the necessary tests were conducted for the suitability of the drug and even after all that the complication occurred. The doctor cannot be held liable for that.

(*f*) Where the case has already been completed between the two parties. Once the case has been completed between the two parties, it cannot be filed again (*Res Judicata* the thing, has been decided).

19. Role of medical expert's opinion

No case of criminal negligence should be registered without medical opinion from expert committee of doctors and it should be given within a reasonable time. Indian Medical Association (IMA), Punjab claimed "They had secured a directive from Director General of Police (DGP) Punjab that no case of criminal negligence can be registered against a doctor without a report from an Expert Committee (*Sunday Times August 8, 2004: 2*). Similar situation exist in the case of State of Delhi where Lieutenant Governor issued to the Delhi Police regarding how to arrest a doctor in medical negligence case. The Delhi High Court also decided to form guidelines for lower judiciary as well as the police to deal with such cases ("Fresh Rules in Negligence Arrests", The Times of India, August 23, 2003: 3).

Hon'ble Supreme Court endorsed the same view as "Criminal Prosecution of doctors without adequate medical opinion would be great disservice to the community as it would shake the very fabric of doctor-patient-relationship with respect to mutual confidence and faith the doctors would be more worried about their own safety instead of giving best treatment of their patients" (*Dr Suresh Gupta* case).

20. Confusion of doctors over the issue of criminal negligence

Doctors are victims of Trial by media or post mortem of Court's judgment done by the media or misinformation spread through the media and technicality of legal words used in the matter of 'criminal negligence'. As reported by various leading national news papers after the decision of Supreme Court (*Dr Suresh Gupta Case*) "Doc not criminally liable of patient dies" (*Hindustan Times, August 6, 2004: 1*), "Saving the Doctors" (*Hindustan Times August 9, 2004: 6*), "S.C. Judgment Qualifies medical negligence" (*The Times of India August 6, 2004: 6*) "S.C. Insures Does against patient Death" (*The Times of India August 6, 2004: 6*), S.C. Ruling a Deliverance for Medical Fraternity" (*Sunday Times August 8, 2004: 2*) SC comes to the Rescue of doctor" (*The Tribune, August 12, 2004: 10)* etc. "This would mean that the relief the doctors had got due to the judgment (*Dr Suresh Gupta* case), would not be available to them till the larger Bench give its opinion. (*SC Judgment on Doctor's criminal liability for larger Bench", The Tribune September 10, 2004: 1*).

Doctors relying on these media reports without verifying the facts from original judgment or through discussion with the legal experts on the issue may fall prey of this misinformation perceived through the eyes of media and may propagate same feeling and knowledge to other colleagues and junior doctors and always remain confused on the issue of criminal negligence, while Supreme Court judgments mention nothing, new except verifying the previous established fact that "error of judgment is not negligence".

21. Role of media

The freedom of information is implicitly covered by Article 19 and Article 21 under the Indian Constitution. (*Narendar Kumar, "Constitutional Law of India" Edition 1997: 146*). Disposing off a case of contempt of Court against the editors of two newspapers recently, the Supreme Court remarked— "It is the duty of a true and responsible journalist to inform the people with accurate impartial presentation of news and his views after dispassionate evaluation of the facts and information received by him to be published as a news item". (*State of Human Rights in India,* (3:3): 94-95).

Since the 1970s, Indian media has played an extremely important role in sensitizing people with information about governance, development, science and technology, foreign relations and so on.

However, lately it has also come in for criticism, as highlighted by the above Supreme Court decision. There is a decline in journalistic credibility, as noted by the Chairman of the Press Council of India as well as the then President Sri K.R. Narayanan.

Recently, due to the media preoccupation with the Trivia, personality cult, one sidedness, and instant in depth investigation, 51 senior journalists feel that the media sides away from important people's issues that it is losing social content and becoming a consumer product with a manager overshadowing the editor. The media has a tendency to launch "trial by the media", even sentencing by the media, while a Court proceeding is underway.

CHAPTER 8

Euthanasia and Doctor

SYNOPSIS

1. Introduction

The word "euthanasia" comes from the Greek — "eu" meaning "goodly or well" + "thanatos" meaning "death". So, euthanasia is literally the "good death".

In 18th-century England, that was what euthanasia meant, a "good" death, a welcome way to depart quietly and well from life. Today the most commonly understood meaning of euthanasia is more than this old dictionary definition of dying well a good and easy death. Euthanasia refers, for example, to the situation when a doctor induces the death with a lethal injection, of a patient who is suffering unrelievably and has persistently requested the doctor to do so.

The most commonly understood meaning of euthanasia today is more than the old dictionary definition of dying well — a good and easy death. It refers, for example, to the situation when a doctor induces the death with a lethal injection, of a patient who is suffering unrelievably and has persistently requested the doctor to do so.

Suicide, whether irrational or rational, for unrelated reasons is not euthanasia. Nor is the forced killing of another person.

The Netherlands is currently the only country in the world in which euthanasia is openly and legally practiced. There, euthanasia and assisted suicide are defined by the State Commission on Euthanasia. It is not specifically allowed by statute, but Dutch law accepts a standard defense from doctors who have adhered to official guidelines. These guidelines hinge on the voluntariness of the request and the unrelievableness of the suffering. Euthanasia is the intentional termination of life by somebody other than the person concerned at his or her request. Assisted suicide means intentionally helping a patient to terminate his or her life at his or her request. Euthanasia is the termination of life by a doctor at the express wish of a patient. The request to the doctor must be voluntary, explicit and carefully considered and it must have been made repeatedly. Moreover, the patient's suffering must be unbearable and without any prospect of improvement.

Pain relief administered by a Dutch doctor may shorten a patient's life. As is the case in other countries, this is seen as a normal medical decision in terminal care and not as euthanasia.

The term normally implies an intentional termination of life by another at the explicit request of the person who wishes to die. Euthanasia is generally defined as the act of killing an incurably ill person out of concern and compassion for that person's suffering. It is sometimes called mercy killing, but many advocates of euthanasia define mercy killing more precisely as the ending of another person's life without his or her request. Euthanasia, on the other hand, is usually separated into two categories: passive euthanasia and active euthanasia. In many jurisdictions, active euthanasia can be considered murder or Manslaughter, whereas passive euthanasia is accepted by professional medical societies, and by the law under certain circumstances.

Euthanasia is a matter of continuing controversy, a tinderbox for debate, an issue on which positions range widely and include enthusiastic advocacy, guarded acceptance, outright rejection and vehement condemnation, equating euthanasia with murder.

2. Passive euthanasia

Hastening the death of a person by altering some form of support and letting nature take its course is known as passive euthanasia. Examples include such things as turning off respirators, halting medications, discontinuing food and water so as to allowing a person to dehydrate or starve to death, or failure to resuscitate.

Passive euthanasia also includes giving patient large doses of morphine to control pain, in spite of the likelihood that the painkiller will suppress respiration and cause death earlier than it otherwise would have happened. Such doses of painkillers have a dual effect of relieving pain and hastening death. Administering such medication is regarded as ethical in most political jurisdictions and by most medical societies.

These procedures are performed on terminally ill, suffering persons so that natural death will occur sooner. They are also commonly performed on persons in a persistent vegetative state; for example, individuals with massive brain damage or in a coma from which they likely will not regain consciousness.

3. Active euthanasia

Far more controversial, active euthanasia involves causing the death of a person through a direct action, in response to a request from that person. The active acceleration of a "good" death by use of drugs, etc, whether by oneself or with the aid of a doctor is therefore, active euthanasia. A well-known example of active euthanasia was the death of a terminally ill Michigan patient on September 17, 1998. On that date, Dr. Jack Kevorkian videotaped himself administering a lethal medication to Thomas Youk, a 52-year-old Michigan man with amyotrophic lateral sclerosis. CBS broadcast the videotape on 60 Minutes less than a week later. Authorities subsequently charged Kevorkian with first-degree premeditated murder, criminal assistance of a suicide, and delivery of a controlled substance for administering lethal medication to a terminally ill man. There was no dispute that the dose was administered at the request of Mr. Youk, nor any dispute that Mr. Youk was terminally ill. A jury found Kevorkian guilty of second-degree murder in 1999. He was sent to prison.

4. Physician-assisted suicide

Somewhat of a hybrid between passive and active euthanasia is physician-assisted suicide (PAS), also known as voluntary passive euthanasia. In this situation, a physician supplies information and/or the means of committing suicide (*e.g.*, a prescription for lethal dose of sleeping pills, or a supply of carbon monoxide gas) to a person, so that that individual can successfully terminate his or her own life.

Physician-assisted suicide received greater public attention after Dr. Kevorkian, a retired pathologist from Michigan, participated in his first such procedure in 1990. Kevorkian set up a machine that allowed a 54-year-old woman suffering from Alzheimer's disease (a degenerative neurological condition) to press a button that delivered a lethal poison into her veins. Kevorkian went on to assist in the suicides of dozens of individuals suffering from terminal, debilitating, or chronic illnesses. In 1992, Michigan passed an assisted-suicide bill (Mich. Comp. Laws § 752.1021) that was specifically designed to stop Kevorkian's activities, but technicalities and questions as to its constitutionality delayed its implementation, thus allowing Kevorkian to continue assisting suicides — often in direct opposition to Court injunctions.

Kevorkian was charged with murder several times but was not initially found guilty. When murder charges were brought against him for his first three assisted suicides, for example, they were dismissed because Michigan, at that time, had no law against assisted suicide. In 1994, Kevorkian was tried and found not guilty of assisting in the August 1993 suicide of Thomas W. Hyde Jr. In December 1994, however, Michigan's Supreme Court ruled in *People* v *Kevorkian* 447 Mich. 436, 527 N.W. 2d 714, that there is no constitutional right to commit suicide, with or without assistance, and upheld the Michigan statute that made assisted suicide a crime. The following year, the U.S. Supreme Court refused to hear Kevorkian's appeal from the state Supreme Court's ruling.

Observers disagree about the humanity of Kevorkian's activities. Some see him as a hero who sought to give suffering people greater choice and dignity in dying. Others point to his lack of procedural precautions and fear that the widespread practice of assisted suicide will lead to the unnecessary death of people who could have been helped by other means, including treatment for depression. Many opponents of assisted suicide find the same faults in the practice that they see in other forms of euthanasia. They envision its leading to a devaluation of human life and even to a genocidal killing of vulnerable or so-called undesirable individuals.

The U.S. Supreme Court has made two important rulings on assisted suicide. In *Washington* v *Glucksberg* 521 U.S. 702, 117 S.Ct. 2258, 138 L.Ed.2d 772, 65 (1997), three terminally ill patients, four physicians, and a non-profit organization had brought action against the state of Washington for Declaratory Judgment, that a statute banning assisted suicide violated due process clause. On June 26, 1997, the Supreme Court unanimously upheld the right of states to prohibit assisted suicide, holding that: (1) asserted right to assistance in committing suicide was not a fundamental liberty interest protected by due process clause, and (2) Washington's ban on assisted suicide was rationally related to legitimate government interests. In *Vacco* v *Quill* 521 U.S. 793, 117 S.Ct. 2293, 138 L.Ed.2d 834 (1997), physicians challenged the constitutionality of New York statutes making it a crime to aid a person in committing suicide or attempting to commit suicide. The Supreme Court held that New York's prohibition on assisting suicide did not violate the equal protection clause of the Fourteenth Amendment.

5. Involuntary euthanasia

The term involuntary euthanasia is used to describe the killing of a person who has not explicitly requested aid in dying. This term is most often used with respect to patients who are in a persistent vegetative state and who probably will never recover consciousness.

6. Euthanasia considerations

Euthanasia is a divisive topic, and different interpretations of its meaning, practice, and morality abound. Those who favour active euthanasia and a patient's right to die do not acknowledge a distinction between active and passive euthanasia. They assert that the withdrawal of life-sustaining treatment cannot be distinguished in principle from affirmative steps to hasten a patient's death. In both situations, they argue, a person intends to cause the patient's death, acts out of compassionate motives, and causes the same outcome. In their view, turning off a life-sustaining respirator switch and giving a lethal injection are morally equivalent actions.

Opponents of active euthanasia argue that it undermines the value of, and respect for, all human life; erodes trust in physicians; desensitizes society to killing; and contradicts many people's religious beliefs. Moreover, they maintain that the intentions and natures of active and passive euthanasia are not essentially the same. In active euthanasia, a person directly intends to cause death and uses available means to achieve this end. In passive euthanasia, a person decides against using a certain form of treatment and then directs that such treatment be withdrawn or withheld, accepting but not intending the patient's death, which is caused by the underlying illness.

While people cite differing reasons for choosing to end their own lives, those suffering from a terminal illness typically state that a serious disorder or disease has adversely affected their quality of life to the point where they no longer wish to continue living. Under such circumstances, patients may have been diagnosed with a degenerative, progressive illness such as ALS, Huntington's disease, multiple sclerosis, AIDS or Alzheimer's disease. Patients with such illnesses often fear, with good reason, a gradual loss of the quality of life in the future as the disease or disorder progresses, or they might already have lost a good deal of their independence and thus might require continuous care. Some feel that this loss of autonomy causes an unacceptable loss of personal dignity. Others realize that they will be dying in the near future and simply want to have total control over the process. Some point out that in addition to physical considerations, they do not want to diminish their assets by incurring large medical costs as their death approaches. They feel that they ought to have the option to die sooner and to pass on their assets to their beneficiaries.

7. Euthanasia and physician-assisted suicide

Imagine that you are suffering from a disease that is terminal, debilitating, and very painful. Should you have the right to die when you wish rather than live in continued agony? Should your doctor be legally free to help you take your own life, perhaps by prescribing some pills and telling you their fatal dosage? Or should the law forbid anyone — including doctors — to assist in the suicide of another human being? These are just some of the questions that surround the issue of physician-assisted suicide, a widely debated ethical issue in modern medicine.

Physician-assisted suicide is a form of voluntary euthanasia. In other words, it involves a patient voluntarily acting to end his or her life. Physician-assisted suicide differs from conventional suicide in that it is facilitated by a physician who confirms the patient's diagnosis, rules out conditions such as depression that may be clouding the patient's judgment, and finally provides the means for committing suicide. Such action usually consists of taking a lethal overdose of prescription medication. However, over 130 patients who were assisted by Dr. Jack Kevorkian between 1990 and 1998 chose to press a button which delivered a lethal poison into their veins, or to put on a mask that emitted carbon monoxide into their lungs. Assisted suicide is a felony offense in most states and is also expressly forbidden in the American Medical Association's (AMA's) Code of Medical Ethics. In 1999, Kevorkian was found guilty of second-degree murder in an assisted suicide case. He was sentenced to serve 10 to 25 years.

The debate surrounding physician-assisted suicide in the United States has been influenced by medical practices in other countries, particularly the Netherlands, which legalized both active euthanasia and physician-assisted suicide, in April 2001 (effective 2002). Physician-assisted suicide in the Netherlands is conducted within strict guidelines that include the following requirements: the patient's request for assisted suicide must be voluntary, the patient must be experiencing intolerable suffering, all other alternatives for treatment must have been explored, and the physician must consult another independent physician before proceeding. A study commissioned by the Dutch government indicated that, in 2001, about 3,500 deaths, or 2.5 percent of the 140,000 death cases that were reported in the Netherlands that year, occurred by active euthanasia. The study, known as the Remmelink Report, defined euthanasia as the termination of life at the patient's request. Figures also indicated that 300 deaths, or 0.2 per cent, were caused by physician-assisted suicide.

In the United States, the debate on legalizing assisted suicide began in earnest in the 1970s. On one side of the debate have been Patients' Rights groups who have lobbied for what they call the right to die — or the right to choose to die, as some have clarified it — of terminally ill patients. The strongest opposition to the legalization of physician-assisted suicide has come from physicians' groups such as the AMA and from religious groups that are morally opposed to the practice.

One person who has done much to make the case for physician-assisted suicide is Derek Humphry, a former journalist who founded the Hemlock Society, in 1980, after seeing the pain and suffering his first wife experienced when she died from cancer. In 2003, the organization changed its name to End-of-Life Choices, which encompasses more clearly the issues supported by its members. With a new name and a new motto, "Dignity Compassion Control," the organization continues to advocate for the right of terminally ill people to choose voluntary euthanasia, or what Humphry has termed self-deliverance.

Humphry has written several books on the subject of voluntary euthanasia, including Jean's Way (1978), which recounts his struggle to assist his wife's death in 1975; Final Exit: The Practicalities of Self-Deliverance and Assisted Suicide for the Dying (1991), a controversial book that gives detailed advice on how terminally ill people may take their own life; and Lawful Exit: The Limits of Freedom for Help in Dying (1993), which contains Humphry's own recommendations for legislation that would legalize physician-assisted suicide and active voluntary euthanasia. In Humphry's words, the "right to choose to die" is "the ultimate civil liberty."

Humphry presents physician-assisted suicide as a merciful, dignified option for people whose illness has eroded their quality of life beyond the limits of tolerance. He also points out that what he calls beneficent euthanasia occurs every day in medical facilities as physicians make decisions regarding the end of life. Others, including some medical euthicists, go so far as to claim that a decision to withhold antibiotics, oxygen, or nutrition from a terminally ill patient is no less "active" a form of euthanasia than is administering a fatal dose of morphine. Indeed, they see the common practice of withholding life support as more open to potential abuse than the practice of physician-assisted suicide. The former, they argue, is a less visible, less easily regulated decision. Proponents of physician-assisted suicide also claim that diseases kill people in far more cruel ways than would any means of death that a physician might provide for an irreversibly ill patient. As a result, they see the action of assisting in suicide as entirely compatible with the physician's duty to the patient.

However, Humphry has been an open critic of Kevorkian's work. He has described Kevorkian's theory and practice of assisted suicide as open-ended euthanasia 'Nothing'.

Kevorkian's lack of precautionary measures such as the use of waiting periods and second opinions, Humphry sees any wider application of Kevorkian's methods as potentially leading to abuse and tragedy. "The thinking people in our movement are appalled by it," Humphry said. "If you have Kevorkian's type of euthanasia, it will be a slippery slope. Kevorkian's is a recipe for skiing down a glacier."

Detractors of physician-assisted suicide also use the familiar "slippery slope" argument, proposing that once physician-assisted suicide is legalized, other forms of euthanasia will more likely be practiced as well. They see assisted suicide as potentially leading to situations in which elderly, chronically ill, and handicapped people, along with others, are killed through active, nonvoluntary euthanasia. Related to this idea is the view that widespread practice of physician-assisted suicide might claim the lives of those whose intolerable suffering is caused by treatable depression. They point out that terminally ill people or others in pain are often also suffering from depression, and that despite their illness, their feelings of hopelessness can often be addressed through means such as counseling and anti-depressant medication.

The Catholic Church is one of many religious organizations that oppose euthanasia and assisted suicide. In Pope John Paul II's words, medical killings such as those caused by assisted suicide are "crimes which no human law can claim to legitimize." Basing its arguments on passages from the Bible, Catholic theology has for many centuries opposed all forms of suicide. Catholicism argues that innocent human life may not be destroyed for any reason whatsoever.

The debate over physician-assisted suicide eventually reached the Supreme Court. In 1994, an advocacy group known as Compassion in Dying filed two lawsuits (*Compassion in Dying et al* v *Washington* and *Quill et al* v *Vacco*) challenging the constitutionality of state laws banning assisted dying in Washington and New York. Compassion in Dying won in the District Court in Washington. Chief Judge Barbara Rothstein wrote, "There is no more profoundly personal decision, nor one which is closer to the heart of personal liberty, than the choice which a terminally ill person makes to end his or her suffering and hasten an inevitable death." In New York, Compassion in Dying lost and filed an appeal in the Second Circuit.

In 1995, Washington's Compassion ruling was overturned by the Ninth Circuit Court of Appeals, reinstating the anti-suicide law. In 1996, however, after reconsideration, the Ninth Circuit Court of Appeals issued a reversal decision in *Compassion* v *Washington*. That decision held that assisted dying was protected by liberty and privacy provisions of the U.S. Constitution. The majority wrote that, "Those who believe strongly that death must come without physician assistance are free to follow that creed, be they doctors or patients. They are not free, however, to force their views, their religious convictions, or their philosophies on all the other members of a democratic society, and to compel those whose values differ with theirs to die painful, protracted, and agonizing deaths."

In April 1996, the Second Circuit joined the Ninth in recognizing constitutional protection for assisted dying in the Quill case, holding that the New York statutes criminalizing assisted suicide violate the equal protection clause of the Fourteenth Amendment. However, on June 26, 1997, the U.S. Supreme Court reversed both the Ninth and *Second Circuit Court in Washington* v *Glucksberg* 521 U.S. 702, 117 S.Ct. 2258, 138 L.Ed.2d 772 (1997) and *Vacco* v *Quill* 521 U.S. 743, 117 S.Ct. 2293, 138 L.Ed.2d 834 (1997). The Court ruled that state laws against assisting a suicide are not unconstitutional, but also stated that patients have a right to aggressive treatment of pain and other symptoms, even if the treatment hastens death. The Court wrote, "Throughout the Nation, Americans are engaged in an earnest and profound debate about the morality, legality and practicality of physician assisted suicide. Our holding permits this debate to continue, as it should in a democratic society."

Ultimately then, the voters and representatives of the states and the legal system itself will have to decide whether or not physician-assisted suicide will be legalized. Regardless of what side prevails in the debate, the exchange of ideas that it creates may lead to a greater understanding of the difficult choices surrounding death in our time.

8. Death and dying; physicians and surgeons

Some patients who decide that they wish to commit suicide are unable or unwilling to accomplish the act without assistance from their physician. Physician-assisted suicide helps them to die under conditions, and at the time, that they wish. PAS is currently legal in the U.S., only in the state of Oregon, under severe restrictions. In other states, a terminally ill patient who wishes to die must continue living until their body eventually collapses, or until a family member or friend commits a criminal act by helping them to commit suicide.

9. Historical considerations

Traditional Christian beliefs concerning all forms of suicide were well documented by Thomas Aquinas during the thirteenth century. He condemned all suicide (whether assisted or not) on the theory that it violated one's natural desire to live. Among European writers, Michel de Montaigne was the first major dissenter on this issue. During the sixteenth century, he wrote a series of essays arguing that suicide should be a matter of personal choice, a human right. He concluded it to be a rational option under certain circumstances.

Attempting to commit suicide was once a criminal act. It has been decriminalized for many decades in most jurisdictions. However, assisted suicide remains a criminal act throughout the United States, with the exception of the state of Oregon. In that state, it is permitted under tightly controlled conditions.

10. Oregon's euthanasia law

In 1994, voters in the state of Oregon approved a ballot measure that would have legalized euthanasia under limited conditions. Under the Death With Dignity law, a person who sought physician-assisted suicide would have to meet certain criteria:

- The person must be terminally ill.
- The person must have six months or less to live.
- The person must make two oral requests for assistance in dying.
- The person must make one written request for assistance in dying.
- The person must convince two physicians that he or she is sincere and not acting on a whim and that the decision is voluntary.
- The person must not have been influenced by depression.
- The person must be informed of "the feasible alternatives," including, but not limited to, comfort care, hospice care and pain control.
- The person must wait for 15 days.

Under the proposed law, a person who met all requirements could receive a prescription of a barbiturate that would be sufficient to cause death. Physicians would be prohibited from inducing death by injection or carbon monoxide.

The National Right to Life Committee, supported by the Roman Catholic Church, obtained a Court Injunction to delay implementation of the measure. The law stalled in the appeals process. In the meantime, the measure was not enacted. In 1997, there was a second public Referendum, and the law was enacted. Within 24 hours of the announcement of the results, state officials had forms for physicians to record instances of assisted suicide. These were later distributed to physicians in the state. The form is entitled "Request for Medication to End My Life in a Humane and Dignified Manner."

Immediately after the law was affirmed, Thomas Constantine, the administrator of the Federal Drug Enforcement Administration (DEA), wrote a policy statement which said that prescribing drugs to help terminally ill patients kill themselves would be a violation of the Controlled Substances Act. Nevertheless, on March 26, 1998, a woman in her mid-eighties died from a lethal dose of barbiturates, which had been prescribed by her doctor under the Oregon law. She was the first person to publicly use the law to commit suicide. She had been fighting breast cancer for 20 years and recently had been told by her doctor that she had less than two months to live. She had been experiencing increased difficulty breathing. She made a tape recording in which she stated, "I'm looking forward to it. I will be relieved of all the stress I have." Her personal doctor would not help her end her life, so she turned to an advocacy group, Compassion in Dying. That group located a doctor to assist her. She fell into a deep sleep about five minutes after taking the lethal dose of pills, and she died peacefully about 25 minutes later. Attorney General Janet Reno officially reversed Constantine's ruling a few weeks later, stating that doctors who use the law to prescribe lethal drugs to terminally ill patients will not be prosecuted and that drug laws were intended to block illegal trafficking in drugs, not to cover situations like the Oregon suicide law.

Despite significant controversy, by the end of 1998, one prediction of the anti-choice forces had not materialized: there was no rush of people to Oregon to seek an easy end to life. While it was predicted that many would take advantage of the law, of the 23 terminally ill individuals who applied to end their own lives in 1998, 15 committed suicide, usually within a day of receiving the prescription. Six died from their illnesses without using the medication. Two remained alive at the end of 1998. From 1998 to 2002, 129 people have opted for physician-assisted suicide.

In early 2001, Oregon State Senator Ron Wyden wrote Attorney General John Ashcroft asking that the George W. Bush administration not mount an attack on the state law permitting assistance in suicide. Ashcroft wrote a letter to Asa Hutchinson, Chief of the Drug Enforcement Administration. He declared that assisting a terminally ill patient to commit suicide is not a "legitimate medical purpose" for federally controlled drugs. He said that physicians who use drugs to help patients die face suspension or revocation of their licenses to prescribe federally controlled drugs. This was contrary to the position taken by Janet Reno, his predecessor. The attorney general of Oregon, Hardy Myers, quickly initiated a lawsuit to have the Ashcroft's directive declared unconstitutional. The Federal District Court in Oregon issued a temporary injunction, which prevents the federal government from enforcing Ashcroft's interpretation of the Controlled Substances Act, (CSA). The state of Oregon requested that the Court block the federal department of justice from taking legal action against Oregon doctors who prescribe medication to help their patients commit suicide. A federal judge ruled in favour of the state law in 2002, and the Department of Justice appealed the decision to the U.S. Court of Appeals for the Ninth Circuit. Both sides have stated that they will appeal the decision if they lose.

11. Other countries

According to the online website, Euthanasia.com, 35 states have legislated against assisted suicide, while nine other states have cited it as a crime under Common Law. Still more states have introduced or passed statutes criminalizing assisted suicide. These statutes forbid a person to knowingly assist or aid another in committing suicide. Some also prohibit soliciting, advising, or encouraging another to commit suicide. Some statutes penalize assisted suicide under guidelines established for murder or manslaughter, whereas others make it a unique offense with separate penalties. Few Courts have interpreted the assisted-suicide statutes, because prosecutions for assisted suicide are rare. In cases of assisted suicide, a state usually prosecutes individuals for murder or manslaughter. The Ohio state Supreme Court, however, ruled in 1996 that assisted suicide is not a crime.

12. Euthanasia in India

Dr. A.K. Tharien, President of the Indian Academy of Social Sciences in Medicine Christian Fellowship Hospital Oddanchatram, Tamil Nadu, who founded and built up this hospital in rural Tamil Nadu 40 years ago, after returning from European medical training has his views regarding euthanasia as follows:

"Medical science and technology have made great strides in recent years. The medical profession has today more power over life and death than they would chosen to have. They have power to prolong life where life seems to have lost its meaning and have power to terminate life without suffering. There are many points of view on euthanasia; legal, social and compassionate.

The debate on Euthanasia has again become a live issue in India as the Supreme Court of India in 1994 passed a verdict that attempted suicide is not a crime. According to the Indian Penal Code, which was mainly adopted from British Penal Code, attempted suicide was a crime, punishable with years of imprisonment. With the recent medical knowledge gained by researchers and the opinions expressed by eminent psychiatrists all over the world, the judges in their verdict were sympathetic to those who attempted suicide. The Supreme Court of India is the highest Court, authorised to interpret the Constitution of India for legal matters. They gave the verdict that attempting suicide is a mental derangement and hence not to be considered as a crime. This signifies social approval of suicide and euthanasia which is assisted suicide.

13. What is euthanasia?

Euthanasia is the deliberate bringing about a gentle and easy death, making the last days of the patient as comfortable as possible. This is to ensure a calm and peaceful death, within the context of relieving incurable suffering in terminal illness or disability. Euthanasia is voluntary, when requested by the sufferer; involuntary or compulsory if it is against the will of the patient; and passive when death is hastened by deliberate withdrawal of effective therapy or nourishment.

14. The dilemma

While I was working in England, I was resuscitating an elderly lady who was admitted in the hospital emergency ward with severe demonstrable cerebral damage. My chief of surgery an Englishman and devout Christian told me gently, "I don't want to interfere with your procedures but if it were my mother I wouldn't do all that you are doing and would allow her to die peacefully". This is often our dilemma. Should one prolong the act of dying in a case of irreversible death or when life is effectively over? One of the achievements of modern medical technology is the use of artificial life support systems like artificial feeding, dialysis, controlled respiration, pump circulation, etc. In some cases it can be so dehumanising, painful, hazardous or costly that other considerations outweigh the aim to conserve life. Euthanasia supporters raise the question, how long to sustain life? A patient might say "I do not want a vegetative existence by drips, drugs and dialysis. I want to die with dignity. I have a right to lay down my life just as I have a right to live".

In the well known Dr. Arthur trial, where Dr. Arthur in U.K. had prescribed an overdose of codeine to a baby, born with Down syndrome with the object of hastening his death, Dr. Arthur was charged with murder. Many eminent witnesses were called to the trial. Most of them justified the procedure. Finally the Court acquitted Dr. Arthur as his motive was compassion. There is an argument that if a foetus is found to be abnormal and severely handicapped it should be sought out and eliminated before birth as such children are socially valueless. Do not the physically handicapped and mentally retarded have as much right to life like others and deserve to get the needed care?

15. Death and dying

The concept of death in the light of new knowledge, is changing. It may be obtained by redefining life. Descriptions of life are organised at many different levels of complexity like molecular, cellular, organ, system, corporal, mental spiritual, etc. Human life may be described as the ability, actual or potential to respond to others, or to be self-aware. This is based on cerebral function. Silverman and others in 1969 have established this by extensive studies and confirming it by encephalogram findings. Once cerebral death is confirmed there is no chance for survival though heart and lung functions continue. So it would be quite unnecessary to continue supportive measures after cerebral death.

16. The Christian concept

According to religious concept Almighty God has created man in his image. He is the giver and sustainer of life. He alone has the right to withdraw life. Life is not a right but a gift of God belonging to God and at all times in His hand. So we have no right to take away deliberately a human life, even one's own.

Euthanasia requests may come out of depression and confusion or out of a feeling of worthlessness, or due to persuasion of interested parties with ulterior motives. Respect for the person of the patient and concern for the family should lead us to use our resources as best as we can to promote life. The essence of our approach to a dying patient is to give ourselves in loving care to meet his need. A patient is not merely a biological unit but a person before God with social and family connections.

17. Suffering

Suffering can sometimes be redemptive and purposeful. It is as much as God's opportunity as health and an opportunity for a creative outcome or a witness or an amendment of life.

Let me share with you the experience of two of my friends who faced the issue of caring for children with disability. One was a hospital Chaplain. When a child with disability was born to him, he asked God why this happened to him, but he could not get an immediate answer. He loved that child but the child could not adequately respond to his love in the normal way. This helped the pastor to realize how God loves us in spite of us not being responsive to His love. The other was a colleague of mine and a highly qualified paediatrician. When a child with disability was born to him and his doctor wife, they did their very best to sustain her life. The child became critically ill immediately after birth, needing exchange blood transfusions. Though their colleagues questioned the wisdom of taking such an extreme step for such a child, they chose to have the exchange transfusions. The child recovered and subsequently brought a new purpose to their life before she finally died at 4 months of age. Through this the parents realised that God had a purpose in bringing her to their home. This experience was an act of God to make them aware of the need of caring for many neglected children with disability in our society. So they resigned from their busy clinical work and offered their lives to start a centre for children with mental handicap and special needs. An apparent traumatic experience became the rallying point for a new mission for compassion.

18. Our guiding principle

Ever since the time of Hippocrates in the fifth century B.C. the medical profession has been guided by the concept of the worth of each individual human life, which was recently reaffirmed by the Geneva Code in 1948, which states, "I will show the utmost respect for human life from the time of conception". "Suffering is evil, and we should take every step to mitigate or relieve it." In the extreme, Hitler had a utilitarian philosophy of life. Any person who had a utilitarian value, he preserved, and others he eliminated. But we respect the unique value of human life. Scriptures says man is made in the image of God. This gives human life, a unique dignity and value. Life should be cherished, supported and cared.

19. Some practical suggestions

1. Doctors should serve and care for their patients in love.
2. Deliberate attempt to end or shorten life, whether by omission or commission is unethical in my personal view and should be restrained.
3. Our society's leaders should proclaim the way of righteousness and truth, against taking innocent lives, and provide compassionate care.

4. Education of medical personnel and people with moral and spiritual values should be done, which may lead to sound legislation.
5. Bring in the principle of love as the motive and mainspring.

Views and ideas and even concepts of ethics are fast changing in the context of the progress of science and technology. The traditional institutions in our society, which protect human life and spiritual values are gradually being pushed aside or getting eliminated. Love is the foundation of ethics. Loving our God with all our heart, soul and mind and loving our neighbour as ourselves, and the two foundations for our ethical practice. Only a code of ethics based on sound principles, can lead our society to lasting happiness, harmony and peace."

20. Should euthanasia be legalized in India?

Euthanasia or mercy killing or Physician Assisted Suicide (PAS) is the bringing about of the gentle death of a patient in the case of a painful, chronic and incurable disease. Now, all these adjectives are of equal importance. A painful disease is one in which the patient suffers unbearable and excruciating pain. A chronic disease is a long lasting one and an incurable disease is one whose cure has not been found till date.

Netherlands was one of the first countries to legalize euthanasia followed by Canada, state of Oregon in USA and Columbia. The state of Oregon has a 'Death with Dignity' law, which has been in place for almost 10 years. It has allowed terminally ill patients to take legal, proscribed medication to end their suffering. The legalizing of euthanasia has been a bone of contention throughout the world and will continue to do so but no one asks a terminally ill patient the kind of pain he goes through. The individual should have at least the right to choose a graceful death for himself. Why should he be allowed to keep suffering day and night?

The essence of human life is to be able to live a dignified life but when some law forces you to live in intense pain and humiliation, there is something wrong with our society. Who are we to prolong the life of one who is suffering and has decided without any undue pressure that he would like to be put to rest? Obviously, legalization of euthanasia should not include anyone wanting to end their life at the flimsiest of excuses but a patient should be allowed to decide when he has suffered enough.

Apart from the miserable pain, that the patient goes through, the trauma and the emotional turmoil his relatives go through is also immense. To see your close ones suffering and going through pain is not an easy sight. You wish the laws should be changed. After all as an individual, you decide where to marry; you decide where to work, and at the last hurdle of your life, you should be allowed to choose how you want to end your life.

But this question cannot be answered so easily. The science of medicine has over the years seen miracles taking place. As long as the patient lives, there is hope. And as long as there is hope, anything can happen. With the new technological advancements taking place all around the globe, we could have cures for diseases like AIDS, cancer, etc.

On the other hand, the chances of the legalization being misused are also very high. What if the patient is in coma and is unable to make a decision, should the relatives be allowed to make it? This is the era of family disputes over property and money. People could also get away with cold-blooded murder. Legalising voluntary Euthanasia would lead to involuntary euthanasia. In this society, full of greed and corruption anything is possible.

In a country like ours, the religious aspects also have to be considered before taking such decisions. The Bible says, "Thou shalt not kill" And even Islam does not allow anyone to take away life. Is our society mature enough to understand the implications of this? We have cases, where doctors are often beaten up if the patient was not treated properly, what would happen to a doctor if he merely suggested Euthanasia to the relatives? Will the relatives be able to understand the suffering of the patient?

Life is a gift, and even a life of pain is a life at least. Some people feel we don't choose when to be born and we should not be given the right to choose when to die. On the contrary, others feel that a life of pain is not a life but an imposition and we should be at least allowed to end it in a dignified peaceful manner. Euthanasia could be legalized, but the laws would have to be very stringent. Every case will have to be carefully monitored taking into consideration the point of views of the patient, the relatives and the doctors. But whether Indian society is mature enough to face this, after all it's a matter of life and death, is yet to be seen.

21. Right to die "To be or not to be?"

In the advent of delving into what has unfurled into one of the most controversial issues that could have tremendous ramifications on basic ethical concepts and most importantly, the sanctity of life.... The precious words of Thomas Jefferson strike a chord.

> "The care of human life and happiness and not their destruction is the first and only legitimate object of good governance."

In juxtaposition, the words "Right to Die" evoke an exactly opposite sentiment. How can it be a right if you are using it to give up your rights? The above right has been used as a guise or a camouflage to include various concepts that are opposed to preservation of life. Euthanasia, Physician-Assisted Suicide (PAS), Suicide, though conceptually different, are species of the same genre.

22. The Indian perspective

In India, the sanctity of life has been placed on the highest pedestal. " The right to life" under Article 21 of the Constitution has received the widest possible interpretation under the able hands of the judiciary and rightly so. This right is inalienable and is inherent in us. It cannot and is not conferred upon us. This vital point seems to elude all those who keep on clamoring for the "Right to Die".

The stance taken by the judiciary in this regard is unquestionable.

In *Gian Kaur* v *State of Punjab*, a five judge Constitutional Bench held that the "right to life" is inherently inconsistent with the "right to die" as is "death" with "life". In furtherance, the right to life, which includes right to live with human dignity, would mean the existence of such a right up to the natural end of life. It may further include "death with dignity" but such existence should not be confused with unnatural extinction of life curtailing natural span of life. In progression of the above, the constitutionality of section 309 of the IPC, which makes "attempt to suicide" an offence, was upheld, overruling the judgment in *P. Rathinam's* case.

The factor of immense significance to be noted here is that suicide, euthanasia, mercy killing and the like amount to unnatural ebbing of life. This decision thereby overruling *P. Rathinam's* case establishes that the "Right to life" not only precludes the "right to die" but also the "right to kill."

Interestingly in *P. Rathinam's* case, even when a Division bench affirmed the view in *M.S. Dubal* v *State of Maharashtra* that the "right to life" provided by the Constitution may be said to bring into its purview, the right not to live a forced life, the plea that euthanasia be legalized was discarded. It was held that as euthanasia involves the intervention of a third person, it would indirectly amount to a person aiding or abetting the killing of another, which would be inviting section 306 of the IPC.

In *Naresh Marotrao Sakhre* v *Union of India,* Lodha J. affirmed that "Euthanasia or mercy killing is nothing but homicide whatever the circumstances in which it is effected." (Emphasis added).

The above inferences lead to one irresistible conclusion i.e. any form that involves unnatural termination of life, whether an attempt to suicide, abetment to suicide/assisted suicide or euthanasia, is illegal. The fact that even an attempt to suicide is punishable goes to show the extent of credibility accorded to the sanctity of life and the right to life as a whole. This apart, the decriminalization of euthanasia is unworkable in the Indian perspective, even on humanitarian grounds, as it involves a third person.

Though, there has been no legislation pertaining to euthanasia in India, the term keeps on coming back for public approval like a recurring decimal.

23. An impracticable solution

The implication of the term "euthanasia" is itself shrouded in ambiguity. It is derived from the Greek word "Euthanatos" meaning "good death". To reiterate the judicial pronouncements in the Indian context, good or happy death would imply the ebbing of life the natural way.

In its earlier form, it was used as an omnibus term to signify a painless death. In its modern context, the term is used a deliberate euphemism to reduce the culpability of an act". An act which is a subset of murder by injecting the term "mercy". The fact remains" Euthanasia/Mercy killing is about giving license for the right to kill.

Euthanasia is defined as an "intentional killing by an act/omission of person whose life is felt is not to be worth living." The above attribution consequentially includes just about any one who has a suicidal impulse. Moreover the term "person" is inclusive of any and everybody and is not solely restricted to "patients." The legalization of the above would result in nothing but pandemonium.

There have been views propagating the practice of passive euthanasia (letting some one die) to be morally permissible and active euthanasia (killing someone), morally impermissible. It is submitted that these distinctions are irrelevant and unnecessary as of both acts inevitably center around a single element — an intention to kill.

The above premise has been aptly summed up by Professor James Rachels who believes.... The active and passive dichotomy is a distinction without a difference.

Proponents and "Right to die" groups argue that, a patient in unbearable agony and excruciating pain or "terminally ill", the saving- grace is euthanasia on compassionate grounds.

It is submitted that the problem here is" the term "terminally ill" has no precise definition. For instance, Jack Kervorkian, a famous proponent of euthanasia, defined "terminal illness" as "any disease that curtails life even for a day". Some laws define "terminal" as one from which death will occur in a "relatively short time" or "within a span of six months".

The nub of the point is that all these definitions scream ambiguity and medical experts have acknowledged that it is virtually impossible to predict the life expectancy of a particular individual.

Interestingly, euthanasia activists have dropped references to terminal illness, replacing them with such phrases as "gentle landing", "hopelessly ill'" "desperately ill" and "meaningless life."

It is reinforced that this issue hovers around an invaluable asset called "life". Just as a mistaken diagnosis is possible, so is a mistaken prognosis. It must be remembered that death is final and a chance of error too great to approve the practice of euthanasia.

24. Technology has come of age

On the flip side of the coin, an undeniable transition is evidenced in the augmentation of medicine and technology. What was excessive in medicine fifty years ago may be ordinary and routine today. The idea here is that what is excessively burdensome and offers little hope for one may be less burdensome and more hopeful for a second patient in a different state of health.

A startling revelation...... Research has shown that ninety-percent of the pain can be alleviated by proper pain control methods. Appropriate care can make a huge difference. This goes to show that medicine and technological break throughs have a fitting reply to almost every problem and the extent of medical commitment is unassailable.

In contradistinction, if every terminal patient were prodded to a "gentle landing", impetus to research, which is the answer to curative medicine, would be foiled. If legalized, doctors would be forced to perform such acts against their consent that would amount to a violation of the Hippocratic Oath. Incidentally, it was as early as 400 B.C., when the renowned Greek physician stipulated in his Oath........" I will give no deadly medicine to anyone if asked, nor suggest any such course."

The fact remains that the practice of euthanasia has been ostracized since time immemorial and Oregon, Belgium and The Netherlands are the only jurisdictions in the world where laws specifically permit euthanasia or assisted suicide.

It may be pertinent to mention that the most vital point is the repercussions that could take place once something as controversial is legalized. The matter is not an issue of force but an issue of the way laws can be expanded once something is declared legal. In India, where abuse of the law is the rule rather than the exception and where conniving relatives clamor to lap up an heirloom, the abovementioned argument holds great weightage.

To elucidate, in England, the House of Lords in *Airedale NHS Trust* v *Bland* permitted non-voluntary euthanasia in case of patients in a persistent vegetative state. Subsequently, the Supreme Court of Ireland in *Re a Ward of Court* expanded the persistent vegetative state to include cases where the patient possessed limited cognitive faculties.

In Netherlands, the Supreme Court in a 1984 ruling held that euthanasia could be lawful only in cases of physical illness. However, a decade down the line, the Supreme Court in *Chabot's* case held that it could even extend to cases of mental illness.

Thus, there is evidenced a conceptual degradation of the right to live with dignity.

The sole qualitative argument in favour of euthanasia, is the fact that if procedures are stringent and foolproof and with proper mechanisms in place, then the legalization of the same could be effected in India. For instance, in The Netherlands the request for euthanasia should come only from the patient and be free, voluntary and persistent; it should be the last resort and should be performed by a physician in consultation with an independent physician colleague who has experience in the field.

25. Poles apart

It is humbly submitted that the implementation of the above mechanism in India is utopian and thus the two situations incomparable. It is ironical to note that ninety per cent of the patients succumb to death without receiving any primary health care. Thus the logical derivation of this aspect would be that India does not have an appropriate health-care mechanism in place, let alone foolproof procedures for euthanasia.

In the presence of the above bottlenecks and policing rampant in our country, the appropriate course of action would be to develop proper "care ethics", ensuring a "dignified existence and termination" of life. Let us augment the above and resultantly, the concept of euthanasia will be nothing but a distant reality.

Aruna Shanbaug, a former nurse, has been brain dead and paralysed for the last 36 years after she was raped in November 1973 in Bombay. Writer and her well wisher Pinki Virani, has approached the Supreme Court of India seeking respite for her and has appealed that Aruna be allowed to die.

According to Experts, when a person carries out an act of euthanasia, he brings about the death of another person because he believes the latter's present existence is so bad that she would be better off dead, or believes that unless he intervenes and ends her life, it will become so bad that she would be better off dead. To deny people the choice of death by active euthanasia is to force them to do something that is against their will and may well prolong their suffering, and therefore lose human dignity and decency. These are the arguments about euthanasia.

Those against euthanasia claim that patients are often too affected by their illness to make adequate decisions about their future. The New Jersey Supreme Court (USA) rules in 1976 that 21 year old Karen Quinlan can be detached from her respirator. According to experts, the *Quinlan* case becomes a legal landmark, drawing national and international attention to end-of-life issues. In 2004,K. Venkatesh died in a hospital in India. He was severely ill with muscular distrophy, and had requested an assisted suicide. He was denied, but he died from his disease. In April 2002, the Dutch Parliament legalised it making the Netherlands the only country in the world to legalise Euthanasia.

Dr. Jack Kevorkian who claimed that he had helped more than 130 people die since 1990. He was known as Dr. Death. In April 1999, he was awarded 10-25 year prison sentence for murder under the law of State of Michigan (USA). In 2001 the Patna High Court in India dismissed Tarakeshwar Chandravanshi's plea seeking mercy killing for his 25-year-old wife Kanchan, who had been suffering for over a year. In the same year, the Kerala High Court rejected the plea of BK Pillai, who had an uncurable illness, to die.

26. Euthanasia and Law

A two judge bench of Supreme Court held that a person has a right not to live a forced life and attempt to suicide is not illegal (*Dr. Pinnamenani Narsimha Rao* v *Gundavarapu Jayaprakasu* AIR 1990 AP 207). But this view has been overruled by a Constitutional Bench of the Supreme Court (*Smt Gian Kaur* v *State* AIR 1996 SC 946). The result is that sections 306 and 309 of the Penal Code which respectively make attempt to suicide and abetment to suicide punishable offences remain constitutionally valid. It is thus now clear that a doctor would be liable for abetting, suicide under section 306 of IPC, if he by taking positive steps, e.g. by administration of drugs, although with the consent of the patient, ends the patients life. To permit euthanasia is a matter of policy within the domain of the legislature.

Court held in the case of *Gian Kaur* that Article 21 speaks of right to life. However the supporters of euthanasia emphasize that when a person suffering with a terminal disease can't even take care of himself, then how can we think for him a dignified life. In that case it will be better if he is allowed to end his life as Article 21 speaks for a dignified life. But the Court made it clear that according to Article 21, a person has a right to live a dignified life which also includes right to die with dignity. But here right to die means dying a natural death. Therefore, Article 21 nowhere mentions about right to die an unnatural death. Curtailing the natural span of life of a person who has a certain end to life cannot in any case be read into Article 21. If a person is terminally ill, it doesn't mean he himself or anyone else can end his life. It will surely be a violation of the 'sanctity of life'. Living a dignified life doesn't at all mean that a person can end his life unnaturally. Our Constitution nowhere provides for it. Thus, right to life does not include right to die. If a person's life is being ended unnaturally it will surely be a violation of human right. By virtue of being a human being a person has right to live a life as he wishes to. But that doesn't allow him to end his life as and when he wants. This life is given to him by God and thus, it should be ended at its natural span.

There is always prevailing the rival claims of the society and the individual and the question lies that which claim should prevail. Mostly in the cases of health concerns, the claims of the society prevail over the individual claim. But it has to be kept in mind while deciding that which side should the balance bend that how will this decision affect the society and the individual. In most of the health concerns, the whole society gets affected, but here individual himself and affected family are getting more influenced by such a decision. Individual liberty is the hallmark of any free society. Thus, we should here consider the rights which accrue to the individual in such cases.

In India, euthanasia is absolutely illegal. If a doctor tries to kill a patient, the case will surely fall under section 300 of Indian Penal Code, 1860. But this is only so in the case of voluntary euthanasia in which such cases will fall under the exception 5 to section 300 of Indian Penal Code, 1860 and thus the doctor will be held liable under section 304 of Indian Penal Code, 1860 for culpable homicide not amounting to murder. Cases of non-voluntary and involuntary euthanasia would be struck by proviso one to section 92 of the IPC and thus be rendered illegal. There has also been a confusion regarding the difference between suicide and euthanasia. It has been clearly differentiated in the case *Naresh Marotrao Sakhre* v *Union of India,* J. Lodha clearly said in this case. "Suicide by its very nature is an act of self-killing or self-destruction, an act of terminating one's own act and without the aid or assistance of any other human agency. Euthanasia or mercy killing on the other hand means and implies the intervention of other human agency to end the life. Mercy killing thus is not suicide and an attempt at mercy killing is not covered by the provisions of section 309. The two concepts are both factually and legally distinct. Euthanasia or mercy killing is nothing but homicide whatever the circumstances in which it is effected."

The question whether Article 21 includes right to die or not first came into consideration in the case *State of Maharashtra* v *Maruti Shripathi Dubal*. It was held in this case by the Bombay High Court that 'right to life' also includes 'right to die' and Section 309 was struck down. The Court clearly said in this case that right to die is not unnatural; it is just uncommon and abnormal. Also the Court mentioned about many instances in which a person may want to end his life. This was upheld by the Supreme Court in the case *P. Rathinam* v *Union of India*. However in the case *Gian Kaur* v *State of Punjab*, it was held by the five judge bench of the Supreme Court that the "right to life" guaranteed by Article 21 of the Constitution does not include the "right to die". The Court clearly mentioned in this case that Article 21 only guarantees right to life and personal liberty and in no case can the right to die be included in it.

27. Debate regarding euthanasia

27.1 'In favour'

Euthanasia means killing a person rather ending the life a person who is suffering from some terminal illness which is making his life painful as well as miserable or in other words ending a life which is not worth living. But the problem lies that how should one decide whether the life is anymore worth living or not. Thus, the term euthanasia is rather too ambiguous. This has been a topic for debate since a long time i.e. whether euthanasia should be allowed or not. In the present time, the debate is mainly regarding active euthanasia rather than passive euthanasia. The dispute is regarding the conflicts of interests: the interest of the society and that of the individual. Which out of these should prevail over the other? According to the supporters of euthanasia the decision of the patients should be accepted. If on the other hand we weigh the social values with the individual interest then we will clearly see that here the interest of the individual will outweigh the interest of the society. The society aims at interest of the individuals rather it is made with the purpose of assuring a dignified and a peaceful life to all. Now if the individual who is under unbearable pain is not able to decide for himself then it surely will hamper his interest. In that case it will surely be a negation of his dignity and human rights. Regarding this debate from legal point of view, Article 21 clearly provides for living with dignity. A person has a right to live a life with at least minimum dignity and if that standard is falling below that minimum level then a person should be given a right to end his life. Supporters of euthanasia also point out to the fact that as passive euthanasia has been allowed, similarly active euthanasia must also be allowed. A patient will wish to end his life only in cases of excessive agony and would prefer to die a painless death rather than living a miserable life with that agony and suffering. Thus, from a moral point of view it will be better to allow the patient die painlessly when in any case he knows that he is going to die because of that terminal illness. So the question arises why to let increase that period of pain for him when in any case he is going to die. Another important point on which the supporters of euthanasia emphasize is that a lot of medical facilities which amount a lot are being spent on these patients which are in any case going to die.

Thus, they argue that rather than spending those on such patients, it will be much better to use such facilities for those who have even fair chances of recovery. Thus, again the question lies that whom do we want to save using these medical facilities; those who are in any case going to die today or tomorrow or those who have fair chances of recovery. A point which is often raised against the supporters of euthanasia is that if such right will be granted to the terminally patients then there will be chances of abuse of it. But the supporters argue that every right involves a risk of being abused but that doesn't mean that the right itself should be denied to the people. We should rather look at the brighter side of it than thinking of it being abused.

27.2 'Against'

There is an intense opposition from the religious groups and people from the legal and medical profession. According to them it's not granting 'right to die' rather it should be called 'right to kill'. According to them it is totally against the medical ethics. Medical ethics call for nursing, care giving and healing and not ending the life of the patient. In the present time, medical science is advancing at a great pace. Thus even the most incurable diseases are becoming curable today. Thus instead of encouraging a patient to end his life, the medical practitioners should encourage the patients to lead their painful life with strength which should be moral as well as physical. The decision to ask for euthanasia is not made solely by the patient. Even the relatives of the patient pay an important role in doing that. Thus, it is probable that the patient comes under pressure and takes such a drastic step of ending his life. Of course in such cases the pressure is not physical, it is rather moral and psychological which proves to be much stronger. Also added to that is the economical pressure. The patient starts feeling him to be a burden on the relatives when they take such a decision for him and finally he also succumbs to it. Opponents also point out that when suicide is not allowed then euthanasia should also not be allowed. A person commits suicide when he goes into a state of depression and has no hope from the life. Similar is the situation when a person asks for euthanasia. But according to the opponents, such tendency can be lessened by proper care of such patients and showing hope in them. Another argument of the opponents is regarding the slippery slope. According to this argument, if voluntary euthanasia will be allowed, then surely it will lead to consequently allowing involuntary and non-voluntary euthanasia also. Also, as has been pointed out earlier, euthanasia in itself is an ambiguous term. The term 'terminally ill' has nowhere been properly defined. Thus even the medical fraternity is not clear as to who are the terminally ill patients, leave aside the legal practitioners. Thus, opponents strongly argue that euthanasia should be allowed only in rarest of the rare cases. If this is not done then surely it will lead to its abuse.

If we carefully examine the opposition to the legalization of euthanasia, we can conclude that the most important point that the opponents raise is that it will lead to its misuse by the doctors. Thus, it is humbly submitted that when a patient or his relatives can willingly put his life in the hands of the doctor trusting him, then why can't a doctor be given such discretion to decide what will be in favour of his patient. Another doubt that is often raised is that if the doctors will be given discretion to practice voluntary euthanasia then surely it will gradually lead to asking for involuntary or non-voluntary euthanasia. But it is humbly submitted that a separate legislation should be made allowing only voluntary euthanasia and not involuntary or non-voluntary euthanasia. As has already been pointed out earlier, we also have to keep in mind the limited medical facilities available in India and the number of patients. This question still lies open that who should be provided with those facilities; a terminally ill patient or to the patient who has fair chances of recovery. As the patient himself out of his pain and agony is asking for death, doctor should not increasing that pain of his should allow euthanasia. It has been ruled in the *Gian Kaur* case that Article 21 does not include right to die by the Supreme Court. But one may try to read it as is evident in the rights of privacy, autonomy and self-determination, which is what has been done by the Courts of United State and England. Thus, we can see that as the said right has been included in the ambit of Article 21, so this can also be included in Article 21. This question was not raised in the case earlier. Again the point that remains unanswered is regarding the abuse of this right by the doctors. But relevant safeguards can be put on this right and thus its abuse can be avoided. One of the safeguards can be that a proper quasi-judicial authority having a proper knowledge in the medical field can be appointed to look into the request of the patient and the steps taken by the doctor. To make it more foolproof some two or three assistant officials including one from the legal field can also be appointed. This will avoid any abuse of this right granted to the terminally ill patients. Here, we have to regard the painful situation in which the patient is and top priority should be lessening his pain. Now when we already know that he is anyway going to die today or tomorrow and he himself is asking for death, there is no point that he should be denied with this right of at least leading a life with minimum dignity and willingly. Otherwise his life will be no better in that situation. Thus, considering the financial and medical facilities also, the question still lies open that what will be better-allowing euthanasia or not allowing euthanasia.

India split over euthanasia in a case involving a woman in coma for the past 36 years by Nirmala Carvalho.

The case of Aruna Shanbhag, 59, sparks a heated debate across India. For writer Pinki Virani, stop feeding and giving the patient water would be a humanitarian act, not euthanasia. India's Supreme Court says, "Under the law of the country, we cannot allow a person to die." For Mgr Dabre, a "culture of death" is increasingly taking hold in India.

A request to stop giving food and water to a 59-year-old coma patient is generating a heated debate across India. The woman, Aruna Shanbhag, was a nurse at the King Edward Memorial Hospital (KEM) in Mumbai when she was raped in 1973. As a result of the traumatic event, she went into a coma, without relatives to care for her. In a permanent vegetative state for the past 36 years in the same hospital where she worked, she has been cared for and fed by hospital nurses.

An attorney, Shekhar Nafde, has petitioned the Court on behalf of writer Pinki Virani, who wrote about Aruna Shanbhag, to allow Aruna to die. Nafde explained that the request could not be construed as a plea for euthanasia. "This is no human right," he said. "Her life is worse than animal existence."

Euthanasia is illegal in India but the *Aruna Shanbhag's* case and Pinki Virani's request are causing a stir in the country.

Public opinion is divided between those who say that withdrawing food does not constitute euthanasia and those who believe that it would set a dangerous precedent and could lead euthanasia being treated as a humanitarian act.

In responding to the petition, the Supreme Court issued a notice, saying, "Under the law of the country, we cannot allow a person to die."

Mgr Thomas Dabre, bishop of Pune and president of the Bishops' Commission on Doctrine, welcome the Court's statement recognising that the dignity of human life is not determined by a person's physical condition.

Speaking to Asia News, the prelate did not hide his real concern about the case raised by Virani, because there are "dangerous trends in [Indian] society".

For the bishop of Pune, support for euthanasia contradicts "Indian Scriptures and Indian traditions, [which] have for centuries propagated the values of life and [...] stood for [its] preservation".

For Mgr Dabre, the fight for the right to die shows that man today "considers suffering as evil." For him, "It is most unfortunate that medical and technological advances are used to end life."

More importantly, "It is specious to argue that ending [Aruna Shanbhag's] life, when persons are in such a state, is a manifestation of mercy and respect for the person".

For Pascoal Carvalho, a physician and a member of the Pontifical Academy for Life, the request to suspend treatment plays on two ambiguous notions, namely that food and water constitute a special form of healthcare, and that the request itself is not about euthanasia.

"As our society progresses towards a culture of death, the so-called 'right-to-die'" could become "an obligation-to-die," involving "for example, anyone who believes that they are a burden to someone else — either financially or otherwise." Instead, "Life is valuable from its beginning to natural end," he explained.

In a first step towards legalising euthanasia, The Law Commission of India, Ministry of Law and Justice has decided to recommend to the Indian Government to allow terminally ill to end their lives.

All in all....... "No life that breathes with human breath has ever truly longed for death."

People still practise euthanasia in India for their near and dear one.

28. Bibliography

Websites:

1. 'Euthanasia in India' by A.K. Tharien retrieved from http://www.eubios.info/EJ52/EJ52F.htm.
2. 'Euthanasia seeker dies in India' retrieved from http://www.bbc.co.uk.
3. 'Euthanasia and Human Rights Law: Compatible or Contradictory?' retrieved from http://www.independentliving.org/Library/content2.html.
4. 'Voluntary euthanasia' retrieved from "http://plato.stanford.edu/cgi-bin/encyclopedia/archinfo.cgi".
5. 'Frequently-Asked-Questions (FAQs) on Euthanasia' by Nikhil Goyal and Raju Easwaran retrieved from http://www.spandan.com/index.php.
6. 'the issue of euthanasia' by Omayer Hashmi retrieved from http://www.chowk.com/gulberg_home.cgi.
7. 'The Hindu: Is euthanasia ethical?' retrieved from http://www.hindu.com/thehindu/hindu.htm
8. 'IIPM Cicero's Challenge, 2006' retrieved from http://www.iipm.edu/IIPM-Research-Publication.html
9. 'International Perspectives on Euthanasia and Assisted Suicide — Euthanasia ProCon.org.' retrieved from http://www.euthanasiaprocon.org/biosorg/euthanasiadotcom.htm
10. 'Is it time to legalise euthanasia? — In News — Express Healthcare Management' retrieved from http://www.expresshealthcaremgmt.com/20050115/innews.shtml
11. 'The constitutional and legal provisions in Indian law for limiting life support Balakrishnan S, Mani RK' retrieved from http://pagead2.googlesyndication.com.
12. 'Amardeep Singh: The Right to Die in India (and everywhere)' retrieved from http://timesofindia.indiatimes.com/articleshow/962771.cms.
13. 'Euthanasia — Wikipedia, the free encyclopedia' retrieved from http://en.wikipedia.org/wiki/Terminal_illness.

CHAPTER 9

Various Indian Legal Systems *vis-a-vis* Medical Negligence

SYNOPSIS

1. Introduction

Public awareness of medical negligence in India is growing. Hospital managements are increasingly facing complaints regarding the facilities, Standards of professional competence, and the appropriateness of their protection Act, 1986, has come into force some patients have filed legal cases against doctors, have established that the doctors were negligent in their medical services and have claimed and received compensation. As a result, a number of legal decisions have been, made on what constitutes negligence and what is required to prove it.

With the amendment of 2003 in the Consumer Protection Act, 1986, the major significance relates to deficiency in medical services. These amendments have brought the medical service and medical professionals too within the ambit of the Act. Hence, it becomes imperative to discuss this particular aspect also in relation to other law's related to consumerism.

2. Negligence

Before discussing the medical negligence, it would be in order to understand the concept of negligence as such.

Negligence may be defined as the "breach of duty caused by omission to do something which a reasonable man, guided by those considerations which ordinarily regulate the conduct of human affairs would reasonable man would and do". A shorter definition is that "negligence as a tort is the breach of legal duty to take care which results in damage undesired by the defendant to the plaintiff". The definition involves three constituents of negligence: (1) A legal duty to exercise the due acre on the part of he party complained towards the party complaining the formers conduct within the scope of the duty; (2) Breach of the said duty and (3) consequential damage.

3. Medical negligence

Professionals such as doctors are persons having special skill and knowledge and possess such requisite qualifications that they will proffer their skill with reasonable degree of care and caution.

Medical negligence is defined as want of reasonable degree of care or skill or willful negligence on the part of medical practitioners in the treatment of patient with whom a relationship of professional attendance is established, so as to bodily injuries or to loss of life. (*Whitehouse* v *Jordan* (1981) I All ER 267 The House of Lords).

A medical professional would be liable only where his conduct fell below that of the standards of a reasonably competent practitioner in his field. At least three weighty considerations can be pointed out which any Forum trying the issue of medical negligence in any jurisdiction must keep in mind, these are:

(*i*) That legal and disciplinary procedures should be properly founded on firm, moral and scientific grounds.

(*ii*) That patients will be better served if the real causes of harm are properly identified and appropriately acted upon, and

(*iii*) That many incidents involve a contribution from more than one identifiable element in the chair of causation the person holding the 'smoking gun'. Thus to establish a medical negligence, the abovementioned position must be kept in mind.

4. Where negligence is a crime

Section 88 of the Indian Penal Code, 1860 provides exemption for acts not intended to cause death, done by consent in good faith for person's benefit, section 92 provides for exemption for acts done in good faith for person's benefit of a person without his consent through the acts cause harm to a person and that person has not consented to suffer such harm. Section 9 saves from criminality certain communications made in godfather. The national behind these provisions is that no man can so conduct him as to make at absolutely certain that he shall not be as unfortunate as to cause the death of a fellow-creature. The almost that he can do is to abstain from everything which is at all likely to cause death.

Thus when a person engaged in the commission of an offence within the meaning of Indian Penal Code causes death by rashness or negligence, but without either intending to cause death. Or thinking it likely that he causes death, he should be liable for the punishment of the offence which he was engaged in committing, superadded to the ordinary punishment of involuntary culpable homicidal. The involuntary causing of death, without either rashness or negligence, should under no circumstances be punished as murder. The following statement of law on criminal negligence by reference so surgeons, doctor, etc. and unskillful treatment contained in Roseoe's Law of Evidence is classic in his regard:

> "Where a person on acting as a medical man, another licensed or unlicensed, is so negligent in his treatment of a patient that death results, it is manslaughter is the negligence was so great as to amount to a crime, and whether or not there was such a degree of negligence is a question in each case for the jury. In explaining to juries the test which they should apply as to amount to a crime, and whether or not there was such a degree of negligence in question in each case for the jury. In explaining to juries the test which they should apply to determine whether the negligence in the particular case amounted or did not amount to a crime, judges have used many epithets, such as culpable, criminal, gross, wicked, elder, complete, but whatever epithet be used and whether an epithet be used or not, in order to establish criminal liability the facts must be such that, in the opinion of the jury, the negligence of the accused went beyond a more matter of compensation between subject and showed such disregard for the life and safety of others as to amount to a crime against the state and conduct deserting punishment."

5. Deficient medical services amounting to negligence

Over the last many years, there has been increased speculation on whether medical services are expressly or categorically included in the definition of term 'Services' under section 2(1)(*o*) of the Consumer Protection Act.

In *Indian Medical Association* v *V.P. Shantha* AIR 1996 SC 550, the principal issue which arose for decision before the Supreme Court was whether a medical practitioner renders 'services' and can be proceeded against for deficiency in service before a Forum under the Consumer Protection Act, 1986. The Court dealt with how a 'professional' defers from an 'occupation' especially in the context of performance of duties and hence the occurrence of negligence. The Court noticed that medical professional do not enjoy any immunity from being sued in contract or fort (*i.e.* in civil jurisdiction) on the ground of negligence.

However, in the observation made in the context of determining professional liability as distinguished from occupation liability, the Court has reference to authorities, in particular, Jacklon and Powell and have so stated the principles, party quoted from the authorities.

> "In the matter of professional liability professions differ from occupations for the reason that professions operate in spheres where success or failure depends upon factors beyond the professional man's control. In devising a rational approach to professional liability which must provide proper protection to the consumer while allowing for the factors mentioned above. The approach of the Courts is to require that professional men should possess a certain minimum degree of competence and that they should

exercise reasonable care in the discharge of their duties. In general, a professional man owes to his client a duty fort as well as in contract to exercise reasonable care in giving advice fort or performing services."

The Court held that even though services rendered by medical practitioners are of a personal nature they cannot be treated as contract of personal services (which are excluded from the Consumer Protection Courts.)

A 'contract for service' implies a contract whereby one party undertakes to render services (such as professional or technical services) to another, in which the service provider in not subjected to a detailed direction and control. The provider exercises professional or technical skill and used his or her own knowledge and discretion. A contract of service implies a relationship of master and servant and involves an obligation to obey orders in the work to be performed and as to its mode and manner of performance. The contract of service implies a relationship of master and servant and involves an obligation to obey order in the work to be performed and as to its mode and manner of performance. The contract of services is beyond the ambit of the Consumer Protection Act, 1986, under section 2(1)(*o*) of the Act. The Consumer Protection Act will come in the rescues of patients if the services are rendered free of charge, or if they have paid only nominal registration fee. However, if patient's charges are waved because of their incapacity to pay, they are considered to be consumers and can run under the Consumer Protection Act.

The remedy under Consumer Protection Act, 1986, is in addition to civil remedy and it cannot be denied to a consumer merely on the ground that either the facts are too complicated or the complainants claim is unreasonable.

6. Claim of compensation under Law of Torts

The law of torts applies even if medical professionals provide free services. In cases where the services offered by the doctor or hospital do not fall in the ambit of service as defined in the Consumer Protection Act. Patient can take recourse to the law relating to negligence under the law of tort and successfully claim compensation. The onus is on the patients to prove that the doctor was negligence and that the injury was a consequence of the negligence. Such cases of negligence may include transfusion of blood of incorrect blood groups, leaving a mop in the patient's abdomen after operating, unsuccessful sterilization resulting in the birth of child, removal of organs without taking consents, operating on a patient without giving Anaesthesia, administering wrong medicine resulting in injury, etc.

7. Are doctors infallible?

There are after cases which show genuine malpractice on bentest of the medico but due to the new ruling, they after escape. Their negligence goes unnoticed by all excepted errant doctors. Voltaire, an eminent philosopher had once said, " Doctor's are men who prescribe medicines of which they know little, to cure diseases of which they know less, in human being of whom they know nothing". Though the medical professions, there regarded as one of the noblest taking advantage of the legal protection provided to them. This is one profession that has on a continuous basis dodged the jurisdiction of the Courts of India; another view taken of the *Jacob Mathew's* case is that when the Supreme Court held that a doctor can not be held liable for the death of the patient, it had undermined equality before the eyes of law.

In the case of *Bhajan Lal Gupta* v *Moolchand Khairati Ram* 2000 I CPJ 31, the judgment of the Supreme Court stated that: " One of the test of medical negligence is that something which is required under medical practitioner to be done was not done or what was done was contradicted at the same time. It is also a settled principle of law that a specialist is supposed to know the latest technique for management of the patient and if he is ignorant about it, then he could be considered to be negligent in his profession.

Courts are of the view that the evidence may not always depend on the testimony of a medical personal alone. Sometimes the negligence deals with the basic requirements of a patient which even a normal witness with no medical background may know about. Therefore, the question that comes to one's mind is that there is such a negligence which is testified to have happened by a witness, should it not be taken into account? Such issue can be put to rest by a testimony of such a witness instead of a medical professional. Taking this view into account by Supreme Court acquitted Dr. Jacobs of all charges taking the *Dr. Suresh Gupta* v *Govt. of NCT of Delhi* (2004) 6 SCC 422 case as a precedent.

Though the constitution does not provide for some special privileges given to patients, Article 21 thrusts an obligation upon the medical professional to project life. It was head by the Supreme Court in the case of *State of Punjab* v *Maninder Singh Chawla* AIR 1997 SC 1225. That Article 21 of the Constitution of India provides for the protection of life and personal liberty. The right to life enshrined in this article includes right to health and the right to live it dignity. No one can violate the right of life. If any body including a medical professional causes harm and injury to any person without his consent, he commits a criminal wrong giving rise to criminal liability.

It becomes clear that a doctor has certain duties towards his patients which he needs to fulfill. If he falls in them he may be sued by the patient for an act of negligence.

8. Extent of liability of medical professionals

In the case of *Indian Medical Association* v *V.P. Shantha* AIR 1996 SC 550, in the year of 1995, the Supreme Court judgment proved to be a monumental one it changed the way one viewed the medical profession from a totally legal point of view. The Judgment brought the medical profession within the ambit of the Consumer Protection Act. Patient could now sue the doctors for injuries sustained by them, in consumer Courts. The judgment bound the doctors to their patients in a contractual way. The Supreme Court further specified that even though the service provided by the doctors was that of a personal nature, it can not be supposed to fall within the purview of contract of personal services it was held that such contractual obligation should be treated as a contract of service.

Where free services are rendered to the patient by medical professionals, it will not fall within the ambit of the farm 'service' unless the payment of the lees was waived due the patient's inability to pay. Under civil law, where the territory of Consumer Protection Act ends, the field of the law of Torts takes over to protect the interest of the patients. Where the patient can not sue under Consumer Protection Act because of the limitation under the term 'Service' the patient can do so under the law of Torts suing the doctor for injuries sustained by him due to the doctor's negligence.

9. Threat of criminal proceedings

Sometimes the negligence on the part of doctor is so grave and obvious that the doctor then faces the threat of criminal proceedings. A doctor can be tried under section 304A of that Indian Penal Code for causing death by negligent act. It most be remembered that there are high standards to mater up to, for providing a doctor grossly negligent. He can not be proved negligent merely because there was lack of necessary care. Often cases test the well established principles of law. It does not happen after that a doctor is tried for murder, because doctor do not intended to kill their patients. Therefore the guilty mind (*mens rea*) that needs to be proved in such cases test the law. When doctor administer treatment to the patient, they do so in good faith for the patient benefit's benefit, and not with an intention to kill. For this reason sections 87, 88, 89 and 92 of the Indian Penal Code provide immunity to the medical professionals. The onus of the proof lies on the doctor. The doctor ought to prove that the treatment was done with the patient's benefit in mind and in good faith.

The Courts in India, following England's practice are inclined to the paternalistic model of physician-patient relationship. Paternalism means "interference with a person's liberty of action justified by reasons referring exclusively to the welfare, good, happiness, needs and interests or value of the person coerced". This has been further supported by the famous *Bolam* principle, which states that a doctor can not be held liable when he acted as any other established and responsible medical man would act.

10. Doctor's liability regarding medical negligence

However, the law does not aim to punish all acts of a doctor that caused injury to a patient. It is concerned only with negligent acts. Medical negligence arises from an act or omission by a medical practitioner, which no reasonably competent and careful practitioner would have committed. What is expected of a medical practitioner is reasonably 'skilful behaviour' adopting the ordinary skills' and practices of the professional with ordinary care. There is, however, room for ambiguity and judicial interpretation as what is 'reasonable and ordinary' is a question of fact. Essentially, doctors are generally bound to exercise an ordinary degree, care and not the highest possible degree of care. If a medical practitioner has taken a reasonable care, then he can not be held liable. A mere difference in opinion is not a ground for fostering liability on doctor. (*Santosh Kumar Sodhi* v *Dr. Vijay Maroo* 2003 I CPJ 344).

Doctor' duties to their patients are clear. They must decide whether or not to undertake the case they must decide what treatment to give, and they must take care in the administration of that treatment. (*L.B. Joshi* (*Dr.*) v *T.B. Godbole* (*Dr.*) AIR 1969 SC 128).

A breach of any of these duties gives the patient a right to action for negligence.

11. Liability under the Consumer Protection Act

In 1995, the Supreme Court decision in *Indian Medical Association* v *V.P. Santha* AIR 1996 SC 550: 1995 (Section 651), brought the medical profession within the ambit of a 'service' as defined the relationship between patients and medical professional as contractual. Patients who had sustained injuries in the course of treatment could now and doctors in 'procedure free' Consumer Protection Courts for compensation.

The Court held that even though services rendered by medical practitioners are of a personal nature they can not be treated as contract of personal services (which are excluded from the Consumer Protection Act). They are contracts for services under which a doctor too can be used in Consumer Protection Courts.

A contract for services implies a contract whereby one party undertake to render services (such as professional or technical services) to another, in which the service provider is not subjected to a detailed direction and control. The provider exercises professional or technical skill and uses his or her own knowledge and discretion. A 'contractor of service' implies as relationship of master and servant and involves an obligation to obey orders in the work to be performed and as to its made and manner of performance. The 'contract of service' is beyond the ambit of the Consumer Protection Act, 1986, under section 2(1)(*o*) of the Act.

The Consumer Protection Act will not come to the resume of patients if the services is rendered free of charge, or if they have paid only a nominal registration fee. However, if patients charged are waived because of their incapacity to pay, they are considered to be consumers and can sue under the Consumer Protection Act.

12. Liability under Law of Tort

Under civil law, at a point where the Consumer Protection Act ends. The law of torts takes over and protects the interests of patients. This applies even if medical professionals provide free services. In cases where the services offered by the doctor or hospital do not fall in the ambit of 'service' as defined in the Consumer Protection Act. Patients can take recourse to the law relating to negligence under the law of torts and successfully claim compensation. The onus is on the patients to prove that the doctor was negligent and that the injury was as consequence of that the injury was a consequence of the doctor's negligence (*Philips India Ltd.* v *Kunju Panma* AIR 1975 Bom 306), Such cases of negligence may include transfusion of blood of incorrect blood groups (*Kalra Satyanarayana* v *Laxmi Nursing Home* 2003 I CPJ 262), leaving a map in the patients abdomen after operating (*Aehutrao Haribhao Khodwa* v *State of Maharashtra* (1996) 2 SCC 834), unsuccessfully sterilization resulting in the birth of child (*State of Haryana* v *Sant Santara* AIR 2000 SC 1888), removal of organs without taking consent (*Lakshmi Rajan* v *Malar Hospital* 1998 III CPJ 586), operating on a patient without giving Anaesthesia (*P.N. Rao* v *G. Jayaprakash* AIR 1950 AP 201), administering wrong medicine resulting in injury (*Spring Meadows Hospital* v *Harjal Abbuwalia* AIR 1998 SC 1801), etc.

13. Liability under Criminal Law

In certain causes, negligence is so blatant that it invites criminal proceedings. A doctor can be punished under section 304A of the Indian Penal Code (IPC) for causing death by a rash or negligent act, say in a case where death of a patient is caused during operation by a doctor not qualified to operate. According to Supreme Court decision. (*Suresh Gupta* (*Dr.*) v *Govt. of NCT of Delhi* 2004 (Sec 422), the standard of negligence required to be proved against a doctor. In case of criminal negligence (especially that under section 304A of the IPC) should be so high that it can be described as 'gross negligence or recklessness' merely lack of necessary care. Criminal liability will not be attracted if the patient dies due to error in judgment or accident. Every civil negligence is not criminal it should be of such a nature that it could be termed as gross negligence.

Very rarely can a doctor be prosecuted for murder or attempt to murder as doctors never intend to kill their patients, and hence do not possess the required level of guilty intention. When doctors administer a treatment involving the risk of death, they do so in good faith and for the patients benefit. A doctor can be punished for causing hurt or grievous hurt under the IPC. However sections 87, 88, 89 and 92 of the IPC provide immunity from criminal prosecutions to doctors who act in good faith and for the patients benefit. For example, a doctor who consciously or knowingly did not use sterilized equipment for an operation can not be said to have acted in good faith.

14. Legal position of medical negligence in India

As regards medical negligence, the legal position has been described in several leading judgments. Some of these are given below.

1. In the leading case *Bolam* v *Friern Hospital Management Committee* (1957) 2 All ER, The Queen's Bench Division of the British Court held: A doctor is not guilty of negligence if he has acted in accordance with a practice accepted as proper by a responsible body of medical men skilled on that particular art.

In this leading case judge Mc Nair J. Has stated as follows.

"........... Where you get a situation which involves the use of some special skill or competence then the test whether there has been negligence or not is not the test of the man on the top of a elepham omnibus, because he has not got this special skill. The test is the standard of the ordinary skilled man exerting and professing to have that special skill. A man need not possess highest expert skill at the risk of being found negligent. It is well established law that it is caffeine if he exercises the ordinary skill of an ordinary competent man exercising that particular art. Causes for the plaintiff put it in this way, that in the case of a medical man, negligence means failure to act in accordance with the standards of reasonably competent medical man at the time. That is perfectly accurate statement, as long as it is remembered that there may be one or more perfectly proper standards, and if medical man conforms with one of those proper standards then he is not negligent A doctor is not guilty of negligence if he has acted in accordance with the practice accepted as a proper by a responsible body of medical man skilled in that particular art. Putting in the other way round, a doctor is not negligent, if he is acting in accordance with a practice merely because there is body of opinion that takes a contrary view. At a same time, that does not mean that a medical man obstinately and pigheadedly carry on with some old technique if it has been proved to be contrary to what is really substantially the whole of informed medical opinion."

The question of degree of negligence has always been considered as relevant to a distinction between negligence in civil law and negligence in criminal law. *In Kurban Hussein Mohamedalli Rangawalla* v *State of Maharashtra* (1965) 2 SCR 622. While dealing with section 304A of IPC, the following statement of law by Sir Lawrence Junking in *Emperor* v *Omkar Rampratap* 4 Bom LR 679 was sited with approval:

> "To impose criminal liability under section 304A, it is necessary that the death should have been the direct result of rash and negligent act of the accused, and that act must be the proximate and efficient cause without the intervention of another's negligence. It must be the *causa causans*, it is not enough that it may have been the *causa sine qua non*."

Dr. Laxman Balakishna Joshi v *Dr. Trimbak Bapu Godbole* AIR 1969 SC 128, was a case of Fatal Accidents Act, 1855. The duties which a doctor owes to his patients came up for consideration.

> "The duties which a doctor owes to his patient are clear. A person who held himself out really to give medical advice and treatment implacably undertakes that he is possessed of skill and knowledge for the purpose. Such a person when consulted by a patient owes him certain duties viz., a duty of care in deciding whether to undertake the case, a duty of care in deciding what treatment to give or a duty of acre I the administration of that treatment. A breach of any of those duties gives a right of action for negligence to the patients. The practitioner must bring to his task a reasonable degree of care. Neither the very highest nor very low degree of care and competence judged in the light of the particular circumstances of each case is what the law requires."

In *Achutrao Haribhau Khodwa* v *State of Maharashtra,* AIR 1996 SC 2377, the Supreme Court noticed that in every nature of medical profession, skills differs from doctor to doctor and more than one alternative course of treatment are available, all admissible. Negligence can not be attributed to a doctor so long he is performing his duties to the best of his ability and with due care and caution. Merely because the doctor chooses one course of action in preference to other one available, he would not be liable if the course of action chooses by him was acceptable to the medical profession.

It was a case where a map was left inside the lady patient's abdomen during operation peritonitis developed which led to a second surgery being performed on her, but she could not survive. Liability for negligence was fastened on the surgeon because no valid explanation was forthcoming of the map having being left inside the abdomen of the lady. The doctrine of *res ipsa loquitur* was held applicable in a case like this.

Poonam Verma v *Ashwin Patel* (1996) 4 SCC 332, In this case a doctor registered as medical practitioner and entitled to practice in homeopathy only, prescribed an allopathic medicine to patient. The patient died. The doctor was held to be negligent and liable to compensate the wife of the deceased for the death of her husband on the ground that the doctor who was entitled to practice in homeopathy only, was under a statutory duty not to enter the field of any other system of medicine and since he trespassed up to the prohibited field and prescribed allopathic medicine to the patient causing the death, his contact amounted to negligence *per se* actionable in civil law.

Dr. Suresh Gupta v *Government of NCT of Delhi* (2004) 6 Scale 432. In this case the legal decision is almost firmly established that where a patient dies due to negligent medical treatment of the doctor, the doctor can be made liable in civil law for paying compensation and damages in tort and some time, if the degree of negligence so gross and his act was reckless as to endanger the life of the patient. He would also made criminal liable to offence under section 304A IPC.

> "Thus a doctor cannot be held criminally responsible for patient death unless his negligence or incompetence showed such disregard for life and safety of his patient as to amount to a crime against the state."

In *Spring Meadows Hospital* v *Harjo Ahluwalia* (1998) 4 SCC 39, the Supreme Court was concerned with the right of patients when a child dies due to medical negligence. It was argued by the hospital that the parents were not consumers under by the Act so could not get any relief. The Court rejected this argument and observed that even parents were covered under the Act and there was nothing in the law which prevented the parents as well as the child from recovering damages.

In this case, a child patient was treated for seven days in the Spring Meadows Hospital (Noida) for typhoid. The consultant physician prescribed "Chloramphenicol Injection," but the unqualified nurse misread it is choloroquince" and indented, for the purchase of injection, "Lariago" (i.e. chloroquine). She injected Chloroquine 5 mg IV, Which was at least 3-1/2 times of the normal paediatric dose. The patient suffered irreversible brain damage. Treatment for was compelled to live in a vegetable state.

The National Consumer Commission, whose judgment was confirmed by the Supreme Court, came to the conclusion, that the attending doctor was negligent, as he allowed an unqualified nurse to administer the injection, even though the consultant doctor had advised administration by the attending doctor himself.

The hospital and the nurse were jointly and severally liable. The Apex Court has specifically paid down the following principles for holding doctor negligent:

> "Gross medical mistake will always result in a finding of negligence, use of wrong drug or wrong gas during the course of anesthetic will frequently lead to the imposition of liability and in some situations even the principle of *res ipsa loquitur* can be applied. Even delegation of responsibility to another may amount to negligence in certain circumstances. A consultant could be negligent where delegates. The responsibility to his junior with the knowledge that the junior was incapable of performing his duties properly we are indicating those principles since in the case in hand certain arguments had been advanced in this regard, which will be dealt with while answering the questions posed by us.

The Court ordered the following compensation:

(*a*) ₹12.50 lakhs to the child (₹10 Lakhs compensations plus ₹2.5 Lakhs for equipment).

(*b*) ₹5 lakhs to the parents for mental agony.

The Supreme Court further held that when a young child is taken to a hospital and treated by a hospital, then.

(*c*) The child's parents would come within the definitions of "consumer" and.

(*d*) The child also becomes a "consumer" being a benefiting of such services.

In *Jacob Mathew* v *State of Punjab* (2005) 6 SCC 1 case, the Supreme Court saved medical professionals from being harassed by the state through its prosecution authorities.

A patient died because of cancer. The relatives of patient, highly influence in politics, brought criminal proceedings against the doctor who was working in CMC, Ludhiana. The bail petitions filed before the District Sessions Court and High Court were dismissed. Thus paving way for his imminent arrest. While he filed a revision petitions before Supreme Court, it quashed the prosecution of a medical professional under section 304A/34, IPC and disposed of all the interlocutory applications that doctor should not be held criminally responsible unless there is a *prima facie* evidence before the Court in the form of a credible opinion from another competent doctor, preferably a government doctor in the same field of medicine supporting the charges of rash and negligent act.

While dealing with the tests to be kept in mind by the Courts in dealing with cases of medical negligence, the Honourable Supreme Court observed as follows:

"................So long as it can be found that the procedure which was infact adopted was one which was acceptable to medical science as on that date, the medical practitioner cannot be held negligent merely because he chose to follow one procedure and not another and the result was a failure."

Indiscriminate prosecution of medical professionals for criminal negligence is counter-productive and does no service or good to the society.

The result of these decisions can be summed up as under:

(1) Negligence is the breach of a duty caused by omission to do something which a reasonable man guided by those considerations which ordinarily regulate the conduct of human affairs would do, or doing something which a prudent and reasonable man would not do. Negligence becomes actionable on account of injury resulting from the act or omission amounting to negligence attributable to the person sued. The essential components of negligence are three: 'duty', 'breach' and 'resulting damage'.

(2) Negligence in the context of medical profession necessarily calls for a treatment with a difference. To infer rashness or negligence on the part of a professional, in particular a doctor, additional considerations apply. A case of occupational negligence is different from one of professional negligence. A simple lack of care, an error of judgment or an accident, is not proof of negligence on the part of a medical professional. So long as a doctor follows a practice acceptable to the medical profession of that day, he cannot be held liable for negligence merely because a better alternative course or method of treatment was also available or simply because a more skilled doctor would not have chosen to follow or resort to that practice or procedure which the accused followed. When it comes to the failure of taking precautions what has to be seen is whether those precautions were taken which the ordinary experience of men has found to be sufficient; a failure to use special or extraordinary precautions which might have prevented the particular happening cannot be the standard for judging the alleged negligence.

(3) A professional may be held liable for negligence on one of the two findings: either he was not possessed of the requisite skill which he professed to have possessed, or, he did not exercise, with reasonable competence in the given case, the skill which he did possess. The standard to be applied for judging, whether the person charged has been negligent or not, would be that of an ordinary competent person exercising ordinary skill in that profession. It is not possible for every professional to possess the highest level of expertise or skills in that branch which he practices.

(4) The jurisprudential concept of negligence differs in civil and criminal law. What may be negligence in civil law may not necessarily be negligence in criminal law. For negligence to amount to an offence, the element of *mens rea* must be shown to exist. For act to amount to

criminal negligence, the degree of negligence should be much night gross or of a very high degree. Negligence which is neither gross nor of a higher degree n provide a ground for action in civil law but cannot form the basis for prosecution.

(5) The word 'gross' has not been used in section 304A of IPC, yet it is settled to criminal law negligence or recklessness, to be so held, must be of such a high degree a 'gross'. The expression 'rash or negligent act as occurring in section 304A of the IPC has to be read as qualified by the word 'grossly'.

(6) To prosecute a medical professional for negligence under criminal law, it must be shown that the accused did something or failed to do something which in the given facts and circumstances no medical professional in his ordinary senses and prudence would have done or failed to do. The hazard taken by the accused doctor should be of such a nature that the injury which resulted was most likely imminent.

(7) *Res ipsa loquitur* is only a rule of evidence and operates in the domain of civil law especially in cases of torts and help in determining the onus of proof in actions relating to negligence. It cannot be pressed in service for determining *per se* the liability for negligence within the domain of criminal law. *Res ipsa loquitur* has, if at all, a limited application in trial on a charge of criminal negligence.

In *Dr. Kunal Saha* v *Dr. Sukumar Mukherjee* 2006 II CLD 609 (NC), the National Consumer Commission summarized the medical negligence law as follows:

Tests for determining deficiency in service laid down are—

Whether there is failure to act in accordance with standard of a reasonable competent medical practitioner?

(*i*) Whether there were expiries of reasonable degree of care?

(*ii*) The degree of standard or reasonable care varies in each case depending upon expertise of medical man and the circumstances of each case. On this aspect, it would be worthwhile to refer to the enunciation from Halsbury's Laws of England.

With regard to degree of skill and care required by the doctors, it has been stated as under in (Pr. 36, P 38, vol. 30, Halsbury's Laws of England, 4th Edn)

"The practitioner must bring to his task a reasonable degree of skill and knowledge, and must exercise a reasonable degree of care. Failure to sue due skill in diagnosis with the result that very treatment is given is negligence. Neither the very highest nor a very low degree of care and competence, judge in the light of particular circumstances of each case, is what the law requires, and a person is not liable in negligence because someone else of greater skill and knowledge would have prescribed deferent treatment or operation in a different way, nor is he guilty of negligence or he has acted in accordance with one responsible body of medical opinion in preference to another in relation to the diagnosis and treatment of a certain condition, provided that the practice of that body of medical opinion is treasonable."

The Apex Court aptly stated the said principles further in *Dr. Laxman Balkrishna Joshi* v *Dr. Trimbak Bapu Godbole* AIR 1969 SC 128, which reads as under:

> "The practitioner must bring to his task a reasonable degree of skill and knowledge and must exercise a reasonable degree of care. Neither the very highest nor a very low degree of care and competence judged in the light of the particular circumstances of each case is what the law requires (if Halsbury's Law of England 3rd vol. 26 P.M.) The doctor no doubt has desertion in choosing treatment which he propose to give to the patient and such secretion is relatively ampler in cases of emergency."

The deficiency in medical negligence is to be judged on the following principles:

(*i*) It is to be remembered that a doctor or a surgeon does not undertake that he will positively cure a patient nor does he undertake to use the highest possible degree of skill, as there may be persons more learned and skilled than himself, but he definitely undertakes to use a fair, reasonable and competent degree of skill.

(*ii*) It is to be stated that if there are several modes of treatment and if a doctor adopts one id them and conducts the same with due care and caution then no negligence can be attributed towards him.

(*iii*) Secondly, in the case of medical man, negligence means, failure to act in accordance with the standards of reasonable competent medical men at the time.

(*iv*) A medical practitioner is expected to exercise reasonable degree of care and exercise skill and knowledge which he possesses.

(*v*) No doubt, failure to use due skill in diagnosis with the result that wrong treatment is given in negligence.

(*vi*) Medical opinion may differ with regard to diagnosis or treatment, but in a complicated case if they occur and Court will be slow in attributing negligence on the part of the doctor if he has performed his duties to the best of his ability and with due care and caution.

In *Nizam Institute of Medical Sciences* v *Prasanth S. Dhanaka* Civil appeal No. 4119 of 1999 and *Civil Appeal No. 3126 of 2000, Judgment delivered on 14-5-200.* the complainant is about 40 years of age, a soft ware IT engineer and earning a sum of ₹28 Lakh per annum. In September 1990 he had been admitted to Nizam Institute of Medical Sciences (NIMS) after test showed that he had a tumor in his chest. A Surgery was conducted on him to remove a sample of tumor to examine if it was malignant. Complainant alleged that the surgeon found the tumor to be benign, but without consulting a neurosurgeon, he went ahead and removed the tumour, damaging blood vessels connected to the spine, leaving him paralyzed below the waist.

National Commission had awarded ₹14 Lakh to be paid to the patient, ₹1.5 Lakh to his father and ₹25,000 as costs.

NIMS had appealed the Supreme Court against the award of National Commission. The Apex Court asked NIMS to pay ₹1 crore to complainant as compensation for medical negligence.

The judgment is a bench mark and highest ever award for damages in a case of medical negligence.

CHAPTER 10

Some General Clarifications on Medical Negligence

SYNOPSIS

1. What is meant by negligence?

Negligence means: The omission to do something which is reasonable man guided, by those ordinary considerations which ordinarily regulate human affairs, would do or the doing of something which a reasonable and prudent man would not do. (Black's Law Dictionary 6th Edition).

Negligence does not always mean absolute carelessness, but want of such a degree of care as is required in particular circumstances. Negligence is failure to observe, for the protection of the interests of another person, the degree of care, precaution and vigilance which the circumstances justly demand, whereby such other person suffers injury. The idea of negligence and duty are strictly correlative. Negligence means either subjectively a careless state of mind, or objectively a careless conduct. Negligence is not an absolute term, but is a relative one; it is rather a comparative term. No absolute standard can be fixed and no mathematically exact formula can be laid down by which negligence or lack of it can be infallibly measured in a given case. What constitutes negligence varies under different conditions and in determining whether negligence exists in a particular case, or whether a mere act or course of conduct amounts to negligence all the attending and surrounding facts and circumstances have to be taken into account to determine whether an act would be taken into account. To determine whether an act would be or would not be negligent, it is relevant to determine if any reasonable man would foresee that the act would cause damage or not. The omission to do what the law obligates or even the failure to do anything in a manner, mode or method envisaged by law would equally and *per se* constitute negligence on the part of such person. If the answer is in the affirmative, it is a negligence act. (*Municipal Corporation of Greater Bombay* v *Laxman Iyer* 2003 (8) SCC 731 — A Case of Motor Accident).

2. What is the meaning of professional negligence?

Professional negligence is the negligence committed by a professional person during the course of their profession. A professional is one engaged in one of the learned professions or in an occupation requiring a high level of training and proficiency. (*As quoted in Black's Law Dictionary*)

The following specific occupations have been accorded professional status.

1. Surveyors
2. Solicitors
3. Medical Practitioners
4. Barristers (In India Advocates)
5. Insurance Broker
6. Architects, Engineers and Quantity Surveyors
7. Accountants

3. What is medical negligence and what are the incidents thereof?

Medical negligence is lack of reasonable care and skill or willful negligence on the part of a doctor in respect to acceptance of a patient, history taking, examination, diagnosis, investigation, treatment medical or surgical, etc. resulting in injury or damage to the patient. The term 'damage' means physical, mental or functional injury to the patient.

> "The law requires that the practitioner must bring to his task a reasonable degree of skill and knowledge and must exercise a reasonable degree of care. The law does not expect the very highest nor a very low degree of care and competence judged in the light of the particular circumstances of each case." (*Halsbury's Laws of England,* 3rd edn vol. 26 P 17).

The Bolam Test: The classic statement of the test of professional negligence is the direction to the jury of Me Nair, J in *Bolam* v *Friern Hospital Management Committee* now widely known as the "Bolam test" which reads as under:

> "But where you get a situation which involved the use of some special skill or competence, then the test whether there has been negligence or not is not the test of the man on the clap ham omnibus, because he has not got this special skill. The test is the standard of the ordinary skilled man exercising and professing to have that special skill. A man need not passes the highest expert skill at the risk of being found negligent. .... it is sufficient if he exercises the ordinary skill of an ordinary competent man exercising that particular art."

His lordship agreed that counsel's statement that "negligence means failure to act in accordance with the standards of reasonably competent medical men at the time." was a perfectly accurate statement of the law, provided that it was remembered that there may be one or more perfectly proper standards:

> "A doctor is not guilty of negligence if he has acted in accordance with a practice accepted as proper by a responsible body of medical men skilled in particular art. ...... pulling it the other way round, a doctor is not negligent, if he is acting in accordance with such a practice, merely because there is a body of opinion that takes a contrary view."

The decision of the House of Lords [*Bolitho* v *City and Hackney H.A.* (1997 4 All ER 771)] has modified the approach to the concept of "accepted practice" in the *Bolam* case in the following words of Lord Brown — Wilkinson:

> "The use of these adjectives — responsible, reasonable and respectable — all show that the court has to be satisfied that the exponents of the body of opinion relied on can demonstrate that such opinion has a logical basis. In particular, in cases involving, as they often do, the weighing of risks against benefits, the judge before accepting a body of opinion as being responsible, reasonable or respectable, will need to be satisfied that, in forming their views, the experts have directed their minds to the question of comparative risk and benefits and have reached a defensible conclusion on the matter."

It is submitted that what Lord Browne — Wilkinson has done is to correctly hand back to the courts the jurisdiction to objectively declare an accepted medical practice as not being able to provide a defence if the practice is found to be lacking of logical basis.

It is important and relevant to mention what the Supreme Court has observed in *Vinitha Ashok* v *Lakshmi Hospital* (2001 (8) SCC 731).

"....... In a large majority cases, it has been demonstrated that a doctor will be liable for negligence in respect of diagnosis and treatment in spite of a body of professional opinion approving his conduct where it has not been established to the court's satisfaction that such opinion relied on his reasonable or responsible. If it can be demonstrated that the professional opinion is not capable of withstanding the logical analysis, the court would be entitled to hold that the body of opinion is not reasonable or responsible."

In *Derr* v *Bonney* (231 P2d 637 Wash 731) an American case, the court's definition of negligent treatment is an excellent statement of general definition of a physician's legal responsibility in treatment:

(1) An individual licensed to practice medicine is presumed to possess that degree of skill and learning which is possessed by the average members of the profession in the community in which he practices, and it is presumed that he has applied that skill and learning with ordinary and reasonable care to those who come to him for treatment.

(2) The contract which the law implies from the employment of a physician or surgeon is that the doctor will treat his patient with that diligence and skill just mentioned.

(3) He does not incur liability for his mistakes if he has used methods recognized and approved by those reasonably skilled in the profession.

(4) Before a physician or surgeon can be liable for malpractice/negligence he must have done something in the treatment of his patient which the recognized standard of medical practice in his community forbids in such cases or he must have neglected to do something required by these standards.

(5) In order to obtain a judgment against the physician or surgeon, the standard of medical practice in the community must be shown and further that the doctor failed to follow the method prescribed by that standard.

(6) It is not required that physicians and surgeons guarantee results, nor that the result be what is desired.

(7) The testimony of other physicians that they would have followed a different courses of treatment than that followed by the defendant or a disagree or a disagreement of doctors of equal skill and learning as to what the treatment should have been, does not establish negligence.

In Canada, one of the most widely cited statements is that of Schroeder J.A. in *Crits* v *Sylvester* 1956 1DLR (2d) 502, 508.

"Every medical practitioner must bring to his task a reasonable degree of skill and knowledge and must exercise a reasonable degree of care and skill which could reasonably be excepted to a normal, prudent practitioner of the same experience and standing and if he holds himself out as a specialist, a higher degree of skill is required of him than of one who does not profess to be so qualified by special training and ability."

The Supreme Court in India, in *Dr. Laxman Balakrishna Joshi* v *Dr. Trimbak Bapu Godbole* AIR 1969 SC 128 which case has been followed in various decisions, including the land mark decision — *Indian Medical Association* v *V.P. Shantha* AIR 1996 SC 550 observed as under:

> "The duties which a doctor owes to his patient are clear. A person who holds himself out ready to give medical advice and treatment impliedly undertakes that he is possessed of skill and knowledge for the purpose. Such a person when consulted by a patient owes him certain duties, viz., a duty of care in deciding whether to undertake the case, a duty of care in deciding what treatment is to give or a duty of care in the administration of that treatment. A breach of any of those duties gives a right of action for negligence to the patient. The practitioner must bring to his task a reasonable degree of skill and knowledge and must exercise a reasonable degree of care. Neither the very highest nor a very low degree of care and competence judged in the light of particular circumstances of each case is what the law requires. The doctor, no doubt, has discretion in choosing treatment which he proposes to give to the patient and such discretion is relatively ampler in cases of emergency."

In the above case what the doctor did was to reduce the fracture without anesthesia to the patient who died. This was held to be negligence and carelessness, the elementary precaution being giving of anesthesia.

Medical negligence can also result from an act of omission. The classical Indian case which illustrates this in the case of *T.T. Thomas* v *Smt. Elisa* AIR 1987 Ker 52 where the patient died due to negligent failure of the surgeon to act, and the surgeon was held liable. The surgeon diagnosed the case as one of perforated appendix and peritonitis and advised emergency operation but failed to perform the same and the next day the condition of the patient was so bad that he could not undergo the operation and later died. The defence of the surgeon was want of consent of the patient to undergo the operation which fact was not noted on the case sheet by the surgeon. The following observations of Peter Parks, J in *Clark* v *Maclenna* (1983) 1 All ER 416 were relied up in holding that burden of proof of absence of consent lay upon the surgeon or medical man, specially so where the patient is dead and not alive to give evidence:

> "Although in an action in negligence the onus of proof normally rested on the plaintiff, in a case where general duty of care arose and there was a failure to take recognized precaution and that failure was followed by the very damage which that precaution was designed to prevent, the burden of proof lay on the defendant to show, first, that he was not in breach of any duty, that the damage suffered by the plaintiff did not result from the breach. Accordingly, a doctor owed a duty of his patient to observe the precautions which were normal in the course of the treatment that he gave."

The Kerala High Court laid down that consent was implicit in the case of a patient who submits to the doctor, and absence of consent must be made out by the person alleging it. In case of emergency operation of the doctor cannot wait for the consent of his patient or where the patient is a minor. Even if he is in a fit condition to give voluntary answer, the surgeon has a duty to inform him of the damages ahead or the risk involved by going without an operation at the earliest.

The Court arrived at the conclusion that the failure to perform the emergency operation amounted to negligence. While doing so it noticed *inter alia*, the following observations of Mc Nair, J. in *Bolam* v *Friern Hospital Management Committee* (1987) 2 All ER 118:

> "Counsel for the plaintiff put it in this way that in the case of a medical man, negligence means failure to act in accordance with the standards of reasonable competent medical man at the time. That is a perfectly accurate statement as long as it is remembered that there may be one or more perfectly proper standards, and if a medical man conforms with one of those proper standards then he is not negligent."

Mc Nair, J. referred in the same case to the following observation of Lord Clyoe in Scottish case *Hunter* v *Hamlay* (1955) SLT 213 at 217.

> "The true test for establishing negligence in diagnosis or treatment on the part of the doctor of ordinary skill would be guilty of acting with ordinary care."

It is wrong to assume negligence on the part of the doctor merely because something went wrong with the patient. There must be direct connection between injury suffered and the treatment given. Sometimes there is scope for adopting different methods of treatment, both are known and acceptable and if the doctor has followed one course of action no case of negligence can be made out. Sometimes decision have to be taken instantaneously and it is difficult to visualize situations and what type of action the situation demands the doctor alone Is the best judge, and accordingly decide the course of action. Even genuine or *bona fide* mistakes committed while exhibiting due care and diligence may have to be kept out of the purview of negligence. After all, negligence is failure to perform to duty cast on him and so long as he performs the said duty with care and caution no negligence can be attributed to him and no doctor of ordinary skill would be guilty of the said conduct resulting in negligence if reasonable care is taken.

4. What is the difference between deficiency in service and medical negligence?

Under section 2(1)(*g*) of the Consumer Protection Act, 1986 the word 'deficiency' means any fault, imperfection, shortcoming or inadequacy in the quality, nature and manner of performance which is required to be maintained by or under any law for the time being in force or has been undertaken to be performed by a person in pursuance of a contract or otherwise in relation to any service.

The Haryana State Consumer Dispute Redressal Commission has held in *Dr. Ravinder Gupta* v *Ganga Devi* (1993) 3 CPR 255 (Har) that there is a clear distinction between medical negligence in the law of tort (civil law) and a deficiency in the medical services undertaken to be rendered within the consumer jurisdiction. Definition under the Consumer Protection Act casts the nest very wide and transcends the somewhat narrower concept of negligence in the law of tort. The commission admitted that there would remain a grey penumbral area between the tort till the matter crystallizes filling in the as yet nascent consumer jurisdiction.

The Supreme Court has now categorically held in *Indian Medical Association* v *V.P. Shantha* AIR 1996 SC 550 as under:

> "A determination about deficiency in service under section 2(1)(*g*) of the Consumer Protection Act is to be made by applying the same test as is applied in an action for damages for negligence."

It would thus be seen deficiency in medical service has been equated with medical negligence.

However there may be instances whether there is no negligence in treatment but only deficiency in service is there. Non-handling over of medical records, undue delay in conducting investigations. Loss of Pathological samples excessive or wrong billing, are some of the instances which would come within the purview of 'deficiency of service' and would certainly not be 'negligence'.

5. What is meant by 'circumstances of the case' in judging cases of medical negligence?

'Circumstances of the case' means the time, place and the opportunities available to the practitioner when he undertook the care of a patient. Depending on these circumstances, different standards may become applicable while judging cases of alleged medical negligence.

It would be unreasonable, for example, to judge by the same criteria the conduct of a doctor who by necessity, performs operation in a remote country, district or in the patient's own house and the conduct of one who operates in a modern hospital with expert assistance and every upto date appliance to hand. (*Ziker* v *Robertson* (1897) 30 NSR 61 – Canadian Case).

Similarly, where a compliant could have been successfully diagnosed by the use of particular instruments regard must be had to the availability of the instruments amounts to negligence (*Whiteford* v *Hunter* (1950) 94 Sol Jo7 58).

Again it will also be unreasonable to expect the same standard from a doctor or surgeon when he is faced with a dilemma in dealing with dangerous case. Thus, where there is an urgent need for immediate action, a practitioner will not necessarily be held for negligence if in the agony of the moment he adopts a course or omits a precaution which he might not perhaps have adopted or omitted had he had time to consider the matter. The conduct of the practitioner in such a case must be judged in the light of the emergency of the occasion and in the light of the facts known to him which compelled him to act. (*Mohan* v *Osborne* 1993 (2) CPJ (Guj)).

Swanson v *Wilson* (1953) 3 DLR 171, a Canadian case will illustrate this principle. As a result of medical examination and X-rays of plaintiff, a man of 77 years of age, two doctors had come to different opinions. One doctor held the view that it was a case of presumptive cancer and the other diagnosed the case as that of gastric ulcer. A third doctors, a surgeon, to whom the matter was referred, after considering different reports and after an examination of the patient, recommended an operation. The operation was conducted with the patient's approval, and it was discovered that it was a case of gastric ulcer. Upon exercising the ulcer, the surgeon who performed the operation, became doubtful whether cancer was not also present. He then called in an experienced pathologist to make a rapid histological examination of specimen. The examination took about ten to twenty minutes and the pathological reported that cancer was probably present though could not be definite about it. Since time was precious and the surgeon could not proceed with a radial operation or to terminate the operation decided to sew up immediately, with a view to await the result of a more detailed and lengthier examination. In doing so, he removed large portions of the patient's stomach pancreas and the entire spleen. It was, however ultimately discovered that the surgeon was not guilty of negligence, because, as it was found that before operation, he had done and secured all information that could reasonably be expected. He was quite justified in the circumstances in proceeding with the radical operation even though it turned out that there was no malignancy.

In *Vaghri Gopal Bhai* v *Parmar Navalben Balabhai* (1993 I CPR 526), the Gujarat State Commission dismissed the complaint on ground of medical services being provided in rural set up where minimal facilities and expert assistance were available and under the attending circumstances doctors had given full medical attention.

In *S. Iqbal Khan* v *Child Trust Hospital Madras* (1994 III CPR 233 (TN)), the hospital was not held negligent when it transfused B positive blood to an A2B positive child because the child was gravely ill and B positive blood was transfused as a life saving measure because A2B positive blood was not available.

6. Define *novus actus interveniens* and how can it affect a case of medical negligence?

It means 'new act' coming between the original negligence act and the ultimate damage, thereby breaching the chain of causation.

The complainants own *novus actus* is also known as contributory negligence. If the *novus actus* was by a third person and the defendant is able to prove it he could escape liability completely or partially.

Damage resulting to plaintiff after the chain of causation set in the motion and does not qualify for award of damages against the defendant's wrongful act snapped is too remote, and does not qualify for award of damages against the defendant (*Weld Blundell* v *Stephens* 1920 AC 956. 86 (HL) per Lord Summer). Such wrongful act may also be a third party as was the case in *Predergast* v *Sam and Dee* (1989) 1 Med LR 36, where a doctor prescribed a drug and though he was negligent in not writing the name of the drug legibly, the doctor contended that there had been a *novus actus* on the part of the chemist for his failure to telephone him about the illegible handwriting which constituted a break in the chain of causation. However, the argument failed because the court ruled that it was foreseeable that the pharmacist would prescribe the wrong drug because of the doctor's illegible writing.

In *Thumu Padma* v *Dr. Hemlatha* 2003 (6) CLD 108 (AP), an MTP case where the patient got perforation and developed peritonitis ten days after MTP, it came to light that the patient had a fall on a cot and her abdomen came into contact with the leg of the cot which could have caused the perforation. This new occurrence/act (*novus actus interveniens*) broke the chain of causation and the doctor was held not negligent.

7. Does refusing to attend constitute negligence?

A doctor is free to choose whom he will serve. Not only this he should exercise due care before deciding to accept a patient for treatment. He must not accept a task beyond his level of competence. But his liberty does not extend to accident, injury and emergency cases as the answer to the next question will clarify.

Hospitals, nursing homes, clinics or doctors, who declare or profess in writing that they provide emergency services 24-hours services, are legally bound to attend all cases. Failure to have the requisite equipment in working order, and non-availability of competent staff within reasonable time would be inferred as medical negligence.

8. Can refusal of medical care to injury and emergency cases constitute negligence?

In order to obtain a clear answer to this question it is essential to understand two Supreme Court rulings on this important issue.

The first ruling was in public interest litigation in the case of *Parmanand Katara* v *Union of India* 1989 ACJ 1000 (SC) where, while approving the decision of the High Power Committee under the chairmanship of Director General of Health Services, the Supreme Court observed:

(1) There are no provisions in the Indian Penal Code, criminal procedure code, Motor Vehicle Act, etc, which prevent doctors from promptly attending seriously injured persons and accident cases before the arrival of the police.

(2) The treatment of the patient would not wait for the arrival of the police or competing legal formalities.

(3) All government hospitals, medical institutions, should be asked to provide immediate medical aid to all the cases-medico-legal or not.

The Supreme Court further observed:

> "There can be no second opinion that preservation of human life is of paramount importance. That is so on account of the fact that once life is lost, the *status quo ante* cannot be resorted as resurrection in beyond the capacity of man.

Article 21 of the Constitution casts the obligation on the state to preserve life. A doctor at the Government Hospital positioned to meet this state obligation is, therefore duty bound to extend medical assistance for preserving life.

Every doctor whether at the Government Hospital or otherwise has the professional obligation to extend his services with due expertise for protecting life. No law or state action can intervene to avoid/delay the discharge of the paramount obligation cast upon numbers of the medical profession. The obligation being Total, absolute and paramount, laws of procedure whether in statute or otherwise which would interfere with the discharge of this obligation cannot be sustained and must therefore give way.

In *Paschim Bengal Khet Mazdoor Samity* v *State of West Bengal* AIR 1996 SC 2426, Hakim Seikh, a member of Paschim Bengal Khet Mazdoor Samity, an organisation of agricultural labourers, fell off a train and suffered serious head injuries and brain hemorrhage. He was taken to a primary health center, but since necessary facilities for the treatment were not available he was referred to higher centre. He was taken to NRS Medical College Hospital, but was refused admission as there was no vacant bed. He was then taken to other state hospitals, who also refused admission on the grounds of no vacant bed. He was then taken to other state hospital, where he recovered after incurring heavy expenditure on his treatment.

The question considered by the Supreme Court was whether the non-availability of facilities (bed/neuro-surgeon) had resulted in denial of his fundamental right guaranteed under Article 21 of the Constitution. The Supreme Court held:

> "The Constitution envisages the establishment of welfare state at the federal level as well as the state level. In a welfare state the primary duty of the government is to secure the welfare of the people. Providing adequate medical facilities for the people is an essential part of the obligation by running hospitals and health centers which provide medical care to the persons seeking to avail these facilities, Article 21 imposes an obligation on the state to safeguard the right to every person. Preservation of human life is thus of paramount importance. The government hospitals run by the state and the medical officers employed therein are duty bound to extend medical assistance for preserving human life. Failure on the part of government to provide timely medical treatment to a person in need of such treatment results in violation of his right to life guaranteed under article 21."

In the present case, there was breach of such right of Hakim Seikh guaranteed under Article 21 when he was denied treatment at various

Government hospitals and state could not avoid its responsibility for such denial of the constitutional right of Hakim Seikh. The Supreme Court awarded ₹25,000 as compensation to Hakim Seikh.

Remedial measures to rule out recurrence of such incidents in future, to ensure medical treatment to person in real need were made and copy of the judgment was directed to be sent to the centre and to all states to take necessary steps to implement these —

The court further observed that in order that proper medical facilities are available for dealing with emergency cases it must be that:

1. Adequate facilities at the primary health centers where the patient can be given immediate primary treatment so as to stabilize his condition.
2. Hospitals at the district level and sub-division level are upgraded so that serious cases can be treated there.
3. Facilities for giving specialist treatment are increased and are available at the hospitals at District level and sub-division level having regard to the growing needs.
4. In order to ensure availability of beds in an emergency at state level hospitals there is a centralized communication system so that the patient can be sent immediately to the hospital where bed is available in respect of the treatment which is required.
5. Proper arrangement of ambulance is made for transport of a patient from the primary health centre to the district hospital or sub-division hospital and from the district hospital or sub-division hospital to the state hospital.
6. The ambulance is adequately provided with necessary equipment and medical personnel.
7. Health centers and hospitals and the medical personnel attached to these centers and hospitals are geared to deal with larger number of patients needing emergency treatment on account of higher risk of accident on certain occasions and in certain seasons.

The casualty officer in a hospital, which is open for receiving patients, who fails to see and examine a person would be negligent in as much as he does not discharge the duty of care owed by the hospital authority to the person who suffers by his negligence.

9. When does duty of care of hospital/doctor start and when does it end?

The moment a doctor/hospital accepts to treat a patient who has submitted himself for such treatment, the duty of care starts irrespective of monetary considerations. This duty ends when:

1. The patient was recovered from that particular illness, for which the treatment was initiated.
2. Patient fails to re-attend for further treatment.

3. Patient abandons the treatment.
4. Patient or the treating doctor dies, in case of treatment in a hospital the duty of care will still exist inspite of death of the treating doctor,
5. In an emergency case requiring critical care ambulance service, preferably equipped with ICU facilities, if available is advised.
6. Patient is referred elsewhere for further treatment. It may be noted that in case of referral the duty of care of the referring doctor continues till the time the patient departs for going to the doctor/hospital to which the patient has been referred. It is the duty of referring doctor to ensure that:
   (*a*) Proper referral note is given.
   (*b*) Proper guidance regarding transportation, care to be taken in transmit, etc, is provided.
   (*c*) In an emergency case requiring critical care ambulance service, preferably equipped with ICU facilities, if available, is advised.
   (*d*) All life saving drugs are given before departure, and
   (*e*) The centre where the referral is being made is informed in advance.

Patient who register with doctors/hospitals and patient who enter the accident and emergency ward of a hospital, are allowed a duty of care, because they either have a legal right to be treated or have actually been treated, in short, their treatment has been undertaken. The word 'treatment' includes diagnosis and any suggested courses of action which ought to be followed, whether the patient has been seen or has not been seen by the doctor for example, the doctor in the causality department of a busy hospital who instructs a nurse *via* the telephone of the treatment which the patient is to undergo, or in the case of what has been referred to as telemedicine, where the patient is treated at a long distance using modern technological methods of communication. It may be noted that telemedicine is now being resorted to in India as well.

10. What is meant by an emergency?

The word 'emergency' means, a sudden, unexpected happening, an unforeseen occurrence or condition. (*Black's Law Dictionary, 6th Edn.*)

Therefore, to qualify as medical emergency, it must be a sudden, unforeseen condition of the patient and/or where according to the patient or his attendants or the doctor, question of life and death is there.

11. When is the duty of care of doctor/hospital towards the patient not established?

Where a doctor examines a patient for some purpose other than providing advice and treatment, no doctor-patient relationship is established in the strict sense and thus to a certain extent on duty of care exists. Some examples are of medical examination for insurance, fitness, medical legal cases, disability, visa and causal advice.

Doctors rendering first aid in an emergency were previously considered outside the purview of doctor-patient relationship, but courts are increasingly holding doctors liable for negligence under the circumstances, although the standard of care expected would be less and the margin of error permitted would be more.

It must be remembered that if the doctor is negligent during examination, *e.g.* using wrong eye drops during eye examination or puncturing artery during taking of blood samples, etc, a claim of negligence may be brought against him.

12. Is abandonment of patient negligence?

Abandon means "to desert", "to relinquish" "to give up" (*Black's Law Dictionary, 6th Edition*). This can occur only after the establishment of doctor-patient relationship. A doctor who happens to be a passerby at an accident or any other emergency site, his failure to react would not be abandonment. To provide abandonment, the following must be established:

1. that there was existing a doctor-patient relationship which was terminated by the doctor without obtaining the consent of patient, and/or without giving time or notice (oral or written),
2. the doctor discontinued the treatment even while the patient had not recovered from the illness for which treatment was initiated, and
3. The abandonment must be the proximate cause of injury/death.

The defence against such charge of negligence may be:

(*a*) Patient was not co-operating/following instructions,

(*b*) Patient has gone under some other responsible care, *e.g.* under care of professional colleague, etc.

(*c*) The doctor was convicted that the illness was fictitious one, and

(*d*) Adequate notice was given.

The defence by the doctor/hospital of non-payment of fees is usually a weak one.

13. Define the kinds of negligence with illustration?

Depending upon the circumstances the negligence may be:

13.1 Gross negligence

The intentional failure to perform a manifest duty is reckless disregard of the consequences. (*Black's Law Dictionary*) ordinary negligence, dealt with under an earlier question is based on the fact that one ought to have known results of his acts, while gross negligence rests on the assumption that one knew results of his acts, but was recklessly or wantonly indifferent to results.

13.2 Criminal negligence

Negligence of such a character, or occurring under such circumstances as to be punishable as a crime by a statute, or such a flagrant and reckless disregard of the life and safety of others, or willful indifference to the injury liable to follow, as to convert an act, otherwise lawful, into a crime against the state when it results in personal injury or death. Here the negligence is so great as to go beyond matter of mere compensation.

Not only has to the doctor made a wrong diagnosis and treatment, but also that he has shown such gross ignorance, gross carelessness or gross neglect for the life and safety of the patient that a criminal charge is brought against him. For this, he may be prosecuted in a criminal court for having caused injury to or the death of his patient by a rash and negligent act amounting to culpable homicide under section 304 of the Indian Penal Code. Some instances which may amount to criminal negligence may include;

Injecting Anaesthesia in fatal dosage or in wrong tissues.

- Amputation of wrong finger, operation on wrong limb, removal of wrong organ or errors in legation of ducts.
- Operation of wrong patient.
- Applying too tight plaster or splints which may cause gangrene or paralysis.
- Leaving instrument or sponges inside the part of body operate upon.
- Transfusing wrong blood.
- Performing a criminal abortion.
- Performing an act which is prohibited or punishable by law.
- Unqualified person conducting operation.

In an attempt to avoid misuse of the word 'reckless', Lord Taylor of Gosforth suggested four categories of attitude which would constitute the required state of mind to bring the case within the realm of the criminal law, they are:

(*a*) Indifference to an obvious risk of injury to health,

(*b*) Actual foresight of the risk coupled with determination nevertheless to run it,

(*c*) Appreciation of the risk coupled with an intention to avoid it but also coupled with such a high degree of negligence in the attempted avoidance as the jury consider justifies action,

(*d*) Inattention or failure to advert to a serious risk which goes beyond mere inadvertence in respect of an obvious and important matter which the defendant's duty demanded he should address.

Needless to emphasize that where the doctor is found criminally negligent, in addition to his being prosecuted under criminal law, the patient/attendant can also bring an action against him for claiming compensation for the negligence, under the law of tort or the Consumer Protection Act.

The Andhra Pradesh High Court in *Shanta* v *State of A.P.* 1997 III CPJ 481 (AP), while granting compensation against a government hospital for negligence of leaving a mop in the womb for violating fundamental right of right to life under Article 21 of the Constitution observed that the petitioner shall be free to take action in tort for the damages under the private law against the hospital and others and also to make complaint for any criminal act of the hospital, if so advised.

When no criminal negligence?

Where a serious patient was taken to a hospital and the doctor did not attend to him immediately it was held by the Supreme Court that if there was delay on the part of the doctor to attend on the patient, that may at worst be a case of civil negligence and not one of culpable negligence falling under section 304A, IPC.

13.3 Negligence per se

Conduct, whether of action or omission, which may be declared and treated as negligence without any argument or proof as to the particular surrounding circumstances, either because it is in violation of a statute or valid municipal ordinance or because it is so palpably opposed to the dictates of common prudence that it can be said without hesitation or doubt that no careful person would have been guilty of it. As a general rule the violation of the public duty, enjoined by the law for the protection of person or property, so constitutes (*Black's Law Dictionary*).

While quoting Black's above definition the Supreme Court in *Poonam Verma* v *Ashwini Patel* AIR 1996 SC 2111, has applied the principal of negligence *per se* which is summarized hereunder as:

> "Respondent, Ashwani Patel, a homeopath, not having studied allopathy, treated the patient suffering from viral fever and then typhoid with allopathic medicines, and the patient died within two weeks. The law under which he was registered as medical practitioner permitted the respondent to practice homeopathy only, hence he was under the statutory duty not to enter the field of any other systems of medicine. His trespassing of this duty constituted negligence *per se*, and he was held liable."

In *Dr. CD Bajaj* (*Fauji Doctor — Cancer Hospital*) v *Hari Chand,* 2003 (1) CPR 328 (Punj), where a cancer patient was treated by a doctor who was not qualified to treat that disease (in this case he was not even an MBBS), it was held this amounted to negligence *per se* by following the case of *Poonam Verma* as *Ashwini Patel* (*Supra*). A compensation of ₹80,000 was awarded.

13.4 Contributory negligence

In many cases, a doctor needs the patient's attendant's cooperation in diagnosis and a treatment. The doctor will need reasonably accurate information regarding the patient's symptoms and medical history. Similarly, cooperation is usually needed in administering the treatment, *e.g.* with regard to taking medication in the right quantity and at proper intervals or returning for follow up. However, it is the doctor's duty to give clear and unambiguous instructions, and to explain in intelligible terms what is required of the patient and to give him any necessary warning if the patient fails to follow these instructions and this is a cause of his injuries then it will be possible to argue that the patient/attendant had been contributory negligent, or in an extreme case, that his conduct was the sole cause of the damages.

Where the damages is attributable partly to the fault (negligence) of the complainant and partly to the fault of the doctor the compensation may be reduced to such an extent as the court thinks just and equitable, having regard to the patient's share the responsibility for the injury.

When the defence is raised in a clinical negligence claim, the defendant doctor will have to establish that the claimant's conduct contributed to the damage and that he has failed to take reasonable care for his own safety. The claimant need not owe any duty to the defendant doctor. The standard of care expected of the claimant is measure objectively and is the same as for negligence itself, although there is of course some discretion in relation to children and those claimants under a disability.

If a doctor wishes to rely on this defence, then he should look to the Canadian Courts for guidance on how the principle may be applied. In *Crossman* v *Stewart* (1997) 82 DLR (3d) 677, a patient was rendered almost blind from chloroquine retinopathy, the drug having been prescribed for a skin disorder. However, the claimant's damages were reduced by two-thirds because she had obtained some of her supplies of the drug from an unknown source and failed to obtain prescription renewals or to consult her treating physician. (*adopted from Malcolm Khan, et al; Clinical Negligence 2nd, edn. 2002 P242*).

Whether the defence would be appropriate in, for example a situation where the claimant fails to return to his doctor surgeon for follow up visits is debatable and it could only be invoked where the claimant has been specifically and repeatedly warned to return if certain symptoms are of serious nature, other than that, it would be unwise to place too much emphasis on this defence, primarily because the court will always view the doctor's duty to his patient as paramount and will reluctant to hold the patient culpable because of his lack of knowledge and lack of control over any given situation. Also any defendant-doctor who pleads contributory negligence may find that the burden of proof is back on him. For example, if the defendant-doctor alleges that the claimant failed to read the prescription properly or return to the doctor if his condition deteriorated, the court may question what advice the defendant-doctor gave to the patient regarding the medication condition and whether this advice was adequate.

14. Contributory negligence must be pleaded as a defence

It is important that when a complaint is filed against a doctor negligence, the defendant doctor must plead that there was contributory negligence on the part of the complainant or his attendant. If it is not pleaded it is not open to the court to find that the complainant had been contributory negligent.

15. Delegation of duties to patient or his attendants

Such delegation may not be justifiable in every case. It depends upon the circumstances of the case, condition of patient, degree of risk involved if instructions are not followed, intelligence and capacity of the patient attendant to carry them out. Failure on the part of the patient/attendant to carry out the instructions may not constitute contributory negligence in certain cases.

Examples

In *R.K. Agarwal* v *Dr. B. Mukhopadhyay* 1995 I CPJ 260, the complainant sustained fracture in his left elbow. Treatment given and advised follow up. Instead he consulted other doctors who advised operation. The court held that the complainant obviously changed doctors and did not follow treatment suggested by Dr. Mukhopadhyay (contributory negligence). The case came to be dismissed.

In *Consumer Education Research Society* v *Dr. Ratilal B. Patel* 1994 II CPJ 342 (Guj), the complainant was suffering from long duration fever and was given injection by the doctor. Infection and septicemia developed, and he had to be operation. Suppression of history of prior illness and treatment taken from a previous doctor was cited in the judgment. The state commission observed:

> "............. We do not say that merely because there was no disclosure the complaint should be dismissed. It has some consideration and relevance only."

In *Md. Aslam* v *Ideal Nursing Home* 1997 III CPJ 81 (NC), wife of the complainant underwent hysterectomy (removal of uterus). During the post-operation period, despite repeated caution to take only liquid and semi-solid diet, she continued to consume ice cream, roti, meat, dal, puri and fried eggs. This led to burst abdomen, but she died the next day. The state commission dismissed the case on the ground that the patient was not following the advice repeatedly given to her (a case of contributory negligence).

In *Dr. R.V. Rao* v *Dr. Y.R. Krishna* 2003 I CPJ 210 (MP), in laparoscopic cholecystectomy the operating surgeon had fixed the clip at the common bile duct (CBD) resulting in obstruction to passing bile from duct to stomach in accumulating the bile at liver resulted in post-cholocystecystectomy CBD structure, obstructive jaundice and an anterior abdominal wall abscess.

When the complications developed, the complainant consulted doctors of Medical College hospital, and other doctors who suggested surgical legation. But, the complainant did not care to abide the medical advice and got the second operation done to correct the mistake which occurred during operation performed by the opposite party, the life of the patient would have been saved. Therefore, the complainant was held equally responsible for prolonging the pain and agony which his wife had to suffer.

Therefore, it was not only the opposite party doctor but the complainant himself who was responsible for his negligence behavior, therefore the state commission was not in favour towards a huge amount of compensation as claimed by the complainant. He had incurred lot of money for treatment. In the circumstances, compensation of ₹1,00,000 was awarded as against ₹9.25 lakh claimed.

In *Mohd. Azeemuddin* v *Dr. M. Nagabhushanam* 2003 (5) CLD 653 (AP), a case of cholecystectomy, the patient developed complications, she was advised for post-surgical follow up and corrective treatment but she did not follow the advice and treatment and ultimately died. The opposite party doctor was held not negligent.

16. Does the duty of care of doctor/hospital extend to persons other than the patient or third parties?

Suppose a paediatrician sees a child with chicken-pox should his advice to the treatment of that child or also think of other family members in contract with the child? The answer is yes. A similar situation would exist whenever a doctor is treating a case of open tuberculosis, other contagious diseases, etc.

In *Tarasoff* v *Regents of the University of California* 551 P (2d) 334 (1976), it was held by the Supreme Court of California (USA) that the psychiatrist was held liable to the third person who was attacked by one of his patients on the ground that the patient had confide his intention to attack the third party but the doctor had failed to take steps to avoid injury to the third party.

There may well be circumstances in which it is foreseeable that the patient could be a potential hazard to third parties where a doctor would be held to owe a duty of care. If, for example, a patient's medical condition (such as epilepsy) or the side effects of a drug that the doctor has prescribed render certain conduct (such as driving a motor vehicle) hazardous, the doctor will be under a duty to warn the patient. If he fails to do so and as a result the patient causes an accident injuring others there could be little doubt that the doctor would owe a duty of care, both to the patient and the third parties.

17. When consent is not required?

The consent is not required when firstly, the patient's balance of mind is distributed, secondly when the patient is incapable of giving consent by reason of unconsciousness, and finally when the patient is minor. [*Punjab Nursing Home* v *Kailash Marodia* 2003 (2) CLD 852 (MP)].

There may be cases where a surgery or a procedure has to be conduct without waiting for the consent, *i.e.*, where the same has to be performed without seeking consent as the same is not feasible because to wait for consent is not in the interest of the patient as it is so emergent (*Dr. Janki S. Kumar* v *Mrs. Sarafunisa* 2000 I CPJ 66).

In an obstetrics case the doctor was not negligent when she removed the uterus of the patient without consent. In the circumstances, as evidence in the case, the removal of uterus without getting the consent of the second plaintiff did not give rise to any actionable claim. Patient was incapable of giving consent as she was anaesthetized when the emergency arose; therefore, the only alternative for doctor was to get the consent from her husband which was obtained. That apart, the doctors had the right as well as the duty to perform any such additional operation which was considered as therapeutically necessary in the course of treatment and it has to be proved that such a necessity arose during the operation. (*Arun Balkrishnan Iyer* v *Soni Hospital* AIR 2003 Mad 389).

18. Can compensation be awarded for want of consent?

In medical field the word "consent" carries a great importance. The concept of consent is not new to the modern world. Consent plays a remarkable legitimate role in the medical field especially in the field of medical negligence. The "consent" should be a free consent as envisaged by section 10 of the Indian Contract Act in the context of medical negligence. A duty is cast upon the medical practitioner to prove that he did not use any undue influence in order to get a legally valid consent from a patient and he has at no point of time utilized his dominant and superior position in obtaining consent from patient who is always practically in a precarious needy and difficult position. In case the consent is not obtained that will give rise to cause of action for seeking the remedy criminally for making any invasive procedure without consent of patient amounting to assault, with criminal force under section 350 of the Indian Penal Code and he can also seek a civil remedy for compensation for the injury occurred to the patient in accordance with law of Torts. According to Law of Torts, if the doctor not seek a legally valid consent, and even if there are no damages in the form of negligence, the patient can sue the doctor for injury upon his personal or private right encroached upon which has been endowed upon him by legislative enactments. The principle of requiring consent applies in all the cases except in certain circumstances in which the doctor may be entitled to proceed without his consent, firstly when the patient's balance of mind is disturbed. Secondly, when the patient is incapable of giving consent by reason of unconsciousness, and finally when the patient is minor but none of the conditions exists in the present case. In the case in hand the doctor had come with a case of proxy consent, *i.e.* of not of the close relative but of a friend. In such circumstances, real consent was not taken which certainly amounts to negligence for giving rise to cause of action irrespective of the fact that medical negligence or deficiency has not been established. It was held that for want of real consent, the complainant is entitled to compensation, which was qualified at ₹12,000 [*Punjabi Nursing Home* v *Kailash Marodia* 2003 (2) CLD 852 (MP)].

When one speaks of consent, that should be informed consent, the person who given the consent should understand the risk involved and on that awareness the patient should have given consent is legally valid. [*Dr. Janki S. Kumar* v *Sarofunnisa* 2000 I CPJ 66].

In *Dr. T.T. Thomas* v *Elisa* AIR 1987 Ker 52 the Kerala High Court laid down that consent was implicit in the case of patient who submits to the doctor, and absence of the consent must be made out by the person alleging it. In the case of emergency operation the doctor cannot wait for the consent of his parent or where the patient is not in fit state of mind to give a conscious answer regarding consent or where the patient is a minor. Even if he is in a fit condition to give voluntary answer, the surgeon has a duty to inform him of the dangers ahead or the risk involved by going without an operation at the earliest.

19. Define acts of commission and omission may make consent legally not valid?

Act of 'commission' which may make consent legally not valid:

— Consent given taken from a person who is under sedation, intoxicated or not fully conscious,

— blanket consent at the time of admission,

— Consent obtained from a person less than 18 years of age,

— Consent given under fear, fraud, misrepresentation of facts, etc.

— Insertion in consent of a clause exonerating the staff/doctor/hospital for liability arising out of any negligence which may occur.

Act of omission which may make consent legally not valid:

— Not providing adequate information before obtaining consent,

— Failure to obtain consent for a specific procedure before the procedure,

— Not ascertaining whether person is fit tc give consent,

— Not obtaining consent in language understood by the person giving consent,

— Not noting date and time on the consent,

— Non-witnessing of consent (in certain circumstances).

20. Does a doctor have a right to decide which patient he would examine first?

It has been held by the National Commission in *B.S. Hegde* v *Dr. Sudhanshu Bhattacharya* 1993 (3) CPR 414 (NC) that a doctor has the absolute right to decide which patient he would examine first even out of turn depending upon the condition of the patient. It cannot be maintained that a patient must be examined by the doctor at the appointed time.

21. Does failure to have equipment in working order constitute negligence?

In case of damage occurring to a patient due to absence/non-working equipment, e.g. oxygen cylinder, suction machine, insulator, ventilator, etc., the doctor/hospital could be held liable. The excuse that the equipment had gone for repairs may not be acceptable.

22. Is failure to write prescription legibly negligence/deficiency in service?

Yes. In an English case — *Prender Gast* v *Sam and Dee* 1989 1 Med LR 36, a doctor had written an illegible prescription for a patient of asthma wherein he had actually prescribed amoxil tablets (an anti biotic) which was misread by the pharmacist as daonil (a hypoglycemic agent) which, when taken by the patient, lowered his blood sugar level causing permanent brain damage.

The doctor and the pharmacist were held negligent to the extent of 25% and 75% respectively. It was also held that the pharmacist had been negligent in failing to refer back to the doctor in case of uncertainty.

23. Does the inherent risk of treatment amount to negligence?

In *Charan Singh* v *Healing Touch Hospital* 2003 (2) CPR 95, an urologist performed an operation for removal of stone urethra under spinal anesthesia. After surgery reticulates and paralysis of left side of body occurred. It was held that what was done by the anesthetist was as per accepted medical practice which carries an inherent and accepted risk of one per cent developing reticulates in 1% cases of spinal anesthesia. The anaesthetist, therefore, was not held to be negligent.

In a case of congenital heart problem the patient had left ventricle perforation during balloon dilation and the doctor aspirated pericardial fluid and the patient was immediately shifted to Operation Theater and subjected to emergency open heart surgery for excision of sub-aortic membrane and Myomectomy. Surgery was conduct for closing the perforation and also for removing the obstructing bands of muscles in the ventricle and after the patient was shifted to intensive care unit he had cardiac arrest. Though cardiac massage/resuscitation was done the patient did not respond and died. Merely because the patient had perforation of left ventricle during the procedure it cannot be presumed that there is negligence on the part of doctor when the risk is inherent in the said procedure [*G. Suresh Kumar* v *Director, Nizam Institute of Medical Sciences* 2003 (3) CLD 377 (AP)].

24. Does failure to foresee risk of treatment and failure to take necessary precaution or make necessary arrangement to avoid damage in the event of that foreseeable risk occurring constitute negligence?

Failure to take precautions to avoid a risk will not be characterized as negligent unless the risk is of a reasonably substantial nature. Where the risk is negligible, failure to take precautions will not be incompatible with exercise of proper care and skill. In *Warren* v *Greig and White, the Lancet,* 1935, Vol LP 330, case reported in the Lancet, a patient underwent an operation for the removal of twenty-eight of his teeth. Following the operation there was excessive bleeding on account of which the patient died. It was however, found afterwards that the patient was suffering from acute mycloid leukemia. It was held that neither the doctor nor the dentist was negligent in failing to test the patient's blood, because the disease being a rare one and it could not be said in the circumstances that a blood test should have been carried out before the operation as a safeguard against the bare possibility that such a condition existed. In any given case precautions are expected to be taken to guard against known risks, that is, risks which were known or ought reasonably to have been known the ordinary skilled intelligent and careful practitioner belongs. A classical case of not anticipating blood requirement and keeping blood in where deceased was admitted in the hospital on 20-11-1995 with labour pains and delivered her second baby there was profuse bleeding after the delivery. When the blood grouping was tested and it was found to be A negative and when A negative blood was not available 2 units of A positive blood were given to the patient followed by 6 units of 'A' negative blood along with dopamine drip, etc, to revive her condition and in spite of that the patient did not recover and died.

No literature of medical opinion was found supporting transfusion of A positive blood when A negative blood was not available. The respondents did not take precaution, even when the patient was admitted, to keep and procure the necessary blood after grouping typing and cross-matching.

There was lack of diligence on the part of doctors in being prepared for caesarean section in case of emergency and also for not acquiring the requisite 'A' negative blood and keeping in ready in case of emergency since the first delivery was by caesarean section and in the second case a normal delivery was being attempted, there could be haemorrhage at any state specially post-partum haemorrhage and not keeping 'A' negative blood ready showed lack of diligence. [*Katra Satyanarayana* v *Lakshmi Nursing Home* 2003 (3) CLD 532].

25. Does failure to warn about inherent risks/special risks or risk of failure of treatment before taking consent constitute negligence? Can a plea be raised against a doctor that he was negligent in failing to disclose the risk involved in the treatment?

In case the risk is known to occur commonly, it should be explained even if it is a minor problem. If a risk is extremely rare but in case of its occurrence it could be serious problem, it should be explained, *e.g.* a person who has been blind in one eye for many years is offered an operation in hope of restoring some degree of vision, should be warned of the one in 14000 chance of sympathetic ophthalmia developing in the other eye, which could render him blind in both the eyes.

Another example may be that of a neuro-paralytic reaction occurring after conventional anti-rabies vaccine course. Before initiating such a course this risk, though rare, ought to be explained in writing to every patient or his attendants.

It is important that not only the inherent and special risks involved in any surgery or treatment must be explained to the patient/attendant and consent obtained, it is equally important to document such consent. In the absence of such documentation it may be difficult for the doctor to defend himself if such a risk occurs and damage is caused.

If the claim is that the doctor failed to disclose the risk involved in the treatment/surgery and the risk actually occurs, the claimant can raise a plea that had such risk been disclosed he would not have agreed to such treatment/surgery. Of course, he has to have a plausible argument as to why he would not have accepted such treatment.

In principle there seems to be little difficult in attributing causative responsibility to a doctor who has in breach of duty failed to draw a particular risk to his parent's attention if in the event that particular risk materializes.

The purpose of the rule requiring doctors to give appropriate information to their patients is to enable the patient to exercise the right to choose whether or not to have the particular operation to for which consent it asked for. Liability lies in negligence rather than trespass. But the patient does still have right to choose what will and will not be done with her body and the doctor must take the care except of a reasonable doctor in the circumstances in giving her the information relevant to that choice. The law is designed to require doctors properly to inform their parents of the risks attendant on their treatment and to answer questions put to them as to that treatment and its dangers, such answers to be judged in the context of good professional practice, which has tended to a greater degree of frankness over the years, with more respect having given to the patient autonomy. The object is to enable the patient to decide whether or not to run the risks of having that operation at that time. If the doctor's failure to take that care results in her consenting to an operation to which she would not otherwise have given her consent, the purpose of that rule would be thwarted if he were not to be held responsible when the very risk about which he failed to warn her materializes and causes her any injury which she would not have suffered then and there (*Chester* v *Afshar* (2002) 3 All ER 552).

In an ophthalmic case, the doctor did not note in the prescription or in any document about the risk involved while undertaking cataract operation. The doctor of course said during his examination in court hat he had explained the danger inherent in the operation because of want of B-scan report, but there was nothing in writing in the prescription nor anywhere in the treatment sheet. The complainant had eventually got one B-scan report done when everything was over and he had become completely blind of his right eye. Had the complainant been told about the exact position of the matter he might not have opted of the operation or might have obtained second medical opinion about the advisability of such an operation. It is noticed that because of failure of the doctor to enlighten the complainant about the entire matter, the complainant was denied of all the opportunities of having a better expert opinion in this regard. Therefore it can be said without any hesitation that the doctor acted in a rash and negligent manner. Therefore it is to be held that there has been deficiency in service on the part of the doctor and as such he is liable to pay compensation to the complainant which was assessed as ₹1,00,000. [*Sourinder Mohan Ghose* v *Dr. D.V. Pahwa* 2002 II CPJ 243 (WB)]

In English Law, patients are not entitled to the fullest possible information about the treatment they receive. Instead it is up the doctor to decide how much information to give, and the test to be applied in deciding whether a doctor had acted reasonably in the amount of information given in that in (*Bolam* v *Friern Hospital Management Committee* (1957) 2 All ER 118). If a doctor is liable to demonstrate that he acted in accordance with a responsible body of medical opinion, he will not be negligent.

In *Sidaway* v *Governors of Bethlem Royal Hospital* (1985) 2 WLR 480, the House of Lords gave long and detailed consideration as to how much a doctor is required to explain to a patient about the possible side effects and risks involved in a particular treatment before the patient agrees for the procedure to begin. In that case the risks inherent in surgery to the plaintiff's arm of long-term damage to the nerves were put at 1% and the House of Lords did not consider that it was necessary for the plaintiff to have been informed of so small a risk. The House of Lords decided that the Bolam test should apply in these circumstances, and that the doctor should assess how much information it is necessary to give a patient in the circumstances of each individual case. As long as the advice of the doctor gives conforms with the advice which would be given by a responsible body of medical practitioners in the same filed, there will be no negligence.

This case demonstrates that it is difficult for the patient to succeed in an action for negligence based on the consent given through lack of information.

However, a recent Australian case departs from this principle. In *Rogers* v *Whitaker* (1992) Aust Torsts Rep 81, a woman who had repeatedly asked an eye surgeon about the risks involved in a particular operation, and who was not informed of a one in 14000 risk of total blindness succeeded in an action for negligence. The High Court of Australia held that *Bolam* only applies in connection with treatment and diagnosis, not to the decision to inform of inherent risks.

In *Smith* v *Barking Havering and Brentwood HA* (1994) 5 Med LR 285, the claimant had undergone an operation as a child to drain a cyst on her spinal cord. At the age of 18, she began to experience problems again and she was advised to have a further operation in the hope of alleviating her condition, without which she would have been in a wheel chair within three months and a tetraplegic with in six months. It was accepted there was a 50% chance that the second operation could immediately worsen the condition, this is fact happened and the claimant was rendered a tetraplegic immediately. It was admitted that the defendant was negligent in failing adequately to disclose to the claimant the risk involved in the procedure.

In *Thake* v *Mauriee* 1986 Q.B. 644, the claimant underwent a vasectomy operation. The operation failed and claimant's wife gave birth to a fifth child. The claimant sued the defendant in contract and negligence for failing to warn him of the possibility that the vasectomy might not render him irreversibly sterile. The claim in contract failed, the court ruling that a reasonable man would not have understood the defendant as giving an absolute guarantee that the operation would be successful. The claim in negligence succeeded the court ruled the defendant had fallen below the standard of care and had the claimant appreciated that the operation was not fool proof, then Mrs. Thake would have suspected she was pregnant at an earlier stage and consequently sought an abortion.

26. Can record be called for by the court or police or Consumer Forum/ Commission?

It must be remembered that under section 91 of Code of Criminal Procedure, 1973 it would be necessary to hand over the records to the relevant authority when asked to do so. This section reads as under:

"*91. Summons to procedure document or other thing*—

(1) Whenever any court or any officer in charge of a police station considers that the production of any document or other thing is necessary or desirable for the purposes of any investigation, inquiry, trial or other proceeding under this Code by or before such court or officer, such court may issue a summons, or such officer a written order, to the person in whose possession or power such document or thing is believed to be requiring him to attend and procedure it, or to produce it, at the time and place stated in the summons or order.

(2) Any person required under this section merely to procedure a document or other thing shall be deemed to have complied with the

requisition if he causes such document or thing to be produced instead of attending personally to produce the same.

(3) Nothing in this section shall be deemed —

(*a*) to effect sections 123 and 124 of the Indian Evidence Act, 1872 or the Banker's Books Evidence Act, 1891, or

(*b*) to apply to a letter, postcard, telegram or other documents or any parcel or thing in the custody of the postal or telegraph authority".

To more or less similar effect, a provision is made in the Consumer Protection Rules, 1987 under rule 10, which reads as under:

"*10. Additional power to the National Commission, State Commission and District Forum*—

(1) The National Commission, State Commission and the District Forum shall have power to require any person,

(*a*) to produce before, and allow to be examined and kept by an officer of the National Commission, the State Commission or the District Forum, as the case may be, specified in this behalf, such books, accounts, documents or commodities in the custody or under the control of the person so required as may be specified or described in the requisition, if the examination of such books, accounts, documents or commodities are required for the purpose of this Act,

(*b*) to furnish to an officer so specified, such information as may be required for the purpose of this Act.

(2) (*a*) Where during any proceeding under this Act, the National Commission, the State Commission or the District Forum as the case may be, has any ground to believe that any book, paper, commodity or document which may be required to be produced in such proceedings are being or may be, destroyed, mutilated, altered, falsified, or secreted, it may, by written order, authorize any officer to exercise the power to entry and search of any premises. Such authorized officer may also seize such books, papers, documents or commodities as are required for the purpose of the Act.

(*b*) The National Commission, the State Commission or the District Forums, as the case may be, on examination of such seized documents or commodities, as the case may be, may order the retention or may return it to the party concerned."

27. Can practicing defensive medicine constitute negligence?

Defensive medicine is a reaction by a doctor to the perceived threat of litigation. It consists of "adopting procedures which are not for the benefit of the patient but safeguard against the possibility of the patient making a claim for negligence" (*White House* v *Jordan* (1980) All ER 650). This has two aspects:

27.1 Positive defensive medicine

This involves undertaking additional procedures such as diagnostic tests and X-rays, sophisticated diagnostic imaging, endoscopies, repeated investigations which, in the doctor's professional judgment are unnecessary. Some classical examples are:

- Undertaking caesarean section even when not necessary,
- Over prescription of drugs,
- Referral to other consultants,
- Prolonging stay in hospital,
- Insisting for hospitalization/frequent follow up visits, and
- Excess record keeping at times leading to anticipatory forgery of the data.

27.2 Negative defensive medicine

This involves:

- Fixed practice hours and fixed number of patients,
- Avoiding emergency and high risk cases,
- Avoiding procedures because of the risk of something giving wrong, which in the doctor's professional judgment are necessary in the patient's best interest, and
- Early retirement from practice.

Positive defensive medicine is a waste of time, money and sources and possibly increases the risk of medical intervention to patients and negative defensive medicine deprives patient of potentially beneficial treatment.

It is important to appreciate that the term "defensive medicine" is used in a perjurative sense, to indicate that the risk of liability includes doctors to adopt practices which are "legally safe" but are not medically required or justified. The charge is that law dictates medical practice, indeed medical practice.

Medical professionals must remember that their frequent argument about defensive medicine does not make sense as a legal concept. The standard of care also applies to defensive medicine. In a case of alleged medical negligence, if a defendant's follow professionals opine that a specific procedure was unnecessary and wasteful, doctor cannot be held negligent for omitting to carry it out. On this basis, it is difficult to see how a doctor can protect himself for a claim in negligence by carrying out an unnecessary procedure or test. If it could be proved on application of principle standard and reasonable care that the doctor fell below it, he could be held liable for practicing defensive medicine.

28. Can a harm occurring following a telephonic advice constitute negligence?

The word causal means 'uncertain' unpremeditated (*Black's Law Dictionary*). Unless and until it is in writing, and causal advice by a doctor to a patient does not establish doctor-patient relationship. Hence duty to care is not established thereby the question of breach of that duty does not arise.

An advice given causally, which may or may not be followed, does not entail liability even though it was given carelessly. (*Kamleshwar Rao Law of Negligence, 1991 Edn.*)

29. If due to other causes any disease occurs, how do the courts decide the question of negligence?

The State Commission held that when the disease can occur due to other causes as well it is for the complainant to prove that the particular act of the opposite party, was the proximate cause of his ailment. [*S.M.N. Consumer Protection Council* v *Ganga Hospital* (1994) III CPJ 237 (TN)].

30. Is adverse reaction of a medicine negligence?

No, reaction to a medicine in itself does not constitute negligence because the response of the patient to the medicine differs from person to person. But in case the doctor has failed to take all necessary precautions which any other reasonably prudent doctor of same level could have taken, *e.g.* asking for history of allergy, performing sensitivity test, checking the dose, route and mode of administration, etc, he may be held liable.

At the same time, it is must that the doctor/hospital equips himself/itself fully to deal with such an eventuality.

In *State of Gujarat* v *Maltiben Valji Bhai Shah* 1994 ACJ 375 (Guj), doctor in order to treat a patient, gave her an injection which reacted and despite anti-reaction treatment, the patient died. The High Court set aside the judgment and conviction under section 304A of IPC of the trail court on the grounds:

(1) Doctor has given a test dose before giving the injection and there was no reaction,

(2) When reaction was noted, the doctor immediately gave anti-reaction treatment, and

(3) The anti-reaction treatment given as testified by another doctor was proper.

In *Consumer Education Research Society* v *Dr. Rati Lal B. Patel* 1994 II CPJ 342 (Guj), following an intramuscular injection in right upper arm, infection and septicemia developed. It was not established that injection was given by unsterilized needle. All standard precautions were observed. As patient was all ready suffering from infection and a number of other injections were given it was difficult to establish that the danger was caused due to that particular injection.

31. Does failure to hand over medical record, X-rays, constitute negligence?

The information regarding patient's illness, prepared or collected by the doctor and indoor patient register, outdoor prescription, investigation reports, X-rays, indoor case sheets, other reports including medico-legal records, certificates, etc.

In the UK there are various acts like the Data Protection Act, 1984, Medical Records Act, 1988 and Health Record Act, 1990 which deal with the issue of handing over medical records to the patient.

In India provision in respect of medical record has been made in the Indian Medical Council (Professional Conduct, Etiquette and Ethics) Regulations, 2002, Regulations 1.3.1 and 1.3.2 whereof provide as under:

> "1.3.1 Every Physician shall maintain the medical records pertaining to his/her indoor patient for a period of 3 years from the date of commencement of the treatment in a standard Performa laid down by medical council of India ...."
>
> "1.3.2 If any request is made for medical records either by the patients/ authorized attendant or legal authorities involved, the same be duly acknowledged and document shall be issued within a period of 72 hours."

Also it must be forgotten that to obtain in writing about his medical illness, investigations and treatment given on a prescription/discharge ticket is the right of every patient.

Non-providing of medical records to the patients/attendants may amount to deficiency in service under the Consumer Protection Act, 1986.

In *Poona Medical Foundation Ruby Hall Clinic* v *Maruti Rao L. Titkare* 1995 I CPJ 232, National Commission has held that there can be no question of negligence by reason of failure to supply hospital records pertaining to the surgical operation performed (unless a legal duty was cast on the hospital to furnish such documents to the patient). It would be sufficient if a discharge card wherein the particulars of diagnosis and treatment administered is mentioned.

In a cardiac surgery the complainant alleged that refusal to give cassettes and photographs of angiogram and angioplasty along with discharge report amounted to deficiency in service on the part of the opposite party Hospital. It was held that such refusal does not amount to deficiency in service on their part when especially the complainant had been furnished with a discharge summary containing the relevant details such as investigation, diagnosis, treatment given and advice on discharge. (*V. Chandrasekar* v *Madar Hospital Ltd.* 2001 I CPJ 137).

In *Mrs. Vijayamma* v *Apollo Diagnostic Centre* 2002 I CPJ 230 (AP), non-issue of discharge card after death of the patient was held to be a deficiency in service.

A special word about handing over x-rays and reports to the patient. Many a time, x-rays and pathological reports are given to the patient at the time of discharge. When a complaint is filed he does not have the X-rays or pathological reports. So, if the X-rays are not retained, it is mandatory that the doctor must write down name, number and date on every X-ray and enter the findings of every X-ray in the indoor record. He should also obtain the signature of the patient at the time of handing over the x-rays and other reports.

32. Is not giving of a test dose prior to local anaesthesia negligence?

No, provided the Anaesthesia used is a common local Anaesthesia that is normally given to all patients and it is not an indication of rashness or negligence. [*Dr. Krishna Prasad* v *State of Karnataka* 1989 ACJ 393 (Karn)].

33. Is giving of local anaesthesia by a surgeon /dentist negligence?

For minor surgery, by practice or convention, the Anaesthesia is not called. It may constitute negligence if some mishap occurs provided the doctor possesses the required knowledge, skill, drugs and equipment to deal with any adverse reaction.

In the changing circumstances, one may prefer to call an Anaesthetist (though this would push up the cost of treatment). Another alternative would be to explain to the patient about the procedure being done without an Anaesthetist being present and act only after taking informed consent in writing.

34. Does giving a wrong report of blood group constitute negligence?

Not necessarily. In the case of *Dharmendra K. Mishra* v *Dr. Akhnri S. Sinha, Medico Lab,* 1996 (2) CPR 192 (Bih.) the blood group report given by opponent as "A" positive. Test from other two hospitals gave blood group as "B" positive. Doctor produced evidence through authoritative books on the subject that fine clumping of red blood cells takes place some times leading to an error in conclusion. Held, a mistaken report in this respect is not necessarily a negligent report.

In regard to the above decision of the Bihar State Commission, it may be submitted that the view that a mistaken report about blood grouping is not necessarily a negligent report cannot be acceptable in all cases. In this particular case because no damage was caused to the patient, the State Commission, taking a lenient view, held that there was no negligence.

There may be cases where on account of wrong report about blood group damage is caused, e.g. occurrence of kernicterus (brain damage as a result of excessive jaundice because of Rh incompatibility in a new born) due to giving of Rh-positive blood report in a pregnant woman when in fact she was Rh-negative.

In *Prafulla K. Sahoo* v *Dr. B.B. Patnaik* (CD Case No. 185 of 1991, decided on 20-5-1993 – unreported), complainant alleged negligence in testing for blood grouping report of which was later cross-checked and found to be wrong. As there was no transfusion of blood based on the erroneous blood group report and as the blood sample which had been drawn somewhere else the State Commission held that no negligence could be proven and dismissed the complaint.

In *Hilarious Institute and Clinical Laboratories* v *Mohan Das,* (Appeal No. 497/95, decided on 20-4-1995 unreported), the complainant was given a wrong report of his blood group test. On the basis of this report, he immediately travelled from Madurai to Calicut to donate blood of his ailing sister-in-law only to find that his blood group was different from that mentioned in the report. The State Commission upheld the decision of the District Forum that deficiency in Service had been committed and order compensation of ₹1,000.

In *Bharat Pathology Laboratory* v *Mangilal Vyas* 2003 III CPJ 94 (NC), where a wrong report of blood was given, there was a concurrent finding at the level of District Forum and State Commission that this amounted to negligence. It was not disturbed by the National Commission.

35. Does improper maintenance or unhygienic condition of hospital premises amount to negligence?

Yes. In *M. Ramesh Reddy* v *State of Andhra Pradesh* 2003 (1) CLD 81 (AP), the hospital authorities were held to be negligent, *inter alia*, for not keeping the bathroom clean (in this case the bathroom was covered with fungus and slippery) which resulted in the fall of an obstetrics patient in the bathroom leading to her death. Compensation of ₹1 lakh was awarded against the hospital.

36. In case of referral can the doctor to whom the case has been referred be held against if he fails to communicate with the referring doctor regarding the patient illness and treatment?

Yes, in certain circumstances the doctor to whom the case is referred is required to communicate with referring doctor and *vice versa* in respect of patient illness and treatment already given.

In *Coles* v *Reading and District HMC* (1993) 107 SJ 115, the deceased suffered a finger injury and went to the local cottage hospital for treatment. He was advised to go to the main hospital for a tetanus injection but failed to do so and instead visited his G.P. His G.P. failed to inquire what treatment he had undergone at the cottage hospital. The patient died of toxaemia, neither the treating hospital nor the G.P. gave the patient a tetanus injection. The cottage hospital was found negligent in failing to communicate the claimant's symptoms and the G.P. for not inquiring what treatment to claimant had received and for not contracting the cottage hospital.

37. Does giving a wrong report of a pathological test amount to negligence?

Yes. In *Chandrasagar D. Rajput* v *Dinesh J. Shah* 1999 I CPJ 434 (Mah.), in an antenatal examination the doctor had given a positive report of VDRL test on taking another confirmatory test in another laboratory, the report turned out to be negative. The State Commission held that giving of wrong VDRL positive report was a deficiency in service and awarded compensation of ₹50,000 for the social trauma which the couple had undergone.

38. Can a non-specialist doctor/surgeon conduct specialist surgeon? Can a surgeon of particular specialty conduct surgeon of any other specialty?

Even if a doctor or surgeon does not have the specialist's qualifications, he is considered competent to treat patients or conduct specialist surgeries on the basis of his training and experience. It will be pertinent to quote a few examples:

The Tamil Nadu State Commission in *Lakshmi Rajan* v *Malar Hospital Ltd* 1997 III CPJ 242, held that general surgeons are competent to do hysterectomy. Many times, they are called to help the gynecologists in cases of complications because of their experience in all the fields. The question whether hysterectomy was indicated or not was not disputed because a gynaecologist had advised immediate hysterectomy because of profuse bleeding per vagina. Hence, it may be concluded that if the question of indication for hysterectomy is not disputed, it is safe for a general surgeon to perform hysterectomy all by himself.

The Madhya Pradesh State Commission in *Study Circle Society* v *Choithram Hospital and Research Centre* 2000 II CPJ 436, did not fined fault with an M.S. (Gen-Surgery) doctor performing Cardiac Surgery on the basis of his experience and frequent study of latest techniques by going abroad.

An MBBS doctor having obtained degree from the university was competent to practice medicine, surgery and obstetrics. Caesarean operation is part of the surgery. It may be that the persons obtaining diploma like DGO may be more qualified to conduct caesarean operation. Further, doctor was qualified as well as eligible for conducting caesarean operation, on the basis of her experience also. [*Surendra Kumar* v *Dr. Santosh Menon* 2000 (1) CPR 23 (Pun)].

39. When should a doctor/hospital refer a patient or consult a specialist?

A doctor/hospital is under a duty to refer patient or consult a specialist/ expert:

(*i*) when the patient/attendant requests the referral or the consultant,

(*ii*) In doubtful or difficult case when the quality of care and management can be conceivably enhanced by referral on consultation.

In some cases, the allegation of negligence is not that the diagnosis was incorrect but that the claimant's condition appeared so serious that the defendant should have referred the claimant to a specialist or, at the very least, carried out further tests. It is advisable for the doctor that, where he suspects that the condition is more serious, he must carry out further tests, even though there is a view point which suggests that he could be sued for over testing such cases would be few and far between and in view of the consequences if he failed to test, he should always err on the side of caution.

In determining whether the doctor has failed to reach the requisite standard of care, he would do well to bear in mind that diagnosis is an on-going factor. A doctor, who refuses to budge from his initial assessment of the claimant's condition, notwithstanding the patient's apparent deterioration, is at risk of being negligent. At all stages, the treating doctor should be alert to the patient's response to the treatment prescribed and whether he has the expertise to continue to treat the patient, that is, should the patient be referred to a specialist?

In *Gordon* v *Wilson* (1992) 3 Med L.R. 401, the claimant had visited her G.P. on several occasions complaining of deafness and difficulties with balance, impaired vision and difficulty in eating and drinking. She was eventually referred to a specialist who removed a benign melanoma from her brain. She sued the G.P. alleging that her symptoms were such that she should have been referred at an earlier stage. The court accepted that her combination of symptoms should have prompted her GP to refer her to a specialist at an early stage.

40. Is relying only on the reports of the investigations justified?

No. In *Rahul Sinha* v *Dr. Alok Mitra* 1995 II CPJ 227, the CT scan report stated that everything was normal, and there was no trace of cancer, which subsequently turned out to be recurrence of cancer. The National Commission, while dismissing the appeal against the Radiologist, from wrong report of CT scan observed that it is prudent before proceeding treatment on the basis of scan report. Relying totally on the impression of the radiologist, in such cases, is not correct particularly when the medical history does create a suspicion of malignancy.

In *Stacey* v *Chiddy* (1993) 4 Med LR 345, a Australian case, the claimant visited her GP after finding two lumps in her breast. The GP arranged a mammogram and an ultrasound scan, which gave normal results but did not confirm that the lumps were cystic. She reattended her G.P. on several occasions. However he failed to re-examine her breasts for lumps and relied on the inconclusive ultrasound scan. Eventually she was referred to a specialist, where it was established that the cancer had spread to her spine. In the New South Wales Supreme Court, the GP was held negligent for placing too much reliance on inconclusive results and for failing to re-examine the claimant. The court held that, although the defendant had not acted irresponsibly with his advice, he should have taken into consideration the magnitude of the risk to which the appellant was exposed if the diagnosis was incorrect.

41. Define the liability of a junior doctor. Is a doctor liable for negligence of his junior doctor?

Doctors have a duty to satisfy themselves that the persons to whom the task is delegated are qualified and/or have the appropriate experience, knowledge and skill to discharge the duties which have been delegated to them. improper delegation would itself qualify as negligence. In case of proper delegation, the senior doctor would be vicariously liable for the negligence of junior doctor during this delegation.

It should be emphasized that the legal duty of care is owed by all categories of health careers, *e.g.* doctor, nurses, physiotherapists, irrespective of their experience. Thus, the junior colleague, this must be correct, since the patient has a right to expect a certain standard of care when he put himself in the hands of the hospital authority or health career. From a practical stand point, this means that the hospital or health authority should avoid placing the health career in a position where unassisted; he will have to do things which are beyond his abilities. Furthermore, the employer of such health careers, that is, the health authority or most owes a direct, as opposed to a various duty of care to the patient.

In case of junior staff working independently, and is competent for that job the senior may not be held liable, *e.g.* running of OPD separately by the junior staff. In such a case, hospital may still be liable.

In case of negligence of a nurse, the doctor or the hospital employing the nurse is held vicariously liable with no liability being fixed on the nurse in almost all cases as will be borne out from the following cases.

In *Spring Meadows Hospital* v *Harjot Ahluwalia* 1998 (2) SCC 620, it was held that even delegation of responsibility to another may amount to negligence in certain circumstances. A consultant could be negligent where he delegates the responsibility to another may amount to negligence in certain circumstances. A consultant could be negligent where he delegates the responsibility of his junior was incapable for performing his duties properly.

In *Dr. K.G. Krishnan* v *Praveen Kumar* (*Minor*), 2003 (3) CLD 705, a minor girl was paralysed because of injection given by the nurse. The main contention of the petitioner doctor before the National Commission was that the allegations main in the complaint are against the nurse and the nurse was not made a party to the proceedings before the fora and hence the complaint should be dismissed for the non-joinder of necessary parties. But the nurse administered the injection under the direction and supervision of the respondent/doctor and the nurse was employed by the doctor himself. Even if the nurse cannot escape liability. He is responsible for the treatment given and also for the actions in administering such treatment by his employees who did so under his direction and supervision and is vicariously liable for their such actions.

In *Foster* v *Englewood Hospital Association* 313 NE 24, 255, III 1974, a case from USA, a young man had an operation for a dislocated shoulder. The orthopedist left the operating room when he had finished, but while the patient's breathing was still being totally assisted. The nurse-anesthetist decided to move him to the recovery room without attaching a respirator. When they arrived she realized he was in difficulty and called for a physician but the patient died from oxygen deprivation almost immediately. The court found the surgeon vicariously liable for the nurse's negligence and negligent in his own right for having failed to remain in surgery with his patient was breathing normally.

With regard to the junior doctor, inexperience is no defence, he must meet the standard of care expected of his rank/status. This is nothing new in the law of tort, where the same standard of care expected of a learner driver as of an experience driver.

The leading authority in England on this point in clinical negligence is *Wilsher* v *Esses AHA* (1986) 3 All ER 801, Mortin Wilsher was born prematurely, suffering from various illnesses including oxygen deficiency. He was placed in a special care baby unit at the hospital. While he was in the unit a catheter was twice inserted into a vein rather than an artery and on both occasions he was given excess oxygen. The doctors administering the oxygen were junior and inexperienced doctors. The position of the catheter was not in itself negligent, as it was a mistake that a reasonably competent doctor could have made. The catheter could have been checked by means of an x-ray which was infact done in this case, however, the senior registrar failed to spot the mistake. The baby was subsequently found to be suffering from retrolental fibroplasia, which causes blindness. In court of appeal it was argued that the standard of the care expected of the junior doctor was not same as that of his experienced counter part. It was suggested that a junior doctor had to learn, otherwise it would be impossible for medicine to develop and function, it was therefore unavoidable that mistakes would be made. Sir Nicholas Browne-Wilkinson VC agreed with this argument.

What about the legal position of the nurse? The nurse should show the standard expected of a reasonably competent nurse. If she finds herself in a difficult position, she should always seek the advice of her superiors; this could be senior nursing staff or a doctor depending on the nature of the difficulty. The nurse should act on the doctor's instructions but should not follow those instructions if they are clearly erroneous or criminal.

The doctor or the hospital, as the case may be held vicariously liable for the negligence of the nurse.

In *Fraster* v *Vancouter General Hospital* (1951) 3 WWR 337, affirmed in (1952) 3 DLR 785 a Canadian case, a patient was admitted to casualty after being involved in a road accident. He was examined by junior doctors, x-rays were taken and examined, and the claimant was sent home. The patient subsequently died. Held, the junior doctors were negligent in attempting to read the x-rays themselves and in failing to consult a specialist. They should have sought the advice of the radiologist and not relied on their own knowledge.

42. Is a doctor vicariously liable for negligence committed by his *locum tenens*?

Black's Law Dictionary 6th edn, 1990 edn, defines *locum tenens* as: holding the place, a deputy, a substitute, lieutenant or representative.

General practitioner often employs a locum to look after their clinics in case of their sickness or holiday. If the appointment is on a causal basis (as is usually the case) the doctor may find it difficult to deny vicarious liability. If the appointment is on certain agreed terms and conditions and the locum is competent enough to provide health care independently, he puts himself in a position of an independent contractor rather than an employee and the appointing doctor may therefore not be vicariously liable.

However the responsibility of the general practitioner or the specialist is to ensure that a suitable qualified person is appointed to deputies, failure to do so may result in direct (not vicarious liability) of the general practitioner.

43. What is the liability in case of polyclinic?

Polyclinic means a place where doctors of different practice with common staff and other facilities. Since, every doctor is practicing individually; he would be responsible for his own negligence of staff of the polyclinic if the negligence occurs during the care of his particular patient in addition to the polyclinic being held liable for negligence of its staff. The other doctor may get involved as partners of the Polyclinic depending upon the agreement.

44. Can lack of proper post-operative advice amount to negligence?

Yes. In *Ram Kali* v *State of Haryana* 2000 ACJ 752 HC, there was not an iota for suggestion given to the plaintiff that at the time of discharge the plaintiff has advised not to share the bed with her husband for a period of three months. On the contrary, the plaintiff who was an illiterate lady could always conceive an idea in her mind that after performing the family planning operation upon her she is secured. A sense of security is involved when a woman or a male person undertakes such type of operation. It is a common case of the parties that a plaintiff could conceive a child.

It was difficult for the plaintiff to say or prove as to what had happened inside her body or uterus at the time of operation. The delivery of the child itself is a suggestion and proof of negligence on the part of the doctor who performed the operation.

Appeal allowed, setting aside decree of the First Appellate Court and granted a money decree of ₹50,000 in favour of plaintiff against defendants.

45. What is liability of an ambulance service?

Where an ambulance service provider professes that the ambulance is equipped with life saving equipment and such equipment is either absent or not working properly it may be liable for negligence.

Kenti v *Griffiths* (2000) 2 All ER 474, a case from the UK establishes that, in appropriate circumstances, an ambulance service could owe a duty of care to a member of public on whose behalf an emergency call was made if, due to carelessness, if failed to arrived within a reasonable time. In this case the claimant had suffered an asthma attack and was seen at home by her general practitioner, who telephoned for an ambulance to take her as an emergency to hospital. The ambulance took 40 minutes to arrive. During that period the claimant suffered a respiratory arrest. The ambulance could and should have arrived at least 14 minutes earlier. A record prepared by a member of the ambulance crew falsely indicated that the ambulance had arrived within 22 minutes. The claimant brought proceedings for negligence against the ambulance service. At the trial the doctor stated that she would have asked the claimant's husband to driver her to the hospital if she had known the ambulance's arrival had been falsified, that no satisfactory reason had been given for the delay and that, had the ambulance arrived within a reasonable time, the respiratory arrest would in all probability not have occurred. In those circumstances the delay was culpable. He awarded damages of £ 362,377.

46. Is a hospital liable for negligence of its doctor and other staff?

This question is best answered by quoting the statement of Lord Denning in *Cassidy* v *Minister of Health* (1951) 1 All ER 574 C.A.

> "...... the hospital authorities are responsible for the whole of their staff, not only for the nurses and doctors but also for the Anaesthetist and the surgeon. It does not matter whether they are permanent or temporary, resident or visiting. Whole time or part time. The hospital authorities are

responsible for all of them. The reason is because, even if they are not servant, they are the agents of the hospital to give the treatment. The only exception to the case of consultants or Anaesthetist selected and employed by the patient itself."

In *Kunhikrishnan P.V.* v *Sreechitra Tirunal Institute of Medical Science and Technology* (2001) III CPJ 86 (Ker), The Kerala State Commission held that if the death of the patient was due to negligence of any of the staff of the institution, the institution cannot escape liability.

In *Aleyamma Varghese* v *Diwan Bahadur Dr. Varghese* 1997 III CPJ 165 (Kar), the complainant's wife underwent caesarean operation, but a large sponge was left behind as was proved by the evidence. The scrub nurse was responsible for counting the sponges and negligence was held on the part. The hospital as employer was vicariously held liable to compensation.

In *Arpana Dutta* v *Apollo Hospital Enterprises Ltd.* 2002 ACJ 954 (Mad), it was held by the Madras High Court that it was hospital which was offering medical services. The terms under which the hospital employs the doctors and surgeons are between them but because of this it cannot be stated that the hospital cannot be held liable so far as. Third party patients are concerned. It is expected from the hospital, the prove such a medical service and in case where there is deficiency of service or in case, where the operation has been done negligently without bestowing, normal care and caution, the hospital also must be held liable and it cannot be allowed to escape from the liability by stating that there is no master and servant relationship between the hospital and surgeon, who did the operation. The hospital is liable in case of established negligence and it is no more a defence to say that the surgeon is not a servant employed by the hospital.

In case of *Smt. Rekha Gupta* v *Bombay Hospital Trust* 2003 II CPJ 160 (NC) related to negligence of consultant doctor, wherein National Commission observed that the hospital has employed all of them whatever the inferred rules are, they have to own up the conduct of all their employees. It cannot escape liability by mere statement that it only provides infrastructural facilities, services of nursing staff, supporting staff and technicians and that it cannot *suo motu* perform or recommended any operation/amputation. All bills including consultant doctor's consultation fee are raised by the hospital on the patient and it deducts 20% commission from the bills which is deducted cannot say otherwise and are thus accountable. Whatever be the outcome of the case, hospital cannot disown their responsibility on these superficial grounds.

47. What is the liability of a visiting surgeon for post-operative care?

In many instances senior and super specialty surgeons *e.g.* Cardio thoracic surgeons, plastic surgeons, neuro surgeons, pediatric surgeons etc may perform surgery in a centre where such expertise is not locally available. After the surgery, the post operative care is left to the local doctor. Failure of the surgeon to personally supervise the post operative care may not constitute negligence provided that the doctor to whom the responsibility of the post-operative care lies is competent. The same would apply to a visiting physician.

The National Commission in *Sudhanshu Bhattacharya* v *B.S. Hegde* 1993 (3) CPR 414 (NC), observed that in the case of the operation being performed in an institution it is the duty of the institution to render post-operative treatment and care to the hospitals patients. Quite often foreign doctors undertake operations in hospitals or nursing homes in India and it cannot be maintained that the post-operative care and treatment will continue to be provided by the foreign doctor who may no longer be in the country.

However, it has been held otherwise by the Chandigarh – UT Commission wherein a visiting Cardio-thoracic surgeon took part in a cardiac surgery and left thereafter, did not enquire about the condition of patient and left the matter of post operative care and follow up treatment to the competence of the other Cardiac surgeon and cardiologist of the hospital who were unable to properly treat and look after the post-operative care and the patient died of profuse bleeding and cardiac arrest, the visiting surgeon was held liable for negligence. He was required to pay compensation in the ration of 1/3rd of total compensation of ₹3 lakh awarded against the hospital and the said surgeon. (*Kuljit Kaur* v *BRS Heart Institute and Research Centre* 2003 (6) CLD 317)

48. Define the rule known as respondent superior?

Under this rule, the principal is held liable for the acts of his agents. This doctrine is manifested in the operation room in the form of the "captain of the ship" doctrine. *Example:* In *M.P. Agarwal* v *Dr. MR Jain decided on 9-1-96 by Rajasthan SCDRC – unreported),* the doctor was held liable for what occurred in the OT on account of negligence of the anaesthetist as it was he who had engaged the anaesthetist.

However, in *Mumbai Grahak Panchayat* v *Dr (Mrs.) Rashmi B. Fadnavis* 1996 (1) CPR 137 (NC), it was held by the National Commission that the anaesthetist who participates in the process of delivery of medical services to the beneficiary is as much liable as the main surgeon, if the anaesthetist's negligence established.

49. What is the liability of a nursing home/hospital where a consultant/ surgeon who is participating independently operates a case?

The hospital authorities are not only responsible for their nursing and other staff, doctor, etc. but also for the Anaesthetist and surgeons. It does not matter whether they are permanent or temporary, resident or visiting consultants, whole time or part time. The hospital authorities are usually held liable for the negligence occurring at the level of any of such personnel.

In *K.K. Radha* v *Dr. Shekhar* 1994 III CPJ 376 (Ker), there was negligence on the part of the surgeon in an orthopedics case and the surgeon was held liable as also the hospital was held vicariously liable and asked to pay compensation since doctor's address was not available. This decision was affirmed in appeal to the National Commission (*PP Ismail* v *KK Radha* 1998 I CPJ 16) where an operation was performed in a hospital by a consultant surgeon who was not in employment of the hospital and negligence occurred, it was held that it is the hospital which was offering medical services. The term under which the defendant hospital employs the doctors and surgeons are between them but because of this it cannot be stated that the hospital cannot be held liable so far as third party patients are concerned. The patients go and get themselves admitted in the hospital relying upon the hospital to provide them the medical service for which they pay necessary fee. It is expected from the hospital, to provide such a medical service and in case where there deficiency of service or in cases like this, where the operation has been done negligently without bestowing normal care and caution, the hospital also must be held liable and it cannot be allowed to escape from the liability by stating that there is no master and servant relationship between the hospital and the surgeon, who did the operation. [*Aparna Dutta* v *Apollo Hospitals Enterprises Ltd* 2002 ACJ 954 (Mad)]

Hospital cannot escape their liability by mere statement that they only provide infrastructural facilities, services of nursing staff and technicians and that they cannot *suo motu* perform or recommended any operation/amputations to the patients. All bills including doctor's consultation fee are raised by the hospital on the patient and the hospital deduct 20% commission while remitting fee to the consultant. Hospital has employed the medical staff, registrars, resident doctors etc, and also take 20% commission from the bills which is deducted now cannot say otherwise and are thus accountable, whatever be the outcome of the case, hospital cannot disown their responsibility on these superficial grounds [*Smt. Rekha Gupta* v *Bombay Hospital Trust* 2003 (2) CPJ 160 (NC)].

50. What should a doctor do if death occurs during surgical procedures? Is post mortem necessary in such cases?

In case death on table during surgical procedures it is mandatory to report the same to the authorities/police immediately. In such cases post mortem is mandatory irrespective of the fact whether death occurs in a government or private hospital. Consent of the attendants is not necessary. [*Arunaben D. Kothari* v *Navdeep Clinic* 1996 III CPJ 605 (Guj)].

It is stated in Gradwohl's Legal Medicine, 3rd edn., that autopsy is a must when death of person is sudden, unexplained, unexpected or violent.

51. Does law recognize anything like team negligence or team liability?

No. The law, in dealing with cases of negligence of doctors, does not recognized any doctrine of team liability and the case of each doctor in the team has to be considered separately. It was so held in *Wilsher* v *Essex Area Health Authority* (1985) 3 All ER 801 (CA), where the plaintiff an infant, who suffered near blindness sued for negligence while he was placed after premature birth in 24 hours special care unit of the defendant hospital. A junior doctor inserted a catheter to monitor oxygen but the catheter was inserted in a vein in place of an artery. The junior doctor consulted the senior doctor who failed to detect the mistake and he himself committed the same mistake while replacing the catheter. The excess oxygen given as a mistake could have caused damage to the retina resulting in near blindness. The junior doctor was held not to have been negligent as he consulted the senior doctor was held to be negligent in not being able to detect the mistake and in repeating the same mistake. The defendant was vicariously held liable for the negligence.

52. What is the liability of an anaesthetist? Is a surgeon/hospital vicariously liable for negligence of anaesthetist?

The anesthetist is held liable irrespective of the fact whether he is a full time employee or part time or visiting consultant of the doctor/hospital or he has been called by the patient/attendant. In addition, the hospital and surgeon are held vicariously liable for the negligence of the anesthetist. In some cases the courts apportion the liability of the anesthetist, the surgeon and the hospital in a particular ratio, or hold them jointly or severely liable depending on facts and circumstances of each case. There is a term in law known as "respondent superior." It holds the principal liable for the acts of his agents. The doctrine is manifested in an operation theatre in the form of the so called "captain of the ship" doctrine. As a captain of the ship the surgeon holds the responsibility for negligent injury to the patient while the surgeon is directing the operation. It is exercise of control over others by the surgeon that is the key to the application of the doctrine. For this reason, the actions of the anaesthetist are generally not imputed to the surgeon. (*M.P. Agarwal* v *Dr. M.P. Jain Complaint No. 125 of 1993, decided on 9-1-1996 by Rajasthan State Commission – unreported*).

But in *Dr. J.N. Shrivastav* v *Rambiharilal* AIR 1982 MP 132, it was held that with regard to the anesthetic, the person ultimately responsible for the surgeon to direct and supervise its administration. Merely because a surgeon insists upon a particular anesthetic procedure would not exonerate the anesthetist. It was also held that it is the anesthetist's duty to see that the patient was safe until he/she returned to consciousness.

In *Mumbai Grahak Panchayat* v *Dr.* (*Mrs.*) *Rashmi B Fadnavis* 1996 (1) CPR 137, the National Commission held:

.... the words "in pursuance of a contract or otherwise in the section 2(1)(g) Consumer Protection Act, 1986, make it amply clear that a privity of the contract is not needed for a claim to be made under the act as long as there is hiring or availing of services to the beneficiary is as much liable as the main surgeon himself if his/he negligence has be established".

In *Dr. Lakshmanan Prakash* v *State* 2001 ACJ 1204 Mad, the opinion given by the doctors was that the death was due to lung shock and acute respiratory failure – sequela to spinal anesthetist administration. So the cause of death was directly attributed to the act of the anesthetist. The part played by the anesthetist by having failed to check-up during the pre-operative anesthesia test as to whether the patient would withstand 3 ml local anesthesia drug was administered through spinal cord to the patient, especially when he had sustained injuries both the head of leg may amount to criminal negligence which would warrant him facing the proceedings under section 304A of IPC. But such a criminal negligence cannot be attributed to the operating doctors, who were responsible for the medical treatment of the patient, have not checked whether all the medical checkup formalities including anesthesia test were properly performed by the anesthetist before the operation. The anesthetist and the operating doctors were also held liable for damages under civil law for their negligence which caused death of the patient.

53. Can a case of medical ethics be entertained by the Consumer Forums under the Consumer Protection Act? Before whom can a complaint be filed against such branch?

The consumer forums have no jurisdiction to entertain such a complaint as was the case in *Mr. X* v *Hospital Z* 1998 (8) SCC 296 where the complaint regarding claim of damages on the ground that the information which was required to be kept secret under medical ethics was disclosed illegally was rejected by National Commission and it directed the complainant to seek his remedy in a civil court.

However, as per Indian Medical Council Regulations, 2002, the complaint for breach of medical ethics can be filed before the Medical Council of India or the appropriate State Commission Council, which have power to award any punishment which includes (*i*) removal altogether or for a specified period, from the register of medical practitioners, the name of the delinquent registered medical practitioner, (*ii*) giving a warning, (*iii*) award of compensation to the aggrieved person.

54. What is quack?

The Supreme Court in *Poonam Verma* v *Ashwini Patel* AIR 1996 SC 2111, has defined a 'quack' as a person who does not have knowledge of a particular system of medicine but practices in the system and is a mere pretender to medical knowledge or skill or put it differently, a charlatan.

55. Under what circumstances does the Code of Medical Ethics permit overriding the rule of confidentiality and disclosure of the fact that a person is suffering from HIV infection/AIDS?

In the doctor-patient relationship, the most important aspect is the doctor's duty of maintaining secrecy. A doctor cannot disclose to a person any information regarding his patient which he has gathered in the course of his treatment nor can the doctor disclose to any one else the mode of treatment or the advise given by him to the patient.

The code of medical ethics, however, craves out an exception to the rule of confidentiality and permits the disclosure in the circumstances under which public interest would override the duty of confidentiality, particularly where is an immediate future health risk to others (*Mr. X* v *Hospital Z* 1998 (8) SCC 296).

The Supreme Court in the above case has quoted with approval from guidelines on HIV infection and AIDS of the General Medical Council of Great Britain as under:

> "When diagnosis has been made by a specialist and the patient after appropriate counseling, still refuses permission for the General Practitioner to be informed of the result that request for privacy should be respected. The only exception would be when failure to disclosure would put the health of

the health care team at serious risk. All the people receiving such information must consider themselves to be under the same obligations of confidentiality as the doctor principally responsible for the patient's care. Occasionally, the doctor may wish to disclose a diagnosis to a third party other than a health care professional. The council thinks the only grounds for this are when there is a serious and identifiable risk to a specific person, who if not so informed, would be exposed to infection ..... A doctor may consider it a duty to ensure that any sexual partner is informed regardless of the patient's own wishes." (Emphasis supplied by the court)

56. Is "right of privacy/confidentiality" absolute?

No. Under both the Constitution of India and Basic Human Rights this right is not absolute. The Right to Privacy which includes Right of confidentiality is an essential component of right to life envisaged by Article 21 of the Constitution. However the right is not absolute and may be lawfully restricted for:

(*i*) the prevention of crime and disorder, or

(*ii*) protection of health, or

(*iii*) protection of morals, or

(*iv*) protection of rights and freedom of others, this right may include right of the doctor who is defendant in a medical negligence case to disclose information about the patient in his own defence.

As one of the basic human rights, the right to privacy is not treated as absolute. The Supreme Court made reference to Article 8 of the European Convention on Human Rights which defines this right as follows:

"(1) Every one has the right to respect for his private and family life, his home and his correspondence.

(2) There shall be no inference by a public authority with the exercise of this right except such as in accordance with the law and is necessary in democratic society in the interests of national security, public safety or the economic well being of the country, for the prevention of the rights and freedoms of others". (Emphasis supplied by the Court)

A court in the course of legal proceeding may order to a doctor who is either a witness or a defendant to disclose information about his patient. In doing so, the court will have to strike a balance between the need for all relevant information to be disclosed, thereby ensuring justice is done, against the need to keep the patients confidence secret.

Further if, pre-trail disclosure is required of such things as expert medical reports on which one or other party is seeking to rely, then again to doctor has no choice, his report will be made public.

57. Would a person suffering from HIV/AIDS who knowingly marries a woman and thereby transmits infection to her, be guilty of any offence?

Yes. The Supreme Court has held that he would be guilty of offences indicated in sections 269 and 270 of Indian Penal Code. These provisions impose a duty upon the person knowing that he is suffering from HIV infection/AIDS not to marry, as the marriage would have the effect of spreading the infection of his own disease to the woman whom he marries and is dangerous to life. (*Mr. X* v *Hospital Z* 1998 (8) SCC 296).

58. Is case of clash of two fundamental rights, which would be enforced through the process of Court?

Where there is a clash of two fundamental rights, the right which would advance the public morality or public interest would be enforced through the process of court.

Where there was a clash between an HIV (+ve) person's right to privacy as part of right to life and a woman's (with whom the marriage of that person was settled) right to healthy life which is her fundamental right under Article 21, the latter's right has to be protected in preference to right to privacy of the person infected with HIV (+ve) the Court cannot assist a person to spoil the health and consequently the life of an innocent woman.

59. Would doctor/hospital's maintenance of strict secrecy and failure to a sexual partner/potential sexual partner (*e.g.* a person who is to get married) about a person having HIV infection/AIDS amount to an offence?

Yes. The Supreme Court has held that in such a situation the silence of the doctor/hospital would make them participles criminals, (a participant in a crime) (*Mr. X* v *Hospital Z* 1998 (8) SCC 296).

Having regard to the fact that the appellant was found to be HIV (+ve), its disclosure would not be violative of either the rule of confidentiality of the appellant's right to privacy as the woman with whom the appellant was likely to be married was saved in time by such disclosure, or she too would have been infected with the dreaded disease of marriage had taken place and consummated.

60. Can a person suffering from a communicable venereal disease or impotency, claim right to marry?

The Supreme Court has observed that so long as the person is not cured of the communicable venereal disease or impotency, the right to marry cannot be enforced through a court of law and shall be treated to be suspended right. [*Mr. X* v *Hospital Z.* 1998 (8) SCC 296]

It is the basic principle of jurisprudence that every right has a correlative duty and every duty has a correlative right. But the rule is not absolute. It is subject to certain exceptions in the sense that a person may have a right but there may not be correlative duty. The case of HIV (+ve) falls within the exceptions.

61. Will prescribing allopathic medicines by Homeopathic practitioner or *vice versa* be considered negligence/deficiency in service?

Yes. Prescribing Ayurvedic/Allopathic medicines by a Homeopathic practitioner or *vice versa* is negligence *per se.* If no damage results, but if it can be shown that damage occurred due to these medicines compensation may be awarded.

In a case of *Poonam Verma* v *Ashwini Patel* 1996 II CPJ 1 (SC), respondent Dr. Patel a homeopath, not having studied allopathic system of medicine, treated the patient, suffering from viral fever and then typhoid with allopathic medicines and the patient died within two weeks. Since the law under which he was registered, the Bombay Homeopathic Practitioner's Act, 1959, sub-section (12)(*a*) of section 20 require him to practice in homeopathy only. Doctor held guilty of negligence *per se*, and damages of ₹3 lakh awarded. Action also under section 15(3) of the Indian Medical Council Act, 1959 section 2(*d*) of Maharashtra Medical Council Act, 1965 and section 2(8), 2(12), 14A, 20(1)(*g*) and 28 of Bombay Homeopathic Practitioners Act, 1959 directed to be taken.

62. Can complaint be filed before the State Medical Council/Indian Medical Council for negligence or professional misconduct of a medical practitioner?

Yes. Provision is made in regulation 8.2 of the Indian Medical Council (Professional Conduct, Ethics) Regulations, 2002 for filing of a complaint by any person, including a patient in respect of professional misconduct of medical practitioner. A professional misconduct in a variety of cases may also amount to negligence/deficiency in service and a detailed discussion on the said regulations.

Some states have framed their own Medical Council Acts e.g. Delhi Medical Council Act, 1997 and rules thereunder have been framed by Delhi State which provide that complaints may be filed before the Delhi Medical Council by patients. Procedure prescribed therein for filing and hearing of complaints is akin to the procedure under the Consumer Protection Act, 1986.

63. Who can file a complaint under Consumer Protection Act, 1986?

The following can file a complaint under the Consumer Protection Act, 1986:

(*i*) A consumer is: (*a*) a patient who pays to get services of doctor/hospital, (*b*) any person who pays for the patient, (*c*) spouse, parents and children of the patient.

(*ii*) Any voluntary consumer association registered under the Companies Act, 1956 or under any other law for the time being in force, or

(*iii*) The Central Government or State Government, and

(*iv*) One or more consumer, where there are numerous consumers having the same interest,

(*v*) In case of death of a consumer, his legal heir or representative.

64. Can a complaint be filed against ESI, hospital for medical negligence under Consumer Protection Act, 1986?

Yes. Under section 3 of the Employees State Insurance Act, 1948 a corporation was set up and the Act applies to all factories whether belonging to Government or not. Under section 38 all employees in the factories or establishments to which the Act applies shall be insured. Sections 39 and 42 contemplate contribution by both the employer and employee. In view of this, the ESI hospitals do not render service free of cost. Hence they are amenable to the jurisdiction under Consumer Protection Act [*Mr. Ramesh Reddy* v *State of Andhra Pradesh* 2003 (1) CLD 81 (AP)]

65. Can practitioner of Indian Medicine (Ayurveda/Unani/Sidha) practice allopathy?

In case of *Dr. Mukhtar Chand* v *State of Punjab* 1998 (5) SCALE 501, the Supreme Court held that:

> "The right to practice modern scientific medicine (allopathic medicine) or Indian System of medicine cannot be based on the provisions of Drug Rules and declarations made there under by State Governments. Indeed, the right to practice a system of medicine is derived from the Act under which a Medical Practitioner is registered."

It further observed that there is no scope for a person who is registered under the Indian Medicine Central Council Act, 1970 and enrolled on the State register of Indian Medicine or Central Register of Indian Medicine to practice modern scientific medicine (allopathy) in any of its branches. All that is allowed to such practitioners is to make use of the various modern advances, such as Radiology report (x-rays, etc.) complete blood picture report, lipids report, ECG, etc, for purposes of practicing in their own system. However, if any state law recognises the qualifications of integrated courses or other qualifications of integrated courses or other qualifications as "sufficient qualification" for registration in the State Medical Register, within the meaning of the Indian Medical Council Act, 1956 on being registered in a State Medical Register, he is eligible to practice allopathic medicine. This benefit would be available only in states where the privilege of such right to practice any system of medicine is conferred by the State law which is for the time being in force, under which practitioners of Indian Medicine are registered in their State Medical Register. In such states the prescriptions of allopathic medicines by such practitioner of allopathic medicines by such practitioner shall have to be honoured by a pharmacist or the chemist under the Pharmacy Act and the Drugs Act.

"State Medical Register; within the meaning of the Indian Medical Council Act, 1956, means a register maintained under any law for the time being in force in any state regulating the registration of practitioners of allopathic medicine.

The benefit of Rule 2(*e*)(III) under the Drug and Cosmetics Rules, 1945 as effective from May 14, 1960, and the notification issued thereunder would be available from 16-6-1964 only in those states where the state law which is for the time being in force recognises their qualification as sufficient for registration in the State Medical Register. In such cases the prohibition under section 15(2)(*b*) of the 1956 Act will not apply.

However, in the states where to such privilege is available this will not debar them from prescribing or administering allopathic drugs sold across the counter for common ailments.

Implications of this judgment are:

— right to practice allopathic medicine is available to registered practitioners of Indian Medicine only if they are enrolled on a State Medical Register in terms of any provision in their State law within the meaning of Indian Medical Council Act, 1956,

— even if they are not enrolled on the State Medical Register they: (*i*) can make use of modern advances such as x-ray, ECG, blood report, etc. for purposes of practicing in their own system and (*ii*) are eligible to prescribe or administer allopathic drugs sold across the counter for common ailments.

66. In case of negligence of doctors and other staff in government hospitals, can the state be held vicariously liable for the occurrence of any negligence?

In case of negligence in Government hospital it has been held in most of the cases that the state is vicariously liable for negligence of its doctors or staff or even primarily liable where there is lack of proper equipment or staff. In a few cases the court passes the order that the compensation paid to the complainant may be recovered from the government doctors whose negligence has been established.

The Supreme Court in *Achutrao Haribbhau Khodwa* v *State of Maharashtra* AIR 1996 SC 2377, observed that running a hospital in a welfare activity undertaken by the Government but is not exclusive function or activity of the Government so as to be regarded as being in exercise of its sovereign power. Hence, the state would be vicariously liable for the damages which may become payable on account of negligence of its doctors or other employees.

Again in *State of Haryana* v *Smt Santra* AIR 2000 SC 1888, the contention that the State is not vicariously liable for the negligence of its officers in performing the sterilization operation was not accepted in view of the law settled by the Supreme Court in *N. Nagendra Rao* v *State of AP* AIR 1994 SC 2663, Common cause, *A registered Society* v *Union of India* (1999) 6 SCC 667 and *Achutrao Haribhau Khodwa* v *State of Maharashtra* AIR 1999 SC 2979. The last case, which related to the fallout of a sterilization operation deals, like the two previous cases, with the question of vicarious liability of the State on account of medical negligence of a doctor in a government hospital. The theory of sovereign immunity was rejected.

In *Dr. M.K. Gourikutty* v *M.K. Madhavan* AIR 2001 Ker 398, the Medical Board constituted by the government examined a case of post mortem sterilization where it was found that the patient had a cardiac arrest following the operation. It was a case where if proper care had been taken, damage to the brain could have been avoided whether proper care had been taken was not proved. Hence, the court below was correct in holding that there was negligence on the part of the defendants. Compensation under different heads was awarded against the government hospital, anaesthesiologist and other staff.

It may be noted that in this case liability was fixed of the government, the anesthesiologist and the staff simultaneously instead of holding only the state vicariously liable for negligence of its staff.

In *Punjab State* v *Surinder Kaur* 2001 ACJ 1266 (P&H), on behalf of the State it was submitted that it a was case of negligence on the part of the doctor also who operated upon the plaintiff. Rejecting the contention the Punjab and

Haryana High Court observed that the doctor who operated upon the plaintiff was performing the duty when he/she was under the employment of the State and in these circumstances, the master is always responsible for vicarious liability of the acts committed on the part of the employee. It is for the state to determine the liability of erring doctor/doctors. It is their internal departmental affair. But so far as the plaintiff is concerned, she can recover the amount from the state and its functionaries.

It is the duty of the authorities under the state to see that the employees are available in time in the hospital. If for any reason, a doctor or an expert is not available, the hospital authorities would have known it before-hand and some other persons should be posted. In a case where absence of an anaesthetist prevented the surgeons in the women and children hospital to conduct operation on the patient and there are very possibility that had the Anaesthetist been available and the operation been conducted early, probably, the patient would have been saved. [*Leela Bai* v *Sebastian* 2002 II CPJ 363 (Ker)].

In many of the cases, there has been a tendency to treat the question of a hospital authority's liability not as one of vicarious liability only but also as one of the primary liability of the authority for beach of its own duty to the patient.

In *R.P. Sharma* v *State of Rajasthan* AIR 2002 JPR Bench 104, the death of the wife of petitioner was as a result of the negligence and carelessness in performance of their duties by the two doctors, the servants of the State of Rajasthan. Also from the report of the committee it was clear that the cause of death of wife of the petitioner was mismatched blood transfusion. The committee further reported that the onus of the responsibility lies on the resident doctor in the blood bank who allowed a wrong bottle of blood to leave the blood bank. The last share of the blame has also been reported to rest on the doctor who transfused the blood.

The respondent State of Rajasthan was directed to pay compensation to the petitioner for the lose of his wife due to negligence in performance of duties by its servants. It was further held that the State of Rajasthan is free to recover the amount from those doctors.

In *Rukmani* v *State of Tamilnadu* AIR 2003 Mad 352, the Madras High Court observed that in India where the population is increasing each second and family planning is a national programme, the doctor as also the state must be held responsible in damages if the sterilization operation performed by him is a failure on account of his negligence which is directly responsible for another birth in the family, creating additional economic burden on the person who had chosen to be operated upon for sterilization. The vicarious liability of the state for the negligence of its officers in performing the sterilization operation should be seen keeping in view of the law settled by the Supreme Court vide *State of Haryana* v *Sentra* (2000) 5 SCC 182.

67. Does insertion of a Standard Clause in consent forms or contracts, exonerating a hospital or an institution and the persons working under them, from every possible and foreseeable liability arising out of medical negligence have a legal validity?

Public policy requirements under section 23 of the Indian Contract Act, 1872 prohibits such an exonerating clause. If the object or any term of contract is opposed to public policy, such a contract is void and cannot be enforced in a court of law, since no one can be allowed to exonerate himself from legal liability absolutely. By permitting such exclusion or exoneration, the possibility of holding a person liable for negligence, etc, despite plausible grounds will be ruled out. Any consent containing such clause is not valid in law.

In *Devendra Kumar Sharma* v *Post Graduate Institute of Medical Education and Research* 2002 I CPJ 211 (Cha.), it was held that the consent cannot be taken to be valid defence where the complainant is able to show that there was negligence and carelessness on the part of the opposite parties at the time of surgery. Therefore, it cannot be taken as an absolute defence that since complainant had given his written consent for the risk involved in the surgery of his wife, hence, he cannot now raise a plea of negligence or carelessness, if any, taking place at the time of operation.

68. Does 'error of judgment' constitute negligence?

In *White House* v *Jordon* (1981) 1 All ER 267 HL, Denning M.R. commented:

> "In professional man, an error of judgment is not negligent."

This statement was not accepted by the House of Lords. Lord Edmund Davies and subsequently Lord Firaser commented that, an error of judgment may or may not be negligent, it all depends on the nature of the error. If it is one that would not have been made by a reasonably competent professional man professing to have the standard and type of skill that the defendant held himself out as having and acting with ordinary care, then this error of judgment is negligent. If, on the other hand, it is an error that a man acting with ordinary care, might have made, then this error of judgment is not negligent.

So the plea that the medical mishap was due to an error of judgment is no defence and the term is redundant as a guide to what constitute negligence.

69. Is failure to keep knowledge up to date negligence?

It is the duty of medical practitioner to keep his professional knowledge up to date. This does not mean that he is bound to read every new publication on medical science or every new publication on medical science or every article in every medical journal. He cannot be charged with negligence if he had failed to read a particular article in the medical press which might have warned him the existence of risks in the method of treatment he adopts (*McQuary Eastwood* (1886) 12 OR 402). It would be putting much too high a burden on a medical man to say that he must read every article in the medical press. His duty must be limited to taking reasonable steps to keep himself abreast of modern developments in medical teaching and the question whether he has failed in his duty must be decided upon the facts. A failure to read a particular article will be excusable, but disregard of a serious of warnings in the medical press will undoubtedly be evidence of negligence.

A practitioner cannot however; excuse himself by sticking on to a practice once approved but now become outworn and discredited. But a practitioner cannot go on experimenting upon his patient with every new development, until its efficiency and safety has been tested by experience (*Slater* v *Baker* (1767) 2 Wils 359). It seems reasonable to allow the practitioner a certain amount of discretion in the use and application of new techniques and methods of treatment within reasonable limits. As Denning L.J. observed:

> "Doctors like the rest of us have to learn by experience and experience often teaches in a hard way. Something goes wrong and shows up a weakness and then it is put right."

70. What does breach of duty imply?

By breach of duty on part of defendant would imply that his activity fell below the standard that could reasonably have been expected of him. The question would be whether the doctor's management of the case in its widest sense was in accordance with currently accepted practice.

71. In a case of accident, injury and emergency cases, after providing necessary first-aid, patient is referred to the higher centre but the patient dies during transport, will this amount to negligence on the part of the referring doctor/hospital?

No. if after providing medical care upto his level of competence, the doctor makes a proper referral note and refers the patient to a higher centre, and any mishap occurring during transport would not be the liability of the doctor. Rather, non referral or delay in referral by the doctor could constitute negligence. Remember, not to forget to inform the police if it is a medico-legal case.

In *Payne* v *St. Heliera Group of Hospitals* 1952 CLV 2442, the patient came with an abdominal injury. The doctor attended him but did not care to refer him to a consultant (surgeon). Latter, the patient died due to a "General peritonitis" the medical officer was held liable.

72. Is difference of opinion/diagnosis or resorting to one of the two or more options available for treatment/surgery amount to negligence?

No, provided that opinions, though different, are given in accordance with accepted medical practice prevailing at that time in the medical profession. It is now well established that where the doctors have two options and they exercise one it can not described to be negligence unless the other party is able to show that the option exercised by the doctor was probably wrong. [*Kiran Bala Rout* v *Christian Medical College and Hospital* 2003 (1) CPR 238 (NC)].

Medical opinion may differ with regard to the course of action to be taken by a doctor treating a patient but as long as a doctor acts in a manner which is acceptable to the medical profession and the court finds that he has attended on the patient with due care, skill and diligence and if the patient still does not survive or suffers a permanent aliment, it would be difficult to hold the doctor to be guilty of negligence. [*Achutrao Haribhau Khadwa* v *State of Maharashtra* 1996 (2) SCC 634].

Even, if there is a difference of opinion amongst the experts on the procedure adopted by a doctor, but a procedure which is commonly in practice in an idea if adopted by a doctor, it cannot be said that there is difference of opinion amongst the experts on the procedure adopted by a doctor, it cannot be said that there is negligence on his part. [*Vinitha Ashok* v *Lakshmi Hospital* 2001 (8) SCC 731].

If it is found that two opinions were there and the doctor adopted one, this cannot amount to medical negligence. [*S.K. Shama* v *Dr. Praful B. Desai* 2003 (2) CPJ 90 (NC)].

The opinion of doctors may vary from doctor to doctor and wrong diagnosis, in itself, is no ground to hold the doctor negligent. [*Badri Prasad Rai* v *Dr. M.L. Peshin* 2003 (3) CPR 119].

73. Can "omission" during medical practice constitute medical negligence?

This is illustrated in certain decided cases:

In *Dr. T.T. Thomas* v *Elisa* AIR 1987 Ker 52, the Kerala High Court held that the surgeon negligent of his omission to perform an emergency operation (appendectomy) resulting in death of the patient on the next itself, owing to bursting of the appendix.

In *Dr. Laxman Balakrishna Joshi* v *Trimbak Bapu Godbole* AIR 1969 SC 128, the Supreme Court held the orthopaedician negligent for his fetal omission of not giving anaesthesia to the patient before attempting reduction of the fracture. The omission of this elementary caution resulted in shock and death of the patient.

In an English case *Selfe* v *Ilford and District Hospital Management Committee* 1970 Times, 26 November, a hospital authority was held liable for injury suffered by a patient when attempting suicide on the ground that it had omitted to provide supervision of the patient which was identified suicide risk. Omission on the part of an ophthalmologist to check vision and intra-ocular pressure (IOP) diabetes before conducting cataract surgery would be negligence. [*Christian Medical Centre* v *A. Shajahan* 1998 III CPJ 242 AP].

In a case of overdose of Amikacin to a patient of chronic kidney disease awaiting kidney transplant there was omission on the part of the treating doctor in not advising audiometry tests of patient as part of overall monitoring of the death of the patient, which is done, would have made it possible to take steps to reverse the hearing impairment at the initial stages such omission was held be negligent. [*Mohd. Ishfaq* v *Dr. Mortin D.Souza* 2003 I CPJ 116 NC].

74. In medical practice some cases are easy to diagnose but some are difficult, is there any difference in the margin of error allowed in a difficult case?

Yes, when diagnosis is accepted by reasonable body to be difficult, the margin of error has to be accepted to be more, example diagnosis of case of ectopic pregnancy rupture. *K Vasantha* v *Teja Hospital* 1993 (1) 30 CPR (TN).

In *Vinitha Ashok* v *Lakshmi Hospital* 2001 (8) SCC 731 a case of ectopic pregnancy having profuse bleeding was operated and dilatation and curettage was done with removal of uterus. The court noted that it was a case difficult to diagnose and held the doctor not negligent for removal of uterus by quoting with approval from the principles and practice of ultrasonography in obstetrics and gynaecology at 412, wherein it is noticed that the rarest types of ectopic pregnancy are cervical and ovarian and because of their rarity these types of ectopic pregnancy are usually not prospectively diagnosed. It further quoted from Linder's operative Gynaecology, 6th edn. By Richard F. Mattingly — wherein it was observed that "the treatment of cervical pregnancy is surgical and the condition usually requires an abdominal hysterectomy."

75. Can trauma (accident and injury) patients be categorised in some way so as to determine the degree of urgency (promptness) required of the doctor to operate/provide treatment?

In cases of trauma, there are three categories of patients, according to immediacy of injury as described by Seymour I. Shwariz MD in his standard textbook: Principles of surgery as quoted in *Haribhajan Singh* v *Dayanand Medical College and Hospital* 1996 III CPJ 263 (Pun):

> "Priority by injury — The first group includes injuries which interfere with vital physiologic function and therefore immediately threaten life, such as obstruction of an airway or bleeding from a gunshot wound. The primary treatment for massive internal bleeding within 5 to 10 minutes following arrival in the emergency room. The operating room should be alerted when the patient is admitted to the emergency room, and no time is wasted in getting the patient into 'operative' condition. Often the control of haemorrhage is dependant on a rapid thoractomy or laparotomy to occlude injured major vessels.
>
> The second groups of patients are those with injuries which offer immediate threat to life. These include patients who have received gunshot wounds, stab wounds, or blunt trauma to the chest and abdomen but whose vital signs are stable. The majority of injured patients are in this category. Although they will require surgical procedures within 1 to 2 hours, there is time for additional information to be obtained. Blood for typing and cross matching is drawn and blood is made available if there is any possibility that the patient will require surgical intervention. If vital sign are stable, x-rays may be obtained to determine the course of the missile and the extent of possible associated injuries, such as fractures. Cystography and pyclography may be done to asses' haematuria. Since patients with penetrating and blunt

abdominal injuries may develop shock at any moment, a physician must be in constant attendance during all evaluations. Patients who suddenly go into shock are immediately taken to the operating room without additional diagnostic procedures.

The third categories of patients are those who injuries produce occult damage. This group is composed primarily of patients who have sustained blunt trauma to the abdomen, which may or may not require surgical intervention and in whom the exact nature of the injury is not apparent. These patients usually have time for extensive laboratory studies, x-rays and more complete physical examination. Surgical intervention in this group may be delayed by hours or days, as with delayed rapture to the spleen."

It will also be worthwhile to reproduce from another standard text book – Love and Bailey Surgery, 22nd edn, P.19, Triage which means the allocation of injured patients into certain categories:

"Triage (after the French 'triager' to sort) means the allocation of injured patients into certain categories for action by the emergency team. A common scheme of assessment would be as follows:

1. Critical: within seconds, *e.g.* acute laryngo-tracheal obstruction.
2. Immediate: within minutes, *e.g.* tension pneumothorax or major arterial or venous haemorrhage.
3. Urgent: within the golden hour, *e.g.* major burns or multiple organ injuries.
4. Deferred: as soon as practical, *e.g.* injury not life threatening, or patient beyond hope of recovery or already dead.

In both major civil disasters and military engagements it is essential to make an accurate judgment of the category which each patient occupies, so that resources are used most efficiently to benefit the maximum number. This assessment must be made by a senior doctor will possess the knowledge combined with sufficient authority to direct the other team members who are essential to success. It is vital that the team is familiar with the systems that are used for the handling of a group of severely injured patients, and are used to working with each other in the emergency reception environment.

Following upon the admirable examples of Germany and USA, it is now recognized that severely traumatised patients must be expertly resuscitated within a hour (the 'Golden hour') of the injury to have the best chance for both life and good functional recovery. To this end, the expert teams of doctors, paramedical personnel and nurses must be available at the scene of the accident. Helicopter facilities are a necessary back up for the emergency team."

Triage may be necessary both in the field and in the hospital setting. In hospital, triage may be used in three situations:

1. on arrival of patients at the accident and emergency department,
2. in the radiography department,
3. in determining priorities for operative intervention.

76. What is an accepted medical practice?

An accepted medical practice is also known as 'Scientific Medical Practice'. It is defined as a practice which is mentioned in (the latest editions of) standard text books or in various issues of leading medical journals or is recognized by a responsible body of medical profession. In many instances there may be more than one accepted method. In cases of medical negligence the outcome of treatment is of secondary importance, the method adopted is of primary and much grater importance. It is imperative that the doctor uses one of the recognized/acknowledged methods of treatment currently accepted by the medical profession at that time. In case the doctor fails to follow one of the accepted methods and instead departs from the conventional course of treatment, the burden of proof lies upon the doctor to show to the court whether he had taken all proper factors into account before deciding to depart and that he had informed the patient of this departure and obtained his consent the accepted practice must be a current practice. This means that the doctor has to keep upto date with new developments in his field of medicine. The medical practitioner cannot stick steadfastly to the principles learnt in his training, he must endeavour to keep up with new developments. But this does not mean he must read everything published within a few weeks of its publication, all he is required to do is to act responsibly and reasonably. Like any other practice, medical practice will be judged by the standard of care prevailing at the time of incident, not at the time of the trial.

The Supreme Court has observed in *Vinitha Ashok* v *Lakshmi Hospital* 2001 (8) SCC 731:

> "...... in a large majority of cases, it has been demonstrated that a doctor will be liable for negligence in respect of diagnosis and treatment in spite of a body of professional opinion approving his conduct where it has not been established to the court's satisfaction that such opinion relied on is reasonable or responsible. If it can be demonstrated that the professional opinion is not capable of withstanding the logical analysis, the court would be entitled to hold that the body of opinion is not capable of withstanding the logical analysis, the court would be entitled to hold that the body of opinion is not reasonable or responsible."

New practice when to adopt? – the problem of any complainant who alleges that the defendant doctor has been negligent in failing to adopt a new practice is to determine when the defendant should have knowledge thereof before he is found negligent in not adopting a new technique? Each case will have to be judged on its own facts but it is the court that looks at:

— how widespread the knowledge is,

— the length of time it has been available, and

— if the new practice is a precaution, the expense of adopting that precaution, the practicality of doing so and the benefit to the patient.

In *Dr. N.T. Subramanyam* v *Dr. B. Krishnarao* 1993 III CPJ 1557 (TN), complainant was admitted in the nursing home for haemalemesis (blood in vomiting). Negligence alleged was that instead of doing endoscopy and selerotherapy, sengstaken's tube was introduced with traction. This cause physical pain and torture.

The State Commission observed that there are three recognized and accepted methods of treatment:

(*i*) balloon tamponade with sengsitaken's tube,

(*ii*) selero therapy, and

(*iii*) surgery.

The doctor had selected one of these accepted methods, hence there is no negligence.

In *R.K. Agarwal* v *Dr. B. Mukhopadhya* 1995 I CPJ 260 (Bih), complainant sustained fracture on left elbow. A particular procedure was adopted, and advised follow up. He consulted other doctors instead. Complainant alleged that other doctor told him that if other method had been adopted he would have been cured.

The State Commission held that when there are two genuinely responsible schools of thought about the method to be adopted the court shall not place hall mark of legality on any one of the treatments. Merely because one of the treatments available was chosen, it could not be held as negligence.

77. What is meant by competence?

Legally, the word competence means "duly qualified" (*Black's Law Dictionary P 284*). It also means "having sufficient capacity" which is determined by one's qualifications, training and/or experience.

78. Whether the liability of a doctor for negligence/deficiency in service under the Consumer Protection Act falls under the category of tort or contract?

In general, a professional man owes to his client a duty in tort as well as in contract in advice or performing service.

Medical practitioners do not enjoy and immunity and they can be sued in contract or tort on the ground that they failed to exercise reasonable skill and care. (*Black's Law Dictionary, 6th edn*).

79. What is meant by contract?

The term 'contract' has been defined in Black's Law Dictionary (6th edn.) as under:

> "Contract, An agreement between the two or more persons which creates an obligation to do or not to do a particular thing. As defined in Restatement, second contracts: A contract is a promise or a set of promises for the breach of which the law is some way recognizes as a duty." A legal relationship

consisting an agreement between the parties that gives each a legal duty to the other and also the right to seek a remedy for the breach of those duties. Its essential are competent parties, subject-matter, a legal consideration, mutuality of agreement, and mutuality of obligation.

Express or implied: An express contractor is an actual agreement of the parties, the terms of which are openly uttered or declared at the time of making it, being stated in distinct and explicit language, either orally or in writing.

As implied contract is one not created or evidenced by the explicit agreement of the parties, but inferred by the law, as a matter of reason and justice from their acts or conduct, the circumstances surrounding the transaction making it a reasonable, or even a necessary assumption that a contract existed between them by tacit under standing.

As implied contract is one inferred from conduct of parties and arises where plaintiff, without being requested to do so, renders services under circumstances indicating that he expects to be paid therefore, and defendant knowing such circumstances avails himself of benefit of those services. It is an agreement which legitimately can be inferred from intention of parties as evidenced by circumstances and ordinary course of dealing and common understanding of men."

80. What is tort?

The word 'tort' is derived from 'tortus' meaning twisted. From there, it came to mean 'wrong' and it is still so used in French. In English, the word 'tort' has a purely technical legal meaning, a legal civil wrong for which the law provides a remedy. In Ballentine's Law Dictionary (3rd edition 1969) the term has been defined comprehensively as under:

"Tort. A wrong independent of contract. A breach of duty which the law, as distinguished from a mere contract, has imposed. An injury or wrong committed, either with or without force, to the person or property of another.

Such injury may arise by the non-feasance, by malfeasance or by the misfeasance by the wrong-doer. In a general way, a tort is distinguished from a breach of contract in that the latter arises under an agreement of the parties, whereas the tort, ordinarily, is a violation of a duty fixed by law, independent of contractor or the will of the parties, although it may sometimes have relation to obligations growing out of, or coincident with a contract, and frequently the same facts will sustain either class of action. Although the same act may constitute both a crime and a tort, the crime is an offense against the public pursued by the sovereign while the tort is a private injury which is pursued by the injured party."

81. How can contract and tort be distinguished? Are there any similarities between them?

There is a well marked distinction between a contract and a tort. A contract is founded upon consent; a tort is infected against or without consent. A contract necessitates privity between the parties to it, in tort no privity is needed. A tort must also be distinguished from a pure breach of contract. First, a tort is a violation of a right *in rem*, *i.e.*, of a right vested in some determinate person, either personally or as a member of community, and available against the world at large, whereas a breach of contract is an infringement of a right *in personam*, *i.e.* of a right available only against some determinate person or body, and in which the community at large has no concern. The distinction between the two lies in the nature of the duty that is violated. In the case of a tort, the duty is one imposed by the law and is owed to the community at large. In the case of a contract, the duty is one imposed by the law and is owed to the community at large. In the case of a contract, the duty is fixed by the will and consent of the parties, and it is owed to a definite person or persons. [*Jay Laxmi Salt Works* (*P*) *Ltd* v *State of Gujarat* (1994) 4 SCC 1]. Thus, if A assaults B, or damages B's property without lawful cause or excuse, it is a tort. Here the duty violated is a duty imposed by the law, and that is the duty not to do unlawful harm to the person or property of another. But if A agrees to sell goods to B for a price, and either party fails to perform the contract, the case is one of breach of contract. Here there is no duty owed by A except to B, and none owed by B except to A. the duty that is violated is a specific duty owed by either party to the other alone, as distinguished from a general duty owed to the community at large. Secondly, in a breach of contract, the motive for the breach is immaterial: in a tort, it is often taken into consideration. Thirdly, in a breach of contract, damages are only a compensation. In an action for tort to the property, they are generally the same. But where the injury is to the person, character or feelings, and the facts disclose improper motive or conduct such as fraud, malice, violence cruelty or the like which aggravate the plaintiff's injury, he may be awarded aggravated damages. Exemplary damages to punish the defendant and to deter him in future can also be awarded in certain cases in tort but rarely in contract. [*Rookes* v *Bornard* (1964) AC 1129 (1221) (HL)]. A clause in contract limiting liability cannot be relied upon by a person who is not a party to that contract and incurs liability in tort. Another distinction that may be mentioned is that the law of torts is aimed at allocation or prevention of losses whereas the law of contract aims to see that the promises made under a contract are performed.

The same act may amount to a tort and breach of contract. Person such as carriers, solicitors, or surgeons, who undertake to discharge certain duties and voluntarily enter into contracts for the performance thereof, will be liable for neglect or unskillful ness either in an action for a breach of contract or in tort to a party to the contract or in tort only to a person not a party to the contract who suffers injury. The breach of such contracts amounts also to a tort because such persons would be equally liable even if there was no contract as they undertake a duty independently of any contract. A father employs a surgeon to attend on his son. The son was injured by unskillful treatment. Hence there is a contract between the father and the surgeon. The father therefore may sue the surgeon in contract, but the son can sue him only in tort. In the celebrated case of *Donoghue* v *Stevonson* (1932) AC 562 (HL), a manufacturer who sold sub-standard article to a retailer who sold it to a customer who after consuming it become ill. The manufacturer was under a contractual duty to the retailer and was in breach was of that duty but he also owed a duty in tort to take reasonable care not to harm the consumer.

The aforesaid distinctions between a tort and a contract though fundamentally sound are getting blurred in certain areas. Although normally a duty in tort is independent of any consent or agreement and is fixed by the law there are cases where some sort of prior consent or agreement on the part of the defendant is necessary.

The duty of care owed to a person advised by a gratuitous advisor, who is placed in such a position that others may reasonably rely upon his judgment or skill, has been described as equivalent to contract and is dependent upon the advisor's agreeing to give advice in circumstances in which but for the absence of consideration there would be a contract.

It may be observed that the fundamental duty in a contract to perform the promise like a tort duty comes into being by mere force of law. Another similarity that may be noticed is that although at the initial stage a duty in tort is towards persons generally but after there is a breach of that duty to pay compensation in tort is like a duty in contract owed to a determinate person to persons.

It is now accepted that there may be concurrent contractual and tortuous duties owed to the same plaintiff who has a choice of proceeding either in tort or contract. [*Coupland* v *Arabian Gulf Petroleum Co.* (1963) 3 All ER 226 (CA)].

Recent advances in the law of negligence allows a plaintiff, although his person or property has not been injured, to recover economic loss suffered by him by the negligent act of the defendant in committing a breach of contract entered into between him and a third party provided there is a close degree of proximity and the loss suffered is a direct and foreseeable result of the defendants negligence [*Junior Books Ltd.* v *Veichi Co. Ltd.* (1982) 3 All ER 201 (HL)]. All this led to the observation that we are moving towards the principle that every breach of contract which might with reasonable care have been avoided is also a tort to a person foreseeably affected thereby including even the parties to the contract.

Thus liability for negligence may sometimes be fixed by the courts simultaneously under contract and tort, as is the case with cases under Consumer Protection Act.

82. What is limitation period prescribed for filing a case under the Consumer Protection Act or under Civil law of tort for medical negligence? Can an action for negligence be brought against a doctor even after the limitation period for filing a case has expired long before?

For filing a case under civil law of tort the limitation period is three years from the date of cause of action as prescribed under the Limitation Act, 1963.

In terms of section 24A of the Consumer Protection Act, 1986, the consumer disputes redressal agencies shall not admit a case unless it has been filed within 2 years from the date on which the cause of action arose.

Limitation starts from the date on which cause of action arises therefore the date on which the complainant comes to know about the failure may be condoned by the court/consumer forum/commission on showing sufficient cause by the complainant. Reason for condonation of delay have to be recorded in writing by the court/consumer forum/commission.

Under section 24A(2) of the Consumer Protection Act, 1986 the words "Satisfies" and "Sufficient Cause" care in *pari materia* (of the same matter) with the words used in section 5 of the Limitation Act, 1963. Hence, the principles laid down in section 5 of the Limitation Act, 1963 can be invoked for condonation of delay in filing a complaint in consumer courts. The consumer court exercising discretion to condone the delay, must record its reasons for condonation of such a delay.

Doctor's negligence may not cause harm until very much later, or at least the patient may not be aware of it until much later. For instance, a 5 years old girl, due to negligence of a doctor/hospital, suffers from perforated appendix. Fifteen years later she gets married and finds herself unable to conceive. Investigations reveal that multiple adhesions had followed the peritoneal sepsis which had occurred due to perforation of the appendix, and that these had obstructed her fallopian tubes she may attempt to get condonation so as to sue the doctor as she had taken all these years to realise that doctor's alleged negligence had caused her infertility.

In the case of *Suvarna Baljekar* v *Rohit Bhatt* (1996) II CPJ 75 (NC), the National Commission upheld the decision of the Maharashtra State Commission. Mr. Rohit Bhatt had taken treatment from Suvarna Baljekar from 1986 to 1988, while the complaint was filed somewhere in 1992. Hence the complaint was hopelessly barred by times as it was filed after more than 3 years of the alleged treatment.

Medical cases are probably the commonest type of negligence on which the complainant may be aware of any damage until long after it has been inflicted. This is explained the intricacies of caution and the latent nature of the damage in medical cases. Medical treatment may extend over a long period of time. The damage may be cumulative and not apparent to the patient until it is well established many years later. A patient is far less likely to notice damage if it has a gradual rather than a sudden onset.

A particularly useful illustration of latent damage occurred in *Plydell* v *Aubyn* (1993) unreported, wherein a two years old girl was seen by her general practitioner several times over the course of a week in 1966. At the end of the week she was admitted to hospital and found to have perforated appendicitis and the recovery process was complicated by adhesions in the long term. After a year or two of the marriage (20 years later) she found herself unable to conceive. On investigation by a gynecologist it was found that the pelvic adhesions from the appendicitis had caused the infertility. The alleged negligence had occurred more than 20 years ago. However the knowledge of the existence of harm was acquired only when she found herself unable to conceive. Hence the court exercised its discretion to condone this delay in filing of the case.

83. Can a case on which compensation has been awarded by Motor Accident Claims Tribunal (MACT) be agitated before Consumer Forum/ Commission? Are the findings of the MACT binding on the State Commission?

In the case of *Harbhajan Singh* v *Dayanand Medical College and Hospital* 1996 III CPJ 263 (Punj.), it was held:

"The cause for entertaining claims under the Motor Vehicles Act is in relation to the use of Motor vehicles whereas under the Consumer Protection Act it is in relation to the deficiency in rendering service by the opposite parties, where the subject-matter is not identical, the case be independently taken up for hearing and the question raised have to be decided on the evidence produced on these questions.

The finding of MACT are not binding on the Consumer Fora, though on the question of assessing the quantum of damages, since the principle of assessment remain the same whether such a question is to be determined under the civil law or under the Motor Vehicle Act or under the Consumer Protection Act, this may be of assistance, though not binding."

84. Where a doctor is found criminally negligent, can a complaint for medical negligence claiming compensation under the Consumer Protection Act or the Law of Tort be filed?

Needless to emphasize that where the doctor is found criminally negligent, in addition to his prosecuted under criminal law, the patient/attendant can also bring an action against him for claiming compensation for the negligence, under the law of tort or the Consumer Protection Act.

The AP High Court in *Mrs. Shanta* v *State of AP* 1997 III CPJ 481 (AP-HC) (DB) while granting compensation against the government hospital for negligence of leaving a mop in the womb for violating fundamental right to life under Article 21 of the Constitution, observed that the petitioner shall be free to take action in tort for the damages the private law against the hospitals and others and also to make complaint for any criminal act of the hospital, if so advised.

85. Is a complaint under the Consumer Protection Act maintainable if a case has already been adjudicated by a civil court? Can a complaint be adjudicated (heard) concurrently in civil and consumer court?

It is firmly established that if adjudication of a case has been made by a civil court then in respect of the same subject matter and relief the Redressal Forums are precluded from adjudicating them again. [*Bhairu Lal* v *Rajasthan State Electricity Board* 1993 III CPJ 1656].

When the subject-matter of the complaint is similar and is *sub-judice* before an ordinary court, as a matter of policy and principle, a concurrent adjudication in respect of the same should not be conducted by a Redressal Agency under the Consumer Protection Act. [*Special Machines* v *Punjab National Bank* 1991 I CPJ 79 (NC)].

86. Can a Consumer Forum entertain a complain of medical negligence involving examination and recording of voluminous evidence and where complicated issues are involved?

In a case of *Indian Medical Association* v *VP Shantha* AIR 1996 SC 550, the Supreme Court held:

> "There may be classes which do not raise such complicated questions and deficiency in service may be due to obvious faults which can be easily established such as:
>
> — removal of wrong limb,
>
> — the performance of an operation on the wrong patient,
>
> — giving injection of a drug to which the patient is allergic without looking into the OPD card containing the warning,
>
> — use of wrong gas during the course of anesthesia
>
> — and leaving inside the patient swabs, forceps or other items of operating equipment after surgery.
>
> Issues raising in the complaints in such cases can be speedily disposed of by the procedure that is being followed by the Consumer Disputes Redressal Agencies and there is no reason why complaints regarding deficiency in service in such cases should not be adjudicated by the agencies under the Act.
>
> In complaints involving complicated issues requiring recording of evidence of experts, the complainant can be asked to approach the civil court for appropriate relief."

The Supreme Court has recently held in the case of *Dr. J.J. Merchant* v *Shrinath Chaturvedi* 2002 CTJ 757, that a plea regarding non-maintainability of a complaint in summary proceedings before the Consumer Forum on the ground that it involves disputed questions of facts, etc. is not legally tenable by observing as under:

> "It was next contended that such complicated questions of fact cannot be decided in summary proceedings. In our view this submission also requires to be rejected because under the Act, for summary or speedy trial, exhaustive procedure in conformity with the principles of natural justice is provided. Therefore, merely because it is mentioned that commission or forum is required to have summary trial to be just and reasonable long draw delayed procedure, giving ample opportunity to the litigant to harass the aggrieved other side, is not necessary. It should be kept in mind that Legislature has provided alternative efficacious, simple, inexpensive and speedy remedy to the consumers and that should not be curtailed on such ground it would also be totally wrong assumption that because summary trial is provided, justice

cannot be done when some questions of facts are required to be dealt with or decided. The Act provides sufficient safe grounds."

87. Whether a pending criminal proceeding in a case is a bar to file complaint under the Consumer Protection Act or seek civil remedy for damages under the law of tort?

The National Commission in *Punjab National Bank* v *K.B. Shetty* 1991 (2) CPR 633, held that where the case is *sub-judice* in a criminal court it cannot be maintained that the complaint could not be entertained by the state commission on the ground that the case was *sub-judice* and under investigation by the Metropolitan Magistrate.

But in the case of *Savita Y. Chaudhari* v *Ghanshyam G. Kochure,* Complaint No. 672/92, decided on 1-2-1994 Mah (unreported), complainant alleged negligence on the part of the opposite party in a case of roadside accident with fracture hand which was in plaster developing gas gangrene for which amputation of the hand had to be done later in order to save her life. In view of the fact that the complainant had already filed a criminal case under section 388 of the IPC and a special civil suit for compensation and had also complained to the medical council of India, decisions of all of which were pending, the state commission declined to adjudicate upon the matter.

It may be stated here that the State Commission might have declined to adjudicate because a special civil suit for compensation was pending *i.e.* for the same cause of action for which complaint under the Consumer Protection Act was filed and not because a criminal case was pending.

It has been held by the Jharkhand State Commission in *Dr. Sunil Rungta* v *Dr. Chandra Shekhar Agarwal* 2002 (3) CPR 30, that scope and ambit of the proceedings in two different statutes are entirely different. The complaint under the Consumer Protection Act is filed for grant of compensation and damages for defective supply of goods and/or deficiency in service on the part of the opposite party whereas the proceeding under the Code of Criminal Procedure is initiated for awarding punishment to the wrong-doers. The Consumer Protection Act has been passed by the Parliament for giving instant relief to the victims who have cheated by the unscrupulous traders/manufacturers and/or to the consumer who suffers loss due to deficiency in service on the part of the opposite parties. The State Commission while arriving at the aforesaid conclusion found support from the following observation of the Supreme Court in *Pratibha Rani* v *Suraj Kumar* (1995) 2 SCC 370.

"There are large numbers of cases where criminal law and civil law run side-by-side. The two remedies are not mutually exclusive but clearly co-extensive and essentially differ in their content and consequence. The object of the criminal law is to punish an offender who commits an offence against persons, property or the State for which the accused, on proof of the offence, is deprived of his liberty and in some cases even his life. This does not however effect the event of his life. This does not however affect the civil remedies at all for suing the wrong-doer in cases like anathema to suppose that when a civil remedy is available, a criminal prosecution is completely barred. The two types of actions are quite different in content, scope and import."

88. Can a complainant file an application to summon expert witnesses (doctors) under the Consumer Protection Act? Can such witnesses be summoned and their attendance enforced by the court/consumer forum/commission?

Yes, section 13(4) authorises the forum established under the Consumer Protection Act to exercise powers which are vested in a civil court under the Code of Civil Procedure with respect to summoning and enforcing the attendance of any defendant or witness and examining the witness an oath. This section further provides receipt of evidence on affidavits. In case of medical negligence, if affidavits are not forthcoming of such expert witnesses, the forums can be requested to summon such expert witnesses as provided under section 13(4)(1) of the Act.

In the case of *Darshan Singh Barsa* v *Dr. Jasbir Singh* 1998 I CPJ 45 (Punj.), the complainant filed the complaint claiming ₹4 lakh on account of death of his wife alleging negligence. An application was filed in the complaint for summoning 2 experts along with records of the patient. The application was rejected by the District forum on the ground that in the application it was not stated that the complainant failed to secure their affidavits and in the summary proceedings as contemplated under Consumer Protection Act evidence on affidavits could be led.

In the case of *Khairati Lal* v *Dr. Kewal Krishnan* 1998 (1) CPJ 181 (Punj.), the complainant had abdominal pain for which Dr. Kewal Krishnan had wrongly administered some I.V. injection which led to gangrene and amputation of three fingers of right hand. During appeal Kharait Lal filed an application to record statement of Dr. Mohan Varghese, professor of cardio thoracic surgery, CMC Ludhiana. This was allowed by the State Commission and his evidence proved vital.

89. Who is an expert?

An expert is one who has been established competence in a particular field, it being for the judge to decide whether a witness can be so rated. Section 45 of Indian Evidence Act, 1872 defines an expert as:

> "***45 Opinion of experts***.—when the court has to form an opinion upon a point of foreign law, or of science, or art, or as to identity of hand writing or finger impressions, the opinion upon that point of persons specially skilled in such foreign law, science or art, or in questions as to identify of hand writing or finger impressions are relevant facts.
>
> Such persons are called experts."

Expert witness has been defined in Black's Law Dictionary (6th edn), *inter alia*, in the following terms:

"One who by reason of education or specialised experience possesses superior knowledge respecting a subject about which persons having no particular training are incapable of forming, an accurate opinion or deducting correct conclusion...... one skilled in any particular art, trade or profession being possessed o particular knowledge concerning the same, and one who has given subject in question particular study, practice or observation."

90. What are the duties and responsibilities of an expert witness?

In *National Justice Compania Navira SA* v *Prudential Assurance Company Ltd.,* "The Ikarian Reefer" Cresswell, J. set out the duties and responsibilities of expert witnesses in civil cases. (1993 2 Lloyd's Rep 68, 81-82 Q.B.D.)

— Expert evidence presented to the court should be and should be seen to be the independent product of the expert uninfluenced as to form or content by the exigencies of litigation.

— An expert witness should provide independent assistance to the court by objective unbiased opinion in relation to matters within his expertise. An expert witness in the High Court should never assume the role of an advocate.

— An expert witness should state the facts or assumptions upon which his opinion is based. He should not omit to consider material facts which could detract from his concluded opinion.

— An expert witness should make it clear when a particular question or issue falls outside his expertise. An expert witness in High Court should never assume the role of the advocate.

— An expert witness should state the facts or assumptions upon which his opinion is based. He should not omit to consider material facts which should not omit to consider material facts which could detract from his concluded opinion.

— An expert witness should make it clear when a particular question or issue falls outside his expertise.

— If an expert opinion is not properly researched because he considers that insufficient data is available, then this must be stated with an indication that the opinion is no more than a provisional one. In cases where an expert witness who has prepared a report, cannot assert that the report contains the truth, the whole truth and nothing but the truth without some qualification, the qualification should be stated in the report.

— In, after exchange of reports, an expert witness changes his view on a material matter having read the other sides expert's report or for any other reason, such change of view should be communicated (through legal representative) to the other side without delay and when appropriate to the court.

— Where expert evidence refers to photographs, plans, calculations, analysis, measurements, survey reports or other similar documents, these must be provided to the opposite party at the same time as the exchange of reports.

91. Can standard material literature be relied in deciding a case of medical negligence?

Yes. In the case of *P. Venkata Lakshmi* v *Dr. Y. Savitha Devi* 2003 (5) CLD 207, absence of expert evidence had been referred to as one of the grounds of 'no-proof' of negligence. While no expert witness had been produced/examined by the appellant complainant, this has to be seen in 'ground reality' terms, that very rarely, if ever, any other doctor comes forward to give evidence in person or by way of evidence against other doctor. In this case this gap was amply made good by producing literature on all the points at issue and on host of other points associated with the decision making process on the issues included in the case. There is no reference to any of the literature produced by the appellant-complainant, on which she relied upon the support her complaint.

Accordingly, the case was remanded to the State Commission for rehearing and passing order as per law after taking into consideration the medical literature produced by the complainant in support of complaint and cross-examination of witnesses, if the State Commission is so inclined on request from the parties examination of an independent expert witness.

In *Suyash Hospital (P) Ltd* v *Prasanna Kumar Ojha* 2003 (2) CLD 451, the State Commission held that there was negligence on the part of the hospital and the death was due to negligence of the hospital authorities which decision was based solely on affidavits and standard text book. The decision was affirmed by the National Commission.

92. With whom does the burden of proving negligence lie?

All medical negligence cases concern various questions of fact. When we say that the patient bears the burden of proof it means that he has the task of convincing the court that his version of the facts in the correct one. The converse does not apply. Thus, the doctor does not produce any acceptable alternative to defend himself although to do so would clearly strengthen his case. The doctor needs to do no more than to undermine his opponent's version sufficiently to prevent it from being accepted.

The burden of proof is not fixed; it keeps shifting from the complainant to the defendant. The initial burden of proof rests with the person alleging it, but the burden shifts to the defendant doctor, and the same principle applies to him. If the defendant doctor makes a statement and the burden to prove that there was no negligence shifts to him.

An exception to the general rule that the burden of proof rests upon the plaintiff in the application of the doctrine of *res ipsa loquitur* (fact speaks for itself) in cases where the facts are so obvious that the onus is shifted to the doctor to prove that he was not negligent.

93. Can the evidence/opinion of an expert (doctor) be relied upon merely on the basis of documents?

The opinion of expert unless he is subjected to the test of examination and cross-examination in court cannot be considered as authentic and such evidence cannot be relied and form a basis of a finding. Merely the proof of documents does not mean that the contents thereof are necessarily true. [*Mohan Mohindrao* v *New India Assurance Company* 1997 (1) CPJ 585].

94. Is it necessary that the court should accept the evidence of an expert and decide the case accordingly?

Expert witnesses have a vital function in medical negligence actions, but the emphasis that is sometimes placed on accepted professional practice can observe their true role, which is to provide the evidence upon which the court decides whether there has been negligence or not. This is not for the witnesses to determine. This was forcefully expressed by Bollen. J, in the Australian case of *F* v *R*, (1992) 33 SASR 189.

> "Expert evidence will assist the court. But in the end, it is court will have been guided and assisted by the expert evidence. It will not produce an answer merely at the dictation of the expert evidence. Sometimes its decision will be the same as it would have been had it accepted dictation. But the court does not merely follow expert evidence slavishly to a decision. The court considers and weighs up all admissible evidence which it has received. If the court did merely follow the path apparently pointed by expert evidence with no critical consideration of it and the other evidence, it would abdicate its duty to decide, on the evidence, whether in law a duty existed and had not been discharged."

The Himachal Pradesh State Commission in *Smt. Ramesh Goyal* v *Senior Divisional Manager, Life Insurance Corporation of India* 1997 (1) CCC 66, while deciding insurance claim has held:

> "We are of the opinion that only in case of the doctors who have given their opinion – expert opinion had supported their versions by means of an affidavit or otherwise in examination before the court, only then the evidence regarding the ailment of the patient could have been given weight."

In an appeal against the decision of the West Bengal State Commission, which had awarded compensation of ₹2 lakh against the appellant for negligence and deficiency in service in transfusing blood of wrong group to the complainant, the National Commission set aside the order of the State Commission on the ground that reliance was placed on certificate issued by a doctor who was neither hematologist nor a pathologist, thus, not an expert and his opinion lacked in all requisite technical details and was absolutely vague.

The expert evidence though can be accepted as proper there may be circumstances in which expert evidence cannot be relied upon as establishing proper level of skill and competence. If the record discloses expert evidence both for and against a particular procedure, whether the evidence adduced is reasonable and responsible and whether such evidence is capable of withstanding the logical analysis is for the court to decide. [*Vinitha Ashok* v *Lakshmi Hospital* 2001 (8) SCC 731].

95. What is meant by causation in cases of medical negligence?

'Causation' means "to bring about" (*Black's Law Dictionary 6th Edn.*). In order to obtain compensation in a case of medical negligence, it is not sufficient to prove that negligence was the cause of the damage which occurred. The more proximate the causation (proximate cause) to the damage the greater is the chance in succeeding in a claim for compensation. The more remote the causation (remote cause), the lesser is the chance of success in getting compensation.

In order to succeed in a medical negligence case the claimant must prove, on a balance of probabilities, that the doctor's breach of duty to care i.e. negligence caused the damage. He has to show that:

— the damage would not have occurred but for the defendant's negligence, or

— the defendant's negligence materially contributed to or materially increased the risk of injury,

— further, if the claim is that the doctor failed to disclose the risk involved in the treatment/surgery and the risk actually occurs, the claimant can raise a plea that had such risk been disclosed he would not have agreed to such treatment/surgery.

— Sometimes, the courts apply the 'but for' test to determine the closeness of the negligence to the damage (causation). Under this test the court's address to the question, could the harm to patient have occurred but for the doctors/hospitals negligence, or could the harm have been suffered anyway?

This 'but for' test is very well illustrated in an English case. In *Barnete* v *Chelsea and Kensignton Hospital Management Committee* (1968) 1 All ER 1068, a night watchman was taken to hospital vomiting and suffering from sever stomach pain, but the casualty doctor on duty sent him away to see his own G.P. He died soon afterwards of arsenic poisoning, and it was discovered that an unknown person had put arsenic to the tea of the watchman on duty on a particular site. There was no dispute about the fact that the doctor had been negligent. What was in issue there was whether that negligent act has caused the man's death. It was held that it had not. The man would have died anyway. Much of the evidence turned upon the question of whether he would have survived if he had been given an antidose as soon as possible after arriving to the hospital and it was proved that he would not. The defendants were held not liable.

In a case of *Ramji Lal* v *Sarvodaya Medical* 1995 (1) CPR 833 (NC), the chemist supplied pectokab MF instead of Darzin with neomycin prescribed by the doctor for diarrhea. But causation could not be established between the negligent act of the chemist and the death of child, who was suffering from cyanotic congenital heart disease with congestive heart failure which was the cause of his death. Hence the national commission held that no compensation would be awarded.

In the case of *Anup Kumar* v *S.M. Kanwar* 1993 1 CPJ 45 (NC), the complaint of fly infected bottle of osto-calcium leading to the alleged deformity was dismissed,, because the causation of the alleged deformity due to the consumption of the medicine in question could not be proved.

The complainant than only claim for the damage which results from the doctor's negligence. Causation is often difficult to prove in a medical negligence cases by a complainant, example a patient who is already ill before he enters the doctors consulting room and fails to survive the illness, his widow may argue that he died because of the treatment but the doctor will argue that he died in spite of it. Some illness are to resistant to treatment that the patient will die even if he is a attended by the most skilled and careful doctor, on the other hand, there are many conditions that are self limiting and the patient will recover even with the worst possible treatment.

96. What is *res ipsa loquitur* and who and where it is possible in medical negligence cases?

In all civil cases (including consumer ones) the onus of proof is on the complainant. By this it means that the complainant had to convenience the court that his version of the event is more than 50% likely to be correct. This can be very difficult. However, there is a method by which a patient can occasionally overcome this difficulty by resorting to the legal maxim *res ipsa loquitur*.

Literally translated *res ipsa loquitur* means "the thing (situation) speaks for itself." Put another way common sense dictated that the accident could happen only if someone (a doctor or a nurse) was negligent. Application of this maxim places on the defendant the onus of disproving this presumption of negligence, i.e. it has the effect of revering the burden of proof.

The presumption is not readily available to any complainant who is having difficulty with his evidence. It is not a rule of any law but rather a maxim upon which a judge may agree to allow a complainant to rely for the purpose of his evidence if the circumstances of the case justify it.

On application of this maxim it is for the doctor to satisfy the court that there was some other cause for the damage, or that the act which he did was not negligent.

The criteria considered essential to make the doctrine of *res ipsa loquitur* applicable are:

- The cause of accident must be the unknown or unascertainable,
- Common knowledge or expert evidence suggesting that the injury, by its very nature, cannot occur without negligence,
- The doctor (defendant) must have been in control of the situation (instrumentalities),
- Patient/attendant must not have contributed to the injury.

Some instances of *res ipsa loquitur* are:

(*a*) rapture of ear drum after ear syringing,

(*b*) development of meningitis after spinal Anaesthesia,

(*c*) permanent brain damage following appendectomy,

(*d*) amputation of wrong limb or wrong digit at operation,

(*e*) burning of the skin caused by a strong antiseptic solution,

(*f*) leaving swabs or surgical instruments inside the patient after an operation,

(*g*) Patient loses use of the arm after a minor surgery to remove a sebaceous cyst on the back of his neck.

Where a girl child aged seven years, suffering from cold and fever was given an injection in the thigh which resulted in paralysis of left lower limb, it was for the doctor to rule out the possibility of faulty administration of injection or a reactible medicine administered by injection. When he sat silent the case was clearly of *res ipsa loquitur*. Another finding that could have been given is about faulty administration of the injection, it would necessarily mean that the injection might have been given at some wrong place of the body which might have been affected the nerve or other avoidable part of the body. All that was a matter for explanation by the doctor. Having failed to do so, only conclusion would be that the doctor would be liable for deficiency in service on the principle of *res ipsa loquitur*. Compensation of ₹1.5 lac was awarded. [*Dr. G.D. Hadia* v *Minor Dharmitha Chotubhai Goswami* 2003 (2) CPR 490].

In *Arpana Dutta* v *Apollo Hospital Enterprises Ltd.* 2002 ACJ 945 (Mad-HC), the evidence adduced by the patient conclusively established that an abdominal pack was left behind in the abdominal region at the time of operation done by the hospital doctor and this was only an act of negligence and due to want of sufficient care and caution of conducting the operation which is expected of a surgeon. So there can be no scope for the hospital and surgeon and they must be made answerable to the suffering and pain undergone by the plaintiff due to carelessness and negligence of the first operating surgeon, while doing the operation in the hospital the doctrine of res ipsa loquitur squarely applies to the facts of the present case. Damages (compensation) of ₹5,80,000 awarded against defendant hospital.

Res ipsa loquitur not applied — In *Air Commodore Satyanarayana* v *L.V. Prasad Eye Institute* 1998 (1) CPJ 110 (AP), the complainant aged 75 years lost sight of his right eye after cataract surgery sought to apply the doctrine of *res ipsa loquitur*, but after considering the material facts and circumstances of the case the court refused to apply the principle.

97. Can the finding in a departmental enquiry be produced as an evidence in a claim under the Consumer Protection Act? Are these findings binding on the court?

In a case of *Harbhajan Singh* v *Dayanand Medical College and Hospital* 1996 III CPJ 203 (Pun), it was held that State Commission has to decide independently the question of negligence on the evidence produced before it, the finding of the departmental enquiry cannot be considered as binding on the judicial authority.

98. Will the following absolve the doctor/hospital of negligence: (1) if fee charged is refunded or (2) if the doctor/hospital reimburses the expenses incurred for carrying out treatment or corrective surgery for rectifying their mistake?

In the case of *Asha Rani* v *Dr. Rohit Grover* 1996 III CPJ 290 (Chd.), the complainant was operated upon his left eye, for glaucoma but her condition did not improve. The doctor refunded the sum of ₹3,600 which he had received from the complainant.

The state commission held that this refund is a circumstance which itself does go against him and at the same time does not absolve him from the liability, if negligence is established.

The state commission, however, gave finding of no negligence on merits and dismissed the complaint.

In *Kunhi Krishnan P. V.* v *Sreechitra Tiruman Institute for Medical Science and Technology* 2001 III CPJ 86 (Ker.), the fee charged by the hospital were refunded on death of the patient and as such contention was raised by the opposite parties hospital that the patient availed of service fee of charge and hence was not a consumer under the Consumer Protection Act, 1986. Rejecting the contention the State Commission held on facts as under:

> "The status of the deceased at the time of availing the service being as a person who availed service for consideration, the said position cannot be altered. Admittedly, service was availed on payment of consideration, the deceased, therefore, was a consumer under section 2(1)(*d*)(II) of the Act. The return of the consideration cannot make the service anything other than service for consideration."

In *Dr. Anil Nadir* v *Dr. Rakesh Dullu* 2003 (3) CPR 308 (Del.), a guide wire was left in the body of the respondent while performing operation by the appellant doctor. The fact that the expenses for the operation which was conducted by another doctor for removing the guide wire from the body of the respondent were borne by the appellant doctor about the deficiency in service (negligence). Hence the doctor/hospital were held negligent and liable to pay compensation.

99. Can *ipse dixit* (he himself said it, asserting on his own) of the complainant be accepted to hold charge of negligence on the part of the doctor?

No. In *Satwant Kaur* v *Dr. Kanwaljit Kaur* 1998 (2) CPR 458 (Punj.), the complainant was that a cotton swab was left in the colon of the patient while performing caesarean or tubectomy operation. It was observed that since there was no injury to the colon the sponge could not have entered the colon without injury. *Ipse dixit* of the complainant is such like matter could not be accepted to hold the change of negligence on the part of the doctor in such circumstances.

100. Can new material facts be filed as rejoinder to the original complaint?

The Punjab State Commission in *Nita Singla* v *Dr. Karnail Singh* 1998 (3) CPJ 39 (Punj), held that there is no provision contained under section 13 of the Consumer Protection Act, 1986 for filing rejoinder to the pleadings of the parties. May be, if a rejoinder is filed only in order to explain the pleas taken in the complaint, the same can be looked into. However, additional pleas, as such taken in the rejoinder which are on material facts cannot be permitted to be raised therein.

101. What is the implication of hiding 'material facts' about the case in cases of medical negligence?

Material fact means: any fact which is going to influence or effect the case. Material fact is one upon which outcome of litigation depends. In medical negligence cases, duration of illness; investigations, previous treatment, etc. are examples of material facts. If the patient or the doctor hides any material facts before the court, it is described as: "not coming with the clean hands" and it may significantly weaken in the case of the person who commits this lapse.

The case of *Gurpreet Kaur* v *Dr. R.K. Bhutani* 1993 (3) CPJ 355 (NC), was a case of suppression of fact, complainant's minor daughter alleged of facts, to have lost her left eye because of negligence on part of Dr. Bhutani performing an operation.

Dr. Bhutani denied the allegations and contended that the child was already operated upon in AIMS when she was only 10 months old, and complainant had suppressed these facts in the complaint. It was held that the complainant had suppressed material facts and accordingly the complaint was dismissed with costs fixed at ₹7,500.

In the case of *Subhlata* v *Christian Medical College* 1995 (1) CPJ 365 (Punj.), complainant's husband died after conducting kidney biopsy, patient was suffering from other life threatening diseases which were not disclosed in the complaint. The court held that this amounted to suppression of material facts and the complaint to claim compensation was dismissed.

In the case of *Baldev Singh* v *Arya Hospital cum Daulat Ram Memorial Medical Centre* 1997 (3) CPJ 528 (Chd.), the complainant was suffering from pain in stomach and he was examined and ultra sonography was done on the same day. He was prescribed some medicines and subsequently asked to stay as an indoor patient but against his advice the complainant left the premises. After 16 or 17 days Baldev was examined at some other hospital where lever cancer was detected and he died on 1-10-96. It was alleged that had his disease been detected earlier his life could have been saved.

The court held that the complainant had not brought on record what treatment the patient received and where during the period 2-8-1996 till 1-10-1996. This showed that material evidence had been withheld. The complaint was dismissed.

102. What are the safeguards against frivolous and vexatious complaints?

Section 26 of the Consumer Protection Act was amended by the Amendment Act of 1993, w.e.f. 18-6-1993.

The amended section 26 reads as under:

> "*26. Dismissal of frivolous and vexatious complaints.*—Where a complaint instituted before the District Forum, the State Commission or, as the case may be, the National Commission is found to be frivolous or vexatious it shall, for reasons to be recorded in writing, dismiss the complaint and make an order that the complainant shall pay to the opposite party such cost, not exceeding Ten thousand rupees, as may be specified in the order."

This section provides for levy of penal cost upto ₹10,000 on the complainant to be paid to the opposite party (doctor) in case of a complaint being found to be frivolous or vexatious.

Even before the section was amended, the National Commission had awarded costs of ₹7,500 against the complainant in the case of *Miss Gurpreet Kaur* (*Minor*) v *Dr. R.K. Bhutani* 1993 III CPJ 355 (NC), wherein it was held that the complainant had put forward a false plea, suppressed material facts resulting to earlier operation and had failed to prove any negligence on the part of the opposite party – ophthalmic surgeon.

In the case of *R. Gopinathan* v *Eskaycee-Medical Foundation Pvt. Ltd.* 1994 I CPJ 147 (NC), the National Commission had awarded costs of ₹7,500 against the complainant where the complaint of negligence against the doctor was found to be without any proof.

In the case of *Brij Mohan Kher* v *Dr. N.H. Banka* 1995 (1) CPJ 99 (NC), the National Commission levied against the complainant heavy cost of ₹10,000 to be paid to each of the two opposite parties (total ₹20,000).

The Commission put forward a plea to the lawmakers to amend the law for adequately compensating the parties who are maliciously and perhaps with a view to blackmail, arraigned under the Act so as to ensure that the Act is not misused.

103. Government doctors get pathological tests and investigations done privately or at nominal charge in the Government hospitals prior to operation/treatment. Further treatment/operation in the hospital is done without any charges. Will such payment for pathological tests, etc. qualify as "Consideration" for treatment or surgery and will the patient be a consumer within the meaning of section 2(1)(*d*) of the Consumer Protection Act for maintaining a complaint under the said Act?

In *Rabinarayan Shaoo* v *Dr. B. Jayaram Patra* 2004 1 CPJ 3 (NC), the National Commission held that the patients paying for pathological tests but no paying any charges for the treatment/operation are not consumers by observing as under:

> "No fee was paid for operation as it was not a Government Hospital, nor any fee for operation is charged from any other patient in this hospital."

The Supreme Court in the case of *Indian Medical Association* v *V.P. Shantha* AIR 1996 SC 550, interpreted the same in Para 56(10):

"Service rendered at a Government Hospital Health Centre/dispensary where services are rendered on payment of charges and also rendered free to charge to other persons availing such services would fall within the ambit of the expression 'service' as defined in section 2(1)(*o*) of the Act irrespective of the fact that the service is rendered free of charge to persons who do not pay for such service would also be 'service' and the recipient a 'consumer' under the Act.

The argument that payment of charges for tests prior to the operation for which no negligence or deficiency of service was attributed cannot be extend to a later event (operation) which is done without any fee. This cannot be clubbed together while claiming that consideration was paid for the operation. Hence in the absence of payment of consideration the complaint is not maintainable under the Consumer Protection Act, 1986."

104. What is the meaning and object of compensation?

The 'rule of law' requires that the wrong should not remain unredressed. All the individuals or persons committing wrongs should be liable in an action for damages for breach of civil law or for criminal punishment. 'Compensation' means anything given to make things equivalent, a thing given or to make amends for loss, recompensation, remuneration or pay, it need not, therefore necessarily be in terms of money, because law may specify principles on which and the matter in which compensation is to be determined and given. Compensation is an act which a court orders to be done, or money which a court orders to be paid by a person whose acts or omissions have caused loss or injury to another in order that thereby the person indemnified may receive equal value for his loss or be made whole in respect of his injury, something given or obtained as an equivalent, rendering of equivalent in value or amount, an equivalent given for property taken or for an injury done to another, a recompense in value, a recompense given for a thing received, recompense for whole injury suffered, remuneration or satisfaction for injury or damage of every description.

The expression 'compensation' is not ordinarily used as an equivalent to 'damages', although compensation may often have to be measured by the same rule as damages in an action for a breach. The term 'compensation' as pointed out in the oxford dictionary signifies that which is given in recompense, an equivalent rendered, "damages" on the other hand constitute the sum of money, claimed or adjudged to be paid in compensation for loss or injury sustained 'compensation' is a return for the loss or damage sustained. Justice requires that it should be equal in value, although not alike to kind [*Divisional Controller, KSRTC* v *Mahadeva Shetty* 2003 (7) SCC 197].

It is true that perfect compensation is hardly possible and money cannot renew a physique or frame that has been battered and shattered as stated by Lord Morris in *West* v *Shephard* 1964 AC 326. The object of providing compensation is to place the claimant as far as possible in the same position financially as he was before the accident. Broadly speaking, in the death of the basis of compensation is loss of pecuniary benefits to the dependents of the deceased in the accident. Compensation awarded should not be inadequate and should neither be unreasonable, excessive nor deficient. There can be no exact uniform rule for measuring the value of human life and the measure of damage cannot be arrived at by precise mathematical calculation, but amount recoverable depends on broad facts and circumstances of each case. It should neither be punitive against whom claim is decreed nor should it be a source of profit for the person in whose favour it is awarded. [*Divisional Controller, KSRTC* v *Mohadeva Shetty* 2003 (7) SCC 197.].

The word compensation is of very wide connotation. It has not been defined in the Consumer Protection Act, 1986. When the Consumer Disputes Redressal Forum has been vested with the jurisdiction to awards value of goods or services as compensation it has to be construed widely enabling the Forum/Commission to determine compensation for any loss or damage suffered by a consumer, which in law is otherwise included in wide meaning of compensation. The provision enables a consumer to claim and empowers the commission to redress any injustice done to him. Any other construction would defeat the very purpose of the Consumer Protection Act. The Commission or the Forum in the Act is thus entitled to award not only value of the goods or services but also to compensate a consumer for injustice suffered by him, [*Lucknow Development Authority* v *M.K. Gupta* AIR 1994 SC 787].

Under civil and consumer law, compensation paid for medical negligence is neither punishment nor reward. The principle on which damages for medical negligence are assessed in that they are to be regarded as compensation for the injury sustained or death and not a punishment for the wrong inflicted. There is no difference in the principles applied to the assessment of damages in a medical negligence case and other actions for personal injuries *e.g.* in motor accidents claims.

105. Will proof of negligence be enough for award of compensation? What are the essentials to be proved before compensation is awarded?

In order to obtain compensation or any other action under the law it is essential to prove that:

(1) negligence occurred,

(2) damage ensued, and

(3) the proximate cause of damage was that negligence

Negligence occurred, but because of it no damage ensured, it will not qualify as actionable negligence, *i.e.* no compensation or any other punishment may be awarded.

In the case of *Suvarna Baljekar* v *Rohit Bhatt* 1996 (2) CPR 13 (NC), complainant Rohit Bhatt took treatment from opposite party for acidity, nasal problem and mental irritation. Homeopathic medicines were given by opposite party for 3 years which were alleged to have caused several problems. State Commission found opposite party not a registered Homeopathic Practitioner. Compensation of ₹20,000 was awarded on appeal the National·Commission held that:

(*a*) there was no evidence that complainant suffered from alleged ailment after taking the medicine prescribed by the opposite party, and

(*b*) no evidence was there that medicines prescribed by the opposite party were likely to cause those ailments.

The National Commission accepted the appeal, set aside the impugned order and dismissed the complaint.

106. What is egg shell skull rule?

Where the complainant suffers from a latent physical or physiological pre-disposition a particular illness or injury which has been activated by the damage inflicted did by the defendant doctor the complainant is entitled to damages to the full extent of his injuries, even if they are exacerbated by the pre-disposition and this is more sever than an ordinary individual would have experienced.

This is usually referred to as the 'thin skull' or the 'egg shell skull' if the complainant has an unusually thin skull, the defendant cannot complain if the injury is much more serious than would have been the case with a normal person.

A tortfeasor takes his victim as he finds him. If the plaintiff suffers personal injury from the wrongful act of the defendant, it is no answer to the claim that the plaintiff would have suffered less injury "if he had not unusually thin skull or an unusually weak heart" [*Dulieu* v *White* (1901) 2 KB 669].

107. In case negligence occurs but that negligence was not related to the course of injury/death, can compensation be awarded?

No, In case of *Ramji Lal* v *Sarvodaya Medical* 1995 (1) CPR 833 (NC), the complainant's infant son was admitted to Sir Padampat Mother And Child Health Institute, Jaipur for cyanotic congenital heart disease. Since he also had diarrhoea, darzin with neomycin was prescribed but instead the opposite party (chemist) gave Pectokab-MF, but as in the death certificate, cause of death was mentioned clearly as cyanotic congenital heart disease with congestive heart failure and not diarrhoea, no compensation was awarded under section 14(1)(*d*) of the Consumer Protection Act, the complainant has to establish not only negligence of the opposite party but also that as a consequence of that negligence loss or injury was suffered by him. In this case the negligence of the opposite party (dispensing wrong medicine) was not the cause of the death of the child. Hence no compensation was awarded.

In the case of *Punam Verma* v *Dr. Ashwini Patel* 1995 (1) CPR 833 (NC), complainant alleged negligence in treatment of her husband by homeopathic doctor for using allopathic drugs to treat his fever leading to his death. The National Commission on basis of material on record and testimony of expert witnesses held that there was no negligence in treatment and dismissed the complaint.

But the Supreme Court in *Poonam Verma* v *Dr. Ashwini Patel* 1996 (2) CPJ 1 (SC), held that a homeopath registered only under Homeopathic Practitioner Act cannot practice allopathy and would be guilty of negligence *per se* for practicing allopathy. In such cases no further proof was needed and such conduct would amount to actionable negligence and awarded ₹3 lakh as a compensation.

108. What is meant by nervous shock?

"Nervous Shock" means the sudden appreciation by sight or sound of a horrifying event which violently agitates the mind. It does not include psychiatric illness caused by the accumulation, over a period of time, of more gradual assaults on the nervous system.

There can be no claim for emotional distress anguish or grief unless this leads to a positive Psychiatric illness (such as an anxiety, nervous or reactive depression) or physical illness (such as miscarriage or heart attack)

It is now well established that a *tort feasor* who has negligently killed or injured A may be liable to B for a psychiatric illness resulting from A's death or injury.

109. In claims for compensation, are the calculations for the quantum of compensation by the complainant enough to determine which consumer forum or commission has the pecuniary jurisdiction?

No. It is seen sometimes that the complainant inflates his assessment in order to bring the matter within the pecuniary jurisdiction of the state or National Commission. The court, on its own, can assess this even at a preliminary stage, and if it finds that there are no sufficient grounds to justify the quantum of compensation claimed, the case may be relegated to the remedy before a forum which has this pecuniary jurisdiction.

In the case of *Jagan Nath* v *Jindal Dental and Orthopaedic Clinic of Kaithal* 1994 (1) CPJ 119 (Har), complainant fell down and fractured his forearm. Orthopedic treatment with surgery was given. Plate inserted got infected, and he had to seek medical assistance in P.G.I., Chandigarh. Compensation of ₹14 lakh claimed. This claim was computed mainly on the basis of the apprehended suffering and injury on the assumption that the infection could have led to the amputation of the arm and patiently remote damage on the ground of the alleged loss of business by the supposed closure of the complainant's cloth shop.

The Commission was of the firm opinion that even when viewed with utmost liberality, the compensation awardable in the case could not come even remotely to the figure of ₹5 Lakh, which was the minimum for entertaining the complaint of the State Commission. The complaint was directed to be returned for presentation before the competent District Forum.

110. What is the mode of assessment of quantum of compensation under the Consumer Protection Act?

The question awarded as to how the 'award of compensation for damages' is to be calculated under section 14(1)(*d*) of the Consumer Protection Act, 1986? The award of compensation by forums established under the Act has to be made only on well recognized legal principles governing the qualification of damages or compensation. The compensation to be awarded has to be qualified on a rational basis on a consideration of the material produced before the adjudicating forums showing the extent of injury suffered and the manner in which and the extent of which monetary loss has been caused thereby to the complainant.

Under section 14(1)(*d*) of the Consumer Protection Act, compensation is payable to the consumer for the loss or injury suffered by the consumer 'due to negligence of the opposite party'. Where there is no evidence of negligence on the part of the opposite party, it has been held that the consumer forum was not entitle to grant any compensation under the Act without proof of negligence on the part of the opposite party resulting in loss or injury to the complainant.

The actual monetary (pecuniary) loss of each individual can only be ascertained by balancing, on the one hand and on the other hand, any pecuniary advantage which from whatever source comes to him by reason of death.

But in a later decision, the Supreme Court in *Helen C. Rebello* v *Maharashtra State Road Transport Corporation* AIR 1998 SC 319, a case of death by motor accident, observed that under the common law it is settled that the pecuniary loss can be ascertained only by balancing on one hand, the loss of the claimant of future pecuniary benefits that would have accrued to him but for the death with the "pecuniary advantage" from whatever source come to him by reason of the death. But when death occurs in a motor accident, only such amounts as become payable to the claimant only on account of accidental death and not other form of death can be deducted from the amount becoming payable in a motor accidents claim. The receipts from provident fund, life insurance policies, family pensions and any other benefits occurring/becoming payable to the claimant, such as, cash balance, fixed deposit, shares, etc, cannot be detected from amount becoming payable to the claimant.

It may be submitted that the same principle can be applied in case of death by medical negligence while awarding compensation under the Consumer Protection Act.

111. Should an insurance company be impleaded as party in a case of medical negligence where a doctor/hospital has obtained a medical indemnity insurance policy?

In a case of medical negligence where a doctor or hospital is insured for indemnity insurance, it is necessary to implead the insurance company as a party (co-respondent) so that the claim against the doctor would be covered if there is any medical negligence found against him and there would be no difficulty for the complainant to get the amount of the claim from the insurance company. [*Dr. C.C. Choubal* v *Punkaj Srivastava* 2003 (3) CPR 20 (NC)].

It may be submitted that if compensation is awarded without making insurance company as a party and without hearing it, it may be challenged the same on the ground that claim was awarded without hearing it.

Whenever of complaint for medical negligence is filed and if a doctor/ hospital has`obtained medical indemnity insurance policy, it is in the interest of such doctor/hospital to request the Consumer Forum/Court to implead the insurance company.

112. How is the quantum of damage/compensation in personal injury or medical negligence cases calculated?

The Supreme Court in *R.D. Hallangadi v. Pest Control (India) Ltd. (1995) 1 SCC 551*, laying down the principles of damages and compensation observed:

> "Broadly speaking while fixing an amount of compensation payable to the victim of an accident, the damages have to be assessed separately as pecuniary damages and special damages. Pecuniary damages are those which the victim has actually incurred and which are capable of being calculated in terms of money, whereas no pecuniary damages are those which are incapable of being accessed by arithmetical calculations. In order to appreciate two concepts pecuniary damages may include expenses incurred by the claimant:
>
> (*a*) Medical attendance,
>
> (*b*) Loss of earning of profit up to the date of trial,
>
> (*c*) Other medical loss
>
> So far as non-pecuniary damages are concerned there may include
>
> (*a*) Damages for mental and physical shock, pain and suffering already suffered or likely to be suffered in future,
>
> (*b*) Damages to compensate for the loss of amenities of life which may include a variety of matters i.e., on account of injury the claimant may not be able to walk, run or sit,
>
> (*c*) Damages for the loss of expectation of life, i.e. on account of injury the normal longevity of the person concerned is shortened.
>
> (*d*) Inconvenience, hardship, discomfort, disappointment, frustration and mental stress in life".

A person not only suffers injuries on account of accident but also suffers in mind and body on account of the accident throughout his life and a feeling is developed that he is no more a normal man and cannot enjoy the amenities of life as another normal person can. While fixing compensation for pain and suffering as also for the loss of amenities of life features like his age, marital status and unusual deprivation he has undertaken in his life have to be reckoned. (*Divisional Manager, KSRTC* v *Mahadev Shetty* 2003 (7) SCC 197).

The damages under the Consumer Protection Act are generally restricted to compensation for the injury/damage caused which under the civil/tort law these may be extended and punitive damages may also be awarded. Punitive damages are, in a sense, a form of punishment and they are divided into an aggravated and an exemplary variety.

If the judge comes to the conclusion that doctor's negligence is of a senior nature he may, in addition to awarding compensation for the injury, also awarded exemplary damages as a measure of punishment for his negligence. In some cases some patients will bring a case mainly to see that the doctor is punished rather than to gain a financial settlement. He feels the award should reflect a sense of upset he has suffered from the way in which his case was handed by the doctor. Damages are awarded in such cases are termed as aggravated damages. Such damages are awarded in such cases are termed as aggravated damages. Such damages are awarded not as a measure of compensation but generally to vindicate the stand of the complainant.

The court can grant any amount as compensation not exceeding the amount claimed in the patient, though not under the very same head they claimed but under other heads which they omitted to claim. The only restriction is that total compensation shall not exceed the total amount claimed in the suit. [*Arun Balakrishnan Iyer* v *Soni Hospital* AIR 2003 Mad 389].

Again in *Dr. U.K. Kini* v *V. Vasudeva Pal* 2001 ACJ 2141 (Ker), the Kerala High Court held that quantum of compensation to be awarded cannot exceed the amount claimed at the trial stage even if the court comes to the conclusion that the complainant is entitled to a higher compensation where the court held that the plaintiffs were entitled to ₹2,50,000 as compensation but it was confined to ₹2 lakh therefore, the amount claimed by him at the trial stage.

Compensatory damages may be categorized into general damages and special damages.

113. General damages

These are awarded for the more subjective factor of the injury, such as:

- Pain and suffering, whether physical or internal,
- Loss of enjoyment of life, from any physical or mental consequences of the negligent act,
- Reduction in the expectation of life apart from the financial aspect,
- Physical defects and disabilities, such as, loss of limb, the loss of sight of an eye, the loss of ability to walk, presence of scar as a result of an unnecessary operation – especially in case of woman — which might reduce the chance of marriage,
- Future suffering, example a reduction in fertility from a failed diagnosis of pelvic inflammatory disease, and an increased chance of arthritis in failed diagnosis of congenital dislocation of hip etc, and
- Loss of life itself may be actionable for the benefit of the dependents, the criteria applied to measure such damage being the loss of potential future earning power, any offsetting by life insurance or pension being taken into account. In this regard, the damage for the death of a child tends to be low.

114. Not pecuniary general damages

These can be classified under the following heads:

- Pain and suffering
- Loss of estate
- Loss of amenities of life
- Loss of consortium
- Damages for the injury itself

115. Pain and suffering

Pain and suffering are subjective and are difficult to measure in terms of money. However, an award can be made to cover physical pain and suffering, psychiatric symptoms and nervous shock.

In *Spring Meadows Hospital* v *Harjot Ahluwalia* 1998 (3) CPJ 1 (SC), the Supreme Court upheld the award of ₹5 lakh by the National Commission given separately to the parents of the minor child for their acute mental agony caused by reason of their only son having been reduced to a vegetative state requiring life long care and attention. The amount awarded in the instant case is among the highest under his head.

In *Rambihari Lal* v *Dr. J.N. Srivastava* AIR 1985 MP, 150, ₹1,000 was awarded for mental agony and physical suffering.

It is believed that the people who are unconscious do not appreciate any pain and the unconsciousness eliminates the damage for pain and suffering which exits by being felt, thought or experienced. In such cases, however, there is very high award for the loss of amenity. (*Wise* v *Kaye* (1962) 1 Q.B. 638).

Particularly in the UK in the failed sterilization cases, there is an award to the mother for the discomfort of pregnancy and the pain and anxiety of childbirth. (*Allen* v *Bloomsbury Health Authority* (1993) 1 All ER 65).

In the UK, since the administration of the Justice Act, 1982, and there is no separate head of damages for loss of expectation of life. Instead, that is now absorbed into the general head of 'pain and suffering' caused the knowledge that one's life has been shortened by the accident. (*Law of Torts, Lecture by Vivienne Harpwood, 1993, P-308*).

116. Loss of amenities of life

The complainant is entitled to damages for the inability to enjoy life in various ways, example inability to play football, sing, dance and enjoy sexual functions or marriage. In unconscious persons the award is very high under this head (*Wise* v *Keye* (1962) QB 638).

The following facts are to be considered in assessment of damages for loss of enjoyment of life.

- The dependence of the injured on the help of others in his daily life.
- The inability to look after, care for and render services to the dependant by the injured,

— Sexual impotency,
— The premature consent of menopause,
— The loss of prospects of marriage,
— Inability to lead the life which the injured used to lead or which he might have led or wanted to lead.

117. Damages for the injury itself

Injuries are itemized and particular sums are awarded for those on the basis of precedents example a broken arm will be worth a certain amount, loss of eye a certain figure, a scar would be worth a certain sum and so on.

118. Loss of estate

In the case of *Aruna Ben D. Kothari* v *Navdeep Clinic* 1996 (3) CPJ 605 (Guj.), ₹40,000 was awarded under this head.

119. Loss of consortium

In the case of *Maharaj Prasad Agarwal* v *Dr. M.R. Jain,* Complaint No. 125 of 1993 decided 9-1-1996 (Rajasthan-unreported), ₹2 lakh was awarded under this head.

120. Special damages

These can be more easily computed and are in generally for longer than general damages. They include:

— The cost of best available medical treatment,
— Loss of earning, whether do not forced absence from work or prevention or impairment of his ability to carry on his previous occupation, so that he is forced to take employment at a lower level of salary or from the loss of expectation of life and the consequent shortening of the earning period,
— Nursing care in case of a badly disabled person a 24 hour care may be required making it vastly expensive,
— Cost of modifying the house, example wheel chair, ramps, modifying toilet, etc, where the person has suffered a sever disabilities necessitating such modifications,
— Cost of special equipment and cost of taxi of taxi fares to attend for treatment/physiotherapy, etc.

In the case of *Spring Meadows Hospital* v *Marjot Ahluwalia* 1998 (1) CPJ 1, a nurse of the Spring Meadows Hospital, on advice of the Senior Consultant Paediatrician, asked the father of the minor patient to fetch injection larigo (Chloroquine). The father of the child purchased the medicine which was written down by nurse and gave it to her. The nurse injected the same to the child upon which the child collapsed. He had cardiac arrest and suffered brain damage and continuous to survive in a vegetative estate.

The nice pleaded as the child was already taking Lariago Syrup and when the doctor advised that injection should be given she thought that the same Lariago injection was to be given. It was the duty of the resident doctor, who was on the round to write, give the injection and take all care.

The Supreme Court held that a consultant would be neglect where he delegates the responsibilities of his junior with the knowledge that the junior was incapable of carrying out his duties properly.

121. Loss of future earnings

The way in which the courts arrive at the sum is to employ the principle of 'multiplicant' and 'multiplier'.

The multiplicant is an annual sum to represent the complainants/deceased annual lost earnings at the date of trial. This essentially is a question of fact.

The multiplier is a notional figure which represents a number of years by which the multiplicand must be multiplied in order to calculate the future losses. The figure is arbitrary and ranges from 10 to 20 depending upon the approach of the court in each case.

The multiplier method of assessing damages to calculate the net pecuniary loss upon an annual basis and to arrive at the total award by multiplying the figure, therefore the number of years the benefit was expected to last taking into consideration the imponderable factor in fixing either the multiplier or the multiplicand. [*Madhya Pradesh State Road Transport Corporation* v *Sudhakar* AIR 1977 SC 1189].

When a person is on the threshold of his career his income is less but he has a longer period to serve and as such a higher 'multiplier is called for. A lower "multiplier" is justified as the person grows old. A multiplier of 16 is commonly used if the deceased is in twenties and multiplier of 15 is used if the deceased is in thirties. [*Krishna Kumari Gupta* v *Gurbax Sheresh Singh* AIR 1985 All 85].

The court also taken into account any possible promotions and salary increases from which the complainant/deceased may have benefited during his career, marriage of widow, children being to earn while growing up, etc. [*Laxman Singh* v *Gurmit Kaur* AIR 1979 P&H 50].

Calculations for children and young people who have not yet started to earn and usually very low. Exceptionally, a larger award may be given if child showed great promise/talent. [*Gurusewak Singh* v *Dr. Jaskaran Singh* 1996 (3) CPJ 300 (Punj.)].

A multiplier of 20 was used in the case of *Rambabu* v *Dr. Anjani Kishor Prasad* 1998 (2) CPR 224 wherein the complainant was 40 years old who lost vision of one eye.

A multiplier of 10 was used in the case of *J.N. Lal* v *Dr. R.K. Akhaury* 1997 (3) CPJ 112 (Bih.), to calculate loss of the profit of profession on account of loss of vision of right eye of complainant whose age was over 40 years.

In *P. Narasimha Rao* v *Gundavarapu Jaya Prakash* AIR 1990 AP 207, ₹2 lakh was awarded for 'future pecuniary loss' on account of permanent brain damage of 27 years old boy.

A young man of 25 years suffering disability of 30% as certified by medical board was awarded compensation amount was arrived at ₹1,08,000 being 30% of the earnings as calculated. [*National Hospital* v *Mohammad Navi* 2003 (1) CPR 653 (Ker)].

122. Cost of future care

Cost of future care, nursing fees, doctor's and specialists fees, cost of travelling for attending physiotherapy sessions, etc, cost of paying a reasonable sum to a husband, wife or other person who gives up work to give her fulltime care to the complainant, etc, can also be claimed.

In the case of *K.N. Lal* v *Dr. RK Akhaury* 1997 (3) CPJ 112 (Bihar), ₹1 lakh was awarded to engage a driver for his car.

If a child is born as a result of negligent sterilization the parent may be awarded costs as to his/her reasonable upbringing. [*State of Haryana* v *Smt Shanta* 2000 (1) CPJ 53 (SC)].

123. Interest and amount awarded

The court sometimes awarded interest on damages in respect of future losses not attract any interest.

The object of payment of interest is to compel the person concerned to make payment without any delay. [*Ramesh Chandra* v *Randhir Singh* AIR 1977 All 330].

The interest may be calculated from the time to offer injury to time of injury to the time of realization of the sum awarded at the rate of 12%.

Interest is usually awarded from the date of the order till the payment is made if the amount is not paid within a specified period. The dictum of Supreme Court of India is that the amount of compensation will carry interest at the rate of 12% per annum from the date of order, if the compensation is not deposited within certain period allowed by the court. [*Pushpa Thakur* v *Union of India* 1984 ACJ 559 (SC)].

Consumer forums are usually awarding interest at the rate of 18% from the date of order, if payable is not made within a specified period (one of three months) [*Aruna Ben D. Kothari* v *Navdeep Clinic* 1996 (3) CPJ 605 (Guj)].

In the case of *Bhiwani Dutt* v *PGI, Chandigarh* 1998 (2) CPJ 102 (Chd.), the court ordered that in case the compensation was not paid within one month, the respondent was not paid within one month, the Respondents No. 1 (Director P.G.I.) Chandigarh shall be liable to pay interest at the rate of 18% from the date of institution of the complaint till realization.

124. Can manufacturers of drugs, vaccines, medical equipment is held negligent?

Yes. The case of *Donoghue* v *Stevension* 1932 AC 562 (HC), establishes that manufacture may owe a duty of care in tort to the ultimate user of his product. This duty will also apply to those professional persons whose expertise is used to design, test or manufacture these products respective of whether such person's act as employees of the manufacturer or as independent consultants.

With respect to manufacturer's liabilities their products it will be patient to quote from Michael A Jones: Medical Negligence (IInd edition 1996) as under:

> "Doctors must take account of manufacturers and known side effects when prescribing drugs, although they should not necessarily rely on the manufacturer's information unthinkingly, since it is known that manufacture's are not always entirely frank about the contraindications or risks associated with their products, where a doctor ignores the manufacturer's instructions and warning it is the doctor who is responsible for any adverse reactions. The manufacturer will not be liable since a warning addressed to the doctor will normally discharge the manufacturer's duty of care to the patient in the case of prescription drugs."

It is not necessary that the warning be addressed directly to the consumer where a product is intended to be used under the supervision of experts. A warning gives to the expert from normally be sufficient to discharge the manufacturer's duty of care. In the case of prescription products the prescribing doctor is clearly in the position of intermediary.

In *Buchan* v *Ortho Pharmaceuticals* (*Canada*) *Ltd. Robins* (1986) 25 DLR (4th) 658, 669 (Ont HC).

J.A. commended that:

> "......... The manufacture of drugs, like the manufacturer of other products has duty to provide consumers with adequate warning of the potentially harmful side effects that the manufacturer knows or has reason to know may be produced by the drug............ In the case of prescription drugs the duty of manufacturers to warn consumers is discharged if the manufacturer provides prescribing Physician, rather than consumer with adequate warning of the potential danger."

The defendant manufacturers in that case were held liable in negligence on the basis of a failure to give sufficient information to the medical profession about the risks of oral contraceptive. The fact that the manufacturers were in a position to learn about the risks inherent in the products from other sources. In *Davidson* v *Connaught Laboratories* (1990) 14 CCLT 251, 276 (Ont HC) Linden. J. observed:

> "A drug company cannot rely upon doctors to read all the scientific dangers involved in the many drugs they have to administer each day.......... They have little time for deep research into the medical literature. They rely on the drug companies to supply them with necessary data."

In the case of *Chaman Singh Fauzdar* v *German Remedies Ltd.* 1992 (2) CPJ 915 (Raj.), the complainant has purchased deriphyline injection to be injected in his mother intravenously. The doctor concerned certified that ampoule had foreign material and was unfit for use. On hearing this his mother was greatly upset and fell unconscious. The state commission directed the manufacturer (German Remedies Ltd.) to pay ₹500 as compensation besides cost of injection.

In *Common Cause* v *Drug Controller of India* 1991 (2) CPJ 698, a public interest litigation petition was filed by common cause regarding manufacturing defects intravenous (IV) fluids. The National Commission issued directions to the drug controller of India for the basis of which an expert committee was constituted which submitted it's report containing recommendations regarding the steps to protect the public from contamination of IV fluids which are either sold through chemists or supplied to hospitals for administration to patients.

In *Jagdeep Mohanlal Kakadia* v *Ophthalmics and Drugs India* 1997 (3) CPR 229 (Guj.), wherein due to defective 'Irrisol' I drop as many patients who had undergone cataract surgery lost their vision, the manufacturer of the drug was held liable. The complainant, who was the operating surgeon, was awarded ₹15 lakh as compensation against the manufacturers of these eye drops by the State Commission. On appeal, the National Commission dismissed the complaint on the technical ground that the drug was not got tested from an independent laboratory as also on the ground that the complaint was not got tested from an independent laboratory as also on the ground that the complainant was not pressed. However, compensation of ₹20,000 was awarded to each of the respondents. Complainants on compensation of ₹20,000 was awarded to each of the respondents complainants on compassionate grounds.

In *Murari Lal Maurya* v *Rallis India Ltd.* 1993 (3) CPR 396 (MP), a 'B-Complex' injection administered to the complainant resulted in reaction. It was subsequently found that the injection vial contained some foreign substance and ₹3,000 was awarded as compensation to be paid by the pharmaceutical company.

125. Can it be said that when a pharmaceutical concern manufactures and sells a pharmaceutical product or drug it is rendering 'service' in the context of section 2(1)(*o*) of the Consumer Protection Act?

Yes, in the case of *Dr. Jagdip Mohan Lal Kakadia* v *Ophthalmic and Drugs India* 1997 (3) CPR 229 (Guj.), the State Commission observed:

The word 'service' is defined in clause (*o*) of sub-section (1) of section 2 of the Act. It among other things means service of any description. As observed by the Supreme Court in *Lucknow Development Authority* v *M.K. Gupta* 1994 (1) CPR 56 (SC), the word service may mean any benefit or any Act resulting in promoting interest or happiness. It may be contractual, professional, public, domestic, legal, statuary, etc. The concept of service thus is very wide. It was observed that the definition of service in clause (*o*) referred to above is in three parts. The main part is followed by inclusive clause and ends by exclusionary clause. The main clause itself is very wide. It applies to any service made available to potential users. The word 'any' and 'potential' are significant. Both are of wide amplitude. Dictionary meaning of word 'any' means 'one or same for all'. In Black's Law Dictionary it is explained thus, word 'any' has a diversity of meaning and may be employed to indicate all or every as well as 'same' or 'one' and its meaning in a given statute depends upon the context and subject-matter of the statute: The use of word 'any' in the context it has been used in clause (*o*) indicates that it has been used in wider sense extending from one to all. The other word 'potential' is again very wide. In Oxford dictionary it is defined as capable of coming into being, possibility. In Black's Law Dictionary it is defined as extending in possibility but not in Act. Naturally and probably expected to come into existence at some future time, though not now existing for example, the future product of gain or trees already planted, or the successive future installments or payments on a contract or engagement, already made'. In other words, service which is not only expanded to actual users but those who are capable of using it are covered in the definition. The Supreme Court went onto observe that this clause is thus very wide and extended to, any or all actual or potential users. The aforesaid observations of the Supreme Court in the case of *Lucknow Development Authority Association* v *V.P. Shanta* 1995 (3) CPJ 1 (SC):

> "This is not the case mere purchase of defective goods. Pharmaceutics is a science of pharmacy, Pharmacology and person skilled in or engaged in pharmacology is known as pharmaceutics. Opponent number 1 is engaged in the business of manufacturing pharmaceutical products. Such business could not be done without the knowledge of science of pharmacy and skilled in pharmacy. Therefore, pharmacist not only does business but also renders service to the medical profession and general public when it manufacturers and sells the drugs. It has to maintain quality control and strict standards prescribed by Indian pharmacology and other recognized pharmacology. Unless the manufacturer of pharmaceutical drugs adheres to the prescribed strict standards, he would be guilty of not only manufacturing and selling defective, impure or spurious drug but he would be guilty of negligence in rendering service or deficiency in service so far as users and potential users of the drugs, be it medical practitioner, be it general public, are concerned. Therefore, manufacture and sale of defective, impure or spurious drugs would amount to deficiency in service. When the complainant or patient purchased drug manufactured by opponent no. 1 which was not upto the standard of defective or impure or spurious, he or his patient could hold manufacturers guilty of deficiency in service. So far as deficiency in service is concerned, purpose of the use, even if commercial would not take the complainant out of the definition of consumer. His case would fall under section 2(1)(*d*)(*ii*) of the Act."

126. Can the question regarding doctor's fee being reasonable or excessive be decided by the consumer forums?

A doctor has a right to fix his fees. The National Commission in *Sudhanshu Bhattacharya* v *B.S. Hegde,* 1993 (3) CPR 414 (NC), held that it is not for the consumer forums to adjudicate on the question where the consideration (fees) charged was reasonable and excessive.

Again, Haryana State Commission in *R.B. Kapoor* v *Phool Dev Prasad* 1996 (3) CPJ 477 (Har.), has held that:

> "It is for the doctor — a medical practitioner to fix his fee for various services and the patient has no legal right to determine as to whether the fee charged is reasonable or exorbitant, as the amount of the fee charged by the

medical practitioner depends on number of factors therefore, this technical qualification, experience in the profession and the nature of quality of services rendered by him. So there can't be a hard and fast yard stick as it differs from a doctor to doctor."

127. Can compensation be awarded for a doctor's negligent advice?

Yes, if it results in any loss (damage) to the patient. Pure economic loss resulting from negligent advice is also recoverable.

In an English case *Hedley Byrne and Co. Ltd.* v *Heller and Partner Ltd.* 1964 AC 465, the doctor was asked to compensate for wrongly advising bed rest, when not necessary, may amount to negligent advice.

128. Can compensation be awarded in a case where there was no negligence in treatment but there were only certain deficiencies in service?

Yes. In *Mrs. Vijayamma* v *Apollo Diagnostic Centre* 2002 (1) CPJ 230 (AP), a cardiac case on taking of E.C.G. to assess the condition of the patient having breathlessness and non-issue of discharge card after death of the patient were held to be deficiency in service although the opposite parties were not held negligent in treating the deceased and administering medicines. A compensation of ₹50,000 was awarded for the above mentioned deficiencies in service.

In *Chandra Sagar D. Rajput* v *Dr. Dinesh J. Shah* 1999 (1) CPJ 434 (Mah.), an antennal examination the doctor had given a positive report of VDRI test. On taking another conformity test in another laboratory, the report turned up to be negative. The State Commission held that giving of a wrong VDRI, positive report was a deficiency in service and awarded compensation of ₹50,000 for the social trauma which the couple had undergone.

129. Can a Consumer Forum award token compensation and even substantial compensation from an Insurance company even after giving finding of negligence?

In a few cases the consumer forums/commissions have awarded compensation on compassionate grounds even where no negligence was found.

In the case of *Hari Bhai Leghar Bhai Solanki* v *Dr. Suresh Parikh* 1994 (1) CPJ 373 (Guj.), the doctor was founded to be not guilty, but on compassionate grounds the insurance company was persuaded to pay ₹75,000 for which Dr. Parikh was covered under the insurance policy.

In the case of *Renu Jain* v *Escorts Heart Institute and Research Centre* 1992 (2) CPJ 391 (NC), the court gave the finding of no negligence, but purely on compassionate grounds the hospital agreed to refund ₹20,000.

130. Can a Consumer Forum/Commission cancel or get cancelled the medical practice certificate of a medical practitioner or direct doctors/ hospitals to stop rendering medical services to patients in future on being held negligent in a particular case?

No. It has been held by the Andhra Pradesh state commission in *RORCE* v *Dr. M. Ganaeswara Rao* 1998 (1) CPJ 413 (AP), that it is beyond the scope of the AP Act to issue such directions.

The forums or commissions established under the Consumer Protection Act, 1986 have no jurisdiction to cancel or get cancelled the medical practice certificate of a medical practitioner. [*Ashok Kumar Aneja* v *Dr. Harish Kohli* 2003 (2) CPJ 290 (Uttaranchal)].

131. Can levying of excess/wrong charges be considered as deficiency in service?

Charging for a bed facility which was not provided was considered as deficiency in service by the Maharashtra State Commission. [*R M Joshi* v *Dr. P. B. Tahilramani* 1993 (3) CPJ 12 (Mah.)]. But the National Commission held that this alone is no sufficient to constitute negligence in service. [*Dr. P.B. Tahilramani* v *R.M. Joshi RP No. 339 of 1993 decided on 3-2-1994 - unreported*]

In the case of *Moti Bai Dalvi* v *M.L. Govilkar* 1991 (1) CPR 334 (Mah.), the state commission directed the hospital to refund ₹1,164 taken as surcharge and ₹1,000 was awarded as compensation for causing harassment.

In the case of *Champaben Babu* v *C.V. Shah Medical Centre* 1992 (1) CPR 667 (Guj.), the State Commission ordered refund of ₹200 which was taken as medico-legal charges because it had no relation with the given treatment.

Allegation on the escalation of hospital fees, certainly cannot be viewed as medical negligence. Cost of surgery, on which the complainant relied related to 1989, whereas the cost of surgery was revised by the hospital and only current/prevalent charges were some proposed to be recovered. It is not even remotely connected with medical negligence resulting in the death of the complainant's husband. However keeping in view the facts of the case respondent hospital was asked not to press for the recovery of outstanding dues. [*Mrs. Kiran Bala Rout* v *Christian Medical College Hospital* 2003 (1) CPR 238 (NC)].

A complaint can be filed in a consumer forum where the doctor/hospital charges or displayed, as for example, the hospital charges more amount than that mentioned in the brochure/list/notice board as a package for a particular surgery/ procedure or charges more amount than agreed. (Section 2(1)(*iv*) of Consumer Protection Act, 1986)

132. Can compensation be awarded in a case of criminal negligence?

Yes. The court can award compensation in a case of criminal negligence of the doctor to the injured party and in case of death, to the legal heirs of the deceased.

Section 357 of the Code of Criminal Procedure, 1973 provides for award of compensation, out of fine if imposed as sentences or part of sentence, imposed in case of a doctor be held criminally liable for any offence. Medical negligence being both a tort as well as a crime, the condition that the compensation for criminal liability was can be awarded only in such cases where compensation can be recovered by civil process gets fulfilled in cases involving criminal negligence.

The power under section 357, Cr.P.C. is a measure of responding appropriately to the crime as well as reconciling the victim with the offender, which, to some extent, is the measure to rehabilitate to an extent the beleaguered victims. (*Hari Shanker Singh* v *Sukhbir Singh* (1988) 4 SCC 561). If compensation is ordered to be paid, then, while arriving at the quantum, courts are under obligation to keep into account the capacity of the accused to pay besides taking into account also the nature of crime in each case, the justness of the claim for compensation and the need for it in the context of the victim or members of the family of the victim and other relevant circumstances. (*Sarwan Singh* v *State of Punjab* AIR 1978 SC 1525).

Sub-section (1) of section 357 deals with a situation where a court imposes a fine or a sentence (including sentence of death) of which fine also forms a part. It confers of discretion on the court to order as to how the whole or any part of fine recovered is to be paid. Sub-section (3) deals with the situation where fine dose not form part of sentence imposed by the court and in such case, the court when passing a judgment can order the accused persons to pay by way of compensation such amount as may be specified in the order to the person who has suffered loss or injury by reason of the Act for which the accused has been convicted and sentenced. Such power is available also to the appellate or High Court or the court of session while exercising revisional power, sub-section (5) deals with the situation when the court fixes the compensation, the Civil Court is required to take into account any sum paid or recovered under this section [*Mangli Lal* v *State of M.P.*, JT 2004 (1) SC 81].

133. Whether compensation can be claimed by and awarded to an injured person for not being provided treatment in a government hospital or for death or injury caused to therein because of any negligence? Whether these amount to breach of right of life under Article 21 of the Constitution?

Yes. In case of *Paschim Banga Khet Mazdoor Samity* v *State of West Bengal* AIR 1996 SC 2426, it has been held by the Supreme Court as under:

> "In respect of deprivation of constitutional rights guaranteed under Part III of the Constitution, the position is well settled that adequate compensation can be awarded by the court for violation by way of redress in proceedings under Articles 32 and 226 of the Constitution."

In this case a person got head injury by falling down from a train. He was taken to various government hospitals but he was not admitted/not given treatment for want of the beds therein. This was held to be breach of right to life guaranteed under Article 21. A compensation of ₹25,000 was awarded by the Supreme Court was such breach. It was also held that providing adequate medical facilities for the people is an essential part of the obligations undertaken by the government in a welfare state failure on the part of Government hospital to provide timely medical treatment to a person in need of such treatment in violation of his right to life guaranteed under Article 21.

Similarly, compensation was ordered by A.P. High Court in *Mrs. Shanta* v *State of Andhra Pradesh* 1997 (3) CPJ 481, against the Government Hospital for negligence of leaving a mop inside the womb was held to be violation of right to life under Article 21 of the Constitution.

134. Can a Consumer Forum/Commission grant a relief which is not specifically prayed for?

The relief's with the consumer forum can grant, are specified in section 14 of the Act, it is up for a consumer forum to pay an appropriate amount by way of compensation of a consumer for any loss or injury suffered by him due to the negligence of the opposing party. In other words, it is not mandatory or obligatory on the part of the complainant to ask for a specific relief of the compensation and the consumer forums are not debarred from granting relief not prayed for by complainant in the complaint. It may be expedient that a complainant prays for a particular relief and this may facilitate expeditious disposal of complaint under the Act, but it is clear that under the scheme of the Consumer Protection Act, the Consumer Forums can grant relief not paid for by the complainant provided the same are justified on merits. [*District Manager, Telephones, Patna* v *Dr. Tarun Bhatnagar* 1992 (1) CPJ 47 (NC)].

However some State Commissions has refused to grant compensation where it is not specifically claimed by the complainant.

135. Can a complaint for medical negligence filed against the doctor during his lifetime be adjudicated and compensation awarded if the doctor dies before culmination of proceedings? Can legal representatives of the deceased doctor be made parties and would such claims survive?

No. In such a case right against the deceased doctor does not survive if the claim is against more than one doctor or against hospital and doctors, then the claim will survive against the hospital and surviving doctors.

In a tort of medical negligence, the cause of action is personal against the doctor discharging his duties and cause of action does not survive against his estate of the legal representatives. However, in case the trial has been completed and the decree/judgment had been passed against the deceased doctor, that amount payable under the decree could be removed from the estate and in such event the legal preventatives of the deceased could be brought on record. But that did not happen in present case and even the question where he had not negligent in the discharge of his duties as a surgeon could not be adjudicated upon. In this view of the matter, the maxim *actio personalis moritum cum* (personal actions dies with the person) as a general rule is applicable to actions in torts and therefore, the cause of action against the party against whom an action in tort is brought is extinguished on his death.

However, in the UK all clauses of action for the defamation, now survive against or, as the case may be for the benefit of his estate.

136. Can misleading signboards, prescriptions slips and advertisements of the doctors/hospitals be construed as deficiency in service or 'unfair trade practice, under the Consumer Protection Act, 1986 and can damages/ compensation be awarded for awarding such practice?

Yes, they are professing misleading facts, some examples are:

The wrong claim of availability of certain facilities – There are some doctors/hospitals, who claim in the signboards/prescriptions slips that 24 hours emergency service are available in their setup but in fact they lack basic emergency facilities like providing the services of a duty doctor round the clock, necessary equipment in working order, intensive care facilities.

Wrongly depicting competence of doctor — In *Dr. Sr. Louie* v *Smt. Kannolil* 1993 (1) CPR 422 (NC), the name would be exhibited by the hospital mentioned M.D. (Gyn) against a doctor's name creating an impression and misleading the patients that the doctor possessed P.G. Degree in Gynaecology. The degree of MD Gyn. was obtained from Freiburg, Germany which as per rules and directions from MCI should have been mentioned. This degree is equal to MBBS in India. Although the doctor had undergone practical training in Gynaecology, she had not acquired any qualification in the form of degree or diploma in that discipline, hence she was not entitled to claim that she was M.D. (Gyn.) in India. Hence she was not qualified to undertake the procedure in question and the resultant vacuum slip and led to complications. Also held liable for misrepresentation of facts. Compensation of ₹77,000 was awarded.

In *Dr. B. Ashok Kumar* v *Kamma Narsimha Swamy* 2003 (3) CLD 670 (AP), by an advertisement that doctor assured the public that any type of Elephantiasis will be operated upon and the leg would be made normal. Therefore, it can be assumed that the opposite party doctor had misled the complainant that his leg would become like any other normal leg after the operation. Such an advertisement amounts to unfair trade practices. Had such a notice not being displayed at the nursing home of the opposite party doctor, the complainant would not have ventured to undergo surgery. Therefore such false notice amounts to unfair trade practice. Therefore, the state commission held that unfair trade practice was adopted by the first opposite party and awarded damages of ₹20,000.

In *Ram Singh A. Parmar* v *Sampat Raj Shah* [1993 (2) CPR 495 (Guj)], it was held that the advertisement given in newspapers was neither untrue nor misleading. The complainant suffering from enlargement of prostrate gland, read the advertisement in the newspaper published by the opponents Thermal Control Unit (T.C.U.) which removes the obstructions of enlarged prostate gland microcomputer electronic system. On reading this advertisement, he books three settings but was not relieved of pain and the problem. The court held that the advertisement nowhere invited any person to take the treatment, but merely described the TCU system. It was just unfortunate that in his case the treatment did not give proper benefit. There can no claim of guarantee of results.

In *Charanjeet Kaur* v *Manjeet Kaur* 1999 (1) CPR 559 (Punj), does one running a clinic unauthorizedly and were conducting delivery, which was held to be not proper by the district forum and as such compensation was awarded to the complainant. But the complaint of complainant was held not mentionable by the state commission further observed that in the case of unfair trade practice; the direction for stopping such a practice can be given. Still compensation, if any, that could be granted has to be under section 14(1)(*d*) of the Consumer Protection Act, that is no proof of negligent Act of the opposite party, to reimburse the loss suffered by the complainant. In order to bring the case under section 14(1)(*d*) of Consumer Protection Act, that is, no proof of negligent act of opposite parties resulting in causing loss of the complainant and in the facts of the case, it could be established only by producing medical expert witness. In the absence of any expert evidence in this respect, no presumption could be drawn that the complications in the matter of delivery of male child to the complainant occurred on account of any negligent act of the opposite parties.

137. Should medical indemnity insurance be made compulsory for medical professionals and should compensation be awarded under the concept of "no fault liability"?

It has been suggested by Dr. D.K. Gaur, in his book: A textbook on the Indian Panel Code (3rd edn 2004 P. 443), that medical indemnity insurance should be compulsory for medical professionals in the following words:

"Perhaps it would be desirable if compulsory medical insurance scheme is introduced that would take care of amount of damages against third party on similar lines as in the case of section 146 of the Motor Vehicles Act, 1988. A system of liability to pay compensation on the principle of "no fault liability" to give some relief in the case of death or permanent disablement of the patient as provided under section 140 of the Motor Vehicles Act, 1988, as provided.

A compulsory medical insurance will not only be of great help to the doctors, hospitals, nursing homes, private clinics and medical practitioners, etc., but also to the patients and their dependents, because the insurance company will take care of the amount of compensation in case of medical negligence."

As stated above, compensation is awarded under the concept of "no fault liability" in motor accident cases as provided in the Motor Vehicles Act, 1988. Competition for no fault liability is also provided in Public Liability Insurance Act, 1991.

In a medical negligence case, as an unusual gesture, the Jammu and Kashmir High Court awarded compensation of ₹50,000 under the concept of "No fault liability" even where there was no fault. In this case the patient had died because of injection Diazepam being given intravenously. [*Bholi Devi* v *State of Jammu And Kashmir* AIR 2002 J and K HC 65].

138. Can Chemist/Druggist be held negligent for wrong dispensing of medicines?

Yes. In *Sunakar Bhol* v *Amar Drug House* 1992 (2) CPJ 938 (Ori), the discharge ticket had prescribed tablet Globiron but the Chemist substituted it with Globac Capsules. Cash memo did not mention the name of the person who prescribed. The chemist was held negligent in dispensing wrong medicine and compensation was awarded.

In *Sai Medical Stores* v *R.D. Gupta* 1993 (2) CPJ 515 (MP), the complainant's wife underwent cataract surgery. The eye specialist had prescribed

"Arbidin" tablets to be taken for a month for improvement of the eyesight, but the medical store instead supplied "Avana" tablets. Compensation of ₹2,000 was awarded.

In the case of *Hari Mohan and Co.* v *Kailash Pati Pandey* 1994 (1) CPJ 344 (Bih.), it was alleged by the complainant that the injection given (Tidigestic) by the salesman of the medical shop was different from the prescribed by the doctor. The same was infected by a compounder to the complainant's wife resulting in adverse reaction. It was held that it is also the duty of the literate person (an advocate in the present case) to ascertain that the injection supplied is a same as prescribed by the doctor or a different one. The compounder should also before injecting verify not only the dose but also whether the injection the same one as prescribed by the doctor. Complaints against salesman of the medical shop not allowed.

In the England case *Prendergant* v *San and Due* 1989 1 Mad LR 36, our doctor had written an illegible prescription for a patient of Asthama wherein he had actually prescribed amoxil tablets (an antibiotic) which was misread by the pharmacist as dionil (a hypoglycaemic agent), which when taken by the patient, lowered his blood sugar level causing permanent brain damage. The doctor and the pharmacist were held negligent and to the extent of 25% and 75% respectively. It was also added that the pharmacist had been negligent in failing to refer back to the doctor in case of uncertainty.

139. Can a doctor who purchases equipment, instrument, article or a drug for professional use be said to have made "commercial" use of the product and is therefore not a "consumer" as laid down in section 2(1)(*d*)(1) of the Consumer Protection Act?

In the case of *Dr. Jagpit Mohanlal Kakadia* v *Ophthalmics and Drug India* 1997 (3) CPJ 229 (Guj), it was submitted that the complainant was regarding Irrisol (an eye drop) being impure or spurious and harmful to human cornea and, therefore they use which he had made the drug was commercial. It was submitted that section 2(1)(*d*)(1) clearly lays down that the person who approaches as goods for commercial purpose is not a consumer and he cannot bring action or file complaint under the Act. Therefore the question which the State Commission considered was whether the complainant had used the drug for commercial purpose. It is settled position of the law that word or expression used in statute has to be given in plane grammatical meaning and it has to be understood in the sense as understood in common parlance. The universal dictionary of English, for short, gives the following meaning to the word of commerce so far as they are relevant to our purpose, legal capacity to buy and sell trade traffic............. business of buying and selling, exchanging and distributing goods of all kinds (used especially of larger transactions) also of financial business involved in this traffic." The meaning of the word "purpose" given in the dictionary is "design, plan, proposal." If these dictionary meanings are kept in mind, the design or object of using the goods has to be far buying selling or business of buying and selling to bring it within the common parlance also, when one talks about commercial purpose, what is meant is purpose of buying and selling goods.

Now in the instant cases, what was the purpose for which the drug was brought? Was it for the purpose of buying and selling? The answer is no. Was it for the purpose of business or was it for the financial purpose? Again the answer is no. The purpose was to use drugs at the time of operation for irrigating and cleaning the capsule to prevent cornea from becoming dry. The complainant was not carrying on any business or commerce. He was carrying on profession of an ophthalmic surgeon. The relevant meaning of profession given in the dictionary is that which one professes or practices as a calling specifically, one of the learned or liable vocations which is sharply contrasted with trade or commerce. What the complainant is carrying on his profession and not business or trade. Therefore, it depends, instruments, articles, drugs, etc, which he uses to carry on his profession or in the course of his profession could not be said to have been used for the purpose of commerce, business or trade. Therefore, the drug could not be used for commercial purpose.

In order to bring goods within the meaning of commerce and purpose, there has to be nexus between the goods and the business. Such goods have to be part of profit generating apparatus or mechanism. In the instant case, the drug which was used by the complainant had no direct link or nexus with the profit earning apparatus or mechanism of the complainant. This data is incidentally used for the purpose stated above for the aforesaid reasons also, the drug could not be said to have been used for commercial purpose, the complainant is not a consumer was not accepted by the State Commission observing that the complainant had purchased the drug for using it in the course of eye or cataract operation and having regard to the purpose of the use, it could not be said to be commercial.

In the case of *Dr.* (*Mrs.*) *Kusum Bakshi Aklawat* v *G.P. Singh, Manager, Administration* 1993 (2) CPJ 1135 (Har.), it was held that a self employed medical professional purchasing equipment for his clinical requirements would not come in the exclusion clause of a purchase for the "commercial purpose".

CHAPTER 11

How Doctors to Avoid Litigation

SYNOPSIS

1. Introduction

It is a primary duty for medical professionals to provide effectively better service to their patients and avoid maximum possibility of litigation. To achieve this object, the following 4 steps could be taken at different levels.

2. Level I – Basic prevention

Human element in medical care determines the patient's and attendant's reaction to an uncovered event. Sources of discontent, such as, tactless handling, trivial indignations or casual unpleasant remarks, etc, are the causes of a large number of legal actions brought against the doctors and hospitals.

Behaviour of the entire system including receptionist, junior staff, cleaners, etc, should be continuously monitored, especially in stressful circumstances. "Commercial attitude/behaviour" should be discouraged. Prescription heads, sign boards, advertisements should be mentioned true qualifications, training, experience, designation and facilities. Guarantee of result should be avoided.

It is desirable that all the queries of the patients and attendants are answered without minding their repeated questioning. The doctor should be brief, to the point and clear in his articulation and language and should maintain moderate behaviour and calm face even while rebuking them for their inattentiveness, carelessness, repeated questioning, etc. He should not mind their questioning the diagnoses/treatment.

He should not be adverse to any suggestion of seeking a second opinion. Doctors who are open minded and communicative and much less to be complained against as patient/attendants generally are extremely forgiving of errors made by a friendly and concerned medical practitioner.

Report with nursing/paramedical staff is crucial; otherwise they could place the medical professionals in jeopardy.

The entire encounter with attendants should be one of open communication and shared decision making. Risk should be discussed and the family should be made aware of the possible outcome of diagnostic and treatment efforts. Paediatrician should tell the patient about the relevant risk, i.e. the serious ones, that may have only have a slight chance of occurring as well as the minor ones, that may only have a slight chance of occurring as well as the minor ones that might occur with significant frequency or regularity.

Make appreciative and kind oral statements of the child, his family members and to the other members of the treatment team. In some situations, a stern warming, a bit of forceful advice, perhaps even righteous indignation may be appropriate recourse in handling the recalcitrant uncooperative child/attendants. But harshness, excessive criticism, profanity or an injudicious unwarranted trade will do more to interfere with good patient rapport than almost any other action by a paediatrician. Be cautious in passing remarks against another doctor, especially in the presence of the attendants.

A high proportion of complaints is precipitated or escalated into legal action by a progressive breakdown of the doctor-patient communication. Try to keep in mind the mental state of the close relatives/friends. Be compassionate. Be careful while informing about 'functional cases', 'bad news and remember not to refuse patient's right to examine and receive an explanation about the bill.

In order to keep up with the 'current accepted practice' doctors and a staff should update their knowledge and skills, and facilities should be updated according to the claims made by the clinic/hospitals. It is the responsibility of every doctor to keep himself generally informed or mainstream changes in diagnosis, treatment and practice through the mainstream literature, such as the leading text books and the leading journals of his specialty. A doctor cannot realistically be expected to read every article in every learned medical journal, or to acquaint himself with the content of the moral of the obscure journals, yet there is an obligation on him a reasonable effort to keep up to date, example where a particular risk has been highlighted on a number of occasions the doctor will ignore it only at his own peril.

Knowledge of medical ethics and law in practice of medicine is very useful in improving practicing attitude and methods of doctors. Medical professionals are advised to carefully study the Indian Medical Council (Professional Conduct, Etiquette and Ethics) Regulations, 2002.

3. Secondly prevention

The important steps are:

3.1 Systematic documentation

A systematic documentation of the date, time and history (in brief), positive physical findings, investigations, treatment and instructions to the junior staff and the patient are necessary. Record history of drug allergy, take care of your handwriting, major drug interactions, mention: where patients should contact in case of your non-availability/emergency, diagnoses under revision until the diagnosis is finally settled, and to rule out a certain disease. Write investigations asked for on the same slip. In a difficult case, it is advisable to refer the patient to a specialist, but if this is not feasible, further testing should be advised to be carried out considering the serious condition of the patient even at the risk of being sued for over testing. Record advice for diagnostic tests and referrals properly.

The prognosis should be explained to the patient/attendant in comprehensible language and in complicated cases it should be done in writing and signatures of the patient/attendant obtained with at least one witness, if possible. A note should be recorded in case of erring patients on any count, example unreliable history, refusing investigations, refusing admission, not complying with instructions, etc., which is mandatory.

The Physician should neither exaggerate not minimize the gravity of the patient's conditions. He should ensure himself that the patient, his relatives or his responsible friends have such a knowledge of the patient's condition as will serve the best interests of the patient and the family. (Regulation 23 of the Indian Medical Council — (Professional Conduct, Etiquette and Ethics Regulations, 2002 – Appendix -1)

3.2 Maintenance of record and supply

Every Physician is required to maintain the medical records pertaining to his/her indoor patients for a period of three years from the date of commencement of the treatment in a standard Performa laid down by the medical council of India. Thus, hospitals and nursing homes should preserve records of patient for not less than three years, so that when a case is filed, (*a*) under the Consumer Protection Act where the limitation for filing a complaint is 2 years, (*b*) are under law of tort where the limitation is 3 years, record can be produced in defense of your case, or it may be required to be produced by the consumer forum or civil court, (*c*) in new-born cases and in case of minors, this should be preserved for not less than 3 years after the child attaining majority age of eighteen years, the reason being that such minors cause of action subsists up to two years after attaining majority under the Consumer Protection Act and up to 3 years under the civil law.

If any request is made for medical records either by the patient/authorised attendant or legal authorities involved, the same may be duly acknowledged and the documents are required to be issued/supplied within the period of 72 hours.

3.3 Valid consent

Most of the consents being obtained in government and private hospitals and nursing homes are legally valid.

The necessity of obtaining a legally valid consent from the Patient/Parents/ Guardian/Attendant need hardly be emphasized.

3.4 Tertiary Prevention

To meet the claim of compensation which may be awarded against a doctor for medical negligence which is called deficiency in service under the Consumer Protection Act, 1986, it has now became essential for every doctor to obtain a professional Indemnity Insurance cover from any one of the Insurance Companies.

4. Formation of Medical Defence Societies

The professional, social and physiological aspects of such litigations and its absence can be fought only by providing a strong peer support and by formation of medical defense organizations/societies at the local, state and national levels and assist in such situations and if necessary take up cover of defence on behalf of doctors against alleged medical negligence. However, no attempt should be made in diagnoses and treatment to defend cases of gross negligence or glaring deviations from the accepted norms of code of ethics for medical professionals.

5. Nine R's preventive steps

The Medical Liability Mutual Insurance Company, New York has published a booklet wherein following nine R's of malpractice prevention have been enumerated:

5.1 Rapport

The lack of rapport makes the patient believe that the Physician is not leading within as a mature intelligent individual and the minute there is a bad result the reaction would be to sue first and ask questions later.

The Physician therefore must maintain a healthy rapport and communication not only with the patients but also with their families, with fellow physicians, with the office staff and with nurses and other personnel at the hospital.

The consultants who were called in deserve the courtesy of complete clinical data. There should be an understanding of what aspects of the patient's care is whose responsibility. Otherwise the patient's might "fall through the cracks" as each Physician is this disowning his responsibility.

Likewise the rapport with the office staff is also crucial, otherwise they can play the Physician in jeopardy. This extends to nurses and para-medical personnel at the hospital.

5.2 Rationale

It is a short hand way of saying that the Physician must understand what he is doing or trying to accomplish with each and every patient and why? He must have in mind a treatment planned, or at least a differential diagnosis, attempting to pinpoint the source of the patients problem and to find the best way of handling it, eliminating it if possible or controlling it if that is the only feasible alternative.

Demonstration of the Physician rational provides proof of compensation and application of the "medical model" needless to say that diagnostic and therapeutic rational should be adequately documented in the medical record. A court that can be expected to understand and follow the Physicians thought process if there is at least some indication of it in the record.

5.3 Record

In a trial the record is the most important evidence. A good record speaks of good care; sloppy incomplete records suggest a sloppy Physician who provides incomplete care.

The record should be carefully prepared, complete, accurate, legible, germane, relevant, timely and generously informative.

5.4 RxS

The Physician must constantly remind himself that it is ill advised to prescribe or administer to a patient any medication without an appropriate medical indication. The Physician must be aware of possible contraindications to the use of any drug: (*a*) because of other medical problems the patient has, (*b*) because of interference with other medications the patient is already taking, and (*c*) because of any allergies to related drugs, carefully detailed histories regarding drug allergies must be taken and documented in the medical record where such data that is easily identifiable and retrievable.

5.5 Res ipsa loquitur

This phrase has been applied by our courts to refer to situations in which even the untrained layman could presume malpractice without the testimony of an expert witness. Examples are the case in which a lap pad or hemostat is left in the abdomen of the patient who undergoes laparotomy, the situation in which the right hip is broken but the left one has the Jewett's nail inserted, the instance in which the patient has sustained a tear in the right medical meniscus but the left knee is opened and repaired.

5.6 Remarks

The word, 'remarks' refers to gratuitous oral statements made to the patient and the patient's family as well as to other members of the treatment team. In some situations, a stern warning, a bit forceful advice, perhaps even righteous indignation may be appropriate recourse in handling the recalcitrant, uncooperative patient. But harshness, excessive criticism, profanity or an injudious unwarranted trade will do more to interfere with good patient report than almost any other action by a Physician.

A doctor should be cautious in passing remarks against another doctor who had treated the patient. Remark should be avoided in the presence of the patient. The complaint of the patient about the other doctors should be verified from the other and the record of the patients should be carefully examined. The doctor should always keep the patient's ailments confidential.

5.7 Risks

Risks should also be discussed with a patient as part of informing him before obtaining him consented to proceed. This requires a careful, thoughtful, individualized approach to each patient. Obviously, the risks for one patient may not be exactly the same as they are for another. Nor should the physician embark on a laundry list or litany of remote risks, or even those of minor consequences. Such a discussion may well cause the patient to refuse the particular diagnostic tests or treatment recommended. It is not necessary to make a nervous or an anxious patient that much more nervous or an anxious. To the contrary, Physicians should tell the patient about the relevant risks, the seriousness, that may only have a slight chance of occurring as well as the minor ones that might occur with significant frequency or regularity. Obviously, any procedure or test that might culminate in death or significant permanent disability should be delineated even if its chances of occurring are relatively small.

5.8 Respect

Many malpractice cases are triggered by the concurrence of a bad medical result or untoward outcome and the patient perception that the Physician lacks respect or concern for him as an individual, as a human being, as the person. Patients resent being treated as experimental animals or as 'disease entities' that happen to be housed in the human bodies. The Physician must remember to treat the patient as he would wish himself or a member of his family to be treated. An attitude of care and concern, a relationship that be speaks thoughtful professionalism and a humanistic approach, solves more problems, malts more hostilities and eliminate more law suits than almost anything else.

5.9 Result

The patient and family should be made aware of the possible outcome of diagnosis and treatment efforts. Such advice may well fall under the heading of 'informed consent', although that term is really a misnomer since a 'consent' cannot be informed. The Physician offers information to the patient, the patient than bases decisions related to his health care on that information. The entire encounter is one of the open communications and shared the decision-making.

CHAPTER 12

The Consumer Protection Act, 1986 with Short Comments

SYNOPSIS

Chapter I

Preliminary

THE CONSUMER PROTECTION ACT, 1986[1]

[68 of 1986]

[As amended upto-date]

[24th December, 1986]

An Act to provide for better protection of the interests of consumers and for that purpose to make provision for the establishment of consumer councils and other authorities for the settlement of consumers' disputes and for matters connected therewith.

BE it enacted by Parliament in the Thirty-seventh year of the Republic of India as follows:

INTRODUCTION

The industrial revolution and the development in the international trade and commerce has led to the vast expansion of business and trade, as a result of which a variety of consumer goods have appeared in the market to cater to the needs of the consumers and a host of services have been made available to the consumers like insurance, transport, electricity, housing, entertainment, finance and banking. A well organised sector of manufacturers and traders with better knowledge of markets has come into existence, thereby affecting the relationship between the traders and the consumers making the principle of consumer sovereignty almost inapplicable.

---

1 Passed by Lok Sabha on 9-12-1986 and Rajya Sabha on 10-12-1986, Assented by the President of India on 24-12-1986. Published in the Gazette of India, Extra. Part II, section 1 dated 26-12-1986, pp. 1-12.

The advertisements of goods and services in television, newspapers and magazines influence the demand for the same by the consumers though there may be manufacturing defects or imperfections or short comings in the quality, quantity and the purity of the goods or there may be deficiency in the services rendered. In addition, the production of the same item by many firms has led the consumers, who have little time to make a selection, to think before they can purchase the best. For the welfare of the public, the glut of adulterated and sub-standard articles in the market has to be checked. Inspite of various provisions providing protection to the consumer and providing for stringent action against adulterated and sub-standard articles in the different enactments like Code of Civil Procedure, 1908, the Indian Contract Act, 1872, the Sale of Goods Act, 1930, the Indian Penal Code, 1860, the Standards of Weights and Measures Act, 1976 and the Motor Vehicles Act, 1988, very little could be achieved in the field of Consumer Protection. Though the Monopolies and Restrictive Trade Practices Act, 1969 arid the Prevention of Food Adulteration Act, 1954 have provided relief to the consumers yet it became necessary to protect the consumers from the exploitation and to save them from adulterated and sub-standard goods and services and to safe guard the interests of the consumers. In order to provide for better protection of the interests of the consumer the Consumer Protection Bill, 1986 was introduced in the Lok Sabha on 5th December, 1986.

COMMENT ON INTRODUCTION

The moment a person comes into this would, he starts consuming. He needs clothes, milk, oil, soap, water and many more things and these needs keep taking one form or the other all along his life. Thus we all are consumers in the literal sense of the term. When we approach the market as a consumer, we expect value for money, *i.e.*, right quality, right quantity, right prices, information about the mode of use, etc. But there may be instances where a consumer is harassed or cheated.

The Government understood the need to protect consumers from unscrupulous suppliers and several laws have been made for this purpose. We have the Indian Contract Act, the Sale of Goods Act, the Dangerous Drugs Act, the Agricultural Produce (Grading and Marketing) Act, the Indian Standards Institution (Certification Marks) Act, the Prevention of Food Adulteration Act, the Standards of Weights and Measures Act, etc. which to some extent protect consumer interests. However, these laws require the consumer to initiate action by way of a civil suit involving lengthy legal process which is very expensive and time consuming.

Every civilized nation of the world has its own legislation which protects the consumers. In India it was at the end of twentieth century, the Consumer Protection Act, 1986 was enacted. The main object of the Act is to provide a better, inexpensive and speedy remedy to the consumers. It seeks to provide for better protection of the interest of consumers and for the said purpose, to make provision for the establishment of

Consumer Councils and other authorities for the settlement of consumer disputes and for matters connected therewith.

The year 1986 is a 'Magna Carta' in the history of Consumerism. It was this year that witnessed the enactment of the Consumer Protection Act. The first ever legislation in India of its kind which solely aimed at the grief-stricken consumers who the victims of the unfair trade practices and sub-standard services rendered to them. The preamble to this Act reads as follows: An Act to provide for better protection of the interests of the consumers and to make provisions for the establishment of consumer councils and other authorities for the settlement of consumers' disputes and for matter connected therewith. Thus the preamble to this Act makes the intention of the framers of this Act crystal clear.

The Consumer Protection Act, 1986 is a social welfare legislation which was enacted as a result of widespread consumer protection movement. The main object of the legislature in the enactment of this Act is to provide for the better protection of the interests of the consumer and to make provisions for establishment of consumer councils and other authorities for settlement of consumer disputes and matter therewith connected.

In order to promote and protect the rights and interests of consumers, quasi judicial machinery is sought to be set up at district, state and central levels. These quasi judicial bodies have to observe the principles of natural justice and have been empowered to give reliefs, of specific nature and also to impose penalties for non compliance of the orders given by such bodies.

The main object of these bodies is to provide speedy and simple redressal to consumer disputes. It is one of the benevolent pieces of legislation intended to protect the consumers at large from exploitation. The Consumer Protection Act, 1986, provides for the better protection of consumers. Unlike existing laws which are punitive or preventive in nature, the provisions of this Act are compensatory in nature. The Act is intended to provide simple, speedy and inexpensive redressal to the consumers' grievances, award relief and compensation wherever appropriate to the consumer.

The setting up of the dispute redressal machinery was only to secure and enable speedy justice to the aggrieved consumers. But the only point on which this mission could not give back its 100% waste short-sightedness in visualising the problem which occur at the post-implementation period of the orders/decrees of the redressal Foras. This was ultimately realised by the legislature though not much expediently, as an outcome of which the Consumer Protection (Amendment) Bill was presented before the House.

Now we understand that the Consumer Protection Act provides means to protect consumers from getting cheated or harassed by suppliers. The question arises how a consumer will seek protection? The answer is the Act has provided machinery whereby consumers can file their complaints which will be entertained by the Consumer Forums with special powers so that action can be taken against erring suppliers and the possible compensation may be awarded to consumer for the hardships he has undergone. No court fee is required to be paid to these forums and there is no need to engage a lawyer to present the case.

After including the amendments made *vide* the Consumer Protection (Amendment) Act, 2002 (62 of 2002) which was passed by Rajya Sabha on 11-4-2002, Lok Sabha on 30-7-2002 {with some amendments} and again by Rajya Sabha on 22-11-2002 and the President of India gave assent on 17-12-2002 and the notification was issue on 18-12-2002.The provisions of the Act are being brought into force w.e.f. 15-3-2003.

The Act has been amended in 1993 and 2002 extends coverage and scope to enhance the powers of the redressal machinery. The problem in India is that there are no stringent laws on consumer rights. Even though the Consumer Protection Act stipulates that consumer courts settle all cases within 90 days, it usually takes up to a year, given the previous backlog.

STATEMENT OF OBJECTS AND REASONS

The Consumer Protection Bill, 1986 seeks to provide for better protection of the interests of consumers and for the purpose, to make provision for the establishment of Consumer councils and other authorities for the settlement of consumer disputes and for matter connected therewith.

2. It seeks, *inter alia*, to promote and protect the rights of consumers such as—

(*a*) the right to be protected against marketing of goods which are hazardous to life and property;

(*b*) the right to be informed about the quality, quantity, potency, purity, standard and price of goods to protect the consumer against unfair trade practices;

(*c*) the right to be assured, wherever possible, access to an authority of goods at competitive prices;

(*d*) the right to be heard and to be assured that consumers interests will receive due consideration at appropriate forums;

(*e*) the right to seek redressal against unfair trade practices or unscrupulous exploitation of consumers; and

(*f*) right to consumer education.

3. These objects are sought to be promoted and protected by the Consumer Protection Council to be established at the Central and State level.

4. To provide speedy and simple redressal to consumer disputes, a quasi-judicial machinery is sought to be setup at the district, State and Central levels.

These quasi-judicial bodies will observe the principles of natural justice and have been empowered to give relief of a specific nature and to award, wherever appropriate, compensation to consumers. Penalties for non-compliance of the orders given by the quasi-judicial bodies have also been provided.

5. The Bill seeks to achieve the above objects.

ACT 68 of 1986

The Consumer Protection Bill, 1986 was passed by both the Houses of Parliament and it received the assent of the President on 24th December, 1986. It came on the Statutes Book as the Consumer Protection Act, 1986 (68 of 1986).

LIST OF AMENDING ACTS

1. The Consumer Protection (Amendment) Act, 1991 (34 of 1991).
2. The Consumer Protection (Amendment) Act, 1993 (50 of 1993).
3. The Consumer Protection (Amendment) Act, 2002 (62 of 2002).

Amendment Act 34 of 1991 — Statement of Objects and Reasons.—In view of the recent decision of the National Consumer Disputes Redressal Commission (National Commission) regarding the order under sub-section (2) of section 14 of the Act, it was felt that the said Act required certain modifications.

2. Accordingly, the Consumer Protection (Amendment) Ordinance, 1991, was promulgated to provide *inter alia*,—

(*a*) for amendment of sub-section (2) of section 14 to provide that every proceeding of the District Forum shall be conducted by the President and at least one Member thereof sitting together;

(*b*) that every order made by the District Forum shall be signed by its President and Member or Members who conducted the proceeding;

(*c*) that where the proceeding is conducted by the President and a Member of the District Forum and they differ on any point or points, the same shall be referred to the other Member on such point or points and the opinion of the majority shall be the order of the District Forum;

(*d*) to validate the orders which have been signed by the President and one Member of the District Forum or the State Commission before amendment; and

(*e*) that in the case of vacancy in the office of the President, the person who is qualified to be appointed as President of the District Forum or the State Commission may be temporarily appointed to hold such office.

Amendment Act 50 of 1993 — Statement of Objects and Reasons.—In 1986, the Consumer Protection Act was enacted to provide for better protection of the interests of consumers and for that purpose to make provisions for the establishment of consumer councils and other authorities for the settlement of consumer disputes and matters connected therewith. The working of the redressal agencies set up under the Act has helped to arouse the expectations of the people and also brought to focus certain inadequacies in the coverage of the Act. The

Consumer Protection (Amendment) Bill, 1993 seeks to plug these loopholes and enlarge the scope of areas covered and entrust more powers to the redressal agencies under the Act. Accordingly, the Bill *inter alia*, seeks to provide for following:

(*i*) to enlarge the scope of the Act so as to enable the consumers to file class action complaints where such consumers have a common interest and to file complaints relating to restrictive trade practices adopted by a trader;

(*ii*) to enable the consumers who are self-employed to file complaints before the redressal agencies where goods bought by them exclusively for earning their livelihood, suffer from any defect;

(*iii*) to add "services" relating to housing constructions;

(*iv*) to enable filing of class action complaints on behalf of groups of consumers having the same interest;

(*v*) to provide for the constitution of selection committees for the selection of non-judicial Members of various redressal agencies;

(*vi*) to increase the monetary jurisdiction of District Fora/State Commissions/ National Commission;

(*vii*) to confer additional powers on the redressal agencies by way of awarding costs to the parties, for ordering removal of defects or deficiency from the services, and for empowering to recall of goods likely to endanger the safety of the public, etc.;

(*viii*) to impose punishment on the complainant in cases of frivolous or vexatious complaints; and

(*ix*) to provide for a limitation period of one year for filing complaints.

Amendment Act 62 of 2002 — Statement of Objects and Reasons.—The enactment of the Consumer Protection Act, 1986 was an important milestone in the history of the consumer movement in the country. The Act was made to "provide for the better protection and promotion of consumer rights through the establishment of Consumer Councils and quasi-judicial machinery. Under the Act, consumer disputes redressal agencies have been set up throughout the country with the District Forum at the district level, State Commission at the State level and National Commission at the National level to provide simple, inexpensive and speedy justice to the consumers with complaints against defective goods, deficient services and unfair and restrictive trade practices. The Act was also amended in the years 1991 and 1993 to make it more effective and purposeful.

2. Although the consumer disputes redressal agencies have, to a considerable extent, served the purpose for which they were created, the disposal of cases has not been fast enough. Several bottlenecks and shortcomings have also come to light in the implementation of various provisions of the Act. With a view to achieving quicker disposal of consumer complaints by the consumer disputes redressal agencies securing effective implementation of their orders, widening

the scope of some of the provisions of the Act to make it more effective, removing various lacunae in the Act and streamlining the procedures, amendments are proposed in the Act, which, *inter alia*, include the following, namely:—

(*i*) provisions for creation of Benches of the National Commission and State Commissions as well as holding of circuit Benches of these Commissions;

(*ii*) prescribing the period within which complaints are to be admitted, notices are to be issued to opposite party and the complaints are to be decided. Similar provisions have been proposed also in respect of appeals;

(*iii*) no adjournment to be ordinarily allowed and a speaking order giving reasons would be made;

(*iv*) enhancing the pecuniary limits of jurisdiction of the consumer disputes redressal agencies so that the District Forums are unable to deal with complaints involving value of goods or services and claims compensation up to ₹20 lakhs (against ₹5 lakhs at present), fixing the pecuniary limits of jurisdiction of State Commissions from ₹20 lakhs upto ₹1 crore (as against above ₹5 lakhs upto ₹20 lakhs at present) and National Commission above ₹1 crore (as against above ₹20 lakhs at present);

(*v*) enabling provision for charging of fee in respect of complaints filed before the consumer disputes redressal agencies;

(*vi*) provision for depositing, either fifty per cent of the amount of compensation or fine or the amounts mentioned below whichever are less, before the admission of appeal, namely:—

(*a*) ₹25,000 in case of appeal to a State Commission from the District Forum;

(*b*) ₹35,000 in case of appeal to the National Commission from a State Commission; and

(*c*) ₹50,000 in case of appeal to the Supreme Court from the National Commission;

(*vii*) exclusion of services availed for commercial purposes from the purview of the consumer disputes redressal agencies;

(*viii*) prescribing minimum qualifications as well as disqualifications for Members of the consumer disputes redressal agencies;

(*ix*) provision for re-appointment of President and Members of the District Forum, State Commissions and the National Commission, for another term of five years;

(*x*) extending the provisions of the Act to service providers indulging in unfair or restrictive trade practices or offering services which are hazardous;

(*xi*) bringing sale of spurious goods or services within the meaning of unfair trade practices;

(*xii*) expressly conferring the powers of a Judicial Magistrate of the first class on the consumer disputes redressal agencies with a view to trying offences under the Act;

(*xiii*) provision for recovery of amounts ordered to be paid by the consumer disputes redressal agencies as arrears of land revenue;

(*xiv*) provision for issue of interim orders by the consumer disputes redressal agencies, in cases where it is considered necessary by such agencies;

(*xv*) provision for substitution of legal heir or representative as a parts to the complaint in the event of the death of the complainant or the opposite party.

3. The Consumer Protection Councils at the Central and State levels are important bodies for the promotion and protection of consumer rights. It is proposed to make the establishment of these Councils a necessary requirement. It is also proposed to provide for the establishment of District Consumer Protection Councils for promotion and protection of consumer rights at the district level.

COMMENTS ON OBJECTS & REASONS

The Consumer Protection Act, 1986 was enacted as a result of widespread consumer protection movement. With reference to the consumer movement and the international obligations for protection of the rights of the consumer, provision has been made in the said Act with the object of interpreting the relevant law in a rational manner and for achieving the objective set forth in the Act. A rational approach and not a technical approach is to mandate of law. [*India Photographic Co. Ltd.* v *H.D. Shourie* AIR 1999 SC 2453]

The Consumer Protection Act is one of the benevolent pieces of legislation intended to protect a large body of consumers from exploitation. The Act provides for an alternative system of consumer justice by summary trial. The authorities under the Act exorcise *qua judicial* powers for redressal of consumer disputes and it is one of the postulates of such body that it should arrive at a conclusion based on reason. Obligation to give reasons not only introduces clarity but it also excludes, or at any rate minimises, the chances of arbitrariness and the higher forum can test the correctness of those reasons. [*Charan Singh* v *Healing Touch Hospital* (2000) 7 SCC 668]

CHAPTER I

Preliminary

1. Short title, extent, commencement and application.—(1) This Act may be called the Consumer Protection Act, 1986.

(2) It extends to the whole of India except the State of Jammu and Kashmir.

(3) It shall come into force on such date[1] as the Central Government may, by notification, appoint and different dates may be appointed for different States and for different provisions of this Act.

(4) Save as otherwise expressly provided by the Central Government by notification, this Act shall apply to all goods and services.

COMMENTS ON SECTION 1

Having due regard to the scheme of the Act and purpose sought to be achieved to protect the interest of the consumers better, the provisions are to be interpreted broadly, positively and purposefully in the context of the present case to give meaning to additional/extended jurisdiction, particularly when section 3 seeks to provide remedy under the Act in addition to other remedies provided under other Acts unless there is clear bar. Under the Consumer Protection Act, 1986 the Court has to consider as regards the additional jurisdiction conferred on the Consumer Forums and not their exclusion. In *Dhulabhai* case AIR 1969 SC 78 consideration was whether the jurisdiction of the Civil Court was excluded. Propositions (1) and (2) set out therein indicate that where the statute gives finality to the orders of the Special Tribunals, the jurisdiction of the Civil Courts must be held to be excluded if there is adequate remedy to do what the Civil Courts would normally do in a suit. Further, where there is an express bar on the jurisdiction of the Court, an examination of the scheme of the particular Act to find the adequacy or the sufficiency of the remedies provided may be relevant but is not decisive to sustain the jurisdiction of the Civil Court. The remedies that are available to an aggrieved party under the Consumer Protection Act, 1986 are wider. For instance, in addition to granting a specific relief the forums under the Consumer Protection Act, 1986 have jurisdiction to award compensation for the mental agony, suffering, etc. which possibly could not be given under the Act in relation tc dispute under section 90 of the Act. Merely because the rights and liabilities are created between the Members and the management of the society under the Act and forums are provided, it cannot take away or exclude the jurisdiction conferred on the forums under the Consumer Protection Act, 1986 expressly and intentionally to serve a definite cause in terms of the objects and reasons of the Consumer Protection Act, 1986. When the decision of *Dhulabhai case* was rendered, the provisions similar to the Consumer Protection Act, 1986 so providing additional remedies to parties were neither available nor considered. If the argument of the appellant is accepted, it will lead to

---

1. The provisions of Chapters I, II and IV of this Act shall come into force in the whole of India except the State of Jammu & Kashmir on 15-4-1987 *vide* Notification No. SO 390(E), dated 15-4-1987, Gazette of India, Extraordinary, 1987, part II, section 3(*ii*). The provisions of Chapter III of this Act shall come into force in the whole of India except the State of Jammu & Kashmir on 1-7-1987 *vide* Notification No. SO 568(E), dated 10-6-1987, Gazette of India, Extraordinary, 1987, part II, section 3(*ii*).

taking away the additional remedies and forums expressly provided under the Consumer Protection Act, 1986, which is not acceptable: *Secretary Rumurugan Cooperative Agricultural Credit Society* v *M. Lalitha* (2004) 1 SCC 305. **See also** [*H.K. Shankara Shastry* v *Asstt. Director of Agriculture* (2004) 6 SCC 230]

It appears appropriate to ascertain the purpose of the Act, the objective it seeks to achieve and the nature of social purpose it seeks to promote as it shall facilitate in comprehending he issue involved and assist in construing various provisions of the Act effectively. To begin with the preamble of the Act, which can afford useful assistance to ascertain the legislative intention, it was enacted, "to provide for the protection of the interest of consumers". Use of the word "protection" furnishes key to the minds of makers of the Act. Various definitions and provisions which elaborately attempt to achieve this objective have to be construed in this light without departing from the settled view that a preamble cannot control otherwise plain meaning of a provision. In fact the law meets long-felt necessity of protecting the common man from such wrongs for which the remedy under ordinary law for various reasons has become illusory. Various legislations and regulations permitting the State to intervene and protect interest of the consumers have become a haven for unscrupulous ones as the enforcement machinery either does not move or it moves ineffectively, inefficiently and for reasons "which are not necessary to be stated. The importance of the Act lies in promoting welfare of the society by enabling the consumer to participate directly in the market economy. It attempts to remove the helplessness of a consumer which he faces against powerful business, described as "a network of rackets" or a society in which, "producers have secured power" to "rob the rest" and the might of public bodies which "are degenerating into storehouses of inaction where papers do not move from one desk to another as a matter of duty and responsibility but for extraneous consideration leaving the common man helpless, bewildered and shocked. The malady is becoming so rampant, widespread and deep that the society instead of bothering, complaining and fighting against it, is accepting it as part of life. The enactment in these unbelievable yet harsh realities appears to be a silver lining, which may in course of time succeed in checking the rot": *H.N. Shankara Shastry* v *Asstt. Director of Agriculture* (2004) 6 SCC 230. **See also** [*Lucknow Development Authority* v *U.K. Gupta* (1994) 1 SCC 243]

So long as the cause of action is not barred under the general law of limitation as on the date of institution of the consumer disputes before the statutory redressal forum, the mere fact that the date of accrual of the cause of action was prior to the date of coming into force of Chapter m is total irrelevant and it will not operate to deprive the aggrieved consumer of his right under the Act to seek relief before the statutory redressal forum. In other words, the only requirement to be satisfied is that as on the date when the consumer dispute is filed before a redressal forum, the cause of action should not have become time barred under the law of the limitation. [*S. Elhence* v *Raghomal Nahar Singh (P) Ltd* (1991)1 CPR 419 (NC)]

The provisions of Chapters I, II and IV of this Act have come into force in the whole of India except the State of Jammu and Kashmir on 15-4-1987 *vide* Notification No. S.O. 390(E), dated 15th April, 1987, published in the Gazette of India,

The provisions of Chapter III of this Act have come into force in the whole of India except the State of Jammu and Kashmir on 1-7-1987 *vide* Notification No. S.O. 568(E), dated 10th June, 1987, published in the Gazette of India, 1987, Ext, Pt II, Section 3(*ii*).

2. Definitions.—(1) In this Act, unless the context otherwise requires,—

[1][(*a*) "appropriate laboratory" means a laboratory or organisation—

(*i*) recognised by the Central Government;

(*ii*) recognised by a State Government, subject to such guidelines as may be prescribed by the Central Government in this behalf; or

(*iii*) any such laboratory or organisation established by or under any law for the time being in force, which is maintained, financed or aided by the Central Government or a State Government for carrying out analysis or test of any goods with a view to determining whether such goods suffer from any defect;]

[2][(*aa*) "branch office" means—

(*i*) any establishment described as a branch by the opposite party; or

(*ii*) any establishment carrying on either the same or substantially the same activity as that carried on by the head office of the establishment;]

(*b*) "complainant" means—

(*i*) a consumer; or

(*ii*) any voluntary consumer association registered under the Companies Act, 1956 (1 of 1956) or under any other law for the time being in force; or

(*iii*) the Central Government or any State Government, who or which makes a complaint; or

[3][(*iv*) one or more consumers, where there are numerous consumers having the same interest;]

---

1 Substituted for "appropriate laboratory" means a laboratory or organisation recognised by the Central Government and includes any such laboratory or organisation established by or under any law for the time being in force, which is maintained, financed or aided by the Central Government or a State Government for carrying out analysis or test of any goods with a view to determining whether such goods suffer from any defect" by the Consumer Protection (Amendment) Act 1993, w.e.f. 18-6-1993.

2 Inserted by the Consumer Protection (Amendment) Act, 1993, w.e.f. 18-6-1993.

3 Inserted, *ibid.*

[1][(*v*) in case of death of a consumer, his legal heir or representative;]

(*c*) "complaint" means any allegation in writing made by a complainant that:

[2][(*i*) an unfair trade practice or a restrictive trade practice has been adopted by [3][any trader or service provider;]

(*ii*) [4][the goods bought by him or agreed to be bought by him] suffer from one or more defects;

(*iii*) [5][the services hired or availed of or agreed to be hired or availed of by him] suffer from deficiency in any respect;

[6][(*iv*) a trader or the service provider, as the case may be, has charged for the goods or for the services mentioned in the complaint, a price in excess of the price—

(*a*) fixed by or under any law for the time being in force;

(*b*) displayed on the goods or any package containing such goods;

(*c*) displayed on the price list exhibited by him by or under any law for the time being in force;

(*d*) agreed between the parties;]

[7][(*v*) goods which will be hazardous to life and safety when used are being offered for sale to the public,—

(A) in contravention of any standards relating to safety of such goods as required to be complied with, by or under any law for the time being in force;

(B) if the trader could have known with due diligence that the goods so offered are unsafe to the public;]

[8][(*vi*) services which are hazardous or likely to be hazardous to life and safety of the public when used, are being offered by the service provider which such person could have known with due diligence to be injurious to life and safety;]

with a view to obtaining any relief provided by or under this Act;

---

1 Inserted by the Consumer Protection (Amendment) Act, 2002, w.e.f. 15-3-2003.

2 Substituted for "(*i*) as a result of any unfair trade practice adopted by any trader, the complainant has suffered loss or damage;" by the Consumer Protection (Amendment) Act, 1993, w.e.f. 18-6-1993.

3 Substituted for 'any trade' by the Consumer Protection (Amendment) Act, 2002, w.e.f. 15-3-2003.

4 Substituted for the words "the goods mentioned in the complaint", by the Consumer Protection (Amendment) Act, 1993, w.e.f. 18-6-1993.

5 Substituted for the words "the services mentioned in the complaint", *ibid.*

6 Substituted for "(*iv*) a trader has charged for the goods mentioned in the complaint a price in excess of the price fixed by or under any law for the time being in force or displayed on the goods or any package containing such goods;" by the Consumer Protection (Amendment) Act, 2002, w.e.f. 15-3-2003.

7 Substituted for "(*v*) goods which will be hazardous to life and safety when used, are being offered for sale to the public in contravention of the provisions of any law for the time being in force requiring trader to display information in regard to the contents, manner and effect of use of such goods;" by the Consumer Protection (Amendment) Act, 2002, w.e.f. 15-3-2003.

8 Inserted, *ibid.*

(*d*) "consumer" means any person who:

(*i*) buys any goods for a consideration which has been paid or promised or partly paid and partly promised, or under any system of deferred payment and includes any user of such goods other than the person who buys such goods for consideration paid or promised or partly paid or partly promised, or under any system of deferred payment when such use is made with the approval of such person, but does not include a person who obtains such goods for resale or for any commercial purpose; or

(*ii*) [1][hires or avails of] any services for a consideration which has been paid or promised or partly paid and partly promised, or under any system of deferred payment and includes any beneficiary of such services other than the person who [2][hires or avails of] the services for consideration paid or promised, or partly paid and partly promised, or under any system of deferred payment, when such services are availed of with the approval of the first mentioned person [3][but does not include a person who avails of such services for any commercial purpose.]

[4][*Explanation.*—For the purposes of this clause, "commercial purpose" does not include use by a person of goods bought and used by him and services availed by him exclusively for the purposes of earning his livelihood by means of self-employment;]

(*e*) "consumer dispute" means a dispute where the person against whom a complaint has been made, denies or disputes the allegations contained in the complaint;

(*f*) "defect" means any fault, imperfection or shortcoming in the quality, quantity, potency, purity or standard which is required to be maintained by or under any law for the time being in force or [5][under any contract, express or implied, or] as is claimed by the trader in any manner whatsoever in relation to any goods;

(*g*) "deficiency" means any fault, imperfection, shortcoming or inadequacy in the quality, nature and manner of performance which is required to be maintained by or under any law for the time being in force or has been undertaken to be performed by a person in pursuance of a contract or otherwise in relation to any service;

---

1 Substituted for the word "hires", by the Consumer Protection (Amendment) Act, 1993, w.e.f. 18-6-1993.

2 *Ibid.*

3 Inserted by the Consumer Protection (Amendment) Act, 2002, w.e.f. 15-3-2003.

4 Substituted for "*Explanation.*—For the purpose of sub-clause (*i*), 'commercial purpose' does not include use by a consumer of goods bought and used by him exclusively for the purpose of earning his livelihood, by means of self-employment;" by the Consumer Protection (Amendment) Act, 2002, w.e.f. 15-3-2003.

5 Inserted by the Consumer Protection (Amendment) Act, 1993, w.e.f. 18-6-1993.

(*h*) "District Forum" means a Consumer Disputes Redressal Forum established under clause (*a*) of section 9;

(*i*) "goods" means goods as defined in the Sale of Goods Act, 1930 (3 of 1930);

[1][(*j*) "manufacturer" means a person who—

(*i*) makes or manufactures any goods or parts thereof; or

(*ii*) does not make or manufacture any goods but assembles parts thereof made or manufactured by others; or

(*iii*) puts or causes to be put his own mark on any goods made or manufactured by any other manufacturer;]

[2][(*jj*) "member" includes the President and a member of the National Commission or a State Commission or a District Forum, as the case may be;]

(*k*) "National Commission" means the National Consumer Disputes Redressal Commission established under clause (*c*) of section 9;

(*l*) "notification" means a notification published in the Official Gazette;

(*m*) "person" includes—

(*i*) a firm whether registered or not;

(*ii*) a Hindu undivided family;

(*iii*) a co-operative society;

(*iv*) every other association of persons whether registered under the Societies Registration Act, 1860 (21 of 1860) or not;

(*n*) "prescribed" means prescribed by rules made by the State Government, or as the case may be, by the Central Government under this Act;

[3][(*nn*) "regulation" means the regulations made by the National Commission under this Act;

---

1 Substituted for "(*j*) "manufacturer" means a person who:

(*i*) makes or manufactures any goods or parts thereof; or

(*ii*) does not make or manufacture any goods but assembles parts thereof made or manufactured by others and claims the end-product to be goods manufactured by himself; or

(*iii*) puts or causes to be put his own mark on any goods made or manufactured by any other manufacturer and claims such goods to be goods made or manufactured by himself.

Explanation.—Where a manufacturer despatches any goods or part thereof to any branch office maintained by him, such branch office shall not be deemed to be the manufacturer even though the parts so despatched to it are assembled at such branch office and are sold or distributed from such branch office;" by the Consumer Protection (Amendment) Act, 2002, w.e.f. 15-3-2003.

2 Inserted by the Consumer Protection (Amendment) Act, 1993, w.e.f. 18-6-1993.

3 Clauses (*nn*) and (*nnn*) substituted for "(*nn*) 'restrictive trade practice' means any trade practice which requires a consumer to buy, hire or avail of any goods or, as the case may be, services as a condition precedent for buying, hiring or availing of other goods or services;" by the Consumer Protection (Amendment) Act, 2002, w.e.f. 15-3-2003.

(*nnn*) "restrictive trade practice" means a trade practice which tends to bring about manipulation of price or its conditions of delivery or to affect flow of supplies in the market relating to goods or services in such a manner as to impose on the consumers unjustified costs or restrictions and shall include—

(*a*) delay beyond the period agreed to by a trader in supply of such goods or in providing the services which has led or is likely to lead to rise in the price;

(*b*) any trade practice which requires a consumer to buy, hire or avail of any goods or, as the case may be, services as condition precedent to buying, hiring or availing of other goods or services;]

(*o*) "service" means service of any description which is made available to potential [1][users and includes, but not limited to, the provision of] facilities in connection with banking, financing, insurance, transport, processing, supply of electrical or other energy, board or lodging or both, [2][housing construction,] entertainment, amusement or the purveying of news or other information, but does not include the rendering of any service free of charge or under a contract of personal service;

[3][(*oo*) "spurious goods and services" means such goods and services which are claimed to be genuine but they are actually not so;]

(*p*) "State Commission" means a Consumer Disputes Redressal Commission established in a State under clause (*b*) of section 9;

(*q*) "trader" in relation to any goods means a person who sells or distributes any goods for sale and includes the manufacturer thereof, and where such goods are sold or distributed in package form, includes the packer thereof;

[4][(*r*) "unfair trade practice" means a trade practice which, for the purpose of promoting the sale, use or supply of any goods or for the provision of any service, adopts any unfair method or unfair or deceptive practice including any of the following practices, namely:—

(1) the practice of making any statement, whether orally or in writing or by visible representation which,—

(*i*) falsely represents that the goods are of a particular standard, quality, quantity, grade, composition, style or model;

---

1 Substituted for the words "users and includes the provision of", by the Consumer Protection (Amendment) Act, 2002, w.e.f. 15-3-2003.

2 Inserted by the Consumer Protection (Amendment) Act, 1993, w.e.f. 18-6-1993.

3 Inserted by the Consumer Protection (Amendment) Act, 2002, w.e.f. 15-3-2003.

4 Substituted for "(*r*) the expression 'unfair trade practice' shall have the same meaning as in section 36A of the Monopolies and Restrictive Trade Practices Act, 1969 (54 of 1969), but shall not include an unfair trade practice adopted by the owner of an undertaking to which Part A of Chapter III of that Act applies or by any person acting on behalf of, or for the benefit of, such owner," by the Consumer Protection (Amendment) Act, 1993, w.e.f. 18-6-1993.

(*ii*) falsely represents that the services are of a particular standard, quality or grade;

(*iii*) falsely represents any re-built, second-hand, renovated, reconditioned or old goods as new goods;

(*iv*) represents that the goods or services have sponsorship, approval, performance, characteristics, accessories, uses or benefits which such goods or services do not have;

(*v*) represents that the seller or the supplier has a sponsorship or approval or affiliation which such seller or supplier does not have;

(*vi*) makes a false or misleading representation concerning the need for, or the usefulness of, any goods or services;

(*vii*) gives to the public any warranty or guarantee of the performance, efficacy or length of life of a product or of any goods that is not based on an adequate or proper test thereof:

Provided that where a defence is raised to the effect that such warranty or guarantee is based on adequate or proper test, the burden of proof of such defence shall lie on the person raising such defence;

(*viii*) makes to the public a representation in a form that purports to be—

(*i*) a warranty or guarantee of a product or of any goods or services; or

(*ii*) a promise to replace, maintain or repair an article or any part thereof or to repeat or continue a service until it has achieved a specified result,

if such purported warranty or guarantee or promise is materially misleading or if there is no reasonable prospect that such warranty, guarantee or promise will be carried out;

(*ix*) materially misleads the public concerning the price at which a product or like products or goods or services, have been, or are, ordinarily sold or provided, and, for this purpose, a representation as to price shall be deemed to refer to the price at which the product or goods or services has or have been sold by sellers or provided by suppliers generally in the relevant market unless it is clearly specified to be the price at which the product has been sold or services have been provided by the person by whom or on whose behalf the representation is made;

(*x*) gives false or misleading facts disparaging the goods, services or trade of another person.

Explanation.—For the purposes of clause (1), a statement that is—

(*a*) expressed on an article offered or displayed for sale, or on its wrapper or container; or

(*b*) expressed on anything attached to, inserted in, or accompanying, an article offered or displayed for sale, or on anything on which the article is mounted for display or sale; or

(*c*) contained in or on anything that is sold, sent, delivered, transmitted or in any other manner whatsoever made available to a member of the public,

shall be deemed to be a statement made to the public by, and only by, the person who had caused the statement to be so expressed, made or contained;

(2) permits the publication of any advertisement whether in any newspaper or otherwise, for the sale or supply at a bargain price, of goods or services that are not intended to be offered for sale or supply at the bargain price, or for a period that is, and in quantities that are, reasonable, having regard to the nature of the market in which the business is carried on, the nature and size of business, and the nature of the advertisement.

Explanation.—For the purposes of clause (2), 'bargaining price' means—

(*a*) a price that is stated in any advertisement to be a bargain price, by reference to an ordinary price or otherwise; or

(*b*) a price that a person who reads, hears, or sees the advertisement, would reasonably understand to be a bargain price having regard to the prices at which the product advertised or like products are ordinarily sold;

(3) permits—

(*a*) the offering of gifts, prizes or other items with the intention of not providing them as offered or creating impression that something is being given or offered free of charge when it is fully or partly covered by the amount charged in the transaction as a whole;

(*b*) the conduct of any contest, lottery, game of chance or skill, for the purpose of promoting, directly or indirectly, the sale, use or supply of any product or any business interest;

[1][(3A) withholding from the participants of any scheme offering gifts, prizes or other items free of charge, on its closure the information about final results of the scheme.

1 Inserted by the Consumer Protection (Amendment) Act, 2002, w.e.f. 15-3-2003.

Explanation.—For the purposes of this sub-clause, the participants of a scheme shall be deemed to have been informed of the final results of the scheme where such results are within a reasonable time, published, prominently in the same newspapers in which the scheme was originally advertised;]

(4) permits the sale or supply of goods intended to be used, or are of a kind likely to be used, by consumers, knowing or having reason to believe that the goods do not comply with the standards prescribed by competent authority relating to performance, composition, contents, design, construction, finishing or packaging as are necessary to prevent or reduce the risk of injury to the person using the goods;

(5) permits the hoarding or destruction of goods, or refuses to sell the goods or to make them available for sale or to provide any service, if such hoarding or destruction or refusal raises or tends to raise or is intended to raise, the cost of those or other similar goods or services;

[1][(6) manufacture of spurious goods or offering such goods for sale or adopting deceptive practices in the provision of services.]

(2) Any reference in this Act to any other Act or provision thereof which is not in force in any area to which this Act applies shall be construed to have a reference to the corresponding Act or provisions thereof in force in such area.

COMMENT ON SECTION 2

Objects and Reasons.—Clause 2(old) of the Bill seeks to amend sub-section (1) of section 2 of the Consumer Protection Act, 1986 so as to define various expressions used in the Act.

The scope of some of the definitions has been broadened and some new definitions have been added.

Sub-clause (*a*) of clause 2(old) seeks to include the legal heir or representative of a consumer, in case of death of the consumer within the meaning of "complainant". Sub-clause (*b*) seeks to broaden the definition of "complaint" to include allegations against service providers of adopting unfair or restrictive trade practices, or charging of excess price or offering services which are hazardous to life and safety. Sub-clause (*c*) seeks to exclude from the definition of "consumer" any person who avails of services for commercial purposes. Commercial undertakings which are already excluded from approaching the redressal agencies in respect of defective goods will thus be excluded from seeking relief from such agencies in respect of deficient services as well. The Consumer Protection Act, 1986 is intended primarily to serve the interests of individual consumers. Sub-clause (*d*) of this clause seeks to amend the definition of "manufacturer" to include any manufacturer who assembles

---

1 Inserted by the Consumer Protection (Amendment) Act, 2002, w.e.f. 15-3-2003.

goods from parts made by others or puts his mark on any goods made or manufactured by any other manufacturer whether he claims such goods to be manufactured by himself or not. Sub-clause (*e*) of this clause seeks to enlarge the definition of "restrictive trade practice". to mean manipulation of price or delivery or flow of supplies leading to unjustified cost and restriction on the consumers and includes delay beyond the agreed period which has led or is likely to lead to rise in the price. Sub-clause (*h*) of this clause also seeks to enlarge the definition of "unfair trade practice" to include withholding of information about final results of any scheme offering gifts, prizes, or other items free of charge, and manufacture of spurious goods and sale of spurious goods or adoption of deceptive practices in the provision of services. Sub-clause (*g*) seeks to define "spurious goods and services" as goods and services which are claimed to be genuine but are actually not so. Sub-clause (*e*) seeks to define "regulation" as regulation made by the National Commission. Sub-clause if) further seeks to bring more clarity to the definition of "service" by clarifying that the services mentioned are only illustrative.

COMMENT ON SECTION 2(1)(*a*)

What is an appropriate laboratory under the Act

Section 2(1)(*a*) of the Act defines an "appropriate laboratory" as a laboratory or organisation—

(*i*) recognised by the Central Government;

(*ii*) recognised by a State Government, subject to such guidelines as may be prescribed by the Central Government in this behalf; or

(*iii*) any such laboratory or organisation established by or under any law for the time being in force, which is maintained, financed or aided by the Central Government or a State Government for carrying out analysis or test of any goods with a view to determining whether such goods suffer from any defect.

Note.—Rule 2A of the Consumer Protection Rules, 1987 provides the procedure to be followed by the laboratories in order to get recognition from the States.

COMMENT ON SECTION 2(1)(*a*)(*iii*)

Where Laboratory Test is Required to Determine the Defect in Goods

A consumer is supposed to file as many copies of the complaint as there are number of judges, with all essential information, supporting papers like correspondence and specifying the compensation demanded.

On receipt of such complaint—

(*a*) The District Forum should refer a copy of the complaint to the opposite party directing him to give his version of the case within a period of thirty days which can be extended to forty five days.

Where the opposite party on receipt of a complaint referred to him denies or disputes the allegations contained in the complaint, or omits or fails to take any action to represent his case within the time given by the District Forum, the District Forum would take the following steps to settle the dispute:

(*b*) The District Forum may require the complainant to deposit specified fees for payment to the appropriate laboratory for carrying out the necessary analysis or test in relation to the goods in question.

(*c*) The District Forum will obtain a sample of the goods, seal it, authenticate it and refer the sample so sealed to the appropriate laboratory for an analysis or test, whichever may be necessary, with a view to finding out whether such goods suffer from any defect.

The District Forum will remit the fees to the appropriate laboratory to enable it to carry out required analysis or test.

The laboratories supposed to report its findings to the District Forum within a period of fifty-five days. This period is extendible by the District Forum.

(*d*) Upon receiving laboratory's report, its copy will be forwarded by the District Forum to the opposite party along with its own remarks.

(*e*) In the event of any party disputing the correctness of the findings, or the methods of analysis or test adopted by the appropriate laboratory, the District Forum shall require the objecting party to submit his objections in writing.

(*f*) The District Forum will give an opportunity of hearing to the objecting party.

(*g*) The District Forum shall issue appropriate order after hearing the parties.

Where No Laboratory test is Required to Determine the Defect in Goods or the Complaint Relates to Services

(*a*) On receiving the complaint, the District Forum should refer a copy of the complaint to the opposite party directing him to give his version of the case within a period of thirty days which can be extended to forty-five days.

(*b*) The opposite party on receipt of a complaint referred to him may—

(*i*) Admit the complaint,

(*ii*) Deny or dispute the allegations contained in the complaint, or

(*iii*) Omits or fails to respond within the time given by the District Forum.

(*c*) Where the opposite party admits the allegation, the District Forum should decide the matter on the basis of the merits of the case and the documents before it.

Where the opposite party denies or disputes the allegations made in the complaint, the District Forum will proceed to settle the dispute on the basis of evidence brought to its notice by both the parties.

Where the opposite party omits or fails to respond within the time given by the Forum, the District Forum will proceed to settle the dispute on the basis of evidence brought to its notice by the complainant.

(*d*) The District Forum shall issue an appropriate order after hearing the parties and taking into account available evidence.

Note.—Although this procedure may be followed by all — the District Forum, State Commission, and National Commission, we have used the name of 'District Forum' while describing the procedure.

COMMENT ON SECTION 2(1)(*b*)

Complaint

An aggrieved consumer seeks redressal under the Act through the instrumentality of complaint. It does not mean that the consumer can complain against his each and every problem. The Act has provided certain grounds on which complaint can be made. Similarly, relief against these complaints can be granted within the set pattern.

COMMENT ON SECTION 2(*b*)

Who can file a complaint [Sections 2(*b*) and 12]?

At the outset it is clear that a person who can be termed as a consumer under the Act can make a complaint. To be specific on this account, following are the persons who can file a complaint under the Act:

(*a*) a consumer; or

(*b*) any voluntary consumer association registered under the Companies Act, 1956 or under any other law for the time being in force, or

(*c*) the Central Government or any State Government,

(*d*) one or more consumers, where there are numerous consumers having the same interest.

In addition to the above following are also considered as a consumer and hence they may file a complaint:

Legal representative of the deceased consumer: The Act does not expressly indicate that the LRs of a consumer are also included in its scope. But by operation of law, the legal representatives get clothed with the rights, status and personality of the deceased. Thus the expression consumer would include legal representative of the deceased consumer and he can exercise his right for the purpose of enforcing the cause of action which has devolved on him. [*Cosmopolitan Hospital* v *Smt. Vasantha P. Nair* (1) 1992 CPJ NC 302]

Legal heirs of the deceased consumer: A legal heir of the deceased consumer can well maintain a complaint under the Act. [*Joseph Alias Animon* v *Dr. Elizabeth Zachariah* (1) 1997 CPJ 96]

Husband of the consumer: In the Indian conditions, women may be illiterate, educated women may be unaware of their legal rights, thus a husband can file and prosecute complaint under the Consumer Protection Act on behalf of his spouse. [*Punjab National Bank, Bombay* v *K.B. Shetty* 1991 (2) CPR 633]

A relative of consumer: When a consumer signs the original complaint, it can be initiated by his/her relative. [*Motibai Dalvi Hospital* v *M.I. Govilkar* 1992 (1) CPR 408]

Insurance company: Where Insurance Company pays and settles the claim of the insured and the insured person transfers his rights in the insured goods to the company, it can file a complaint for the loss caused to the insured goods by negligence of goods/service providers. For example, when loss is caused to such goods because of negligence of transport company, the insurance company can file a claim against the transport company. [*New India Assurance Company Ltd.* v *Green Transport Co.* II 1991 CPJ (1) Delhi]

COMMENT ON SECTION 2(1)(*c*)

What constitutes a complaint

Complaint is a statement made in writing to the National Commission, the State Commission or the District Forum by a person competent to file it, containing the allegations in detail and with a view to obtain relief provided under the Act.

What a complaint must contain

A complaint must contain any of the following allegations:

(*a*) An unfair trade practice or a restrictive trade practice has been adopted by any trader;

Example: A sold a six months old car to B representing it to be a new one. Here B can make a complaint against A for following an unfair trade practice.

(*b*) The goods bought by him or agreed to be bought by him suffer from one or more defects;

Example: A bought a computer from B. It was not working properly since day one. A can make a complaint against B for supplying him a defective computer.

(*c*) The services hired or availed of or agreed to be hired or availed of by him suffer from deficiency in any respect.

Example: A hired services of an advocate to defend himself against his landlord. The advocate did not appear every time the case was scheduled. A can make a complaint against the advocate.

(*d*) A trader has charged for the goods mentioned in the complaint a price in excess of the price fixed by or under any law for the time being in force or displayed on the goods or any package containing such goods.

Example: A bought a sack of cement from B who charged him ₹100 over and above the reserve price of the cement declared by the Government. Here A can make a complaint against B.

(*e*) Goods which will be hazardous to life and safety when used are being offered for sale to the public in contravention of the provisions of any law for the time being in force requiring traders to display information in regard to the contents, manner and effect of use of such goods.

Example: 'A' bought a tin of disinfectant powder. It had lid which was to be opened in a specific manner. Trader did not inform 'A' about this. While opening the lid in ordinary way, some powder flew in the eyes of A which affected his vision. Here 'A' can make a complaint against the trader.

COMMENT ON SECTION 2(1) (*c*)(*v*)

Hazardous Goods

The term "Hazardous goods' has not been defined in the Act. The dictionary meaning of the term is — dangerous or risky. However, the term is used in context of 'goods' only, i.e., a person can make a complaint if he is not informed about the hazardous nature of the goods but the same is not true in case of hazardous services.

The rationale behind this provision is to ensure physical safety of the consumers. The law seeks to ensure that those responsible for bringing goods to the market, in particular, suppliers, exporters, importers, retailers and the like should ensure that while in their care these goods are not rendered unsafe through improper handling or storage.

Consumers should be instructed in the proper use of goods and should be informed of the risks involved in intended or normally foreseeable use. Vital safety information should be conveyed to consumers.

Example: 'A' bought an insecticide from 'B'. 'B' did not inform 'A' that touching this insecticide with bare hands can create skin problem. 'A', while using the insecticide came in contact with it and suffered from skin problem consequently. Here 'B' can be held liable under the Act.

COMMENT ON SECTION 2(1)(*d*)

Beneficiary of the goods/services

The definition of consumer itself includes beneficiary of goods and services. [*K.B. Jayalaxmi* v *Government of Tamil Nadu* 1994 (1) CPR 114]

(*i*) Where a young child is taken to the hospital by his parents and the child is treated by the doctor, the parents of such a minor child can file a complaint under the Act. [*Spring Meadows Hospital* v *Harjot Ahluwalia* JT 1998 (2) SC 620]

(*ii*) Persons buying goods either for re-sale or for use in large scale profit making activity will not be `consumers' entitled to protection under the Act. [*Raj Kumar* v *S.C. Verma* 2001 (1) CPR 437]

(*iii*) The government servants and the staff of the Accountant General Office of the Comptroller and Auditor General maintains the records of provident fund of government servants, issue slips of deposits of fund and on retirement final payments are made to the subscribers. The government servants and the staff of the Accountant General in discharging their duties does not render any service for consideration, nor hiring of any service is involved hence, maintenance of General Provident Fund Accounts does not fall within the meaning of 'service'. [*Hari Vallabh Vijay* v *Administration Officer* 2001 (1) CPR 529]

(*iv*) When the National Commission as a matter of fact, recorded the findings as to the discharge of the liability of the carrier, the Supreme Court did not interfere on the issue. [*Saddler Shoes Pvt. Ltd.* v *Air India* (2001) 8 SCC 390]

(*v*) The insurance company is not a consumer. Hence the consumer complaint by insurance company is not maintainable. [*Savani Road Lines* v *Sundaram Textiles Ltd.* AIR 2001 SC 2630]

(*vi*) The repudiation of the claim by the Insurance Company on the ground that the driver was not holding a valid driving license at the time of the accident could not be termed as deficiency in service or negligence on the part of the Insurance Company within the meaning of section 2(*g*) of the Act. [*New India Assurance Co. Ltd.* v *Pushpa Yashwant Ghatge* I996 NCJ 195]

(*vii*) Medical services are covered under the definition of "service". Service includes rendering of consultation, diagnosis and treatment, both medical and surgical. [*Indian Medical Association* v *V.P. Shantha* 1995 SCALE 273]

(*viii*) "Contract of personal service" has to be distinguished from a "contract for personal service". In the absence of relationship of master and servant between the patient and the medical practitioner, the service rendered by a medical practitioner to the patient cannot be regarded as service rendered under a contract of personal service. It is "contract for personal services". Wherever, there is relationship like that of master and servant it is a "contract of personal service" and is excluded from the purview of the Act. [*Indian Medical Association* v *V.P. Shantha* 1995 SCALE 273]

(*ix*) A licensee to run a phone is not a consumer. [*Technocombine Associates* v *Union of India* I (1994) CPJ 481: 1994 (I) CPR 298]

(*x*) A lottery ticket holder is not "consumer" within the ambit of the definition of "consumer" under the Act. [*Jagdish Chand* v *Director, Sikkim State Lottery* 1994 (I) CPR 213]

(*xi*) Applicant who merely applies for allotment of shares is not a consumer. [*HG Bhatia* v *ABC Computers Pvt. Ltd.* 1994 (I) CPR 316]

(*xii*) The beneficial consumer jurisdiction cannot be extended to lotteries and wagering transactions or consequential rights flowing from void contracts. [*Jagdish Chand* v *Director, Sikkim State Lotteries* 1994 (I) CPR 213]

(*xiii*) If somebody does not perform his part of the contract, it amount/s to deficiency in service. [*Ramala Roy* v *Rabindra Nath Sen* 1994 (I) CPR 66]

(*xiv*) The agreement for hypothecation does not create the ownership right, and as such no complaint can be maintained for deficiency in service. [*Jayantial Keshavlal Chauhan* v *National Insurance Co. Ltd.* 1994 (I) CPR 390]

(*xv*) Undue delay in declaration of examination result is obviously deficiency in service. [*Secretary, Board of School Education, Haryana* v *Mukesh Chand* 1994 (I) CPR 269]

(*xvi*) The student is a consumer of service of educational institute. [*Sushant Yuvaraj Rode* v *Shri Ramdeobaba Engineering College* 1993 (III) CPR 624]

(*xvii*) A person who receives medical treatment in a Government hospital is not a consumer under the Act; *Consumer Unity & Trust Society* v *State of Rajasthan* (1991) I CPR 241. However, the State Commission of Orissa held that a patient is a Consumer being the beneficiary of services in as much as the State Government is paying the consideration amount in the form of salary to the doctors and hospital staff. [*Sukanti Behera* v *Dr. Sashi Bhusan Rath* II (1993) CPJ 633]

(*xviii*) Subscriber of a law reporter, is not a consumer. [*Delhi Law Times Office* v *Jagdish Prasad* (1996) 2 CPJ 78 (Bihar)] (*xix*) A doctor will not be guilty of negligence if he has acted in accordance with the practice accepted as proper by a responsible body of medical men skilled in that particular art and if he has acted in accordance with such practice then merely because there is a body of opinion that takes a contrary view will not make him liable for negligence. [*Vinitha Ashok* v *Lakshmi Hospital* (2001) 8 SCC 731]

(*xx*) An insurer compensating the consignor for loss of goods during transit and having as assignment, is not beneficiary of the services hired by the consignor from the carrier; insurer being not a consumer, could not maintain a complaint against the carrier of the goods. Even the addition of the consignor as a co-complainant would not enable the insurer to maintain such a complaint. [*Oberai Forwarding Agency* v *New India Assurance Co. Ltd.* AIR. 2000 SC 855; *Savani Road Lines* v *Sundaram Textiles Ltd.* AIR 2001 SC 2630]

(*xxi*) Institution of suit or other proceedings in a Civil Court after payment of "Court-fee" cannot be said to be equal to "hiring" or "availing of" service of a Court after paying consideration and, thus, complaint is not maintainable before consumer forum on ground that there were deficiencies in set up of the civil judicial administration. [*Akhil Bhartiya Grahak Panchayat* v *State of Gujarat* (1994) 1 CPJ 114 (NC)]

(*xxii*) In absence of terms in lease for cleaning, repairing and maintenance of building by the landlord, held, tenant cannot be said to be a consumer so as to maintain a claim for compensation against the landlord for omission to render said services. [*Laxmiben Laxmichand Shah* v *Sakerben Kanji Chandan* (2001) 9 SCC 604]

(*xxiii*) Consumer forums have jurisdiction to entertain complaint against common carrier regarding loss of or damage to goods entrusted to carrier for transportation. [*Patel Roadways Ltd.* v *Birla Yamaha Ltd.* AIR 2000 SC 1461]

(*xxiv*) An employee, who is a Member of Employees' Provident Fund Scheme, is a consumer and duties performed by Regional Provident Fund Commissioner under such scheme is "service" and, thus, in case of delay in release of provident fund, complaint for deficiency in service, is maintainable. [*Regional Provident Fund Commissioner* v *Shiv Kumar Joshi* AIR 2000 SC 331]

(*xxv*) C.T. scan machine, etc., of a charitable trust, running a diagnostic centre wherein patients taking advantage of C.T. scan, etc., are required to pay for the same and only ten per cent, of them are provided free service, can be said to be meant for "commercial purpose". [*Kalpavruksha Charitable Trust* v *Toshniwal Brothers (Bombay) (Fvt.) Ltd.* AIR 1999 SC 3356] (*xxvi*) Where Advocate had rendered service free of charge and without compensation, held, a claim for compensation against him for deficiency in service, was not maintainable. [*G. Swaminathan* v *E. Kumar* (1991) 1 MWN (CP) 71 (TN)]

(*xxvii*) A Railway passenger is a "consumer". [*Basanta Kumar Sahoo* v *Chief Commercial Manager* (1998) 3 CPJ 286 (Ori.)]

(*xxviii*) A person registering himself for release of LPG connection with the distributor is a "consumer", though at that time he pays nothing and the payment is deferred till the time of release of gas connection. [*Dharam Chand* v *Mandeep Gas Service* (1993) 2 CPJ 985 (Punj.)]

(*xxix*) Nominee under a policy of life insurance is a "consumer". [*Jagdish Prasad Dagar* v *Senior Divisional Manager, LIC* (1992) 2 CPJ 493 (NC)]

(*xxx*) A person using electricity for a commercial purpose is a "consumer". [*Sub-Divisional Officer, H.S.E.B.* v *Sita Ram* (1992) 2 CPJ 819 (Haryana)]

(*xxxi*) A person who purchased large quantity of rice, cannot considered as a "consumer", as such a large quantity cannot be for self-consumption but for re-sale. [*Shri Lakshmi Narayan Rice Mill* v *Food Corporation of India* (1996) 1 CPJ 161 (NC)]

Following are some of instances of "commercial purpose" and, thus, not treated as "consumer":—

(*i*) Purchase of vehicle for running it as taxi. [*Pushpa Meena* v *Shah Enterprises* (*Rajasthan*) *Ltd.* (1992) 1 CPJ 271 (Raj.)]

(*ii*) Purchase of goods for re-sale. [*Zohia Starlinger Ltd.* v *Zenith Computers Ltd.* (1991) 1 CPJ 145 (NC)]

(*iii*) Purchase of V.C.R. for running video parlour. [*Assistant Manager, BPL India* v *S.R. Tushar* (1991) 1 CPJ 155]

(*iv*) Grant of Stage carriage permit. [In re *State Transport Authority* (1992) 2 CPJ 677 (Cal)]

(*v*) Purchase of Photocopier for commercial purpose. [*Ram Singh* v *Branch Manager, Kores India Ltd.* (2001) 1 CPJ 480 (Raj)]

(*vi*) Purchase of Ultra Sound Scanner Machine. [*Network Ltd.* v *Vijay Prakash Goyal* (1998) 3 CPJ 674 (UP)]

(*vii*) Persons buying goods either for re-sale or for use in large scale profit making activity will not be 'consumers' entitled to protection under the Act. [*Raj Kumar* v *S.C. Verma* 2001 (1) CPR 437]

(*viii*) The insurance company is not a consumer. Hence the consumer complaint by Insurance Company is not maintainable. [*Savant Road Lines* v *Sundaram Textiles Ltd.* AIR 2001 SC 2630] (*ix*) A licensee to run a phone is not a consumer. [*Technocombine Associates* v *Union of India* I (1994) CPJ 481: 1994 (I) CPR 298]

(*x*) A lottery ticket holder is not "consumer" within the ambit of the definition of "consumer" under the Act. [*Jagdish Chand* v *Director, Sikkim State Lottery* 1994 (I) CPR 213]

(*xi*) Applicant who merely applies for allotment of shares is not a consumer. [*H.G Bhatia* v *ABC Computers Pvt. Ltd.* 1994 (I) CPR 316]

However the following are also consumers:

The beneficial consumer jurisdiction cannot be extended to lotteries and wagering transactions or consequential rights flowing from void contracts. [*Jagdish Chand* v *Director, Sikkim State Lotteries* 1994 (I) CPR 213]

The student is a consumer of service of educational institute. [*Sushant Yuvaraj Rode* v *Shri Ramdeobaba Engineering College* 1993 (III) CPR 624]

A person who receives medical treatment in a Government hospital is not a consumer under the Act; *Consumer Unity & Trust Society* v *State of Rajasthan* (1991) 1 CPR 241. However, the State Commission of Orissa held that a patient is a Consumer being the beneficiary of services in as much as the State Government is paying the consideration amount in the form of salary to the doctors and hospital staff. [*Sukanti Behera* v *Dr. Sashi Bhusan Rath* II (1993) CPJ 633]

COMMENT ON SECTION 2(1)(*g*)

What is meant by "deficiency" in service

Section 2(1)(*g*) of the Act provides that, "deficiency" means any fault, imperfection, shortcoming or inadequacy in the quality, nature and manner of performance which is required to be maintained by or under any law for the time being in force or has been undertaken to be performed by a person in pursuance of a contract or otherwise in relation to any service.

Reading the above definition by breaking it into elements, we get—

(*a*) "deficiency" means any fault, imperfection, shortcoming or inadequacy in the quality, nature and manner of performance.

Examples:

1. 'A' boarded a train. The compartment in which he and his wife travelled was in a bad shape-fans not working, shutters of windows were not working, rexin of the upper berth was badly torn and there were rusty nails which caused some injuries to the wife of 'A'. 'A' made a complaint against the railway department. It was held that the complaint constituted 'deficiency in service' and the compensation of ₹1500 was

awarded to 'A'. [*General Manager, South Eastern Railway* v *Anand Prasad Sinha* I (1991) CPJ 10 (12) NC]

2. Dr. 'A' treated 'P' under Allopathic system, though he himself was a Homoeopathic practitioner. Later on 'P' alleged 'A' for wrong treatment. The Commission held it as deficiency in service. [*Poonam Verma* v *Ashwin Patel* (1996) II CPJ 1 SC]

3. 'A' booked a car for 'B' and promised to deliver it within one month of booking. The car was not delivered even after four months. Here 'A' could be held liable for deficiency in service. One interesting aspect is that deficiency in service should occur during the happening of performance. Thus it is crucial to determine when the performance of a service commenced.

   Example: 'A' contracted with 'B' to supply, erect and commission cold rolling mill. 'A' supplied the mill, but failed to erect and commission the mill. B filed a suit alleging deficiency of service on 'A's' failure to elect and commission the mill. The National Commission observed that the deficiency must pertain to performance of service. Since 'A' never started erecting and commissioning the mill, the question of performance did not arise. Thus the case is not that of deficiency of service. [*Jaipur Metals & Electricals Ltd.* v *Laxmi Inds.* (1991) II CPJ 602 (NC)]

(*b*) Such quality and manner of performance of service should have been required to be maintained by or under any law for the time being in force or undertaken to be performed by a person in pursuance of a contract or otherwise.

Example: 'A', the builder, promised under written agreement to provide a flat to 'B'. Subsequently, he expressed his inability to give possession of the flat and entered into a fresh agreement to pay ₹9,51,000 to 'B' in place of flat. 'A' didn't even pay this money. 'B' sued 'A'. The Commission held that since 'A' had not even paid the money as per subsequent contract, the rights of earlier contract can be involved by 'B'. And that there was a deficiency of service on the part of builders. [*Lata Construction* v *Dr. Rameshchandra Ramniklal Shah* AIR 2000 SC 380 (384)]

(*c*) The deficiency must be in relation to a service. The words '.... in relation to any service' in the definition signifies that the deficiency is always in terms of service. Thus if the grievance pertains to a matter which does not fall in the definition of service, the concept of deficiency would not apply.

Example: 'A' deposited ₹100 with 'B' as application fee and executed bond for the purpose of drilling tubewell. 'B' did not drill the tubewell because it was not feasible. 'A' alleged deficiency in service. It was held that depositing ₹100 as application fee and executing a bond does not amount to hiring of services, thus the deficiency of service cannot be complained of in the matter. [*Mangilal* v *Chairman, District Rural Development Agency* (1991) 1 CPJ 474 (Raj.)]

Deficiency in service due to circumstances beyond control

In normal course, if the service is found deficient as per the above criteria, it is held deficient and the compensation is awarded. However there may be abnormal circumstances beyond the control of the person performing service. If such circumstances prevent a person from rendering service of the desired quality, nature and the manner, such person should not be penalized for the same.

Example: 'A' undertook to supply water to 'B' for irrigation of crops. Due to power grid failure of the State, 'A' could not get sufficient power to perform the service. Here 'A' cannot be held liable for deficiency in service.

However, negligence on the part of performer may not be excused under the cover of circumstances beyond control.

Example: 'A' agreed to supply water to 'B' for irrigation of crops. He failed to do so because of a power breakdown due to burning of transformer. As a result crops damaged. 'B' sued 'A' for providing deficient service. The National Commission held that it was duty of 'A' to get the transformer repaired immediately. Since he was negligent in doing so, he is liable for the deficiency in service. [*Orissa Lift Irrigation Corpn. Ltd.* v *Birakishore Raut* (1991) 2 CPJ 213 (NC)]

COMMENT ON [SECTION 2(1)(*i*) AND (*f*)]

Goods and Defect

A consumer can make complaint when he comes across defective goods. Here it is required to understand what are the items, which can be considered as 'goods' and what constitutes 'defect' under the Act.

Goods: The Consumer Protection Act does not define the term 'Goods'. It says that — "goods" means goods as defined in the Sale of Goods Act, 1930.

Section 2(7) of the Sale of Goods Act, 1930, defines 'goods' as — "Goods means every kind of movable property other than actionable claims and money; and includes stock and shares, growing crops, grass, and things attached to or forming part of the land which are agreed to be severed before sale or under the contract of sale."

The definition reveals that—

(*a*) Goods must be movable;

(*b*) Things attached to or forming part of land which can be severed satisfy the movability criteria;

(*c*) Actionable claim and Money have been specifically excluded from definition of goods.

Defect: Section 2(1)(*f*) of the Act provides that, "defect" means any fault, imperfection or shortcoming in the quality, quantity, potency, purity or standard which is required to be maintained by or under any law of the time being in force under any contract, express or implied or as is claimed by the trader in any manner whatsoever in relation to any goods.

This is an exhaustive definition. It means that the Act recognizes only those defects which are covered by the definition. Any type of defect not mentioned here will not be entertained by Consumer Forums. Moreover the defect has to be in relation to goods only, i.e., if an item does not fall within the definition of 'Goods', no defect can be complained therein. However, the coverage of this definition is very wide.

Examples:

1. A Pressure Cooker burst and caused injury to the user. It was held to be a manufacturing defect. [*T.T. (P.) Ltd.* v *Akhil Bhartiya Grahak Panchayat* II (1996) CPJ 239 NC]
2. Failure to handover registration book along with jeep purchased by complainant is a defect. [*Ramesh Chandra* v *Commercial Tax Officer* (1993) 3 CPR 182 (Ori.)]
3. Where laboratory test report showed that soft drink was not fit for human consumption, it was held defective. [*Narayanan Vyankatkrishnan Iyengar* v *Shakti Foods* (1994) 2 CPJ 652 (Mah)]
4. Rape seed oil adulterated with toxic substances, which led to paralysis of limbs and other disabilities, has been considered as defective. [*Barsad Ali* v *MD, West Bengal Essential Commodities Supply Corporation Ltd.* (1993) 1 CPR 217 WB]
5. Electric household appliances which are not in accordance with the standards prescribed by ISI, being unsafe are defective. [*Farooq Hazi Ismail Saya* v *Gavabhai Bhesania* (1991) 2 CPJ 452 (Guj)]
6. Gas Cylinder with excessive gas is defective goods. [*Dayanand A Avasare* v *Bharat Petroleum Corporation Ltd.* (1993) 1 CPR 278 (Mah)]
7. Development of cracks of half inch to three and a half inch in walls and mosaic floor in a flat after taking possession from a Housing Board. [*R. Shanmugasundaram* v *Tamil Nadu Housing Board* (1998) 1 CPJ 96 NC]
8. A supplied white marble to B. Later on the colour of the marble changed. B sued a alleging supply of defective marble. It was held that A should have expressly told B that the marble would not retain its colour when polished. In the absence of such assertion,

it is deemed that A made B to understand that the marble would retain its white colour and when the colour changed, it comes within the scope of 'defect' in goods under the Act. [*Chitranjan Sahu* v *N.C. Jain* II (1993) CPJ 1127 (Ori)]

9. 'A' sold a stolen car to 'B'. 'B' wanted to sue 'A' for defect in the title of the car. Here 'B' cannot sue 'A' under the Consumer Protection Act as the defect in title of goods would not constitute defective goods as defined under the Act.

Consumer of goods: The provision of section 2(*d*) of the Consumer Protection Act reveals that a person claiming himself as a consumer of goods should satisfy that—

THE GOODS ARE BOUGHT FOR CONSIDERATION — There must be a sale transaction between a seller and a buyer; the sale must be of goods; the buying of goods must be for consideration. The terms sale, goods, and consideration have not been defined in the Consumer Protection Act. The meaning of the terms 'sale', and 'goods' is to be construed according to the Sale of Goods Act, and the meaning of the term 'consideration' is to be construed according to the Indian Contract Act.

ANY PERSON WHO USE THE GOODS WITH THE APPROVAL OF THE BUYER IS A CONSUMER — When a person buys goods, they may be used by his family members, relatives and friends. Any person who is making actual use of the goods may come across the defects in goods. Thus the law construes users of the goods as consumers although they may not be buyers at the same time. The words "....with the approval of the buyer" in the definition denotes that the user of the goods should be a rightful user.

Example: 'A' purchased a scooter which was in 'B's' possession from the date of purchase. 'B' was using it and taking it to the seller for repairs and service from time to time. Later on 'B' had a complaint regarding the scooter. He sued the seller. The seller pleaded that since 'B' did not buy the scooter, he was not a consumer under the Act. The Delhi State Commission held that B, the complainant was using it with the approval of A, the buyer, and therefore he was consumer under the Act. [*Dinesh Bhagat* v *Bajaj Auto Ltd.* (1992) III CPJ 272]

Note.—This is an exception to the general rule of law that a stranger to a contract cannot sue.

ANY PERSON WHO OBTAINS THE GOODS FOR 'RESALE' OR COMMERCIAL PURPOSES' IS NOT A CONSUMER — The term 'for resale' implies that the goods are brought for the purpose of selling them, and the expression 'for commercial purpose' is intended to cover cases other than those of resale of goods. When goods are bought to resell or commercially exploit them, such buyer or user is not a consumer under the Act.

Examples:

1. A jeep was purchased to run it as a taxi. The question was whether the buyer of the jeep was a consumer under the Act. The Rajasthan State Commission held that to use the jeep as a taxi with the object to earn profits was a commercial purpose, and therefore, the buyer/user was not a consumer within the meaning of the Act. [*Smt. Pushpa Meena* v *Shah Enterprises* (*Rajasthan*) *Ltd.* (1991) 1 CPR 229]
2. 'L Ltd.' purchased a computer system from 'Z'. The computer system was giving constant trouble and 'Z' was not attending it properly. 'L Ltd.' filed a complaint against 'Z' with the National Commission. 'Z' contended that 'L Ltd.' was not a consumer under the Act because computer system was used for commercial purposes. 'L Ltd.' argued that computer system was not directly used of commercial purposes rather it was used to facilitate the work of the company. The Commission rejected the argument on the grounds that the system made part of the assets of the company, and its expenses were met by it out of business income. Thus the said purchase was a purchase for commercial purposes and 'L Ltd'. was held not to be a consumer under the Act.

One thing is plain and clear from the decided cases that what is important to decide is — Whether a particular good is used for commercial purposes. If it is the buyer/user is not a consumer and if it is not — the buyer/user is a consumer.

PERSON BUYING GOODS FOR SELF EMPLOYMENT IS A CONSUMER — When goods are bought for commercial purposes and such purchase satisfy the following criteria:

— the goods are used by the buyer himself;

— exclusively for the purpose of earning his livelihood;

— by means of self-employment,

then such use would not be termed as use for commercial purposes under the Act, and the user is recognised as a consumer.

Examples:

1. 'A' buys a truck for plying it as a public carrier by himself, 'A' is a consumer.
2. 'A' buys a truck and hires a driver to ply it, 'A' is not a consumer.
3. 'A' has one cloth shop. He starts another business of a photocopier and buys a photocopy machine therefore. He hasn't bought this machine exclusively for the purpose of earning livelihood. He is not a consumer under the Act.

Note.—That this is an exception to the rule that a buyer of commercial goods is not a consumer under the Act.

The intention of the legislature is to exclude big business houses carrying on business with profit motive from the purview of the Act. At the same time it is pertinent to save the interests of small consumers who buy goods for self employment to earn their livelihood, like a rickshaw puller buying rickshaw for self employment, or a farmer purchasing fertilizer for his crops, or a taxi driver buying a car to run it as a taxi, etc.

Example: 'A' was running a small type institute to earn his livelihood. He purchased a photocopy machine-Canon NP 150. It proved defective. He sued the seller who contended that A is not a consumer under the Act as he purchased the photocopier for commercial use. The Commission held that by no stretch of imagination it can be said that the photocopier would bring large scale profits to A. It was a part of his small scale enterprise. He was construed as consumer under the Act.

However, if such a buyer takes assistance of two or more persons to help him in operating the vehicle or machine, etc., he does not cease to be a consumer.

Examples:

1. 'A' buys a truck, ply it himself and hires a cleaner who accompany him all the time and at times drives also when 'A' is busy otherwise, 'A' is a consumer.
2. 'P', an eye surgeon, purchased a machine from 'R' for the hospital run by him. The machine was found to be a defective one. 'R' contended that 'P' was not a consumer under the Act as the machine was bought for commercial purposes. The National Commission rejected this contention and held that 'P' is a medical practitioner, a professional working by way of self employment by using his knowledge and skill to earn his livelihood. It was not proved by any evidence that 'P' is running a huge hospital. Thus the purchase of machinery is in the nature of self employment. [*Rampion Pharmaceuticals* v *Dr. Preetam Shah* (1997) I CPJ 23 (NCDRC)]

(*i*) Persons who are allotted plots or houses by the Housing and Development Board for consideration are consumer under the Act. [*U.P. Avas Evam Vikas Parishad* v *Garima Shukla* (1991) 1 CPR 387]

(*ii*) A person who receives medical treatment in a Government hospital is not a consumer under the Act. *Consumer Unity & Trust Society* v *State of Rajasthan* (1991) 1 CPR 241. However, the State Commission of Orissa held that a patient is a Consumer being the beneficiary of services in as much as the State Government is paying the consideration amount in the form of salary to the Doctors and hospital staff. [II (1993) CPJ 633] (*iii*) A person who purchases goods for consideration for any commercial purpose is not a consumer under the Act. [*M/s Lohia Starlings Ltd.* v *Zenith Computers Ltd.* (1991) 1 CPR 389]

(*iv*) A patient getting treatment at a private nursing home is availing services. [(1992) I CPR 41]

(*v*) A purchase made for use in self-employment is not for commercial purpose and the purchaser is a Consumer. [1992 (2) CPR 355]

(*vi*) Payment of tax which goes into the general revenue of the State or local authority will not legally constitute payment of consideration for any specific service. [*A Srinivas Murthi* v *Hariman, Bangalore Development Authority,* (1991) 1 CPR 529 (NO); *Consumer Unity and Trust Society* v *State of Rajasthan* (1991) 1 CRP 241 (NC)]

(*vii*) The maintenance of public roads and highways by the Government may be considered to be a service but the road using public cannot be considered to have hired this service for consideration. [*S.M.N. Consumer Protection Council* v *Chief Engineer, Highways and Rural Works* (1992) 1 CPR 107 (Mad)]

(*viii*) A person who goes to receive medical treatment in a Government Hospital is not a consumer. [*Consumer Unity and Trust Society* v *State of Rajasthan* (1991) I CPR 241 (NC). **See also** *V.P. Kunhikannan* v *E.K. Varghese* (1991) 2 CPR 41 (Ker)]

(*ix*) The word "hire" means to acquire the temporary use of a thing or the services of a person in exchange for payment (Collins English Dictionary), to engage the temporary use for a fixed sum (Webster), to procure the use of services of, at a price; to grant temporary use of for compensation (Chambers). This is the ordinary, plain, grammatical meaning of the expression hire and it is only in this sense the word has been used in section 2(1)(*d*)(*ii*) of the Act. [*Consumer Unity and Trust Society* v *State of Rajasthan* (1991)1 CPR 241 (NC)]

(*x*) The exception contained in relation to goods purchased for commercial purpose or for resale contained in sub-clause (*i*) is not applicable to sub-clause (*ii*) of clause (*d*) in section 2 of the Act. *Universal Health Services Pvt. Ltd.* v *Pertech Computers Ltd.* (1991) 1 CPR 506 (Bom). In order that the exclusion clause should apply, it is necessary that there should be a close nexus between the transaction of purchase of goods and the large scale activity carried on for earning profit. [*Synco*

Textiles Pvt. Ltd. v *Greaves Cotton and Co.* (1991) 1 CPR 165 (NC)]

(*xi*) The definition of consumer contemplates pre-existence of completed transaction of sale. Mere agreement for purchase is not enough. [*M.N. Narsimha Reddy* v *Managing Director, Maruti Udyog Ltd., F.A.No. 67* of 1990, decided on 20-12-1990 (NC)]

(*xii*) A person, other then the original consumer who hires any services, namely a beneficiary thereof, can also maintain a complaint under the Act. *B.S. Sidhu* v *Secretary, Central Government Post & Telegraph Department* (1991) 2 CPJ 90 (Har). A person who availed the service with the approval of person who hired the services is also protected under the Act. [*D.V. Lakshminarayana* v *Divisional Electrical Engineer* (1991) 1 CPR 9O (AP)]

(*xiii*) The following are consumers:

(*a*) S.B. Account holder of Bank. [*Branch Manager, Canara Bank* v *K.R. Hanumantha Rao* (1992) 1 CPR 134 (Mah)]

(*b*) A person who hires services of a travelling company. [*Aradhna Travel Services* v *Ramchandra* (1991) 1 CPR 134 (Mah)]

(*c*) Patient in a private nursing home is 'consumer'. [*Navaneethan* v *Rathinasami* (1992) 1 CPR 41 (Mad)]

(*d*) Holder of insurance policy. [*Akhil Bhartiya Grahak Panchayat* v *Chairman, LIC* (1991) 1CPJ171 (Bom); *Life Insurance Corporation of India* v *V. Krishnamoorthy* (1991) 2 CPR 160 (Ker)]

(*e*) Person availing service of Postal Department by paying postal charges. [*Koku Rajendra Prasad* v *Union of India*, (1991) 1 CPR 299 (AP)]

(*f*) Complainant who had deposited the amount at the time of booking the scooter. [*S. Rajashekar* v *Lohia Machine Ltd.* (1991) 1 CPR 480 (Kant)]

(*g*) An allottee of a flat from the Development Authority. [*Sneh Chanda* v *Delhi Development Authority* (1991) 1 CPR 532 (NC); *Civilal Sreedharan* v *Regional Engineer, Kerala State Housing Board* (1991) 2 CPR 243 (Ker); *Narayanan Unni* v *Administrative Officer, Kerala State Housing Board* (1991) 1 CPR 65 (Ker)]

(*h*) A person who takes insurance policy of goods booked through transport carrier. [*K.M. Ahmad Koya* v *United India Insurance Company Ltd.* (1991) 2 CPR 132 (TN)]

CONSIDERATION MUST BE PAID OR PAYABLE — Consideration is regarded necessary for hiring or availing of services. However, its payment need not necessarily be immediate. It can be in installments. For the services provided without charging anything in return, the person availing the services is not a consumer under the Act.

Examples:

1. 'A' hires an advocate to file a suit for recovery of money from his employer. He promises to pay fee to the advocate after settlement of the suit. 'A' is a consumer under the Act.
2. 'A' goes to a Doctor to get himself treated for a fracture. The Doctor being his friend charged him nothing for the treatment. 'A' is not a consumer under the Act.
3. 'B' issued an advertisement that a person could enter the contest by booking a Premier Padmini car. 'S' purchased the car and thus entered the contest. He was declared as winner of the draw and was thus entitled to the two tickets from New Delhi to New York and back. 'S' filed a complaint alleging that the ticket was not delivered to him. The National Commission held that 'S' was not a consumer in this context. He paid for the car and got it. 'B' was not liable so far as the contract of winning a lottery was concerned. [*Byford* v *S.S. Srivastava* (1993) II CPR 83 (NCDRC)]

The Direct and Indirect taxes paid to the State by a citizen is not payment for the services rendered.

Example: 'T' was paying property tax for his house to the local corporation. This corporation was responsible for proper water supply to the premises under its work area. 'T' raised a consumer dispute over the inadequacy of water supply by the corporation. The National Commission held that it was not a consumer dispute as water supply was made by the corporation out of its statutory duty and not by virtue of payment of taxes by 'T.'. [*Mayor, Calcutta Municipal Corporation* v *Tarapada Chatterjee* (1994) 1 CPR 87 (NCDRC)]

BENEFICIARY OF SERVICES IS ALSO A CONSUMER — When a person hires services, he may hire it for himself or for any other person. In such cases the beneficiary (or user) of these services is also a consumer.

Example.—'A' takes his son 'B' to a doctor for his treatment. Here 'A' is hirer of services of the doctor and 'B' is beneficiary of these services. For the purpose of the Act, both 'A' and 'B' are consumers.

Note.—This is an exception to the rule of privity to the contract.

Note that in case of goods, buyer of goods for commercial purpose ceases to be a consumer under the Act. On the other hand, a consumer of service for commercial purpose remains a consumer under the Act.

Example: 'A' applied to Electricity Board for electricity connection for a flour mill. There was a delay in releasing the connection. 'A' made a complaint for deficiency in service. He was held a consumer under the Act. [*Shamsher Khan* v *Rajasthan State Electricity Board* (1993) II CPR 6 (Raj)]

COMMENT ON SECTION 2(1)(*nn*)

What is a Restrictive Trade Practice

The Act provides that, "restrictive trade practice" means "any trade practice which requires a consumer to buy, hire or avail of any goods or, as the case may be, services as a condition precedent for buying, hiring or availing of other goods or services".

An analysis of above definition reveals that where sale or purchase of a product or service is made conditional on the sale or purchase of one or more other products and services, it amounts to restrictive trade practice.

Technically, this type of arrangement is called 'tie-up sales' or 'tying arrangement'. The effect of such an arrangement is that a purchaser is forced to buy some goods or services which he may not require alongwith the goods or services which he wants to buy. Thus where a buyer agrees to purchase product 'X' upon a condition that he will also purchase product 'Y' from the seller, the sale of product 'Y' (tied product) is tied to the sale of product 'X' (tying product).

The buyer has to forego his free choice between competing products. This results in neutralizing healthy competition in the 'tied' market.

Example: 'A,' a gas distributor instead his customers to buy gas stove as a condition to give gas connection. It was held that it was a restrictive trade practice. [Re. *Anand Gas* RTPE 43/1983 (MRTPC)]

However, where there is no such pre-condition and the buyer is free to take either product, no tying arrangement could be alleged even though the seller may offer both the products as a single unit at a composite price.

Example: 'A' is a furniture dealer. He is selling Sofa at ₹20,000 and Bed at ₹15,000. He has an offer that whoever will buy Sofa and Bed both, he will charge ₹30,000 only. Here the choice is open to the customer to buy the products single or composite. This is not a restrictive trade practice.

Note.—The term 'restrictive trade practice' has a very wide meaning when read in context of the MRTP Act, 1969. However under Consumer Protection Act, 1986, it has been used in a narrower sense.

COMMENT ON SECTION 2(1) (*o*) AND (*g*)

Service and Deficiency

When a service is found deficient by a consumer, he can make a complaint under the Act. Thus the prime requirement is that the matter must fall within the definition of service, and it must entail a deficiency as per the norms given by the Act.

What can be termed as a service

Section 2(1)(*o*) of the Act provides that "service" means service of any description which is made available to potential users and includes the provision of facilities in connection with banking, financing, insurance, transport, processing, supply of electrical or other energy, board or loading or both, housing construction, entertainment, amusement or the purveying of news or other information, but does not include the rendering of any service free of charge or under a contract of personal service.

The definition provides a list of eleven sectors to which service may pertain in order to come under the purview of the Act. The list of these sectors is not an exhaustive one. Service may be of any description and pertain to any sector if it satisfies the following criteria:

1. service is made available to the potential users, *i.e.*, service not only to the actual users but also to those who are capable of using it;
2. it should not be free of charge, *e.g.*, the medical service rendered free of charge in Government hospital is not a service under the Act;
3. it should not be under a contract of personal service.

When we talk about 'service' under the Consumer Protection Act, we take it as a regular commercial transaction. Thus the services rendered under the contract of personal service are specifically excluded from the definition.

The expression 'contract of personal service' is not defined under the Act. In common parlance, it means — a contract to render service in a private capacity to an individual. For example, where a servant enters into an agreement with a master for employment, or where a landlord agrees to supply water to his tenant, these are the contracts of personal service. The idea is that under a personal service relationship, a person can discontinue the service at any time according to his will; he need not approach Consumer Forum to complaint about deficiency in service.

There is a difference between 'contract of personal service' and 'contract for personal service'. In case of 'contract of personal service', the service-seeker can order or require what is to be done and how it should be done. Like a master can tell his servant to bring goods from a particular place. But in a 'contract for personal service', the service-seeker can tell only what is to be done. How the work will be done is at the wish of the performer. Like when a person gives a suit to the tailor for stitching, he does not tell him which method he should use to stitch it.

Note.—That it is 'contract of personal service' is excluded from the definition of service, 'contract for personal service' is recognised as service under the Act.

It does not make a difference whether the service provider is a Government body or a Private body. Thus even if a statutory corporation provides a deficient service, it can be made liable under the Act.

Example: 'A' applied for electricity connection for his flour mill to Rajasthan State Electricity Board. The Board delayed in releasing the connection. It was held deficient in performing service.

Some other sectors/professionals/services which are not specified in the definition of service but which have been considered by the Consumer Forums as service sectors from time to time are listed below:

Advocates, Airlines, Chartered Accountants, Courier, Chit Fund, Education, Gas Cylinder/LPG, Medical services, Postal services, Railways, Investment related services and Telephone services.

Thus, the test is — whether the person against whom the complaint is made performs a service for consideration which is sought by a potential user.

Consumer of services — A person is a consumer of services if he satisfies the following criteria:

SERVICES ARE HIRED OR AVAILED OF — The term 'hired' has not been defined under the Act. Its Dictionary meaning is — to procure the use of services at a price. Thus the term 'hire' has also been used in the sense of 'avail' or 'use'. Accordingly it may be understood that consumer means any person who avails or uses any service.

Example: 'A' goes to a doctor to get himself treated for a fracture. Here 'A' is hiring the services of the doctor. Thus, he is a consumer.

What constitutes hiring has been an issue to be dealt with in many consumer disputes. If it is established that a particular act constitutes hiring of service, the transaction falls within the net of the Consumer Protection Act, and *vice versa*.

Examples:

1. 'A' passenger getting railway reservation after payment is hiring service for consideration.
2. 'A' landlord neglected and refused to provide the agreed amenities to his tenant. He filed a complaint against the landlord under the Consumer Protection Act. The National Commission dismissed the complaint saying that it was a case of lease of immovable property and not of hiring services of the landiord. [*Smt. Laxmiben Laxmichand Shah* v *Smt. Sakerben Kanji Chandan* (1992) 1 Comp. LJ 177 (NCDRC)]
3. 'A' presented before the Sub-Registrar a document claiming it to be a will for registration who sent it to the Collector of Stamps for action. The matter remains pending for about six years. In the meantime. A filed a complaint under the Consumer Protection Act

alleging harassment by the Sub-Registrar and Collector and prayed for compensation. The National Commission held the view that 'A' was not a "consumer" under the CPA. because there was no hiring of services by the complainant for consideration and because a Government official doing his duty as functionary of the State under law could not be said to be rendering a service to the complainant. [*S.P. Goel* v *Collector of Stamps* (1995) III CPR 684 (SC)]

Further it has been held as:

(*i*) The telephone service falls within the definition of the word service, as contained in Consumer Protection Act, 1986. [*M/s Mahaveer Electricals* v *Bistt. Engineer, Tele Communications* (1991) 1 CPR 85]

(*ii*) Service rendered by hospitals and members of medical profession for consideration constitutes service as defined in the Act. Service rendered by a medical officer cannot be described as personal service. [*Cosmopolitan Hospitals* v *Vasantha P. Nair* 1993 CCJ 198 (NC); *Dr. Sr. Louie* v *Kannolil Pathumma* 1993 CCJ 294 (NC)]

(*iii*) Medical services provided by a doctor for consideration answer the description of' service within the meaning of the Act. *Gulam Abdul Husain* v *Katta Pullaiah Choudhary* (1991) 1 CPR 499; *Motibai* v *M.I. Govikar* (1991) 1 CPR 334 (Bom); *M.A. Azeez* v *Naguru Rajanna,* F.A. 3/90 dated 5-4-1990 (NC); *Mappooyan* v *Premvathy Illango* (1991) 1 CPR 78 (Mad). But facility of medical treatment offered in Government hospital does not constitute 'service'. [*Consumer Unity & Trust Society* v *State of Rajasthan* (1991) 1 CPR 241 (NC)]

(*iv*) Repudiation of claim in insurance contract whether deficiency in service. [*United India Insurance Co. Ltd.* v *Pushpalaya Printers* (2003) 4 SCC 694]

(*v*) The relationship of teacher and student of an educational institution is not a service on hire because student is not such a consumer which is linked any way with the buyer of any economic goods and hire has not been linked with education, teacher and student. [*N. Taneja* v *Calcutta Distt. Forum* AIR 1992 Cal 95]

(*vi*) Grant of overdraft facility by bank to its customer, being not without consideration, amounts to providing of "service". [*Vimal Chandra Grover* v *Bank of India* AIR 2000 SC 2181]

(*vii*) Institution of suit or other proceedings in a Civil Court after payment of "Court-fee" cannot be said to be equal to "hiring" or "availing of" service of a Court after paying consideration and, thus, complaint is not maintainable before consumer forum on ground that there were deficiencies in set up of the civil judicial administration. [*Akhil Bhartiya Grahak Panchayat* v *State of Gujarat* (1994) 1 CPJ 114 (NC)]

(*viii*) The services rendered by the Government servant under the Central Government Health Scheme are not covered by the term "service" as defined in the Act .[*Additional Director, CGHS* v *R.L. Butani* (1996) 1 CPJ 255 (NC)]

(*ix*) An employee, who is a Member of Employees' Provident Fund Scheme, is a consumer and duties performed by Regional Provident Fund Commissioner under such scheme is "service" and, thus, in case of delay in release of provident fund, complaint for deficiency in service, is maintainable. [*Regional Provident Fund Commissioner* v *Shiv Kumar Joshi* AIR 2000 SC 331]

(*x*) ESI medical service are covered under Consumer Protection Act.

Held. The medical service rendered in an ESI hospital/dispensary to an insured employee fails within the ambit of section 2(1)(*o*) of the Consumer Protection Act, and, therefore, the Consumer Protection Act have jurisdiction to adjudicate upon a dispute arising between the insured and the Employees' State Insurance Corporation. Following is the summery of judgment pronounced by Apex Court.

Legal Pronouncement by Supreme Court: Medical services in ESI Hospital/Dispensary to an insured employee fall within the ambit of Consumer Protection Act, 1986.

Law laid down: (*i*) The medical services rendered in an ESI Hospital/ dispensary to an insured employee under ESI Act, 1948 falls within the ambit of Section 2(1)(*o*) of Consumer Protection Act, 1986.

(*ii*) Apex court held that the corporation is required to establish and maintain hospitals and dispensaries to provide medical and surgical services. The expenses incurred come from contribution made by employer and employee. It is not free of cost, hence despite it is under a policy, it may not be said to be of gratuitous in nature and allowed to be out of purview of Consumer Protection Act.

(*iii*) Appellant insured employee is thus a 'CONSUMER' within the meaning of Section 2(1)(*d*) and activity rendered by corporation is 'SERVICES' under section 2(1)(*o*) of Consumer Protection Act, 1986. And such claims shall not fall within the purview of Employee Insurance Court.

(*iv*) It was further held that jurisdiction of consumer forum is not ousted by virtue of section 75 of ESI Act, 1948.

(*c*) Effect: Now insured employees, if aggrieved and not satisfied by the services of corporation may file complaint before District Consumer Forum seeking various relief invoking provisions of Consumer Protection Act, 1986.

(*d*) Employer's concern: In course of adjudication of such complaint, the principal employer is generally made a party as primary witness in consumer forums or proforma respondents in Higher Courts. Thereby the judicial review of the Courts creeps in to the compliances, being done by concerned employer. [*Chairman, Employees' State Insurance Corporation* 2007 LLR 740]

When the allegation relates to deficiency in 'banking service', it is trite to hold that 'banking service' is a service as defined under the Consumer Protection Act and the opposite party having hired the said banking service provided by the writ petitioner for consideration, he squarely comes under the definition of a "Consumer", as defined in section 2(*d*). [*Biratunga S.C.S. Ltd.* (*Mini Bank*) v *Sangram Keshari Pati* AIR 2006 Ori 97]

Mere non-admission of a patient as an indoor patient in the hospital when there was no vacant bed available does not tantamount to medical negligence or deficiency in service. [*Sukumari Sahu* v *Tata Memorial Hospital* AIR 2006 (NOC) 520 (All)]

The government servants and the staff of the Accountant General Office of the Comptroller and Auditor General maintains the records of provident fund of government servants, issue slips of deposits of fund and on retirement final payments are made to the subscribers. The government servants and the staff of the Accountant General in discharging their duties does not render any service for consideration, nor hiring of any service is involved hence, maintenance of General Provident Fund Accounts does not fall within the meaning of 'service'. [*Hari Vallabh Vijay* v *Administration Officer* 2001 (1) CPR 529]

Medical services are covered under the definition of "service". Service includes rendering of consultation, diagnosis and treatment, both medical and surgical. [*Indian Medical Association* v *V.P. Shantha* 1995 SCALE 273]

"Contract of personal service" has to be distinguished from a "contract for personal service". In the absence of relationship of master and servant between the patient and the medical practitioner, the service rendered by a medical practitioner to the patient cannot be regarded as service rendered under a contract of personal service. It is "contract for personal services". Wherever, there is relationship like that of master and servant it is a "contract of personal service" and is excluded from the purview of the Act. [*Indian Medical Association* v *V.P. Shantha* 1995 SCALE 273]

If somebody does not perform his part of the contract, it amounts to deficiency in service. [*Ramala Roy* v *Rabindra Nath Sen* 1994 (I) CPR 66]

The agreement for hypothecation does not create the ownership right, and as such no complaint can be maintained for deficiency in service. [*Jayantial Keshavlal Chauhan* v *National Insurance Co. Ltd.* 1994 (I) CPR 390]

Undue delay in declaration of examination result is obviously deficiency in service. [*Secretary, Board of School Education, Haryana* v *Mukesh Chand* 1994 (I) CPR 269]

The repudiation of the claim by the Insurance Company on the ground that the driver was not holding a valid driving licence at the time of the accident could not be termed as deficiency in service or negligence on the part of the Insurance Company within the meaning of section 2(*g*) of the Act. [*New India Assurance Co. Ltd.* v *Smt. Pushpa Yashwant Ghatge* 1996 NCJ 195]

COMMENT ON SECTION 2(1)(*q*) AND (*j*)

Trader and Manufacturer

When a person finds any defect in the goods, be it manufacturing defect, or excessive price, or lack of information about hazardous nature, or restrictive or unfair trade practice, he can make a complaint against the trader. Thus it is very important to know who can be termed as a trader under the Act.

Trader

Section 2(1)(*q*) of the Act says that 'trader' means any person who sells or distributes any goods for sale and includes the manufacturer thereof, and where such goods are sold or distributed in package form, includes the packer thereof.

Generally speaking, 'trader' means any person who carries on a trade. Under the Consumer Protection Act, even a packer has been included in the definition of trader. Packer means one who packs the goods.

Examples:

1. 'A' got an agency of 'Indana' products. He sells and distributes these products in North India. He is a trader under the Act.
2. 'A' manufactures combs. He is a trader under the Act.
3. 'A' provides bottles to pack the perfume manufactured by 'B'. Here 'A' is also a trader under the Act.

Note.—"Trader" is a wider term which includes a manufacturer also.

Manufacturer

In terms if clause (*j*) of section 2(1) of the Act, "manufacturer" means a person who—

(*i*) makes or manufactures any goods or parts thereof; or

(*ii*) does not make or manufacture any goods but assembles parts thereof made or manufactured by others and claims the end-product to be goods manufactured by himself; or

(*iii*) puts or causes to be put his own mark on any goods made or manufactured by any other manufacturer and claims such goods to be goods made or manufactured by himself.

Thus manufacturer is a person who either himself manufactures goods, or assemble any goods manufactured by others, or puts his own mark or trade mark on the goods manufactured by others.

Examples:

1. 'A Ltd'. was into manufacturing of Pressure Cookers. 'B' bought a Cooker which burst out while using. 'B' sued 'A Ltd'. for compensation. Here 'A Ltd'. being manufacturer of the Cooker is liable for the loss.
2. 'A Ltd'. used to buy components and assemble computers therefrom. They were selling them under the brand name 'Rotal'. 'B' bought a Rotal computer which turned out to be defective. Here 'B' can hold 'A Ltd.' Liable for the loss as they will be considered manufacturer of Rotal computer under the Act.
3. 'N' bought H-4 Cotton seeds from the market which were labeled as produced and marketed by the Hindustan Levers Ltd. N established that the seeds were defective. He sued HLL. HLL contended that it did not manufactured the seeds but had only marketed them, and that some company based in Gujarat produced the same. The Commission held that in this case HLL comes under the third limb of the definition of manufacturer under the Act. Thus it is liable for the loss suffered by 'N'. [*Namdeo Baijrao Raut* v *Hindustan Lever Ltd.* (1993) 3 CPR 346 (Mah. CDRC)]

It may be noted that where a manufacturer despatches any goods or part thereof to any branch office maintained by him, such branch office shall not be deemed to be the manufacturer even though the parts so despatched to it are assembled at such branch office and are sold or distributed from such branch office.

Example: A Ltd. based in Delhi was having a branch office in Chennai. It used to sent components of computers to its Chennai branch which was assembling and selling them. B purchased a computer from Chennai branch which turned out to be defective. Here A Ltd. is responsible for the loss, and not the Chennai branch.

Who should be sued by a consumer — manufacturer or seller

Generally when a consumer finds defect in the goods, he sues the person from whom he bought the goods. Reason being privity of contract.

If the defect is a manufacturing defect, the consumer may sue the manufacturer also along with the seller. This is an option with the consumer. Thus the manufacturer is a possible party and not a necessary party.

Example: A was manufacturer of "X" brand cars and B was a dealer for them. 'C' bought a car from 'B' and found it defective. Here he may sue B alone, or 'A' and 'B' both.

Charging Excessive Price

A complaint may be made against a trader who has charged a price in excess of the price:

(*a*) fixed by or under any law for the time being in force, or

(*b*) displayed on the goods, or

(*c*) displayed on any package containing the goods.

Examples:

1. Government fixed control rate of milk at ₹15 per litre in the month of June 2001. 'A' sold it at the rate of ₹18 per litre in the same period. Price charged by 'A' are excessive.
2. The price displayed on a one Kg. packet of salt was ₹4. Suddenly there was paucity of salt in the market. 'A' started selling the same @ ₹6 per kg. The price charged by 'A' is excessive.

It may be noted that when price of an article is not fixed by law, or when the same is not displayed on goods or on the package containing goods, no complaint can be made under the Act for excess pricing.

Example: Mahaboobnagar Milk Chilling Centre charged 15 paise extra per half litre of milk supplied in sachets in comparison to the other varieties of milk. The National Commission held that in the absence of any law requiring an article to be sold at or below a particular price fixed thereunder, and when there was no declaration of the price on the packet containing the goods, a case for excessive pricing may not be construed.

(*viii*) makes to the public a representation in a form that purports to be—

Both manufacturer as well as dealer of a car are jointly responsible for post-sale service. [*Padma V. Amrapukar* v *J. Williams & Co.* (1991) 1 CPR 287]

COMMENT ON [SECTION 2(1)(*r*) AND (*nnn*)]

Unfair Trade Practice and Restrictive Trade Practice

We have discussed that a consumer can make a complaint when an unfair or a restrictive trade practice is followed by a trader. What can be termed as an unfair or a restrictive trade practice is another question of law.

What is an Unfair Trade Practice

The Act says that, "unfair trade practice" means a trade practice which, for the purpose of promoting the sale, use or supply of any goods or for the provision of any service, adopts any unfair method or unfair or deceptive practice including any of the following practices, namely—

(1) The practice of making any statement, whether orally or in writing or by visible representation which—

(*i*) falsely represents that the goods are of particular standard, quality, quantity, grade, composition, style or model;

(*ii*) falsely represents that the services are of a particular standard, quality or grade;

(*iii*) falsely represents any re-built, second-hand, renovated, reconditioned or old goods as new goods;

(*iv*) represents that the goods or services have sponsorship, approval performance, characteristics, accessories, uses or benefits which such goods or services do not have;

(*v*) represents that the seller or the supplier has a sponsorship or approval or affiliation which such seller or supplier does not have;

(*vi*) makes false or misleading statement concerning the need for, or the usefulness of, any goods or services;

(*vii*) gives to the public any warranty or guarantee of the performance, efficacy or length of life of a product or of any goods that is not based on an adequate or proper test thereof;

(*viii*) makes to the public a representation in a form that purports to be a warranty or guarantee of a product or of any goods or services; or a promise to replace, maintain or repair an article or any part thereof or to repeat or continue a service until it has achieved a specified result, if such purported warranty or guarantee or promise is materially misleading or if there is no reasonable prospect that such warranty, guarantee or promise will be carried out;

(*ix*) materially misleads the public concerning the price at which a product or like products or goods or services, have been or are, ordinarily sold or provided, and, for this purpose, a representation as to price shall be deemed to refer to the price at which the product or goods or services has or have been sold by sellers or provided by suppliers generally in the relevant market unless it is clearly specified to be the price at which the product has been sold or services have been provided by the person by whom or on whose behalf other representation is made;

(*x*) gives false or misleading facts disparaging the goods, services or trade of another person.

Note.—A statement is said to be made to public when it is—

(*a*) expressed on an article offered or displayed for sale, or on its wrapper or container; or

(*b*) expressed on anything attached to, inserted in, or accompanying, an article offered or displayed for sale, or on anything on which the article is mounted for display or sale; or (*c*) contained in or on anything that is sold, sent, delivered, transmitted or in any other manner whatsoever made available to a member of the public, by the person who had caused the statement to be so expressed, made or contained.

(2) Permits the publication of any advertisement whether in any newspaper or otherwise, for the sale or supply at a bargain price, of goods or services that are not intended to be offered for sale or supply at the bargain price, or for a period that is, and in quantities that are, reasonable, having regard to the nature of the market in which the business is carried on, the nature and size of business, and the nature of the advertisement.

Note.—"Bargain price" means—

(*a*) a price that is stated in any advertisement to be a bargain price, by reference to an ordinary price or otherwise, or

(*b*) a price that a person who reads, hears or sees the advertisement, would reasonably understand to be bargain price having regard to the prices at which the product advertised or like products are ordinarily sold.

(3) Permits the offering of gifts, prizes or other items with the intention of not providing them as offered or creating impression that something is being given or offered free of charge when it is fully or partly covered by the amount charged in the transaction as a whole; or the conduct of any contest, lottery, game of chance or skill, for the purpose of promoting, directly or indirectly, the sale, use or supply of any product or any business interest.

(4) Permits the sale or supply of goods intended to be used, or are of a kind likely to be used, by consumers, knowing or having reason to believe that the goods do not comply with the standards prescribed by competent authority relating to performance, composition, contents, design, constructions, finishing or packaging as are necessary to prevent or reduce the risk of injury to the person using the goods.

(5) Permits the hoarding or destruction of goods, or refuses to sell the goods or to make them available for sale or to provide any service, if such hoarding or destruction or refusal raises or tends to raise or is intended to raise, the cost of those or other similar goods or services.

The definition of the expression "unfair trade practice" applies not merely to the sale or supply of any goods but to the provision of any service. [*Montora Oil Products* (*P*) *Ltd.* v *Oriental Insurance Co.* (1991) 1 CPR 181 (NC)]

3. Act not in derogation of any other law.—The provisions of this Act shall be in addition to and not in derogation of the provisions of any other law for the time being in force.

COMMENT ON SECTION 3

The Act seeks to provide remedy under the Consumer Protection Act in addition to other remedies provided under other Acts unless there is a clear bar. [*Secretary, Thirumurugan Co-operative Agricultural Credit Society* v *M. Lalitha* AIR 2004 SC 448]

(*i*) The remedy provided under the Act is in addition to the provisions of any other law for the time being in force. The provisions of this Act give the consumer an additional remedy besides those that may be available under other existing laws. [*Consumer & Citizens Forum* v *Karnataka Power Corporation* 1994 (I) CPR 130]

(*ii*) When a case is pending in a court in which full evidence is to be recorded the Forums constituted under the Consumer Protection Act, 1986 should not entertain the complaint with respect to the same cause of action. [*Hanuman Prasad* v *New India Assurance Co. Ltd.* I (1994) CPJ I (NC)]

(*iii*) It is nowhere laid down that whenever the examination and cross-examination is involved, the proper forum for adjudication of the dispute is only Civil Court. [*S.K. Lakhotia* v *National Insurance Co. Ltd.* 1994 (I) CPR 43]

(*iv*) It is authoritatively settled that the arbitration clause is not a bar to the entertainment of the complaint by the Redressal Agency constituted under the Act, even if the arbitration provision has been laid down in a statute. [*Ram Nath* v *Improvement Trust, Bathinda* 1994 (I) CPR 357]

(*v*) In *Suraj Steel Hazaribagh* v *R.R Sharma, F.A. No. 488* decided on 25-7-1989 by National Commission, it was held that the matter was purely in the realm of breach of contract and it did not constitute a 'consumer dispute', therefore, the complainant should have been referred by the State Commission to pursue his ordinary remedy by way of instituting a civil suit and no relief should have been granted to him under the Act-Again in *M.X. Joseph* v *State Bank of India,* O.P. No. 12/89, decided on 23-8-1989 by the National Commission it was held that the matter in that case fell in the realm of a civil dispute which had to be settled by a civil court. Relying on the above decisions the State Commission Rajasthan in *Shankar Birmiwal* v *Jaipur Development Authority* (1991) 2 CPR 86, held that where the matter falls within the realm of the civil court it will not be appropriate for the consumer agencies to entertain and decide the complaint.

(*vi*) Where the subject-matter of a complaint is *sub-judice* before the ordinary civil court, a concurrent adjudication in respect of the same will not be conducted by the authorities constituted under the Act. The objection is not really on the ground of lack of jurisdiction but is one based on consideration of propriety and prudence keeping in view the necessity for avoidance of collecting decisions and multiplicity of proceedings. [*Special Machines, Karnal* v *Punjab National Bank* (1991) 1 CPR 52 (NC); *Oswal Fine Arts* v *H.M.T. Madras, O.P. 1 of 1988,* dated 27-4-1989]

(*vii*) The consumer agencies are in addition and not in derogation of the provisions of any other law. [*Patel Laljibhai* v *Adarsh Welding Works* (1991) 1 CPR 641 (NC)]

(*viii*) When the matter is pending before the arbitrator appointed by the civil court the Consumer Forum cannot enter upon adjudication. [*Hotel Gandharva* v *Bharat Bijlee Ltd.* (1991) 1 CPR 138 (NC)]

(*ix*) An arbitration clause in an insurance policy is no bar to a proceeding under the Consumer Protection Act. Consequently, the complainant has an option to seek redress either under the Consumer Protection Act or under any other law including through arbitration as provided in the contract of insurance. [*New Jaipur Dyeing and Tents Works* v *Oriental Insurance Co. Ltd.* (1991) 2 CPR 149 (NC)]

(*x*) The mere fact that the default or deficiency may also amount to a breach of contract under the general law will not in any way affect the jurisdiction of the Forums set up under the Consumer Protection Act. [*Synco Textiles Pvt. Ltd.* v *Economic Transport Organization* (1991) 1 CPJ 40 (NC)]

(*xi*) Where the complainant's case involves a determination of complex questions of law and fact which cannot be satisfactorily determined by the Consumer Forum in the time frame provided under the Act it would be better for the complainant to seek redress of his grievances in a civil court. *Pannalal* v *Bank of India* (1992) 1 CPR 34 (NC). The Act does not contemplate the determination of complicated issues of fact involving taking of elaborate oral evidence and adducing of voluminous documentary evidence and a detailed scrutiny and assessment of such evidence by the *Consumer Redressal Forums.* [*Industrial Products, Karnal* v *Punjab National Bank* (1992) I CPR 70 (NC); *Special Machine Karnal* v *Punjab National Bank* (1991)1 CPR 52 (NC)]

(*xii*) In view of the provisions of Railway Claims Tribunal Act, 1987 the Consumer Forum have no jurisdiction to entertain a complaint in respect of matters referred to in section 13 of the said Act. [*Union of India* v *Derby Textile* 1993 CCI 120 (Raj)]

(*xiii*) Billing dispute — Existence of a remedy by way of arbitration under section 7B of the Telegraph Act does not preclude an aggrieved consumer from seeking redressal before the Forums constituted under Consumer Protection Act which is a special statue enacted by Parliament for the specific purpose of providing a speedy, cheap and efficacious remedy to consumers before the special Forums created for that purpose. [*Commercial Officer, Office of the Telecom Distt. Manager, Patna* v *Bihar State Warehousing Corporation* (1991) 1 CPR 142: (1991) 1 CPJ 42 (NC); *Jagdamba Rice Mills* v *Union of India* (1991) 1 CPJ 273 (Har)]

(*xiv*) In *Union of India* v *Nilesh Aggarwal* (1991) 1 CPJ 203 (NC), the National Commission was of the view that a telephone subscriber can invoke the remedies provided under the Act.

(*xv*) However there is absolutely no bar in appropriate case to refer the dispute to arbitration under section 7B of the Telegraph Act. [*Chief General Manager* v *M.K. Gupta* (1991) 2 CPJ 116 (WB)]

(*xvi*) If the billing disputes require adequate investigation which is not possible for the authorities under the Consumer Protection Act to do, the only course open is to refer the billing dispute to the arbitration under section 7B of the Telegraph Act [*Chief General Manager* v *M.K Gupta* (1991) 2 CPJ 116 (WB)]

(*xvii*) Criminal proceedings launched by the complainant on same cause of action is no bar to maintainability of complaint under the Consumer Protection Act. [*M.K.S. Balasubramanian* v *Jayalakshmi Planners* (1992) 1 CPR 133 (Mad)]

(*xviii*) The remedy provided under the Act is in addition to the provisions of any other law for the time being in force. The provisions of this Act give the consumer an additional remedy besides those that may be available under other existing laws. [*Consumer & Citizens Forum* v *Karnataka Power Corporation* 1994 (I) CPR 130]

(*xix*) When a case is pending in a court in which full evidence is to be recorded the Forums constituted under the Consumer Protection Act, 1986 should not entertain the complaint with respect to the same cause of action. [*Hanuman Prasad* v *New India Assurance Co, Ltd.* I (1994) CPJ 1 (NC)]

(*xz*) It is nowhere laid down that whenever the examination and cross-examination is involved, the proper forum for adjudication of the' *dispute is only Civil Court. [S.K. Lakhotia* v *National Insurance Co. Ltd.* 1994 (I) CPR 43]

(*xxi*) It is authoritatively settled that the arbitration clause is not a bar to the entertainment of the complaint by the Redressal Agency constituted under the Act, even if the arbitration provision has been laid down in a statute. [*Ram Nath* v *Improvement Trust, Bathinda* 1994 (I) CPR 357]

CHAPTER II

Consumer Protection Councils

4. The Central Consumer Protection Council.—(1) [1][The Central Government shall], by notification, establish with effect from such date as it may specify in such notification, a Council to be known as the Central Consumer Protection Council (hereinafter referred to as the Central Council).

(2) The Central Council shall consist of the following members, namely:—

(*a*) the Minister in charge of [2][Consumer Affairs] in the Central Government, who shall be its Chairman, and

(*b*) such number of other official or non-official members representing such interests as may be prescribed.

COMMENT

Objects and Reasons.—Clauses 3 and 4 (old) seek to amend sections 4 and 7 respectively so that establishment of the Central Consumer Protection Council and the State Consumer Protection Council which is in the larger interests of consumers becomes a necessary requirement. Clause 4 also seeks to provide for inclusion of up to ten official and non-official Members nominated by the Central Government in the State Council.

5. Procedure for meetings of the Central Council.—(1) The Central Council shall meet as and when necessary, but [3][at least one meeting] of the Council shall be held every year.

(2) The Central Council shall meet at such time and place as the Chairman may think fit and shall observe such procedure in regard to the transaction of its business as may be prescribed.

COMMENT ON SECTION 5

Meetings

The State Council meets at least twice a year. In addition, it may meet as and when necessary. The council may meet at such time and place as the Chairman may think fit.

Procedure in regard to the transaction of its business is prescribed by the State Government.

Working Groups [Rule 3]

For the purpose of monitoring the implementation of the recommendations of the Central Council and to suggest the working of

---

1 Substituted for the words "The Central Government may" by the Consumer Protection (Amendment) Act, 2002, w.e.f. 15-3-2003.

2 Substituted for the words "the Department of Food and Civil Supplies", by the Consumer Protection (Amendment) Act, 1993, w.e.f. 18-6-1993.

3 Substituted for the words "not less than three meetings", by the Amendment Act, 1993, w.e.f. 18-6-1993.

the Council, the Central Government may constitute from amongst the members of the Council, a Standing Working Group, under the chairmanship of the Member Secretary of the Council. The Standing Working Group shall consist of not exceeding 30 members and shall meet as and when considered necessary by the Central Government.

6. Objects of the Central Council.—The objects of the Central Council shall be to promote and protect the rights of the consumers such as,—

(*a*) the right to be protected against marketing of goods [1][and services] which are hazardous to life and property;

(*b*) the right to be informed about the quality, quantity, potency, purity, standard and price of goods [2][or services, as the case may be,] so as to protect the consumer against unfair trade practices;

(*c*) the right to be assured, wherever possible, access to a variety of goods [3][and services] at competitive prices;

(*d*) the right to be heard and to be assured that consumers' interests will receive due consideration at appropriate forums;

(*e*) the right to seek redressal against unfair trade practices [4][or restrictive trade practices] or unscrupulous exploitation of consumers; and

(*f*) the right to consumer education.

7. The State Consumer Protection Councils.—(1) [5][The State Government shall], by notification, establish with effect from such date as it may specify in such notification, a Council to be known as the Consumer Protection Council for .... (hereinafter referred to as the State Council).

[6][(2) The State Council shall consist of the following members, namely:—

(*a*) the Minister incharge of Consumer Affairs in the State Government who shall be its Chairman;

(*b*) such number of other official or non-official members representing such interest as may be prescribed by the State Government;]

[7][(*c*) such number of other official or non-official members, not exceeding ten, as may be nominated by the Central Government.]

[8][(3) The State Council shall meet as and when necessary but not less than two meetings shall be held every year.

---

1 Inserted by the Consumer Protection (Amendment) Act, 1993, w.e.f. 18-6-1993.

2 Inserted, *ibid.*

3 Inserted, *ibid.*

4 Inserted, *ibid.*

5 Substituted for the words, "The State Government may" by the Consumer Protection (Amendment) Act, 2002, w.e.f. 15-3-2003.

6 Substituted for "(2) The State Council shall consist of such number of members as may be specified by the State Government by notification from time to time." by the Consumer Protection (Amendment) Act, 1993, w.e.f. 18-6-1993.

7 Inserted by the Consumer Protection (Amendment) Act, 2002, w.e.f. 15-3-2003.

8 Inserted by the Consumer Protection (Amendment) Act, 1993, w.e.f. 18-6-1993.

(4) The State Council shall meet at such time and place as the Chairman may think fit and shall observe such procedure in regard to the transaction of its business as may be prescribed by the State Government.]

8. Objects of the State Council.—The objects of every State Council shall be to promote and protect within the State the rights of the consumers laid down in clauses (*a*) to (*f*) of section 6.

[1][**8A. The District Consumer Protection Council.**—(1) The State Government shall establish for every district, by notification, a council to be known as the District Consumer Protection Council with effect from such date as it may specify in such notification.

(2) The District Consumer Protection Council (hereinafter referred to as the District Council) shall consist of the following members, namely:—

(*a*) the Collector of the district (by whatever name called), who shall be its Chairman; and

(*b*) such number of other official and non-official members representing such interests as may be prescribed by the State Government.

(3) The District Council shall meet as and when necessary but not less than two meetings shall be held every year.

(4) The District Council shall meet at such time and place within the district as the Chairman may think fit and shall observe such procedure in regard to the transaction of its business as may be prescribed by the State Government.]

[2][**8B. Objects of the District Council.**—The objects of every District Council shall be to promote and protect within the district the rights of the consumers laid down in clauses (*a*) to (*f*) of section 6.]

COMMENT ON SECTIONS 6 AND 8

Objects and Reasons

Clauses 6 (old) seeks to insert new sections 8A and 8B to provide for the setting up a District Consumer Protection Council for every district with objects similar to those of the Central and State Councils. This will provide a forum for promoting and protecting the rights of the consumers at grass root level.

Consumer Forums

Ram, a resident of Panipat district, took his son Shyam to a doctor for eye treatment. Due to negligence of the doctor, Shyam lost sight of his left eye. Ram filed a suit against the doctor in District Forum claiming ₹4 lakh as compensation. The District Forum dismissed his complaint on the ground that negligence of the doctor could not be proved.

Ram appealed to Haryana State Commission against this order. State Commission also upheld the decision of District Forum. Now Ram

---

1 Inserted by the Consumer Protection (Amendment) Act, 2002, w.e.f. 15-3-2003.

2 Inserted, *ibid.*

approached the National Commission and made an appeal therein. Ram knew that after National Commission also, he is still left with an option to approach the Supreme Court against the order of the Commission. However, the National Commission decided in favour of Ram.

The Consumer Protection Act provides for a 3 tier approach in resolving consumer disputes. There are three levels of consumer courts—

First, there is the District Court, called District Consumer Disputes Redressal Forum (District Forum),

Next comes the State Consumer Disputes Redressal Commission (State Commission),

At the national level, there is National Consumer Disputes Redressal Commission (National Commission).

District Forum and State Commission are formed by States with the permission of the Central Government while the National Commission is formed by the Central Government. These forums have not taken away the jurisdiction of the civil courts but have provided an alternative remedy.

The Consumer Protection Act, 1986 has given powers to the Central and State Governments to make rules with regard to various aspects of the consumer protection machinery. In our discussion, we have included the Consumer Protection Rules, 1987 made by the Central Government, wherever required.

Objects of the Councils

There is one basic thought that 'consumer needs to be protected'. Another thought is — how he can be protected? Definitely, there has to be some agency to work towards this protection. The Act has provided for constitution of Consumer Councils for this purpose.

Now, when we say that these councils are there to protect the consumers, a question arises — consumers are protected against what? Thus the Act has detailed some rights of consumers which need to be protected by the councils. These are:

Right to safety

It is right to be protected against the marketing of goods and services which are hazardous to life and property.

Unsafe goods may cause death or serious injury to the user due to defective ingredients, defective design, poor workmanship, or any other reason. At times safety hazards are found due to absence of proper instructions to use the product. Thus it is to be ensured that—

Manufacturers and traders ensure that the goods are safe for the users, in case of hazardous goods, they give clear instructions as to mode of use, consumer is informed of the risk involved in improper use of goods, and vital safety information is conveyed to consumers.

Manufacturers or distributors who become aware of the unforeseen hazards after the goods are supplied must inform the authorities and the public in order to forewarn consumers about such hazards.

Where a product is found such as is likely to be hazardous even when properly used, traders should either recall it and modify the same, or replace it with a new product, or adequately compensate for it.

Right to information

It is right to be informed about the quality, quantity, potency, purity, standard and price of goods or services, with a view to protect the consumer against unfair trade practices.

Adequate information is very important in order to make a right choice. In our country, however, consumers do not get adequate comparative information about the quality, quantity, potency, purity, standard and price of different kinds of goods or services which are available. As a result buying decisions become difficult. Therefore consumers need to be given maximum information about the wide variety of competing goods available in the market.

Right to choose

The right to choose can be made meaningful by ensuring access to a variety of goods and services at competitive prices.

Fair and effective competition must be encouraged so as to provide consumers with the widest range of products and services at the lowest cost.

Right to represent

It is right to be heard and to be assured that consumer's interests will receive due consideration at appropriate forums.

The Consumer Protection Act, 1986 has well taken care of this right by making available the instrumentality of Redressal Forums. Every consumer has a right to file complaint and be heard in that context.

Right to redressal

It is a right to seek redressal against unfair trade practices or restrictive trade practices or unscrupulous exploitation of consumers.

When consumers are wronged in a market place transaction, appropriate and adequate redress must be available. The Act has ensured this right by establishing Consumer Forums and recognising restrictive and unfair trade practices as a ground to make a complaint.

Right to education

The right to consumer education is a right which ensures that consumers are informed about the practices prevalent in the market and the remedies available to them.

For spreading this education, media, or school curriculum, or cultural activities, etc. may be used as a medium.

Note that the Central Council's object is to ensure these rights of the consumers throughout the country while the State Councils look to ensure these rights to consumers within their territories persons capable of representing consumer interest not specified above—not exceeding fifteen;

(*i*) One or more consumers can file complaint. [*Chief General Manager, Calcutta Telephones* v *International Packers & Movers* I (1994) CPJ 132: 1994 (I) CPR 252]

(*ii*) When no objection was taken to the territorial jurisdiction of District Forum by filling written version, the objection cannot be entertained in appeal raised orally. [*Essen Computers Ltd.* v *Tagore Gracias* 1992 (II) CPR 556]

(*iii*) If a redressal forum has no jurisdiction, it cannot entertain the complaint on merits. [*Solvochen Intermediates Pvt. Ltd.* v *Boilertech Engineers Pvt. Ltd.* 1992 (II) CPR 322]

(*iv*) A petition of complaint can be field against corporation carrying on business within the territory or District Forum or commission even though its sole or principal office is situated outside state limits. [*Consumer Education and Research Society* v *Canara Bank* (1991) 1 CPR 405]

(*v*) The question of pecuniary jurisdiction can be decided only on the claim made by the complainant and will not affect the ultimate relief granted. [*S.A. Purani* v *Executive Engineer* (1992) 1 CPR 131 (Guj.)]

(*vi*) A suit against Corporation will lie only in the court within the local limits of whose jurisdiction the sole or principal office of the Corporation is situated except in cases where a cause of action has arisen at any other place where the Corporation has a subordinate office in which event the suit can be instituted in a court within whose jurisdiction such subordinate office is situated. [*Indian Airlines Corporation* v *Consumer Education and Research Society* (1992) 1 CPR (NC)]

(*vii*) A consumer can file a petition of complaint against a corporation which is carrying on its business in the local limits of the State but whose sole or principal office is situated outside the State limits even if the cause of action has arisen outside the territory of the State. [*Consumer Education and Research Society* v *Canara Bank* (1991) 1 CKP 405 (Guj)]

(*viii*) Where the car was booked at Pondicherry but actual delivery was made at Madras, the District Forum at Madras had territorial jurisdiction to entertain the complaint. [*M.O. Hasan* v *Joseph K.Thomas* (1991) 1 CPR 650 (Mad)]

CHAPTER III

Consumer Disputes Redressal Agencies

9. Establishment of Consumer Disputes Redressal Agencies.—There shall be established for the purposes of this Act, the following agencies, namely:—

(*a*) a Consumer Disputes Redressal Forum to be known as the "District Forum" established by the State Government [1][* * *] in each district of the State by notification:

[2][Provided that the State Government may, if it deems fit, establish more than one District Forum in a district.]

(*b*) a Consumer Disputes Redressal Commission to be known as the "State Commission" established by the State Government [3][* **] in the State by notification; and

(*c*) a National Consumer Disputes Redressal Commission established by the Central Government by notification.

COMMENTS ON SECTION 9

Constitution of the Forums

The composition of the District Forum and the State Commission has been detailed out by the Consumer Protection Act, 1986. As for the National Commission, the Consumer Protection Rules, 1987, elaborates upon its composition.

Wherever a sitting District Judge is functioning as the President of a District Forum if the workload exceeds the minimum monthly load of 150 cases consistently for a six months period, the High Court will convey the same to the State Government/U.T. administration which will within a period of six months from the date of receipt of the communication, appoint a regular independent District Forum as envisaged by section 9 of the Act. After the expiry of the said six months period, the High Court will be free to terminate the *ad hoc stopgap* arrangement of loaning the services of a sitting District Judge to work as the President of the District Forum under intimation to the State Government/U.T. administration and it will then be the responsibility of the latter to make provision for carrying out the purposes of the Act. [*Common Cause, A Registered Society* v *Union of India* AIR 1993 S.C 1403]

(*i*) One or more consumers can file complaint. [*Chief General Manager, Calcutta Telephones* v *International Packers & Movers* I (1994) CPJ 132: 1994 (I) CPR 252]

(*ii*) When no objection was taken to the territorial jurisdiction of District Forum by filling written version, the objection cannot be entertained in

---

1 The following words"with the prior approval of the Central Government" omitted by the Consumer Protection (Amendment) Act, 1993, w.e.f. 18-6-1993.

2 Inserted by the Consumer Protection (Amendment) Act, 1993, w.e.f. 18-6-1993.

3 The following words "with the prior approval of the Central Government" omitted, *ibid.*

appeal raised orally. [*Essen Computers Ltd.* v *Tagore Gracias* 1992 (II) CPR 556]

(*iii*) If a redressal forum has no jurisdiction, it cannot entertain the complaint on merits. [*Solvochen Intermediates Pvt. Ltd.* v *Boilertech Engineers Put. Ltd.* 1992 (II) CPR 322]

10. Composition of the District Forum.—[1][(1) Each District Forum shall consist of,—

(*a*) a person who is, or has been, or is qualified to be a District Judge, who shall be its President;]

[2][(*b*) two other members, one of whom shall be a woman, who shall have the following qualifications, namely:—

(*i*) be not less than thirty-five years of age,

(*ii*) possess a bachelor's degree from a recognised university,

(*iii*) be persons of ability, integrity and standing, and have adequate knowledge and experience of at least ten years in dealing with problems relating to economics, law, commerce, accountancy, industry, public affairs or administration:

Provided that a person shall be disqualified for appointment as a member if he—

(*a*) has been convicted and sentenced to imprisonment for an offence which, in the opinion of the State Government involves moral turpitude; or

(*b*) is an undischarged insolvent; or

(*c*) is of unsound mind and stands so declared by a competent court; or

(*d*) has been removed or dismissed from the service of the Government or a body corporate owned or controlled by the Government; or

(*e*) has, in the opinion of the State Government, such financial or other interest as is likely to affect prejudicially the discharge by him of his functions as a member; or

---

1 Substituted for "(1) Each District Forum shall consist of—

(*a*) a person who is or has been, or is qualified to be a District Judge to be nominated by the State Government, to be its President;

(*b*) a person of eminence in the field of education, trade or commerce;

(*c*) a lady social worker." by the Consumer Protection (Amendment) Act, 1993, w.e.f. 18-6-1993.

2 Substituted for "(*b*) two other members, who shall be persons of ability, integrity and standing, and have adequate knowledge or experience of, or have shown capacity in dealing with, problems relating to economics, law, commerce, accountancy, industry, public affairs or administration, one of whom shall be a woman;" by the Consumer Protection (Amendment) Act, 2002, w.e.f. 15-3-2003.

(*f*) has such other disqualifications as may be prescribed by the State Government.]]

[1][(1A) Every appointment under sub-section (1) shall be made by the State Government on the recommendation of a selection committee consisting of the following, namely:—

(*i*) the President of the State Commission — Chairman

(*ii*) Secretary, Law Department of the State — Member

(*iii*) Secretary incharge of the Department dealing with consumer affairs in the State — Member:]

[2][Provided that where the President of the State Commission is, by reason of absence or otherwise, unable to act as Chairman of the Selection Committee, the State Government may refer the matter to the Chief Justice of the High Court for nominating a sitting Judge of that High Court to act as Chairman.]

[3][(2) Every member of the District Forum shall hold office for a term of five years or up to the age of sixty-five years, whichever is earlier:

Provided that a member shall be eligible for re-appointment for another term of five years or up to the age of sixty-five years, whichever is earlier, subject to the condition that he fulfils the qualifications and other conditions for appointment mentioned in clause (*b*) of sub-section (1) and such re-appointment is also made on the basis of the recommendation of the Selection Committee:

Provided further that a member may resign his office in writing under his hand addressed to the State Government and on such resignation being accepted, his office shall become vacant and may be filled by appointment of a person possessing any of the qualifications mentioned in sub-section (1) in relation to the category of the member who is required to be appointed under the provisions of sub-section (1A) in place of the person who has resigned:

Provided also that a person appointed as the President or as a member, before the commencement of the Consumer Protection (Amendment) Act, 2002 shall continue to hold such office as President or member, as the case may be, till the completion of his term.]

(3) The salary or honorarium and other allowances payable to, and the other terms and conditions of service of the members of the District Forum shall be such as may be prescribed by the State Government:

---

1 Inserted by the Consumer Protection (Amendment) Act, 1993, w.e.f. 18-6-1993.

2 Inserted by the Consumer Protection (Amendment) Act, 2002, w.e.f. 15-3-2003.

3 Substituted for the following: "(2) Every member of the District Forum shall hold office for a term of five years or up to the age of 65 years, whichever is earlier, and shall not be eligible for re-appointment:

Provided that a member may resign his office in writing under his hand addressed to the State Government and on such resignation being accepted, his office shall become vacant and may be filled by the appointment of a person possessing any of the qualifications mentioned in sub-section (1) in relation to the category of the members who has resigned." *ibid.*

[1][Provided that the appointment of a member on whole-time basis shall be made by the State Government on the recommendation of the President of the State Commission taking into consideration such factors as may be prescribed including the work load of the District Forum.]

COMMENTS ON SECTION 10

Objects and Reasons

Clause 7 (old) seeks to make amendments in section 10 to provide minimum age of thirty-five years, minimum qualification of graduation and minimum experience of ten years for Members of the District Forum. It also seeks to provide disqualifications for the office of Member. It seeks to make a new proviso to sub-section (1A) to provide that where the President of the State Commission is, by reason of absence or otherwise, unable to act as Chairman of the Selection Committee, the State Government may refer the matter to the Chief Justice of the High Court who shall nominate a sitting Judge of that High Court to act as a Chairman to avoid delay in selection. It also seeks to amend sub-section (2) to provide for re-appointment of Presidents and Members to enable utilisation of their experiences for a longer period. It also seeks to provide that persons already holding office of President or Member will continue to hold such office till the completion of their term. It further seeks to amend sub-section (3) to provide that the State Government shall appoint a Member on whole-time basis on the recommendations of the President of the State Commission taking into consideration to workload and other factors as may be prescribed.

Composition

District Forum consists of one president and two other members (one of whom is to be a woman).

The president of the Forum is a person who is, or has been qualified to be a District Judge, and other members are persons of ability, integrity and standing, and have adequate knowledge or experience of, or have shown capacity in dealing with, problems relating to economics, law, commerce, accountancy, industry, public affairs or administration.

The object underlying the inclusion of non-judicial members appears to be to impart a balance to the functioning of the District Forum by ensuring that the members are able to understand the economic and social impact of the matters. Further inclusion of one female members ensures that the matters are viewed from a woman's angle also.

The pension received by the Presidents of the District Consumer Forum in respect of their previous services as District Judges is subject to deduction from their salary as President of the Forum fixed under provisions of the Act. [*M.S. Chawla* v *State of Punjab* AIR 2001 SC 1706]

---

1 Inserted by the Consumer Protection (Amendment) Act, 2002, w.e.f. 15-3-2003.

11. Jurisdiction of the District Forum.—(1) Subject to the other provisions of this Act, the District Forum shall have jurisdiction to entertain complaints where the value of the goods or services and the compensation, if any, claimed [1][does not exceed rupees twenty lakhs].

(2) A complaint shall be instituted in a District Forum within the local limits of whose jurisdiction,—

(*a*) the opposite party or each of the opposite parties, where there are more than one, at the time of the institution of the complaint, actually and voluntarily resides or [2][carries on business or has a branch office] or personally works for gain, or

(*b*) any of the opposite parties, where there are more than one, at the time of the institution of the complaint, actually and voluntarily resides, or [3][carries on business or has a branch office] or personally works for gain, provided that in such case either the permission of the District Forum is given, or the opposite parties who do not reside, or [4][carry on business or have a branch office] or personally work for gain, as the case may be, acquiesce in such institution; or

(*c*) the cause of action, wholly or in part, arises.

COMMENTS ON SECTION 11

Under section 17 of the Consumer Protection Act, a State Commission has jurisdiction to decide the complaints of the value between rupees five and twenty lakhs but there is no such provision as contained in section 11(2) of the Act applicable to the State Commission. Section 18 of the Act does not make provision of section 11(2) applicable to the State Commission. Each State has its own State Commission. There is a purpose for it. The first appeal of the District Forum situated within the State lies to the State Commission and then the State Commission can take cognizance of the dispute arising within that State. It cannot be the intention of the Legislature that the dispute arising in one State could be taken cognizance of by the State Commission of another State. [*Union Bank of India* v *Seppo Rally Oy* (1999) 8 SCC 357]

(*i*) Consumer forums have jurisdiction to entertain complaint against common carrier regarding loss of or damage to goods entrusted to carrier for transportation. [*Patel Roadways Ltd.* v *Birla Yamaha Ltd.* AIR 2000 SC 1461]

(*ii*) Objection and regarding territorial jurisdiction should be taken at the earliest opportunity or the same deemed to have been waived.

---

1 Substituted for the words "does not exceed rupees five lakhs", by the Consumer Protection (Amendment) Act, 2002, w.e.f. 15-3-2003.

2 Substituted for the words "carries on business", by the Consumer Protection (Amendment) Act, 1993, w.e.f. 18-6-1993.

3 Substituted for the words "carries on business", *ibid.*

4 Substituted for the words "carry on business", *ibid.*

[*Kurukshetra University* v *Vinay Prakash Verma* II (1993) CPJ 647]

(*iii*) A petition of complaint can be filed against corporation carrying on business within the territory of District Forum or Commission even though its sole or principal office is situated outside state limits. [*Consumer Education and Research Society* v *Canara Bank* (1991 I CPR 405]

(*iv*) Voluntary consumer associations should be permitted to file one complaint covering the persons similarly situated, when the cause of action arises out of the same act or transaction against the same opponents. *Consumer Protection Council* v *Lohia Machines Ltd.* (1992) 1 CPR 127 (Guj). In *Mumbai Grahak Panchayat* v *Lohia Machines Ltd.* (1991) 1 CPR 184, the National Commission not only granted the relief of 934 consumers represented by the voluntary consumer association, but directed the company to submit list of all other unascertained persons who are similarly situated by treating that application as a public interest litigation.

(*v*) Where the remedy of the complainant by means of a civil suit is barred by law of limitation, complaint under the Consumer Protection Act is not maintainable. [*Teesta Fruit & Vegetable Processing Ltd* v *Chinmoy Ghosh* (1992) 1 CPR 121 (NC)]

(*vi*) The only requirement to be satisfied is that on the date when the consumer dispute is filed before the Redressal Forum the cause of action should not have become time barred under the law of the limitation. [*S. Elhence* v *Raghomal Nahar Singh Ltd.* (1991)1 CPR 419 (NC)]

(*vii*) Where the claim had become time barred under the law of limitation long prior to the coming into force of the Act, the Consumer Forum cannot entertain a stale claim. [*Oswal Fine Arts* v *H.M.T., Madras* O.P. No. 1 of 1988 decided on 27-4-1989 (NC)]

(*viii*) In view of the definition of 'untoward incident' provided under section 123(*c*) of the Railway Claims Tribunal Act, 1987, it is beyond any doubt that the compensation on account of untoward incident can be decided by the Railway Tribunal and none else. Therefore, the District Forum under the Consumer Protection Act, 1986, could not decide the dispute. [*Union of India* v *Ashok Shankar Sarkale* AIR 2006 Bom 198]

(*ix*) Objections regarding territorial jurisdiction should be taken at the earliest opportunity or the same deemed to have been waived. [*Kurukshetra University* v *Vinay Prakash Verma* II (1993) CPJ 647]

(*x*) A petition of complaint can be filed against corporation carrying on business within the territory of District Forum or Commission even though its sole or principal office is situated outside state limits. [*Consumer Education and Research Society* v *Canara Bank* (1991) 1 CPR 405]

[1][**12. Manner in which complaint shall be made.**—(1) A complaint in relation to any goods sold or delivered or agreed to be sold or delivered or any service provided or agreed to be provided may be filed with a District Forum by—

(*a*) the consumer to whom such goods are sold or delivered or agreed to be sold or delivered or such service provided or agreed to be provided;

(*b*) any recognised consumer association whether the consumer to whom the goods sold or delivered or agreed to be sold or delivered or service provided or agreed to be provided is a member of such association or not;

(*c*) one or more consumers where there are numerous consumers having the same interest, with the permission of the District Forum, on behalf of, or for the benefit of, all consumers so interested; or

(*d*) the Central Government or the State Government, as the case may be, either in its individual capacity or as a representative of interests of the consumers in general.

(2) Every complaint filed under sub-section (1) shall be accompanied with such amount of fee and payable in such manner as may be prescribed.

(3) On receipt of a complaint made under sub-section (1), the District Forum may, by order, allow the complaint to be proceeded with or rejected:

Provided that a complaint shall not be rejected under this sub-section unless an opportunity of being heard has been given to the complainant:

Provided further that the admissibility of the complaint shall ordinarily be decided within twenty-one days from the date on which the complaint was received.

---

1 Substituted by the Consumer Protection (Amendment) Act, 2002, w.e.f. 15-3-2003. The old section read as under:

"*12.* A complaint in relation to any goods sold or delivered or agreed to be sold or delivered or any service provided or agreed to be provided may be filed with a District Forum by—

(*a*) the consumer to whom such goods are sold or delivered or agreed to be sold or delivered or such service provided or agreed to be provided;

(*b*) any recognised consumer association whether the consumer to whom the goods sold or delivered or agreed to be sold or delivered or service provided or agreed to be provided is a member of such association or not;

(*c*) one or more consumers, where there are numerous consumers having the same interest, with the permission of the District Forum, on behalf of, or for the benefit of, all consumers so interested; or

(*d*) the Central or the State Government.

Explanation.—For the purposes of this section, "recognised consumer association" means any voluntary consumer, association registered under the Companies Act, 1956 or any other law for the time being in force."

(4) Where a complaint is allowed to be proceeded with under sub-section (3), the District Forum may proceed with the complaint in the manner provided under this Act:

Provided that where a complaint has been admitted by the District Forum, it shall not be transferred to any other court or tribunal or any authority set up by or under any other law for the time being in force.

Explanation.—For the purposes of this section, "recognised consumer association" means any voluntary consumer association registered under the Companies Act, 1956 (1 of 1956) or any other law for the time being in force.]

COMMENTS ON SECTION 12

Objects and Reasons

Clause 9 (old) seeks to substitute section 12 to provide that every complaint filed with the District Forum shall be accompanied with such amount of fee as may be prescribed. It also seeks to provide that the admissibility of the complaint shall ordinarily be decided within twenty-one days from the date on which the complaint is received and that once admitted a complaint shall not be transferred to any other Court or Tribunal. This will help to quicken disposal of complaints.

Sitting of the Forums

The law has provided certain norms as to the number of judges who will handle a dispute. The rationale must have been to make the decisive body as broad as possible.

Sitting of the District Forum

For conducting any proceedings to resolve a consumer dispute at least two members of the Forum must be there one of whom should be the president.

Where the member, for any reason, is unable to conduct the proceeding till it is completed, the President and the other member shall conduct such proceeding *de novo* i.e. from the beginning.

Example: A District Forum has three members, 'P' the President, and 'X' and 'Y', the other two members. 'P' and 'X' started dealing with a particular case. In the meantime, 'X' fell ill and dropped out. Now the proceedings in the given case will be started afresh by 'P' and 'Y' (or any other member appointed in place of 'X'.

Sitting of the State Commission: Every proceeding is required to be conducted by the president of the State Commission and at least one member thereof sitting together.

However, if for any reason the member is unable to conduct the proceeding till it is completed, the president and the other member shall conduct such proceeding afresh.

Sitting of the National Commission: The disputes must be disposed of by at least three members of the National Commission, one of whom must be the president (or the senior most members authorised to work as president).

Where the member(s) for any reason are unable to conduct the proceeding till it is completed, the president (or the senior most member acting as president) shall conduct the proceeding afresh.

Note that the rules regarding sitting are mandatory. Any failure to comply with the same may invalidate the order.

13. [1]**[Procedure on admission of complaint]**.—(1) The District Forum shall, [2][on admission of a complaint], if it relates to any goods,—

[3][(*a*) refer a copy of the admitted complaint, within twenty-one days from the date of its admission to the opposite party mentioned in the complaint directing him to give his version of the case within a period of thirty days or such extended period not exceeding fifteen days as may be granted by the District Forum;]

(*b*) where the opposite party on receipt of a complaint referred to him under clause (*a*) denies or disputes the allegations contained in the complaint, or omits or fails to take any action to represent his case within the time given by the District Forum, the District Forum shall proceed to settle the consumer dispute in the manner specified in clauses (*c*) to (*g*);

(*c*) where the complaint alleges a defect in the goods which cannot be determined without proper analysis or test of the goods, the District Forum shall obtain a sample of the goods from the complainant, seal it and authenticate it in the manner prescribed and refer the sample so sealed to the appropriate laboratory along with a direction that such laboratory make an analysis or test, whichever may be necessary, with a view to finding out whether such goods suffer from any defect alleged in the complaint or suffer from any other defect and to report its findings thereon to the District Forum within a period of forty-five days of the receipt of the reference or within such extended period as may be granted by the District Forum;

(*d*) before any sample of the goods is referred to any appropriate laboratory under clause (*c*), the District Forum may require the complainant to deposit to the credit of the Forum such fees as may be specified, for payment to the appropriate laboratory for carrying out the necessary analysis or test in relation to the goods in question;

---

1 Substituted for the words "Procedure on receipt of complaint" by the Consumer Protection (Amendment) Act, 2002, w.e.f. 15-3-2003.

2 Substituted for the words "on receipt of a complaint," ibid.

3 Substituted for clause (*a*) which read as under:

"(*a*) refer a copy of the complaint to the opposite party mentioned in the complaint directing him to give his version of the case within a period of thirty days or such extended period not exceeding fifteen days as may be granted by the District Forum;" ibid.

(*e*) the District Forum shall remit the amount deposited to its credit under clause (*d*) to the appropriate laboratory to enable it to carry out the analysis or test mentioned in clause (*c*) and on receipt of the report from the appropriate laboratory, the District Forum shall forward a copy of the report along with such remarks as the District Forum may feel appropriate to the opposite party;

(*f*) if any of the parties disputes the correctness of the findings of the appropriate laboratory, or disputes the correctness of the methods of analysis or test adopted by the appropriate laboratory, the District Forum shall require the opposite party or the complainant to submit in writing his objections in regard to the report made by the appropriate laboratory;

(*g*) the District Forum shall thereafter give a reasonable opportunity to the complainant as well as the opposite party of being heard as to the correctness or otherwise of the report made by the appropriate laboratory and also as to the objection made in relation thereto under clause (*f*) and issue an appropriate order under section 14.

(2) The District Forum shall, if the [1][complaint admitted] by it under section 12 relates to goods in respect of which the procedure specified in sub-section (1) cannot be followed, or if the complaint relates to any services,—

(*a*) refer a copy of such complaint to the opposite party directing him to give his version of the case within a period of thirty days or such extended period not exceeding fifteen days as may be granted by the District Forum;

(*b*) where the opposite party, on receipt of a copy of the complaint, referred to him under clause (*a*) denies or disputes the allegations contained in the complaint, or omits or fails to take any action to represent his case within the time given by the District Forum, the District Forum shall proceed to settle the consumer dispute,—

(*i*) on the basis of evidence brought to its notice by the complainant and the opposite party, where the opposite party denies or disputes the allegations contained in the complaint, or

(*ii*) [2][ex parte on the basis of evidence] brought to its notice by the complainant where the opposite party omits or fails to take any action to represent his case within the time given by the Forum;

[3][(*c*) where the complainant fails to appear on the date of hearing before the District Forum, the District Forum may either dismiss the complaint for default or decide it on merits.]

---

1 Substituted for the words "complaint received" by the Consumer Protection (Amendment) Act, 2002, w.e.f. 15-3-2003.

2 Substituted for the words "on the basis of evidence" by the Consumer Protection (Amendment) Act, 2002, w.e.f. 15-3-2003.

3 Inserted by the Consumer Protection (Amendment) Act, 2002, w.e.f. 15-3-2003.

(3) No proceedings complying with the procedure laid down in sub-sections (1) and (2) shall be called in question in any court on the ground that the principles of natural justice have not been complied with.

[1][(3A) Every complaint shall be heard as expeditiously as possible and endeavour shall be made to decide the complaint within a period of three months from the date of receipt of notice by opposite party where the complaint does not require analysis or testing of commodities and within five months if it requires analysis or testing of commodities:

Provided that no adjournment shall be ordinarily granted by the District Forum unless sufficient cause is shown and the reasons for grant of adjournment have been recorded in writing by the Forum:

Provided further that the District Forum shall make such orders as to the costs occasioned by the adjournment as may be provided in the regulations made under this Act.

Provided also that in the event of a complaint being disposed of after the period so specified, the District Forum shall record in writing, the reasons for the same at the time of disposing of the said complaint.

(3B) Where during the pendency of any proceeding before the District Forum, it appears to it necessary, it may pass such interim order as is just and proper in the facts and circumstances of the case.]

(4) For purposes of this section, the District Forum shall have the same powers as are vested in a civil court under the Code of Civil Procedure, 1908 (5 of 1908), while trying a suit in respect of the following matters, namely:—

(*i*) the summoning and enforcing attendance of any defendant or witness and examining the witness on oath;

(*ii*) the discovery and production of any document or other material object producible as evidence;

(*iii*) the reception of evidence on affidavits;

(*iv*) the requisitioning of the report of the concerned analysis or test from the appropriate laboratory or from any other relevant source;

(*v*) issuing of any commission for the examination of any witness; and

(*vi*) any other matter which may be prescribed.

(5) Every proceeding before the District Forum shall be deemed to be a judicial proceeding within the meaning of sections 193 and 228 of the Indian Penal Code (45 of 1860), and the District Forum shall be deemed to be a civil court for the purposes of section 195, and Chapter XXVI of the Code of Criminal Procedure 1973 (2 of 1974).

[2][(6) Where the complainant is a consumer referred to in sub-clause (*iv*) of clause (*b*) of sub-section (1) of section 2, the provisions of rule 8 of Order I of the

---

1 Inserted by the Consumer Protection (Amendment) Act, 2002, w.e.f. 15-3-2003.
2 Inserted by the Consumer Protection (Amendment) Act, 1993, w.e.f. 18-6-1993.

First Schedule to the Code of Civil Procedure, 1908 (5 of 1908) shall apply subject to the modification that every reference therein to a suit or decree shall be construed as a reference to a complaint or the order of the District Forum thereon.]

[1][(7) In the event of death of a complainant who is a consumer or of the opposite party against whom the complaint has been filed, the provisions of Order XXII of the First Schedule to the Code of Civil Procedure, 1908 (5 of 1908) shall apply subject to the modification that every reference therein to the plaintiff and the defendant shall be construed as reference to a complainant or the opposite party, as the case may be.]

COMMENTS ON SECTION 13

Objects and Reasons

Clause 10 (old) seeks to amend section 13 to require the District Forum to refer a copy of the admitted complaint within twenty-one days from the date of its admission to the opposite party to give his version. It also seeks to make explicit the provision for *ex parte* order. It seeks to include a new sub-section (3A) to provide that complaint shall be heard as expeditiously as possible and endeavour made to decide the complaints within the prescribed period. Adjournments would ordinarily not be granted, and if granted for reasons to be recorded in writing by the Forum, an order as to the costs occasioned by the adjournment would also be made by the Forum. It further seeks to include a new sub-section (3B) to enable the District Forum to pass interim orders where required. It also seeks to include a new sub-section (7) for the substitution of parties in accordance with the provisions of Order XXII of the First Schedule to the Code of Civil Procedure, 1908 in the event of death of the complainant or opposite party. These amendments will facilitate quicker disposal of cases, enable complainants to get immediate relief where required, and streamline procedures.

Powers of the Consumer Forums

For the purpose of adjudicating a consumer dispute, section 13(4) has vested the Consumer Forums with certain powers of a civil court. Apart from these powers, the Central Government has provided some additional powers to them under Rule 10 of the Consumer Protection Rules, 1987. Finally section 14 of the Act has provided them with the power to issue orders.

Powers akin to those of Civil Court [Section 13(4)]

The Forums are vested with the Civil Court powers with respect to the following:

(*a*) summoning and enforcing the attendance of any defendant or witness and examining the witness on oath;

---

1 Inserted by the Consumer Protection (Amendment) Act, 2002, w.e.f. 15-3-2003.

(*b*) discovery and production of any document or other material object producible as evidence;

(*c*) receiving of evidence on affidavits;

(*d*) requisitioning of the report of the concerned analysis or test from the appropriate laboratory or from any other relevant source;

(*e*) issuing of any commission for the examination of any witness; and

(*f*) any other matter which may be prescribed.

Additional powers of the consumer forums [Rule 10]

The National Commission, the State Commission and the District Forum have following additional powers:

(*a*) Requiring production of any books, accounts, documents, or commodities from any person, examining and retaining them.

(*b*) Obtaining information required for the purpose of the proceedings from any person.

(*c*) enter and search any premises and seize from such premises books, papers, documents, commodities required for the purpose of proceedings under the Act.

(*i*) In section 13(4) of the Consumer Protection Act the provisions of Civil Procedure Code which have been made applicable to the complaints have been given. Order II, Rule 2 has not been made applicable to such proceedings. It is thus clear that the Legislature in its wisdom did not make applicable the provisions of Order II, Rule 2 to the proceedings under the Consumer Protection Act, 1986. [*Oriental Insurance Co.* v *Sh. Lekh Raj Dang* (1991) 1 CPR 307]

(*ii*) When the case is not a simple case of deficiency in service and involves determination of complex questions of facts and law, which cannot be satisfactorily determined by the redressal agency. In the time frame provided under the Rules, it would be better for the complainant to seek redressal of his grievances in a Civil Court, if so advised. [*Harbans & Co.* v *State Bank of India* II (1994) CPJ 476: 1994 (1) CPR 381]

(*iii*) If "fraud" is alleged, it is desirable that the complainant should be directed to Civil Court as investigation about such fraud is required to be done. [*Jayantilal Keshavlal Chauhan* v *National Insurance Co. Ltd.* 1994 (I) CPR 396]

(*iv*) A consumer knocking at the door of the redressal agencies under the Act for relief in a consumer dispute must do so with clean hands. [*Sagli Ram* v *General Manager, United India Insurance Co. Ltd. II* (1994) CPJ 444: 1994 (I) CPR 434]

(*v*) Compensation is to be given for loss or injury suffered by a consumer, due to negligence of the opposite party. [*S.K. Lakhotia* v *National Insurance Co. Ltd.* 1994 (I) CPR 43] (*vi*) The party to be awarded compensation has not only to show deficiency in service but also the negligence of the other party and without the finding of negligence there cannot be any award. [Director, *Himachal Institute of Engineering & Technology* v *Ani1 Kumar Gupta* 1994 (I) CPR 182]

(*vii*) If a consumer sustained any loss or damage actually, he is entitled to compensation. [*Padmana Dash* v *Divisional Rly. Manager, S.E. Rly.* 1994 (I) CPR 77]

(*viii*) The Consumer Disputes Redressal Agencies/which are not vested with power of a Civil Court, are not entitled to exercise review jurisdiction as envisaged under section 114 of the Code of Civil Procedure. [*Eureka Estates Pvt. Ltd.* v *A.P. State Consumer Dispute Redressal Commission* AIR 2005 AP 118]

(*ix*) Application for amendment of complaint can be entertained by District Forum, though there is no specific provision for amendment, there is also no bar in allowing amendment. [*Manimalan* v *K. Subrayan* AIR 2004 Mad 446]

(*xi*) When the case is not a simple case of deficiency in service and involves determination of complex questions of facts and law, which cannot be satisfactorily determined by the redressal agency in the time frame provided under the Rules, it would be better for the complainant to seek redress of his grievances in a Civil Court, if so advised. [*Harbans & Co.* v *State Bank of India, II* (1994) CPJ 456: 1994 (I) CPR 381]

(*xii*) If "fraud" is alleged, it is desirable that the complainant should be directed to Civil Court as investigation about such fraud is required to be done. [*Jayantilal Keshavlal Chauhan* v *National Insurance Co. Ltd.* 1994 (I) CPR 396]

(*xii*) A consumer knocking at the door of the redressal agencies under the Act for relief in a consumer dispute must do so with clean hands. [*Sagli Ram* v *General Manager, United India Insurance Co. Ltd. II* (1994) CPJ 444: 1994 (I) CPR 434]

14. Finding of the District Forum.—(1) If, after the proceeding conducted under section 13, the District Forum is satisfied that the goods complained against suffer from any of the defects specified in the complaint or that any of the allegations contained in the complaint about the services are proved, it shall issue an order to the opposite party directing him to [1][do] one or more of the following things, namely:—

(*a*) to remove the defect pointed out by the appropriate laboratory from the goods in question;

---

1 Substituted for the word "take" by the Consumer Protection (Amendment) Act, 1993, w.e.f. 18-6-1993.

(*b*) to replace the goods with new goods of similar description which shall be free from any defect;

(*c*) to return to the complainant the price, or, as the case may be, the charges paid by the complainant;

(*d*) to pay such amount as may be awarded by it as compensation to the consumer for any loss or injury suffered by the consumer due to the negligence of the opposite party:

[1][Provided that the District Forum shall have the power to grant punitive damages in such circumstances as it deems fit;]

[2][(*e*) to [3][remove the defects in goods] or deficiencies in the services in question;

(*f*) to discontinue the unfair trade practice or the restrictive trade practice or not to repeat them;

(*g*) not to offer the hazardous goods for sale;

(*h*) to withdraw the hazardous goods from being offered for sale;]

[4][(*ha*) to cease manufacture of hazardous goods and to desist from offering services which are hazardous in nature;

(*hb*) to pay such sum as may be determined by it if it is of the opinion that loss or injury has been suffered by a large number of consumers who are not identifiable conveniently:

Provided that the minimum amount of sum so payable shall not be less than five per cent of the value of such defective goods sold or service provided, as the case may be, to such consumers:

Provided further that the amount so obtained shall be credited in favour of such person and utilized in such manner as may be prescribed;

(*hc*) to issue corrective advertisement to neutralize the effect of misleading advertisement at the cost of the opposite party responsible for issuing such misleading advertisement;]

[5][(*i*) to provide for adequate costs to parties.]

[6][(2) Every proceeding referred to in sub-section (1) shall be conducted by the President of the District Forum and at least one member thereof sitting together:

---

1 Inserted by the Consumer Protection (Amendment) Act, 2002, w.e.f. 15-3-2003.
2 Inserted by the Consumer Protection (Amendment) Act, 1993, w.e.f. 18-6-1993.
3 Substituted for the words "remove the defects" by the Consumer Protection (Amendment) Act, 2002, w.e.f. 15-3-2003.
4 Inserted, ibid.
5 Inserted by the Consumer Protection (Amendment) Act, 1993, w.e.f. 18-6-1993.
6 Substituted by the Consumer Protection (Amendment) Act, 1991, w.e.f. 15-6-1991.

[1][Provided that where a member, for any reason, is unable to conduct a proceeding till it is completed, the President and the other member shall continue the proceeding from the stage at which it was last heard by the previous member].

[2][(2A) Every order made by the District Forum under sub-section (1) shall be signed by its President and the member or members who conducted the proceeding:

Provided that where the proceeding is conducted by the President and one member and they differ on any point or points, they shall state the point or points on which they differ and refer the same to the other member for hearing on such point or points and the opinion of the majority shall be the order of the District Forum.]

(3) Subject to the foregoing provisions, the procedure relating to the conduct of the meetings of the District Forum, its sitting and other matters shall be such as may be prescribed by the State Government.

COMMENTS ON SECTIONS 14(1) AND RULE 10

Objects and Reasons

Clause 11 (old) seeks to amend section 14 to empower the District Forum if it is satisfied that the allegations contained in the complaint are proved, also to issue orders directing the opposite party, *inter alia*, to pay punitive damages, cease manufacture of hazardous goods and desist from offering services which are hazardous in nature, pay such sum not less than five per cent, of the value of defective goods sold or services provided where loss or injury has been suffered by a large number of consumers who are not conveniently identifiable, and to issue corrective advertisement to neutralise the effect of misleading advertisement. It also seeks to amend sub-section (2) to do away with the requirement of *de novo* proceedings if a Member is unable to conduct the proceeding till it is completed and allow the proceeding to continue from the stage it was last heard by the previous Member. This will avoid delay in disposal of such cases.

Rule 5(5) of the West Bengal Consumer Protection Rules, 1987 overrides section 14 of the Consumer Protection Act, 1986 and as such the said Rule 5(5) is bad, illegal and inoperative. [*N. Taneja* v *Calcutta Distt. Forum* AIR 1992 Cal. 95]

While quantifying damages, Consumer Forums are required to make an attempt to serve the ends, of justice so that compensation is awarded, in an established case, which not only serves the purpose of

---

1 Substituted by the Consumer Protection (Amendment) Act, 2002, w.e.f. 15-3-2003 for the following proviso:

"Provided that where the member, for any reason, is unable to conduct the proceeding till it is completed, the President and the other member shall conduct such proceeding *de novo*."

2 Inserted by the Consumer Protection (Amendment) Act, 1991, w.e.f. 15-6-1991.

recompensing the individual, but which also at the same time, aims to bring about a qualitative change in the attitude of the service provider. Indeed, calculation of damages depends on the facts and circumstances of each case. No hard and fast rule can be laid down for universal application. While awarding compensation, a Consumer Forum has to take into account all relevant factors and assess compensation on the basis of accepted legal principles, on moderation. [*Charan Singh* v *Healing Touch Hospital* (2000) 7 SCC 668]

Interest can be awarded on equitable grounds. [*Sovintorg* (*India*) *Ltd.* v *State Bank of India* AIR 1999 SC 2963]

Power to issue order [Section 14(1)]

If, after the proceedings, the Forum is satisfied that the complainant suffer from any defect in goods or deficiency in service, it may issue an order to the opposite party directing him to do one or more of the following things, namely:—

(*a*) to remove the defect pointed out by the appropriate laboratory from the goods in question;

(*b*) to replace the goods with new goods of similar description which shall be free from any defect;

(*c*) to return to the complainant the price, or, as the case may be, the charges paid by the complainant;

(*d*) to pay such amount as may be awarded by it as compensation to the consumer for any loss or injury suffered by the consumer due to the negligence of the opposite party;

(*e*) to remove the defects or deficiencies in the services in question;

(*f*) to discontinue the unfair trade practice or the restrictive trade practice or not to repeat it;

(*g*) not to offer the hazardous goods for sale;

(*h*) to withdraw the hazardous goods from being offered for sale;

(*i*) to provide for adequate costs to complainant.

(*i*) A consumer knocking at the door of the redressal agencies under the Act for relief in a consumer dispute must do so with clean hands. [*Sagli Ram* v *General Manager, United India Insurance Co. Ltd.* II (1994) CPJ 444: 1994 (I) CPR 434]

(*ii*) The Fora have no jurisdiction to pass interim order. The complaint was filed to restrain a public issue. It was also held that unsuccessful applicants, who have not been allotted any shares can not prefer a complaint under the Act. [*Morgan Stanley* v *Kartlk Das, II* (1994) CPJ 7 (SC)]

(*iii*) Delay in delivery after booking of a car is no deficiency. [*M/s. Maruti Udyog Ltd* v *Mrs. Bhuvana Viswanathan* II (1993) CPJ 172 (NC)] (*iv*) Redressal forums have no jurisdiction in matters involving outright sale of immovable property at an auction. [*Allied (Garments) Exports Industries Pvt, Ltd.* v *D.D.A.* II (1992) CPJ 505 (NC)]

(*v*) Consumer Forums have no jurisdiction to pass interim orders. [*District Manager, Telephones* v *M/s. Munilal Erij Mohan* 1 (1993) CPJ 41 (NC)]

(*vi*) It is well settled that if the District Forum has no jurisdiction to entertain the complaint, the order passed by it, regarding *status quo* is without jurisdiction. [*Jaipur Stock Exchange Ltd.* v *C.O.Mehta* (1991) 1 CPR 26]

(*vii*) The delay in filing an appeal should not have been for reasons which indicate the party's negligence in not taking necessary steps, which he could have or should have taken. What would be such necessary steps will depend upon the circumstances of a particular case and each case will have to be decided by the courts on the facts and circumstances of the case. Any observation of an illustrative circumstance of fact will only tend to be a curb on the free exercise of the judicial mind by the court in determining whether the facts and circumstances of a particular case amount to sufficient cause or not. It is for the court to exercise its judicial discretion soundly in the interest of justice. But the expression 'sufficient cause' cannot be constructed too liberally, merely because the party in. default is the Government. It cannot also be gainsaid that the same consideration that will be shown by courts to a private party when he claims the protection of section 5 of the Limitation Act should also be available to the State. The words 'sufficient cause' should receive a liberal construction so as to advance substantial justice when no negligence or inaction or want of bona fide is imputable to a party. [*State of W.B,* v *Administrator, Howrah Municipality* (1972) 1 SCC 366, 367, 373, 374: AIR 1972 SC 749: (1972) 2 SCR 874]

(*viii*) In dealing with question of condoning the delay under section 5 of the Limitation Act the party seeking relief has to satisfy the court that it had sufficient cause for not preferring the appeal or making the application within the prescribed time and this has always been understood to mean that the explanation has to cover the whole period of delay. It is not possible to lay down precisely as to what facts or matters would constitute sufficient cause under the section but those words should be liberally construed so as to advance substantial justice where no negligence or any inaction or want of *bona fides* is imputable to the party; that is, the delay in filing the appeal should not have been for reasons which indicated the party's negligence in not taking necessary steps which he would have or should have taken. Discretion is conferred on the High Court before which an application for condoning the delay is made and if the court after keeping in view relevant principles exercises its discretion granting relief, unless it is shown to be manifestly unjust or perverse, the Supreme Court would be loathe to interfere with it. [*Sandhya Rani Sarker* v *Sudha Rani Debi* (1978) 2 SCC 116: AIR 1978 SC 537]

(*ix*) The words "sufficient cause" and "satisfied" used in proviso to section 15 are in *pari materia* with the words used in section 5 of the Limitation Act. The appellant is required to explain delay beyond the terminus line of the prescribed period of limitation and further that he had acted diligently for the purpose of filing the appeal. It is settled that if anything is not done with due care and attention, it cannot be said to have been done diligently. [*Mahendra Thaker* v *Devendra Kothari* (1992) 1 CPR 23 (Rai)]

(*x*) Cross-objections, as commonly understood, are only a creature of Order 41, Rule 22, of the Civil Procedure Code, 1908 and can be preferred only in areas where the said provision is applicable *stricto sensu*. There can be no little doubt that Order 41, Rule 22 is not attached to the field of consumer legislation under the Act. [*Haryana State Electricity Board* v *Dinesh Kumar* (1991) 2 CPJ 30 (Har); *Anand Motor Agents Pvt. Ltd.* v *Sweta Kaura* (1991) 1 CPR 356 (NC)]

(*xi*) Cross-objection cannot be filed in an appeal field before the. [*National Commission Manjulaben* v *LIC* 1992) 1 CPR 227 (NC)]

(*xii*) Providing cross-objections at appellate stage cannot be made applicable to the proceedings under the Act, hence cross-objections are not maintainable as these were not filed before the District Forum. [*Arvinder Singh Chawla* v *Kulbhushan* 2001 (1) CPR 387]

(*xiii*) the words "sufficient cause", though deserves to receive a liberal interpretation, yet, a just and equitable balance has to be maintained between the right secured by the respondent as a result of expiry of the prescribed period of limitation and the injustice of depriving the appellant of a adjudication of his grievances on the merit of his appeal for causes beyond his reasonable control, which means the cause in *bona fide* and beyond the control of the appellant. Though, no hard and fast line can be drawn as to what affords 'sufficient causes' in a given case, yet, again as per settled law, any cause which prevents a person from approaching the court within the time is 'sufficient cause'. In doing so, it is the test of a reasonable man in normal circumstances which has to be applied. [*Pradeep Kumar* v *Assistant Finance Officer, Delhi Vidhut Board* 2001 (1) CPR 9]

(*xiv*) The Appellate Fora constituted under the Act should not dismiss the appeal merely on the ground of default of appearance of the appellant but the merits of the case should be considered on the basis of the material available before them and thereafter pass appropriate order in the appeal. [*General Manager. Telecom* v *Jyantilal Hemchand Gandhi* 1993 (III) CPR 155]

(*xv*) Ordinarily, the Appellate Court does not interfere with the compensation awarded unless it is too inadequate or too excessive. [*Namlada* v *Suresh Chandra Mittal* 1993 (I) CPR 631]

(*xvi*) For award of compensation the loss or injury must have been caused due to negligence of the opposite party. [*Consumer Unity Trust Society* v *Chairman & Managing Director, Bank of Baroda* (1991) 1 CPR 263]

(*xvii*) Award of compensation on account of non-availability of vehicle during the period of its repair by dealer is not justified. [*Western India State Motors* v *Sobhag Mai Meena* (1991) 1 CPR 413]

(*xviii*) In *Maruti Udyog Ltd.* v *V.K. Jain* (1991) 1 CPR 162: (1991) 1 CPJ 50, the National Commission held that the provisions of Section 14(2) are mandatory in that every order passed by the District Forum has to be signed by all the three members (President and two Members) all of whom together constitute the District Forum and its not competent for a Bench consisting of only two Members or even a single Member to validly hear and dispose of any complaint field before the District Forum. The National Commission was fully conscious of the serious inconvenience and delay that would result from the insistence on the presence of all the Members at every sitting of the District Forum. To avoid this situation it was suggested that an appropriate amendment should be urgently carried out in section 14 so that the objective of assuring cheap and speedy redressal of consumer grievances should not be hampered — Consequently, present sub-sections (2) and (2A) have been substituted for old sub-section (2) by Ordinance 6 of 1991 which has been replaced by Act 34 of 1991, with effect from 15-6-1991.

(*xix*) Under section 14(2) as amended by Act 34 of 1991, it is not necessary that all the members of the State Commission should participate in the hearing of a case or singing the order, the section requires that a case must be heard and disposed of by at least two members of the State Commission. This requirement is mandatory. [*H.K. Purohit* v *Registrar, University of Jodhpur, Revision Petition Nos. 61 and 62 of 1991*, decided on 22-10-1991 (NC)]

(*xx*) A casual absence on account of illness or any other cause does not create a vacancy among the Members of the District Forum. A vacancy can be said to exist only when the post of the Member is unoccupied and remains to be filled by appointment of a substitute. [*United India Insurance Co. Ltd.* v *Ram Rattan* (1992) 1 CPR 162 (Raj)]

(*xxi*) In *General Manager, M.T.N.L. Ltd.* v *Nazar J. Irani* (1992) 1 CPR 110 (NC) the case was disposed of by the District Forum before coming into operation of Act 34 of 1991. There was a difference of opinion between the President and the other Member and they delivered separate divergent judgments. By invoking Rule 11(4) of Maharashtra Rules the decision of the President was treated as the decision of the District Forum. The National Commission held that the order of the District Forum was not valid since it was not in conformity with mandatory procedure prescribed in provision to sub-section (2A) of section 14. The order could not be validated by invoking section 5 of the Amending Act 34 of 1991.

(*xxii*) Compensation is to be given for loss or injury suffered by a consumer, due to negligence of the opposite party. [*S.K. Lakhotia* v *National Insurance Co. Ltd.* 1994 (I) CPR 43]

(*xxiii*) The party to be awarded compensation has not only to show deficiency in service but also the negligence of the other party and without the finding of negligence there cannot be any award. [*Director, Himachal Institute of Engineering CV Technology* v *Anil Kumar Gupta* 1994 (I) CPR 182]

(*xxiv*) If a consumer sustained any loss or damage actually, he is entitled to compensation. [*Padmanav Dash* v *Divisional Rly. Manager, S.E. Rly.* 1994 (I) CPR 77]

(*xxv*) The Fora have no jurisdiction to pass interim order. The complaint was filed to restrain a public issue. It was also held that unsuccessful applicants, who have not been allotted any shares can not prefer a complaint under the Act. [*Morgan Stanley* v *Kartik Das* II (1994) CPJ 7 (SC)] (*xxvi*) Delay in delivery after booking of a car is no deficiency. [*Maruti Udyog Ltd.* v *Mrs. Bhuvana Viswanathan* II (1993) CPJ 172 (NC)]

(*xxvii*) Redressal forums have no jurisdiction in matters involving outright sale of immovable property at an auction. [*Allied (Garments) Exports Industries Pvt. Ltd.* v *D.D.A.* II (1992) CPJ 505 (NC)]

(*xxviii*) Consumer Forums have no jurisdiction to pass interim orders. *District Manager, Telephones* v *Munilal Brij Mohan* I (1993) CPJ 41 (NC)]

Orders of the Forums

The orders of the Consumers Forums are like orders of the Civil Court and are enforceable like a decree of the court. The order of a junior Forum is appealable with the senior Forum, and when no appeal is instituted, the order is final. However, the law has prescribed certain norms as to the signing of orders without complying which the orders cannot be made.

District Forum

Signing requirement — Section 14(2A) provides that every order made by the District Forum shall be signed by its President and the member or members who conducted the proceeding.

Example: A complaint was dismissed by the President of a District Forum where other members of the Forum were not parties to it. On appeal, the State Commission held that section 14(2) of the Act makes it abundantly clear that for the decision on a complaint, one member of the Forum is must besides the President. Thus in the present case, the President of the Forum alone is not competent to dismiss the claim. [*Pankaj* v *Chairman, Central Secondary Education Board* (1991) 1 CPR 711 Delhi (CDRC)]

If there is difference of opinion between any two members, matter should be referred to the third member for a decision. And the decision of the majority would be final. Thus any order passed by a single member of the District Forum is not warranted.

State Commission

Signing requirement — Every order made by the State Commission shall be signed by its President and the member or members who conducted the proceeding.

If there is difference of opinion between any two members, matter should be referred to the third member for a decision. And the decision of the majority would be final.

National Commission

Signing requirement — Every order made by the National Commission must be signed by the president (or the senior most member acting as president), and at least two members who conducted the proceeding, and in case of any difference of opinion, the opinion of the majority shall be the order of the Commission.

15. Appeal.—Any person aggrieved by an order made by the District Forum may prefer an appeal against such order to the State Commission within a period of thirty days from the date of the order, in such form and manner as may be prescribed:

Provided that the State Commission may entertain an appeal after the expiry of the said period of thirty days if it is satisfied that there was sufficient cause for not filing it within that period:

[1][Provided further that no appeal by a person, who is required to pay any amount in terms of an order of the District Forum, shall be entertained by the State Commission unless the appellant has deposited in the prescribed manner fifty per cent, of that amount or twenty-five thousand rupees, whichever is less.]

COMMENTS ON SECTION 15

Objects and Reasons

Clause 12 (old) seeks to insert a new proviso in section 15 to provide that no appeal by a person, who is required to pay any amount in terms of an order of the District Forum, shall be entertained by the State Commission unless the appellant deposits fifty per cent of the amount or twenty-five thousand rupees, whichever is less.

The date of pronouncement of the order in the open Court by itself cannot be the starting point for determining the period of limitation under section 15 of the Act. It has also to be shown that the order of the District Forum so pronounced was duty signed and dated by the Members of the District Forum constituting the Bench and the same was communicated to the parties free of charge. But under the scheme of the Haryana Consumer Protection Rules, 1988 a copy of the said order has also to be communicated to the parties affected by the said order and the period of limitation in view of the above discussion will commence from the date on which the copies of the order were ready and made available. [*Housing Board, Haryana* v *Housing Board Colony Welfare Association* AIR. 1996 SC 92]

If the order of the Forum goes wrong and is made palpably without jurisdiction then certainly a citizen has the right to come under the protection of Article 226 of the Constitution. [*N. Taneja* v *Calcutta Distt. Forum* AIR 1992 Cal. 95]

---

1 Inserted by the Consumer Protection (Amendment) Act, 2002, w.e.f. 15-3-2003.

(*i*) Providing cross-objections at appellate stage cannot be made applicable to the proceedings under the Act, hence cross-objections are not maintainable as these were not filed before the District Forum. [*Arvinder Singh Chawla* v *Kulbhushan* 2001 (1) CPR 387]

(*ii*) The words "sufficient cause", though deserves to receive a liberal interpretation, yet, a just and equitable balance has to be maintained between the right secured by the respondent as a result of expiry of the prescribed period of limitation and the injustice of depriving the appellant of a adjudication of his grievances on the merit of his appeal for causes beyond his reasonable control, which means the cause in *bona fide* and beyond the control of the appellant. Though, no hard and fast line can be drawn as to what affords 'sufficient causes' in a given case, yet, again as per settled law, any cause which prevents a person from approaching the court within the time is 'sufficient cause'. In doing so, it is the test of a reasonable man in normal circumstances which has to be applied. [*Pradeep Kumar* v *Assistant Finance Officer, Delhi Vidyut Board* 2001 (1) CPR 9]

(*iii*) The Appellate Fora constituted under the Act should not dismiss the appeal merely on the ground of default of appearance of the appellant but the merits of the case should be considered on the basis of the material available before them and thereafter pass appropriate order in the appeal. [*General Manager, Telecom* v *Jyantilal Hemchand Gandhi* 1993 (III) CPR 155]

(*iv*) Ordinarily, the appellate court does not interfere with the compensation awarded unless it is too inadequate or too excessive. [*Narmada* v *Suresh Chandra Mittal* 1993 (I) AJR 631]

16. Composition of the State Commission.—(1) Each State Commission shall consist of,—

(*a*) a person who is or has been a Judge of a High Court, appointed by the State Government, who shall be its President:

[1][Provided that no appointment under this clause shall be made except after consultation with the Chief Justice of the High Court;]

[2][(*b*) not less than two, and not more than such number of members, as may be

---

1 Inserted by the Consumer Protection (Amendment) Act, 1993, w.e.f. 18-6-1993.

2 Substituted by the Consumer Protection (Amendment) Act, 2002, w.e.f. 15-3-2003, for the following clause:

"(*b*) two other members, who shall be persons of ability, integrity and standing and have adequate knowledge or experience of, or have shown capacity in dealing with, problems relating to economics, law, commerce, accountancy, industry, public affairs or administration, one of whom shall be a woman: →→

prescribed, and one of whom shall be a woman, who shall have the following qualifications, namely:—

(*i*) be not less than thirty-five years of age;

(*ii*) possess a bachelor's degree from a recognised university; and

(*iii*) be persons of ability, integrity and standing, and have adequate knowledge and experience of at least ten years in dealing with problems relating to economics, law, commerce, accountancy, industry, public affairs or administration:

Provided that not more than fifty per cent of the members shall be from amongst persons having a judicial background.

Explanation.—For the purposes of this clause, the expression "persons having judicial background" shall mean persons having knowledge and experience for at least a period of ten years as a presiding officer at the district level court or any tribunal at equivalent level:

Provided further that a person shall be disqualified for appointment as a member if he—

(*a*) has been convicted and sentenced to imprisonment for an offence which, in the opinion of the State Government, involves moral turpitude; or

(*b*) is an undischarged insolvent; or

(*c*) is of unsound mind and stands so declared by a competent court; or

(*d*) has been removed or dismissed from the service of the Government of a body corporate owned or controlled by the Government; or

(*e*) has, in the opinion of the State Government, such financial or other interest, as is likely to affect prejudicially the discharge by him of his functions as a member; or

(*f*) has such other disqualifications as may be prescribed by the State Government.]

[1][(1A) Every appointment under sub-section (1) shall be made by the State Government on the recommendation of a Selection Committee consisting of the following members, namely:—

(*i*) President of the State Commission — Chairman;

(*ii*) Secretary of the Law Department of the State — Member;

(*iii*) Secretary, incharge of the Department dealing with Consumer Affairs in the State — Member:

→ → Provided that every appointment under this clause shall be made by the State Government on the recommendation of a selection committee consisting of the following, namely:—

(*i*) President of the State Commission — Chairman,

(*ii*) Secretary of the Law Department of the State — Member,

(*iii*) Secretary, incharge of the Department dealing with consumer affairs in the State — Member."

1 Inserted by the Consumer Protection (Amendment) Act, 2002, w.e.f. 15-3-2003.

Provided that where the President of the State Commission is, by reason of absence or otherwise, unable to act as Chairman of the Selection Committee, the State Government may refer the matter to the Chief Justice of the High Court for nominating a sitting Judge of that High Court to act as Chairman.

(1B)(*i*) The jurisdiction, powers and authority of the State Commission may be exercised by Benches thereof.

(*ii*) A Bench may be constituted by the President with one or more members as the President may deem fit.

(*iii*) If the members of a Bench differ in opinion on any point, the points shall be decided according to the opinion of the majority, if there is a majority, but if the Members are equally divided, they shall state the point or points on which they differ, and make a reference to the President who shall either hear the point or points himself or refer the case for hearing on such point or points by one or more or the other members and such point or points shall be decided according to the opinion of the majority of the members who have heard the case, including those who first heard it.]

(2) The salary or honorarium and other allowances payable to, and the other terms and conditions of service [1][* * *] of the members of the State Commission shall be such as may be prescribed by the State Government:

[2][Provided that the appointment of a member on whole-time basis shall be made by the State Government on the recommendation of the President of the State Commission taking into consideration such factors as may be prescribed including the work load of the State Commission.]

[3][(3) Every member of the State Commission shall hold office for a term of five years or up to the age of sixty-seven years, whichever is earlier:

Provided that a member shall be eligible for re-appointment for another term of five years or up to the age of sixty-seven years, whichever is earlier, subject to the condition that he fulfils the qualifications and other conditions for appointment mentioned in clause (*b*) of sub-section (1) and such re-appointment is made on the basis of the recommendation of the Selection Committee:

Provided further that a person appointed as a President of the State Commission shall also be eligible for re-appointment in the manner provided in clause (*a*) of sub-section (1) of this section:

Provided also that a member may resign his office in writing under his hand addressed to the State Government and on such resignation being accepted, his

---

1 The words and brackets "(including tenure of office)" omitted by the Consumer Protection (Amendment) Act, 1993, w.e.f. 18-6-1993.

2 Inserted by the Consumer Protection (Amendment) Act, 2002, w.e.f. 15-3-2003.

3 Substituted by the Consumer Protection (Amendment) Act, 2002, w.e.f. 15-3-2003 for the following sub-section:

"(3) Every member of the State Commission shall hold office for a term of five years or up to the age of sixty-seven years, whichever is earlier and shall not be eligible for re-appointment."

office shall become vacant and may be filled by appointment of a person possessing any of the qualifications mentioned in sub-section (1) in relation to the category of the member who is required to be appointed under the provisions of sub-section (1A) in place of the person who has resigned.]

[1][(4) Notwithstanding anything contained in sub-section (3), a person appointed as the President or as a member, before the commencement of the Consumer Protection (Amendment) Act, 2002 shall continue to hold such office as president or member, as the case may be, till the completion of his term.]

COMMENT ON SECTION 16

Objects and Reasons

Clause 13 (old) seeks to make amendments in section 16 to make the same provisions with regard to qualifications and disqualifications of Members, chairmanship of the Selection Committee, re-appointment of Presidents and Members, resignation of Members, completion of term of existing Members and appointment of Members on whole-time basis in respect of the State Commission as in the case of the District Forums. It also seeks to make provision to enable appointment of more than two Members in the State Commission and creation of Benches. This will facilitate quicker disposal of cases in State Commissions having a large number of cases.

State Commission [Section 16]

After the District Forum, State Commission is next in the hierarchy of Consumer Redressal Forums under the Act.

Composition: State Commission consists of a president and two members one of whom is to be a woman. President is a person who is or has been a Judge of a High Court and the member, are persons of ability, integrity and standing and have adequate knowledge or experience of, or have shown capacity in dealing with, problems relating to economics, law, commerce, accountancy, industry, public affairs or administration.

Appointing Authority: President of a State Commission is appointed by the State Government after consultation with the Chief Justice of the High Court.

Other members of the Commission are made by the State Government on the recommendation of a selection committee consisting of the following, namely—

(*i*) President of the State Commission — Chairman.

(*ii*) Secretary of the Law Department of the State — Member.

---

1 Substituted by the Consumer Protection (Amendment) Act, 2002, w.e.f. 15-3-2003 for the following sub-section:

"(4) Notwithstanding anything contained in sub-section (3), a person appointed as a President or as a member before the commencement of the Consumer Protection (Amendment) Act, 1993, shall continue to hold such office as President or member, as the case may be, till the completion of his term."

(*iii*) Secretary, incharge of Department dealing with consumer affairs in the State — Member.

TERM OF OFFICE [SECTION 16(3)]: Every member of the State Commission shall hold office for five years or upto the age of 67 years whichever is earlier and he shall not be eligible for re-appointment.

VACANCY: Rules as to the vacancy related in the office of the president or any member are similar to those discussed in context of the members of the District Forum.

TERMS AND CONDITIONS OF SERVICE [SECTION 16(2)]: The salary or honorarium and other allowances payable to, and the other terms and conditions of service of, the members of the State Commission shall be such as may be prescribed by the State Government.

17. Jurisdiction of the State Commission.—[1][(*1*)] Subject to the other provisions of this Act, the State Commission shall have jurisdiction—

(*a*) to entertain—

(*i*) complaints where the value of the goods or services and compensation, if any, claimed exceeds rupees [2][twenty lakhs but does not exceed rupees one crore;] and

(*ii*) appeals against the orders of any District Forum within the State; and

(*b*) to call for the records and pass appropriate orders in any consumer dispute which is pending before or has been decided by any District Forum within the State, where it appears to the State Commission that such District Forum has exercised a jurisdiction not vested in it by law, or has failed to exercise a jurisdiction so vested or has acted in exercise of its jurisdiction illegally or with material irregularity.

[3][(2) A complaint shall be instituted in a State Commission within the limits of whose jurisdiction,—

(*a*) the opposite party or each of the opposite parties, where there are more than one, at the time of the institution of the complaint, actually and voluntarily resides or carries on business or has a branch office or personally works for gain; or

(*b*) any of the opposite parties, where there are more than one, at the time of the institution of the complaint, actually and voluntarily resides, or carries on business or has a branch office or personally works for gain, provided that in such case either the permission of the State Commission is given or the opposite parties who do not reside or carry on business or have a branch office or personally works for gain, as the case may be, acquiesce in such institution; or

(*c*) the cause of action, wholly or in part, arises.]

---

1 Section renumbered as sub-section (1), ibid.

2 Substituted for the words "five lakhs but does not exceed rupees twenty lakhs", by the Consumer Protection (Amendment) Act, 2002, w.e.f. 15-3-2003.

3 Inserted, *ibid*.

[1][**17A. Transfer of Cases.**—On the application of the complainant or of its own motion, the State Commission may, at any stage of the proceeding, transfer any complaint pending before the District Forum to another District Forum within the State if the interest of justice so requires.

17B. Circuit Benches.—The State Commission shall ordinarily function in the State Capital but may perform its functions at such other place as the State Government may, in consultation with the State Commission, notify in the Official Gazette, from time to time.]

COMMENTS ON SECTION 17

Objects and Reasons

Clause 14 (old) seeks to amend section 17 so as to clarify the jurisdiction of the State Commission and also to raise its jurisdiction to entertain complaints where the value of goods or services and compensation claimed exceed rupees twenty lakh but does not exceed rupees one crore. At present the jurisdiction of the State Commission is above rupees five lakhs and up to rupees twenty lakhs. This will be convenient for the complainants and will reduce the number of complaints filed before the National Commission

Under section 17 of the Consumer Protection Act, a State Commission has jurisdiction to decide the complaints of the value between rupees five and twenty lakhs but there is no such provision as contained in section 11(2) of the Act applicable to the State Commission. Section 18 of the Act does not make provision of section 11(2) applicable to the State Commission. Each State has its own State Commission. There is a purpose for it. The first appeal of the District Forum situated within the State lies to the State Commission and then the State Commission can take cognizance of the dispute arising within that State. It cannot be the intention of the legislature that the dispute arising in one State could be taken cognizance of by the State Commission of another State. [*Union Bank of India* v *Seppo Rally Oy* (1999) 8 SCO 357]

Clause 15 (old) seeks to insert a new section 17A to empower the State Commission to transfer a case from one District Forum to another District Forum within the State. if required for the ends of justice. It also seeks to insert another new section 17B to enable the State Commissions to hold Circuit Benches.

Ram, an engineer by profession shifted to Delhi. He bought a computer from Shyam, a dealer who gave him all guarantees and warranties. The moment he plugged in the computer, some noise came and the computer was shut down. He called up Shyam, but got no response from him. After making many calls to him, he understood that he was cheated of his money.

---

1 Inserted by the Consumer Protection (Amendment) Act, 2002, w.e.f. 15-3-2003.

Ram could have gone to courts, but knowing the lengthy and expensive procedures involved, he preferred not to initiate any action against Shyam. One day while watching television he came across a programme on consumer protection. Ram got interested in it and noted the address of consumer council which was sponsoring the programme. Thereafter he contacted the Council and talked about his computer affair. The Council made him aware that there is a speedy and inexpensive way to assert his right as a consumer, and that where and how a complaint can be filed for that, and that he need not hire an advocate for the suit, and assured him of any assistance he may need for the same.

The Consumer Councils are created to advise and assist the consumers in seeking and enforcing their rights. We have Consumer Protection Councils both at Centre level and State level that is one Central Council and many State Councils.

These councils work towards the promotion and protection of consumers. They make investigations and give publicity to the matters concerning consumer interests, take steps towards furthering consumer education and protecting consumer from exploitation, advice the Government in the matter of policy formulation keeping consumer interest as pivotal concern, etc. Although their suggestions are recommendatory in nature but they have significant impact in policy making.

While deciding about the composition of these councils, the State keeps in mind that it should have proper representation from all the possible areas affecting consumer interests. Again the rules as to when should these councils meet, what should they aim at, how they conduct their business are framed by the Government with a view to balance the efficacy and practicability of its business.

APPELLATE JURISDICTION [Section 17(*a*)(*ii*)]: State Commission has power to adjudicate upon the appeals made against the order of the District Forums. Any person aggrieved by an order made by the District Forum may prefer an appeal against such order within 30 days from the date of order. However, the State Commission may entertain an appeal after the expiry of 30 days if it is satisfied that there was sufficient cause for delay.

Note.—30 days are counted not from the date of order but from the date when the order is communicated to the appellant.

REVISIONAL JURISDICTION [Section 17(*b*)]: State Commission may call for the records and pass appropriate orders in any consumer dispute which is pending before or has been decided by any District Forum within the State, where State Commission is of the view that the District Forum—

— has exercised jurisdiction which it was not entitled to, or

— has failed to exercise such jurisdiction which it was entitled to, or

— has exercised its jurisdiction illegally or with material irregularity.

Such revisional jurisdiction may be exercised by the Commission on its own or on the application of a party.

(*i*) The State Commission has the Jurisdiction to award cost. [*Mahaboobnagar Citizens Council* v *Manager, Milk Chilling Centre* (1991) 1 CPR 220]

(*ii*) Section 11 of the Act deals with the jurisdiction of the District Forum but there is no separate corresponding provision relating to a State Commission. The jurisdiction of the State Commission will, therefore, be governed by the general principle of law with reference to which jurisdiction of courts and tribunals are ordinarily determined. The best guidance in respect of this matter is contained in the relevant provision of the CPC and more particularly section 20 which directly deals with the matter. [*Indian Airlines Corporation* v *Consumer Education and Research Society, Ahmedabad* (1992) 1 CPR 4 (NC)]

(*iii*) The jurisdiction is to be found on the basis of the claim laid by the party and not on the basis of relief granted. [*Akhil Bhartiya Grahak Panchayat* v *Chairman, LIC* (1991) 1 CPJ 171: (1991) 1 CPR 50 (NC)]

(*iv*) Where the compensation claimed by the complainant is less than rupees one lakh, the State Commission has no jurisdiction under Section 17 of the Act to entertain and adjudicate upon fee complaint. [*Suraj Steel Hazaribagh* v *R.P. Sharma* (1991) 1 CPR 331 (NC)]

(*v*) But where no objection as to jurisdiction was taken before the State Commissioner in memorandum of appeal before the national Commission and no miscarriage of justice resulted, the National Commission would not interfere with order of the State Commission. [*S.K. Trading and Co.* v *R. Sharma* (1991) 1 CPR 385 (NC)]

(*vi*) The State Commission has no power to review its earlier order. [*Usha Rani Gupta* v *General Manager* (1991) 2 CPJ 87]

(*vii*) If, in respect of the same subject-matter, proceedings before the Civil Forum had been instituted prior to the institution of the proceedings before the Fora constituted under the Act definitely gets ousted of jurisdiction. [*M/s. Sh. Jagannath Constructions Ltd.* v *M/s. Kotak Mahindra Pvt. Ltd.* 2001 (1) CRP 1]

(*viii*) The State Consumer Disputes Redressal Commission has no jurisdiction to entertain complaints regarding the transactions of shops/kiosks having been purchased in auction from the Delhi Development Authority. [*Kashyap Constructions (Pvt.) Ltd.* v *Delhi Development Authority* 2001 (1) CPR. 128] (*ix*) Even if the appeal is not maintainable, the State Commission can still treat and decide the same as revision in exercise of its power under section 17(*b*) of the Act. [*C.R. Kataria, Telecom District Manager* v *Consumer Disputes Redressal District Forum* 1991 (II) CPJ 682]

(*x*) If a party is aggrieved by the order passed by the District Forum, his remedy is to prefer an appeal before the State Forum and not to invoke the jurisdiction to the High Court under Article 227 of the Constitution. [*Manimalan* v *K. Subrayan* AIR 2004 Mad 446]

(*xi*) If, in respect of the same subject matter, proceedings before the Civil Forum had been instituted prior to the institution of the proceedings before the fora constituted under the Act and such proceedings are pending, the fora constituted under the Act definitely gets ousted of jurisdiction. [*M/s. Shree Jagannath Constructions Ltd.* v *M/s. Kotak Mahindra Private Limited* 2001 (1) CRP 1]

(*xii*) The State Consumer Disputes Redressal Commission has no jurisdiction to entertain complaints regarding the transactions of shops/kiosks having been purchased in auction from the Delhi Development Authority. [*Kashyap Constructions* (*Pvt.*) *Ltd.* v *Delhi Development Authority* 2001 (1) CPR 128]

(*xiii*) Even if the appeal is not maintainable, the State Commission can still treat and decide the same as revision in exercise of its power under section 17(*b*) of the Act. [*C.R. Kataria, Telecom District Manager* v *Consumer Disputes Redressal District Forum* 1991 (II) CPJ 682]

18. Procedure applicable to State Commissions.—[1][The provisions of sections 12, 13 and 14 and the rules made thereunder] for the disposal of complaints by the District Forum shall, with such modifications as may be necessary, be applicable to the disposal of disputes by the State Commission.

[2][***18A. Vacancy in the office of the President.***—*Omitted by the Consumer Protection* (*Amendment*) *Act, 2002*].

---

1 Substituted for the words, "The procedure specified in sections 12, 13 and 14 and under the rules made thereunder", by the Consumer Protection (Amendment) Act, 1993, w.e.f. 18-6-1993.

2 Omitted by the Consumer Protection (Amendment) Act, 2002, w.e.f. 15-3-2003. Prior to its omission, it provided as under:

'*18A. Vacancy in the office of the President.*—When the office of the President of the District Forum or of the State Commission, as the case may be, is vacant or when any such President is, by reason of absence or otherwise, unable to perform the duties of his office, the duties of the office shall be performed by such person, who is qualified to be appointed as President of the District Forum or, as the case may be, of the State Commission, as the State Government may appoint for the purpose."

19. Appeals.—Any person aggrieved by an order made by the State Commission in exercise of its powers conferred sub-clause (*i*) of clause (*a*) of sub-section (1) of section 17 may prefer an appeal against such order to the National Commission within a period of thirty days from the date of the order in such form and manner as may be prescribed:

Provided that the National Commission may entertain an appeal after the expiry of the said period of thirty days if it is satisfied that there was sufficient cause for not filing it within that period:

[1][Provided further that no appeal by a person, who is required to pay any amount in terms of an order of the State Commission, shall be entertained by the National Commission unless the appellant has deposited in the prescribed manner fifty per cent of the amount or rupees thirty-five thousand, whichever is less.]

[2][**19A. Hearing of Appeal.**—An appeal filed before the State Commission or the National Commission shall be heard as expeditiously as possible and an endeavour shall be made to finally dispose of the appeal within a period of ninety days from the date of its admission:

Provided that no adjournment shall be ordinarily granted by the State Commission or the National Commission, as the case may be, unless sufficient cause is shown and the reasons for grant of adjournment have been recorded in writing by such Commission:

Provided further that the State Commission or the National Commission, as the case may be, shall make such orders as to the costs occasioned by the adjournment as may be provided in the regulations made under this Act.

Provided also that in the event of an appeal being disposed of after the period so specified the State Commission or the National Commission, as the case may be, shall record in writing the reasons for the same at the time of disposing of the said appeal.]

COMMENT ON SECTION 19

Objects and Reasons

Clause 17 (old) seeks to insert a new proviso in section 19 so that no appeal by a person, who is required to pay any amount In terms of an order of the State Commission, shall be entertained by the National Commission unless the appellant has deposited in the manner as prescribed by the State Governments fifty per cent, of the amount or rupees thirty-five thousand, whichever is less.

Clause 18 (old) seeks to insert a new section 19A to provide that endeavour shall be made to dispose of appeals filed before the State Commission or the National Commission within ninety days from the date of admission. It also further seeks to provide that no adjournment shall ordinarily be granted unless for sufficient reason for grant of adjournment

---

1 Inserted by the Consumer Protection (Amendment) Act, 2002, w.e.f. 15-3-2003.

2 Inserted, *ibid*.

has been recorded in. writing and costs for such adjournment have also been specified in order.

Section 11(2)(*c*) is not made applicable under section 18 of the Act. However, principle in respect of territorial jurisdiction of a State Commission would be governed under the Code of Civil Procedure. [*Arisetty Sanyasi Raju* v *Hindustan Motors Ltd.* 1992 (I) CPR 689]

Appeals against orders

'Appeal' is a legal instrumentality whereby a person not satisfied with the findings of a court has an option to go to a higher court to present his case and seek justice. In the context of Consumer Forums:—

1. An appeal can be made with the State Commission against the order of the District Forum within 30 days of the order which is extendable for further 15 days. [Section 15]
2. An appeal can be made with the National Commission against the order of the State Commission within 30 days of the order or within such time as the National Commission allows. [Section 19]
3. An appeal can be made with the Supreme Court against the order of the National Commission within 30 days of the order or within such time as the Supreme Court allows.

If a party is aggrieved by the order passed by the State Commission, his remedy is to approach the National Commission and not to invoke the jurisdiction of the court under Article 227 of the Constitution. [*P. Subramanian* v *Oriental Insurance Co. Ltd.* AIR 2004 Mad 494]

20. Composition of National Commission.—(1) The National Commission shall consist of,—

(*a*) a person who is or has been a Judge of the Supreme Court, to be appointed by the Central Government, who shall be its President:

[1][Provided that no appointment under this clause shall be made except after consultation with the Chief Justice of India;]

[2][(b) not less than four, and not more than such number of members, as may be prescribed, and one of whom shall be a woman, who shall have the following qualifications, namely:—[2]

---

1 Inserted by the Consumer Protection (Amendment) Act, 1993, w.e.f. 18-6-1993.

2 Substituted by the Consumer Protection (Amendment) Act, 2002, w.e.f.15-3-2003, for the following clause:

"(*b*) four other members, who shall be persons of ability, integrity and standing and have adequate knowledge or experience of, or have shown capacity in dealing with, problems relating to economics, law, commerce, accountancy, industry, public affairs or administration, one of whom shall be a woman:

Provided that every appointment under this clause shall be made by the State Government on the recommendation of a selection committee consisting of the following, namely:— →→

(*i*) be not less than thirty-five years of age;

(*ii*) possess a bachelor's degree from a recognised university; and

(*iii*) be persons of ability, integrity and standing, and have adequate knowledge and experience of at least ten years in dealing with problems relating to economics, law, commerce, accountancy, industry, public affairs or administration:

Provided that not more than fifty per cent of the members shall be from amongst persons having a judicial background.

Explanation.—For the purposes of this clause, the expression "persons having judicial background" shall mean persons having knowledge and experience for at least a period of ten years as a presiding officer at the district level court or any tribunal at equivalent level:

Provided further that a person shall be disqualified for appointment as a member if he—

(*a*) has been convicted and sentenced to imprisonment for an offence which, in the opinion of the Central Government, involves moral turpitude; or

(*b*) is an undischarged insolvent; or

(*c*) is of unsound mind and stands so declared by a competent court; or

(*d*) has been removed or dismissed from the service of the Government or a body corporate owned or controlled by the Government; or

(*e*) has, in the opinion of the Central Government, such financial or other interest, as is likely to affect prejudicially the discharge by him of his functions as a member; or

(*f*) has such other disqualifications as may be prescribed by the Central Government:

Provided also that every appointment under this clause shall be made by the Central Government on the recommendation of a selection committee consisting of the following, namely:—

(*i*) a person who is a Judge of the Supreme Court, to be nominated by the Chief Justice of India — Chairman;

(*ii*) Secretary in the Department of Legal Affairs in the Government of India — Member;

(*iii*) Secretary of the Department dealing with Consumer Affairs in the Government of India.] — Member;

→→ (*i*) a person who is a Judge of the Supreme Court, to be nominated by the Chief Justice of India — Chairman;

(*ii*) Secretary in the Department of Legal Affairs in the Government of India — Member:

(*iii*) Secretary of the Department dealing with consumer affairs in the Government of India — Member."

[1][(1A)(*i*) The jurisdiction, powers and authority of the National Commission may be exercised by Benches thereof.

(*ii*) A Bench may be constituted by the President with one or more members as the President may deem fit.

(*iii*) If the Members of a Bench differ in opinion on any point, the points shall be decided according to the opinion of the majority, if there is a majority, but if the members are equally divided, they shall state the point or points on which they differ, and make a reference to the President who shall either hear the point or points himself or refer the case for hearing on such point or points by one or more or the other Members and such point or points shall be decided according to the opinion of the majority of the Members who have heard the case, including those who first heard it.]

(2) The salary or honorarium and other allowances payable to and the other terms and conditions of service [2][* * *] of the members of the National Commission shall be such as may be prescribed by the Central Government.

[3][(3) Every member of the National Commission shall hold office for a term of five years or up to the age of seventy years, whichever is earlier:

Provided that a member shall be eligible for re-appointment for another term of five years or up to the age of seventy years, whichever is earlier, subject to the condition that he fulfils the qualifications and other conditions for appointment mentioned in clause (*b*) of sub-section (1) and such re-appointment is made on the basis of the recommendation of the Selection Committee:

Provided further that a person appointed as a President of the National Commission shall also be eligible for re-appointment in the manner provided in clause (*a*) of sub-section (1):

Provided also that a member may resign his office in writing under his hand addressed to the Central Government and on such resignation being accepted, his office shall become vacant and may be filled by appointment of a person possessing any of the qualifications mentioned in sub-section (1) in relation to the category of the member who is required to be appointed under the provisions of sub-section (1A) in place of the person who has resigned.]

[4][(4) Notwithstanding anything contained in sub-section (3), a person

---

1 Inserted by the Consumer Protection (Amendment) Act, 2002, w.e.f. 15-3-2003.

2 The words and brackets "(including tenure of office)", omitted, by the Consumer Protection (Amendment) Act, 1993, w.e.f. 18-6-1993.

3 Substituted by the Consumer Protection (Amendment) Act, 2002, w.e.f. 15-3-2003 for the following sub-section:

"(3) Every member of the National Commission shall hold office for a term of five years or up to the age of seventy years, whichever is earlier and shall not be eligible for re-appointment."

4 Substituted by the Consumer Protection (Amendment) Act, 2002, w.e.f. 15-3-2003 for the following sub-section:

"(4) Notwithstanding anything contained in sub-section (3), a person appointed as a President or as a member before the commencement of the Consumer Protection (Amendment) Act, 1993, shall continue to hold such office as President or member, as the case may be, till the completion of his term."

appointed as a President or as a member, before the commencement of the Consumer Protection (Amendment) Act, 2002 shall continue to hold such office as President or member, as the case may be, till the completion of his term.]

COMMENTS ON SECTION 20

Objects and Reasons

Clause 19 (old) seeks to make amendments in section 20 to make the same provisions in respect of qualifications and disqualifications for Members, re-appointment of the Presidents and Members, resignation of Members and completion of term of existing Members with regard to the National Commission as in the case of the State Commission and District Forum. Clause 16 also seeks to make provision to the appointment of more than four Members and also creation of Benches of the National Commission.

National Commission [Section 20]

The National Commission is the topmost layers in the three level hierarchies of the Consumer Forums.

COMPOSITION

The National Commission consists of a President, and four other members (one of whom is to be a woman).

The president should be the one who is or has been a Judge of the Supreme Court, and the members should be the persons of ability, integrity and standing and have adequate knowledge or experience of, or have shown capacity in dealing with, problems relating to economics, law, commerce, accountancy, industry, public affairs or administration.

APPOINTING AUTHORITY

The President is appointed by the Central Government after consultation with the Chief Justice of India.

The appointment of other members of the Commission is made by the Central Government on the recommendation of a selection committee.

This selection committee consists of, namely:—

(*a*) a person who is a Judge of the Supreme Court, to be nominated by the Chief Justice of India — Chairman.

(*b*) the Secretary in the Department of Legal Affairs in the Government of India — Member.

(*c*) Secretary of the Department dealing with consumer affairs in the Government of India — Member.

Note that before appointment, the President and Member(s) of the National Commission have to take an undertaking that he does not and will not have any such financial or other interest as is likely to affect prejudicially his functions as such member.

Term of Office [Section 20(3)]: Every member of the National Commission is to hold office for a term of five years or up to the age of seventy years, whichever is earlier and is not eligible for re-appointment.

Vacancy: A vacancy in the office of President or a Member may occur after the expiry of his term, or by his death, resignation or removal.

In terms of proviso to rule 12(3), the President or a Member may resign his office in writing under his hand addressed to the Central Government, or he can be removed from his office in accordance with the provisions of Rule 13.

Removal of the President and Members in certain circumstances: In terms of Rule 13 of the Consumer Protection Rules, 1987, the Central Government may remove from office, the President or any member, who—

(*a*) has been adjudged as an insolvent; or

(*b*) has been convicted of an offence which, in the opinion of the Central Government, involves moral turpitude; or

(*c*) has become physically or mentally incapable of acting as the President or the member; or

(*d*) has acquired such financial or other interest as is likely to affect prejudicially his functions as the President or a member; or

(*e*) has so abused his position as to render his continuance in office prejudicial to the public interest; or

(*f*) remain absent in three consecutive sittings except for reasons beyond his control.

Note that the President or any Member shall not be removed from his office on the grounds specified in clauses (*d*), (*e*) and (*f*) above except on an inquiry held by Central Government in accordance with such procedure as it may specify in this behalf and finds the President or a member to be guilty of such ground.

A casual vacancy caused by resignation or removal of the President or any other member of the National Commission is filled by fresh appointment.

When the President of the National Commission is unable to discharge the functions owing to absence, illness or any other cause, the senior most member of the National Commission with judicial background, if authorised so to do by the President in writing, shall discharge the functions of the President until the day on which the President resumes the charge of his functions.

TERMS AND CONDITIONS OF SERVICE [SECTION 20(2)]: In terms of rules 11 and 12 made by the Central Government in pursuance of the powers given under the Act, the terms and conditions of service of the President and the Members of the Commission are as follows:

(*a*) The President of the National Commission is entitled to salary, allowances and other perquisites as are available to a sitting Judge of the Supreme Court.

(*b*) The Members, if sitting on whole-time basis, are entitled to a consolidated honorarium of ten thousand rupees per month or if sitting on part-time basis, a consolidated honorarium of five hundred rupees per day of sitting.

(*c*) The President and the Members are entitled to travelling and daily allowances on official tours at the same rates as are admissible to group 'A' Officers of the Central Government.

(*d*) The President and the Members of the National Commission are entitled to conveyance allowance of one hundred fifty rupees per day of its sitting or a sum of one thousand and five hundred rupees per month, as may be opted by them.

Notes.—1. The terms and conditions of service of the President and the members should not be varied to their disadvantage during their tenure of office.

2. The money payable to these Members and the President shall be defrayed out of the Consolidated Fund of India.

Further it is worth noting that in case any defect lies in the constitution of the District Forum, or State Commission or National Commission, or any vacancy remains therein while proceedings are made for any dispute, such defect or vacancy shall not affect the validity of the order of the Forum. [Section 29A].

Jurisdiction

The term jurisdiction may be defined as authority or legal power to hear and decide the cases. Thus a court may adjudicate only those matters which fall under its jurisdiction. The question of jurisdiction has to be considered with reference to the value, place and nature of the subject matter.

Example: 'A' and 'B' reside in Bombay. They have some dispute. Here the dispute may be subjected to the jurisdiction of the Bombay courts (except matters pertaining to Supreme Court). Courts of Delhi, or Chennai, or any other place for that matter cannot adjudicate the issue.

The general rule is that if the court rendering the judgment suffers from want of jurisdiction, its judgment is nullity and may be ignored.

Jurisdiction of Consumer Forums (*i.e.* consumer courts) differs in terms of monetary value of claims, geographical area and appellate powers.

District Forum

PECUNIARY JURISDICTION: District Forum entertains the cases where the value of claim is upto ₹5 Lakh. Where a claim exceed this limit, the matter is beyond the jurisdiction of the Forum.

This limit of ₹5 lakh is as to the value of claim filed by the party. Value of goods or services in question or value of relief granted is not relevant for this purpose.

Example: 'A' purchased machinery for ₹7 lakhs. After working for some time, the machine broke down due to some manufacturing defect. 'A' filed a claim for compensation worth ₹4.5 lakh. Since the value of claim is less than ₹5 Lakh, it will fall under the jurisdiction of District Forum.

The complainant has a right to reduce value of his claim in order to bring his claim within the jurisdiction of a junior forum.

Example: 'A' filed a complaint with a District Forum claiming ₹6,00,000 as against a supplier of machinery. The complaint was rejected on the ground that it was beyond the jurisdiction of the District Forum. 'A' revised his claim to ₹4,99,999 and filed the plaint again with the same District Forum. The plaint was accepted and tried.

TERRITORIAL JURISDICTION: Every District Forum has definite geographical limits within which it can exercise its jurisdiction. A case is supposed to fall within such territory when at the time of the institution of the complaint —

(*a*) The party against whom the claim is made actually and voluntarily resides or carries on business or has a branch office or personally works for gain in that area, or

(*b*) Where there are more than one opposite party, each such party actually and voluntarily resides or carries on business or has a branch office or personally works for gain in that area, or

(*c*) Where there are more than one opposite party, and any such party actually and voluntarily resides or carries on business or has a branch office or personally works for gain in that area, provided the other parties not so residing or working agrees, or the District Forum gives permission in this regard,

(*d*) The cause of action, wholly or in part, arises in that area.

APPELLATE JURISDICTION: District Forum is the lowest rung of the ladder of the consumer courts. Thus this is not an appellate court, i.e., no appeal lies in this court.

State Commission

PECUNIARY JURISDICTION: State Commission entertains the cases where the value of claim exceeds ₹5 lakh. But where value of a claim exceed ₹20 lakh, the matter is beyond the jurisdiction of the Commission.

Example: A of Delhi bought a house from housing board for ₹4 lakh. Due to defect in the house, its wall fell down on the daughter of 'A' and she dies. 'A' sue the Housing Board claiming ₹15 lakh as compensation. This matter will lie with the State Commission of Delhi.

Note: That although the value of house is less than 5 lakh, the decisive factor regarding jurisdiction is the value of claim.

TERRITORIAL JURISDICTION: The Consumer Protection Act does not specifically provide for the territorial jurisdiction of the State Commission. Thus it is governed by the general principle of the law which is contained in section 20 of the Civil Procedure Code.

Broadly these principles are on the similar lines on which the territorial jurisdiction of District Forum is based. Thus a suit can be instituted in the State Commission within whose local limits—

(*a*) the party against whom the claim is made actually and voluntarily resides or carries on business or personally works for gain, or

(*b*) where there are more than one opposite party, each such party actually and voluntarily resides or carries on business or personally works for gain, or

(*c*) where there are more than one opposite party, and any such party actually and voluntarily resides or carries on business or has a branch office or personally works for gain, provided the other parties not so residing or working agrees, or the State Commission gives permission in this regard, or

(*d*) the cause of action, wholly or in part, arises.

so vested, or has acted in the exercise of its jurisdiction illegally or with material irregularity.

NATIONAL COMMISSION

PECUNIARY JURISDICTION: Since National Commission is the highest level of Consumer Forums, it may entertain all the matters where the value of claim exceeds ₹20 lakh.

TERRITORIAL JURISDICTION: The territorial jurisdiction of the National Commission is whole of India except the State of Jammu & Kashmir.

However, the Consumer Protection Act is applicable only if the cause of action arise in India. If the cause of action arises out of India, National Commission has no jurisdiction over the matter as it cannot be tried in India under the Act.

Example: The complainant alleged that they were not properly treated by the Egyptian Airlines authorities at Barcelona. It was held that the cause of action arose at Barcelona, so the complaint under the Act is not maintainable in India. [*Gulab Hotchand Bhagchandaney* v *Egyptian Airlines* III 1994 CPJ 172 (NC)]

APPELLATE JURISDICTION: The National Commission has jurisdiction to entertain appeals against the order of any State Commission. The appeal may be made within 30 days from the date of the order of the State Commission. However the National Commission may entertain an appeal filed after the expiry of 30 days if it is satisfied that there was sufficient cause for not filing the appeal within the given time.

21. Jurisdiction of the National Commission.—Subject to the other provisions of this Act, the National Commission shall have jurisdiction,—

(*a*) to entertain,—

(*i*) complaints where the value of the goods or services and compensation, if any, claimed exceeds rupees [1][one crore;] and

(*ii*) appeals against the orders of any State Commission; and

(*b*) to call for the records and pass appropriate orders in any consumer dispute which is pending before or has been decided by any State Commission where it appears to the National Commission that such State Commission has exercised a jurisdiction not vested in it by law, or has failed to exercise a jurisdiction so vested, or has acted in the exercise of its jurisdiction illegally or with material irregularity.

COMMENTS ON SECTION 21

Objects and Reasons

Clause 20 (old) seeks to amend section 21 to provide that complaints may be filed before the National Commission where the value of the goods or services and compensation, if any, claimed exceeds rupees one crore. This is consequential to changes sought in the jurisdiction of the District Forums and State Commissions.

REVISIONAL JURISDICTION [Section 21(*b*)]: National Commission can call for the records and pass the appropriate orders in any consumer dispute which is pending before or has been decided by any State Commission it is of the view that the State Commission —

— has exercised jurisdiction which it was not entitled to, or

— has failed to exercise such jurisdiction which it was entitled to, or

— has exercised its jurisdiction illegally or with material irregularity.

Note that the revisional jurisdiction is available to the National Commission only in the cases where there has been wrongful, illegal and improper exercise of jurisdiction or failure to exercise jurisdiction on the part of State Commission.

Example: K made an appeal to the National Commission against the order of the State Commission whereby the State Commission had made an order against him although he was not a made a party to the dispute by the complainant. The National Commission observed that the order of the State Commission was vitiated by illegal exercise of jurisdiction resulting immaterial irregularity and accordingly, the same was liable to

1 Substituted for the words "twenty lakhs" by the Consumer Protection (Amendment) Act, 2002, w.e.f. 15-3-2003.

be set aside. [*Kinetic Engineering Ltd.* v *Samasi Saunand* (1993) II CPR 409 (NC)]

When the National Consumer Forum can have the jurisdiction to call for the records from the State Commission and to set aside the order containing any perverse finding, the naturally alternative remedy is available to approach the National Consumer Forum and when that remedy is not exhausted, approaching High Court under Article 227 cannot be considered as maintainable. [*R. Jaivet* v *State of Tamil Nadu* AIR 2006 Mad 215]

The powers of National Commission are very limited. [*Kangara Ananth Ram* v *Telecom Visit. Engineer* (1991) 1 CPR 391]

[1][**22. Power of and procedure applicable to the National Commission.**—(1) The provisions of sections 12, 13 and 14 and the rules made thereunder for the disposal of complaints by the District Forum shall, with such modifications as may be considered necessary by the Commission, be applicable to the disposal of disputes by the National Commission.

(2) Without prejudice to the provisions contained in sub-section (1), the National Commission shall have the power to review any order made by it, when there is an error apparent on the face of record.]

[2][**22A. Power to set aside ex parte Orders.**—Where an order is passed by the National Commission ex parte against the opposite party or a complainant, as the case may be, the aggrieved party may apply to the Commission to set aside the said order in the interest of justice.

22B. Transfer of Cases.—On the application of the complainant or of its own motion, the National Commission may, at any stage of the proceeding, in the interest of justice, transfer any complaint pending before the District Forum of one State to a District Forum of another State or before one State Commission to another State Commission.

22C. Circuit Benches.—The National Commission shall ordinarily function at the New Delhi and perform its functions at such other place as the Central Government may, in consultation with the National Commission, notify in the Official Gazette, from time to time.

22D. Vacancy in the office of the President.—hen the office of President of a District Forum, State Commission, or of the National Commission, as the

---

1 Substituted by the Consumer Protection (Amendment) Act, 2002, w.e.f. 15-3-2003 for the following section:

22. The National Commission shall, in the disposal of any complaints or any proceedings before it, have—

(*a*) the powers of a civil court as specified in sub-sections (4), (5) and (6) of section 13;

(*b*) the power to issue an order to the opposite party directing him to do any one or more of the things referred to in clauses (*a*) to (*i*) of sub-section (1) of section 14,

and follow such procedure as may be prescribed by the Central Government.

2 Sections 22A to 22D inserted by the Consumer Protection (Amendment) Act, 2002, w.e.f. 15-3-2003.

case may be, is vacant or a person occupying such office is, by reason of absence or otherwise, unable to perform the duties of his office, these shall be performed by the senior most member of the District Forum, the State Commission or of the National Commission, as the case may be:

Provided that where a retired Judge of a High Court is a member of the National Commission, such member or where the number of such members is more than one, the senior most person among such members, shall preside over the National Commission in the absence of President of that Commission.]

COMMENTS ON SECTION 22

Objects and Reasons

Clause 21 (old) seeks to substitute section 22 so that the provisions of sections 12, 13 and 14 and the rules made there under for the disposal of complaints by the District Forum, shall, with such modifications as may be considered necessary by the Commission, be applicable to the disposal of disputes by the National Commission. It also seeks to empower the National Commission to review any order made by it, when there is an error apparent on the face of record. These provisions will make the powers and procedures in respect of National Commission more explicit. It also seeks to insert new sections 22A, 22B, 22C and 22D. New section 22A empowers the National Commission to set aside *ex-parte* orders against the opposite party or complainant in the interest of justice. New section 22B empowers the National Commission to transfer any complaint pending before the District Forum of one State to a District Forum of another State or before one State Commission to another State Commission in the interest of justice. New section 22C enables the National Commission to hold Circuit Benches in any part of the country. New section 22D provides for the senior most members to preside in the absence of the President of the District Forum, State Commission and National Commission, as the case may be, to ensure un-interrupted functioning of the Forum or Commission. However, in the case of National Commission, it provides that where a retired Judge of a High Court is a Member or where number of such Members is more than one, the senior most amongst them shall preside over the Commission. These provisions will streamline the functioning of the Consumer Redressal Forums and also reduce the number of appeals to the Supreme Court from orders of the National Commission.

Relief available against complaint [Sections 14 and 22]

A complainant can seek any one or more of the following relief under the Act:

(*a*) to remove the defect pointed out by the appropriate laboratory from the goods in question;

(*b*) to replace the goods with new goods of similar description which shall be free from any defect;

(*c*) to return to the complainant the price, or, as the case may be, the charges paid by the complainant;

(*d*) to pay such amount as may be awarded by it as compensation to the consumer for any loss or injury suffered by the consumer due to the negligence of the opposite party;

(*e*) to remove the defects or deficiencies in the services in question;

(*f*) to discontinue the unfair trade practice or the restrictive trade practice or not to repeat it;

(*g*) not to offer the hazardous goods for sale;

(*h*) to withdraw the hazardous goods from being offered for sale;

(*i*) to provide from adequate costs to complainant.

When a complaint cannot be filed — A complaint on behalf of the public which consists of unidentifiable consumers cannot be filed under the Act.

Example: A complaint was filed on the basis of a newspaper report that passengers travelling by flight No. 1C-401 from Calcutta to Delhi on May 13, 1989 were made to stay at the airport and the flight was delayed by 90 minutes causing great inconvenience to the passengers. It was held that such a general complaint cannot be entertained. No passenger who boarded that plane came forward or authorised the complainant to make the complaint. [*Consumer Education and Research Society* v *Indian Airlines Corporation* (1992) 1 CPJ 38 NC]

A complaint by an individual on behalf of general public is not permitted. [*Commissioner of Transport* v *Y.R. Grover* 1994 (1) CPJ 199 NC]

An unregistered association cannot file a complaint under the Act.

Example: The complainant was an association formed in the Gulf and was unregistered in India. It was held that since the petitioner was not a voluntary organization registered under any law in force in India, cannot come within clause (*d*) of section 2(1) of the Act and hence can't file a complaint. [*Gulf Trivandrum Air Fare Forum* v *Chairman & Managing Director* 1991 (2) CPR 129]

A complaint after expiry of limitation period is not permitted. A complaint cannot be filed after the lapse of two years from the date on which the cause of action arise unless the Forum is satisfied about the genuineness of the reason for not filing complaint within the prescribed time.

Example: 'A' supplied defective machinery to 'B' on 12-1-1998. B filed a suit against 'A' on 10-3-2001. It was not admitted before the Forum for the reason that the time available to make complaint lapsed.

Dismissal of frivolous and vexatious complaints — Since the Act provides for an inexpensive procedure (Court fees are not charged in consumer complaints under the Act) for filing complaints, there is a possibility that the Act is misused by people for filing vexations claims. To discourage frivolous and vexatious claims, the Act has provided that such complaints will be dismissed and the complainant can be charged with the costs not exceeding ₹10,000.

Example: A filed a complaint against 'B' to recover compensation of ₹55,99,000 with the motive of indulging in speculative litigation taking undue advantage of the fact that no court fee was payable under the Consumer Protection Act. The National Commission held that the complainant has totally failed to make a case against 'B', and dismissed the complaint as frivolous and vexatious imposing ₹10,000 as costs to 'A'. [*Brij Mohan Kher* v *Dr. N.H. Banka* I 1995 CPJ 99 NC]

Procedure to be followed by the National Commission [Section 22]

Section 22 of the Act provides that the National Commission shall follow such procedure as prescribed by the Central Government. The Consumer Protection Rules, 1987 framed by the Central Government lay down the procedure which is as follows:

(1) A complaint containing the following particulars shall be presented by the complainant in person or by his agent to the National Commission or be sent by registered post, addressed to the National Commission:

(*a*) the name, description and the address of the complainant;

(*b*) the name, description and address of the opposite party or parties, as the case may be, so far as they can be ascertained;

(*c*) the facts relating to the complaint and when and where it arose;

(*d*) documents in support of the allegations contained in the complaint;

(*e*) the relief which the complainant claims.

(2) The National Commission shall, in disposal of any complaint before it, as far as possible, follow the procedures laid down and section 13 of the Act.

(3) On the date of hearing, it shall be obligatory on the parties or their agents to appear before the National Commission. Where the complainant or his agent fails to appear, the National Commission may either dismiss the complaint for default or decide it on merits. Where the opposite party or its agent fails to appear on the date of hearing the National Commission may decide the complaint *ex parte*.

(4) The complaint shall be decided as far as possible within a period of three months from the date of notice received by opposite party where complaint does not require analysis or testing of commodities and within five months if it requires analysis or testing of commodities.

(5) After the proceedings, the National Commission shall issue the orders accordingly.

The meaning of the expression "person aggrieved" may vary according to the context of the statute and the facts of the case, nevertheless, normally, a "person aggrieved" must be a man who has suffered a legal grievance, a man against whom a decision has been pronounced which has wrongfully deprived him of something or wrongfully refused him something, or wrongfully affected his title to something. [*Thammanmna* v *Veera Reddy* (1980) 4 SCC 62, 68]

(*i*) Where the complaint is mala fide, vexatious and frivolous and the opposite party has to incur expenses for contesting the complaint, the Redressal Fora should saddle the complainant with costs. [*K. Jayaraman* v *The Poona Hospital & Research Centre* 1994 (1) CPR 23]

(*ii*) Merely because no court fee is payable for lodging a complaint before the consumer forums, parties have a tendency to misuse the provisions of the Consumer Protection Ac tin respect of matters not falling within its purview. This tendency must be discouraged. [*Orissa Vegetable Oil Complex Ltd.* v *State of Orissa* 1994 (1) CPR 32]

(*iii*) Where the issue involved is a legal issue, the complaint cannot said to be frivolous. [*Rasikalal Mohanlal* v *Apollo Tyres Ltd.* 1992 (II) CPR 327]

(*iv*) Cost can be saddled with only in case of fraudulent or vexatious complaints. [*Vihol Jaswant Singh Shivaji* v *Asstt. Branch Manager, New India Insurance Co. Ltd.* 1994 (I) CPR 417]

(*v*) Where the issue involved is a legal issue, the complaint cannot be said to be frivolous. [*Rasikalal Mohanlal* v *Apollo Tyres Ltd.* 1992 (II) CPR 327]

(*vi*) The District Forum and the State Commission have no power to pass any ad interim order to exercise inherent power as embodied in CPC. [In the *State Transport Authority* (1992) 1 CPR 28 (Cal HC)]

(*vii*) The District Forum has no power to review its orders. [*Rajasthan State Industrial Development Corporation* v *Premier Paints* (1991) 1 CPR 614]

(3) All offences under this Act may be tried summarily by the District Forum or the State Commission or the National Commission, as the case may be.)

The Central Government has notified that the National Commission shall perform its functions at the following places other than New Delhi:—

1. Ahmedabad	5. Chennai	9. Lucknow
2. Allahabad	6. Hyderabad	10. Nagpur
3. Bangalore	7. Jodhpur	11. Pune
4. Bhopal	8. Kolkata	

Vide S.O. 974(E), dated 31st August, 2004, published in the Gazette of India, Extra., Pt. II, Sec. 3(11), dated 31st August, 2004.

23. Appeal.—Any person, aggrieved by an order made by the National Commission in exercise of its power conferred by sub-clause (*i*) of clause (*a*) of section 21, may prefer an appeal against such order to the Supreme Court within a period of thirty days from the date of the order:

Provided that the Supreme Court may entertain an appeal after the expiry of the period of thirty days if it is satisfied that there was sufficient cause for not filing it within that period:

[1][Provided further that no appeal by a person who is required to pay any amount in terms of an order of the National Commission shall be entertained by the Supreme Court unless that person has deposited in the prescribed manner fifty per cent of that amount or rupees fifty thousand, whichever is less.]

COMMENTS ON SECTION 23

Objects and Reasons

Clause 22 (old) seeks to insert a new proviso in section 23 so that no appeal by a person, who is required to pay any amount in terms of an order of the National Commission, shall be entertained by the Supreme Court unless the appellant has deposited in the manner as prescribed by the Central Government fifty per cent, of that amount or rupees fifty thousand, whichever is less.

24. Finality of Orders.—Every order of a District Forum, the State Commission or the National Commission shall, if no appeal has been preferred against such order under the provision of this Act, be final.

[2]**[24A. Limitation Period.**—(1) The District Forum, the State Commission or the National Commission shall not admit a complaint unless it is filed within two years from the date on which the cause of action has arisen.

(2) Notwithstanding anything contained in sub-section (1), a complaint may be entertained after the period specified in sub-section (1), if the complainant satisfies the District Forum, the State Commission or the National Commission, as the case may be, that he had sufficient cause for not filing the complaint within such period:

Provided that no such complaint shall be entertained unless the National Commission, the State Commission or the District Forum, as the case may be, records its reasons for condoning such delay.]

[3]**[24B. Administrative Control.**—(1) The National Commission shall have administrative control over all the State Commissions in the following matters, namely:—

---

1 Inserted by the Consumer Protection (Amendment) Act, 2002, w.e.f. 15-3-2003.
2 Inserted by the Consumer Protection (Amendment) Act, 1993, w.e.f. 18-6-1993.
3 Inserted by the Consumer Protection (Amendment) Act, 1993, w.e.f. 18-6-1993.

(*i*) calling for periodical returns regarding the institutions, disposal, pendency of cases;

(*ii*) issuance of instructions regarding adoption of uniform procedure in the hearing of matters, prior service of copies of documents produced by one party to the opposite parties, furnishing of English translation of judgments written in any language, speedy grant of copies of documents;

(*iii*) generally overseeing the functioning of the State Commissions or the District Fora to ensure that the objects and purposes of the Act are best served without in any way interfering with their quasi-judicial freedom.

(2) The State Commission shall have administrative control over all the District Fora within its jurisdiction in all matters referred to in sub-section (1).]

COMMENTS ON SECTION 24

Time frame within which a complaint can be filed

Section 24A of the Act provides that a consumer dispute can be filed within two years from the date on which the cause of action arises.

Since this provision was inserted in the Act in 1993, before that the Consumer Forums were following the Limitation Act, 1963, which says that a suit can be filed within three years after the cause of action arises.

The point of time when cause of action arises is an important factor in determining the time period available to file a complaint. There are no set rules to decide such time. It depends on the facts and circumstances of each case.

Examples:

1. A got his eye operated by B in 1989. He got a certificate of blindness on 18th December, 1989. He was still in hope of gaining his sight and went from second operation in 1992 and was discharged on 21-1-1992. He filed a complaint against B on 11-1-1994. B opposed on the ground that more than 2 years were over after 18-12-1989, thus the complaint is not maintainable. The Commission held that here the cause of action for filing the complaint would arose after the second operation when A lost entire hope of recovery. Thus the suit is maintainable. [*Mukund Lal Ganguly* v *Dr. Abhijit Ghosh* III 1995 CPJ 64]
2. A house was allotted on 1-1-1999. Defects appeared in the house on 10-1-1999. Here the cause of action will arise on 10-1-1999.

It may be noted that these time frames are not absolute limitations. If the Consumer Forum is satisfied that there was sufficient cause for not filing the complaint within the prescribed period, it can entertain a complaint beyond limitation time. However the Forum must record the reasons for condonation of delay.

Example: A deposited some jewellery with a bank. Bank lost it. Bank kept giving her false sense of hope to retrieve the jewellery, and thus A was put in a state of inaction. Later on when A filed a suit on the Bank, it claimed that the suit was not maintainable as the limitation time after the cause of action arose has lapsed. The Commission reprimanded the bank and admitted the case. [*Agnes D'Mello* v *Canara Bank* (1992) I CPJ 335 (NCDRC)]

According to section 24A there should have been an application filed within two years from the date of cause of action. Complaint was made on 30-11-1998 and in order to make the complaint dated 30-11-1998 as within time/the cause of action should have been shown as occurred on or after 30-11-1996. While there is acknowledgment of liability made on 9-12-1996 and if that is taken into account, the complaint could have been filed even later, that is up to 9-12-1998, that would be the exterior time; the complaint was found filed in time on 30-11-1998; So the question of limitation is of no substance in favour of the opposite party. [*R. Jawel* v *State of Tamil Nadu* AIR 2006 Mad 215]

[1][**25. Enforcement of Orders of the District Forum, the State Commission or the National Commission.**—(1) Where an interim order made under this Act, is not complied with the District Forum or the State Commission or the National Commission, as the case may be, may order the property of the person, not complying with such order to be attached.

(2) No attachment made under sub-section (1) shall remain in force for more than three months at the end of which, if the non-compliance continues, the property attached may be sold and out of the proceeds thereof, the District Forum or the State Commission or the National Commission may award such damages as it thinks fit to the complainant and shall pay the balance, if any, to the party entitled thereto.

(3) Where any amount is due from any person under an order made by a District Forum, State Commission or the National Commission, as the case may be, the person entitled to the amount may make an application to the District Forum, the State Commission or the National Commission, as the case may be, and such District Forum or the State Commission or the National Commission

---

1 Substituted by the Consumer Protection (Amendment) Act, 2002, w.e.f. 15-3-2003 for the following section:

"*25. Enforcement of orders by the Forum, the State Commission or the National Commission.*— Every order made by the District Forum, the State Commission or the National Commission may be enforced by the District Forum, the State Commission or the National Commission, as the case may be, in the same manner as if it were a decree or order made by a court in a suit pending therein and it shall be lawful for the District Forum, the State Commission or the National Commission to send, in the event of its inability to execute it, such order to the court within the local limits of whose jurisdiction,—

(*a*) in the case of an order against a company, the registered office of the company is situated, or

(*b*) in the case of an order against any other person, the place where the person concerned voluntarily resides or carries on business or personally works for gain, is situated,

and thereupon, the court to which the orders is so sent, shall execute the order as if it were a decree or order sent to it for execution."

may issue a certificate for the said amount to the Collector of the district (by whatever name called) and the Collector shall proceed to recover the amount in the same manner as arrears of land revenue.]

COMMENTS ON SECTION 25

Objects and Reasons

Clause 23 (old) seeks to substitute section 25 to provide for attachment by the District Forums, State Commission or National Commission, as the case may be, of the property of a person not complying with an interim order. It also seeks to provide that on application from any person entitled to receive any amount from another person under an order made by a District Forum, State Commission and National Commission which remains due, the District Forum, State Commission and National Commission, as the case may be, may issue a certificate to the Collector for recovery of the amount as arrears of land revenue. These new provisions are expected to overcome the delays and other difficulties faced in execution of orders of the redressal agencies through civil Courts.

State Commission while exercising appellate jurisdiction cannot entertain application for executing order passed by the District Forum. In the event the decree is modified by the Appellate Court then the decree of the Appellate Court shall be executed. [*Chief General Manager, Calcutta Telephone* v *State Consumer Disputes Redressal Commission* AIR 2004 Cal 141]

[1][**26. Dismissal of frivolous or vexatious complaints.**—Where a complaint instituted before the District Forum, the State Commission or, as the case may be, the National Commission is found to be frivolous or vexatious, it shall, for reasons to be recorded in writing, dismiss the complaint and make an order that the complainant shall pay to the opposite party such cost, not exceeding ten thousand rupees, as may be specified in the order.]

COMMENTS ON SECTION 26

(*i*) Where the complaint is *mala fide,* vexatious and frivolous and the opposite party has to incur expenses for contesting the complaint, the Redressal Fora should saddle the complainant with costs. [*K. Jai/araman* v *Poona Hospital & Research Centre* 1994 (I) CPR 23]

(*ii*) Merely because no court fee is payable for lodging a complaint before the consumer forums, parties have a tendency to misuse the provisions of the Consumer Protection Act in respect of matters not falling within its purview. This tendency must be

---

1 Substituted for the old section 26. "Where a complaint instituted is found to be frivolous or vexatious, the District Forum, the State Commission or, as the case may be, the National Commission, may dismiss the complaint", by the Consumer Protection (Amendment) Act, 1993, w.e.f. 18-6-1993.

discouraged. [*Orissa Vegetable Oil Complex Ltd.* v *State of Orissa* 1994 (I) CPR 32]

(*iii*) Cost can be saddled with only in case of fraudulent or vexatious complaints. [*Vihol Jashvantsingh Shivaji* v *Asstt. Branch Manager, Nezu India Insurance Co. Ltd.* 1994 (I) CPR 417]

(*iv*) Where the issue involved is a legal issue, the complaint cannot be said to be frivolous. [*Rasikalal Mohanlal* v *Apollo Tyres Ltd.* 1992 (II) CPR 327]

27. Penalties.—[1][(1)] Where a trader or a person against whom a complaint is made [2][or the complainant] fails or omits to comply with any order made by the District Forum, the State Commission or the National Commission, as the case may be, such trader or person [3][or the complainant] shall be punishable with imprisonment for a term which shall not be less than one month but which may extend to three years, or with fine which shall not be less than two thousand rupees but which may extend to ten thousand rupees, or with both.

[4][* * *]

[5][(2) Notwithstanding anything contained in the Code of Criminal Procedure, 1973 (2 of 1974), the District Forum or the State Commission or the National Commission, as the case may be, shall have the power of a Judicial Magistrate of the first class for the trial of offences under this Act, and on such conferment of powers, the District Forum or the State Commission or the National Commission, as the case may be, on whom the powers are so conferred, shall be deemed to be a Judicial Magistrate of the first class for the purpose of the Code of Criminal Procedure, 1973 (2 of 1974).

(3) All offences under this Act may be tried summarily by the District Forum or the State Commission or the National Commission, as the case may be.]

[6][**27A. Appeal against order passed under section 27.**—(1) Notwithstanding anything contained in the Code of Criminal Procedure, 1973, an appeal under section 27, both on facts and on law, shall lie from—

(*a*) the order made by the District Forum to the State Commission,

---

1 Section 27 renumbered as sub-section (1) by the Consumer Protection (Amendment) Act, 2002, w.e.f. 15-3-2003.

2 Inserted by the Consumer Protection (Amendment) Act, 1993, w.e.f. 18-6-1993.

3 *Ibid.*

4 The following *proviso* to section 27 omitted by the Consumer Protection (Amendment) Act, 2002, w.e.f. 15-3-2003:

"Provided that the District Forum, the State Commission or the National Commission, as the case may be, may, if it is satisfied that the circumstances of any case so require, impose a sentence of imprisonment or fine, or both, for a term lesser than the minimum term and the amount lesser than the minimum amount, specified in this section."

5 Inserted by the Consumer Protection (Amendment) Act, 2002, w.e.f. 15-3-2003.

6 Inserted by the Consumer Protection (Amendment) Act, 2002, w.e.f. 15-3-2003.

(*b*) the order made by the State Commission to the National Commission, and

(*c*) the order made by the National Commission to the Supreme Court.

(2) Except as aforesaid, no appeal shall lie to any court from any order of a District Forum or a State Commission or the National Commission.

(3) Every appeal under this section shall be preferred within a period of thirty days from the date of an order of a District Forum or a State Commission or, as the case may be, the National Commission:

Provided that the State Commission or the National Commission or the Supreme Court, as the case may be, may entertain an appeal after the expiry of the said period of thirty days, if it is satisfied that the appellant had sufficient cause for not preferring the appeal within the period of thirty days.]

COMMENTS ON SECTION 27

Objects and Reasons

Clause 24 (old) seeks to amend section 27 to empower the District Forum, State Commission and National Commission, as the case may be, "with the powers of a Judicial Magistrate of the first class for the summary trial of offences under the Act notwithstanding anything contained in the Code of Criminal Procedure. This is considered necessary to clarify that the District Forums or State Commissions or National Commission can themselves try offences under the Act and impose penalty of imprisonment. It also seeks to delete the proviso to section 27 which empowers the redressal agencies to impose a sentence of imprisonment or fine lesser than the minimum prescribed.

CHAPTER IV

Miscellaneous

28. Protection of action taken in good faith.—No suit, prosecution or other legal proceedings shall lie against the members of the District Forum, the State Commission or the National Commission or any officer or person acting under the direction of the District Forum, the State Commission or the National Commission for executing any order made by it or in respect of anything which is in good faith done or intended to be done by such member, officer or person under this Act or under any rule or order made thereunder.

[1][**28A. Service of Notice, etc.**—(1) All notices required by this Act to be served shall be served in the manner hereinafter mentioned in sub-section (2).

(2) The service of notices may be made by delivering or transmitting a copy thereof by registered post acknowledgment due addressed to opposite party against whom complaint is made or to the complainant by speed post or by such courier service as are approved by the District Forum, the State Commission or the National Commission, as the case may be, or by any other means of transmission of documents (including FAX message).

---

1 Inserted by the Consumer Protection (Amendment) Act, 2002, w.e.f. 15-3-2003.

(3) When an acknowledgment or any other receipt purporting to be signed by the opposite party or his agent or by the complainant is received by the District Forum, the State Commission or the National Commission, as the case may be, or postal article containing the notice is received back by such District Forum, State Commission or the National Commission, with an endorsement purporting to have been made by a postal employee or by any person authorized by the courier service to the effect that the opposite party or his agent or complainant had refused to take delivery of the postal article containing the notice or had refused to accept the notice by any other means specified in sub-section (2) when tendered or transmitted to him, the District Forum or the State Commission or the National Commission, as the case may be, shall declare that the notice had been duly served on the opposite party or to the complainant:

Provided that where the notice was properly addressed, pre-paid and duly sent by registered post acknowledgment due, a declaration referred to in this sub-section shall be made notwithstanding the fact that the acknowledgment has been lost or mislaid, or for any other reason, has not been received by the District Forum, the State Commission or the National Commission, as the case may be, within thirty days from the date of issue of notice.

(4) All notices required to be served on an opposite party or to complainant shall be deemed to be sufficiently served, if addressed in the case of the opposite party to the place where business or profession is carried and in case of complainant, the place where such person actually and voluntarily resides.]

29. Power to remove difficulties.—(1) If any difficulty arises in giving effect to the provisions of this Act, the Central Government may, by order in the Official Gazette, make such provisions not inconsistent with the provisions of this Act as appear to it to be necessary or expedient for removing the difficulty:

Provided that no such order shall be made after the expiry of a period of two years from the commencement of this Act.

(2) Every order made under this section shall, as soon as may be after it is made, be laid before each House of Parliament.

[1][(3) If any difficulty arises in giving effect to the provisions of the Consumer Protection (Amendment) Act, 2002, the Central Government may, by order, do anything not inconsistent with such provisions for the purpose of removing the difficulty:

Provided that no such order shall be made after the expiry of a period of two years from the commencement of the Consumer Protection (Amendment) Act, 2002.

(4) Every order made under sub-section (3) shall be laid before each House of Parliament.]

---

1 Inserted by the Consumer Protection (Amendment) Act, 2002, w.e.f. 15-3-2003.

[1][**29A. Vacancies or defects in appointment not to invalidate orders.**—No act or proceeding of the District Forum, the State Commission or the National Commission shall be invalid by reason only of the existence of any vacancy amongst its members or any defect in the constitution thereof.]

COMMENTS ON SECTION 29

Objects and Reasons.—Clause 26 (old) seeks to insert a new sub-section 29 to enable the Government to make orders to remove any difficulty with respect to the amended provisions of the Act for a period of two years after their coming into force.

[2][**30. Power to make rules.**—(1) The Central Government may, by notification, make rules for carrying out the provisions contained in clause (*a*) of sub-section (1) of section 2, clause (*b*) of sub-section (2) of section 4, sub-section (2) of section 5, sub-section (2) of section 12, clause (vi) of sub-section (4) of section 13, clause (*hb*) of sub-section (1) of section 14, section 19, clause (*b*) of sub-section (1) and sub-section (2) of section 20, section 22 and section 23 of this Act.

(2) The State Government may, by notification, make rules for carrying out the provisions contained in clause (*b*) of sub-section (2) and sub-section (4) of section 7, clause (*b*) of sub-section (2) and sub-section (4) of section 8A, clause (*b*) of sub-section (1) and sub-section (3) of section 10, clause (c) of sub-section (1) of section 13, clause (*hb*) of sub-section (1) and sub-section (3) of section 14, section 15 and clause (*b*) of sub-section (1) and sub-section (2) of section 16 of this Act.]

[3][**30A. Power of the National Commission to make regulations.**—(1) The National Commission may, with the previous approval of the Central Government, by notification, make regulations not inconsistent with this Act to provide for all matters for which provision is necessary or expedient for the purpose of giving effect to the provisions of this Act.

(2) In particular and without prejudice to the generality of the foregoing power, such regulations may make provisions for the cost of adjournment of any proceeding before the District Forum, the State Commission or the National Commission, as the case may be, which a party may be ordered to pay.]

---

1 Inserted by the Consumer Protection (Amendment) Act, 1991, w.e.f. 15-6-1991.

2 Substituted by the Consumer Protection (Amendment) Act, 2002, w.e.f. 15-3-2003 for the following section:

"*30.* (1) The Central Government may, by notification, make rules for carrying out the provisions contained in clause (*a*) of sub-section (1) of section 2, clause (*b*) of sub-section (2) of section 4, sub-section (2) of section 5, clause (*iv*) of sub-section (4) of section 13, section 19, sub-section (2) of section 20 and section 22 of this Act.

(2) The State Government may, by notification, make rules for carrying out the provisions contained in clause (*b*) of sub-section (2) and sub-section (4) of section 7, sub-section (3) of section 10, clause (*c*) of sub-section (1) of section 13, sub-section (3) of section 14, section 15 and sub-section (2) of section 16."

3 Inserted by the Consumer Protection (Amendment) Act, 2002, w.e.f. 15-3-2003.

COMMENTS ON SECTION 30

Objects and Reasons

Clause 28 (old) seeks to substitute a new section for section 30 to deal with the powers of the Central Government and the State Governments to make rules.

Clause 29 (old) seeks to insert a new section 30-A to empower the National Commission to make regulations with the previous approval of the Central Government where required for the purpose of giving effect to the provisions of the Act, and in particular to make provisions for the cost of adjournment of any proceedings before the District forum, the State Commission or the National Commission, as the case may be, which a party maybe ordered to pay.

[1][**31. Rules and Regulation to be laid before each House of Parliament.**— (1) Every rule and every regulation made under this Act shall be laid, as soon as may be after it is made, before each House of Parliament, while it is in session, for a total period of thirty days which may be comprised in one session or in two or more successive sessions, and if, before the expiry of the session immediately following the session or the successive sessions aforesaid, both Houses agree in making any modification in the rule or regulation or both Houses agree that the rule or regulation should not be made, the rule or regulation shall thereafter have effect only in such modified form or be of no effect, as the case may be; so, however, that any such modification or annulment shall be without prejudice to the validity of anything previously done under that rule or regulation.

(2) Every rule made by a State Government under this Act shall be laid as soon as may be after it is made, before the State Legislature.]

COMMENTS ON SECTION 31

Objects and Reasons

Clause 30 (old) seeks to substitute section 31 in respect of procedures for laying of rules and regulations made under the Act before each House of Parliament or the State Legislature, as the case may be.

---

1 Substituted by the Consumer Protection (Amendment) Act, 2002, w.e.f. 15-3-2003 for the following section:

"*31. Laying of Rules.*—(1) Every rule made by the Central Government under this Act shall be laid, as soon as may be after it is made, before each House of Parliament, while it is in session, for a total period of thirty days which may be comprised in one session or in two or more successive sessions, and if before the expiry of the session immediately following the session or the successive sessions aforesaid, both Houses agree in making any modification in the rule or both Houses agree that the rule should not be made, the rule shall thereafter have effect only in such modified form or be of no effect, as the case may be; so, however, that any such modification or annulment shall be without prejudice to the validity of anything previously done under that rule.

(2) Every rule made by a State Government under this Act shall be laid as soon as may be after it is made, before the State Legislature."

CHAPTER 13

Consumer's Checklist & Tips

SYNOPSIS

Yes its time to brush up our consumer right. Consumer is considered to be the King of the Market but when it comes to consumer's protection it is *vice versa* and we consumers are made to stake at mind. Consumer awareness is actually the need of the hour. With the increasingly large number of new products springing up in the market there is need to educate the community. Consumer Awareness program focuses on breaking the barriers of Consumer ignorance.

1. Consumer must ask for a receipt

The consumers must always insist on an invoice, receipt/bill of purchase/cash memo and must retain the same carefully. This serves as proof of purchase and can be helpful, if any defect in the quality/quantity of product purchased from the particular trader is discovered at a later stage. It is very difficult to attach liability on the seller/trader in absence of bill of purchase or where bill of purchase is lost or destroyed. Further, this will establish that he is a 'consumer' of the product or services in question. This is very important as only consumers can file a complaint under the Consumer Protection Act, 1986.

2. One way traffic

The consumers can question the stipulation made in the cash memos and other such documents of the seller that goods once sold will not be taken back. Such a stipulation is not consistent with the valuable rights of the consumers under the Sale of Goods Act, 1930.

3. All that glitters is not gold

Where the sale is by description, the consumer should see that the goods supplied by the seller in correspond with the description or claim made by the seller in respect of its quality/quantity/measurement/specification/number, as the case may be. If the sale is by sample, the goods supplied should correspond to the sample in quality and standard. In case the sale is by sample as well as description, the bulk should correspond to both. The consumers should also be vigilant against any tall claims and representations made by the seller for the purpose of promoting the sale, use or supply of any goods or for the provisions of any services. Those representing that the goods are of a particular quality or standard or model when they do not possess the said characteristics or benefits 3r standard. Any misrepresentation of the seller in this regard can be called into question under the MRTP Act, 1969 as well as under the Consumer Protection Act, 1986 as an unfair trade practice. The consumers must always read the fine print of all contracts, warranties and guarantees carefully.

4. Is it under guarantee?

The consumers should also ensure that all warranties/guarantees/relevant papers/instruction manuals etc. are delivered to him along with the goods.

5. A stitch in time saves nine?

The consumers must also check the batch number, date of manufacture, etc. when buying the goods. This is very important particularly in case of food items. The consumers must also check the date of expiry when buying medicines canned/tinned foods or tetra packed drinks which have a limited shelf life. In case of canned/tinned food items, the consumers must check for cans bulging due to microbial contamination.

6. This is ISI marked

The consumers must always insist of' 'ISI' marked goods. In case of items like spices, condiments and other food commodities, the consumers must insist on properly packaged and sealed foods preferably with as 'AGMARIK' certificate. In case of canned foods and bottled food items like ketchup, etc., the consumer should see that the same have a Fruits Products Order (FPO) certification. The consumer has a right to insure that the goods are free from any defects which render them unfit for "consumption even if the defect is not apparent on reasonable visual examination of the same. In regard to foodstuffs, the consumer is entitled to compensation for inedible food articles even if he buys it from governmental machinery like F.C.I, or public distribution system.

7. Shoppe from Shop — *Caveat emptor*

The consumers should also make sure that the seller has a right to sell goods. In other words, the seller should have a clear title to the goods. In this connection, the consumers must ensure that they purchase the goods from reputed shops and not from wayside stalls or buyers. This also applies to an immovable property purported to be sold by the seller if he does not have a clear title to such property. The property represented by the seller to be owned by him should also be free from any charge or encumbrance in buyer/consumer before or at the time of sale.

8. Testing authorities

In case any food stuff are found to be adulterated, the consumers should get it tested and should approach the authorities at the District, State or the National level, as the case may be.

9. Penny wise, Pound foolish!

The consumers also have a right to insist on the supply of goods in reasonable price. In the case of packed commodities, the price should not exceed the one shown on the packet.

10. Prevention is better than cure

Consumers should know that although the Act has come into existence and it has dealt with so many kinds of goods and services, traders and institutions, yet, it is equally important that apart from the statutory machinery, at public service, what forms the basis of consumerism? It is AWARENESS. Consumers should know their rights. Fight for them. Fight for them so well that situation for going to the courts becomes the last resort. Know the law since ignorance of it is no excuse. And remember, nobody is above the law, NOBODY. If consumers know what to purchase, what is good for health, what are the responsibilities of the sellers and traders, that there are institutions for standardization, that there are standard weights and measures, that the edible oils, drinks, milk, food items and other consumable are to conform to certain specifications, then consumers cannot be taken for a ride in the market so easily. So the consumers should wake up and help the law help them.

11. Excess of anything is bad

Awareness is alright. But consumers should not also jump to premature conclusions. One may have suffered a wrong but one should give the other party a chance to make amends. May be the lapse is only through inadvertence and oversight. The consumers should not try to abuse the process of the law. The consumers should not try to blackmail. The consumers should not try to be vindictive. A vexatious or frivolous complaint is also liable to be dismissed and sometimes with costs, which may extend to ₹10,000 and rest assured, if the Act is armed to defend the *bona fide* consumers, it does not contemplate that every person should be put on the alter merely because he happens to be a trader. By filing such complaints, the valuable time of the Courts is wasted, cases are piled up and *bona fide* litigant suffers on that account. So, when the consumer really happens to suffer, it may be too late.

12. Give him a chance

It is always better to try to negotiate. Consumer awareness and conviction may at the outset force the trader to make good the loss. If he is far away, one should write to him. If that is also fruitless and high stakes are involved, one should get him served with a legal notice through a lawyer. That may click the issue. Even if it doesn't, do not get disheartened. All the said communications shall be part and parcel of the subsequent complaint and help to make a *prima facie* case depicting callousness and blatantly not business like disposition of the opposite party. This will not only substantiate your relief but may also be considered by the Court, while awarding the damages, costs, amount of compensation, incidental expenses and interest on the amount as may have accrued in favour of the consumer. It will also explicitly show that consumers have come with clean hands and after exhausting other avenues.

13. Speech is silver, silence is gold and being precise is a blend of both

Consumers should try to be as brie£ precise and to the point in the complaint. It should be a concise statement of facts, exact picture of the suffering, naked truth of the dereliction of the trader and an unambiguous inroad to the relief the complainant has claimed. The consumer should not try to raise blind allegations or exaggerate. A complainant may get caught in technicalities and expose himself to avoidable embarrassment.

14. Storm in a tea cup

In a way, yes the Act is of such an exhaustive nature that one stretches one's imagination and at very point of time, one will find himself to be a consumer. And may be a badly cheated one so, next time if a consumer thinks something is wrong, he need not bear with it. That's not like today's consumer.

15. Do it yourself

By now consumers must be brimming with confidence to take up the task of protection of their interests. The proceedings under the Act are not at all to be compared with that of the regular civil or criminal Court. Procedure is such as would encourage general public to approach the Forum & Commissions on their own, argue their own cases and have a face to face reckoning with the trader. So if a consumer has prepared and filed the complaint, he must go forward. By doing it himself he is not only fighting for his rights and setting example for others, he is also enriching the society and the Nation with an enlightened individuality, as a free citizen of the country. It can hit at the root of corruption and curb the abnormal tendencies of the people who matter. And, it will help to get the matter decided at the earliest, nourished by consumer's strict follow up. However, it may be a bit difficult in certain cases. For that matter one may engage a lawyer. He will bring the cases within the parameters of the Act and draft the pleadings in the light of the prevailing intricacies of the law, of course, regularly instructed by the consumer. The first step is that of the consumer. And the last too.

A purchaser should run the following checklist before accepting the seller's offer and placing the purchase order:

- Product or services details such as: Label, Safety and Quality Certification (ISI, ISO certification, etc.)
- Authorization of the dealer by Manufacturer/Service Provider,
- All the accessories that are part of the offer (In case of laptop, it may include battery, power cord and adapter, optical drive (in case detachable), carry-case, etc.)
- Date of manufacturing and expiry date (if applicable)
- Whether product features and specifications are as per instruction/user manual
- method and/or instructions of use of the product
- MRP (Price of a product cannot exceed MRP);

- Discount-if there is any Manufacturer's discount applicable *vis-à-vis.* dealers discount
- Taxes applicable- CST, LST, VAT or any other charges
- Payment terms/acceptable modes of payment,
- If there is any arrangement of finance through some financer. If so, read the terms in the agreement carefully.
- Read the Terms of Guarantee/warranties thoroughly (Keep the Agreement in safe custody)
- Insist on a bill for purchases-check its date, stamp of dealer and terms and conditions contained therein
- Insist on having Sale receipts and keep it in safe custody.
- Whether Packing of the goods is proper
- Whether replacement of goods is applicable and what is availability of spare parts or components
- Contact details of Service/Support centre
- Delivery system and associated charges
- Whether the product is insured. If so, read the terms thoroughly.
- On delivery, check the items and all the accessories against what is mentioned in the bill. In case any defect is detected or any part is missing, point out at that very instance.

Remember filing of any complaint by the consumer before the court must be in chronological order and supported by evidence. Hence running the above checklist at the time of purchase not only helps consumer in detecting deficiencies, but also in terms of furnishing strong evidence in case defect or deficiency is detected at a later date and consumer decides to file a complaint before appropriate forums.

In case any defect/deficiency is detected in the product, first you should approach the seller and preferably submit the complaint in writing giving complete details. In case the seller agrees to rectify the problem to your satisfaction, ask for time it should take to do the same and have a copy of acknowledgement of receipt of complaint for your records. If the Seller fails to attend the complaint in due course of time or creates dispute, the buyer can approach Consumer Court, MRTP Commission, Weight and Measurement department, or file criminal complaint in case of cheating. Now-a-day, consumer courts are very effective in helping the consumer to resolve the dispute.

(1) In case where the value of goods and services is less than Rupees Twenty Lakh, complaint can be filed in the District Consumer Forum constituted in the specified districts of the State.

(2) In case where the value of goods and services is more than Rupees Twenty Lakhs, but does not exceed Rupees One Crores, complaint can

be filed in the State Consumer Forum constituted in the capital cities of different states.

(3) In case where the value of goods and services is more than ₹1 Crores, complaint can be filed in the National Consumer Forum constituted in the Capital of India.

"Consumer" means any person who buys any goods and services for a consideration which has been paid or promised or partly paid and partly promised, or under any system of deferred payment other than the person who buys such goods for resale or for any commercial purpose.

"Defect" means any fault, imperfection or short-coming in the quality, quantity, potency, purity or standard which is required to be maintained by or under any law for the time being in force or [under any contract, express or] implied, or as is claimed by the trader in any manner whatsoever in relation to any goods.

"Deficiency" means any fault, imperfection or inadequacy in the quality, quantity, nature and manner of performance which is required to be maintained by or under any law for the time being in force or has been undertaken to be performed by a person in pursuance of a contract or otherwise in relation to any service.

A complainant can be —

(1) a consumer; or

(2) any voluntary consumer association registered under the Companies Act, 1956 (1 of 1956) or under any other law for the time being in force; or

(3) the Central Government or any State Government,

(4) One or more consumers, where there are numerous consumers having the same interest.

"Complaint" means any allegation in writing made by a complainant that —

(1) an unfair trade practice or a restrictive trade practice has been adopted by any trader or service provider

(2) the goods bought by the complainant or agreed to be hired or availed of by him suffer from one or more defect

(3) the services hired or availed of or agreed to be hired suffer from deficiency in any respect.

The Consumer Protection Act, 1986, guarantees the following statutory rights to the consumers —

(1) The right to be protected against the marketing of goods and services which are hazardous to life and property. It is the duty of the manufacturers and the distributor not to supply any goods to the consumers which fail to comply with the general safety requirements. Consumers should know about safety standards published from time to time by the relevant authorities in relation to different types of consumer

goods. They should insist on looking at quality marks like ISI, ISO, AGMARK, etc.

(2) The right to be informed about the quality, quantity, potency, purity, standard and price of goods or services, as the case may be, so as to protect the consumer against unfair trade practices: This is intended to save the consumers from unfair trade practices like false and misleading advertisements selling defective or sub-standard articles, or exaggerated statements about power or potency of a product. It's important to note that a victim of unfair trade practices would be able to avail protection through Consumer Forum only if he is a consumer within the meaning of the Act. Otherwise he will have to go to the Monopolies Commission under MRTP Act.

(3) The right to be assured, wherever possible, access to a variety of goods and services at competitive prices: The Central Council has been entrusted responsibility of organizing markets and market practices in such a way that firstly all dealers are supplied with a variety of goods for the benefit of the consumers and secondly goods are offered at competitive prices. Only then the consumers will have access to variety of goods and services at competitive prices.

(4) The right to be heard and to be assured that consumer's interest will receive due consideration at appropriate forums: Right to be heard is a principle of natural justice as well. The Central Council is entrusted with the responsibility of assuring consumers that they can approach appropriate forums and forums would give due attention and consideration to their concerns or grievances. This also includes right of consumers to form non-political and non-profitable community welfare organizations to represent on appropriate forums.

(5) The right to seek redressal against unfair trade practices or restrictive trade practices or unscrupulous exploitation of consumers: The right can be explained clearly by the following example – Buyer pays an advance sum for supply of a particular good within a month, but the laptop is delivered much later, say in six months. In such a situation retention of money beyond a month is an unfair trade practice and the consumers can claim proper interest on the advance amount for the period of delay.

(6) The right to consumer education. This is one of the most important rights, which consumers can exercise to prevent exploitation by manufacturers and traders. The Central Council is responsible for educating consumers on their rights under the Act and remedies available for redressal.

This Need of the hour is for consumers to be aware of their rights and exercise them whenever any seller indulges in unfair trade practices or adopts unscrupulous methods.

16. Buying insurance?

Since the nationalisation of the life insurance business in 1956, the state-owned Life Insurance Corporation of India had been the only source of life insurance to the Indian consumer for over 40 years.

With the opening up of the insurance industry in 2000 and the activation of private participation, the Indian insurance landscape has changed entirely. Today the consumer is presented with unprecedented choice and will benefit from the liberalization and competition in numerous ways.

This aims to help customers select their insurance from the abundance of choices available.

LIC has done an admirable job in the past 40+ years. Nonetheless by its own admission, market penetration in insurance has stagnated at 12-15 per cent. India has a 250-million strong middle class segment, much of which is uninsured or underinsured. As a result, life insurance premia has been contributing a mere 1.4 per cent of the GDP.

Obviously, there is need to raise this figure to globally competitive standards of two-digit share percentages. As in every sector of world economies, competition will benefit the consumer through enhanced market savvy and consumer responsiveness of players. With the entry of the private players, the Indian insurance individual retail market is estimated to be worth $25-27 billion in the next 7-8 years.

Most certainly, premium contribution to our GDP will increase to double-digit share percentages, up from the current 1.4 per cent of GDP.

In many international markets, the product offerings of the insurance industry are fairly similar. The true differentiators come from delivery and service. Consumers while studying the market for an insurance plan should certainly look at an innovative and comprehensive product line in companies. This helps in times of repeat sale and for addressing differing needs at various stages of one's life.

Certainly, the service of the company offers is an important criterion for careful examination. An agent trained to consider long time needs, who is helpful and believes in full disclosures for a consumer to make informed decisions about his/her financial planning, will help in making the choice.

Global experience has shown that life insurance is never bought but always sold and the only real way of reaching consumers is face to face. Hence personalized service that includes regular reviews, updates and the flexibility to adapt insurance solutions to suit consumer's changing needs are also important.

A strong business foundation and a robust distribution network are some of the essentials while considering any life insurance company. The reputation and standing of a company are also indicators that reveal the kind of products and service one can expect.

Insurance companies are periodically rated by international rating agencies for their financial stability and ability to settle claims. Large insurance companies receive high ratings from rating agencies, like Standard & Poor's, Moody's Investors Services and A M Best.

A company's reputation will also indicate its ethics, its integrity and best practices. These metrics too are significant and go a long way to inspire confidence in consumers and also shareholders. Companies with solid a reputation usually believe in fairness to all stakeholders (consumers, shareholders, employees and agents) and it is reflected in all aspects of the business including financial prudence in all its dealings.

Insurance coverage is essential for every individual. How much and what type of insurance one needs will differ with every individual. Review the following with your financial advisor to arrive at the life insurance solutions that suits your needs:

- Review your own insurance needs and circumstances. Choose the kind of policy that offers benefits that most closely fit your needs.
- Make sure you can afford the premium payments. If the premium amount increases later, can you still afford it?
- Do not sign an insurance application until you review it carefully to be sure all the answers are complete and accurate.
- Do not buy life insurance unless you intend to stick with your plan. It may be very costly if you quit during the early years of the policy.
- Do not drop one policy and buy another without a thorough study of the new policy and the existing one. Replacing your insurance may be costly.
- Read your policy documents carefully. Ask your advisor or company about anything that does not appear clear to you.
- Review your life insurance programme with your financial advisor or company every few years to keep up with your changing requirements.
- Your insurance policy gives you long-term protection while offering immediate tax benefits. Your insurance needs are usually greater than the need for a tax benefit in the current financial year.

Insurance in the future will no longer be bought as a savings tool but will be sold for protection. An insurance policy offers much more than returns from tax planning and investment. It offers one the ability to plan for unforeseen events that could affect the individual and the family's financial well being adversely.

Life insurance is universally acknowledged as an effective tool to eliminate risk, substitute certainty for uncertainty and ensure timely aid of the family in the unfortunate event of the death of the breadwinner. Hence life insurance provides assistance if premature death occurs which may leave a dependent family to fend for itself and also for old age without visible means of support.

Buying life insurance cannot be compared with other investment decisions especially stock market investments where one waits for the right time to buy or sell. As far as life insurance goes, the best time to buy it is right *now!*.

17. Be a wise consumer

How many times have you felt cheated when you came from the market? How many times have you wished that you could make a complaint but did not know how and to whom?

Your answer probably would be, 'Yes, many times." Most of us consumers have been cheated some time or the other while making a purchase. Many of us wish that we had more knowledge that would help us become wiser consumers.

Do we go on in this state of ignorance? Certainly not. We can and need to educate ourselves on our rights and responsibilities as consumers.

As consumers, we first need to be aware of all the different products available in the market. You probably know some or most of them. In today's scenario, it may not be possible to know all the products that exits, but what is more important is to be aware of the products that could be useful to you. If you are a working mother, you may be interested in different ready-mixes or masalas that make your job easier. If you are at home, you would probably be interested in some other products. So keep your eyes an ears open, to increase your knowledge of the many choices available to you today.

Apart from the many products that exist, there are many brands for each type of category. Cooking oils, for instance. There are oils made from different sources like groundnut, sunflower and various other seeds. In each type, both the refined and filtered varieties are available.

You may ask yourself, "If there is so much to know, where do I start? What are the essentials that I need to know that would help me make better purchases?

All food manufacturers require a license. The Prevention of Food Adulteration Act (PFA) stipulates the information that is to be given on every food product that is above a certain minimum weight. This information could be used by you while making your purchase.

18. To start with, look out for the following details on the packaging

The date of manufacture. This gives you an idea of when the product was manufactured and is of particular importance for ready-to eat and canned foods. In most cases, the month of manufacture is stated. For some products the date of packing may be given. The date of manufacture does not have to be printed on fast moving perishable goods like milk, butter and ice-cream.

Expiry date is another important piece of information to consider when buying a food product. However, under the PFA Act, it is not mandatory for the manufacturer to print the expiry date on the packaging. This provision is currently under consideration and is, likely to be incorporated under the Act in the near future.

In Europe and America, the scenario is quite different. It is mandatory for all perishable commodities to have the date of expiry clearly visible on its label. Every one customarily checks that expiry date before buying any item, making rough calculations of the shelf life of his product. Neither the retailer, nor the dealer there, would stock anything which has a current expiry date. In India, the expiry date rule only applies to pharmaceutical drugs. In all other commodities, the mention of it is not mandatory. This could be one of the major reasons why Indian food products are not popular in EEC markets. The risk of contamination and staleness is high. A few manufacturers, particularly multinationals, print 'best before date' on their products. This is another way of stating the expiry date.

You may have noticed that canned and bottled food products like jams, pickles, sauces and jellies have the letters FPO and a number printed on them. FPO stands for Fruits Product Order and is the act that governs the manufacture and packing of fruit products. Every licensed fruit product will have the FPO number printed on its label.

Another important factor for any food product is the ingredients used in it. Every packaged food product has to have an ingredient list on its label. The ingredients are mentioned in descending order of quantity. The ingredient list for a soup powder would be as follows — dehydrated vegetables, salt, corn flour, etc. This means that dehydrated vegetables are the largest item, by weight in the soup powder. The ingredient list is of particular importance to those who cannot eat certain foods like eggs, for example.

The PFA Act stipulates the type and quantity of flavours and colours that can be used in food products. The label of every food product must mention that it contains 'permitted colours and flavours'. The FDA regularly checks products for the type and quantity of colours and flavours sued.

19. How do we know the quality of ingredients that go into the product?

We can only depend on the reputation of the manufactures. In most cases, it is preferable to buy a product of a known or reputed manufactures rather that that of an unknown one. The former is likely to have undertaken quality checks than his smaller counterpart.

Price is another important parameter that we need to check when buying a food product, particularly a high value one, like oil. In today's competitive scenario, prices may not differ too much between brands but we still need to make comparisons to satisfy ourselves.

The price of a product is stated as MRP (incl. of all taxes). This is an all-inclusive price. A retailer can charge you a lower price but not more than the MRP that is printed on the product.

The packaging act specifies the various sizes in which products can be packages and sold. Some manufactures charge a higher price by selling in a non-standard pack size. Any product that is of a different size needs to mention the unit price so that the consumer can make her own comparisons.

Packaging is another important element of a product. One of the important functions of packaging is to protect a product. Avoid buying or refuse to accept a product with a soiled or damaged packaging as the product it contains may have been pilfered or contaminated. You may choose to accept a product with damaged packaging only if you are sure that the product inside is unaffected by the damage to its packaging.

Having seen what we need to know as a consumer, we also need to know the procedure to be followed to make a complaint. Vanmana Manjure, a consumer rights activist and panelist of the Consumer Disputes and Redressal Forum (CDRF), an arbitrating body, elaborates on the procedure. "When a consumer is dissatisfied with a product, he should dispatch an acknowledgement due registered letter to the marketing division of the concerned company. If the matter is very serious, the consumer can send the letter to the MDs of the company too. Send in details of your complaint, along with the mention of the shop from where you purchased the products, the details about the packaging and also what kind of compensation you are seeking.

The penalties on the company will depend on the nature of the consumer's complaint. If the consumer is seeking a replacement of the product or a money-back response, the company will have to comply. In case of money-back, the amount will be refunded along with 18 per cent interest.

If the company does not respond, the consumer will have to take his grievance to the Consumer Guidance Society of India (CGSI) or in Mumbai, to the Mumbai Grahak Panchayat. The CGSI is based in Mumbai and has branches in the following cities — Calicut, Goa, Hyderabad, Kottayam, Pune, Trichur and Udaipur. If the need arises you can contact their local office.

These organizations will make a representation to the company concerned, on behalf of the consumer. If the company fails to respond, then through these bodies, the consumer can approach the CDRF which will hold a Consumer Court, summoning all parties involved and arbitrate on the issue. In the event of any complaint, all the costs of litigation have to be borne by the company. The consumer is not charged anything."

Vijay Jathan, Hon Gen Secretary of the CGSI, calls the process "righting a wrong'.

You as a consumer have been wronged and now it has to be set right." Every consumer should be aware of his or her rights and responsibilities and should exercise them accordingly. Next time you have a grievance, act immediately and refuse to be short changed. If the country requires an active consumer movement it will be effective only through vigilant consumers.

20. When buying a car

Once you have decided on the car model that you want to buy, there are a few things that you need to keep in mind before you drive away in it. Ideally, you should have two checks on the vehicle — the pre-registration check and then the pre-delivery check. Both these checklists consist of the same check points. The idea is to ensure that the car you choose is the car you drive out of the dealership.

Visit the dealer and check the car prior to registering it in your name. Call the dealer ahead of time and let him know that you plan to perform a very detailed inspection to ensure that the car has been prepared and is ready. Take a knowledgeable relative or friend along, for suggestions, observations, or comments. Insist that no invoice is made in your name till you complete the inspection. Another check to be done is for any body damage or repair jobs.

21. Visual inspection of vehicle

Remember, a careful inspection is critical. After the car leaves the dealership lot, the dealer can reasonably claim that any damage or lack has been caused by you. So, take your time on the inspection.

1. Do a walk-around on the car — to get a first impression on how clean the car looks.
2. Check the car's manufacturing month/year.
3. Check for body damage or repair jobs done, such as difference in paint shade, dents, etc.
4. Check that the chassis no. and engine no. matches the one mentioned on the invoice or challans.
5. Check the mileage on the car — ideally it should be very close to zero. But reasonably, anything less than 50 kms is okay.
6. Check to see if seams and door lines are straight. Overuse at the dealership will definitely tell on these parts — they will be worn or dented.
7. Engine Check
    - Open the bonnet and check if the engine is in perfect shape.
    - Check if every dipstick, plastic cover and wiring is present and properly attached.
    - Check that all fluids — transmission fluid, engine oil, coolant, brake oil, power steering oil, windscreen water and battery water are at optimal level.
    - Check for fluid leakage. There should be none. The same applies for dirt or grime.
    - Check for signs of exterior wear and tear on engine components. For instance, a spark plug wire that is a different shade of black should be immediately questioned.
    - Check the battery — you shouldn't find any corrosion on the electrodes. It should be properly connected and fastened to wire leads and properly secured.

Check if the battery has a separate warranty.

1. Tyre-Check

   Check that the spare wheel is fresh and that all related tools (spanner, jack, etc.) are present.

- Are there wheel locks?
- Ensure that the lug key is present in the car.
- What should the proper air pressure be?
- What is the tyre warranty and is it present?
- The tyres should show no signs of wear, and should be properly inflated.
- Tyres should be scuff-free and the hubcaps should be fixed properly.

2. Check if all the doors, hoods, trunks, deck lids and lift gates work properly.
3. Do the locks work properly? If they are automatic, can they be operated by remote?
4. Make sure that the power window controls, rapid down operation, wipers and rear window defroster are all working properly.
5. Carry your own audio cassettes or CDs to test the music system in the car.
6. Interior Check - You have the right to expect spic and span interiors
   - Check for stains on the carpet, head rest and seats
   - Check if all seatbelts work properly.
   - Check if floor mats are all in place.
   - Driver's seat - do you know how to work the seat position controls, such as wheel positioning, tilt, telescope, lock, horn and cruise control?
   - Keys — Ensure that you have more than one set of keys. Check if the remote entry key is working.
   - Check for child protection on door locks.
   - How does the alarm work? How do you activate and disarm it? Is there a cut off switch?

22. Documentation

Read the paperwork properly. Do not take anybody's word for anything. Make sure all the blanks in the contract are filled in. Your paperwork should include:

1. Sales certificate
2. All payment receipts
3. Registration certificate (RC) or temporary registration certificate

Is your name spelt correctly?

Is the number same on the number plate and the RC book?

1. Check if insurance is adequate, valid and active.

2. Check for original pollution under control (PUC) certificate. This should be valid for one year.
3. Owner's manual.
4. Warranty card for car — check to see if warranty details are properly counter-signed by the dealership.
5. Check to ensure that you have all the free service coupons in place.
6. Ensure that you collect the warranty cards for batteries, tyres and all other accessories.
7. Check extended warranty details (if opted for).
8. Check roadside assistance contact details.
9. Collect dealership and service personnel business cards.

Payment: If any payment formalities still remain to be completed, carry along the relevant post-dated cheques (PDCs) or cash or credit card.

Date of delivery: If you have a preference for a particular day/time (for auspicious reasons), inform the dealer well in advance. Always take delivery in broad daylight, since artificial lighting or insufficient lighting at night can be misleading.

23. Consumer protection while shopping Online — Tips!

You may be apprehensive about shopping online? Why? It could be the rate of phishing, internet scams, etc. which is raising these concerns. How do you protect your payment or any information divulged on the internet? It is simple, apply for a 3d secure pass word from your bank through which you are doing all the financial transactions while shopping. Once, this is requested, you can type your favourite statement which appear every time you shop online as if to reassure you that it is safe. Any time you shop you will be asked to type this pass word and if you see your statement appearing you are safe.

In case the product delivered to you does not match what was displayed on the shopping site, then you can file a case in the resolution centre. This is a platform which brings together both the supplier and purchaser. They can communicate in the presence of a customer support and make sure that all the transactions are carried out online and not offline. If it is carried out offline, then there is no proof of the communication. Once, the problem is resolved and the supplier agrees to send a better product he can close the case. If it is not resolved by the supplier then under the Consumer Protection Act, you will be reimbursed your amount.

Whatever transaction you carry out has to be done on the same site. This provides enough proof of what you have communicated and your money will be protected. You will be paid back the whole amount and the supplier will have a poor rating which will further affect his account. Hence, he will never again try to deceive another person like the way he did to you. Be aware of all your rights and know how to deal with a situation like this. Cyber crimes are very common and should not be overlooked. You should always take precautions before you make any transaction over the web. This makes it hard for anyone to see and steal your information. Some websites have fake yellow locks on their websites to make their sites look secure. In order to see if a lock is authentic, you should click on the lock. A pop-up window should appear verifying its authenticity.

Always check for anti virus updates on your system. This will prevent hackers from entering your system and hacking all the bank information and other confidential details. This way you can have safe transactions!

24. Travel tips — How do you lodge a formal complaint with an Airline?

Imagine that you're sitting in first class for the first time. You've used a combination of frequent flyer miles from your spouse's business travels and points earned through a rewards program with your credit card to book the two of you on a nonstop flight to a romantic destination for the weekend. You're excited about your first time in first class — having enough room to be comfortable and getting the extra perks that come along with the prestigious seating.

As the flight attendant walks by for the first time you ask him, "Excuse me, do you have any magazine's I can look at." He turns and says, "I'm sorry. Haven't you heard about 9/11, airlines in bankruptcy, employee layoffs, overworked flight attendants? Of course, we don't have any magazines. You should have brought your own." You think to yourself, "But I thought I was in first class. I thought I'd get waited on hand and foot." Then your spouse, who is a very frequent air traveler, lets you know that first class isn't what it used to be.

Next, you try to put up your tray only to find out that it's broken. It sits right in your lap, making it useless. When you point this out to the same flight attendant (actually, the only flight attendant it seems), he tells you that you must be doing something wrong. It's not broken. When you show him it is broken he says, "Huh," and walks away. You spend your flight with food in your lap and a huge disappointment over your "first class" treatment.

This, of course, is a true story that was relayed by a friend of mine, and one many air travelers can probably believe and most likely top. It seems that the service you get on an airline truly isn't what it used to be, and most air travellers have learned to adjust. But what should you do if you're met with rude airline employees or unacceptable amenities on the plane?

25. Complain

It would have done my friend no good to complain to the flight attendant. He clearly didn't care and most likely wasn't in a position to change anything even if he had cared. So who should you complain to and how should you go about doing so?

Situations like this are best left to filing a formal complaint with the airline after the air travel experience is done. The best way to file a formal complaint is in writing — either by written letter or e-mail.

Before writing your complaint, attempt to get a hold of the airline's passenger's rights statement, often called a "conditions of carriage" or "contract of carriage" statement. It will spell out the airline's policy on how passengers are to be treated. If you can find that your treatment or situation was against what is mentioned in their statement, it is best to include that in your letter. Copy the specific wording from their statement in your letter and relay exactly how your situation is in violation of their policy.

Your written complaint should be professional and to the point and include the following information:

Your flight information so that the airline knows exactly which flight you were on and which seat you were sitting in

Focused details about your complaint explain what the situation was and why it was specifically a problem for you. Include the names of any airline employees who were rude, disrespectful or just plain made the situation worse. Also, if there were any employees who tried to make the situation better, but couldn't, include their names also. Sometimes, your complaint has nothing to do with employee conduct.

Choose which aspects of your experience to complain about and keep your letter to the point. In my friend's case, the rudeness of the employee was much more of a problem than the fact that there were no magazines available for the passengers. The rudeness of the flight attendant should have been the focus of the incident.

If you are a frequent traveller with that airline, state it in the letter. If the experience has made you rethink your relationship with the airline, state that also. It will get their attention.

Send a copy of your complaint to The Department of Transportation and the Aviation Consumer Action Project and let the airline know you're doing so. This will also get their attention.

An explanation of how you would like the airline to go about remedying the situation. You could ask for monetary compensation, frequent flyers miles added to your account, discounts, free travel, or perhaps just an apology. Don't get greedy, however. Is an overworked, disgruntled employee's snip about no magazines really worth a free ticket?

Before writing a formal letter of complaint, you may try making a phone call to complain and remedy your situation, but most experts agree that writing a formal letter of complaint is a much more effective way of getting satisfaction from the airline.

You may wish to include a photocopy of your tickets, but NEVER send your original documents.

If you have not heard from the airline within 30 days of your initial complaint, resend the letter. This time send it by registered mail

It is best to write and send your letter of complaint in a timely manner, as close to the date of the flight as possible. Unfortunately for my friend with the disappointing first class experience, the complaints were heard by friends but never by the airline. It is now a year past the experience and too much time has passed for the complaint to seem important to either the traveler or the airline.

TIPS: CONSUMER LOAN

26. Getting it right

So, Mrs. Gupta has a new 3D cooling, super fast ice making fridge while you have your old but hey, dependable fridge (burn, burn). And Mr. Chaman (the old so and so codger) got the Surround Sound, PIP, Super bazooka Plasma TV with 124 channels while you have just your 64 channel TV (more heartburn)? Before you reach out for the antacid pills for your ulcers or call the IT officials to raid your neighbour (where did he get the money, huh, huh?), hang on to your horses folks. Keeping up with the Jones, R. Guptas et al aint very trying nowadays. Think no more of the sweat and toil of saving up for ages to get the desired gizmos to grace your kitchen and sundry other rooms.

Go in for a consumer loan from any non-banking finance company (NBFC) and banks. Bring home your manpasand gizmos and having the fun of seeing your neighbours, colleagues, friends turn a delicate shade of green. Do you want to hear more?

It is structured in various sections so that you get all your fundamental queries on where and how to get a loan.

27. The Loan ranger

With the section that deals with getting the loan for the entire range of white goods.

The Loan Ranger Consumer loans probably encompass the widest range of goods ~ your TV, fridge, washing machine, microwave oven, dishwashing machine and loads of other gadgets which we missed out on. Getting a loan for these goods is many respects very different from that for getting loans for a car or home. Here ~Rs what you have to watch out for while on the prowl for consumer loans.

28. No moans and groans just plain loans

The best thing about consumer loans is that you don't even need a guarantor or collateral. The only criterion the bank must be assured of is your ability to repay the loan. Save money by avoiding bulk payment. If you're unsure about whether or not to take out a new consumer loan, this basic calculation can be helpful.

(*i*) Add all sources of income for a month.

(*ii*) Total all monthly living expenses and your savings requirements, debt, and insurance payments.

(*iii*) Avoid a loan that requires monthly payments that are bigger than the balance left when you subtract expenditures from monthly income.

Banks can give loans upto ₹1 lakh. The extent of funding depends on the product, model that you wish to purchase and the repayment period you are opting for. You can get a loan upto 85 per cent of the product price for consumer durables and upto 70 per cent for two-wheelers. You can choose your repayment tenors from 6 months to 60 months.

29. Norms for availing the loan

The ability to repay must be justified in your loan package. Since this loan doesn't require any collateral, banks want to see sources of repayment. For this you have to produce proof of your income. If you are salaried you would need to produce: Form 16 (Tax Deducted at Source) and/or income-tax returns for the last two years; Last two salary slips from the employer; Bank statements for the past 6 months. If you are self-employed you would need to produce: Income-tax returns for the past two years OR an assessment order Computation of income OR balance sheet and profit & loss account for the past two years OR A bank statement for the past 6 months:

- You should also satisfy the age criteria of being within 21 to 58 years
- You should also reside within the prescribed city limits of the banks

SHOPPING FOR THAT LOAN

Ideally, you should find a loan when you start looking for your product. This will help in speeding up the delivery of the product to your home. Much like the best bargain being around the corner, there is scope for reducing your loan costs further, if you spend some time shopping around for them. Keep these points in mind while shopping around for the loan.

30. Calculate EMI

EMI is the first scale on which you should measure different loans. Don't get swayed by the interest rate quoted by the lender, instead look at the EMI for the same repayment tenure. Besides the quoted interest rate, the effective interest rate depends on the reducing balance method used. Reducing balance is the method of reducing the principal amount repaid, from the outstanding loan amount. Every time you make a payment, the interest you pay is calculated on balance outstanding principal.

The reducing balance can be of 4 types: daily, monthly, quarterly and yearly.

Daily reducing: The principal is reduced every day as if you were making repayment of the principal on a daily basis..

Monthly reducing: In this system, the principal on which you pay interest reduces every month as you pay your EMI.

Quarterly reducing: On a quarterly basis.

Annual Reducing: The principal is reduced at the end of the year. You thus continue to pay interest on a certain portion of the principal, which you have actually paid back to the lender. This simply translates to this: the EMI under the monthly reducing system effectively being a smaller amount than under the annual reducing method

The catch lies in the method of computation. The more frequently the rate is calculated, the better the deal. Going by this principle, a daily reducing balance calculation is better than a monthly, which in turn is better than a quarterly and so on.

There are also different EMI finance options available:

Margin money scheme: In this kind of scheme, the financier finances up to 75-90% of the cost of the product. You have to repay it back in equated EMIs'.

Advance EMI scheme: In this scheme, the financier provides upto 100% of the cost of the product but you would have to pay anywhere between 2-7 EMIs in advance. Indirectly you are paying the financier margin money as the EMIs paid in advance which is deducted from the loan amount.

Deposit scheme: In this kind of scheme, the financer provides 100% finance but you have to provide the financer with 15-35% of the loan amount as a deposit. Your deposit will earn interest for the loan tenure while you repay your loan in EMIs.

31. Processing and other fee

While applying for a loan, you have to pay a certain charge on the amount applied for. The charge is calculated on the amount of loan applied for and not on the amount actually sanctioned. This charge varies with the lender and may be a fixed amount irrespective of the amount applied for or may be a percentage of the loan applied for. This amount, paid upfront, effectively reduces the money you get.

If the processing charge is 2% of loan applied for, and you apply for ₹10,000, you will have to pay ₹200 as processing fee upfront. And if the loan sanctioned is ₹8,000, the money you actually receive is 7,800 (8,000 minus 200 processing fee you paid), but you have to pay the interest on ₹8,000.

This can make big difference in the real cost of the loan. Look for the lowest fees lenders. Use our tools for finding the actual cost of a loan

32. Prepayment penalty

Try to get a lender who doesn't charge a prepayment penalty. This is a great way of getting rid of your debt in case your fiscal fitness improves. Also if the interest rates fall, you can go for replacing the higher cost loan with a lower cost one.

Also keep in mind that when the bank offers you the option of pre-payment, it does not give the flexibility of part payment. If you decide to repay the loan earlier than the pre-determined period, you have to pay the whole outstanding principal. So perish the thought of paying a part of your loan when you have a surplus as the bank does not allow it.

TIPS FOR CHOOSING PHONE SERVICE

Though most of these companies offer excellent deals, no single rate plan is best for everyone. Be sure to compare these programs carefully to determine which plan is the best for you. Some tips on choosing the right long distance program for your needs:

1. ***Check for monthly service charges:*** If you have a relatively small long distance bill, even a monthly service charge of $3-$6 may make a huge difference in how much you actually save. Consumers spending less than

$20 monthly should generally look for a plan that has no monthly service charges.

2. ***Check for monthly minimums:*** Some carriers have a minimum amount that they will bill you for, otherwise your bill will be raised to that amount. If you are a low biller, make sure that you will spend at least as much as the monthly minimum, taking discounted rates into consideration.
3. ***Check your intrastate rate:*** If you make many calls within your state, it is important to choose a rate plan which gives you the best rate for in-state calls. Some programs will lure you with a low interstate (state-to-state) rate, but will hit you with high charges to make calls just a few miles away. Make sure that you take intrastate rates into account when choosing your service provider.
4. ***Check billing increments:*** This is a must for those who use the phone for business, faxes and make many short phone calls. Most long distance carriers simply "round up" the charge for your phone calls to the next full minute. If your call lasts 1 minute and 5 seconds, you will probably be billed for two minutes. Full minute billing does not affect most residential customers who make calls lasting an average of 6 minutes or more that greatly. However, if you make many short duration calls, it pays to find a long distance carrier who bills in six second increments. Be sure to check the fine print.

CONSUMER CREDIT TIPS

33. Checking accounts

Important points to remember

1. Do not write checks unless you have enough funds in your account, and make sure you write clearly and always with a pen.
2. Always record all checks written in your check book and keep checks in a save place.
3. To help minimize the chances of bouncing a check, many banks provide overdraft protection.
4. Overdraft protection draws from available funds in savings, line of credit, or credit card if you overdraw your account.
5. Use the telephone, Internet, or ATM to get the most current information about your account.
6. Utilize direct deposit for a convenient and secure way to get access to your money without making a trip to the bank.
7. Enough time to make certain the checks clear (usually 3-5 days, depending on the institution).
8. If your checks are lost or stolen, report it immediately to your financial institution. Check periodically for missing checks from your checkbook.

9. Keep all financial information including banking/checking statements for 3-5 years. If you are writing more than 10 checks a month consider online banking to save time.

TIPS TO SMART ONLINE BIDDING

For a whole generation of people, malls are a place where you go to eat, catch a movie or just hang out. Serious shopping, especially for books, clothes and electronic gizmos, is something you do online.

However, those who do not understand the ways and pitfalls of the vast e-mall that is online shopping, end up angry, frustrated or simply feeling cheated; and more so when they shop on auction sites.

They are the ones who have the most complaints about e-commerce and auction sites not providing a local address where they can send a written complaint in triplicate and seek a stamped acknowledgement.

Last week, a member of my consumer group was seriously angry at eBay for not posting a local address on its site. I, however, discovered that review sites report a fairly high users satisfaction level of 76 per cent; most satisfied customers tell people to take time to understand how auction sites work.

The good news is that the proposed amendments to the Consumer Protection Act will insist on publishing a local address and phone number. But if you want to buy online, you must be prepared to complain online too; without first exercising that option, you can't dash off to the nearest branch office.

Online shoppers have plenty of practical tips for extracting the best out of auction sites on review sites such as mouthshut.com; the most important one is to use good old common sense.

Here is what experts advise about smart buying online.

Don't use an auction site for something you need urgently. Instead, watch the auctions closely for a couple of months before narrowing down on a product and seller.

Ignore all sellers with a rating of under 95 per cent.

Read the listing carefully for hidden caveats and conditions and check the cost of insurance, warranty, shipping charges and return policies.

Before zeroing in on a seller, pay some attention to his/her location — some cities are notorious for dubious dealings.

Avoid those who do not want credit card payments and do not hesitate to ask the seller for any additional information you need (save that correspondence in case you have need for it later).

There are three types of sellers:

Those who run a business and want to make money (they are cordial and prompt).

Those who are cheats and want to make a fast buck.

And, ordinary folk who have something to sell. It may be a good idea to figure them out with a test bid for a low-priced item to understand how the system works.

Once you get the hang of bidding online, place your bid in the last five minutes or preferably even at the last minute. For those who use paypal, the very fact that a customer has moved to cancel an order sometimes galvanises the seller into delivering the product.

What do you do when things still go wrong? First, ensure that the hitch is not due to poor communication. Secondly, you can cancel a transaction, since most credit card companies provide that option. E-commerce sites also have a 'Standard Purchase Protection Programme' which is ₹10,000 in case of eBay and ₹50,000 for purchases under Paisa Pay.

Most websites also have a clear privacy policy and spend a lot of money on e-security because safe commerce is the core of their business. They also have a system of investigating allegations regarding cheating, non-delivery of purchases and 'significantly not as described' products.

Disciplinary action ranges from warnings to suspension of user accounts, but only when inappropriate behaviour is proven. Clearly, online auctions do have plenty of checks and balances, but ultimately a careful buyer has a better chance of being a satisfied customer.

CHECKLIST FOR BUYING LAND/HOUSE

There are many incentives to buying your own property. You may want to live in your own place after living in a rented property, or you may want to buy property as an investment mechanism, or to take advantage of some of the tax laws. At the same time, while buying a property, it is necessary that you ensure that everything is above board, that you are not investing a large sum of money if things are not clear or the legal title is not clear. Here is an attempt to prepare a checklist for cross-checking before buying a property.

— Call for original property documents. The non-availability of such documents should be taken as a red signal. It could mean that the title of the seller is not clear and there could be a lien, mortgage or other encumbrance on the property.

— Ask for photocopies of all deeds of title related to the property to be purchased. A legal opinion through a good standing advocate is advisable. The legal counsel will examine the deeds to establish the ownership of the property by seller, preferably through an advocate. Ascertain the survey number, village and registration district of the property as these details are required for registration of the sale. Previous encumbrances and loans, if any on the property must be cleared before completion of purchase of the property. The title of the Vendor to the property must be clear and marketable.

— For apartment. Check for approved layout plan and approved building plan with number of floors.

— Check the building bye-laws in that area to verify any issue with setback, side setback, height, etc.

— Confirm transfer fees, stamp duty and registration charges to be paid on purchase of the property as well as outgoings to be paid for the property *i.e.* property tax, water and electricity charges, society charges, maintenance charges.

— The original sale agreement should have the municipal-approved plan of the flat, carpet area with the area of the balconies shown separately, price of the property including the proportionate price of common areas and facilities shown separately and intervals at which installments may be paid.

— Check if proper stamp duty has been paid.

— If the property is in a co-operative society, examine the original share certificate. It mentions the latest owner's name.

— Obtaining a society's NOC may not be mandatory under the new Model Bye-laws of the Co-operative Housing Society, but it is advisable as it offers clarity about the title of the property, pending society dues, property disputes and hypothecation, if any.

— An income-tax clearance certificate would ensure that the seller has discharged his income tax liabilities to avoid attachment of the property.

— If possible, consult a property lawyer, especially where the sale is through a power of attorney. A good lawyer will undertake proper investigation and issue prominent public notices to clear interest of other properties in the property concerned.

— Getting a home loan sanctioned ensures that the documents are in place as banks or institutions conduct due diligence before disbursing loans.

— Ensure payment and discharge of encumbrances that are to be cleared before purchase.

— Obtain physical delivery of the property and of the title deeds.

— Complete the transaction of sale by executing and registering the deed. An unregistered sale agreement has no validity in a court of law.

— Financing capability. The debt-service ratio helps you assess to what extent you can take financial risks. For every ₹100 earned, your EMI should not exceed ₹40, and that includes EMI's taken for other purposes. Maintaining this ratio is important as it helps you deal with other expenses easily.

— Accessibility. Access to the property is critically important. If access is difficult, re-sale values will be affected and may cause day-to-day inconvenience.

— Locality: Proximity to transport hubs, schools, hospitals, market, central business district, entertainment centres, hotels, restaurants, pollution levels, safety records of the neighbourhood.

— Reputation of the builder or seller. Check around with local sources to find out more of the builders reputation.

— Get a good idea of the costs of various components like price, stamp duty, registration charges, transfer fees, monthly outgoings, society charges and costs of utilities. These are not immediately available, but should be factored in to the total cost.

— Facilities. Adequate water, electricity and other utilities should be an important factor.

— If you believe in beliefs such as Vaastu, get consultation done before buying the property.

— If you are buying property on loan, get an insurance so that in case of your fatality, your family can clear the outstanding loan.

These may seem like a cumbersome steps, but it is better safe than to be sorry before buying a property.

SAFEGUARD YOUR INTERESTS AS A CONSUMER WHILE SEEKING ADMISSIONS IN EDUCATIONAL INSTITUTIONS

The Demand for professional education has risen steeply in the last few years. This cannot be met fully by state-funded or state-aided institutions alone. This is why a new category of private, self-financing institutions have registered a phenomenal growth. They offer courses in engineering and technology, computer, medicine, dentistry, pharmacy, management, teacher education and law, for which there is great demand. Many of these institutions are deficient in matters like infrastructure, competent faculty and even a congenial campus environment. Hence there arises a need for both students and their parents to be aware of their rights and undertake comprehensive assessment of the infrastructure facilities and validity of the courses before committing their hard-earned money to such institutes.

34. Crucial role of regulatory bodies

Education, including university education is in the State list of the Constitution. However, the Centre is entrusted with the responsibility of coordinated development and maintenance of prescribed standards of education. Accordingly, the University Grants Commission was set up in 1956 followed by the establishment of a number of regulatory bodies called Councils in the field of professional education through parliamentary enactments. While in the pre-independence days there was only one such Council — the Medical Council of India established in 1933 — three are now more than dozen.

Besides the Councils, there are three other statutorily constituted regulatory bodies, viz., the Institute of Chartered Accountants of India (ICAI), the Institute of Company Secretaries of India (ICSI) and the Institute of Cost and Works Accountants of India (ICWAI). They are responsible for regulating the standards of education and profession in their respective areas. Unlike the Councils, they themselves conduct the examinations and admit the qualified students as Associate Members as professionals.

The most widely known regulatory Council is the All India Council for Technical Education (AICTE), because of the large number of professional and technical disciplines it controls.

A medical student must qualify from a medical college recognised by the Medical Council of India and after fulfilling the specified conditions (e.g., internship in hospitals) becomes eligible for registration with the State level Medical Council to undertake practice legally. In professions, where no such registration is necessary, students qualifying from recognised institutions only are eligible for employment or can pursue further education. For example, the National Council for Teacher Education, which regulates education, has issued a sort of 'statutory warning' that "qualification in teacher education obtained pursuant to courses offered by unrecognised institutions will not be treated as a valid qualification for purposes of employment under Central/State government institutions, universities, colleges, schools or other educational bodies aided by Central/State Governments".

It is therefore, essential that students must first ascertain whether the institutions in which they are seeking admission are recognised by the concerned regulatory authority.

The AICTE which has a comparatively larger number of institutions under its umbrella, publish several directories, each dealing with a group of courses. National Council for Teacher Education (NCTE) and the Rehabilitation Council of India (RCI) have established their own websites. Lists of recognised institutions and courses are available from these sites.

35. Consumer Protection Act — Boon for the students

The issue of recognition of professional educational institutions and course by the concerned regulatory authorities become the subject of dispute under the Consumer Protection Act, 1986 had led to far reaching verdict awarded by the National Consumer Dispute Redressal Commission. The apex consumer court has resolved the basic question whether

Educational institutions come under the ambit of consumer courts and held that they too are liable for deficient services rendered. The verdict was in response to complaint field by 12 students, who joined the Buddhist Mission Dental College in Bihar. The College in its admission advertisements for the BDS Course, gave an impression that it is affiliated to Magadh University and recognized by the Dental Council of India. After joining the College the students to their dismay found that it was neither affiliated to Magadh University nor it is recognized by the Council. As a result, they not only lost two academic years but also the money spent on fees, hostel charges, etc. Holding the service rendered by the College to be deficient, the Commission directed it to refund all admission expenses with interest and pay compensation for the loss of two years and, also the cost of the petition.

Apart from the redressal of the grievances of students, the importance of the award lies in the fact, that it brought educational institution under the ambit of the Consumer Protection Act. The Commission observed, "Imparting of education by an educational institution for consideration falls within the ambit of 'service' as defined in the Consumer Protection Act. Fees are paid for service to be rendered by way of imparting education by the educational institutions. If there is no rendering of service, the question of payment of fee world not arises. The complaints (the student in this case) had hired the service of the respondents (the College) for consideration and so they are consumers as defined in Consumer Protection Act".

Educational institutions that collect fee are thus service providers and Students and their parents who are paying for these services can seek compensation for such deficiencies.

36. What constitutes deficiency of services

Some of the instances that can be considered as deficiency of services are listed below:—

(*i*) Running Un-recognised schools and colleges

(*ii*) Employing under qualified and untrained teachers.

(*iii*) Inadequate infrastructure facilities like library, laboratory, accommodations, furniture and playground

(*iv*) Adopting of syllabi which is not prescribed or standard syllabi

(*v*) Issuing of misleading advertisements promising placements/practical training

(*vi*) Delay in providing provisional certificates, resulting in denying admission to the students during the academic year in to the next higher course.

(*vii*) In case the management runs an unrecognised educational institute due to which students become ineligible to appear in the examination having studied for the whole year or even a few months the institution can be held responsible.

(*viii*) Promise of placements in India and abroad that are not fulfilled can also make such institutions liable for compensation. Such a promise of guaranteed placement which is not fulfilled later on is a clear case of unfair trade practice and such managements are liable to sue for the loss sustained by the students.

(*ix*) Inadequate computer lab

(*x*) Lack of adequate space and facilities to undertake projects as required under the course curriculum

(*xi*) Laboratory facilities being inadequate with requisite books often not available

(*xii*) Frequent shuffling of classes

(*xiii*) Hostel facility not in close proximity of the campus

(*xiv*) High student-faculty ratio that is detrimental to students' interest.

(*xv*) Non-supply of hall tickets for examination which may result in loss of one year.

(*xvi*) When promised practical training is not given even though the course is completed.

(*xvii*) A student though present in the examination hall but is shown as being absent.

(*xviii*) Failure of institutions to offer facilities that were promised at the time of collecting fees.

(*xix*) Failure to provide hygienic food in residential school where boarding facilities are offered

(*xx*) Suffering of students due negligent driving of the driver of private buses/transport employed by the institute

(*xxi*) In respect of pre-nursery and play schools failure of the institutions to ensure suitable safety measures for children below 5 years especially with regard to fire, water, electricity

(*xxii*) Non-following of prescribed or standard syllabi

(*xxiii*) Refusal to issue transfer certificate and conduct certificate when demanded by students or parents on account of poor services offered by the institute

(*xxiv*) Refusal by the institute to refund the deposit amount when request for transfer certificate has been made by the student on account of genuine and unavoidable circumstances.

(*xxv*) Collection of the entire fees for the whole year in advance and refusal to refund the part fees when a student wants to leave the institute mid-term on account of genuine unavoidable circumstances.

(The list given above is purely suggestive and indicative and the actual interpretation of what constitutes a "Deficiency in Service" shall have to be analysed and interpreted on a case by case basis)

Safeguards required to be adopted by parents:—

(*i*) Take bills for all the payments made to the school or college.

(*ii*) Keeping a copy of the prospectus handy during the entire tenure of the course.

(*iii*) Ask for copies of certification of academic degrees offered by the institute

(*iv*) Check the infrastructure facilities provided by the institute before finalising admissions

(*v*) Examine the "minimum standards" in respect of infrastructural facilities as prescribed by AICTE, UGC, MCI, etc.

37. Checking the validity of academic degrees – The most crucial aspect

Elaborate rules and procedures have been prescribed by Government for establishment of private education institutions. The validity and recognition status of degrees awarded by the institution becomes extremely important since getting a degree which is not recognised by the Government is not only a financial loss but results in a valuable loss of time and almost ruins the career of such students who may have taken admission to such institutions. Consumer Courts have taken very serious note of such institutions in which the brochures/ prospectus/advertisements of the institutions claimed that the courses were recognised by AICT and UGC, etc. but when the candidates who passed out from such institutes it was found that the degrees awarded to them were not recognised. Such instances not only destabilise the financial position of the parents but very importantly the students are devastated mentally and are at loss to decide about their future.

Parents and students must therefore check the validity of the degrees by logging on to the Website for All India Council for Technical Education (AICTE) (www.aicte.ernet.in), University Grants Commission (www.ugc. ac.in), National Council of Teacher Education (www.ncte-in.org) and Medical Council of India (www.mciindia.org). The list is indicative.

38. Role of educational institutions

While the ultimate responsibility lies on the students and their parents, the educational institutions themselves can play a very important role in ensuring that the rights of students and parents as consumer of their services are not violated. It is the responsibility of these institutions to make available all the information in the form of brochures, prospectus and their respective website. If the prospectus gives all the terms and conditions associated with a course and provides all the relevant information about the status of the institute the validity of the course and also gives the relevant information about the source of recognition i.e. whether UGC or AICT, it should impart confidence in the minds of students. In case a prospectus/brochure contains very lofty promises without adequate background information of facts to support such promises the students and their parents should think twice about admissions to such institutes.

It would be in the fittest of things if education institutions play a positive role in spreading consumer awareness by a combination of activities such as seminars, workshops, literature, discussions, essay competitions, quizzes, etc.

Simultaneously, students and parents should behave as Smart Consumers and ensure they get the 'services' for which they have made the payment to the respective Educational Institutions.

39. How do you file a consumer complaint?

(The following is NOT legal advice and is purely for informational purposes only. We are not competent to give any legal advice. For legal advice please contact a competent lawyer. Any reliance that you place on this information is at your own risk. We do not guarantee the accuracy of this information and are not responsible for any consequences, actions, lack of actions, results or lack of results that you may or may not face from following information in this section.)

Stage 0: Decide To File

Stage 1: Collect Necessary Documentation

Stage 2: Send a Notice to the Company

Stage 3: Get Legal Representation

Stage 4: Prepare Your Complaint

(*a*) How much time do I have?

(*b*) What format should I use to prepare a complaint?

(*c*) Which court should I file the complaint in?

(*d*) How to find the address of the court?

Stage 5: File your Complaint

Stage 6: Attend the Admission Hearing

Stage 7: Attend Subsequent Hearings till the Verdict

Stage 8: After the Verdict

Stage 0: Decide to file

The most common emotions when you have been duped, ignored, insulted or cheated by a company from whom you bought a product is that of helplessness, anger or revenge. You may also hear yourself threatening the company about going to consumer court.

We fully understand and appreciate these emotions. However, a word of caution that decision to go to consumer court is one that should be taken without emotion, rationally. No matter how much the government blows its trumpets about consumer rights and consumer protection, long story short is that consumers are a helpless lot in the legal system of India. The consumer court system of our country is one of the most putrid, decadent, impersonal and sluggish systems in the world.

Of course, this is not the news you want to hear and you may still have the question whether you should go to court. If you have a case with merit against the company, the answer is a big **YES**.

However this yes is not without warning. For you should not expect quick results; expect to spend up to the next 5-10 years in a legal battle against the company, the long waits and to stand in long lines, to deal with corrupt court clerks and court officials, to deal with harassment from consumer court officials, to stand helplessly in over-crowded rooms without ventilation or air-conditioning, to have patience beyond you have ever known to have, and to understand the true meaning of the common politician maxim "the law will take its own course".

Even then, the merits of filing a complaint are overwhelming. At the end, the company will be made to pay for its mistakes and you (or your children or grandchildren can have the satisfaction with a full refund, and even collecting punitive damages from the company.

Whatever your decision is about filing a complaint in a consumer court, we still would encourage you to take a few steps to ensure that the company pays for its mistakes and to ensure other innocent customers do not walk into the same trap of buying a product from this company. These include:

- Filing a complaint at the Consumerdaddy website www.consumerdaddy.com
- Filing a complaint at other popular consumer blogs in India
- Filing a complaint with various consumer advocacy groups in your city
- Filing a complaint with the local police as applicable
- Filing a complaint with the controller of legal metrology in your state as applicable
- Opting to move your complaint to lok adalats (after you have already filed) as applicable
- Filing a complaint with your state's Human Rights Commission
- Filing a complaint with Ombudsman (for Insurance and Banking issues)
- Filing a complaint with Insurance Regulatory and Development Authority (for Insurance issues)
- Filing a complaint with TRAI (Telecom Regulatory Authority of India) (for Telecom issues)
- Filing a complaint with Bureau of Indian Standards (BIS) as applicable
- Sending a detailed report of the incident to Press/Television and Radio media companies

Remember, your action of doing as suggested above and filing a complaint against the company will prevent up to 3000 other customers from buying any product from the company. What other better way to make the company pay for its mistake?

If your decision after reading this section is to file a complaint in a consumer court, the following will inform you in a concise manner the various stages involved in filing a consumer complaint in the Legal System in India.

Stage 1: Collect necessary documentation

Before a consumer complaint can be filed against a company, you need to ensure that you have all the supporting documentation that you need. These may include the following documents related to the purchase of the product from the company:

- An invoice or bill for the purchase (Preferably with an invoice number and Tax ID of the company)
- Warranty card for products and SLA for services (This is optional)
- Proof of payment such as copy of the cheque or credit card statement (This is optional)
- Any other communication or record from the company that can show negligence, insensitivity or lack of attention from the company (Telephone call logs made to the company with long wait times, letters from company expressing uncaring attitude, etc.)

- The registered address of the company. You should be able to find this either in the above documentation, website of the company or from third party sources such as directories. Consumerdaddy itself has a large database of registered addresses of companies that you can search and find from the home page of www.consumerdaddy.com/home.htm

There are great chances that you are likely to misplace such documentation. In such cases, you can simply obtain a duplicate copy of the invoice/bill of purchase from the company itself by informing them that you need it for "record keeping" or "accounting purposes". More than often the company will give you a copy without knowing your intention

In case you cannot get a copy of the bill, do not worry or feel helpless. Most of the billed purchases are entered into the ledger and accounting books of the company. So when you reach a court, you may be able to retrieve the purchase information from the company's accounting system merely by quoting the serial number of the product that you purchased or even an approximate purchase date.

Stage 2: Send a notice to the company

In this step, you will be required to "officially" notify the company of your grievance. Be detailed about what it is that you are complaining about and what you expect the company to do. Be fair in your demands to the company. For example, if a product you purchased for ₹10,000 is broken due to no fault of yours, ask to either replace the product or refund ₹10,000 + a small additional sum for any inconveniences caused; do not place unreasonable demands for ₹50,000 or so:. You are also entitled to ask for interest on any amount paid, if you think you are eligible for it.

Also, when it comes to making demands, be sure to give the company more than one option. For example, company policy might prevent them from giving you a full refund, but they may be open to giving you a replacement product that is superior to the one you purchased. In other words, the more options you give the company, the better your chances are to get your grievance addressed without going to court. When you think of the hassles of going to court, being flexible here will ultimately help you out a lot!

Your notice can be printed in English on a regular A4 size page, signed by you and sent by post to the registered address of the company. Be sure to use either **registered post** with acknowledgement due or speed post with tracking feature. This is important as you will need legal proof that the company has received your notice.

In your notice, you will also need to give the company some time to redress your grievance. This time should be specified as after the receipt of the notice. Again, be fair when providing time to the company. Anywhere between 15 to 45 days should be adequate depending on the gravity of the matter.

You should also be sure to mention, in a non-threatening manner, your intention to pursue the matter legally should the company fail to address your problem in the given time. The statement could be merely something like this;

"You are hereby given fifteen (15) days from the receipt of this letter, to grant and process this demand, failing which, I will be forced to pursue other legal measures including filing a petition with the State Consumer Disputes Redressal Commission (or other competent court or forum with jurisdiction) on this matter".

Important points to take care of in the notice include the following:

- Providing clarity to the company on the nature of your grievance
- Providing clarity to the company on how you expect the company to solve your complaint
- Providing the time frame in which you expect the company to rectify your grievance
- Providing a polite and stern notification that you intend to pursue the matter legally.

With luck on your side, the company will respond to your notice with willingness to resolve the issue. We wish that all the consumer complaints in this country get solved in this manner, but then the chances are that you will have to read on to the next step.

Stage 3: Get legal representation

There are people who would advice you for and against hiring an advocate or lawyer to represent you.

The biggest advantage or hiring a lawyer is that you do not have to read the remaining of this boring article. The advocate will know what to do from here on.

The biggest disadvantage of hiring a lawyer is that good ones don't come free.

Put simply, if your case is complicated, you have less time to spare and the compensation you seek is large, hire one. If your case is simple, you can spend up to 5 full days in a year for this purpose and you are seeking low to medium compensation from the company, do it yourself.

Also, it is important to note that more than likely your city is bound to have powerful consumer advocacy and consumer action groups who, in many cases, will provide you excellent legal representation free of cost or at a very nominal rate. There are also a multitude of consumer lawyers who are dedicated to consumer rights and consumer protection issues who may pursue your case for very reasonable, if any, fees.

If you decide to get legal representation, then the remaining steps will be followed through by your lawyer.

Stage 4: Prepare your complaint

As you prepare your complaint, here are a few questions that may come to your mind.

(*a*) *How much time do I have?*

According to the Indian Consumer Protection Act of 1986, clause 24A(*i*) a consumer court shall not admit a complaint unless it is filed within two years from the date on which the cause of action has arisen'. Interestingly it mentions only the date on which the 'cause of action' has arisen and not the date of purchase of the product from the company. So this can lead to the disputed interpretation that you need to file the complaint within two years from the time the customer has got the grievance, i.e., the time the customer started to be unsatisfied with the product of the company. For further interpretation of this clause, we recommend that you talk to a qualified legal expert.

(*b*) *What format should I use to prepare a complaint?*

It is too much legal jargon to explain the nitty gritty details of preparing a complaint to file in the court. So we will just point you to a few good web pages that have this information already provided. You will need to prepare a complaint and an affidavit as per these suggestions. You need not file the complaint in a stamp paper. It can be filed in a regular legal size sheet or as suggested by your advocate.

(*a*) ICRPC

(*b*) Consumer Help India

(*c*) *Which court should I file the complaint in?*

Depending on convenience, you can file the complaint in the area you purchased the product from or the area the company did the action to grievance you or any area where the company does business in. Depending on the amount of compensation you claim, you must file the complaint at appropriate courts. If the total amount (of cost and compensation) in your complaint is below ₹20 Lakhs, you must file the complaint with the District Consumer Disputes Redressal Forum. If it is between ₹20 Lakhs and ₹1 Crore, then you must file the complaint with the State Consumer Disputes Redressal Commission. If it is more than ₹1 Crore, then you must file with the National Consumer Disputes Redressal Commission.

(*d*) *How to find the address of the court?*

The National Consumer Disputes Redressal Commission's (NCDRC) address can be found at its website.

(*a*) Vakilno1

(*b*) NCRDC

(*c*) ICRPC

Here are a few web pages that give the address of the district forums:

(*a*) NCRDC

(*b*) Consumer Help India

(*c*) ICRPC

Stage 5: File your complaint

There are several actions involved in this step as listed below:

1. Along with your complaint and the affidavit, attach a list of documents you are submitting as part of the complaint file. You will need to attach

copies of the evidentiary documents. Ensure that you attach only photocopies of the evidentiary documents and not the original. You may also need to sign and attach a Vakalatnama , which is similar to a power of attorney authorizing your lawyer to represent you in court on this case, should you decide to hire a lawyer.

2. You will need to approach a Notary and get your complaint file and the affidavit notarized. The Notary who, unless known to you, will require you to show a proof of identification such as your driver's license, PAN card, passport, ration card or election ID. You will then need to sign the complaint and the affidavit in front of the Notary after which he/she will notarize the document with his/her Notary seal and signature. Notarization is a process by which the consumer court can ascertain that you are the person you claim you are and that you have actually signed the complaint.
3. You will then be required to make a specific number of copies of the complaint. In most cases, you will need to make a total of five copies including three for the court, one for the court to send to the company and one for yourself. We recommend that you visit the court in which you intent to file the complaint and find out exactly how many copies are needed.
4. The next action is preparing the court fee payment. Most courts accept Demand Drafts (DD) through a Nationalized Bank duly crossed, drawn in favor of the person as shown in the table as the mode of payment. The recent fee structure is also shown in the following table. We HIGHLY recommend that you visit the court to validate these amounts and to verify the mode of payment.

Amount of Compensation Sought	Court Fee to be Paid	Court with Jurisdiction	Demand Draft drawn in the Favor of
Up to ₹1 Lakh	₹100	District Consumer Disputes Redressal Forum	President, Consumer Disputes Redressal Forum, (District Name)
₹1 Lakh to ₹5 Lakhs	₹200	District Consumer Disputes Redressal Forum	President, Consumer Disputes Redressal Forum, (District Name)
₹5 Lakhs to ₹10 Lakhs	₹400	District Consumer Disputes Redressal Forum	President, Consumer Disputes Redressal Forum, (District Name)
₹10 Lakhs to ₹20 Lakhs	₹500	District Consumer Disputes Redressal Forum	President, Consumer Disputes Redressal Forum, (District Name)
₹20 Lakhs to ₹50 Lakhs	₹2,000	State Consumer Disputes Redressal Commission	Registrar, State Consumer Disputes Redressal Commission, (State Name)

Amount of Compensation Sought	Court Fee to be Paid	Court with Jurisdiction	Demand Draft drawn in the Favor of
₹50 Lakhs to ₹1 Crore	₹4,000	State Consumer Disputes Redressal Commission	Registrar, State Consumer Disputes Redressal Commission, (State Name)
Above ₹1 Crore	₹5,000	National Consumer Disputes Redressal Commission	Registrar, National Consumer Disputes Redressal Commission

5. The last and the most tedious action in this step is to go to the court, locate the receiving clerk, deposit your complaint file and make the court fee payment. Be sure to obtain a receipt of the payment. At this time, the clerk will also give the date a judge will first hear your case (admission hearing) and a complaint reference number.
6. The court will then send the complaint to the company and ask them to respond to the complaint within 30 days and also to attend the admission hearing.

Stage 6: Attend the admission hearing

Till this point you might have got a rosy picture of the concept of consumer protection in India. From this point of time, be warned that it is going to change because you ultimately will have to lay hands on the infamous consumer court system of India.

Most of the consumer courts such as District Consumer Disputes Redressal Forums in the country operate from shacks that are in high probability a little, if not any, better than a cattle shed. Many of them do not have presiding officers for weeks, if not months continuously due to the inefficiency and irresponsibility of our government and bureaucracy. This has been raised repeatedly by consumer advocacy groups and media time and time again with very little if not any effect.

Also, it is a public secret that merely depositing the court fee will not get you a complaint reference number or the admission hearing date. You will also have to pay the unofficial "fee" or the bribe to the court clerk. It is not a secret either that the more the "unofficial fee" you are willing to pay, the higher your chances are of getting an earlier hearing date, although this is unverifiable information.

Lastly, if you are one of the most unlucky, you will also get a judge who will require you to pay the "unofficial fee" to get your case admitted, heard or disposed. There are yet others who will simply push the date of the hearing, indefinitely, before they receive their "unofficial fee". If you come across such judges, we recommend that you contact the court vigilance officers, CBI, vigilance commissions, the chief justices of the high courts or the chief justice of India, although we are very doubtful about the outcome of a complaint against a judge.

If your case has merits (and you're lucky not to fall in front of an unscrupulous, lazy or corrupt judge), at the admission hearing, the consumer court will admit your complaint and you will be given the date for the subsequent hearings.

We highly recommend that you do not miss the admission hearing or the subsequent hearings as if you are absent, your case will be decided in your absence (*ex-parte*) based on its merits. This is highly risky as the judge may fail to read some relevant portions of your complaint, or may misunderstand certain others. Remember that companies have vast resources, so it is very likely that the lawyer of the company will attend the hearing. Without you there to explain, clarify and express your grievance in person, it is very likely that the verdict will be in favor of the company.

On the date of the admission hearing, or any court hearing for that matter, we recommend you plan to spend the full day patiently in court, as it is HIGHLY UNPREDICTABLE as to when during the day your case will be called for hearing. Even a 5 minute rest room visit may cost you the hearing if you are waiting alone to be called into the court room. When attending the admission hearing, ensure that you have a copy of your complaint and all the originals of the evidentiary documents.

When called to the court room, ensure that you are earnest in your appearance and polite, respectful, and stern in your tone of voice. If you have not hired a lawyer, when asked be sure to make that clear to the judge. Remember that a judge's job is highly monotonous as they listen to hundreds of people in a day, day after day. Their attention span is very short and their patience is very low. So if you expected a pleasant smiling judge, who will give you all the time in the world, change your expectations.

Typically, your judge will review the case file and use one or both of the following two ways to gain clarity into your case:

- Narrative: Judges using these ways will ask you to give an explanation of the problem and what solution you seek. Be sure to explain the case in a short concise manner as you have described in your complaint. Ensure that you do not contradict anything you have written in your complaint.
- Probing: Judges using these ways will ask you short questions to clarify the merits of your case. Be short and precise in your answers. Again, be certain not to contradict yourself or your complaint.

The judge may also ask you for additional evidence or for the originals of the documents if there are any disputes regarding the authenticity of the documents. If this is the case, ensure that the documents are handed over only to court officials and not to any company official, including the company lawyer.

If your case has the merit, it will be admitted. If so, you will be given the date of the next hearing remember, the sole purpose of the admission hearing is to decide if you have a case or not. The actual arguments or counter arguments will all happen in the subsequent hearings.

Stage 7: Attend subsequent hearings till the verdict

This shall depend on the complexity of your case, and the number of times the judge decides to postpone or conduct hearings. Typically, it could be anywhere from one to seven hearings before which your case is disposed. Be sure to attend each hearing to avoid an *ex-parte* verdict.

The consumer court will finally reach a verdict on your case and send you and the company the court order. If the verdict is in your favor, you may be eligible for a refund, and the company may also have to pay for punitive damages that include compensating you for any mental agony, insult, inconvenience, or damage you may have suffered. In many cases, the court will also direct the company to pay for your legal and court expenses.

Stage 8: After the verdict

Most lawyers will tell you that your actual legal battle with a company starts only after you obtain a verdict from a consumer court. Consumer court system in our country has no stalwart statutory powers to enforce their verdicts on any company. If the company does not follow the verdict of the consumer court, and neither does it file appeal within 30 days, to get a company to abide by the verdict of a consumer forum, you will have to file another proceeding to "execute the verdict" in the consumer court. Put simply, after you get a verdict from a consumer court, you will have to approach it again to issue a judgment to the company to follow the verdict of the consumer court or to face other civil and criminal penalties including attachment of properties or arrest. Sadly, this could mean another 2-5 years of your life fighting a legal battle against this company to remedy your problem. So, we wind up this article by encouraging you to check Stage 0 of this article and undertake the other recommended measures mentioned in that section. Good luck with your complaint and thank you for visiting our website.

40. A step-by-step guide to formulating a consumer complaint

1. Find out who is responsible for the problem
2. Collect the name and address of the dealer/seller and the manufacturer
3. Write letters of complaint to the concerned authorities clearly stating
   (*a*) The nature of your problem
   (*b*) Evidence of having purchased goods or services to be provided
   (*c*) In what way you hold him/her responsible
   (*d*) The relief claimed — repair/replacement/refund/compensation
   (*e*) Give the person a deadline for replying
   (*f*) Send the letter by registered post with acknowledgement due
   (*g*) Always insist on a written reply from the opposite party
   (*h*) After expiry of deadline you must notify the authorities involved, for example — if the trader has sold you goods using uncaliberated weights you can complain to the Controller of Weights and Measures.

(*i*) If there is no response from the concerned authorities you may have to consider your next step.

(*j*) Contact your local consumer group for help/or for help to initiate legal action.

(*k*) If you have taken legal action, publicise the result in public interest.

Problems can often be solved over the telephone but this will leave no record of your complaint especially if the trader/service provider denies that the matter was brought to his/her notice

If you do make a telephone complaint, keep a record of the time, date and outcome.

It would be difficult to imagine life without labels. In today's pre-packed world they're essential to provide the customer, with enough basic information to identify one product from another. More recently countries have adopted eco-labelling to promote eco-friendly products and recycled products.

Quite a few products carry labels which state:

- What the goods are made from
- Quality or safety
- Advise you on how to look after goods
- tell you where they were made
- give you instructions for use.
- Use symbols
- Warning labels

41. What you can do as a consumer

When you buy food products check the labels for the following details:

1. Ingredients
2. Weight,
3. Name & address of manufacturer,
4. Date of manufacture - use before, best before,
5. Batch number
6. Certification of standard such as AGMARK, FPO,ISI.
7. Instructions for use and storage
8. Check out for symbols such as — Vegetarian and Non-Vegetarian Food
9. Imported food products must contain the name and address of the Indian Importer

42. Drugs and medicines

The Drugs Controller in every State regulates production, supply and distribution of Drugs and Cosmetics.

When purchasing medicines from a pharmacy:

(*a*) Check the date of manufacture/expiry date/Batch Number.

(*b*) Check if the name and address of the manufacturer is printed.

(*c*) Verify the name of the medicine with the prescription.

(*d*) Always check the Maximum Retail Price on the medicines being purchased.

(*e*) Read carefully directions for use/dosage/storage

(*f*) The red vertical line on the left side of the medicine strip indicates that the medicine will be available only on prescription.

(*g*) Always insist on a bill.

43. Cosmetics

When buying cosmetics always check for its quality. Also check for details such as name and address of manufacturer, cost, weight, ingredients, manufacturing date and batch number. All finished cosmetics must have the "Best use before" date printed on them such as skin powder, baby powder, skin cream, shampoo-soap based, nail polish and lipstick.

Beware of Cosmetics such as:

Fairness creams - since with prolonged use these are known to cause damage to the skin

Eye make up such as 'Kajal' or 'Surma' which often has a high lead content

Always check the advertisement details especially those which offer gifts or exchange offers before purchasing a product.

44. Vague commercial persuasion

Marketing techniques ever more sophisticated more effective more intriguing more attractive more — Pied Pipers of Hamelin

Advertising is all around us and is often striking, thought provoking or amusing, and many slogans and catchphrases find their way into everyday language. Advertising creates social trends and often influences people to spend money on goods that they do not necessarily need. Advertising today is a major industry. Most advertising is communication between sellers and potential buyers [consumers and other producers].

Advertisements should be informative but some advertisements contain no words, only colours and pictures and the brand name. Consumers must be provided with information to make 'informed choices'.

WATCH OUT, many advertisements are:

- Highly exaggerated – example –'full of vitamins' for shoes — special shock absorption techniques – in shoes often have an exaggerated sense of the protection offered – lulled in to a false sense of security and take risks

- Make false claims — example 'rebuilds hair' or 'health foods' Super refined extra refined, cholesterol-free
- Give incomplete description of products
- Make misleading comparisons
- Bait and switch advertisements to switch to another product which is costlier

Advertisements should be truthful and accurate. Must be aware of the effect it has on the safety health and nutrition of children.

Always check the advertisement details especially those which offer gifts or exchange offers before purchasing a product.

CHAPTER 14

Other Laws Showing Spirit of Consumerism

SYNOPSIS

The Consumer Protection Act is in addition to and not in derogation of provisions of any other law. The Indian Government has passed many laws and they have been amended from time to time to put more teeth into the enforcement machinery to ensure better protection for the consumer. Infact if a particular defect or deficiency is cognizable under some special enactment then while considering the consumer complaint the connotation of that enactment would also be taken into view to award such relief as is deemed fit in the facts and in the circumstances of the case. Various statutes intended to protect the consumer against different forms of deceit, injury and exploitation have been enacted. Some of these enactments provide for consumer protection in some way or the other. The following enactments may be referred by the consumers.

1. The Agricultural Produce (Grading and Marketing) Act, 1937.
2. The Air (Prevention and Control of Pollution) Act, 1981.
3. The Code of Civil Procedure 1908.
4. The Drugs and Cosmetics Act, 1940.
5. The Hire Purchase Act, 1972.
6. The Code of Criminal Procedure 1973.
7. The Environment (Protection) Act, 1986.
8. The Drugs and Magic Remedies (Objection and Advertisement) Act, 1954.
9. The Export (Quality Control and Inspection) Act, 1963.
10. The Indian Contract Act, 1872.
11. The Essential Commodities Act, 1955.
12. The Indian Penal Code, 1860.
13. The Prevention of Food Adulteration Act, 1954.
14. The Protection of Civil Right Act, 1955.
15. The Sale of Goods Act, 1930.
16. The Monopolies and Restrictive Trade Practices Act, 1969.
17. The Prevention of Black Marketing and Maintenance of Supplies of Essential Commodities Act, 1980.
18. The Trade and Merchandise Marks Act, 1958.
19. The Usurious Loans Act, 1918.
20. The Specific Relief Act, 1963.
21. The Transplantation of Human Organs Act, 1994 Act No. 42 of 1994
22. The Pre-Natal Diagnostic Techniques (Regulation And Prevention of Misuse) Act, 1994 Act No. 57 of 1994
23. The Medical Termination of Pregnancy Amendment Act, 2002 (No. 64 of 2002)
24. Medical Termination of Pregnancy Regulations, 2003

BRIEF DISCUSSION ON ABOVE MENTIONED LAWS

1. The Agricultural Produce (Grading and Marketing) Act, 1937

The legislation provide for the grading and marketing of agricultural and other produce under the Act. The central government is empowered to make rules regarding prescription of grade designation as indicative of the quality of any scheduled article including in the schedule to the Act. An article is deemed to be misgraded if:

(I) The article is not of the quality prescribed for the grade designation with which it is marked.

(II) The composition of the article offered for grading is altered in any way after a sample has been drawn for analysis and determination of the grade designation of the article in accordance with the Rules made under the Act.

(II) Any false claim is made for the quality prescribed for the grade designation, upon the label or through advertisement or in any other manner.

(IV) The article is tampered with in any manner penalties are provided for

(*i*) unauthorised marking with grade designation mark

(*ii*) counterfeiting grade designation mark, and

(*iii*) Selling misgraded articles.

The Act is implemented by Directorate of Marketing and Inspection (DMI) (Section 3.1). Various manufacturers and producers of agricultural products interested in markings their products under AGMARK are required to apply for a licence to implement the AGMARK scheme which is based on an availability of internal quality control systems created *by* the manufacturer or producer and overseeing by D.M.I by checking quality of the samples taken from time to time.

The following persons are entitled to make a complaint for taking cognizance of an offence punishable under the Act:

(*i*) the Central Government or the State Government or any officer authorised by it in writing, or

(*ii*) the aggrieved person, or

(*iii*) a recognised consumer association, whether the person aggrieved is a member of that association or not.

2. The Air (Prevention and Control of Pollution) Act, 1981

This Act was brought on the statute book for the following reasons:

(*i*) To provide for the prevention, control and abatement of air pollution,

(*ii*) To establish Boards for carrying out the purposes given in.

(*iii*) To confer on and assign to such Boards powers and functions relating thereto.

Section 2 of Act defines certain terms. Air pollution means any solid, liquid or gaseous substance including noise present in the atmosphere in such concentration as **may** be or tend to be injurious to human beings or other living creations or plants or property or environment. Air pollution means the presence in the atmosphere of any air pollutant. Emission means any solid or liquid or gaseous substance carrying out of my chimney, duct or fuel or any other outlet. Occupier, in relation to any factory or premises and includes in relation to any substance, the person in possession of the substance. Section 3 of the Act authorises the Central Pollution Central Board constituted under the Water

(Prevention and Control of Pollutions) Act, 1974 to exercise the powers and perform the functions of the Central Pollution Control Board for prevention and Control of air pollution under this Act. Similarly, if State Pollution Control Board has been constituted under that Act, it shall be deemed to be the State Board for the prevention of air pollution under this Act. Otherwise, the State Government shall constitute a State Board for prevention and control of air pollution. In the case of Union Territories, the Central Board shall exercise the powers and perform the functions of a State Board.

Functions of the Central Board: Section 16 enumerates the functions of the Central Board. These are:

(*i*) To advise the Central Government on any matter concerning improvement of the quality of air and prevention, control or abatement of air pollution,

(*ii*) To plan and cause to be executed a nation-wide programme for the prevention, control or abatement of air pollution,

(*iii*) To co-ordinate the activities of the state Board and resolve disputes among them.

(*iv*) To provide technical assistance and guidance to the state Board, carry out and sponsor investigations and research relating to problems of air pollution and prevention, control or abatement of air pollution,

(*v*) To perform such of the functions of any Stats Boards as may be specified in an order made under section 18(2).

(*vi*) To plan and organise the trainings of persons engaged or to be engaged in programmes for the prevention, control and abatement of air pollution on such terms and conditions as the Central Board may specify,

(*vii*) To organise, through mass media, a comprehensive programme regarding the prevention, control or abatement of air pollution,

(*viii*) To collect, compile and publish technical and statistical data to air pollution and the measures devised for its effective prevention, control and abatement and to prepare manuals, codes or guides relating to prevention, control or abatement of air pollution.

(*ix*) To lay down standards for the quality of air.

(*x*) To collect and disseminate information in respect of matters relating to air pollution,

(*xi*) To perform such other functions as may be prescribed.

Section 17. Enumerates the functions of a State Board. These are:

(*i*) To plan a comprehensive programme for the prevention, control, abatement of air pollution and to secure the exceution thereof.

(*ii*) To advise the State Government on any matter concerning the prevention control or abatement of air pollution.

(*iii*) To collect and disseminate information relating to air pollution, (*iv*) To collaborate with Central Board in organising the trainings of the persons engaged or to be engaged in programmes relating to prevention control or abatement of air pollution and to organise mass education programme relating thereto.

(*v*) To inspect, at all reasonable times, any control equipment, industrial plant or manufacturing process and to give by order, such directions to such personas as it may consider necessary to 'take steps for prevention, control or abatement of air pollution.

(*vi*) To inspect air pollution control areas at such intervals as it may think necessary, assess the quality of air therein and take steps for prevention control or abatement of pollution in such areas.

(*vii*) To advise the State Government with respect to the suitability of any premises or location for carrying on any industry which is likely to cause air pollution,

(*viii*) To perform such other functions as may be prescribed or as may from time to time, be entrusted to it by the Centre or State Government.

(*ix*) To do such other things and to perform such other acts, as it may think necessary, for the proper discharge of its functions and generally for the purpose of carrying into effect the purposes of this Act.

Section 19. Empowers the State Government to declare any or areas within the State as air pollution control area for the purposes of this Act.

Section 20. Provides that with a view to ensure that standards for emission of air pollution from automobiles, laid down by the State Board, are complied with, the State Government shall give such instructions as may be deemed necessary to the concerned authority incharge of registration of motor vehicles under the Motor Vehicles Act, 1988.

Section 21. Provides that no person shall, without the consent of the State Board, establish or operate any industrial plant in any air pollution control area.

Section 22. Provides that no person operating any industrial plant, in any air pollution control area, shall discharge or cause or permit to be discharged the emission of any air pollution in excess of the standards laid down by the State Board.

Section 23A empowers the Board to make application to court for restraining persons from causing air pollution.

Section 23 provides as follows: where in any area, the emission of any air pollution into the atmosphere, in excess of the standards laid down by the State Board, occurs or is apprehended to occur due to accident or other unforeseen act or event, the person in charge of the premises from where such emission occurs or the premises from where such emission occurs or is apprehended to occur shall, forthwith intimate the fact of such occurrence or the apprehension of such occurrence to the state board. On receipt of information, the State Board shall as early as practicable, cause such remedial measures to be taken as are necessary to mitigate the emission of such sir pollutants. Expenses, if any, incurred by the State Board, authority or agency with interest (at such reasonable rate, as the State Government, by order, fix) from the date when a demand for the expenses is made until it is paid, may be recovered by that Board, from the person concerned, as arrears of land revenue or of public demand.

Section 26. Empowers a State Board to take for the purpose of analysis, samples of air or emission from any chimney, flue or duct or any other outlet.

Section 27. Provides the reports of the result of analysis of samples taken under section 26.

Section 31A. Provides that a Board may issue any directions in writing to any person, officer authority. This power includes authority to direct (*a*) the closure, prohibition or regulation of any industry, operation or process, or (*b*) the stoppage o: regulation of supply of electricity, water or any other service.

Section 37. Provides for imprisonment and fine in case of failure to comply with certain provisions.

Section 38. Makes certain acts to be punishable with imprisonment with fine or with both.

Section 39. Provides penalty for contravention of certain provisions of this Act.

Section 40. Makes provisions as regards offence by companies. Section 41 is concerned with offence by government department.

3. The Code of Civil Procedure, 1908

Section 94 of this Code provides that in order to prevent the ends of justice from being defeated the court may, if it is so prescribed:

(*a*) Issue a warrant to arrest the defendant and bring him before the court to show cause why he should not give security for his appearance, and if he fails to comply with any order for security, commit him to the civil prison.

(*b*) Direct the defendant to furnish security to produce any property belonging to him and to place the same at the disposal of the court or order the attachment of any property;

(*c*) Grant a temporary injunction and in case of disobedience commit the person guilty thereof to the civil prison and order that his property be attached and sold;

(*d*) Appoint a receiver of any property and enforce the performance of his duties by attaching and selling his property;

(*e*) Make such other interlocutory orders as may appear to the court to be just and convenient.

Section 95 provides that where, in any suit in which an arrest or attachment has been affected or a temporary injunction granted under the last preceding section:

(*a*) It appears to the court that such arrest, attachment or injunction was applied for on insufficient grounds, or

(*b*) The suit of the plaintiff fails and it appears to the court that there was no reasonable or probable ground for instituting the same the defendant may apply to the court and the court may, upon such application award against the plaintiff by its order such amount not exceeding one thousand rupees, as it deems reasonable compensation to the defendant for the expense or injury (including injury to reputation) caused to him:

Provided that a court shall not award, under this section an amount exceeding the limits of its pecuniary jurisdiction.

An order determining any such application shall bar any suit for compensation in respect of such arrest, attachment or injunction.

4. The Drugs and Cosmetics Act, 1940

This Act provides for regulation of import, manufacture, sale and standards of drugs and cosmetics thereby protecting the interests of consumer in the area of drug and cosmetic industries in India. The main objective of the Act is to ensure that the drugs and cosmetics are of the required standards of quality, purity and strength and are packed in containers giving all necessary information about them and, their manufacture under the Act drugs used in different systems of medicine viz Allopathy, Ayurvedic, Siddha and Unani are covered.

Section 18 provides for prohibition of manufacture and sale of certain drugs and cosmetics, the State Government may provide that no person shall himself or by any other person on his behalf:

(*a*) manufacture for sale or for distribution or sell or stock or exhibit or offer for sale or distribute:

(*i*) any drug which is not of a standard quality or is misbranded, adulterated or spurious,

(*ii*) any cosmetic which is not of a standard quality or is misbranded or spurious,

(*iii*) any patent or proprietary medicine, unless there is displayed in the prescribed manner on the label, or container thereof the true formula of list of active ingredients contained in it together with the quantities thereof.

(*iv*) any drug which by means of any statement, design or device accompanying it, or by any other means, purports, or claims to prevent, cure or mitigate any such disease or ailment or to have any such other effect as may be prescribed,

(*v*) any cosmetic containing any ingredient which may render, it unsafe or harmful for use under the directions indicated or recommended.

(*b*) Sell or stock or exhibit or offer for sale or distribute any drug or cosmetic which has been imported or manufactured in contravention of any of the provisions of this Act or any sale made there under.

(*c*) Manufacture for sale or for distribution or sell, or stock or exhibit or offer for sale or distribute any drug or cosmetics except under, and in accordance with the condition of, a licence issued for such purpose under this chapter IV.

5. The Hire Purchase Act, 1972

A hire purchase agreement is a hybrid transaction which, starting as a contract of hire may culminate in on out and out sale. It is an agreement for hire with an option to the hirer to purchase the goods.

Sections 3, 4 & 22 stipulate that the hirer understands the true nature and implications of the agreement in real sense. Further more, he has a right to obtain, from time to time, the current state of his account in relation to the agreement.

Section 6 implies that every hire-purchase agreement does contain certain conditions and warranties in favour of the hirer. It makes provision for two implied warranties and reads as follows:

"Notwithstanding anything contained in any contract, in every hire-purchase agreement there shall be an implied warranty (I) That the hirer shall have and enjoy quiet possession of the goods, and (II) that the goods shall be free from any charge or encumbrance in favour of any third party at the time when the property is to pass".

Section 9 deals with purchase at any time with rebate.

Section 10 deals with termination of agreement at any time.

Sections 15 and 16 provide obligation of hirer in respect of use of goods and to give information as to where about of goods respectively.

Section 17 ensures the rights of hirer in case of seizure of goods by owner.

Section 20 puts a restriction on owner's right to recover possession of goods otherwise than by proceeding through court of law after a specified proportion of hire-purchase price has been paid or tendered. From those provisions it is obvious that this Act has extended special protection to a hirer. (i.e. consumer)

6. The Code of Criminal Procedure, 1973

This Code protects the consumer in some degree or so.

Section 153 entitles any officer in charge of a police station to enter, without warrant, any place within the limits of such station for the purpose of inspecting or searching for any weights or measures or instruments for weighting, used or kept therein. Further, whenever there is a reason to believe that in such place weights, measures or instruments for weighting are false, he may seize the same and send information of such seizure to a magistrate having" jurisdiction.

Section 406 empowers the Supreme Court to direct transfer of cases and appeals from High Court to another criminal court of equal or superior jurisdiction subordinate to another High Court. The court is to be satisfied that the order of the transfer is necessary for the ends of justice i.e. to protect the interest of litigants.

Section 407 empowers a High Court to transfer (*i*) cases and appeals if it is made to appear to it that a fair and impartial enquiry or trial cannot be had in any criminal court subordinate thereto, or (*ii*) that some question of law of unusual difficulty is likely to arise, or (*iii*) that an order under this section is required by any provision of the Code, or will tend to the general convenience of the parties or witnesses or is expedient for the ends of justice. Then the court may order (*i*) that any offence be inquired into or tried by any court not qualified under sections 177 to 185 (both inclusive) but in other respects competent to inquire into or try such offence, (*ii*) that any particular case or appeal, or class of cases or appeals, be transferred from a criminal court subordinate to its authority to any other such criminal court of equal or superior jurisdiction, (*iii*) that any particular case be committed for trial to a court of session or (*iv*) that any particular case or appeal be transferred to and tried before itself.

Section 408 empowers sessions judge to transfer cases and appeals. It provides that whenever it is made to appear to a session judge that an order under the sub-section is expedient for the ends of justice, he may order that any particular case be transferred from one criminal court to another criminal court in session division. The session judge may act either on the report of the lower court, or on the application of a party interested in, or on his own initiative.

Section 409 provides for withdrawal of cases and appeals by session judge. A session judge may withdraw any case or appeal from or recall any raise or appeal which he had made over to, any Assistant Session Judge or Chief Judicial Magistrate subordinate to him.

Section 410 empowers the Chief Judicial Magistrate to withdraw cases from any Magistrate subordinate to him and may enquire himself or refer it or enquiry to any other magistrate subordinate to him.

Section 482 saves the inherent powers of the High Court from all the provisions of code, to make such orders as may he necessary to give effect to any order under this Code, or to prevent abuse of the process of any court or otherwise to secure the ends of justice.

7. The Environment (Protection) Act, 1986

The objective of the Act is to provide for the protection and improvement of environment and for matters connected therewith. The Act came into force with effect from 19th November, 1986. This Act is in addition to the two allied Acts viz Water and Air (Prevention and Control of Pollution). The genesis of the Act is in Articles 48A and 51A of the Indian Constitution.

This Act is the most comprehensive piece of legislation relating to environment as it (*i*) contains a very wide definition of environment, (*ii*) empowers the Central Government to take strict actions and (*iii*) provides for penalties for various offences.

Section 3 empowers the Central Government to take all such measures as it deems necessary or expedient for the specific purposes which are: (*i*) Protecting and improving the quality of the environment and (*ii*) Preventing, controlling and abating environmental pollution, This Act empowers the Central Government to initiate an authority and delegate the following powers to it:

(*i*) Such of its powers and functions under this Act. as may be mentioned in the order,

(*ii*) Power of Central Government to issue directions,

(*iii*) The power to take fourteen measures as enumerated in section 3. Section 11 empowers the Central Government or any officer empowered by it in this behalf, to take for the purpose of analysis, samples of air, water, soil or other substance from any factory, premises or other place in such manner as may be prescribed.

Section 12 empowers the Central Government to (*a*) establish one or more laboratories, (*b*) recognise one or more laboratories or institutions as environmental laboratories to carry out the functions entrusted to an environmental laboratory under this Act.

Section 16 provides for penalty in case of offences by companies. Section 17 provides for penalty when an offence under this Act is committed by any Department of Government.

Environment Audit Report

In March 1992, Rule 14 was introduced in Environment (Protection) Rules, 1992. Every person carrying on an industry, operation or process requiring consent under section 25 of the Water (Protection and Control of Pollution) Act, 1981", or both or authorization under the Hazardous Wastes (Management and Handlings) Rules, 1989 issued under the Environment (Protection) Act, 1986 shall submit an Environmental Audit Report for the financial year ending 3ist March in Form V to concerned State Pollution Control Board on or before the 10th day of May every year, beginning 1993.

8. The Drugs and Magic Remedies (Objection and Advertisement) Act, 1954

This legislation was enacted for the laudable objection of controlling advertisements of drugs, in newspapers or magazines or otherwise, relating to a (*i*) alleged cures for general diseases, and diseases peculiar to woman and (*ii*) Sexual stimulants such type of advertisement led the ignorant, the gullible and the unwary to restore to self-medication with useless, and sometimes harmful, having side and after-effects, drugs and appliances.

Section 2(C) defines the term "magic remedy" as to include a talisman, mantra, kavacha and any other charm of any kind which is alleged to possess miraculous powers for or in the diagnosis, cure, mitigation, treatment or. prevention of any disease in human beings or animals or for affecting or influencing in any way the structure of any organic function of the body of human beings or animals.

Section 3 prohibits the advertisement of certain drugs. No person can take any part in the publication of any advertisement referring to any drug in terms which suggests or is calculated to lead to the effect of the drug for—(*a*) the procurement of miscarriage in women or' prevention of conception in women or (*b*) the maintenance or improvement of the capacity of human beings for sexual pleasure, or (*c*) the correction of menstrual disorder in women, or (*d*) the diagnosis, care, mitigation, treatment or prevention of any disease, disorder or condition specified in the Schedule of Act or any other disease, disorder or condition which may be specified in the rules made under this Act. However, no such rules shall be made except (*i*) in respect of any disease, disorder or condition which requires timely treatment in consultation with a registered medical practitioner or for which there are normally no accepted remedies and (*ii*) after consultation with the Drugs Technical Board constituted under the Drugs and Cosmetics Act, 1940 and if the Central Government considers necessary, with such other persons having special knowledge or practical experience in respect of Ayurvedic or Unani systems of medicines, as the government deems fit.

Section 4 prohibits misleading advertisement relating to drugs. No person can take any part in the publication of any advertisement relating to drug if the advertisement contains any matter which (*i*) directly or indirectly gives a false impression regarding true character of the drug, or (*ii*) makes a false claim for the drug or (*iii*) is otherwise false or misleading in any material particular.

Section 5 prohibits the advertisement of magic remedies for treatment of certain diseases and disorders. No person carrying on or purporting to carry on the profession of administering magic remedies can take any part in the publication of any advertisement referring to any magic remedy which directly or indirectly claims to be efficacious for any of the purpose specified in section 7 provides penalties for contravention of the provisions of the Act.

9. The Export (Quality Control and Inspection) Act, 1963

Under this Act, a certificate of export worthiness is issued to commodity by the export inspection agency. The Central Government is empowered to notify the commodities, which are prohibited from export unless they are accompanied by certificates issued by export inspection agencies.

When the decision to subject a product to quality control, or inspection or both is made, a notification is issued under section 6. This notification has to specify the type of quality control and it has to establish, adopt or recognise one or more standard specifications for a notified commodity.

Under section 17 of the Act, rules are framed which let a standard for the export of products which are subject to quality control under the Act,

10. Indian Contract Act, 1872

Under this Act, ail agreements are contracts if they are made by the "free consent" of the parties competent to contract, for a lawful consideration and with a lawful object and are not expressly declared to be void under the Act. Consent is said to be free when it is not caused by coercion, or undue influence, fraud, misrepresentation or mistake. In certain cases when consent to an agreement is caused by coercion, fraud, misrepresentation or undue influence, the agreement is a contract voidable at the option of the party whose consent was so caused, which the agreement is void where both the parties are under a mistake as to matter of fact.

11. The Essential Commodities Act, 1955

In the interest of the general public, this Act empowers the Central Government to (*i*) regulate production, supply, distribution, storage, transport etc., and (*ii*) control prices of commodities which have been declared under the Act as essential. In particular, the objects of the Act are: (*i*) Control of production, supply and distribution of essential commodities, (*ii*) Check of inflationary trends in prices, (*iii*) Ensure equitable distribution of the essential commodities.

Under this Act, section 2(*a*) enumerates classes of commodities which are essential. These are:

(*i*) Cattle fodder including oil cakes and other concentrates,
(*ii*) Coal including coke and other derivatives,
(*iii*) Component, parts and accessories of automobiles,
(*iv*) Cotton and woollen textiles,
(*v*) Drugs,
(*vi*) Foodstuffs, including edible oil seeds, oils and cooked food,
(*vii*) Iron and steel. including manufactured products of iron and steel
(*viii*) Paper including news print, paper board of straw board.
(*ix*) Petroleum and petroleum products,
(*x*) Raw cotton, whether ginned or unginned and cotton seed,
(*xi*) Raw jute.

In addition, the Central Government may, by notified order, declare any other class of commodities for the purposes of this Act, being a commodity with respect to which Parliament has power to make laws by virtue of entry 33 in list III in Seventh Schedule to the Constitution.

Section 3 empowers the Central Government to regulate or prohibit the production, supply and distribution of any essential commodity or trade and commerce therein:

(*i*) Where it is necessary or expedient so to do for maintaining or increasing supplies of any essential commodity,
(*ii*) Where it is necessary to secure their equitable distribution and availability at fair prices, and
(*iii*) Where it is necessary to secure it for the defence of India or the efficient conduct of military operations.

Confiscation of Essential Commodity

Section 6A provides that where any essential commodity is seized, a report of such seizure must, without delay, be made to the collector of the area in which such essential commodity is seized. The collector, on receipt of the report, may if he thinks it expedient so to do — so direct the commodity, so seized to be produced for inspection before him, and if he is satisfied that there has been a contravention of the order, may order confiscation of:

(*a*) the essential commodity so seized,

(*b*) any package, covering or receptacle in which such essential commodity is found, and

(*c*) any animal, vehicle, vessel or other conveyance used in carrying such essential commodity.

The award of any confiscation by the collector shall not prevent the infliction of any punishment to which the person affected thereby is liable under the Act (Section 6D).

Penalty (Section 7)

Section 7 of the Act provides that the person found guilty of contravention of certain orders made under provisions of Act can be punished *inter alia* with imprisonment which may extend to seven years and the subject property may be forfeited.

Furthermore, it is provided that no court shall take cognizance of any punishable under this Act except on a report in writing of the facts constituting such offence made by a person who is a public servant as defined in section 21 of the Indian Penal Code or any person aggrieved or any recognised consumer association, whether such person is a member of that association or not.

Explanation.—For the purposes of section 12AA,"recognised consumer association" means a voluntary consumer association registered under the Companies Act, 1956 (1 of 1956) or under any other law for the time being in force.

12. The Indian Penal Code, 1860

Under the Code, there are several provisions aimed at protecting the interest of the consumers such as:

Fraudulent use of false instruments for — weighing-whoever fraudulently uses any instrument for weighing which he knows to be false, shall be punished with imprisonment of either description for a term which may extend to one year or with fine, or with both. (Section 264)

Fraudulent use of false weight or measure — whoever fraudulently uses any false weight or false measure of length or capacity as a different weight or measure it shall be punished with imprisonment of either description for a term which may extend to one year or with fine, or with both. (Section 265)

Being in possession of false weight or measure — whoever is in possession of any instrument for weighing or of any weight, or of any measure of length or capacity which he knows to be false, intending that the same may be fraudulently used, shall be punished with imprisonment of either description for a term which may extend to one year or with fine, or with both. (Section 266)

Making or selling false weight or measure — whoever makes, sells or disposes of any instrument for weighing or any weight or any measure of length or capacity which he knows to be false, in order that the same may be used as true. Shall be punished with imprisonment of either description for a term which may extend to one year or with fine, or with both. (Section 267)

Adulteration of food or drink — intended for sale whoever adulterates any article of food or drink, so as to make such article noxious as food or drink, intending to sell such article as food or drink, or knowing it to be likely that the same will be sold as food or drink, shall be punished with imprisonment of either description for the term which may extend to six months or with fine which may extend to one thousand rupees, or with both. (Section 272)

Sale of noxious food or drink — whoever sells or offers or exposes for sale, as food or drink, any article, which has been rendered or has become noxious, or is in a state unfit for food or drink, knowledge or having reason to believe that the same is noxious as food or drink, shall be punished with imprisonment of either description for a term which may extend to six months or with fine which may extend to one thousand rupees or with both. (Section 273)

Adulteration of drugs — whoever adulterates any drug or medical preparation in such a manner as to lessen the efficacy or changes the operation of such drug or medical preparation, or to make it noxious, intending that, it shall be sold or used, for or knowing it to be likely that it will be sold or used, for any medicinal purpose, as if it had not undergone such adulteration, shall be punished with imprisonment of either description for a term which may extend to six months or with fine which may extend to one thousand rupees, or with both. (Section 274)

Sale of adulterated drugs — whoever knowing any drug or medicinal preparation to have been adulterated in such a manner as to lessen its efficacy, to change its operation, or to render it noxious, sells the same or offers or exposes it for sale, or issues it from any dispensary for medicinal purposes *by* any person net knowing of the adulteration, shall be punished with imprisonment of either description for a term which may extend to six months or with fine which may extend to one thousand rupees, or with both. (Section 275)

Sale of drug as a different drug or preparation — whoever knowingly sells, or offers or exposes for sale or issues from a dispensary for medicinal purposes any drug or medicinal preparation as a different drug of medicinal preparation, shall be punished with imprisonment of either description for a term which may extend to six months or with fine which may extend to one thousand rupees, or with both. (Section 276)

13. The Prevention of Food Adulteration Act, 1954

The Prevention of Food Adulteration Act, 1954 was enacted to eradicate the anti-social evil of food adulteration and ensuring purity in the articles of food.

Section 5 prohibits the import into India of any food article which is adulterated of misbranded or is in contravention of the conditions of licence.

Section 6 provides that the custom officer or any officer of the Central Government duly authorised in this behalf, may detain any imported package which he suspects to contain any article of food, the import of which is prohibited by section 5. He shall forthwith report to the Director of Central Food Laboratory, and if required by him, forward the package or send samples of any suspected article of food found therein to the said laboratory.

Section 7 specifically prohibits the "manufacturing" for sale, storing, selling, or distributing of—

(*i*) any adulterated, or

(*ii*) misbranded, or

(*iii*) any other article of food, for the sale of which licence is required, export in accordance with the conditions of licence, or

(*iv*) any article of food the sale of which is for the time being prohibited by the Food (Health) Authority in the interest of public health, and

(*v*) any article of food in contravention of any other provision of this Actor any rules made thereunder, or

(*vi*) any adulterant.

Section 8 empowers the Central and State Government to appoint any person having requisite qualification, as public analyst for a specified area. However a person having any financial interest in the manufacture, import or sale of any article of food, shall not be eligible for appointment as a public analyst. Section empowers the Central and State Governments to appoint such persons, having the prescribed qualifications, to be Food Inspectors for such local area as may be assigned to them by the Central or the State Government. However, a person having financial interest in the manufacture, import or sale of any food article is not eligible to be appointed as a Food Inspector. A Food Inspector is a public servant within the meaning of section 21 of the Indian Penal Code, 1860.

Section 10 enumerates a number of powers of a Food Inspector. Section 15 empowers the Central Government or the State Government to cast a duty upon the medical practitioners in any local area to report all cases of food poisoning coming within their cognizance.

to the authority specified in that behalf.

Section 18 provides that any person, who has been convicted under this Act for the contravention of any of the provisions of this Act or any rule thereunder, will be deprived of the entire quantity of food in respect of which the offence was committed. The forfeiture of property is in addition of fine, imprisonment and publication of the name of the offender against the violation of the provisions of the Act or the rules made thereunder.

14. The Protection of Civil Rights Act, 1955

This legislation was enacted with the objective of protecting the civil rights of *Harijans* by prohibiting enforcement of any religious disability in any religious place like a temple and social and in public places and restaurants. Thus they are equally entitled to the enjoyment of and use of wells, water taps, public conveyance, educational institutions, hotels, hospitals, parks, shops, etc. Anyone denying these rights to non-Harijans will attract penalty under the Act.

Section 4 provides that an enforcement of any disability against any person with regard to the following would attract penalty under the Act; (*i*) access to any shop, public restaurant, hotel or place of public entertainment, or (*ii*) the use of any utensils and other articles kept in any public restaurant, hotel, dharamshala, sarai or musafirkhana for the use of general public or of any section thereof, or (*iii*) the practice of any profession or the carrying on of any occupation, trade or business or employment in any job, or (*iv*) the use of, or access to, any river, stream, spring, well, tank, cistern water tap or other watering place or any bathing ghat, burial or cremation ground, any sanitary convenience, any road, or passage or any other place of public resort which other members of the public, or persons professing the same religion or belonging to the same religious denomination or any section thereof, as such person, have a right to use or have access to, or (*v*) the use of, or access to, any place used for a charitable or public purpose maintained wholly or partly out of state funds or dedicated to the use of the general public, or any section thereof, or (*vi*) the enjoyment of any benefit under a charitable trust created for the benefit of the general public or of any section thereof, or (*vii*) the use of, or access to any public conveyance or (*viii*) the construction, acquisition or occupation of any residential premises in any locality, whatsoever, or (*ix*) the use of any dharamshala, sarai or musafirkhana, which is open to the general public or to any section thereof, or (*x*) the observance of any social or religious custom, usage or ceremony or taking part in, or taking out, any religious, social or cultural procession, or (*xi*) the use of jewellery and finery.

Section 8 provides that any refusal to sell any goods or any refusal to render any service to any person, at the time and place and on the same terms and conditions at or on which such goods are sold or services rendered to other" persons (i.e.-non Harijans) in the ordinary course of business, on the ground of untouchability, will attract penalty.

15. The Sale of Goods Act, 1930

Under this Act, in a contract of sale, unless the circumstances of the contract are such as to show a different intention, there is:

(*a*) an implied condition on the part of the seller that, in the case of a sale, he has a right to sell the goods and that in the case of an agreement to sell the goods at the time when the property is to pass;

(*b*) an implied warranty that the buyer shall have and enjoy quiet possession of the goods;

(*c*) an implied warranty that the goods shall be free from any charge and encumbrance in favour of any third party not declared or known to the buyer before or at the time when contract is made. (Section 14)

Furthermore, regarding the implied condition as to the quality or fitness of the goods, it says that there is no implied warranty or condition as to the quality or fitness for any particular purpose of goods supplied under a contract of sale, except as follow:

(1) Where the buyer, expressly or by implication, makes known to the seller the particular purpose for which the goods are required so as to show that the buyer relies on the seller's skill or judgment, and the goods are of a description which it is in the course of the seller's business to supply (whether he is the manufacturer or producer or not), there is an implied condition that the goods shall be reasonably fit for such purpose:

Provided that, in the case of a contract for the sale of a specified article under its patent or other trade name, there is no implied condition as to its fitness for any particular purpose.

(2) Where goods are bought by description from a seller who deals in goods of that description (whether he is the manufacturer or producer or not), there is an implied condition that the goods shall be of merchantable quality:

Provided that, if the buyer has examined the goods, there shall be no implied condition as regards defects which such examination ought to have revealed.

(3) An implied warranty or condition as to quality or fitness for a particular purpose may be annexed by the usage of trade.

(4) An express warranty or condition does not negate a warranty or condition implied by this Act unless inconsistent therewith. (Section 16)

As regards sale by sample, it provides that in the case of a contract for sale by sample, there is an implied condition:

(*a*) that the bulk shall correspond with the sample in quality:

(*b*) that the buyer shall have a reasonable opportunity of comparing the bulk with the sample;

(*c*) that the bulk shall be free from any defect, rendering them unmerchantable, which would not be apparent on reasonable examination of the sample.

Where the seller wrongfully neglects or refuses to deliver the goods to the buyer, the buyer may sue the seller for damages for non-delivery. (Section 57)

Subject to the provisions of Chapter II of the Specific Relief Act, 1963 in any suit for breach of contract to deliver specific or ascertained goods, the Court may, if it thinks fit, on the application of the plaintiff, by its decree direct that the contract shall be performed specifically without giving the defendant the option of retaining the goods on payment of damages. The decree may be unconditional, or upon such terms and conditions as to damages, payments of the price or otherwise, as the Court may deem just, and the application of the plaintiff may be made at any time before the decree. (Section 58)

Where there is a breach of warranty by the seller or where the buyer elects/or is compelled to treat any breach of a condition on the part of the seller as a breach of warranty entitled to reject the goods, but may —

(*a*) set up a case against the seller for the breach of warranty in diminution or extinction of the price: or

(*b*) sue the seller for damages for breach of warranty.

The fact that a buyer has set up a case for breach of warranty in diminution or extinction of the price does not prevent him from suing for the same breach of warranty if he had suffered further damage. (Section 58)

Where either party to a control of sale repudiates the contract before the date of delivery, the other may either treat the contract as subsisting and wait till the date of delivery, or he may treat the contract as rescind and sue for damages for the breach. (Section 60)

Nothing in this Act shall affect the right of the seller or the buyer to recover interest or special damages in any case where by law interest or special damages may be recoverable, or to recover the money paid where the consideration for the payment of it has failed. In the absence of a contract to the contrary, the Court may award interest at such rate, as it thinks fit, on the amount of price —

(*a*) to the seller in a suit by him for the amount of the price, from the date of the tender of the goods or from the date on which the price was payable;

(*b*) to the buyer in a suit by him for the refund of the price in a case of a breach of the contract on the part of the seller, from the date on which the payment was made. (Section 61)

16. The Monopolies and Restrictive Trade Practices Act, 1969

This Act, was brought on the statute with a view (*i*) to ensure that (*a*) the operation of the economic system does not result in the concentration of economic power to the common detriment, (*b*) there are no monopolies, and (*ii*) to prohibit monopolistic, restrictive' and unfair trade practices, which are prejudicial to public interest.

This Act in its broad outline, is a measure to arrest the development of huge monopolies having an adverse effect on market and to prevent concentration of economic power in the hands of a few to the detriment of many. The Act desires that there should be no (*i*) economic monopolies, (*ii*) monopolistic trade practices, (*iii*) restrictive trade practices and (*iv*) unfair trade practices.

Clause (*i*) of section 2 defines the terms "monopolistic trade practice". A monopolistic trade practice means a trade practice, which has or is likely to have, the effect of:

(*i*) maintaining price at an unreasonable level by limiting, reducing or otherwise controlling the production, supply or distribution of goods of any description or the supply of any services or in any other manner,

(*ii*) unreasonably preventing or lessening competition in the production, supply or distribution of any goods or in the supply of any services, (*iii*) limiting technical development or capital investment to the common detriment or allowing the quality of any goods produced, supplied or distributed or any service rendered in India to deteriorate,

(*iv*) increasing unreasonably—

(*a*) the cost of production of any goods, or

(*b*) charges for the provision, or maintenance, or any service,

(*v*) increasing unreasonably—

(*a*) the price at which goods are, or may be sold or resoled or charged at which the services are or may be provided, or

(*b*) the profits which are, or may be derived by the production, supply or distribution (including the sale or purchase) of any goods or by the provision of any services, or

(*iv*) preventing or lessening competition in production, supply or distribution of any goods or in the provision or maintenance of any services by the adoption or unfair method of unfair or deceptive practices.

Control of Monopolistic Trade Practices

The Act provides a mechanism of enquiry and suitable action to remove the undesirable effects of the monopolistic trade practice. Section 18 provides that the Commission is empowered to regulate the procedure and conduct of its business regarding inquiry. The Commission has also the "entire" discretion to determine the extent to which the person interested or claiming to be interested in the subject-matter of any proceeding before it are allowed to be present or to be heard either by themselves or by their representatives or to cross-examine witness or otherwise to take part in the proceeding.

The Commission is however, empowered to exercise the following powers in respect of monopolistic trade practices:

(*i*) To grant a temporary injunction (Section 12A)

(*ii*) To award compensation. (Section 12B)

The Commission may initiate an inquiry into a monopolistic trade practice.

17. The Prevention of Black-marketing and Maintenance of Supplies of Essential Commodities Act, 1980

The Essential Commodities Act, 1955 could not deal effectively with certain malpractices indulged in and try unscrupulous elements like — black marketers, hoarders, profiteers. Hence it was felt necessary to supplement the Act by legislation i.e., the Prevention of Black Marketing and Maintenance of Supplies of Essential Commodities Act, 1980. Section 3 provides for ordering a person to be detained with the object of preventing him from acting in a manner which might be prejudicial to maintenance of supplies of commodities considered essential to the community.

The power to make detention orders have been conferred on the Union as well as State Government, District Magistrate and Commissioners of Police. The detention orders are to be executed at any place within India in the manner prescribed for execution of warrants of arrest under the Criminal Procedure Code, 1973. Section 5 empowers the appropriate government to regulate the place and conditions of detention. Section 8 provides for disclosure of grounds of detention order to the person affected thereby. Sections 9 and 10 provide that the appropriate government shall place before the Advisory Board the grounds of the detention order and any representation, if so made, by the detained person. Section 11 sets out the procedure of the Advisory Board. The Board is required to submit its report to the appropriate government, specifying therein its opinion as to the existence of a sufficient cause of detention. Sections 12 and 13 set out the action to be taken on the report of the Board about the detention. Accordingly, the appropriate government may confirm the order of detention or the order be revoked and the detained person to be forthwith released.

18. The Trade and Merchandise Marks Act, 1958

This Act provides a comprehensive law in tune with consumer protection relating to registration and better protection of trade marks in the country.

Main Objectives of the Act:

(i) *To provide for the registration of trade marks*

This Act provides for the registration of trade marks. Once a person gets a trade mark registered, he acquires certain rights under the Act. If his trade mark is infringed, he has certain remedies. A trade mark is registered by the competent authority only if it is not likely to injure the public interest.

(ii) *Better protection of trade marks*

However, the registration of trade mark could be attacked on the ground of invalidity of registration or the defendant could establish honest concurrent user, or acquiescence on the part of the registered, then the plaintiff has to establish that the defendant's mark is deceptively similar, *i.e.*, the similarity is such as to be likely to deceive or cause confusion in the minds of the public. This may not be very easy for the plaintiff to establish. In the case of unregistered marks and marks which are not registrable, no protection under the Act is provided to the owner thereof. However an action for passing off may be maintained by the plaintiff if he proves sufficient use of the mark so as to create a valuable goodwill of the business connected with the goods bearing the mark.

(iii) *Prevention of the use of fraudulent marks on merchandise*

One of the functions of the trade mark is to give an indication of the source of goods. Thus the public in general will associate a particular trade mark on certain goods with a particular manufacture. The law provides for the prevention of the use of fraudulent marks on merchandise in the public interest.

Deceptively Similar

A mark shall be deemed to be deceptively similar to another mark if it so nearly resembles that other mark as to be likely to deceive or cause confusion.

Section 96 lays down an implied warranty on sale of marked goods. It provides that on the sale or in the contract for sale of any goods to which a trade mark or mark or trade description has been applied, there shall be deemed to be an implied warranty on the part of the seller that the mark is a genuine mark and not falsely applied, or that the trade description is not a false trade description unless the contrary is expressed in some writing signed by or on behalf of the seller and delivered at the time of the sale of contract to sell and accept by the buyer.

Section 78 provides that a person shall be deemed to apply a trade mark or mark or trade description to goods who—

(*a*) applies to the goods themselves, or

(*b*) applies it to any package in or with which the goods are sold, or exposed for sale, or had in possession for sale or for any purpose of trade or manufacture, or

(*c*) places, encloses or annexes any goods which are sold, or exposed for sale or it had in possession for sale or for any purpose of trade description has been applied, or

(*d*) uses a trade mark, or mark or trade description in any manner reasonably likely to lead to the belief that the goods in connection with which it is used are designed and described by that trade mark or mark or trade description, or

(*e*) in relation to the goods, uses a trade mark or trade description, in any sign, advertisement, invoice, catalogue, business letters, business papers, price list, or other commercial document and goods are delivered to a person in pursuance of a request or order made by reference to the trade mark or trade description as so used.

Further a trade mark or mark or trade description shall be deemed to be applied to goods whether it is woven in or impressed on, or otherwise worked into, or annexed or affixed to, the goods or to any package or other thing.

Section 77 provides that:

(*i*) When is a person deemed to falsify a trade mark? A person shall be deemed to falsify a trade mark who, either

  (*a*) without the assent of the proprietor of the trade mark applies that trade or a deceptively similar mark, or

  (*b*) falsify any genuine trade mark, whether by alteration, addition, effacement or otherwise.

(*ii*) When a person is deemed to falsely apply to goods a trade mark? A person shall be deemed to falsely apply to goods a trade mark who, without the assent of the proprietor of the trade mark—

  (*a*) applies such trade mark or a deceptively similar mark, to goods or any package containing goods, (*b*) uses any package bearing a mark which is identical with deceptively similar to the trade mark of such proprietor, for the purpose of packing, filling, or wrapping therein any goods other than the genuine goods of the proprietor of the trade mark.

Penalty

Under the Act, penalties are provided for the following:

(*i*) for applying false trade marks, trade description, etc., (Section 78)

(*ii*) for selling goods to which false trade marks is applied

(*iii*) for removing piece goods (Section 80)

(*iv*) for falsely representing a trade mark as registered (Section 81)

(*v*) for improperly describing a place of business as connected with the trade mark office. (Section 82)

(*vi*) for offences by companies. (Section 88)

19. The Usurious Loans Act, 1918

Many a times, we come across loans carrying interest at usurious rate, these loans may be in money or in kind. Such loans are very harsh for the borrower and can be termed as unconscionable. The Usurious Loans Act, 1918 give some powers to courts while they are dealing with such type of transaction.

Section 3 provides that where in any suit to which this Act applies, whether heard *ex parte* or otherwise, the court has reason to believe that (*i*) the interest rate is excessive and (*ii*) the transaction was, as between the parties thereto, substantially unfair, the Court may exercise all or any of the powers mentioned below. These are:

(*i*) reopen the transaction, take an account between the parties and relieve the debtor of all liability in respect of any excessive interest,

(*ii*) notwithstanding any agreement, purporting to close previous dealings and to create a new obligation, reopen any account already taken between them and relieve the debtor of all liability in respect of any excessive interest, and if anything has been paid or allowed in account in respect of such liability, order the creditor to repay any sum which it considers to be repayable in respect thereof,

(*iii*) set aside either wholly or in part or revise or alter any security given or agreement made in respect of any loan, and if the creditor, has parted with security, order him to indemnify the debtor in such manner and to such extent as it may deem just.

However, in exercise of these powers, the Court shall not:

(*i*) reopen any agreement purporting to close previous dealings and to create a new obligation which has been entered into by the parties or any person from whom they claim at a date more than 12 years from the date of the transaction, (*ii*) do anything which affects any decree of a Court. In this case which the court deems to be reasonable having regard to the risk recurred has it appeared or must be taken to have appeared to the creditor at the date of the Loan.

In considering whether interest is excessive under this section, the court shall take into account any amounts charged or paid, whether in money or in kind, for expenses, in queries, fines bonus premium renewals or any other charges, and if compound interest is charged, the periods at which it is calculated, and the total advantage which may reasonably so taken to have been expected from the transaction.

In considering the question of risk, the court shall take into account the presence or absence of security and the value thereof, the financial condition of the debtor and the result of any previous transactions of the debtor, by way of loan, so far as the same were known, or must be taken to have been known, to the creditor.

In considering whether a transaction was substantially unfair, the court shall take into account all circumstances materially affecting the relations of the parties at the time of the loan to tending to show that the transaction was unfair, including the necessities or supposed necessities of the debtor at the time of the loan so far as the same were known, or must so taken to have been known, to the creditor. Further, interest may itself be sufficient evidence that the transaction was substantially unfair.

This section shall apply to any suit whatever its form may be, if such suit is substantially one for the recovery of a loan or for the enforcement of any agreement or security in respect of a loan or for the redemption of any such security.

Nothing in this section shall affect the right of any transferee for value which satisfies the court that the transfer to him was *bona fide* and that he had at the time of such transfer no notice of any fact which would have entitled the debtor as against the lender to relief under this section.

20. The Specific Relief Act, 1963

Under this Act, enactment underlines the various reliefs to be granted by the Civil Court. Section 4 clearly postulates that specific relief can be granted only for the purpose of enforcing individual civil right and not for the mere purpose of enforcing a penal law.

Section 5 lays down that a person entitled to the possession of specific immovable property may recover it in the manner provided by the Code of Civil Procedure, 1908. Immovable Property can be recovered under Order 21 and Rules 35 and 36 in execution of a decree providing for the delivery of the property. Such a decree can be passed in an ejectment suit. A plaint till suing for ejection can succeed only on the basis of his own title.

Furthermore, section 6 of the Act provides that if any person is dispossessed without his consent of immovable property otherwise than in due course of law, he or any person claiming through him may by suit, recover possession thereof, notwithstanding any other titles may be set up in such suit. However, such suit shall be brought within six months from the date of dispossession. It is a summary and speedy remedy since a right of possession receives protection from the statute. The question of ownership or title to the property is irrelevant in a suit of this kind. Even if the defendant has a superior title, he must first put the plaintiff back in possession and later file his own suit on the basis of title. Recovery of specific movable property is provided under section 7. Specific performance of any contract may in the discretion of the Court, be enforced under section 10 when there exists no standard for ascertaining the actual damage caused by the non-performance of the act agreed to be done or when the act agreed to be done is such that the compensation in money for its non-performance would not afford adequate relief.

Specific performance of part of a contract has been enshrined in section 12 of the Act as under:

(1) Except as otherwise hereinafter provided in this section, the court shall not direct the specific performance of a part of a contract.

(2) Where a party to a contract is unable to perform the whole of it, but the part which must be left unperformed bears only a small proportion to the whole in value and admits of compensation in money, the court may at the suit of either party, direct the specific performance of so much of contract as can be performed, and award compensation in money for the deficiency.

(3) Where a party to a contract is unable to perform the whole of this part, and the part which must be left unperformed either—

(*a*) forms a considerable part of the whole though admitting of compensation in money; or

(*b*) does not admit of compensation in money, he is not entitled to obtain a decree for specific performance; but the court may; at the suit of the other party, direct the party in default to perform specifically so much of his part of the contract as he can perform, if the other party — (*i*) in a case falling under clause (*a*), pays or has paid the agreed consideration for the whole of the contract reduced by the consideration for the part which must be left unperformed and in a case falling under clause (*fa*) pays or has paid, the consideration for the whole of the contract without any abatement; and (*n*) in either case, relinquishes all claims as to the performance of the remaining part of contract and all right to compensation either for the deficiency or for the loss or damage sustained by him through the default of the defendant.

(4) When a part of a contract which, taken by itself, can and ought to be specifically performed, stands on a separate and independent footing from another part of the same contract which can not or ought to be

specifically performed, the Court may direct specific performance of the former part.

Explanation.—For the purpose of this section, a party to a contract shall be deemed to be unable to perform for the whole or his part of it if a portion of its subject-matter existing at the date of the contract has ceased to exist at the time of its performance.

Specific performances of contracts which cannot be specifically enforced as enshrined in section 14 are:

(*a*) a contract for the non-performance of which compensation in money is an adequate relief;

(*b*) a contract which runs into such minute or numerous details or which is so dependant on the personal qualification or volition of the parties, or otherwise from its nature is such, that the Court cannot enforce specific performance in its material terms;

(*c*) a contract which in its nature is determinate:

(*d*) a contract with performance of which involves the performance of a continuous duty which the Court cannot supervise.

Save as provided by the Arbitration Act, 1940 (10 of 1940) no contract to refer present or future differences to arbitration shall be specifically enforced; but if any person who has made such a contract (the then arbitration agreement to which the provisions of the said Act apply) and has refused, to perform it, sues in respect of any subject which he has contracted to refer, the existence of such contract shall bar the suit.

Notwithstanding anything contained in clause (*a*) or clause (*d*) of sub-section (I) the Court may enforce specific performance in the following cases:

(*a*) Where the suit is for the enforcement of a contract —

(*i*) to execute a mortgage or furnish any other security for securing the repayment of any loan which the borrower is not willing to repay at once:

Provided that where only a part of the loan has been advanced the lender is willing to advance the remaining part of the loan in terms of the contract: or

(*ii*) to take up and pay for any debentures of a company.

(*b*) where the suit is for —

(*i*) the execution of a formal deed of partnership. The parties having commenced to carry on the business of the partner in a firm;

(*c*) where the suit is for the enforcement of contract for the construction of any building or execution of any other work on land:

Provided that the following conditions are fulfilled, namely:

(*i*) the building or other work is described in the contract in terms sufficiently precise to enable the Court to determine the exact nature of the building or work;

(*ii*) the plaintiff has substantial interest in the performance of the contract and the interest is of such a nature that the compensation in money for non-performance of contract is not an adequate relief; and

(*iii*) the defendant has, in pursuance of the contract obtained possession of the whole or any part of the land on which the building is to be constructed or other work is to be executed.

The Court has been vested with powers under section 22 to grant relief in a case of a specific performance of a contract for transfer of immovable property for possession or partition and separate possession of such property or any other relief including refund of any earnest money or deposit paid in case the relief of specific performance is declined.

Any person entitled to any legal character or to any rights as to any property if denied or apprehends to be denied the same, may invoke section 34 to seek a decree of declaration to that effect.

The relief of preventive nature in the form of injunctions is available in the discretion of the Court under section 36. In common parlance, it is called 'Stay'. The order may be temporary or perpetual. In the former case, it continues till a specified time or till further orders of the Court while the latter can only be granted *by* the *decree* on merits whereby the defendant is perpetually restrained from infringing on the rights of plaintiff.

In case defendant is to be compelled to do certain acts then positive directions are issued by the Court in the form of mandatory injunctions provided under section 39. Damages may also be awarded in addition to or as an alternate relief of injunction under section 40. However, the Court cannot grant an injunction in the following cases enshrined under section 41:

(*a*) to restrain any person from prosecuting any "judicial proceeding" pending at the institution of the suit in which injunction is sought, unless such restraint is necessary to prevent a multiplicity of proceedings;

(*b*) to restrain any person from instituting or prosecuting any proceeding in a Court not subordinate to that from which the injunction is sought;

(*c*) to restrain any person from applying to any legislative body;

(*d*) to restrain any person from instituting or prosecuting any proceedings in a criminal matter;

(*e*) to prevent the breach of contract the performance of which would not be specifically enforced;

(*f*) to prevent on the ground of nuisance an act of which it is not reasonably clear that it will be a nuisance;

(*g*) to prevent a continuing breach in which the plaintiff has acquiesced;

(*h*) when equally efficacious relief can certainly be obtained by any other usual mode of proceeding except in case of trust;

(*i*) when the conduct of the plaintiff or his agents has been such as to disentitle him to be of the assistance of the Court;

(*j*) when the plaintiff has no personal interest in the matter.

21. The Hire Purchase Act, 1972

The statement of objects and reasons of the Act candidly states as follows:

A hire-purchase agreement is a hybrid transaction which, starting as a contract of hire, may eliminate in an out and out sale. It is an agreement for hire with an option to the hirer to purchase the goods its socio-economic importance can hardly be overestimated as it is convenient and useful legal device for acquiring consumer durable goods.

Sections 3,4 and 22 stipulate that the hirer understands the true nature and implications of the agreement in real sense. Furthermore, he has a right to obtain, from time to time, the current state of his account in relation to the agreement.

Section 6 implies that every hire purchase agreement does contain certain conditions and warranties in favour of the hirer. It makes provision for two implied warranties and reads as follows:

Notwithstanding anything contained in any contract, in every hire purchase agreement there shall be an implied warranty—

(*i*) that the hirer shall have and enjoy quiet possession to the goods, and

(*ii*) that the goods shall be free from any charge or encumbrance in favour of any third party at the time when the property is to pass".

Section 8 deals with passing of property.

Section 9 deals with purchase at any time with rebate.

Section 10 deals with termination of agreement at any time.

Sections 15 and 16 provide obligation of hirer in respect of use of goods and to give information as to whereabouts of goods respectively.

Section 17 ensures the right of hirer in case of seizure goods by owner.

Section 20 puts a restriction, on owner's right to recover possession of goods otherwise than by proceeding through court of law after a specified proportion of hire purchase price has been paid or tendered. From these provisions, it is obvious that this Act has extended a special protection to a hirer (*i.e.*, a consumer).

22. The Transplantation of Human Organs Act, 1994

(42 of 1994)

[*8th July, 1994*]

An Act to provide for the regulation of removal, storage and transplantation of human organs for therapeutic purposes and for the prevention of commercial dealings in human organs and for matters connected therewith or incidental thereto.

WHEREAS it is expedient to provide for the regulation of removal, storage and transplantation of human organs for therapeutic purposes and for the prevention of commercial dealings in human organs;

AND WHEREAS Parliament has no power to make laws for the States with respect to any of the matters aforesaid except as provided in Articles 249 and 250 of the Constitution;

AND WHEREAS in pursuance of clause (1) of Article 252 of the Constitution, resolutions have been passed by all the Houses of the Legislatures of the States of Goa, Himachal Pradesh and Maharashtra to the effect that the matters aforesaid should be regulated in those States by Parliament by law;

BE it enacted by Parliament in the Forty-fifth Year of the Republic of India as follows:—

Chapter I

PRELIMINARY

1. Short title, application and commencement.—(1) This Act may be called the Transplantation of Human Organs Act, 1994.

(2) It applies, in the first instance, to the whole of the States of Goa, Himachal Pradesh and Maharashtra and to all the Union territories and it shall also apply to such other State which adopts this Act by resolution passed in that behalf under clause (1) of Article 252 of the Constitution.

(3) It shall come into force in the States of Goa, Himachal Pradesh and Maharashtra and in all the Union territories on such date as the Central Government may, by notification, appoint and in any other State which adopts this Act under clause (1) of Article 252 of the Constitution, on the date of such adoption; and any reference in this Act to the commencement of this Act shall, in relation to any State or Union territory, means the date on which this Act comes into force in such State or Union territory.

2. Definitions.—In this Act, unless the context otherwise requires,—

(*a*) "advertisement" includes any form of advertising whether to the public generally or to any section of the public or, individually to selected persons;

(*b*) "Appropriate Authority" means the Appropriate Authority appointed under section 13;

(*c*) "Authorisation Committee" means the committee constituted under clause (*a*) or clause (*b*) of sub-section (4) of section 9;

(*d*) "brain-stem death" means the stage at which all functions of the brain-stem have permanently and irreversibly ceased and is so certified under sub-section (6) of section 3;

(*e*) "deceased person" means a person in whom permanent disappearance of all evidence of life occurs, by reason of brain-stem death or in a cardiopulmonary sense, at any time after live birth has taken place;

(*f*) "donor" means any person, not less than eighteen years of age, who voluntarily authorises, the removal of any of his human organs for therapeutic purposes under sub-section (1) or sub-section (2) of section 3;

(*g*) "hospital" includes a nursing home, clinic, medical centre, medical or teaching institution for therapeutic purposes and other like institution;

(*h*) "human organ" means any part of a human body consisting of a structured arrangement of tissues which, if wholly removed, cannot be replicated by the body;

(*i*) "near relative" means spouse, son, daughter, father, mother, brother or sister;

(*j*) "notification" means a notification published in the Official Gazette;

(*k*) "payment" means payment in money or money's worth but does not include any payment for defraying or reimbursing;

(*i*) the cost of removing, transporting or preserving the human organ to be supplied; or

(*ii*) any expenses or loss of earnings incurred by a person so far as reasonably and directly attributable to his supplying any human organ from his body;

(*l*) "prescribed" means prescribed by rules made under this Act;

(*m*) "recipient" means a person into whom any human organ is, or is proposed to be, transplanted;

(*n*) "registered medical practitioner" means a medical practitioner who possesses any recognised medical qualification as defined in clause (*h*) of section 2 of the Indian Medical Council Act, 1956, and who is enrolled on a State Medical Register as defined in clause (*k*) of that section;

(*o*) "therapeutic purposes" means systematic treatment of any disease or the measures to improve health according to any particular method or modality; and

(*p*) "transplantation" means the grafting of any human organ from any living person or deceased person to some other living person for therapeutic purposes.

Chapter II

AUTHORITY FOR THE REMOVAL OF HUMAN ORGANS

3. Authority for removal of human organs.—(1) Any donor may, in such manner and subject to such conditions as may be prescribed, authorise the removal, before his death, of any human organ of his body for therapeutic purposes.

(2) If any donor had, in writing and in the presence of two or more witnesses (at least one of whom is a near relative of such person), unequivocally authorized at any time before his death, the removal of any human organ of his body, after his death, for therapeutic purposes, the person lawfully in possession of the dead body of the donor shall, unless he has any reason to believe that the donor had subsequently revoked the authority aforesaid, grant to a registered medical practitioner all reasonable facilities for the removal, for therapeutic purposes, of that human organ from the dead body of the donor.

(3) Where no such authority as is referred to in sub-section (2), was made by any person before his death but no objection was also expressed by such person to any of his human organs being used after his death for therapeutic purposes, the person lawfully in possession of the dead body of such person may, unless he has reason to believe that any near relative of the deceased person has objection to any of the deceased person's human organs being used for therapeutic purposes, authorise the removal of any human organ of the deceased person for its use for therapeutic purposes.

(4) The authority given under sub-section (1) or sub-section (2) or, as the case may be, sub-section (3) shall be sufficient warrant for the removal, for therapeutic purposes, of the human organ; but no such removal shall be made by any person other than the registered medical practitioner.

(5) Where any human organ is to be removed from the body of a deceased person, the registered medical practitioner shall satisfy himself, before such removal, by a personal examination of the body from which any human organ is to be removed, that life is extinct in such body or, where it appears to be a case of brain-stem death, that such death has been certified under sub-section (6).

(6) Where any human organ is to be removed from the body of a person in the event of his brain-stem death, no such removal shall be undertaken unless such death is certified, in such form and in such manner and on satisfaction of such conditions and requirements as may be prescribed, by a Board of medical experts consisting of the following, namely:

(*i*) the registered medical practitioner in charge of the hospital in which brain-stem death has occurred;

(*ii*) an independent registered medical practitioner, being a specialist, to be nominated by the registered medical practitioner specified in clause (*i*), from the panel of names approved by the Appropriate Authority;

(*iii*) a neurologist or a neurosurgeon to be nominated by the registered medical practitioner specified in clause (*i*), from the panel of names approved by the Appropriate Authority; and

(*iv*) the registered medical practitioner treating the person whose brain-stem death has occurred.

(7) Notwithstanding anything contained in sub-section (3), where brain-stem death of any person, less than eighteen years of age, occurs and is certified under sub-section (6), any of the parents of the deceased person may give authority, in such form and in such manner as may be prescribed, for the removal of any human organ from the body of the deceased person.

4. Removal of human organs not to be authorised in certain cases.—(1) No facilities shall be granted under sub-section (2) of section 3 and no authority shall be given under sub-section (3) of that section for the removal of any human organ from the body of a deceased person, if the person required to grant such facilities, or empowered to give such authority, has reason to believe that an inquest may be required to be held in relation to such body in pursuance of the provisions of any law for the time being in force.

(2) No authority for the removal of any human organ from the body of a deceased person shall be given by a person to whom such body has been entrusted solely for the purpose of interment, cremation or other disposal.

5. Authority for removal of human organs in case of unclaimed bodies in hospital or prison.—(1) In the case of a dead body lying in a hospital or prison and not claimed by any of the near relatives of the deceased person within forty-eight hours from the time of the death of the concerned person, the authority for the removal of any human organ from the dead body which so remains unclaimed may be given, in the prescribed form, by the person in charge, for the time being, of the management or control of the hospital or prison, or by an employee of such hospital or prison authorized in this behalf by the person in charge of the management or control thereof.

(2) No authority shall be given under sub-section (1) if the person empowered to give such authority has reason to believe that any near relative of the deceased person is likely to claim the dead body even though such near relative has not come forward to claim the body of the deceased person within the time specified in sub-section (1).

6. Authority for removal of human organs from bodies sent for postmortem examination for medicolegal or pathological purposes.—Where the body of a person has been sent for postmortem examination.—(*a*) for medico-legal purposes by reason of the death of such person having been caused by accident or any other unnatural cause; or

(*b*) for pathological purposes, the person competent under this Act to give authority for the removal of any human organ from such dead body may, if he has reason to believe that such human organ will not be required for the purpose for which such body has been sent for postmortem examination, authorise the removal, for therapeutic purposes, of that human organ of the deceased person provided that he is satisfied that the deceased person had not expressed, before his death, any objection to any of his human organs being used, for therapeutic purposes after his death or, where he had granted an authority for the use of any of his human organs for therapeutic purposes, after his death, such authority had not been revoked by him before his death.

7. Preservation of human organs.—After the removal of any human organ from the body of any person, the registered medical practitioner shall take such steps for the preservation of the human organ so removed as may be prescribed.

8. Savings.—(1) Nothing in the foregoing provisions of this Act shall be construed as rendering unlawful any dealing with the body or with any part of the body of a deceased person if such dealing would have been lawful if this Act had not been passed.

(2) Neither the grant of any facility or authority for the removal of any human organ from the body of a deceased person in accordance with the provisions of this Act nor the removal of any human organ from the body of a deceased person in pursuance of such authority shall be deemed to be an offence punishable under section 297 of the Indian Penal Code (45 of 1860).

9. Restrictions on removal and transplantation of human organs.—(1) Save as otherwise provided in sub-section (3), no human organ removed from the body of a donor before his death shall be transplanted into a recipient unless the donor is a near relative of the recipient.

(2) Where any donor authorizes the removal of any of his human organs after his death under sub-section (2) of section 3 or any person is competent or empowered to give authority for the removal of any human organ from the body of any deceased person authorizes such removal, the human organ may be removed and transplanted into the body of any recipient who may be in need of such human organ.

(3) If any donor authorises the removal of any of his human organs before his death under sub-section (1) of section 3 for transplantation into the body of such recipient, not being a near relative, as is specified by the donor by reason of affection or attachment towards the recipient or for any other special reasons, such human organ shall not be removed and transplanted without the prior approval of the Authorisation Committee.

(4) (*a*) The Central Government shall constitute, by notification, one or more Authorisation Committees consisting of such members as may be nominated by the Central Government on such terms and conditions as may be specified in the notification for each of the Union territories for the purposes of this section.

(*b*) The State Government shall constitute, by notification, one or more Authorisation Committees consisting of such members as may be nominated by the State Government on such terms and conditions as may be specified in the notification for the purposes of this section.

(5) On an application jointly made, in such form and in such manner as may be prescribed, by the donor and the recipient, the Authorisation Committee shall, after holding an inquiry and after satisfying itself that the applicants have complied with all the requirements of this Act and the rules made thereunder, grant to the applicants approval for the removal and transplantation of the human organ.

(6) If, after the inquiry and after giving an opportunity to the applicants of being heard, the Authorisation Committee is satisfied that the applicants have not complied with the requirements of this Act and the rules made thereunder, it shall, for reasons to be recorded in writing, reject the application for approval.

Chapter III

REGULATION OF HOSPITALS

10. Regulation of hospitals conducting the removal, storage or transplantation of human organs.—(1) on and from the commencement of this Act,—

(*a*) no hospital, unless registered under this Act, shall conduct, or associate with, or help in, the removal, storage or transplantation of any human organ;

(*b*) no medical practitioner or any other person shall conduct, or cause to be conducted, or aid in conducting by himself or through any other person, any activity relating to the removal, storage or transplantation of any human organ at a place other than a place registered under this Act; and

(*c*) no place including a hospital registered under sub-section (1) of section 15 shall be used or cause to be used by any person for the removal, storage or transplantation of any human organ except for therapeutic purposes.

(2) Notwithstanding anything contained in sub-section (1), the eyes or the ears may be removed at any place from the dead body of any donor, for therapeutic purposes, by a registered medical practitioner.

Explanation.—For the purposes of this sub-section, "ears" includes ear drums and ear bones.

11. Prohibition of removal or transplantation of human organs for any purpose other than therapeutic purposes.—No donor and no person empowered to give authority for the removal of any human organ shall authorise the removal of any human organ for any purpose other than therapeutic purposes.

12. Explaining effects, etc., to donor and recipient.—No registered medical practitioner shall undertake the removal or transplantation of any human organ unless he has explained, in such manner as may be prescribed, all possible effects, complications and hazards connected with the removal and transplantation to the donor and the recipient respectively.

Chapter IV

APPROPRIATE AUTHORITY

13. Appropriate Authority.—(1) The Central Government shall appoint, by notification, one or more officers as Appropriate Authorities for each of the Union territories for the purposes of this Act.

(2) The State Government shall appoint, by notification, one or more officers as Appropriate Authorities for the purposes of this Act.

(3) The Appropriate Authority shall perform the following functions, namely:

(*i*) to grant registration under sub-section (1) of section 15 or renew registration under sub-section (3) of that section;

(*ii*) to suspend or cancel registration under sub-section (2) of section 16;

(*iii*) to enforce such standards, as may be prescribed, for hospitals engaged in the removal, storage or transplantation of any human organ;

(*iv*) to investigate any complaint of breach of any of the provisions of this Act or any of the rules made thereunder and take appropriate action;

(*v*) to inspect hospitals periodically for examination of the quality of transplantation and the follow-up medical care to persons who have undergone transplantation and persons from whom organs are removed; and

(*vi*) to undertake such other measures as may be prescribed.

Chapter V

REGISTRATION OF HOSPITALS

14. Registration of hospital engaged in removal, storage or transplantation of human organs.—(1) No hospital shall commence any activity relating to the removal, storage or transplantation of any human organ for therapeutic purposes after the commencement of this Act unless such hospital is duly registered under this Act:

Provided that every hospital engaged, either partly or exclusively, in any activity relating to the removal, storage or transplantation of any human organ for therapeutic purposes immediately before the commencement of this Act, shall apply for registration within sixty days from the date of such commencement:

Provided further that every hospital engaged in any activity relating to the removal, storage or transplantation of any human organ shall cease to engage in any such activity on the expiry of three months from the date of commencement of this Act unless such hospital has applied for registration and is go registered or till such application is disposed of, whichever is earlier.

(2) Every application for registration under sub-section (1) shall be made to the Appropriate Authority in such form and in such manner and shall be accompanied by such fees as may be prescribed.

(3) No hospital shall be registered under this Act unless the Appropriate Authority is satisfied that such hospital is in a position to provide such specialised services and facilities, possess such skilled manpower and equipments and maintain such standards as may be prescribed.

15. Certificate of registration.—(1) The Appropriate Authority shall, after holding an inquiry and after satisfying itself that the applicant has complied with all the requirements of this Act and the rules made there under, grant to the hospital a certificate of registration in such form, for such period and subject to such conditions as may be prescribed.

(2) If, after the inquiry and after giving an opportunity to the applicant of being heard, the Appropriate Authority is satisfied that the applicant has not complied with the requirement, of this Act and the rules made there under, it shall, for reasons to be recorded in writing, reject the application for registration.

(3) Every certificate of registration shall be renewed in such manner and on payment of such fees as may be prescribed.

16. Suspension or cancellation of registration.—(1) The Appropriate Authority may, suo moto or on complaint, issue a notice to any hospital to show cause why its registration under this Act should not be suspended or cancelled for the reasons mentioned in the notice.

(2) If, after giving a reasonable opportunity of being heard to the hospital, the Appropriate Authority is satisfied that there has been a breach of any of the provisions of this Act or the rules made thereunder, it may, without prejudice to any criminal action that it may take against such hospital, suspend ills registration for such period as it may think fit or cancel its registration:

Provided that where the Appropriate Authority is of the opinion that it is necessary or expedient so to do in the public interest, it may, for reasons to be recorded in writing, suspend the registration of any hospital without issuing any notice.

17. Appeals.—Any person aggrieved by an order of the Authorisation Committee rejecting an application for approval under sub-section (6) of section 9, or any hospital aggrieved by an order of the Appropriate Authority rejecting an application for registration under sub-section (2) of section 15 or an order of suspension or cancellation of registration under sub-section (2) of section 16, may, within thirty days from the date of the receipt of the order, prefer an appeal, in such manner as may be prescribed, against such order to—

(*i*) the Central Government where the appeal is against the order of the Authorisation Committee constituted under clause (*a*) of sub-section (4) of section 9 or against the order of the Appropriate Authority appointed under sub-section (1) of section 13; or

(*ii*) the State Government, where the appeal is against the order of the Authorisation Committee constituted under clause (*b*) of sub-section (4) of section 9 or against the order of the Appropriate Authority appointed under sub-section (2) of section 13.

Chapter VI

OFFENCES AND PENALTIES

18. Punishment for removal of human organ without authority.—(1) Any person who renders his services to or at any hospital and who, for purposes of transplantation, conducts, associates with, or helps in any manner in, the removal of any human organ without authority, shall be punishable with imprisonment for a term which may extend to five years and with fine which may extend to ten thousand rupees.

(2) Where any person convicted under sub-section (1) is a registered medical practitioner, his name shall be reported by the Appropriate Authority to the respective State Medical Council for taking necessary action including the removal of his name from the register of the Council for a period of two years for the first offence and permanently for the subsequent offence.

19. Punishment for commercial dealings in human organs.—Whoever—

(*a*) makes or receives any payment for the supply of, or for an offer to supply, any human organ;

(*b*) seeks to find a person willing to supply for payment any human organ;

(*c*) offers to supply any human organ for payment;

(*d*) initiates or negotiates any arrangement involving the making of any payment for the supply of, or for an offer to supply, any human organ;

(*e*) takes part in the management or control of a body of persons, whether a society, firm or company, whose activities consist of 10 or include the initiation or negotiation of any arrangement referred to in clause (*d*); or (*f*) publishes or distributes or causes to be published or distributed any advertisement,—

(*i*) inviting persons to supply for payment of any human organ;

(*ii*) offering to supply any human organ for payment; or

(*iii*) indicating that the advertiser is willing to initiate or negotiate any arrangement referred to in clause (*d*), shall be punishable with imprisonment for a term which shall not be less than two years but which may extend to seven years and shall be liable to fine which shall not be less than ten thousand rupees but may extend to twenty thousand rupees:

Provided that the court may, for any adequate and special reason to be mentioned in the judgment, impose a sentence of imprisonment for a term of less than two years and a fine less than ten thousand rupees.

20. Punishment for contravention of any other provision of this Act.—Whoever contravenes any provision of this Act or, any rule made, or any condition of the registration granted, thereunder for which no punishment is separately provided in this Act, shall be punishable with imprisonment for a term which may extend to three years or with fine which may extend to five thousand rupees.

21. Offences by companies.—(1) Where any offence, punishable under this Act has been committed by a company, every person who, at the time the offence was committed was in charge of, and was responsible to, the company for the conduct of the business of the company, as well as the company, shall be deemed to be guilty of the offence and shall be liable to be proceeded against and punished accordingly:

Provided that nothing contained in this sub-section shall render any such person liable to any punishment, if he proves that the offence was committed without his knowledge or that he had exercised all due diligence to prevent the commission of such offence.

(2) Notwithstanding anything contained in sub-section (1), where any offence punishable under this Act has been committed by a company and it is proved that the offence has been committed with the consent or connivance of, or 'is attributable to any neglect on the part of, any director, manager, secretary or other officer of the company, such director, manager, secretary or other officer shall also be deemed to be guilty of that offence and shall be liable to be proceeded against and punished accordingly.

Explanation.—For the purposes of this section,—

(*a*) "company" means any body corporate and includes a firm or other association of individuals; and

(*b*) "director", in relation to a firm, means a partner in the firm.

22. Cognizance of offence.—(1) No court shall take cognizance of an offence under this Act except on a complaint made by—

(*a*) the Appropriate Authority concerned. or any officer authorised in this behalf by the Central Government or the State Government or, as the case may be, the Appropriate Authority; or

(*b*) a person who has given notice of not, less than sixty days, in such manner as may be prescribed, to the Appropriate Authority concerned, of the alleged offence and of his intention to make a complaint to the court.

(2) No court other than that of a Metropolitan Magistrate or a Judicial Magistrate of the first class shall try any offence punishable under this Act.

(3) Where a complaint has been made under clause (*b*) of sub-section (1), the court may, on demand by such person, direct the Appropriate Authority to make available copies of the relevant records in its possession to such person.

Chapter VII

MISCELLANEOUS

23. Protection of action taken in good faith.—(1) No suit, prosecution or other legal proceeding shall lie against any person for anything which is in good faith done or intended to be done in pursuance of the provisions of this Act.

(2) No suit or other legal proceeding shall lie against the Central Government or the State Government for any damage caused or likely to be caused for anything which is in good faith done or intended to be done in pursuance of the provisions of this Act.

24. Power to make rules.—(1) The Central Government may, by notification, make rules for carrying out the purposes of this Act.

(2) In particular, and without prejudice to the generality of the foregoing power, such rules may provide for all or any of the following matters, namely:—

(*a*) the manner in which and the conditions subject to which any donor may authorize removal, before his death, of any human organ of his body under sub-section (1) of section 3;

(*b*) the form and the manner in which a brain-stem death is to be certified and the conditions and requirements which are to be satisfied for that purpose under sub-section (6) of section 3;

(*c*) the form and the manner in which any of the parents may give authority, in the case of brain-stem death of a minor, for the removal of any human organ under sub-section (7) of section 3;

(*d*) the form in which authority for the removal of any human organ from an, unclaimed dead body may be given by the person incharge of the management or control of the hospital or prison, under sub-section (1) of section 5; 12

(*e*) the steps to be taken for the preservation of the human organ removed from the body of any person, under section 7;

(*f*) the form and the manner in which an application may be jointly made by the donor and the recipient under sub-section (5) of section 9;

(*g*) the manner in which all possible effects, complications and hazards connected with the removal and transplantation is to be explained by the registered medical practitioner to the donor and the recipient under section 12;

(*h*) the standards as are to be enforced by the Appropriate authority for hospitals engaged in the removal, storage or transplantation of any human organ under clause (*iii*) of sub-section (3) of section 13;

(*i*) the other measures as the Appropriate Authority shall undertake in performing its functions under clause (*vi*) of sub-section (3) of section 13;

(*j*) the form and the manner in which an application for registration shall be made and the fee which shall be accompanied, under sub-section (2) of section 14;

(*k*) the specialised services and the facilities to be provided, skilled manpower and the equipments to be possessed and the standards to be maintained by a hospital for registration, under sub-section (3) of section 14;

(*l*) the form in which, the period for which and the conditions subject to which certificate of registration is to be granted to a hospital, under sub-section (1) of section 15;

(*m*) the manner in which and the fee on payment of which certificate of registration is to be renewed under sub- section (3) of section 15;

(*n*) the manner in which an appeal may he preferred under section 17;

(*o*) the manner in which a person is required to give notice to the Appropriate Authority of the alleged offence and of his intention to make a complaint to the court, under clause (*b*) of sub-section (1) of section 22; and

(*p*) any other matter which is required to be, or may be, prescribed.

(3) Every rule made under this Act shall be laid, as soon as may be after it is made, before each House of Parliament, while it is in session, for a total period of thirty days which may be comprised in one session or in two or more successive sessions, and if, before the expiry of the session immediately following the session or the successive sessions aforesaid, both Houses agree in making any modification in the rule or both Houses agree that the rule should not be made, the rule shall thereafter have effect only in such modified form or be of no, effect, as the case. may be; so, however, that any such modification. or annulment shall be without prejudice to the validity of anything previously done under that Rule 13.

25.Repeal and savings.—(1) The Ear Drums and Ear Bones (Authority for Use for Therapeutic Purposes) Act, 1982 (28 of 1982) and the Eyes (Authority for Use for Therapeutic Purposes) Act, 1982 (29 of 1982) are hereby repeated. (2) The repeal shall, however, not affect the previous operation of the Acts so repealed or anything duly done or suffered thereunder.

23. The Pre-Natal Diagnostic Techniques (Regulation and Prevention of Misuse) Act, 1994

57 of 1994

[*20th September, 1994*]

An Act to provide for the regulation of the use of pre-natal diagnostic techniques for the purpose of detecting genetic or metabolic disorders or chromosomal abnormalities or certain congenital malformations or sex linked disorders and for the prevention of the misuse of such techniques for the purpose of pre-natal sex determination leading to female foeticide and for matters connected therewith or incidental thereto.

BE it enacted by Parliament in the Forty-fifth Year of the Republic of India as follows:—

Chapter I

PRELIMINARY

1. Short title, extent and commencement.—(1) This Act may be called the Pre-natal Diagnostic Techniques (Regulation and Prevention of Misuse) Act, 1944.

(2) It shall extend to the whole of India except the State of Jammu and Kashmir.

(3) It shall come into force on such date as the Central Government may, by notification in the Official Gazette, appoint.

2. Definitions.—In this Act, unless the context otherwise requires,—

(*a*) "Appropriate Authority" means the Appropriate Authority appointed under section 17;

(*b*) "Board" means the Central Supervisory Board constituted under section 7;

(*c*) "Genetic Counseling Centre" means an institute, hospital, nursing home or any place, by whatever name called, which provides for genetic counselling to patients;

(*d*) "Genetic Clinic" means a clinic, institute, hospital, nursing home or any place, by whatever name called, which is used for conducting pre-natal diagnostic procedures;

(*e*) "Genetic Laboratory" means a laboratory and includes a place where facilities are provided for conducting analysis or tests of samples received from Genetic Clinic for pre-natal diagnostic test;

(*f*) "Gynaecologist" means a person who possesses a post-graduate qualification in gynaecology and obstetrics;

(*g*) "medical geneticist" means a person who possesses a degree or diploma or certificate in medical genetics in the field of pre-natal diagnostic techniques or has experience of not less than two years in such field after obtaining—

(*i*) Any one of the medical qualifications recognised under the Indian Medical Council Act, 1956 (102 of 1956); or

(*ii*) a post-graduate degree in biological sciences;

(*h*) "paediatrician" means a person who possesses a post-graduate qualification in paediatrics;

(*i*) "pre-natal diagnostic procedures" means all gynaecological or obstetrical or medical procedures such as ultrasonography foetoscopy, taking or removing samples of amniotic fluid, chorionic villi, blood or any tissue of a pregnant woman for being sent to a Genetic Laboratory or Genetic Clinic for conducting pre-natal diagnostic test;

(*j*) "pre-natal diagnostic techniques" includes all pre-natal diagnostic procedures and pre-natal diagnostic tests;

(*k*) "pre-natal diagnostic test" means ultrasonography or any test or analysis of amniotic fluid, chorionic villi, blood or any tissue of a pregnant woman conducted to detect genetic or metabolic disorders or chromsomal abnormalities or congenital anomalies or naemoglobinopathies or sex-linked diseases;

(*l*) "prescribed" means prescribed by rules made under this Act;

(*m*) "registered medical practitioner" means a medical practitioner who possesses any recognized medical qualification as defined in clause (*h*) of section 2 of the Indian Medical Council Act, 1956 (102 of 1956) and whose name has been entered in a State Medical Register;

(*n*) "Regulations" means regulations framed by the Board under this Act.

Chapter II

REGULATION OF GENETIC COUNSELLING CENTRES GENETIC LABORATORIES AND GENETIC CLINICS

3. Regulation of Genetic Counselling Centres, Genetic Laboratories and Genetic Clinics.—*On and from the commencement of this Act.*—(1) no Genetic Counselling Centre, Genetic Laboratory or Genetic Clinic unless registered under this Act, shall conduct or associate with, or help in, conducting activities relating to pre-natal diagnostic techniques;

(2) no Genetic Counselling Centre, Genetic Laboratory or Genetic Clinic shall employ or cause to be employed any person who does not possess the prescribed qualifications;

(3) no medical geneticist, gynaecologist paediatrician registered medical practitioner or any other person shall conduct or cause to be conducted or aid in conducting by himself or through any other person, any pre-natal diagnostic techniques at a place other than a place registered under this Act.

Chapter III

REGULATION OF PRE-NATAL DIAGNOSTIC TECHNIQUES

4. Regulation of pre-natal diagnostic techniques.—On and from the commencement of this Act,—

(1) no place including a registered Genetic Counselling Centre or Genetic Laboratory or Genetic Clinic shall be used or caused to be used by any person for conducting pre-natal diagnostic techniques except for the purposes specified in clause (2) and after satisfying any of the conditions specified in clause (3);

(2) no pre-natal diagnostic techniques shall be conducted except for the purposes of detection of any of the following abnormalities, namely:—

(*i*) Chromosomal abnormalities;

(*ii*) Genetic metabolic diseases;

(*iii*) Haemoglobinopathies;

(*iv*) Sex -linked genetic diseases;

(*v*) Congenital anomalies;

(*vi*) Any other abnormalities or diseases as may be specified by the Central Supervisory Board;

(3) no pre-natal diagnostic techniques shall be used or conducted unless the person qualified to do so is satisfied that any of the following conditions are fulfilled, namely:—

(*i*) age of the pregnant woman is above thirty-five years;

(*ii*) the pregnant woman has undergone two or more spontaneous abortions or foetal loss;

(*iii*) the pregnant woman had been exposed to potentially teratogenic agents such as drugs, radiation, infection or chemicals;

(*iv*) the pregnant woman has a family history of mental retardation or physical deformities such as spasticity or any other genetic disease;

(*v*) any other condition as may be specified by the Central Supervisory Board;

(4) no person, being a relative or the husband of the pregnant woman shall seek or encourage the conduct of any pre-natal diagnostic techniques on her except for the purpose specified in clause (2).

5. Written consent of pregnant woman and prohibition of communicating the sex of foetus.—(1) No person referred to in clause. (2) of section 3 shall conduct the pre-natal diagnostic procedures unless—

(*a*) he has explained all known side and after effects of such procedures to the pregnant woman concerned;

(*b*) he has obtained in the prescribed form her written consent to undergo such procedures in the language which she understands;

(*c*) a copy of her written consent obtained under clause; and

(*b*) is given to the pregnant woman.

(2) No person conducting pre-natal diagnostic procedures shall communicate to the pregnant woman concerned or her relatives the sex of the foetus by words, signs or in any other manner.

6. Determination of sex prohibited.—On and from the commencement of this Act,—

(*a*) no Genetic Counselling Centre or Genetic Laboratory or Genetic Clinic shall conduct or cause to be conducted in its Centre, Laboratory or Clinic, pre-natal diagnostic techniques including ultrasonography, for the purpose of determining the sex of a foetus;

(*b*) no person shall conduct or cause to be conducted any pre-natal diagnostic techniques including ultrasonography for the purpose of determining the sex of a foetus.

Chapter IV

CENTRAL SUPERVISORY BOARD

7. Constitution of Central Supervisory Board.—(1) The Central Government shall constitute a Board to be known as the Central Supervisory Board to exercise the powers and perform the functions conferred on the Board under this Act.

(2) The Board shall consist of—

(*a*) The Minister in charge of the Ministry or Department of Family Welfare, who shall be the Chairman, ex officio;

(*b*) the Secretary to the Government of India in charge of the Department of Family Welfare, who shall be the Vice-Chairman, ex-officio;

(*c*) two members to be appointed by the Central Government to represent the Ministries of Central Government in charge of Woman and Child Development and of Law and Justice, ex-officio;

(*d*) The Director General of Health Services of the Central Government, ex officio;

(*e*) ten members to be appointed by the Central Government, two each from amongst —

(*i*) eminent medical geneticists;

(*ii*) eminent gynaecologists and obstetricians;

(*iii*) eminent paediatricians;

(*iv*) eminent social scientists; and

(*v*) representatives of women welfare organisations;

(*f*) three women Members of Parliament, of whom two shall be elected by the House of the People and one by the Council of States;

(*g*) four members to be appointed by the Central Government by rotation to represent the States and the Union territories, two in the alphabetical order and two in the reverse alphabetical order:

Provided that no appointment under this clause shall be made except on the recommendation of the State Government or, as the case may be, the Union territory;

(*h*) an officer, not below the rank of a Joint Secretary or equivalent of the Central Government, in charge of Family Welfare, who shall be the Member-Secretary, ex officio.

8. Term of office of members.—(1) The term of office of a member, other than an ex officio member, shall be,—

(*a*) In case of appointment under clause (*e*) or clause (*f*) of sub-section (2) of section 7, three years; and

(*b*) In case of appointment under clause (*g*) of the said sub-section, one year.

(2) If a casual vacancy occurs in the office of any other members, whether by reason of his death, resignation or inability to discharge his functions owing to illness or other incapacity, such vacancy shall be filled by the Central Government by making a fresh appointment and the member so appointed shall hold office for the remainder of the term of office of the person in whose place he is so appointed.

(3) The Vice-Chairman shall perform such functions as may be assigned to him by the Chairman from time to time.

(4) The procedure to be followed by the members in the discharge of their functions shall be such as may be prescribed.

9. Meetings of the Board.—(1) The Board shall meet at such time and place, and shall observe such rules of procedure in regard to the transaction of business at its meetings (including the quorum at such meetings) as may be provided by regulations:

Provided that the Board shall meet at least once in six months.

(2) The Chairman and in his absence the Vice-Chairman shall preside at the meetings of the Board.

(3) If for any reason the Chairman or the Vice-Chairman is unable to attend any meeting of the Board, any other member chosen by the members present at the meeting shall preside at the meeting.

(4) All questions which come up before any meeting of the Board shall be decided by a majority of the votes of the members present and voting, and in the event of an equality of votes, the Chairman, or in his absence, the person presiding, shall have and exercise a second or casting vote.

(5) Members other than ex officio members shall receive such allowances, if any, from the Board as may be prescribed.

10. Vacancies, etc., not to invalidate proceedings of the Board.—No act or proceeding of the Board shall be invalid merely by reason of—

(*a*) any vacancy in, or any defect in the constitution of, the Board; or (*b*) any defect in the appointment of a person acting as a member of the Board; or

(*c*) any irregularity in the procedure of the Board not affecting the merits of the case.

11. Temporary association of persons with the Board for particular purposes.—(1) The Board may associate with itself, in such manner and for such purposes as may be determined by regulations, any person whose assistance or advice it may desire in carrying out any of the provisions of this Act.

(2) A person associated with it by the Board under sub-section (1) for any purpose shall have a right to take part in the discussions relevant to that purpose, but shall not have a right to vote at a meeting of the Board and shall not be a member for any other purpose.

12. Appointment of officers and other employees of the Board.—(1) For the purpose of enabling it efficiently to discharge its functions under this Act, the Board may, subject to such regulations as may be made in this behalf, appoint (whether on deputation or otherwise) such number of officers and other employees as it may consider necessary:

Provided that the appointment of such category of officers, as may be specified in such regulations, shall be subject to the approval of the Central Government.

(2) Every officer or other employee appointed by the Board shall be subject to such conditions of service and shall be entitled to such remuneration as may be specified in the regulations.

13. Authentication of orders and other instruments of the Board.—All orders and decisions of the Board shall be authenticated by the signature of the Chairman or any other member authorised by the Board in this behalf, and all other instruments issued by the Board shall be authenticated by the signature of the Member-Secretary or any other officer of the Board authorised in like manner in this behalf.

14. Disqualifications for appointment as member.—A person shall be disqualified for being appointed as a member if, he—

(*a*) has been convicted and sentenced to imprisonment for an offence which, in the opinion of the Central Government, involves moral turpitude; or

(*b*) is an undischarged insolvent; or

(*c*) is of unsound mind and stands so declared by a competent court; or

(*d*) has been removed or dismissed from the service of the Government or a Corporation owned or controlled by the Government; or

(*e*) has, in the opinion of the Central Government, such financial or other interest in the Board as is likely to affect prejudicially the discharge by him of his functions as a member; or

(*f*) has, in the opinion of the Central Government, been associated with the use or promotion of pre-natal diagnostic technique for determination of sex.

15. Eligibility of member for reappointment.—Subject to the other terms and conditions of service as may be prescribed, any person ceasing to be a member shall be eligible for reappointment as such member.

16. Functions of the Board.—The Board shall have the following functions, namely:—

(*i*) To advise the Government on policy matters relating to use of pre-natal diagnostic techniques;

(*ii*) To review implementation of the Act and the rules made thereunder and recommend changes in the said Act and rules to the Central Government;

(*iii*) To create public awareness against the practice of pre-natal determination of sex and female foeticide;

(*iv*) to lay down code of conduct to be observed by persons working at Genetic Counseling Centers, Genetic Laboratories and Genetic Clinics;

(*v*) any other functions as may be specified under the Act.

Chapter V

Appropriate Authority and Advisory Committee

17. Appropriate Authority and Advisory Committee.—(1) The Central Government shall appoint, by notification in the Official Gazette, one or more Appropriate Authorities for each of the Union territories for the purposes of this Act.

(2) The State Government shall appoint, by notification in the Official Gazette, one or more Appropriate Authorities for the whole or part of the State for the purposes of this Act having regard to the intensity of the problem of pre-natal sex determination leading to female foeticide.

(3) The officers appointed as Appropriate Authorities under sub-section (1) or sub-section (2) shall be,—

(*a*) When appointed for the whole of the State or the Union territory, or of above the rank of the Joint Director of Health and Family Welfare; and

(*b*) when appointed for any part of the State or the Union territory, of such other rank as the State Government or the Central Government, as the case may be, may deem fit.

(4) The Appropriate Authority shall have the following functions, namely:—

(*a*) To grant, suspend or cancel registration of a Genetic Counselling Centre, Genetic Laboratory or Genetic Clinic;

(*b*) To enforce standards prescribed for the Genetic Counselling Centre, Genetic Laboratory and Genetic Clinic;

(*c*) To investigate complaints of breach of the provisions of this Act or the rules made there under and take immediate action; and

(*d*) To seek and consider the advice of the Advisory Committee, constituted under sub-section (5), on application for registration and on complaints for suspension or cancellation of registration.

(5) The Central Government or the State Government, as the case may be, shall constitute an Advisory Committee for each Appropriate Authority to aid and advise the Appropriate Authority in the discharge of its functions, and shall appoint one of the members of the Advisory Committee to be its Chairman.

(6) The Advisory Committee shall consist of—

(*a*) Three medical experts from amongst gynaecologist, obstetricians, pediatricians and medical geneticists;

(*b*) One legal expert;

(*c*) One officer to represent the department dealing with information and publicity of the State Government or the Union territory, as the case may be;

(*d*) Three eminent social workers of whom not less than one shall be from amongst representatives of women's organisations.

(7) No person who, in the opinion of the Central Government or the State Government, as the case may be, has been associated with the use or promotion of pre-natal diagnostic technique for determination of sex shall be appointed as a member of the Advisory Committee.

(8) The Advisory Committee may meet as and when it thinks fit or on the request of the Appropriate Authority for consideration of any application for registration or any complaint for suspension or cancellation of registration and to give advice thereon:

Provided that the period intervening between any two meetings shall not exceed the prescribed period.

(9) The terms and conditions subject to which a person may be appointed to the Advisory Committee and the procedure to be followed by such Committee in the discharge of its functions shall be such as may be prescribed.

Chapter VI

REGISTRATION OF GENETIC COUNSELLING CENTRES, GENETIC LABORATORIES AND GENETIC CLINICS

18. Registration of Genetic Counselling Centers, Genetic Laboratories or Genetic Clinics.—(1) No person shall open any Genetic Counselling Centre, Genetic Laboratory or Genetic Clinic after the commencement of this Act unless such Centre, Laboratory or Clinic is duly registered separately or jointly under this Act.

(2) Every application for registration under sub-section (1), shall be made to the Appropriate Authority in such form and in such manner and shall be accompanied by such fees as may be prescribed.

(3) Every Genetic Counselling Centre, Genetic Laboratory or Genetic Clinic engaged, either partly or exclusively, in counselling or conducting pre-natal diagnostic techniques for any of the purposes mentioned in section 4, immediately before the commencement of this Act, shall apply for registration within sixty days from the date of such commencement.

(4) Subject to the provisions of section 6, every Genetic Counselling Centre, Genetic Laboratory or Genetic Clinic engaged in counseling or conducting pre-natal diagnostic techniques shall cease to conduct any such counseling or technique on the expiry of six months from the date of commencement of this Act unless such Centre, Laboratory or Clinic has applied for registration and is so registered separately or jointly or till such application is disposed of, whichever is earlier.

(5) No Genetic Counselling Centre, Genetic Laboratory or Genetic Clinic shall be registered under this Act unless the Appropriate Authority is satisfied that such Centre, Laboratory or Clinic is in a position to provide such facilities, maintain such equipment and standards as may be prescribed.

19. Certificate of registration.—(1) The Appropriate Authority shall, after holding an inquiry and after satisfying itself that the applicant has complied with all the requirements of this Act and the rules made thereunder and having regard to the advice of the Advisory Committee in this behalf, grant a certificate of registration in the prescribed form jointly or separately to the Genetic Counseling Centre, Genetic Laboratory or Genetic Clinic, as the case may be.

(2) If, after the inquiry and after giving an opportunity of being heard to the applicant and having regard to the advice of the Advisory Committee, the Appropriate Authority is satisfied that the applicant has not complied with the requirements of this Act or the rules, it shall, for reasons to be recorded in writing, reject the application for registration.

(3) Every certificate of registration shall be renewed in such manner and after such period and on payment of such fees as may be prescribed.

(4) The certificate of registration shall be displayed by the registered Genetic Counselling Centre, Genetic Laboratory or Genetic Clinic in a conspicuous place at its place of business.

20. Cancellation or suspension of registration.—(1) The Appropriate Authority may suo moto, or on complaint, issue a notice to the Genetic Counselling Centre, Genetic Laboratory or Genetic Clinic to show cause why its registration should not be suspended or cancelled for the reasons mentioned in the notice.

(2) If, after giving a reasonable opportunity of being heard to the Genetic Counselling Centre, Genetic Laboratory or Genetic Clinic and having regard to the advice of the Advisory Committee, the Appropriate Authority is satisfied that there has been a breach of the provisions of this Act or the rules, it may, without prejudice to any criminal action that it may take against such Centre, Laboratory or Clinic, suspend its registration for such period as it may think fit or cancel its registration, as the case may be.

(3) Notwithstanding anything contained in sub-sections (1) and (2), if the Appropriate Authority is, of the opinion that it is necessary or expedient so to do in the public interest, it may, for reasons to be recorded in writing, suspend the registration of any Genetic Counselling Centre, Genetic Laboratory or Genetic Clinic without issuing any such notice referred to in sub-section (1).

21. Appeal.—The Genetic Counselling Centre, Genetic Laboratory or Genetic Clinic may, within thirty days from the date of receipt of the order of suspension or cancellation of registration passed by the Appropriate Authority under section 20, prefer an appeal against such order to —

(*i*) The Central Government, where the appeal is against the Order of the Central Appropriate Authority; and

(*ii*) The State Government, where the appeal is against the order of the State Appropriate Authority, in the prescribed manner.

Chapter VII

OFFENCES AND PENALTIES

22. Prohibition of advertisement relating to pre-natal determination of sex and punishment for contravention.—(1) No person, organisation, Genetic Counselling Centre, Genetic Laboratory or Genetic Clinic shall issue or cause to be issued any advertisement in any manner regarding facilities of pre-natal determination of sex available at such Centre, Laboratory, Clinic or any other place.

(2) No person or organisation shall publish or distribute or cause to be published or distributed any advertisement in any manner regarding facilities of pre-natal determination of sex available at any Genetic Counselling Centre, Genetic Laboratory, Genetic Clinic or any other place.

(3) Any person who contravenes the provisions of sub-section (1) or sub-section (2) shall be punishable with imprisonment for a term which may extend to three years and with fine which may extend to ten thousand rupees.

Explanation.—For the purposes of this section, "advertisement" includes any notice, circular, label wrapper or other document and also includes any visible representation made by means of any light, sound, smoke or gas.

23. Offences and penalties.—(1) Any medical geneticist, gynaecologist, registered medical practitioner or any person who owns a Genetic Counselling Centre, a Genetic Laboratory or a Genetic Clinic or is employed in such a Centre, Laboratory or Clinic and renders his professional or technical services to or at such a Centre, Laboratory or Clinic, whether on an honorary basis or otherwise, and who contravenes any of the provisions of this Act or rules made thereunder shall be punishable with imprisonment for a term which may extend to three years and with fine which may extend to ten thousand rupees and on any subsequent conviction, with imprisonment which may extend to five years and with fine which may extend to fifty thousand rupees.

(2) The name of the registered medical practitioner who has been convicted by the court under sub-section (1), shall be reported by the Appropriate Authority to the respective State Medical Council for taking necessary action including the removal of his name from the register of the Council for a period of two years for the first offence and permanently for the subsequent offence.

(3) Any person who seeks the aid of a Genetic Counselling Centre, Genetic Laboratory or Genetic Clinic or of a medical geneticist, gynaecologist or registered medical practitioner for conducting pre-natal diagnostic techniques on any pregnant woman (including such woman unless she was compelled to undergo such diagnostic techniques) for purposes other than those specified in clause (2) of section 4, shall, be punishable with imprisonment for a term which may extend to three years and with fine which may extend to ten thousand rupees and on any subsequent conviction with imprisonment which may extend to five years and with fine which may extend to fifty thousand rupees.

24. Presumption in the case of conduct of pre-natal diagnostic techniques.—Notwithstanding anything in the Indian Evidence Act, 1872 (1 of 1872), the court shall presume unless the contrary is proved that the pregnant woman has been compelled by her husband or the relative to undergo pre-natal diagnostic technique and such person shall be liable for abetment of offence under sub-section (3) of section 23 and shall be punishable for the offence specified under that section.

25. Penalty for contravention of the provisions of the Act or rules for which no specific punishment is provided.—Whoever contravenes any of the provisions of this Act or any rules made thereunder, for which no penalty has been elsewhere provided in this Act, shall be punishable with imprisonment for a term which may extend to three months or with fine, which may extend to one thousand rupees or with both and in the case of continuing contravention with an additional fine which may extend to five hundred rupees for every day during which such contravention continues after conviction for the first such contravention.

26. Offences by companies.—(1) Where any offence, punishable under this Act has been committed by a company, every person who, at the time the offence was committed was in charge of, and was responsible to, the company for the conduct of the business of the company, as well as the company, shall be deemed to be guilty of the offence and shall be liable to be proceeded against and punished accordingly:

Provided that nothing contained in this sub-section shall render any such person liable to any punishment, if he proves that the offence was committed without his knowledge or that he had exercised all due diligence to prevent the commission of such offence.

(2) Notwithstanding anything contained in sub-section (1), where any offence punishable under this Act has been committed by a company and it is proved that the offence has been committed with the consent or connivance of, or is attributable to any neglect on the part of, any director, manager, secretary or other officer of the company, such director, manager, secretary or other officer shall also be deemed to be guilty of that offence and shall be liable to be proceeded against and punished accordingly.

Explanation.—For the purposes of this section,—

(*a*) "company" means any body corporate and includes a firm or other association of individuals, and

(*b*) "director", in relation to a firm, means a partner in the firm.

27. Offence to be cognizable, non-bailable and non-compoundable.—Every offence under this Act shall be cognizable, non-bailable and non-compoundable.

28. Cognizance of offences.—(1) No court shall take cognizance of an offence under this Act except on a complaint made by—

(*a*) the Appropriate Authority concerned, or any officer authorised in this behalf by the Central Government or State Government, as the case may be, or the Appropriate Authority; or

(*b*) A person who has given notice of not less than thirty days in the manner prescribed, to the Appropriate Authority, of the alleged offence and of his intention to make a complaint to the court.

Explanation.—For the purpose of this clause, "person" includes a social organisation.

(2) No court other than that of a Metropolitan Magistrate or a Judicial Magistrate of the first class shall try any offence punishable under this Act.

(3) Where a complaint has been made under clause (*b*) of sub-section (1), the court may, on demand by such person, direct the Appropriate Authority to make available copies of the relevant records in its possession to such person.

Chapter VIII

MISCELLANEOUS

29. Maintenance of records.—(1) All records, charts, forms, reports, consent letters and all other documents required to be maintained under this Act and the rules shall be preserved for a period of two years or for such period as may be prescribed:

Provided that, if any criminal or other proceedings are instituted against any Genetic Counselling Centre, Genetic Laboratory or Genetic Clinic, the records and all other documents of such Centre, Laboratory or Clinic shall be preserved till the final disposal of such proceedings.

(2) All such records shall, at all reasonable times, be made available for inspection to the Appropriate Authority or to any other person authorised by the Appropriate Authority in this behalf.

30. Power to search and seize records, etc.—(1) If the Appropriate Authority has reason to believe that an offence under this Act has been or is being committed at any Genetic Counselling Centre, Genetic Laboratory or Genetic Clinic, such Authority or any officer authorised thereof in this behalf may, subject to such rules as may be prescribed, enter and search at all reasonable times with such assistance, if any, as such authority or officer considers necessary, such Genetic Counselling Centre, Genetic Laboratory or Genetic Clinic and examine any record, register, document, book, pamphlet, advertisement or any other material object found therein and seize the same if such Authority or officer has reason to believe that it may furnish evidence of the commission of an offence punishable under this Act.

(2) The provisions of the Code of Criminal Procedure, 1973 (2 of 1974) relating to searches and seizures shall, so far as may be, apply to every search or seizure made under this Act.

31. Protection of action taken in good faith.—No suit, prosecution or other legal proceeding shall lie against the Central or the State Government or the Appropriate Authority or any officer authorised by the Central or State Government or by the Authority for anything which is in good faith done or intended to be done in pursuance of the provisions of this Act.

32. Power to make rules.—(1) The Central Government may make rules for carrying out the provisions of this Act.

(2) In particular and without prejudice, to the generality of the foregoing power, such rules may provide for—

(*i*) the minimum qualifications for persons employed at a registered Genetic Counselling Centre, Genetic Laboratory or Genetic Clinic under clause (1) of section 3;

(*ii*) the form in which consent of a pregnant woman has to be obtained under section 5;

(*iii*) the procedure to be followed by the members of the Central Supervisory Board in the discharge of their functions under sub-section (4) of section 8;

(*iv*) allowances for members other than ex officio members admissible under sub-section (5) of section 9;

(*v*) the period intervening between any two meetings of the Advisory Committee under the proviso to sub-section (8) of section 17;

(*vi*) the terms and conditions subject to which a person may be appointed to the Advisory Committee and the procedure to be followed by such Committee under sub-section (9) of section 17;

(*vii*) the form and manner in which an application shall be made for registration and the fee payable thereof under sub-section (2) of section 18;

(*viii*) the facilities to be provided, equipment and other standards to be maintained by the Genetic Counselling Centre, Genetic Laboratory or Genetic Clinic under sub-section (5) of section 18;

(*ix*) the form in which a certificate of registration shall be issued under sub-section (1) of section 19;

(*x*) the manner in which and the period after which a certificate of registration shall be renewed and the fee payable for such renewal under sub-section (3) of section 19;

(*xi*) the manner in which an appeal may be preferred under section 21;

(*xii*) the period up to which records, charts, etc., shall be preserved under sub-section (1) of section 29;

(*xiii*) the manner in which the seizure of documents, records, objects, etc., shall be made and the manner in which seizure list shall be prepared and delivered to the person from whose custody such documents, records or objects were seized under sub-section (1) of section 30;

(*xiv*) any other matter that is required to be, or may be, prescribed.

33. Power to make regulations.—The Board may, with the previous sanction of the Central Government, by notification in the Official Gazette, make regulations not inconsistent with the provisions of this Act and the rules made thereunder to provide for—

(*a*) the time and place of the meetings of the Board and the procedure to be followed for the transaction of business at such meetings and the number of members which shall form the quorum under sub-section (1) of section 9;

(*b*) the manner in which a person may be temporarily associated with the Board under sub-section (1) of section 11;

(*c*) the method of appointment, the conditions of service and the scales of pay and allowances of the officer and other employees of the Board appointed under section 12;

(*d*) generally for the efficient conduct of the affairs of the Board.

34. Rules and regulations to be laid before Parliament.—Every rule and every regulation made under this Act shall be laid, as soon as may be after it is made, before each House of Parliament, while it is in session, for a total period of thirty days which may be comprised in one session or in two or more successive sessions, and if, before the expiry of the session immediately following the session or the successive sessions aforesaid, both Houses agree in making any modification in the rule or regulation or both Houses agree that the rule or regulation should not be made, the rule or regulation shall thereafter have effect only in such modified form or be of no effect, as the case may be; so, however, that any such modification or annulment shall be without prejudice to the validity of anything previously done under that rule or regulation.

24. The Medical Termination of Pregnancy (Amendment) Act, 2002

(64 of 2002)

(18th December 2002)

An Act to provide for the termination of certain pregnancies by registered Medical Practitioners and for matters connected therewith or incidental thereto.

Be it enacted by Parliament in the Fifty-third Year of the Republic of India as follows:—

1. Short title, extent and commencement.—(1) This Act may be called the Medical Termination of Pregnancy (Amendment) Act, 2002.

(2) It extends to the whole of India except the State of Jammu and Kashmir.

(3) It shall come into force on such date as the Central Government may, by notification in the Official Gazette, appoint.

2. Definitions.—in this Act, unless the context otherwise requires,—

(*a*) "guardian" means a person having the care of the person of a minor or a "mentally ill" (Substituted by Amendment of 2002);

(*b*) "mentally ill person" means a person who is in need of treatment by reason of any mental disorder other than mental retardation;' (Substituted by Amendment of 2002).

(*c*) "minor" means a person who, under the provisions of the Indian Majority Act, 1875 (9 of 1875), is to be deemed not to have attained his majority;

(*d*) "registered medical practitioner" means a medical practitioner who possesses any recognized medical qualification as defined in clause (*h*) of section 2 of the Indian Medical Council Act, 1956 (102 of 1956), whose name has been entered in a State Medical Register and who has such experience or training in gynaecology and obstetrics as may be prescribed by rules made under this Act.

3. When pregnancies may be terminated by registered medical practitioners.—(1) Notwithstanding anything contained in the Indian Penal Code (45 of 1860), a registered medical practitioner shall not be guilty of any offence under that Code or under any other law for the time being in force, if any pregnancy is terminated by him in accordance with the provisions of this Act.

(2) Subject to the provisions of sub-section (4), a pregnancy may be terminated by a registered medical practitioner, —

(*a*) Where the length of the pregnancy does not exceed twelve weeks if such medical practitioner is, or

(*b*) Where the length of the pregnancy exceeds twelve weeks but does not exceed twenty weeks, if not less than two registered medical practitioners are, of opinion, formed in good faith, that—

(*i*) the continuance of the pregnancy would involve a risk to the life of the pregnant woman or of grave injury to her physical or mental health; or

(*ii*) there is a substantial risk that if the child were born, it would suffer from such physical or mental abnormalities to be seriously handicapped.

Explanation 1.—Where any pregnancy is alleged by the pregnant woman to have been caused by rape, the anguish caused by such pregnancy shall be presumed to constitute a grave injury to the mental health of the pregnant woman.

Explanation 2.—Where any pregnancy occurs as a result of failure of any device or method used by any married woman or her husband for the purpose of limiting the number of children, the anguish caused by such unwanted pregnancy may be resumed to constitute a grave injury to the mental health of the pregnant woman.

(3) In determining whether the continuance of a pregnancy would involve such risk of injury to the health as is mentioned in sub-section (2), account may be taken of the pregnant women's actual or reasonable foreseeable environment.

(4) (*a*) No pregnancy of a woman, who has not attained the age of eighteen years, or, who, having attained the age of eighteen years, is a mentally ill (Substituted by Amendment of 2002), shall be terminated except with the consent in writing of her guardian.

(*b*) Save as otherwise provided in clause (*a*), no pregnancy shall be terminated except with the consent of the pregnant woman.

4. Place where pregnancy may be terminated.—No termination of pregnancy shall be made in accordance with this Act at any place other than —

(*a*) a hospital established or maintained by Government, or

(*b*) a place for the time being approved for the purpose of this Act by Government or a District Level Committee constituted by that Government with the Chief Medical Officer or District Health Officer as the Chairperson of the said Committee:

Provided that the District Level Committee shall consist of not less than three and not more than five members including the Chairperson, as the Government may specify from time to time."

5. Sections 3 and 4 when not to apply.—(1) The provisions of section 4, and so much of the provisions of sub-section (2) of section 3 as relate to the length of the pregnancy and the opinion of not less than two registered medical practitioners, shall not apply to the termination of a pregnancy by a registered medical practitioner in a case where he is of opinion, formed in good faith, that the termination of such pregnancy is immediately necessary to save the life of the pregnant woman.

'(2) Notwithstanding anything contained in the Indian Penal Code, the termination of pregnancy by a person who is not a registered medical practitioner shall be an offence punishable with rigorous imprisonment for a term which shall not be less than two years but which may extend to seven years under that Code, and that Code shall, to this extent, stand modified.

(3) Whoever terminates any pregnancy in a place other than that mentioned in section 4, shall be punishable with rigorous imprisonment for a term which shall not be less than two years but which may extend to seven years.

(4) Any person being owner of a place which is not approved under clause (*b*) of section 4 shall be punishable with rigorous imprisonment for a term which shall not be less than two years but which may extend to seven years. (Substituted by Amendment of 2002)

Explanation 1.—For the purposes of this section, the expression "owner" in relation to a place means any person who is the administrative head or otherwise responsible for the working or maintenance of a hospital or place, by whatever name called, where the pregnancy may be terminated under this Act. (Substituted by Amendment of 2002)

Explanation 2.—For the purposes of this section, so much of the provisions of clause (*d*) of section 2 as relate to the possession, by registered medical practitioner, of experience or training in gynaecology and obstetrics shall not apply'. (Substituted by Amendment of 2002)

6. Power to make rules.—(1) The Central Government may, by notification in the Official Gazette, make rules to carry out the provisions of this Act.

(2) In particular, and without prejudice to the generality of the foregoing power, such rules may provide for all or any of the following matters, namely —

(*a*) the experience or training, or both, which is registered medical practitioner shall have if he intends to terminate any pregnancy under this Act; and

(*b*) Such other matters as are required to be or may be, provided by rules made under this Act.

(3) Every rule made by the Central Government under this Act shall be laid, as soon as may be after it is made, before each House of Parliament while it is in session for a total period of thirty days which may be comprised in one session or in two successive sessions, and if, before the expiry of the session in which it is so laid or the session immediately following, both Houses agree in making any modification in the rule or both Houses agree that the rule should not be made, the rule shall thereafter have effect only in such modified form or be of no effect, as the case may be; so, however, that any such modification or annulment shall be without prejudice to the validity of anything previously done under that rule.

7. Power to make regulations.—(1) The State Government may, by regulations —

(*a*) require any such opinion as is referred to in sub-section (2) of section 3 to be certified by a registered medical practitioner or practitioners concerned, in such form and at such time as may be specified in such regulations, and the preservation or disposal of such certificates;

(*b*) require any registered medical practitioner, who terminates a pregnancy, to give intimation of such termination and such other information relating to the termination as may be specified in such regulations;

(*c*) prohibit the disclosure, except to such purposes as may be specified in such regulations, of intimations given or information furnished in pursuance of such regulations.

(2) The intimation given and the information furnished in pursuance of regulations made by virtue of clause (*b*) of sub-section (1) shall be given or furnished, as the case may be, to the Chief Medical Officer of the State.

(3) Any person who willfully contravenes or willfully fails to comply with the requirements of any regulation made under sub-section (1) shall be liable to be punished with fine, which may extend to one thousand rupees.

8. Protection of action taken in good faith.—No suit or legal proceedings shall lie against any registered medical practitioner for any damage caused or likely to be caused by anything, which is in good faith done or intended to be done under this Act.

25. Medical Termination of Pregnancy Regulations, 2003[1]

G.S.R. 486(E).—In exercise of powers conferred by section 7 of the Medical Termination of Pregnancy Act, 1971 (34 of 1971), the Central Government hereby makes the following regulations, namely;

1. Short title, extent and commencement.—(1) These regulations may be called the Medical Termination of Pregnancy Regulations, 2003.

(2) They extend to all the Union territories.

(3) They shall come into force on the date of their publication in the Official Gazette.

2. Definitions.—In these regulations, unless the context otherwise requires,—

(*a*) "Act" means the Medical Termination of Pregnancy Act, 1971 (34 of 1971)

(*b*) "Admission Register" means the register maintained under regulation 5;

(*c*) Chief Medical Officer of the **District** means the Chief Medical Officer of the **District** by whatever name called;

(*d*) "Form" means a form appended to these regulations;

(*e*) "hospital" means a hospital established or maintained by the Central Government or the Government of Union territory;

(*f*) "section" means a section of the Act.

3. Form of certifying opinion or opinions.—(1) Where one registered medical practitioner forms or not less than two registered medical practitioners form such opinion as is referred to in sub-section (2) of section 3 or 5, he or she shall certify such opinion in Form I.

(2) Every registered medical practitioner who terminates any pregnancy shall, within three hours from the termination of the pregnancy certify such termination in Form I.

4. Custody of forms.—(1) The consent given by a pregnant woman for the termination of her pregnancy, together with the certified opinion recorded under section 3 or section 5, as the case may be and the intimation of termination of pregnancy shall be placed in an envelope which shall be sealed by the registered medical practitioner or practitioners by whom such termination of pregnancy was performed and until that envelope is sent to the head of the hospital or owner of the approved place or the Chief Medical Officer of the State, it shall be kept in the safe custody of the concerned registered medical practitioner or practitioners, as the case may be.

(2) On every envelope referred to in sub-regulation (1), pertaining to the termination of pregnancy under section 3, there shall be noted the serial number

---

1 Notification No. GSR 486(E), dated 13-6-2003.

assigned to the pregnant woman in the Admission Register and the name of the registered medical practitioner or practitioners by whom the pregnancy was terminated and such envelope shall be marked "SECRET".

(3) Every envelope referred to in sub-regulation (2) shall be sent immediately after the termination of the pregnancy to the head of the hospital or owner of the approved place where the pregnancy was terminated.

(4) On receipt of the envelope referred to in sub-regulation (3), the head of the hospital or owner of the approved place shall arrange to keep the same in safe custody.

(5) Every head of the hospital or owner of the approved place shall send to the Chief Medical Officer of the State. In Form II a monthly statement of cases where medical termination of pregnancy has been done.

(6) On every envelope referred to in sub-regulation (1), pertaining to the termination of pregnancy under section 5, there shall be noted the name and address of the registered medical practitioner by whom the pregnancy was terminated and the date on which the pregnancy was terminated and such envelope shall be marked "SECRET".

Explanation.—The columns pertaining to the hospital or approved place and the serial number assigned to the pregnant woman in the Admission Register shall be left blank in Form I in the case of termination performed under section 5.

(7) Where the Pregnancy is not terminated in an approved place or hospital, every envelope referred to in sub-regulation (6) shall be sent by registered post to the Chief Medical Officer of the State on the same day on which the pregnancy was terminated or on the working day next following the day on which the pregnancy was terminated:

Provided that where the pregnancy is terminated in an approved place or hospital, the procedure provided in sub-regulations (1) to (6) shall be followed.

5. Maintenance of Admission Register.—(1) Every head of the hospital or owner of the approved place shall maintain a register in Form III for recording there in the details of the admissions of women for the termination of their pregnancies and keep such register for a period of five years from the end of the calendar year it relates to.

(2) The entries in the Admission Register shall be made serially and a fresh serial shall be started at the commencement of each calendar year and the serial number of the particular year shall be distinguished from the serial number of other years by mentioning the year against the serial number, for example, serial number 5 of 1972 and serial number 5 of 1973 shall be mentioned as 5/1972 and 5/1973.

(3) Admission Register shall be a secret document and the information contained therein as to the name and other particulars of the pregnant woman shall not be disclosed to any person.

6. Admission Register not to be open to inspection.—The Admission Register shall be kept in the safe custody of the head of the hospital or owner of the approved place, or by any person authorized by such head or owner and save as otherwise provided in sub-regulation (5) of regulation 4 shall not be open for inspection by any person except under the authority of law:

Provided that the registered medical practitioner on the application of an employed woman whose pregnancy has been terminated, grant a certificate for the purpose of enabling her to obtain leave from her employer:

Provided further that any such employer shall not disclose this information to any other person.

7. Entries in registers maintained in hospital or approved place.—No entry shall be made in any case-sheet, operation theater register, follow-up card or any other document or register other than the admission Register maintained at any hospital or approved place indicating therein the name of the pregnant woman and reference to the pregnant woman shall be made therein by the serial number assigned to the woman in the Admission Register.

FORM I

[*See* Regulation 3]

I____

(Name and qualifications of the Registered Medical practitioner in block letters)

____

(Full address of the Registered Medical practitioner)

I____

(Name and qualifications of the Registered Medical practitioner in block letters)

____

(Full address of the Registered Medical practitioner) hereby certify that *I/We am/are of opinion, formed in good faith, that it is necessary to terminate the pregnancy of

____

(Full name of pregnant women in block letters) resident of

____

(Full address of pregnant women in block letters)

For the reasons given below**.

* I/We hereby give intimation that *I/We terminated the pregnancy of the woman referred to above who bears the serial no. ______________ in the Admission Register of the hospital/approved place.

Place : Signature of the registered Medical Practitioner

Date : Signature of the registered Medical Practitioners

*Strike out whichever is not applicable.

** of the reasons specified items (*i*) to (*v*) write the one which is appropriate.

(*i*) in order to save the life of the pregnant women,

(*ii*) in order to prevent grave injury to the physical and mental health of the pregnant women,

(*iii*) in view of the substantial risk that if the child was born it would suffer from such physical or mental abnormalities as to be seriously handicapped,

(*iv*) as the pregnancy is alleged by pregnant women to have been caused by rape,

(*v*) as the pregnancy has occurred as a result of failure of any contraceptive device or methods used by married woman or her husband for the purpose of limiting the number of children

Note.—Account may be taken of the pregnant women's actual or reasonably foreseeable environment in determining whether the continuance of her pregnancy would involve a grave injury to her physical or mental health.

Place:

Date:

Signature of the Registered Medical Practitioner

Signature of the Registered Medical Practitioners

FORM II

[*See* Regulation 4(5)]

1. Name of the State
2. Name of the Hospital/approved place
3. Duration of pregnancy (give total No. only)
   (*a*) Up to 12 weeks.
   (*b*) Between 12-20 weeks
4. Religion of woman
   (*a*) Hindu
   (*b*) Muslim
   (*c*) Christian
   (*d*) Others
   (*e*) Total
5. Termination with acceptance of contraception.
   (*a*) Sterilization.
   (*b*) I.U.D.
6. Reasons for termination:
   (give total number under each sub-head)
   (*a*) Danger to life of the pregnant woman.

(*b*) Grave injury to the physical health of the pregnant woman.

(*c*) Grave injury to the mental health of the pregnant woman.

(*d*) Pregnancy caused by rape.

(*e*) Substantial risk that if the child was born, it would suffer from such physical or mental abnormalities as to be seriously handicapped.

(*f*) Failure of any contraceptive device or method.

Signature of the Officer
Incharge with Date

FORM III

(*See* Regulation 5)

ADMISSION REGISTER

(To be destroyed on the expiry of five years from the date of the last entry in the Register)

1	2	3	4	5	6	7
S. No.	Date of Admission	Name of the Patient	Wife/Daughter of	Age	Religion	Address

8	9	10	11	12	13	14
Duration of Pregnancy	Reasons on which Pregnancy is terminated	Date of termination of Pregnancy	Date of discharge of patient	Result and Remarks	Name of Registered Medical Practitioner (s) by whom the opinion is formed	Name of Registered Medical Practitioner (s) by whom Pregnancy is terminated

Various Indian Legal Systems Regarding Medical Negligence

With the amendment of 2003 in the Consumer Protection Act, the major significance relates to deficiency in medical services. These amendments have brought the medical services and medical professionals too within the ambit of the Act. Hence it becomes imperative to discuss this particular aspect also in relation to other laws related to consumerism.

With the awareness in the society and the people in general gathering consciousness about their rights, measures for damages in tort, civil suits and criminal proceedings are on the augment. Not only civil suits are filed, the accessibility of a medium for grievance redressal under the Consumer Protection Act, 1986 (CPA), having jurisdiction to hear complaints against medical professionals for 'deficiency in service', has given rise to a large number of complaints against doctors, being filed by the persons feeling aggrieved. The criminal complaints are being filed against doctors alleging commission of offences punishable under section 304A or sections 336/337/338 of the Indian Penal Code, 1860 (IPC) alleging rashness or negligence on the part of the doctors resulting in loss of life or injury of varying degree to the patient. This has given rise to a situation of great distrust and fear among the medical profession and a legal assurance, ensuring protection from unnecessary and arbitrary complaints, is the need of the hour. The liability of medical professionals must be clearly demarcated so that they can perform their benevolent duties without any fear of legal sword. At the same time, justice must be done to the victims of medical negligence and a punitive sting must be adopted in deserving cases. This is more so when the most sacrosanct right to life or personal liberty is at stake.

Nature of Medical Negligence

In the law of negligence, professionals such as lawyers, doctors, architects and others are included in the category of persons professing some special skill or skilled persons generally. Any task which is required to be performed with a special skill would generally be admitted or undertaken to be performed only if the person possesses the requisite skill for performing that task. Any reasonable man entering into a profession which requires a particular level of learning to be called a professional of that branch, impliedly assures the person dealing with him that the skill which he professes shall be exercised with reasonable degree of care and caution. On the same analogy, this assures the patients that a doctor possesses the requisite skill in the medical profession which he is practicing and while undertaking the performance of the task entrusted to him he would be exercising his skill with reasonable competence. Judged by this standard, a professional including medical professional may be held liable for negligence on one of two findings: either he was not possessed of the requisite skill which he professed to have possessed, or, he did not exercise, with reasonable competence in the given case, the skill which he did possess.

The standard to be applied for judging, whether the person charged has been negligent or not, would be that of an ordinary competent person exercising ordinary skill in that profession. It is not necessary for every professional to possess the highest level of expertise in that branch which he practices. Where a profession embraces a range of views as to what is an acceptable standard of conduct, the competence of the professional is to be judged by the lowest standard that would be regarded as acceptable. The test is the standard of the ordinary skilled man exercising and professing to have that special skill. A man need not possess the highest expert skill; it is well established law that it is sufficient if he exercises the ordinary skill of an ordinary competent man exercising that particular art.

Thus, a professional man should command the corpus of knowledge which forms part of the professional equipment of the ordinary member of his profession. He should not lag behind other ordinary assiduous and intelligent members of his profession in knowledge of new advances, discoveries and developments in his field. He should have such awareness as an ordinarily competent practitioner would have of the deficiencies in his knowledge and the limitations on his skill. He should be alert to the hazards and risks in any professional task he undertakes to the extent that other ordinarily competent members of the profession would be alert. He must bring to any professional task he undertakes no less expertise, skill and care than other ordinarily competent members of his profession would bring, but need bring no more.

To establish liability on that basis it must be shown —

(1) that there is a usual and normal practice;

(2) that the defendant has not adopted it; and

(3) that the course in fact adopted is one no professional man of ordinary skill would have taken had he been acting with ordinary care.

A medical practitioner cannot be held liable simply because things went wrong from mischance or misadventure or through an error of judgment in choosing one reasonable course of treatment in preference of another. A medical practitioner would be liable only where his conduct fell below that of the standards of a reasonably competent practitioner in his field. At least three weighty considerations can be pointed out which any forum trying the issue of medical negligence in any jurisdiction must keep in mind. These are: (*i*) that legal and disciplinary procedures should be properly founded on firm, moral and scientific grounds; (*ii*) that patients will be better served if the real causes of harm are properly identified and appropriately acted upon; and (*iii*) that many incidents involve a contribution from more than one person, and the tendency is to blame the last identifiable element in the chain of causation the person holding the 'smoking gun'. Thus, to establish a medical negligence, the abovementioned position must be kept in mind

Criminal Law: Where Negligence Amounts To Crime

The criminal law has invariably placed the medical professionals on a pedestal different from ordinary mortals. The Indian Penal Code, 1860 sets out a few vocal examples. Section 88 in the Chapter on General Exceptions provides exemption for acts not intended to cause death, done by consent in good faith for person's benefit. Section 92 provides for exemption for acts done in good faith for the benefit of a person without his consent though the acts cause harm to a person and that person has not consented to suffer such harm. Section 93 saves from criminality certain communications made in good faith. The rationale behind these provisions is that no man can so conduct himself as to make it absolutely certain that he shall not be so unfortunate as to cause the death of a fellow-creature. The utmost that he can do is to abstain from every thing which is at all likely to cause death.

No fear of punishment can make him do more than this; and therefore, to punish a man who has done this can add nothing to the security of human life. Thus, when a person engaged in the commission of an offence within the meaning of IPC causes death by rashness or negligence, but without either intending to cause death, or thinking it likely that he shall cause death, he should be liable for the punishment of the offence which he was engaged in committing, superadded to the ordinary punishment of involuntary culpable homicide. The involuntary causing of death, without either rashness or negligence, should under no circumstances be punished as murder. The following statement of law on criminal negligence by reference to surgeons, doctors, etc. and unskillful treatment contained in Roscoe's Law of Evidence is classic in this regard:

> "Where a person, acting as a medical man, whether licensed or unlicensed, is so negligent in his treatment of a patient that death results, it is manslaughter if the negligence was so great as to amount to a crime, and whether or not there was such a degree of negligence is a question in each case for the jury. In explaining to juries the test which they should apply to determine whether the negligence in the particular case amounted or did not amount to a crime, judges have used many epithets, such as 'culpable,' 'criminal', 'gross', 'wicked', 'clear', 'complete.' But whatever epithet be used and whether an epithet be used or not, in order to establish criminal liability the facts must be such that, in the opinion of the jury, the negligence of the accused went beyond a mere matter of compensation between subjects and showed such disregard for the life and safety of others as to amount to a crime against the State and conduct deserving punishment."

Deficiency in Services Amounting To Negligence

Practice of medicine is as old as existence of human race. Originally, the priest functioned as preacher, teacher, judge as well as healer. He was the first physician and his relationship with his patients was unique and unquestioned. With the passage of time not only has practice of medicine graduated to become independent and noble profession, but his relationship has slowly shifted from 'Next to God' to 'Friend, Philosopher and Guide', to 'respected professional' and, today, to service provider. With increased consumer awareness, rising expectation, western trend of medical liability litigation, Consumer Protection Act, and judicial activism, increasing number of complaints are being filed by dissatisfied patients resulting in growing distrust between patients and doctors and increased cost of medical treatment.

Over the last fifteen years there has been increased speculation on whether "Medical Services" are expressly or categorically included in the definition of term "services" under section 2(1)(*o*) of the Consumer Protection Act.

In *Indian Medical Association* v *V.P. Shantha*, the principal issue which arose for decision before the Supreme Court was whether a medical practitioner renders 'service' and can be proceeded against for 'deficiency in service' before a forum under the Consumer Protection Act, 1986. The Court dealt with how a 'profession' differs from an 'occupation' especially in the context of performance of duties and hence the occurrence of negligence. The Court noticed that medical professionals do not enjoy any immunity from being sued in contract or tort (i.e. in civil jurisdiction) on the ground of negligence.

However, in the observation made in the context of determining professional liability as distinguished from occupational liability, the Court has referred to authorities, in particular, Jackson & Powell and have so stated the principles, partly quoted from the authorities.

In the matter of professional liability professions differ from occupations for the reason that professions operate in spheres where success cannot be achieved in every case and very often success or failure depends upon factors beyond the professional man's control. In devising a rational approach to professional liability which must provide proper protection to the consumer while allowing for the factors mentioned above, the approach of the Courts is to require that professional men should possess a certain minimum degree of competence and that they should exercise reasonable care in the discharge of their duties. In general, a professional man owes to his client a duty in tort as well as in contract to exercise reasonable care in giving advice or performing services.

The Court held that even though services rendered by medical practitioners are of a personal nature they cannot be treated as contracts of personal service (which are excluded from the Consumer Protection Act). They are contracts for service, under which a doctor too can be sued in Consumer Protection Courts.

A 'contract for service' implies a contract whereby one party undertakes to render services (such as professional or technical services) to another, in which the service provider is not subjected to a detailed direction and control. The provider exercises professional or technical skill and uses his or her own knowledge and discretion. A 'contract of service' implies a relationship of master and servant and involves an obligation to obey orders in the work to be performed and as to its mode and manner of performance. The 'contract of service' is beyond the ambit of the Consumer Protection Act, 1986, under section 2(1)(*o*) of the Act. The Consumer Protection Act will not come to the rescue of patients if the service is rendered free of charge, or if they have paid only a nominal registration fee. However, if patients' charges are waived because of their incapacity to pay, they are considered to be consumers and can sue under the Consumer Protection Act.

Torts Law: Recourse to Claim Compensation

Under civil laws, at a point where the Consumer Protection Act ends, the law of torts takes over and protects the interests of patients. This applies even if medical professionals provide free services. In cases where the services offered by the doctor or hospital do not fall in the ambit of 'service' as defined in the Consumer Protection Act, patients can take recourse to the law relating to negligence under the law of torts and successfully claim compensation. The onus is on the patient to prove that the doctor was negligent and that the injury was a consequence of the doctor's negligence. Such cases of negligence may include transfusion of blood of incorrect blood groups, leaving a mop in the patient's abdomen after operating, unsuccessful sterilisation resulting in the birth of a child, removal of organs without taking consent, operating on a patient without giving anaesthesia, administering wrong medicine resulting in injury, etc

Review of Judicial Pronouncements In India

A review of Indian decisions on medical negligence would be relevant in this regard. In *John Oni Akerele* v *The King a duly* qualified medical practitioner gave to his patient the injection of Sobita which consisted of Sodium Bismuth Tartrate as given in the British Pharmacopoeia. However, what was administered was an overdose of Sobita. The patient died. The doctor was accused of manslaughter, reckless and negligent act. He was convicted. The matter reached in appeal before the House of Lords. Their Lordships quashed the conviction and summed up the position as under:

That a doctor is not criminally responsible for a patient's death unless his negligence or incompetence went beyond a mere matter of compensation between subjects and showed such disregard for life and safety of others as to amount to a crime against the State;

That the degree of negligence required is that it should be gross, and that neither a jury nor a court can transform negligence of a lesser degree into gross negligence merely by giving it that appellation. There is a difference in kind between the negligence which gives a right to compensation and the negligence which is a crime.

It is impossible to define culpable or criminal negligence, and it is not possible to make the distinction between actionable negligence and criminal negligence intelligible, except by means of illustrations drawn from actual judicial opinion. The most favourable view of the conduct of an accused medical man has to be taken, for it would be most fatal to the efficiency of the medical profession if no one could administer medicine without a halter round his neck

The question of degree has always been considered as relevant to a distinction between negligence in civil law and negligence in criminal law. In *Kurban Hussein Mohamedalli Rangawalla* v *State of Maharashtra* while dealing with section 304A of IPC, the following statement of law by Sir Lawrence Jenkins in *Emperor* v *Omkar Rampratap*, was cited with approval:

"To impose criminal liability under section 304A, it is necessary that the death should have been the direct result of a rash and negligent act of the accused, and that act must be the proximate and efficient cause without the intervention of another's negligence. It must be the *causa causans*; it is not enough that it may have been the *causa sine qua non*."

The above said view of the law has been generally followed by High Courts in India. The same view has been reiterated in *Kishan Chand* v *State of Haryana. Juggankhan* v *State of Madhya Pradesh*, the accused, a registered Homoeopath, administered 24 drops of Stramonium and a leaf of Dhatura to the patient suffering from guinea worm. The accused had not studied the effect of such substances being administered to a human being. The poisonous contents of the leaf of dhatura were not satisfactorily established by the prosecution. The Supreme Court exonerated the accused of the charge under section 302, IPC. However, on a finding that stramonium and dhatura leaves are poisonous and in no system of medicine, except perhaps Ayurvedic system, the Dhatura leaf is given as cure for Guinea Worm, the act of the accused who prescribed poisonous material without studying their probable effect was held to be a rash and negligent act. It would be seen that the profession of a Homoeopath which the accused claimed to profess did not permit use of the substance administered to the patient.

The accused had no knowledge of the effect of such substance being administered and yet he did so. In this background, the inference of the accused being guilty of rash and negligent act was drawn against him. Thus the principle which emerges is that a doctor who administers a medicine known to or used in a particular branch of medical profession impliedly declares that he has knowledge of that branch of science and if he does not, in fact, possess that knowledge, he is prima facie acting with rashness or negligence.

Dr. Laxman Balkrishna Joshi v *Dr. Trimbak Bapu Godbole* was a case under Fatal Accidents Act, 1855. The duties which a doctor owes to his patients came up for consideration. The Supreme Court held that a person who holds himself out ready to give medical advice and treatment impliedly undertakes that he is possessed of skill and knowledge for that purpose. Such a person when consulted by a patient owes him certain duties, viz., a duty of care in deciding whether to undertake the case, a duty of care in deciding what treatment to be given or a duty of care in the administration of that treatment. A breach of any of those duties gives a right of action for negligence to the patient.

The practitioner must bring to his task a reasonable degree of skill and knowledge and must exercise a reasonable degree of care. Neither the very highest nor a very low degree of care and competence judged in the light of the particular circumstances of each case is what the law requires. The doctor no doubt has discretion in choosing treatment which he proposes to give to the patient and such discretion is relatively ampler in cases of emergency. In this case, the death of patient was caused due to shock resulting from reduction of the fracture attempted by doctor without taking the elementary caution of giving anesthetic to the patient. The criminal negligence or liability under criminal law was not an issue before the Court as it did not arise and hence was not considered.

In *Poonam Verma* v *Ashwin Patel*, a doctor registered as medical practitioner and entitled to practice in Homoeopathy only, prescribed an allopathic medicine to the patient. The patient died. The doctor was held to be negligent and liable to compensate the wife of the deceased for the death of her husband on the ground that the doctor who was entitled to practice in homoeopathy only, was under a statutory duty not to enter the field of any other system of medicine and since he trespassed into a prohibited field and prescribed the allopathic medicine to the patient causing the death, his conduct amounted to negligence *per se* actionable in Civil Law.

In *Achutrao Haribhau Khodwa* v *State of Maharashtra,* the Supreme Court noticed that in the very nature of medical profession, skills differs from doctor to doctor and more than one alternative course of treatment are available, all admissible. Negligence cannot be attributed to a doctor so long as he is performing his duties to the best of his ability and with due care and caution. Merely because the doctor chooses one course of action in preference to the other one available, he would not be liable if the course of action chosen by him was acceptable to the medical profession. It was a case where a mop was left inside the lady patient's abdomen during an operation. Peritonitis developed which led to a second surgery being performed on her, but she could not survive. Liability for negligence was fastened on the surgeon because no valid explanation was forthcoming for the mop having been left inside the abdomen of the lady. The doctrine of *res ipsa loquitur* was held applicable 'in a case like this'.

In *Dr. Suresh Gupta* v *Govt. of NCT of Delhi* the legal decision is almost firmly established that where a patient dies due to negligent medical treatment of the doctor, the doctor can be made liable in Civil Law for paying compensation and damages in tort and the same time, if the degree of negligence so gross and his act was reckless as to endanger the life of the patient, he would also be made criminally liable to offence under section 304A IPC. "Thus a doctor can not be held criminally responsible for patient's death unless his negligence or incompetence showed such disregard for life and safety of his patient as to amount to a crime against the State".

In the case of *Jacob Mathew* v *State of Punjab* three Judge Bench of Supreme Court by order quashed prosecution of a medical professional under sections 304A/304, IPC and disposed of all the interlocutory applications that doctors should not be held criminally responsible unless there is a *prima facie* evidence before the Court in the form of a credible opinion from another competent doctor, preferably a Government doctor in the same field of medicine supporting the charges of rash and negligent act.

The result of these decisions can be summed up as:

(1) Negligence is the breach of a duty caused by omission to do something which a reasonable man guided by those considerations which ordinarily

regulate the conduct of human affairs would do, or doing something which a prudent and reasonable man would not do. Negligence becomes actionable on account of injury resulting from the act or omission amounting to negligence attributable to the person sued. The essential components of negligence are three: 'duty', 'breach' and 'resulting damage'.

(2) Negligence in the context of medical profession necessarily calls for a treatment with a difference. To infer rashness or negligence on the part of a professional, in particular a doctor, additional considerations apply. A case of occupational negligence is different from one of professional negligence. A simple lack of care, an error of judgment or an accident, is not proof of negligence on the part of a medical professional. So long as a doctor follows a practice acceptable to the medical profession of that day, he cannot be held liable for negligence merely because a better alternative course or method of treatment was also available or simply because a more skilled doctor would not have chosen to follow or resort to that practice or procedure which the accused followed. When it comes to the failure of taking precautions what has to be seen is whether those precautions were taken which the ordinary experience of men has found to be sufficient; a failure to use special or extraordinary precautions which might have prevented the particular happening cannot be the standard for judging the alleged negligence.

(3) A professional may be held liable for negligence on one of the two findings: either he was not possessed of the requisite skill which he professed to have possessed, or, he did not exercise, with reasonable competence in the given case, the skill which he did possess. The standard to be applied for judging, whether the person charged has been negligent or not, would be that of an ordinary competent person exercising ordinary skill in that profession. It is not possible for every professional to possess the highest level of expertise or skills in that branch which he practices.

(4) The jurisprudential concept of negligence differs in civil and criminal law. What may be negligence in civil law may not necessarily be negligence in criminal law. For negligence to amount to an offence, the element of men rea must be shown to exist. For an act to amount to criminal negligence, the degree of negligence should be much higher i.e. gross or of a very high degree. Negligence which is neither gross nor of a higher degree may provide a ground for action in civil law but cannot form the basis for prosecution.

(5) The word 'gross' has not been used in section 304A of IPC, yet it is settled that in criminal law negligence or recklessness, to be so held, must be of such a high degree as to be 'gross'. The expression 'rash or negligent act' as occurring in section 304A of the IPC has to be read as qualified by the word 'grossly'.

(6) To prosecute a medical professional for negligence under criminal law it must be shown that the accused did something or failed to do something which in the given facts and circumstances no medical professional in his ordinary senses and prudence would have done or failed to do. The hazard taken by the accused doctor should be of such a nature that the injury which resulted was most likely imminent.

(7) *Res ipsa loquitur* is only a rule of evidence and operates in the domain of civil law especially in cases of torts and helps in determining the onus of proof in actions relating to negligence. It cannot be pressed in service for determining *per se* the liability for negligence within the domain of criminal law. *Res ipsa loquitur* has, if at all, a limited application in trial on a charge of criminal negligence.

Conclusions

An indiscriminate prosecution of medical professionals for criminal negligence is counter-productive and does no service or good to the society. There must be a link between fault, blame and justice requirements. The learned authors of Errors, Medicine and the Law highlight the link between moral fault, blame and justice in reference to medical profession and negligence. These are of significance and relevant to the issues before us. These are:

(*i*) The social efficacy of blame and related sanctions in particular cases of deliberate wrongdoings may be, a matter of dispute, but their necessity in principle from a moral point of view, has been accepted. Distasteful as punishment may be, the social and possibly moral, need to punish people for wrongdoing, occasionally in a severe fashion, cannot be escaped. If we are constantly concerned about whether our actions will be the subject of complaint, and that such complaint is likely to lead to legal action or disciplinary proceedings, a relationship of suspicious formality between persons is inevitable.

(*ii*) Culpability may attach to the consequence of an error in circumstances where substandard antecedent conduct has been deliberate, and has contributed to the generation of the error or to its outcome. In case of errors, the only failure is a failure defined in terms of the normative standard of what should have been done. There is a tendency to confuse the reasonable person with the error-free person. While nobody can avoid errors on the basis of simply choosing not to make them, people can choose not to commit violations. A violation is culpable.

(*iii*) A correct balance of the interests of the plaintiff and the interests of the defendant should ensure that tort liability is restricted to those cases where there is a real failure to behave as a reasonably competent practitioner would have behaved. An inappropriate rising of the standard of care threatens this balance. While expectations from the professionals must be realistic and the expected standards attainable, this implies recognition of the nature of ordinary human error and human limitations in the performance of complex tasks.

(*iv*) Conviction for any substantial criminal offence requires that the accused person should have acted with a morally blameworthy state of mind. Recklessness and deliberate wrongdoing are morally blameworthy, but any conduct falling short of that should not be the subject of criminal liability. Common-law systems have traditionally only made negligence the subject of criminal sanction when the level of negligence has been high a standard traditionally described as gross negligence. In fact, negligence at that level is likely to be indistinguishable from recklessness.

(*v*) Blame is a powerful weapon. Its inappropriate use distorts tolerant and constructive relations between people. Distinguishing between (*a*) accidents which are life's misfortune for which nobody is morally responsible, (*b*) wrongs amounting to culpable conduct and constituting grounds for compensation, and (*c*) wrongs calling for punishment on account of being gross or of a very high degree requires and calls for careful, morally sensitive and scientifically informed analysis; else there would be injustice to the larger interest of the society.

This may not be understood as holding that doctors can never be prosecuted for an offence of which rashness or negligence is an essential ingredient. There is a need for care and caution in the interest of society; for, the service which the medical profession renders to human beings is probably the noblest of all, and hence there is a need for protecting doctors from frivolous or unjust prosecutions. Such malicious proceedings have to be guarded against and genuine complaints must be ensued with extreme punitive stings. Thus, a complainant has to produce prima facie evidence before the Court to support the charge of rashness or negligence on the part of the accused doctor.

CHAPTER 15

Consumer Sovereignty in India

SYNOPSIS

Consumer sovereignty in the Indian market milieu is virtually a myth. The Indian consumer is only nominally a King, and in reality a person of no consequence. The root causes the average Indian consumer's plight are many: the generally low standard of living, widespread illiteracy, ignorance of the legitimate rights of consumers, lack of sufficient knowledge of the market milieu, and a persistent and negative tendency to resign him to the exploitation in sheer helplessness.

Invariably, consumers are a vulnerable lot for exploitation, more so in a developing country with the prevalence of mass poverty and illiteracy. India too is no exception to it. Instances like overcharging, black marketing, adulteration, profiteering, lack of proper services in trains, telecommunication, water supply, airlines, etc. are not uncommon here. From time to time, the government has attempted to safeguard consumer's interests through legislations and the CPA 1986 is considered as the most progressive statute for consumer protection. Procedural simplicity and speedy and inexpensive redressal of consumer grievances as contained in the CPA are really unique and have few parallels in the world. Implementation of the Act reveals that interests of consumers are better protected than ever before. However, consumer awareness through consumer education and actions by the government, consumer activists and associations are needed the most to make consumer protection movement a success in the country.

Even though strong and clear laws exist in India to protect consumer rights, the actual plight of Indian consumers could be declared as completely dismal. Very few consumers are aware of their rights or understand their basic consumer rights. Of the several laws that have been enacted to protect the rights of consumers in India, the most significant is the Consumer Protection Act, 1986. Under this law, everyone, including individuals, a Hindu undivided family, a firm, and a company, could exercise their consumer rights for the goods and services purchased by them. It is important that, as consumers, we know at least the basis of our rights and about the courts and procedures that deal with the infringements of our rights.

In general, the rights of consumers in India can be listed as under:

- The right to be protected from all types of hazardous goods and services
- The right to be fully informed about the performance and quality of all goods and services
- The right to free choice of goods and services
- The right to be heard in all decision-making processes related to consumer interests
- The right to seek redressal, whenever consumer rights have been infringed
- The right to complete consumer education

A complaint for infringement of consumer rights could be made under the following circumstances in the nearest designated consumer court:

- The goods or services bought by a person or agreed to be bought by a person suffer from one or more deficiencies or defects in any respect
- A trader or a service provider resorted to restrictive or unfair trade practices
- A trader or a service provider charged a price in excess of the price displayed on the goods or the price that had been agreed upon between the parties or the price that had been stipulated under any law in force

- Goods or services that pose a hazard to the safety and life of a person offered for sale, knowingly or unknowingly, causing injury to health, safety or life.

Consumers play a vital role in the economic system of a nation because in the absence of effective demand that emanates from them, the economy virtually collapses. Mahatma Gandhi said, "A consumer is the most important visitor on our premises. He is not dependent on us, we are on him. He is not an interruption to our work; he is the purpose of it. We are not doing a favour to a consumer by giving him an opportunity. He is doing us a favour by giving us opportunity to serve him. But, of late, unfortunately cheating by way of overcharging, black marketing, misleading advertisements, etc has become the common practice of greedy sellers and manufacturers to make unreasonable profits. In this context, it is the duty of the government to confer some rights on consumers to safeguard their interests.

1. Consumer rights

1. ***Right to safety:*** The right to be protected against goods which are hazardous to life and property.
2. ***Right to information:*** The right to be informed about the quality, quantity, purity, price and standards of goods.
3. ***Right to choose:*** The right to be assured access to a variety of products at competitive prices, without any pressure to impose a sale, i.e., freedom of choice.
4. ***Right to be heard:*** The right to be heard and assured that consumer interests will receive due consideration at appropriate forums.
5. ***Right to seek redressal:*** The right to get relief against unfair trade practice or exploitation.
6. ***Right to education:*** The right to be educated about rights of a consumer.

2. Protection of consumer rights

Consumer protection means safeguarding the rights and interests of consumers. It includes all the measures aimed at protecting the rights and interests of consumers.

Consumers need protection due to the following reasons:

1. ***Illiteracy and ignorance:*** Consumers in India are mostly illiterate and ignorant. They do not understand their rights. A system is required to protect them from unscrupulous businessmen.
2. ***Unorganised consumers:*** In India consumers are widely dispersed and are not united. They are at the mercy of businessmen. On the other hand, producers and traders are organized and powerful.
3. ***Spurious goods:*** There is increasing supply of duplicate products. It is very difficult for an ordinary consumer to distinguish between a genuine product and its imitation. It is necessary to protect consumers from such exploitation by ensuring compliance with prescribed norms of quality and safety.

4. ***Deceptive advertising:*** Some businessmen give misleading information about quality, safety and utility of products. Consumers are misled by false advertisement and do not know the real quality of advertised goods. A mechanism is needed to prevent misleading advertisements.
5. ***Malpractices of businessmen:*** Fraudulent, unethical and monopolistic trade practices on the part of businessmen lead to exploitation of consumers. Consumers often get defective, inferior and substandard goods and poor service. Certain measures are required to protect the consumers against such malpractices.
6. ***Freedom of enterprise:*** Businessmen must ensure satisfaction of consumers. In the long run, survival and growth of business is not possible without the support and goodwill of consumers. If business does not protect consumers' interests, Government intervention and regulatory measures will grow to curb unfair trade practices.
7. ***Legitimacy for existence:*** Business exists to satisfy the needs and desires of consumers. Goods are produced with the purpose of selling them. Goods will, in the long run, sell only when they meet the needs of consumers.
8. ***Trusteeship:*** Businessmen are trustees of the society's wealth. Therefore, they should use this wealth for the benefit of people.

3. Consumer awareness

Consumer awareness is about making the consumer aware of his/her rights. It is a marketing term which means that consumers are aware of products or services, its characteristics and the other marketing P's (place to buy, price and promotion). Though the first consumer movement began in England after the Second World War, a modern declaration about consumer's rights was first made in the United States of America in 1962, where four basic consumer rights (choice, information, safety and to be heard) were recognized. Ralph Nadar, a consumer activist, is considered as the father of 'consumer movement'. March 15 is now celebrated as the World Consumer Rights Day. The United Nations in 1985 adopted certain guidelines to achieve the objectives of maintaining protection for consumers and to establish high level ethical conduct for those engaged in production and distribution of goods and services.

High prices, duplicate articles, underweight and under-measurements, rough behaviour, undue conditions, artificial scarcity are some of the ways by which consumers are exploited by manufacturers and traders. Limited information, limited supplies and low literacy are factors causing exploitation of consumers.

According to the Longman Business English Dictionary, consumer awareness is a term used to describe the awareness of a potential or current buyer about a particular product or company. Consumer awareness can be as simple as a shopper remembering a television commercial or as specific as a customer delving into the manufacturing origins of a specific product.

Consumer awareness plays a key role in customer decision making. By increasing a potential or current customer's knowledge about a product, service or business, a healthy economic environment is established in which customers are informed and protected and businesses are accountable.

The need for empowerment of consumers as a class cannot be over emphasized and is already well recognized all over the world. The advancement of technology and advent of sophisticated gadgets in the market and aggressive marketing strategies in the era of globalization have not only thrown open a wide choice, for the consumer but all the same also rendered the consumer vulnerable to a plethora of problems concomitant to such rapid changes. There is an urgent and increasing necessity to educate and motivate the consumer to be wary of the quality of the products, and also the possible deficiencies in the services of the growing sector of public utilities. In short, the consumer should be empowered with respect to his rights as a consumer. He should be equipped to be vigilant with a discerning eye so as to be able to protect himself from any wrongful act on the part of the trader. In order to be able to position the consumer in such a state, there is every need not only to evolve legal remedies but also provide reliable and exhaustive information, which he can access without much effort and expense. Recognizing the importance of the problem, the Government of India and State Government have initiated steps to introduce dispute redressal mechanism by way of Consumer Protection Act, but a lot more has to be done in the area of creating awareness on the part of the consumer to facilitate his seeking suitable remedy wherever there is a need. This becomes more important in the rural areas, where there is wide spread illiteracy.

He should undertake steps to create a facilitative mechanism with the following objectives:

1. Promote General Awareness of the rights of the consumer by encouraging consumer education and supplying information.
2. Publish periodical and product specific booklets, pamphlets, cassettes, CDs, slides, documentary films and other devices of mass communication for promoting consumer awareness in English and regional languages, highlighting the problem in specified areas like real estate, public utilities, non-banking financial agencies, etc.
3. Enlighten the business community on its ethical and legal obligations to maintain quality of the products or services and to be transparent in dealing with consumers.
4. Encourage consumer activities to strengthen the existing institutional set up of consumer dispute redressal by acting as a facilitator between consumer and the institution.
5. Study the available legal remedies, analyze and suggest new measures for the effective and better consumer protection.
6. Bring together the consumer, traders and policy makers to exchange information of mutual interest for better coordination. Bring together the

NGO's/Consumer activities operating in different areas and equip them with suitable and required information and knowledge to enable them to act as nodal agents of change in rural areas.

7. Organize and conduct seminars, workshops and group discussions and thus provide a platform for threadbare discussion of the issues and evolve suitable remedial action. Conduct motivational campaigns for groups of potential customers both in urban and rural areas.
8. Coordinate programmes organized by Central and State Governments, State Legal Aid Authorities, Academic Institutes, National and International Consumer Organizations.
9. Periodic interaction with electronic & print media on success stories of consumers.
10. Establish links with educational institutions like universities, colleges, high schools to emphasize the need for improving consumer education in the curriculum. Consumer clubs would go a long way in achieving this.
11. Interact with national level organizations like NISIET, NIRD, ASCI, etc. to explore possible collaboration and organize awareness programmes for their clientele and undertake research projects.
12. Organize a database enabling the consumer retrieve the required information in a less expensive and quick way. Set up a website to publish information, news including judgments, articles, on product analysis and related matters for the guidance of consumers to have informed choice of product services, redressal agencies and mechanisms.

4. Consumer awareness: Rights & responsibilities

Liberalisation is paving way for a market-driven economy, where the manufacturers seek to maximise profits. Manufacturers are not often concerned about the quality of goods and services and their impact on the health of people and the environment. Instead of the consumer guiding the producer about what should be produced, it is the producer who decides what the consumer should want. The plight of a consumer is further worsened by the use of advertising techniques. Consumers are saddled with the problem of choosing between too many products with too less information. With the concentration of market in the hands of a few large corporations, it becomes important that the consumers are aware of their rights in order to ensure proper standards for the goods and services for which they make payment.

There are many goods which are sold in the market without much information about their quality, quantity and purity. In case of goods meant for mass consumption like, food, milk products, edible oil, etc. the ingredients are not known. Manufacturers or producers seldom follow the safety regulations in the products like, lamps, batteries, footwear, electrical equipments, wires, cement, LPG cylinders, stoves, switches, plugs, sockets, etc. leading to many fatal accidents. Adulteration of food is another major problem. Milk can contain detergent, refined oil, caustic soda or urea. Mustard oil can be adulterated with argemone oil and arhar dal with yellow colour. Vegetables and fruits are artificially coloured. Indiscriminate use of pesticides by farmers and untreated effluents by industries, have led to the problem of food contamination by pesticide residues and toxic heavy metals.

Although in Kautilya's Arthashastra, strict rules were set for the trade and industry and punishments for exploitation were prescribed. But, there was no organised and systematic movement safeguarding the interests of the consumers in India. Rampant food shortages, hoarding, black marketing, adulteration of food and edible oil gave birth to the consumer movement in an organised form in the sixties. Consumers started voicing their concerns and demanding better products and services. Till mid seventies, consumer organisations were largely engaged in writing articles and holding exhibitions. They formed consumer groups to work on the malpractices in ration shops and overcrowding in the road passenger transport. The eighties witnessed an upsurge in the number of consumer groups.

Consumers have the social responsibility of exposing the manufacturer/ supplier or the service provider for resorting to illegal trade practices. Unethical notings like "Goods once sold will never be taken back" are in sharp contrast to the practice in some of the developed countries, where the sellers declare, "In case you are not fully satisfied with our product, you can bring the same to us within a month for either replacement or return of your money."

This is the result of consumer consciousness. Consumers have to realize their role and importance. The consumer movements can be winner movements only with our active involvement by knowing our rights and enforcing them. It requires a voluntary effort involving the participation of one and all. If the consumers remain passive, they will continue to be exploited. It is necessary that consumers take action with solidarity to get a fair deal and timely redressal. An alert consumer is a safe consumer.

Consumer protection laws are designed to ensure fair competition and the free flow of truthful information in the marketplace. The laws are designed to prevent businesses that engage in fraud or specified unfair practices from gaining an advantage over competitors and may provide additional protection for the weak and those unable to take care of themselves. Consumer Protection laws are a form of government regulation which protects the interests of consumers. For example, a government may require businesses to disclose detailed information about products — particularly in areas where safety or public health is an issue, such as food. Consumer protection is linked to the idea of "consumer rights" (that consumers have various rights as consumers), and to the formation of consumer organizations which help consumers make better choices in the marketplace.

Consumer is defined as someone who acquires goods or services for direct use or ownership rather than for resale or use in production and manufacturing.

Consumer interests can also be protected by promoting competition in the markets which directly and indirectly serve consumers, consistent with economic efficiency, but this topic is treated in Competition law.

Consumer protection can also be asserted *via* non-government organizations and individuals as consumer activism.

The Consumer Protection Act, 1986 and various other laws like the Standards, Weights & Measures Act have been formulated to ensure fair competition in the market place and free flow of true information from the providers of goods and services to those who consume them. However, the success of these laws would depend upon the vigilance of consumers about their rights, as well as their responsibilities. In fact, the level of consumer protection in a country is considered as the correct indicator of the extent of progress of the nation.

The production and distribution systems have become larger and more complicated today. The high level of sophistication achieved by the providers of goods and services in their selling and marketing practices and various types of promotional activities like advertising resulted in an increased need for higher consumer awareness and protection. In India, the government has realized the plight of Indian consumers and the Ministry of Consumer Affairs, Food and Public Distribution established the Department of Consumer Affairs as the nodal organization for the protection of consumer rights, redressal of all consumer grievances and promotion of standards governing goods and services offered in India.

5. Methods of consumer protection

There are four main methods of protecting the interests of consumers:

1. ***Business self-regulation:*** The business community itself can help in achieving consumer protection and satisfaction through self-discipline. Businessmen can regulate their own behaviour and actions by adopting higher ethical standards. Trade associations and chambers of commerce can check unfair trade practices used by some businessmen.
2. ***Consumer self-help:*** Every consumer must be alert as self-help is the best help. He should educate himself and know his rights. He should not allow unscrupulous businessmen to cheat him.
3. ***Consumers' Associations:*** Consumers should form voluntary associations. These associations can educate and awaken consumers. They can take organized action and put pressure on businessmen to adopt fair trade practices.
4. ***Government Regulations:*** The State can ensure consumer protection through legislative, executive and judicial actions. The laws enacted by the Government must be strictly enforced by the executive. Government of India has enacted several laws to protect the interests and rights of consumers. Some of these laws are as follows:

    (*a*) The Essential Commodities Act, 1955 which aims to regulate and control the production, supply and distribution and prices of essential commodities.

(*b*) The Prevention of Food Adulteration Act, 1954 which aims to check adulteration in food items and eatables.

(*c*) The Drugs and Cosmetics Act, 1940 which seeks to ensure purity and quality in drugs and cosmetics.

(*d*) The Standards of Weights and Measures Act, 1956 which aims at ensuring that consumers get the right weight and measurement in products.

(*e*) The Household Electrical Appliances (Quality Control) Order, 1976 which seeks to ensure safety and quality in the manufacture of electrical appliances.

(*f*) The Consumer Protection Act, 1986 which seeks to provide speedy and inexpensive redressal to the grievances of consumers.

6. Historical evolution of Consumer Protection Law in India

In this age of consumers, the regime of Indian consumer law will undoubtedly rule Indian markets and bestow a new phase on the existing Indian legal structure with its strong ancient legal foundations.

Consumer Protection has its deep roots in the rich soil of Indian civilization, which dates back to 3200 B.C. In ancient India, human values were cherished and ethical practices were considered of great importance. However, the rulers felt that the welfare of their subjects was the primary area of concern. They showed keen interest in regulating not only the social conditions but also the economic life of the people, establishing many trade restrictions to protect the interests of buyers. This article examines the historical perspective of consumer protection in India from the Vedic age (ancient period) to the modern period. 5000B.C. to 2500 B.C. though different versions give different dates for the actual period of the *Vedic* age. However, it is said that "The Vedic age in India which is considered to be the first literary source of civilization, is seen as a glorious period of cultural evolution in the ancient world. The Vedas are not books of law but are the repository of culture delineating the feelings and habits of the people of the time which indicate and give vivid ideas of legal concepts in a developed civilization." *Veda* means knowledge. There are four *Vedas*: the *Rigveda,* the *Yajurveda,* the *Samaveda* and the *Atharvaveda.*

7. Consumer protection in ancient India: A historical perspective

In ancient India, all sections of society followed *Dharma-sastras* ("*Dharma*") Codes of Morals. They also deal with the rules of conduct, law and customs, which laid out social rules and norms, and served as the guiding principle governing human relations. The principles of *Dharma* were derived from *Vedas. Vedas* were considered the words of God, and law was said to have divine origin which was transmitted to society through sages. Thus, *Vedas* were the primary sources of law in India.

Many writers and commentators of the ancient period documented the living conditions of the people through their innovative and divine writings, including *Smriti* (tradition) and *sruti* (revelation), and also prescribed codes to guide the kings and rulers about the method of ruling the State and its subjects. Consumer protection was also a major concern in their writings.

Among the *Dharmas*, the most authoritative texts are:—

(*a*) the *Manu Smriti* (800 B.C. to 600 B.C.);

(*b*) the *Yajnavalkya Smriti* (300 B.C. to 100 B.C);

(*c*) the *Narada Smriti* (100 A.D to 200 A.D.);

(*d*) the *Bruhaspati Smriti* (200A.D. to 400 A.D.); and

(*e*) the *Katyayana Smriti* (300 A.D. to 600 A.D).

Among these, *Manu Smriti* was the most influential.

7.1 Manu Smriti

Manu Smriti describes the social, political and economic conditions of ancient society. Manu, the ancient law giver, also wrote about ethical trade practices. It is interesting to note that Manu was the first to write about the eighteen heads or titles of litigation and matters pertaining to buyers and consumers, including money lending, deposits and pledges, sale without ownership of property, non-performance of contracts and breach of contract of sale, etc. He prescribed a code of conduct to traders and specified punishments to those who committed certain crimes against buyers. For example, he referred to the problem of adulteration and said "one commodity mixed with another must not be sold (as pure), nor a bad one (as good) not less (than the property quantity or weight) nor anything that is at hand or that is concealed." The punishment "for adulterating unadulterated commodities and for breaking gems or for improperly boring (them)" was the least harsh.. Severe punishment was prescribed for fraud in selling seed corn: "he who sells (for seed-corn that which is) not seed-corn, he who takes up seed (already sown) and he who destroys a boundary (mark) shall be punished by mutilation." Interestingly, Manu also specified the rules of competency for parties to enter into a contract. He said "a contract made by a person intoxicated or insane or grievously disordered (by disease and so forth) or wholly dependent, by an infant or very aged man, or by an unauthorized (party) is invalid."

During the ancient period, the king had the power to confiscate the entire property of a trader in two instances: (1) when the king had a monopoly over the exported goods; and (2) when the export of the goods was forbidden. There was also a mechanism to control prices and punish wrongdoers. The king fixed the rates for the purchase and sale of all marketable goods. Manu said "man who behaves dishonestly to honest customers or cheats in his prices shall be fined in the first or in the middle most amercement." There was a process to inspect all weights and measures every six months and the results of these inspections were duly noted.

All these measures show how effective ancient society was in regulating the many wrongs of the market place. These measures also show how developed the system was in identifying the market strategies of traders. Thus, *Manu Smriti* effectively dealt with various consumer matters, many of which remain of great concern in modern legal systems.

7.2 Kautilya's Arthasastra

Written subsequent to *Manu Smriti*, Kautilya's *Arthasastra* (400 B.C. to 300 B.C) is considered to be a treatise and a prominent source, describing various theories of statecraft and the rights and duties of subjects in ancient society. Though its primary concern is with matters of practical administration, consumer protection occupies a prominent place in *Arthasastra*. It describes the role of the State in regulating trade and its duty to prevent crimes against consumers.

Between 400 and 300 B.C., there was a director of trade whose primary responsibility was to monitor the market situations. Additionally, the director of trade was made responsible for fair trade practices. The director of trade was required to be "conversant with the differences in the prices of commodities of high value and of low value and the popularity or unpopularity of goods of various kinds whether produced on land or in water [and] whether they... arrived along land-routes or water-routes, [and] also [should know about] suitable times for resorting to dispersal or concentration, purchase or sale." The director of trade advised to "Avoid even a big profit that would be injurious to the subjects.... He should not create a restriction as to time or the evil of a glut in the market in the case of commodities constantly in demand."

During this period, several measures were taken to maintain official standards of weights and measures. Kautilya observed: "The superintendent of standardization should cause factories to be established for the manufacture of standard weights and measures." He further said "[the superintendent] should cause a stamping [of the weights and measures] to be made every four months. The penalty for unstamped [weights] is twenty-seven *panas* and a quarter. [Traders] shall pay a stamping fee amounting to one *kakani* every day to the superintendent of standardization."

According to Kautilya, 'the trade guilds were prohibited from taking recourse to black marketing and unfair trade practice." Severe punishments were prescribed for different types of cheating. For example, "for cheating with false cowrie-shells, dice, leather straps, ivory-cubes or by sleight of hand, [the punishment shall be] cutting-off of one hand or a fine." The rights of the traders were also well protected. Kautilya said, "On the subject of the return of an article purchased or payment of price thereof, there was fixed rule of time, after which an article could not be returned."

During Chandragupta's period, (Chandragupta Maurya ranks as one of the India's greatest rules. The period dates back to 323 B.C.) in which Kautilya lived, good trade practices were prevalent. For example, "Goods could not be sold at the place of their origin, field or factory. They were to be carried to the appointed markets (*panya sala*) where the dealer had to declare particulars as to the quantity, quality and the prices of his goods which were examined and registered in the books." Every trader was required to take a license to sell. A trader from outside had to obtain permission. The superintendent of commerce fixed the whole-sale prices of goods as they entered the Customs House. He allowed a margin of profit to fix retail prices. Speculation and cornering to influence prices were prohibited. Thus, the State bore a heavy responsibility for protecting the public against unfair prices and fraudulent transactions. There were severe punishments for smuggling and adulteration of goods. For example, public health was guarded by punishing adulteration of food products of all kinds, including grains, oils, alkalies, salts, scents and medicines.

Also during Chandragupta's period, (Chandragupta Maurya ranks as one of the India's greatest rules. The period dates back to 323 B.C.), easy access to justice for all, including consumers, was considered of great importance. The king was the central power to render justice. According to Kautilya, "The king should look to the complaints of the people [of the town and village] in the second part of the day. The mobile and circuit courts worked at night, when necessity arose. They also must have worked on holidays in urgent matters." The king was required to pay full attention to the truth and he was primarily responsible for administering justice. Everyone could approach the king's court for justice. However, standing was strictly followed. The king only entertained cases if the aggrieved presented a valid complaint. The king was directed not to "foster litigation by starting an action without a complainant, and moreover, [the king was told that] no complaint should be taken notice of when it proceeded from a person altogether unconnected with the person aggrieved." In addition to this, different set of courts were prevalent in ancient India.

The court system during Kautilya's time was well organized. There were two different benches comprising judges and magistrates to try civil and criminal cases. In civil matters, the judges themselves were empowered to take cognizance of the cases of disadvantaged persons who could not approach the court, for example, the cases concerning ascetics, women, and minors, old, sick and helpless people. Thus, rendering justice was regarded as one of the essential duties of the rulers, and care was taken to ensure that justice was accessible to all. Indeed, this emphasis on justice for all remains a cornerstone of India's legal system.

8. Consumer protection in medieval and modern periods

In the medieval period, consumer protection continued to be of prime concern of the rulers. During Muslim rule, a large number of units of weights were used in India. During the Sultanate period, the prices used were determined by local conditions. During the rule of Alauddin Khilji, strict controls were established in the market place. In those days, there was unending supply of grain to the city and grain-carriers sold at prices fixed by the Sultan. There was a mechanism for price-enforcement in the market. Similarly, shop-keepers were punished for under-weighing their goods.

In the modern period, the British system replaced the age old traditional legal system of India. However, one of the outstanding achievements of British rule in India was "the formation of a unified nationwide modern legal system. During the British period, from 1600 to 1947. The Regulating Act of 1773 was passed by the British Parliament and one of its objectives was to bring the management of the East India Company under the control of the British Parliament and British Crown., the Indian legal system was totally revolutionized and the English legal system was introduced to administer justice. However, it is important to note that the traditions and customs of the Indian legal system were not ignored. "The law itself underwent considerable adaptation. The British institutions and rules were combined with structural features [e.g. a system of separate personal laws] and rules [e.g. *Dharma,* and local custom] which accorded with indigenous understanding. The borrowed elements underwent more than a century and a half of pruning in which British localisms and anomalies were discarded and rules [were] elaborated to deal with new kinds of persons, property and transactions." To administer justice, "they were confronted [with] the problem of the value suitable to attach in practice to the [Indian traditions and customs]." Despite the challenges of combining the British and Indian legal systems, "the fabric of modern Indian Law... is unmistakably Indian in its outlook and operation" and consumer protection is not an exception to this perception.

Some of the laws which were passed during the British regime concerning consumer interests are: the Indian Contract Act of 1872, the Sale of Goods Act of 1930, the Indian Penal Code of 1860, the Drugs and Cosmetics Act of 1940, the Usurious Loans Act of 1918, and the Agriculture Procedure (Grading and Marketing Act) of 1937. These laws provided specific legal protection for consumers.

For fifty-five years, the Sale of Goods Act of 1930 [SGA] was the exclusive source of consumer protection in India. The SGA, drafted with precision, is "an admirable piece of legislation." It is also praised as a "Consumer's Charter." The main protection for the buyer against the seller for defective goods is found in section 16 of the Act. Section 16 of Sale of Goods Act says " Subject to the provisions of this Act and of any other law for the time being in force, there is no implied warranty or condition as to the quality or fitness for any particular purpose of goods supplied under a contract of sale, except as follows:

(1) Where the buyer, expressly or by implication, makes known to the seller the particular purpose for which goods are required, so as to show the that the buyer relies on the seller's skill or judgment and the goods are of a description which it is in the course of the seller's business to supply (whether he is the manufacturer or producer or not), there is an implied condition that the goods shall be reasonably fit for such purpose:

Provided that, in the case of a contract for the sale of a specified article under its patent or other trade name, there is no implied condition as to its fitness for any particular purpose.

(2) Where the goods are bought by description from a seller who deals in goods of that description (whether he is the manufacturer or producer or not), there is an implied condition that the goods shall be of merchantable quality:

Provided that, if the buyer has examined the goods, there shall be no implied condition as regards defects which such examination ought to have revealed.

(3) An implied warranty or condition as to quality or fitness for a particular purpose may be annexed by the usage of trade.

(4) An express warranty or condition does not negative a warranty or condition implied by this Act unless inconsistent therewith. Sale of Goods Act, No. 3 of 1930; India Code (1930), ch. 2 § 16.

It provides exceptions to the principle of *Caveat emptor* ("let the buyer beware") and the interests of the buyer are sufficiently safeguarded. Phrases such as "skill and judgment of the seller", "reliance on sellers' skill", and the test of "merchantable quality" provide effective remedies to buyers. Courts interpreted these rules in the consumer's favor. The SGA was the exclusive consumer legislation until 1986, with the passage of the Consumer Protection Act of 1986, designed to supplement the remedies already provided under the SGA.

Consumer protection was also provided within India's criminal justice system. The Indian Penal Code of 1860 has a number of provisions to deal with crimes against consumers. It deals with offenses related to the use of false weights and measures, the sale of adulterated food or drinks, the sale of noxious food or drink, and the sale of adulterated drugs.

Consumer protection legislation enacted after India's independence from Britain include: the Essential Commodities Act of 1955, the Prevention of Food Adulteration Act of 1954 and the Standard of Weights and Measures Act of 1976. A benefit of these Acts is that they do not require the consumer to prove *mens rea.* Rather, "the offenses are of strict liability, and not dependent on any particular intention or knowledge." Criminal law in the field of consumer protection has acquired much significance, as consumers are less inclined to go to civil court for small claims. It has been said that "the functional value of criminal law in the field of consumer protection is a high one and it has a respectable pedigree." Another view is that there has been an attempt to look at consumer protection as "a public interest issue rather than as a private issue" to be left to individuals for settlement in court.

In addition to the remedies under contract and criminal law, consumers have rights under tort law. Based on its numerous legal intricacies, however, tort law is not the ideal remedy for injured consumers in India. For example, the traditional doctrine of negligence imposes heavy responsibility on the plaintiff to prove each of its required elements. These traditional legal requirements naturally encourage injured consumers to pursue legal remedies under different laws. Not surprisingly, it is estimated that for about half a century from 1914 to 1965, only 613 tort cases came before the appellate courts.

The orthodox legal requirements under the law of torts and contracts forced the policy makers to craft specific legislation to protect consumers. As a result, the Consumer Protection Act of 1986 was enacted with the objective of providing "cheap, simple and quick" justice to Indian consumers. It is said, due to the congestion of courts with heavy arrears, it may take 5 to 15 years for a claimant to wade through the different levels of courts in tort litigation in India.

9. The Indian Consumer Protection Act of 1986 and the evolution of a new legal culture

The Indian legal system experienced a revolution with the enactment of the Consumer Protection Act of 1986 ["CPA"], which was specifically deigned to protect consumer interests. The CPA was passed with avowed objectives. It is intended to provide justice which is "less formal, [and involves] less paper work, less delay and less [expense]". The CPA has received wide recognition in India as poor man's legislation, ensuring easy access to justice. However, the CPA simply gives a new dimension to rights that have been recognized and protected since the ancient period. It is rightly said that "the present-day concern for consumer rights... is not new and that consumer's rights like the right to have safe, unadulterated and defect-free commodities at appropriate prices has been recognized since ancient times."

Four decades of experience with the operation of the CPA shows its popular acceptance and the legal preference of injured consumers to enforce their rights under it. The CPA commands the consumer's support because of its cost-effectiveness and user-friendliness. In fact, the CPA creates a sense of legal awareness among the public and at the same time, brings disinterest to approach traditional courts, especially on consumer matters. It has changed the legal mindset of the public and made them think first of their remedies under the CPA, regardless of the nature of their case. In short, the CPA has instilled confidence among the "teeming millions" of impoverished litigants. The way in which the consumer Fora are flooded with cases and the mode in which these cases are being disposed off creates an impression of "judicial populism" in India in the arena of consumer justice.

The greatness of the CPA lies in its flexible legal framework, wider jurisdiction and inexpensive justice. One can find in the CPA a mixture of principles of torts and contracts. Simply speaking, it is "a shorthand term to indicate all the many different aspects of general law." Basically, the CPA liberalizes the strict traditional rule of standing and empowers consumers to proceed under the CPA. Consumer groups, the central or any state government are all empowered to lodge complaints under the CPA. This liberalization shows the care that has been taken to represent and fight for the cause of weak, indifferent and illiterate consumers. The novelty of the CPA is the inclusion of both goods and services within its ambit. The consumer can bring suit for defective products as well as for deficiency of services. In the event of any deficiency, all services, whether provided by the government or private companies, can be questioned under the CPA.

The CPA also liberalized rigid procedural requirements and introduced simple and easy methods of access to justice. To proceed under the CPA, the consumer need only pay a nominal fee and need not send any notices to the opposite party. A simple letter addressed to the consumer forum draws enough attention to initiate legal action. Another major procedural flexibility is the option the consumer has to engage a lawyer. If the consumer prefers, he can represent himself. The simple measures of action drive consumers to avail themselves of the benefits of the CPA.

The CPA initiated a legal revolution by ushering in the era of consumers and developing a new legal culture among the masses to take recourse under the CPA regardless of their grievance. The Consumer Disputes Redressal agencies, the National Commission, the State Commission and the District Fora are working together in a way that is revolutionizing the present Indian legal system and challenging the traditional system of delivering justice. With easy access to the courts guaranteed by the CPA, consumers now wage legal battles against unscrupulous traders or service providers without any hesitation. The Indian government is also taking an active interest in protecting consumer rights and promoting effective consumer movements. In 2003, the Planning Commission of India identified "Consumer Awareness, Redressal and Enforcement of the Consumer Protection Act of 1986" as a priority, and as a result, a national action plan was prepared.

The Consumer Fora created by the CPA have proven to be effective, disposing of thousands of cases with few legal formalities and leading the way toward well-founded consumer jurisprudence in India. The traditional Indian legal system, in addition to a huge backlog of cases, is experiencing a litigation explosion in the area of consumer protection. According to one report, the total number of consumer cases pending in different fora was 359,469 cases as of June, 2004.[60] Around 45,798 cases have been filed before the national commission since its inception. At present, 8,884 cases are pending disposal. The huge backlog of consumer cases before consumer Fora is forcing the Indian legal systems to think of "alternatives" for speedy disposal of consumer cases. India, home to the majority of the world's consumers, is committed to working for the welfare of consumers through new legal innovations.

Consumer protection is always a matter of great concern. In ancient India, effective measures were initiated to protect consumers from crimes in the market place. Ancient law givers ably described various kinds of unfair trade practices and also prescribed severe punishments for wrong-doers. Mainly, acts of adulteration and false weights and measures were seriously dealt with. In ancient India, the king was the supreme authority to render justice, but his authority was circumscribed by the rules of *Dharma*. In the medieval period, some Muslim rulers developed well organized market mechanisms to monitor prices and the supply of goods to the markets. During the British period, the modern legal system was introduced in India and many laws were enacted to protect the interests of consumers generally. Today, the civil justice system is tainted with deficiencies that discourage the consumer from seeking legal recourse. However, the Consumer Protection Act of 1986, which provides easy access to justice, has brought a legal revolution to India as a result of its cost-effective mechanisms and popular support. At the same time, these mechanisms pose a great legal challenge to the traditional courts which conduct litigation in orthodox ways. In this age of consumers, the regime of Indian consumer law will undoubtedly rule Indian markets and bestow a new phase on the existing Indian legal structure with its strong ancient legal foundations.

10. The Consumer Protection Act, 1986

The Act provides following remedies to an aggrieved consumer:

1. Removal of defects in goods or deficiency in service.
2. Replacement of defective goods with new goods of similar description which shall be free from any defect.
3. Return of price paid by the consumer.
4. Payment of compensation for any loss or injury suffered by the consumer.
5. Discontinue the restrictive, or unfair trade practice, and not to repeat it.
6. Withdraw the hazardous goods from being offered for sale and not to offer them for sale.
7. Provide for adequate cost to the aggrieved party.

The Consumer Production Act provides for a three-tier system of redressal agencies: one at district level known as District Forum, second at state level known as 'State Commission', and third at national level known as 'National Commission'. A complaint is to be made to the district forum of the concerned district where the value of goods and services and compensation, if any, is up to ₹20 lakhs, to the 'State Commission' between ₹20 lakhs and ₹100 lakhs, and to the National Commission for more than ₹100 lakhs. Interestingly, there is provision for appeals against the orders of a particular redressal forum by the aggrieved party before the next higher echelon and even from the findings of the National Commission before the Supreme Court.

In India, the concept of consumer protection is not new. References to the protection of consumer's interest against exploitation by trade and industry, underweight and measurement, adulteration and punishment for these offences, were made in Kautilya's 'Arthashastra'. However, an organized and systematic movement to safeguard the interest of consumers, is a recent phenomenon. The consumers have to be aware not only of the commercial aspects of sale and purchase of goods, but also of the health and security aspects. Food safety has become an important element of consumer awareness these days. In case of food products, its quality depends not only on its nutritional value, but also on its safety for human consumption. Consumption of contaminated or adulterated food is a major cause of human illness and suffering.

This called for strong legal measures to ensure that the manufacturers and sellers observe uniformity and transparency in prices, stocks and quality of their goods. Enactment of Consumer Protection Act, 1986 was one of the most important steps taken to protect the interests of consumers. The provision of the

Act came into force, with effect from July 1, 1987. The Act recognizes consumer's right to seek redresses and right to consumer education. The salient features of the Act are as follows:—

- Applies to all goods and services unless specifically exempted by the Union Government;
- Covers all the sectors whether private, public or cooperative;
- Enshrines the consumer's rights related to safety, information, choice, representation and redress and consumer education;
- The Act gives consumers an additional remedy besides those which may be available to them under the provisions of other existing laws and they are free to choose the remedy;
- Empower consumers seeking discontinuance of certain unfair and restrictive trade practices, defects or deficiencies in services and stopping in services or withdrawal of hazardous goods from the market.

There are no legal formalities for filing the complaint. Suppose, you find yourself cheated by trader or a manufacturer and wish to make a complaint to consumer court, you can write the details on a plain paper. Attach the supporting documents, that is, guarantee or warrantee card and cash memo with the complaint and submit it in the district consumer court. You do not have to go to any lawyer or professional for legal assistance. You yourself can plead the case in the Consumer Court. Since, the enactment of the Consumer Protection Act and even before that, newspapers and magazines have been responding to the needs of consumers. Apart from publishing articles, columns, etc. newspapers have also tried to come to the rescue of harassed consumers. The Indian Express was one of the first newspapers to start a consumer complaint column.

There are 500 consumer associations, which are working in the field of consumer protection. They deal with various aspects of consumer exploitation. Some of the prominent ones are: Consumer Guidance Society of India, Mumbai; Citizens Action Group, Mumbai; Common Cause, New Delhi; Voice, New Delhi; Consumer Utility and Trust Society, Jaipur.

So next times you find yourself at the wrong end of a purchase don't just sit back and blame, go to a consumer court and make your claim.

11. Responsibilities of consumers

1. BEFORE BUYING
   - Planning in advance
   - Enquiring past performance of product/service
   - Enquiring about reputation and past performance of producer/seller/ service provider

2. WHILE BUYING

    - Asking for demonstration regarding how to operate/use the product/ service
    - Enquiring about after-sales service and ensuring availability, phone number, address and e.mail of service center
    - Reading and knowing the contents of guarantee/warranty card
    - Insisting for approved sale bill with serial number, address, phone number, etc.
    - Obtaining guarantee/warranty card and getting it signed/sealed by dealer

3. AFTER BUYING

    - Using products as per instruction given in user manual
    - Keeping bills and guarantee card safely
    - In case of fault inform dealer and service center. Do not meddle or repair yourself
    - Keeping record for all correspondences
    - Seek immediate redressal of deficiency in product

12. Points for consumer attention

12.1 Purchasing under Public Distribution System

Public Distribution System Outlets (ration shops) are distributing commodities against family cards at subsidized rates. Consumer should ensure that—

- Commodities are provided in correct weight without denial
- Display board is placed in front of every shop indicating available commodities and their quantity with selling price of each product
- Samples of commodities are placed for notice of card holders
- In the absence of any of above complaint can be made to Civil Supplies and Consumer Protection Department.

12.2 Purchase of cosmetics

- While buying cosmetics consumer should
- Not be carried away through Colorful misleading advertisements
- Check manufacturing date and date of expiry
- Keep in mind that Colors are almost Chemicals

- Keep in mind that following statements are mostly false "100% Natural", "Chemicals not used", "Oil free"
- Consult other users

If you have any grievance/complaint, you may file it with the Local Drug Inspector or with the Controller of Drugs

12.3 Purchase of drugs

- Purchase to be made only as per prescription by Registered Medical Practitioner
- Self medication is dangerous
- Checking for manufacturing date/expiry date
- Checking name of medicine purchased with prescription
- Checking availability of Maximum Retail Price on the strips/containers
- Insisting for bill with details of batch number, etc. printed over strips/ containers
- Checking for dosage and perseverance details of medicines
- If you have any grievance/complaint, you may file it with the Local Drug Inspector or with the Controller of Drugs

12.4 Purchase of clothes

- Checking whether clothes withstand normal washing habits
- Insisting and obtaining bills and preserving them
- Insisting for "silk mark" while purchasing costly silk sarees
- If you have any grievance you may send a notice to the seller/manufacturer or file a petition in the District Consumer Forum

12.5 Purchase of gold

Checking for "Hall Mark"—

- Weight of stones to be separately noted down in bills while purchasing ornaments with precious stones
- Obtaining purchase bills and keeping it safely
- In case of grievances you may issue a notice to the seller or file a complaint with Bureau of Indian Standards

12.6 Misleading advertisements

Consumer should always—

- be alert about the advertisements while going for purchase of goods afresh or in exchange of old product

- not be carried away by statements like free offers/discounts, etc. since they are not the deciding factors for the requirement of consumers
- not be misled through colourful glamorous advertisements
- In case of grievances, please issue a notice to the newspaper or complain to Advertisement Standards Council of India (ASCI) at 219, Bombay Market, Tardeo Road, Mumbai 400 034, ph 23521066/23516863, Web: www.ascionline.org and Email: ascia@vsnl.com.

12.7 Purchase of food products

- Don't buy spoilt products. It is dangerous to health
- Check manufacturing and expiry date, weight, manufacturer address, etc.
- If perishables, check if it has been stored in freezer/cold storage properly.
- Avoid cheap and colourful food with hazardous colour additives
- Avoid products without manufacturer address.
- You have no recourse in case of any problem
- Avoid purchase of unbranded products like oil without sealed packs
- In case of any complaint, including adulteration, call up your Local Food
- Inspector or Joint Director (PFA)

12.8 Packaged commodities

- Every packed commodity has to carry the following information
- Name and address of packer/manufacturer
- Name of commodity
- Net quantity/Weight
- Month and year of packing and expiry date
- Maximum Retail selling price
- Quality assurance symbols like AGMARK, FPO, ISI, etc.
- Other relevant information (regarding ingredients of product)

12.9 Sustainable consumption

Every alert consumer has a duty to be a responsible consumer too. This means:

- Consume only what one needs. Remember the poor and underprivileged
- Don't waste products/service, natural resources. Someone else may badly need it

- Avoid polluting products such as plastics, chemicals. Instead, use environmentally friendly degradable materials such as cloth, jute bags/materials
- Help keeping the environment safe and healthy. Recycle degradable waste in your house

12.10 Remember the ₹3 of a dutiful consumer

- Reduce: Consume only what you need, if possible reduce consumption of water, electricity, fuel and other non-renewables
- Reuse: If a product can serve you for a longer period, use it instead of buying a new one.
- Recycle: Don't litter the environment, please recycle degradable or recyclable materials through scrap dealers

The Consumer Protection Act, 1986 envisages a three-tier quasi-judicial system. They are known as:

(*i*) District Consumer Disputes Redressal Forum

(*ii*) State Consumer Disputes Redressal Commission, and

(*iii*) National Consumer Disputes Redressal Commission

13. Disputes Redressal Commission

Features of Consumer Protection Act, 1986 and filing of complaints —

1. Simple formalities
2. Advocates not compulsory
3. Consumers themselves can conduct cases
4. Complaints may be sent even through Registered Post
5. Registered Consumer Organizations or Government can also file complaint on behalf of consumer(s)
6. Less expensive
7. Compensation can be claimed for the loss suffered including mental agony

Protection offered by Consumer Protection Act, 1986 against:

(*a*) Deficiency in product or service

(*b*) Poor aftersales service

(*c*) Damage/Loss to health, life and property due to product

(*d*) Hazards arising out of product/service

(*e*) Unjust enrichment through unfair means

(*f*) Misleading advertisements

(*g*) Unfair Trade Practices

(*h*) Restrictive Trade Practices (like tie-up sales)

(*i*) Violations of any other applicable laws or regulations

14. Grievance redressal

- Consumer should send a detailed petition to the dealer/service provider through registered post pointing out the defect/deficiency and details regarding relief sought for.
- Copy of the petition with postal acknowledgement card to be preserved.
- If the dealer/service provider not responded in time consumer may approach District Consumer Protection Council headed by District Collector or Commissioner of Civil Supplies and Consumer Protection or Reputed Consumer Organisation who will be sending notices to the dealer/service provider on behalf of consumer.
- If no remedy available through all above agencies, then relevant Consumer Disputes Redressal Commission/Forum as the case may be approached to file a complaint against dealer/service provider.

15. Future course of action

The battle for consumer protection has to be fought by many agencies. The Government has to play an important role, by enacting suitable laws and enforcing them effectively. India has been observing 15th March since 1989 as the National Consumers' Day. This day has a historic importance as it was on this day in 1962, that the Bill for Consumer Rights was moved in the US Congress. Steps have been taken by the Government of India by way of enactment of various Acts and other measures to help consumers. Indian Penal Code, Standards of Weights and Measures Act, Motor Vehicles Act, are some of the Acts.

Despite these Acts, the fact remains that very little could be achieved in the field of consumer protection. A major breakthrough came during 1986 when Parliament passed a law for Consumer Protection Act, 1986. Three-tier quasi-judicial machinery at the district, state and national levels was set up with a view to provide speedy and simple redressal to consumer disputes. The District Forum deals with the cases involving claims upto ₹20 lakhs, the State Commission between ₹20 lakhs to one crore and the National Commission deals with the cases involving claims exceeding ₹ one crore. The objective of the consumer courts is to ensure speedy justice to the consumers against various malpractices and negligence without involving any cost, as no court fees is charged. Consumer courts have been set up as special courts, as it was expensive and time consuming to get justice through civil courts.

The Consumer Protection Act, which has been defined as "the Magna Carta of Consumers", spells out six consumer rights: Right to Safety, Right to

Information, Right to Choice, Right to Representation, Right to Redress, and Right to Consumer Education. India has the biggest consumer movement today due to the efforts of consumer organisations and the establishment of consumer courts. India is the only country in the world which has exclusive courts for consumer redressal. This has been internationally praised including the developed countries. The Consumer Protection Act (COPRA) has succeeded in bringing about fair play in the supply of goods and services to a large extent. The Act applies to almost all goods and services.

Still, the present scenario is not very encouraging. Unfortunately, the consumer courts have become replica of legal courts, as the procedure is no longer simple and quick. The consumer redressal process is relatively cumbersome and more expensive and time- consuming than desired. The process involves engaging a professional personnel, requires time for filing the case and attending the court proceeding and certain other formalities like producing the bill, warranty cards, etc. These procedures need to be made simpler and quicker for making the process more meaningful and realistic.

CHAPTER 16

Consumerism and Consumer

SYNOPSIS

Consumerism is regarded as a movement by consumers and consumer organizations intended to ensure fair and ethical practices by producers and marketing intermediaries for the whole body of consumers. The success of a consumer movement depends not only on the ability of consumer organizations to curb the unfair trade practices and prevent the sellers from exploiting the buyers' ignorance but also on the behavior of the consumers themselves. It calls for a high degree of awareness on the part of the consumers about their various rights including product quality, information and safety.

In the good olden days the principle of 'Caveat Emptor', which meant buyer beware governed the relationship between seller and the buyer. In the era of open markets buyer and seller came face to face, seller exhibited his goods, and buyer thoroughly examined them and then purchased them. It was assumed that he would use all care and skill while entering into transaction.

The maxim relieved the seller of the obligation to make disclosure about the quality of the product. In addition, the personal relation between the buyer and the seller was one of the major factors in their relations. But with the growth of trade and its globalization the rule no more holds true. It is now impossible for the buyer to examine the goods beforehand and most of the transactions are concluded by correspondence. Further on account of complex structure of the modern goods, it is only the producer/seller who can assure the quality of goods. With manufacturing activity becoming more organized, the producers/sellers are becoming stronger and organised whereas the buyers are still weak and unorganized. In the age of revolutionized information technology and with the emergence of e-commerce related innovations the consumers are further deprived to a great extent. As a result buyer is being misled, duped and deceived day in and day out. Mahatma Gandhi, the father of nation, attached great importance to what he described as the "poor consumer", who according to him should be the principal beneficiary of the consumer movement. He said "A Consumer is the most important visitor on our premises. He is not dependent on us we are on him. He is not an interruption to our work; he is the purpose of it. We are not doing a favour to a consumer by giving him an opportunity. He is doing us a favour by giving an opportunity to serve him."

Inspite of these views consumerism is still in its infancy in our country, thanks to the sellers market and the government monopoly in most services. Consumer awareness is low due to the apathy and lack of education among the masses. No one has told them about their rights to be informed about product quality, price, protection against unsafe products, access to variety of goods at competitive prices, consumer education etc. What consumerism lacks here are education and information resources, testing facilities, competent leadership, price control mechanism and adequate quasi-judicial machinery. The providers of goods and services have been reluctant to give due consideration to consumer interest protection.

1. Consumerism — The origin and growth

The protection of people against economic exploitation has existed for several centuries. England established standard measurements for wool and the first regulations regarding bread sizes were established in 1226 A.D. Sale of adulterated food and drink was subject to criminal penalties in the 14th century. The first consumer law was enacted in 1784 in Massachusetts followed by the law on weights and measures in 1790. In U.K. Merchandise Marks Act was passed in 1852 and in 1878, the first Weights and Measurement Act was passed. The well known Sale of Goods Act came into force in 1893.

In the middle of the 19th century, a section of consumers in England organized themselves to protest against exploitation of labour by the textile industry and they gave a call to boycott the buying of textiles manufactured by such erring companies. There were also similar moves by another section against employment of child and women labour and slavery. Towards the end of 19th century, there were sporadic attempts by consumers in the U.K., America and

Europe to form buyers clubs in order to avoid middlemen and profiteering. These Buyers Clubs were like informal consumer co-operatives. In India the origin of Consumer Movement was in the form of consumer co-operatives. Therefore, co-operatives are sometimes mentioned as the starting point of the Consumer Movement.

Consumerism merits the attention of one and all because it affects all of us as consumers. Consumerism arises from widely shared feelings of consumers that they are ill served by their economy. In its most vigorous form, it produces outrage, sometimes stemming from the abuse of powers by the sellers, a situation that holds in many developing countries in a more visible form. Often this discontent arises from the market failure, unsafe products, dishonored promises, misrepresentation, deceptive advertising, frauds and failures of communication between buyer and seller. We know that most of the consumer problems originate in the inability or unwillingness of producers to satisfy consumer needs and interests. Some consumer problems are self-inflicted. Consumer needs and interests are extremely varied, differing among cultures and also within cultures, from one individual group to another. In fact, the word consumerism implies a certain activist behaviour or attitude which is appropriate in recent times because consumers are paying more attention to their decision making in the market place. Therefore, we may say that this term consumerism also connotes awareness among people to raise their voice and demand a safe and better living. However, consumerism as a movement of consumers makes them well aware of their rights and responsibilities and fight against odds.

2. Consumer protection and the Manu Smriti

Protection of consumers has had relevance since the existence of consumers in India. It is surprising to see the roots of matters relevant to consumer protection in the Manu Smriti, a text which came into existence between 800 to 200 BC. Manu Smriti or Manusmriti is a semi-religious Hindu text recording the traditions narrated by Brahma to Manu, who is the first man to have lived on earth. The word Manu Smriti means the traditions as laid out by Manu (based on Brahma's wisdom).

The significance of Manu Smriti in matters of consumer protection is in the fact that it heeds immense importance to the economical aspects of the society and in particular unethical trade practices. Manu Smriti lays out a charter of ethics for sellers on how to sell consumer products to consumers. It also specifies the penalties that must be handed out to sellers who are unethical in their actions.

Focus on prevention of adulteration is a key consumer protection issue even in those days and ages. Manu Smriti specifically prohibits the sale of any commodity that has been mixed with another commodity. This is particularly significant on purchase of items such as gold where by the purity of it becomes questionable due to adulteration. It is also significant in commodities the consumption of which could have a detrimental effect on the health of the consumer; commodities include pharmaceuticals, food or personal care supplies.

Manu Smriti also mandates proper disclosure of quality and quantity of all items that are sold to consumers and prohibits the concealment of any aspects related to the product sold. This is particularly significant as the majority of consumer complaints arise around issues related to the quantity and quality of the consumed product. Manu Smriti gives guidelines on how often weights and measures have to be calibrated, inspected and also lays out the manner in which the results of inspections have to be dissipated.

3. Consumer protection in Medieval India

Consumer protection was of paramount importance in the medieval period in India ranging from 1000 AD to 1750 AD. Several prominent Muslim rulers had ruled India during this period from their capital in Delhi. The Delhi Sultanate, being the start of such a long period of Islamic rule in India, laid the foundation to the economic, financial and commercial backbone of the Indian medieval period.

The most notable achievements in Consumer Protection during the Delhi Sultanate were during the period of Alauddin Khilji (1296 AD to 1316 AD). Alauddin Khilji was the second ruler of the Khilji dynasty. During his reign, there were unprecedented improvements in the weights and measures standardization process bringing about dramatic changes in the transparency practices of traders with consumers. Commodities were weighed and measured through standards established by the Sultan and people who did not follow standards were punished through fines and even capital punishment. The Sultan had judges who were omnipotent in enforcing the rights of the consumers and approaching the courts when injustice occurred was simple and without bureaucracy.

Several generations of rulers following the Khilji did not contribute much to the consumer protection cause until Sher Shah Suri who ruled during the brief period between 1540 and 1545 AD. Sher Shah Suri was a visionary in matters related to commerce. He envisioned that an economy is always dependant on how well its consumers are treated. He emphasized on standardized measures and set forth decimal and centenary systems with respect to measures. He also published quality guidelines especially for produce, grocery, confectionaries and pharmaceuticals. The financial system he introduced along with the currency Rupiyah forms the foundation of the monetary system of modern India. Although his reign was brief, he is thought to be one of the most important medieval ruler who has influenced consumer protection policies of modern India.

During the reign of Akbar (1556-1605), the third Mughal Emperor of India, several significant achievements were made in matters related to consumer protection. The right of the consumer to be informed perhaps found its earliest roots during the period. All traders were required to publish details regarding the quality and quantity of their merchandise including weights, measures, adulteration if any, age, grade and usability. This law was strictly enforced through prefects and secret service personnel employed by the emperor. Violations and deceitful behaviour were dealt with the harshest of punishments including amputation of limbs. Consumers also enjoyed the right to return merchandise which did not meet the standard requirements related to quality and quantity. Akbar's contribution is notable in that his rule improved accountability and transparency in commodity transactions which were perhaps non-existent in the medieval days in India.

Although the Mughal kings that came afterwards did continue the achievements laid by their forefather, they concentrated more on literary, architectural and military pursuits. Eventually by the time the British gained control over the whole Indian peninsula, consumer issues had deteriorated into a stage that needed a rigorous revival. Nevertheless, the awareness, vision and perseverance through which the medieval rulers of India preserved the importance of consumer protection issues has been a source of fascination for international historians and economists.

4. Consumer protection in Modern India

In the modern day, business contracts are significant to consumer protection. Very often we can see consumers and consumable companies engaging in Service Level Agreements (SLA) to safeguard consumer interests especially when purchasing services that are consumed regularly over extended periods of time. Interestingly, the text of Manu Smriti also provides guidelines on how business contracts may be executed and when such contracts may be deemed void.

The most significant tenet of consumer protection is given absolute importance in the Smriti. The text explicitly prohibits any form of collusions in the market which could lead to monopoly or oligopoly. The king had the absolute right and the moral obligation to control the prices keeping in mind the absolute interest of the consumer. When viewed in the background of today's anti-trust laws and agencies, price conspiracies had its due share of attention even in the pre-Christ period in India.

Although in itself Manu Smriti's sole focus is not consumer protection, this work seems to focus broadly on several aspects related to the well being of the consumer. It also shows how concerned the ancient society was in matters related to consumerism. It is also surprising that despite having such a pro-consumer oriented culture 2500 years or so ago, the consumer protection movement has still not evolved to meet the challenges that Indian consumers face in this day and age.

In present situation, consumer protection, though as old as consumer exploitation, has assumed greater importance and relevance. Consumerism is a recent and universal phenomenon. It is a social movement. Consumerism is all about protection of the interests of the consumers. According to McMillan Dictionary (1985) "Consumerism is concerned with protecting consumers from all organisations with which there is exchanged relationship. It encompasses the set of activities of government, business, independent organisations and concerned consumers that are designed to protect the rights of consumers". The Chamber's Dictionary (1993) defines Consumerism as the protection of the interests of the buyers of goods and services against defective or dangerous goods, etc. "Consumerism is a movement or policies aimed at regulating the products or services, methods or standards of manufacturers, sellers and advertisers in the interest of buyers, such regulation may be institutional, statutory or embodied in a voluntary code occupied by a particular industry or it may result more indirectly from the influence of consumer organisations".

As commonly understood consumerism refers to wide range of activities of government business and independent organisations designed to protect rights of the consumers. Consumerism is a process through which the consumers seek redress, restitution and remedy for their dissatisfaction and frustration with the help of their all organised or unorganised efforts and activities. It is, in-fact a social movement seeking to protect the rights of consumers in relation to the producers of goods and providers of services. Infact consumerism today is an all-pervasive term meaning nothing more than people's search for getting better value for their money. Consumer is the focal point of any business. Consumers' satisfaction will benefit not only business but government and society as well. So consumerism should not be considered as consumers' war against business. It is a collective consciousness on the part of consumers, business, government and civil society to enhance consumers' satisfaction and social welfare which will in turn benefit all of them and finally make the society a better place to live in.

5. Components of consumerism

There are various components of consumerism. First and foremost is self-protection by consumers. Consumer must be aware of his rights, raise voice against exploitation and seek redressal of his grievances. Consumers' consciousness determines the effectiveness of consumerism. It is the duty of the consumer to identify his rights and to protect them. Voluntary Consumer Organisations engaged in organising consumers and encouraging them to safeguard their interests is another important element of consumer movement The success of consumerism lies in the realisation of the business that there is no substitute for voluntary self-regulations. Little attention from the business will not only serve consumers interest but will also benefit them. Some businesses in India have come together to adopt a code of conduct for regulating their own activities. Regulation of business through legislation is one of the important means of protecting the consumers. Consumerism has over the time developed into a sound force designed to aid and protect the consumer by exerting, legal, moral and economic pressure on producers and providers in some of the developed countries.

The consumer movement in India is as old as trade and commerce. In Kautilya's Arthashastra, there are references to the concept of consumer protection against exploitation by the trade and industry, short weighment and measures, adulteration and punishment for these offences. However, there was no organised and systematic movement actually safeguarding the interests of the consumers. Prior to independence, the main laws under which the consumer interests were considered were the Indian Penal Code, Agricultural Production,

Grading and Marketing Act, 1937, Drugs and Cosmetics Act, 1940. Even though different parts of India exhibited different levels of awareness, in general, the level of awareness was pretty low.

An average Indian consumer is noted for his patience and tolerance. Perhaps because of these two traditional traits and due to the influence of the Mahabharata, the Ramayana and the Bhagavad Gita, he considers the receipt of defective goods and services as an act of fate or unfavourable planetary position in his horoscope. When a new television or refrigerator purchased by him turns out to be defective from day one, he takes it reticently, blaming it on his fate or as the consequence of the wrongs committed by him in his previous birth. Very often he is exploited, put to avoidable inconveniences and suffers financial loss. It is rather paradoxical that the customer is advertised as the "king" by the seller and service provider; but in actual practice treated as a slave or servant. Goods are purchased by him along with the label "Items once sold by us will never be received back under any circumstances whatsoever."

This unethical, illegal and unilateral declaration has to be viewed in the light of the practice in developed countries where the seller declares, "In case you are not fully satisfied with our product, you can bring the same to us within a month for either replacement or return of your money." This will clearly indicate the level of consumer consciousness. However, things are changing — slowly but steadily and the momentum has increased considerably since the establishment of consumer courts and due to the efforts of a number of consumer organisations and the media. The next millennium will witness a high degree of consumer awareness and the concepts of "comparative costs", "consumer preference/resistance/abstinence" and "consumer choice" will become vital aspects of the economy.

An analysis of the data from the consumer courts in different States shows that there is a direct relationship between literacy and consumer awareness. Statistics relating to Kerala and Bihar will justify this. The question to be considered is what can the Government do to improve the position?

The Government wears three hats to deal with cases of three different categories. The first one is dealing with the ministries and departments of government. The Standing Committee of Parliament on Health said Government hospitals should be brought under the purview of the Consumer Court. To this, it may be pointed out the latest ruling of the Supreme Court which lays down that the Consumer Protection Act will apply only when the consumer pays for the goods and services and on this count the government hospital, where the services are not charged on the consumer, will not come under the Act. For such cases the government has developed the concept of "Citizen's Charter". All government departments dealing with the public are to publish a "Citizen's Charter" clearly indicating the services offered and the procedure to be followed. All the information has to be made available in a single window. This programme is in its incipient stage and has a long way to go to achieve the desired levels of consumer satisfaction. The general reaction of the consumer to this is: what happens if what is stated in the Citizen Charter is not adhered to? Unless and until this is clarified, the responsibility fixed and those held accountable are dealt with, the purpose will not be achieved.

The second area is where the services/utilities are provided and charged either by the government department or the agencies under its control. At present, a number of regulatory authorities have been constituted and the country is entering a new regime of "regulatory economies" in the services sector. It is heartening to note that the regulatory bodies like the Telecom Regulatory Authority of India (TRAI) have given importance to the interests of consumers and this has been publicly declared as one of the main objectives. In the field of telecom, power, transport and water supply, the consumers today are going through a number of problems not knowing how to get their grievances redressed. The numbers of cases relating to these sectors are increasing in the consumer courts. It must be possible for the government to take steps to see that the areas of grievances are identified and remedial steps taken through proper systematisation of procedure and working style.

There are a number of areas where the procedure has to be made simple and consumer-friendly. For example, when it was felt that the quality of bottled water purchased by the consumer has to be ensured by fixing standards, it came out that even though it is necessary and desirable, under the existing laws it cannot be done. The Ministry of Law pointed out and rightly so, that water is not "food" as per the provisions in the Food Adulteration Act. The process of getting statutory notification in the interest of the consumer in this case, where all concerned are agreeable, is likely to take 12 to 18 months. In such a situation, the only answer is to prevail upon the manufacturers to go for voluntary ISI (Indian Standards Institution) certification. This method is working in the case of bottled water, thanks to the cooperation of producers and the clear preference expressed by the active consumer groups.

Similarly in the area of "investor protection" inspite of several steps taken by the regulatory authorities such as the Reserve Bank of India and the Securities and Exchange Board of India, the case of exploitation of consumers is increasing. This is an area of grave concern and requires concerted action by the regulators, government and the consumer organisations. We must find a way out to save the consumers from the unscrupulous functioning of Non-banking finance companies.

The third category is the protection of consumers from the private sector dealing with goods and services. It is not to be construed that the entire business sector is keen on exploiting the consumers. These are established business firms which really care for consumer satisfaction, their own reputation and goodwill. Voluntary bodies like the Fair Business Practices Forum are functioning effectively and are quick in removing the grievances of the consumers. These can go a long way in reducing the number of cases in the consumer courts.

If the Government is to take a pro-active role in increasing consumer awareness, encourage consumer education, training and research and administer the infrastructural need of the consumer courts — then it should have enough funds. It is not easy to get adequate budget allocations for obvious reasons. The best way appears to be to work out methods by which the Central Consumer Welfare Fund is augmented and a similar fund is set up at State level also. It is gratifying to note that action has been initiated in this direction and there is every reason to hope that the future will be better.

The consumer has to be aware of his rights and play a key role. The success of "consumerism" is a strong function of consumer awareness and the assistance the movement gets from the government. The consumer movement got a boost and moral support from the late U.S. President John F. Kennedy in the historic declaration in Congress on March 15, 1962, declaring four basic consumer rights (choice, information, safety and the right to be heard). Subsequently, March 15 every year is celebrated as World Consumer Rights Day. However this annual ritual observation does not appear to have produced the desired results. A sub-continent like India with regional imbalances and diversity of languages requires not one but several Ralph Nadars. A survey has revealed that a number of consumers in the urban as well as rural areas are not very much aware of the consumer movement and the rights of the consumers. It is in this context that it is considered relevant to quote the objectives adopted by the General Assembly of United Nations in 1985.

The U.N. guidelines for consumer protection are meant to achieve the following objectives:

(*a*) To assist countries in achieving or maintaining adequate protection for their population as consumers;

(*b*) To facilitate production and distribution patterns responsive to the needs and desires of consumers;

(*c*) To encourage high levels of ethical conduct for those engaged in the production and distribution of goods and services to consumers;

(*d*) To assist countries in curbing abusive business practices by all enterprises at the national and international levels which adversely affect consumers;

(*e*) To facilitate the development of independent consumer groups;

(*f*) To further international cooperation in the field of consumer protection;

(*g*) To encourage the development of market conditions which provide consumers with greater choice at lower prices.

It is interesting to note that in spite of U.N. recognition, encouragement from the developed countries and the pro-active role played by the Government, the consumer in India still does not get his due. It is time that he wakes up and realizes his rights. Even the great Hanuman required someone older and wiser to remind him of his potential strength. It will be useful if voluntary consumer organisations take up this role and make way for the realisation of the objectives of the U.N. guidelines and the Consumer Protection Act.

In the next millennium, every consumer in his own interest has to realise his role and importance in the right perspective. Each citizen in a democracy derives his power at the time of elections and exercises it through the ballot. In a competitive economic environment the consumer has to exercise his choice either in favour of or against the goods and services. His choice is going to be vital and final. He should realise his importance and prepare himself to exercise his rights with responsibility. It is very often stated "Customer is sovereign and consumer is the King." If that is really so, why do we have the Consumer Protection Act? Why is there a need for protecting the King? Should it not be rightly called "Consumer Sovereignty Act"? It is for the consumers to decide. After all the dictum in democracy is, the citizens get a government they deserve. Similarly the consumers in society get a position in the market depending upon what they do or do not do. It is agreed on all hands that "consumer empowerment" in India has a long way to go. This is the right time to act. Let us prepare for the next millennium and usher in a new era of "Consumerism". When we cross the winter, spring cannot be far behind.

6. Raising consumerism in India

It is an accepted fact that this globalization has brought about a tremendous change in consumption pattern at all levels across countries and the overall purchasing power of consumers has increased. Prior to the enactment of different Consumer Protection Acts, laws and growth of consumer activists and organizations in India., the doctrine of "Caveat Emptor" (buyer beware) was prevailing. But now the time has come for the doctrine "Caveat Venditor"(seller beware) to rule.

Consumerism merits the attention of one and all because it affects all of us as consumers. All of us enjoy shopping. Whether we like it or not, spend a lot of time as consumers of goods and services. When we buy goods, eat in a restaurant, travel or seek the help of doctors, engineers or repairmen, we act as consumers.

We know that very often we do not get what we seek. Therefore, the so-called Consumerism arises from widely shared feelings of consumers that they are ill served by their economy. In its most vigorous form, it produces outrage, sometimes stemming from the abuse of powers by the sellers, a situation that holds in many developing countries in a more visible form. Often this discontent arises from the market failure, unsafe products, dishonored promises, misrepresentation, deceptive advertising, frauds and failures of communication between buyer and seller. We know that most of the consumer problems originate in the inability or unwillingness of producers to satisfy consumer needs and interests. Some consumer problems are self-inflicted. Consumer needs and interests are extremely varied, differing among cultures, and also within cultures, from one individual group to another.

In fact, the word consumerism implies a certain activist behavior or attitude which is appropriate in recent times because consumers are paying more attention to their decision making in the market place. Therefore, we may say that this term consumerism connotes awareness among the people to raise their voice and demand a safe and better living. However, consumerism is a movement of consumers which makes them well aware of their rights and responsibilities and fight against odds.

We know that the new waved Globalization is creating new inequalities and challenges in every nook and corner of the world. Therefore, consumers' world over need to organize themselves to secure proper justice and to fight for their rights. The loud alarms, Consumer unite! Should be heard by consumers' world over, otherwise, everywhere, throughout the world, across the countries, consumers are taken for a ride mercilessly.

First, consumer luxuries have got democratised during this decade. Products that were considered for a few started to reach larger and larger masses of consumers — from colas to shampoos to ready wear to mobile to airlines. Categories that started in the 90s began to expand their footprint and became a part of mass life. Consumption and consumerism reached more people than it did in the 90s. Social inequity continues to be part of India's economic, but the capitalistic principle that "open up from the top to a few, and the benefits will flow down to many" has come true. Consumerism is truly mass!

Along with this, has come a culture of upgrade and step movement rather than lifetime ownership and gradual movement. I think technology, mobile handsets in particular, made consumers get used to constant change — buying a new product even when the old one was "functional", thus breaking the barrier of the "replace when it's broke" mindset. And then this extended to other categories in life — from clothes to televisions to homes. Every Indian market presents an opportunity to marketers to get consumers to move up. As technology improves and consumers' disposable income increases, the willingness and propensity of consumers to make leaps from unbranded to branded and pay significant premia is also increasing. There is no longer "lifetime ownership", but "lifetime consumer value"!

Third, there has been a shift from product to services and experiences. And this is taking place across categories. Coffee has become Cafes, beauty products are transiting into Parlours — and this is going into small towns too with local "aunties" sensing business opportunities opening parlours and beauty counselling centres at home — and home videos have become multiplexes. And in every case, it provides marketers an opportunity to extract more value.

7. Consumer Organizations: What are they?

Consumers unite! Fight for your rights! Put an end to adulteration! Say 'No' to deceptive advertising! Grow as green consumers! Achieve sustainable consumption! Are some of the slogans that all of us as consumers should learn to speak, spread and achieve. Indeed, it is a matter of great urgency that the consumers world over should be organized to face this changing and challenging Globalized world.

Consumer organizations are those organizations which are formed and framed by consumers to fight for their rights, to create awareness among fellow consumers about their responsibilities, to enhance consumer welfare through proper co-ordination with the governments and institutions. They might be working under different names such as Residents Welfare Associations, Associations for Consumer Guidance, Consumers Welfare Agency, Residents Union, Civic societies and Non-governmental organizations. Such organizations are found throughout the world in almost all countries.

But in some countries they are more united and aggressive and effective in safeguarding the interests of the consumer. The consumer organizations anywhere in the world should work with one point formula — Consumer Safety and Welfare through an active participation of consumer.

Like the utterance of great scientific socialist Karl Marx's Workers Unite World Over! consumers should be made to unite world over. This great task can be made possible only through the effective consumer organizations.

When a consumer organization is formed, its first job is —

1. To provide consumer education which includes their rights and responsibilities
2. To share and exchange consumer related information.
3. To promote co-operation and collaboration of all activities related to consumer protection and interests.
4. To conduct research and product testing.
5. To ensure the basic needs such as food, housing, health care and clean environment to every consumer.
6. To develop the spirit and confidence among the consumers to represent their grievances.
7. To educate consumers to think critically to make their own decisions and to gain strength to resist hazardous trends and practices.
8. To work with communities to help them to solve their problems.
9. To provide counseling and guidance in case of grievances. To organize programmes of public interest.
10. Any consumer organization with abovesaid features will be an effective and successful organization. The developing world has been in quest of such effective consumer organizations which will be very pragmatic and beneficial to all sections of the society.

8. Rights and responsibilities of consumers

Every year, March 15, is observed as World Consumers' Rights Day. It commemorates a historic declaration of four basic consumer rights by former US President John F. Kennedy on March 15, 1962. Those declarations eventually lead to international recognition by governments and the UNO. Over the years, these rights have been expanded and formulated precisely in the form of seven demands by the Consumers International, Malaysia.

8.1 The right to safety

This means the right to be protected against products, production processes and services which are hazardous to health or life.

8.2 The right to be informed

This means the right to be informed of the facts needed to make an informed choice or decision. The right to be informed now goes beyond avoiding deception and the protection against misleading advertising, labeling or other practices. Consumers should be provided with adequate information, enabling them to act wisely and responsibly.

8.3 The right to choose

This right refers to the right to have access to a variety of products and services at competitive prices and in the case of monopolies to have an assurance of satisfactory quality of goods and services at a fair price.

The right to choose has been reformulated to mean the right to basic goods and services. This is because the unrestrained right of a minority to choose can mean a denial of share to the majority.

8.4 The right to be heard

This means the right to be represented so that consumer's interests receive full and sympathetic consideration in the formulation and execution of economic policy. The right is being broadened to include the right to be heard and represented in the development of products and services before they are produced or set up: it implies a role, not only in formulating government policies, but also in economic fora and other organizations.

8.5 The right to redressal

This means the right to fair settlement of just claims.

The right has been generally accepted since the early 1970's. It involves the right to receive compensation for misrepresentation or supply of shoddy goods or services where needed, free legal aid or an accepted form of redress for small claims should be available.

8.6 The right to consumer education

This means the right to acquire the knowledge and skills to be an informed consumer throughout life.

The right to consumer education incorporates the right to the knowledge and skills needed for taking action to influence factors that affect consumer decisions.

8.7 The right to a healthy environment

This means the right to a physical environment that will enhance the quality of life.

This right involves protection against environmental problems over which the individual consumer has no control. It acknowledges the need to provide and improve the environment for present and future generations.

For exercising rights, the consumers should know their following responsibilities:

- Consume less and not give into over consumption.
- To consume all kinds of energy and not to waste.
- To pay a reasonable price and not to encourage black marketing. To cooperate in a situation of shortage and not to hoard. To be alert and not be apathetic.
- To complain systematically and await redressal.
- Obtain full information regarding quality and price before making any purchase. Be careful about false and misleading advertisements.
- Purchase goods having ISI mark, Agmark, etc. as and where available for safety and quality.
- Obtain proper receipt/cash memo for the purchase made and guarantee/warranty card duly stamped and signed by the seller wherever applicable.
- Approach district forum, state commission or national commission for redressal of consumer grievances against sale of defective goods or deficient services or adoption of unfair or restrictive trade practices.

However, the Consumer Protection Act of 1986 gives the following strength to the Indian consumer:

- To know about the quality and price of goods and services being paid for, so that you are not cheated by unfair trade practices.
- To be heard and be assured that consumer interest will receive due consideration at appropriate fora.
- To seek legal redressal against unfair or restrictive trade practices or exploitation.
- To be protected against the sale of goods and services which are spurious and hazardous for life and property?
- To be assured, wherever possible, access to a variety of goods and services at competitive prices.

9. Present status of Indian consumerism

The consumerism in India is as old as trade and commerce itself. Indian history reveals that in various periods and regimes of different Kings and dynasties prior to the British rule, there were enactments to punish the dishonest and unfair traders and producers. During the middle ages, the dishonest traders had their hands cut-off and a trader selling shoddy goods was dragged around town with his wares tied around his neck! Indeed in 200 B.C. there were laws in India against food adulteration. The laws of Manu (a great classical philosopher) and Arthasastra of Kautilya (a great classical economist) also refer to the punishment to be awarded to dishonest traders. The British introduced some laws in India such as the Sale of Goods Act, Weights and Measurement Act which were being followed in England. Some organized efforts to protect consumers from the middlemen were made in the 1940s by eminent freedom fighters such as Sri. Tanguduri Prakasam, C. Rajagopalacharie in southern India. They started consumer co-operative stores to supply retail essential commodities. This became a social movement and the concept of consumer co-operative movement spread to different parts of the country. Today consumer organizations such as Mumbai Grahak Panchayat, Consumer Education and Research Center (CERC) in Ahmedabad under the guidance of Indian Ralph Nader, Professor Manu Bhai Shah are continuing this approach to consumer welfare by organizing seminars and workshops.

The origin and growth of consumer movement in India has many similarities to the movement elsewhere. In the 1960s, organizations such as Consumer Guidance Society of India, Mumbai was formed to inform and educate consumers on the quality of goods and services and to conduct simple tests on goods of daily consumption. Shortage in supply of essential commodities and unsatisfactory functioning of the public distribution system led activists to form consumer organizations in their towns and localities to ventilate their grievances to the authorities concerned. Several such organizations which were formed between 1970 and 1980 were concerned with the problems of inflation, food adulteration and public distribution system. These consumer organizations serve a useful purpose as voluntary vigilance groups in the market place.

The third phase of growth covering the period from 1981 to 1990 signifies the expansion and consolidation of the consumer movement in India. Especially after the enactment of Consumer Protection Act of 1986, there has been a spurt in the number of new organizations in the country.

The period from 1991 to 2000 A.D. is being considered as a period that empowered the Indian consumer. Consumer education, product testing, product safety and promotion were well activated.

Hence, the consumer movement in India has come of age. Consumer organizations have always felt since the movement started picking up in the 1970s, that there were benefits in numbers. Beginning with less than 10 organizations in 1965, by 1996 established over 900 consumer organizations and today there are more than 2000 active consumer organizations all over the country.

Following Are Some Consumer Groups and Organizations established during different years:

1. Passengers and Traffic Relief Association (PATRA) 1915
2. Women Graduate Union (WGU) 1915
3. Women's India Association (WGU) 1917
4. Triplicane Urban Co-operative Stores (TUCS) 1949
5. Indian Association of Consumers 1956

6. Gayathri Charitable Trust 1960
7. Jyoti Sang Grahak Suraksha Vibhag 1962
8. Bombay Civil Trust 1963
9. Consumer Guidance Society of India (CGSI) 1966
10. Baroda Citizen Council (BCC) 1966
11. All India Bank Depositors Association 1968
12. Surat Consumers Association 1969
13. Karnataka Consumers Service Society 1970
14. Visaka Consumer Council 1973
15. Akhil Bharat Grahak Panchayat 1974.
16. Trichy District Consumer Council 1976
17. Consumer Education and Research Center 1978
18. Mumbai Grahak Panchayat 1979
19. Grahak Panchayat 1979
20. Jagrut Grahak 1980
21. Consumer Forum 1980
22. Consumer Education Center1982
23. Voluntary Organization in the Interest of Consumer Education 1984
24. Consumer Unity and Trust Society 1984
25. National Center For Human Settlements and Environment 1984
26. Consumer Guidance Society of Jamshedpur 1984
27. Consumer Action Group 1985
28. Consumer Cause 1985
29. SMN Consumer Protection Council 1986
30. Bombay Telephone Users Association 1989
31. Federation of Consumer Organization of Tamil Nadu 1990
32. Confederation of Indian Consumer Organizations 1991
33. Gujarat Federation of Consumer Organizations 1992
34. Consumer Coordination Council 1992

(*Source:* Emergence and Formation of Consumer Groups-published by CERC, Ahmedabad, India, 1992, page 29)

In 1974, the then existing consumer organizations at the Second All India Consumer Conference had convened at Bangalore, stated that a time has come for the consumer organizations in India, not only to work in small groups but also to work with the help and guidance of a central agency so that Indian consumers can organize and voice their opinion to the government and act as a cohesive force to defend and faster their interests. This conference was determined to form a federation and its purpose would be to inform, educate and guide its affiliates to the greater advantage of the Indian consumer. Unfortunately, the central agency could not take off at that time because they did not have 7 members needed to sign as founder members. In 1989 some consumer activists once again tried to form central agency and in February 1991, the Confederation of Indian Consumer Organizations was formed in the Second National Convention of Consumer Activists in Delhi. The primary objective of CICO was to make the consumer movement a popular grass-roots movement. It was felt that the primary target of CICO should be facilitating the formation of state level federation of consumer organizations.

Consumers in India need more exposure to consumerism and consumer education. In a developing country like India, the consumer is at special risk while taking market decisions. As a consumer, one has to grapple with the problems of undernourishment, over population, poverty, unemployment, ill health and a host of other problems. Most often, poverty which is considerably widespread, does not lend the consumer the necessary strength to question and to resist the attempts of victimization.

Today, an average Indian consumer is mostly poor, illiterate, ignorant, apathetic or just defeatist and continues to be at the receiving end. A recent study indicated that Indian consumers are cheated to the tune of Rs.20,000 million a year, either by poor quality or less quantity or by overcharging the poor chap who is always at the receiving end. A survey conducted by Consumers Guidance Society of India in collaboration with the Health Department of Mumbai** Municipal Corporation revealed that almost half of the samples of groundnut oil collected from various parts of the city were adulterated. Another report indicates that 20 to 50% of foodstuffs sold in the market are adulterated. The gradual increase in the liver cancer cases in certain parts of India has even been attributed to the adulteration in edible oil.

The condition of rural consumers is very miserable as they buy goods mostly in loose form and in small quantities without weighment. Most of these goods may not be of standard quality. It has generally been experienced by buyers in sub-urban areas. Shops in villages and hilly areas charge even more than Maximum Retail Price (MRP) on one pretext or the other. In urban areas also a lot of spurious goods are sold at the rates of genuine goods. Thus cheating the consumers by rate difference by supplying low quality goods. However, much would depend upon the consumers to unite for awareness about their rights. Consumer King a concept of Benham, an economist of England is a myth in India because consumers are totally in the dark for reasons which are evident in developing countries. The reasons being:

1. Illiteracy
2. Lack of consumer education
3. Age old inherent submissiveness among consumers
4. Lack of knowledge about consumer rights
5. Innocence and implicit faith
6. Economic backwardness

All abovesaid factors lead to take unwise decisions and improper purchasing.

In today's globalized era the problem of a consumer is of very crucial importance. Protection connotes someone is there as protector and protected. Consumer problem often is depicted as trader *versus* consumer but the trader himself is also a consumer. In Satyuga no violation took place as all performed their purest duties dictated by the divine law.

However, an unmistakable duality exists in the way the consumer has been represented in the literature on consumerism. The dominant position is that all consumers function as free, discriminating and happy individuals, making rational choices while consuming goods and services in the market. Diametrically opposed is the view that the consumer is an irrational being irresistibly drawn to the market, but unaware of the imminent threat posed by it. Sometimes this distinction is made to differentiate between consuming communities among which high information and awareness prevail, from those where they are low. All consumer awareness/protection movements ideally aim to create an 'informed' consumer. It seems that with the gradual transition of the feudal into a market society, the term consumer began to earn greater respectability. By the nineteenth century consumer came to be used as a counterpoint to the term producer. The nineteenth century view of the consumer has survived in most capitalist democracies. In fact, consumers have a 'secondary relationship' with goods and services, because they are forced to live with and through services and goods that they themselves did not create. Thus, the consumer still remains as a 'marginal group' in today's dominant market economy of the world.

Indian market today is dominated by the consumerism, particularly after a decade from economic reforms process. It is gradually being transformed from a predominantly sellers market to a buyers market where exercised choice by the consumers depends on their awareness level. Consumer rights could be protected in a competitive economy only when right standards for goods and services for which one makes payment are ensured by evolving a network of institutions and legal protection system. Ensuring consumer welfare is the responsibility of the government as every citizen of the country is a consumer in one way or the other.

However, the present day's world is generating impurities of all kinds. The consequences of today's mass consumption are leading to generation of these impurities in basic livelihood resources and the degrading environment badly. Therefore, the production of good human beings is more important than production of goods and services only. He suggested that the issue of protecting the consumers calls for evolving healthy Institutional back up system, awareness generation and grievances redressal system. Our school curriculum should include consumer rights and traders obligations to the society.

The healthy markets only could maximize welfare of the consumers with certain underlying assumptions. However, in most of the developing countries the markets are imperfect and sick. Net result in such situation is the exploitation of the consumers. In a rudimentary economy, commodities were exchanged for commodities as per their use value. This situation changed to the exchange of commodities for money further leading to commodities production as per the requirements of the consumers. In present days world the situational is diametrically changed to profit maximization by resorting to investment in terms of money for commodity production and earning more money as per the exchange value of goods and services. Commodities and services under these circumstances are primarily produced for exchange value. It is desirable for assigning due consideration to the traditional Indian view point of Bhoga.

The efficient and effective programme of Consumer Protection is of special significance to all of us, as we all are consumers.

Even a manufacturer or provider of a service is a consumer of some other goods or services. If both producers/service providers and consumers realize the need for co-existence, adulterated products, spurious goods and other deficiencies in services would become a thing of the past.

The active involvement and participation from all quarters i.e. the central and state governments, the educational Institutions, the NGO's, the print and electronic media and the adoption and observance of a voluntary code of conduct by the trade and industry and the citizen's charter by the service providers is not only necessary but a *sine qua non* for the success of the Consumer movement. The need of the hour is for total commitment to the consumer cause and social responsiveness to consumer needs. This should, however, proceed in a harmonious manner so that our society becomes a better place for all of us to live in.

The existing consumer protection initiatives in India address only to the needs of the elite and empowered consumers. A disempowered consumer on the other hand, has no alternative choice except to agitate or may resort to violent resistance sometimes. Many problems arise only when consumption is regarded as a derivative of production. Numerous deceptive, disruptive and misleading tendencies are followed mainly through advertisements to mould the needs of consumers.

The average Indian consumer is susceptible to capitalist controlled media influences and is self-depreciated and unsure of his needs and wants. Indian consumers need to be understood and their problems resolved through law and other devices. He discussed theory of commodity fetishism deployed to explain subjective feelings towards consumer goods. Indian consumer needs to be taught, trained and should be made to learn to consume. Consumer should not ask what the government can do for them but first think what they can do for themselves.

The problem of protecting consumer rights that requires in the first place existence of basic minimum rights as individuals. Secondly, the basic minimum entitlements need institutional acceptance as rights. In underdeveloped countries like India rights based institutional approach is often missing, either because of non-existence or improper functioning of intuitions and because of weak bargaining power of individuals.

10. Consumer Organizations and attitude of Government

Enactment of law itself is not enough to safeguard the rights of consumers unless it is followed up by the creation of awareness of such legislation and sustained efforts for its effective enforcement. It is in these areas that the role of consumer organizations assumes greater significance.

Awareness is essential for consumers and it is equally important for the shopkeepers, traders and manufacturers of consumer items. To be made aware of the rights of consumers, relevant regulations and powers of intervention granted to consumers and consumer organizations. The mission of consumer organizations in India is the promotion and protection of rights and interests of consumers. They are actively engaged with related issues at the local and national levels. These include;

1. Violations under the Food Adulteration Act
2. Deficiencies in public distribution system
3. Environmental pollution
4. Awareness programme in educational institutions
5. Consumer awareness and publicity campaigns
6. Publication of books and literature on consumer activism
7. Free advice regarding redressal of consumer complaints
8. National workshop on women empowerment
9. National workshop on fertilizers and pesticides
10. Convention of WTO negotiations and consumer
11. Symposium on globalization and consumer in India
12. Street plays and dramas on deceptive ads, short weights, adulteration, price cheating and a number of such day-to-day consumer problems.

Consumer organizations represent consumer problems through the following government and non-government bodies:

1. Central Consumer Protection Council
2. State Consumer Protection Council
3. National Consumer Disputes Redressal Commission
4. Consumer District Forum
5. Patent Officer
6. Bureau of Indian Standards
7. Federation of Indian Chamber of Commerce and Industry
8. Confederation of Indian Industries
9. Confederation of Indian Consumer Organizations

In India, consumer organizations no doubt have registered an impressive growth. In quantitative terms, the growth seems to be quite encouraging. But the way they are functioning is quite disappointing. Most of these organizations suffer from lack of funds, potential volunteers, continued support of the members, leadership with vision, etc.

Once the objectives are framed, the consumer organizations have to enroll members which will not only help the organization to expand but also to strengthen financially. A large membership will add to the collective strength for effective working. It is important that a nominal fee has to be charged as membership fee at the time of enrollment and also periodically, as monthly or annually. If an expanding organization requires more money for its activities, it can take up some research projects and get them sponsored by the Consumer Affairs Departments of the state or central government. Organizations can run a laboratory through which it gets income by testing the suspected products brought by the consumers. Other sources can be from publications and fund raised from the public.

The most important requirement for an organization is the manpower. Therefore, it requires a good number of active volunteers to carry out its activities. Any organization with good intention would attract more people to join the organization.

Since the consumer movement is basically a Demand for Justice Movement, every consumer has a right to protest such as:

- Written protest
- Protest march
- Fasting in protest

Street plays and dramas. If it is made through consumer organizations, it will be more effective.

It was with the passage of pro-consumer legislation and the setting up of relevant agencies and councils, even at the highest levels in the government that consumers could rest assured that, for the most part, the products that reach them have been produced and distributed under conditions which take account of the health and safety of consumers and the old law of the jungle. Let The Buyer Beware has been partially replaced. In India, unlike the developed countries, problems are not merely of the quality of goods and services produced but even greater problem is that of the availability of these goods to the masses. Thus rationing of essential commodities is a daily occurrence, not restricted to wartime scarcities and shortages.

Indeed, quite a lot of initiatives have been taken by the government enacting a number of laws to protect the consumer. The Prevention of Food Adulteration Act of 1954 and the Essential Commodities Act of 1955 were the early enactments that independent India gave to its consumers. In 1956, it also started a national agency called the Indian Association of Consumers with the financial backing of the Planning Commission and the involvement of many eminent personalities like Mr. G.L. Nanda, Mr. Shegal and Mrs. Susheela Nayar.

The Government of India has been playing a very vital role in protecting consumers and encouraging consumer organizations. The louder voice of some dissatisfied consumers made the government at last to implement a separate comprehensive piece of legislation protecting the consumer, and in 1986 the Consumer Protection Act was passed.

In 1986, the Government of India amended a number of laws to empower the consumer and registered consumer organizations to file complaint in the court. Among them, the Drugs and Cosmetics Act, 1940, the Agricultural Produce, Grading and Marketing Act, 1937, the Prevention of Food Adulteration Act, 1954, the Essential Commodities Act, 1955, the Monopolies and Restrictive Trade Practices Act, 1969 and Standards of Weights and Measures Act, 1976.

In 1991, the Parliament amended the central excise and customs laws to provide for the establishment of Consumer Welfare Fund for making available grants for reimbursing legal expenses incurred by a complainant or class of complaints in a consumer dispute after its final adjudication and for making any other purpose recommended by the central consumer protection council. The Ministry of Consumers Affairs and Public Distribution has started awarding First, Second and Third cash prizes to the tune of Rs 50,000, Rs 25,000 and Rs. 10,000 respectively to the best performing consumer organizations in India. Thus the Government of India has been encouraging consumerism and consumer organizations in the country.

The various measures taken by the Government has aroused a lot of expectation among the consumers. In the last few years, a major thrust has been given to the consumer protection programme and a number of additional steps have been taken to protect the interests of the consumers. The Department of Consumer Affairs along with the Department of Administrative Reforms and Public Grievances has brought out 62 citizens charters in ministries having public contacts. The department regularly monitors retail prices, wholesale prices of essential commodities as part of its monitory activity to safeguard the interests of the consumers.

Indeed, the laudable effort of the Government of India is the great enactment of Consumer Protection Act of 1986 which provided for the establishment of central consumer protection council, the state consumer protection councils and the district consumer protection councils. Overall, the attitude of Indian Government towards consumerism and consumer organizations is encouraging.

Though India has an ancient history of consumer protection, consumer movement had its beginning only in the early part of this century. But they were mainly highlighted as freedom movement agitations. For e.g. The Swadeshi Movement 1905 to 1911- boycott of foreign goods with the slogan "Be Indian Buy Indian" and Dandi March, March 12, 1930 to May 18, 1930- protest march on the imposition of tax on the manufacturer of salt. These two agitations were lead by Mahatma Gandhi, the father of India. In the later part of the twentieth century that is after gaining independence in the year 1947 consumer organizations slowly started emerging.

11. Guidelines for Consumer Organizations to face the globalized world

Due to Globalization and fast advancement in technology, new economic issues are emerging making the market place more complex. In such a market place consumer is get confused and mislead in decision making. This problem of consumer, inevitably, has to be tackled by the consumer organizations. Hence, the consumer organizations world over should develop an effective Think Tank to plan a taskforce to face the challenges ahead. The probable guidelines that could be followed by the consumer organizations of India and Japan to face the challenges of globalized world are:

1. The United Nations Guidelines on the Protection of Consumers, endorsed at the United Nations General Assembly in 1999, added the principle of promoting sustainable consumption. It says: "All members and organizations of the entire society share responsibilities for sustainable consumption."
2. Consumers can play a necessary role in promoting consumption based on a sustainable environment, economy and society. Consumer organizations are responsible for promoting public participation in sustainable consumption and should work together with the Government and the industrial and business communities to promote the same.
3. Consumer organizations throughout the world should affiliate with Consumers International based in Malaysia to tackle international consumer issues. Consumers should be made known all about Consumers Interpol which was launched by Consumers International in the year 1981 as an international consumer policy network.
4. Consumers International aim is to be fast, comprehensive and truly international, corresponds from a number of countries who have joined this network to inform the Consumer Interpol of a suspected hazardous products withdrawal in their home market as well as international.
5. The spirit of consumer education that is to be followed by consumer organizations and the concerned authorities are given below by Consumers International as a charter for consumer action;
6. Critical awareness with consumers learning, how to distinguish needs from wants, how to ask informed question about price, availability, quality of goods and services.
7. Action and involvement with consumers being able to act on their own behalf backed by the confidence of knowledge and learning how to get a fair deal.
8. Social responsibility, consumers acting with concern and sensibility, aware of the impact of their actions on other citizens, particularly on disadvantaged groups.
9. Ecological responsibility with consumers thinking about the effects of their decisions on the physical environment, aware of the possible conflict between their desire to own things and the spoiling of our environment.

10. Solidarity with consumers realizing that their most effective action is through the information of citizen groups. Together such groups can acquire the strength and influence to make sure that adequate attention is given to consumer interests.

    - Consumer organizations should insist the concerned governments to introduce compulsory consumer education as a part of education system. It helps younger generation with requisite skills in today's complex market place. The basics of consumerism should be taught at school level itself. Certificates, Diploma and Degree courses must be offered in consumer affairs with an assurance of employment.
    - We know that pen is mightier than sword. No organization is complete without publications. A regular newsletters and magazines should be brought out periodically as the media communication between the consumer activists and consumers. Besides this, TV interviews of consumer activists and their programs, plan of action to solve consumer problems should be broadcasted.
    - Consumer organizations should join their hands to establish World Institute of Consumers (WIC) exclusively to carry out research in all kinds of consumer problems world over.
    - Consumer organizations should insist industrialists to set up a council for fair business practices which in turn will avoid mal-practices of traders. These councils should lay down a code of ethics for the traders.
    - Obviously, producer is also a consumer. Hence, organization should enroll more and more manufacturers, traders and business community considering them as consumers which would make the organization more effective. However, such members should not violate the aims and objectives of organization.
    - The list of dos and don'ts of the organization should be updated according to the changes of the economy.
    - Organizations should take initiative to organize Industry Trade Consumer Interface for a dialogue between consumer bodies and traders organizations. If it provides workable results, it is indeed a thing of beauty and joy for consumers.
    - Organizations should lobby the government to set up mobile consumer courts for rural consumers and special consumer courts for quick disposal of consumer complaints. Many economic policies as they exist today are working against the consumer. For example, if the banking industry decides to go on strike, the employees do not lose as they get their wages, the employer too has nothing to lose, and it is only the consumer who faces the inconveniences. Therefore, organizations should insist concerned authorities to change such policies.

- Despite the package of legal measures, it is found that the trading and manufacturing lobby tries to subvert the protective laws. Government officials are often bullied into pressure to use their discretionary powers. The quality control inspection staff is also put under pressure not to prosecute offenders. Such things should be brought to public notice by the consumer organizations to safeguard consumers.
- Since it is a computer age, organizations should try to computerize for quick interaction.
- Organizations should celebrate World Consumers Rights Day on March 15, every year to convey their solidarity. On the day, programmes arranged should be constructive and educative such as symposiums, workshops, exhibitions, rallies and discourse by experts especially on environmental awareness, which is the need of the hour.
- The organization should be willing to admit a mistake if proved with facts. The organization should be impartial and transparent.
- The members should set an example by practicing what they advice to consumers.
- Consumer activists should avoid loses talks. One should not give vague impression about what they speak and act.
- Organizations should be non-violent.
- Ignorance of law is not an excuse. So it must be the bounded duty of the organizations to study the existing consumer protection laws and amendments and enlighten the consumers.
- In most countries, services like telephone, electricity, water supply and public distribution system are managed by government agencies but there are so many complaints pertaining to these public utility services. Therefore, organizations should form a vigilance group to watch them.
- Organizations should act as a strong watch dogs and lobby governments to implement effective consumer protection laws when and where required instantly. Organizations should put pressure on governments to extend financial help for their activities since what they are working for consumers actually should have to be done by the governments. However, the organizations should try to finance themselves. The meetings of the organization should be regular, frequent and informal where the members are allowed to express freely and openly.
- There is too much political interference which misleads the organization. Most of the time the aims and objectives of the organization are disturbed by the political interference and weaken

the strength of the organization. Therefore they should be non-political.

- Consumer organizations world over should campaign for the reduction of Global Burden of Malnutrition.

Last but not the least, organizations should interact and co-ordinate with co-organizations. Co-ordination and working with national and international bodies will create Collective Consumer Search Capital (CSK) which would be useful for every consumer organization to spread the consumer movement world over and to face this changing and challenging globalize market scenario.

12. Kerton's concept of consumer search capital and Neelakanta's concept of Consumer Decision Capsule — The two new gadgets of consumerism

Robert R. Kerton, Professor of Economics, University of Waterloo has developed a concept, which has come to be known as Consumer Search Capital (CSK). There is great hope for using this concept for our conditions in India to help make better consumer decisions.

The concept CSK is defined as "the accumulated stock of decision making principles and data which can be used to increase the effectiveness of consumer decisions". Since the concept CSK consists of a collection of searching and bargaining strategy that the consumer can employ in the market place, it ultimately determines the quantity received per unit of currency. The value of CSK is far larger than what seems to be at first examination.

The concept obliges us to give explicit attention to these consumer skills and strategies.

The CSK must be regarded as a capital because first the skill give services overtime, and second time and resources are used to create this capital. The process of accumulation of decision-making principles must be viewed as an investment. Such investments are of two types i.e., private and collective CSK. The private CSK is created on an individual basis, where as collective CSK is in the form of consumer associations and government departments.

Collective CSK is often far more economical compared to individual CSK, especially when there are economies of scale in the collection of information. To be more precise, some government departments would serve as collective CSK. The accumulation of CSK provides a better decision-making status to a consumer. This accumulation is possible through an organized system of consumer oriented education and information gathering.

As a prelude to this accumulation of CSK, let us take a look at existing conditions in India, which is still a developing country. Here we are constantly confronted with a number of unscrupulous market practices. Quality of products is always poor. Cost curve is on a constant upward move. Nefarious activities like adulteration and duplicating and faking with no exception to price cheating have become too common. If the consumer in India were to face such a complex developing situation he is to be initiated by individual and collective bodies including government agencies who act directly to mitigate the sufferings of the consumer, organizations who take on the role of a liaison between the individual consumer and government agencies. Part of the responsibility of educating the consumer lies more with the voluntary agencies as they have a better consumer problem and accumulate more CSK through experience and information.

In a developing country like India, the consumer is at greater risk while taking market decisions. Because consumer in a developing country is exposed to the glittering and colourful standard of living that his counterpart in an advanced country enjoys and would desire to be placed in a similar situation. There is constant conflict between desire prompted wants and need based requirements. "Wants are insatiable", says the economist. It is sure, but in our Indian situation wants are many and resources are few. The gap between production and consumption, cost of production and price level has never been bridged and a balanced coordination of these factors, of production, resources, prices and management and distribution, etc. have not been commensurate with each other.

In India more than 2/3rd of the population is still illiterate and ill informed according to Central Statistical Report of India, 2004. As consumer at large has to grapple with problems of under nourishment, over population, poverty, unemployment ill-health and host of other problems, so the CSK has special importance. At the same time it needs special formulation to be lamented that, poor as we habitually become passive as an economic group with low CSK. Poverty does not lend the consumer the desired strength to question and to resist the attempts of victimization. We just let things pass and resign to a status of apathetic situation of futility. It is suggested earlier in this paper that voluntary organizations can do as much to be of service to the consumer as government agencies. And it is also economical and more effective to raise voices in a collective manner, which is bound to be heard, whereas a single voice ends up in thin air. When consumers are united there is strength to be reckoned with which ultimately wins. The Consumers International in Malaysia, Australian Consumer Association and Consumer Education and Research Centre in India are some of the examples that could be cited for organized consumer movement which go to prove the importance of collective CSK as being useful in a developing country.

The theory of CSK could be very profitable when applied to our conditions through consumer associations where collective CSK is embodied and this collective CSK does have significant effects on the progress of developing countries. This is also especially significant to people with low incomes. In a developing economy the market is flooded with an ever-increasing variety of goods, which also leads to more competition and subsequent dubious market transactions. This situation is again a better care for application of CSK concept. While trying to adopt Kerton's CSK methods to our developing situation, it is imperative to suggest certain more practical and adoptable techniques for consumer movement in our country. These techniques could be adopted at broadly three levels:

1. Individual
2. Collective

3. Government Sponsored

In the first place, awareness among consumer fraternity about their rights and privileges has to be created. This is best done through providing education followed by information. As an individual, a consumer can do well by gathering more information about the commodity market; the standards and quality, production and distribution and unscrupulous market practices, allocation of budget based on priorities and needs. He should also make competitive studies of commodities he buys through available information and consultation with knowledgeable people and neighbours and make his purchases worthwhile. His principle should be that what he has bought is worthy of the unit of money spent.

As a collective example several organizations devoted to consumerism already exist in this country though in a very small number. According to Kerton, it is this collective CSK gathered through voluntary organizations can do yeoman service in our country. If consumer associations were to be more effective under an Indian condition they will have to be on a wider and more decentralized pattern. That means every individual consumer should have easy access to the organizations. The programmes of organization should be such that the consumers are primarily educated in matters of consumerism and get suitable and adequate information, which ultimately places them in a good state of defense. The consumer body should also try to use all available sources to disseminate useful information to the consumer in a better and acceptable fashion. This entails the production of simple, readable and illustrated materials which is helpful for the consumer.

The State Government should have a greater responsibility towards the consumer. The consumer protection activity put forth by the governments is far too inadequate considering the magnitude of the problems that the consumer has to face today. It would be more appropriate that each state in our country has an autonomous, well-organized and adequately staffed expertise formed. The governments also on the other hand should examine the possibility of remodeling the existing educational structure to be more consumers oriented. In short it would be highly ideal if every consumer who goes to school has an opportunity to learn and as a consumer he has every right to safety, to be informed about protection and education. The government should also instruct the communication media under its control to intensify consumer-oriented programmes.

We know that active consumerism started from the US through high thinking great men like, John F. Kennedy, former President of the US in 1962. But the consumer guidelines being developed then were not much useful for consumers in the under privileged in developing countries. It is vital that we have to find a useful technique available to India; Consumer Search Capital is one technique we must deploy.

13. Consumer Decision Capsule: A similar concept like CSK

We need not say that present day market is complex with inconsistent information, highly fluctuating prices and stock positions. Consumer public is bound to be misled owing to these constrains. Decision-making is highly complicated and absolutely impossible. Therefore, Professor Neelakanta felt that the decision making of consumer would have been easier if there could be a readymade model to provide him authenticated product information. In this article, an attempt is made to develop a model, which suits the consumer public in general.

It is evident that consumerism today has become a way of life for a citizen anywhere in the world. Whether well informed or ignorant, a consumer has to behave positively and register an economic gain in his day-to-day participation in the market place. Today's market is such a complex phenomena that a consumer is bound to get misled confused, react negatively and regret his unwise shopping. True, there are varieties of information sources, through ads that highlight and project a colorful image of the product range. But all that is unilateral in the sense that the fund of information at hand to the consumer today through ads is only commercial and profit oriented. A consumer before he actually buys a product has to scan the information available and use to his best advantage in making the most economical buying in relation to his budget. Because, today's market is so complex, with inconsistent information and highly fluctuating prices and stock positions. Decision-making is almost impossible or utterly difficult. This sort of complexity does not help the consumer in either planning his budget or making the purchase. His budget calculation may go wrong.

Due to advancement of science and technology there has been a fast changing market structure and the subsequent ruthless bombardment of audio-visuals to project the products through ads has put the consumer in a great dilemma. To understand the present day market situation, to plan his buying selectively and economically a consumer needs proper, processed product information at hand to help him make the purchase with proper decisions and have the satisfaction of good buying. His decision making would have been easier if only a consumer has access to a well prepared readymade model to provide him authenticated product information and help him make the decision, so that without much confusion he could buy the product and get the satisfaction of having made the most economic need based buying.

But that question is how and where such authentic information is available to make proper decision. Hence, to solve this problem an attempt is made to collect information, process the same and make available to the consumer for the asking in a ready to use form. This we prefer to call Consumer Decision Capsule (CDC).

14. What is Consumer Decision Capsule (CDC)

To a layman a capsule mean a highly potent drug (antibiotic or otherwise) filled in an easily consumable form. To be more precise, to present anything in a capsule means a more complex material is simplified for use even by a child. On the same analogy a loud thinking is made in order to help consumer make wise decisions with the help of brief and precise information in capsules. These capsules are supposed to be in the form of handouts.

The ongoing reforms in the direction of Globalization are emerging as a potential challenge to consumers both in India and Japan. The Globalization paved the way for the advent of multinational corporations into the domestic economic scenario. The markets are now flooded with a number of products claiming each of their product as best one. The advertisement costs are mounting up, placing an unnecessary burden on consumers. The consumer today is a lot confused one struggling very hard for safeguarding his interests. Therefore, there is a great need for effective consumer organizations in India.

Now the question is; how to evolve effective consumer organizations and who could do that?

The answer to this is a joint effort of consumers, organizations and the governments concerned.

There is a tendency that it is the bounded duty of a government to look after the welfare of the consumers. But the consumers should realize that they too have a role to play by following their responsibilities along with the rights. These rights and responsibilities should be made known to consumers by consumer organizations. The organizations should be made strong with the dedicated participation by the consumer clan. Simultaneously, government should take consumers into account while making policy decisions.

15. Some suggestions

The large business houses especially those who are producing consumer products must have a consumer affairs cell at the highest level in their own business organization. This should be made compulsory by the concerned ministry. If necessary, ordinance has to be passed and asked to follow the directions very strictly.

Consumer meets should be organized regularly by traders and business houses on open invitation through advertisements published in newspapers and customers attending these meets should be invited to offer their complaints and suggestions in regard to the products and services of the company. The concerned governments should direct all the business houses to organize meets regularly and should be watched constantly.

Business organizations and consumer bodies should regularly provide information in regard to self-regulatory or consumer protection activities to the media and that should persuade important newspapers to publish a regular feature on consumer affairs so as to promote consumer awareness.

The concerned governments should instruct the concerned authorities through proper guidelines to introduce compulsory consumer education in schools and colleges to create consumer awareness among younger generation. Besides, it should also insist to conduct workshops and seminars on consumer problems like, deceptive ads, price cheating, food and drug adulteration and environmental pollution. More information should be provided on existing consumer protection laws in the country, changing market scenario, globalization and consumer, multinational organizations and consumer as well as activities of Consumers International, Malaysia.

Consumer organizations should provide counseling and guidance to the consumer, especially the needy one to handle a complaint either by arriving at a pre-trial negotiated settlement with the opposite party or by restoring to redressal mechanism effectively in an innovative way.

Training programmes, workshops and orientation courses should be conducted by the consumer organizations to develop the understanding, knowledge and expertise on consumer protection provisions and keep abreast of the most recent facts or developments in the field with the support of the government.

Arrangements should be made by both consumer organizations and governments for collaborative, participative and responsive relationship between the two for safeguarding consumer rights and promoting their welfare.

The consumer organizations should be provided with adequate funds by the central and state governments to undertake consumer welfare programmes. It is appreciable to note that the government of Korea is doing this great job and the researcher wishes that the same should be followed by the governments of Japan and India. In the meantime, the governments should not expect the organizations to come under their clusters.

The governments should encourage consumer organizations by awarding cash prizes to those who are highly dedicated. Swami Vivekananda Award in India is one such example to be noted here.

Consumer the world over is being mercilessly exploited by not one but several agencies reducing him to nothingness. Some advanced economies called consumer a king, but this term ends up in sarcasm. This worldwide melody of consumer exploitation that has turned from an academic to epidemic stage needs to be halted. But a consumer himself has to be more aware and active in his defense.

Indeed, a day will come that a good number of Ralph Naders will emerge not only in India but also in the whole world and consumer awareness will spread and consumer organizations will gain momentum to safeguard the interests of consumers. The term Consumer Sovereignty gains meaning and momentum in an economy only when consumer become sovereign and only when he can fulfill the dream of Benham (Consumer Is King).

However, as consumers, all of us should join our hands and remember the bold words of Sri Swami Vivekananda, a famous saint and philosopher of India- Arise! Awake! Stop not till the goal is reached.

In a recent verdict pertaining to a consumer dispute case, the Supreme Court of India ruled that the liability of a common carrier is absolute and it is not for the consumer to prove negligence. This indicates that consumer protection is becoming an area of increasing concern as the economy becomes more consumer and market centric. Consumers in India as a breed lack knowledge about their rights and the legal provisions for redressal.

Though India has had a Consumer Protection Act in place since 1986, it has been felt time and again that the provisions of the law were insufficient to protect consumer interests. To this end, the Act has been amended twice, in 1991 and in 1993. But the provisions are still insufficient to cope with some practical difficulties that have a bearing on the consumer courts' working. The government is considering amending the Act again this year to protect consumers from "aggressive product advertisement" and "the presence of duplicate goods bearing bogus ISI marks".

The Consumer Protection Act promotes and protects the interests and rights of consumers against deficiencies in goods or services purchased and against unfair or restrictive trade practices. The Act defines any person or entity buying goods or hiring a service for personal use as a "consumer". But disputes pertaining to goods or services bought for commercial purposes or resale are excluded from the purview of the Act. This means that in case of a dispute, the appellant will have to prove that he bought the goods or hired the service for personal use exclusively. However, a person who consumes goods or uses services that he has not bought, but using them with the consent of the person who has bought them, also comes under the definition of a consumer under the Act. Services rendered for free are not included under the Consumers Protection Act.

The term "deficiency" in goods or services should be understood as any fault, imperfection or inadequacy in the quality, nature of goods and performance of a service. In order to file a complaint against deficiency in service, such a service should necessarily have been rendered for a consideration. An "unfair trade practice" occurs when any unfair or deceptive method or practice is adopted by a seller for the purpose of promoting the sale (advertisement), use or supply of any goods or for the provision of any service. These include:

- False or misleading representations of the quality or quantity of goods or services,
- Misrepresentation of characteristics or uses or accessories or sponsorships, etc, which they do not have. If any guarantee is promised by the seller as to the performance or efficacy of the goods or services, which is not based on adequate or proper tests, this too comes under the unfair trade practices tag,
- Misleading the consumer about the price at which the product is to be sold, like advertising the supply of goods or services at bargain prices, when that is not the case,
- Offering of gifts, prizes with the intention of not providing them as offered or if the price of the gift or prize is included in the item sold,
- Non-compliance with product safety standards, and finally,
- Hoarding or destruction of goods.

A "restrictive trade practice" includes any trade practice that requires a consumer to buy or hire any goods or services with a prior condition attached for such buying or hiring. The Consumer Protection Act applies to all goods and services, irrespective of private, public or cooperative enterprises, unless the goods or services are specifically exempted by the Central Government.

The provisions of the Act are compensatory in nature. This means that the consumer is not legally required to deposit a court fee, which used to deter consumers earlier from approaching the courts; the court's rulings come in the form of ordering a compensation in case of a default.

Before purchasing a product, one should check its quality and guarantee. It is always better to purchase quality products bearing government approval marks like ISI and AGMARK. A complaint can be launched with the pecuniary judiciary if a deficiency in goods or services consumed is found and the complaint should bear the value of the relief that is being sought. If the value of the concerned goods and services is less than Rs 5 lakh, the complaint must be filed in the District Forum. And if the value of the concerned goods and services is between Rs 5 lakh and Rs 20 lakh, the complaint should be filed with the State Commission. If the value of the goods and services exceeds Rs 20 lakh, the complaint has to be filed with the National Commission.

CHAPTER 17
Consumer Protection & Guidance

SYNOPSIS

Importance of the consumer to the business has yet to be realised fully. Business makes profit only when goods are consumed or services utilised. This presupposes consumer existence. Business is entirely dependent on the consumer not only for its very survival but also for its growth.

1. Consumer movement

The problem of consumers have been felt and recognised with the growth of industrialisation, and urbanisation and along with the rapid growth of industrialisation,, new market techniques were developed which influenced the economic and social culture. The common law maxim "Caveat Emptor, ('let the buyer beware') which placed once on the buyer to protect his own interest, protected the seller against any action for damages sustained due to defects in goods. However, with the growth of liaise faire competition, it was accepted that the interest of buyer served best by free competition between sellers. With farther increase in the volume of production and distribution, the problem of consumers became prominent and consumer groups started asserting their claims. Consequently both at national and international level the consumer protection movement started.

Consumer seeks protection, advice and information when his rights are adversely affected. The shift from buyer beware to seller beware has increased the role of Government in promoting the consumer's right to safety, the right to be informed, the right to choose, the right to be heard, the right to redress and right to represent. These consumer rights constitute Consumer Bill of Rights. In 1962, President John F. Kennedy, in his consumer message, summed up these rights of consumers and paved the way for organised consumerism in the U.S.A. and all over the world.

2. Consumer protection in India

In general, consumers are scattered over the country. They are highly disorganised. Individually, they have very weak bargaining power. They are not professional or shrewd buyers. Besides, in India, they have an additional handicap, namely, majority of consumers are ignorant and usually lack information to make intelligent purchases. In many cases, they are incompetent to protect their interests, particularly when they deal with fully organised, united and well-informed professional sellers. Above all, apathy, indifference and inertia of the public are the perpetual enemies and they are simply appalling. These are serious obstacles to the sound and sustained development of consumerism and consumer protection in India.

In India where the majority of consumer is illiterate and ill-informed, and has limited purchasing power and are not in a position to meet the basic necessities of life. A number of non-essential, traders by means of unfair practices and deceptive methods, competition in the market is often reduced to competition in advertising, as companies spend more and more money on exaggerated, misleading and deceptive advertising claims, rather than improving and functional features, making the distribution system more efficient or reducing the price.

In economics, it is said that the act of production is not complete until the commodity is in the hands of the ultimate consumer. All production is, in fact, for consumption directly or indirectly. It is true that consumption should be the sole end and purpose of all production. In a free market economy, it is said that consumer is the king. He communicates his decision or wish through price, every rupee representing a ballot paper and the prime regulator of our economic life. He rules the economy through pricing. He brings about the so-called optimum allocation of scarce economic resources through the all powerful mechanism of pricing governed by the impersonal and, therefore, impartial general relations of demand and supply.

In reality, consumer is not a king. At the most, he is a prince without a privy purse and is often indistinguishable from a serf or a pauper. He is the main sufferer of inflation, sometimes controlled or otherwise naked. He pays more and earns much less in the real terms. He is the one to suffer most from acute shortages (man-made or god-made) of essential commodities. He is the one who is often cheated and fleeced-even given shoddy and adulterated goods. Short weights and measures, deceptive packaging, misleading advertising, hoarding, profiteering and countless frauds committed by trade on the poor and innocent consumers clearly indicate gross exploitation of the consumer by industry, trade and by organised labour. By and large, during the last 25 years, the consumer in India has been a victim of Central Government's various policies. It resorted to enhancing from time to time excise duties and commodity taxes which heavily leaned on the consumer. Indirect taxes hit the consumers most particularly when they can be easily transferred to consumers in the form of price rise. In the seller's market, the producer can do so without any danger of reduction in demand. Heavy investment in capital goods industry and the neglect of consumer goods industry led to an era of scarcity, rising prices and misery for the consumer. Extraordinary finance for financing huge projects under planned economy was secured through deficit financing. Of all the taxes perhaps, inflation is the most ruthless and its impact on the low-income consumers is probably the highest. Above all, extraordinary growth of populating in India further complicates the problem of distribution.

During inflation, we have a persistent rise in prices. When there is a labour dispute, and bonuses are increased, immediately employers and managements conveniently raise prices due to higher cost of production. If the price is controlled, they demand Government's sanction for a price hike or rise. In any event, the price spiral (rise) is in full swing and inflation is accentuated. The victim of inflation once again is the consumer.

The foregoing state of affairs incidentally happens to be the profile of Indian economic situation for the last thirty years and strongly emphasizes the immediate need for consumer protection, consumer guidance and consumer education in India.

Unless there is a general awakening in the consumer-public, consumer movement and consumer guidance or protection cannot have firm and strong foundation. Consumer education assumes considerable importance in evolving a favorable climate for exercising the sovereign right to demand, justice and fair trade practices. Businessmen usually take full advantage of general apathy, indifference and helplessness on the part of the consumer and adopt anti-consumer policies to earn larger profits.

We have monuments to the unknown soldier, statues for martyrs, and tableaux for freedom fighters. But so far, in no country there is a single memorial for the conveniently forgotten man and the victim of our society — the poor and helpless consumer.

3. What is consumer protection?

Consumer protection is essential for a healthy economy.

1. We need physical protection of the consumer, for instance, protection against products that are unsafe or endanger the health and welfare of consumer.
2. We need protection of the consumer against deceptive and unfair trade practices. Consumer must have adequate rights and means of redress against business malpractices and frauds.
3. Ecological and environmental effects of chemical, fertilizer or refinery complexes will have to be seriously considered because they pollute water, air and food and endanger human life. Consumer wants due protection against all types of pollution, he wants a healthy environment free from pollution.
4. We must have adequate protection of consumer public against the abuse of monopoly position and/or restrictive trade practices. Protection delayed is protection denied.

Greater and free competition in the market is of definite advantage to the consumer. Competition can reduce prices, enhance Quality and stimulate innovation in product-mix and marketing-mix. Innovation means progress and progress means life, a prosperous life. Competition is the dispenser of justice to the consumer and producer alike.

4. Why consumer protection?

The 'why' of consumer protection is evident at least in India?

1. Consumer has no voice in the product which is manufactured for his consumption. Hence, consumer naturally demands the existence of fair trade practices which would ensure physical safety when he consumes the product. Similarly, fair trade practices will enable him to get the real value for his money.
2. It is very difficult to effectively organize consumers in country as vast as India. The backwardness of people is a further obstacle to consumer organization.
3. A majority of the population is illiterate and ignorant.
4. Poverty, lack of education, lack of information, traditional outlook of Indians to suffer in silence, considering poverty and misery as a god-given thing—all these negative sides of our life have enabled unscrupulous businessman to exploit consumers in India. To prevent this ruthless exploitation, we need a forceful well-organised consumerism or consumer movement coupled with Government support and patronage in the form of special legislation. Of course, legislation can protect consumers only when consumers themselves assert their rights and exert pressure on the producers, dealers and the Government. Then only the prevailing malpractice like profiteering, black marketing, hoarding, adulteration, short measures and weights, misleading advertisement, faulty packaging, mail-order frauds, etc., can be cured or reduced to the minimum.

5. The march of science and technology has increased the difficulties of the consumer along with his opportunities of selection from a very wide variety of goods (many of them highly sophisticated and complicated). Increasing technical complexity of consumer goods, especially those containing machinery clearly points out that consumers (who are not professional buyers) cannot know the ins and outs of such goods. Rational choice between and among such goods would require the skills of amateur electrician, mechanic dietician, mathematician, etc. Marketing is now becoming increasingly impersonal (professional).

The consumer choice is influenced by mass advertising and other promotional devices, utilising highly developed art of persuasion. Commercial sources are the core of the existing information system. But consumers find that most advertising and promotion today are deceptive or misleading. Hence, consumer cannot know whether drug preparations meet the minimum standards of safety, quality and efficacy. He usually does not know whether one processed food has more nutritional value than another. He may not know whether the performance of a product will in fact meet his needs or whether the large economy size, or the best buy is really a bargain.

Consumers wish to meet producers as equals. They want value for money, reasonable quality, prices related to the cost of production, transport, etc. Too many producers are bringing out products that people do not really need and cannot afford. But aggressive advertising and salesmanship make people want the things. In many cases people spend the money they otherwise need for food, clothing and shelter on gadgets that are not really needed. The advertising industry in the U.S.A. spent $ 150 per person per year (in 1978) to push up goods on consumers. The consumer wants protection against deceptive and misleading advertisements and sales promotion devices.

Therefore, in the present intricate and complicated market, he is just an amateur. In short, consumers do need protection and guidance under the present circumstances.

After evaluating the scope, need and significance of consumer protection, let us now deal with the alternative ways and means of securing reasonable consumer guidance and protection.

There are three agencies for ensuring consumer protection:

(1) Self-help, *i.e.* consumer organisation itself.

(2) Business, by self-regulation and by giving a fair deal to the retailers.

(3) Government, by having special Acts and implementing those laws strictly. Mere legislation is not enough. More important is their enforcement not only in letter but also in spirit. The legislation ensures competition, provision of information to buyers and regulation of unfair trade practices.

5. How to provide consumer protection?

The consumer interest in the market place is the focus or the heart of enlightened marketing mix. The business and consumerism both aim at the protection of consumer interest-business through self-regulation and consumerism through self-help. Consumerism invokes Government assistance when business misbehaves and fails to fulfill special responsibilities.

In exchange relationship normally, we have only two parties: (1) Seller and (2) Buyer. However, in the modern market, the seller is organised and has professional skill, whereas the buyer is usually unorganised and amateur. Hence, we need consumer legislation and consumerism.

6. Consumer legislation

If business morality is high and if moral values are at a premium, there is no reason why self-regulation by traders and their associations should fail to give meaningful guarantee or money back to consumers. In reality, the problem of consumer protection is bilateral. (1) Organised consumer movement inducing consumers to take intelligent interest in consumer democracy, and (2) Self-regulation and self-discipline by producers and traders. Government intervention takes place only to protect the weaker party *in* the market (consumer) and to prevent exploitation by the stronger party (businessmen).

It should be noted the consumer legislation is a rough substitute for self-regulation of business. It appears as a last resort, when consumerism is recognised as a shame on marketing. Consumer legislation offer insurance against business malpractice and ensures distributive justice to amateur consumers.

7. Consumer Ombudsman (Lokayukta)

7.1 What is the Consumer Ombudsman?

The Consumer Ombudsman (a Consumer Protection Agency) is the Commissioner for Consumers- a chief officer of Central Consumer Council appointed by the Government He is in charge of enforcing and administering the Consumer Protection Acts. He can speed up legal processes in dealing with trade practices.

The aim of Fair Trade Practices Act is to protect consumers against misleading advertising, deceptive packaging, misbranding, mislabeling, false warranties and other undesirable commercial marketing *i.e.*, all activities undertaken in order to increase the sale of goods and services by greedy sellers.

The cleaning up of advertising, sales promotion and other marketing practices, which can be achieved with the aid of the consumer legislation, may in turn help to make it easier for consumers to make their decisions when buying goods and services.

The consumer Ombudsman (at the Central and State levels) checks that advertising contains no misleading information about products, prices, quality, etc. The supervision of the Ombudsman covers all kinds of commercial marketing carried out by all business enterprises. He scrutinizes advertisements in newspapers and periodicals and on packages, as well as direct mail advertising, outdoor advertisement, film radio and TV. advertisements, etc.

Consumer Ombudsman protects consumers from undesirable conditions which may appear in the printed sales agreement forms which are used when capital goods such as household appliances, television sets, books, etc,, are sold. For instance, these contracts may have small prints improperly favouring the seller at the cost of the buyer — a clause reserving the right of the seller alone to decide whether to goods sold are defective or there may be a price increase clause, giving unilateral right to the seller to raise the agreed price.

(1) He tries to get the matter put right voluntarily, by discussing in with the seller or his representative, *e.g.* advertising agency.

(2) If correction by a voluntary agreement is impossible, the case is referred to a special court dealing with unfair trade practices. The court's decision is final.

(3) In matters of minor importance, the consumer Ombudsman can himself issue 'cease and desist' order prohibiting a misleading marketing action.

Consumer Ombudsman is accessible to all consumers or their associations. In Sweden, we have consumer Ombudsman since 1971 under the Marketing Practices Act and under the Act Prohibiting improper contract terms.

A consumer Ombudsman or a consumer protection authority (Lokayukta) can survey the whole field of consumer protection in consultation with consumer associations and take necessary steps for speeding up legal processes in dealing with trade malpractice. There is a compelling need for a thorough survey of the real as opposed to the theoretical protection offered to the consumer by present legislation. A consumer Ombudsman may be the answer to our consumer problems is India. He can act as a statutory agency empowered to enforce genuine claims on behalf of Indian consumer.

8. The Act: A historical step

In India, until the advent of independence, there were hardly any laws which were directed to the protection of consumer interest. The Sale of Goods Act, the Drugs and Cosmetics Act did not directly deal with the subject of consumer interest. Under Constitution of India, fundamental rights have been declared and procedure for their enforcement has been laid down. Many civil and criminal statutes define and deal with the right of the citizens and courts and tribunal have been set up for remedying the wrongful acts done to them. However, in context of the growing needs of the citizens many problems relating to their routine necessities, do not find effective measure for verifying wrongful acts and for compensation due to consequent loss to them. For example, the supplier of adulterated or spurious articles of food can be prosecuted and punished but the victim or consumer will not get any compensation or awards for the damage or loss done to him.

Likewise, under Civil Procedure Code, a person may file suit for recovering the damages but due to complexities of the procedure delay in disposal and expensive litigation, such procedure was not considered desirable, particularly for the enforcement of the rights of the protection of the rights of the consumers who are the victim of the delay and negligence on the part of the supplier of goods or services and sustained personal loss while consuming goods or utilizing services.

After the report of Sachhar Committee, the Consumer Protection Bill, 1986 was introduced in the Parliament and received the assent of the President on December 24,1986.

The Act became effective from January 7, 1987. It provided better protection of the interests of consumer and for establishment of consumer council and other authority for the speedy settlement of the consumer disputes and matters connected therewith.

9. Objects of Consumer Protection Act, 1986

In the statement of objects and reasons, it is said that the Act seeks to provide speedy and simple redressal to consumer dispute, a quasi-judicial machinery is sought to be set up at the District, State and Central levels. The quasi-judicial body will observe the principles of natural justice and have been empowered to give relief of a specific nature and to award, wherever appropriate, compensation to consumer, penalty for non compliance of orders given by the quasi-judicial body have also been provided.

The Act seeks to protect the consumers in the following respects. Section 6 of the Act spells out these objects as follows:

(*a*) The right to be protected against the marketing of goods and services which are hazardous to life and property.

(*b*) The right to be informed about the quality, quantity, potency, purity, standard and price of goods to protect the consumer against unfair trade practices.

(*c*) The right to be assured whenever possible, with regard to access to a variety of goods at the competitive prices.

(*d*) The right to be heard and to be assured that consumer's interest will receive due consideration at the appropriate forums.

(*e*) The rights to redressal against unfair trade practices of unscrupulous exploitation of consumers, and

(*f*) The right to consumer education.

9.1 Protection against hazardous goods

The Act says that the consumer has a right to be protected against the marketing of those goods which are hazardous to life and property *e.g.* gas cylinder, if not sealed and delivered properly, may cause injury to life.

There are many laws intended to safeguard these interests, *e.g.* Food Adulteration Act, 1954. Besides, there is provision for I.S.I, and Agmark in order to secure these interests.

But the problem is of honest and efficient enforcement of standards laid down in these laws.

Consumer Protection Act, 1986 provides protection to consumers from such goods if any how they have got place in the market and have caused any injury to consumer or his property.

Donoghue v *Stevenson* quotes where a bottle of drink sprang the remains of a dead shell to the fright of the consumer at a restaurant, who had already taken a part of the contents, aggravating her illness and the manufacturer was held liable to the distant user [(1932) Ac 562].

9.2 Right to information

The consumer has the right to be informed about the quality, quantity, potency, purity standard and prices of goods.

In *Indian Photographic Film Co.* v *H.D. Shourie* case (1990 CPJ 142), it was held that the importer of film was not able to print the price of the film on the film, because the nature of trade was such that it did not permit him to do so. He was directed to make it a condition with his retailers to attach price tag to each film before they delivered the same.

This has been done in order to save consumer from unfair trade practices and to save them from false and misleading description about the quality and nature of the product.

9.3 Right of access to variety

Consumer has right to choose from a variety at competitive prices. For this objective all the dealers are supplied with the variety of goods so that they can offer variety of goods to consumer and to resist monopoly of a dealer or manufacturer. It is the duty of the Central Council, constituted under this Act, to ensure that consumer enjoys variety of goods at competitive prices and they are not being cheated by a dealer.

9.4 Right to be heard

The right to be heard pertain to the post-purchase. It has two aspects, One is that the supplier of goods or services should attend to the complaint and the other is that the consumer should have a legal remedy in the event of non-redress by the supplier.

To be heard, appropriate forum has been constituted under this Act, so that consumers receive due consideration at the hands of the appropriate redressal forums.

9.5 Unscrupulous exploitation

The consumer has been given right to seek redressal against unfair trade practices or unscrupulous exploitation.

Angela Fonese v *Corol Lawn* [(1991) CPJ 670] states, Plaintiff booked the lawn for marriage and this booking was done on a non-refundable deposit. It was held to be unfair trade practice and deposited money was ordered to be refunded with interests when plaintiff, due to pre-ponement of marriage date, was not allowed to use the lawns though lawn was free on that date.

9.6 Consumer education

It has been found that despite of various remedies, people do not exercise their legal remedies and thus do not get any benefits of such Acts. Thus it was felt consumers should be informed about the remedies available under this Act, so that they can exercise this legal right. The Consumer Protection Act, 1986 assigns to the central council set-up under the Act, the task of organizing consumer education.

Once people are rendered conscious of their rights they may feel energised to struggle against exploitation by manufacturers and traders.

10. Consumer rights

(1) ***Right to protection of health and safety:*** There are unsafe products, unstated dangers in product performance and inadequate services after sale. Right to safety means protection against the marketing of goods that are unsafe to health and life.

Products should not cause any physical danger to consumers or put them in difficulty due to sudden failure. Consumers must have assurance regarding quality, reliability and performance. There are so many common household items now available to consumers containing potentially harmful substances. Food additives, food colouring and pesticides further add new potential dangers.

In the case of food and drugs, we need safety to consumers. In many sophisticated products, *e.g.*, toys, appliances, flammable fabrics, etc, we need considerable safety. Fortunately, the recent trend in legislation for consumer safety shows a continuous shift in emphasis for consumer buyer responsibility to seller-trader responsibilities for damages and losses arising out of unsafe and dangerous products. Food and Drug Acts now hold the seller responsible for product safety. With the advance of science and technology, consumer products have become highly complex and intricate. In many instances, responsibility for safety of finished products is directly placed on producers and distributors. Legislation to achieve consumer protection against unsafe products is only the first step. Equally important is vigorous and sincere imaginative enforcement of law by adequately-staffed agencies.

By misleading advertisement consumers are led to expect higher performance levels than the product can deliver. For instance, Zippers jam, food products are adulterated, wash and wear clothes need ironing, appliance do not perform as advertised, cosmetics fail to fulfill even the minimum expectation, etc. Not only is the product quality poor but also after sales service is deplorable. In all these respects, consumers have a right of reasonable protection.

(2) ***Right to be informed:*** Consumers demand positive obligation of full disclosure to be placed on the manufacturer and dealer. We must have adequate, accurate and up-to-date information on the quality, performance and other vital characteristics of products.

Full information will enable consumers to exercise intelligently their decision to buy before they part with their money in exchange of good. The consumer must be protected against fraud. The establishment of standard weights and measures, truth in labeling and packaging, performance testing in drugs, grade labeling, tel-tags (informative labels), standardization and so on will help consumers to get reliable information. Consumer must have all facts needed to make informed choices. We have frequently inadequate and misleading information, deceptive advertising, deceptive packing, misleading warranties, scanty information on product contents and operating instruction, or care of the products, collusive pricing, deceptive credit terms, etc. The trader takes undue advantage of consumer ignorance and he is deceived as to quality, quantity, price, weight, size and any other factor involved in buying. Once the right to information is legally recognised, many of the aforesaid malpractices will be reduced to the minimum.

The seller should ensure that his advertisement mean what they say and what they really mean. Unfortunately, such sincere seller are rare in the market. Advertising causes us to buy goods which we do not want at prices, we cannot pay, and on terms we cannot meet. Want of objective information is a great obstacle in consumer satisfaction and many a time, they have a bad bargain. A housewife buys what is showed to her. It is packaged. She buys it on good faith. Unscrupulous sellers may exploit such a situation.

(3) ***Right to choose:*** It should be the keystone of dealer's policy. The widest possible section of quality brand names at fair price should be offered to the customers.

Right to choose implies that monopoly is disliked by consumers. They want to buy a product of their will. They want to exercise their option to choose a particular brand or to decide about the quantity. If the market has ample quantity and variety of products at competitive price, buyers have an opportunity of wise selection. Collusion among sellers, price fixing understanding among leading competitors, cartel movement, etc. cannot give wider choice to consumers. Competition assures consumers the right to choose.

Competition and consumer legislation provide ample protection for the consumers. More efficient information system will enable consumers to make a satisfactory choice. Competition provides wider choice of goods and services. Consumer legislation and Government regulations provide official system to make a wise selection or best bargain.

(4) ***Right to be heard:*** Consumer has a right to dissatisfaction and get his complaint heard and weighed. This gives greater importance. Even if consumer have the right to safety, to be informed and to choose, but do not enjoy the right to be heard, would be of no real control on the other three rights. If this right to be heard is denied to consumers, there would be no body to listen to their complaints and the very purpose of granting them other rights would be simply defeated. The right to be heard implies the existence of a legal framework and Government intervention to safeguard consumer interest. Many business firms are utterly indifferent to consumer's grievances and protests.

(5) ***The right to redress:*** Today, a new right is being recognised. It is the right to redressal or to settlement of just and deserving claims or grievances of consumer. This consumer right was not part of the original consumer's bill of rights. It is a good addition. This is the right to expect every product to perform as advertised when it is used as directed. If the performance and quality is short of expectation, a consumer has a right of redress. The product must be repaired, replaced or taken back by the seller. Warranties such as money back guarantee, if dissatisfied must be meaningful. Then only consumers will have confidence in the seller.

In fact, the right to be heard further implies the existence of a mechanism through which other rights can be asserted: in particular, by ensuring the right of redressal (to set right or rectify) of legitimate consumer grievances. The consumer adviser of Ombudsman (Lokayukta) and the Government authorities often receive complaints and attempt to resolve them. If we have standing grievance machinery for listening to the complaints of consumers and for the settlement of their grievances, consumer relation with the business will be very cordial and harmonious. Such a bridge of understanding or communication is necessary for assuring protection. A business firm should have a consumer affairs department to receive customer complaints and problems and to resolve them amicable. The new department should be directly attached to the top management.

(6) ***The right to a physical environment that will enhance the quality of life:*** This right has been recently incorporated to the consumer bill of rights thereby considerably enhancing the scope and significance of modern consumerism. Indeed, consumerism is now defined broadly as an organised expression for an improved quality of life. The environmental problems do affect the life of consumers. Air pollution, water pollution, food pollution and noise pollution are the legacies of reckless industrialization. The social costs of the aforesaid forms of pollution are at the cost of social benefits. Please note that each form of pollution destroys the social benefits already existing. Industry is directly responsible for many forms of pollution. Investment decisions of industry, *e.g.* chemical and fertilizer complex, refineries, etc., must ensure quality of community life by preventing or reducing the evil effects of air, water and food pollution.

11. Consumer, guidance or education

Consumer education has been defined as conscious preparation of the individual in the skills, concepts and understandings that are required for everyday living to achieve, within the framework of his/her own values and culture, the maximum satisfaction and utilization of his/her resources.

Consumer education is necessary when we have in the marketplace varied and numerous consumer goods and services demanding adequate information regarding safety and performance or correct use of the products. Consumer awareness and education will be necessary to bring about balanced control among buyers and sellers.

Consumer education will also enable buyers to protect themselves against exploitation by unscrupulous sellers indulging in unfair trade practices. In the modern complicated retail markets, we must make consumer aware of business malpractices and sales gimmicks. Consumer should be enabled to discern deceptive advertising, deceptive packaging and misleading labels. Consumer must be aware of the tactics of high pressure salesmanship and high powered advertising.

Consumer welcomes education and guidance so that he/she cannot be fooled and cannot be made to pay more than what he/she has to pay by law. Consumer education gives confidence to the buyer that he cannot be cheated in the market by fraudulent sellers.

12. Scope of consumer education

(1) Consumer education should cover efforts to give opportunities in acquiring an understanding of market economy, knowledge of consumer and agencies serving consumer interest.

(2) It should also cover a general familiarity with legal rights and responsibilities of consumers and those of manufacturers and dealers. A buyer should know the implication involved in a purchase contract specially in durable goods.

(3) Consumer should have adequate information on standard of quality, knowledge of technical and commercial terms used in the market of goods and services.

(4) He should have a general awareness of fraudulent and misleading advertisements, deceptive packaging and labeling, misbranding and adulteration and such other common dishonest practices prevalent in business. Such awareness prevents consumer victimisation to a great extent.

Consumer education and awareness will be necessary for self-insurance against sharp selling practices and usual unfair trade practices. To accomplish all these skills effectively, consumer education must focus on everyday living situations of a given group of consumers.

Consumers in India need more knowledge about nutrition and food use (cooking recipes and substitute food) and their corresponding food value. They should know the ways and means to reduce waste, to find out low cost housing materials, low cost clothing, etc. They should be educated in safety on roads and streets, and they should have overall ability to assess and judge critically the comparative values of goods in the current market in order to get maximum satisfaction in all their daily wants.

13. How to become a better buyer?

Buymanship: We have ample literature on advertisement, salesmanship; marketing, etc. filled with numerous ways and means for successful selling. Hence, we have professional sellers in the market. However, we have comparatively limited literature on buymanship particularly for consumers. Books on purchasing invariably concentrate on industrial purchasing or merchandise useful for industrial buyers and merchants.

Better buymanship substitutes rational or intelligent action for emotional consumer action in the market. An alert and informed consumer is his own best friend and needs no consumer advocates or world savers to protect him. He needs no protection from big, bad business, which is incidentally the producer of largest variety and best quality of goods and services in the world. Better buymanship is insurance against high pressure salesmanship advertising and high powered sales promotion. Remember, however, that the consumer-buyer is an amateur while the seller, by and large, is a professional. Better buymanship is the counterpart of modern salesmanship and to the extent it will certainly ensure more equal and balanced contest in the market.

14. Ingredients of better buymanship

(1) Be prepared with adequate and up-to-date information. Professional purchasing agent is always an informed buyer. One can collect relevant information from consumer magazines, *e.g.* 'Keemat', from informative labels and advertisements and from other buying guides.

(2) Watch for lures and traps, such as bait and switch advertising, deceptive levels, etc. Bad advertising is used to lure innocent consumers into a store. The low-priced advertised item may not be shown on the sales counters and the salesman may urge you to see more expensive item and persuade you to buy it. Buymanship helps you to guard against such deceptive and fraudulent sales methods.

(3) Avoid Impulse buying: Average consumer buys on impulse at least on 50 per cent occasions. The sellers exploit the buyer's tendency to purchase impulsively. You should be aware of impulse purchase traps.

(4) Watch for Sales: During certain seasons, buying is profitable. Seasonal purchases can give you 20 per cent savings. In addition to seasonal sales, we have annual sales, special sales, one-day sales, reduction sales and so on.

(5) Shopping around before actual buying can save easily 20 per cent of your income. It is desirable to have price comparison study of a product in several stores. Consumers who shop around, comparing quantity, quality and price get definite reduction in their purchase bill. One can save easily fifty rupees per month on all monthly purchases (worth ₹300), through shopping around. A careful shopper does this with interest.

It is not true that you get what you pay for. There is no close correlation between price and quality. Seller wants us to believe that higher price means higher quality. Out of 100 items surveyed in one market survey, only 25 had significant price correlation, 20 items actually had negative correlation, *i.e.* lower price was associated with higher quality. The remaining 55 items had very low correlation. Hence, shopping around is justifiable particularly in buying costly - articles.

(6) Bargain for lower prices arid other concessions or services. This is possible even under the so-called one price system. In retail trade, retailer would not allow himself to be undersold. He is prepared to meet competitor's prices. Careful buyer must compel him to give price reductions directly or indirectly (for example free home delivery or free installation).

(7) When we have normal supplies, careful buyer can buy in bulk and secure special price concession in bulk purchase.

(8) Read carefully labels, warranties and the freshness date or the expiry date particularly in foods and medicines.

(9) Check the quantity; do not be fooled by the size of the package. Label points out net weight, measure or count. Find out whether the package is full or semi-empty.

(10) Always adopt cash and carry system. Credit costs more money. Cash purchases are economical and free from future worries. As far as possible daily necessaries should be bought on cash at competitive prices.

(11) Check prices and totals on the bills. When unit pricing becomes universal, price checking will be easier. There may be clerical errors in calculations and totals.

(12) Keep records and receipts of purchases. This will help you to protest and get quick redress against your complaints.

In case you decide to exercises your protest and get redress, *e.g.*, the article bought is defective, follow the procedure given below:

(*a*) Give the seller opportunity to redress.

(*b*) If he is not prepared to give justice to you, approach the Consumer Organization for further action.

(*c*) You may write to the manufacturer direct and send a copy of your protest to the concerned Government authority.

(*d*) You may also approach Fair Price Trade Practices Association and lodge your complaint formally.

15. How to manage consumer problem

Let us change the way consumers are treated in India. Persistence pays. Keep on keeping on. Your one hour per week for consumer protection will make a huge difference in long run. If you are having problem with goods or services, purchased by you, then you need to initiate following steps:

1. Make oral complaint to the local dealer and customer care contact number of the company, which is available on its website or with the local dealer. Note down name of person, date, time and complaint number.
2. If no satisfactory action is initiated in a week, lodge detailed written complaint with the company, by sending email/complaint with copy to the local dealer. Visit customer care or contact us link on the website of the company for address. In case of telephone, banks, insurance companies, address complaint to Nodal Officer at its H. O.
3. After 15 days, scale-up the complaint to Chairman of the Company with copy to local dealer and claim compensation for mental tension, agony in addition to refund of price of goods or services, with interest and expenses. Give him 15 days time for redressal. Invoke warranty/ guarantee in complaint.
4. If the problem continues, write to national and local NGOs who are working for consumer protection and send copies to the Chairman of the company, its local dealer and consumer protection council which works under the District Collector at Collectorate Office.
5. Simultaneously, post your complaint at www.corecentre.co.in or contact toll free No. 1800-11-4000 from bsnl/mtnl land line.
6. If problem pertains to central govt. department or public sector undertaking, lodge complaint at www.pgportal.gov.in. If problem is pertaining to share or securities, email complaint to SEBI and NSE by visiting their websites.
7. Keep date-wise record of visit of technician or oral discussion with the dealer or customer care executive of service provider. In case if any paper is required to be signed by company representative, obtain a photocopy of the same, before signing.
8. If the problem still continues, you should file complaint with Ombudsman wherever Ombudsman Scheme [banking, insurance, electricity, etc.] exists for details, visit websites of RBI, IRDA, etc. This is fast, cost effective system.
9. If nothing works for a month, lodge a complaint with District Consumer Forum for claims upto ₹20 lakhs. Claim amount as per notice stated in para 3 above. You can yourself plead your case if amount is not substantial, otherwise it is advisable to have services of an advocate practicing in consumer protection. In Consumer Forum fees are nominal, procedure is simple and comparatively fast.
10. If the supplier of goods or service provider is a govt. department or undertaking, follow-up your complaint with The Right to Information Act, 2005. For this, visit my article "Any thing pending with Govt?" posted in RTI label at my blog www.jps50.blogspot.com and at jps50 blog at www.rtiindia.org

11. Following are websites which are useful for consumer protection:
    01. www.fcamin.nic.in
    02. www.corecentre.co.in
    03. www.ncdrc.nic.in
    04. www.consumerhelpline.in
    05. www.cgsiindia.org
    06. www.consumeronline.org
    07. www.icrpc.org
    08. www.consumer-voice.org
    09. www.cai-india.org
    10. www.cercindia.org
    11. www.cccindia.net
    12. www.ngpnet.org
    13. www.core.nic.in
    14. www.watchoutinvestor.com
    15. www.consumercom.nic.in
    16. www.pgportal.gov.in
    17. www.bankingombudsman-rbi.org.in
    18. www.confonet.nic.in
    19. www.cag.org.in
    20. www.investorhelpline.in
    21. www.iepf.gov.in
    22. www.sebi.gov.in
    23. www.nse-india.com

16. Use of RTI in consumer protection

The Right to Information Act, 2005 [RTI] enables a citizen to access information from government departments, offices and organisations. It also allows access to information of private entity through government authority.

To effectively present his case, the aggrieved consumer needs to have information and documents. For example, if there are unauthorised or fraudulent debits to your account with a bank, you first should have details of such debits. If insurance claim is rejected, you must know not only reasons but also the process followed to arrive at decision of rejection. In case if your application to a government department is not being attended, you should know why it is pending and what action has so far been taken. If a road is repaired by municipal corporation and the same gets washed away in first rains, you should be in a position to find out reasons thereof by getting details of contract and material actually used, etc. If you get exorbitant electricity bills, you need to get all the details and causes for such bills from records of service provider. Without having necessary and authentic information and papers with you, it would not be possible to effectively exert your right as a consumer.

RTI lays down a cost effective, time bound and simple procedure for extracting information, papers and samples from government authorities. It has conferred a right to this effect in Indian citizen and it flows from fundamental rights guaranteed under Article 19 of the Constitution of India.

RTI has been successful in reducing corruption to some extent. Any wrong doing by public servants can be exposed with simple application under RTI. Thus the public and consumers of government services and goods are benefited. RTI has also alerted government servants to attend citizens' work in prescribed time limit, lest questions will be asked under RTI. RTI has also made government machinery to efficiently discharge their duties, lest citizens will seek and divulge information pertaining to their dereliction of duties. A sense of accountability has been infused in government working through RTI, which has positive effect on users of government services.

Aggrieved consumers should resort to RTI for redressal of their consumer problems. In fact, RTI should precede action under Consumer Protection.

For information about RTI citizens can access www.rti.gov.in, www.cic.gov.in, www.rtiindia.org, www.prajanet.org or www.jps50.blogspot .com.

17. How to address problems with banks?

If you are having problem with any bank, initiate following steps:

1. Lodge a complaint on phone/mobile with the customer care helpline of the bank and note down complaint number, date, time and name of the person who attended your call. Details of contact numbers of customer care can be had from website of the bank.
2. If nothing transpires to your satisfaction, send a detailed written complaint, with copies of papers held by you to the branch of the bank and obtain acknowledgement or send by registered/speed post ad. Simultaneously if possible, send an email by visiting bank's website. Now most of the banks are having branch wise contact details and email IDs.
3. If no action is initiated or you are not satisfied with the reply, address the complaint to Nodal Officer at Head Office of the bank. Give details of your complaint to customer care and bank branch and their reply or no reply. Contact details are available on bank's website under customer service/care icon. Send it by registered/speed ad post and also email the same.
4. If you do not get proper reaction within a month from the bank, file a complaint with banking ombudsman of your state by visiting www.bankingombudsman.rbi.org.in. Procedure is simple, cost effective and prompt.

5. You have one year time from date of cause of action to approach banking ombudsman. If you are not satisfied with the decision of banking ombudsman, you can file appeal to Dy. Governor of RBI at its H.O. in Mumbai.
6. If you are still not satisfied, you can resort to Consumer Protection Act. You have maximum two years time from date of cause of action.
7. If you are not having necessary papers, in case of nationalized banks you can simultaneously resort to The Right to Information Act for getting the papers.
8. You need not hire any advocate for approaching nodal officer or banking ombudsman. You can communicate in English, Hindi or regional language. Even for Complaint under Consumer Protection Act there is no need of advocate, but it is advisable if amount involved is substantial.
9. If possible, you can take assistance of a serving or retired officer of the bank for properly drafting the complaint.
10. You can also refer the matter to NGOs working for consumer protection in your area and also www.core.nic.in [central govt helpline]. They also take up the matter with banks on your behalf. You can get details of NGOs by searching on yahoo/google, etc.
11. Whenever you personally discuss your problem with bank officer, note down his name and designation with date, place and time of discussion. Send an email giving gist of discussion. This is necessary, as the officer cannot retract later on unless he refutes your gist sent by email by return post.

CHAPTER 18

Consumer Protection Act — Quick Review

SLIDE 1

The Consumer Protection Act, 1986
A QUICK REVIEW

PREPARED BY:
Dr. NIRAJ KUMAR

Introduction

- Caveat Emptor Rule **(let the buyer beware)** in Sale of Goods Act of 1930, sprout the root of consumer interest protection.
- United Nations passed resolution of consumer protection in April 1985.

- In India, Consumer Protection Act was enacted in 1986 and it became effective from January 7, 1987.
- Aimed at providing simple, quick and cheap protection of consumers' interest.
- Till date there have been three amendments in the Act:
  - 2002 — perennial problems of delay.
  - 2003 — exclusion of services for commercial purposes from the CPA.
  - 2004 — commercial purposes.

SLIDE 2

The Consumer Protection Act, 1986

An Act to provide for better protection of the interests of consumers and for that purpose to make provision for the establishment of consumer councils and other authorities for the settlement of consumers' disputes and for matters connected therewith.

SLIDE 3

UN Guidelines for the Consumer Protection

- Promote and protect economic interests;
- Provide adequate information for informed choice;
- Consumer education;
- Protect from hazard to health and safety;
- Provide effective redress — formal and informal procedures;
- Freedom to form groups and present views in decision-making affecting consumers;

SLIDE 4

Introduction

- For the welfare of the public, the gluts of adulterated and sub-standard articles in the market have to be checked. Inspite of various provisions providing protection to the consumer and providing for stringent action against adulterated and sub-standard articles in the different enactments like Code of Civil Procedure, 1908, the Indian Contract Act, 1872, the Sale of Goods Act, 1930, the Indian Penal Code, 1860, the Standards of Weights and Measures Act, 1976 and the Motor Vehicles Act, 1988, very little could be achieved in the field of Consumer Protection.

SLIDE 5

Introduction

- Though the Monopolies and Restrictive Trade Practices Act, 1969 and the Prevention of Food Adulteration Act, 1954 have provided relief to the consumers yet it became necessary to protect the consumers from the exploitation and to save them from adulterated and sub-standard goods and services and to safeguard the interests of the consumers.
- In order to provide for better protection of the interests of the consumer the Consumer Protection Bill, 1986 was introduced in the Lok Sabha on 5th December, 1986.

SLIDE 6

Statement of Objects and Reasons

- The Consumer Protection Bill, 1986 seeks to provide for better protection of the interests of consumers and for the purpose, to make provision for the establishment of Consumer councils and other authorities for the settlement of consumer disputes and for matters connected therewith.

SLIDE 7

Statement of Objects and Reasons

2. It seeks, *inter alia,* to promote and protect the rights of consumers such as—

(*a*) the right to be protected against marketing of goods which are hazardous to life and property;

(*b*) the right to be informed about the quality, quantity, potency, purity, standard and price of goods to protect the consumer against unfair trade practices;

(*c*) the right to be assured, wherever possible, access to an authority of goods at competitive prices;

(*d*) the right to be heard and to be assured that consumers interests will receive due consideration at appropriate forums;

(*e*) the right to seek redressal against unfair trade practices or unscrupulous exploitation of consumers; and

(*f*) right to consumer education.

SLIDE 8

Statement of Objects and Reasons

3. These objects are sought to be promoted and protected by the Consumer Protection Council to be established at the Central and State level.

4. To provide speedy and simple redressal to consumer disputes, quasi-judicial machinery is sought to be setup at the District, State and Central levels. These quasi-judicial bodies will observe the principles of natural justice and have been empowered to give relief of a specific nature and to award, wherever appropriate, compensation to consumers. Penalties for non-compliance of the orders given by the quasi-judicial bodies have also been provided

SLIDE 9

Act 68 of 1986

The Consumer Protection Bill, 1986 was passed by both the Houses of Parliament and it received the assent of the President on 24th December, 1986. It came on the Statute Book as the Consumer Protection Act, 1986 (68 of 1986).

SLIDE 10

CHAPTER I
PRELIMINARY

1. Short title, extent, commencement and application.—(1) This Act may be called the Consumer Protection Act, 1986.

(2) It extends to the whole of India except the State of Jammu and Kashmir.

(3) It shall come into force on such date as the Central Government may, by notification, appoint and different dates may be appointed for different States and for different provisions of this Act.

(4) Save as otherwise expressly provided by the Central Government by notification, this Act shall apply to all goods and services.

SLIDE 11

2. Definitions.—(1) In this Act, unless the context otherwise requires,

SLIDE 12

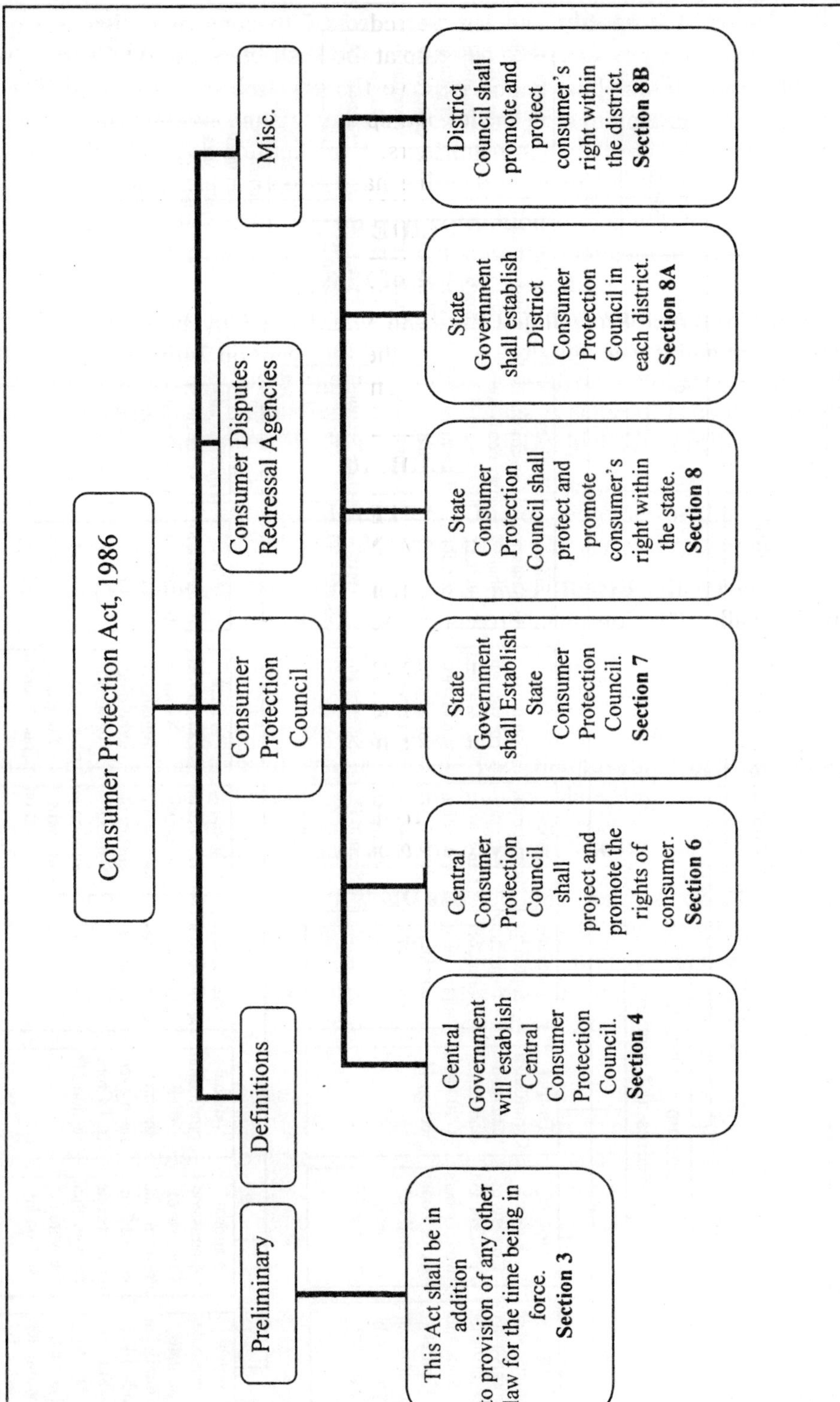
Consumer Protection Act, 1986
Preliminary
Definitions
Consumer Protection Council
Consumer Disputes Redressal Agencies
Misc.
This Act shall be in addition to provision of any other law for the time being in force. Section 3
Central Government will establish Central Consumer Protection Council. Section 4
Central Consumer Protection Council shall project and promote the rights of consumer. Section 6
State Government shall Establish State Consumer Protection Council. Section 7
State Consumer Protection Council shall protect and promote consumer's right within the state. Section 8
State Government shall establish District Consumer Protection Council in each district. Section 8A
District Council shall promote and protect consumer's right within the district. Section 8B

SLIDE 13

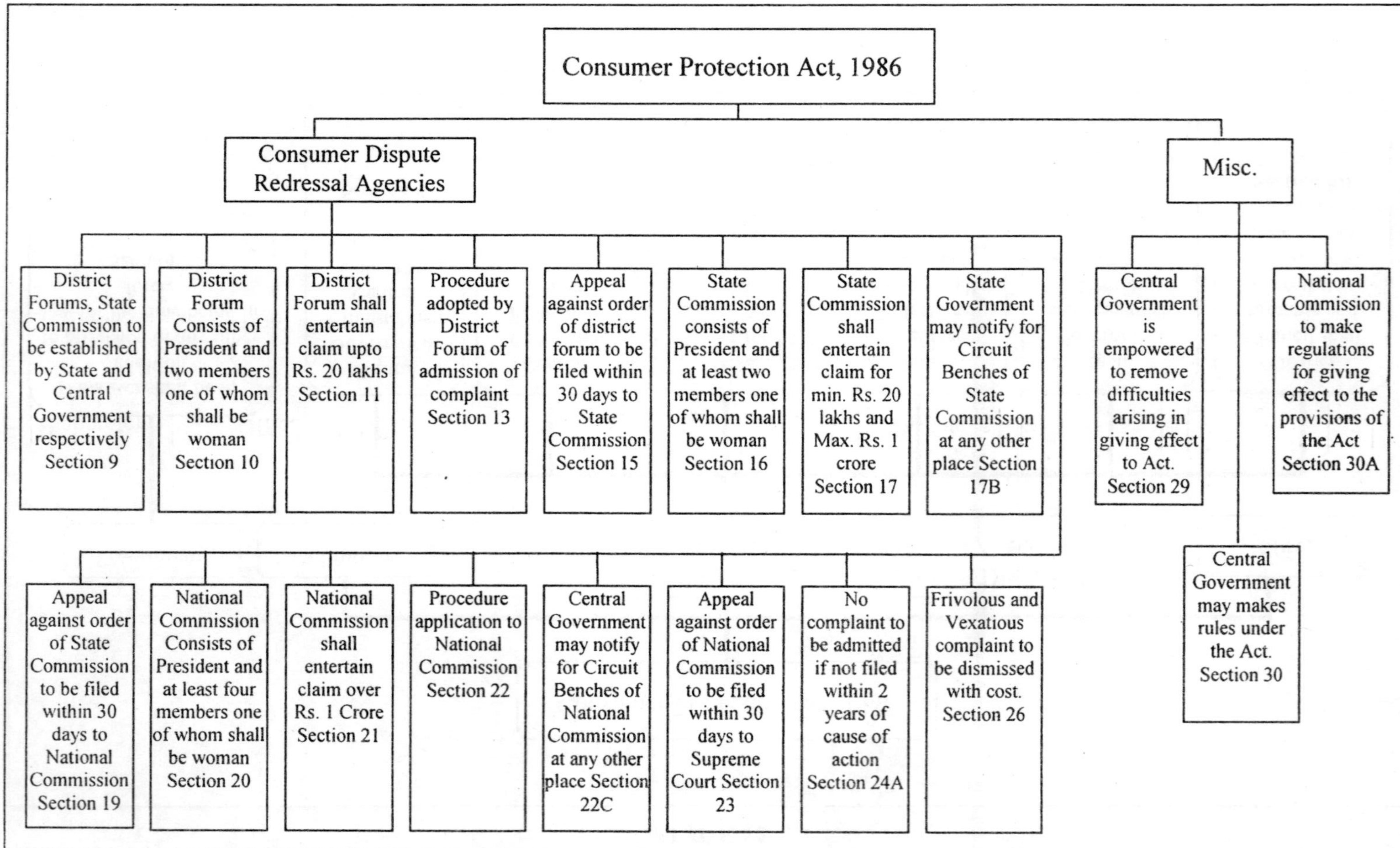

Consumer Protection Act, 1986
Consumer Dispute Redressal Agencies
Misc.
District Forums, State Commission to be established by State and Central Government respectively Section 9
District Forum Consists of President and two members one of whom shall be woman Section 10
District Forum shall entertain claim upto Rs. 20 lakhs Section 11
Procedure adopted by District Forum of admission of complaint Section 13
Appeal against order of district forum to be filed within 30 days to State Commission Section 15
State Commission consists of President and at least two members one of whom shall be woman Section 16
State Commission shall entertain claim for min. Rs. 20 lakhs and Max. Rs. 1 crore Section 17
State Government may notify for Circuit Benches of State Commission at any other place Section 17B
Appeal against order of State Commission to be filed within 30 days to National Commission Section 19
National Commission Consists of President and at least four members one of whom shall be woman Section 20
National Commission shall entertain claim over Rs. 1 Crore Section 21
Procedure application to National Commission Section 22
Central Government may notify for Circuit Benches of National Commission at any other place Section 22C
Appeal against order of National Commission to be filed within 30 days to Supreme Court Section 23
No complaint to be admitted if not filed within 2 years of cause of action Section 24A
Frivolous and Vexatious complaint to be dismissed with cost. Section 26
Central Government is empowered to remove difficulties arising in giving effect to Act. Section 29
National Commission to make regulations for giving effect to the provisions of the Act Section 30A
Central Government may makes rules under the Act. Section 30

SLIDE 14

CONSUMER PROTECTION ACT, 1986

DEFICIENCY – Section 2

- Sec. 2(1)(*a*) – Appropriate Laboratory
- Sec. 2(1)(*aa*) – Branch Office
- Sec. 2(1)(*b*) – Complainant
- Sec. 2(1)(*c*) – Complaint
- Sec. 2(1)(*d*) – Consumer
- Sec. 2(1)(*e*) – Consumer Dispute
- Sec. 2(1)(*f*) – Defect
- Sec. 2(1)(*g*) – Deficiency
- Sec. 2(1)(*h*) – District Forum
- Sec. 2(1)(*i*) – Goods
- Sec. 2(1)(*j*) – Manufacturer
- Sec. 2(1)(*jj*) – Member
- Sec. 2(1)(*k*) – National Commission
- Sec. 2(1)(*l*) – Notification
- Sec. 2(1)(*m*) – Person
- Sec. 2(1)(*n*) – Prescribed
- Sec. 2(1)(*nn*) – Regulation
- Sec. 2(1)(*nnn*) – Restrictive Trade Practice
- Sec. 2(1)(*o*) – Service
- Sec. 2(1)(*oo*) – Spurious Goods & Services
- Sec. 2(1)(*p*) – State Commission
- Sec. 2(1)(*q*) – Trader
- Sec. 2(1)(*r*) – Unfair Trade Practices

SLIDE 15

Section 2(1)(*a*) "appropriate laboratory" means a laboratory or organisation—

(*i*) recognised by the Central Government;

(*ii*) recognised by a State Government, subject to such guidelines as may be prescribed by the Central Government in this behalf; or

(*iii*) any such laboratory or organisation established by or under any law for the time being in force, which is maintained, financed or aided by the Central Government or a State Government for carrying out analysis or test of any goods with a view to determining whether such goods suffer from any defect;

SLIDE 16

Section 2(1)(*aa*) "branch office" means—

(*i*) any establishment described as a branch by the opposite party; or

(*ii*) any establishment carrying on either the same or substantially the same activity as that carried on by the head office of the establishment.

SLIDE 17

Section 2(1)(*b*) "complainant" means—

(*i*) a consumer; or

(*ii*) any voluntary consumer association registered under the Companies Act, 1956 (1 of 1956) or under any other law for the time being in force; or

(*iii*) the Central Government or any State Government;

(*iv*) one or more consumers, where there are numerous consumers having the same interest;]

(*v*) in case of death of a consumer, his legal heir or representative;

who or which makes a complaint;

SLIDE 18

Section 2(1) (*c*) "Complainant" means—

Any allegation in writing made by a complainant that—

(*i*) an unfair trade practice or a restrictive trade practice adopted by any trade or service provider,

(*ii*) the goods bought by him or agreed to be bought by him suffers from one more defect, (*iii*) the services hired or availed of or agreed to be hired or availed of suffer from deficiency in any respect,

(*iv*) a trader or the service provider, as the case may be, has charged for the goods or for the services mentioned in the complaint, a price in excess of the price—

(*a*) fixed by or under any law for the time being in force,

(*b*) displayed on the goods or any package containing such goods,

(*c*) displayed on the price list exhibited by him by or under any law for the time being in force,

(*d*) agreed between the parties;

SLIDE 19

Section 2(1)(*c*) "Complainant" means—

(*v*) goods which will be hazardous to life and safety when used, are being offered for sale to the public—

(*a*) in contravention of any standard relating to safety of such goods as required to be complied with, by or under any law for the time being in force;

(*b*) if the trader could have known with due diligence that the goods so offered are unsafe to the public;

(*vi*) services which are hazardous or likely to be hazardous to life and safety of the public when used, are being offered by the service provider which such person could have known with due diligence to be injurious to life and safety; with a view to obtaining any relief provided by or under this Act;

SLIDE 20

WHO IS A CONSUMER?

Two kinds of consumer under the Act

Consumer of goods

buys or agrees to buy goods

any user of such goods

Consumer of services

hires or avails any services

any beneficiary of such service

SLIDE 21

Section 2(1)(*d*) "consumer" means any person who—

(*i*) buys any goods for a consideration which has been paid or promised or partly paid and partly promised, or under any system of deferred payment and includes any user of such goods other than the person who buys such goods for consideration paid or promised or partly paid or partly promised, or under any system of deferred payment when such use is made with the approval of such person, but does not include a person who obtains such goods for resale or for any commercial purpose; or

SLIDE 22

Section 2(1)(*d*) "consumer" means any person who—

(*ii*) hires or avails of any services for a consideration which has been paid or promised or partly paid and partly promised, or under any system of deferred payment and includes any beneficiary of such services other than the person who hires or avails of] the services for consideration paid or promised, or partly paid and partly promised, or under any system of deferred payment, when such services are availed of with the approval of the first mentioned person; (but does not include a person who avails of such services of any commercial purpose).

Explanation.—for the purposes of sub-clause (*d*)

(*i*) "commercial purpose" does not include use by a consumer of goods bought and used by him exclusively for the purpose of earning his livelihood, by means of self-employment;

SLIDE 23

Who are not consumers?

1. A person who purchased goods for resale
2. A person who purchased goods for commercial purpose
3. A person who obtains services without consideration
4. A person who obtains services under a contract of personal service
5. Tax payers to municipality
6. Contractors
7. Applicants for jobs
8. Persons who filed suits in courts

SLIDE 24

Consumer *versus* Customer

- A consumer and customer are commonly used in the same context at times in business literature. However, they are not the same. Consumers are just one sub-group of customers. Consider this example with the

Racold Company. If a restaurant buys a Racold mixie (blender) for making juice to serve its patrons, then the restaurant is just a customer and NOT a consumer. But if you go and buy a Racold mixie to make juice for your children at home, you are a consumer.

SLIDE 25

Consumer *Versus* Customer

- What does this example mean? It means that if you buy a product for any commercial purposes you are not a consumer. If you buy a product purely for your own consumption, you are a consumer.
- The Consumer Protection Act, 1986 of India, is a little more generous with the word 'Consumer'. According to this law, consumer is not only a person who uses the product for domestic personal use, but also one who uses the product to earn his daily livelihood. So if your restaurant is a proprietorship company, you are the sole proprietor and the purchase of the mixie is in your name, then you could be deemed a consumer according to the Consumer Protection Act, 1986.

SLIDE 26

Consumer *Versus* Customer

- There are organizations that call customers who buy products for personal use 'consumers' and customer who buy products for commercial use 'clients'. In short, there are two categories of customers based on how they intend to use the product; consumers and clients
- Obviously, Consumer Protection Act, 1986 provides protection only for consumers. If you think about it, buying a product for commercial purposes is a business transaction as you have no intention to consume the product for personal use. Like any other business transactions that goes sore, contractual law/civil legislation/arbitration clauses should guide how disputes are resolved. Summarily, consumer protection is only for consumers. You cannot go to a consumer disputes redressal forum (consumer court) if a business transaction goes sour.

SLIDE 27

Consumer *Versus* Customer

- The Consumer Protection Act, 1986 is further expansive of the term consumer. You don't necessarily have to buy a product for personal use to be a consumer. Just the intention makes you a consumer. In other words, you are a consumer if you intend to buy the product
- Let's consider the following as an example. Say a consumer walked into a shop, and tried to buy a product with a maximum retail price

(MRP) of ₹670. However, just as the consumer is about to pay, he realizes

that the seller wants to charge him ₹700. The consumer refuses to buy the product and walks off without buying the product. Can such a consumer seek protection as per the provisions of Consumer Protection Act? The answer is yes. As a consumer, it is your right not to be overcharged more than the MRP.

SLIDE 28

Consumer *Versus* Customer

- Consider another example. A consumer observes a newspaper advertisement claiming a TV has a specific feature. The consumer visits the TV dealer to buy the TV. However, while discussing the product, the consumer notices that the TV doesn't have the advertised feature. The consumer therefore walks off without buying the TV. Can such a consumer seek protection as per the provisions of Consumer Protection Act? The answer is again a resounding Yes. As a consumer, it is your right not to be misinformed about any products capability.

SLIDE 29

Consumer *Versus* Customer

- But sadly, the chances that you as a consumer will ever win a case in the first example is slim to none. Since you refused to purchase the product, you have no proof that the shopkeeper tried to charge you ₹700. In the second case, you stand a good chance of winning a case if you have a certified copy of the newspaper advertisement claiming the product feature and any product literature that shows the lack of availability of the feature.

SLIDE 30

Consumer *Versus* Customer

- Now what does winning as a consumer mean in the second case. Since you have not bought the TV, it is hard to prove any damages. You can try to get punitive damages against the company for trying to defraud you as a consumer. However, this is not something to bet on. Your relief as a consumer is that you can request the consumer court to order the company to correct the advertisement, or withdraw the product with such claims. You are very likely to win the former relief, the latter again is uncertain.

SLIDE 31

Consumer *Versus* Customer

- The larger question is, to obtain such a relief, should you as a consumer approach a consumer court staking your financial resources, or should there be an effective government (sigh!) watchdog consumer agency that should resort to action on your behalf? This has been a question that has been the core of consumer issues in this country for the last four decades since the inductment of Consumer Protection Act, 1986. It also throws light on the deficiencies of Consumer Protection Act in India.

SLIDE 32

Section 2(1)(*e*) "consumer dispute" means —

- a dispute where the person against whom a complaint has been made, denies or disputes the allegations contained in the complaint;

SLIDE 33

Section 2(1)(*f*) "defect" means

- any fault, imperfection or shortcoming in the quality, quantity, potency, purity or standard which is required to be maintained by or under any law for the time being in force or under any contract, express or implied or as is claimed by the trader in any manner whatsoever in relation to any goods;

SLIDE 34

Section 2(1)(*g*) "deficiency" means —

- any fault, imperfection, shortcoming or inadequacy in the quality, nature and manner of performance which is required to be maintained by or under any law for the time being in force or has been undertaken to be performed by a person in pursuance of a contract or otherwise in relation to any service;

SLIDE 35

Section 2(1)(*i*) "goods"

- means goods as defined in the Sale of Goods Act, 1930 (3 of 1930);

SLIDE 36

Section 2(1)(*j*) "manufacturer" means a person who —

- makes or manufactures any goods or parts thereof; or

- does not make or manufacture any goods but assembles parts thereof made or manufactured by others and claims the end-product to be goods manufactured by himself; or
- puts or causes to be put his own mark on any goods made or manufactured by any other manufacturer and claims such goods to be goods made or manufactured by himself.

SLIDE 37

Section 2(1)(*m*) "person" includes,—

- a firm whether registered or not;
- a Hindu undivided family;
- a co-operative society;
- every other association of persons whether registered under the Societies Registration Act, 1860 (21 of 1860) or not;

SLIDE 38

Section 2(1)(*nnn*) "restrictive trade practice" means —

- a trade practice which tends to bring about manipulation of price or its conditions of delivery or to affect flow of supplies in the market relating to goods or services in such a manner as to impose on the consumers unjustified costs or restrictions and shall include;
- delay beyond the period agreed to by a trader in supply of such goods or in providing the services which has led or is likely to lead to rise in the price;
- any trade practice which requires a consumer to buy, hire or avail of any goods or, as the case may be, services as condition precedent to buying, hiring or availing of other goods or services;

SLIDE 39

Section 2(1)(*o*) "service" means —

- service of any description which is made available to potential users and includes the provision of facilities in connection with banking, financing, insurance, transport, processing, supply of electrical or other energy, board or lodging or both, housing construction, entertainment, amusement or the purveying of news or other information, but does not include the rendering of any service free of charge or under a contract of personal service;

SLIDE 40

Section 2(1)(*o o*) "spurious goods and services" mean

- such goods and services which are claimed to be genuine but they are actually not so;

SLIDE 41

Section 2(1)(*q*) "trader" in relation to any goods means —

- a person who sells or distributes any goods for sale and includes the manufacturer thereof, and where such goods are sold or distributed in package form, includes the packer thereof;

SLIDE 42

Section 2(1) (*r*) "unfair trade practice" means—

a trade practice which, for the purpose of promoting the sale, use or supply of any goods or for the provision of any service, adopts any unfair method or unfair or deceptive practice including any of the following practices, namely;—

Section 2(1)(*r*)(1) the practice of making any statement, whether orally or in writing or by visible representation which,—

(*i*) falsely represents that the goods are of a particular standard, quality, quantity, grade, composition, style or model;

(*ii*) falsely represents that the services are of a particular standard, quality or grade;

(*iii*) falsely represents any re-built, second-hand, renovated, reconditioned or old goods as new goods;

SLIDE 43

Section 2(1)(*r*) "unfair trade practice" means —

(*i*) represents that the goods or services have sponsorship, approval, performance, characteristics, accessories, uses or benefits which such goods or services do not have;

(*ii*) represents that the seller or the supplier has a sponsorship or approval or affiliation which such seller or supplier does not have;

(*iii*) makes a false or misleading representation concerning the need for, or the usefulness of, any goods or services;

(*iv*) gives to the public any warranty or guarantee of the performance, efficacy or length of life of a product or of any goods that is not based on an adequate or proper test thereof:

Provided that where a defence is raised to the effect that such warranty or guarantee is based on adequate or proper test, the burden of proof of such defence shall lie on the person raising such defence;

SLIDE 44

Section 2(1)(*r*) "unfair trade practice" means—

(*i*) makes to the public a representation in a form that purports to be—

(*a*) a warranty or guarantee of a product or of any goods or services; or

(*b*) a promise to replace, maintain or repair an article or any part thereof or to repeat or continue a service until it has achieved a specified result, if such purported warranty or guarantee or promise is materially misleading or if there is no reasonable prospect that such warranty, guarantee or promise will be carried out;

SLIDE 45

Section 2(1) (*r*) "unfair trade practice" means —

(*ii*) materially misleads the public concerning the price at which a product or like products or goods or services, have been or are, ordinarily sold or provided, and, for this purpose, a representation as to price shall be deemed to refer to the price at which the product or goods or services has or have been sold by sellers or provided by suppliers generally. In the relevant market unless it is clearly specified to be .the price at which the product has been sold or services have been provided by the person by whom or on whose behalf the representation is made;

(*iii*) gives false or misleading facts disparaging the goods, services or trade of another person.

SLIDE 46

Section 2(1) (*r*) "unfair trade practice" means —

Explanation.—For the purposes of clause (1), a statement that is—

(*a*) expressed on an article offered or displayed for sale, or on its wrapper or container; or

(*b*) expressed on anything attached to, inserted in, or accompanying, an article offered or displayed for sale, or on anything on which the article is mounted for display or sale; or

(*c*) contained in or on anything that is sold, sent, delivered, transmitted or in any other manner whatsoever made available to a member of the public, shall be deemed to be a statement made to the public by, and only by, the person who had caused the statement to be so expressed, made or contained;

SLIDE 47

Section 2(1) (*r*) "unfair trade practice" means

Section 2(1)(*r*)(2) permits the publication of any advertisement whether in any newspaper or otherwise, for the sale or supply at a bargain price, of goods or services that are not intended to be offered for sale or supply at the bargain price, or for a period that is, and in quantities that are, reasonable, having regard to the nature of the market in which the business is carried on, the nature and size of business, and the nature of the advertisement.

SLIDE 48

Section 2(1) (*r*) "unfair trade practice" means—

For the purpose of clause (2), "bargaining price" means—

(*a*) a price that is stated in any advertisement to be a bargain price, by reference to an ordinary price or otherwise, or

(*b*) a price that a person who reads, hears or sees the advertisement, would reasonably understand to be a bargain price having regard to the prices at which the product advertised or like products are ordinarily sold;

SLIDE 49

Section 2(1) (*r*) "unfair trade practice" means —

Section 2(1)(*r*)(3) permits —

(*a*) the offering of gifts, prizes or other items with the intention of not providing them as offered or creating impression that something is being given or offered free of charge when it is fully or partly covered by the amount charged ,in the transaction as a whole; the conduct of any contest, lottery, game of chance or skill, for the purpose of promoting, directly or indirectly, the sale, use or supply of any product or any business interest;

Section 2(1)(*r*)(3A) withholding from the participants of any scheme offering gifts, prizes or other items free of charge on its closure the information about final results of the scheme.

Explanation.—For the purpose of this sub-clause, the participants of a scheme shall be deemed to have been informed of the final results of the scheme where such results are within a reasonable time published, prominently in the same newspaper in which the scheme was originally advertised;

SLIDE 50

Section 2(1) (*r*) "unfair trade practice" means —

Section 2(1)(*r*)(4) permits —

the sale or supply of goods intended to be used, or are of a kind likely to be used, by consumers, knowing or having reason to believe that the goods do not comply with the standards prescribed by competent authority relating to performance, composition, contents, design, constructions, finishing or packaging as are necessary to prevent or reduce the risk of injury to the person using the goods;

Section 2(1)(5) permits —

the hoarding or destruction of goods, or refuses to sell the goods or to make them available for sale or to provide any service, if such hoarding or destruction or refusal raises or tends to raise or is intended to raise, the cost of those or other similar goods or services.

SLIDE 51

Section 2(1) (*r*) "unfair trade practice" means —

Section 2(1)(r)(6) permits —

Manufacture of spurious goods or offering such goods for sale or adopting deceptive practices in the provision of services;

(2) Any reference in this Act to any other Act or provision thereof which is not in force in any area to which this Act applies shall be construed to have a reference to the corresponding Act or provision thereof in force in such area.

SLIDE 52

Consumer Disputes Redressal Forums

The aims and objectives of the Act are achieved by the constitution and creation of

- District Forum
- State Commission, and
- National Consumer Disputes Redressal Commission.

SLIDE 53

A District Forum shall have the powers

1. to remove the defect pointed out by the appropriate laboratory from the goods in question
2. to replace the goods with new goods of similar description which shall be free from any defect
3. to return to the complainant the price, or as the case may be, the charges paid by the complainant

4. to pay such amount as may be awarded by it as compensation to the consumer for any loss or injury suffered by the consumer due to the negligence of the opposite party.

SLIDE 54

District Forum

- Each District Forum shall consist of a person who is or has been or is qualified to be a District Judge who shall be its President two other members, one of whom shall be a woman possessing a bachelor's degree from a recognized university, be a person of ability, integrity and standing and have adequate knowledge and experience
- Every member of the District Forum shall hold office for a term of 5 years or up to the age of 65 years whichever is earlier.
- Subject to the other provisions of the Act a District forum shall have jurisdiction to entertain complaints where the value of the goods or services and the compensation, if any, claimed does not exceed ₹20 Lakh.

SLIDE 55

State Commission

- Each State Commission shall have jurisdiction to entertain complaints where the value of the goods or services and compensation, if any, claimed exceeds ₹20 Lakhs but does not exceed ₹1 crore and appeals against the orders of any District Forum within the State.

SLIDE 56

National Commission

- The 'National Commission' shall consist of a person who is or has been a Judge of the Supreme Court, shall be its President. Not less than 4 and not more than such number of members as may be prescribed and one of whom shall be a woman with similar qualifications as required in the case of appointment as a member to a District Forum or a State Commission.
- Every member of the National commission shall hold office for a term of 5 years or up to the age of 70 years whichever is earlier.
- The National Commission shall have jurisdiction to entertain complaints where the value of the goods or services and compensation, if any, the claim exceeds ₹1 Crore and appeals against the orders of any State Commission.

SLIDE 57

Consumer Disputes Redressal Forums

- The District Forum, State Commission or the National Commission shall not admit a complaint unless it is filed within 2 years from the date on which the cause of action has arisen.
- Where a trader or a person against whom a complaint is made fails or omits to comply with any order made by the District Forum, the State Commission, the National Commission, as the case may be, such trader or person shall be punished with imprisonment for a term which shall not be less than 1 month but which may extend to 3 years, or with fine which shall be not less than ₹2,000 but which may extend to ₹10,000 or with both.

SLIDE 58

A complaint may be filed by

1. The consumer to whom such goods are sold
2. Any recognized consumer association, where the consumer to whom goods are sold or delivered is a member
3. One or more consumers, where there are numerous consumers having same interest
4. The Central and State Government

SLIDE 59

Procedure of Complaint — Section 13

Complaint relating to goods

1. Reference of sample to laboratory
2. Deposit of fees
3. Remission of fees to lab and forwarding of report to opposite party
4. Objections
5. Reasonable opportunity to parties

SLIDE 60

Complaint relating to services

1. Reference of claim to opposite party
2. Denial of allegations by the opposite party
3. Settlement of dispute
4. Proceedings of district forum final

5. Death of complainant
6. Period

SLIDE 61

Essential Information in the Application

— Name and full address of opposite party

— Description of goods and services

— Quality and quantity

— Price

— Date and proof of purchase

— Name and full address of complainant

— Nature of deception

— Type of redressal prayed for

SLIDE 62

Findings and Verdicts — Section 14

(*a*) To remove the defect

(*b*) To replace the goods with new goods of similar description.

(*c*) To return the complainant the price

(*d*) To pay compensation to the consumer for any loss or injury suffered

(*e*) To remove the defects in the goods

(*f*) To discontinue the unfair trade practices

(*g*) Not to offer hazardous goods for sale

(*h*) To provide adequate costs to parties

SLIDE 63

Benefits and Reliefs

Benefit

— Disposal within 90 days

— No adjournment shall ordinarily be granted — Speedy trial

Relief

— Removal of defects in goods or deficiency in services.

— Replacement of defective goods.

— Refund against defective goods or deficient services.

— Compensation.

— Prohibition on sale of hazardous goods.

SLIDE 64

Appeals — Section 15

Appeal to the State Commission

any person aggrieved by an order made by the district forum may prefer an appeal against such order to the State Commission within a period of 30 days

Appeal to the National Commission

any person aggrieved by an order made by the State Commission in exercise of its powers may prefer an appeal against such order to the National Commission within a period of 30 days

SLIDE 65

Hearing of Appeal — Section 19(A)

- No adjournment shall be ordinarily granted by the State Commission or the National Commission as the case may by unless sufficient cause is shown and the reasons for grant of adjournment have been recorded.
- The State Commission and the National Commission as the case may be shall make such orders as to the costs occasioned by the adjournment.

SLIDE 66

Miscellaneous

- Protection of action taken in good faith — Section 28
- Service of Notices — Section 28A
- Power to remove difficulties — Section 29
- Power to make rules — Section 30
- Laying of rules — Section 31

CHAPTER 19
EPILOGUE

SYNOPSIS

1. Few words

A quack is a person who pretends to have knowledge which he does not possess; who promises to do what he is either not sure he can perform or what he is certain he cannot perform; who represents his practice to be more successful than that of other men; who pretends to cure diseases known and admitted to be incurable; whose manner is confident and imposing; whose tone and language are unhesitating and boastful; who employs remedies, the nature and composition of which he keeps unknown and who deals in specifics and universal remedies. He is addicted to handbills, newspapers and similar modes of making known his pretensions and proceedings. This is the quack and the conduct of this man is quackery.

(*From Edinburgh Medical and Surgical Journal 1845; 63: 176*)

There is no denying the fact that no citizen of the country, be that an Engineer, an Architect, an Advocate or for that matter a Doctor, or even a Judge or the Prime Minister, is above the law of the land. All the professionals are already liable for scrutiny of their work under the existing laws.

The National Consumer Disputes Redressal Commission has observed in the case of *Cosmopolitan Hospitals Pvt. Ltd.* v *Vasantha P. Nair* [I (1992) CPJ 302 (NC)], that: "There is no provision in the Indian Medical Council Act, 1956 for the protection of the interests of the persons who may have suffered on account of negligence or deficiency in the service rendered by the medical profession. The field left open by the said Act is covered by the Law of Tort in general and by the Consumer Protection Act in particular".

The Consumer Protection Act provides for machinery which aims at dispensing speed and inexpensive justice.

The Doctor-patient relationship in our country has undergone a sea change in the last decade and a half. The lucky doctors of the past were treated like God and people revered and respected them. We witness today a fast pace of commercialization and globalization on all spheres of life and the medical profession is no exception to these phenomena. As a result, the doctor-patients relationship has deteriorated considerably. Earlier too, doctors were covered by various laws, *i.e.* the Law of Torts, IPC, etc., but since the passing of the Consumer Protection Act in 1986, litigation against doctors is on the increase. The medical profession is definitely perturbed by this and a rethink is necessary on standards of medical practice or 'defensive medicine'.

Surgeons busy themselves in acquiring knowledge, perfecting operative techniques and assimilating the newest technologies that are evolving so rapidly. The Physicians also do not lack behind in their constant endeavour in getting new knowledge. Sometimes the course of the disease or therapeutic decisions does not run along predictable lines. The patient-doctor relationship is then put to test.

Doctors practicing ethically and honestly should not have any reason for fear. Law whether civil, criminally or consumer law, can only set the outer limits of acceptable conduct *i.e.* minimum standards of professional care and skill, leaving the question of ideal to the profession itself.

The landmark judgment by the Supreme Court, stating that medical services to patients, for which fees are charged, come under the purview of Consumer Protection Act, 1986, has put a curtain on the long- drawn-out debate between doctors and consumers on the issue. Whilst the matter was still under deliberation by the Court, several claims were made from within the medical profession, probably as part of a strategy. Consumer courts were not equipped or competent to judge on intricate medical matters involved in medico-legal litigation, implying that there was wide scope for injustice. Once their powers were augmented, medical councils and not Consumer Courts, should take these matters up. The Consumer Protection Act would ultimately be against the interests of patients because there would be defensive medicine. These arguments release a lot of hot air but shed no light. Now that the dust has settled it is worth examining how the medical community has responded to the very positions it tried to take.

2. Doctor-patient relationship

Since the ancient times, certain duties and responsibilities have been cast on persons who adopt the sacred profession as exemplified by *Charak's Oath* (1000 B.C.) and Hippocratic Oath (460 B.C.).

In order to understand the complexities of the doctor-patient relationship it is necessary to know about the Duties and Obligations of a Doctor, Doctor-Patient contract and what constitutes Professional Negligence.

3. Prerequisites of medical practice

A duly qualified medical professional, *i.e.* a doctor has a right to seek to practice medicine, surgery and dentistry by registering himself with the Medical Council of the State of which he is a resident, by following the procedure as prescribed under the Medical Act of the State.

The State Medical Council has the power to warn, refuse to register/remove from register the name of the doctor who has been sentenced by any court for any non-bailable offence or found to be guilty of infamous conduct in any professional respect. The State Medical Council has also the power to re-enter the name of the doctor in the register.

The provisions regarding offences and professional misconduct which may be brought before the appropriate Medical Council (State/Medical Council of India) have been stated in the Code of Medical Ethics formulated by the Medical Council of India. The appropriate Medical Councils are empowered to award such punishment as deemed necessary or direct the removal of the name of the delinquent registered practitioner from the register either permanently or for a specified period, if he has been found guilty of serious professional misconduct. No action against a medical practitioner can be taken unless an opportunity has been given to him to be heard in person or through an advocate.

4. Duties and obligations of a doctor

Duties and obligations of doctors are enlisted in ordinary laws of the land and various Codes of Medical Ethics and Declarations — Indian and International, which are: (*i*) Code of Medical Ethics of Medical Council of India; (*ii*) Hippocratic Oath; (*iii*) Declaration of Geneva; (*iv*) Declaration of Helsinki; (*v*) International Code of Medical Ethics; (*vi*) Government of India Guidelines for Sterilization.

These Codes and Declarations are being printed in the Appendices. On the basis of these various Codes of Ethics and Declarations, the duties can be summarised as under —

1. Duties to Patient.
2. Duties to Public.
3. Duties towards Law Enforcers.
4. Duties not to violate Professional Ethics.
5. Duties not to do anything illegal or hide illegal acts.
6. Duties to each other.

4.1 Duties to patient

These are: Standard Care, Providing Information to the Patient/Attendant Consent for Treatment and Emergency Care.

4.1.1 Standard care

This means application of the principles of standard care which an average person takes while doing similar job in a similar situation:

- Due care and diligence of a prudent Doctor.
- Standard, suitable, equipment in good repair.
- Standard assistants: Where a senior doctor delegates a task to a junior doctor or paramedical staff, he must assure himself that the assistant is sufficiently competent and experienced to do the job and fulfills the prescribed qualifications.

- Non-standard drug is a poison by definition.
- Standard procedure and indicated treatment and surgery.
- Standard premises, *e.g.* Nursing Home, Hospital, must comply with all laws applicable as imposed by the State and these must be registered wherever required.
- Standard proper reference to appropriate specialist.
- Standard proper record keeping for treatment given, surgery done, X-ray and pathological reports.
- Standard of not to experiment with patient (See Declaration of Helsinki).
- Anticipation of standard risks of complications and preventive actions taken in time.
- Observe punctuality in consultation.

4.1.2 Duty to provide information to patient/attendant

- Regarding necessity of treatment.
- Alternative modalities of treatment.
- Risks of pursuing the treatment, including inherent complications of drugs, investigations, procedure, surgery, etc.
- Regarding duration of treatment.
- Regarding prognosis. Do not exaggerate nor minimize the gravity of patient's condition.
- Regarding expenses and break-up thereof.

4.1.3 Consent for treatment

Various types of consent and implications thereof are requisite for treatments are specifically in operative cases. These have been dealt previously by us.

4.1.4 Emergency care

A doctor is bound to provide emergency care on humanitarian grounds; unless he is assured that others are willing and able to give such care. It may be noted that prior consent is not necessary for giving emergency/first-aid treatment. In emergency medico-legal cases, condition of first aid being seen by medical jurist is not essential.

4.2 Duties to the public

- Health Education
- Medical help when natural calamities like drought, flood, earthquakes, etc. occur.
- Medical help during train accidents.
- Compulsory notification of births, deaths, infectious diseases, food poisoning, etc.
- To help victims of house collapse, road accidents, fire, etc.

4.3 Duty towards law enforcers, police, Courts, etc.

To inform the police all cases of poisoning, burns, injury, illegal abortion, suicide, homicide, manslaughter, grievous hurt and its natural complications like tetanus, gas-gangrene, etc. This includes vehicular accidents, fractures, etc.

- To call a Magistrate for recording dying declaration.
- To inform about bride burning and battered child cases.

4.4 Duty not to violate professional ethics (Only important ones given)

- Not to associate with unregistered medical practitioner and not allow him to practice what he is not qualified for.
- Not to indulge in self-advertisement except such as is expressly authorized by the M.C.I. Code of Medical Ethics.
- Not to issue false certificates and bills.
- Not to run a medical store/open shop for sale of medical and surgical instruments.
- Not to write secret formulations.
- Not to refuse professional service on grounds of religion, nationality, race, party politics or social status.
- Not to attend patient when under the effect of alcohol
- No fee sharing (Dichotomy).
- Not to talk loose about colleagues.
- Information given by patient/attendant to be kept as secret. Not to be divulged to employer, insurance company, parents of major son/daughter without consent of patient. Even in court this information is given only if ordered by the Court.
- Recovering any money (in cash or kind) in connection with services rendered to a patient other than a proper professional fee, even with the knowledge of the patient.

4.5 Duty not to do anything illegal or hide illegal acts

- Perform illegal abortions/sterilizations
- Issue death certificates where cause of death is not known.
- Not informing police a case of accident, burns, poisoning, suicide, grievous hurt, gas gangrene.
- Not calling Magistrate for recording dying declaration.
- Unauthorized, unnecessary, uninformed treatment and surgery or procedure.
- Sex determination (in certain States).

4.6 Duty to each other

- A doctor must give to his teachers respect and gratitude.

- A doctor ought to behave to his colleagues as he would like them to bêhave to him.
- A doctor must not entice patients from his colleagues, even when he has been called as a specialist.
- When a patient is referred to another doctor, a statement of the case should be given. The second doctor should communicate his opinion in writing/over telephone/fax direct to the first doctor.
- Differences of opinion should not be divulged in public.
- A doctor must observe the principles enunciated in 'The Declaration of Geneva' approved by the World Medical Association.

5. Duties of the patient/attendant

When a patient (consumer) hires or avails of services of a doctor for treatment, he has the following duties:—

- He must disclose all information that may be necessary for proper diagnosis and treatment.
- He must co-operate with the doctor for any relevant investigations required to diagnose and treat him.
- He must carry out all the instructions as regards drugs, food, rest, exercise or any other relevant/necessary aspect.

In the case of a private medical practitioner he must compensate the doctor in terms of money and money alone. Moral considerations apart, failure on the part of the patient/attendant to do his duty: (*a*) will enable the doctor to terminate patient-physician contract and that would free him from his legal responsibilities, (*b*) will be construed as contributory negligence and weaken the case of the patient for compensation enhanced.

6. Doctor-patient contract

Contract is defined as an agreement between two or more persons which creates an obligation to do or not to do a particular thing. Contract may be implied or express.

An implied contract is one inferred from conduct of parties and arises where one person renders services under circumstances indicating that he expects to be paid therefore and the other person knowing such circumstances avails himself of benefit of those services.

An express contract is an actual agreement of the parties, the terms of which are openly uttered or declared at the time of making it, being stated in distinct and explicit language, either orally (oral agreement) or in writing (written agreement). The doctor-patient contract is almost always of the implied type, except where a written informed consent is obtained.

While a doctor cannot be forced to treat any person, he has certain possibilities for those whom he accepts as patients. It is an implied contract. Implied contract is not established when: (*i*) the doctor renders first-aid in an emergency; (*ii*) he makes a pre-employment medical examination for a prospective employer; (*iii*) he performs an examination for life insurance purpose; (*iv*) he is appointed by the trial court to examine the accused for any reason; and (*v*) when he makes an examination at the request of an attorney for last suit purposes.

A doctor-patient contract requires that the doctor must: (*i*) continue to treat such a person; (*ii*) with reasonable care; (*iii*) reasonable skill; (*iv*) not undertake any procedure/treatment beyond his skill and (*v*) must not divulge professional secrets.

These various requirements will now be discussed in the succeeding paragraphs.

(*i*) ***Continue to treat***

Responsibility towards a patient It begins the moment a doctor agrees to examine the case. He must not, therefore, abandon his patient except under the following circumstances—

- The patient has recovered from the illness, for which treatment was initiated.
- The patient/attendant do not pay the doctor's fees (in case of a private practitioner).
- The patient/attendant consults another doctor (of any branch of medicine) without the knowledge of the first attending doctor.
- The patient/attendants do not co-operate and follow the doctor's instructions.
- The patient is under some other responsible care, *e.g.*, the patient, after admission in a hospital, comes under care of senior doctors/unit
- head.
- The doctor has given due notice (orally or written) for discontinuing treatment.
- The doctor is convinced that the illness is a fictitious one.

(*ii*) ***Reasonable care:*** A doctor must use clean and proper instruments and provide his patients with proper and suitable medicines if he dispenses them himself. If not, he should write the prescriptions legibly, using standard abbreviations and mention instructions for the pharmacist in full. He should give full directions to his patients as regards administration of drugs and other measures, preferably in local written language. He must suggest/insist on consultation with a specialist in the following circumstances:

- When the case is complicated.
- When the question arises about performing an operation which may be dangerous to life or requiring amputation.
- Operating on a case in which there has been a criminal assault.

- Performing an operation which may affect the intellectual or reproductive functions of a patient.
- In cases where there is suspicion of poisoning or other criminal act.
- When desired by the patient/attendants.
- When it appears that the quality of medical service is required to be
- When there is no one from whom informed consent can be obtained upon.

(*iii*) ***Reasonable skill***: The degree of skill a doctor undertakes is the average degree of skill possessed by his professional brethren of the same standing as himself. The best form of treatment may differ when different choices are available. There is an implied contract between the doctor and the patient when the patient is told in effect: "Medicine is not an exact science. I shall use my experience and best judgment and you take the risk that I may be wrong. I guarantee nothing."

(*iv*) ***Not to undertake any procedure beyond his skill***: This depends upon his qualifications, special training and experience. The doctor must always ensure that he is reasonably skilled before undertaking any special procedure/treating a complicated case. To quote an example, a doctor who is not sufficiently trained or qualified should not administer anaesthesia.

(*v*) ***Professional secrets***: A professional secret is one which a doctor comes to learn in confidence from his patients, on examination, investigations or which is noticed in the ordinary privacies of domestic life. A doctor is under a moral and legal obligation not to divulge any such secret except under certain circumstances. This is known as privileged communication which is defined as a communication made by a doctor to a proper authority who has corresponding legal, social and moral duties to protect the public. In must be *bonafide* and without malice, *e.g.*, as a witness in a court of law; warning partners or spouses of AIDS patients and those found infected with HIV; informing public health authorities of food poisoning from a hotel, etc; assisting apprehension of a person who has committed a serious crime; informing law enforcers about medico-legal cases, etc.

During the past few years — whilst the case was before the Supreme Court — there was a public uproar on the kidney transplant racket. How did the medical community and the medical councils in our various states respond to it? Many doctors knew of those who had indulged in such practices but chose to be tight-lipped bystanders. The medical councils stirred into a semblance of activity only after the media turned on the heat. Their activity seems to have conveniently petered out. But then, historically, the medical councils, meant to be the guardians of ethical standards in medical practice, have chosen to look the other way, avoiding taking action and even neglecting to exercise the powers they already have. How, then, can the argument — that the medical community in general and medical councils in particular would provide adequate regulation and redressal to safeguard the plight of patients were they granted extra powers — inspire confidence?

A heated debate started relating to the pros and cons of the application of the Consumer Protection Act, 1986 to the Medical Profession. The Medical Professionals are against the inclusion of patients under the category of consumers. They feel that for them their patients are something more than mere clients or source of profit making. To them the mention of 'patient' as 'consumer' is nauseating and inclusion of medical services within the ambit of Consumer Protection Act is equivalent to degrading the nobleness of their profession. They feel that in a poor country like ours, this will increase the hardships to the common patient and harassment to doctors.

While agreeing broadly with these aspects, I think doctors should not forget that medical accountability has been in existence since the birth of this sacred profession. This accountability has taken the latest shape in the form of Consumer Protection Act. Fears of doctors stem from what is perceived by them as the 'unknown'. If this 'unknown' becomes 'known' the same would appear much less fearsome, in whatever form it exists. This is exactly what I have attempted to achieve through this book.

Human element in medical care sometimes determines the patient's/ attendant's reaction to an untoward event. Sources of discontent, such as, tactless handling or unnecessary unpleasant remarks, trivial indignation's are the cause of a large number of legal actions brought against the doctors and the hospitals. One strongly recommend that appropriate behavioral aspects of patient-care should be regularly stressed upon all healthcare personnel including all levels of hospital employees.

7. Professional negligence (Malpractice, Malpraxis)

Professional negligence is defined as the breach of a duty caused by the omission to do something which a reasonable man guided by those considerations which ordinarily regulate the conduct of human affairs would do or doing something which a prudent and reasonable man would not do.

Medical negligence or malpractice is defined as lack of reasonable care and skill or wilful negligence on the part of a doctor in the treatment of a patient whereby the health or life of a patient is endangered.

The term 'damage' means physical, mental or functional injury to the patient, while 'damages' are assessed in terms of money by the court on the basis of loss of concurrent and future earnings, treatment costs, reduction in quality of life, etc.

In order to achieve success in an action for negligence, the consumer must be able to establish to the satisfaction of the court that: (*i*) the doctor (defendant) owed him a duty to conform to a particular standard of professional conduct; (*ii*) the doctor was derelict and breached that duty; (*iii*) the patient suffered actual damage; and (*iv*) the doctor's conduct was the direct or proximate cause of the damage.

The burden of establishing all four elements is upon the patient/consumer. Failure to provide substantive evidence on any one element may result in no compensation.

8. Criminal negligence

Here the negligence is so great as to go beyond matter of mere compensation. Not only has the doctor made a wrong diagnosis and treatment, but also that he has shown such gross ignorance, gross carelessness or gross neglect for the life and safety of the patient that a criminal charge is brought against him. For this he may be prosecuted in a criminal court for having caused injury to or the death of his patient by a rash and negligent act amounting to culpable homicide under section 304A of the Indian Penal Code. Some examples are as follows:

- Injecting anesthetic in fatal dosage or in wrong tissues.
- Amputation of wrong finger, operation on wrong limb, removal of wrong organ, or errors in ligation of ducts.
- Operation on wrong patient.
- Leaving instruments or sponges inside the part of body operated
- Leaving tourniquets too long, resulting in gangrene.
- Transfusing wrong blood.
- Applying too tight plaster or splints which may cause gangrene or paralysis.
- Performing a criminal abortion.

9. Issues before the medical profession

Legal aspects of medical practice have always constituted an important component of medical education. Standard books on Medical Jurisprudence contain excellent Chapters on 'The Law in Relation to Doctors.' Thus, from an early stage the words 'would be doctors' are made conversant with the legal issues inherent in medical practice. The application of the Consumer Protection Act to the Medical Professionals has only served to bring into focus some of the legal liabilities of the doctors.

Mere mention of the Consumer Protection Act at any get-together or scientific meeting of doctors evokes their instant attention and all other conversation cases, giving rise to passionate exchange of opinion, experiences, fears, etc. and questions being asked about the implications of the application of the Act to the Medical Profession.

It is these questions and fears which are sought to be discussed in the following paragraphs. By going through this section of the book conscientiously, much of the dread of the 'unknown' that is inherent in legal aspects of medical practice, especially in relation to the Consumer Protection Act, will be mitigated.

1. What was the necessity of the Consumer Protection Act and its application to the medical profession?

This is the foremost question which comes to the mind of the doctors. This necessity arose because the existing laws of the land which provide for action in cases of medical negligence under the Law of Tort and Indian Penal Code have some well documented problems. These include the following: (*i*) Delay, which, in medical negligence cases, tends to be greater; (*ii*) the cost of bringing an action, which is notoriously high in relation to the sums recovered in damages; (*iii*) limited access to the courts; (*iv*) success depends on proof of both negligence and causation (which can be particularly difficult in cases of medical negligence).

Hence necessity to provide for an alternate system which would be easily accessible, speed and cheap, gave birth to the Consumer Protection Act. This Act was made applicable to the doctors because there are no provisions in the Indian Medical Council Act, 1956; (*i*) to entertain any complaint from the patient; (*ii*) to take action against the Medical Practitioner in case any negligence has been committed; (*iii*) to award any compensation, etc. in case the negligence is proved.

2. ***Who is a consumer?***

   Consumer is: (*a*) a patient who pays to get services of doctor/hospital; (*b*) any person who pays for the patient; (*c*) legal heirs/representatives of such patients; (*d*) spouse, parents and children of the patient.

3. ***Does the service rendered by doctors/hospitals stand excluded because it is under a contract of personal service as distinguished from a contract for service?***

   This is the key clause being disputed by the doctors.

10. Master -servant relationship

The judgments till date have held that the medical services rendered by doctors/hospitals for payment are covered under this Act as they are not Contract of Personal Services but Contract for Services. Contract of Personal Service involves Master-Servant relationship which must satisfy four criteria stated in the column 'Master-Servant Relationship' hereunder:—

Master-Servant Relationship (as per National Commission Decision)	**Doctor-Patient Relationship (as per doctors' contention)**
(*i*) The employer's (master's) power of selection of his employee (servant).	(*i*) A patient/guardian has full power of selecting his doctor/hospital. He is not under any compulsion
(*ii*) The payment of wages or other remuneration.	(*ii*) A doctor is also paid remuneration and steps into the shoes of an 'employee' during the period he gives treatment or performs operation.
(*iii*) The employer's right of suspension or dismissal	(*iii*) The patients/guardians also have the right to reject the services of doctor/hospital (which is equivalent to suspension/dismissal) any

Master-Servant Relationship (as per National Commission Decision)	Doctor-Patient Relationship (as per doctors' contention)
	moment they are not satisfied, they feel that they have a better alternative without any reason. On the basis of these three criteria the relationship between doctor and patient is similar to master and servant. Patient can choose any doctor/hospital, go for treatment if the charges are suitable and reject the services at any moment without assigning any reason.
(*iv*) The employer's right to control the method of doing the work.	(*iv*) Coming to the 4th criteria, which has been considered as cardinal in distinguishing between Contract of personal service and Contract for Service is the EXISTENCE OF THE RIGHT TO CONTROL. This control is never 100% even in Master-Servant contract, as servant is not a machine. You can order a servant to suspend all other work and clean the utensils but cannot control his response, how quick and well he will clean the utensils, how many utensils he will break etc. We all know how much exactly, we can control the servant We all know the consequences, if we are rude, harsh, physically or verbally abusive with the servant. We have got to be polite with him and respect his sensibilities. We must distinguish between Master-Servant and Master-Slave relationship.

Medical professionals strongly feel that the relationship between Doctor - Patient is that of 'Contract of Personal Service', where they consider patient to be the master and themselves as servants with the exception that God has bestowed them with professional skill to serve the master (human body) with a difference. They do not deny accountability, nor do they deny existence of erring hospitals, deviant doctors and malpractice. But, the percentage of this is too small to give to the general public daggers to run after doctors.

Medical professionals fully agree that efforts should continue so that the master (human body) can be served even better. If the master losses faith in them, their very existence will be threatened. What exactly is the degree of control a doctor has over his patient?

11. Points to ponder

- A patient may show up very late in course of illness — sometimes in terminal stages.
- If consulting time/waiting time for consultation/treatment does not suit patient he is free to approach someone else.
- Patient may come without any record whatsoever of treatment already taken.
- Patient may be hiding facts from the doctor. The Doctor does not have any foolproof method to know whether the history is true.
- Patient may question the probable diagnosis, drugs prescribed, their role, side-effects, cost, interaction, etc. and may avoid taking the prescribed medicine.
- After the consumer (patient) leaves the doctor's clinic with the prescription, can a doctor control subsequent actions?
- Will all the prescribed medicines be purchased?
- Will the prescribed doses be administered at correct intervals?
- Will the full course of treatment be given? What if patient takes treatment for only 2 days instead of 7?
- Will other precautions advised be taken by him?

Can the doctor control follow-up of patient? Patient may not come at all or come according to convenience. Doctor does not know he has improved/deteriorated/gone elsewhere. Follow-up, which is cardinal component of medical management, is entirely beyond the control of the doctor. Irregular treatment is tubercular patients, rheumatic heart disease, epileptics, etc. is well known.

Patient may comply with doctor's prescription but concomitantly use Homeopathic, Ayurvedic or Unani medicines, the interactions of which are not known. Patient may resort to magic/faith healing. How can a doctor control this? A case of jaundice is advised certain tests, precautions and medicines. Patient may not bother about these and after leaving doctor's clinic may go for "Jhara" (Magic healing). In case of deterioration, how can a doctor's service be held deficient?

Some patients refuse investigations without which at times correct management is not possible.

Whenever a patient feels that he is not getting well with the treatment of a doctor/hospital he is free to leave any moment, or to consult any other doctor. Most private hospitals permit consultation with any doctor the patient/attendants wish to. They can always question the rationale of treatment, progress of illness during the course of treatment.

Doctor does not guarantee a diagnosis. It may be a provisional diagnosis or a differential diagnosis on which the treatment may be based.

Doctor never guarantees a cure. He makes his best efforts because he knows that much more than anything else, his professional reputation is at stake.

12. Meaning of service

The judgment of Honorable Supreme Court of India dated 13-11-1995 gave a new meaning to the term "Service". On the meaning of the word "service" in relation to medical profession, the Supreme Court in *Indian Medical Association* v *V.P. Shantha* (*supra*) came to the following conclusions:

- Service rendered to a patient by a medical practitioner (except) where the doctor rendered service free of charge to every patient or under a contract of personal service), by way of consultation, diagnosis and treatment, both medicinal and surgical, would fall within the ambit of 'service' as defined in section 2(1)(*o*) of the Act.
- The expression 'contract of personal service' in section 2(1)(*o*) of the Act cannot be confined to contracts for employment of domestic servants only and the said expression would include the employment of a medical officer for the purpose of rendering medical service to the employer. The service rendered by a medical officer to his employer under the contract of employment would be outside the purview of 'service' as defined in section 2(1) (*o*) of the Act.
- Service render at a Government hospital/health centre/dispensary or at non-government hospital/nursing home where no charge whatsoever is made from any person availing the service and all patients (rich and poor) are given free service — is outside the purview of the expression "service" as defined in section 2(1)(*o*) of the Act. The payment of a token amount for registration purpose only at the hospital/nursing home would not alter the position.
- Service rendered at a non-government hospital/nursing home where charges are required to be paid by the person availing such services falls within the purview of the expression 'service' as defined in section 2(1)(*o*) of the Act.
- Service rendered at Government hospital/Health centre/Dispensary or at a non-government Nursing home where charges are required to be paid by persons who are in a position to pay and persons who cannot afford to pay are rendered service free of charge would fall within the ambit of the expression 'service' as defined in section 2(1)(*o*) of the Act irrespective of the fact that the service is rendered free of charge to persons who are not in a position to pay for such services. Free service, by such doctors and hospitals would also be 'service' and the recipient a 'consumer' under the Act.
- Service rendered by a medical or hospital/nursing home cannot be regarded as service rendered free of charge, if the persons availing the service has taken an insurance policy for medical care where under the policy charges for consultation diagnosis and medical treatment are

borne by the insurance company and such service would fall within the ambit of 'service' as defined in section 2(1)(*o*) of the Act.

- Similarly, where as a part of the conditions of service, the employer bears the expenses of medical treatment of an employee and his family member dependent on him, the service rendered to such an employee and his family members by a medical practitioner or a hospital/nursing home would not be free of charge and would constitute 'service' under section 2(1)(*o*) of the Act.

13. Preventive steps against litigation

It is not as if this aspect has not crossed the minds of doctors before the application of Consumer Protection Act (CPA) to medics. Complaints have been lodged with State Medical Councils and M.C.I. and there have been instances of action taken against doctors. More frequently, patients have been suing and prosecuting doctors in Civil and Criminal Courts. The medical professionals have been exercising due caution while dealing with patients. With the coming into existence of compensation oriented Consumer Forums, the medical profession has been suddenly made to sit-up. What they were doing till the other day in mutual trust could land them into trouble, if they do not exercise extra precautions.

Where the doctor feels that the patient is suffering from some major illness in which complications are pre-existing or are likely to occur, he should take proper precautions. The precautions desired to be taken may be summarised as "Do's and Don'ts" which are as follows.

14. Some dos'

Mention your qualifications on the prescription. Qualifications mean recognized degrees/diplomas as regulated by the Indian Medical Degrees Act, 1916 as amended from time to time. Mention of scholarships/training/membership/awards which are not qualifications should be avoided.

Always mention date and timing of the consultation.

14.1 Mention age, sex, weight (If child)

In complicated cases record precisely history of illness and substantial physical findings about the patient on your prescription.

If the patient/attendants are erring on any count (history not reliable, refusing investigations, refusing admission) make a note of it or seek written refusal preferably in local language with proper witness.

Mention the condition of patient in specific/objective terms. Avoid vague/non-specific terminology.

14.2 Record history of drug allergy

Write name of drugs clearly. Use correct dosages (by revising knowledge periodically) and mention clearly method and interval of administration. Here one must use local or sign language. Do not forget writing precautions like Ast./p.c./a.c./locally/with milk/h.s. etc.

If a drug is a poison (*e.g.*, certain local applications), warn in writing. Mention additional precautions *e.g.*, food, rest, avoidance of certain drugs, allergens, alcohol, smoking, etc. if indicated.

Mention whether prognosis explained. If necessary take a signature of patient/attendant, after explaining the prognosis in written local language. In case of any deviation from standard care, mention reasons.

14.3 Specifically mention review, SOS/or follow-up schedule

Mention if patient/attendant are/is under effect of alcohol/drugs. In case a particular drug/equipment is not available, make a note. Mention where the patient should contact in case of your non-availability/ emergency.

Keep updating your knowledge. Read again what you think you already know. You will be in for surprises. Routinely advice X-rays in injury to bones/joints.

15. Some don'ts

Do not hesitate to discuss the case with your colleagues.

Do not hesitate to discuss the case with patients/attendants.

Do not write Ayurvedic formulations.

Do not allow substitutions.

For goodness sake do not examine a patient if you are sick, exhausted, under effect of alcohol.

Never talk loose of your colleagues, despite intense professional rivalry. *Never* criticize your brother in profession. The patient/attendants may incite you to say/do something. They may seek your comments on the other doctor's treatment. There is always a polite way to set aside their queries. Remember if you had seen the case from start you would done the same. If your colleague has made error of judgment regarding diagnosis or treatment, you never know under what circumstances this happened.

Do not adopt experimental method in treatment. If there is some rationale do it only after informed consent.

If you to back and read the Duties and Obligations of Doctors carefully and apply them religiously in your day to day practice, you are safe.

Insurance protection against outcome of litigation: A tertiary level of protection against outcome of litigation would be to go for Insurance cover. PROFESSIONAL INDEMNITY INSURANCE cover became available for Doctors and Medical establishments only recently, *i.e.* from December, 1991.

The term "indemnity" means reimbursement, to compensate. The principle of indemnity is strictly observed in liability insurances. These insurances (*e.g.*, Professional Indemnity Insurance) are designed to provide the insured person protection against the financial consequences of legal liability. If the insured is legally liable to pay damages to others, the policy will indemnify him subject to the terms, conditions and limitations of the contract. Indemnity is also available in respect of legal costs awarded against the insured as well as legal costs and expenses incurred by the insured with the written consent of the insurers in the defence of settlement of claims.

16. Professional Indemnity Insurance

16.1 General Rules and Regulations

Applicability: The policy provides insurance cover in respect of ERRORS and OMISSIONS on the part of the professionals whilst rendering their services. This applies to Doctors and Medical Establishments, Engineers, Financial Consultants, Management Consultants, Lawyers, Advocates, Solicitors and Counsels. The agreeable limits within India and including Nepal/Bhutan, for any one year/during the policy period, shall not exceed ₹2 crores.

Standard Proposal Form: Insurers shall obtain duly completed Standard Proposal Form from the prosecutors at inception and subsequent renewals. No cover shall be granted unless a declaration as provided for in the proposal form is obtained from the proposer to the effect that all statutory requirements relating to the business activities are complied with.

Standard Policy Form: All policies — fresh and renewals issued shall be in the Standard Policy Form prescribed by the insurance company/corporation.

Liabilities Covered: Policies issued under this scheme shall cover all sums which the Insured becomes legally liable to pay as damages to third party in respect of ERRORS and/or OMISSIONS on the part of the Insured whilst rendering professional services, arising out of claims first made in writing against the insured during the policy period, including legal costs and expenses incurred with the prior consent of insurer, subject always to the limits of indemnity and other terms, conditions and exceptions of the policy. It shall not be permissible to issue any Professional Indemnity Insurance Policy with unlimited liability.

Premium: The rates of premium under the Agreement are annual rates. Full premium under the policy shall be paid at inception. It is not permissible to accept premium in installments. Turnover figure whenever required shall be as far as possible accurately assessed and declared by the proposer at inception of the policy. In case the insured anticipates any increase/decrease in turnover during the policy period such fluctuations should be immediately notified to the Insurer and necessary adjustments made. Under no circumstances it shall be permissible to adjust the premium for the turnover after expiry of the policy.

Retroactive Date: Retroactive Date is the date when the risk is first incepted under a claim-made policy and thereafter renewed without break in the period of cover.

16.2 Revision in limits of indemnity

No revision (increase/decrease) shall be allowed in the limits of Indemnity during the currency of the policy. For any upward revision in indemnity limits at renewals, the retroactive date shall be the inception date of the Policy renewal, so far as the increased limits are applicable.

Compulsory excess: All policies issued under the Agreement shall be subject to compulsory excess of certain fixed percentage of the limit of indemnity for any one accident or any one year subject to a minimum of ₹1,000 and maximum of ₹1,00,000 (Rupees One Lakh Only). The Insured shall bear this Compulsory Excess which is applicable to property damage claims and death/bodily injury claims inclusive of defence costs arising out of any one accident. This excess is not applicable for Doctors and Medical Practitioners.

Voluntary excess: The following discounts on the premium may be allowed for Voluntary Excess opted by the Insured except for policy for Doctors and Medical Practitioners. But these are applicable in case of insurance policies obtained by Hospitals and Medical Establishments.

Voluntary Excess (percentage) of limit of Indemnity per any one Accident	Discount (%)
1.	2.5
2.	5.0
4.	7.5
6.	10.0
8.	12.5
10.	15.0

The Voluntary Excess shall be in addition to the Compulsory Excess and shall be applicable to property damage claims and/or death/bodily injury claims inclusive of defence costs arising out of any one accident.

16.3 Short period premiums

It shall not be permissible to issue Policies for periods more than 12 months. The following short period scale of premium shall apply to: (*i*) policies issued for periods less than 12 months and (*ii*) policies cancelled during the currency at the request of the insured subject to no claims:

Period	Rate
Not exceeding one month	1/4th of the annual premium
Not exceeding two months	3/8th of the annual premium
Not exceeding three months	1/2nd of the annual premium
Not exceeding four months	5/8th of the annual premium
Not exceeding six months	3/4th of the annual premium
Exceeding six months	Full annual premium

For annual policies cancelled during the currency at the request of the insured, premium should be adjusted at the Short Period Scales for the actual period of cover subject to no claims. No refund is permissible in case of any claim under the policy.

The short period premium is subject to the minimum premium in the Rating Schedule.

17. Doctors and medical practitioners (Guidelines)

The policy will indemnify any act committed by the insured, who shall be a Registered Medical Practitioner, giving rise to any legal liability to Third Parties. The Insured includes the policy holder and his qualified assistants or employees named in the proposal.

The act has to be committed during the period of insurance commencing from the retroactive date.

In the normal course all claims for compensation have to be legally established in a court of law. However, insurers may arrive at compromised settlement if *prima-facie* liability exists under the policy.

Jurisdiction applicable will be Indian Courts.

The limit of indemnity granted under the policy for any one accident or any one year (per accident per policy year) will be identical.

No short period policies are permitted. However, in case of cancellation of the policy by the Insured short period scale rates as provided for will be applicable.

Registered Medical Practitioners shall be classified as:

1. (*a*) Physicians without dispensing and other facilities General Pathologist/Radiologist	₹0.5 per 1000 on AOY limit.
(*b*) General Physicians with facilities like dispensing/ pathological/radiological, etc	7.5% additional premium for each facility subject to maximum of 20%.
2. (*a*) Specialists/Consulting Physician (Non-surgical)	₹1.0 per 1000 on AOY limit
(*b*) For other facilities (Specify) such as E.C.G., X-ray, Scanning, Sonography, etc.	7.5% extra for each facility subject to facility subject to maximum of 20%.
3. (*a*) Surgeons excluding specialists in Plastic Surgery, Lithotripsy, Dentists and similar extra corporeal methods of treatment would fall within this category.	₹2.0 per 1000 on AOY limit
(*b*) For other facilities (specify) such as E.C.G., X-Ray, Scanning, Sonography, etc.	7.5% extra for each facility subject to a maximum of 20%.
4. (*a*) Diagnostic Centres	₹1.0 per 1000 on AOY limit.
(*b*) For other facilities (specify) such as E.C.G., X-Ray, Scanning, Sonography, etc	7.5% extra for each facility subject to a maximum of 20%.

5. (*a*) Surgeons (Plastic Surgery) Anaesthetics.	₹3 per 1000 on AOY limit
(*b*) For other facilities (specify) such as E.C.G., XRay, Scanning, Sonography, etc.	7.5% extra for each facility subject to a maximum of 20%.

(1) Physicians, (2) Pathologists, (3) Oncologists, (4) Cardiologists, (5) Psychiatrists, (6) Radiologists or Roentgenologists, (7) General Surgeons, (8) Plastic Surgeons, (9) Orthopaedic Surgeons, (10) Urologists, (11) Abdominal Surgeons, (12) Thoracic Surgeons, (13) Neuro-Surgeons, (14) Cardio-Vascular Surgeons, (15) Otorhinolaryngologists, (16) Protologists, (17) Ophthalmologic Surgeon, (18) Ophthalmologic Physician, (19) Obstetrician and Gynaecologist (Excluding Surgery), (20) Physician and non-specialist, (21) Other Practitioner-describe Surgeon. fully.

Insurance Rating for Doctors and Medical Practitioners [To be charged on Any One Year (AOY) limit]

Minimum Premium ₹100.

No Compulsory or Voluntary Deductibles are applicable.

Insurance Rating for Medical Establishments

₹3 per 1000 on AOY limits plus ₹5 per each in patient plus Re. 1 per out-patient.(Number of patients to be as per previous year's record or the anticipated number of patients during the year whichever is higher.)

Radioactive treatment Additional premium of 15% (other than X-ray) on total premium.

The indemnity in respect of any one person would be limited to 25% of the Any One Year (AOY) limit under the policy.

Minimum Premium under one policy: ₹1,000.

Compulsory Excess and Voluntary Excess are applicable.

Exclusions:

- no liability shall attach to the Company in respect of—
- any criminal act or any act committed in violation of any law or ordinance:
- services rendered while under the influence of intoxicants or narcotics;
- the performance by dentists and dental surgeons of: (1) general anaesthesia; or (2) any procedure carried out under general anaesthesia unless performed in a Hospital:
- the use of drugs for weight reduction;
- cosmetic surgery
- third party public liability;
- claims arising from any condition directly or indirectly caused by or associated with Human T-Cell Lymphotropic Virus Type III (HTLV III)

or Lymphadenopathy Associated Virus (LAV) of the mutants derivatives or variations thereof or in any way related to Acquired Immune Deficiency Syndrome (AIDS) or any Syndrome or condition of a similar kind howsoever it may be named.

The Policy does not cover liability —

- assumed by the Insured by agreement and which would not have attached in the absence of such agreement;
- arising out of deliberate, wilful or intentional non-compliance of any Statutory provision;
- arising out of loss of pure financial nature such as loss of goodwill, loss of market, etc;
- arising out of all personal injuries such as libel, slander, false arrest, wrongful eviction, wrongful detention, defamation, etc. and mental injury, anguish or shock;
- arising out of fines, penalties, punitive or exemplary damages;
- directly or indirectly occasioned by happening through or in consequence of war, invasion, act of foreign enemy, hostilities (whether war be declared or not), civil war, rebellion, revolution, insurrection or military or usurped power;
- directly or indirectly caused by or contributed by: ionising radiations or contamination by radioactivity from any nuclear fuel or from any nuclear waste from the combustion of nuclear fuel;
- the radioactive, toxic, explosive or other hazardous properties of any explosive nuclear assembly or nuclear component thereof;
- arising out of genetic injuries caused by X-ray treatment/diagnosis or treatment/diagnosis with radioactive substances, in respect of professional services rendered by the Insured prior to the Retroactive Date in the Schedule.
- the deliberate conscious or intentional disregard of the insured's technical or administrative management of the need to take all reasonable steps to prevent claims;
- injury/death to any person under a contract of employment or apprenticeship with the Insured when such injury/death arises out of the execution of such contract.

It may be noted that the amount paid as premium for obtaining a Professional Indemnity Insurance Policy qualifies as deductible expense under section 36 of the Income-tax Act.

The doctors/hospitals may contact the Insurance Companies or their Agents for obtaining more information on the subject.

18. Selected Indian landmark judgments

In the case of *Consumer Unity and Trust Society* v *State of Rajasthan* [*Gurbax Singh's Law of Consumer* p.389: 1991 (1) CPR 241 (NC)], complaint was regarding a tubectomy operation at a Government Hospital. The patient developed serious complication after the surgical operation and she became physically invalid person and suffered continuous physical pain as well as great mental agony. It was alleged in the complaint that on account of negligence on the part of the surgeon and due to lack of post-operative care and attention, serious complication had resulted and claim for compensation for the loss and injury suffered by the patient was lodged.

The National Commission rejected the claim for compensation and held that persons who availed themselves of the facility of medical treatment in a Government Hospital are not "consumers" as defined in Consumer Protection Act and the said facility cannot be regarded as service "hired" for "consideration".

It was contended on behalf of the complainant that direct and indirect taxes paid to the State by a citizen constituted "consideration" for the services and facility provided to a citizen by the State. The National Commission, making a distinction between "tax" and "fee" held that a tax is levied as part of common burden while fee is for payment of specific benefit or privilege. Unlike "fee", "tax" in its true nature is a levy made by the state for the general purposes of the Government and it cannot be regarded as payment for any particular or specific service.

On the question whether contributors to the CGHS Scheme and patients in a "paying ward" in a Government Hospital are "consumers" within the meaning of the Act, it observed that contribution to CGHS should be taken to be in lieu of free treatment in the diverse dispensaries, as well as the free provisions of medicines from these dispensaries. In regard to "paying wards", it further observed that these payments are specifically related to special rooms/beds for which the separate charge is made; the (free) medical facilities are common to all patients, inclusive of those in the paying wards, without discrimination.

In the case of *Cosmopolitan Hospital Pvt. Ltd.* v *Vasantha P. Nair* and *Cosmopolitan Hospital Pvt. Ltd.* v *V.P. Santha,* decided on 21st April, 1992, [I, 1992) CPJ 302 (NC)], the National Commission has decided some important points regarding maintainability of complaints regarding medical services under the Consumer Protection Act, 1986 and held that:

When a patient goes to a hospital which provides treatment to patients for payment and avails himself of the facility of treatment on payment of consideration, he is dealing only with an institution carrying on the activity of providing medical service for payment and no element of "personal service" does enter into the picture in such a case. Thus, the activity of providing medical assistance for payment by hospitals and members of medical profession falls within the scope of "service" as defined in section 2(1)(*o*) of the Act and in the event of any deficiency in the performance of such service the aggrieved party file a complaint under the Act (Consumer Protection Act).

In the case of death of a patient; legal heirs of the deceased have '*locus standi*' to file complaint under the Act and they are held to be "consumers."

There is no provision in the Indian Medical Council Act, 1956, for the protection of the interests of the persons who may have suffered on account of negligence or deficiency in the service rendered by the medical profession. The field left open by the said Act is covered by the Law of Tort in general and by the Consumer Protection Act in particular.

In the case of *Dr. T.T. Thomas* v *Elisa* AIR 1987 Ker. 52, the question was regarding the liability of a doctor not performing an emergency operation for want of patient's consent and consequent death of the patient. In that case, on complaint of severe abdominal pain by the patient, the general practitioner, after diagnosis, found it to be a case of appendicitis and the patient was admitted to the hospital. The operation was not performed on that very day and on the subsequent day the patient died owing to bursting of the appendix. The plaintiff's case was that had the operation been performed immediately, on the very day of admission, the patient's life would, most probably have been saved.

The defendant-surgeon took the plea of refusal by patient to give his consent to the operation which was the reason why operation could not be performed on the very first day. But this argument was not accepted either by the trial court or the High Court, as there was no mention in the case sheet of the patient that consent was sought and the same was refused by the patient.

The Kerala High Court held that the burden of proof that consent was sought and it was refused was upon the one who takes such a plea particularly when the patient himself has died and held the doctor negligent for failure to perform an emergency operation.

The doctor has a discretion in choosing treatment he proposes to give and such discretion is amplified in cases of emergencies. [*Joshi* v *Godbole* 1968 AC J 183, p. 187 (SC)].

In the case of *R. Lalitha* v *M. Jeeva* [1992 (2) CPR 409 (Tamil Nadu State Commission)], the complaint was regarding negligence of a private doctor's hospital which the complainant attended for pre-natal treatment, etc. Her uterus got ruptured on account of delayed labour and the male child, who was born, died. The State Commission observed: "Here is a case where the opposite party who is merely a nurse and mid-wife, has taken upon herself, the management of a situation pregnant with dire consequences as this was a case of second caesarean operation and her management has ultimately led to the rupture of the uterus, removal of it and to the death of her male child. The opposite party has acted rashly, recklessly and with culpable negligence," It held the opposite party guilty of gross negligence and awarded compensation of ₹2,50,000 as under:

1. Rupees one lakh for rupture and removal of the uterus which is a permanent injury of a grave character.
2. Rupees one lakh for the pain and agony suffered.
3. Rupees fifty thousand for the death of a male child.

In another case which was decided by the National Commission on 16-11-1992, [*Dr. Sr. Louie* v *Smt. Kannolil Pathumma* 1993 (I) CPR 422], it was held that:

As fee was charged for room rent, treatment, etc., the service rendered falls within the scope of the Act.

Heirs/legal representatives of deceased consumer are entitled to file complaint.

Medical negligence existed on following grounds:

Patient was known to have complications during her first delivery in same hospital and after admission, to induce labour she was started on syntocinon drip. Artificial rupture of membranes was done. At this point the doctor left the patient to attend patients in the OPD. This was against standard medical recommendations (of reasonable care and skill).

The condition of patient became bad. Doctor was called who applied vacuum extractor. The baby extracted was asphyxiated and mother started bleeding severely. Both died subsequently. Was the doctor employed by the hospital qualified to do this procedure? The name board exhibited by the hospital mentioned M.D. (Gyn.) against her name creating an impression and misleading the patients that the doctor possessed P.G. degree in Gynecology. The degree M.D., Gyn. was obtained from Freiburg, Germany which, as per the rules and directions from M.C.I., should have been mentioned. This degree is equal to M.B.B.S., in India. Although the doctor had undergone practical training courses in Gynecology, she had not acquired any qualification in the form of degree or diploma in that discipline, hence she was not entitled to claim that she is M.D. (Gyn.) in India. Hence, she was not qualified to undertake this procedure and the resultant vacuum slip had led to complications. Also held liable for misrepresentation of facts. Complainant was awarded ₹77,000 as compensation, to be paid by the society which is running the hospital.

In the case of *Bansidhar Panigrahi* v *Chief Medical Officer, Ganjam* [1993 (I) CPR 94 (Orissa State Commission)], a tubectomy operation was performed on the patient and she left the Hospital at her accord inspite of knowing that there are possibilities of complications after the operation. Later on she had developed tetanus and she died.

The State Commission held that disease contributed to her death in not keeping the operation wound clean for which she got infection from her home, as others who were operated on the same day were not affected by the disease and there was no negligence on the part of operation surgeon, paramedical persons and the treatment at the Hospital.

In the case of *Sir Gangaram Hospital* v *D.P. Bhandari* [II (1992) CPJ 397 (NC)], it was held by the National Commission that there was no negligence or deficiency on the part of the Hospital in not transferring the patient to I.C.U. on account of non-availability of vacant bed in the I.C.U. and it was also not negligence or deficiency on the part of the Hospital merely on account of their omission to inform the relative of the patient to shift the patient to some other Hospital if they so chose in view of non-availability of vacant bed in the I.C.U.

In the case of *Renu Jain* v *Escorts Heart Institute and Research Centre* [III (1992) CPJ 391 (NC)], a complaint was filed wherein it had been alleged that the patient who had undergone coronary by-pass surgery was discharged after a major surgery negligently, wrongly and prematurely and that a post-operation infection had occurred which was not properly treated and as a result the patient suffered from Thromboambolism phenomenon which resulted in patient going into coma.

The opposite party, *i.e.*, the Hospital disclaimed altogether the charge of deficiency in service and negligence in treatment which would have possibly either directly or indirectly caused the death of the patient. It was contended that infection in the wound was superficial and mild. There was no evidence of severe infection. There was no fever, no discharge. Consequently, the antibiotics prescribed on 14th March at the time of discharge after the patient had undergone Coronary bye-pass surgery were withdrawn on 21st March. The Blood Reports of the patient on 4th April when he went in to coma were also normal. After examination by different Neurologists of the Hospital it was established that the cause of the patient going into coma was Brain-stem Hemorrhage which eventually resulted into death of the patient on 15-4-1991.

The National Commission accepted the contention of the Hospital and held that the patient's death was caused by Brain-stem Hemorrhage and there was no negligence on the part of the Hospital in treating the patient.

On the point of conducting of autopsy by the Hospital, the National Commission observed that it is essential to conduct autopsy in case where death has been caused due to criminality, as an aid to preventive medicine or when death is caused by an accident, etc. or when the precise cause of death is to be determined, etc. As it was not a medico-legal case and the cause of death, Brain-Stem Hemorrhage was not in doubt, the Hospital Authorities should not have advised the relatives of the patient for having autopsy done.

In the case of *Vinitha Ashok* v *Lakshmi Hospital* [II (1992) CPJ 372 (NC), the National Commission has observed:

> "... the law does not require that a doctor in the discharge of his duty of a case should use the highest degree of skill. Since that may never be acquired, it is enough for the doctor to show that he acted in accordance with the general and approved practice. A mistake diagnosis is not necessarily a negligent diagnosis. A practitioner can be held liable in this respect only if his diagnosis is so palpably wrong as to prove negligence, that is to say if his mistake is of such a nature as to imply an absence of reasonable skill and care on his part, regard being had to be ordinary level of skill in the profession."

A unit of blood was purchased by the complainant for his wife from opposite party which was found to be contaminated and had virus of Hepatitis B. The

State Commission held that the blood bank has failed to observe the fundamental requirement of ensuring that the blood supplied to the complainant was free from any contamination, the complainant's wife suffered from viral Hepatitis B which was later communicated by her to her husband, the complainant. Both the complainant and his wife suffered for a few months due to defective and contaminated blood supplied by the Blood Bank (the opposite party). The State Commission held the Blood Bank guilty of supply of contaminated blood and awarded a sum of ₹20,000 as damages to the complainant for ill health and discomfort caused to him and his wife. The Commission held that the Doctor who recommended the particular blood bank was not held responsible, since there is no procedure for testing the blood at the time of transfusing the blood and further that the blood bank is under obligation to ensure that it did not stock contaminated blood. [*Harish Kumar* v *Sunil Blood Bank Ltd.* 1 (1991) CPJ 645 (Delhi SC)].

In the case of *Mappooyan* v *Dr. Premavathy Elango* [(1991)] II CPR 460 (Tamil Nadu State Commission)], wife of the complainant got treatment from a doctor who was a family friend. The doctor administered some test injection following which the patient fell unconscious and subsequently died. It was held by the State Commission, since the doctor gave the treatment free of charge, the patient was not a consumer and the complaint is outside the purview of the Consumer Protection Act.

In the case of *M Arunachala Vadivel* v *Dr. N. Gopalkrishnan* [II (1992) CPJ 764 (Tamil Nadu State Commission], the complaint was regarding alleged negligence of the doctor in thyroidectomy operation on account of which the patient had died.

The State Commission, after going through and examining the case history and treatment record of the patient, came to the conclusion, "A perusal of Exhibit B-6 and the treatment given to the patient after she failed to revive, show that nothing has been let undone to her. Despite this emergent treatment, the patient has collapsed. We are not able to find any negligence in the management of this patient after the operation."

The State Commission also held that when oral consent of the patient and the relative is taken, it is enough.

The State Commission while dealing with this case, have discussed and analysed a good number of Indian and Foreign decided cases on Medical Negligence which are being reproduced here for the benefit of the readers:

Medical Negligence is defined as want of reasonable degree of care and skill or wilful negligence on the part of the medical practitioners in the treatment of a patient with whom a relationship of professional attendant is established so as to lead to his bodily injury or permanent disability or loss of life. As pointed out by this Commission in a very recent decision rendered in *R. Gopinath* v *Eskaycee Medical Foundation* (O.P. 199/91, dated 10-4-92), the law on the subject is very considerate to medical profession. In *Hatcher* v *Black* (Lancet 154-2-1980), Lord Danniel opined that the jury must not find a doctor negligent simply because one of the risks inherent in an operation actually took place or because as a matter of opinion he made an error of judgment. They should find him guilty only when he had fallen short of reasonable medical care. Similarly Lord Justice Denning observed that we should be doing a disservice to the community at large, if we were to impose liability on hospitals and doctors for every thing that happens to go wrong. We must insist on due care for the patient at each point, but we must not condemn as negligence that which is only a misadventure, *Roe* v *Ministry of Health* [1954-2-All E.R. 131], Mr. Justice Barrie in *Moore* v *Lewisham Group HMC* (1959) observed that "when there are two genuinely responsible schools of thought about the management of a clinical situation, the Courts could do no great disservice to the community or the advancement of medical science than to place the hall-mark of the legality upon one form of treatment." As observed by Lord Nathan in his Medical Negligence, a mistake diagnosis is not necessarily a negligent diagnosis. In *Mitchel* v *Dicksen* (1954-AP PD -519), Innes, ACJ observed, "No human being is infallible and in the present state of science even the most eminent specialist may be at fault in detecting the true nature of the deceased condition. A practitioner can only be liable in this respect if his diagnosis is so palpably wrong as to prove negligence, that is to say, if his mistake is of such a nature as to imply absence of reasonable skill and care on his part, regard being had to the ordinary level of skill in the practitioner." A reference to some of the decided authorities would explain the legal position better. In *Wood* v *Thurston* (1953-1-C.L.C. 687) a drunken man was brought to the causality ward of a hospital with a history of having been run over by a motor lorry, with 18 broken ribs, a fractured collar-bone and badly congested lung. The surgeon did not examine him as closely as the case required and had even failed to use his stethoscope which could have enabled him to discover the patient's true condition. Added to that, he permitted the patient to return home who after a few hours died. The surgeon was found negligent in failing to make a proper diagnosis. Another typical instance of negligence is diagnosis is *Edler* v *Greenwich and Deptford Hospital* (1953 The Times March 7) where a child complained of severe abdominal pain and vomiting. On being asked by the doctor where the pain was, she indicated generally her stomach and winced the right side of the abdomen was palpated. The doctor failed to diagnose appendicitis, the existence of which the circumstances clearly indicated. He was rightly held negligent in failing to exercise proper care and diagnosis. Now-a-days where injection therapy has become so common, there may arise many situations in which a doctor may find himself guilty of negligence. He may, for instance, inject a wrong solution by mistake or oversight. He may inject the fluid into artery instead of a vein or use a solution intended to be injected intramuscular as one intravenous, or break the needle in the body of the patient. Any one of these mistakes may result in disaster to the patient and there can be no two opinions as to the civil liability of the practitioner for the consequences. [Kameswararao's Law of Negligence, 1991 — Edition page 709]. The case of *Antonny* v *Grey* (1936 1 All E.R. 540) may be taken as an illustration of the type of cases where an injection was given at a wrong place, that is, into an artery instead of into a vein, or into vein instead of into the muscle. There a patient succeeded in an action for negligence against a medical man who was treating him for malaria by giving quinine injections in the buttocks. On one occasion in giving the injection he travelled beyond the safe area for injection and injured the patient's sciatica nerve, with the result that the patient was prematurely lamed. Again, in a case reported in the *British Medical Journal* [(dated 27-3-1954, page 767) (*Peters* v *Fulhar*)] where the complaint was that thiopentone had been injected into an artery, the hospital authorities admitted the negligence. In *Collins* v *Hertfordshire County Council* (1947-1-All E.R. 633) a patient while undergoing an operation was killed by an injection of cocaine which was given by the operating surgeon in the mistake belief that it was procaine. The operation surgeon had ordered procaine on the telephone, but the resident house surgeon had misheard "procaine" as "cocaine" and had told the pharmacist to dispense a mixture which was in fact lethal. The mixture prepared by the pharmacist according to instructions was administered by the operating surgeon without checking. It was held that the operating surgeon was liable in negligence. The responsibility of the surgeon for things done or left undone in the operation theater has been the subject-matter of consideration in what are known as "Swab Cases" and "Forceps cases." Leaving behind the "Swab" and "Forceps" in the body of the patient at the end of an abdominal operation is a real and grave danger and the liability of the surgeon for negligence, has never been in doubt. In *Urry* v *Bierer* (1955-The Times, 16th March), a 10 inch square pack was left in the patient's abdomen after a cesarean operation. The operating surgeon did not take any special precautions to guard against the possibility of a pack being overlooked, but relied entirely upon the sister's count. Lord Pierson held that the surgeon was negligent. In a Canadian Case *Gloning* v *Miller* (1954-IDLR, 372), the surgeon was found negligent when a pair of forceps was left behind in the patient's abdomen after a caesarean operation. It is thus well settled that negligence can be attributed to a surgeon only if his mistakes are of such a nature as to imply absence of reasonable care and skill on his part. It is also equally well settled that the burden of establishing negligence is on the complainant. He has not only to establish negligence on the part of the medical practitioner, but also the proximate causal connection between the alleged negligence and injury. (*vide* 1984-SC-1570).

In the case of *B.S. Hegde* v *Dr. Sudhansu Bhattacharya* [II (1992) CPJ 449], the State Commission of Maharashtra held the doctor guilty of gross negligence for failure to render necessary post-operative care which was undertaken by him for consideration (fee). This fee of ₹40,000 was paid by cheque a few days after the open-heart by-pass operation performed on the complainant at the Bombay Hospital, for rendering post-operative care and treatment for a period of three months. The fee was excessive, unreasonable and unjustifiable though conceding that the amount to be charged as fee for medical services is the choice of the medical practitioner. The State Commission further observed that the complainant badly needed post-operative care as pus was formed in his chest region for want of post-operative care, which could have caused death. The doctor examined the patient reluctantly on one of the post-operative follow-ups and on another occasion did not grant interview to the patient. Hence it was held that the doctor had charged disproportionately and there was imperfection, short-coming and inadequacy in the nature and performance of post-operative care and awarded a sum of ₹2 lacs by way of compensation to the patient.

On appeal against this order of the State Commission, the National Commission, in *Sudhanshu Bhattacharya* v *B.S. Hegde* decided on 7-10-1993, 1993 (3) CPR 414, held that:

There is no evidence of any deficiency in service on the part of the doctor or in rendering adequate care and treatment, because there was no cardiac or any other serious complication during the post-operative period. Pus formation in the stitches is a normal occurrence in the post-operation period of coronary by-pass surgery. It also noted the statement of other doctors who had subsequently attended on the patient that the discharge from the sternum was serious, there was no tenderness, patient was a febrile and vital parameters were within normal limits and the treatment given was of a superficial nature and could not in ordinary course cause death.

The National Commission also agreed in general with the observation of the State Commission that fee paid for an operation also includes post-operative care. But in the case of the operation being performed in an institution (hospital), it is the duty of the institution to render post-operative care and treatment. The private doctor, who is performing the operation for a fee in the hospital, cannot be expected to undertake and provide post-operative treatment and care to the hospital's patient. Quite often foreign doctors undertook operations in hospitals or nursing homes in India and it cannot be maintained that the post-operative care and treatment will continue to be provided by the foreign doctors who may no longer be in the country.

Regarding the charging of ₹40,000 for post-operative care and treatment, it found it to be clearly unreasonable. But, however, important it may be, the demand and acceptance of an exorbitant fee cannot be deemed to be deficiency in service and hence, it is not for the consumer forums to adjudicate on the question whether the consideration charged was reasonable.

It also conceded that a doctor has the absolute right to decide which patient he would examine first and even out of turn depending upon the condition of the patient. He also has the right to examine patients in their turn and it cannot be maintained that a patient must be examined by the doctor at the appointed time irrespective of the time he may have to spend in examining the previous patient.

In the light of above discussion, the order passed by the State Commission was set aside and complaint was dismissed.

In the case of *Smt. Chanchal Oswal* v *SDM Hospital and Dr. Nimish A. Shah,* decided on 28-11-1992 by the Rajasthan State Consumer Disputes Redressal Commission, the complainant had undergone heart surgery in the hospital and it was alleged that a surgical gauze was left in her body at the time of operation, on account of which she suffered great pain and had to undergo second operation at Bangalore. The complainant claimed compensation against the negligence of the Hospital and the Surgeon.

It was contended by the opposite parties that the heart operation was successful but the post-operative X-ray examinations carried out showed a collection of fluid on the left side of the chest and the complainant was advised for operation to remove the fluid which the complainant refused although it was to be done free of charge. However she went to Bangalore and got herself operated upon where the surgical gauze was allegedly got removed.

The State Commission while dismissing the complaint held that, "there is no evidence on record to prove that during the operation by opposite party No. 2 a surgical gauze was left in the chest which was removed at Bangalore. There is not the slightest evidence of any deficiency in service and consequent negligence of the opposite party No. 2, when he performed operation of the complainant. "

19. Doctors and the Consumer Protection Act

As regards defensive medicine, by its very nature, it will be intended to safeguard the interests of the doctor.

Transferring the expenses incurred on this account to patients will constitute an unfair practice under the Consumer Protection Act. Does this mean that the doctor is to be defenseless? The need for such defense would be minimised if we had standard protocols for the investigation and treatment of common diseases. We understand that the Indian Academy of Paediatrics is evolving protocols for paediatric problems. This is a step in the right direction. As long as the doctor follows nationally accepted protocols, normally he cannot be accused of negligence or malpractice.

The bench of the Consumer Court is headed by a retired judge who can avail of expert services if and when needed. In Bombay, the court requires the complainant to provide attestments from two medical doctors that there is a basis for admitting the case. This means that when the case against a doctor is before the CPA court, at least two medical doctors feel there is prima facie merit in it: What is more, if the complaint proves to be frivolous, the complainant can be fined upto ₹10,000 Surely, there is no room for apprehension. The judgment, by itself, does not encourage the filing of suits against doctors. By and large, the Indian citizen does not like to litigate.

Is the Consumer Protection Act a dampener for medical practice? I do not think so. On the contrary, taken in the right spirit, it is a boon for ethical, patient-oriented doctors. Doctors claiming to adhere to ethics have always lamented that colleagues stooping to unethical practices have an unfair advantage because there is no control over these practices. The CPA should help in curbing this unfair advantage.

If doctors would like fewer legal restrictions on themselves, they must regulate — and be seen to regulate themselves through adherence to the principles of medical ethics.

20. International code of medical ethics

20.1 Duties of doctors in general

A DOCTOR MUST always maintain the highest standards of professional conduct.

A DOCTOR MUST practice his profession uninfluenced by motives of profit.

THE FOLLOWING PRACTICES are deemed unethical:

- Any self advertisement except such as is expressly authorised by the national code of medical ethics.
- Collaboration in any form of medical service in which the does not have professional independence.
- Receiving any money in connection with services rendered to a patient other than a proper professional care, even with the knowledge of the patient.
- ANY ACT OR ADVICE which could weaken physical or mental resistance of a human being may be used only in his interest.
- A DOCTOR IS ADVISED to use great caution in divulging discoveries or new techniques of treatment.
- A DOCTOR SHOULD certify or testify only to that which he has personally verified.

20.2 Duties of doctors to the sick

A DOCTOR MUST always bear in mind the obligation of preserving human life.

A DOCTOR OWES to his patient complete loyalty and all the resources of his science. Whenever an examination or treatment is beyond his capacity he should summon another doctor who has the necessary ability. A DOCTOR SHALL preserve absolute secrecy on all he knows about his patients because of the confidence entrusted in him. DOCTOR MUST give emergencies care as a humanitarian duty unless he is assured that others are willing and able to give such care. Duties of Doctors to Each Other

- A DOCTOR OUGHT to behave to his colleagues as he would have them behaved to him.
- A DOCTOR MUST NOT entice patients from his colleagues.
- A DOCTOR MUST OBSERVE the principles of 'The Declaration of Geneva' approved by the World Medical Association.

21. Consent

Another major and important thing to do for a doctor is to obtain proper consent of the patient/attendant/relative.

The term 'consent' is defined thus: When two or more persons agree upon the same thing in the same sense they are said to consent as per the definition of 'consent' given in section 13 of Indian Contract Act, 1872.

22. Who can give consent

For the purpose of clinical examination, diagnosis and treatment consent can be given by any person who is conscious, mentally sound and is of and above twelve years of age as provided under sections 88 and 90 of the Indian Penal Code, 1860.

Doctors are reminded that consent is taken under section 13 of the Indian Contract Act, 1872. This Act, however also provides under section 11 that only those persons who are of and above 18 years of age are competent to enter into a contract. Since doctor-patient relationship amounts to entering into a contract, it is advisable that consent should be obtained, specially written consent, from parents/guardian of a patient who is below 18 years so that validity of the contract is not challengeable.

23. When consent is not valid

Consent given under fear, fraud or misrepresentation of facts, or by a person who is ignorant of the implications of the consent, or who is under 12 years of age is invalid (Section 90, IPC).

In most of the cases filed against the doctors it is alleged that no consent was obtained. Obtaining of consent will thus be a cornerstone of protection against litigation. Depending upon the circumstances in each and every case consent may be implied, express or informed.

24. Implied consent (Tacit consent)

This is by far the most common variety of consent in both general practice and hospital practice. The fact that a patient comes to a doctor for an ailment implies that he is agreeable to medical examination in the general sense. This, however, does not imply consent to procedures more complex that inspection, palpation, percussion, auscultation and routine sonography for other examinations, notably rectal and vaginal and withdrawal of blood for diagnostic purpose, express consent (oral or written) should be obtained. For more complicated diagnostic procedures, *e.g.*, lumbar puncture, radiology, endoscopy, C.T. Scan, etc. express written consent should be obtained.

25. Express consent

Anything other than the implied consent is express consent. This may be either oral or written. Express oral consent is obtained for relatively minor examinations or therapeutic procedures, preferably in the presence of a disinterested third party. Express written consent is to be obtained for: (*i*) all major diagnostic procedures, (*ii*) general anesthesia, (*iii*) for surgical operations, (*iv*) intimate examinations, (*v*) examination for determining age, potency and virginity and in medico-legal cases.

26. Informed consent

The concept of informed consent has comes to the fore in recent years and many actions have been brought by patients who alleged that they did not understand the nature of the medical procedure to which they gave consent. All information must be explained in comprehensible non-medical terms preferably in local language about the (*a*) diagnosis, (*b*) nature of treatment, (*c*) risks involved, (*d*) prospects of success, (*e*) prognosis if the procedure is not performed and (*f*) alternative methods of treatment. The physician's duty to disclosure is subject to the exceptions: (*a*) if the patient prefers not be informed and (*b*) if the doctor believes in the exercise of coming to a sound medical judgment, that the patient is so disturbed or anxious that the information provided would not be processed rationally or that it would probably cause significant psychological harm. This is known as *Therapeutic Privilege.* In such a case it is advisable that the doctor should consult the patient's family physician. Revelation of risk is always a compromise between reasonable information and the danger of frightening off the patient from beneficial treatment. The three important components of such consent are information, voluntariness and capacity. (See *Model Form of Informed Consent at the end of this Chapter*).

27. Proxy consent (Substitute consent)

All the above types of consent can take the shape of Proxy Consent. Parent for child, close relative for mentally unsound/unconscious patient, etc.

28. Situations where consent may not be obtained

1. Medical Emergencies. The well being of the patient is paramount and medical rather than legal considerations come first.
2. In case of person suffering from a notifiable disease. In case of AIDS/HIV positive patients, the position in India regarding its being a notifiable disease or not is not yet clear. However, in England the Public Health (Infectious Diseases) Regulations, 1988 extend the provisions of notifiable diseases to AIDS but not to persons who are HIV positive.
3. Immigrants.
4. Members of Armed Forces.
5. Handlers of food and dairymen.
6. New admission to Prisons.
7. In case of a person where a court may order for psychiatric examination or treatment.
8. Under section 53(1) of the Code of Criminal Procedure, a person can be examined at request of the police, by use of force. Section 53(2) lays down that whenever a female is to be examined, it only by, or under the supervision of a female doctor.

29. Situations requiring extra caution

Doctors should keep in mind certain high risk situations which are common causes for medical negligence actions and require extra caution Shall be made.

29.1 Failure to attend

These are particularly frequent where children are concerned, especially in relation to acute abdominal emergencies, meningitis and chest infections.

29.2 Retention of objects in operations sites

Swabs, packs, instruments or towels may be left behind in the field of operation. The responsibility remains with the surgeon.

29.3 Accident and Emergency Departments

This is the most hazardous part of the hospital and senior staff must be readily available to supervise the work.

29.4 Amputation of the wrong limb, digit or operation of wrong eye/tooth

This is a common mishap. Carelessness in hospital notes, errors in pre-operative skin marking and failure to check notes against the patient in the operating theater are the common reasons for the misadventure.

29.5 Emergency, orthopaedics and obstetrics

Surgery, Orthopedics, obstetrics, plastic-surgery and gynaecology are 'high-risk specialities. Missed fractures (especially the scaphoid) tight plaster casts and poor results from spinal procedures are common complaints in orthopedics. In obstetrics, damage to the newborn from anoxia or forceps procedures major damage claims. Failed sterilisation/Vasectomy is again a common cause for litigation.

29.6 Anesthesia

Anesthetists along with surgeons, present a common target for litigation; the actual administration of the anesthetic is not usually the cause of complaint, but the many ancillary responsibilities such as transfusions, injections, airways, i.v. catheters, diathermy and hot water bottle burns may form grounds for allegations of negligence. One of the serious mishaps is the production of cerebral damage from hypoxia due to failure to maintain oxygenation during the operation. Inattention rather than failure to maintain oxygenation is the more common cause, and recent surveys have shown that inexperienced junior anesthetists are a major cause of problems.

29.7 Therapeutic hazards

These can be avoided by:

(*i*) Administering the right drug, the right dose, *via* the right route, *e.g.*, in case of potassium chloride, insulin, antibiotics, spinal anesthesia.

(*ii*) Informing patients/attendants of the potential risks of treatment.

(*iii*) Taking all possible steps to avoid undesirable consequences.

29.8 Failure of communication

A doctor should inform about the patient's medical condition in comprehensible language. In case of reference to another doctor, it is his responsibility to communicate directly with the second doctor and not rely on the patient to carry any informal message.

30. What should a doctor do in the event of a medical mishap?

When something untoward happens following a diagnostic or therapeutic procedure, or when a patient or relative makes a complaint, the doctor must take appropriate steps, some of which may be:

1. Complete the patient's record and recheck the written notes.
2. Be frank enough and inform clearly of the mishap. Show that you were genuinely concerned about the unfortunate mishap. Answer all the queries of patient/relative and do not mind their repeated questioning, harsh attitude and at times even abusive language. Keep in mind the mental state of the close relatives/friends. Be compassionate. Try to remain on the scene as long as possible. Try to engage less excited attendants into discussion on the mishap and indirectly try to bring into focus the circumstances under which the mishap occurred. Doctors who are open-minded and communicative are much less likely to be complained against as patients/attendants are extremely forgiving of errors made by a friendly and concerned medical attendant. A high proportion of complaints are precipitated or escalated into legal action by a progressive breakdown of the doctor-patient communication.
3. After these initial responses, the doctor should contact some other doctor/protection organization to seek advice. The Medical Associations, Medical Practitioners' Society, Hospitals and Nursing Homes' Associations, etc. could form groups/cells to advise and assist in such situations. In future Medical defence organizations could be formed to take up cases of defence on behalf of doctors against alleged medical negligence.

----

31. Model Form of informed consent

I.................................. son of.....................................aged............... resident of .... being under the treatment of .... (*state here name of doctor/hospital/nursing home*) *do hereby* give consent to the performance of medical/surgical/anesthesia/diagnostic procedure of .... (*mention nature of procedure/treatment to be performed, etc.*) upon myself/upon .... aged .... who is related to me as .... (*mention here relationship, e.g. son, daughter, father, mother, wife, etc.*).

I declare that I am more than 18 years of age. I have been informed that there are inherent risks involved in the treatment/procedure. I have signed this consent voluntarily out of my free will without any pressure and in my fell senses.

Place:

Date: *SIGNATURE*

Time: (To be signed by parent/guardian in case of minor)

Notes:

1. This Consent Form should be signed BEFORE the treatment is started. These formats may be modified as per individual requirements or experiences of Hospitals/Nursing Homes.
2. These formats should be in local language and in certain cases it would be prudent to record a proper witness to signature consent.

3. Informed consent forms for various situations can be made for Nursing Homes/Hospitals. Help of lawyers may have to be taken. Detailed forms on Medical history can also be maintained. Keep all records in order and safely.
4. It is important to note that written consent should refer to one specific procedure. Obtaining 'blanket' consent on admission does not have legal validity.

32. Parting words

The support which medical professionals render to us is the noblest. Aryans embodied the rule that, *vidyo narayano harihi* (which means medical doctors are equivalent to Lord Vishnu). However the points are changing on both sides viz. the doctor is no more God and patients are merely the consumers.

The really nature from the Hospital — industry/healthcare profession creates it vulnerable to civil and criminal suits. Many suits are filed to harass doctors, or are filed to evade the payment of bills. It is simpler for individuals to force doctors to Consumer Protection Forums. While It is necessary to punish guilty medical doctors. It can also be essential to protect medical doctors who act in great faith from harassment.

The Supreme Court as soon as observed that the doctor's job is to protect existence and also the courts should aid in this cause so far as feasible. It is also the duty from the courts to determine that medical doctors aren't harassed in the course of overall performance of such duty. The law does not goal to punish all acts of the hospital/doctor that caused injury to some patient. It's concerned only with negligent acts.

Healthcare negligence arises from an act or omission by a medical practitioner, which no reasonably competent and cautious practitioner would have committed. What's anticipated of the medical practitioner is 'reasonably skilful behavior' adopting the 'ordinary skills' and practices of the profession with 'ordinary care'. There's, nevertheless, room for ambiguity and judicial interpretation as what is 'reasonable' and 'ordinary' is really a question of truth.

Essentially, medical doctors are generally bound to exercise an ordinary degree of treatment and not the highest feasible degree of treatment. If a medical practitioner has taken reasonable care, then he cannot be held liable. A mere distinction in opinion isn't a ground for fastening liability on doctor.

Doctors' duties to their sufferers are clear. They should choose whether or to not undertake the situation; they should decide what treatment to provide and they must take treatment in the administration of that treatment. A breach of any of these duties provides the patient a correct to action for negligence.

APPENDIX I

Consumer Protection Regulations, 2005

NOTIFICATION

In exercise of the powers conferred by section 30A of the Consumer Protection Act, 1986 (68 of 1986), the National Consumer Disputes Redressal Commission with the previous approval of the Central Government, hereby makes the following regulations, namely:—

1. Short title and commencement.—(1) These regulations may be called the Consumer Protection Regulations, 2005.

(2) They shall come into force on the date of their publication in the Official Gazette.

2. Definitions.—In these regulations unless the context otherwise requires,—

(*a*) "Act" means the Consumer Protection Act, 1986 (68 of 1986);

(*b*) "Consumer Forum" means a District Forum. a Consumer Disputes Redressal Commission established in a State under clause (*b*) of section 9 (hereafter called the State Commission) or the National Consumer Disputes Redressal Commission;

(*c*) "Registrar" means the head of the ministerial establishment of the Consumer Forum and exercising such powers and functions as are conferred upon him by the President of the Consumer Forum:

(*d*) "rules" means the rules made under the Act;

(*e*) "section" means a section of the Act:

(*f*) words and expressions used in these regulations and not defined herein but defined either in the Act or in the rules shall have the same meaning respectively assigned to them either in the Act or in the rules, as the case may be.

3. Arrangements in Consumer Forum.—(1) A Consumer Forum, being not a regular court, shall have the arrangements as to depict it distinct from a court.

(2) In the hall in which the Consumer Forum shall hear the parties, the dais may not be kept more than 30c.m. in height than the place earmarked for the parties to occupy.

(3) At the dais of the hall, the President and the members of the Consumer Forum shall use the same type of chairs at the same level and these chairs need not have high backs.

4. Dress code.—(1) The President and members of every Consumer Forum while presiding over the Benches,—

(*a*) shall wear simple and sober dress;

(*b*) shall not wear—

(*i*) flashy dress or dress display any affluence;

(*ii*) Jeans or T-shirts.

(*iii*) as if they are holding Courts as Judges of a High Court or a District Court.

(2) The advocates shall be allowed to appear in the usual dress as prescribed by the High Court but without the gown.

5. Hearing hours.—Subject to the provisions of the rules, the normal working hours of the Consumer Forum for hearing matters shall be from 10.30 a.m. to 1.00 p.m. and 2.00 p.m. to 4.00 p.m. on all working days of the Central Government is the case of the National Commission and on all working days of the State Government in the case of the State Commission and the District Forum.

6. Cause List.—(1) Cause list of the Consumer forum for the following entire week shall be made ready before the close of the working hours of the preceding week and displayed on the notice board. The cause list in respect of a Consumer Forum having a website shall also be hosted on the website.

(2) Cause list shall be split into three different parts, namely:—

(*i*) Admission and after notice matters;

(*ii*) Matters where evidence is to be recorded;

(*iii*) Final disposal matters.

(3) Every cause list shall contain the following particulars, namely:—

Sl.No.	No. of the matter	Name of the parties	Name of the party or Counsel or agent appearing

(4) If a date of hearing is given in the presence of parties or their agents, it shall not be a ground for non-appearance for the reason that the cause list for the concerned date does not show the matter or contains incorrect entry or there is omission of the particulars of the matter.

7. Institution of complaints, appeals and revision petitions.—(1) Where a complaint is filed in District Forum or State Commission it shall be filed in three sets and where it is filed in the National Commission it shall be filed in four sets with additional sets equal to the number of opposite party(ies)/respondent(s).

(2) Every complaint shall clearly contain particulars of dispute and the relief claimed and shall also be accompanied by copies of such documents as are necessary to prove the claim made in the complaint.

8. Nomenclature to be given to the complaints, appeals and revision petitions.—(1) A complaint shall hereinafter be referred to as Consumer Complaint (C.C.) instead of O.P., *e.g.*, C.C. No. 2 of 2005.

(2) An appeal shall be referred to as F.A., Revision Petition as R.P., Execution. Application as E.A, Transfer Application T.A. and Review as RA containing the number and the year of filing.

9. Scrutiny of complaint, appeal, petition and revision petition.—(1) Every complaint, appeal, or revision petition shall after it is filed be numbered by the Registrar.

(2) If there is any defect in the filing of the complaint, appeal or revision petition, the particulars of such defects shall be recorded and the party or his agents shall be informed of the defects asking them for removing the defects within 15 days.

(3) In case the party disputes in the correctness of the defects pointed out the matter shall be placed before the Consumer Forum for appropriate orders.

(4) After the expiry of the time given, the matter shall, irrespective of the fact as to whether the defects have been removed or not, be placed before the Consumer Forum for appropriate orders.

(5) If the objections raised by the Registrar are substantial and are not removed within the time allowed for the purpose, those days shall not be excluded for counting the period of limitation.

(6) As required by the second proviso to sub-section (3) of section 12, the admissibility of the complaint shall ordinarily be decided within twenty-one days from the date on which the complaint was received.

(7) In case any defect is pointed out by the Registrar, twenty-one days from the date on which such defect was removed shall be reckoned for the purpose of sub-regulation (5).

(8) All pending complaints, appeals and revision petitions which have not come up for admission till the date of commencement of these regulations and are pending for admission for more than 21 days shall be listed immediately by the Consumer Forum for admission and not later than 21 days from the date of commencement of these regulations.

10. Issue of notice.—(1) Whenever the Consumer Forum directs the issuance of a notice in respect of a complaint, appeal or revision petition, as the case may be, to the opposite party(ies)/respondent(s), ordinarily such notice shall be issued for a period of 30 days and depending upon the circumstances of each case even for less than 30 days.

(2) When there is a question of raising presumption of service, 30 days notice shall be required.

(3) Whenever notices are sought to be effected by a courier service, it shall be ascertained that the courier is of repute.

(4) While appointing the courier for the purpose of effecting service, security deposit may also be taken.

(5) Along with the notice, copies of the complaint, memorandum of grounds of appeal, petitions as the case may be and other documents filed shall be served upon the opposite party(ies)/respondent(s).

(6) After the opposite party or respondent has put in appearance, no application or document shall be received by the Registrar unless it bears an endorsement that a copy thereof has been served upon the other side.

11. Adjournment.—(1) Every proceeding before a Consumer Forum shall be conducted as expeditiously as possible and as per the requirements of the Act.

(2) The Consumer Forum shall record the reasons for any adjournment made by it.

(3) The cost of adjournment, if asked by the opposite party or parties, shall not be less than five hundred rupees per adjournment and could be more depending upon the value and nature of the complaint as may be decided by the Consumer Forum.

(4). The complainant, appellant or petitioner, as the case may be, may also be burdened with cost unless sufficient cause is shown for seeking adjournment:

Provided that in the circumstances of a particular case, the amount of cost imposed may be less than five hundred rupees but in no case less than one hundred rupees.

(5) The cost imposed may be given to the other party or parties to defray his or their expenses or be deposited in the Consumer Legal Aid Account to be maintained by the respective Consumer Forum, as the Consumer Forum may order.

(6) If any adjournment is granted without awarding cost, the order sheet shall mention the reasons thereof.

(7) All orders adjourning the matter shall be signed by the President and members constituting the Bench and not by the Court Master or Bench Clerk.

(8) Non-availability of a lawyer who is representing the party shall not be a ground for seeking adjournment of the matter unless absence is beyond the control of the lawyer such as his sudden illness or bereavement in the family.

12. Hearing by Benches.—Where a Bench, constituted by the President of the State Commission or the National Commission as provided under section 16 or section 20, as the case may be, does not have a member with judicial background and any complex question of law arises and there is no precedent to decide the law point, the Bench so constituted may refer the matter to the President of the State Commission or the National Commission as the case may be to constitute another Bench of which the President shall be a member.

13. Arguments.—(1) Arguments should be as brief as possible and to the point at issue.

(2) Where a party is represented by a counsel, it shall be mandatory to file a brief of written arguments two days before the matter is fixed for arguments.

(3) In case of default to file briefs, the cost shall be imposed at the same rates as laid down for grant of adjournments.

14. Limitations.—(1) Subject to the provisions of sections 15, 19 and 24A, the period of limitation in the following matters shall be as follows:—

(*i*) Revision Petition shall be filed within 90 days from the date of the order or the date of receipt of the order as the case may be;

(*ii*) Application for setting aside the *ex-parte* order under section 22A or dismissal of the complaint in default shall be maintainable if filed within thirty days from the date of the order or date of receipt of the order, as the case may be;

(*iii*) An application for review under sub-section (2) of section 22 shall be filed to the National Commission within 30 days from the date of the order or receipt of the order, as the case may be;

(*iv*) The period of limitation for filing any application for which no period of limitation has been specified in the Act, the rules of these regulations shall be thirty days from the date of the cause of action or the date of knowledge.

(2) Subject to the provisions of the Act, the Consumer Forum may condone the delay in filing an application or a petition referred to in sub-regulation (1) if valid and sufficient reasons to its satisfaction are given.

15. Review.—(1) It shall set out clearly the grounds for review.

(2) Unless otherwise ordered by the National Commission, an application for review shall be disposed of by circulation without oral arguments, as far as practicable between the same members who had delivered the order sought to be reviewed.

16. Appearance of Voluntary Consumer Organisations.—(1) Recognised Consumer Organisations have a right of audience before the Consumer Forum.

(2) An authorisation of a Voluntary Consumer Organisation may be by way of special power of attorney executed on a non-judicial paper or even on plain paper duly attested by a Gazetted Officer or a Notary Public.

(3) The Power of Attorney holder shall be entitled to engage a counsel, if authorised to do so.

(4) A Voluntary Consumer Organisation can engage a counsel or an advocate of its choice or it can itself represent through one of its office bearers as per the rules governing it.

(5) In case of a complaint where the Voluntary Consumer Organisation is a complainant along with the consumer himself and the dispute affects the complainant individually, he can withdraw the complaint:

Provided that if the issue involves unfair trade practice or restrictive trade practice a Voluntary Consumer Organisation may continue to proceed with the complaint even if the complainant wishes to withdraw the same.

(6) A Consumer Forum has to guard itself from touts and busybodies in the garb of power of attorney holders or authorised agents in the proceedings before it.

(7) While a Consumer Forum may permit an authorised agent to appear before it, but authorised agent shall not be one who has used this as a profession:

Provided that this sub-regulation shall not apply in case of advocates.

(8) An authorised agent may be debarred from appearing before a Consumer Forum if he is found guilty of misconduct or any other malpractice at any time.

17. *Ex-parte* interim order.—Any *ex-parte* interim order issued by the Consumer Forum shall stand vacated after 45 days if in the meanwhile the objections to the interim order are not heard and disposed of.

18. Final order.—(1) An order on the top right hand corner shall show as to when the complaint was filed and the date of the order.

(2) The cause title of the order shall contain the names of all the parties with their addresses.

(3) In the body of the order it is desirable that after mentioning the complainant or the opposite party, their names as shown in the title be mentioned and parties thereafter may not be mentioned as complainant or opposite party No.1 or opposite party No. 2, etc.

(4) The cause title shall also clearly show if the appellant or respondent was the complainant or opposite party.

(5) The order of a Consumer Forum disposing of a matter shall be as short and precise as practicable and unnecessary long quotations from the judgments of the higher courts or otherwise shall be avoided.

(6) When a copy of the order is sent to a party, the mode by which it is sent and the date on which it is sent shall be stamped on the last page of the order.

(7) The Consumer Forum shall pass final order invariably within fifteen days of the conclusion of the arguments.

19. Return on institution and disposal of cases.—(1) A Consumer Forum is expected to dispose of at least 75 to 100 matters every month.

(2) A periodic monthly return of institution and disposal of cases shall be sent by the District Forum to the State Commission.

(3) The State Commission shall submit a periodic monthly return of institution and disposal of cases to the National Commission.

(4) Notwithstanding anything contained in this regulation, the President of the National Commission may, at any time, call for any return or information relating to its functioning from a State Commission or District Forums.

20. Preservation of records.—(1) In the case of complaint, the record containing main files with original order sheet shall be preserved for a period of five years.

(2) In the case of records of first appeal and revision petitions, it shall be preserved for three years from the date of disposal of the appeal or revision as the case may be.

(3) Immediately after the consumer complaint, first appeal or revision petition, as the case may be, is disposed of, extra sets shall be given to the parties who may use the same for filing of appeal or revision petition and in that case the necessity to summon the record from the forums below can be dispensed with.

(4) The Registrar shall inform the parties while forwarding the certified copy of the final order, where they do not appear in person at the time of finally disposing of the matter to arrange to collect the extra sets.

(5) A period of at least one month shall be given for the purpose of collection of records by the party and in case of default the extra sets shall be weeded out.

21. Certified copy.—(l) A copy of the order is to be given to the parties free of cost as required under the Act and the rules made thereunder.

(2) In case a party requires an extra copy, it shall be issued to him duly certified by the Registry on a payment of ₹ 20 irrespective of number of pages.

(3) A certified copy of an order shall clearly specify the date when free copy was issued, date of application, date when the copy was made ready and the date when it was so delivered to him.

(4) A fee of ₹ 20 shall be paid for obtaining another certified copy.

(5) Any party desiring to get a certified copy of any document on the file of the Consumer Forum, may get the same on payment of certification fee of twenty rupees per copy. Provided that if any such document of which certified copy is sought, is over and above 5 pages, an extra amount of one rupee per page shall be charged over and above the fee of twenty rupees.

(6) Certified copy of any miscellaneous order passed by the Consumer Forum shall be supplied on payment of ₹ 5 per copy.

22. Inspection of records.—Parties or their agents can inspect the records of any matter by filing an application on payment of ten rupees as fee.

23. Filing of criminal complaint.—Wherever a complaint is required to be filed by the Consumer Forum under sub-section (5) of section 13, the Consumer Forum may authorise its Registrar to file the complaint.

24. Practice Directions.—The National Commission shall be entitled to issue practice directions from time to time as may be necessary for the proper conduct of the cases before Consumer Forum including prescribing forms for complaints, notices, returns, certificate to be issued to the collector and the like.

25. Paresha Yad-dast.—Where a party appears in person and is illiterate, the Court Master or Bench Clerk shall give to that party the next date of hearing in writing.

26. Miscellaneous.—(1) In all proceedings before the Consumer Forum, endeavour shall be made by the parties and their counsel to avoid the use of provisions of Code of Civil Procedure, 1908 (5 of 1908):

Provided that the provisions of the Code of Civil Procedure, 1908 may be applied which have been referred to in the Act or in the rules made thereunder.

(2) Every State Commission and every District Forum shall take steps for its computerisation and networking.

(3) The Consumer Forum shall give proper respect and courtesy to the parties who appear in person and shall provide separate accommodation in the Hall for the convenience of the parties.

(4) The Consumer Forum shall not insist upon the parties to engage advocates.

(5) The Fees collected for inspection of the documents and supply of certified copies shall be deposited in the account maintained for the purpose of depositing fee for filing a complaint as prescribed by the Central Government by rules.

(6) The cases filed by or against the senior citizens, physically challenged, widows and persons suffering from serious ailments shall be listed and disposed of on a priority basis.

APPENDIX II

The Consumer Protection Rules, 1987

In exercise of the powers conferred by sub-section (1) of section 30 of the Consumer Protection Act, 1986 (68 of 1986), the Central Government hereby makes the following rules, namely:—

1. Short title and commencement.—(1) These rules may be called the Consumer Protection Rules, 1987.

(2) They shall come into force on the date of their publication in the Official Gazette.

2. Definitions.—In these rules, unless the context otherwise requires—

(*a*) "Act" means the Consumer Protection Act, 1986 (68 of 1986);

(*b*) "agent" means a person duly authorised by a party to present any complaint, appeal or reply on its behalf before the National Commission;

(*c*) "appellant" means a party which makes an appeal against the order of the State Commission;

(*d*) "chairman" means a chairman of the Central Consumer Protection Council established under sub-section (1) of section 4 of the Act;

(*e*) "memorandum" means any memorandum of appeal filed by the appellant;

(*f*) "opposite party" means a person who answers complaint or claim;

(*g*) "president" means the President of the National Commission;

(*h*) "respondent" means the person who answers any memorandum of appeal;

(*i*) "section" means section of the Act;

(*j*) "state" includes Union territories also;

(*k*) words and expressions used in the rules and not defined but defined in the Act shall have the meanings respectively assigned to them in the Act.

[1][**2A. State Governments to recognise a laboratory as an appropriate Laboratory.**—(1) For the purpose of obtaining recognition as an appropriate laboratory, the applicant shall send application, in triplicate, in the proforma prescribed by the Bureau of Indian Standards with the relevant details to the Department concerned with the consumer protection work in the State Government.

(2) The State Government on receiving the application from the applicant, shall forward its two copies to the Bureau of Indian Standards to assess the suitability of the laboratory from the standards prescribed by them (Bureau of Indian Standards). The fee charged by the Bureau of Indian Standards, for this purpose, shall be paid by the applicant.

(3) The State Government on receiving the recommendations and approval of the Bureau of Indian Standards, shall notify that laboratory as an "appropriate laboratory" for the purpose of Consumer Protection Act, 1986 for a period of three years.]

---

1 Inserted by the Consumer Protection (Amendment) Rules, 1995, *vide* GSR 605(E), dated 30-8-1995.

3. The Constitution of the Central Consumer Protection Council and the Working Groups.—(1) The Central Government shall, by notification in the Official Gazette constitute the Central Consumer Protection Council (hereinafter referred to as the Central Council) which shall consist of the following members, not exceeding [1][35], namely:—

[2][(*a*) [the Minister in-charge of Consumer Affairs in the Central Government] who shall be the Chairman of the Central Council;

(*b*) the Minister of State (where he is not holding independent charge) or Deputy Minister [3][in charge of Consumer Affairs in the Central Government] who shall be the Vice-Chairman of the Central Council;

[4][(*c*) the Minister in-charge of Consumer Affairs of two of the States from each region as mentioned in Schedule I to be changed by rotation on expiration of the term of the Council on each occasion;

(*ca*) an administrator (whether designated as administrator or Lieutenant Governor), of a Union Territory, to represent a Union Territory, as mentioned in Schedule II, to be changed by rotation on expiration of the term of the Council on each occasion;]

(*d*) [5][two] Members of Parliament [6][one] from the Lok Sabha and [7][one] from the Rajya Sabha;

[8][(*e*) * * *]

(*f*) representatives of the Central Government Departments and autonomous organisations concerned with consumer interests — not exceeding [9][five];

[10][(*fa*) The Registrar, National Consumer Disputes Redressal Commission, New Delhi;]

[11][(*g*) representatives of Consumer Organisations from amongst the Indian members of the International Organisation, namely, Consumer International — not exceeding six, to be nominated by the Central Government;

(*ga*) representatives with proven expertise and experience who are capable of representing consumer interests, drawn from amongst consumer organizations, consumer activists, women, farmers trade and industry — not exceeding five, one from each of the regions specified in Schedule annexed to these rules;]

---

1 Substituted for "150" by the Consumer Protection (Amendment) Rules, 2006, vide GSR 273(E), dated 5-5-2006.

2 Substituted for "the Minister in-charge of Department of Civil Supplies" by the Consumer Protection (Amendment) Rules, 1993, published in the Gazette of India, Extra., Pt. II, Sec. 3(*i*), dated 30-12-1993.

3 Substituted for "in the Department of Civil Supplies," *ibid.*

4 Substituted for "the Minister In-charge of Consumer Affairs in States" by the Consumer Protection (Amendment) Rules, 2006, *vide* GSR 273(E), dated 5-5-2006.

5 Substituted for "eight", *ibid.*

6 Substituted for "five", *ibid.*

7 Substituted for "three", *ibid.*

8 The words "the Secretary of the National Commission for Scheduled Castes and Scheduled Tribes" omitted, *ibid.*

9 Substituted for "twenty", *ibid.*

10 Inserted by the Consumer Protection (Amendment) Rules, 2004, *vide* GSR 175(E), dated 5-3-2004.

11 Substituted for "representatives of the Consumer Organisations or Consumers — not less than thirty-five" by the Consumer Protection (Amendment) Rules, 2006, *vide* GSR 273(E), dated 5-5-2006.

(*h*) [1][* * *]

(*i*) [2][* * *]

[3][(*j*) the Secretaries in-charge of Consumer Affairs in the States to be nominated by the Central Government — not exceeding three;]

(*k*) [4][the Secretary in-charge of the Consumer Affairs in the Central Government] shall be the Member-Secretary of the Central Council.

(2) The term of the Council shall be three years:

[5][Provided that the Council shall continue to function for a further period of three months or till it is constituted, whichever is earlier.]

(3) Any member may, by writing under his hand to the Chairman of the Central Council, resign from the Council. The vacancies, so caused or otherwise, shall be filled from the same category by the Central Government and such person shall hold office so long as the member whose place he fills would have been entitled to hold office, if the vacancy had not occurred.

[6][(4) * * *]

4. Procedure of the Central Council.—Under sub-section (2) of section 5, the Central Council shall observe the following procedure in regard to the transaction of its business,—

(1) The meeting of the Central Council shall be presided over by the Chairman. In the absence of the Chairman, the Vice-Chairman shall preside over the meeting of the Central Council. In the absence of the Chairman and the Vice-Chairman, the Central Council shall elect a member to preside over that meeting of the Council.

(2) Each meeting of the Central Council shall be called by giving, not less than ten days from the date of issue, notice in writing to every member.

(3) Every notice of a meeting of the Central Council shall specify the place and the day and hour of the meeting and shall contain statement of business to be transacted thereat.

(4) No proceedings of the Central Council shall be invalid merely by reasons of existence of any vacancy in or any defect in the constitution of the Council.

(5) For the purpose of performing its functions under the Act, the Central Council may constitute from amongst its members, such working groups as it may deem necessary and every working group so constituted shall perform such functions as are assigned to it by the Central Council. The findings of such working groups shall be placed before the Central Council for its consideration.

---

1 The words "representative of women — not less than ten" omitted by the Consumer Protection (Amendment) Rules, 2006, *vide* GSR 273(E), dated 5-5-2006.

2 The words "representative of farmers trade and industries — not exceeding twenty" omitted, *ibid.*

3 Substituted for "persons capable of representing consumers interest not specified above — not exceeding fifteen", *ibid.*

4 The words "Minister of Food and Civil Supplies or" omitted by the *Consumer Protection (Amendment) Rules, 1997 vide* GSR 95(E), dated 27-2-1997.

5 Inserted by the *Consumer Protection (Amendment) Rules, 2011 vide* GSR 385(E), dated 12-5-2011.

6 The words "For the purpose of monitoring the implementation of the recommendations of the Central Council and to suggest the working of the Council, the Central Government may constitute from amongst the members of the Council, a Standing Working Group, under the chairmanship of the Member-Secretary of the Council. The Standing Working Group shall consist of not exceeding 30 members and shall meet as and when considered necessary by the Central Government," omitted by the *Consumer Protection (Amendment) Rules, 2006 vide* GSR 273(E), dated 5-5-2006.

[1][(6) In connection with the journey undertaken to and fro by the non-official members for attending the meeting of the Central Consumer Protection Council or its working group, they shall be entitled to [2][economy class air fare]. The non-official members shall be entitled to a sum of [3][[4][₹2,000] per each day of the meeting] day as incidental charges to cover the expenditure towards their daily allowance, lodging, local conveyance from residence to the station/airport and from station/airport to the venue of meeting and *vice-versa.* Every claim made under this sub-rule shall be subject to certifying that the member will not claim any benefit from any other Central Government Ministry, Department or Organization during his visit for attending the meeting of the Central Consumer Protection Council or any of its Working Group. Local non-official members residing at the place of the venue of the meeting, shall be paid [5][consolidated conveyance and hire charges] to the tune of [6][₹500] *per diem* irrespective of the classification of the city. Members of Parliament attending meetings of the Council or its Working Group shall be entitled to travelling and daily allowances at such rates as are admissible to such members.]

(7) The resolutions passed by the Central Council shall be recommendatory in nature.

5. Place of the National Commission.—The office of the National Commission shall be located in the Union Territory of Delhi.

6. Working days and office hours of the National Commission.—The working days and office hours of the National Commission shall be the same as that of the Central Government.

7. Seal and emblem.—The official seal and emblem of the National Commission shall be such as the Central Government may specify.

8. Sittings of the National Commission.—The sitting of the National Commission as and when necessary, shall be convened by the President.

---

1 Substituted for "The non-official members shall be entitled to first class or second Air-Conditioned by all trains (including Rajdhani Express) to and fro Railway fare or actual mode of travel whichever is less. Outstation non-official members shall be entitled to a daily allowance of one hundred rupees per day for attending the meetings of the Central Council or any working group. Local non-official members shall be paid actual conveyance, hire charges subject to a ceiling of ₹75.00 per day irrespective of the classification of the city. Members of Parliament shall be entitled to travelling and daily allowances at such rates as are admissible to such members." by the *Consumer Protection (Amendment) Rules, 2004, vide* GSR 175(E), dated 5-3-2004.

2 Substituted for "avail first class or two-tier air-conditioned class of railway accommodation by all trains (including Rajdhani Express) and claim such fare or cost of actual mode of travel, whichever is less. The non-official members from Island territories shall be entitled to, to and fro air journey (economy class) in domestic airlines from the Islands to the nearest main-land airport and thereafter rail fare by entitled class. The non-official members who are senior citizens shall be entitled to, to and fro air-journey (economy class) in domestic airlines on availing senior citizen concessional air fare for their journeys provided the distance being travelled is 1000 kms or above" by the *Consumer Protection (Second Amendment) Rules, 2009 vide* GSR 591(E), dated 20-8-2009.

3 Substituted for the words "₹1,000 per day" by the *Consumer Protection (Second Amendment) Rules, 2005 vide* GSR 64(E), dated 10-2-2005.

4 Substituted for "₹1,000" by the *Consumer Protection (Second Amendment) Rules, 2009 vide* GSR 591(E), dated 20-8-2009.

5 Substituted for the words "consolidated conveyance, hire charges and incidental charges to cover the daily allowances", *ibid.*

6 Substituted for "₹200" by the *Consumer Protection (Second Amendment) Rules, 2009 vide* GSR 591(E), dated 20-8-2009.

9. Staff of the National Commission.—The Central Government shall appoint such staff as may be necessary to assist the National Commission in its day-to-day work and to perform such other functions as are provided under the Act and these rules or assigned to it by the President. The salary payable to such staff shall be defrayed out of the Consolidated Fund of India.

9A. Fee for making complaints before District Forum.—[1][(1) Every complaint filed under sub-section (1) of section 12, sub-section (1) of section 17 and clause (*a*) in sub-clause (*i*) of section 21 of the Act shall be accompanied by a fee as specified in the table given below in the form of crossed Demand Draft drawn on a nationalised bank or through a crossed Indian Postal Order in favour of the President of the District Forum, Registrar of the State Commission or the Registrar of the National Commission as the case may be, and payable at the respective place where the District Forum, State Commission or the National Commission is situated.

(2) The concerned authority referred to in sub-rule (1) shall credit the amount of fee received by it into the Consumer Welfare Fund of the respective State and where such fund is not established into the Receipt Account of the State Government and in the case of the National Commission, to the Consumer Welfare Fund of the Central Government.

TABLE

Sl. No.	**Value of goods or services and the compensation claimed**	**Amount of fee payable**
(1)	(2)	(3)
	District Forum	
(1)	Upto one lakh rupees — For complainants who are under the Below Poverty Line holding Antyodaya Anna Yojana Cards	Nil
(2)	Upto one lakh rupees — For complainants other than Antyodaya Anna Yojana card holders.	₹100
(3)	Above one lakh and upto five lakh rupees	₹200
(4)	Above five lakh and upto ten lakh rupees	₹400
(5)	Above ten lakh and upto twenty lakh rupees	₹500

1 Substituted by the *Consumer Protection* (*Second Amendment*) *Rules, 2005 vide* GSR 64(E), dated 10-2-2005 for the following Rule 9A inserted by the *Consumer Protection* (*Amendment*) *Rules, 2004 vide* GSR 175(E), dated 5-3-2004:

"(1) Every complaint filed under sub-section (1) with a District forum shall be accompanied by fee, as specified in the table given below in the form of crossed Demand Draft drawn on a nationalized bank or through a crossed Indian Postal Order drawn in favour of the Registrar of the State Commission and payable at the respective place where the State Commission is situated. The concerned District Forum shall deposit the Amount of fee so received in the State Government Receipt Account.

TABLE

Sl. No.	*Value of goods or services and the compensation claimed*	*Amount of fee payable*
(1)	(2)	(3)
	District Forum	
1.	Upto one lakh rupees	₹100
2.	One lakh rupees and above but less than five lakh rupees	₹200
3.	Five lakh rupees and above but less than ten lakh rupees	₹400
4.	Ten lakh rupees and above but not exceeding twenty lakh rupees	₹500"

(1)	(2)	(3)
	State Commission	
(6)	Above twenty lakh and upto fifty lakh rupees	`2,000
(7)	Above fifty lakh and upto one crore rupees	`4,000
	National Commission	
(8)	Above one crore rupees	`5,000

(3) The complainants who are under the Below Poverty Line shall be entitled for the exemption of payment of fee only on production of an attested copy of the Antyodaya Anna Yojana cards.]

10. Additional powers of the National Commission, State Commission and District Forum.—(1) The National Commission, the State Commission and the District Forum shall have power to require any person,—

(*a*) to produce before, and allow to be examined and kept by an officer of the National Commission, the State Commission or the District Forum, as the case may be, specified in this behalf, such books, accounts, documents or commodities in the custody or under the control of the person so required as may be specified or described in the requisition, if the examination of such books, accounts, documents or commodities are required for the purpose of this Act;

(*b*) to furnish to an officer so specified, such information as may be required for the purpose of this Act.

(2) (*a*) Where during any proceedings under this Act, the National Commission, the State Commission or the District Forum, as the case may be, has any ground to believe that any book, paper, commodity or document which may be required to be produced in such proceedings, are being or may be, destroyed, mutilated, altered, falsified or secreted, it may, by written order, authorise any officer to exercise the power of entry and search of any premises. Such authorised officer may also seize such books, papers, documents or commodities as are required for the purpose of this Act:

Provided that such seizure shall be communicated to the National Commission, the State Commission or the District Forum, as the case may be, as soon as it is made or within a period not exceeding 72 hours of making such seizure after specifying the reasons in writing for making such seizure.

(*b*) The National Commission, the State Commission or the District Forum, as the case may be, on examination of such seized documents or commodities, as the case may be, may order the retention thereof or may return it to the party concerned.

[1][**10A. Credit of the fine into the Consumer Welfare Fund when consumers are not identified conveniently.**—(1) Where an order is passed by the National Commission in exercise of the powers vested under clause (*hb*) of sub-section (1) of section 14 directing the opposite party to pay such amount as determined by it on account of loss or injury suffered due to defects in goods complained against or alleged deficiency of service to a large number of consumers, who are not identifiable conveniently; such sum shall be credited by the National Commission in the Consumer Welfare Fund established by the Central Government under section 12C of the Central Excise Act, 1944 (1 of 1944).

(2) Any amount credited to the said Fund shall be utilized in accordance with the provisions of the Consumer Welfare Fund Rules, 1992.

10B. Number of Members in the National Commission.—The National

1 Inserted by the *Consumer Protection (Amendment) Rules, 2004, vide* GSR 175(E), dated 5-3-2004.

Commission shall consist of not less than four members and not more than [1][eleven] members and at least one of them shall be a woman.]

11. Salaries, honorarium and other allowances of the President and Members of the National Commission.— [2][(1) The President of the National Commission shall be entitled to salary, allowances and other perquisites as are available to a sitting Judge of the Supreme Court.

(1A) The other members of the National Commission appointed on whole time basis shall be entitled to the following honorarium and other allowances with effect from the 1st day of April, 2006, namely:—

(*a*) the members shall be paid twenty-three thousand rupees per month by way of honorarium:

Provided that the members, who are retired Judges of High Courts or retired Secretaries to the Government of India shall have the option to either receive consolidated honorarium of twenty-three thousand rupees per month or receive remuneration of last pay drawn less pension;

(*b*) a woman who has not held an office of profit earlier, on appointment as a member shall be entitled to a pay in the scale of ₹ 24,050-26,000 per month along with other benefits;

(*c*) the members shall be provided with Government accommodation or receive house rent allowance of [3][twenty-five thousand rupees per month with effect from 1st September, 2008] in lieu thereof;

(*d*) the members shall be paid conveyance allowance at the rate of ten thousand rupees per month, if no chauffeur driven government vehicle is provided in which event one hundred fifty liters of petrol shall be supplied or the price thereof shall be paid:

[4][*Explanation.*—For the purpose of this clause, if the members are not provided with chauffeur driven government vehicle or if the members do not opt for hired vehicle in lieu of conveyance allowance, the members shall be paid conveyance allowance per month at the rate of ten thousand rupees and the cost of one hundred fifty litres of petrol.]

(*e*) the members shall be entitled to one thousand free calls for the telephone installed at their residence, with STD and ISD facilities; and

---

1 Substituted for "nine" by the *Consumer Protection (Amendment) Rules, 2010 vide* GSR 579(E), dated 5-7-2010. Earlier, "nine" was substituted for "six" by the *Consumer Protection (Second Amendment) Rules, 2005, vide* GSR 64(E), dated 10-2-2005.

2 Sub-rule (1) substituted by the *Consumer Protection (Amendment) Rules, 2006*, w.e.f. 4-8-2006 *vide* Notification No. 462(E), dated 4-8-2006 for the following:

"(1) The President of the National Commission shall be entitled to salary, allowances and other perquisites as are available to a sitting Judge of the Supreme Court and the other members, appointed on whole-time basis, shall receive a consolidated honorarium of fifteen thousand rupees per month."

Earlier, sub-rule (1) was substituted by the *Consumer Protection (Third Amendment) Rules, 2005 vide* GSR 67(E), dated 11-2-2005 for "(1) The President of the National Commission shall be entitled to salary, allowances and other perquisites as are available to a sitting Judge of the Supreme Court and other members, if sitting on whole-time basis, shall receive a consolidated honorarium of ten thousand rupees per month or if sitting on part-time basis, a consolidated honorarium of five hundred rupees per day for sitting."

3 Substituted for "eight thousand rupees per month" by the *Consumer Protection (Amendment) Rules, 2010 vide* GSR 579(E), dated 5-7-2010. Earlier, "nine" was substituted for "six" by the *Consumer Protection (Second Amendment) Rules, 2005, vide* GSR 64(E), dated 10-2-2005.

4 Inserted, *ibid*.

(*f*) the members shall be entitled to fifteen days casual leave in a year.]

(2) [1][The members] shall be entitled to traveling and daily allowances on official tours at the same rates as are admissible to group 'A' Officers of the Central Government.

[2][* * *]

(3) The honorarium or the salary, as the case may be, and other allowances shall be defrayed out of the Consolidated Fund of India.

12. Terms and conditions of service of the President and members of the National Commission.—(1) Before appointment, the President and a member of the National Commission shall have to take an undertaking that he does not and will not have any such financial or other interest as is likely to affect prejudicially his functions as such member.

[3][(2) * * *]

(3) Notwithstanding anything contained in sub-rule (2), the President or a member may.—

[4][(*a*) by writing under his hand and addressed to the Central Government resign his office at any time but his office shall become vacant only when such resignation is accepted by the Central Government,]

(*b*) be removed from his office in accordance with the provisions of rule 13.

(4) The terms and conditions of service of the President and the members shall not be varied to their disadvantage during their tenure of office.

(5) A casual vacancy caused by resignation or removal of the President or any other member of the National Commission under sub-rule (3) or otherwise shall be filled by fresh appointment.

[5][(6) When the office of the President of the National Commission is vacant or a person occupying such office is by reason of absence or otherwise, unable to perform the duties of his office, the same shall, save as otherwise provided in the proviso to section 22D be performed by the seniormost member of the National Commission.]

---

1 Substituted for "The President and the members" by the *Consumer Protection (Second Amendment) Rules, 2006,* w.e.f. 4-8-2006 *vide* GSR No. 462(E), dated 4-8-2006.

2 Omitted by *Consumer Protection (Second Amendment) Rules, 2006* w.e.f. 4-8-2006 *vide* GSR No. 462(E), dated 4-8-2006. Prior to omission, it read as under:

"(2A) The President and the members of the National Commission shall be entitled to conveyance allowance of one hundred and fifty rupees per day of its sitting or a sum of one thousand and five hundred rupees per month, as may be opted by them."

Earlier, it was inserted by the *Consumer Protection (Amendment) Rules, 1998, vide* GSR No. 88(E), dated 24-12-1998.

3 Omitted the following sub-rule (2) by the *Consumer Protection (Amendment) Rules, 2004, vide* GSR 175(E), dated 5-3-2004:

"Every member of the National Commission shall hold office for a term of five years or up to the age of seventy years, whichever is earlier, and shall not be eligible for re-appointment."

4 Substituted for "by writing under his hand and addressed to the Central Government resign his office at any time;" *ibid.*

5 Substituted by the *Consumer Protection (Amendment) Rules, 2004, vide* GSR 175(E), dated 5-3-2004 for

"When the President of the National Commission is unable to discharge the functions owing to absence, illness or any other cause, the senior most member of the National Commission with judicial background, if authorised so to do by the President in writing, shall discharge the functions of the President until the day on which the President resumes the charge of his functions."

[1][(7)] The President or any member ceasing to hold office as such shall not hold any appointment in or be connected with the management or administrations of an organisation which have been the subject of any proceeding under the Act during his tenure for a period of 5 years from the date on which he ceases to hold such office.

[2][**12A. Procedure for selection of members.**—(1) Save as otherwise provided in sub-rule (2), the process of appointment of a member shall be initiated at least three months before the vacancy arises.

(2) If a post falls vacant due to resignation or death of a member or creation of a new post, the process for filling the post shall be initiated immediately after the post has fallen vacant or is created, as the case may be.

(3) An advertisement of a vacancy inviting applications from eligible candidates may be published in leading newspapers in India or by vacancy circulars or both, as may be decided by the Central Government.

(4) After scrutiny of the applications received till the last date specified for receipt of applications, a list of eligible candidates alongwith their applications shall be placed before the Selection Committee constituted under the third proviso to sub-section (1) of section 20.

(5) The Selection Committee shall consider all the applications of eligible applicants referred to it.

[3][(6) The Selection Committee shall, subject to the provisions of sub-rule (6A), assess the suitability of the candidates for the post of Member:

Provided that the Selection Committee may, if it considers necessary, depending on the number of candidates, short-list them on the basis of comparative merit and experience of such candidates for selection.

(6A) The Selection Committee shall assess the suitability of the candidates and where short listing is done, from among the short-listed candidates, for the post of Member in the following manner, namely:—

(*a*) in the case of candidates having judicial background, by assessing them on the basis of the judgments and other judicial orders passed by such candidates;

(*b*) in the case of candidates having experience of working under the Central Government or any State Government or an undertaking under the Central Government or a State Government, by assessing such candidates on the basis of their Annual Confidential Reports and their experience relevant to the post applied for;

(*c*) in other cases, the suitability of the short listed candidates shall be assessed by the Selection Committee on the basis of personal interview conducted by it:

Provided that notwithstanding anything contained in this sub-rule, the Selection Committee may, for assessing the suitability of a class or category of candidates, if it considers necessary, call such class or category of candidates for interview for assessing their suitability for the post of Member.]

---

1 Sub-rules (7), (8) and (9) are omitted and sub-rule (10) re-numbered as sub-rule (7) by the *Consumer Protection (Amendment) Rules, 1991, vide* GSR 533(E), dated 14-8-1991.

2 Inserted by the *Consumer Protection (Amendment) Rules, 2005 vide* GSR 50(E), dated 1-2-2005.

3 Substituted by the *Consumer Protection (Third Amendment) Rules, 2006*, w.e.f. 13-10-2006 *vide* Notification No. 637(E), dated 13-10-2006 for the following:

"(6) The Selection committee may, if it considers necessary, depending on the number of candidates, short list them on the basis of merit and call such short listed candidates for personal interview to consider their suitability for the post of Member."

(7) The Selection Committee may, on the basis of its assessment made by it, recommend a panel of names of candidates for appointment as members from amongst the applicants referred to in sub-rule (5) in order of merit for the consideration of the Central Government.

(8) The Central Government shall, before seeking approval of the Appointments Committee of the Cabinet, verify or cause to be verified the credentials and antecedents of the candidates selected by the Central Government from the panel recommended by the Selection Committee and satisfy the suitability of such candidates for appointment as members.

(9) Every appointment of a member shall be subject to his medical fitness.]

13. Removal of President or members from office in certain circumstances.—(1) The Central Government may remove from office, the President or any member, who,—

(*a*) has been adjudged as an insolvent; or

(*b*) has been convicted of an offence which, in the opinion of the Central Government, involves moral turpitude; or

(*c*) has become physically or mentally incapable of acting as the President or the member; or

(*d*) has acquired such financial or other interest as is likely to affect prejudicially his functions as the President or a member; or

(*e*) has so abused his position as to render his continuance in office prejudicial to the public interest; or

[1][(*f*) remain absent in three consecutive sittings except for reasons beyond his control.]

[2][(2) Notwithstanding anything contained in sub-rule (1), the President or any member of the National Commission shall not be removed from his office except by an order made by the Central Government on the grounds specified in clauses (*d*), (*e*) and (*f*) of that sub-rule and after an inquiry held by a sitting Judge of the Supreme Court nominated by the Chief Justice of India in which the President or member of the National Commission, as the case may be, has been informed of the charges against him and given a reasonable opportunity of being heard in respect of those charges and found guilty.]

14. Procedure to be followed by the National Commission.—(1) A complaint containing the following particulars shall be presented by the complainant in person or by his agent to the National Commission or be sent by registered post, addressed to the National Commission:

(*a*) the name, description and the address of the complainant;

(*b*) the name, description and address of the opposite party or parties, as the case may be, so far as they can be ascertained;

(*c*) the facts relating to the complaint and when and where it arose;

(*d*) documents in support of the allegations contained in the complaint;

(*e*) the relief which the complainant claims.

---

1 Inserted by the *Consumer Protection (Amendment) Rules, 1997, vide* GSR 95(E), dated 27-2-1997.

2 Substituted for the following sub-rule (2) by the *Consumer Protection (Amendment) Rules, 2004, vide* GSR 175(E), dated 5-3-2004.

"Notwithstanding anything contained in sub-rule (1), the President or any member shall not be removed from his office on the grounds specified in clauses (*d*), (*e*) and (*f*) of that sub-rule except on an inquiry held by Central Government in accordance with such procedure as it may specify in this behalf and finds the President or a member to be guilty of such ground."

[1][(1A) Every complaint under sub-rule (1) shall be filed in quadruplicate or with such number of copies as may be required by the National Commission.]

[2][(2) The National Commission shall, in disposal of any complaint before it, as far as possible, follow the procedure and conditions including the provisions governing adjournments as laid down in sections 12 and 13 in relation to the complaints received by the District Forum, with such modification as may be considered necessary by the Commission.]

(3) On the date of hearing or any other date to which hearing could be adjourned, it shall be obligatory on the parties or their agents to appear before the National Commission. Where the complainant or his agent fails to appear before the National Commission on such days, the National Commission may in its discretion either dismiss the complaint for default or decide it on merits. Where the opposite party or its agent fails to appear on the date of hearing the National Commission may decide the complaint *ex-parte.*

(4) The National Commission may, on such terms as it deems fit and at any stage of the proceedings, adjourn the hearing of the complaint but the complaint shall be decided as far as possible within a period of three months from the date of notice received by opposite party where complaint does not require analysis or testing of commodities and within five months if it requires analysis or testing of commodities.

[3][(4A) In the event of a complaint being disposed of after the period specified in sub-rule (4), the National Commission shall record in writing, the reasons for the delay in such disposal.]

(5) If after the proceedings conducted under sub-rule (3), the National Commission is satisfied with the allegations contained in the complaint, it shall issue orders to the opposite party or parties, as the case may be, directing him or them to take one or more of the things as mentioned in sub-section (1) of section 14. The National Commission shall also have the power to direct that any order passed by it, where no appeal has been preferred under section 23 or where the order of the National Commission has been affirmed by the Supreme Court under that section, be published in the Official Gazette or through any other media and no legal proceedings shall lie against the National Commission or any media for such publication.

[4]**[14A. Appeals before National Commission.**—Every appeal filed in terms of section 19 shall be accompanied by such amount as specified in the second proviso to the said section and such amount may be remitted in the form of a crossed Demand Draft drawn on a nationalized bank in favour of the Registrar, National Commission, payable at Delhi. The National Commission dealing with the appeals filed before them shall follow the provisions of sections 19 and 19A as may be required to hear the appeals filed before the Commission.

Explanation.—In this rule, "nationalized bank" means a corresponding new bank specified in the First Schedule to the Banking Companies (Acquisition and Transfer of

---

1 Inserted by the *Consumer Protection (Second Amendment) Rules, 2005 vide* GSR 64(E), dated 10-2-2005.

2 Substituted for the following sub-rule (2) by the *Consumer Protection (Amendment) Rules, 2004, vide* GSR 175(E), dated 5-3-2004.

"The National Commission, shall, in disposal of any complaint before it, as far as possible, follow the procedures laid down in sub-sections (1) and (2) of section 13 in relation to complaint received by the District Forum."

3 Inserted, *ibid.*

4 Inserted, *ibid.*

Undertakings) Act, 1970 (5 of 1970) or a corresponding new bank specified in the First Schedule to the Banking Companies (Acquisition and Transfer of Undertakings) Act, 1980 (40 of 1980).]

15. Procedure for hearing the appeal.—(1) Memorandum shall be presented by the appellant or his agent to the National Commission in person or be sent by registered post addressed to the Commission.

(2) Every memorandum filed under sub-rule (1) shall be in legible handwriting preferably typed and shall set forth concisely under distinct heads, the grounds of appeal without any argument or narrative and such grounds shall be numbered consecutively.

(3) Each memorandum shall be accompanied by a [1][crossed demand draft as referred to in rule 14A and by a certified copy of the order of the State Commission appealed against and such of the documents as may be required to support grounds of objection mentioned in the memorandum.

(4) When the appeal is presented after the expiry of the period of limitation as specified in the Act, the memorandum shall be accompanied by an application supported by an affidavit setting forth the facts on which the appellant relies to satisfy the National Commission that he has sufficient cause for not preferring the appeal within the period of limitation.

(5) The appellant shall submit [2][four copies or such number of copies] of the memorandum to the Commission for official purpose.

(6) On the date of hearing or on any other day to which hearing may be adjourned, it shall be obligatory for the parties or their agents to appear before the National Commission. If appellant or his agent fails to appear on such date, the National Commission may in its discretion either dismiss the appeal or decide *ex-parte* on merits. If the respondent or his agent fails to appear on such date, the National Commission shall proceed *ex-parte* and shall decide the appeal on merits of the case.

(7) The appellant shall not, except by leave of the National Commission, urge or be heard in support of any ground of objection not set forth in the memorandum but the National Commission, in deciding the appeal, may not confine to the grounds of objection set forth in the memorandum:

Provided that the Commission shall not rest its decision on any other ground other than those specified in the memorandum unless the party who may be affected thereby, has been given, an opportunity of being heard by the National Commission.

[3][(8) No adjournment shall ordinarily be granted by the National Commission, unless sufficient cause is shown and the reasons for grant of adjournment have been recorded in writing by the Commission. The National Commission may also adjourn the hearing of the appeal *suo motu*, on such terms as it may think fit and at any stage of the proceedings for reasons to be recorded in writing. The appeal shall be decided, as far as possible, within ninety days from the date of its admission. In the event of an appeal being disposed of after the period so specified, the National Commission shall record in writing the reasons of the same at the time of disposal of the said appeal.]

---

1 Substituted for the words 'certified copy', *ibid.*

2 Substituted for "six copies" by the *Consumer Protection (Second Amendment) Rules, 2005 vide* GSR 64(E), dated 10-2-2005.

3 Substituted for the following sub-rule (8) by *Consumer Protection (Amendment) Rules, 2004 vide* GSR 175(E), dated 5-3-2004.

"The National Commission, on such terms as it may think fit and at any stage, adjourn the hearing of the appeal, but not more than one adjournment shall ordinarily be given and the appeal should be decided, as far as possible within 90 days from the first date of hearing."

[1][(9) The order of the National Commission shall be communicated to the parties concerned free of cost.]

[2][**15A. Sitting of the National Commission and signing of orders.**—(1) Every proceeding of the National Commission shall be conducted by the President [3][or the seniormost member] and at least two members thereof sitting together except when a bench is constituted by the President of the National Commission with one or more members as he may deem fit.]

[4][Provided that where the member or members for any reason are unable to conduct the proceeding till it is completed, the President or the seniormost member, as provided in section 22D of the Act, shall conduct such proceedings from the state at which it was last heard by the previous member.]

(2) Every order made by the National Commission shall be signed by the President or the seniormost member [5][as provided under section 22D] and at least two members who conducted the proceeding and if there is any difference of opinion among themselves, the opinion of majority shall be the order of the National Commission:

Provided that where the proceeding is conducted by the President or the seniormost member [6][as provided in section 22D] and three members thereof and they differ on any point or points, they shall state the point or points on which they differ and refer the same to the other member for hearing on such point or points and such point or points shall be decided accordingly to the opinion of the majority of the National Commission.

[7][**16. Manner of deposit of amount in appeals before Supreme Court.**— Every appeal filed before the Supreme Court in terms of section 23 shall be accompanied by an amount as provided in the second proviso to that section and such amount may be remitted in the form of a crossed Demand Draft drawn on a nationalized bank in favour of Registrar, Supreme Court, payable at Delhi.

Explanation.—In this rule, "nationalized bank" means a corresponding new bank specified in the First Schedule to the Banking Companies (Acquisition and Transfer of Undertakings) Act, 1970 (5 of 1970) or a corresponding new bank specified in the First Schedule to the Banking Companies (Acquisition and Transfer of Undertakings) Act, 1980 (40 of 1980).]

[8][SCHEDULE I

[See rule 3(*l*)(*c*)]

1. Eastern Region — to consist of the States of Bihar, Chhattisgarh, Jharkhand, Orissa, and West Bengal.

---

1 Substituted by the *Consumer Protection (Amendment) Rules, 1991, vide* GSR 533(E), dated 14-8-1991.

2 Inserted by the *Consumer Protection (Amendment) Rules, 1991, ibid.*

3 Substituted for "the senior most member authorised under Rule 12" by the *Consumer Protection (Second Amendment), Rules, 2005, vide* GSR 64(E), dated 10-2-2005.

4 Substituted by the *Consumer Protection (Second Amendment) Rules, 2005 vide* GSR 64(E), dated 10-2-2005 for "Provided that where the member or members for any reason are unable to conduct the proceeding till it is completed, the President or the seniormost member authorised under Rule 12 shall conduct such proceeding *de novo*.

5 Substituted for authorised under Rule 12" *ibid.*

6 *ibid.*

7 Inserted by the *Consumer Protection (Amendment) Rules, 2004, vide* GSR 175(E), dated 5-3-2004.

8 Inserted by the *Consumer Protection (Amendment) Rules, 2006 vide* GSR 273(E), dated 5-5-2006.

2. Western Region — to consist of the States of Goa, Gujarat, Maharashtra, Madhya Pradesh and Rajasthan.
3. Northern Region — to consist of the States of Haryana, Himachal Pradesh, Jammu & Kashmir, Punjab, Uttar Pradesh and Uttaranchal.
4. Southern Region — to consist of the States of Andhra Pradesh, Karnataka, Kerala and Tamil Nadu.
5. North Eastern Region — to consist of the States of Arunachal Pradesh, Assam, Manipur, Meghalaya, Mizoram, Nagaland, Tripura and Sikkim.

SCHEDULE II

[See rule 3(*l*)(*ca*)]

The Union Territories of the Andaman and Nicobar Islands, Chandigarh, Dadra and Nagar Haveli, Daman and Diu, Lakshadweep, Pondicherry and the National Capital Territory of Delhi.]

APPENDIX III

Twelfth Report Standing Committee on Food, Civil Supplies and Public Distribution (2001)

(*Thirteenth Lok Sabha*)

Chapter I

INTRODUCTORY

The Consumer Protection (Amendment) Bill, 2001 as introduced in Rajya Sabha on 26-4-2001 was referred to the Standing Committee on Food, Civil Supplies and Public Distribution for examination and report.

1.2 Giving an account of the history of consumer movement in India, the Department of Consumer Affairs in a note furnished to the Committee informed that the consumer movement in India is as old as trade and commerce. In Kautilya's Arthshastra, there are references to the concept of protection of the consumer against exploitation by trade and industry, short weighment and measurements, adulteration and punishment of these offences. However, there was no organized and systematic movement actually safeguarding the interests of the consumers. Prior to independence, consumer interests were considered mainly under laws like the Indian Penal Code, Agricultural Produce (Grading and Marking Act, 1937), Drugs and Cosmetics Act, 1940, etc. Even though, different parts of India had different levels of awareness, in general, the level of awareness was low.

2. Consumer Welfare Related Legislations

1.3 Activities and functions of many Ministries/Departments have a bearing on consumer welfare. Several legislations have been framed to safeguard the interests of the consumers either directly or indirectly and these Legislations are administered by different Ministries/Departments in the Central and State Governments, *e.g.* the Drugs and Cosmetics Act, 1940, the Prevention of Food Adulteration Act, 1954 (Ministry of Health), the Monopolies and Restrictive Trade Practices Act, 1969 (Department of Company Affairs), Agricultural Produce (Grading and Marking) Act, 1937 (Ministry of Agriculture), the Trade and Merchandise Act, 1958 (Ministry of Industry and Commerce), etc. The Department of Consumer Affairs, being the nodal Ministry in the field of consumer protection, takes up consumer related matters with different Ministries/Departments in order to take care of the interest of the consumers.

3. The Consumer Protection Act, 1986

1.4 One of the most important milestones in the consumer movement in the country has been the enactment of the Consumer Protection Act, 1986. This Act was necessitated because the well organized sectors of manufacturers, traders and service providers, armed with knowledge of the market and manipulative skills, often attempt to exploit the consumers, despite the existence of provisions in different laws protecting their interests. Moreover, various factors including increase in the population resulted in enormous pendency and delay in disposal of cases in the Civil Courts. Consumers cannot be asked to wait for years for settlement of even small claims. Hence, the Consumer Protection Act, 1986 was enacted to better protect the interest of the consumers. It is one of the most progressive and comprehensive piece of legislation and it is an umbrella legislation covering all goods and services. The Act provides for a separate three-tier quasi-judicial consumer dispute redressal machinery at the National, State and District levels and is intended to provide simple, speedy and inexpensive redressal for consumers' grievances.

4. Brief Background relating to the Consumer Protection Act, 1986

1.5. The Consumer Protection Act, 1986 "which provides for the setting up of a three-tier quasi-judicial machinery at the National, State and District level to deal with consumer complaints against defective or hazardous goods, deficient services, unfair trade practices, etc. and also provides for the setting up of Consumer Protection Councils at the Central and State level which are Advisory Bodies to promote and protect the rights of consumers. The Act was amended in 1991 and 1993 in the light of the experience gained during the implementation of the provisions of the Act.

1.6 Although effective use of the redressal agencies has been made by consumers, a number of practical difficulties have been brought to the notice of the Central Government including the pronouncements of Consumer Redressal Forums, High Courts and the Supreme Court which has bearing on the working of the redressal agencies. On the recommendation of the Central Consumer Protection Council, a Working Group was constituted by Government in June, 1994 under the Chairmanship of Shri Naren De, Minister of Food and Civil Supplies, Government of West Bengal, to examine the need for further change in the Consumer Protection Act, 1986. Suggestions were also invited from the State Governments, members of the Central Consumer Protection Council, Presidents of the State Commission and District Forums and Voluntary Consumer Organizations. All these suggestions were considered by then Working Group, which submitted its report in May, 1995.

1.7 Proposals for amendment of the Consumer Protection Act, 1986 were formulated on the basis of the recommendations of the Working Group and also those of an Expert Group set up in July, 1997. Extensive consultations were held with representatives of consumer interests, President of the National Commission and State Commissions and all the concerned Ministries of the Central Government. The Amendment Bill was finally introduced in the Rajya Sabha on 26-4-2001.

5. Major Objectives of the Amendments

1.8 The major objectives of the present amendments being proposed are:—

(*i*) Facilitating quicker disposal of complaints. Delay in disposal of cases by the redressal agencies at the District, State and National level which were expected to undertake speedy disposal of consumer complaints has been a cause of major concern.

(*ii*) Enhancing the capability of the redressal agencies.

(*iii*) Widening the scope of various provisions of the Consumer Protection Act to make it more effective.

(*iv*) Strengthening or clarifying the powers of the redressal forums.

(*v*) Streamlining the procedure, removing lacunae and bringing clarity to certain provisions.

1.9 The Committee examined the Consumer Protection (Amendment) Bill, 2001 at its various sittings. The Committee invited representatives of the Ministry of Consumer Affairs, Food and Public Distribution (Department of Consumer Affairs) and Ministry of Law, Justice and Company Affairs (Legislative Department). The Committee also heard the views of the: (*i*) Citizen Consumer and Civil Action Group; (*ii*) Voluntary Organization in the Interest of Consumer Education; (*iii*) Consumer Coordination Council; (*iv*) Consumer Columnist (Smt. Pushpa Girimaji); (*v*) Consumer Association of India; (*vi*) Justice Lokeshwar Prasad, President, Delhi State Consumer Disputes Redressal Commission; (*vii*) Justice K.C. Baraga, President, U. P. State Consumers Disputes Redressal Commission; (*viii*) Shri A.C. Nirankar, Advocate; and (*ix*) Shri U.P. Sharma, Advocate-Legal Advisor.

1.10 During the course of discussions on the Bill, the main aim of the Committee has been to facilitate the consumers with quicker disposal of their complaints and to remove the hindrances that are causing delay in disposal of cases by the redressal agencies at the District, State and National levels. The Committee sought clarifications from the representatives of the Ministry of Consumer Affairs, Food and Public Distribution in this regard.

1.11 The Committee note that the Consumer Fora were established to protect a large number of consumers from exploitation. However, the device adopted by the Government to help the consumers has failed for want of proper receipt for the goods sold or services rendered to them. It has been observed that not only in remote and rural areas but also in towns, the consumers do not get the receipt for goods purchased and services availed by them and thus they are deprived of their rights to go to a Consumer Court in case of cheating. The Committee, therefore, strongly recommend that the Central Government in consultation with the State Governments should devise ways and means to make it mandatory for goods sellers and service providers to issue receipts for the items sold and services rendered. For this, vigorous efforts should be made to awaken the consumers about their rights.

1.12 The Committee note with concern that a large number of District Fora which were established for the redressal of grievances of the consumers within stipulated time are still non-functional. The Committee is of the opinion that if the grievance of a consumer is not timely redressed, the very purpose of establishment of Consumer Court is defeated as "justice delayed is justice denied". The Committee has, therefore, come to the conclusion that the Government should make efforts to make the non-functional District Fora functional without further loss of time.

1.13 The Committee is also of the opinion that vigorous efforts should be made to ensure that in no case the vacancy of member in Courts should be for more than one month. However, in case of unavoidable procedural delay, the present incumbent of the Court should be allowed to continue till new appointment is made which in turn will check the piling of cases of Consumer Courts.

1.14 The Committee further note that the Consumer Disputes Redressal Agencies established under the Consumer Protection Act, 1986 lack infrastructural facilities such as proper building, adequate secretarial assistance, etc. which in turn affects the efficiency of these agencies and ultimately results in reduction of their output/disposal of cases. Also, the Consumer Disputes Redressal Agencies have not been provided with financial and administrative autonomy. Even in routine matters and petty sanction, the redressal agencies have to look to the Administrative Departments which in turn hamper day-to-day functioning of these agencies. The Committee, therefore, strongly recommends that in order to check delays in disposal of cases by the redressal agencies the Government should persuade the State Governments to provide necessary infrastructural facilities to the District Fora and State Commissions without further delay. Also administrative and financial powers should be vested in the Presidents of the State Commissions and the District Fora so that day-to-day functioning of these redressal agencies do not suffer. The Committee, therefore, desires that section 24B of the Consumer Protection Act, 1986 should be suitably amended.

Chapter II

REPORT

2.1 The Committee considered the Bill clause by clause.

Clause 2

Section 2(*o*) of the Consumer Protection Act, 1986 states as under:

"Service" means service of any description which is made available to potential users and includes the provision of facilities in connection with banking, financing, insurance, transport, processing, supply of electrical or other energy, board or loading or both, housing construction, entertainment, amusement of the purveying of news or other information, but does not include the rendering of any service free of charge or under a contract of personal service.

2.2 Clause 2 of the Consumer Protection (Amendment) Bill, 2001 proposes to substitute the words "users and includes the provisions of" by the words "users and includes, but not limited to, the provisions of".

2.3 The Committee considered the amendment proposed by the Government in detail and felt that some of the services like Medical Services, Employees Provident Fund, General Provident Fund, Education, Educational Institutions, Postal Service, Basic Amenities, Provision and Maintenance of Streets, Street Lights, Drainage, etc. should be included in the list and recommend that after the words "news" the word "Health and medical Services; Employees Provident Fund, General Provident Fund, Education, Postal Service, Basic Amenities, etc." and the matter incidental thereto should be added. The Committee are also of the opinion that uninterrupted advertisements in this regard should be given to make the consumer of the remote and rural areas aware of their rights."

Clause 3

2.4 Section 3 of the Consumer Protection Act, 1986 states that "the provisions of this Act shall be in addition to and not in derogation of the provisions of any other law for the time being in force". Clause 3 of the Consumer Protection (Amendment) Bill, 2001 proposes to substitute the aforesaid section of the Principal Act which says "The provisions of this Act shall apply to all claims except claims in respect of which corresponding remedies of judicial nature are available under any special law for the time being in force."

2.5 The Committee deliberated the amendment proposed by the Government in detail. After hearing the views of the experts, the Committee has noted that the proposed substitution of section 3 is against the consumer interest. In the opinion of the Committee, exclusion of cases from the purview of Consumer Courts in regard to which similar remedies are available under special laws, will harass the consumer in getting quick and inexpensive justice instead of helping him. For instance a consumer will have to move a long distance and incur heavy expenditure as Tribunals, etc. set up by the Government are in State capitals only whereas District Fora are available in Every District. In view of the Committee, as per proposed amendment, a consumer will have to move a long distance for redressal of his grievances which will be very expensive. Thus, the very purpose of the establishment of District Fora for providing quick and less expensive grievance redressal machinery to a consumer will be defeated.

The Committee, therefore, strongly recommend that the proposed amendment to section 3 of the Consumer Protection Act, 1986 should be withdrawn.

Clause 7

2.6 Clause 7(*b*) of the Consumer Protection (Amendment) Bill, 2001 states that "two other members, one of whom shall be a woman, who shall have the following qualifications, namely:—

(*i*) be not less than thirty-five years of age,

(*ii*) possess a bachelor's degree from a recognized University,

(*iii*) be persons of ability, integrity and standing, and have adequate knowledge and experience of at least ten years in dealing with problems relating to economics, law, commerce, accountancy, industry, public affairs or administration."

In the opinion of the Committee the qualifications prescribed under this clause is for all the members including the woman member, The Committee, therefore, recommend that the word "who" from clause 7(*b*) of the Bill should be deleted.

Clause 7(2)

2.7 Clause 7(2) of the Consumer Protection (Amendment) Bill, 2001 'states that "Every member of the District Forum shall hold office for a term of five years or up to the age of sixty-five years, whichever is earlier:

"Provided that a member shall be eligible for re-appointment of another term of five years or up to the age of sixty-five years, whichever is earlier, subject to the condition that he fulfills the qualifications and other conditions for appointment mentioned in clause (*b*) of sub-section (1) and such re-appointment is also made on the basis of the recommendation of the Selection Committee."

2.8 During discussion on clause 7(2) of the Amendment Bill, the Ministry has clarified that the purpose of said substitution is to provide for re-appointment of Presidents/Members for utilisation of the experience of the existing Presidents/Members for a longer period. The Ministry further clarified that the said provisions have also been substituted in case of State Commissions and the National Commission. The Committee, therefore, urge the Government to include the word "President" wherever the word "Member" has been reflected in clause 7(2) of the Bill for the sake of clarity.

Clause 12(2)

2.9 Clause 12(2) of the Consumer Protection (Amendment) Bill, 2001 provides that "Every complaint filed under sub-section (1) shall be accompanied with such amount of fee and payable in such manner as may be prescribed."

2.10 The Committee discussed the issue in detail. In their opinion, Consumer Courts have been established with a view to provide justice to poor consumer free of cost. Through this insertion the Government has sought to change the basic objective of the establishment of these Courts and thus Consumer Courts will also run more or less on the pattern of Civil Courts. The reasons given by the Ministry that to expedite the disposal of complaints, collection of fee with the complaints is necessary to cover at least a part of the costs relating to process, service of notices, etc. is not acceptable to the Committee. The Committee is of the opinion that in case the Central Government wants to help the State Governments to earn some revenue for running these Courts they may issue instructions to the Courts to levy cost on decree with the defaulters.

2.11 The Committee, therefore, strongly recommends that proposed clause 12(2) of the Bill should be withdrawn in order to provide inexpensive justice to poor consumers.

Clause 13

2.12 Section 16(l)(*a*), 16(1)(*b*) and 16(2) of the Consumer Protection Act, 1986 states that:—

"(1) Each State Commission shall consist of—

(*a*) a person who is or has been a Judge of a High Court, appointed by the State Government, who shall be its President:

[Provided that no appointment under this clause shall be made, except after consultation with the Chief Justice of the High Court.]

(*b*) two other members, who shall be persons of ability, integrity and standing and have adequate knowledge or experience of, or have shown capacity in dealing with, problems relating to economics, law, commerce, accountancy, industry, public affairs or administration, one of whom shall be a woman.

(2) The salary or honorarium and other allowances payable to, and the other terms and conditions of service of the members of the State Commission shall be such as may be prescribed by the State Government."

Clause 13 of the Bill proposes that

2.13 (*a*) In sub-section (1), for clause (*b*) and the proviso thereunder, the following clause shall be substituted, namely:—

"(*b*) not less than two, and not more than such number of members, as may be prescribed, and one of whom shall be a woman, who shall have the following qualifications, namely:—

(*i*) be not less than thirty-five years of age;

(*ii*) possess a bachelor's degree from a recognized university; and

(*iii*) be persons of ability, integrity and standing, and have adequate knowledge and experience of at least ten years in dealing with problems relating to economics, law, commerce, accountancy, industry, public affairs or administration:

Provided that not more than fifty per cent, of the members, shall be from amongst persons having judicial background."

2.14 The Committee discussed the proposed amendment in detail and arrived at the conclusion that for the words "not more than fifty per cent" occurring in proposed proviso of sub-clause (1) of clause 13, the words "not less than fifty per cent" be substituted as each additional bench consisting of two members shall have to consist of one judicial member otherwise the constitution of such bench may indirectly come into conflict.

2.15 The Committee has been informed that the salaries and other perks for the Presidents of Courts are being governed by the existing laws in force whereas in case of salaries of Members it is left at the discretion of the State Governments. In the opinion of the Committee, this causes a lot of hindrance in quick disposal of cases in the Consumer Courts. Keeping in view the fact, the committee strongly recommend that the Central Government should persuade the State Governments to come out with a suitable scale of pay and allowances for the Members also, which should be commensurate to their working and also should be uniform in all the States as far as possible which in turn will attract qualified and talented persons to accept the post of Members.

APPENDIX IV

Addresses of Consumer Disputes Redressal Forums in India

(IN ALPHABETICAL ORDER)

STATE COMMISSION/DCDRF IN THE STATE OF ANDHRA PRADESH

Adilabad

District Consumer Forum, Court Complex, Adilabad-504 001
Phone: (O)(08732)225078 — e-mail: dist.forum_adb@ap.nic.in
District Consumer Forum,

Ananthapur

District Court Premises, Ananthapur-515001
Phone: (O)(08554)220893 — e -mail: dist.forum_atpr@ap.nic.in

Chittoor-I

District Consumer Forum, District Court Compound, Chittoor-517 501.
Phone: (O)(08572)233577 — e-mail: dist.forum_ctr@ap.nic.in
District Consumer Forum, 7-131, Shanti Nagar, M.R. Palle
Tirupathi, Chittoor-517 501.
Phone: (O) (0884)2378821 — e-mail: dist.forum_eg@ap.nic.in

Chittoor-II

District Consumer Forum,
Chittoor-II at Tirupathi
Phone: (O)(08577)2246744 — e-mail: dist.forum_tpr@apsu.ap.nic.in

Kakinada

District Consumer Forum, Ground Floor, D.No. 12-21-13/3, 2nd Floor
Near Court Complex, Aaryapuram, Rajahmundry, E.G. District, East Godavari-I at Kakinada

Rajahmundry

District Consumer Forum,
East Godavari-II at Rajahmundry
Phone: (O)(0863)2241500 — e-mail: dist.forum_gtr@ap.nic.in

Guntur

District Consumer Forum, District Court Compound, Guntur

Hyderabad-I

District Consumer Forum-I, 9th Floor, Chandravihar,
M.J. Road, Nampally, Hyderabad-500 001.
Phone: (O)(040)24733368 — e-mail: dist.forum_hyd1@ap.nic.in

Hyderabad-II

District Consumer Forum-II, 9th Floor, Chandravihar, M.J. Road, Nampally, Hyderabad
Phone: (O)(040)24747733 — e-mail: dist.forum_hyd2@ap.nic.in

Kadapa

District Consumer Forum, Collectorate Compound, Kadapa-516 001.
Phone: (O)(040)24746001 — e-mail: dist.forum_hyd3@apsu.ap.nic.in

Karimnagar

District Consumer Forum, Collectorate Complex, Karimnagar
Phone: (O) (0878)2232577 — e-mail: dist.forum_krgn@ap.nic.in

Kurnool

District Consumer Forum, Junior Civil Judges Court Compound, Kurnool
Phone: (O)(08518)245688 — e-mail: dist.forum_knl@ap.nic.in

Khammam

District Consumer Forum, Varadhaiah Nagar, Khammam-507 002.
Phone: (O)(08742)25434 — e-mail: dist.forum_khm@ap.nic.in
District Consumer Forum-I,

Krishna Dist

Near Pinnamaneni Teachers Guild Association Edepalli, Machilipatnam, Krishna Dist.
Phone: (O) (08672) 229832 — e-mail:dist.forum_mpatnam@ap.nic.in

Medak

District Consumer Forum, Collectorate Premises Sanga Reddy, Medak Dist.
Phone: (O)(08455)275355 — e-mail: dist.forum_mdk@ap.nic.in
District Consumer Forum, Collectorate Compound, Mahaboobnagar
Phone: (O)(08542) 245633 — e-mail: dist.forum_mbng@ap.nic.in

Nellore

District Consumer Forum, Golden Jubilee Bhavan, Collectorate Compound, Nellore.
Phone: (O) (0861) 2337063 — e-mail: dist.forum_nlr@ap.nic.in

Nizamabad

District Consumer Forum, Old L.I.C. Buildings, Yellamagunta Chowrasta Nizamabad-503 003.
Phone: (O) (08462) 233275 — e-mail: dist.forum_nzm@ap.nic.in

Nalgonda

District Consumer Forum, District Court Compound, Nalgonda-001
Phone: (O) (08682) 232979 — e-mail: dist.forum_nlg@ap.nic.in

Prakasam District

District Consumer Forum, Prakasam Dist.
Gadalaguntapalem, Opp: S.S.N. Junior College, Ongole, Prakasam District
Phone: (O) (08592) 231292 — e-mail: dist.forum_ong@ap.nic.in

Srikakulam

District Consumer Forum, District Court Complex, Srikakulam
Phone: (O) (08942) 224468 — e-mail: dist.forum_srk@ap.nic.in

Hyderabad

District Consumer Forum, N.T.R. Nagar, L.B. Nagar, Hyderabad,

Ranga Reddy

Ranga Reddy District
Phone: (O) (040)24047675 — e-mail: dist.forum_rrd@ap.nic.in
District Consumer Forum, 3rd Floor, Criminal Court Complex

Visakapatnam-I

District Court Complex, Prakasa Rao Pet, Visakapatnam
Phone: (O)(0891) 2746026 — e-mail: dist.forum_vsp@ap.nic.in
District Consumer Forum, 3rd Floor, Criminal Court Complex
Prakasa Rao Pet, Visakapatnam

Visakapatnam-II

District Court Complex, Prakasa Rao Pet, Visakapatnam
Phone: (O)(0891)2734128 — e-mail: dist.forum_vsp2@apsu.ap.nic.in

Vizianagaram

District Consumer Forum, Pradeep Nagar, Near District Court Complex
Vizianagaram-535 003.
Phone: (O)(08922)221640 — e-mail: dist.forum_viz@ap.nic.in

Warangal

District Consumer Forum, H.No. 1/706-1, I Floor, Samata Sadan
Near Ekashila Park, Balasamudram Hanamkonda, Warangal-506 001.
Phone: (O)(0870) 2567995 — e-mail: dist.forum_wgl@ap.nic.in
District Court Premises, Eluru-534 006, WEST GODAVARI District
Phone: (O) (08812)239670 — e-mail: dist.forum_wg@ap.nic.in

STATE COMMISSION/DCDRF IN THE STATE OF ARUNACHAL PRADESH

Arunachal Pradesh State Consumer
Disputes Redressal Commission,
Near Pawan Hans Office,
(Old Secretariat Complex)
Naharlagun, ITANAGAR
STD CODE: 0360
E-mail: arp-sforum@nic.in

STATES/DISTRICT FORUM ARUNACHAL PRADESH

UPPER SUBANSIRI DISTRICT FORUM

P.O. Daporijo Arunachal Pradesh
03792-223223
Fax-223330

LOWER SUBANSIRI DISTRICT FORUM

P.O. Ziro Arunachal Pradesh
03788-224255
Fax-224325

TAWANG DISTRICT FORUM
P.O. Tawang Arunachal Pradesh
03794-222221 • Fax-222250

WEST KAMENG DISTRICT FORUM
P.O. Bomdila Arunachal Pradesh
03782-222021 • Fax- 222378

EAST KAMENG DISTRICT FORUM
P.O. Seppa Arunachal Pradesh
03787-222338 • Fax-222427

EAST SIANG DISTRICT FORUM
P.O. Pasighat Arunachal Pradesh
0368-2222340 • Fax-2222302

WEST SIANG DISTRICT FORUM
P.O. Along Arunachal Pradesh
03783- 222221 • Fax-222785

UPPER SIANG DISTRICT FORUM
P.O. Yuhgkiong
Arunachal Pradesh
03777-222221 • Fax-222324

LOHIT DISTRICT FORUM
P.O. Tezu
Arunachal Pradesh
03804-223666 • Fax-222540

TIRAP DISTRICT FORUM
P.O. Khonsa
Arunachal Pradesh
03786-222222
Fax-222224

CHANGLANG DISTRICT FORUM
P.O. Changlang
Arunachal Pradesh
03808-222221
Fax-222221

LOWER DIBANG VALLEY DISTRICT FORUM
P.O. Roing
Arunachal Pradesh
03803-222223
Fax-222380

PAPUM PARE
District Forum
P.O. Yupia Via-Naharlagun
Arunachal Pradesh
0360-2284900
Fax-2284901

KURING KUMEY DISTRICT FORUM
(Newly established)
P.O. Koloriang
Arunachal Pradesh
03788-225512

DIBANG VALLEY
(Newly Established)
P.O. Anini
Arunachal Pradesh
03801-222222
Fax-222222

STATE COMMISSION/DCDRF IN THE STATE OF ASSAM

Assam State Consumer Disputes Redressal Commission,
Housefed Complex,
Central Block,
5th Floor, Front Portion,
Beltola Bashistha Road,
Guwahati-781 006 • STD CODE: 0361
E-mail: asm-sforum@nic.in

States/District Forum Assam

Barpeta DF
03665-252223

Bongaigaon DF
03664-221060

Cachar DF
03842-232597

Darrang DF
03713-222238

Dhemaji DF
037532-224213

Dhubri DF
03662-230024

Dibrugarh DF
0373-95712

Goalpara DF
03663-240181

Golaghat DF
03762-2480072

Guwahati DF
0361-2668616

Hailakandi DF
03844-222719

Jorhat DF
0376-2371414

Karbi-Anglong DF
03671-
Karimganj DF
03843-262636
Kokrajhar DF
03661-70741
Lakhimpur DF
03752-222337
Morigaon DF
03678-240311
N. C. Hills DF
03673-
Nagaon DF
03372-234002
Nalbari DF
03624-220320
Sibsagar DF
03762-2222146
Sonitpur DF
03712-957112, 231431
Tinsukia DF
0374-2331258

STATE COMMISSION/DCDRF IN THE STATE OF ANDAMAN & NICOBAR ISLANDS

State Commissions Andaman & Nicobar Islands
Andaman & Nicobar Islands State Consumer Disputes Redressal Commission,
Dte of Civil Supplies,
Civil Supplies Complex,
PORT BLAIR-744102
STD CODE: 03192
E-mail: an-sforum@nic.in
Andaman & Nicobar Islands
Andaman & Nicobar Islands District Forum
District Forum District Court Complex, Port Blair-744101.

STATE COMMISSION/DCDRF IN THE STATE OF BIHAR

Bihar State Consumer Disputes Redressal Commission,
R-Block, Road No.2,
South of Daroga Prasad Rai Memorial Trust,
PATNA-800 001
STD CODE: 0612
E-mail: scdrc@sancharnet.in & bih-sforum@nic.in
States/District Forum Bihar
Araria District Forum
Collectorate Compound Araria
06453-224421
Aurangabad District Forum
Collectorate Compound Aurangabad
06186-225266
Banka District Forum
Collectorate Compound Banka
06424-233613
Begusarai District Forum
Collectorate Compound Begusarai
06243-210678
Bhagalpur District Forum
Collectorate Compound Bhagalpur
0641-2403419
Bhojpur District Forum
Collectorate Compound Ara
06182-242280
Buxar District Forum
Collectorate Compound Buxar
06183-224258
Darbhanga District Forum
Collectorate Compound Darbhanga
06272-240430
E. Ch. Motihari District Forum
Collectorate Compound Motihari
06252-2234126
Gaya District Forum
Collectorate Compound Gaya
0631-2429321
Gopalganj District Forum
Collectorate Compound Gopalganj
06156-227476
Jehanabad District Forum
West Gandhi Maidan Jehanabad
06114-226420
Jamui District Forum
Collectorate Compound Jamui
06345-223946
Kaimur District Forum
S.D.O. Court Compound Bhabhua
06189-224439
Katihar District Forum
Collectorate Compound Katihar
06452-249234

Khagaria District Forum
Collectorate Compound Khagaria
06244-226452

Kishanganj District Forum
Collectorate Compound Kishanganj
06456-226140

Lakhisarai District Forum
Collectorate Compound Lakhisarai
06346-233033

Madhepura District Forum
Collectorate Compound Madhepura
06476-224967

Madhubani District Forum
Collectorate Compound Madhubani
06276-226845

Mungher District Forum
Collectorate Compound Mungher
06344-226390

Muzaffarpur District Forum
Collectorate Compound Muzaffarpur
0621-2210609

Nalanda District Forum
Collectorate Compound Bihar Sharif
06112-227629

Nawadah District Forum
Collectorate Compound Nawadah
06324-210355

Patna District Forum
Biscomaun Tower 3Rd Floor Patna
0612-2221896

Purnia District Forum
Collectorate Compound Purnia
06454-241699

Rohtas District Forum
Collectorate Compound Sasaran
06184-227591

Saharsa District Forum
Collectorate Compound Saharsa
06478-222500

Samstipur District Forum
Collectorate Compound Samstipur
06274-221431

Saran District Forum
Collectorate Compound Chapra
06152-244156

Shaikhpura District Forum
Collectorate Compound Shaikhpura
06341-223410

Sheohar District Forum
Collectorate Compound Sheohar
06222-257195

Sitamarhi District Forum
Collectorate Compound Sitamarhi
06226-255055

Siwan District Forum
Collectorate Compound Siwan
06154-227740

Supaul District Forum
Collectorate Compound Supaul
06473-225426

Vaishali District Forum
Block Campus Hajipur
06224-276014

W. Ch. Bettiah District Forum
Collectorate Compound Bettiah
06254-237184

STATE COMMISSION/DCDRF IN THE STATE OF CHANDIGARH

Chandigarh State Consumer Disputes Redressal Commission,
Plot No.5-B, Madhya Marg,
Sector-19, B,
Chandigarh –160 019
STD CODE: 0172
E-mail: stcomm@chd.nic.in & cdg-sforum@nic.in

States/District Forum Chandigarh

District Forum-I Union Territory, Chandigarh
District Consumer Forum-I,
Plot No.5-B, Sector
19B, Madhya Marg, CHANDIGARH
0172-2549196

District Forum-II Union Territory, Chandigarh.
District Consumer Forum-II,
Plot No.5-B, Sector
19B, Madhya Marg, CHANDIGARH
0172-2549196

STATE COMMISSION/DCDRF IN THE STATE OF CHHATTISGARH

Chhattisgarh State Consumer Disputes Redressal Commission,
Behind New Bus Stand,
Pandri,
RAIPUR-492 004
STD Code: 0771
E-mail: chg-sforum@nic.in

States/District Forum Chhattisgarh

RAIPUR

District Forum
RDA Building,
Phool Chowk, Raipur
0771-2435190
0771-2535190
0771-2443015 (Resi)

BILASPUR

District Forum
Near Composite Office Complex,
Bilaspur
0775-226113
0775-226113
07752-227542 (Resi)

DURG

District Forum
Shopping Complex, Near New Bus
Stand, Durg.
0788-2328507
0788-2328507
0788-2328278 (Resi)

RAJNANDGAON

District Forum
Behind Collectorate Rajnandgaon.
07744-227344

SARGUJA

District Forum
Near Collectorate, Sarguja
07774-235094
07774-235094

BASTAR

District Forum
District Court Premises, Jagdalpur.
07782-231082
07782-231084 (Fax)

RAIGARH

District Forum
Collectorate Premises, Raigarh.
07762-223733
07762-223644 (Fax)

KORIA

District Forum.
Collectorate, Koria.
Attached with Sarguja DCDRF.

JASHPUR NAGAR

District Forum
Collectorate, Jashpurnagar.
Attached with Sarguja DCDRF.

KANKER

District Forum
Jilla Panchayat Office Campus,
Kanker.
Attached with Bastar DCDRF.

DHAMTARI

District Forum
New Collectorate Compus, Dhamtari.
Attached with Raipur DCDRF.

KORBA

District Forum
Near Additional District & Judge
Court, Korba.
Attached with Bilaspur DCDRF.

JANJGIR-CHAMPA

District Forum
Additional District & Session Court,
Janjgirchampa.
Attached with Bilaspur DCDRF.

MAHASAMUND

District Forum
Old Collectorate Compus,
Mahasamund.
Attached with Raipur DCDRF.

KAWARDHA

District Forum
Tehsil Office, Kabirdham, Kawardha.
Attached with Rajnandgaon DCDRF.

DANTEWADA

District Forum
Collectorate Compus (Food Section)
Dhantewada.
Attached with Bastar DCDRF

UNION TERRITORY OF DELHI

STATE CONSUMER DISPUTES REDRESSAL COMMISSION

A-Block, First Floor, Vikas Bhawan, I.P.
Estate, New Delhi-110002
Registrar, Phone: 23370799
Supdt. (Registry): 23378564
PS to the Hon'ble President
Phone: 23370258, Fax: 23378566
E mail: statecommission@vsnl.net

UNION TERRITORY OF DELHI,

DISTRICT CONSUMER DISPUTES REDRESSAL COMMISSION NORTH

Room Nos. 2 & 3, Old Civil Supplies Bldg., Tis Hazari, Delhi. Tel: (Office) 23912675/23969372

Jurisdiction of cases pertaining to police station

Kamla Market, Darya Ganj, Civil Lines, Timarpur, Roop Nagar, Maurice Nagar, Subzi Mandi, Gulabi Bagh, Pratap Nagar, Sarai Rohilla, Bara Hindu Rao, Sadar Bazar, Kashmere Gate, Kotwali, Lahore Gate, Town Hall (Chandni Chowk), And Any Other Police Station Which May Be Created In Future.

SOUTH

C-22 & 23,
Udyog Sadan,
Qutub Institutional Area,
Behind Qutub Hotel, Mehrauli, Delhi. Tel.:(Office) 26565666/26961433

Jurisdiction of cases pertaining to police station

Parliament Street, Mandir Marg, Tilak Marg, Chanakya Puri, Tuglak Road, Hauz Khas, Malviya Nagar, Mahrauli, Defence Colony, Lodhi Colony, Kotla Mubarakpur, Lajpat Nagar, Sriniwaspuri, Hazarat Nizamuddin, Greater Kailash, Chittaranjan Park, And Any Other Police Station which may be created in future.

WEST

C-Block, Community Centre, Pankha Road, Janak Puri, New Delhi.
Tel.: (Office) 25541281/25505036

Jurisdiction of cases pertaining to police station

Patel Nagar, Anand Parbat, Moti Nagar, Tilak Nagar, Janak Puri, Vikas Puri, Punjabi Bagh, Paschim Vihar, Nangloi, Rajouri Garden, Hari Nagar, Kirti Nagar, And Any Other Police Station which may be created in future.

NORTH-EAST

Bunkar Vihar Complex (Weavers Complex), Nand Nagri, Delhi.
Tel.: (Office) 22121591

Jurisdiction of cases pertaining to police station

Seelampur, Gokalpuri, Bhajanpura, Welcome Colony, New Usmanpur, Khajuri Khas, Dilshad Garden, Maansarover Park, Seemapuri, Nand Nagari, And Any Other Police Station which be created in future.

NORTH-WEST

Convenient Shopping Centre, Block-C, Pocket-C, Shalimar Bagh, Delhi.
Tel.: (Office) 27494833/27492650

Jurisdiction of cases pertaining to police station

Sultanpuri, Mangolpuri, Kanjahanwala, Ashok Vihar, Saraswati Vihar, Keshav Puram Shalimar Bagh, Jahangir Puri, Rohini, Narela, Samaipur Badli, Alipur, Mukherjee Nagar, Adarsh Nagar, Model Town, Bawana, Parshant Vihar, And Any Other Police Station which may be created in future.

NEW DELHI

Barracks, Kasturba Gandhi Marg, New Delhi
Tel.: (Office) 23389323

Jurisdiction of cases pertaining to police station

Connaught Place and Any Other Police Station which may be created in future.

SOUTH-WEST

Local Shopping Centre, Sheikh Sarai, Phase-Ii, Delhi.
Tel.: (Office) 29259612/29259613

Jurisdiction of cases pertaining to police station

Vasant Vihar, Vasant Kunj, R.K.Puram, Sarojini Nagar, Vinay Nagar, Delhi Cantt., Dabri, Naraina, Mayapuri, Inderpuri, Najafgarh, Jaffarpur Kalan, Dwarka, Kapashera, Ambedkar Nagar, Greater Kailash, Sarita Vihar & Okhla and Any Other Police Station which may be created in furture

Central

Mezannine Floor, ISBT, Kashmere Gate, Delhi
Tel.(Off).: 23866727/23866728

Jurisdiction of cases pertaining to police station

Chandni Mahal, Jama Masjid, Hauz Quasi, I.P. Estate, Pahar Ganj, D.B.G. Road, Nabi Karim, Karol Bagh, Prasad Nagar, Rajinder Nagar and Any Other Police Station which may be created in future.

EAST

Convenient Shopping Centre, Saini Enclave, Delhi.
Tel. Office: 22373093/22379588

Jurisdiction of cases pertaining to police station

Kalyanpuri, Mandwali Parsh Bazar, Ashok Nagar, Mayur Vihar, Trilokpuri, Vivek Vihar, Anand Vihar, Preet Vihar, Shakarpur, Gandhi Nagar, Krishna Nagar, Geeta Colony And Any Other Police Station which may be creating in future

SOUTH-II

C-22 & 23, Udyog Sadan, Qutub Institutional Area,
Behind Qutub Hotel, Mehrauli, Delhi.

Jurisdiction of cases pertaining to police station

Chitranjan Park, Ambedkar Nagar, Kalkaji, Badarpur, New Friends Colony, Sanjom Vihar, And Any Other Police Station which may be created in future.

STATE COMMISSION/DCDRF IN THE STATE OF GUJARAT

Gujarat State Consumer Disputes Redressal Commission,
4th Floor, 'A' Block and Ground Floor,
'C' Block, Multistoried Building,
Laldarwaja,
AHEMDABAD-380009
STD CODE: 079
E-mail: guj-sforum@nic.in

States/District Forum Gujarat

Ahmedabad (City) District Forum
New Bhagwati Complex, B/s. Badsha Dairy, Near Jainmarchant Society, Paldi, Ahmedabad (City)
079-26608959/079-26608969

Ahemdabad (Rural) District Forum
11th Floor, 'C' Wing, Apna Bazar, Ahemdabad (Rural)
079-25511278

Ahmedabad (City Additional) District Forum
M. S. Building, 'C' Block, 11th Floor, Laldarwaja, Ahmedabad
079-25501774

Gandhinagar
District Forum
Block No. 26/2, 'GH' Type Nr. C.N.I. Church, Sector-20, Gandhinagar.
079-23262262

Sabarkantha District Forum
Himatnagar
District Court Compound, Ground Floor Himatnagar Sabarkantha.
02772-247678

Mehsana District Forum
Juna Raj Mahal Building, Electrision Branch, Mehsana Distt., Mehsana.
02762-221322

Palanpur District Forum
No. 1/2, R.R.P. Building, Palanpur (B.K.), Disttt. Banaskantha
02742-254138

Kutch-Bhuj District Forum
Near Circuit House
Kutch- Bhuj.
02832-250723

Rajkot District Forum
District Collector Office, Block No. 1, 7th Floor M.S. Bldg. Rajkot.
0281-2474565

Rajkot (Additional) District Forum
District Collector Office, Block No. 1, 7th Floor M.S. Bldg. Rajkot.
0281-2478723

Jamnagar District Forum
Opp. Juna Railway Station, Jamnagar.
0288-2552977

Amreli District Forum
Room No. 106,
C-Block, 1st Floor, Rajmahal Compd, Amreli.
02792-230625

Bhavnagar District Forum
Block No. G-1, Anax Ground Floor, M.S. Building, Bhavnagar.
0278-2422726

Surendranagar District Forum
M. S. Building, Block-A, Ground Floor, Room No. 3-4, Kherali Road, Ratanpur, Surendranagar.
02752-282142

Junagadh District Forum
Smruti Bhavan. 2nd Floor, Opp. Narsingh Vidhya Mandir, M.K. Road, Nr. Court Junagadh.
0285-2625593

Vadodra District Forum
Room No. 70, 2nd Floor, Old Kothi Building, Raopura, Vadodra.
0265-2422098

Vadodra (Additional) District Forum
Room No. 70, 2nd Floor, Old Kothi Building, Raopura, Vadodra.
0265-2421717

Panchmahal District Forum
Room No. 33/4, 2nd Floor, M.S. Buldg. Collector Office Compd., Godhra, Panchmahal.
02672-246016

Nadiad District Forum
Room No. 15/16, 2nd Floor, Sardar Patel Bhawan, Nadiad.
0268-2569301

Bharuch District Forum
Panchbatt, Panam Plaza Building, No. 132 to 135, Ist floor, Opp. Relief Cinema Station Road, Bharuch.
02642-251604

Surat District Forum
"A" Block, 1st Floor, M.S. Building, Nanpura, Surat.
0261-2472683

Surat (Additional) District Forum
"A" Block, 1st Floor, M.S. Building, Nanpura, Surat.
0261-2460182

Valsad District Forum
Damanganga Bhavan 3rd Floor, B/H. Collector Office, Valsad.
02632-242824

Anand District Forum
1, Ajanta Society, Mahavir Marg, District Anand
02692-266022

Navsari District Forum
Collector's Office Compound, 'C' Block, 2nd Floor, Junathana, Navsari
02637-240251

Patan District Forum
Sardar Complex, 1st Floor, Above Hotel Kapil, Near Sipur Char Rasta, Patan
02766-233339

STATE COMMISSION/DCDRF IN THE STATE OF GOA

Goa State Consumer Disputes Redressal Commission,
Junta House, 1st Lift,
4th Floor, Vivekanand Road,
PANAJI-403 001
STD CODE: 0832
E-mail: gcdrc@goa.nic.in &
goa-sforum@nic.in

States/District Forum Goa

District Consumer Disputes Redressal Forum, North Goa

Flat No.F-F-1, Goa Housing Board, Commercial-Cum-Residential Complex, Block No. A, Alto Betim, Porvorim, Bardez-Goa-403521.
0832-2411148
dcfs@goa.nic.in

District Consumer Disputes Redressal Forum, South Goa.

Ist Floor, Blessings Pioneer Commercial Complex, Opposite District Court, Old Market, Margo-Goa. 403601.
0832-2713073
dcfs@goa.nic.in

STATE COMMISSION/DCDRF IN THE STATE OF DADRA & NAGAR HAVELI & DAMAN & DIU

Dadra & Nagar Haveli & Daman & Diu State Consumer Disputes

Redressal Commission,
Department of Civil Supplies,
Collectorate, DAMAN-396220
STD CODE: 0260
Email: daman@guj.nic.in & dnh-sforum@nic.in

States/District Forum Dadra & Nagar Haveli & Daman & Diu

Daman District Forum

Office of the Collector, Civil Supplies Department, Collectorate, Fort Area, Moti Daman- 396 220
0260 2230698
0260 2230689

Diu District Forum

Office of the Collector, Civil Supplies Department, Collectorate,
Diu- 362 520.
02875- 252444
02875- 252333 (Fax)

STATE COMMISSION/DCDRF IN THE STATE OF HIMACHAL PRADESH

H.P. State Commission
Block No. 33, 2nd Floor,
H.P.N.V.P. Commercial Complex,
Kasumpti
Shimla- 171009
Tel:(O): 0177-2620854/(R): 0177-2624315 Fax:(O): 0177-2622491

DISTRICT FORUMS/COURTS IN HIMACHAL PRADESH

District Consumer Disputes Redressal Forum Shimla District
Block No. 33 IInd Floor, HPNVP Commericial Complex
Kasumpti,Shimla-171009

Solan District

District Consumer Disputes Redressal Forum Solan District
Block No. 33 IInd Floor, HPNVP Commericial Complex
Kasumpti,Shimla-171009

Sirmaur District

District Consumer Disputes Redressal Forum Sirmaur District
Block No. 33 IInd Floor, HPNVP Commericial Complex
Kasumpti,Shimla-171009

Una

District Consumer Disputes Redressal Forum Una District
District & sessions Judge, Una-174303

Bilaspur

President District Consumer Disputes Redressal Forum Bilaspur District C/o District & Sessions Judge, Bilaspur-174841

Chamba

District Consumer Disputes Redressal Forum Chamba District
District & Sessions Judge, Kangra for Chamba

Mandi

District Consumer Disputes Redressal Forum Mandi District
District & Sessions Judge, Mandi-175001

Dharamshala

District Consumer Disputes Redressal Forum Kangra District
District & Sessions Judge, Dharamshala-176001

Mandi for Kullu

District Consumer Disputes Redressal Forum Kullu District
District & Sessions Judge, Mandi for Kullu

Lahaul Spiti and Kullu

District Consumer Disputes Redressal Forum Lahaul & Spiti
District C/o District & Sessions Judge, Kullu-175001

Hamirpur

District Consumer Disputes Redressal Forum Hamirpur District
District & Sessions Judge, Hamirpur-177001

Kinnaur

District Consumer Disputes Redressal Forum Kinnaur District
Block No. 33 IInd Floor, HPNVP Commericial Complex
Kasumpti, Shimla-171009

STATE COMMISSION/DCDRF IN THE STATE OF JAMMU & KASHMIR

J & K State Consumer Disputes Redressal Commission,

(*i*) 3, Manda Hill, Rehari, Jammu Tavi,
Jammu & Kashmir
(*ii*) Near Municipality Office,
Municipality Complex,
SRINAGAR
STD CODE: Jammu-0191,
Srinagar- 0194
E-mail: jk-sforum@nic.in

States/District Forum Jammu & Kashmir

Jammu District Forum

District Court Premises,
Jani Pore, Jammu (J&K)
Telefax: 0191-2533137

Srinagar District Forum

Stone Building, Old Secretariate,
Srinagar (J&K)
Telefax: 0194-2452912

STATE COMMISSION/DCDRF IN THE STATE OF JHARKHAND

Jharkhand State Consumer Disputes Redressal Commission,

Near High Court, Dauranda,
RANCHI-834002
E-mail: jkh-sforum@nic.in

States/District Forum Jharkhand

Gumla District Forum

Besides Civil SDO Office,
Gumla-835207
06524-222098

Ranchi District Forum

Collectorate Campus,
Ranchi-834001
0651-2208817

Lohardagga District Forum

Near Sub-Divisional Office,
Lohardagga-835302
06526-222898

W. Singhbhum
(Chaibasa) District Forum
E. Singhbhum
(Jamshedpur) District Forum
Sakchi Court Campus, Sakchi-831001
0657-2435597

Dumka District Forum
Collectorate Campus, Dumka-814101
06434-226122

Sahebganj District Forum
In front of District Treasury,
Sahebganj-816109
06436-224587

Pakur District Forum
Besides Civil Court, Pakur-816107
06435-220746

Palamau District Forum
Collectorate Campus,
Palamau-822101
06562-227893

Hazaribagh District Forum
Collectorate Campus,
Hazaribagh-825301
06546-261465

Chatra District Forum
Besides Collectorate Campus,
Chatra-825401
06541-223392

Kodarma District Forum
Collectorate Campus,
Kodarma-825410
06534-252599

Giridih District Forum
Near Collectorate Campus,
Giridih-815301
06532-224633

Dhanbad District Forum
Collectorate Campus,
Dhanbad-826001
0326-2312209

Bokaro District Forum
Collectorate Campus,
Bokaro-827001
06542-223363

Deoghar District Forum
Collectorate Campus, Deoghar-814112
06432-231718/
06432-2237248

Garhwa District Forum
Collectorate Campus, Garhwa-822114
06561-223733

Godda District Forum
Near SDO Residence, Godda
06422-220614

Jamtara District Forum
Officers Club, Near Dak Bungalow,
Jamtara-815351
06433-223397

Saraikela District Forum
Collectorate Campus,
Saraikela-833210
06597-234843

Simdega District Forum
Near Civil Court, Simdega-835223
06525-225992

Latehar District Forum
Near SDM Office, Latehar-829206
06565-248158

STATE COMMISSION/DCDRF IN THE STATE OF KARNATAKA

Karnataka State Consumer Disputes Redressal Commission
Basava Bhavan, High Grounds,
Bangalore-560 001.
Telephone 080-22262865/080-22260590/080-26763749

Bangalore Urban District Consumer Disputes Redressal Forum,
Cauvery Bhavan, 8th Floor,
BWSSB Wing, K.G. Road,
Bangalore-560 009.
080-22211137/080-25715747

Bangalore Rural & Bangalore Urban 1 Addl DCDRF,
Swathi Complex, Seshadripuram,
Bangalore-560020.
TEL. 080-23442670

Bangalore Urban II Addl. DCDRF,
Swathi Complex, Seshadripuram,
Bangalore-560020.
080-23468596/080-23335589

Bangalore Urban III Addl DCDRF,
No.8, VI Floor,Cunningham Road,
Bangalore-560052.
080-22352623/080-5710011

Bangalore Urban IV Addl DCDRF,
No.8, VII Floor, Cunningham Road,
Bangalore 560052.
080-22352624/080-7725399

Bellary DCDRF,
D.C Office Premises,
Bellary-583 101.
08392-276589/08392-268444

Belgaum DCDRF,
Mahathma Gandhi Bhavan,
College Road, Belgaum-590 001.
0831-2426140/0831-2481067

Bidar DCDRF,
No.8-11-16, Chatrapathi Shivaji
Road, Bidar-585401.
08482-225463/08482-224661

Bijapur DCDRF,
Near Tahsildar Office,
Bijapur-586 101
08352-250200/08352-255390

Chickmagalur DCDRF,
Nagarathna Building, Vijayapura
Main Road,
Chickmagalur-577 101.
08262-234864/08262-239232

Chitradurga DCDRF,
3rd Cross, J.C.R Layout,
Upstairs of the Merchants,
Co-op.Bank Building, Chitradurga.
08194-231451/9448567526

Dakshina Kannada DCDRF,
Mangalore City Corporation,
Building, Lalbagh,
Mangalore-575 008.
0824-2457498/0824-2475266

Dharwad DCDRF,
Shinge Building,
Opp. Vidyagiri Post Office,
Vidyagiri, Dharwad-580 004.
0836-2460842/0836-2461227

Gulbarga DCDRF,
Compound of Vikas Bhavan,
I Floor, Above Labour Court,
Station Road,
Gulbarga-585 102.
08472-256033/09448333744

Hassan DCDRF,
1097, 11th Cross, K.R. Puram,
Hassan-573 201.
08172-266892/08172-251912

Kolar DCDRF,
K.No. 419, 1st Floor, M.B. Road,
Kolar-563 101.
08152-241121/080-23507772

Kodagu DCDRF,
Shekar Complex,
Mahadeva Pete,
Madikere-571 201. Kodagu Dist.
08272-229852/09448587806

Mandya DCDRF,
2062, 2nd Cross, Subhashnagar,
Mandya-571 401.
08232-222100

Mysore DCDRF,
No. 845, New Kantharaj Urs Road,
G.C.S.T. Layout, Kuvempu Nagar,
Mysore-570023.
0821-2344902/0821-2341911

Raichur DCDRF,
D.C. Office Compound
Raichur-584 101.
08532-233006/08532-223516

Shimoga DCDRF,
1st Floor, Gandhinagar Main Road,
Shimoga-577 201.
08182-220058/08182-277752

Tumkur DCDRF,
Old D.C. Office Compound,
Tumkur-572 101.
0816-2273037/09886766013

Uttara Kannada DCDRF,
M.G. Road,
Karwar-581 301. U.K. Dist.
08382-227404/08382-231331

Haveri DCDRF,
C.D. Haveri Building,
Parameshwara Complex,
P.B. Road
Haveri-581 110.
08375-832509/08192-223902

Chamarajanagar DCDRF,
B.C. Manjunath Shastri Building,
Shops Street,
Chamarajanagar-571 313.
08226-226502/080- 28565970

Davanagere DCDRF,
842, Opp. Shankar Mill, P.B. Road,
Davangere-577 006.
08192-256618/08192-222255

Koppal DCDRF,
Old Civil Court Building,
Koppal-583 231.
08539-220770/08539-221768

Gadag DCDRF,
Sri Siddalingeswara Nilaya, Near
Marata Mandhir, Vakeela Chala,
Gadag-528 101.
08372-532515/08372-221668

Bagalkot DCDRF,
No. 1, Sector No. 33, Navanagar,
Bagalkot-587 102.
08354-235778/08354-235778

Udupi DCDRF,
Vadiraja Commercial Complex,
Old Post Office Road,
Udupi-576 101.
0820-2523170/0820-2523876

STATE COMMISSION/DCDRF IN THE STATE OF KERALA

Kerala State Consumer Disputes Redressal Commission,
Sisu Vihar Lane,
Vazhuthacaud,
Thiruvananthapuram-695 010.
STD CODE: 0471
E-mail: ker-sforum@nic.in

States/District Forum Kerala
President,
State Consumer Disputes Redressal Commission,
T.C.14/407,
Extra Police Road,
Palayam, Museum P. O.,
Thiruvananthapuram,
Kerala
Pin-695033.

Alappuzha
President,
Consumer Disputes Redressal Forum,
Beach Road, Bazar P.O., Alappuzha.
Pin-688012. (0477) 242452

Ernakulam
President,
Consumer Disputes Redressal Forum,
Kathrikadavu, Pulleppadi,
Near Govt. Homoeo Hospital,
Ernakulam. Pin-682017. (0484) 403316

Idukki
President,
Consumer Disputes Redressal Forum,
Painavu P.O., Idukki. Pin-685603
(0486) 232552

Kannur
President,
Consumer Disputes Redressal Forum,
Near S.N.Park, Kannur. Pin-670001.
(0497) 706632

Kasaragod
President,
Consumer Disputes Redressal Forum,
Bldg. No.12/278, Near SDO Phones Office,
Fort Road,Kasaragod. Pin-671121.(0499) 430845

Kollam
President,
Consumer Disputes Redressal Forum,
Civil Station, Kollam. Pin-691013.
(0474) 795063

Kottayam
President,
Consumer Disputes Redressal Forum,
Civil Station, Collectorate P.O.,
Kottayam. Pin-686002. (0481) 565118

Kozhikkode
President,
Consumer Disputes Redressal Forum,
II Floor,
B-Block,Civil Station, Calicut. Pin-673020. (0495) 370455,

Malappuram
President,
Consumer Disputes Redressal Forum,
Civil Station, Malappuram. Pin-676505. (0493) 734802,

Pathanamthitta
President,
Consumer Disputes Redressal Forum,
12/2956(2), Doctor's Lane,
Pathanamthitta.P in-689645.(0473) 323699

Palakkad
President,
Consumer Disputes Redressal Forum,
Civil Station, Palakkad. Pin-678001.
(0491) 536782

Thiruvananthapuram
President,
Consumer Disputes Redressal Forum,
T.C.No. 9/2159, Faja Bhavan,
Near S.B.T.,
Sasthamangalam,Thiruvananthapuram Pin-695010.
(0471) 329451,
(0471) 331069

Thrissur
President,
Consumer Disputes Redressal Forum,
T.C. 50/931,
Ayyanthole,Thrissur.Pin-680003.
(0487) 361100

Wayanad
President,
Consumer Desputes Redressal Forum,
Civil Station, Kalpetta,Wayanad.
Pin-673122.
(0493) 602755, 07653

STATE COMMISSION/DCDRF IN THE STATE OF LAKSHADWEEP (UT)

Lakshadweep State Consumer Disputes Redressal Commission,
C/o Assistant Controller of Legal Metrology, Department of Legal Metrology & Consumer Affairs,
U.T. of Lakshadweep,
KAVARATTI-682555
STD CODE: 04896
E-mail: lak-accal@hub.nic.in & lak-sforum@nic.in

States/District Forum Lakshadweep Kavaratti
District Consumer Disputes Redressal Forum,
UT of Lakshadweep, Kavaratti-682555
04896-262087/04896-263852
04896-263298 (Fax)
lak-accal@laksha.nic.in

STATE COMMISSION/DCDRF IN THE STATE OF MADHYA PRADESH

Madhya Pradesh State Consumer Disputes Redressal Commission
Plot No.- 76, Arera Hills
BHOPAL-462 001
STD CODE: 0755
E-mail: scdrcbho@mp.nic.in & mp-sforum@nic.in

States/District Forum Madhya Pradesh

Bhopal District Forum
Bhopal Plot No. 76 Area Hills,
Bhopal, M.P.
0755-2551613/0755-2551613 (Fax)

Indore District Forum
Opp. Residency Club, Near Azad Nagar Police Chowki, Indore.
0731-2711030/0731-2711030 (Fax)

Gwalior District Forum
Behind S. P. Office, Civic Centre,
Gwalior.
0751-2231510/0751-2231510 (Fax)

Jabalpur District Forum
Block No.15-K, Scheme No. 18
Civic Centre, Jabalpur-482001.
0761-2310636/0761-2310636(Fax)

Rewa District Forum
Near Venkat Bhawan, Rewa- 486001.
07662-242451/07662-242451 (Fax)

Ujjain District Forum
Vishala Vikas Bhavan, Block-A,
Bharatpuri, Ujjain-456001.
0734-2511435/0734-2511435 (Fax)

Hoshangabad District Forum
Near District Civil Court,
Hoshangabad-461001.
07574-252976/07574-252976 (Fax)

Morena District Forum
H-957, Housing Board Colony, Near Civil Court, Morena-476001.
07532-232221/07532-232221 (Fax)

Mandsaur District Forum
Collectorate Campus,
Old Election Office,
Building Mandsaur-458001.
07422-245502/07422-245502 (Fax)

Dhar District Forum
Near Income Tax Building, Behind District Court, Dhar-454001.
07292-237085/07292-237085 (Fax)

Guna District Forum
Near Collectorate, Guna-473001.
07542-250041/07542-250041 (Fax)

Sagar District Forum
Opp. Commissioner Office, Near Old District Court,
Sagar-470001.
07582-228442
07582-228442 (Fax)

Satna District Forum
Near Collectorate,
Civil Line Satna-485661.
07672-226775/07672-226775 (Fax)

Seoni District Forum
Near Collectorate Jabalpur Road,
Seoni-480661
07692-221891
07692-221891 (Fax)

Khandwa District Forum
Near District Court,
Khandwa-450001.
0733-2230828
0733-2230828 (Fax)

Shivpuri District Forum
District Court Campus, Shivpuri-473551.
07492-233452
07492-233452 (Fax)

Bhind District Forum
District Court Building,
Bhind-470661.
07534-231004
07534-231004 (Fax)

Vidisha District Forum
55, Club Road,
Vidisha-464001.
07592-251207 (Fax)

Damoh District Forum
Near Collectorate,
Damoh-470661.
07812-223450
07812-223450 (Fax)

Chhindwara District Forum
District Court Campus, Chhindwara-480001.
07162-222444/07162-222444 (Fax)

Khargone District Forum (clubbed with Khandwa)
Near District Court,
Khandwa-450001.
0733-2230828/0733-2230828 (Fax)

Jhabua
(Clubbed with District Forum Dhar)
District Court Building,
Jhabua-457661
07392-244252

Dewas
(Clubbed with District Forum Ujjain)
District Court Building,
Dewas-455001
07272

Ratlam
(Clubbed with District Forum Mandsour)
Near Collectorate Rambag,
Ratlam-457001.
07412-221790/07412-221790 (Fax)

Shajapur
(Clubbed with District Forum Ujjain)
District Court Building Shajapur-465001.
07364

Datia
(Clubbed with District Forum Shivpuri)
District Court Building Datia-475661.
07522

Shahdol
IIIrd Floor, Collectorate Compound,
Shahdol.
07652

Sidhi
(Clubbed with District Forum Satna)
District Court Building Sidhi.
07822

Panna
(Clubbed with District Forum **Satna)**
District Court Building Panna.
07732

Chhatarpur District Forum
(Clubbed with Damoh)
Front of Maharaja Chhatrashal College, Chhatarpur.
07682-240700/07682-240700 (Fax)

Tikamgarh
(Clubbed with District Forum Sagar)
District Court Building Tikamgarh.
07683-247045/07683-247045(Fax)

Sehore
(Clubbed with District Forum Bhopal)
District Court Building Sehore.
07562

Raisen
(Clubbed with District Forum Vidisha)
District Court Building, Raisen-464551.
07482

Rajgarh
(Clubbed with District Forum Guna)
District Court Building Rajgarh-465661.
07372

Betul
(Clubbed with District Forum Hoshangabad)
District Court Building, Betul-460001.
07141

Narsinghpur
(Clubbed with District Forum Chhindwara)
District Court Building Narsinghpur-487001.
07792

Mandla
(Clubbed with District Forum Jabalpur)
Opp. Forest Rest House, Mandla-481661.
07642-251841
07642-251841 (Fax)

Balaghat
(Clubbed with District Forum Seoni)
District Court Building Balaghat-481001.
07632

Barwani
(Clubbed with District Forum Khandwa)
Collectorate Building Barwani-451551.
07290

Neemuch
(Clubbed with District Forum Mandsour)
District Court Building Neemuch-458441.
07732

Harda
(Clubbed with District Forum Hoshangabad)
District Court Building Harda-461331
07577

Sheopurkalan
(Clubbed with District Forum Shivpuri)
District Court Building Sheopurkalan-476337
07530

Katni
(Clubbed with District Forum Jabalpur)
District Court Campus, Katni-483501
07622-231000,
07622-231000

Dindori
(Clubbed with District Forum Jabalpur)
District Court Building Dindori-481880
07644

Umaria
Government Hospital Compound, Umaria-484661

STATE COMMISSION/DCDRF IN THE STATE OF MAHARASHTRA

Maharashtra State Consumer Disputes Redressal Commission,
Old Administrative Staff College Bldg., Opp. C.S.T. Station, Hazarimal Somani Marg,
MUMBAI-400 001
STD CODE: 022
E-mail: mah-sforum@nic.in

States/District Forum Maharashtra

South Mumbai Dist. Consumer Dispute Forum
Arun Chember, 6th Floor, Tardeo, Mumbai Central (W), Mumbai.
022-23511737

Central Mumbai Dist. Forum
Arum Chember, 6th Floor, Tardeo, Mumbai Central(W), Mumbai.
022-23521770

Mumbai Suburban Dist. Forum
Administrative Bldg. 3rd Floor, Bandra Govt. Colony, Near C.B.D. Bandra (E), Mumbai-400 034.
022-26551625

Thane Dist. Forum
Room No. 214, 2nd Floor, Collector's Office Thane-400 601.
022-25344069

Addl. Thane Distt. Forum
Konkan Bhawan Annexe Bldg. 4th Floor, Room Nos. 428 & 429, Opp. C.B.D. Belapur Rly. Station, Navi Mumbai-400 614
022-27574074

Raigad Dist. Forum
Patil Sadan, Block No. 6 & 8, Ist Floor, New By-Pass Road, Chandhare, Alibag, Distt Raigad- 402 201.
02141-224225

Ratnagiri Dist. Forum
Collector Office Compound, Ratnagiri Distt. Ratnagiri-415 601.
02352-223745

Sindhudurga Dist. Forum
Main Admn. Bldg, "C" Block, Gr. Floor, At. Post Sindhudurga Nagari, Tal-Kudal, Dist. Sindhudurga.
02362-228825

Pune Dist. Forum
Pushpa Hights, Duggada Family Trust, Pune-Satara Road, Bibewadi, Pune.
020-24217489

Addl. Pune Dist. Forum
Pushpa Hights, Duggada Family Trust, Pune Satara Road, Bibewadi, Pune- 411037.
020-24210364

Satara Dist. Forum
524/1-A, Sadar Bazar, Near Co-Operative Court, Koregaon Road, Satara-415001.
02162-237469

Sangli Dist. Forum
Behind Circuit House, (Madhav Nagar Road), Near New Pride Multiplex Theatre, Sangli.
0233-2311313

Kolhapur Dist. Forum
Shri Pant Balekundri Market, 1st Floor Shahupuri, 6th Lane Gavat Mandi,Kolhapur-416001.
0231-2651327

Solapur Dist. Forum
Collector Office Compound
Solapur-3.
027-2622003

Nasik Dist. Forum
Collector Office Compound, Nasik-2.
0253-2580142

Dhule Dist. Forum
New Admn. Bldg. Compound, Dhule.
02562-237110

Nandurbar Distt. Forum
Room No. 205-206, Collector Office Compound, Nandurbar
02564-261119

Jalgaon Dist. Forum
New Admn. Bldg., Besides All India Radio Station, Jalgaon.
0257-2221868

Ahmednagar Dist. Forum
Parag Bldg., Near Collector Office, Ahmednagar-414001.
0241-2347917

Aurangabad Dist. Forum
Collectorate Bldg. 2nd Floor,Aurangabad-431001.
0240-2321202

Beed Dist. Forum
House No. 1/6/266, Near Chhatrapati Shahu Bank, Pangeri Road, Shahu Nagar, Beed-431122.
02442-230501

Parbhani Dist. Forum
Admn. Bldg., Compound, Parbhani-431401.
02452-222640

Hingoli Distt. Forum
Admn. Bldg. G-8, Collector Office Compound, Hangoli
02456-223888

Nanded Dist. Forum
V.I.P. Road, Opp. Telephone Exchange, Nanded- 431 602.
02462-254729

Latur Dist. Forum
Latur.
Admn. Bldg., 2nd Floor, Collector Office Compound, Latur.
02382-242319

Osmanabad Dist. Forum
Collector Office Compound, Osmanabad- 431 501.
02472-223478

Jalna Dist. Forum
Survey No. 488 (62), By-Pass Road, Opp. Sports Complex, Jalna- 431 203.
02482-225473

Amravati Dist. Forum
Ramyana Bldg., Biyani Chowk, Camp, By-pass Road, Amravati-444602.
0721-2662158

Akola Dist. Forum
Collector Office Compound, Akola- 444 002.
0724-2438281

Washim Distt. Forum
Patni Chowk, Balaji Complex, Near "Deshonnati" Office, Washim.
07252-235545

Buldhana Dist. Forum
Govt. Admn. Bldg Compound, Opp. S.T. Bus Stand, Buldhana- 443001.
07262-243045

Yavatmal Dist. Forum
Grahak Nyay Bhavan, Near Admn. Bldg.,Yavatmal.
07232-243015

Nagpur Dist. Forum
Lines, Nagpur.
New Admn. Bldg., 5th Floor, Civil Lines, Nagpur.
0712- 2548522

Addl. Nagpur Dist. Forum
New Admn Bldg., 3rd Floor Civil Lines, Nagpur-440001.
0712-2546884

Wardha Dist. Forum
Sewagram Road, Near Yashwant College, Wardha- 442001.
07152- 243550

Bhandara Dist. Forum
Before Akhil Sabhagriha, Ganeshpur, Bhandara- 441904.
07184-254467

Gondia Distt. Forum
Collector Admn. Building, Room No. 214, Gondia
07182-232250

Chandrapur Dist. Forum
"Grahak Nyay Bhawan", Near Bachat Saphlya Bhavan, Collector Compound, Chandrapur- 442401.
07172-251010.

Gadchiroli Dist. Forum
District Complex, Barrack No. 1, Room Nos. 17,18,19 and 20, Gadchiroli- 442605.
07132- 222735

STATE COMMISSION/DCDRF IN THE STATE OF MANIPUR

State Commissions Manipur

Manipur State Consumer Disputes Redressal Commission,
Deptt of Food & Civil Supplies, Sangaiprou, IMPHAL
STD CODE: 0385
E-mail: man-sforum@nic.in

STATE COMMISSION/DCDRF IN THE STATE OF MIZORAM

Mizoram State Consumer Disputes Redressal Commission,
Zodian Square,
AIZWAL-796 001
STD CODE: 0389
E-mail: miz-sforum@nic.in

States/District Forum Mizoram

Aizawl
Tuikhuahtlang, Aizawl-796001
0389-2329202

Lunglei
Office of the Deputy Commissioner, Lunglei-790701
0372-2324020

Saiha
Office of the Deputy Commissioner, Saiha-796901
0835-22024

Serchhip
Office of the Deputy Commissioner, Serchhip-796181
0389-22285

Lawngtlai
Office of the Deputy Commissioner, Lawngtlai-796891
03835-232805

Champhai
Office of the Deputy Commissioner, Champhai-796321
03831-234402

Kolasib
Office of the Deputy Commissioner, Kolasib Office of the Deputy Commissioner, Kolasib-796081
03837-21063

Mamit
Office of the Deputy Commissioner, Mamit-796441
0389-2565221

STATE COMMISSION/DCDRF IN THE STATE OF MEGHALAYA

Meghalaya State Consumer Disputes Redressal Commission,
Horse Shoe Building,
Lower Luchumiere,
SHILLONG-793 001
STD CODE: 0364
E-mail: meg-sforum@nic.in

States/District Forum Meghalaya

Shillong District Forum
East Khasi Hills, Shillong
0364-2224003/0364-2223394 (Fax)

Nongstoin District Forum
West Khasi Hills, Nongstoin
03654-280221/03654-280331 (Fax)

Jowai District Forum
Jaintia Hills, Jowai
03652-220721/03652-220865 (Fax)

Nongpoh District Forum
Ribhoi District, Nongpoh
03638-232221/03638-232503 (Fax)

Williamnagar District Forum
East Garo Hills, Williamnagar
03658-220226/03658-220272 (Fax)

Tura District Forum
West Garo Hills, Tura
03651-223835/03651-222226 (Fax)

Baghmara District Forum
South Garo Hills, Baghmara
03639-222292/03639-222225 (Fax)

STATE COMMISSION/DCDRF IN THE STATE OF NAGALAND

Nagaland State Consumer Disputes Redressal Commission,
Guwahati High Court,
Kohima Bench,
KOHIMA-797 001
STD CODE: 0370
E-mail: nag-sforum@nic.in

STATE COMMISSION/DCDRF IN THE STATE OF ORISSA

Orissa State Consumer Disputes Redressal Commission,
Sector-1, Near Sati Choura Chowk, C.D.A. Bidanasi,
CUTTACK-14
STD CODE: 0671
E-mail: ors-sforum@nic.in

States/District Forum Orissa

ANGUL District Forum
Plot No. 1013 (P) At/PO/Distt-Angul,
PIN-759 122
06764-231454(O)

BALASORE District Forum
Plot No.778, Srikanthapur, PO/Dist. Balasore,
PIN-756 001.
06782-263910(O)

BARGARH District Forum
At-Backside of Civil Court Near Ranibandh, Ward No. 10 Po/Dist. Bargarh PIN-768028.
06646-31532(O)

BHADRAK District Forum
Naripur Chhak PO/Dist. Bhadrak.
PIN-756100.
06784-241942(O)

BOLANGIR District Forum
Near Children Park At/PO/Dist. Bolangir. PIN-767001.
06652-233350(O)

BOUDH District Forum
Boudh Kunja Nivas, PO/Dist. Boudh PIN-762014.
06841-222419(O)

CUTTACK District Forum
Sector-1, C.D.A. Colony, Near Sati Choura Chhak, Cuttack-753014.
0671-2366339(O)

DEOGARH District Forum
Deogarh Near Post Office, Plot No. 231/1337 PO/Dist. Deogarh-762014.
26879(O)

DHENKANAL District Forum
Parikh Sahi Mahabir Bazar PO/Dist. Dhenkanal-759001.
24279(O)

Gajapati (Paralekhemundi) District Forum
Jengaon Street PO-Paralakhemundi Dist. Gajapati-761201.
23127(O)

GANJAM District Forum (Behrampur)
Nehru Nagar-9 PO-Gosani Nuagaon, Dist. Ganjam- 760003.
200860(O)

JAGATSINGHPUR
District Forum
At/Po/Dist. Jagatsinghpur PIN-754103.
06724-220106

JAJPUR District Forum
At Babel Bazar PO/Distt Jajpur-755 001.
06728-223498

JHARSUGUDA District Forum
Jharsuguda Near Collectorate PO-O. M.P. Line Dist. Jharsuguda PIN-768204.
06645-270699

Kalahandi (BHAWANIPATNA) District Forum
At/Po:- Bhawanipatna Dist. Kalahandi-766001.
06670-231008

KENDRAPARA District Forum
Plot No. 209, At-Santa Sahi Dist. Kendrapara, Near Police Station.
Pin-754211
06727-232030

KEONJHARGARH District Forum
At/Po-Keonjhar Dist. Keonjhar. PIN-758001.
06766-253390

KHURDA District Forum
Plot No. 1159, at Jagamara, PO-Khandagiri, Near Khandagiri Chhak, Dist. Khurda-751002.
0674-2350122

KORAPUT District Forum
Koraput At Jeypore At/Po-Jeypore, Dist. Koraput-764004.
06852-230792

MALKANAGIRI District Forum
Old S.B.I. Building, Po/Dist. Malkanagiri-764045.
06861-230337

MAYURBHANJ District Forum
At/Po:- Baripada, Dist. Mayurbhanj-757001.
06792-257574

NABARANGPUR District Forum
Old Sanskrati Bhawan, In the RCD High School Playground Po/Dist-Nabarangpur-764059.
06858-232780

NUAPADA District Forum
Nuapada Rajpur, Near Bhagabat Temple Po/Dist. Naupada- 766 105.
06678-223624

NAYAGARH District Forum
Nayagarh Po/Dist.-Nayagarh-752064.
06753-252913

PHULBANI District Forum
At/PO/Dist- Phulbani-762 001
06842-254363

PURI, District Forum
H.No. 336, Matimandap Sahi, Dwarkanath Das Lane, PO/Dist. Puri-752 001.
06752-224781

RAYAGADA District Forum
New Colony,
PO/Dist-Rayagada –765 001
06855-223025

SAMABALPUR District Forum
At-Nari Seba Sadan,
Building, Municipality Chowk, PO/Dist. Sambalpur-768 001
0663-2410037

SONEPUR District Forum
At-Sonepur Town, PO/Dist. Sonepur-767 017
06654-220401

SUNDARGARH-I Disrict Forum
At/PO/Dist- Sundargarh-770001
06622-273234

SUNDARGARH-II
Rourkela, Qr.No.C/13, Rourkela-2, Distt. Sundargarh-269 002
0661-2642989

STATE COMMISSION/DCDRF IN THE STATE OF PONDICHERRY (NOW PUDUCHERY) (UT)

State Commissions Puducherry
The President, Pondicherry State Consumer Disputes Redressal Commission,
No.46, Gubert Avenue (Beach Road), Pondicherry-605 001

States/District Forum Puducherry
Pondicherry State Consumer Disputes Redressal Commission,
Plot No.3, D.P. Thottam, Behind Hotel Sarguru,
Muthialpet, T.V. Nagar,
PONDICHERRY-605 003
STD CODE: 0413
E-mail: scdrc@pondy.pon.nic.in & pon-sforum@nic.in

STATE COMMISSION/DCDRF IN THE STATE OF PUNJAB

Punjab State Consumer Disputes Redressal Commission,
SCO Nos. 3009-3010,
Sector-22-D,
CHANDIGARH-160 022
STD CODE: 0172
E-mail: pun-sforum@nic.in

States/District Forum Punjab

Amritsar District Forum
SCO No.10, Ist Floor, District Shopping Centre, Ranjit Avenue, Bank of India Bldg., Amritsar
95183-2504499

Bathinda District Forum
Near Bus Stand, Bhatinda
95164-2215855

Faridkot District Forum
Judicial Court Complex, Faridkot
951639-253552

Fatehgarh District Forum
District Court Complex, Fatehgarh Sahib
951763-232101

Ferozepur District Forum
Shaheed Bhagat Singh Stadium, Indore Game Complex, New Railway Bridge,
Ferozepur City-155002
951632-243303

Gurdaspur District Forum

New PWD, Rest House Road, Gurdaspur
951874-234971

Hoshiarpur District Forum

B-17/813, Manwata Nagar, Sutheri Road, Opp. Dr. Kapila's Hospital, Hoshiarpur.
951882-221522

Jalandhar District Forum

Room No.217-220, IInd Floor, Administrative Complex, Jalandhar.
95181-2222360

Kapurthala District Forum

Bldg. No.B-XVII-23, Ist Floor, Fateh Bazar, Opp. Old Hospital, Amritsar Road, Kapurthala.
951822-231886

Ludhiana District Forum

Guru Theg Bahadur Market, Near Clock Tower, Ludhiana.
95161-2747108

Mansa District Forum

Sardar Sita Singh Bldg., Opp. New District Court Complex, Mansa.
951652-228649

Moga District Forum

D.C. Complex, Opp. Geet Cinema, Moga.
951636-235400

Muktsar District Forum

District Court Complex, Kotakapuras Road, Mukatsar.
951633-260129

Nawan Shahr District Forum

Chhokran Mohalla, Nawan Shahr.
951823-222681

Patiala District Forum

239, Shah Bldg., Passy Road, Patiala.
95175-2305407

Ropar District Forum

Room No.4, Ist Floor, Court Complex, Mini Secretariat, Ropar.
01881-220295

Sangrur District Forum

Ist Floor, Old Treasury Office Bldg., Opp. District Court Complex, Sangrur.
951672-231432

STATE COMMISSION/DCDRF IN THE STATE OF RAJASTHAN

Rajasthan State Consumer Disputes Redressal Commission,

Handloom Haveli, Ashok Marg, C-Scheme, 1st Floor,
JAIPUR- 302 001
STD CODE: 0141
E-mail: raj-sforum@nic.in

States/District Forum Rajasthan

Ajmer

Collectorate Premises, Ajmer, Rajasthan-305001
0145-2425228
Fax: 2425228

Alwar

Collectorate Premises, Alwar, Rajasthan-301001.

Telefax: 0144-2337627

Banswara

D.J. Collectorate Premises, Banswara, Rajasthan-327001.
Telefax: 02962-240160

Barmer

Collectorate Premises, Barmer, Rajasthan-344001
Telefax: 02982-221519

Bundi

Collectorate Premises, Bundi, Rajasthan-323001
Telefax: 0747-2442464

Bharatpur

Room No. 53, Collectorate Premises, Bharatpur, Rajasthan-321001.
Telefax: 05644-225090

Bhilwara

IInd Floor, Collectorate Premises, Bhilwara, Rajasthan –311001.
Telefax: 01482-222833

Bikaner

New Court Premises, Public Park, Bikaner, Rajasthan-334001.
Telefax: 0151-2523346

Baran

Collectorate Premises, Baran, Rajasthan-325205
Telefax: 07453-230624

Churu

Collectorate Premises, Churu, Rajasthan-51394
Telefax: 01562-251394

Chittorgarh

Collectorate Premises, Chittorgarh, Rajasthan-312001
Telefax: 01472-241710

Dungarpur

Collectorate Premises, Dungarpur, Rajasthan-314001.
Telefax: 02964-232171

Dholpur

Bari Sepau Road, Dholpur, Rajasthan-328001
Telefax: 05642-221382

Dausa

Collectorate Premises, Dausa, Rajasthan-303303.
Telefax: 01427-223217

Hanumangarh

G.P.F. Office Grieph Road, Hanumangarh Jn., Rajasthan-335512
Telefax: 01552-261140

Jaipur-I

Court Premises, CBI Court Bldg., Banipark, Jaipur-I, Rajasthan-302006.
Telefax: 0141-2200138

Jaipur-II

Mini Secretariat, Banipark, Jaipur-II, Rajasthan-302106
Telefax: 0141-2202872

Jodhpur

High Court Premises, Jodhpur, Rajasthan-342001
Telefax: 0291-2545502

Jaisalmer

Collectorate Premises Jaislmer, Rajasthan-345001.
Telefax: 02992-250012

Jalore

Collectorate Premises, Jalore, Rajasthan-3433001.
Telefax: 02973-223241

Jhalawar

Near Bhawami Natya Shala, Jhalawar, Rajasthan-326001.
Telefax: 07432-230661

Jhunjhunu

Collectorate Premises, Jhunjhunu, Rajasthan, 303301.
Telefax: 01592-232982

Kota

Collectorate Premises, Kota, Rajasthan-342001.
Telefax: 0744-2329200

Nagaur

Manasar Road, Collector Circle, Nagaur, Rajasthan-3341001.
Telefax: 01582-242421

Pali

Room No. 116, Collectorate Premises, Pali, Rajasthan-306401.
Telefax: 02932-222361.

Rajsamand

Collectorate Premises, Rajasamand, Rajasthan-313326.
Telefax: 02952-221726

Sikar

Shiv Singh Pura Navalgarh Road, Sikar, Rajasthan-3332001.
Telefax: 01572-249637

Sawai Madhopur

Collectorate Premises, Sawai Madhopur, Rajasthan-322001.
Telefax: 07462-220592

Sirohi

Swaroop Vilas, Sirohi, Rajasthan-307001.
Telefax: 02972-220652

Sri Ganganagar

Old Hospital Premises, Sri Ganganagar, Rajasthan-335001.
Telefax: 0154-2444416

Tonk

Collectorate Premises, Tonk, Rajasthan-304001.
Telefax: 01432-246550

Udaipur

District & Sessions Judge, Udaipur, Rajasthan-313001.
Telefax: 0294-2411743.

Karauli

Court Premises, Karauli, Rajasthan-322241
Telefax: 07464-250084

STATE COMMISSION/DCDRF IN THE STATE OF SIKKIM

Sikkim State Consumer Disputes Redressal Commission,

Palzor Stadium Road,
Near Sikkim Nationalised Transport,
GANGTOK-737 101
STD CODE: 03592
E-mail: sik-sforum@nic.in,
Statecommission_sikkim@hub.nic.in

States/District Forum Sikkim

District Forum (East District)

District Consumer Disputes Redressal Forum, Secretariat Annexe-I, Sonam Tshering Marg, Gangtok Sikkim
03592-21168
Fax: 03592-202248

District Forum(North)

Office of the District Civil Supplies and Officer,
Food & Civil Supplies and Consumer Affairs Department, Govt. of Sikkim,
Mangan-737116, North Sikkim.

District Forum (South)

Office of the District and Session Judge(S/W) Govt. of Sikkim, Namchi-737126, South Sikkim
03595-264358
250779
Fax: 03592-263360

District Forum(West)

Office of the District and Session Judge (S/W) Govt. of Sikkim, Gayalshing-737111, West Sikkim.
03595-50405

STATE COMMISSION/DCDRF IN THE STATE OF TAMIL NADU

Tamil Nadu State Consumer Disputes Redressal Commission,

Slum Clearance Board Building, II Floor, (Southern Wing), No.212, R.K. Mutt Road, Mylapore,
CHENNAI-600 004
STD CODE: 044
E-mail: scdrc@tn.nic.in &
tn-sforum@nic.in

States/District Forum Tamil Nadu

Chennai South, DCDRF

No. 212, R.K. Mutt Road, III Floor, Mylapore, Chennai – 600 004.
044-24938699

Chennai North, DCDRF

No. 212, R.K. Mutt Road, Ist Floor, Mylapore, Chennai – 600 004.
044-24952458

Chengleppattu DCDRF

Sub-Collector Office Compound, G.S.T. Road, Melamaiyur Village, Chengalpattu
04114-27428832

Coimbatore DCDRF

Collectorate Campus, Coimbatore-641018
0422-2300152

Cuddalore DCDRF

102, Pudupalayam Main Road, Cuddalore-607002
04142-215926

Dindigul DCDRF

D.Nos. 95 & 96, Pensioners' Street, Near Arya Bhawan, Dindigul-624001
0451-2433055

Erode DCDRF

Erode Commercial Complex, Surampatty Naal Road, Erode-638009.
0424-2250022

Karur, DCDRF

Municipal Building, Azad Road, Karur 639 002.
04324-260193

Krishnagiri DCDRF

(clubbed with Salem DCDRF)
Taluk Office Campus, Salem-636002
0427-2213279

Madurai, DCDRF

District Court Campus
Madurai-625001
0452-2533304

Nagapattinam DCDRF

543, Public Office Road, Vellipalayam, Nagapattinam-611001
04365-247668

Nagercoil DCDRF

55, Old No.36/1, Ist Floor, President Sivathanu Road, South of S.L.B. Hr.Sec. School, Nagercoil,
04652-229683

Namakkal DCDRF

3/152, Jeeva Complex, Trichy Main road, Namakkal: 637001.
04286-224716

PERAMBALUR DCDRF

Lakshmi Illam, 345, Rover Nagar, Ist Floor, Ellambalur Road, Perambalur: 621212.
04328-276700

Pudukkottai DCDRF

(Clubbed with Dindigul DCDRF)
D.Nos. 95 & 96, Pensioners' Street, Near Arya Bhawan, Dindigul-624001
0451-2433055

Ramanathapuram DCDRF

Collectorate Complex (Meeting Hall) Ramanathapuram-623501

Salem DCDRF

Taluk Office, Campus Salem: 636002.
0427-2213279

Sivagangai DCDRF

10/25, Thirupathur Road
Sivagangai-630561
04575-241591

Srivilliputhur, DCDRF
Court Hall No. 5, Virudhnagar District Court Complex, Srivilliputhur-626125
04563-260380

Thanjavur DCDRF
Elango Commercial Complex, Court Road, Needhi Nagar, Thanjavur-613 002
04362-272507

The Nilgiris DCDRF
NCMS Complex, Udhagamandalam-643001
0423-2451500

Theni DCDRF
1st Floor, Combined Court Building, Lakshipuram, Periakulam Road, Theni-625523
04546-269801

Tiruchirapalli DCDRF
63A, St.Mary's Complex, Ist floor, Bharathidasan Salai, Tiruchirapalli-62001
0431-2461481

Tirunelveli DCDRF
D.No. 4/993, 2nd Street, Shanthi Nagar, Bel Amrose Colony, Palayamkottai, Tirunelveli: 627002.
0462-2572134

Tiruvallur DCDRF
1-D, C.V. Naidu Salai, 1st Cross Street, Tiruvallur-602001
04116-264823

Tiruvannamalai DCDRF
(Clubbed with Vellore DCDRF)
District Court Campus, Sathuvachari, Vellore-632009
0416-2254780

Tiruvarur DCDRF
52, Kumara Koil Street
Tiruvarur-610001
04366-224353

Tuticorin DCDRF
2/263, 10th St., Valli Illam, P&T Colony, Tuticorin-628008

Vellore DCDRF
District Court Campus, Sathuvachari, Vellore-632009
0416-2254780

Villupuram DCDRF
(Clubbed with Chengleput DCDRF)
Sub-Collector Office Compound, G.S.T. Road, Melamaiyur Village, Chengalpattu
04114-27428832

STATE COMMISSION/DCDRF IN THE STATE OF TRIPURA

Tripura State Consumer Disputes Redressal Commission,
Ramangar Road No.1,
AGARTALA-799 002
STD CODE: 0381
E-mail: tri-sforum@nic.in

States/District Forum Tripura

District Forum, West Tripura, Agartala.
District Judge's Court Complex, Agartala.

District Forum, South Tripura, Udaipur.
District Judge's Court Complex, Udaipur.

District Forum, North Tripura,
Kailashahar.
District Judge's Court Complex, Kailashahar.

STATE COMMISSION/DCDRF IN THE STATE OF UTTARAKHAND

Uttarakhand State Consumer Disputes Redressal Commission,
2nd Floor, F.T.C. Building, District Court Compound,
DEHRADUN-248 001
STD CODE: 0135
E-mail: utr-sforum@nic.in

States/District Forum Uttarakhand

Almora
Choughan Pata,
Almora-263601
05962-230190

Bageshwar
District Court Compound,
Bageshwar-263 642
05963-220394

Champawat
District Court Compound,
Champawat-246401
05965-230878

Chamoli
District Court Compound, Gopeshwar
Chamoli-246401
01372-252i91

Dehradun
District Court Compound,
Dehradun-248001

Haridwar
Collectorate Compound, Room No. 319, 2nd Floor, Roshanabad,
Haridwar-249401
01334-239314

Nainital
District Court Compound,
Nainital-263002
05942-2378040

Pauri Garhwal
District Court Compound,
Pauri Garhwal-246001
01368-222596

Pithorgarh
District Court Compound,
Pithorgarh-262505
05964-224894

Rudraprayag
District Court Compound,
Rudraprayag-246171
01364-233284

Tehri Garhwal
District Court Compound,
Tehri Garhwal-249148
01376-232356

Udhamsingh Nagar
Collectorate Compound, Rudrapur,
Udhamsingh Nagar-263153
05944-244432

Uttarkashi
District Court Compound,
Uttarkashi-249193
01374-222287

STATE COMMISSION/DCDRF IN THE STATE OF UTTAR PRADESH

Uttar Pradesh State Consumer Disputes Redressal Commission,
C-1, Vikrant Block-1,
Near Shaheed Path,
Gomati Nagar,
LUCKNOW-226 010
STD CODE: 0522
E-mail: up-sforum@nic.in

States/District Forum Uttar Pradesh

Moradabad-I District Forum
Civil Court Club Compound,
Moradabad-244001
0591-2425826

Moradabad-II Disrict Forum
Civil Court Club Compound
Moradabad-244001
0591-2428660

Ram Pur District Forum
Room No. 35, Collectorate Compound, Ram Pur-244901
0591-2353707

Bijnor District Forum
Collectorate Compound, Near Krishi Bhawan, Bijnor-246701
01342-260890

J.P. Nagar District Forum
District Court Compound,
J. P. Nagar-244221
05922-259066

Lucknow-I, District Forum
2-A/1, Rana Pratap Marg,
Lucknow-226001
0522-2616246

Lucknow-II District Forum
2-A/1, Rana Pratap Marg,
Lucknow-226001
0522-2230743

Hardoi District Forum
Dharamshala Road, Hardoi-241100
05852-232776

Unnao District Forum
Room No. 43, Collectorate
Compound, Unnao-209801
0515-2820780

Raebareli District Forum
House No. 213, Sarojini Sadan, Field
Hostel Road, Raibareli-229001
0535-2702454

Sitapur District Forum
Collectorate Compound,
Sitapur-261001
05862-245579

Lakhimpur Kheri District Forum
Civil Court Compound, Lakhimpur
Kheri-262701
05872-255614

Agra-I District Forum
Civil Court Compound Agra-282002
0562-2526477

Agra-II District Forum
Civil Court Compound Agra-282001
0562-2263021

Firozabad District Forum
Civil Court Compound Firozabad-
283203
05612-285075

Hathras District Forum
Room No. 9 Collectorate Campus
Hathras-204101
0571-2610810

Aligarh District Forum
Tehsil Koal Parishad Aligarh-202001
0571-2511960

Etah District Forum
IIIrd Floor, Civil Court Campus,
Etah-207001
05742-230399

Mathura District Forum
Collectorate Compound, Opp. SSP
Office, Mathura-281001
0565-2407495

Mainpuri District Forum
Civil Court Compound Mainpuri-
205001
05672-235460

Kanpur Nagar District Forum
15/261 New Civil Lines Kanpur
Nagar-208001
0512-2330466

Kanpur Dehat District Forum
Civil Court Compound, Civil Lines,
Kanpur Dehat-208001
0512-2305638

Etawah District Forum
Civil Court Compound Etawah-
206001
05688-256537

Farrukhabad District Forum
Civil Court Campus Farrukhabad-
209625
05692-235408

Meerut District Forum
Collectorate Compound,
Meerut-245001
0121-2662865

Ghaziabad District Forum
Room No. 202, Collectorate Campus,
Raj Nagar, Ghaziabad-201001
0120-2826770

Bulandshahar District Forum
Civil Court Compound
Bulandshahar-203001
05732-281682

Gautam Budh Nagar District Forum
C-27 Sector-12, Civil Court
Compound, Noida, Gautam Budh
Nagar
0120-2543232

Saharanpur District Forum
Civil Court Compound,
Saharanpur-251003
0132-2722220

Muzaffarnagar District Forum
Civil Court Compound,
Muzaffarnagar-251001
0131-2409044

Faizabad District Forum
Mohda Civil Lines Faizabad-224001
05278-225970

Barabanki District Forum
Civil Court Compound Panchayat Bhawan, Barabanki-225001
05248-227088

Sultanpur District Forum
D.S.O. Office, Sultanpur-228001
05362-227534

Ambedkar Nagar District Forum
102, Meeranpur, Akbarpur,
Ambedkar Nagar-224122
05271-246907

Gonda District Forum
Civil Court Compound, Gonda-271001
05262-232486

Bahraich District Forum
Collectorate Compound Zila Panchayat Bhawan Bahraich-271801
05252-238895

Shravasti District Forum
Near Old Tehsil, Bhinga, Shravasti
05250-222680

Balrampur District Forum
District Court Compound,
Balrampur-271201
05263-236036

Varanasi District Forum
Pcf Plaza Building, IInd Floor, Room No. 10, Ment House, Nadesar,
Varanasi-221001
0542-2509593

Jaunpur District Forum
Civil Court Compound, Jaunpur-222001
05452-260467

Chandauli District Forum
Munsab Katra G.T. Road, Chandauli-232104
05412-260260

Ghazipur District Forum
Civil Court Compound,
Ghazipur-233001
0548-2220218

Bareilly District Forum-I
202-B Civil Lines Bareilly-243001
0581-2429497

Bareilly District Forum -II
202-B Civil Lines Bareilly-243001
0581-2511357

Badaun District Forum
Collectorate Campus Badaun-243601
05832-266053

Sahajahanpur District Forum
Civil Court Compound
Sahajahanpur-242001
05482-233433

Pilibhit District Forum
Civil Court Compound,
Pilibhit-262001
05882-256438

Gorakhpur District Forum
Charuchandrapuri Gorakhpur-273001
0551-2200791

Maharajganj District Forum
Near Sarojininagar District Hospital
Maharajganj-273303
05523-222431

Deoria District Forum
Collectorate Compound, Deoria-274001
05568-222504

Padrauna (Kushinagar)
North Sahabganj, Near Gaushala,
Padrauna/Kushinagar-274403
05564-240062

Basti District Forum
Collectorate Compound, Basti-272001
05542-245917

Sidarthnagar District Forum
Sisahnia Ward No. 6 House No. 7
Behind Police Station Sidarthnagar
05544-222528

Jhansi District Forum
372/36A Civil Lines Jhansi-284001
0510-2449293

Lalitpur District Forum
District Court Compound, Lalitpur-284403
05176-273800

Jalaun District Forum
District Court Compound, Jalaun-285123
05162-252420

Banda District Forum
District Court Compound, Banda-210001
05192-285148

Hamirpur District Forum
Zilla Panchayat Parishad, Hamirpur-210301
05282-222245

Mahoba District Forum
Law Chamber Collectorate Campus Mahoba-210427
05281-255444

Chitrakoot District Forum
District Court Compound, Chitrakoot-210204
05198-235757

Azamgarh District Forum
Harioudh Kala Bhawan Azamgarh-276001
05462-227097

Mau District Forum
Civil Court Compound Mau-284204
0547-2224225

Ballia District Forum
District Court Compound, Ballia-277001
05498-222172

Allahabad District Forum
Civil Court Compound, Allahabad-211002
0532-2548598

Fatehpur District Forum
District Court Compound, Fatehpur-223601
05180-223620

Pratapgarh Disrict Forum
DSO Office, Pratapgarh-230001
05342-223503

Kaushambi District Forum
District Court Compound Kaushambi
05331-232815

Mirzapur District Forum
Behind City Club, New Basti Ramaipatti Mirzapur-231001
05442-253127

Sonbhadra District Forum
Collectorate Compound Sonbhadra
05444-223996

Sant Ravidas Nagar District Forum
Collectorate Campus, Sant Ravidas Nagar-221401
05414-251028

STATE COMMISSION/DCDRF IN THE STATE OF WEST BENGAL

West Bengal State Consumer Disputes Redressal Commission,
Bhabani Bhavan, (Ground Floor), 31, Belvedere Road, Alipore, Kolkata-700 027
STD CODE: 033
E-mail: wb-sforum@nic.in

States/District Forum West Bengal

CDF Kol. Unit-I
8B, Nelie Sengupta, Sarani, 7th Floor, Kolkata-700087.
033-2252-0634

CDF Kol. Unit-II
8B, Nelie Sengupta, Sarani, 7th Floor, Kolkata-700087.
033-2252-0312

CDF Alipore
24 PGS(S), 18, Judges Court Road, Alipore, Kolkata-27.
033-2479-4350

Barasat CDF
24 PGS(N), 2 No., Barrackpore Road, Maya Bhavan (1st Flr), PO Nabapally, Barasat
033-2542-5131

Jalpaiguri
PO Jalpaiguri, Old Court, Near D. M. Office, District Jalpaiguri,
03561-225395

Coochbehar CDF
Sri D.K. Dutta, 2nd Floor, B.S. Road (Opp. Site of the CMO Health Office, Coochbehar-736101
03582-222023.

Maldah CDF
Maldah Sevaniketan, Atul Ch. Kr. Market, PO & Distt. Maldah-732101.
03512-251472

Birbhum CDF
C/o House of Abdur Rashid, Chandnipara, Behind Deaf & Dumb School, P.O. & P.S. Suri, Distt. Birbhum
03462-255559. (Telefax)

Howrah CDF
Red Court Bldg., Rishi Bankim Ch. Road, Howrah-711101.
033-2660-0892

Hooghly CDF
C/o Khadya Bhawan, PO Chinsurah, Hooghly-712102
033-2680-4768

Murshidabad CDF
Murshidabad Cantonment Road, Behrampur, Murshidabad
03482-253207

Purulia CDF
Collectorate Compound, P. O. & Distt. Purulia.
03252-224001

D.Dinajpur CDF
Distt. Judges Office, Dakshin Dinajpur at Balurghat, Balurghat-733 101
03522-271050

U. Dinajpur CDF
PO Raigunj, (Super Market Complex), Block-I, First Floor U. Dinajpur
03523-252006

Nadia CDF
170, Don Bosco Road, Austin Memorial House, P.O. Krishnanagar, Nadia
953472-257788

Siliguri CDF
Kshudiram Basu Bipanan Kendra, (2nd Floor), Hill Cart Road, Pradhannaar, Siliguri-724403.
0353-2517190

Midnapore CDF
At the house of Nemai Kundu, Mohatabpur, PO & Dt. Midnapore
03222-266694

Bankura CDF
Dist. Judge, Kuchkuchia Road, PO 7 Dt. Bankura
953242-241317

Burdwan CDF
Muchipara, G.T. Road, PO Sripally, Distt. Burdwan-713103
0342-2545861

Darjeeling CDRF
New Bldg, CAPT N. Sherpa 24, Mahatih Chand Road, Darjeeling-734101.
0354-2252305

Purba Mednipore
President, DCDRF A. Abasbari, PO Tamluk, Purba Mednipore
953228-270125

APPENDIX V

Address of National/State Consumer Disputes Redressal Commission in India

National Consumer Disputes Redressal Commission
A Wing, 5th Floor, Janpath Bhawan
Cannaught Place
New Delhi 110001
Fax: (011) 23712456

ADDRESSES OF STATE CONSUMER DISPUTES REDRESSAL COMMISSIONS IN INDIA

Andhra Pradesh

The President
State Consumer Disputes Redressal Commission
High Court Building, Hyderabad-500002

Arunachal Pradesh

The President
Arunachal Pradesh State Consumer Disputes Redressal Commission,
65 Vivek Vihar, Itanagar- 795 111,

Assam

The President,
Assam State Consumer Disputes Redressal Commission,
Guwahati High Court, Guwahati.

Bihar

The President,
Bihar State Consumer Disputes Redressal Commission,
12, North Shrikrishnapuri, Patna.

Delhi

Delhi State Consumer Disputes Redressal Commission
A-Block, Vikaas Bhawan
I.P. Estate
New Delhi.
Tel: 23322946, 23322989, 23321558

Goa

The President,
Goa State Consumer Disputes Redressal Commission,
C/o. Directorate of Civil Supplies & Price Control,
Janta House, Panaji, Goa.

Gujarat

The President,
Gujarat State Consumer Disputes Redressal Commision,
4, Vijay Park Society, Opp. Municipal Market,
Navrangpura, Ahemdabad-380 009.

Haryana

President,
Haryana State Consumer Disputes Redressal Commission,
Kothi No. 548, Sector 8B, Chandigarh-160 018.

Himachal Pradesh

The President,
H.P. State Consumer Disputes Commission,
Mini Secretariat, Shimla-171 002

Karnataka

The President,
Karnataka State Consumer Disputes Redressal Commission,
Basava, Basaveswara Circle,
Miller Road, Banglore-560 001

Kerala

The President,
State Consumer Disputes Rerdressal Commission,
T.C.14/407, Extra Police Road,
Palayam, Museum P.O.
Thiruvananthapuram,
Pin-695033.

Madhya Pradesh

The President,
Madhya Pradesh State Consumer Disputes Redressal Commission,
Plot No. N-24, Zone-I Maharana Pratap Nagar,
Bhopal-462 011.

Maharastra

The President,
Maharastra State Consumer Disputes Redressal Commission,
Administrative College, Room Nos. 1 and 2, Hazarimal Somani Marg,
Opp. V.T. Station, Bombay-400 001.

Manipur

The President,
Manipur State Consumer Disputes Redressal Forum,
Post Box No. 64, Imphal.

Meghalaya

The President,
Meghalaya State Consumer Disputes Redressal Commission,
C/o Office of the Transport Commissioner,
Lower Luchumiere, Shillong- 793 001.

Mizoram

The President,
Mizoram State Consumer Disputes Redressal Commission,
Zodian Squarew, Aizawal-796 001, Mizoram.

Nagaland

The President,
Nagaland State Consumer Disputes Redressal Commission,
Guwahati High Court Building, Guwahati

Orissa

President,
Orissa State Consumer Dispute Redressal Commission,
High Court Building, Cuttack- 753 001.

Punjab

The President,
Punjab State Consumer Disputes Redressal Commission,
SCO No. 3009010, Sector 22-D, Chandiagarh.

Rajasthan

The President,
Rajasthan State Consumer Disputes Redressal Commission,
Room No. 133, 1st Floor, SSO Building, Secretariat
Jaipur (Rajasthan)

Sikkim

The President,
Sikkim State Consumer Disputes Redressal Commission,
C/o O/o Food & Civil Supplies Department, Gangtok.

Tamil Nadu

The President,
Tamil Nadu State Consumer Disputes Redressal Commission,
212, R.K. Mutt Road, Slum Clearence Board Building,
IInd Floor, Southern Wing, Mylapore, Madras -600 004.

Tripura

The President,
Tripura State Consumer Disputes Redressal Commission, 307,
Akhura Road, Agartala-799 001 (Tripura)

Uttar Pradesh

The President,
Uttar Pradesh State Consumer Disputes Redressal Commission,
2A/1, Rana Pratap Marg, Lucknow (U.P.)

West Bengal

The President,
West Bengal State Consumer Disputes Redressal Commission,
Bhabani Bhavan, Ground Floor, Calcutta -700 027.

Andaman & Nicobar Islands

President,
Andaman & Nicobar State Consumer Disputes Redressal Commission,
Andaman & Nicobar Islanda, Port Blair-744 102.

Chandigarh Administration

The President,
Chandigarh State Consumer Disputes Redressal Commission,
District Court Complex, New, IIIrd Floor,
Sector -17, Chandigarh-160 017.

Dadra & Nagar Haveli

The President,
Dadra & Nagar Haveli State Consumer Disputes Redressal Commission,
Nunicipal Council Hall, Daman.

Daman and Diu

The President,
Daman & Diu State Consumer Disputes Redressal Commission,
Bunglows No.45/1, Civil Lines, Nagpur-440 001.

Delhi

The President,
Delhi State Consumer Disputes Redressal Commission,
Vikas Bhawan, Near C.R. Building,
I.P. Estate, New Delhi-110 002.

Lakshadweep

The President,
Lakshadweep State Consumer Disputes Redressal Commission,
U.T. of Lakshadweep, Kavaratti-682 555

Pondicherry

The President, Pondicherry State Consumer Disputes Redressal Commission,
No.46, Gubert Avenue (Beach Road), Pondicherry-605 001

DELHI DISTRICT FORUM (North)

District Consumer Disputes Redressal Forum
Room No. 2 & 3
Old Civil Supplies Building
Tis Hazari
New Delhi.
Telephone No.: 23969372, 22924780

DELHI DISTRICT FORUM (South)

District Consumer Disputes Redressal Forum
C-22 & 23, Udyog Sadan
Institutional Area
Behind Qutab Hotel
Mehrauli
New Delhi.
Telephone No.: 26961433, 26565666

MUMBAI SUBURBAN DISTRICT

Mumbai Suburban District Consumer Disputes Redressal Forum
New Administrative Building, 3rd Floor
Near Chetna College, Opposite Dr. Ambedkar Garden
Government Colony
Bandra, Mumbai 400051
Telephone: 26551625

ADDITIONAL MUMBAI DISTRICT

Consumer Disputes Redressal Forum
Additional Bombay District
Arun Chambers, 6th Floor
Tardeo Road
Mumbai 400034
Telephone: 24911737/24937770

THANE DISTRICT

District Consumer Disputes Redressal Forum
The Collectorate Office Building, 1st Floor,
Thane (West)
Telephone No. 25344069

PUNE DISTRICT

District Consumer Disputes Redressal Forum
692, Pushpa Heights
Bibewadi
Pune 411037
Telephone No.: 4210364 (Registrar), 4217489 (Office)

APPENDIX VI
State Commissions Addresses of Consumer Court

Andhra Pradesh
State Consumer Disputes Redressal Commission,
'Eruvaka' Building, Kahairatabad,
HYDERABAD-500004
STD Code: 040

Arunachal Pradesh
State Consumer Disputes Redressal Commission,
Near Pawan Hans Office,
(Old Secretariat Complex)
Naharlagun, ITANAGAR
STD CODE: 0360

A & N Islands
State Consumer Disputes Redressal Commission,
Deptt of Civil Supplies,
Civil Supplies Complex,
PORT BLAIR-744102
STD CODE: 03192

Assam
State Consumer Disputes Redressal Commission,
Housefed Complex,
Central Block,
5th Floor, Front Portion,
Beltola Bashistha Road,
Guwahati-781 006
STD CODE: 0361

Bihar
State Consumer Disputes Redressal Commission,
R-Block, Road No. 2,
South of Daroga Prasad Rai Memorial Trust,
PATNA-800 001
STD CODE: 0612

Chandigarh
State Consumer Disputes Redressal Commission,
Plot No.5-B, Madhya Marg,
Sector-19B,
Chandigarh –160 019
STD CODE: 0172

Chhattisgarh
State Consumer Disputes Redressal Commission,
Behind New Bus Stand,
Pandri,
RAIPUR-492 004
STD Code: 0771

Dadra & Nagar Haveli & Daman & Diu
State Consumer Disputes Redressal Commission,
Department of Civil Supplies,
Collectorate, DAMAN-396220
STD CODE: 0260

Delhi
State Consumer Disputes Redressal Commission,
'A' Block, First Floor,
Vikas Bhawan, I.P. Estate,
NEW DELHI –110 002
STD CODE: 011

Goa
State Consumer Disputes Redressal Commission,
Junta House, 1st Lift,
4th Floor, Vivekanand Road,
PANAJI-403 001
STD CODE: 0832

Gujarat
State Consumer Disputes Redressal Commission,
4th Floor,' A' Block and Ground Floor,
'C' Block, Multistoried Building,
Laldarwaja,
AHEMDABAD-380009
STD CODE: 079

Haryana
State Consumer Disputes Redressal Commission,
Bays No. 3-6, Sector-4,
Panchkula, Haryana
STD CODE: 0172

Himachal Pradesh
State Consumer Disputes Redressal Commission,
Block No.33, 2nd Floor,
H.P. Nagar Vikas Pradhikaran
Commercial Building,
Kusumpati, SHIMLA-171 009
STD CODE: 0177

J & K
State Consumer Disputes Redressal Commission,
(*i*) 3, Manda Hill, Rehari, Jammu Tavi,
Jammu & Kashmir
(*ii*) Near Municipality Office,
Municipality Complex,
SRINAGAR
STD CODE: Jammu-0191,
Srinagar- 0194

Jharkhand
State Consumer Disputes Redressal Commission,
Near High Court, Dauranda,
RANCHI-834002
STD CODE: 0651

Kerala
State Consumer Disputes Redressal Commission,
Sisu Vihar Lane, Vazhuthacaud,
THIRUVANANTHAPURAM-695 010.
STD CODE: 0471

Madhya Pradesh
State Consumer Disputes Redressal Commission
Plot No.- 76, Arera Hills
BHOPAL-462 001
STD CODE: 0755

Maharashtra
State Consumer Disputes Redressal Commission,
Old Administrative Staff College Bldg.,
Opp. C.S.T. Station, Hazarimal Somani Marg,
MUMBAI-400 001
STD CODE: 022

Manipur
State Consumer Disputes Redressal Commission,
Deptt of Food & Civil Supplies,
Sangaiprou,
IMPHAL
STD CODE: 0385

Meghalaya
State Consumer Disputes Redressal Commission,
Horse Shoe Building,
Lower Luchumiere,
SHILLONG-793 001
STD CODE: 0364

Mizoram
State Consumer Disputes Redressal Commission,
Zodian Square,
AIZWAL-796 001
STD CODE: 0389

Nagaland
State Consumer Disputes Redressal Commission,
Guwahati High Court,
Kohima Bench,
KOHIMA-797 001
STD CODE: 0370

Orissa
State Consumer Disputes Redressal Commission,
Sector-1, Near Sati Choura Chowk,
C.D.A. Bidanasi,
CUTTACK-14
STD CODE: 0671

Puducherry
State Consumer Disputes Redressal Commission,
Plot No.3, D.P. Thottam, Behind Hotel Sarguru,
Muthialpet, T.V. Nagar,
PUDUCHERRY-605 003
STD CODE: 0413

Punjab

State Consumer Disputes Redressal Commission,
SCO Nos. 3009-3010,
Sector-22-D,
CHANDIGARH-160 022
STD CODE: 0172

Rajasthan

State Consumer Disputes Redressal Commission,
Handloom Haveli, Ashok Marg, C-Scheme 1st Floor,
JAIPUR- 302 001
STD CODE: 0141

Sikkim

State Consumer Disputes Redressal Commission,
Palzor Stadium Road,
Near Sikkim Nationalised Transport,
GANGTOK-737 101
STD CODE: 03592

Tamil Nadu

State Consumer Disputes Redressal Commission,
Slum Clearance Board Building, II Floor, (Southern Wing),
No. 212, R.K. Mutt Road, Mylapore,
CHENNAI-600 004
STD CODE: 044

Tripura

State Consumer Disputes Redressal Commission,
Ramangar Road No.1,
AGARTALA-799 002
STD CODE: 0381

Uttar Pradesh

State Consumer Disputes Redressal Commission,
C-1, Vikrant Block-1,
Near Shaheed Path,
Gomati Nagar,
LUCKNOW-226 010
STD CODE: 0522

Uttarakhand

State Consumer Disputes Redressal Commission,
2nd Floor, F.T.C. Building, District Court Compound,
DEHRADUN-248 001
STD CODE: 0135

West Bengal

State Consumer Disputes Redressal Commission,
Bhabani Bhavan,
(Ground Floor),
31, Belvedere Road, Alipore,
Kolkata-700 027
STD CODE: 033

APPENDIX VII

List of Voluntary Consumer Organistions

ANDAMAN & NICOBAR ISLANDS

• President

Citizen's Allian Council for PM's 20-Point Programme, Rajendra Bhawan, P.O. Junglighat Port Blair.

• President

Pradesh Consumer Council Andaman & Nicobar Islands, Port Blair.

• President

Nehru Yuvak Kendra, Port Blair

• President

All India Food Council, Port Blair

• President

Andaman & Nicobar Consumers Council, Port Blair

ANDHRA PRADESH

• President

Consumer Education Centre No. 4 Sesna Vilas, 3-6293, 1st floor, Hyderguda, Hyderabad-500029 Ph: 231833.

• President

Consumer Guidance Society of India (Hyderabad Branch), 3-5-815, Hyderguda, Hyderabad-29 Ph: 237458

• President

Consumers' Forum 12-1-508/75, Laxminagar, North Lalguda, Secunderabad-17

• President

Akhil Bhartiya Grahak Panchayat, 5-1-560, Jambagh Road, Navrang Cinema Compound, Hyderabad-500 195.

• President

Federation of Andhra Pradesh Consumer Organisation (FAPCO) No. 4, Sesha VIlas, 3-6-293, 1st Floor, Hyderguda, Hyderabad-29

• President

Consumer Care Centre (A.P. Consumer Guidance and Protection Society), 3-5-273, VIttalwadi, Narayanaguda, Hyderabad-29 Ph: 231915

• President

Sanathangar Residents Consumer Association SRT 484, Sanathanagar, Hyderabad-18 Ph: 261372

• President

Consumer Forum of India (A.P. Chapter) Koorma House, 90, Road No. 9, Mahindra Hills, East Mahinda Hills, East Maredpally, Secunderabad-500026

• President

Vittalwadi Welfare Association 3-5-275, Vittalwadi, Narayanaguda, Hyderabad-29.

• President
Citizen Consumer Council, H. No. 250/SRT, Chandulal Baradari Colony, Hyderabad-500 264 Ph: 526727

• President
Motinagar, Erragadda, Hyderabad-18

• President
Consumer Research Information and Education Society (CRIES) 3-4-497, Barkatpura, Hyderabad-500027 Ph: 63486,

• President
Confederation of A.P Consumer Organisations (CAPCO) 3-5-273, Vittalwadi, Narayanaguda Hyderabad -29.

• President
Dilsukhanagar Consumer Council 1-2, Prabhath Nagar, Chaitanyapuri, Hyderabad-500036.

• President
Jeedimetla Consumers Council, 276, Suraram X Roads, I.D.A. Jeedimetla, Hyderabad.

• President
Bharatnagar Consumers Council 142, MIGH, Bharatnagar Colony Rangareddy District, Hyderabad-18. Ph: 263759.

• President Srikakulam Consumers Council 3-6-75, lppolli Street, Srikakulam-532001.

• President
Vizianagaram Consumers Council, 1-9-5-31/32, Kanukurthyvari Street Vizianagaram-531202.

• President
Consumer Protection Council Samarlakota, Vizianagaram District.

• President
Consumer Protection Council, Vizianagaram.

• President
Consumer Protection Council Kothavalasa, Vizianagaram District.

• President
Consumer Protection Council, Gajapathianagaram, Vizianagaram District.

• President
Consumer Protection Council, Nellimarla, Vizianagaram District.

• President
Consumer Protection Council, Cheepurupal'l, Vizianagaram District.

• President
Visakha Consumers Council, 13-28-6(4), KG.H. up Road Vishakahpatnam-530002

• President
Visakha Electricity Consumers Association 16-1-18, Near Naval Cpast Battery, Maharanipet Vishakhapatnam-2,

• President
FORCE (Forum for Consumers and Environmental Welfare), 4th Floor, Maganti Mansions, Jagadamba Junction, Vishakhapatnam-530020.

• President
Vishakhapatnam District Consumers Concil Lingala Colony, Payakaraopt-531126, Vishakhapatnam District.

• President
Chinagadial Consumer Protection Council, Plot No. 308, Vishalakshinagar, Vishakhapatnam-10

• President

The Greater Vishakha Consumers Association, 45-50-1 Abid Nagar, Vishakhapatnam-16

• President

Kakinada Consumers Council, Plot No. 18, Srinagar Apartment, Srinagar, Kakinada-533 105

• President

Rajahmundry Consumers Council, 8-4-34 C/o Pop Musicals Innespeta, Rajahmundry-101.

• President Konaseema Consumers Council H. No. 8-4-34, H/o Bokha Satyanarayana, Ravulapalem -533238 East Godavari District.

• President

Manadapeta Consumers Association, Mandapeta, East Godavari District.

• President

Tuni Town Consumers Society,Tuni-533 401, East Godavari District.

• President

Anaparthy Consumers Council, Anaparthy, East Godavari District.

• President

Nethaji Youth Consumers Society Kathipudi-533 499 (E. G. District)

• President

Razole Consumers Society Ananda Nilayam, D. No. 4-110/2 Razole-533 242

• President

Consumers Association, Sri Mavullamma Temple Street, Bhimavaram-534 201, West Godavari District

• President

Consumers Council Tuni Madal, Tuni-533 401 (E.G. Distt)

• President

East Gcdavari District Aid, Advice & welfare Society Sarada Rama Nivas', 4-2-16A, Kilimavari Street Ramakrishna Raopeta, Kakinada-533001.

• President

Eluru Consumers Council, H.No. 23 A-8-2, Benapudivari Street, Ramachandraraopet Eluru-534002, W. G. District.

• President

Consumer Council NIDADAVOLE. 534303 W.G. District.

• President

Consumer Welfare Association Tadepalilgudem-534001 W.G. District.

• President

Consumers' Association, Achanta, 15-7 Konja Street Achanta-534123 W.G. District

• President

Mandal Consumers' Council, Jungareddygudem-534447 W.G. District.

• President

Narsapur Mandal Consumers Council, Narsapur, W.G. District.

• President

Mogalture Mandal
Consumers Council, Mogaltur, W. G. District.

• President

Elamanchili Mandal Consumers Councils, Elamanchill, W.G. District

• President

Palakol Mandal Consumers Council, Palakol, W.G. District.

• President
Koduru Mandal Consumers Council, Koduru, W.G. District.
• President
Palakoderu Mandal Consumers Council, Palakoderu, W. G. District.
• President
Veeravasaram Mandal Consumers Council Veeravasaram, W. G. District.
• President
Akiveedu Mandal Consumers Council
• President
Kalla Mandal Consumers Council, Kalla, W. G. District
• President
Achanta Mandal Consumers Council, Achanta, W.G. District
• President
Attili Mandal Consumers Council, D. No. 9-40, Mekulaveeranna Street, Attili, W.G. Distt-534134.
• President
Mandal Consumers Council, C/o Lions Club, Chintalpudi-534460, W. G. District.
• President
Consumer Awarness Rural Research Centre 22-10-37, Tatavarjyvari Street, Bhimavaram-534201 (W. G. Distt)
• President
Vijayawada Consumers Council, Upstairs, Visalandar Book House, Eluru Road, Governorpet, Vijayawada-2.
• President
Consumer Protection Centre 26-13-37, Sanyasiraju Road, Gandhinagar, Vjjayawada
• President
Bezwada Consumer Council, 62-2-44, Patamatalanka, Vijayawada-14.
• President
Consumer Protection Council, Door No. 30-518, Mustakanpet, Machilipatnam-521001.
• President
Consumers Council, Avanigadda, Krishna District.
• President
Consumers Council, Guduru, Krishna District.
• President
Consumer Protection Society, Challapalli, Krishna District.
• President
Consumers Council, Koduru, Krishna District.
• President
Consumer Protection Council, Vuyyuru, Krishna District.
• President
Krishna Zilla Viniyogadarual Council Ground Floor, Iswaraya Towers, Kotilingam Street Opp. Rama Corporation Seetharampuram Vijayawada-4 (Krishna District)
• President
Housing Board Colony Residents United Welfare and Consumers Council MIG, Block No. 79/F5, Bhavanipuram, Vijayawada-520012.
• President
The Consumer Communication Centre, Bharat Book House, 3rd Lane, Arundelpet Guntur-2.

• President
Consumer Council Chandramoulinagar, Kalyaru Road, Guntur-7.
• President
Consumer Council, 1-1404, Pedakoneti Street, Managalagirl-522503.
• President
The Guntur Consumers Concil, Bharmananda Municipal Buildings, Guntur-3.
• President
Piduguralla Consumers Society, Piduguralla, Guntur District-522413.
• President
Universal Consumers Association, Ramireddypet Narasaraopet-522 601. Guntur District
• President
Repalle Consumers Council, Railpet, Repalle-522 265, Guntur District.
• President
Rural Consumers Council Kalankonda,Tadepalli(v) Guntur Distt.
• President
Consumer Society Ganapavaram-522418.
• President
Dachepalli Consumers Society Pragatlil Vidyalayam, Srinagar-522414 (Guntur Dist).
• President
Consumer Council Ongole, Prakasam District.
• President
Consumer Council, Santanuthalapadu, Prakasam District.
• President
Consumer Council, Maddipadu, Prakasam Dist.
• President
Consumer Council, Chimakurthy, Prakasam Dist.
• President
Consumer Council, Addanki, Prakasam District-
• President
Consumer Council, Ballikurvava, Prakasam Dist.
• President
Consumer Council, Chirala, Prakasam District.
• President
Consumer Council, Vetapalem, Prakasam Dist.
• President
Consumer Council, Chinaganjam, Prakasam District.
• President
Consumer Council Yeddanapudi, Prakasam District.
• President
Consumer Council, Kanigirl, Prakasam District.
• President
Consumer Council Council Podili, Prakasam District.
• President
Consumer Council, Pedaraveedu, Prakasam District.
• President
The Nellore Town Consumers Council, 16/726, Sankara Agraharam, Nellore-524001,
• President
Nellore Zilla Viniyogadarula, Seva Sangham, 27-75-21, Income Tax Colony, Podalakuru Road, Nellore-524001.

• President

District Consumers Council, H. No. 43/133-A- N.R. Peta, Kumool-518004.

• President

Consumers Council, Gudur, Kurnool District.

• President

Consumers Council Kudumur, Kurnool District.

• President

Consumers Council, Atmakur, Kurnool District.

• President

Consumers Council, Nandikotkur, Kurnool Dist.

• President

Consumers Council, Machavaram Post, Via Adoni, Mantralayam, Kurnool District.

• President

Consumers Council, Rudravaram, Kurnool District.

• President

Consumers Council, G. Singavaram, Kurnoo! District.

• President

Consumers Council, Sanjeeva Nagar, Nandayal, Kurnool District.

• President

Kurnool Town Consumers Council, Narasingropeta, 45/195 Medapaina, Kurnool-

• President

The Jammalamadugu Consumers Council Nagalakatta, Street Jammalamadugu, Cuddapah District.

• President

Cuddapah District Consumer Association, D.No. 4/343, Ravindra Nagar Cuddapah 516003.

• President

Mubarak Consumers Council, High School Street, Chembakur (PO) Rajnasamudram Mandal, Chittoor District

• President

Universal Consumers' Council, 6-187 (upstairs), Bazar Street, Puttur-517 583 Chittoor District

• President

Consumers' Council Madanapalle-517325.

• President

Consumers Council, Kamareddy, Nizamabad District.

• President

Consumers Council, Renzal, Nizamabad District

• President

Consumers Council Nizamsagar, Nizamabac District.

• President

Consumers Council Kammarapall, Nizamabad District.

• President

Consumer Protection Council, Medak, Medak District.

• President

Mahabubnagar Citizen's Counsil, 2-7-3/2, Market Road, Mahabubanagar-509001

• President

Warangal Consumers Council 2-6-44/3, Nakkalagutta, Hanumakonda, Warangal-506010.

• President
The Jangaon Consumers Council, H.No. 2-11-23, Near Swarnakala Mandir, Jangaon, Warangal District
• President
Consumers Council, Gudur, Warangal District.
• President
Consumers Council, Mulugu, Warangal District.
• President
Consumers Council Parkala, Warangal District.
• President
Consumers Council, Yeturunagaram, Warangal District.
• President
Consumers Council, Govindaraopeta, Warangal District.
• President
Consumers Council, Maripeda, Warangal District.
• President
Consumers Council, Nekkonda, Warangal District.
• President
Consumers Council, Kothaguda, Warangal District.
• President
Consumers Council, Hanumakonda, Warangal District.
• President
Consumers Council, Shayampeta, Jagir Village, Warangal District.
• President
Consumers Council, Thimmanapur, Haveli Village, Warangal District.
• President
Consumers Council, Vidipally Village, Warangal District.
• President
Consumers Council, Kadiplkaonda Village, Warangal District
• President
Yellandu Mandal and Town Consumer Council, Yellandu, Khamman District
• President
The A.P. Consumer Rights Protection Council, Gundala Mandal Khammar T District.
• President
The Khammam Viniyogadarula Mandal Khammam.
• President
The Consumer Protection Council, Aswapuram, Khamman District.
• President
The Consumer Protection Council, Amarada, Aswapuram (M) Kharnmam District.
• President
The Consumer Protection Council, Chintriyala, Aswapuram Mandal, Khammam District
• President
The Consumer Protection Council, Gondigudem, Aswapuram (M), Khammam Distt
• President
The Consumer Protection Council, Ammagraripalli, Aswapuram (M), Khammam Distt.
• President
The Consumer Protection Council, Nellipaka, Aswapuram Mandal, Khammam District
• President
The Consumer Protection Council, Tummala Cheruvu, Aswapuram Mandal, Khamman District

• President

The Consumer Protection Council, Mamillabai, Aswapuram Mandal, Khammam District

• President

Andhra Pradesh Viniyogadarula Hakkula Parirakshana Samithi, Bayyaram, Dhammam District.

• President

Andhra Pradesh Viniyogadarula Hakkula Parirakshan Samithi, Ramchandrapuram, Bayyaram (M), Khammam Distt

• President

The Consumer Protection Council, Nelakondapalli, Khammam District.

• President

The Consumer Protection Council, Singareddipalem, Nalakondapalli Mandal, Khammam District

• President

The Consumer Protection Council, Acharalagudem, Nelakondapalli Mandal, Khammam District

• President

The Consumer Protection Council, Sadasivapuram, Nelakondapalli Mandal, Khammam District

• President

The Consumer Protection Council, Aregudem, Nelakondapalli Mandal, Khammam District

• President

The Consumer Protection Council, Anasagaram, Nelakondapalli Mandal, Khammam District

• President

The Consumer Protection Council, Guwalagudem, Nelakondapalli Mandal, Khammam District

• President

The Consumer Protection Council, Kattukacharam, Nelakondapalii Mandal, Khammam District

• President

The Consumer Protection Council Cheruvumadharam, Nelakondapalli Mandal, Khammam District

• President

The Consumer Protection Council, ManagapuramTanda, Nelakondapalli Mandal, Khammam District.

• President

The Consumer Protection Council, Budharam, Nelakondapalli Mandal, Khammam District

• President

The consumer Protection Council, Kongara, Nelakondapalli Mandal Khammam District

• President

The Consumer Protection Council, Appalanarasimhapuram, Nelakondapalli Mandal, Kharnmam District.

• President

The Consumer Protection Council, Bhiravenipalli, Nelakondapalli Mandal, Khammam District

• President
The Consumer Protection Council, Surdepalli, Nelakondapalli Mandal, Khammam District
• President
The Consumer Protection Council, Bodulabanda, Nelakondapalli Mandal, Khammam District
• President
The Consumer Protection Council, Rajeswarapuram, Nelakondapalli Mandal, Khammam District
• President
The Consumer Protection Council, Ammagudem, Nelakondapalli Ammagudem, Nelakondapalli Mandal, Khammam District
• President
The Consumer Protection Council, Komatlagudem, Nelakondapalli Mandal, Khammam District
• President
The Consumer Protection Council, Mandrajupalli, Nelakondapalli Mandal, Khammam District
• President
The Consumer Protection Council, Ramachandrapuram, Nelakondapalli Mandal, Khammam District.
• President
The Consumer Protection Council, Nachesaliy, Khammam District.
• President
The A.P. Viniyogadarula Hakkula Parirakshana Samithi, Singarent Mandal, Khammam District
• President
The A.P. Consumer Eights Protection Council, Penubatli, Khammam District.
• President
The Consumer Protection Council, Kummarigudem, Aswapuram Mandal, Khammam District
• President
Consumer Council, Peddapalli, Karimnagar District.
• President
Consumers Welfare Council, Osmanpura, JAGITIAL, Karimnagar District
• President
Jagitial Consumers Welfare Council, 5-7-71, JAGTOAL-505 327 Karimnagar District.
• President
Karimanagar Consumer Council, Vavllapalli, Karimnagar District.
• President
Anantpur Consumer Protection Council Deptt of Commerce, S.K. University Ananthapur.
• President
Consumer Welfare Association, Pambatwada, Luxettipet-504215 Adilabad District

ASSAM

• President
Dibrugarh Grahak Manch Chiring Chapori, Dibrugarh.
• President
Dibrugarh Mahila Surakshya Samittee Nirmallgaon, Dibrugarh.

• President

Jorhat District Upbhokta Surakshya Samittee Bongal Pukhuri Jorhat.

• President

Grahak Surakshya Sanstha R. G. Baruah Road. Sundarpur. Ghy.

• President

Grahak Surakshya Sanstha, "Adhar" Zoo Narangi Road Guwahati-781024.

BIHAR

• President

Consumer Guidance Society of Jamshedpur, Avatar Building, Bistupur Jamshedpur-831001.

• President

Akhil Bharatiya Grahak Panchayat, Singhbbum Zilla, Road No. 1. Quarter No. LA/2 Farm Area, Kadam, Jamshedpur-831005.

• President

National Consumers' Union for Legal Assistance, Laxman Mission, Bistupur Jamshedpur-831005.

• President

Bihar Pradesh Upbhokta Seva Sangh, Thilling Trishul Temple Lane, Purance Bazar, Muzaffarpur-842001,

• President

Mahila Upbhokta Sangh Bala Gopaldas Sangat Prabhat Cinema Road, Muzaffarpur.

• President

Bihar State Council Federation, Chather Bhavan, South Mandivi, Patna-800001.

• President

Bihar Rajya Upbhokta Sangh 241-C, Kakar Bagh Colony, Patna-800020.

• President

Akhil Bharatiya Grahak Panchayat BI-A,716, Bokaro Steel City, Dhanbad-827003.

• President

National Consumer Union for Legal Asstt, Bimala Bhavan, West Lohanipur, Patna-800003.

• President

Akhil Bharatiya Grahak Panchayat Distt. Sihghbum, F/10, Tayo Colony, P.O. Gamharia, Singhburn.

• President

Akhil Bharatiya Grahak Panchayat Moubhandar, NF-3/6, Moubhandar, Singhbhum-832303.

• President

Kathihar Zilla Upbhokta Sangram Sangh, Mangal Bazar, Bara Chowk, Katihar.

• President

Koshi Division Consumer protection Organisation, Nutan Press, Katihar-854105.

• President

Gramin Upbhokta Sangam, Village Pakri Ismail, P.O. Laddora Parri Muzaffarpur.

• President

Akhil Bharatiya Grahak Panchayat M-34/5, Telco Colony, Jamshedpur.

• President

Mahila Upbhokta Seva Sangh C-27 Punarchik, Patna.

• President

Priti Mahila Sarkari Upbhokta Bhandar Abulas Lane, Machua Tola. Patna.

• President

Akhil Bharatiya Grahak Panchayat, Grahak Bhavan,' 64/2/3, Vagveda Colony P.O. Tata Nagar, Jamshedpur.

• President

Akhil Bharatiya Grahak Panchayat Annumaudal, Ramrekhighat, Buxar, Bhojpur.

• President.

Akhil bhartiya Grahak Panchayat Vaniyapur Prekhaud, VIII; Chetanehhapra P.O. Pukhari, Saran.

• President

Akhil Bharatiya Grahak Panchayat Parry Prakland, VIII & P.O. Devaria Khoti, Muzafiarpur,

• President

Akhil Bharatiya Grahak Panchayat, Shahsupur Mohalla Naka No. 5, Darbanga.

• President

Akhil Bharatiya Grahak Panchayat, VIII & P.O. Sindhurvally, Purniya.

• President

Akhil Bharatiya Grahak Panchayat Tola, Kathar.

• President

Akhil Bharatiya Grahak Panchayat P.O. Vaidhanath Dharam, Devdhar.

• President

Akhil Bharatiya Granhak Panchayat, Kali Jazia Marg, Pilwarpur Mungair.

CHANDIGARH

• President

Consumer Forum, Kothi No. 99, Sector-8-A, Chandigarh-160008.

• President

Consumers Welfare Association (N.R.) 3341, Sector 2 ID, Chandigarh.

• President

Consumers Welfare Organisation (Regd) 1415, Sector-22-B, Chandigarh. PH: 26934.

• President

National Consumer Awareness Group Society SCO 1108-1109 (IInd Floor) Sector 22, Chandigarh.

DELHI

• President

Mahila Dakshata Samiti 1, Telegraph Lane Kasturba, Gandhi Marg, New Delhi.

• President

Indian Federation of Consumer Organisations, 231, Jor Bagh New Delhi-110003.

• President

War Widows Association, C/o Shaheed Bhavan, 18/1 Jeet Singh Marg, Institutional Area, New Delhi.

• President

Guild of Service- 166-A Sainik Farms Khan Pur, New Delhi.

• President

Consumer Service Society, 148, Jor Bagh, New Delhi 110003.

• President

Consumer Federation of India, 343, LIG Flats, Pkt. B. Hastsal Uttam Nagar, New Delhi

• President

Pragatisheel Mahila Samiti Road No. 12. Kothi No. 28, Punjabi Bagh (East) Near Ring Road, New Delhi.

• President

Voice 108, Golf Link New Delhi-110003.

• President

Common Cause, A-31, West End New Delhi 110021.

• President

Consumers Forum, B-24, Maharani Bagh, New Delhi-65.

• President

Society for Civic Rights, J-13 Prasad Nagar, New Delhi-5.

• President

BINTY, B-7/55 (2nd Floor), DDA Flats, Safdarjung Enclave, New Delhi.

• President

All India Women Conferance, 6, Bhagwan Dass Road, New Delhi.

• President

Siddharatha Ladies Welfare Association, 135, Siddhartha Enclave, New Delhi.

• President

Upbhoktas Seva Samiti Block C2-A, Flat No, 265-A, Janakpuri, New Delhi.

• President

South Delhi Housewives Association, A-38, Kailash Colony, New Delhi.

• President

SANCHETNA, Post Box, No. 10524, Jawahar Lal Nehru University, New Delhi

• President

Grahak Panchayat, C- 4A/37C, Janakpuri, New Delhi-110058.

• President

Confederation of Indian Consumer Organisations 10, Institutional Area Lodhi Road, New Delhi-11003.

• President

Defence Colony Welfare Association (Regd) The 'CUMBAD' Defence Colony, New Delhi-110024. Ph. 611464.

GOA

• President

Consumer Guidance Society of India, (Goa Branch), St. Paul Building Church Square, Panaji (Goa)

• President

The Institute of Management Training & Research P.O. Box No. 77, Margao (Goa)

GUJARAT

• President

Consumer Affairs & Protection Agency of Gujarat, 22, Government Servants Housing Society Near Municipal Market, Navrangpura-38009. Ph: 467049.

• President

Consumer Protection Association: Ahmedabad Yuvak Samaj, (Consumer Protection Centre), Jan Saheb's Gali, Relief Road, Ahmedabad-380001. Ph: 350626.

• President

Consumer Education & Research Centre, Thakorbhal Desai Smarak Bhavan, Near Lal College, Ellisbridge, Ahmedabad-380066.

• President

Jyoti Sangh (Consumer Protection Section), Pattarkuwa, Relief Road, Ahmedabad-380001.

• President

Manekchowk Consumer Protection Association Opp. Chhipamavji's Pete, Ahmedabad 380001.

• President
Consumer Protection Committee, Paramdham' Prayag Society, Ankur Char Rasta, Narnapura, Ahmedabad 380013.
• President
Consumer Protection Council, Bldg. No. 11, 1st Floor, Mill Officer's Colony, Behind La Gujar Chamber, Ashram Road, Ahmedabad 380004.
• President
Jagruti Grahak Suraksha Mandal Natraj, 11, Baatnagar Society Gita Mandir Road Ahmeadabad 380022.
• President
Sarvodaya Grahak Suraksha Mandal, Vyayanagar Housing, Soc, Kankaria Road, Ahmedabad-380022.
• President
Jagrut Grahak Mandal, Ratanpole, Patana, Nr. State Bank, Dist-Mehasana North Gujarat 384265.
• President
Consumer protection Association P.N. Institute of Medical Science Compound, Jal Somnath', Himmatnagar, Dist Sabarkantha-383001.
• President
Akhil Bharatiya Grahak Panchayat, 110, Hare Krishna Complex, Nr Apsara Cinema, Kanakaria, Ahmedabad 380028.
• President
Vadodara City Consumers Council, Sharamsadhana', Opp. Police Ground, Raopura, Baroda 390001.
• President
Jagrut Grahak, Sardar Chhatralaya, Karell Baug, Baroda-390018.
• President
Gtahak Suraksha Sangh, Gupta Chambers, Opp. Kothi Bldg., Raopur, Baroda 390001.
• President
Panchamahal Jila Grahak Suraksha Mandal Nareshbhuvan, Dungra Bhint, Lunawada, Dist: Panchamahal.
• President
Bharuch Grahak Suraksha Mandal, B-342, Natthu Thobhan's Khadki, Nava Dera, Bharuch.
• President
Valsad Grahak Suraksha Mandal, A-1/Purab-Pacchim, M.G. Road, Valsad-396001.
• President
Consumer Association, Near Vaijanath Mahadeo, Mahudha, Tal-Nadiad, Disit. Kheda 387335.
• President
Consumer Service & Education Society, Dhruv Faiia, Mehmadavad, Dist: Kheda.
• President
Grahak Suraksha Mandal, Pankaj Society, Chakalla Road, Dohad Distt Panchamahal 389151.
• President
Rajkot City Consumer Council, 11, Ramnik House, IInd Floor, Jubille, Chowk, Rajkot 360001.
• President
Consumer Protection Education & Research Centre, 16, Deobaug, P.B No: 137, Bhavnagar-364002.

• President
Grahak Hit Suraksha Mandal, Pani Darwaja, Kodinar, Via-Veraval, Distt: Amrall 62720.
• President
Shri Bliuj Grahak Suraksha Mandal, Smt Laxmiben Lalbhal Gor Blood Bank's House, LalTakri, Bhuj, Dist: Kutch, 370001.
• President
Mandvi Taluka Grahak Suraksha Mandal, Limdavli Deli, Chapre Sheri, Mandvi, Dist: Kutch.
• President
Grahak Suraksha Mandal, Kothkuwa, Unjha, Dist: Mahesana 384170.

HARYANA

• President
Consumer Welfare Association of Haryana, 3391, Gupt Gary Market Palwal 121120.
• President
Consumer Welfare Association, 400, Qutabpur, Rewari 123 401.
• President
Consumer Forum, C/o Shivadayal & Sons Industrial Area, Ambala Cantt (Haryana).
• President
Upbhokta Sangh of Fateabad Dhariwal Nursing Home, Dhariwalsak Road, Fateabad 125050 (Hissar Distt.)
• President
Consumer Association Ananda Bhavan, Shivaji Park Yamuna Nagar 135001.
• President
Panchkula Consumers Forum (Regd.) 762-A, Sector 8, Panchkula 134109.

HIMACHAL PRADESH

• President
Himachal Upbhokta Jagran Manch, Solan Sadan, Near Todo Ground, Solan.
• President
Consumers Protection Council Crystal Lodge, Shankli (Near UC Guest House) H.P., Simla.

JAMMU & KASHMIR

• President
People's Citizers Council, Vakil Building, Srinagar 190001.
• President
Jammu & Kashmir Alsafah Forum, Near Masjid Building Opp. Old D.A.V. School Saraiballa, Srinagar.

KARNATAKA

• President
BalakedararaVedike, Jain Temple Road, Mudubidare, South Kanara.
• President
BalakedararaVedike, Puttur, South Kanara.
• President
Consumers' Forum, Raina Bilding, Shriya 574116.
• President
Akhila Bharata Grahak Panchayat, No. 25, 91th Cross, Margosa Raod, Malleswaram, Bangalore 5600003.
• President
Consumes' Forum No. 1554, Dhobighat Road, Karwar, Karnataka.

• President
Karnataka Consumers Forum, No. 9 Karnic Street, Shankarapuram, Bangalore-560004.
• President
Grahak Mandala Asthana, Sirsi 581401, North Kanara.
• President
Consumers Forum, Suratkal Mangalore District.
• President
Citizens Froum, Kotta Post, Udupi
• President
Citizens Froum, No. 2 "Nayan' Ashokanagar Road Hubli 580029.
• President
Consumers Froum C/o Dr. D.C. Devadar, S.D.F. College, Ujjare Post, Beltangadi.
• President
Consumer Forum, Upendrabagh, Near Kalpana Theatre, Udupi 576101.
• President
Citizens Froum Near S.T.V. Temple, Basroorf 576211.
• President
Jagrata Mandali, No. 947, 12th Cross, J.P. Nagar, I Phase, Bangalore-560078.
• President
Citizens Forum, Hotel Dharwad, Dharwad.
• President
Consumer Eduction Trust (R) Microwave Station Road, Mangalore 575006.
• President
Grahak Jagrathi, No. 20 Market Road, Basvanagudi Bangalore 560004.
• President
Jagrathi Balakedara Vedike, Sanjeevaiah Compound, Varthur, Bangalore Distt.
• President
Balakedara Vedike, Ananthasayana Road, Karkala.
• President
Balakedara Balaga, C/o Manila Kendra, Surathkal.
• President
Janajagaruti Trust, Suddi Biddgade, Suliya 574239 (D.K).
• President
Consumers Forum C/o Gayathri Nursing Home, Suilya.
• President
Nagarika Samithi, Karkala, Udupi
• President
Praja Jagruti Sangha, Bellary.
• President
Consumer Guidance Society of India, Dandeli Branch, II-Type, 10156, Bangur Nagar, Dande-581362.
• President
Citizen Forum, Gampathi Circle, Bijapur 586101.
• President
Consumer Forum, Sri Kundeshwar Road, Kundapur.
• President
All India Grahak Panchayat, Mysore.
• President
Grahakaa Vedike, F-l-1534, Shakari Pant's House, Venkteshnagar, Gulbarga.

• President

Grahaka Mandaia Asthana. D. No. 7/47 C, South Extn., Kollegal.

• President

Mysore Consumer Awareness Council 600/B, New Knatharaja Urs Road, Kuvernpunagar, Mysore 570023.

• President

Praja Jagruthi Sangha, Bellary.

• President

Citizens Welfare Association, No. 955.41st Cross. Opp. B.S.I. Hospital, 111 Block, Rajajinagar, Bangalore 560010.

• President

The Karnataka Consumers' Forum, "Sadhana" Temple Road, Jayalakshmipuram, Mysore 570012.

• President

Consumers Council Karnataka.

• President

Karnataka Consumer Service Society 32A, Benson Cross Road, Benson Town, Bangqlore 560046.

• President

Akhil Grahak Panchayat, Bangalore Rural District 107, II Kengari, Upanagara, Bangalore 560060.

• President

Karnataka Forum for Consumer Action 160, 36A Cross, 7th Block, Jayanagar, Bangalore-82.

• President

Mysore Consumer Council, 6/1, Vivekananda Road, Yadavagiri, Mysore 570020.

KERALA

• President

Consumer Protection Wing, Centre for Legal Research, Consumer Protection & National Legal Education, 47/20, S.R.M. Road, Cochin-683018.

• President

Kerala State Consumer Guidance Siciety, C/o. Kerala State Civil Supplies Corpn, M.G. Road, Cochin 16.

• President

Kerala Consumer Welfare Association, Door No XXVT 519 Thevara, Cochin-682013.

• President

Cochin Mahila Consumer Vigyan Kendra, Prathibha, 47/855, Ashoka Road, Cochin 682017.

• President

Kerala Consumer Service Society 47/855, Ashoka Road, Cochin 682 017.

• President

Consumer Guidance and Research Society of India, Opp SHHS, Cheral P.O. Earnakulam.

• President

Kerala State Consumer Council, Chirakkal P.O. Cannanore 760011.

• President

Consumer Guidance Forum, Mananthavady Wynad 670645.

• President

Consumer Guidance Society of India (Trichur Branch), Municipal Stadium, Room No. 63, Palace Rd. Trichur-680020.

• President
Consumer Guidance Society of India, (Kerala Branch), Poonithra Puthanangady, Kottayam 686001.
• President
Association for Protection of Consumers 19/1965, Madhuven Mugal, 19/85; Poojapura P.O. Trivandrum 695012.
• President
Centre for Legal Research & Consumer Protection, Layarn Road, Cochin 682011.
• President
Kerala Consumer Protection Council, Principal Jawahar Balbhavan, Trivandurm.
• President
Quilon District Consumer Protection Council, Principal Jawahar Balbhavan, Trivandurm,
• President
Quilon District Consumer Protection Council, QMS 551/VHI, National Highway Parappat Junction, Quilon 91001.
• President
Kerala Consumer Association, Mattapally House, Cheral-83514, Kerala.
• President
Centre for Indian Consumer Protection and Research (CONBAR) 19/2139, Poojapura Trivandrum.
• President
Kerala State Consumer Co-Ordination, Trivandrum District Committee, Pooma, Dr. Palpu Road, Trivandrum.
• President
Consumer Protection Forum, Trivandrum District T.C. 12/1190, Kunnukuzhy, Trivandurm 37.

MADHYA PRADESH

• President
Madhya Pradesh Consumer Council, 8, Gorakund, Indore 452001.
• President
Upbhokta Hitchintika Samh, 567/4, Sai Kutti, Santosh, Rutty Colony, M.G. Marg, Tukoganj, Main Road, Opp: High Court Indore 452001.
• President
Consumer Protection Sangh, Ramkunj, Kothi Road, Ujjain 456010.
• President
Upbhokta Samrakshan Samiti Bhopal E-5/3 Arara Colony, Bhopal 462016 (M.P).
• President
Upbhokta Parishad 32, Karsa Nagar, Mehra Nursing Home, Ratlam, M.P.

MAHARASHTRA

• President
Consumer Guidance Society of India, Hutment, J, Mahapalika Marg, Opp. Cama Hospital, Bombay 400 001.
• President
Akhil Bharatiya Grahak Panchayat, Chanderi Mahal, 601, Budwar Peth, Pune 411002.
• President
Bharatiya Rashtriya Shahakari Upbhokta Sangh Ltd, 3rd Floor, Suresh Bhawan, Near Wilson College, Sea Face, Bombay 400007.
• President
Mumbai Grahak Panchayat Grahak Bhavan (J.V.P. J Market), Sant Dhyaneshwar Marg, Juhu Vila Parle, Bombay 400056.

• President

Grahak Sanstha Manch, 12, Sahawas Kashinath Dhuru Road, Dadar, Bombay 400056.

• President

All India Bank Depositors Association Piramal Mansion 235, D.N. Road Bombay 400001.

• President

Bombay Telephone User's Association 16, Pancharantna, Prof. Almeida Road, Bandra Bombay 400050.

• President

Save Bombay Committee, C/o Kayjay Engineers, 123, M.G. Road Bombay-400001.

• President

Citizen's Front, Bombay Civil Trust, 1st Floor, Jahangir Art Gallery, M.G. Road Bombay-400023.

• President

Western Railway Suburban Passengers Study Group, Topiwala Bungalow, Topiwala Road, Goregaon (West), Bombay 400062.

• President

Woman Graduates Union, (Consumer and Civil Affairs Committee) Women Graduate's Union Road, Near Colaba Bus Station, Bombay 400005.

• President

Akhil Bharatiya Grahak Panchayat, Dharashiv, Osmanabad, District Osmanabad.

• President

Nashik Grahak Panchayat, Aryama, Nava Jakatnaka, Gangapur Road, Nashik.

• President

Akhil Bharatiya Grahak Panchayat, Shri Vasantrao Dandavate's Wada, Jaunamodha Nanded.

• President

Akhil Bharatiya Grahak Panchayat, C/o. Advocate Deshmukh, Balaji Ward, Chandrapur 443402.

• President

Akhil Bharatiya Grahak Panchayat Chikhali District: Bhuldhana 443201.

• President

Akhil Bharatiya Grahak Panchayat Hinganghat District: Bhuldhana 443201.

• President

Akhil Bharatiya Grahak Panchayat, Hinganghat, District-Wardha.

• President

Yuvashakti Pratisthan, Stree-hitwardhini Bldg, Lokmanya Nagar Compound, Near Tilak Bhawan, Dadar, Bombay 400025.

• President

Sangli Jila Grahak Panchayat Telang Bunglo, 318, Radhakrishnan Vasahat, Sangli 416416.

• President

Akhil Bharatiya Grahak Panchayat, at Jalgaon, C/o Alka Printing Press, Visaji Nagar, Jalgaon-425001.

• President

Association for Consumer Action on Safety and Health, 21, Lawyers Chamber, R.S. Sapre Marg, Bombay 400002.

• President

Grahak Margdarshan Kendra C/o. Shri Ashok Higne Gharda Colony Pirlote, Khed, District Ratnagirl.

• President

Express Citizens Forum (Pune) C/o. Indian Express, 3/11, Aurora Towers, 9A, Molediner Road, Pune-411001.

MANIPUR

• President

Manipur Consumers' Protection Society, Paona Bazar, Imphal 765 001, Manipur.

MIZORAM

• President

Central Young Mizo Association, Aizwal Mizoram.

ORISSA

• President

Orisa Consumers Association, Biswanath Lane, Cuttack Distt., Cuttack.

• President

State Consumer Protection League AT/PO-Janti 725 052 Distt. Puri, Orissa.

• President

Consumer Protection Council H-197, Sector-2 Rourkela 769006, ·

• President

Bhubaneswar Citizen's Forum, A/69, Industrial Area, Bhubaneswar 751001.

• President

Nilachala Sebashrama Plot No. 1150/AUnit-9, Bhubaneswar, Puri Distt.

• President

Orissa Sanskrutika Samaj Budharaj, Sambalpur.

• President

Bhubaneswar Nagarika Upabhokta Sangathan, 665, Saheednagar, Bhubaneswar, Puri Distt

• President

Kranti Surakshay Forums Patnaikpada, Sambalpur, 768001.

• President

Jayadurga Club Umachhak Bhatli-Sambalapur 768030.

• President

PathiBkash Chandan Bazar Dhenkanal.

• President

Pragati Club P.O. Odiso Andigods, Dharmsala, Cuttack Distt.

• President

Sarbodoya Samity Gandhi Nagar, Koraput Orissa.

• President

Dibya Jiban Sarigha, Irrigation Colony Bhawanipatna, Kalahandi Distt

• President

Swami Vibekanand Yuba Parish ad Digmara, Kalahandi.

• President

Duarshari Shramik Sangha, P.O. Boden, Kalahandi, Distt.

• President

Jayadev Bihar Sanskrutika Unnauyana Parishad, Jayadevbihar, Bhubaneswar 751013.

• President

Centre for Youth & Social Development, 65 Satyanagar Bhubaneswar 751007.

• President

L.P. Gas Consumer Forum P.O. Berampur, Ganjam Distt.

• President

Utkalmahila Samity Bajrabhati Road, Gamahadia, Cuttack.

• President

Consumers Association for Guidance & Education P.O, V Dist: Balangir (Regadiapara) 767001.

PONDICHERRY

• President
All India Consumer Council, 15, Ayyanakuttipalayam, Pondicherry-9.
• President
Voice of Consumer, 2/47, Cuddalore Road, Mudallarpet, Pondicherry 4.
• President
Pondicherry Consumer Welfare Association, Government Press, Thattachavadi, Pondicherry 9.
• President
Citizens Council, Calve Subhaya Chetty Street, Pondicherry-1.
• President
TIL Pattinam Consumers' Forum, No. 26 Market Street, Thirumalalray Anpatlinath, Pondicherry.
• President
Pulita Youth Welfare Association No. 21 Varudavur Road Dharmapuri Pondicherry 9.
• President
Consumer Care Association, No. 37, V.O.C. Street. Pondicherry 1.
• President
Indian Consumer Welfare Council, 74, Anne Besant Street, V.O.C. Nagar Pondicherry 3.
• President
Kinmbapet Citizens Council, No. 17 Kinmbapet, Ayyankuttipalayam.
• President
Bharathi Nugarvour Muraiyeettu Kazhagam, No. 131 Eswarankll Street, Pondicherry 1.
• President
Association for Consumer Protection Jasin Building, Mahe 673310.

PUNJAB

• President
Rajpoot Bhala Sabha, Barnaja, Sangrur Dist.
• President
Manav Sewa Sangh, Loha Madi Road, Phagwara, Kapurthala Dist.
• President
Laxini Ladies Club Rakh Bagh, Ludhiana.
• President
Shri Sanatan Dharam Sabha, Pathankot, Gurdaspur Dist.
• President
Consumer Protection Society, Bansal Medical Hall Premises, Opp. Civil Hospital, Mansa, Bhatinda Dist
• President
Dainik Prarthana Sabha, Batal, Gurdaspur Dist
• President
Consumer Protection Association 27-Sewak Colony, Patiala.
• President
Consumers Association, Chowk Clock Tower, Fazilka 152123
• President
Consumer Movement Gali No. 3/1047, Abobar 152116, Ferozepur Dist. (Punjab).
• President
Sirhind Consumer Protection Forum Mohala Modian Sirhind 140407.

RAJASTHAN

• President
Varishth Nagrik Parishad, K. 11, Lahuctia Bhawan, C. Scheme, Ashok Marg, Jaipur 302001.

• President
Kota Consumer Education and Research Society 16-B, Civil Lines Kota 324001.
• President
Rajasthan Society for Consumer Education and Research, Adarsh Raj Colony Chora House, C. Scheme, Jaipur-302015.
• President
Rajasthan Uphbokta Sanrakshan Samiti, Hair Marg Tonk Road Jaipur 302001.
• President
Dr. Ambedkar Seva Samiti Sirohi Zilla, Branch Mount Abu, Mount Abu. Ph.: 398.
• President
Sajag Upbhokta Shakti Sanghathan, B-176, Mangal Marg, Bapu Nagar, Jaipur
• President
Upbhokta Manch Maruti Seva Samiti, 57, Loha Bazar, Behind Saraswati Press Near Swapan Lok Cinema, Udaipur.
• President
Zila Upbhokta Sanrakshan Samiti 7-C, Industrial State Sri Ganganagar 335001.
• President
Upbhoktajagaran Samiti "Ujaas" V/P Shimla, Sardar Shaher Distt. (Rajasthan 331403)
• President
Bhilwada Zilla Proad Shiksha Sangh 8/199, Sindhu Nagar, Bhilwada.
• President
Upbhokta Seva Samit, Tahasil Rashmi Gangar Distt. Rashmi, Chittograrh, P.O. Jadana 3122203.
• President
Upbhokta Seva Samiti Gudachanderji, Distt. Sawai Madhowpur Rajastlian 32213.
• President
Federation of Rajasthan Trade & Industry, Federation Bhawan, Johri Bazar, Jaipur: 302003.
• President
Upbhokta Seva Samiti Mani Deep, Bahir Road, Tonk 304001.
• President
Upbhokta Sanrakshan Samiti Rishbh Printers Sarkari Darwaja, Bhopalganj, Bhilwada 311001.
• President
Astha 109, Kharol Colony, Purana Fatehpur Udaipur 313001.
• President
Bal Rashmi Society, A-48, Shanti Path, Tilak Nagar, Jaipur 32004.

TAMIL NADU

• President
Tamil Nadu Consumer Welfare Council, No. 1/38, Housing Unit, Thanjavur 613001.
• President
Tamil Nadu Consumer Council, No. 10 Lakshmi Colony Esvari Nagar, Thanjavur 613007
• President
Consumer Council of India Salem Branch, New Vanniar St., Koundanpatty, Edapadi Village Salem District.
• President
Consumer Awarenese Forum, 9/160-D, East Main Road, Metturdam 636 401, Salem District
• President
Kamarajar District Consumer Council, No. 37, Railway Feeder Road, Rajapalayam, Kamarajar District

• President

Pudukottai District Consumers Association, No 47, Alangudi Road, Usilangulam, Pudukottai.

• President

District Consumers Council, 9/13, Sethupathi Street, Sivaganga 623560, Psumpon Thevar Thirumagan District,

• President

Madurai District Public Welfare and Civil Rights Association, No. 44, Sathyamoorthy Main Road, Meenambalpuram, Madurai 2.

• President

Consumer Rights Protection Council, 57, American College Building.

• President

Consumer Protection Council, 180, Gandhiji Road, Erode 638002,

• President

Periyar District

• President

Kanyakumari District Consumer Protection Council, No. 248 D Arunachalam Colony, Asamla Road, Kanyakumari District 629001.

• President

Consumer Federation Tamil Nadu 68, Pattabiraman Pillai Street, Tennur, Trichy 620017,

• President

Trichy District Consumer Right's Council 208-C Madurai Road, Edamalaipattipudur, TRICHY 620012.

• President

Kudanthal Consumers Right Protection Council, 31, Muslim New Street Melacauvery Rumbokonam 612002.

• President

Consumer Council Seshadri Memoral Hall' Mugvaiurani Mela Them, Bamanthanpura 623501.

• President

Village Consumers Protection 2/132, Railway Station Road, Kavaral Pattal 601206.

• President

Consumer Protection Council, Tamil Nadu; 216B -B Main Road Mettupalayam 641301.

• President

Ma.......Urimal PadukappuKazhagam2/401-B7 Gandhiji Road, Paramukudi 623707. Ramanatha Puram District

• President

Consumer Protection Council 36/1-G P.M. Street, Gudiyattam 632602.

• President

Tirupura Consumer Protection Organisation 34, Krishangiri Road, Tirupara.

• President

Uthangaral Taluk Consumer Protection Organisation, 32A, Chelary Street Uthangir (T.N.) (Dharmapur Distt).

TRIPURA

• President

Consumer Protection Association 29, Central Road, Agartala 799001.

• President

Consumer Protection Organisation, Bhattacharya Villa, Siddhi Ashram, Agartala 799003.

UTTAR PRADESH

• President
Dakshinachal Consumer Council Kobertsganj, Mirzapur 231216.
• President
Akhil Bharirya Grahak Panchayat, 87f B/5, Sarvodaya Nagar, Allahabad.
• President
Consumer Protection Centre 848 Shiv, Puri. Rly. Road, Hapur.
• President
All India Consumer Welfare Society, C-1491, Rajai Puram, Lucknow 226017.
• President
Upbhokta Parishad, Gyan Lok, Hapur, Dist Ghaziabad.
• President
Consumer Forum Khushalnagar, Station Rd., Muradabad 244001.
• President
Mahila Upbhokta Sangathan, C-1613,Talkatora Avas Vikas Colony, Lucknow 226017.
• President
Indian National Consumers' Federation H.No. 124/644, Block-B Asha Ram Misra Bhawan, Govind Nagar, Kanpur 208006.
• President
All India Consumer Council, 755, Rajput Road, Dehradun 248001.
• President
Manilla Upbhokta Parishad, Himdeep, Radhapuri, Hapur.
• President
Upbhokta Manch, 136, Jawahar Ganj Hapur 245101.
• President
Mahila Kalyankari Upbhokta Samiti, 969, Bagh Jankidas, Prem Puri Road, Muzaffar Nagar.
• President
Sevanivrit Karamchari Evam Upbhokta Sanrakshan Samiti 73/59, Sahebganj, P.O. Dadua Bazar, Bargaon Gonda 271002.
• President
Upbhokta Kalyan Parishad 10/215, A, Karta, Bazarikhan, Jamuna Bridge, Agra.

WEST BENGAL

• President
Consumer Action Forum, 5/1 Red Cross Place, Calcutta 700062.
• President
Consumer Protection Centre 24-B, Dr. Rajendra Road, Calcutta 700020.
• President
Consumers Unity and Trust Society 3-B, Camac Street, Calcutta 16.
• President
Women's' Co-ordinating Council 5/1, Red Cross Place, Calcutta 700062.

APPENDIX VIII

Recognised Consumer Associations

1. Consumer Education Centre, No. 4, Sesha Vilas, 3-6-293, 1st Floor, Hyderguda, Hyderabad-29. Ph.228249.
2. Consumer Guidance Society of India (Hyderabad Branch), 3-5-815, Hyderguda, Hyderabad-29 Ph.237458.
3. Consumer Forum, 12-1-508/75, North Lalaguda, Santinagar, Secunderabad-500 017.Ph. 824245.
4. Akhil Bharatiya Grahak Panchayat, 5-1-560, Jambagh Road, Navrang Cinema Compound, Hyderabad. Ph. 64758.
5. Federation of Andhra Pradesh Consumers Organisation, No. 4, Seshavilas, 3-6-293, 1st Floor, Hyderguda, Hyderabad-29. Ph. 36804.
6. A.P. Consumer Guidance and Protection Society, 3-5-273, Vittalwadi, Narayanaguda, Hyderabad-29. Ph. 231915.
7. Consumer Protection Council, 607, Srinivasa Towers, 6th Floor, Begumpet, Hyderabad-38.
8. Sanathnagar Residents' Consumer Association, SRT 484, Sanathnagar, Hyderabad-18.
9. Jeedimetla, Consumer Council, 34-122, Kalavathinagar, I.D.A. Jeedimetla, Hyderabad.
10. Consumer Federation of India, (A.P. Chapter) Koorma House, 90/11, Threemurthy Nagar, Mahindra Hills. East Maredpally, Secunderabad-500026. Ph. 230461/230987/237700.
11. Vittalwadi Welfare Association, 3-5-275, Vittalwadi, Narayanaguda, Hyderabad-29.
12. Citizen Consumer Council, H.No. 250/SRT, Chandulal Baxadari Colony, Hyderabad-500 264. Ph. 526 727.
13. The Consumer Communication Centre, Bharat Book House, 3rd Lane, Arundalpet, Guntur-522 022.
14. Consumer Council, 3rd Lane, Brodipet, Guntur-522022.
15. Consumer's Council, 1-1404, Pedakoneti Street, Mangalagirj-522 503.
16. The Guntur Consumer's Council, Bharamananda Municipal Buildings, Guntur-522 023.
17. Piduguralla Consumers' Society, Distt, Guntur, Piduguralla-522 413.
18. Universal Consumers' Association, 11-8-4, Ramareddpet, Narasaraopet, Guntur-522 601.
19. Repalle Consumers' Council, Railpet, Repalle, Guntur.
20. 'Kakinada Consumers' Council, 59-19-17. Santisadan, Pasterpet Kakinada-2. Ph. 4101

21. Rajahmundry Consumers' Council, 46-7-4, Jampets, Rajahmundary 533103. Ph. 3470.
22. Kondaseema Consumers' Council, H.No. 8-4-34, H O Bokka Satyanarayana, East Godavari Distt. Ravulapalem -533 238.
23. Mandapeta Consumers' Association, Mandapeta, East Godavari Distt.
24. Tuni Tawan Consumers' Society, East Godavari Distt. Tuni-533 401.
25. Consumer Association, Sri Mavullamma Temple St. West Godavari Distt, Godavri, Bhimavaram- 534 201. Ph. 3273.
26. Consumer Council, Nidadavole, West Godavari District.
27. Eluru Consumer Council, H. No,23A-8-2, Bendapudivari St., Ramachandraraopet, Eluru-534 002, Ph. 22543.
28. Consumer Welfare Association, West Godavari Distt, Tadepalligudem -534 101.
29. Consumers' Association, Achanta, 15-7, Konja Street, Achanta-534 123.
30. Mandal Consumers' Council, West Godavari Distt. Jangareddygudem-53447.
31. Narsapur Mandal Consumers' Council, West Godavari District, Mogaltur.
32. Mogaltur Mandal Consumers' Council, West Godavari District, Magaitur.
33. Elamenchili Mandal Consumers' Council, West Godavari District, Elamanchili.
34. Palkol Mandal Consumers' Council, West Godavari District, Palkol.
35. Koduru Mandal Consumers' Council, West Godavari District, Palkol.
36. Palakoderu Mandal Consumers' Council, West Godavari District, Palakoderu.
37. Veeravasaram Mandal Consumers' Council, West Godavari District, Veeravasaram.
38. Akiveedu Mandal Consumers' Council, Akkiveedu, West Godavari District.
39. Kalla Mandal Consumers' Council, Kalla, West Godavari District.
40. Undi Mandal Consumers' Council, Undi, West Godavari District.
41. Achanta Mandal Consumers' Council, Achantamandal, West Godavari District.
42. Vijayawada Consumers' Council, Upstairs Visalandra Book House, Eluru Road, Governorpet, Krishna District, Vijayawada-2.
43. Consumer Protection Centre, 26-13-37, Sanyasiraju Street, Gandhinagar, Vijayawada-3.
44. Consumer Protection Council, Krishna District, Machilipatnam-521001.
45. Consumers' Council, Avanigadda, Krishna District.
46. Consumers' Council, Guduru, Krishna District.
47. Consumers Protection Society, Challapalli, Krishna District.
48. Consumer's Council, Koduru, Krishna District.
49. Consumers' Protection Council, Vuyyuru, Krishna District.
50. Visakha Consumer's Council, 16-3-5, Official Colony, Maharanipet, Visakhapatnam-530 002. Ph. 64871, Ext. 393, Res, 64095.
51. Visakha Electricity Consumers Association, 16-1-18, Near Naval Coast Battery, Maharanipet, Visakhapatnam-530 002.
52. Force (Forum for Consumer & Environment), 4th Floor Meganti Mansions, Jagadamba Junction, Visakhapatnam-530 020.
53. Visakhapatnam District Consumers' Council, Visakhapatnam District, Payakaraopeta-531126.
54. Chinagadila Consumers' Council, Visalakshinagar, Visakhapatnam-10.
55. Consumers' Council, Allipuram, Visakhapatnam District.

56. Mahabubnagar Citizens Council, 2-7-3/2, Market Road, Mahabubnagar-509 001.Ph. 2803.
57. The Vizianagaram Consumers' Council, 19-5-31/32 Kanukurthyuari St.Vizianagaram-531202.
58. Consumer Protection Council, Vizianagaram.
59. Consumer Protection Council, Samarlakota, Vizianagaram. District.
60. Consumer Protection Council, Kothavalassa, Vizianagaram. District.
61. Consumer Protection Council, Gajapathinagaram, Vizianagaram.District.
62. Consumer Protection Council, Neelimarla, Vizianagaram. District.
63. Consumer Protection Council, Cheepurupalli, Vizianagaram.
64. District Consumers' Council, H.No. 43/133-A, N.R. Peta.
65. Consumers' Council, Gudur, Kurnool District.
66. Consumers' Council, Kodumur, Kurnool District.
67. Consumers' Council, Atmakur, Kurnool District.
68. Consumers' Council, Nandikotkur, Kurnool District.
69. Consumers' Council, Mantralayam, Kurnool District.
70. Consumers' Council, Chalagalamarri, Kurnool District.
71. Consumers' Council, Kudravaram, Kurnool District.
72. Consumers' Council, G. Singavaram, Kurnool District.
73. Consumers' Council, Nandyal, Kurnool District.
74. Yellandu Mandal Town Consumers Council, Yellandu, Khammam District.
75. The A.P. Consumer Rights Protection Council, Gundala Mandal, Khammam District.
76. The Khammam Viniyogaarulu Mandali, Khammam.
77. The Consumers' Protection Council, Aswapuram Mandal, Khammam District.
78. The Consumers' Protection Council, Amarda, Aswapuram Mandal, Khamroam District.
79. The Consumers' Protection Council, Chintriyala, Aswapuram Mandal, Khammam District.
80. The Consumer's Protection Council, Gondigudem, Aswapuram Mandal, Khammam District.
81. The Consumers' Protection Council, Pamulapalli, Answapuram Mandal, Khammam District.
82. The Consumers' Protection Council, Kummarigudem, Aswapuram Mandal, Khammam District.
83. The Consumers' Protection Council, Ammagaripalli, Aswapuram Mandal, Khammam District.
84. The Consumers' Protection Council, Neelipaka, Aswapuram Mandal, Khammam District.
85. The Consumers' Protection Council, Mamillabai, Aswapuram Mandal, Khammam District.
86. The Consumers' Protection Council, Tummalacheruvu, Answapuram Mandal, Khammam District.
87. Andhra Pradesh Viniyogadarula Hakkula Parirakshana Samithi, Dayyaram, Khammam District.
88. Andhra Pradesh Viniyogadarula Hakkula Parirakshana Samithi, Kothapeta, Khammam District.

89. Andhra Pradesh Viniyogadarula Hakkula Parirakshana Samithi, Ramachandrapuram, Bayyaram Mandal, Khammam District.
90. The Consumer Protection Council, Nelakondapalli, Khammam District.
91. The Consumer Protection Council, Nelakondapalli, Mandal, Singareddipalem, Khammam District.
92. The Consumer Protection Council, Nelakondapalli, Mandal Acharlagudem, Khammam District.
93. The Consumer Protection Council, Nelakondapalli, Mandal Sadasivapuram, Khammam District.
94. The Consumer Protection Council, Nelakondapalli, Mandal, Aregudem, Khammam District.
95. The Consumer Protection Council, Nelakondapalli, Anasgaram, Khammam District.
96. The Consumer Protection Council, Nelakondapalli, Mandal Mujjugudem, Khammam District.
97. The Consumer Protection Council, Nelakondapalli, Mandal Guvvalagudem, Khammam District.
98. The Consumer Protection Council, Nelakondapalli, Mandal, Kattukacharam, Khammam District.
99. The Consumer Protection Council, Nelakondapalli, Mandal, Cheruvumadharam, Khammam District.
100. The Consumer Protection Council, Nelakondapalli, Mandal, Mangapuram, Khammam District.
101. The Consumer Protection Council, Nela Kondopali Mandal, Cheruvumadharam, Khammam District.
102. The Consumer Protection Council, Nelakondapalli, Mandal, Ravigudem, Khammam District.
103. The Consumer Protection Council, Nelakondapalli, Mandal, Kongara, Khammam District.
104. The Consumer Protection Council, Nelakondapalli, Mandal, Appalanarasimhapuram, Khammam District.
105. The Consumer Protection Council, Nelakondapalli, Mandal, Bhiravenipalli, Khammam District.
106. The Consumer Protection Council, Nelakondapalli, Mandal, Painampalli, Khammam District.
107. The Consumer Protection Council, Nelakondapalli, Mandal, Tirumalapuram, Khammam District.
108. The Consumer Protection Council, Nelakondapalli, Mandal, Konaigudem, Khammam District.
109. The Consumer Protection Council, Nelakondapalli, Mandal, Chennaram, Khammam District.
110. The Consumer Protection Council, Nelakondapalli, Mandal, Surdepalu, Khammam District.
111. The Consumer Protection Council, Bodulabanda, Khammam District.
112. The Consumer Protection Council, Rajeswarapuram, Khammam District.
113. The Consumer Protection Council, Ammagudem, Khammam District.
114. The Consumer Protection Council, Nelakondapalli, Mandal, Motapuram, Khammam District.

115. The Consumer Protection Council, Nelakondapalli, Mandal, Komatlaguderm, Khammam District.
116. The Consumer Protection Council, Nelakondapalli, Mandal, Mandrajupalli, Khammam District.
117. The Consumer Protection Council, Nelakondapalli, Mandal, Ramachandrapuram, Khammam District.
118. The Consumer Protection Council, Nachepalli, Khammam District.
119. The A. P. Viniyogadarula Hakkula Parirakshana Samithi, Singareni Mandal, Khammam District.
120. The AP.Consumer Rights Protection Council, Penuballi, Khammam District.
121. "Warangal Consumers' Council, 2-6-44/3, Nakkalagutta, Hanumakonda, Warangal-506010.
122. The Jangaon Consumers' Council, H.No. 2-11-23, near Swasnakala Mandir, Jangaon, Warangal District.
123. Srikakulam Consumers' Council, 3-8-75, Ippoli St, Srikakulam.
124. Consumers' Council, Srikakulam District, 12-14-20, L. Bahadur Shastry Colony, Srikakulam,
125. The Nellore Town Consumers' Council, 16 726, Sankara Agraharam, Nellore-524 001.
126. Mubarak Consumers' Council, Ramasamudram Mandal, Chembakur, Chittoor District.
127. Consumer Council, Peddapalli, Karimnagar District.
128. Grahak Suraksha Sanstha, Adhar Zoo Narangi Road, Guwahati-781024.
129. Consumer Guidance Society of Jamshedpur, Avtar Building, Bistupur, Jamshedpur-831 001.
130. Akhil Bhartiya Grahak Panchayat, Singbhum Zilla, Road No. 1, Quarter No. L4/2, Farm Area. Kadma, Jamshedpur-831 005.
131. National Consumers' Union for Legal Assistance, Laxmi Mission, Bistupur, Jamshedpur-831 005.
132. Bihar Pradesh Upbhokta Seva Sangh, Thrilling Trishul Temple Lane, Purancee Bazar, Muzaffarpur-842 001.
133. Mahilla Upbhokta Sangh, Bala Gopaldas Sangat, Prabhat Cinema Road, Muzaffarpur.
134. Bihar State Consumer Federation, Chather Bahvan, South Mandivi Patna-800 001.
135. Bihar Rajya Upbhokta Sangh, 241-C, Kakar Bagh Colony, Patna-800 020.
136. Bihar Consumers' Council, Congress Maidan, Kadam Kuan, Patna-800 003.
137. Akhil Bharatiya Grahak Panchayat, III-AJ716, Bokaro Steel city, Dhanbad-827 003.
138. National Consumers' Union for Legal Assistance, Bimala Bhavan, West Lohanipur, Patna-800 003.
139. Akhil Bharatiya Grahak Panchayat, Distt, Singhbhum, F/10,Tayo Colony, P.O.Gamaharia, Singhbhum.
140. Akhil Bharatiya Grahak Panchayat, Moubhandar, NF/3/6, Mounbhandar, Singhbhum-823 303.
141. Katihar Zila Upbhokta Sangram Sangh, Mandal Bazar, Bara Chowk, Katihar.
142. Koshi Division Cosumer Protection Organisation, Nutan Press, Katihar-854 105.

143. Gramin Upbhokta Sangam, Village Pakri Ismail, P.O. Laddora Parri, Muzaffarpur.
144. Ahmedabad Yuvak Samaj, Grahak Surksha Kendra, Jana Sahebni Gali, Relief Road, Ahmedabad.
145. Consumer Education & Research Centre, Thakorbhai Desial Smarak Bhavan, Ellisbridge, Ahmedabad-380 006.
146. Jyotisangh Grahak Suraksha Mandal, C/o.Jyotisangh, Patharkuwa Relief Road, Ahmedabad-380 001.
147. Manekchowk Grahak Suraksha Mandal, C/o Mandvini Pole Seva Sangh, Mandvim Pole, Ahmedabad-380 001.
148. Grahak Suraksha Samiti, Paramadham, Prayag Society, Ankur Char Rasta, Navarangpura, Ahmedabad-380 009.
149. Consumer Protecion Council, Building No. 11,1st Floor, Mill Officer Colony, Behind La Gajjar Chamber, Ashram Road, Ahmedabad-380 009.
150. Adarsh Mahila Samaj, 337-29, Pitampura-2, Girdharnagar, Ahmedabad.
151. Jagruti Grahak Suraksha Mandal, Natraj, 11, Bharatnagar, Geetamandir Road, Ahmedabad.
152. Sarvoday Grahak Suraksha Mandal, Vijaynagar Housing Society, Kankaria Road, Ahmedabad-382 002.
153. Consumer Protection Education & Research Center, 16, Devubag, Bhavan agar.
154. Jagrut Grahak, Amin Building, Gandhi Gate, Baroda.
155. Grahak Suraksha Sangh, Gupta Chambers, Behind Kothi, Ravpura, Baroda.
156. Grahak Suraksha Mandal, Pankaj Society, Chakalia Road, Dahod, Panchamanal.
157. Panchamahal Jilla Grahak Suraksha Mandal, Naresh Bahvan, Dangar Bhint, Lunawada Dist. Panchamahal.
158. Jagrut Gahak Mandal, C/o Bhagini Samaj, Gole Sheri, Patna.
159. Vadodara Sahkar Grahak Suraksha Mandal, Sharamsudhara, Near Police Ground, Ravpura, Baroda.
160. Grahak Hit Surakusha Mandal, Panidarwaja, Kodinara, Distt. Amreli.
161. Grahak Suraksha Mandal, P.N. Institute of Medical Science Compound, Himatnagar.
162. Grahak Association, Near Vaijnath Mahadev, Mahudha, Distt. Kheda.
163. Rajkot Saher Grahak Sangathan, 11, Ramnik House, 2nd Floor, Jubilee Chowk, Rajkot.
164. Shri Valsad Grahak Suraksha Mandal, Shitalamata Sheri, Valsad.
165. Mandvi Taluka Grahak Suraksha Mandal, Limbdavala Deli, Chhapara Sheri; Mandvi Distt. Kutch, Bhuj.
166. Bhuj Grahak Suraksha Mandal, Ulipark Road, Bhuj, District Kutch.
167. Bharuch Grahak Suraksha Mandal, B-342, Natthy Thobhanni Khadki, Dehxa, Bharuch.
168. Consumer Guidance Society of India (Goa Branch), St, Paul Building, Church Square, Panji (Goa).
169. Consumer Welfare Association of Haryana, 3391, Gupta Ganj Market, Palwal-121102.
170. Consumer Welfare Association, 400, Quatabpur, Rewari-123 401.
171. Consumer Forum, Ambala Cantt, Haryana.
172. Himachal Pradesh Upbhokta Samiti, Shimla.

173. Himachal Upbhokta Jagran Manch, Solan Sadan, Near Todo Ground, Solan.
174. People's Citizens Council, Vakil Building, Srinagar-190 001.
175. Consumer Welfare Association, C/o. Charta Suraj Rehari, Jammu.
176. Jammu & Kashmir Alsafah Forum, Near Masjid Building, Opp. Old D.A.V. School, Saraiballa, Srinagar.
177. Karnataka Consumer Service Society, 32-A, Benson Cross, Benson Town, Bangalore-560 046.
178. Grahak Jagrati, 20, Market Rd, Basavangudi, Bangalore-560 004.
179. Jagrf.th Mandeli, 947, 12th Cross, J.P. Nagar, 1st Stange, Bangalore-560 078.
180. Consumer Education Trust of Mangalore, Microwave Station, Bangalore- 575 006.
181. The Citizen's Forura, Nayan, No, 2, Ashokanagar Road, Hubli-581 362.
182. Consumer Guidance Society of India, H Type, 10/56, Bangurnagar, Dandeli-584 362.
183. Citizens Forum, Near Marathi Vidhayala, Bijapur-586 101.
184. Consumers' Forum, Upendra Bang, Near Kalpna Talkies; Udipi-576 101.
185. Consumers' Forum, Near STV Temple, Basrur-576 211.
186. Consumers' Forum, 8/447, Jhansi Lakshmi Devi Road, Kundapur-576207.
187. Consumers' Forum, Naina Building, Shirya-574 116.
188. Gulburga Distt. Consumers' Forum, E-1-1534, Sahakari Pant's House, Venkatesh Nagar, Gulburga-585 102.
189. Consumers' Forum, Balthangdi, C/o. Dr.D.C.Devdhar, SDM College, Ujare, Kamataka.
190. Consumers' forum, C/o, Gayatri Nursing Home, Sullia-574 239.
191. Jan Jagarithi Trust, Near C.A. Bank, Sullia-239.
192. Nagarikarara Vedika, Kotta Post, Udupi, Kamataka.
193. Balakedarara Vedika, Anantha Shayan Road, Karkala, South 570 014.
194. Balakedara Belaga, C/o. Manila Kendra Souratkal, Souratkal, Karnataka.
195. Balakedarara Vedika, Puttur, South Kanara, Karnataka.
196. Kalakedara Vediaka, Surrathkal, Manglore Taluka, Karnataka.
197. Balakedarara Vedika, Jain Temple Road, Mudubidare, South Kanara, Karnataka.
198. Nagarika Samithi, Parkala, Udupi, Karnataka.
199. Praja Jagrithi Sangh, Bcllary, Karnataka.
200. Consumer Welfare Council. Door No. 4/471-C, South Extension, Kolleegal-571440.
201. Jagrathi Balakedarar Vedika, Sanjivayya Compound, Virthur, Banglore, Karnataka.
202. The Citizen Forum, Hostel Dharwad, Dharwad, Karnataka.
203. The Bellary Citizens Forum, 33/B, Venkatachalam Street, IInd Ward Office, Station Road, Bellary-583 101.
204. Consumer Protection Wings, Centre for Legal Research Consumer Protection & Non formal Legal Education, 47/20, S.R.M. Road, Cochin-682 018.
205. Kerala State Consumer Guidance Society, C/o. Kerala State Civil Supplies Corporation, M.G.Road, Cochin-682 016.
206. Kerala Consumer Welfare Association, Door No. XXVt/519, Thevara, Cochin-682013.

207. Cochin Manila Consumer Vigyan Kendara, Prathibha, 47/855, Ashoka Road, Cochin-682017.
208. Kerala Consumer Service Society, 47/855, Ashoka Road, Cochin-682 017.
209. Consumer Guidance and Research Society Of India, Opp. S.H.H.S., Cherai P.O. Ernakulam.
210. Kerala State Consumer Council, Chirakkal P.O., Cannanore-670 Oil.
211. Consumer Guidance Forum, Mananthavady,Wynad-670 645.
212. Consumer Guidance Society of India, Trichur Branch, Municipal Stadium, Room No. 63, Palace Rd, Trichur-680 020.
213. Consumer Guidance Society of India, Kerala Branch, Poonithra Puthanangady, Kottayam-686 001.
214. Association for Protection of Consumers, 19/1965, Mudhavan Mugal, 99/85, Poojapura P.O, Trivandrum-69 012.
215. Centre for Legal Research & Consumer Protection, Layam Road, Cochin-682 Oil.
216. Kerala Consumer Protection Council, C/o. Principal, Jawahar Balbhavan, Trivandrum.
217. Quilon District Consumer Protection Council, Thottumukkathu, Paper Mill. P.O. Quilon Distt, Punalur-691 332.
218. Kerala Consumer Association, Mattappilly House,Cherai-683 514.
219. Madhya Pradesh Consumer Counci., 8, Gorakund. Indore-452 001.
220. Upbhokta Hitchintika Samiti, 567/4, Sai Kutti. Santosh, Kutty Colony, M.G. Marg, Tukoganj, Main Road, Opp. High Court, Indore-452 001.
221. Consumer Protection Sangh, Ramkunj, Kothi Road, Ujjain-456 010.
222. Consumer Guidance Society of India, J.Mahapalika Marg, Opp. Cama Hospital, Bombay-400 001.
223. Akhil Bharatiya Grahak Panchayat, Grahak Bhavan, Tilak Marg, Pune-42.
224. Bharatiya Rashtriya Sahakari Upbhokta Sangh Ltd, 3rd Floor, f iresh Bhavan, Near Wilson College, Sea Face, Bombay-400 007.
225. Mumbai Grahak Panchayat, 42, Kokan Nagar, Lieut Kotnis Marg, Mahim, Bombay-400 016.
226. Grahak Sanstha Manch, 12, Sahawas Kashinath Dhuru Road, Dadar, Bombay-400 028.
227. All India Bank Depositors Association, Piramal Mansion, 235, D.N Road, Bombay-400 001.
228. Bombay Telephone Users' Association, 16, Panchratna, Prof, Almeida Road, Bandra, Bombay-400 050.
229. Save Bombay Committee, C/o, KK Engineers, 123, M.G. Road, Bombay-400 023.
230. Citizen's Front, Bombay Civil Trust, 1st Floor, Jahangir Art Gallery, M.G. Road, Bombay-400 001.
231. Westren Railway Suburban Passengers Study Group, Topiwala Bungalow, Topiwala Road, Goregaon (West), Bombay-400 062.
232. Women Graduates, Union (Consumer and Civil Affairs Committee), Women Graduates "Union Road, Near Colaba Bus Station, Bombay-400 005.
233. Manipur Consumes' Protection Society, Paona Bazar, Imphal-795 001.
234. Orissa Consumers' Association, Biswanath Lane, Cuttack.

235. State Consumer Protection League, AT/PO Jatni Distt. Puri, Orissa-752 052.
236. Consumer Protection Council, H-197, Section-2, Rourkela-769 006.
237. Bhubaneswar Citizens' Forum, A/69, Industrial Area, Bhubaneswar-751 001.
238. Srihind Consumers Protection Forum, Manilla Modian, Sirhind-140 407.
239. Rajasthan State Consumers' Council, Brij Nikunj, Civil Lines, Jaipur-302 006.
240. Rajasthan Society for Consumer Education & Research, D-63, Adarsh Raj Colony, C-Scheme, Jaipur-302 001.
241. Consumers Unity & Trust Society, 8, Mahavir Marg, Jaipur-302 001.
242. Consumers Association, Kamlesh Villa, Post Office St, Falna 306 116.
243. Consumers Service Society, Mani Deep BahirRoad. Tont 304001
244. Consumer Protection & Research Council Jwala Premises, Tiwari Building, Mirza Ismail Road, Jaipur-302 001.
245. The Madras Provincial Consumer Association, No, 89, Big Street Madras-600 005.
246. Consumer Council of India (Central Unit), No. 67, Pidariyar Koil Street, Madras-600 001.
247. Consumer Protection Forum, No. 151, Radhakrishnan Salai, Mylapore, Madras-600 004.
248. Institute of Consumer Protection Studies, No. 4 Venketesa Naickan Street, Madras-600 001.
249. Consumer Action Group, No.l 44, Venkatakrishna Iyer St, Mandaveli, Madras.
250. SMN Consumer Protection Council, No. 22, 2nd Main Road, Kasturba Nagar Adayar, Madras-600 020.
251. Consumer Protection Council, Tamil Nadu, No. 2 Rana Building, Thillainagar, Trichy-18.
252. The Trichy District Consumer Council, No. 68, Pattabiram Pillai Street, P.B. No. 707, Tennur, Trichy-17.
253. Citizens Forum, 6-A, Basdhyakaralu Road, East RS. Puram, Coimbatore 2
254. Citizens Voice Club; Coimbatore Consumer Council, P.B. No. 4606, Coimbatore-23.
255. Coimbatore District Consumer Protection Forum, No.58, Geetar Hall Road, Coimbatore-18.
256. Tamilnadu Consumer Walfare Council, No. 1/38, Housing Unit, Tanjore.
257. Tamilnadu Consumer Welfare Council, Mannargudi Branch, Taluk Office Road, Mannargudi.
258. Tamilnadu Consumer Council, No, 10, Lakshmi Colony, Eswari Nagar Tanjore-7.
259. Civil & Consumer Welfare & General Services, Society of South Arcot, No, 30, Rajaji Street, South Arcot Distt, Tindivanam.
260. The Tamilnadu Consumers' Organisation, 34, Krishnagar Road (North Arcot Disst.) Tirupathur.
261. Consumer Council of India, Salem Branch, New Vanniar St. Koundanpatty, Edapadi Village, Salem.
262. Consumer Awareness Forum, No. 9/160, D. East Main Road, Mettur Dam-636 401. Salem.
263. Pudukottai District Consumers' Association, No. 47, Alangudi Road, Usilangulam, Pudukottai Distt.

264. Consumers' Council No, 25, Gokale Hall Street, Sivagangi, P.M. Distt.
265. District Consumers' Council, No. 6, Sinthamil Nagar, Bose Nagar (P.O.), Sivaganga-624 561, Pasumpon Distt.
266. Kannayakumari District Consumer Protection Cell, No. 95, Big Street, Vadiveswaram, Nagercoil 2, Kanyakumari Distt.
267. Kamarajar District Consumer No, 37, Railway Feeder Road, Rajapalayam, Kamarajar Distt.
268. Madurai District Public Welfare and Civil Rights Association, No. 44, Sathyasamoorthy Main Road, Meenabapuram, Madurai Distt. Madurai-2.
269. Consumer Rights Protection Council, 57, American College Building, Madurai-2.
270. Consumer Protection Cell, Periyar District, No. 198, Cutchery Street, Erode.
271. Consumer Protection Association, No. 643, Gandhiji Road, Thisainovilai, Radhapuram Taluk, T.N. Velli Distt.
272. Consumer Protection Association, 29, Central Road, Agartala-799 001.
273. Consumer Protection Organisation, Bhattacharya Villa, Siddhi Asharam, Agartala-799 003.
274. Dakshinachai Consumer Council, Robertsgunj, Mirjapur-231 216.
275. Akhil Bharatiya Grahak Panchayat, 87, B 5, Sarvodaya Nagar, Allahabad.
276. Consumer Protection Council, 848, Shiv Puri, Rly. Road, Hapur.
277. All India Consumer Welfare Society, C-1491, Rajaji Puram Lucknow-226 017.
278. Upbhokta Parishad, Gyan Lok, Hapur, Distt. Ghaziabad.
279. Consumer Forum, Khushalnagar, Station Road, Moradabad-244 001.
280. Mahila Upbhokta Sangathan, C-1613, Talkatora Avas, Vikas Colony, Lucknow-226017.
281. Indian National Consumers' Federation, H.O. 124 644. Block-B, Asha Ram Misra Bhawan, Kanpur-208 006.
282. All India Consumers Council, 75, Rajput Road, Dehradun-248 001.
283. Mahila Upbhokta Parishad, Himdeep, Radhapuri, Hapur-245 101.
284. Upbhokta Manch, 136 Jawahar Ganj, Hapur-245 101.
285. Mahila Kalyankaree Upbhokta Samiti, 969, Bagh Jankidas Prem Puri Road, Muzzaffar Nagar.
286. Consumers' Action Forum, 5/1, Red Cross Place, Calcutta-700 062.
287. Consumer Protection Centre, 24-B, Dr. Rajendra Road, Calcutta-700 020.
288. Consumers Unity and Trust Society, 3-B, Camac Street, Calcutta-16.
289. Citizen's Alliance Council for PM's 20-Point Programme, Rajendra Bhawan, P.O. Junglighat, Port Blair.
290. Pradesh Consumer Council, Andaman & Nicobar Islands, Port Blair.
291. The Youth Co-ordinator, Nehru Yuvak Kendra, Port Blair.
292. Consumers Forum, Kothi No.99, Sector 8A, Chandigarh-160 008.
293. Consumers Welfare Association (M.R.), 3341, Sector 21D, Chandigarh.
294. Consumer Welfare Association of India, 1116, 2nd Floor, Sector 22B, Chandigarh.
295. Mahila Dakshata Samiti, B-I6B, East of Kailash, Delhi-110 048.
296. Indian Federation of Consumer Organisations, 213, Jor Bagh, New Delhi-110 003.
297. War Widows Association, C/o. Sahheed Bhavan, 18/1, Jeet Singh Marg Institutional Area, New Delhi.

298. Guild of Services, 166A, Sainik Farms, Khanpur, New Delhi.
299. Consumer Service Society, 148, Jor Bagh, New Delhi-110 003.
300. Consumer Federation of India, XZ/K-17, New Mahavir Nagar, New Delhi-110 018,
301. Pragatisheel Mahila Samiti, Road No, 12, Kothi No. 28, Punjabi Bagh (West), Near Ring Road, New Delhi.
302. Voice, 108, Golf Lines, New Delhi -110 003.
303. Common Cause, C-381, Defence Colony, New Delhi-24.
304. Consumers Forum, B-24, Maharani Bagh, New Delhi-65.
305. Society for Civic Rights, J-13, Prasad Nagar, New Delhi-110 005.
306. Binty, B-7/55, 2nd Floor, DDA Flats, Safdarjung Enclave, New Delhi-110 029.
307. All India Women's Conference, 6, Bhagwan Dass Road, New Delhi-110 01.
308. Sidhartha Ladies Welfare Association, 135, Sidharth Enclave, New Delhi.
309. Upbhokta Seva Samiti, Block C2-A, Flat No. 265-A, Janakpuri, New Delhi.
310. All India Consumer Council, 15, Lyenkuttypalayam, Pondicherry-605 001.
311. The Pondicherry Consumer Welfare Association, 9, Big Rue Sufferon, Pondicherry-605 001.
312. Citizens Council, 77, Calve Subbaraya Chetty Street, Pondicherry.
313. Voice of Consumer, 2/47, Cuddalore Road, Mudaliarpet, Pondicherry-605 004.
314. Kurumbhapet Citizen Council, No. 17, Kurumbhapet Rural Housing Complex, Lyenkuttypalayam, Pondicherry.

APPENDIX IX

List of Major NGOs Working for Consumer Rights

Non-Governmental Consumer Organizations are non-profit, non-political (in most cases), non-regulatory, independent advocacy groups promoting consumerism in India. Although they lack statutory powers, they form a critical support network for you when you are a victim of corporate malpractice and/or deceit. Imagining you alone against a corporate powerhouse with 50,000 employees, 50 lawyers, and ₹ 500 Crores at their disposal isn't exactly a comforting thought. With consumer organizations to assist, you don't have to worry; you are not alone in your fight for justice... you have the support of powerful and determined social organizations that can organize protest rallies against corporate entities (no matter how powerful they are), or lobby the government or other statutory agencies to take notice of your grievance.

Consumer organizations improve your awareness of your consumer rights and advice you on the legal recourse you can take when your consumer rights are violated. This provides you information about the salient consumer protection and advocacy groups in India today.

1. Consumer Coordination Council (CCC)

Established in 1993 under the Societies Registration Act, 1860, Consumer Coordination Council (CCC) has been a stalwart proponent of good governance. In 1996, CCC launched a national campaign on citizens' charter to implement transparency, accountability, standards of service and a public grievance redressal system at the government level. CCC has made notable achievements in influencing the making of laws, governmental policy decisions, and providing administrative infrastructure for protecting consumer interest. It also serves as an umbrella organization for all other consumer NGOs in India.

Contact

Phone: +91 9426201611
Fax: +91 120 240 4273
Address: Consumer Coordination Council (CCC) NITS Complex A 20-21, Sector 62
Noida, Uttar Pradesh 201 307
Website: www.cccindia.net
Email: cccdel@del3.vsnl.net.in

2. Consumer Guidance Society of India

Consumer Guidance Society of India (CGSI) was founded in 1966 to eliminate all possible forms of consumer exploitation. It is one of the oldest consumer organizations in the country and has been instrumental in lobbying the government to pass a Consumer Protection Act. It has been a member of Consumers International for several years and 70% of the consumer complaints received by it have been resolved. CGSI has been instrumental in promoting consumerism by publishing its flagship monthly periodical "Keemat", performing product testing, providing consumer education at the grass root level such as schools, and giving legal guidance to consumers with grievances. It won the national award for consumer protection in 1991 for its long, dedicated and effective services to consumers.

Contact

Phone: +91 22 2262 1612
Fax: +91 22 2265 9715
Address: Consumer Guidance Society of India Block 'J', Mahapalika Marg Mumbai, Maharashtra 400 001
Website: http://www.cgsiindia.org
Email: cgsibom@mtnl.net.in

3. Citizen Consumer and Civic Action Group

Established on October 7, 1985, Citizen Consumer and Civic Action Group (CAG) has grown out to be one of the country's leading consumer advocacy groups. Instrumental in running campaigns for greater access to information, improved functioning of public utilities, greater transparency and accountability in governmental and private sector functioning, and protection of our open spaces and natural environment, CAG plays a vital role in the growth of consumerism in our country. CAG specializes in attending issues that affect the common man's life such as lack of hygiene, pollution of our natural resources, inaccessible healthcare facilities, corruption and lack of accountability for the government revenue from tax sources. CAG has been a member of Consumers International since 1990.

Contact

Phone: +91 44 2446 0387
Fax: +91 44 2491 4358
Address: Citizen Consumer and Civic Action Group 9/5, II Street, Padmanabha Nagar, Adyar Chennai, Tamil Nadu 600 020
Website: http://www.cag.org.in
Email: contact@cag.org.in

4. Association for Consumers Action on Safety and Health

Association for Consumers Action on Safety and Health (ACASH) is a consumer organization that focuses on health-related consumer issues. It has programs aimed at the general public promoting consumer rights and overall dispersion of information regarding consumer safety. Founded by a group of doctors, lawyers and other eminent personalities, ACASH today helps consumers in India through education & awareness, training, developing IEC (Information, Education and Communication) material, networking, advocacy and lobbying and follow-up action. A member of Consumers International since 1990, ACASH is also a member of Globalink, International Network of Women Against Tobacco (INWAT), International Baby Food Action Network (IBFAN), International Lactation Consultant Association (ILCA), World Alliance for Breastfeeding Action (WABA), Health Action International (HAI), Breastfeeding Promotion Network of India (BPNI), All India Drug Action Network (AIDAN), Bureau of Indian Standards (BIS) and Voluntary Health Association of India (VHAI).

Contact

Phone: +91 22 2388 6556/2388 7354
Fax: +91 22 2388 7340
Address: Association for Consumers Action on Safety and Health Lawyers Chambers, Room #21, R S Sapre Marg Mumbai, Maharashtra 400 002
Website: http://www.acash.org
Email: acashorg@vsnl.com

5. Consumer Education and Research Centre

Consumer Education and Research Centre (CERC) protects consumer interest in India through consumer research, campaigns through media, creation/monitoring/ enforcement of effective consumer laws, consumer advocacy and information dissemination. An apolitical outfit, CERC has research facilities recognized by the Indian government, and the United Nations has approved CERC as an NGO. CERC's mission includes environmental protection, creating transparency and accountability in the public and private enterprises and agencies in our country, resolving individual consumer complaints, ensuring consumer safety through product research, consumer education, awareness campaigns and product test results dissemination.

Contact

Phone: +91 79 2748 9945/2748 9946/2745 0528/2743 8752/2743 8753/2743 8754
Fax: +91 79 2748 9947
Address: Consumer Education and Research Centre 'Suraksha Sankool', Thaltej, Sarkhej-Gandhinagar Highway Ahmedabad, Gujarat 380 054
Website: http://www.cercindia.org
Email: cerc@cercindia.org

6. Consumer Protection Council

Not to be confused with the governmental bodies established as per the Consumer Protection Act, 1986, the Consumer Protection Council (CPC) is a consumer organization that is non-affiliated to any statutory agency. Instituted in Ahmedabad, the CPC has been instrumental in undertaking consumer issues such as consumer safety, traffic safety and pedestrian safety. It has effectively and successfully pursued legal battles against governmental agencies when they neglect or fail to carry out their duties to the tax payers. CPC has been a member of Consumers International since 1986.

Contact

Phone: +91 79 2754 1472
Fax: +91 79 2754 2786
Address: Consumer Protection Council 501/B, 5th Floor, 'SHAILY', Opp. Loha Bhavan B/h. Old Gujarat High Court, Navrangpura Ahmedabad, Gujarat 380 009
Website: None
Email: cpc_ahd@yahoo.co.in

7. Consumer Unity and Trust Society

Consumer Unity and Trust Society (CUTS) originated from a rural background in Rajasthan. It operates five program centers in India, an advocacy center in New Delhi, and resource centers in several international locations. CUTS's consumer work is focused on consumer protection and consumer safety. With about 20,000 square feet office space, 140 employees, and affiliation to/recognition from major national and international consumer agencies, CUTS is truly equipped to be the champion of consumer causes in our country. It publishes a monthly 'Gram Gadar' which has been effective in ensuring justice for oppressed social masses. CUTS has been a member of Consumers International since 1990.

Contact

Phone: +91 141 228 2821
Fax: +91 141 228 2485
Address: Consumer Unity and Trust Society D-217, Bhaskar Marg, Bani Park Jaipur, Rajasthan 302 016
Website: http://www.cuts-international.org
Email: cuts@cuts.org

8. Consumers Association of India

Consumers Association of India (CAI) was established on the world consumer rights day to be a powerful lobby for the consumer. It has successfully and determinately taken up the mission to spread awareness among consumers, educate them about their responsibilities and rights and to ensure that the consumers' voices can be heard. In the past six years, CAI has successfully settled over 98% of the 7500 complaints it has received through arbitration. For the remaining 2% CAI has supported the consumer in pursuing the complaint through the Indian legal system. CAI has been a member of Consumers International since 2003.

Contact

Phone: +91 44 2449 4576
Fax: +91 44 2449 4578
Address: Consumer Association of India 3/242, Rajendra Garden, Vettuvankeni Chennai, Tamil Nadu 600 041
Website: http://www.cai-india.org
Email: cai.india1@gmail.com

9. Consumers' Forum

Consumers' Forum is one the consumer organizations that existed in India long before the Consumer Protection Act, 1986 was passed. The mission of the organization, at its start, was to promote consumerism by making aware, training and educating the consumers on their rights. This was particularly necessary when there were no stalwart laws in our country to protect the consumers. The forum provides free advice to consumers, conducts brain storming sessions on matters related to consumer protection and ensures the representation of consumers in national, state and district level consumer courts and legally mandated consumer protection councils. Consumer Forum has been a member of Consumers International since 1996.

Contact

Phone: +91 11 2588 7833
Fax: +91 11 4248 8331
Address: Consumers' Forum 12/25 Ground Floor, West Patel Nagar, Delhi 110008
Website: http://www.consumer.org.in
Email: Not available

10. Mumbai Grahak Panchayat

Mumbai Grahak Panchayat (MGP), or Bombay Consumer Forum, started as an agitation against the increase of consumer prices near festival season for fair and free distribution of consumer goods. The distribution system that flourished was registered under the Indian Societies Registration Act, 1960 and Indian Public Trust Act, 1950 in the name of MGP. MGP promotes consumerism by bringing the consumer to the forefront of the logistics and supply chain of consumer goods as decision-makers, executors and monitors. MGP's primary objectives include organizing the consumers for common causes, educating them and protecting consumer interest through legal and other means.

Contact

Phone: +91 22 2628 1832/1839
Fax: +91 22 2625 0916
Address: Mumbai Grahak Panchayat Grahak Bhavan, Sant Dnyaneshwar Marg Road Behind Cooper Hospital, JVPD Market, Vile Parle (West) Mumbai, Maharashtra 400 056
Website: Not available
Email: mgpanchayat@hotmail.com

11. VOICE Society

Voluntary Organization in Interest of Consumer Education (VOICE) strives to be the voice of and for the consumer that the governments and other statutory/regulatory bodies of the country seldom hear. The primary focus of this NGO is to establish informed consumers in India. Information dispersed to consumers through VOICE includes corporate negligence/misconduct on issues such as consumer safety or customer satisfaction, your rights as a consumer to get value for your money, and the recourse that can be taken if your consumer rights are defied. Founded by students and teachers of the University of Delhi in 1983, it was registered as charitable public trust in 1986, the same year the Consumer Protection Act came into being.

Contact

Phone: +91 11 2437 9078/79/80
Fax: +91 11 2437 9081
Address: VOICE Society 441, Jangpura, Bhogal, Mathura Road, Delhi 110 014
Website: http://www.consumer-voice.org
Email: legal@consumer-voice.org

12. Grahak Shakti

Grahak Shakti works towards creating consumer awareness by organizing various programs, street plays and on shows such as 'Hello Geleyere'. The organization has undertaken a number of surveys like the one on spurious drugs in coordination with the Drugs Control Department-Government of India. Its campaign on credit cards and effective liaison with the regulator was an effective way to warn the erring bankers to conduct business ethically. It also participated in joint raids in coordination with the Department of Legal Metrology and some oil companies to check malpractices related to weights and measurement, adulteration and pilferage.

Contact

Phone: +91 9448366360
Fax: +91 8023145998
Address: Grahak Shakti, No. 57,18th Cross, 4th Main Chitrakoot Apartment, Flat No. 19, Malleswaram, Bangalore, Karnataka-560055
Website: http://www.grahakshakti.org
Email: grahakshakti@gmail.com

APPENDIX X

Model Forms

1. CONSUMER COMPLAINT IN CONSUMER FORUM

Consumer Complaint

Consumer Complaint, where value of the goods or services and compensation exceeds Rupees One Crore, can be filed with the Registry of this Commission within a period of Two Years from the date on which the cause of action has arisen. Petition can be filled on all working days between 10.00 A.M. to 4.30 P.M. at (Give address of designated Forum of your City). Consumer Complaint should be signed by the complainant and supported by an affidavit with four copies, and one set each for Opposite Parties. The Consumer Complaint along with all the copies should be paginated and duly indexed in the following *seriatim:*

Consumer Complaint (CC) — 21(*a*)(*i*)

1. Index
2. List of Dates
3. Memo of Parties
4. Complaint with affidavit
5. Limitation, if any (2 years from cause of action)
6. Supporting documents in favour of complaint *e.g.* Receipt, voucher, etc.
7. Fee for ₹ 5,000 for making Consumer Complaint [Demand Draft in the name of "The Registrar, (Give address of designated Forum of your City)"]

Notes:

1. The documents shall be filed in English language only or translated copy of any other language.
2. If the documents are not filed in order in the format mentioned above the same will be returned to the parties at the counter itself without acknowledgement and will only be registered after removing the defects.
3. After admission hearing, any documents if filed in a case the same has to be served on the other side and be filed with proof of service, well in advance of two days earlier from the date of hearing.
4. Henceforth, the review petition/application for recalling of order will be listed before the bench by way of circulation in chambers.
5. No. of copies to be filed in the Commission 1+3 sets + Number of Opposite Parties. (With File cover)

No Strict or complex drafting is required to file a complaint under the Act. It should be in such form that the Court is able to comprehend the facts and the grievance suffered by the complainant and relief which is claimed and ought to be granted thereunder. However in order to make it systematic and befitting the decorum of the Court the following format may be used:

2. COMPLAINT OR FIRST APPEAL IN CONSUMER FORUM

FIRST APPEAL

First Appeal as provided under section 19 of the Consumer Protection Act, 1986 can be filed with the Registry of this Commission on all working days between 10.00 A.M. to 4.30 P.M. at (Give address of designated Forum of your City). First Appeal must be supported by an affidavit along with Four copies for the Commission, and One set for each Respondent. Paper books of First Appeal and all the copies should be paginated and duly indexed in the following *seriatim:*—

3. COMPLAINT OR FIRST APPEAL (FA) – 19

1. Index
2. List of Dates
3. Memo of Parties
4. Appeal with affidavit
5. Stay Application with affidavit, if required
6. Limitation, if any (Within 30 days of receipt of order)
7. Certified copy of order of State Commission
8. Any other documents required
9. Demand Draft (in the name of "The Registrar, NCDRC, New Delhi")

Notes:

1. The documents shall be filed in English language only or translated copy of any other language.
2. If the documents are not filed in order in the format mentioned above the same will be returned to the parties at the counter itself without acknowledgement and will only be registered after removing the defects.
3. After admission hearing, any documents if filed in a case the same has to be served on the other side and be filed with proof of service, well in advance of two days earlier from the date of hearing.
4. Henceforth, the review petition/application for recalling of order will be listed before the bench by way of circulation in chambers.
5. No. of copies to be filed in the Commission 1+3 sets + Number of Opposite Parties. (With File cover).

4. MODEL FORM 'A' THE COMPLAINT

BEFORE THE HON'BLE DISTRICT CONSUMER DISPUTES REDRESSAL FORUM AT..

OR BEFORE THE HON'BLE STATE CONSUMER DISPUTES REDRESSAL COMMISSION AT..

OR

BERORE THE HON'BLE NATIONAL CONSUMER DISPUTES REDRESSAL COMMISSION AT NEW DELHI

IN RE: COMPLAINT NO........OF 200..............

IN THE MATTER OF

(FULL NAME)

(DESCRIPTION)

(COMPLETE ADDRESS)

............COMPLAINANT

CONSUMER PROTECTION

VERSUS

FULL NAME

(DESCRIPTION)

(COMPLETE ADDRESS)

.............OPPOSITE PARTY/PARTIES

COMPLAINT UNDER SECTION 11(*i*) SECTION 17/SECTION 21 OF THE CONSUMER PROTECTION ACT, 1986.

RESPECTFULLY SHOWETH:

(1) INTRODUCTION................................

(In this opening paragraph the complainant should give his introduction as well as that of the opposite party/parties.

(2) TRANSACTION................................

(In this paragraph complainant should describe the transaction complained of *i.e.* particulars and details of goods/services availed; items of goods/kind and nature of service; date of purchase of goods/availing of service; amount paid as price/consideration, full or in part towards the goods/service; Photocopies of the bill/cash memo/voucher or receipt should be attached and properly marked as annexure -AB.C. and so forth or l, 2, 3, and so forth.)

(3) DEFECT/DEFICIENCY..........................

(In this paragraph complainant should explain the grievance *i.e.* whether the loss or damage has been caused by some unfair trade practice or there is some defect in the goods or there has been deficiency in service or the trader has charged excessive price for the goods. One should elucidate the nature of unfair trade practice adopted by the trader *i.e.* relating to the quality of goods/service; sponsorship; warranty or guarantee for such period promised. The nature and extent of defects in goods should be explained and so should be the deficiency in service. In case of excessive price one should specify the details of actual price fixed by or under any law for the time being in force or as set out on goods and their packing *vis-a-vis* the price charged by the trader. You should narrate your grievance and rest assured it is being' read/heard by compassionate and pragmatic judges. Photocopies of relevant documents must be attached.)

(4) RECTIFICATION................................

(In this paragraph complainant should highlight what attempts were made by him to set things right *i.e.* personal visits or negotiations; communication in writing if any; whether any legal notice was got served and/or whether has approached any other agency for redressal like M.R.T.P. Commission Civil or Criminal Court of competent jurisdiction; the stage of its proceedings its outcome, if any, along with copies (certified preferably) of such proceedings. The nature of response which you got from the trader when irregularities were brought to his notice, should be disclosed here).

(5) OTHER PROVISIONS:

(In this paragraph, reference may be made to any other law or rules or regulations of particular procedure which is applicable to the case and/or which has been violated by the trader and Consumer's rights under the same. There are incidental statutory obligations, which traders must fulfill and in case of their failure to do so the case is *prima facie* made out and Forum would take cognizance).

(6) EVIDENCE................................

(In this paragraph complainant should give details of documents and/or witnesses he will rely upon to substantiate his case. The documents attached as Annexures as stated above may be incorporated in a proper list and a list of witnesses (if any) may be filed similarly). The annexure should be attested as "True Copy'.

(7) JURISDICTION............................

(In this paragraph complainant should liquidate the claim in the complaint *i.e.* up to 1 lac; 1 lac to 10 lacs: or above and set out the pecuniary jurisdiction of the Forum/State Commission/National Commission, as the case may be. The territorial jurisdiction should be highlighted to obviate any formal objection),

(8) LIMITATION

That the present complaint is being filed within the period prescribed under, Section 24A of the Act.

(9) RELIEF CLAIMED........................

(In this paragraph complainant should describe the nature of relief he wants to claim *i.e.* for removal of defects in goods or deficiency in service; replacement with new goods; return of the price or charges, etc. paid and/or compensation on account of financial loss or injury or detriment to his interest occasioned by negligence of the opposite party and elucidate how you have calculated the amount of compensation claimed).

(10) PRAYER CLAUSE...........................

It is therefore, most respectfully, prayed that this Hon'ble Forum/Commission may kindly be pleased to..

(Details of relief's which complainants want the Court to grant)

Complainant

Place.................

Date..................

through.......................

(ADVOCATE OR CONSUMER ASSOCIATION, ETC.)

VERIFICATION

I................., the complainant above named, do hereby solemnly verify that the contents of my above complaint are true and correct to my knowledge, no part of it is false and nothing material has been concealed therein.

Verified this..day of..

200............... at..

Complainant

Note.—Although it is not compulsory, complainant may file an affidavit in support of the complaint, which adds to the truth and veracity of allegations and gives credibility to the cause. It need not be a Stamp paper but one should get it attested from an Oath Commissioner appointed by a High Court. The format is just as simple.

OR USE THE FOLLOWING FORMAT

COMPLAINT FORM

(Form for complaint under the Consumer Protection Act, 1986)

In the complaint case no...

....

Before the Hon'ble District Forum ....

....

or Before the State Commission..

or Before the National Commission ....

Complaint

No...of...

....

In the matter of ....

....

Name & address of complainant/complainant..

versus

Name & address of opposite party/parties..

I/we, the above named complainant/complainants respectfully state before the Hon'ble Forum/Commission the complaint as follows:

It is therefore prayed —

(*i*) That opposite party be directed to refund the amount paid by the complainant to the tune of ₹...

(*ii*) Complainant may please be compensated to the tune of ₹.......................... for the mental agony and harassment caused to him/her in the due course

(*iii*) Cost of litigation may also be awarded suitably.

....

Signature of Complainant

Place: ....

Date:...............................

(Name of Complainant)

VERIFICATION

I .... S/o .... aged .... the above named complainant do hereby solemnly declare that the particulars stated above are true to the best of my knowledge and belief and nothing has been concealed therein. I further certify that Annexures I,II and III appealed to the complaint are the true copies of original documents.

Verified at......................................this day of.......................................

(*a*) .... Annexure I **Signature of Complainant**

(*b*) .... Annexure II

(*c*) .... Annexure III **(Name of the Complainant/Deponent)**

AFFIDAVITS

Supporting the application and the complaint with an affidavit gives an added strength to the truth and veracity of averments made in the complaint.

Even otherwise, the evidence is recorded in the Redressal Agencies under the Act mostly by affidavits. Under the Code of Civil Procedure, 1908, affidavits are governed by Order XIX as under.

(1) Power to order any point to be proved by affidavit

Any Court may at any time for sufficient reason, order that any particular fact or facts may be proved by affidavit, or that the affidavit of any witness may be read at the hearing on such conditions as the Court thinks reasonable:

Provided that where it appears to the Court that either party *bona fide* desired the production of a witness for cross-examination and that such witness can be produced, an order shall not be made authorizing the evidence of such witness to be given by affidavit.

(2) Power to order attendance of deponent for cross examination

(*a*) Upon any application evidence may be given by affidavit but the Court may, at the instance of either Party, Order the attendance for cross-examination of the deponent.

(*b*) Such attendance shall be in Court unless the deponent is exempted from personal appearance in Court, or the Court otherwise directs.

(*c*) Matters to which affidavit shall be confined —

(*i*) Affidavit shall be confined to such facts as the deponent is able of his own knowledge to prove, except on interlocutory applications on which statements of his belief may be admitted provided that the grounds thereof are stated.

(*ii*) The costs of every affidavit which shall unnecessarily set forth matters of hearsay or argumentative matter, or copies of extracts from documents, shall (unless the Court otherwise directs) be paid by the party filing the same.

An affidavit is a declaration as to facts made in writing and sworn before a person having authority to administer an oath like Oath Commissioner, Notaries, Magistrates, etc. The solemn affirmation is essential for its validity. It should also correctly state, description and true place of abode of the deponent. Under the rules of practice framed by the High Courts in India, every affidavit should be drawn up in the first person and divided into paragraphs consecutively numbered, each paragraph dealing with a specific portion of the subject as nearly as may be. It should contain only facts and not inferences. The affidavits should be properly verified. The opposite party can file a counter affidavit for the immediate purpose of being used or filed in the court is exempt from stamp duty. Even where allegations in your affidavit are stated to be correct to the best of his/her knowledge, the nature and source of the knowledge must be disclosed. An affidavit is defective if the deponent does not say which part is based on information and which on belief or if he does not state the grounds of his belief.

Remember, an affidavit is to substantiate one's case, not to abuse its credibility. If an affidavit contains scandalous and irrelevant allegations it may be ordered to be taken off the file or the particular passage may be expunged. And not only this the swearing to a false affidavit is an offence of perjury under section 91 of the Indian Penal Code, which is certainly a grave and serious matter and no Court will take any lenient view of such an event.

5. MODEL FORM 'B'-AFFIDAVIT IN SUPPORT OF THE COMPLAINT

BEFORE THE HON'BLE..

IN RE; COMPLAINT NO..................................OF 20.............

IN THE MATTER OF:

.... COMPLAINANT

VERSUS

..................................OPPOSITE PARTY

AFFIDAVIT

Affidavit of Sh..S/o.Sh.. aged .... years, resident of..I, the above, named deponent do hereby solemnly affirm and declare as under:

(1) That I am complainant in the above case, thoroughly conversant with the facts and circumstances of the present case and am competent to swear this affidavit.

(2) That the facts contained in my accompanying complaint, the contents of which have not been repeated herein for the sake of brevity may be read as an integral part of this affidavit and are true and correct to my knowledge.

Deponent

VERIFICATION

I, the above named deponent do hereby solemnly verify that the contents of my above affidavit are true and correct to my knowledge, no part of it is false and nothing material has been concealed therein.

Verified this...day of............. 20...............at..............

Deponent

6. MODEL FORM 'C-APPEAL

An appeal may be preferred in the following format:

BEFORE THE HON'BLE

....CONSUMER

DISPUTES REDRESSAL COMMISSION

AT..

(APPELLATE JURISDICTION)

IN RE; MEMORANDUM OF APPEAL NO.

.................................Of 20...................

IN THE MATTER OF:

....

....

....APPEALLANT(S)

VERSUS

....RESPONDENT(S)

Appeal under section 15/section 19 of the Consumer Protection Act, 1986 against the order date.................................. passed by the district consumer disputes redressal forum at../state consumer disputes redressal commmission at................................in complaint case no...................................of 20..................... respectfully showeth:

(1) That the appellant above, named has preferred this appeal against the order of the.................................Forum/Commission passed in Complaint Case No.................of 20.........on which was received by appellant on......................

(2) FACTS

(In this paragraph details of the case should be given with a brief note of the proceedings and the order of the District Forum/State Commission, as the case may be).

(3) That the impugned order dated......passed by the District Forum/State Commission aforesaid is liable to be quashed/set aside/modified, *inter alia*, on the following:

(3) GROUNDS:

(*i*) ....

(*ii*) ....

(*iii*) ....etc.

(In this paragraph appellant should elucidate the grounds both factual and legal on the basis of which he has challenged the impugned order and which are likely to be accepted in the appeal;.

(4) That the appellant has not preferred any other appeal against the impugned order.

(5) That the present appeal is being filed within the time prescribed by Section 15/Section 19 of the Act.

(In case the appeal is being filed beyond limitation then it should be accompanied an application for condonation of such delay setting out therein the sufficient cause which has occasioned delay to the satisfaction of the court. It should be supported by an affidavit.)

(6) Prayer.................

It is, therefore, most respectfully prayed that this Hon'ble Commission may kindly be pleased to allow the present appeal and set aside/quash' modify the impugned order of the District Forum/State Commission.

Place................. Appellant

Date.................

Through.................

(ADVOCATE)

or.......................

The appeal should be supported by an affidavit (for form see complaint) and certified copy of the order appealed against. You should also file such documents as would substantiate your case in a listed form).

FORM OF NOTICE

There is no prescribed form of notice in Act. It is not even mandatory to serve the other party with a notice. However it is advisable to serve the opposite party with a notice before filing a complaint. Naturally, in each and every case one does not enter into written correspondence with the opposite party. In such a situation one final intimation of one's intention to proceed against him in a Court of law would serve the purpose. In such a notice one should describe the transaction, the grievance, previous attempts to negotiate, previous correspondence, if any, and the passive attitude on the part of the other party. Contents of the notice should be such that it gives an idea to the opposite party of what is in store from him in the Court. A properly and methodically drafted notice would not only help the complainant prepare well the complete but also ensure that there is consistory in the allegations. In other words notice and complaint should be commensurate with each other, the later following the former. Liquidate the relief/claim/compensation to an exact precision so that the opposite party does not have a chance to point out any avoidable disparity between the contentions of the notice and the complaint. Send the notice under Regd. Cover A.D. as well as under Postal Certificate. Retain the reply, if any received and produce it in the documents of reliance. If there is any ambiguity or Consumers feel some more force should be added to the notice it may be sent through a lawyer. If the case is *prima facie* indisputable then may be the opposite party will settle the claim immediately. That may save valuable time and expenses. Remember, principles of natural justice, equity and good conscience postulate that nobody should be condemned unheard *i.e.* a "show cause" is imperative. Serving the opposite party with a notice will give the consumer a *bona fide* character before the Court and also help the consumer as a pre-filing exercise. So "call upon him to call on you or else you will call the law to haul him up."

The notice may be prepared in the style given below, and sent by registered acknowledgement-due post, courier, fax.. The complainant should retain the proof of posting.

One may use the following format and evolve one's own one using your own writing skills.

7. MODEL FORM 'D'-NOTICE BEFORE FILING THE COMPLAINT

Name and address ....

(of the trader, firm, company, etc.)

....

(Complete Address)

IN RE: {Mention the goods/services complained of giving details)

....

Dear Sir,

This is to bring to your kind notice that I had purchased .... from your .... for a consideration of ₹ .... paid in cash *vide* your cash memo/Receipt/Invoice No...or through cheque No.............dated...........drawn on.................... &................bank for a sum of ₹..................).

The said goods are suffering from the following defects:

(*i*) ....

(*ii*) ...., etc.

I have reported the above matter to you several times {give reference of earlier letters, if any) but despite all my pleadings you have not made good the defect in the goods {or deficiency in services) which is indeed regrettable and highly unbusiness like. On account of your aforesaid dereliction of duty and failure and neglect to rectify the same I have suffered losses/incurred expenses..

(Give details)

which you are liable to compensate to me. You are hereby finally called upon to

(*i*) remove the said defects in the goods and/or

(*ii*) replace the goods with new goods and/or

(*iii*) return the price/charges paid

(*iv*) pay compensation for financial loss/injury/interest suffered due to your (give details)

in the sum of ₹............................. with interest @...........................% per annum within....days of the receipt of this notice failing which I shall be constrained to initiate against you for redressal of my aforesaid grievances and recovery of the aforesaid amount such proceedings, both civil and criminal as are warranted by law, besides filing a complaint under the statutory provisions of the Consumer Protection Act, 1986 exclusively at your own risk, cost, responsibility and consequences which please note.

Sd

Place: ....

Date: ....

Name & Address................................

OR YOU MAY USE THE FOLLOWING FORMAT

Dated: dd/mm/yyyy

To,

The Managing Director/Nodal Officer/Manager,

Company Name,

Address of the Parent Company,

Sub: Notice Before Filing Consumer Complaint

Dear Sir,

1. Give details of your purchase of product or service (cash memo number and date).

2. Give information about the warranty or guarantee received by you at the time of purchase.

3. Give details of the deficiency in the product or service.

4. Give the problems you are facing due to this deficiency.

5. Give the details about your efforts to inform about this grievance in the past to which the party has not responded.

6. Give a time limit of at least 15 to 20 days to settle your grievance by asking for refund of full amount with suitable interest (18%), or replacement of the product along with suitable compensation, else you will file a complaint with the Consumer Forum as you are protected under the Consumer Protection Act of 1986.

7. Inform that the consumer complaint will be at his cost and expenses and you will seek compensation for the mental agony caused due to his deficiency in services.

Yours truly,

Your Name,

Your Address

REPLY TO THE COMPLAINT (WRITTEN STATEMENT)

The essential ingredients of a complaint as discussed hereinbefore bringing forward the grievance of a consumer. Now the opposite party may have a very good defence to the complaint, so one need not fear and express himself with out concealing any material facts or technical peculiarities. This is not only contesting a consumer dispute but also developing the law which is going to decide the fate of many a consumer and trader. Although each case has its own given set of facts, circumstances and the law laid down as on even date yet an attempt has been made to include certain general objections or defenses the whole or some of which may be applicable and incorporated in a written statement as under:

8. MODEL FORM 'E' — REPLY BY THE TRADER TO THE COMPLAINT

BERORE THE HONB'BLE.. THE CONSUMER DISPUTES FEDRESSAI, FORUM/COMMISSION AT......................................

IN RE: COMPLAINT NO......................................OF 20...............

IN THE MATTER OF

....COMPLAINANT

VERSUS

.... OPPOSITE PARTY

DATE OF HEARING......................................

WRITTEN STATEMENT ON BEHALF OF RESPONDENTS TO THE COMPLAINT OF THE COMPLAINANT

RESPECTFULLY SHOWETH:

Preliminary Objections:

1. That the present complaint wholly misconceived, groundless and unsustainable in law and is liable to be dismissed as such.
2. That this Hon'ble Court has no jurisdiction to entertain and adjudicate upon the dispute involved in the complaint inasmuch as it is not a consumer dispute and does not fall within the ambit of the provisions of the Consumer Protection Act, 1986, hereinafter called the said Act and is exclusively troubled by a Civil Court and as such the complaint is liable to be dismissed summarily on this score alone.
3. That the dispute raised by the complainant in the present complaint is manifestly outside the purview of the said Act and in any event, the Act is in addition to and not in derogation of the provisions of the .... Act. The proceedings initiated by the complainant under the Act are *non- est*, null and void and without jurisdiction.
4. That the definitions of 'Complainant', 'Complaint', 'Consumer Dispute' and 'Service', as defined in section 2(1) of the said Act do not cover the claims arising under the present dispute and that from the aforesaid definitions, the complainant is not 'consumer' and the controversy involved in the complaint is not a 'consumer dispute'.
5. That the present complaint is baseless and flagrant abuse of process of law to harass and blackmail the answering respondent.
6. That the complainant has no focus stand; to initiate the present proceedings.
7. That the complaint is bad for has non-joinder of necessary and proper party and is liable to be dismissed on this score alone.
8. That the complainant thus already filed a Civil Suit for...in a court of competent jurisdiction which is pending disposal in the Court of....and the present complaint has become infructuous.
9. That the present complaint is hopelessly barred by limitation.
10. That this Hon'ble Forum/Commission has no territorial/or pecuniary jurisdiction inasmuch as the amount involved in the subject-matter exceeds/is less than the limit prescribed by section 11D/Section 17(*a*)(*i*)/Section 21(*a*)(*i*) of the Act.
11. That the present complaint is frivolous and vexatious and liable to be dismissed under section 26 of the Act.
12. That the present complaint has not been verified in accordance with law.

ON MERITS:

In these paragraphs respondent must relay each and every allegations made and contention raised by the complainant, factual and legal as well. In case one should already made good the defect or deficiency, elucidate steps taken. One may have, *inter alia*, following good defence as well:

1. That the transaction entered between the parties to the above dispute is a commercial one and the complainant cannot claim any relief from this authority inasmuch as...
(Give details)

2. That the complainant had purchased the goods as a Seller/retailer/ distributor, etc. for consideration of resale and as such is barred from moving this Hon'ble Court for the alleged defect/deficiency, etc. inasmuch as ....
(Give details)

3. That the complainant has already availed the warranty period during which the answering respondent has repaired/replaced the goods in question. The complainant is thus legally stopped from enforcing this complaint or to take benefit of his own wrong.

4. That the present complaint is an exaggeration beyond proportion despite the fact that the complainant is himself responsible for delay and laches inasmuch as he has on several occasions changed his option for class of goods/type of allotment scheme of flats/model of vehicle, etc. ....
(Give details)

5. That the answering respondent is well within his rights to charge extra price for the subject-matter of the above dispute inasmuch as time was not the essence of delivery thereof. The complainant is liable to pay the increased price w.e.f................on account of escalation due to excise duty/budgetary provisions, etc. inasmuch as...
(Give details)

6. That the complainant has accepted the goods and/or service towards repair/replacement, etc. without protest and the present complaint is merely an after-thought.

7. That without prejudice the answering respondent as a gesture of goodwill is prepared to .... (give details of rectification, if any, which you can do in case of minor or tolerable problems to avoid harassment to consumer and litigation problems)...........

The allegations of defect/default/negligence and/or deficiency in service are wholly misconceived; groundless, false, untenable in law besides being extraneous and irrelevant having regard to the facts and circumstances of the matter under reference.

Prayer clause with all the submissions made therein is absolutely wrong and is emphatically denied complainant is not entitled to any relief whatsoever and is not entitled to claim and recover any thing from the answering respondents in the light of what is stated above. The complaint itself is not maintainable and is beyond the jurisdiction of this Hon'ble Court and is liable to be dismissed summarily on this score alone and more fully set out in the preliminary objections. It is prayed that the complaint may kindly be dismissed with costs.

Sd

Place:
(Opposite party)
Dated.

Through
(Advocate)

VERIFICATION

I..the abovenamed respondent do hereby verify that the contents of Paras..to.. of the written statement on merits are true and correct to my knowledge. While paras.......to..........of preliminary objections and.... to....of reply on merits are true to my information, belief and legal advice received by me and believed to be true while the last para is prayer to this Hon'ble Court.

Verified at....................this....................day of....................20...........

Sd

(Opposite party)

9. MODEL FORM 'F'-APPLICATION FOR CONDONATION OF DELAY

BEFORE THE HON'BLE..

IN RE: COMPLAINT NO....................OF 20............

IN THE MATTER OF:

....

.... COMPLAINANT

VERSUS

....

.... OPPOSITE PARTY

APPLICATION ON BEHALF OF THE COMPLAINANT UNDER SECTION 24A(2) OF THE CONSUMER PROTECTION ACT (AS AMENDED UPTO DATE)

RESPECTFULLY SHOWETH:

1. That the complainant abovenamed has filed the accompanying complaint the contents of which have not been repeated herein for the sake of brevity which may be read as an integral part of this application also.
2. That the complainant has a *bona fide* and *prima facie* case against the opposite party.
3. That the cause of action had arisen in favour of the complainant and against the opposite party on..............................but despite due diligence and prudence the present complaint could not be filed within two years therefrom as envisaged under section 24A(1) of the Act due to..........................

   (Here one may highlight the reason for the delay in filing of the complaint).
4. That the complainant had sufficient cause for not filing present complaint within limitation as stated above and there are just and sufficient grounds justifying and warranting the condonation of delay and deciding the present case on meets.
5. In view of the aforesaid facts and circumstances in order to meet ends of justice and to effectually adjudicate the present dispute, it is, therefore, most respectfully prayed that this Hon'ble Forum/Commission may kindly be pleased to:

   (*a*) Condone the delay in filing the present complaint and admit the same:

   (*b*) Issue notice to the opposite party and entertain and decide the complaint on merits.

Place..................................

Date...................................

Complainant

(A supportive affidavit may be attached)

10. MODEL FORM 'G' — EXECUTION APPLICATION

BEFORE THE HON'BLE.................................

IN RE: COMPLAINT NO..................................OF 20..........

IN THE MATTER:

..................................COMPLAINANT

VERSUS

..............................OPPOSITE PARTY

APPLICATION ON BEHALF OF THE COMPLAINANT FOR EXECUTION

RESPECTFULLY SHOWETH:

1. That *vide* orders dated................passed in complaint No.......of 20.....this Hon'ble Forum/Commission had been pleased to allow the complaint and in terms of the said orders the opposite party was to..................within a period of...............days.
2. That the registered head office of the respondent Company/voluntary residence and/or business/work place of the opposite party is situated at........................
3. That it would be just, proper and in the interest of justice if the aforesaid order is sent to the Hon'ble court of the.. at......................... within the local limits of whose jurisdiction the respondent's head office is situated opposite party resides or works for gain.

   It is prayed accordingly.

Place..................................

Date...................................

Complainant

11. MODEL FORM 'H' APPLICATION IN CASE OF NON-COMPLIANCE

BEFORE THE HON'BLE..

IN RE: COMPLAINT NO..................................OF 20.........

IN THE MATTER OF:

.....................................COMPLAINANT

VERSUS

..................................OPPOSITE PARTY

APPLICATION UNDER SECTION 27 OF THE CONSUMER PROTECTION ACT, 1986 (AS AMENDED UPTO DATE)

1. That *vide* orders dated..............passed in complaint No...........of 20.........this Hon'ble Forum/Commission had been pleased to allow the complaint and in terms of the said orders the opposite party was to... within a period of.................days.
2. That the respondents have flagrantly violated the said orders of this Hon'ble Forum/Commission inasmuch as they have not complied with the same. Wholly or in part, within the prescribed period of.....................days which expired on...........................In fact the respondents have not initiated any steps even in this regard.

3. That the respondents have committed an offence under section 27 of the said Act.

   It is, therefore, most respectfully prayed that the respondents be summoned and tried for having committed the aforesaid offence under section 27 of the Act and be punished accordingly. Any other order which this Hon'ble Forum/Commission may be pleased to grant may also be passed.

Place................

Date.................

Complainant

(Attach supportive affidavit. The above application can also lie against a complainant and necessary modifications can be carried out)

12. MODEL FORM 'I' APPLICATION FOR PRODUCTION OF DOCUMENTS

BEFORE HON'BLE...

IN RE; COMPLAINT NO...........OF 20..............

IN THE MATTER OF:

....

.... COMPLANANT

VERSUS

..............................OPPOSITE PARTY

APPLICATION ON BEHALF OF THE .... UNDER SECTION 13(4)(*ii*) OF THE CONSUMER PROTECTION ACT. 1986 (AS AMENDED UPTO DATE) READ WITH RULE 10(l)(*a*) OF THE CONSUMER PROTECTION RULES. 1987.

RESPECTFULLY SHOWETH:

1. That the present application has filed a detailed complaint/Written statement, the contents of which have not been repeated herein for the sake of brevity which may be read as an integral part of this application also.
2. That the original (description and nature of documents) which is a vital document in the present case is in the custody and possession of the......................................and needs elucidation before this Hon'ble Forum/Commission for the just and proper disposal of the present dispute.

   In view of the aforesaid facts and circumstances, in order to meet the ends of justice and to effectually adjudicate the present dispute it is, therefore, most respectfully prayed that this Hon'ble Forum/Commission may kindly be pleased to direct the..................................to place on record the original...

Place..................................

Date...................................

Applicant

13. MODEL FORM 'J' APPLICATION FOR SEIZURE OF DOCUMENT(S)

BEFORE HON'BLE...

IN RE: COMPLAINT NO............OF 20.....IN THE MATTER OF:

....

......................COMPLANANT

VERSUS

..................................OPPOSITE PARTY

APPLICATION ON BEHALF OF THE............UNDER SECTION 13(4)(*ii*) OF THE CONSUMER PROTECTION ACT, 1986 (AS AMENDED UPTO DATE) READ WITH RULES 10(2)(*a*) OF THE CONSUMER PROTECTION RULES, 1987.

RESPECTFULLY SHOWETH:

1. That the present applicant has filed a detailed complaint/written statement, the contents of which have not been repeated herein for the sake of brevity which may be read as an integral part of this application also.
2. That the original (description and nature of documents) which is a vital document in the present case is in the custody and possession of the..........and needs elucidation before this Hon'ble Forum/Commission for the just and proper disposal of the present dispute.
3. That the applicant apprehends that the respondents may destroy, mutilate, alter, falsify or tamper with the aforesaid document and the purpose of filing of the present case shall be defeated.
4. That the aforesaid documents are presently lying at the (place) situated at

It is, therefore, most respectfully prayed that this Hon'ble Forum/Commission may kindly be pleased to pass an order authorizing a competent officer to:

(*a*) enter the premises situated at..............and effect search for the aforesaid documents,

(*b*) seize the books, papers, documents, etc. as set out above.

Place..................................

Date..................................

Complainant/Respondent

(Attach supportive affidavit. An application can also lie for seizure of commodities and necessary modifications may be carried out.

14. MODEL FORM 'K'- APPLICATION FOR SEEKING PERMISSION TO FILE SINGLE COMPLAINT ON BEHALF OF VARIOUS CONSUMERS HAVING COMMON INTEREST

BEFORE HON'BLE...

IN RE; COMPLAINT NO..................................OF 20............

IN THE MATTER OF:

....

.... COMPLAINANTS

VERSUS

....

.........................OPPOSITE PARTY

APPLICATION UNDER SECTION 2(1)(B)(IV); SECTION 12(C); SECTION 13(6) READ WITH ORDER 1 RULE 8 SUB-RULE (1)(9) OF THE CODE CIVIL PROCEDURE, 1908.

RESPECTFULLY SHOWETH:

1. That the complainants abovenamed have filed the accompanying complaint die contents of which are not being repeated herein for the sake of brevity which may be read as integral part of this application also.

2. That the complainants above named have suffered financial loss/mental agony etc. on account of defect in (goods) purchased from/deficiency in services rendered by.......and the nature of goods/services and the grievance suffered is identical. In fact the evidence which the complainants crave leave to produce at an appropriate stage, is also identical. Accordingly the complainants have same interest in the above complaint.

In the light, of the aforesaid facts and circumstances in order to meet the ends of justice and to effectually adjudicate the present dispute it is, therefore, most respectfully prayed that this Hon'ble Forum/Commission may kindly be pleased to grant permission to complainants to institute and prosecute the present complaint through....................................for and on behalf of and which this Hon'ble Forum/Commission may deem fit and proper may also be passed.

Place....................................

Date....................................

Complainant

REVISION PETITION IN CONSUMER FORUM

REVISION PETITION

Revision Petition as provided under section 21(*b*) of the Consumer Protection Act, 1986 can be filed with the Registry of this Commission on all working days between 10.00 A.M. to 4.30 P.M. at (Give address of designated Forum of your City). Revision Petition must be supported by an affidavit along with Four copies for the Commission, and One set for each Respondent. Paper books of Revision Petition and all the copies should be paginated and duly indexed in the following seriatim:—

Revision Petition (RP) – 21(*b*)

1. Index
2. List of Dates
3. Memo of Parties
4. Revision Petition with affidavit
5. Stay Application with affidavit, if required
6. Limitation, if any (Within 90 days of the receipt of the order)
7. Certified copy of order of State Commission
8. Copy of order of District Forum
9. Supporting documents in favour of RP

Note:

1. The documents shall be filed in English language only or translated copy of any other language.
2. If the documents are not filed in order in the format mentioned above the same will be returned to the parties at the counter itself without acknowledgement and will only be registered after removing the defects.
3. After admission hearing, any documents if filed in a case the same has to be served on the other side and be filed with proof of service, well in advance of two days earlier from the date of hearing.
4. Henceforth, the review petition/application for recalling of order will be listed before the bench by way of circulation in chambers.
5. No. of copies to be filed in the Commission 1+3 sets + Number of Opposite Parties. (With File cover)

Sample Complaint Petitions...

You can draft your complaint as per format given below. And fight in Consumer Court. If you find it difficult or don't have sufficient time to write complaints, Affidavits, rejoinder, etc. or plead your case and study the law applicable in your case than you may inform us in that case we can provide you assistance at two levels at a very reasonable charge. At first level we can undertake all the documentation work rest of the things you may do your self *i.e.* appearing before court. At the second level we can undertake to fight your case and you have to do nothing.

Sample Complaint Petitions

In Consumer Courts (quasi-judicial consumer disputes redressal bodies), formed under the Consumer Protection Act a consumer can seek redress for his/her grievance, relating to defective goods or deficient services. Sample complaint petitions for both the cases are given here. These are just for illustration only. The exact contents of the petition will depend on the facts of the case. Assuming that the pecuniary loss suffered as less than ₹ 20 lakhs, these petitions have been made as applicable to a District Forum. In case the value of loss is more, the petition has to be changed accordingly, as State Consumer Disputes Redressal Commission or the National Consumer Redressal Commission.

1. For defective good
2. For deficient service
3. AFFIDAVIT
4. FORMAT FOR AUTHORISATION

15. SAMPLE COMPLAINT PETITION

For defective good

CASE: Mr. X purchases a mixer grinder from M/s Y & Co. operating in the same town, in December 2009. Even within the warranty period of 1 year the grinder fails. M/s Y & Co. fails to rectify the defect. The manufacturer M/s Z Ltd., was also unable to rectify the mixer grinder. Frustrated, Mr. X finally approaches the District Forum.

COMPLAINT PETITION

BEFORE THE DISTRICT CONSUMER DISPUTES REDRESSAL FORUM, <NAME OF THE DISTRICT>

Consumer Dispute Case No........../200 <Year of filing>

A petition under section 11 of Consumer Protection Act and In the mater of:

Mr. X

<Address of Mr. X> ...... Complainant

Vs.

1. Proprietor,

M/s Y & Co.

<Address of Y & Co.>

2. Managing Director,

M/s Z Ltd.,

<Address of Z> ..... Opposite Parties

To
Hon'ble President and Members of District Forum
<Name of District>
May it please your honours:

This complaint petition is being filed on behalf of Mr. X, <Address of X>, referred hereafter as Complainant, and is as follows:

1.0 That this complaint Petition is being filed under section 2(1)(*b*)(*i*) of the Consumer Protection Act.

2.1 That the opposite party No. 1 is engaged in the business of selling Consumer durables like refrigerator, TV, Mixer Grinder, etc. to the public for a consideration, apart from other activities. (Description about the O.P.)

2.2 That the Opposite Party No. 2 is the manufacturer of 'A' brand mixer grinders and other electrical household gadgets and that the mixer grinders of O.P. No. 2 are sold in retail by O.P. No. 1. (Description about the O.P)

(Narration of the incident)

1. That on 26th December 2009 (date of purchase), the complainant purchased one 'A' brand Mixer Grinder, Sl. No....... (Details about the equipment purchased) manufactured by O.P. No. 2 from the show room of O.P. No. 1, vide Cash memo No...(Cash memo/Cash receipt No.), a photocopy of the said document is furnished at Annexure-I.

3.2 That the mixer grinder abruptly stopped functioning (Nature of problem encountered) on 8th January, 2010 (when) and the matter was immediately reported to O.P. No. 1. As per his advice the defective mixer grinder was handed over in their Service Centre, on 9th January, 2010. A photocopy of the Service Centre receipt is furnished at Annexure-II.

3.3 That the mixer grinder was returned back after rectification on 24th January, 1999.

3.4 That the mixer grinder was put to use on 25th January, 1999. After running hardly for 5 minutes, the mixer grinder once again totally failed.

3.5 That the Complainant immediately reported the matter to O.P. No. 1 and also complained to O.P. No. 2. Copy of the letter is furnished at Annexure-III. (Furnish important relevant documents.)

3.6 That as per the advice of O.P. No. 1 the defective Mixer Grinder was once again handed over to their Service Centre on 30th January, 2010. There was inordinate delay in rectifying the defect by O.P. No. 1. In

April 1999 O.P. No. 2 advised O.P. No. 1 to replace the Mixer Grinder, Copy of the said letter is furnished at Annexure-IV.

3.7 That the O.P. No. 1 did not bother to honour the directive of O.P. No. 2 and till date the Complainant is suffering due to non-availability of the Mixer Grinder.

4.0 That the O.P.s had supplied defective good and they have to make good the losses suffered by the complainant.

PRAYER

In view of the submissions contained in the preceding paragraphs, the complainant most respectfully prays to the Hon'ble Forum to direct the Opposite Parties to:

(*a*) refund the cost of the Mixer Grinder, ₹ <Cost> along with 18% interest;

(*b*) pay a sum of ₹ 10,000 towards the physical strain and mental agony suffered by the complainant and his family members (compensation); and

(*c*) pay a sum of ₹ 1,000 towards cost of this petition (Cost);

for which act of kindness, the complainant shall, as is duty bound, ever pray.

Signature
(X)

(Name)
Complainant

SAMPLE COMPLAINT PETITION

For deficient service

Case: Mr. X invests a sum of money with M/s Y & Co., a NBFC (Non-Banking Finance Company), operating in the same town, in December 2008. The deposit matures in December 2008, but the Company fails to honour its commitment. It does not pay the dues. Frustrated, Mr. X finally approaches the District Forum.

COMPLAINT PETITION

BEFORE THE DISTRICT CONSUMER DISPUTES REDRESSAL FORUM, <NAME OF THE DISTRICT>

Consumer Dispute Case No........../200 <Year of filing>

A petition under Section 11 of Consumer Protection Act

and

In the mater of:

Mr. X

<Address of Mr. X> ...... Complainant

Vs.

Chairman & Managing Director

M/s Y & Co.

<Address of Y & Co.> ...... Opposite Party

To

Hon'ble President and Members of District Forum

<Name of District>

May it please your honours:

This complaint petition is being filed on behalf of Mr. X, <Address of X>, referred hereafter as Complainant, and is as follows:

1.0 That this complaint Petition is being filed under section 2(1)(*b*)(*i*) of the Consumer Protection Act.

2.0 That the opposite party is a NBFC, engaged in the business of accepting deposits from the public, apart from other activities. (Description about the O.P.) (Narration of the incident)

3.1 That on 26th December, 2008 (date of deposit), the complainant deposited a sum of ₹............(amount deposited) with the O.P., for a period of 1 year, *vide* Fixed Deposit receipt No........, a photocopy of the said document is furnished at Annexure-I.

3.2 That the F.D. matured on 25th December, 2008 and the Complainant approached the office of the O.P., on 26th December, 2008, for encashing the FD. But the staff of the Company, on some pretext or the other delayed making the payment (Nature of problem encountered). Hence the Complainant wrote to the O.P., requesting his immediate intervention. A photocopy of the said letter is furnished at Annexure-II. But the Complainant has not been paid his dues till date.

3.3 That the non-payment of the maturity value of FD, by the O.P., on the scheduled date, amounts to deficiency in service as defined under section 2(1)(*g*) of the Consumer Protection Act.

4.0 That the O.P. has inflicted enormous amount of mental agony and financial loss on the Complainant and his family.

PRAYER

In view of the submissions contained in the preceding paragraphs, the complainant most respectfully prays to the Hon'ble Forum to direct the Opposite Party to:

(*a*) pay the maturity value of the fixed deposit, ₹........, along with 18% interest;

(*b*) pay a sum of ₹ 10,000 towards the physical strain and mental agony suffered by the complainant and his family members (compensation); and

(*c*) pay a sum of ₹ 1,000 towards cost of this petition (Cost);

for which act of kindness, the complainant shall, as is duty bound, ever pray.

Signature
(X)

(Name)
Complainant

AFFIDAVIT

I,______________________________, Son of, ____________________, and residing at ______________________________, do hereby solemnly affirm and declare as under:

1. That the facts stated in the complaint petition paras __________ to __________, in ______________________________ Vs. ______________________________, being filed before the Hon'ble (District Consumer Disputes Redressal Forum (, Place)/State Consumer Disputes Redressal Commission (, State)/National Consumer Disputes Redressal Commission, New Delhi are true to the best of my knowledge and based on the records maintained by me, which I believe to be true.

Deponent

Verification

Verified at <Place>, on this __________ day of <Month> <Year> that the contents of the above affidavit are true and correct to the best of my knowledge and belief.

Deponent

Note:

1. The Affidavit has to be sworn before the Notary, on a ₹ 5 non-judicial stamp paper.
2. The details of Place, State, Month, Year are to be filled as per actual.
3. Complainant or Appellant is the Deponent.

FORMAT FOR AUTHORISATION

BEFORE THE NATIONAL COMMISSION, NEW DELHI/
BEFORE THE STATE COMMISSION, <STATE>/
BEFORE THE DISTRICT FORUM, <DISTRICT>.

Consumer Dispute Case/First Appeal/Revision Petition No. ________ of <Year>

BETWEEN

______________________________ <Complainant>

And

______________________________ <Opp. Party/Respondent>

AUTHORISATION

I ____, of <Address>_________________________, Complainant/Appellant in the above case do hereby appoint and retain ______________________________________ to appear for me in the above case and to conduct and prosecute the abovementioned Respondent and in all proceedings that may be taken in respect of any application connected with the same or any decree or order passed therein. I authorise the aforesaid Representative to admit any compromise lawfully entered in the said case.

Dated the : **(Signature of the Complainant)**

MODEL SPECIMEN OF NOTICE, COMPLAINT AFFIDAVIT AND REPLY

NOTICE BEFORE FILLING THE COMPLAINT

Name and address ....

(of the trader, dealer, firm, company, etc.)

(Complete address)

IN RE: (Mention the goods/services complained of giving details)

....

Dear Sir,

This is to bring to your kind notice that I had purchased .... from your .... For a consideration of Rs..................................paid in cash *vide* your cash memo/Receipt/Invoice No...................................(or through cheque No..........................) dated..................drawn on .... bank for a sum of Rs...................

The said goods are suffering from the following defects:-

(*i*) ....

(*ii*) ....etc.

I have reported the above matter to you several times (give reference of earlier letters, if any) but despite all my pleadings you have not made good the defect in the goods (or deficiency in services) which is indeed regrettable and highly unbusiness like. On account of your aforesaid dereliction of duty and failure and neglect to rectify the same I have suffered losses/incurred expenses ....

(give details)

which you are liable to compensate to me.

You are hereby finally called upon to —

- remove the said defects in the goods and/or
- replace the goods with new goods and/or
- return the price/charges paid

(*iv*) pay compensation for financial loss/injury/interest suffered due to your negligence......................

(give details)

in the sum of Rs... with interest @.......................% per annum within ....days of the receipt of this notice failing which I shall be constrained to initiate against you for redressal of my aforesaid grievances and recovery of the aforesaid amount such proceedings, both civil and criminal as are warranted by law, besides filing a complaint under the statutory provisions of the

Consumer Protection Act, 1986 exclusively at your own risk, cost, responsibility and consequences which please note.

Place ....

Dated.................... (Signature)

Name & Address

THE COMPLAINT

BEFORE THE HON'BLE DISTRICT CONSUMER DISPUTES
REDRESSAL FORUM AT..........................

OR

BEFORE THE HON'BLE STATE CONSUMER DISPUTES
REDRESSAL COMMISSION AT....................

OR

BEFORE THE HON'BLE NATIONAL CONSUMER DISPUTES REDRESSAL COMMISSION AT NEW DELHI

IN RE: COMPLAINT NO................OF 20............IN THE MATTER OF

(FULL NAME) (DESCRIPTION) (COMPLETE ADDRESS)

...........................complainant

VERSUS

(FULL NAME) (DESCRIPTION) (COMPLETE ADDRESS)

........................Opposite Party/Parties

COMPLAINT UNDER SECTION 12/SECTION 17/SECTIONS 21 OF THE CONSUMER PROTECTION ACT, 1986

RESPECTFULLY SHOWETH:

• **INTRODUCTION**

(In this opening paragraph the complainant should give his introduction as well as that of the opposite party/parties.)

• **TRANSACTION**

(In this paragraph complainant should describe the transaction complained of, *i.e.*, particulars and details of goods/services availed: items of goods/kind and nature of service: date of purchased of goods/availing of service: amount paid as price/ consideration, full or in part towards the goods/service; Photocopies of the bill/cash memo/voucher or receipt should be attached and properly marked as Annexure – A,B,C and so forth or 1,2,3 and so forth.)

• **DEFECT/DEFICIENCY**

(In this paragraph, complainant should explain the grievance, *i.e.*, whether the loss or damage has been caused by some unfair trade practice or restrictive trade practice adopted by any trader or there is some defect in the goods or there has been deficiency in service or the trader has charged excessive price for the goods. One should elucidate the nature of unfair trade practice adopted by the trader, *i.e.*, relating to the quality of goods/services: sponsorship: warranty or guarantee for such period promised. The nature and extent of defects in goods should be explained and so should the deficiency in service. In case of excessive price one should specify the details of actual price fixed by or under any law for the time being in force or as set out on goods and their packing *vis-a-vis* the price charged by the trader. Complaint can also be filed against offer for sale of goods hazardous to life and safety when used. You should narrate your grievance and rest assured it is being read/heard by compassionate and pragmatic judges. Photocopies of relevant documents must be attached.)

• RECTIFICATION

(In this paragraph, complainant should highlight what attempts were made by him to set things right, *i.e.*, personal visits or negotiations, communication in writing if any: whether any legal notice was got served and/or whether he has approached any other agency for redressal like M.R.T.P. Commission, Civil or Criminal Court of competent jurisdiction; the stage of its proceedings, its outcome, if any, alongwith copies (certified preferably) of such proceedings. The nature of response got from the trader when irregularities were brought to his notice, should also be disclosed here).

• OTHER PROVISIONS

(In this paragraph, reference may be made to any other law or rules or regulations of particular procedure which is applicable to the case and/or which has been violated by the trader and consumer's rights under the same. There are incidental statutory obligations, which traders must fulfill and in case of their failure to do so the case in *prima facie* made out and Forum would take cognizance).

• EVIDENCE

(In this paragraph, complainant should give details of documents and/or witnesses he will reply upon to substantiate his case. The documents attached as Annexures as stated above may be incorporated in a proper list and a list of witnesses (if any) may be filed similarly). The annexures should be attested as "True Copy".

• JURISDICTION

(In this paragraph, complainant should liquidate the claim in the complaint *i.e.*, upto 20 lacs; 20 lacs to 1 crore; or above and set out the pecuniary jurisdiction of the Forum/State Commission/National Commission, as the case may be. The territorial Jurisdiction should be highlighted to obviate any formal objection).

• LIMITATION

That the present complaint is being filed within the period prescribed under section 24A of the Act.

• RELIEF CLAIMED

(In this paragraph, complainant should describe the nature of relief he wants to claim, *i.e*, for removal of defects in goods or deficiency in service; replacement with new goods; return of the price or charges, etc., paid and/or compensation on account of financial loss or injury or detriment to his interest occasioned by negligence of the opposite party and elucidate how you have calculated the amount of compensation claimed).

(10) PRAYER CLAUSE

It is, therefore, most respectfully prayed that this Hon'ble Forum/Commission may kindly be pleased to ....

(Details of reliefs which complainant wants the Court to grant)

Place ....

Dated.................. Complainant

Through..................

(Advocate or Consumer Association, etc.)

VERIFICATION

I .... the complainant abovenamed do hereby solemnly verify that contents of my above complaint are true and correct to my knowledge, no part of it is false and nothing material has been concealed therein.

Verified this .... day of ....20..........at...............

Complainant

Note: Although it is not compulsory, complainant may file an affidavit in support of the complaint which adds to the truth and veracity of allegations and gives credibility to the cause. It need not be on a Stamp paper but one should get it attested from an Oath Commissioner appointed by a High Court. The format is just as simple.

AFFIDAVIT IN SUPPORT OF THE COMPLAINT

BEFORE THE HON'BLE ....IN RE: COMPLAINT NO............OF 20.........

IN THE MATTER OF:

....

....Complainant

Versus

....Opposite Party

AFFIDAVIT

Affidavit of Shri..s/o. Shri .... aged ....years, resident of ....

I, the abovenamed deponent do hereby solemnly affirm and declare as under:—

- That I am complainant in the above case, thoroughly conversant with the facts and circumstances of the present case and am competent to swear this affidavit.
- That the facts contained in my accompanying complaint, the contents of which have not been repeated herein for the sake of brevity may be read as an integral part of this affidavit and are true and correct to my knowledge.

Deponent

VERIFICATION

I, the above named deponent do hereby solemnly verify that the contents of my above affidavit are true and correct to my knowledge, no part of it is false and nothing material has been concealed therein.

Verified this ....day of ....20..............at..................

Deponent

POINTS TO BE TAKEN CARE BEFORE FILING A CASE

- In all cases the burden of proof is always on the complainant to prove his case. Generally consumers believe that filing a complaint with Consumer Forum is enough, it is not so consumer/complainant.
- It should not be presumed that if a doctor/clinic/hospital has done something wrong than just filing a case in consumer court is sufficient. Consumer has to produce medical opinion and decided cases before the consumer court to prove his case.

- As the complainant is required to produce strict evidence of the negligence on the part of opposite party. That is why most of the consumers/complainant lose their case.
- Generally fighting a case in consumer forum is not so easy, the delay adopted by the advocates of opposite party cause a lot harassment to the complainant. So if your case is more than ₹ 50,000 don't hesitate to engage an Advocate otherwise it is risky to stand against the highly experienced Advocates of the opposite party.

APPENDIX XI

Glossary of Common Medical Symbols

#	Fracture
A	Diagnosis
Dx	Diagnosis
Hx	History of
Rx	Treatment
o	Nil/Nothing
↑	Up/increase
↓	Down/decrease
1/7	One day
2/52	Two weeks
3/12	Three months

APPENDIX XII

Expert to Consult in case of Ailments

Disease/Organ/Investigations involved	*Expert*
Alimentary Canal/Liver	Gastroenterologist.
Anaesthetic Cases	Anaesthetist as well as the specialty within which the anaesthetic problem arose.
Baby and Infants	Paediatrician.
Bones	Orthopaedic surgeon/consultant.
Brain/Head injury	Neurologist/neurosurgeon preferably at a hospital with brain scan equipment
Cancer	Haematologist/Physician/Oncologist/Surgeon of the speciality involved/Radiotherapist.
Chest Complaints	Chest physician — most teaching hospitals have large chest clinics with modern equipment and post-graduate expertise.
Children	Paediatrician; Paediatric Surgeon.
Diabetes, Thyroid & Hormonal disorders	Endocrinologist.
Diagnostic examination of blood/ tissues/body secretions & fluids	Haematologist/Pathologist/Microbiologist.
Ear, Nose and Throat	Otoiaryngologist (ENT Surgeon).
Eyes	Ophthalmologist.
GP Cases	An experienced GP and/or Medical College teacher of General Medicine.
Heart & Vascular System	Cardiologist, and Cardio thoracic surgeon.
Kidneys & Urinary Tract	Nephrologist/Urologist.
Mother and Female	Obstetrician and Gynaecologist,
Negligent Surgery	A general surgeon or surgeon expert in the field.
Nursing Cases	A senior nursing officer or GP.
Personality Disorders	Psychiatrist/Clinical Psychologist.
Wrong Drug treatment	Pharmacologist (and Toxicologist if necessary) and appropriate expert.
'Wrongful Birth Cases'	May involve Haematologist, Geneticist.
X-rays/Sonography/CT scan/ MRI, etc.	Radiologist.

Note.—In addition to seeking advice from an expert, it is advisable to rely upon and/or to refer a standard text book on the subject of specialty under which the negligence/mishap occurred.

APPENDIX XIII
Vocabulary of Scientific Medicine

The vocabulary of scientific medicine is built from the following units. Most come from classical Greek. The next most common source is Latin.

Stems	*Meaning*
acanth	spine, prickle
aceto	vinegar
acou	hear
acro	extremity, tip, sharp
actin	ray, beam
acu	sharp, abrupt, sudden
adeno	gland
adipo	fat
aero	air
(a)esth	perception
agogue	leader
agon	contest, struggle
ala	wing
alb	white
algo	pain
alien	stranger, strange
allelo	one another, mutual
amauros	blind
am(o)eb	constantly changing
ambi/amph	both sides
ambly	dim, faint
ambul(o)	walk
amnio	amnion, "bowl"
amylo	starch
andro	male
angio	vessel (blood, bile)
ankyl	bent, crooked; a joint locked in one position
annulus	little ring
anser	goose
anthem	flower
anthrac	black
anthro	man/human
aort	aorta
aphro	froth, sexual love
aqu	water
arachn	spider, spiderweb
archo	ancient, beginning
argy	silver, shiny
artero	artery (as opposed to vein)
arthro	joint
artic	little joint
asthm	panting, short breaths
athero	gruel
atri	entry chamber
axilla	armpit
axo	center, axis
aud	hear
aur	hear
aus	hear
auto	self
aux	make grow
azo	nitrogen
bac(t)	rod
ball	throw
balano	acorn, glans
blast	sprout
blenno	snot
bleph	eyelid
bol	throw
brachi	arm
brady	slow
branch	gill
bronch	bronchus
bucc	cheek (inside)
burs	bursa, purse
caes	cut deep
c(h)ord	notochord
c(o)ele	rupture
carpo	wrist
calci	limestone

Stems	*Meaning*
calco	heel, spur
calyc	cup
campy	bend
canc	crab
capo	head, expanded part
centr	center
carbo	charcoal, carbon
carcin	crab
carcinoma	cancer from epithelium
card	heart, heart-shape
carot	great neck arteries
carpo	wrist
caus	burn
centesis	puncture
cep(h)	head, expanded part
cephal	head
cept	seize, take
cereb(r)	brain
cervic	neck
ch(e)ir	hand
chemo	chemistry
chlor	light green
chol(e)	bile
chondr	cartilage; grain
chorea	dance
chori	chorionic membrane
chrom	color
chron	time, long time
chyle	digested food juice
cide	killing, "falling"
cise	cut deep
cili	eyelash
cion	uvula
clast	break
claustr	barrier
cleido	collarbone, key
clino	bed
clivus	slope
coagul	coagulate, clot
coccus	berry
coccyx	cuckoo, cuckoo bill
collic	hill
collo	glue
collus	neck
conios	dust
cond	hard knob
core	dolly, pupil (of eye)
cori	leather
corn	horn

Stems	*Meaning*
cox(a)	hip
corp	physical body
cre(s)c	grow
cribi	sieve
crine	secretion ("separation")
cubit	elbow
cubo	lay down
cule	little
culpo	vagina
cuneo	wedge
cutis	skin
cyan	dark blue
cycl	circle, wheel
cysto	urinary bladder
cyto	cell
dacr	tear (from the eye)
dacty	finger
demos	people
dens	tooth
dent	tooth
derm	skin
desm	harden, bind together
desis	binding
desmo	hard
dextro	right-sided
diadocho	succeed, take over
didym	twin
digi(t)	finger, toe
diphth	leathery membrane
docho	cup, container
drepan	sickle
dromo	running a race; course
duc, duct	lead, guide
dynia	pain
echin	spiny
ectasia	dilatation
edem(a)	excess tissue fluid/"swelling"
embol	bottle stopper
embryo	embryo, fetus
emesis	vomiting
em(ia)	blood
enceph	brain
enchyme	filling, installation
entero	intestine
ergo	work
erythro	red
esthesia	perception
f(a)eco	feces, refuse

Stems	Meaning
fac	make, build, do, perform
facie	face, countenance, looks
fasc	bundle, fascia
fec	make, build, do, perform
fer	carrying, bearing
fibr	fibrous
fic	make, build, do, perform
fis, fid	split, cleave, divide
fistula	pipe
flagel	whip
flav	yellow
flat	blow
flect	bend
flex	bend
fora/foro	make a hole
fornic	arch
fract	break into pieces
frag	break into pieces
fring	break into pieces
fuge	flee
fun	melt, pour
fus	melt, pour
gala(k)	milk
gam(y)	marry
gangl	knot
gangr	gangrene, gnawing sore
galact	milk
gastr	stomach, belly
gemin	twin
gen	become, beget, produce
genesis	origin
genu	knee
ger	old age
gest	bring forth, produce
glans	acorn
gleno	shoulder
gli(o)	glial cells, literally "glue"
glob	sphere, ball, round body
glomer	tuft
gloss	tongue
glute	buttocks
gnatho	jaw
gnosis	know
gogue	lead
gono	offspring, product, seed, semen
gonio	angle
gracile	slender

Stems	Meaning
gram	record
gran	grain
graph	writing, scratching
gryph	claw
gynec	female
(h)(a)em	blood
habeo	to hold, habit, general state of
halluc	big toe
helic	spiral
helm	worm
hermaphro	male and female in one body
hepat	liver
hernia	rupture, hernia
hidr	sweat
hippo	horse
histo	tissue, web, cloth
hy(a)l	glass, primitive material
hydatid	water drop
hydro	water
hypno	sleep
hystero	uterus
iatric	healing
iatro	physician
ichth	fish
idio	self, personal, private
inguin	part of body from groin to hip
insul	island
irid	rainbow, bright-color circle
ischi	hip joint
islet	island
ject	throw, hurl
jejun	hungry
junc	join together
jug	join together
jux	join together
karyo	nucleus
kera	horny
kern	kernel, deep brain
kerato	skin surface, cornea, horn
kine	set in motion
kyn	dog
lachry	tear (from the eye)
labio	lip
lacto	milk

Stems	*Meaning*
lal	babble, talk
latero	side
lecith	egg yolk
leiomyo	smooth muscle
lein	spleen
lens	lentil
lepros	rough and rotting off
lepto	thin, fine, slender
leuco/leuko	white
levo	left-sided
liga(t)	bind together, bandage
ling	tongue
lith	stone
lumbo	lower back, loin
lumbri	earthworm
lumen	the tube down a hollow organ
lymph	"clear fresh water"
lysis	breaking down
malar	cheek (outside)
mal(i)	abnormal, bad
malacia	soft
malako	soft
malleo	hammer
mania	wild about
medi	middle portion
medulla	soft inner part
meli	sweet
mere	part
manu	hand
mara	wither
mast(*i*)	whip, flog, beat
mast(*o*)	breast
mea	passage
meatus	external opening
meios	lessening
melano	black
melia	limb
mening	meninges
men(i)s	moon, month
ment	mind, chin
meter	measure
metro	uterus
mito	thread
mnem	memory
mnes	memory
mob	move
morb	sick
morph	shapes, dreams

Stems	*Meaning*
mot	move
mur(al)	wall
musc	mouse, muscle
myc(o)	fungus
myelo	soft, pith
myi	fly (insect)
myo	muscle
myxo/muco	slime
narco	sleep
naso	nose
necro	dead
nephelo	cloud
nephr	kidney
nerv	nerve
neuro	nerve
nos, nox	nasty, sickening
nous	mind, spirit
nyct	night
occiput	back of the head
ocul	eye
(h)odo	way, path, road
odon	tooth
odyn	pain
olfact	smell
oma	tumor/lump
omen(t)	omentum
omphalo	belly button
on(e/t)	to be
onco	tumor, mass
onycho	nail (finger/toe)
o”	egg
o”phor	ovary
op/opsy	eye, see, etc.
ophth	eye
opio	poppy juice
opsi	late
opson	relish, meat seasoning
orbi	wheel
orch	testis
org	work
oro	mouth
ortho	straight
os	bone, mouth
osm	smell
ost(eo)	bone
ot(o)	ear
ovin	sheep
oxy	oxygen, acid

Stems	*Meaning*
p(a)ed	child
palpebr	eyelid
pannus	cloth, rag
pap	nipple
par(i)t	have a baby
parietal	wall
partheno	virgin
partum	birth
patho	disease, misery
pect	chest
pelvis	basin
pes/ped	foot
phage	eat
phakos	lentil, lens of the eye
pharmako	sorcery, poison, drug
pheo	ugly, dusky
phero	carry, bear
philo	like, love
phlebo	vein
phleg	flame
phobia	fear
phoco	seal (the animal)
phoro	carry, bear
phos/phot	light
phragm	divide into two, wall off
phren	mind, breath
phth	waste away, wither
phyllo	leaf-like
physio	nature
phyte	a plant
pineo	pine cone
pinna	feather
pino	drink
pisi	pea
pituit	snot
placent	cake, placenta
plak	cake
plantar	sole of the foot
plasm	molded
plast	molded
platy	flat
plegia	stroke, paralysis
pleur	pleura ("side of ribs")
plex	braid, wind together
plexy	stroke
plic	braid, wind together
pn(e)	breath
pod(o)	foot
poie(sis)	making

Stems	*Meaning*
polio	gray; gray matter of the nervous system
pollic	thumb
pomp	precede, parade
porph	purple
porta	door
posthe	foreskin
prac	done
prag	done
prax	done
pre/pro	before
procto	rectum
pron(o)	prone, face down
proto	first
pseud	false
psyche	spirit, mind
psychr	cold, frigid
pter	wing
pto	droop
pty(alo)	spit
pulmo	lung
punct	prick, little spot
pupa	doll, miniature figure
purp	purple
pyelo	vat, basin, pelvis
pykno	shrivelled
pyo	pus
p(u/y)ri	pear
pyr(o)	fever (cognate to "fire")
radi	rod
r(h)ach	backbone
re(i)n	kidney
ret(ic)	net
rhabdo	striated muscle
rhaph	sew together
rheo	flow
rheum	runny stuff
rhino	nose
riso	smile
rrha(g)	discharge from a burst vessel
rub(r)	red
sacc	sack
sacch(ar)	sugar
salpinx	trumpet, oviduct
sang(ui)	blood
sapro	dead
sarc(o)	flesh

Stems	***Meaning***
sarcoma	cancer from connective tissue or muscle
scato	feces, filth
scapho	boat
schi(s/z)	split
sclero	hard
scope	examine carefully
sebo	hard fat, skin grease, suet
sec/seg	cut
sella	saddle
seps/sept	make rotten
septo	fence, partition
sero	whey, wet protein
sial	saliva
sinus	hollow or pocket
skel	dried up, skeleton
soma/somy	body
spasmo	a drawing tight
spondylo	spine
sphinct	bind tight, squeeze shut
sphygno	heartbeat
spir	breathing
splanchn	innards
staphyl	bunch of grapes
stasis	standing up, being stable
stat	stop
statio	standing up, being stable
staxis	drip, drop
stem	standing up, being stable
steato	fat
sterco	feces
sthen	strength
stigm	spot
stole	to pull, to draw
stom(a)	mouth
stomy	mouth
strepto	wavy
stylo	stylus
sudo	sweat
sulco	plowed furrow
syring	pipe, tube, reed
tachy	fast, swift
tact	touch
tainia	band, tapeworm
talo	ankle
tasis	stretch
tarso	flat plate
taxo	arrangement, put in order
telo	the tip, the end

Stems	***Meaning***
temporal	temple
ten(d)o	stretch, tendon
terato	monster
theca	box (sheath, covering)
thel	breast, covering layer
thenar	palm, sole
thym	mind, spirit, mood
thym	warty mass, thymus gland
thyro	oblong shield
toco	have a baby
tom(e)	cut
tono	stretch
topo	place
tort	twist
tox(o)	bow, arrow, poisoned arrow
trema	hole
tricho	hair
trophy	grow/food
tryps	break into many pieces, crush
tuber	bump, potato(e)
typho	smoky, delirious fever
typhl	cecum
unguis	nail (finger, toe)
uro	urine
uvo	grape
vacc	cow
vago	wanderer
valgus	turned outward
varus	turned inward
vaso	blood vessel
velo	veil, curtain, cover
vener	sexual acts, lusty
veno	vein (as opposed to artery)
vert	turn
vesico	bladder
viscero	innards
volv	turn around, twist around
xantho	yellow
xeno	stranger
xero	dry
z(a)o	to live
zo”	animals
zema	boiled
zygo	yoke
zyme	ferment

APPENDIX XIV
List of Medical Combing Forms

These combining forms usually appear at the beginning of terms, but they may certainly sometimes appear within or at the end of a term also. Use this handy table for reference.

Form	Meaning
Adeno –	gland
Adreno –	adrenal gland
Angio –	vessel
Ano –	anus
Arterio –	artery
Arthro –	joint
Balano –	glans penis
Blepharo –	eyelid
Broncho –	bronchus (windpipe)
Cantho –	canthus (angle at either end of Slit between eyelids)
Capit –	head
Cardi or cardio –	heart
Carpo –	wrist
Cephalo –	head
Cerebello –	cerebellurn (part of brain)
Cerebro –	cerebrum (part of brain)
Cheilo –	lip (mouth)
Chole –	bile (Note: Chole plus cyst, meaning bladder, equals gallbladder; chole plus doch, meaning duct, equals choledocho or common bile duct.)
Chondro –	cartilage
Chordo –	cord or string (usually used in connection with the vocal cord or spermatic cord)
Cilia –	hair (Latin)
Cleido –	collarbone
Coccygo –	coccyx (end bone of the spinal column)
Colpo –	vagina
Cordo –	cord (usually vocal cord)
Coxa –	hip (Latin)
Cranio –	head

Form	Meaning
Cysto –	sac, cyst, or bladder (most often used in connection with the urinary bladder)
Cyto –	cell
Dacryo –	tear (used commonly in relation to tear duct or sac)
Dento- or donto –	tooth
Derma –	skin
Duodeno –	duodenum (part of small intestine)
Emia –	blood
Encephalo –	brain
Entero –	intestines
Fascia –	sheet or band of fibrous tissue (Latin)
Fibro –	fibers
Gastro –	stomach
Genu –	knee (Latin)
Gingivo –	gums
Glomerulo –	glomerulus (often a structure of the kidney)
Glosso –	tongue
Gnatho –	jaw
Hallux –	great toe (Latin)
Hem, hema, hemo, hemato –	blood
Hepato –	liver
Hilus –	pit or depression in an organ where vessels and nerves enter (Latin)
Histio –	tissue
Hystero –	uterus (Note: This term may also pertain to hysteria.)
Ileo –	ileum (part of small intestine)
Ilio –	flank or ilium (bone of the pelvis)
Jejuno –	jejunum (part of small intestine)
Kerato –	cornea or horny layer of the skin
Labio –	lips (either of mouth or vulva)
Lacrimo –	tears (used also in connection with tear ducts or sacs)
Laparo –	loin or flank (also refers to abdomen)
Laryngo –	larynx
Linguo –	tongue
Lympho –	lymph
Masto –	breast
Meningo –	meninges (coverings of the brain and spinal cord)
Metra, metro –	uterus
Morpho –	form
Myelo –	bone marrow and also spinal cord (Note: The use of this term will determine which tissue is meant.)

Form	Meaning
Myo –	muscle (Note: The Latin word for muscle is mus.)
Myringo –	eardrum
Naso –	nose
Nephro –	kidney
Neuro –	nerve
Oculo –	eye
Odonto –	tooth
Omphalo –	navel or umbilicus
Onycho –	nails
Oophoro –	ovary
Ophthalmo –	eye
Orchio, orchido –	testis
Oro –	mouth
Os –	bone — or mouth
Osteo –	bone
Oto –	ear
Ovario –	ovary
Palato –	palate of mouth
Palpebro –	eyelid
Pectus –	breast, chest, or thorax (Latin)
Pharyngo –	pharynx
Phlebo –	vein
Pilo –	hair
Pleuro –	pleura of lung (relates also to side or rib)
Pneumo or pneumono	lungs (also used in referring to air or breath)
Procto –	rectum
Pyelo –	pelvis of kidney
Pyloro –	pylorus (part of stomach just be fore duodenum)
Rhino –	nose
Sacro –	sacrum
Salpingo –	fallopian tube or oviduct
Sialo –	saliva (used in connection with a salivary duct or gland)
Splanchno –	viscera
Spleno –	spleen
Sterno –	sternum
Stoma –	mouth
Tarso –	instep of foot; ankle (also edge of eyelid)
Teno, tenonto –	tendon
Thoraco –	thorax or chest
Thyro –	thyroid
Trachelo –	neck, particularly the neck of the uterus

Form	Meaning
Tracheo –	trachea
Unguis –	nail
Uretero –	ureter
Urethro –	urethra
Uro –	urine; urinary
Utero –	uterus
Vaso –	vessel
Veno –	vein
Ventriculo –	ventricle, either of heart or brain
Viscero –	viscera

In medical terminology, many verbs or combining forms of verbs are derived from either Greek or Latin. These verbs may be added to other root words to form words or prefixes and suffixes may be added to them to form words.

Root	Meaning	Examples
Algia	Pain	Cardialgia (heart); gastralgia (stomach); neuralgia (nerve)
Audi, audio	Hear, hearing	Audiometer (measure); audiophone (voice instrument for deaf)
Bio	Live	Biology (study of living); biostatistics (vital statistics); biogenesis (origin)
Cau, caus	Burn	Caustic (suffix added to make adjective); cauterization; causalgia (burning pain); electrocautery
Centesis	Puncture, perforate	Thoracocentesis (chest); pneumocentesis (lung); arthrocentesis (joint); enterocentesis (intestine)
Clas, claz	Smash, break	Osteoclasis (bone); odontoclasis (tooth)
Duct	Draw	Ductal (suffix added to make adjective); oviduct (egguterine tube or fallopian tube); periductal (per means around); abduct (prefix meaning lead away from)
Dynia	Pain	Mastodynia (breast); pleurodynia (chest); esophagodynia (esophagus); coccygodynia (coccyx)
Ecta, ectas	Dilate	Venectasia (dilation of vein); cardioectasis (heart); ectatic (suffix added for adjective)
Edem	Swell	Myo edema (muscle); lymphedema (lymph); (a is a suffix added to make a noun)
Esthes	Feel	Esthesia (suffix added to make noun); anesthesia (an is prefix)
Fiss	Split	Fissure; fission (suffixes added to make nouns)
Flex, flec	Bend	Flexion (suffix added to make noun); flexor (suffix added); anteflect, (prefix added meaning before bending forward)

Root	Meaning	Examples
Flu, Flux	Flow	Fluctuate; fluxion; affluent (abundant flowing)
Geno, genesis	Produce, origin	Genotype; homogenesis (same origin); pathogenesis (disease origin of disease); heterogenesis (prefix added, meaning other alteration of generation)
Iatro, iatr	Treat, cure	Geriatrics (old age); pediatrics (children)
Kine, kino, kineto, kinesio	Move	Kinetogenic (producing movement); kinetic (suffix added to make adjective); kinesiology (study)
Liga	Bind	Ligament (suffix added to make noun) ligat ligature
Logy	Study	Parasitology (parasites); bacteriology (bacteria); histology (tissues)
Lysis	Breaking up, dissolving	Hemolysis (blood); glycolysis (sugar); autolysis (self destruction of cells)
Morph, morpho	Form	Morphology; amorphous (no definite form); pleomorphic (more occurring in various forms polymorphic (many)
Olfact	Smell	Olfactophobia (fear); olfactory (suffix added to make adjective)
Op, opto	See	Amblyopia (dull dimness of vision); presbyopia (old impairment of vision in old age); optic; myopia (myein, meaning shut nearsighted)
Palpit	Flutter	Palpitation
Par, partus	Labor	Postpartum (after birth); parturition (act of giving birth); para i, ii, iii, iv, etc., are symbols of number of births
Pep	Digest	Dyspepsia (bad, difficult); peptic (suffix added to make adjective)
Pexy	Fix	Mastopexy (fixation of breast); nephrosplenopexy (surgical fixation of kidney and spleen)
Phag, phago	Eat	Phagocytosis (eating of cells); phagomania (madness mad craving for food or eating dysphagia (difficult eating or swallowing)
Phan, phas	Appear visible,	Phanerosis (act of becoming visible); phantasia; phantasy; phasmophobia (fear of ghosts)
Phas	Speak, utter	Aphasia (unable to speak); dysphasia (difficulty in speaking)
Phil	Like, love	Hemophilia (blood a hereditary disease characterized by delayed clotting of blood); acidophilia (acid stain liking or staining with acid stains); philanthropy (love of mankind)

Root	Meaning	Examples
Phobia	Fear	Hydrophobia (fear of water); photophobia (fear of light); claustrophobia (fear of close places)
Phrax, phrag	Fence off, wall off	Diaphragm (across partition separating thorax from abdomen); phragmoplast (formed)
Plas	Form, grow	Neoplasm (new growth); rhinoplasty (nose operation for formation of nose); otoplasty (ear); choledochoplasty (common bile duct)
Plegia	Paralyze	Paraplegia (paralysis of lower limbs); ophthalmoplegia (eye); hemiplegia (partial paralysis)
Pne, pneo	Breathe	Dyspnea (difficult breathing); apnea (lack of breathing); hyperpnea. (overbreathing)
Poie	Make	Hematopoiesis (blood); erythropoiesis (red blood cells); leukopoiesis ('white blood cells)
Ptosis	Fall	Proctoptosis (anus prolapse of anus); splanchnoptosis (viscera)
Rhagia	Burst forth, pour	Menorrhagia (abnormal bleeding during menstruation); menometrorrhagia (abnormal uterine bleeding); hemorrhage (blood)
Rhaphy	Suture	Herniorrhaphy (suturing or repair of hernia); hepatorrhaphy (Jiver); nephrorrhaphy (kidney)
Rhea	Flow, discharge	Leukorrhea (white discharge from vagina); galactorrhea (milk discharge); rhinorrhea (nasal discharge)
Rhexis	Rupture	Enterorrhexis (intestines); metrorrhexis (uterus)
Schiz	Split, divide	Schizophrenia (mind split personality); schizonychia (nails); schizotrichia (hair)
Scope	Examine	Microscopic; cardioscope; endoscope (endo means within an instrument for examining the interior of a hollow viscus)
Stasis	Stop, stand still	Hematostatic (pertaining to stagnation of blood); epistasis (checking or stopping of any discharge)
Stazien	Drop	Epistaxis (nosebleed)
Teg, tect	Cover	Tegmen; tectum (rooflike structure); integument (skin covering)
Therap	Treat, cure	Therapy; neurotherapy (nerves); chemotherapy (chemicals); physiotherapy
Tomy	Cut, incise	Phlebotomy (incision of vein); arthrotomy (joint); appendectomy (ectomy, meaning cut out excision of appendix); oophorectomy (excision of ovary); ileocecostomy (ostomy, meaning creation of an artificial opening, and of, pertaining to opening or mouth thus, an anastomosis of ileum and cecum)

Root	Meaning	Examples
Topo	Place	Topography; toponarcosis (numbing hence, numbing of a part, or localized anesthesia
Tropho	Nourish	Hypertrophy (enlargement or overnourishment); atrophy (undernourishment); dystrophy (difficult or bad)
Volv	Turn	Involution; volvulus (twisting of an organ, intestinal obstruction with twisting of bowel, or twisting of the esophagus)

APPENDIX XV

List of Medical Acronyms and Abbreviations for Medical Terms

Abbreviation is a single letter or group of letters, which is derived from a word or words. It is used to represent the words for the sake of briefness. The doctors, medical students, pharmacists and scientists very commonly use some abbreviations in their communication in the healthcare industry. These short-cuts or short forms are known as medical abbreviations.

Medical abbreviations can be found in the medical as well as non-medical literature. Many of the common medical abbreviations are frequently used in physician orders, to write prescriptions, complete the patient charts and medical records as well as in communication. They boost brevity, convenience and efficiency as long as wisely used. They also save the time of medical professionals who would otherwise have to write very lengthy medical terms. However, one needs to avoid certain abbreviations to avoid confusion and mistakes. There are thousands of medical abbreviations and it may be difficult for one to remember all the short forms.

However, we have made an attempt to provide to readers an A to Z list of medical abbreviations and acronyms used as short forms for medical terms. This list contains more than just common medical abbreviations, and would be helpful to you as a reference to know the meaning of abbreviations used in medical fields and specialties.

Abbreviation	*Medical Term*
Ac	Before Meals
a.a.	Amino Acids
A/G	Albumin/Globulin ratio
A-a gradient	Alveolar to Arterial Gradient
AAA	Abdominal Aortic Aneurysm
AAD	Antibiotic-associated Diarrhea
AAO	Alert, Awake and Oriented
AAS	Acute Abdominal Series
AB	Abortion
ab, abs	Abdomen or Abdominal
ABD	Abdomen
ABE	Acute Bacterial Endocarditis
ABG	Arterial Blood Gas
ABI	Acquired Brain Injury
AC	Before Eating
ACB	Aortocoronary Bypass
ACD	Anemia of Chronic Disease
ACE	Angiotensin-Converting Enzyme
ACL	Anterior Cruciate Ligament
ACLS	Advanced Cardiac Life Support
ACS	Acute Coronary Syndrome
ACTH	Adrenocorticotropic Hormone
AD	Alzheimer's Disease
ADA	Adenosine Deaminase

Abbreviation	*Medical Term*
ADD	Attention Deficit Disorder
ADH	Antidiuretic Hormone
ADHD	Attention Deficit Hyperactivity Disorder
ADR	Acute Dystonic Reaction or Adverse Drug Reaction
AE	Hyperkalemia
AED	Antiepileptic Drug
AED	Automated External Defibrillator
AF	Amniotic Fluid
AF	Atrial Fibrillation or Afebrile
AFB	Acid Fast Bacillus (TB)
AFP	Alpha-fetoprotein
AGN	Acute Glomerulonephritis
AI	Artificial Insemination or Aortic Insufficiency
AIDP	Acute Infectious and Parasitical Diseases
AIDP	Acute Inflammatory Demyelinating Polyneuropathy
AIDP	Autoimmune Progesterone Dermatitis
AIDS	Acquired Immune Deficiency Syndrome
AIN	Acute Interstitial Nephritis
AKA	Above the Knee Amputation
ALA	Aminolevulinic Acid
Alc	Alcohol
ALD	Alcoholic Liver Disease
ALG	Antilymphocytic Globulin
ALI	Acute Lung Injury
ALL	Acute Lymphoblastic Leukemia
ALP	Alkaline Phosphatase
ALPS	Autoimmune Lymphoproliferative Syndrome
ALS	Amyotrophic Lateral Sclerosis
ALT	Alanine Transaminase
Amb.	Ambulate
AMI	Acute Myocardial Infarction
AML	Acute Myeloid Leukemia
AMS	Acute Mountain Sickness
ANA	Anti-nuclear Antibody
ANS	Autonomic Nervous System
Anti-D	This gamma globulin must be given by injection to rhesus negative mother who delivers/aborts rhesus positive child/foetus, to prevent mother developing antibodies which would damage a subsequent rhesus positive baby
AODM	Adult-Onset Diabetes Mellitus (Type 2 Diabetes)
AOM	Acute Otitis Media
APC	Atrial Premature Contraction
APD	Adult Polycystic Disease
APECED	Autoimmune Polyendocrinopathy-Candidiasis-ectodermal dystrophy
APH	Antepartum Hemorrhage
APKD	Adult Polycystic Kidney Disease
APLS	Antiphospholipid Syndrome
APR	Abdominoperineal Resection
APS	Autoimmune Polyendocrine/Polyglandular Syndrome
APTT	Activated Partial Thromboplastin Time

Abbreviation	*Medical Term*
Aq	Water
ARC	AIDS-related Complex
ARDS	Acute Respiratory Distress Syndrome
ARF	Acute Renal Failure
Arg	Arginine
ARM	Artificial Rupture of Membranes
ART	Antiretroviral Therapy
ARVC	Arrhythmogenic Right Ventricular Cardiomyopathy
ARVD	Arrhythmogenic Right Ventricular Dysplasia
AS	Aortic Stenosis
ASA	Acetylsalicylic Acid (Aspirin)
ASAP	As soon as possible
ASCAD	Arteriosclerotic Coronary Artery Disease
ASCVD	Arteriosclerotic Vascular Disease (Arteriosclerosis)
ASD	Atrial Septal Defect
ASD	Autism Spectrum Disorder
ASGUS	Atypical Squamous Glandular Cells of Undetermined Significance
ASH, ASHD	Arteriosclerotic Heart Disease (Coronary Heart Disease)
ASIS	Anterior Superior Iliac Spine
ASO	Antistreptolysin-O
AST	Aspartate Transaminase
ATN	Acute Tubular Necrosis
ATNR	Asymmetrical Tonic Neck Reflex
ATP	Acute Thrombocytopenic Purpura
ATP	Adenosine triphosphate
ATS	Anti-tetanus Serum

Abbreviation	*Medical Term*
A-V	Arteriovenous
AV	Arteriovenous/Atrioventricular
AVM	Arteriovenous Malformation
A-VO2	Arteriovenous Oxygen
AVR	Aortic Valve Replacement
AXR	Abdominal X-Ray
AZT	Azidothymidine
b.d./b.i.d.	Twice a day
B.P.	British Pharmacopeia
B/L	Bilaterial
BAC	Blood Alcohol Content
BAL	Blood Alcohol Level
BAL	Bronchoalveolar Lavage
BAO	Basic Acid Output
BAT	Brown Adipose Tissue
BBB	Bundle Branch Block
BBB L	Left Bundle Branch Block
BBB R	Right Bundle Branch Block
BC	Blood Culture
BCAA	Brached Chain Amino Acid
BCC	Basal Cell Carcinoma
BCG	Bacille Calmette-Guerin (Tuberculosis Vaccination)
BCP	Birth Control Pill
BD	Bipolar Disorder
BDD	Body Dysmorphic Disorder
BDI	Beck Depression Inventory
BE	Barium Enema
BEE	Basal Energy Expenditure
BGAT	Blood Glucose Awareness Training
BGL	Blood Glucose Level
Bid	Twice a day
BiPAP	Bilevel Positive Airway Pressure
BiVAD	Bilateral Ventricular Assist Device
BK	Bradykinin

Abbreviation	Medical Term
BKA	below-the-knee amputation
Bld	Blood
BM	Bone Marrow
BM	Bowel Movement
BMC	Bone Mineral Content
BMD	Bone Mineral Density
BMI	Body Mass Index
BMP	Blood Metabolic Profile
BMR	Basal Metabolic Rate
BMT	Bone Marrow Transplant
BNP	Brain Natriuretic Peptide
BOM	Bilateral Otitis Media
BOOP	Bronchiolitis Obliterans Organizing Pneumonia
BP	Blood Pressure
BPAD	Bipolar Affective Disorder
BPD	Borderline Personality Disorder
BPH	Benign Prostatic Hyperplasia
BPM	Beats Per Minute
BPPV	Benign Paroxysmal Positional Vertigo
BRBPR	Bright Red Blood Per Rectum
BRCA 1	Breast Cancer 1 (human gene and protein)
BRP	Bathroom Priviledges
BS	(*i*) Breath Sounds; (*ii*) Bowel Sounds; (*iii*) Blood Sugar
BSA	Body Surface Area
BSE	Bovine Spongiform Encephalopathy
BSL	Blood Sugar Level
BT	Bleeding Time
BTL	Bilateral Tubal Ligation
BTP	Breakthrough pain
BUN	Blood Urea Nitrogen
BVP	Biventricular Vaginosis
BW	Body Weight
BX	Biopsy
C	With (Latin: cum)
C&S	Culture & Sensitivity
C/O	Complaining of
Ca	Calcium
CA	Carcinoma or Cancer
Ca	Carcinoma/cancer
CABG	Coronary Artery Bypass Graft
CABGS	Coronary Artery Bypass Graft Surgery
CAD	Coronary Artery Disease
CADASIL	Cerebral Autosomal Dominant Arteriopathy with Subcortical Infarcts and Leukoencephalopathy
CAG	Coronary Angiography or Coronary Artery Graft
CAH	Chronic Active Hepatitis
CAH	Congenital Adrenal Hyperplasia
CAMP	Cyclic Adenosine Monophosphate
CAPD	Central Auditory Processing Disorder
CAPD	Continuous Ambulatory Peritoneal Dialysis
Caps	Capsules
CAT	Computed Axial Tomography
CAT scan	Computed Axial Tomograph
CBC	Complete Blood Counts
CBD	Common Bile Duct
CBG	Capillary Blood Gas
CBS	Chronic Brain Syndrome
CC	Cardiac Catheter
CC	Chief Complaint
CCF	Congestive Cardiac Failure

Abbreviation	*Medical Term*
CCK	Cholecystokinin
CCR	Cardiocerebral Resuscitation
CC's	Chief Complaints
CCU	Cardiac Care Unit
CCU	Clean Catch Urine
CCU	Coronary Care Unit
CCV	Critical Closing Volume
CDH	Congenital Dislocated Hip
CDP	Cytosine Diphosphate
CEA	Carcinoembryonic Antigen, Carotid Endarterectomy
CF	Cystic Fibrosis
CFS	Chronic Fatigue Syndrome
CGL	Chronic Granulocytic Leukemia
CGMP	Cyclic Guanosine Monophosphate
CGN	Chronic Glomerulonephritis
CH	Congenital Hypothyroidism
CHD	Chronic Heart Disease or Coronary Heart Disease
ChE	Cholinesterase
CHF	Congestive Heart Failure
CHO	Carbohydrate
Chol	Cholesterol
CHT	Congenital Hypothyroidism
CI	Cardiac Index
CICU	Cardiac Intensive Care Unit
CIDP	Chronic Inflammatory Demyelinating Polyneuropathy
Circ	Circumcision
CIS	Carcinoma in situ
CJD	Creutzfeldt-Jakob Disease
CKD	Chronic Kidney Disease
CKMB	MB isoenzyme of creatine kinase
CLL	Chronic Lymphocytic Leukemia
CML	Chronic Myelogenous Leukemia/Chronic Myeloid Leukemia
CMML	Chronic Myelomonocytic Leukemia
CMP	Cytosine Monophosphate
CMS	Chronic Mountain Sickness
CMV	Cyomegalovirus
CN	Cranial Nerves
CNS	Central Nervous System
CO	Cardiac Output, Carbon Monoxide
CO	Complaining Of
CO_2	Carbon Dioxide
COAD	Chronic Obstructive Airways Disease
COCP	Combined Oral Contraceptive Pill
COLD	Chronic Obstructive Lung Disease
Conj	Conjunctiva
COPD	Chronic Obstructive Pulmonary Disease
COX-1	Cyclooxygenase 1
CP	Cerebral Palsy
CP	Chest Pain
CPAP	Continuous Positive Airway Pressure
CPK	Creatine Phosphokinase
CPKMB	Creatine Phosphokinase heart
CPP	Cerebral Perfusion Pressure
CPR	Cardiopulmonary Resuscitation
CPT	Current Procedural Terminology
CrCl	Creatinine Clearance
CREST	Calcinosis Raynaud Esophagus Sclerosis Teleangiectasiae

Abbreviation	*Medical Term*
CRF	Chronic Renal Failure
CRF	Corticotropin-releasing factor
CRH	Corticotropin-releasing hormone
CRI	Chronic Renal Insufficiency
CRNS	Certified Registered Nurse Anesthetist
CRP	C-Reactive Protein
CRT	Cardiac Resynchronization Therapy
CsA	Ciclosporin A
C-Section	Cesarean Section
CSF	Cerebrospinal Fluid
CT	Computed Tomography or Computerized Tomography
CTA	Computed Tomography Angiography
CTMT	Computerised Tread Mill Test
CTP	Cytosine Triphosphate
CTS	Carpal Tunnel Syndrome
CTU	Cancer Treatment Unit
CTX	Ceftriaxone Contractions
CV	Cardiovascular
CVA	Cardiovascular Accident (stroke)
CVA	Costovertebral Angle
CVAT	CVA tenderness
CVC	Central Venous Catheter
CVC	Chronic Venous Congestion
CVD	Cardiovascular Disease
CVI	Cardiovascular incident
CVID	Common Variable Immunodeficiency
CVP	Central Venous Pressure
CVS	Cardiovascular System
Cx	Cervix
CXR	Chest X-Ray
D&C	Dilation and Curettage
D&C/DNC	Dilatation and Curettage
D&E	Dilatation and Evacuation
D&V	Diarrhoea and Vomitting
D.D.	Differential Diagnosis
D/C	Discharge
D/W	Discussed With
D5W	5% dextrose in water
DAT	Diet as tolerated
DAT	Direct Antiglobulin Test
DAW	Dispense as written
DBP	Diastolic Blood Pressure
DBS	Deep Brain Stimulation
DBT	Dialectical Behavioral Therapy
DC	Discharge or Discontinue
DCBE	Double Contrast Barium Enema
DCIS	Ductal Carcinoma in situ
DCM	Dilated Cardiomyopathy
DDD	Daily Defined Doses
DDS	Doctor of Dental Surgery
DDx	Differential Diagnosis
DES	Diethylstilbestrol
Detox	Detoxification
DEXA	Dual Energy X-ray Absorptionmetry
DHE	Dihydroergotamine
DHEA	Dehydroepiandrosterone
DHEA-S	Dehydroepiandrostero ne Sulphate
DHF	Decompensated Heart Failure
DI	Diabetes Insipidus
DIC	Disseminated Intravascular Coagulation

Abbreviation	*Medical Term*
DIC	Disseminated Intra-vascular Coagulation (a serious complication of many conditions-relates to widespread thrombosis)
DID	Dissociative Identity Disorder
Dil	Dilute
DIP	Distal Interphalangeal Joint
DiPer Te	Diphtheria Pertussis Tetanus
Dis	Dislocation
DiTe	Diphtheria Tetanus
DIU	Death in Utero-Stillbirth
DJD	Degenerative Joint Disease (Osteoarthritis)
DKA	Diabetic Ketoacidosis
Dl	Deciliter
DLE	Disseminated Lupus Erythematosus
DLG	Differential Leukocyte Count
DM	Diabetes Mellitus
DMD	Doctor of Dental Medicine
DMD	Duchenne Muscular Dystrophy
DNA	Deoxyribonucleic Acid
DNA	Did Not Attend
DNR	Do not resuscitate
DO	Doctor of Osteopathy
DOA	Dead On Arrival
DOA	Drugs of Abuse
DOB	Date of Birth
DOE	Dyspnea on Exertion
DOPA	Dopamine
DP	Dorsalis Pedis
DPH	Diphenylhydantoin
DPL	Diagnostic Peritoneal Lavage
DPT	Diphtheria Pertussis Tetanus-DPT vaccine
DSA	Digital Subtraction Angiography
DSM	Diagnostic and Statistical Manual
DT	Delirium Tremens
DTA	Descending Thoracic Aorta
DTP	Diphtheria Tetanus Pertussis
DTR	Deep Tendon Reflex
DU	Duodenal Ulcer
DUB	Dysfunctional Uterine Bleeding
DVT	Deep Vein Thrombosis
Dx	Diagnosis
dz	Disease
E. Coli	Escherichia Coli bacteria
EAA	Essential Amino Acids
EACA	Epsilon-aminocaproic acid
EBL	Estimated blood loss
EBM	Expressed Breast Milk
EBT	Electron beam tomography
EBV	Epstein-Barr Virus
ECF	Extracellular fluid
ECG	Electrocardiogram
ECHO	Echocardiogram
ECMO	Extracorporeal Membrane Oxygenation
ECT	Electroconvulsive Therapy
ED	Ectodermal Dysplasia
ED	Erectile Dysfunction
EDC	Expected Date of Confinement
EDD	Expected Date of Delivery
EDH	Epidural Hematoma
EDM	Esophageal Doppler Monitor
EDTA	Ethylene-diamine-tetra-acetic acid
EEG	Electroencephalogram
EEX	Electrodiagnosis
EF	Ejection Fraction
EFAD	Essential Fatty Acid Deficiency

Abbreviation	Medical Term
EGD	Esophagogastroduodenoscopy
EI	Emotional Intelligence
EKG	Electrocardiogram
ELISA	Enzyme-linked Immunosorbent Assay
EmBx	Endometrial Biopsy
EMF	Endomyocardial Fibrosis
EMG	Electromyography
EMR	Electronic Medical Record
EMU	Early Morning Urine Sample
EMV	Eyes, motor, verbal response
ENT	Ear, Nose and Throat
EOM	Extraocular Muscles
EOMI	Extraocular Movements Intact
EPH	Edema Proteinuria Hypertension
EPO	Erythropoietin
EPS	Electrophysiology
EQ	Emotional Intelligence Quotient
ER	Emergency Room
ERCP	Endoscopic Retrograde Cholangio Pancreatography
ERG	Electroretinogram
ESBL	Extended Spectrum Beta-Lactamase
ESR	Erythrocyte Sedimentation Rate
ESRD	End-Stage Renal Disease
ESV	End-systolic Volume
ESWL	Extracorporeal Shock Wave Lithotripsy
ET	Endotracheal
Etiol	Etiology
ETOH	Ethanol
ETS	Endoscopic Thoracic Sympathectomy
ETT	Endotracheal Tube
EUA	Examination under Anesthesia
EUP	Extrauterine Pregnancy
EUS	Endoscopic Ultrasonography
EVAR	Endovascular Aneurysm Repair
EVF	Erythrocyte Volume Fraction
Exam	Examination
Exp Lap	Exploratory Laparotomy
F	Fahrenheit
F/C	Fevers and/or Chills
Fab	Fragment Antigen Binding
FAMMM	Familial Atypical Multiple Mole Melanoma Syndrome
FAP	Familial Adenomatous Polyposis
FB	Finger's Breadth
FB	Foreign Body
FBC	Full Blood Count
FBE	Full Blood Exam
FBG	Fasting Blood Glucose
FBS	Fasting Blood Sugar
FBS	Foetal Blood Sampling (ob)
FDA	Food and Drug Administration
FDC	Follicular Dendritic Cells
FDIU	Foetal Demise in Utero
FDP	Fibrin Degradation Product
Fe	Iron
Fem	Female
FEV	Forced Expiratory Volume
FFA	Free Fatty Acids
FFP	Fresh Frozen Plasma
FH	Family History
FHH	Foetal Heart Heard
FHHR	Foetal Heart Heard Regular
FHR	Fetal Heart Rate
FHS	Fetal Heart Sound
FHT	Fetal Heart Tones

Abbreviation	*Medical Term*
FHx	Family History
Finger-stick	Blood Sugar
Flu	Influenza
FMF	Foetal Movement Felt
FMP	First Menstruation Period (Menarche)
fMRI	Functional Magnetic Resonance Imaging
FNA	Fine Needle Aspiration
FNAB	Fine Needle Aspiration Biopsy
FNAC	Fine Needle Aspiration Cytology
FNC	Full Nursing Care
FNH	Focal Nodular Hyperplasia
FOBT	Fecal Occult Blood Test
FOS	Full of Stool
FPG	Fasting Plasma Glucose
FRC	Functional Residual Capacity
FROM	Full Range of Motion
FSE	Fetal Scalp Electrode
FSH	Follicle-stimulating Hormone
FTA	Fluorescent Treponemal Antibody
FTA-ABS	Fluorescent Treponemal Antibody Absorption
FTT	Failure to thrive
FU	Follow-up
FUO	Fever of Unknown Origin
FVC	Forced Vital Capacity
FWB	Full Weight Bearing
Fx, #	Fracture
G	Gravidity
G6PD	Glucose-6-Phosphate Dehydrogenase
GA	Genera] Anaesthetic/Anaesthes ia
GABA	Gamma-Aminobutyric Acid
GAD	Generalized Anxiety Disorder

Abbreviation	*Medical Term*
GB	Gallbladder
GBM	Glomerular Basement Membrane
GC	Gonorrhea or Gonococcus
GCA	Giant Cell Arteritis
GCS	Glasgow Coma Scale
GDA	Gastroduodenal Artery
GDLH	Glutamate Dehydrogenase
GDP	Guanosine Diphosphate
GERD	Gastroesophageal Reflux Disease
GETT	General by Endotracheal Tube
GFR	Glomerular Filtration Rate
GGT	Gamma Glutamyl Transpeptidase
GH	Growth Hormone
GHFR	Growth Hormone Releasing factor
GI	Gastro-Intestinal
GI	Glycemic Index
GIFT	Gamete Intrafallopian Transfer
GIST	Gastrointestinal Stromal Tumor
GIT	Gastrointestinal Tract
GITS	Gastrointestinal Therapeutic System
GMC	General Medical Condition
GM-CSF	Granulocyte-Monocyte-Colony Stimulating Factor
GMP	Guanosine Monophosphate
GN	Glomerulonephritis (Nephritis)
GnRH	Gonadotropin-Releasing Hormone
GOAT	Galveston Orientation and Amnesia Test
GOD	Glucose Oxidase
Gomer	Get Outta My ER
GORD	Gastroesophageal Reflux Disease

Abbreviation	Medical Term
GOT	Glutamic-oxalacetic Transaminase
GPT	Glutamic-pyruvic transaminase
Gr	Grain
GRAV I	First Pregnancy
GSW	Gun Shot Wound
GTT	Glucose Tolerance Test
GU	Gastric Ulcer
GU	Genitourinary
GUT	Genitourinary Tract
GVHD	Graft-versus-host disease
GXT	Graded Exercise Tolerance (stress test)
Gym	Gymnasium
Gyn	Gynecology
H & E	Hematoxylin and Eosin
H & H	Hemoglobin and Hematocrit
H & M	Hematemesis and Melena
H & P	History and Physical Examination
h.s.	At Bedtime
H/H	Henderson-Hasselbach Equation
h/o	History of
HA	Hypertonia Arterialis
HA, H/A	Headache
HAA	Hepatitis Associated Antigen
HAART	Highly Active Anti-aetroviral Therapy
HACE	High Altitude Cerebral Edema
HAD	HIV-associated dementia
HAE	Hereditary Angioedema
HAPE	High Altitude Pulmonary Edema
HAV	Hepatitis A Virus
Hb	Haemoglobin
HB	Heart Block
HbA	Hemoglobin
HbA1C	Glycosylated hemoglobin
HbF	Fetal Hemoglobin
HBP	High Blood Pressure
HBsAg	Hepatitis B Surface Antigen
HBV	Hepatitis B Virus
HCC	Hepatocellular Carcinoma
hCG	Human Chorionic Gonadotropin
HCL	Hairy Cell Leukemia
Hct	Hematocrit
HCT	Hematopoietic Cell Transplantation
HCTZ	Hydrochlorothiazide
HCV	Hepatitis C Virus
HD	Hodgkin's Disease
HDL-C	High-density lipoprotein-cholesterol
HDU	High Dependancy Unit
HDV	Hepatitis D virus
HEENT	Head, Eyes, Ears, Nose, Throat
HELP, HELLP	Hypertension, Elevated Liver enzymes, Low Platelets
Hema	Hematest
HEMA	Hydroxy Ethyl Methacrylate
HES	Hydroxyethyl Starch
HETE	Hydroxyeicosatetraeno ic Acid
HEV	Hepatitis E Virus
Hgb	Hemoglobin
HGH	Human Growth Hormone
HGPRTase	Hypoxanthine-guanine Phosphoribosyl Transferase
HGV	Hepatitis G Virus
HH	Hiatus Hernia
HHT	Hereditary Hemorrhagic Telangiectisia
HHV	Human Herpesvirus
HI	Homicidal Ideation
Hib	Haemophilus Influenzae B
HIDS	Hyper-IgD Syndrome

Abbreviation	*Medical Term*
HIT	Heparin-induced Thrombocytopenia
HIV	Human Immunodeficiency Virus
HJR	Hepatojugular Reflex
HL	Hearing Level
HL	Hepatic Lipase
HL	Hodgkin's Lymphoma
HLA	Histocompatibility Locus Antigen
HLA	Human Leukocyte Antigen
HLHS	Hypoplastic Left Heart Syndrome
HMD	Hyaline Membrane Disease
HMG-CoA	3-hydroxy-3-methyl-glutaryl-CoA
HMGR	3-hydroxy-30methyl-glutaryl-CoA reductase
HMS	Hyper-reactive Malarial Splenomegaly
HMSN	Hereditary Motor Sensory Neuropathy
HN	Hemagglutinin-neuraminidase
HND	Hemolytic Disease of the Newborn
HNPCC	Hereditary Nonpolyposis Colorectal Cancer
HOB	Head of Bed
HOCM	Hypertrophic Obstructive Cardiomyopathy
HONK	Hyperosmolar Nonketotic Coma
HPA	Hypothalamic-Pituiatary-Adrenal Axis
HPETE	Hydroxyeicosatetraenoic Acid
HPF	High Power Field (Microscopy)
HPI	History of Present Illness
HPL	Human Placental Lactogen
HPOA	Hypertrophic Pulmonary Osteoarthropathy
HPV	Human Papillomavirus
HR	Heart Rate
HRT	Hormone Replacement Therapy
HS	Heart Sounds
H-S	Heel-to-shin test
hs	Hours of Sleep
HSC	Human Chorionic Somatomammotropin
HSG	Hysterosalpingogram
HSM	Hepatosplenomegaly
HSP	Henoch-Schonlein Purpura
HSV	Herpes Simplex Virus
Ht	Height
HT, HTN	Hypertension
HTLV	Human T-lymphotropic Virus
HTN	Hypertension
HTPA	Hypothalamic-pituitary-adrenal axis
HTVD	Hypertensive Vascular Disease
HUS	Hemolytic Uremic Syndrome
HVLT	High-velocity Lead Therapy
HVS	High Vaginal Swab
Hx	History (medical)
Hx/H.O.	History of
I&D	Incision and Drainage
I&O	Inputs and Outputs, Intake and Outputs
I.P.	Indian Pharmacopeia
i.s.q.	No change
I131	Radioactive Iodine
IA	Intra-arterial
IABP	Intra-aortic Balloon Pump
IAI	Intra-amniotic Infection
IBC	Inflammatory Breast Cancer
IBD	Inflammatory Bowel Disease

Abbreviation	Medical Term
IBS	Irritable Bowel Syndrome
IC	Ileocecal
IC	Immune Complex
IC	Immunocompromised
IC	Informed Consent
IC	Intensive Care
IC	Interstitial Cystitis
IC	Intracardiac
ICCU	Intensive Cardiac Care Unit
ICD	Implantable Cardioverter-defibrillator
ICD-10	International Classification of Diseases - 10th revision
ICDS	Integrated Child Development Services Program
ICF	Intracellular Fluid
ICG	Impedance Cardiography
ICH	Intracerebral Hemorrhage
ICP	Intracranial Pressure
ICS	Intercostal Space
ICU	Intensive Care Unit
ID	Infectious Disease or Identifying Data or Identification
IDA	Iron Deficiency Anemia
IDC	Idiopathic Dilated Cardiomyopathy
IDC	Indwelling Catheter
IDC	Infiltrating Ductal Carcinoma
IDDM	Insulin Dependent Diabetes Mellitus
IDL	Intermediate Density Lipoprotein
IDP	Infectious Disease Precautions/Process
IF	Immunofluorescence
IFG	Impaired Fasting Glycaemia
Ig	Immunoglobulin
IgA	Immunoglobulin A
IgD	Immunoglobulin D
IgE	Immunoglobulin E
IgG	Immunoglobulin G
IgM	Immunoglobulin M
IGT	Impaired Glucose Tolerance
IHC	Immunohistochemistry
IHD	Ischemic Heart Disease
IHSS	Idiopathic Hypertropic Subaortic Stenosis
IM	Intramuscular
IM	Intra-muscular
IMA	Inferior Mesenteric Artery
IMB	Inter Menstrual Bleed
IMI	Intramuscular Injection
IMN	Infectious Mononucleosis
IMS	Irritable Male Syndrome
IMT	Intima-media Thickness
IMV	Intermittent Mandatory Ventilation
In aq	In water
Inc	Incomplete
Inf	Injection
INF	Intravenous Nutritional Fluid
INH	Isoniazid
Inj	Injections
IO	Intraosseous Infusion
IOL	Induction of Labor
IOP	Intraocular Pressure
IP	Interphalangeal Joint
IP	Intraperitoneal
IPPB	Intermittent Positive Pressure Breathing
IPPV	Intermittent Positive Pressure Ventilation
IPS	Intra-Peritoneal Sounds
IQ	Intelligence Quotient
IRDM	Insulin Resistant Diabetes Mellitus

Abbreviation	Medical Term
ISA	Intrinsic Sympathomimetic Activity
ISDN	Isosorbide dinitrate
ISH	Isolated Systolic Hypertension
ISMN	Isosorbide Mononitrate
IT	Interthecal
ITP	Idiopathic Thrombocytopenic Purpura
ITU	Intensive Treatment/ Therapy Unit
IU	International Units
IUCD	Intrauterine Contraceptive Device
IUD	Intrauterine Death
IUD	Intrauterine Device
IUFD	Intrauterine Foetal Demise
IUI	Intrauterine Insemination
IUP	Intrauterine Pregnancy
IUS	Intrauterine System
IV	Intravenous
IVC	Inferior Vena Cava
IVC	Intravenous Cholangiogram
IV-DSA	Intravenous Digital Subtraction Angiography
IVDU	Intravenous Drug User
IVF	In vitro fertilization
IVF	Intravenous Fluids
IVI	Intravenous infusion
IVP	Intravenous Pyelogram
IVPB	Intravenous Piggyback
IVU	Intravenous Urogram
IVUS	Intravascular Ultrasound
JIA	Juvenile Idiopathic Arthritis
JMS	Junior Medical Student
JODM	Juvenile-Onset Diabetes Mellitus
JRA	Juvenile Rheumatoid Arthritis
JVD	Jugular Vein Distension
JVP	Jugular Venous Pressure
K	Potassium
KA	Ketoacidosis
KBr	Potassium Bromide
Kcal	Kilocalorie
KCCT	Kaolin Cephalin Clotting Time
kg	Kilogram
KIV	Keep in View
KLS	Kidney, Liver, Spleen
KOR	Keep Open Rate
KS	Kaposi's Sarcoma
KSHV	Kaposi's sarcoma-associated Herpes virus
KUB	Kidney, Ureter and Bladder
KUB	Kidneys, Ureters and Bladder
KVO	Keep Vein Open
L	Leukocytes (White Blood Cells)
L	Litre
L	Lumbar vertebrae
L&D	Labor and Delivery (Childbirth)
LA	Left Atrium, Lymphadenopathy
LA	Local Anaesthetic/ Anaesthesia
Lab	Laboratory
LABBB	Left Anterior Bundle Branch Block
LAD	Left Anterior Descending-Coronary Artery
LAD	Left Axis Deviation-Electrocardiogram
LAD	Leukocyte Adhesion Deficiency
LAD	Lymphadenopathy
LAE	Left Atrial Enlargement
LAHB	Left Anterior Hemiblock
Lam	Laminectomy
Lap	Laparotomy
LAP	Leukocyte Alkaline Phosphatase

Abbreviation	*Medical Term*
LAR	Low Anterior Resection
LARP	Left-Anterior, Right-Posterior
LAS	Lymphadenopathy Syndrome
LASIK	Laser-Assisted In-Situ Keratomileusis
Lat	Lateral
lb, LB	Pound
LBBB	Left Bundle Branch Block
LBO	Large Bowel Obstruction
LBP	Low Back Pain
Lc of ch	Laxative of choice
LCA	Left Coronary Artery
LCIS	Lobular Carcinoma in situation
LCM	Lymphocytic Meningitis
LCX	Left Circumflex Artery
LDH	Lactate Dehydrogenase
LDL	Low Density Lipoprotein
LDL-C	Low Density Lipoprotein Cholesterol
L-DOPA	Levo-Dihydroxyphenylalanine
LE	Lower Extremity
LEC	Lupus Erythematosus Cell
LES	Lower Esophageal Sphincter
LES	Lupus Erythematosus Systemicus
leu	Leukocytes
LFT	Liver Function Tests
LGL	Lown-Ganong-Levine Syndrome
LGM	Lymphogranulomatosis Maligna
LGV	Lymphogranuloma Venereum
LH	Luteinizing Hormone
Lig	Ligament
LIH	Left Inguinal Hernia
lin	Liniments
Linc	Linctus
LLE	Left Lower Extremity
LLL	Left Lower Lobe
LLQ	Left Lower Quadrant
LM	Left Main
LMA	Left Mentoanterior-Fetal Position
LMCA	Left Main Coronary Artery
LMD	Local Medical Doctor
LMP	Last Menstrual Period
LN	Lymph Node
LOA	Left Occipitoanterior
LOC	Loss of Consciousness
LOP	Left Occipitoposterior
LORTA	Loss of Resistance To Air
LOS	Length of Stay
Lot	Lotion
Lp	Lipoprotein
LP	Lumbar Puncture (Spinal Tap)
LPH	Left Posterior Hemiblock
LPL	Lipoprotein Lipase
LPN	Licensed Practical Nurse
LR	Lactated Ringer's Solution
LRTI	Lower Respiratory Tract Infection
LSB	Left Sternal Border
LSCS	Lower Segment Caesarean Section
LSD	Lysergic Acid Diethylamide
LSK	Liver, Spleen, Kidneys
Lt.	Left
LTAC	Long-term Acute Care
LUL	Left Upper Lobe-Lung
LUQ	Left Upper Quadrant
LV	Left Ventricle
LVAD	Left Ventricular Assist Device
LVEDP	Left Ventricular End Diastolic Pressure

Abbreviation	*Medical Term*
LVEF	Left Ventricular Ejection Fraction
LVF	Left Ventricular Failure
LVH	Left Ventricular Hypertrophy
LVOT	Left Ventricular Outflow Track
Ly	Lymphocytes
Lytes	Electrolytes
M	Murmur (heart murmur)
M&M	Morbidity & Mortality
MAE	Moves All Extremities
MAL	Midaxillary Line
MAO-I	Monoamine Oxidase Inhibitor
MAP	Mean Arterial Pressure
MARSA	Methicillin and Aminoglyco side-resistant Staphylococcus aureus
MAS	Morgagni-Adams-Stokes Syndrome
MAST	Medical Antishock Trousres
MAT	Multifocal Atrial Tachycardia
MBT	Maternal Blood Type
MC	Metacarpal Bone
MC&S	Microscopy, Culture and Sensitivity
MCH	Mean Cell Hemoglobin or Mean Corpuscular Hemoglobin
MCHC	Mean Cell Hemoglobin Concentration
MCP	Metacarpophalangeal Joint
MCV	Mean Cell Volume
MDD	Major Depressive Disorder (Clinical Depression)
MDE	Major Depressive Episode
MDI	Metered Dose Inhaler
MDS	Myelodysplastic Syndrome
MEDLINE	Medical Literature Analysis and Retrieval System Online
Meg	Micro gram
MEN	Multiple Endocrine Neoplasia
mEq	Milliequivalent
MeSH	Medical Subject Headings
MET	Metabolic Equivalent
met	Metastasis
Mg	Magnesium
mg	Milligram
$MgSO_4$	Magnesium Sulfate
MGUS	Monoclonal Gammopathy of Undetermined Significance
MI	Myocardial Infraction (Heart Attack)
MIC	Minimum Inhibitory Concentration
MICA	Mental Illness and Chemical Abuse
MICU	Mobile Intensive Care Unit
MIP	Maximum Inspiratory Pressure
ml	Millilitres
MLC	Mixed Lymphocyte Culture
MLE	Midline Episiotomy
MM	Myeloid Metaplasia
MMEF	Maximal Mid Expiratory Flow
Mmol	Millimole
MMPI	Minnesota Multiphasic Personality Inventory
MMR	Measles-Mumps-Rubeila (vaccine)
Mo	Monocytes
mod	Moderate or Modified
MODY	Maturity Onset Diabetes of the Young
MOM	Milk of Magnesia

Abbreviation	Medical Term
Mono	Infectious Mononucleosis (Glandular Fever)
MOPP	Mechlorethamine, Vincristine, Procarbazine and Prednisone
MPD	Myeloproliferative Disease
MPV	Mean Platelet Volume
MR	Mitral Regurgitation
MR	Modified Release
MRA	Magnetic Resonance Angiography
MRCP	Magnetic Resonance Cholangiopancreatography
MRG	Murmurs, Rubs and Gallops
MRI	Magnetic Resonance Imaging
MRSA	Methicillin-resistant Staphylococcus Aureus
MS	Mental Status
MS	Mitral Stenosis
MS	Multiple Sclerosis
MSE	Mental Status Examination
MSH	Melanocyte-Stimulating Hormone
MSM	Methylsulfonylmethane
MSO_4	Morphine or Morphine Sulfate
MSSA	Methicillin-Sensitive Staph Aureus
MSU	Midstream Specimen of Urine
MSUD	Maple Syrup Urine Disease
MT	Metatarsal Bone
MTBI	Mild Traumatic Brain Injury
MTP	Medical Termination of Pregnancy
MTP	Metatarsalphalangeal Joint
MTX	Methotrexate
MVA	Motor Vehicle Accident
MVC	Motor Vehicle Crash
MVI	Multivitamin Injection
MVP	Mitral Valve Prolapse
MVPS	Mitral Valve Prolapse Syndrome
MVR	Mitral Valve Replacement
MVV	Maximum Voluntary Ventilation
N&V	Nausea and Vomiting
N.P.O.	Nothing by Mouth
N.S.	Not Significant
Na	Sodium
NABS	Normoactive Bowel Sounds
NAD	No Abnormality Detected or No Apparent Distress
NAD	Nothing Abnormal Detected
NAS	No Added Salt
NB	Newborn
NBM	Nil by Mouth
NBN	Newborn Baby Nursery or Newborn Nursery
NC	Nasal Cannula
NC	Nerve Action Potential
NCC	Noncompaction Cardiomyopathy
NCS	Nerve Conduction Study
NCT	Nerve Conduction Test
NCV	Nerve Conduction Velocity
ND	Not Done
Ne	Neutrophil Granulocytes
NE	Norepinephrine
NEC	Not Elsewhere Classified
NED	No Evidence of Recurrent Disease
Neg	Negative
Neo	Neoplasm
NES.	Not Elsewhere Specified

Abbreviation	*Medical Term*
NFR	Not for Resuscitation
Ng	Nanogram
NG	Nasogastric
NGT	Nasogastric Tube
NGU	Non-Gonococcal Urethritis
NHL	Non-Hodgkin Lymphoma
NI	Normal
NICU	Neonatal Intensive Care Unit
NIDDM	Non-Insulin Dependent Diabetes Mellitus (Type 2 Diabetes)
NK	Natural Killer Cells
NKA	No Known Allergies
NKDA	No Known Drug Allergies
NLP	Neuro-Linguistic Programming
NLP	No Light Perception
NM	Nuclear Medicine
NMCS	No Malignant Cells Seen
NMR	Nuclear Magnetic Resonance
NNH	Number Needed to Harm
NNT	Number Needed to Treat
NO	Nitric Oxide
No.	Number
Noct.	Of the night
NOF	Neck of Femur Fracture
Non rep.	Do not repeat
NOS	Nitric Oxide Synthase
NOS	Not Otherwise Specified
NPH	Normal Pressure Hydrocephalus
Npl	Neoplasm
NPO	Nil per os
NPTAC	No Previous Tracing Available For Comparison
NRB	Non-Rebreather Mask
NREM	Non-Rapid Eye Movement
NRM	No Regular Medications
NS	Normal Saline
NSA	No Significant Abnormality
NSAID	Non-Steroidal Anti-Inflammatory Drug
NSCC	Non-squamous-cell carcinoma
NSD	Normal Spontaneous Delivery (Natural Childbirth)
NSE	Neurospecific Enolase
NSR	Normal Sinus Rhythm
NST	Non-Stress Test
NSTEMI	Non-ST Elevation Myocardial Infarction
NSU	Non-Specific Urethritis
NT	Nasotracheal
NT	Not Tested
NTG	Nitroglycerin
NTT	Nasotracheal Tube
NVD	Nausea, Vomiting and Diarrhea
NVD	Normal Vaginal Delivery
NVDC	Nausea, Vomiting, Diarrhea and Constipation
O&P	Ova and Parasites
O/E	On examination
O_2	Oxygen
OA	Osteoarthritis
OB-GYN	Obstetrics and Gynecology
Obl	Oblique
OBS	Organic Brain Syndrome
Occ	Occasional
OCD	Obsessive Compulsive Disorder
OCG	Oral Cholecystogram
OCNA	Old Chart Not Available
OCP	Oral Contraceptive Pill

Abbreviation	Medical Term
OCPD	Obsessive Compulsive Personality Disorder
OCT	Optical Coherence Tomography
od	Everyday or Daily
OD	Occupational Disease
Od	once daily
OD	Overdose
OD	Right Eye (Latin: Oculus Dexter)
OE	On Examination
OE	Otitis Externa (Ear Infection)
OGTT	Oral Glucose Tolerance Test
Oint	Ointment
om	Every Morning
OM	Otitis Media (Ear Infection)
OME	Otitis Media with Effusion
on	Every Night
OOB	Out of bed
OPD	Outpatient Department
OPPT	Oriented to Person, Place and Time
OPV	Oral Polio Vaccine
OPV	Outpatient Visit
OR	Operating Room
ORIF	Open Reduction Internal Fixation
ORSA	Oxacillin-resistant Staphylococcus aureus
OS	Left Eye (Ltin-Oculus Sinister)
OS	Orthopedic Surgery
OSA	Obstructive Sleep Apnea
OSH	Outside Hospital
OSHA	Occupational Safety and Health Administration
Osm	Osmolarity
Osteo	Osteomyelitis
OT	Occupational Therapy
OT	Operating Theatre
OTC	Over-the-Counter Drug
OTD	Out the Door
OTPP	Oriented to Time Place and Person
OU	Both eyes (Latin: Oculi Uterque)
oz	Ounce
P	Phosphorus
P	Post
P	Pulse
P&A	Percussion and Auscultation
P&PD	Percussion and Postural Drainage
p.c.	After Food (Latin: Post Cibum)
p.o.	By Mouth
p.r.	Per Rectum
P.R.N.	As Needed
p.v.	Per Vagina
PA	Physician Assistant
PA	Posterior Anterior
PA	Posteroanterior
PA	Pulmonary Artery
PAC	Premature Atrial Contraction
PAC	Pulmonary Artery Catheter
PAD	Peripheral Artery Disease
PAF	Paroxysmal Atrial Fibrillation
PAF	Platelet Activating Factor
PAI-1	Plasminogen Activator Inhibitor 1
PAL	Posterior Axillary Line
PALS	Pediatric Advanced Life Support
PAN	Polyarthritis Nodosa
PAO	Peak Acid Output
PaO2	Peropheral Arterial Oxygen Content
PAOD	Peripheral Artery Occlusive Disease
PAP	Papanicolaou Stain
Pap	Papanicolaou Test (Pap Smear)
PAP	Positive Airway Pressure

Abbreviation	Medical Term
PAP	Pulmonary Artery Pressure
PARA I	Indicating a woman with one child
PAT	Paroxysmal Atrial Trachycardia
pc	After Meals
PCA	Patient Care Report
PCA	Patient-controlled Analgesia
PCa	Prostate Cancer
PCD	Postconcussional Disorder
PCI	Percutaneous Coronary Intervention
PCL	Posterior Cruciate Ligament
PCN	Penicillin
PCNSL	Primary CNS Lymphoma
PCO	Polycystic Ovary
PCOS	Polycystic Ovarian Syndrome
PCP	Pneumocystis Pneumonia
PCP	Primary Care Physician
PCR	Patient Care Report
PCR	Polymerase Chain Reaction
PCS	Post-concussion Syndrome
PCV	Packed Cell Volume
PCV	Polycythemia vera
PCWP	Pulmonary Capillary Wedge Pressure
PD	Parkinson's Disease
PD	Peritoneal Disease
PDA	Patent Ductus Arteriosus
PDD	Pervasive Developmental Disorder
PDE	Phosphodiesterase
PDR	Physician's Drug Reference
PDT	Photodynamic Therapy
PE	Physical Examination

Abbreviation	Medical Term
PE	Pre-eclampsia
PE	Pulmonary Embolism
PEA	Pulseless Electrical Activity
PEEP	Positive End Expiratory Pressure
PEF	Peak Expiratory Flow
PEFR	Peak Expiratory Flow Rate
PEG	Percutaneous Endoscopic Gastrostomy
pen	Penicillin
Per Vag	Per Vaginam
PERLA	Pupils are Equal and React to Light and Accommodation
PERRL	Pupils Equal, Round, Reactive to Light
PET	Positron-emission Tomography
PFO	Patent Foramen Ovale
PFT	Pulmonary Function Test
pg	Picogram
PGCS	Paediatric Glasgow Coma Scale
ph	Acidity/Alkalinity scale
pH	Hydrogen Ion Concentration
PH	Past History
PH	Pulmonary Hypertension
Ph1	Philadelphia Chromosome
PHTLS	Prehospital Trauma Life Support
PHx	Past History (medical)
PI	Present Illness
PI	Pulmonic Insufficiency Disease
PICC	Peripherally Inserted Central Catheter
PID	Pelvic Inflammatory Disease
PID	Prolapsed Intervertibral Disc

Abbreviation	*Medical Term*
PIH	Pregnancy Induced Hypertension
PIP	Proximal Interphalangeal Joint
PK	Pyruvate Kinase
PKA	Protein Kinase A
PKD	Polycystic Kidney Disease
PKU	Phenylketonuria
PLAT	Tissue Plasminogen Activator
PLT	Platelets
PM&R	Physical Medicine and Rehabilitation
PMB	Post-Menopausal Bleeding
PMH	Past Medical History
PMH	Perimesencephalic Subarachnoid Hemorrhage
PMI	Point of Maximal Impulse
PMN	Polymorphonuclear Leukocytes
PMR	Percutaneous Myocardial Revascularisation
PMR	Polymyalgia Rheumatica
PMS	Premenstrual Syndrome
PND	Paroxysmal Nocturnal Dyspnea
PNM	Perinatal Mortality
PNS	Peripheral Nervous System
PO	By Mouth
POD	Postoperative Days
POEMS	Polyneuropathy, Organomegaly, Endocrinopathy, Monoclonal Protein, Skin Changes
poly	Polymorphonuclear Cells
Post	Posterior
POX	Peroxidase
PP	Postpartum or Post-partum

Abbreviation	*Medical Term*
PP	Post-Prandial or Pulsus Paradoxus or Pulse Pressure
PPCS	Prolonged Post-Concussion Syndrome
PPD	(Cigarette) Packs Per Day
PPD	Postpartum Depression
PPD	Purified Protein Derivative or Mantoux Test
PPH	Postpartum Hemorrhage
PPH	Primary Pulmonary Hypertension
PPH	Procedure for Prolapse and Hemorrhoids
PPI	Proton Pump Inhibitor
PPROM	Preterm Premature Rupture of Membranes
PPS	Post-Partum Sterilization
Ppt	Precipitate
PPTCT (HIV)	Prevention of Parent To Child Transmission
PPTL	Post-Partum Tubal Ligation
PR	(*i*) Pulse Rate (*ii*) Per Rectum
PR	Prothrombin Ratio
PRA	Plasma Renin Activity
PRBC	Packed Red Blood Cells
Preme	Premature Baby
Prep	Preparation
PRIND	Prolonged Reversible Ischemic Neurologic Deficit
PRL	Prolactin
PRN	As Necessary
Prog	Prognosis
PROM	Premature Rupture of Membranes
PRP	PanRetinal Photocoagulation
PRV	Polycythemia rubra vera
PS	Pulmonic Stenosis

Abbreviation	*Medical Term*
PSA	Prostate Specific Antigen
PSH	Pscychosocial History
PSP	Phenylsulphtalein
PSS	Progressive Systemic Sclerosis
PSV	Pressure Supported Ventilation
Pt	Patient
PT	Physical Therapy
PT	Prothrombin Time
PTA	Percutaneous Transluminal Angioplasty
PTA	Peritonsillar Abscess
PTA	Post-traumatic Amnesia
PTA	Prior to admission
PTB	Pulmonary Tuberculosis
PTC	Percutaneous Transhepatic Cholangiography
PTCA	Percutaneous Transluminal Coronary Angioplasty
PTD	Prior to Discharge
PTH	Parathyroid Hormone
PTHC	Percutaneous Transhepatic Cholangiography
PTSD	Post-traumatic Stress Disorder
PTSS	Post-traumatic Stress Syndrome
PTT	Partial Thromboplastin Time
PTU	Propylthiouracil
PTx	Pneumothorax
PUD	Peptic Ulcer Disease
PUO	Pyrexia (Fever) of Unknown Origin
PUVA	Psoralen UV A
PV	Per Vagina
PVC	Premature Ventricular Contraction
PVD	Peripheral Vascular Disease

Abbreviation	*Medical Term*
PVFS	Post-viral Fatigue Syndrome
PVR	Pulmonary Vascular Resistance
PVS	Persistent Vegetative State
PVS	Pulmonary Valve Stenosis
PWP	Pulmonary Wedge Pressure
Px	Physical Examination
Px	Prognosis
P-Y	Pack-years
q	Each, every (Latin: Quaque)
q.a.d.	Every Other Day (Latin: Quaque Altera Die)
q.AM	Every morning
q.d.	Each Day
q.d.s.	Four Times Each Day
q.h.	Each Hour
q.h.s.	Every bedtime
q.I.	As much as you like
q.i.d.	Four times a day
q.m.t.	Every Month
q.n.	Every Night
q.o.d.	Every Other Day
q.o.h.	Every Other Hour
q.s.	As much as suffices
q.w.k.	Weekly
q4h, q6h	Every 4 hours, every 6 hours
QALY	Quality-adjusted Life Years
QNS	Quantity Not Sufficient
QOF	Quality and Outcomes Framework
Qs/Qt	Shunt Fraction
qt	Quart
Qt	Total Cardiac Output
R.T.	Radiation Therapy; Reading Test
R/O	Rule Out
RA	Refractory Anemia
RA	Rheumatoid Arthritis
RA	Right Atrium
Rad hys	Radical Hysterectomy

Abbreviation	*Medical Term*
rad	Radian
RAD	Reactive Attachment Disorder
RAD	Reflex Anal Dilatation
RAD	Right Axis Deviation
RAE	Right Atrial Enlargement
RAI	Radioactive Iodine
RAP	Right Atrial Pressure
RAPD	Relative Afferent Pupilary Defect
RBBB	Right Bundle Branch Block
RBC	Red Blood Cells or Red Blood Count
RBP	Retino-binding Protein
RCA	Right Coronary Artery
RCM	Restrictive Cardiomyopathy
RCM	Right Costal Margin
RCT	Randomized Controlled Trial
RD	Retinal Detachment
RDA	Recommended Daily Allowance
RDS	Respiratory Distress Syndrome
RDW	Red Cell Distribution Width
RELP	Restriction Fragment Length Polymorphism
REM	Rapid Eye Movement
RES	Reticuloendothelial System
RF	Rheumatoid Factor
RFT	Renal Function Test
Rh	Rhesus factor
RHD	Rheumatoid Heart Disease
RhF	Rheumatoid Factor
RIA	Radioimmunoassay
RIBA	Radioimmunoblotting Assay
RICE	Rest, Ice, Compression and Elevation
RIH	Right Inguinal Hernia
RIMA	Reversible Inhibitor of Monoamine Oxidase A
RIND	Reversible Ischemic Neurologic Deficit
RL	Ringer's Lactate
RLE	Right Lower Extremity
RLL	Right Lower Lobe-lung
RLN	Recurrent Laryngeal Nerve
RLN	Regional Lymph Node
RLQ	Right Lower Quadrant
RLS	Restless Legs Syndrome
RML	Right Middle Lobe-lung
RNA	Ribonucleioc Acid
RNV	Radionuclear Ventriculography
ROA	Right Occipital Anterior
ROM	Range of Motion
ROM	Range of Movement
ROP	Right Occipital Posterior
ROS	Review of Systems
ROSC	Return of Spontaneous Circulation
RPG	Retrograde Pyelogram
RPR	Rapid Plasma Reagin Test
RQ	Respiratory Quotient
RR	Respiratory Rate
RRR	Regular Rate and Rhythm
RSI	Rapid Sequence Induction
RSV	Respiratory Syncytial Virus
RT	Respiratory Therapy
Rt.	Right
RTA	Renal Tubal Acidosis
RTC	Return to Clinic
RTI	Respiratory Tract Infection
RTS	Revised Trauma Source
RU	Resin Uptake
RUE	Right Upper Extremity
RUG	Retrograde Urethogram

Abbreviation	*Medical Term*
RUL	Right Upper Lobe-lung
RUQ	Right Upper Quadrant
RV	Residual Volume
RV	Right Ventricle
RVAD	Right Ventricular Assist Device
RVF	Right Ventricular Failure
RVH	Right Ventricular Hypertrophy
RVSP	Right Ventricular Systolic Pressure
RVT	Renal Vein Thrombosis
Rx	Prescription Drug or Medical Treatment
S	Sacrum
S&E	Sugar and Acetone
s.c.	Scubcutaneous(ly)
s.d.	Subdermal
S/B	Seen By
S/D	Systolic/Diastolic
S1	First Heart Sound
S2	Second Heart Sound
SA	Sinoatrial Node
SAA	Syntheric Amino Acid
SAB	Spontaneous Abortion (Miscarriage)
SAB	Staphylococcal Bacteremia
SAH	Subarachnoid Hemorrhage
SAN	Sinoatrial Node
SaO2	Oxygen Saturation of Artial Blood
SAPS II	Simplified Acute Physiology Score
SAPS III	Simplified Acute Physiology Score
SARS	Severe Acute Respiratory Syndrome
Sat	Saturation
SB	Small Bowel
SBE	Subacute Bacterial Endocarditis
SBFT	Small Bowel Follow Through

Abbreviation	*Medical Term*
SBO	Small Bowel Obstruction
SBP	Spontaneous Bacterial Peritonitis
SBP	Systolic Blood Pressure
SBS	Short Bowel Syndrome
SCC	Squamous Cell Carcinoma
SCID	Severe Combined Immunodeficiency
Scope	Microscope or Endoscope
SCr	Serum Creatinine
SD	Standard Deviation
SDH	Subdermal Hematoma
Sed	Sedimentation
Segs	Segmented Cells
SEM	Systolic Ejection Murmur
SFA	Serum Folic Acid
SFA	Superficial Femoral Artery
SG cath	Swan-Ganz Catheter
SGA	Small for Gestational Age
SGGT	Serum Gamma-Glutamyl Transpeptidase
SGOT	Serum Glutamic Oxaloacetic Transaminase
SGPT	Serum Glutamic Pyruvic Transaminase
SHBG	Sex Hormone-Binding Globulin
SHx	Social History or Surgical History
SI	International System of Units
SI	Sacroiliacal (Sacroiliac Joints)
SI	Seriously Ill
SI	Suicidal Ideation
SIADH	Syndrome of Inappropriate Antidiuretic Hormone

Abbreviation	Medical Term
SICU	Surgical Intensive Care Unit
SIDS	Sudden Infant Death Syndrome
sig	Write on Label
SIMV	Synchronized Intermittent Mechanical Ventilation
SIT	Stress Inoculation Training
SK	Streptokinase
sl	Sublingual (Below the Tounge)
SLE	Systemic Lupus Erythematosus
SLR	Straight Leg Raise
SM	Multiple Sclerosis
SMA	Sequential Multiple Analysis
SMA	Spinal Muscular Atrophy
SMA	Superior Mesenteric Artery
SMA-6	Six-channel Serum Multiple Analysis
SMA-7	Serum Metabolic Assay
SMO	Slips made out
SMS	Senior Medical Student
SMT	Spinal Manipulative Therapy
SMV	Superior Mesenteric Vein
SN	Student Nurse
SNB	Sentinel Node Biopsy
SNP	Sodium Nitroprusside
SNRI	Serotonin-norepinephrine Reuptake Inhibitor
SOAP	Subjective, Objective, Assessment, Plan
SOB	Shortness of Breath (Dyspnea)
SOBOE	Short of Breath on Exercise
Sol	Solution

Abbreviation	Medical Term
SOL	Space Occupying Lesion
SOOB	Send Out of bed
SOS	Save Our Souls
SOS	Si Opus Sit (if necessary) or See Other Sheet
SP	Status Post
Sp. Fl.	Spinal Fluid
Sp. Gr.	Specific Gravity
Spec	Specimen
SPECT	Single Photon Emission Computed Tomography
SPEP	Single Protein Electrophoresis
SPET	Single Photon Emission Tomography
Sq	Subcutaneous
SR	Slow Release
SROM	Spontaneous Rupture of Membranes
SS	Sickle-cell disease (anemia)
SSRI	Selective Serotonin Reuptake Inhibitor
SSS	Sick Sinus Syndrome
SSSS	Staphylococcal Sclaed Skin Syndrome
St.	Let it stand
Staph	Staphylococcus
Stat	Immediately
STD	Sexually Transmitted Disease
STEMI ST	Elevation MI (Myocardial Infarction)
STH	Somatotropic Hormone
STI	Sexually Transmitted Infection
STI	Soft Tissue Injury
STNR	Symmetrical Tonic Neck Reflex
STOP	Surgical Termination Of Pregnancy (Abortion)
Strep	Streptococcus

Abbreviation	Medical Term
STS	Serological Test for Syphilis
Subq	Subcutaneous
Supp	Suppository
SV	Seminal Vesicle
SV	Stroke Volume
SVC	Superior Vena Cava
SVD	Spontaneous Vaginal Delivery
SVI	Systemic Viral Infection
SVN	Small Volume Nebulizer
SVR	Systemic Vascular Resistance
SVT	Supraventricular Tachycardia
Sx	Surgery
Sx	Symptoms
SXA	Single Energy X-ray Absorptiometer
SXR	Skull X-ray
Syr	Syrup
Sz	Seizure
T	Thoracic Vertebrae
T&A	Tonsillectomy with Adenoidectomy
T&C	Type and cross-match (Blood Transfusion)
T&H	Type and Hold
t.d.s.	Three Times a day
t.i.d.	Three times a day
T.S.T.H.	Too Sick to Send Home
Tab	Tablet
TAB	Therapeutic Abortion
TAH	Total Abdominal Hysterectomy
TB	Tuberculosis
TBC	Total Body Crunch
TBG	Total Binding Globulin
TBI	Total Body Irradiation
TBI	Traumatic Brain Injury
TBLC	Term Birth Living Child
TC	Traffic Crash
TCC	Transitional Cell Carcinoma
TCN	Tetracycline
TCT	Thrombin Clotting Time
Td	Tetanus and Diphtheria
TdP	Torsades de pointes
TEB	Thoracic Electrical Bioimpedance
TEE	Transesophageal Echocardiogram
TEM	Transmission Electron Microscopy
Temp	Temperature
TENS	Transcutaneous Electrical Nerve Stimulator
TERN	Intern
TF, T/F	Transfer
TFTS	Thyroid Function Test
TFTs	Thyroid Function Tests
Tg	Thyroglobulin
TG	Triglycerides
TGA	Transposition of the Great Arteries
THR	Total Hip Replacement
TIA	Transient Ischemic Attack
TIBC	Total Iron Binding Capacity
Tib-Fib	Tibia and Fibula
TIG	Tetanus Immune Globulin
TIPS	Transjugular Intrahepatic Portosystemic Shunt
TKR	Total Knee Replacement
TKVO	To Keep Vein Open
TLC	Tender Loving Care
TLC	Total Leukocyte Count
TLC	Total Lung Capacity
TLR	Tonic Labyrinthine Reflex
TM	Transcendental Meditation
TM	Tympanic Membrane
TMB	Too Many Birthdays

Abbreviation	Medical Term
TME	Total Mesorectal Excision
TMJ	Temporomandibular Joint
TNF	Tumor Necrosis Factors
TNG	Trinitroglycerin
TNM	Tumor-Nodes-Metastases
TNTC	Too numerous to count
TO	Telephone Order
TOA	Tuboovarian Abscess
TOD	Transoesophageal Doppler
TOE	Transoesophageal Echocardiogram
TOP	Termination of Pregnancy (Abortion)
top.	Topically
TOPV	Trivalent Oral Polio Vaccine
TP	Totyal Protein
TPa	Tissue Plasminogen Activator
TPN	Total Parenteral Nutrition
TPR	Temperature, Pulse, Respiration
Tr	Tincture
TR	Tricuspid Regurgitation
TRAM	Transverse Rectus Abdominis Myocutaneous Flap
TRF	Transfer
TRF'd	Transferred
TRH	Thyrotropin Releasing Hormone
TS	Tricuspid Stenosis
TSH	Thyroid Stimulating Hormone
Tsp	Teaspoon
TT	Thrombin Time
TTE	Transthoracic Echocardiogram
TTO	To Take Out
TTP	Thrombotic Thrombocytopenic Purpura
TTR	Transthyretin
TTS	Transdermal Therapeutic System
TTTS	Twin To Twin Transfusion Syndrome
Tu	Tumor
TUR	Transurethral Resection
TURBT	Transurethral Resection of Bladder Tumor
TURP	Transurethral Resection of Prostate
TV	Tridal Volume
TVH	Total Vagina Hysterectomy
tw	Twice a week
Tx	Traction
Tx	Transplatation (Organ Transplant)
Tx	Treatment
U&E	Urea and Electrolytes
UA	Urinanalysis
UAC	Umbilical Artery Catheter
UAC	Uric Acid
UAO	Upper Airway Obstruction
UBD	Universal Blood Donor
UBT	Urea Breath Test
UC	Ulcerative Colitis
UC	Umbilical Cord
UCHD	Usual Childhood Disease
UD	As directed
UDS	Urine Drug Screening
UE	Upper Extremity
UFH	Unfractionated Heparin
UG	Urogenital System
UGI	Upper Gastrointesinal
Ung/ung	Ointment
Unk	Unknown
UOP	Urinary Output
UPJ	Ureteropelvic Junction
URI	Upper Respiratory Infection

Abbreviation	Medical Term
URQ	Upper Respiratory Quadrant
URTI	Upper Respiratory Tract Infection
URTI/URJ	Upper Respiratory Tract Infection
US	Ultrasonogram or Ultrasound
USG	Ultrasonography (Prenatal Ultrasound Imaging)
USP	United States Pharmacopeia
USR	Unheated Serum Reagin
USS	Ultrasound Scan
UTI	Urinary Tract Infection
UUN	Urinary Urea Nitrogen
UVAL	Ultraviolet Argon Laser
V/Q	Ventilation/Perfusion Scan
VA	Visual Acuity
VAD	Venous Access Device
VAD	Ventricular Assist Device
VAD	Vincristine Adriblastine Dexamethasone
Vag	Vaginal
VAMP	Vincristine Adriblastine Methylprednisone
VBAC	Vaginal Birth After Caesarean
VC	Vital Capacity
vCJD	Variant Creutzfeldt-Jakob Disease
VCT	Venous Clotting Time
VCTC	Voluntary Counselling and Testing Centers
VCUG	Voiding Cysourethrogram
VD	Vaginal Delivery
VD	Venereal Disease
VD	Volume of Distribution
VDRF	Ventilator Dependent Respiratory Failure
VDRL	Venereal Diseases Research Laboratory
VE	Vaginal Examination
VEB	Ventricular Ectopic Beat
VF or V-fib	Ventricular Fibrillation
VIP	Vasoactive Intestinal Peptide
VLDL	Very Low Density Lipoprotein
VMA	Vanillylmandelic Acid
VMA	Violent Mechanical Asphyxia
VNPI	VanNuys Prognostic Scoring Index (Ductal Carcinoma)
VO	Verbal Order
VOD	Volume of Distribution
VPA	Valproic Acid
VPAP	Variable Positive Airway Pressure
VPB	Ventricular Premature Beats
VPC	Ventricular Premature Contraction
VRE	Vancomycin-Resistant Enterococcus
VRSA	Vancomycin-resistant Staphylococcus aureus
VS	Vital Signs
VSD	Ventricular Septal Defect
VSR	Ventricular Septal Rupture
VSS	Vital Signs Stable
VT	Ventricular Tachycardia
VTE	Venous Thromboembolism
VV	Varicose Veins
VW	Vessel Wall
VWD	Von Willebrand's Disease
VZV	Varicella Zoster Virus
W	With
W/C	Wheelchair
w/o	without
W/U	Workup

Abbreviation	*Medical Term*
WAP	Wandering Atrial Pacemaker
WAT	white adipose tissue
WB	Whole Blood
WBC	White Blood Cell, White Blood Cell Count
WBR	whole body radiation
WC	white cells
WD	well developed
WDL	within defined limits
WDWN	well developed and well nourished
WF	white female
WH	Well Hydrated (No Dehydration nor Water Intoxication)
WIA	wounded in action
WN	well nourished
WNL	within normal limits
WO	written order, weeks old, wide open.
WOP	without pain
WPW	Wolff-Parkinson-White Syndrome
WS	Waardenburg Syndrome
WS	Water-Soluble
WS	Werner Syndrome
WS	West Syndrome
WS	Williams Syndrome
WS	Wolfram Syndrome
wt	Weight
W-T-D	wet to dry

Abbreviation	*Medical Term*
WWI	Walking while intoxicated
X2d	Times 2 days
XL	Extended Release
XL	Extra Large
XM	Crossmatch
XMM	Xeromammography
XOM	Extraocular Movements
XR	Extended Release
XR	X-ray Radiography (Radiation Therapy)
XRT	Radiation Therapy or X-ray Threapy
XRT XS	Excessive
XULN	Times Upper Limit of Normal
YF	Yellow Fever
YLC	Youngest Living Child
YO/yo	Years Old
YOB	Year of Birth
ytd	Year to Date
ZD	Zinc Deficiency
ZDV	Zidovudine
ZE	Zollinger-Ellison
Z-ESR	Zeta Erythrocyte Sedimentation Rate
ZIFT	Zygote Intrafallopian Transfer
Zn	Zinc
ZnO	Zinc Oxide
ZSB	Zero Stools Since Birth

APPENDIX XVI
List of Medical Prefixes

Prefixes, the most frequently used elements in the formation of Greek and Latin words, consist of one or more syllables (prepositions or adverbs) placed before words or roots to show various kinds of relationships. They are never used independently, but when added before verbs, adjectives, or nouns, they modify the meaning. Many prefixes are added to other words with a hyphen, but medical dictionary publishers are opting to drop the hyphen on many of the more common prefixed medical words.

Most prefixes are a part of words in ordinary speech and do not refer specifically to medical or scientific terminology, but there are many that occur frequently in medical terminology and studying them is an important step in learning medical terms and building a medical vocabulary.

Prefix	*Translation of Greek or Latin*	*Examples*
A ("an" before vowel) Without	lack of	Apathy (lack of feeling); apnea (without breath); aphasia (without speech); anemia (lack of blood)
Ab	Away from	Abductor (leading away from); aboral (away from mouth)
Ad	To, toward, near to	Adductor (leading toward); adhesion (sticking to); adnexia (structures joined to); adrenal (near the kidney)
Ambi	Both	Ambidextrous (ability to use hands equally); ambilaterally (both sides)
Amphi	About, on both sides, both	Amphibious (living on both land and water)
Ampho	Both	Amphogenic (producing offspring of both sexes)
Ana	Up, back, again, excessive	Anatomy (a cutting up); anagenesis (reproduction of tissue); anasarca (excessive serum in cellular tissues of body)
Ante	Before, forward	Antecubital (before elbow); anteflexion (forward bending)
Anti	Against, opposed to, reversed	Antiperistalsis (reversed peristalsis); antisepsis (against infection)
Apo	From, away from	Aponeurosis (away from tendon); apochromatic (abnormal color)

Prefix	*Translation of Greek or Latin*	*Examples*
Bi	Twice, double	Biarticulate (double joint); bifocal (two foci); bifurcation (two branches)
Cata	Down, according to, complete	Catabolism (breaking down); catalepsia (complete seizure); catarrh (flowing down)
Circum	Around, about	Circumflex (winding about); circumference (surrounding); circumarticular (around joint)
Com	With, together	Commissure (sending or coming together)
Con	With, together	Conductor (leading together); concrescence (growing together); concentric (having a common center)
Contra	Against, opposite	Contralateral (opposite side); contraception (prevention of conception); contraindicated (not indicated)
De	Away from	Dehydrate (remove water from); dedentition (removal of teeth); decompensation (failure of compensation)
Di	Twice, double	Diplopia (double vision); dichromatic (two colors); digastric (double stomach)
Dia	Through, apart, across, completely	Diaphragm (wall across); diapedesis (ooze through); diagnosis (complete knowledge)
Dis	Reversal, apart from, separation	Disinfection (apart from infection); disparity (apart from equality); dissect (cut apart)
Dys	Bad, difficult, disordered	Dyspepsia (bad digestion); dyspnea (difficult breathing); dystopia (disordered position)
E, ex	Out, away from	Enucleate (remove from); eviscerate (take out viscera or bowels); exostosis (outgrowth of bone)
Ec	Out from	Ectopic (out of place); eccentric (away from center); ectasia (stretching out or dilation)
Ecto	On outer side, situated on	Ectoderm (outer skin);ectoretina (outer layer of retina)
Em, en.	In	Empyema (pus in); encephalon (in the head)
Endo	Within	Endocardium (within heart); endometrium (within uterus)
Epi	Upon, on	Epidural (upon dura); epidermis (on skin)
Exo	Outside, on outer side, outer layer	Exogenous (produce outside); exocolitis (inflammation of outer coat of colon)
Extra	Outside	Extracellular (outside cell); extrapleural (outside pleura)
He mi	Half	Hemiplegia (partial paralysis); hemianesthesia (loss of feeling on one side of body)

Prefix	*Translation of Greek or Latin*	*Examples*
Hyper	Over, above, excessive	Hyperemia (excessive blood); hypertrophy (overgrowth); hyperplasia (excessive formation)
Hypo	Under, below, deficient	Hypotension (low blood pressure); hypothyroidism (deficiency or underfunction of thyroid)
Im, in	In, Into	Immersion (act of dipping in); infiltration (act of filtering in); injection (act of forcing liquid into)
Im, in	Not	Immature (not mature); involuntary (not voluntary); inability (not able)
Infra	Below	Infraorbital (below eye); infraclavicular (below clavicle or collarbone)
Inter	Between	Intercostal (between ribs); intervene (come between)
Intra	Within	Intracerebral (within cerebrum); intraocular (within eyes); intraventricular (within ventricles)
Intro	Into, within	Introversion (turning inward); introduce (lead into)
Meta	Beyond, after, change	Metamorphosis (change of form); metastasis change (beyond original position); metacarpal (beyond wrist)
Opistho	Behind, backward	Opisthotic (behind ears); opisthognathous (beyond jaws)
Para	Beside, beyond, near to	Paracardiac (beside the heart); paraurethral (near the urethra)
Per	Through, excessive	Permeate (pass through); perforate (bore through); peracute (excessively acute)
Peri	Around	Periosteum (around bone); periatrial. (around atrium); peribronchial (around bronchus)
Post	After, behind	Postoperative (after operation); postpartum (after childbirth); postocular (behind eye)
Pre	Before, infront of	Premaxillary (in front of maxilla); preoral (in front of mouth)
Pro	Before, infront of	Prognosis (foreknowledge); prophase (appear before)
Re	Back, again, contrary	Reflex (bend back); revert (turn again to); regurgitation (backward flowing, contrary to normal)
Retro	Backward, located behind	Retrocervical (located behind cervix); retrograde (going backward); retrolingual. (behind tongue)

Prefix	*Translation of Greek or Latin*	*Examples*
Semi	Half	Semicartilaginous (half cartilage); semilunar (halfmoon); semiconscious (half conscious)
Sub	Under	Subcutaneous (under skin); subarachnoid (under arachnoid); subungual (under nail)
Super	Above, upper, excessive	Supercilia (upper brows); supernumerary (excessive number); supermedial (above middle)
Supra	Above, upper, excessive	Suprarenal (above kidney); suprasternal (above sternum); suprascapular (on upper part of scapula)
Sym, syndrome	Together, with	Symphysis (growing together); synapsis (joining together); synarthrosis (articulation of joints together)
Trans	Across, through, beyond	Transection (cut across); transduodenal (through duodenum); transmit (send beyond)
Ultra	Beyond, in excess	Ultraviolet (beyond violet end of spectrum); ultraligation (ligation of vessel beyond point of origin); ultrasonic (sound waves beyond the upper frequency of hearing by human ear)

SOME OTHER PREFIXES (a(d)-towards)

Stem	*Meaning*
a(n)-	without
ab-	from
ab(s)-	away from
ad-	towards
allo-	other, another
ambi-	both
amphi-	on both sides, around
ana-	up to, back, again, movement from
aniso-	different, unequal
ante-	before, forwards
anti-	against, opposite
ap-, apo-	from, back, again
bi(s)-	twice, double
bio-	life
brachy-	short
cata-	down
circum-	around
con-	together
contra-	against

Stem	*Meaning*
cyte-	cell
de-	from, away from, down from
deca-	ten
di(s)-	two
dia-	through, complete
di(a)s-	separation
diplo-	double
dolicho-	long
dur-	hard, firm
dys-	bad, abnormal
e-, ec-	out, from out of
ecto-	outside, external
ek-	out
em-	in
en-	into
endo-	into
ent-	within
epi-	on, up, against, high
eso-	I will carry

Stem	*Meaning*
eu-	well, abundant, prosperous
eury-	broad, wide
ex-, exo-	out, from out of
extra-	outside, beyond, in addition
haplo-	single
hapto-	bind to
hemi-	half
hept-	seven
hetero-	different
hex-	six
homo-	same
hyper-	above, excessive
hypo-	below, deficient
im-, in-	not
in-	into, to
infra-	below, underneath
inter-	among, between
intra-	within, inside, during
intro-	inward, during
iso-	equal, same
juxta-	adjacent to
kata-	down, down from
macro-	large
magno-	large
medi-	middle
mega-	large
megalo-	very large
meso-	middle
meta-	beyond, between
micro-	small
neo-	new
non-	not
ob-	before, against
octa-	eight

Stem	*Meaning*
octo-	eight
oligo-	few
pachy-	thick
pan-	all
para-	beside, to the side of, wrong
pent-	five
per-	by, through, throughout
peri-	around, round-about
pleo-	more than usual
poly	many
post-	behind, after
pre-	before, in front, very
pros-	besides
prox-	besides
pseudo-	false, fake
quar(t)-	four
re, red-	back, again
retro-	backwards, behind
semi-	half
sex-	six
sept-	seven
sub-	under, beneath
super-	above, in addition, over
supra-	above, on the upper side
syn-	together, with
sys-	together, with
tetra-	four
thio-	sulfur
trans-	across, beyond
tri-	three
uni-	one
ultra-	beyond, besides, over

APPENDIX XVII
List of Medical Suffixes

Suffixes are the one or more syllables or elements added to the root or stem of a word (the part that indicates the essential meaning) to alter the meaning or indicate the intended part of speech.

In order to make a word pronounceable, the last letter or letters of the root to which the suffix is attached may be changed. The last vowel may be changed to an "o," or an "o" may be inserted if it is not already present before a suffix beginning with a consonant, as in "cardiology." The final vowel in the root may be dropped before a suffix beginning with a vowel, as in "neuritis".

Most suffixes are in common use in English, but there are some peculiar to medical science. The suffixes most commonly used to indicate disease are **"itis,"** meaning inflammation; **"oma,"** meaning tumor; and **"osis,"** meaning a condition, usually morbid. The suffixes listed occur often in medical terminology, but they are also used in ordinary language.

Suffix	***Use***	***Examples***
ize, ate	Add to nouns or adjectives to make verbs expressing to use and to act like; to subject to; make into	Visualize (able to see); impersonate (act like); hypnotize (Put into state of hypnosis)
ist, or, er	Add to verbs to make nouns expressing agent or person concerned or instrument	Anesthetist (one who practices the science of anesthesia); dissector (Instrument that dissects or person who dissects); donor (giver)
ent	Add to verbs to make adjectives or nouns of agency	Recipient (one who receives); concurrent (happening at same time)
sia, y, tion	Add to verbs to make nouns expressing action, process, or condition	Therapy (treatment); inhalation (act of inhaling); anesthesia (process or condition of feeling)
ia, ity	Add to adjectives or nouns to make nouns expressing quality or condition	Septicemia (poisoning of blood); disparity (inequality); acidity (condition of excess acid); neuralgia (pain in nerves)
ma, mata, men, -mina, ment, ure	Add to verbs to make nouns expressing result of action or object of action	Trauma (injury); foramina (openings); ligament (tough fibrous band holding bone or viscera together); fissure (groove)
ium, olus, olum, -culus,	Add to nouns to make diminutive nouns	Bacterium; alveolus (air sac) follicle (little bag); cerebellum (little brain);

Suffix	*Use*	*Examples*
culum, cule, -cle		molecule (little mass); ossicle (little bone)
ible, ile	Add to verbs to make adjectives expressing ability or capacity	Contractile (ability to contract); edible (capable of being eaten); flexible (capable of being bent)
al, c, ious	Add to nouns to make adjectives expressing relationship, concern, or pertaining to	Neural (referring to nerve); neoplastic (referring to neoplasm); cardiac (referring heart); delirious (suffering from delirium)
id	Add to verbs or nouns to make adjectives expressing state or condition	Flaccid (state of being weak or lax); fluid (state of being liquid)
tic	Add to a verb to make an adjective showing relationship	Caustic (referring to burn); acoustic (referring to sound or hearing)
oid, form	Add to nouns to make adjectives expressing resemblance	Polypoid (resembling polyp); plexiform (resembling a plexus); fusiform (resembling a fusion); epidermoid (resembling epidermis)
ous	Add to nouns to make adjectives expressing material	Ferrous (composed of iron); serous (composed of serum); mucinous (composed of mucin)

SOME OTHER SUFFIXES

Stems	*Meanings*
acanth	spine, prickle
aceto	vinegar
acou	hear
acro	extremity, tip, sharp
actin	ray, beam
acu	sharp, abrupt, sudden
adeno	gland
adipo	fat
aero	air
(a)esth	perception
agogue	leader
agon	contest, struggle
ala	wing
alb	white
algo	pain
alien	stranger, strange
allelo	one another, mutual
amauros	blind
am(o)eb	constantly changing
ambi/amph	both sides
ambly	dim, faint
ambul(o)-	walk
amnio	amnion, "bowl"
amylo	starch
andro	male
angio	vessel (blood, bile)
ankyl	bent, crooked; a joint locked in one position
annulus	little ring
anser	goose
anthem	flower
anthrac	black
anthro	man/human
aort	aorta
aphro	froth, sexual love
aqu	water
arachn	spider, spiderweb
archo	ancient, beginning
argy	silver, shiny
artero	artery (as opposed to vein)
arthro	joint
artic	little joint
asthm	panting, short breaths
athero	gruel
atri	entry chamber

Stems	Meanings
axilla	armpit
axo	center, axis
aud	hear
aur	hear
aus	hear
auto	self
aux	make grow
azo	nitrogen
bac(t)	rod
ball	throw
balano	acorn, glans
blast	sprout
blenno	snot
bleph	eyelid
bol	throw
brachi	arm
brady	slow
branch	gill
bronch	bronchus
bucc	cheek (inside)
burs	bursa, purse
caes	cut deep
c(h)ord	notochord
c(o)ele	rupture
carpo	wrist
calci	limestone
calco	heel, spur
calyc	cup
campy	bend
canc	crab
capo	head, expanded part
centr	center
carbo	charcoal, carbon
carcin	crab
carcinoma	cancer from epithelium
card	heart, heart-shape
carot	great neck arteries
carpo	wrist
caus	burn
centesis	puncture
centr	center
cep(h)	head, expanded part
cephal	head
cept	seize, take
cereb(r)	brain
cervic	neck
ch(e)ir	hand
chemo	chemistry
chlor	light green

Stems	Meanings
chol(e)	bile
chondr	cartilage; grain
chorea	dance
chori	chorionic membrane
chrom	color
chron	time, long time
chyle	digested food juice
cide	killing, "falling"
cise	cut deep
cili	eyelash
cion	uvula
clast	break
claustr	barrier
cleido	collarbone, key
clino	bed
clivus	slope
coagul	coagulate, clot
coccus	berry
coccyx	cuckoo, cuckoo bill
collic	hill
collo	glue
collus	neck
conios	dust
cond	hard knob
core	dolly, pupil (of eye)
cori	leather
corn	horn
cox(a)	hip
corp	physical body
cre(s)c	grow
cribi	sieve
crine	secretion ("separation")
cubit	elbow
cubo	lay down
cule	little
culpo	vagina
cuneo	wedge
cutis	skin
cyan	dark blue
cycl	circle, wheel
cysto	urinary bladder
cyto	cell
dacr	tear (from the eye)
dacty	finger
demos	people
dens	tooth
dent	tooth
derm	skin
desm	harden, bind together

Stems	*Meanings*
desis	binding
desmo	hard
dextro	right-sided
diadocho	succeed, take over
didym	twin
digi(t)	finger, toe
diphth	leathery membrane
docho	cup, container
drepan	sickle
dromo	running a race; course
duc, duct	lead, guide
dynia	pain
echin	spiny
ectasia	dilatation
edem(a)	excess tissue fluid/"swelling"
embol	bottle stopper
embryo	embryo, fetus
emesis	vomiting
em(ia)	blood
enceph	brain
enchyme	filling, installation
entero	intestine
ergo	work
erythro	red
esthesia	perception
f(a)eco	feces, refuse
fac	make, build, do, perform
facie	face, countenance, looks
fasc	bundle, fascia
fec	make, build, do, perform
fer	carrying, bearing
fibr	fibrous
fic	make, build, do, perform
fis, fid	split, cleave, divide
fistula	pipe
flagel	whip
flav	yellow
flat	blow
flect	bend
flex	bend
fora/foro	make a hole
fornic	arch
fract	break into pieces
frag	break into pieces
fring	break into pieces
fuge	flee

Stems	*Meanings*
fun	melt, pour
fus	melt, pour
gala(k)	milk
gam(y)	marry
gangl	knot
gangr	gangrene, gnawing sore
galact	milk
gastr	stomach, belly
gemin	twin
gen	become, beget, produce
genesis	origin
genu	knee
ger	old age
gest	bring forth, produce
glans	acorn
gleno	shoulder
gli(o)	glial cells, literally "glue"
glob	sphere, ball, round body
glomer	tuft
gloss	tongue
glute	buttocks
gnatho	jaw
gnosis	know
gogue	lead
gono	offspring, product, seed, semen
gonio	angle
gracile	slender
gram	record
gran	grain
graph	writing, scratching
gryph	claw
gynec	female
(h)(a)em	blood
habeo	to hold, habit, general state of
halluc	big toe
helic	spiral
helm	worm
hermaphro	male and female in one body
hepat	liver
hernia	rupture, hernia
hidr	sweat
hippo	horse
histo	tissue, web, cloth

Stems	*Meanings*
hy(a)l	glass, primitive material
hydatid	water drop
hydro	water
hypno	sleep
hystero	uterus
iatric	healing
iatro	physician
ichth	fish
idio	self, personal, private
inguin	part of body from groin to hip
insul	island
irid	rainbow, bright-color circle
ischi	hip joint
islet	island
ject	throw, hurl
jejun	hungry
junc	join together
jug	join together
jux	join together
karyo	nucleus
kera	horny
kern	kernel, deep brain
kerato	skin surface, cornea, horn
kine	set in motion
kyn	dog
lachry	tear (from the eye)
labio	lip
lacto	milk
lal	babble, talk
latero	side
lecith	egg yolk
leiomyo	smooth muscle
lein	spleen
lens	lentil
lepros	rough and rotting off
lepto	thin, fine, slender
leuco/leuko	white
levo	left-sided
liga(t)	bind together, bandage
ling	tongue
lith	stone
lumbo	lower back, loin
lumbri	earthworm
lumen	the tube down a hollow organ
lymph	"clear fresh water"

Stems	*Meanings*
lysis	breaking down
malar	cheek (outside)
mal(i)	abnormal, bad
malacia	soft
malako	soft
malleo	hammer
mania	wild about
medi	middle portion
medulla	soft inner part
meli	sweet
mere	part
manu	hand
mara	wither
mast(i)	whip, flog, beat
mast(o)	breast
mea	passage
meatus	external opening
meios	lessening
melano	black
melia	limb
mening	meninges
men(i)s	moon, month
ment	mind, chin
meter	measure
metro	uterus
mito	thread
mnem	memory
mnes	memory
mob	move
morb	sick
morph	shapes, dreams
mot	move
mur(al)	wall
musc	mouse, muscle
myc(o)	fungus
myelo	soft, pith
myi	fly (insect)
myo	muscle
myxo/muco	slime
narco	sleep
naso	nose
necro	dead
nephelo	cloud
nephr	kidney
nerv	nerve
neuro	nerve
nos, nox	nasty, sickening
nous	mind, spirit
nyct	night

Stems	Meanings
occiput	back of the head
ocul	eye
(h)odo	way, path, road
odon	tooth
odyn	pain
olfact	smell
oma	tumor/lump
omen(t)	omentum
omphalo	belly button
on(e/t)	to be
onco	tumor, mass
onycho	nail (finger/toe)
o"	egg
o"phor	ovary
op/opsy	eye, see, etc.
ophth	eye
opio	poppy juice
opsi	late
opson	relish, meat seasoning
orbi	wheel
orch	testis
org	work
oro	mouth
ortho	straight
os	bone, mouth
osm	smell
ost(eo)	bone
ot(o)	ear
ovin	sheep
oxy	oxygen, acid
p(a)ed	child
palpebr	eyelid
pannus	cloth, rag
pap	nipple
par(i)t	have a baby
parietal	wall
partheno	virgin
partum	birth
patho	disease, misery
pect	chest
pelvis	basin
pes/ped	foot
phage	eat
phakos	lentil, lens of the eye
pharmako	sorcery, poison, drug
pheo	ugly, dusky
phero	carry, bear
philo	like, love
phlebo	vein

Stems	Meanings
phleg	flame
phobia	fear
phoco	seal (the animal)
phoro	carry, bear
phos/phot	light
phragm	divide into two, wall off
phren	mind, breath
phth	waste away, wither
phyllo	leaf-like
physio	nature
phyte	a plant
pineo	pine cone
pinna	feather
pino	drink
pisi	pea
pituit	snot
placent	cake, placenta
plak	cake
plantar	sole of the foot
plasm	molded
plast	molded
platy	flat
plegia	stroke, paralysis
pleur	pleura ("side of ribs")
plex	braid, wind together
plexy	stroke
plic	braid, wind together
pn(e)	breath
pod(o)	foot
poie(sis)	making
polio	gray; gray matter of the nervous system
pollic	thumb
pomp	precede, parade
porph	purple
porta	door
posthe	foreskin
prac	done
prag	done
prax	done
pre/pro	before
procto	rectum
pron(o)	prone, face down
proto	first
pseud	false
psyche	spirit, mind
psychr	cold, frigid
pter	wing
pto	droop

Stems	*Meanings*
pty(alo)	spit
pulmo	lung
punct	prick, little spot
pupa	doll, miniature figure
purp	purple
pyelo	vat, basin, pelvis
pykno	shrivelled
pyo	pus
p(u/y)ri	pear
pyr(o)	fever (cognate to "fire")
radi	rod
r(h)ach	backbone
re(i)n	kidney
ret(ic)	net
rhabdo	striated muscle
rhaph	sew together
rheo	flow
rheum	runny stuff
rhino	nose
riso	smile
rrha(g)	discharge from a burst vessel
rub(r)	red
sacc	sack
sacch(ar)	sugar
salpinx	trumpet, oviduct
sang(ui)	blood
sapro	dead
sarc(o)	flesh
sarcoma	cancer from connective tissue or muscle
scato	feces, filth
scapho	boat
schi(s/z)	split
sclero	hard
scope	examine carefully
sebo	hard fat, skin grease, suet
sec/seg	cut
sella	saddle
seps/sept	make rotten
septo	fence, partition
sero	whey, wet protein
sial	saliva
sinus	hollow or pocket
skel	dried up, skeleton
soma/somy	body
spasmo	a drawing tight
spondylo	spine
sphinct	bind tight, squeeze shut
sphygno	heartbeat
spir	breathing
splanchn	innards
staphyl	bunch of grapes
stasis	standing up, being stable
stat	stop
statio	standing up, being stable
staxis	drip, drop
stem	standing up, being stable
steato	fat
sterco	feces
sthen	strength
stigm	spot
stole	to pull, to draw
stom(a)	mouth
stomy	mouth
strepto	wavy
stylo	stylus
sudo	sweat
sulco	plowed furrow
syring	pipe, tube, reed
tachy	fast, swift
tact	touch
tainia	band, tapeworm
talo	ankle
tasis	stretch
tarso	flat plate
taxo	arrangement, put in order
telo	the tip, the end
temporal	temple
ten(d)o	stretch, tendon
terato	monster
theca	box (sheath, covering)
thel	breast, covering layer
thenar	palm, sole
thym	mind, spirit, mood
thym	warty mass, thymus gland
thyro	oblong shield
toco	have a baby
tom(e)	cut
tono	stretch
topo	place

Stems	*Meanings*
tort	twist
tox(o)	bow, arrow, poisoned arrow
trema	hole
tricho	hair
trophy	grow/food
tryps	break into many pieces, crush
tuber	bump, potato(e)
typho	smoky, delirious fever
typhl	cecum
unguis	nail (finger, toe)
uro	urine
uvo	grape
vacc	cow
vago	wanderer
valgus	turned outward
varus	turned inward
vaso	blood vessel
velo	veil, curtain, cover
vener	sexual acts, lusty
veno	vein (as opposed to artery)
vert	turn
vesico	bladder
viscero	innards
volv	turn around, twist
	around
xantho	yellow
xeno	stranger
xero	dry
z(a)o	to live
zo"	animals
zema	boiled
zygo	yoke
zyme	ferment

LIST OF ADDITIONAL MEDICAL SUFFIXES (-ase fermenter)

Stems	*Meanings*
-ate	do
-cide	killer
-c(o)ele	cavity, hollow
-ectomy	removal of, cut out
-form	shaped like
-ia	got
-iasis	full of
-ile	little version
-illa	little version
-illus	little version
-in	stuff
-ism	theory, characteristic of
-itis	inflammation
-ity	makes a noun of quality
-ium	thing
-ize	do
-logy	study of, reasoning about
-megaly	large
-noid	mind, spirit
-oid	resembling, image of
-ogen	precursor
-ol(e)	alcohol
-ole	little version
-oma	tumor (usually)
-osis	full of
-ostomy	"mouth-cut"
-pathy	disease of, suffering
-penia	lack
-pexy	fix in place
-plasty	re-shaping
-philia	affection for
-rhage	burst out
-rhea	discharge, flowing out
-rhexis	shredding
-pagus	Siamese twins
-sis	idea (makes a noun, typically abstract)
-thrix	hair
-tomy	cut
-ule	little version
-um	thing (makes a noun, typically concrete)

APPENDIX XVIII
Glossary of Common Medical Terms

A-, An-: Prefix meaning without, away from, not.

Ab-: Prefix denoting away from, *e.g.*, Abembryonic (away from or opposite the embryo).

Abscess: A localised collection of pus in the body surrounded and walled off by damaged and inflamed tissues. In a cold abscess, due to tubercle organisms, there is swelling, but little pain or inflammation (as in acute abscesses).

ACE inhibitor: Angiotensin-converting enzyme inhibitor: any one of a group of drugs used in the treatment of raised blood pressure and heart failure. They include Captopril and Enalapril.

Acidosis: A condition in which the acidity of body fluids and tissues is abnormally high and at increased level. This is because of failure of the mechanisms responsible for maintaining a balance between acids and alkalis in the blood.

Acro-: Prefix denoting 1. Extremity; tip, *e.g.* acrohypothermy (abnormal coldness of the extremities (hands and feet)). 2. Height; promontory, *e.g.*, acrophobia (morbid dread of heights). 3. Extreme; intense, *e.g.*, acromania (an extreme degree of mania).

Acute: 1. Describing a disease of rapid onset, severe symptoms, but of brief duration. 2. Describing any intense symptom, such as severe pain.

Adenocarcinoma: A malignant epithelial tumor arising from glandular structures, which are constituent parts of organs of the body. Term is also applied to tumors showing a glandular growth pattern. These tumors may be sub-classified according to the substances that they produce, *e.g.*, mucus-secreting and serous adenocarcinomas, or to the microscopic arrangement of their cells into patterns, *e.g.*, papillary zndfollicular adenocarcinomas. They may be solid or cystic (cystadeno-carcinomas). Each organ may produce tumors showing a variety of histological types, *e.g.*, the ovary may produce both mucinous and serous cystadeno-carcinomas.

Adenoma: A benign tumor of epithelial origin that is derived from glandular tissue or exhibits clearly defined glandular structures. Adenomas may undergo malignant change. Some show recognizable tissue elements, such as fibrous tissue (fibro-adenomas), while others, such as some bronchial adenomas, produce active compounds giving rise to clinical syndromes. Tumors in certain organs, including the pituitary gland, are often classified by their histological staining affinities.

Adhesion: 1. The union of two normally separate surfaces, such as the moving surfaces of joints, by fibrous connective tissue developing in an inflamed or damaged region. (The fibrous tissue itself is also called an adhesion). 2. A healing process in which the edges of a wound fit together. In primary adhesion there is very little granulation tissue, in secondary adhesion the two edges are joined together by granulation tissue.

Adjuvant Therapy: Cytotoxic drug treatment given to patients after surgical removal of, or radiotherapy to, their primary tumor when there is known to be a high risk of future tumor recurrence arising from micrometastases. Adjuvant therapy is aimed at destroying these secondary tumors and is recommended for patients with breast cancer, colorectal cancer and other types of cancer.

Adnexa: Adjoining parts, *e.g.*, the uterine adnexa are the fallopian tubes and ovaries (which adjoin the uterus).

Adrenal gland: A triangular mass of tissue covering the superior surface of each kidney.

Agranulocytosis: Disorders in winch there is a severe acute deficiency of certain blood cells (neutrophils) as a result of damage to the bone marrow by toxic drugs or chemicals. It is characterised by fever, with ulceration of the mouth and throat, and may lead rapidly to prostration and death. When feasible, transfusion of white blood cells may be life-saving.

Agraiphia: Inability to express thoughts in writing.

AIDS: Acquired Immune Deficiency Syndrome: an illness which is caused by infection with a retrovirus - HIV, transmitted in sexual fluids and blood (often if not always fatal) in which opportunism infections or malignant tumors develops as a result of the severe loss of cellular immunity.

Air Bed: A bed with a mattress whose upper surface is perforated with thousands of holes, through which air is forced under pressure. This type of bed is invaluable for the treatment of patients with large areas of burns.

-algia: Suffix denoting pain, *e.g.*, neuralgia (pain in a nerve).

Allantois: The membranous sac that develops as an outgrowth of the embryonic hindgut.

Amenorrhoea: Absence or suppression of menstrual discharge.

Amnesia: Disorders of memory, literally without (*a*) memory (mnesis). May be an imprinting deficit for new material, or a memory retrieval deficit for old material.

Amniocentesis: Withdrawal of a sample of the fluid (amniotic fluid) surrounding an embryo in the uterus by piercing the amniotic sac through the abdominal wall. As the amniotic fluid contains cells from the embryo (mostly shed from the skin), cell cultures enable chromosome patterns to be studied so that prenatal diagnosis of chromosomal abnormalities, such as Down's syndrome, thalassaemia (Cooley's anaemia), can be made. Metabolic error and other diseases, such as spina biflda, can also be diagnosed prenatally from the biochemistry of the cells or that of the fluid. Although the risks of amniocentesis, in skilled hands, are extremely low, there is no point in undertaking it unless the parents agree to a termination of the pregnancy if a serious abnormality is discovered.

Amniotic Fluid: Fluid contained within the amniotic cavity. It surrounds the growing foetus, protecting it from external pressure. The fluid is initially secreted from the amnion and is later supplemented by urine from the foetal kidneys.

Amputation: Removal, usually by surgery or by injury, of a limb, part, or organ.

Anaesthesia: Loss of feeling or sensation in a part or all of the body. Anaesthesia of a part of the body may occur as a result of injury to or disease of a nerve, *e.g.*, in leprosy. The term is usually applied, however, to the technique of reducing or abolishing an individual's sensation of pain to enable surgery to be performed. This is effected by administering drugs or by the use of other methods, such as acupuncture or hypnosis. Local anaesthesia: Abolishes pain in a limited area of the body and is used for minor operations, particularly in dental procedures. It may be achieved by injections of substances such as lignocaine (commonly used in dentistry) close to u local nerve, which deadens the tissues supplied by that nerve. Local anaesthesia may be combined with intravenous sedation. An appropriate injection into the spinal column produces spinal anaesthesia in the lower limbs or abdomen. Regional anaesthesia: usually of a limb, is achieved by encircling local anaesthetic solution and is used in situations where general anaesthesia is not appropriate. General anaesthesia: It is total unconsciousness, usually achieved by administering a combination of injections and gases (the latter are inhaled through 11 mask).

Anaphylaxis: An abnormal reaction to a particular antigen, in which histamine is released from tissues and causes cither local or widespread symptoms. An allergic attack is an example of localized anaphylaxis. Rarer, but much more serious, is anaphylactic shock: an extreme and generalized allergic reaction causes widespread release of histamine causes swelling (oedema), constriction of the bronchioles, heart failure, circulatory collapse and sometimes death, - Adj. Anaphylactic.

Aneurysm: Swelling in the wall of an artery.

Angina Pectoris: Pain in the centre of the chest, which is induced by exercise and relieved by rest and may spread to the jaws and arms. Angina pectoris occurs when the demand for blood by the heart exceeds the supply of the coronary arteries and it usually results from coronary artery atheroma.

Angiography: Diagnostic or therapeutic radiography of the heart and blood vessels, using a radio-opaque contrast by inserting a catheter into any chamber of the heart or great vessels for diagnosis, assessment of abnormalities, etc. of the heart.

Angioplasty: Alteration of blood vessel either surgically or by dilating the vessel using a balloon inside the lumen.

Angulation: Abnormal formation of angles of tubular structures such as the intestine, a blood vessel or ureter.

Ankylosing spondylitis: It predominantly affects young males and the inflammation affects the joint capsules and their attached ligaments and tendons, principally the inter-vertebral joints and sacroiliac joints. The disorder can lead to severe deformities of the spine.

Ankylosis: Obliteration of a joint by fusion, either bony or fibrous. It may be congenital (sometimes hereditary), or it may be result of disease, trauma, surgery or contractures resulting from immobility.

Anorexia: Loss of appetite.

Anosmia: Loss of sense of smell. May also affect the perceived taste of liquid and solid foodstuffs.

Anoxia: Deficiency in Oxygen supply to the brain, if profound, causes permanent brain damage.

Ante-: Prefix denoting before, *e.g.*, antenatal (before birth); anteprandial (before meals).

Antenatal: Occurring before birth. Syn. prenatal.

Antero-: Prefix denoting anterior, front, before.

Anuria: Failure of the kidneys to produce urine.

Aorta (pi. aortae or aortas): The main artery of the body, from which all others derive. It arises from the left ventricle (ascending aorta), arches over the top of the heart and descends in front of the backbone (descending aorta), giving off large and small branches and finally dividing to form the right and left iliac arteries. The part of the descending aorta from the aortic arch to the diaphragm is called the thoracic aorta; the part below the diaphragm is the abdominal aorta.

Aphakia: Absence of the lens of the eye; the state of the eye after a cataract has been removed.

Aphasia: Absence of the capacity for language comprehension, or expression, in the absence of any defect in the voice, sight or hearing.

Aphonia: Inability to make sounds.

Aplastic Anaemia: Anaemia caused by deficient red cell production due to disorders of bone marrow. 40% to 70% of the cases are idiopathic; most common in adolescents and young adults. Exposure to chemical and antineoplastic agents, and ionizing radiation can result in aplastic anaemia; chronic renal failure and infiltration of the bone marrow by cells that are not normally blood producing.

Apnoea: Temporary cessation of breathing from any cause. Attacks of apnoea are common in newborn babies and should be taken seriously although they do not necessarily indicate serious illness.

Arachnoiditis: An inflammatory process causing thickening and scarring (fibrosis) of the membranous linings (meninges) of the spinal canal. The resulting entrapment of nerve roots may result in weakness, pain, and numbness in the affected area.

Arch- (arche-, archi-, archo-): Prefix denoting first; primitive; ancestral, *e.g.*, archinephron (first-formed embryonic kidney).

Areola: 1. Brownish or pink ring of tissue surrounding the nipple of the breast. 2. Part of the iris that surrounds the pupil of the eye. 3. A small space in a tissue.

Arter- (arteri-, arterio-): Prefix denoting an artery, *e.g.*, arteriopathy (disease of); arteriorrhaphy (suture of); arteriovenous (relating to arteries and veins).

Arthr- (arthro-): Prefix denoting a joint, *e.g.*, arihrology (science of); arthrosclerosis (stiffening or hardening of).

Arthritis: Pain and Swelling (inflammation) of joints.

Artrial septal defect: Congenital heart defect in which there is an opening between the atria.

Ascites (hydroperitoneum): Accumulation of fluid in the peritoneal cavity, causing abdominal swelling. Causes include infections (such as tuberculosis), heart failure, portal hypertension, cirrhosis and various cancers (particularly of the ovary, pancreas and liver).

Asepsis: The complete absence of bacteria, fungi, viruses, or other microorganisms that could cause disease. Asepsis is the ideal state for the performance of surgical operations and is achieved by using sterilization techniques.

Asphyxia: Condition caused by insufficient intake of Oxygen.

Aspiration: Sucking out fluid (*e.g.*, from a joint or cavity) through a hollow needle.

Ataxia: Loss of coordination and precision of movement of torso, head or limbs due to a defect in the cerebellum, vestibular or proprioceptive system.

Atel- (atelo-): Prefix denoting imperfect or incomplete development, *e.g.*, atelencephaly (of the brain); atelocardia (of the heart).

Artery: A blood vessel carrying blood away from the heart. All arteries except the pulmonary artery carry oxygenated blood. The walls of arteries contain smooth muscle fibres, which contract or relax under the control of the sympathetic nervous system.

Atheroma: Degeneration of the walls of the arteries due to the formation in them of fatty plaques and scar tissue. This limits blood circulation and predisposes to thrombosis. It may be symptomless but often causes complications from arterial obstruction in middle and late life (such as angina pectoris, heart attack, stroke and gangrene).

Atherosclerosis: A disease of the arteries in which fatty plaques develop on their inner walls, with eventual obstruction of blood flow.

Atri- (airio-): Prefix denoting an atrium, especially the atrium of the heart, *e.g.*, atrioventricular (relating to the atria and ventricles of the heart).

Atrium: Chamber or cavity communicating with another structure, pi. atria; chamber of heart.

Atrophy: A state of wasting due to some interference with tissue nutrition. Atypia,

Atypical: The state of not conforming to a standard or regular type.

Audiometry: An apparatus for measuring hearing at different sound frequencies, so helping in the diagnosis of deafness. The assessment and quantification of hearing function.

Aut- (auto-): Prefix denoting self, *e.g.*, autokinesis (voluntary movement).

Aux- (auxo-): Prefix denoting increase; growth, *e.g.*, auxocardia (enlargement of the heart).

Avasular: Lacking blood vessels or having a poor blood supply. (The term is usually used with reference to cartilage).

Axilla (pi. Axillae): The armpit.

Barium Test: A test involving use of barium sulfate as a radio-opaque material for outlining an anatomical area such as the esophagus and other portions of the intestinal tract by use of radiographic or fluoro-scopic examinations.

Bed Sore: Ulcerated area of skin caused by continuous pressure on part of the body; a hazard to be guarded against in all bedridden (especially unconscious) patients. Healing is hindered by the reduced blood supply to the area and careful nursing is necessary to prevent local gangrene.

Bell's Palsy: Paralysis of the facial nerve causing weakness of the muscles of one side of the face and an inability to close the eye. In some patients hearing may be affected so that sounds seem abnormally loud, and a loss of taste sensation may occur.

Benign: 1. Describing a tumor that does not invade and destroy the tissue in which it originates or spread to distant sites in the body, *e.g.*, a tumor that is not cancerous. 2. Describing any disorder or condition that does not produce harmful effect.

Bi-: Prefix denoting two; double, *e.g.*, biciliate (having two cilia); binucleate (having two nuclei). Bicornuate uterus: Having two hornlike processes or projections. The term is applied to an abnormal uterus that is divided into two separate halves at the upper end.

Bifid: Split or cleft into two parts. Bile duct: Any of the ducts that convey bile from the liver. Bile is drained from the liver cells by many small ducts that unite to form the main bile duct of the liver, the hepatic duct. This joins the cystic duct which leads from the gall bladder, to form the common bile duct, which drains into the duodenum.

Biliary: Relating to or affecting the bile duct or bile.

Bio-: Prefix denoting life or living organisms, *e.g.*, biosynthesis (formation of a compound within a living organism).

Biopsy: The obtaining of representative tissue sample for microscopic examination, usually to establish a diagnosis.

-blast: Suffix denoting a formative cell, *e.g.*, osteoblast (formative bone cell).

Blood Pressure: The pressure of blood against the walls of the main arteries. Pressure is highest during systole, when the ventricles are contracting (systolic pressure), and lowest during diastole, when the ventricles are relaxing and refilling (diastolic pressure). Blood pressure is measured, in millimetres of mercury, by means of a sphygmomanometer at the brachial artery of the arm, where the pressure is most similar to that of blood leaving the heart. The normal range varies with age, but a young adult would be expected to have a systolic pressure of around 120 mm. and a diastolic pressure of 80 mm. These are recorded as 120/80.

Bone Marrow: The soft organic material that fills the cavities of the bone. Boyle's apparatus: An apparatus for giving mixture of nitrous oxide and oxygen and adding to them ether and chloroform or trichloro-ethylene vapour. BPH: Benign prostatic hypertrophy.

Brachi-: Prefix denoting the arm, *e.g.*, brachialgia (pain in).

Brachial: Relating to or affecting the arm.

Brachial Palsy: A condition characterised by a weak, numb or paralysed arm. Often caused by injury to the brachial plexus of nerves which arise from the neck to supply the arm (*e.g.*, birth injury).

Brachy-: Prefix denoting shortness.

Brady-: Prefix indicating slow.

Bradycardia: A slow heart beat characterised by a pulse rate below 60 beats per minute.

Brain Stem: Posterior part of the brain comprising the midbrain, pons and medulla containing vital centres, ascending and descending tracts, nuclei of cranial nerves and the reticular formation. The stem like part of the brain which contains vital centres for control of respiration, heart-rate, etc.

Branch- (broncho-): Prefix denoting the bronchial tree, *e.g.*, bronchoalveolar (relating to the bronchi and alveoli); bronchopulmonary (relating to the bronchi and lungs)

Bronchoscopy: An instrument used to look into the trachea and bronchi. There is a narrow flexible fibreoptic instrument with which bronchi can be inspected. With this instrument, the bronchial tree can be washed out and samples of tissue and foreign bodies can be removed with long forceps.

Buerger's Disease: An inflammatory condition of the arteries, especially in the legs, that predominantly affects young male cigarette smokers. Intermittent claudication (pain due to reduced blood supply) and gangrene of the limbs may develop. Coronary thrombosis may occur and venous thrombosis is common.

Bulbar: Concerning the medulla.

Bulbous Urethra: Bulb shaped; swollen; terminating in an enlargement. A part of urethra (external urinary passage).

Burr-hole: Hole drilled in the skull.

Bursa: A cyst-like sac between a bony prominence and the skin, *e.g.* prepatellar bursa, inflammation in which constitutes "housemaid's knee".

Caecal: Pertaining to caecum.

Caecum: A blind-ended pouch or cul-de-sac that forms the first portion of the large intestine, located below the entrance of the ileum at the ileo-caecal valve.—Adj. caecal.

Caesarean Section: A surgical operation for delivering a baby through the abdominal wall. There are several varieties of caesarean section, differing mainly in the technique employed. In addition to its use in cases of obstructed labour, mal-presentation (breech, brow, and shoulder) and in severe ante-partum haemorrhage, caesarean section is being performed increasingly when the baby is at risk and is exhibiting signs of distress. Because of improved techniques in perinatal care, particularly of the preterm baby, the operation may be performed, if necessary, as soon as the child is viable. It is not necessarily true that once a patient has had a caesarean section all subsequent deliveries must be done in this manner.

Calliper (also called calliper splint, orthosis): A surgical appliance that is used to correct or control deformity of a joint in the leg. It consists of a metal bar that is fixed to the shoe and held to the leg by means of straps. It may be made from a variety of materials, including rubber, leather, canvas, rubber synthetics, and plastic.

Callus: The cement-like new bone formation which produces union of the fragments of a fracture.

Calyx: A cup-shaped part, especially any of the divisions of the pelvis of the kidney. Each calyx receives urine from the urine-collecting tubes in one sector of the kidney.—pi. calyes.

Candida: A genus of yeast like fungi that develop a pseudomycelium and reproduce by budding. Commonly part of the normal flora of the mouth, skin, intestinal tract and vagina. One of the most common causes of vaginitis in women of reproductive age.

Candida Albicans: A small, oval budding fungus that is the primary etiologic organism of moniliasis (candidiasis).

Carcinoma: Cancer that arises in epithelium, the tissue that lines the skin and internal organs of the body. It may occur in any tissue containing epithelial cells. In many cases the site of origin of the tumor may be identified by the nature of the cells it contains. Organs may exhibit more than one type of carcinoma, *e.g.*, an adenocarcinoma and zsquamous carcinoma may be found in cervix (but not usually concurrently).

Cardi- (Cardio-): Prefix denoting the heart.

Cardiac: Pertaining to the heart.

Cardiac Arrest: The cessation of effective pumping action of the heart, which most commonly occurs when the muscle fibers of the ventricles start to beat rapidly without pumping any blood (ventricular fibrillation) or when the heart stops beating completely (asystole). There is abrupt loss of consciousness, absence of the pulse and breathing stops. The most common cause is myocardial infarction. Unless treated promptly, irreversible brain damage and death follow within minutes. Some patients may be resuscitated by massage of the heart, artificial respiration and defibrillation.

Carotid Endarterectomy: Operation on the carotid artery (in the neck) to remove debris blocking the artery and hence reduce the risk of a stroke.

Cartilage: A dense connective tissue composed of a matrix produced by cells called chon-droblasts, which become embedded in the matrix as chondrocytes. It is a semiopaque grey or white substance, consisting chiefly of chondroitin sulphate, which is capable of withstanding considerable pressure. There are three types: hyaline cartilage, elastic cartilage mdfibro-cartilage. In the adult, hyaline cartilage is found in the costal cartilages, larynx, trachea, bronchi, nose and covering the surface of bones at joints, where wear and damage results in osteoarthritis. Elastic cartilage occurs in the external ear and fibrocartilage in the intervertebral discs and tendons.

Cataract: Any opacity in the lens of the eye that results in blurred vision. Cataracts may be congenital or due to metabolic disease (such as diabetes), direct or indirect injury to the lens, or prolonged exposure of the eye to infrared rays or ionizing radiation, but they are most commonly a result of age.

Catheter: A flexible tube for insertion into a narrow opening so that fluids may be introduced or removed. Urinary catheters are passed into the bladder through the urethra to allow drainage of urine in certain disorders and to empty the bladder before abdominal operations.

Cauda Equina: It is a bundle of nerve roots from the lumbar, sacral, and coccygeal spinal nerves that descend nearly vertically from the spinal cord until they reach their respective openings in the vertebral column.

Cauterize: To destroy tissues by direct application of a heated instrument (known as a cautery): used for the removal of small warts or other growths and also to stop bleeding from small vessels.—n. Cautery.

-cele (-ceole): Suffix denoting swelling, hernia or tumour, *e.g.*, gastrocele (hernia of the stomach).

Cellulitis: An infection of the deep dermis of the skin by bacteria. It is most common on the lower legs and there may be associated lymphangitis and lymphadenitis. It is otherwise similar to erysipelas, but the margins are less clearly defined because the infection is deeper.

-centesis: Suffix denoting puncture or perforation, *e.g.*, amniocentesis (surgical puncture of the amnion).

Central Nervous System (CNS): The brain and the spinal cord, as opposed to the cranial and spinal nerves and the autonomic nervous system, which together form the peripheral nervous system. The CNS is responsible for the integration of all nervous activities.

Cephalic: Pertaining to the head.

Cerebr- (cerebri- ,cerebro-): Prefix denoting the cerebrum or brain.

Cerebral: Pertaining to the brain.

Cerebral abscess: The brain and its meninges have a low resistance to infection and a cerebral abscess is liable to follow any penetration of these by micro-organisms. The condition is fatal unless relieved by aspiration or surgical drainage.

Cerebral Palsy: Any of various non-progressive forms of paralysis caused by damage to motor areas of the brain before, during birth or early developmental period of brain manifested in early childhood by weakness and imperfect control of the affected muscles. Occurs due to many reasons.

Cervical: Pertaining to the neck.

Cervical Laminectomy: An operation to remove a prolapsed spinal disc from the neck.

Cheir- (cheiro-): Prefix denoting the hand(s), *e.g.*, cheiralgia (pain in); cheiroplasty (plastic surgery of).

Chemotherapy: The prevention or treatment of disease by the use of chemical substances. The term is sometimes restricted to the treatment of infectious diseases with antibiotics and other drugs or to the control of cancer with anti-metabolites and similar drugs (in contrast to radiotherapy).

Cholangiolitis: Inflammation of the smallest bile ducts.

Cholecystectomy: Excision of gall-bladder.

Cholecystitis: Inflammation of the gall-bladder.

Chondr- (chondro-): Prefix denoting cartilage, *e.g.*, chondrogenesis (formation of).

Chondromalacia: Softening, inflammation, and degeneration of cartilage at a joint. Chondro-malacia patellae is the most common kind, affecting the under surface of the kneecap; it results in pain in the front of the knee and grating, which is made worse by kneeling, squatting, and climbing stairs.

Chorion: The embryonic membrane that totally surrounds the embryo from the time of implantation. It is formed from trophoblast lined with mesoderm and becomes closely associated with the allantois. The blood vessels (supplied by the allantois) are concentrated in the region of the chorion that is attached to the wall of the uterus and forms the placenta.

Chorion Biopsy: Biopsy of tissue which establishes an intimate connection with the inner lining of uterus giving rise to the placenta.

Chorionic Villus Sampling (CVS): A foetal monitoring technique in which a sample of chorionic villus is extracted through the cervix or abdomen under ultrasound visualization. The earliest recommended time for sampling is the ninth week of pregnancy. The cells so obtained are subjected to chromosomal and biochemical studies to determine if any abnormalities are present in the foetus. This enables the prenatal diagnosis of such congenital disorders as Down 's syndrome and thalassaemia,

-cide: Suffix denoting killer or killing, *e.g.*, bactericide (of bacteria); infanticide (of children).

Cirrhosis: A chronic disease of the liver in which destruction and degeneration of liver cells occurs.

Claudication: Pain in the calf muscles resulting from defective blood supply owing to arterial disease.

Club-foot (talipes): Congenital deformity of one or both feet in which the patient cannot stand with the sole of the foot flat on the ground. In the most common variety (congenital talipes equinovarus) the foot points downwards, the heel is inverted, and the forefoot twisted. Other varieties are talipes varus, inward deviation of the hind foot; and talipes valgus, an outward deviation of the hind foot, which is much less common.

Coagulation: The process by which a colloidal liquid changes to a jelly-like mass; clotting (of blood).

Cognition: Mental functions of attention, memory, thinking, perception and intellectual activity.

Col- (coli- colo-): Prefix denoting the colon, *e.g.*, coloptosis (prolapse of).

Colostomy: A surgical operation in which a part of the colon is brought through the abdominal wall and opened in order to drain or decompress the intestine. The part of the colon chosen depends on the site of obstruction. The colostomy may be temporary, eventually being closed after weeks or months to restore continuity, or permanent, usually when the rectum or lower colon has been removed.

Colotomy: Incision of colon.

Colporrhaphy: 1. Repair of a vaginal tear by freshening and suturing the edges. 2. A plastic operation on the vaginal walls in order to narrow the lumen.

Coma: An abnormal deep stupor occurring as a result of illness or injury. Absence of awareness of self and environment even when the subject is externally stimulated.

Comminuted Fracture: A fracture in which the bone is broken into more than two pieces. A crushing force is usually responsible and there is often extensive injury to surrounding soft tissues.

Common Bile Duct (CBD): See Bile duct.

Concussion: A reversible disturbance of consciousness following head trauma.

Confabulation: Filling in gaps in memory with invented and often improbable stories or facts which the patient accepts as true.

Congenital Disease: A disease that is present at birth. It maybe due to heriditary factors, pre-natal infection, injury, or the effect of a drug the mother took in pregnancy.

Conjunctiva: The delicate mucous membrane that covers the front of the eye and lines the inside of the eyelids.

Consciousness: State of awareness of the self and the environment the opposite of coma.

Conservative Treatment: Treatment aimed at preventing a condition from becoming worse, in the expectation that either natural healing will occur or progress of the disease will be so slow that no drastic treatment will be justified. See also Radical treatment.

Contra-: Prefix denoting against or opposite, *e.g.*, contraversion (turning away from).

Contracture: Fibrosis of muscle or connective tissue producing shortening and resulting in deformity of a joint. See also Volkmann's contracture.

Contraindication: Any factor in a patient's condition that makes it unwise to pursue a certain line of treatment, *e.g.*, an attack of pneumonia in a patient would be a strong contraindication against the use of a general anaesthetic.

Contusion: Bruising of neural tissue.

Cooley's Anaemia: See Thalassaemia

Cor: The heart.

Cor Pulmonale: Enlargement of the right ventricle of the heart that results from diseases of the lungs or the pulmonary arteries. Such diseases include those affecting the structure of the lungs (*e.g.*, emphysema) or their function (*e.g.*, obesity) except when these changes result from congenital heart disease or diseases primarily affecting the left side of the heart.

Cornea: The transparent circular part of the front of the eye ball. It refracts the light entering the eye onto the lens which then focuses it onto the retina.—Adj. corneal.

Coronary Artery Bypass Surgery: Surgical establishment of a shunt that permits blood to travel from the aorta to a branch of the coronary artery at a point past an obstruction/biockage. It is used in coronary artery disease.

Coronary artery: One of a pair of arteries which supplies blood to the muscles of the heart.

Coronary artery disease: Narrowing of the coronary arteries sufficient to prevent adequate blood supply to the heart muscle, usually caused by atherosclerosis or any other factor, damaging heart muscle.

Cortical Atrophy: Thinning of cortical tissue.

Crani-(Cranio): Prefix denoting the skull, *e.g.*, cranioplasfy (plastic surgery of).

Cranial Nerves: The nerves of the brain, twelve on each side, arising directly from the brain and the brain stem.

Craniectomy: 1. Surgical removal of a portion of the skull, performed to expose the brain and meninges for inspection or biopsy or to relieve excessive intracranial pressure (as in a subdural haematoma). 2. Surgical perforation of the skull of a dead foetus during difficult labour, so that delivery may continue. 3. Opening in the skull where the bone is not replaced. Craniotomy: Opening in the skull where the bone is replaced.

Creatinine: A substance derived from creatine and creatine phosphate m muscle. It is excreted in the urine.

Crepitations (rale): A soft fine crackling sound heard in the lungs through the stethoscope. Crepitations are made either by air passages and alveoli (air sacs) opening up during inspiration or by air bubbling through fluid. They are not normally heard in healthy lungs.

Crepitus: A crackling sound or grating feeling produced by bone rubbing on bone or roughened cartilage, detected on movement of an arthritic joint. Crepitus in the knee joint is a common sign of chondromalaciapatellae in the young and osteoarthritis in the elderly. 2. A similar sound heard with a stethoscope over an inflamed lung when the patient breathes in.

Cryoprecipitate: A component of blood used to aid coagulation.

CSF: Cerebrospinal fluid, which covers the surface of the brain and spinal cord and circulates inside the ventricles of the brain.

CT(Computed Tomography): A scan which uses a finely collimated moving x-ray beam and computed to construct pictures of a part of the body, which show internal structure as though the organ examined had been sliced open.

Cul-de-sac: 1. A blind pouch or cavity. 2. The rectouterine pouch or pouch of Douglas, an extension of the peritoneal cavity, which lies between the rectum and posterior wall of uterus.

Curettage: The scraping of the skin or the internal surface of an organ or body cavity by means of a spoon-shaped instrument (curette), usually to remove diseased tissue or to obtain a specimen for diagnostic purposes. Curettage of the skin is combined with cauterization; it may be used for the removal of basal cell carcinoma, seborrhoeic keratoscs, etc. and usually causes little scarring.

Cyanosis: A bluish discoloration of the skin and mucous membranes resulting from an inadequate amount of oxygen in the blood. Cyanosis is associated with heart failure, lung diseases, the breathing of oxygen-deficient atmospheres, and asphyxia Cyanosis is also seen in blue babies, because of congenital heart defects.—Adj. Cyanotic.

Cyst- (cysto-): Prefix denoting: 1. A bladder, especially the urinary bladder, *e.g.*, cystoplasty (plastic surgery of). 2. A cyst.

Cystography: Radiography of the bladder.

Cystoscopy: Examination of the bladder by means of an instrument inserted *via* the urethra. The cystoscope consists of a metal sheath surrounding a telescope and light-conducting bundles. Irrigating fluid is conducted via the sheath into the bladder and additional channels are available for the catheters to be inserted into the ureters, diathermy electrodes for removing polyps, etc., or biopsy forceps for taking specimens of tumors or other growths.

Cyto-, Cyt-: Prefix denoting the cell.

De-: Prefix denoting: 1. Removal or loss, *e.g.*, demineralisation (of minerals from bones or teeth); devascularisation (of blood supply). 2. Reversal.

Debridement: The process of cleaning an open wound by removal of foreign material and dead tissue, so that healing may occur without hindrance.

Decortication: 1. Removal of the outside layer (cortex) from an organ or structure, such as the kidney. 2. An operation for removing the blood clot and scar tissue that forms after bleeding into the chest cavity.

Deep vein thrombosis (DVT): In contrast to thrombophlebitis, this affects superficial leg veins. Prolonged bed rest, heart failure, pregnancy, injury and surgery predispose to thrombosis by encouraging sluggish blood flow. Many of these conditions are associated with changes in the clotting factors in the blood that increase the tendency to thrombosis; these changes also occur in some women taking oral contraceptives. The affected leg may become swollen and tender. The main danger is that the clot may become detached and give rise to pulmonary embolism.

Defibrillator: An electric device that stops fibrillation (an abnormal rhythm) of the heart.

Degeneration: Death of tissue

Dementia: Deterioration of intellect, involving a diffuse reduction in cognitive functions and changes in personality.

Dermatitis: An inflammatory condition of the skin caused by outside agents.

Diabetes Insipidus: Passage of uncontrolled amounts of dilute urine.

Diabetes Mellitus: Passage of uncontrolled amounts of urine containing too high a concentration of glucose.

Diabetic Coma: Loss of consciousness occurring in diabetes mellitus caused by lack of insulin, which produces metabolic changes with excess production of acetone bodies and metabolic acidosis.

Dialysis: The passage of a solute through a membrane; the process of diffusing blood across a semi-permeable membrane to remove toxic materials and to maintain fluid, electrolyte and acid-base balance in cases of impaired kidney functions or absence of the kidneys.

Diastematomyelia: Abnormal congenital division of the spinal cord by a bony spicule or fibrous band protruding from a vertebra or two, each of the halves surrounded by a dural sac. Diffuse: 1. Not definitely limited or localised. 2. To pass through or to spread widely through a tissue or substance.

Dilatation and Curettage (D and C): Scraping the inside of the womb; this procedure is often performed in cases of excessive bleeding.

Diplopia: Double vision: The simultaneous awareness of two images of the one object. It is usually due to limitation of movement of one eye so that the two eyes cannot simultaneously look at the same object. Double vision that does not disappear on covering one eye can be caused by early cataract.

Disarticulation: Separation of two bones at a joint. This may be the result of an injury or it may be done by the surgeon at operation in the course of amputation, *e.g.*, of a limb, finger, or toe.

Disseminated Intravascular Coagulation (DIC): A condition resulting from over stimulation of the blood clotting mechanisms in response to disease or injury, such as severe infection, asphyxia, hypothermia, abruptio placentae, or intrauterine foetal death. The over-stimulation results in generalised blood coagulation and excessive consumption of coagulation factors. The resulting deficiency of these may lead to spontaneous bleeding. Transfusions of plasma are given to replace the depleted clotting factors and treatment of the underlying cause is essential.

Dors- (dorsi-dorso-): Prefix denoting: 1. The back, *e.g.*, dorsalgia (pain in). 2. Dorsal.

Duct: A tube like structure or channel specially one of carrying glandular secretions.

Duodenal Ulcer: Damaged mucous membrane, usually accompanied by suppuration. Sometimes a sore that bleeds is present. This creates danger of perforation. It heals slowly due to constant passage of irritating fluids, enzymes and food over it.

Dupuytren's Contracture: Thickened fibrous tissue in the palm of the hand causing contracture of the fingers; Contracture of palmer fascia.

Dura (dura mater, pachymeninx): The thickest and outermost of the three meninges surrounding the brain and spinal cord. It consists of two closely adherent layers, the outer of which is identical with the periosteum of the skull. The inner dura extends downwards between the cerebral hemispheres to form the falx cerebri and forwards between the cerebrum and cerebellum to form the tentorium. A thin film of fluid (not cercbrospinal fluid) separates the inner dura from the arachnoid.—Adj. Dural.

Dys-: Prefix denoting difficult, abnormal, or impaired, *e.g.*, dysbasia (difficulty in walking); dysgeusia (impairment of taste).

Dysarthria: Disturbance of speech articulation.

Dyslexia: A reading disability.

Dysmenorrhoea: Painful menstruation, of which there are two main forms: Primary (spasmodic) dysmenorrhoea and Secondary (congestive) dysmenorrhoea.

Dysphagia: Disturbance of swallowing.

Dysphasia: Disturbance of communication. Receptive component in which the written or spoken word is not perceived correctly. Expressive component in which the patient cannot find the correct word to express himself.

Dyspnoea: Laboured or difficult breathing. (The term is often used for a sign of laboured breathing apparent to the doctor, breathlessness being used for the subjective feeling of laboured breathing.) Dyspnoea can be due to obstruction to the flow of air into and out of the lungs (as in bronchitis and asthma), various diseases affecting the tissue of the lung (including pneumoconiosis, emphysema, tuberculosis and cancer) and heart disease.

Dysrhythmias: Abnormal, disordered or disturbed rhythm.

-ectomy: Suffix denoting surgical removal of a segment or all of an organ or part, *e.g.*, appendicectomy (of the appendix); prostatectomy (of the prostate gland).

Ectopic Pregnancy: The development of a foetus at a site other than in the uterus. This may happen if the fertilised egg cell remains in the ovary or in the tube leading from near the ovary to the uterus (the fallopian tube) or if it lodges in the free abdominal cavity. The most common type of ectopic pregnancy is a tubal (or oviducal) pregnancy, which occurs in fallopian tubes that become blocked or inflamed. The growth of the foetus may cause the tube to rupture and bleed. In many cases the foetus dies within three months of conception and the products are absorbed into the maternal circulation. Rarely, the pregnancy may continue until a live baby can be delivered by caesarcan section. The condition may be diagnosed by ultrasound and the products of conception may be removed by laparoscopy before damage is done to the fallopian tube.

EEG: (electroencephalography) recording the amplified spontaneous electrical activity of the brain from surface electrodes.

Effusion: Escape of fluid (pus, blood, serum, lymph) in any cavity within the body. Extravasation of fluid in a joint (or any cavity), *e.g.*, "water on the knee" (*i.e.* synovitis)

Electrocardiogram (ECG): A tracing which represents the passage of the nervous electrical discharge through the muscle of the heart. The technique involves recording from the leads placed on the limbs and on specified parts of the chest wall. Its main use is to follow the progress of a myocardial infraction (ischaernic death of portions of heart muscle) or to assist in the diagnosis in the event of uncertainty: indigestion is, for example, notorious for mimicking cardiac disease.

Electroconvulsive Therapy (ECT): An accepted treatment for, particularly, depressive psychosis. It consists of the passage of an electric current through the frontal lobes of the brain.

ELISA test: Enzyme linked immunosorbent assay test: an initial screening test for detecting HIV antibodies, etc.

Embolism: The condition in which an embolus a clot which has migrated becomes lodged in an artery and obstructs its blood flow. The most common form of embolism is pulmonary embolism, in which a blood clot is carried in the circulation to lodge in the pulmonary artery. An embolus in any other artery constitutes a systemic embolism. In this case a common source of the embolus is a blood clot within the heart in mitral valve disease or following myocardial infarction. The clinical features depend upon the site at which an embolus lodges (for example, a stroke may result from a cerebral embolism and gangrene caused by a limb embolism). Treatment is by anticoagulant therapy with heparin and warfarin. Major embolism is treated by embolectomy or streptokinase to remove or dissolve the embolus.

Embryo: Child-in-utero before completion of eight weeks of gestation.

Emphysema: Air in the tissues. In pulmonary emphysema the air sacs (alveoli) of the lungs are enlarged and damaged, which reduces the surface area for the exchange of oxygen and carbon dioxide. It is usually associated with chronic bronchitis, smoking and advancing age.

Emphysema, Surgical: Collection of interstitial tissue air in the tissues through puncture of the lung by a fractured rib.

Encephalitis: Inflammation of the brain. A potentially fatal viral or bacterial disease that damages the brain andbrainstem bilaterally.

Encephalopathy: Brain damage due to various (*e.g.* toxic) causes.

End- (endo-): Prefix denoting within or inner.

Endometnosis: The presence of tissue similar to the lining of the uterus at other sites in the pelvis, it is thought to be caused by retrograde menstruation. When the tissue has infiltrated the wall of the uterus (myotnetrium) the condition is known as adenomyosis. The tissue may also be found in the ovary, fallopian tubes, pelvic ligaments, on the pelvic peritoneum and even in the cervix and the vagina. This tissue undergoes the periodic changes similar to those of the endomctrium and causes pelvic pain and severe dysmenorrhoea. The pain continues throughout and after menstruation. Symptoms disappear if pregnancy occurs and after the menopause. The formation of pelvic adhesions is a common sequel to endometnosis. In such circumstances the uterus, fallopian tubes, and ovaries may need to be surgically removed in order to alleviate the symptoms.

Endometritis: Inflammation of the endometrium due to acute or chronic infection. It may be caused by foreign bodies, bacteria, viruses, or parasites. In the acute phase it may occur in the period immediately after childbirth (puerperium) but the chronic phase may not be associated with pregnancy (as in tuberculous endometritis). Chronic endometritis in women with IUDs may be responsible for the contraceptive action.

Endophthalmitis: Inflammation, usually due to infection, within the eye.

Endoscope: Any instrument used to obtain a view of the interior of the body. Examples of endoscopes include the auriscope, used for examining the ear canal and eardrum and the gastroscope, for examining the inside of the stomach. Essentially, most endoscopes consist of a tube with a light at the end and an optical system or a miniature video camera for transmitting an image to the examiner's eye.

Endoscopic Retrograde Cholangiopancreatography (ERCP): The technique in which a catheter is passed through a duodenoscope into the ampulla of Vater of the common bile duct and injected with aradiopaque medium to outline the pancreatic duct and bile ducts radiologically. It is widely used in the diagnosis of obstructive jaundice and pancreatic disease.

Endoscopy: Inspection of body organs or cavities by use of the endoscope.

Endotracheal Tube: Tube used inside the trachea to provide an airway through the trachea while preventing aspiration of foreign material into the bronchus.

ENT: Ear, nose and throat.

Enter- (entero): Prefix denoting the intestine.

Enuresis: Urinary incontinence during the night. Involuntary discharge of urine after the age at which bladder control should have been established.

Ependymoma: A cerebral tumor derived from the glial (non-nervous) cells lining the cavities of the ventricles of the brain. It may obstruct the flow of cerebrospinal fluid, causing a hydrocephalus.

Epi- (ep-): Prefix denoting above or upon.

Epidermis: The outer layer of the skin.

Epidural (Extradural): On or over the dura mater (the outermost of the three membranes covering the brain and spinal cord). The epidural space is the space between the dura mater of the spinal cord and the vertebral canal. The spinal epidural space is used for anaesthetizing spinal nerve roots, especially to provide pain relief during childbirth or to reduce the need for deep general anaesthesia (*e.g.* to relax muscles).

Epilepsy: A disorder of brain function characterised by recurrent seizures that have a sudden brief attacks of altered consciousness, motor activity or sensory phenomena. Convulsive seizures are the most common forms of attack. The different forms of epilepsy can be controlled by the use of antiepilcptic drugs.

Epiphysis: The end of a bone during the period of growth.

Episio-: Prefix denoting the vulva. Episiotomy: An incision into the tissues surrounding the opening of the vagina (perineum) during a difficult birth, at the stage when the infant's head has partly emerged through the opening of the birth passage.

Erb's Palsy: Weakness or paralysis of the shoulder and arm caused by injury to the upper roots of a baby's brachial plexus during birth. This may happen if, during a difficult delivery, excess traction applied to the head damages the fifth cervical root of the spinal cord. The muscles of the shoulder and the flexors of the elbow are paralysed and the arm hangs at the side internally rotated at the shoulder.

Erythema: Flushing of the skin due to dilatation of the blood capillaries in the dermis. It may be physiological or a sign of inflammation or infection.

Erythema multiforme: The eruption, which can take various forms, is characterised by so-called target lesions that may be recurrent and follow herpes simplex infection.

ESR: Eryihrocyte sedimentation rate. A laboratory test upon the blood to detect the presence of an inflammatory process in the body.

Euphoria: A state of optimism, cheerfulness, and well-being. In psychiatry an exaggerated feeling of well-being; mild elation.

Euthanasia: The act of taking life to relieve suffering. In voluntary euthanasia the sufferer asks for measures to be taken to end his life. This may be accomplished by active steps, usually the administration of a drug, or by passive euthanasia.

Ex- (exo-): Prefix denoting outside or outer.

Exfoliative: 1. Flaking off of the upper layers of the skin. 2. Separation of a surface epithelium from the underlying tissue. 3. The natural shedding of primary teeth.

Extravasation: The leakage and spread of blood or fluid from vessels into the surrounding tissues, which follows injury, bums, inflammation and allergy.

Facia-: Prefix denoting the face, *e.g.*, faciobrachial (relating to the face and arm); faciolingual (relating to the face and tongue); facioplegia (paralysis of).

Fallopian Tube (oviduct, uterine tube): Either of a pair of tubes that conduct ova (egg cells) from the ovary to the uterus.

Fascia: Connective tissue forming membranous layers of variable thickness in all regions of the body. Fascia surrounds the softer or more delicate organs and is divided into superficial fascia (found immediately beneath the skin) and deep fascia (which forms sheaths for muscles).

Fasciotomy: Surgical incision and division of a fascia.

Fascids: Inflammation of fascia. It may result from bacterial infection or from a rheumatic disease, such as Reiter's syndrome or ankylosing spondylitis.

Fat Embolism: An embolism caused by globules of fat obstructing blood vessels. It frequently occurs after fracture of long and pelvic bones.

Febrile: Feverish; pertaining to a fever.

Femoral: Of or relating to the thigh or to the femur.

Femur (thigh bone): A long bone between the hip and the knee.

Fibr- (fibro-): Prefix denoting fibres or fibrous tissue.

Fibrillation: Quivering or spontaneous contraction of individual muscle fibres, *e.g.*, of heart, skeletal muscles.

Fibroplasia: The production of fibrous tissue, occurring normally during the healing of wounds.

Fibrosis: Thickening and scarring of connective tissue, most often a consequence of inflammation or injury.

Fine-needle Aspiration Cytology (FNAC): A technique that uses samples obtained by fine-needle aspiration to provide information on the cells of tumors or cysts. It is useful for excluding the presence of malignant cells in cysts of the breast and thyroid.

Fistula: An abnormal tube like passage from a normal cavity or tube to a free surface or to another cavity. May be due to congenital incomplete closure of parts or may result from abscesses, injuries, or inflammatory processes. Many fistulae are caused by infection or injury, *e.g.*, anal fistula may develop after an abscess in the rectum has burst, creating an opening between the anal canal and the surface of the skin. Some fistulae develop as complications of surgery, *e.g.*, a rectovaginal fistula (between the rectum and vagina), a urethrovaginalfistula (between the urethra and vagina) or utero-vesical fistula (between the uterus and bladder), pi. Fistulae.

Flaccidity: Decrease or loss of normal tone in muscles leaving them abnormally limp.

Foetus: The child-in-utero after completion of the eighth gestation week.

Follicle: 1. (In anatomy) a small secretory cavity, sac, or gland, such as any of the cavities in the ovary in which the ova are formed. 2. (In ophthalmology) any of the smooth translucent elevations of the conjunctiva produced by an immune response. They are usually associated with viral inflammation.—Adj. follicular.

Fulminanting, Fulminant, Fulgurant: Describing a condition or symptom that is of very sudden onset, severe and of short duration; coming in lightening-like flashes of pain.

Gangrene: A necrosis, or death, of tissue of bone, usually resulting from deficient or absent blood supply. Total death of a structure through deprivation of blood supply.

Gastrectomy: The surgical removal of part or all of the stomach.

Gastric: Pertaining to the stomach.

Gastritis: Inflammation of the lining (mucosa) of the stomach. Acute gastritis is caused by ingesting excess alcohol or other irritating or corrosive substances, resulting in vomiting. Chronic gastritis is associated with smoking and chronic alcoholism and may be caused by bile entering the stomach from the duodenum, but most cases are caused by the bacterium Helicobacter pylori. It has no definite symptoms, but the patient is liable to develop gastric ulcers or gastric cancer.

Gastroenteritis: Inflammation of the stomach and intestine. It is usually due to acute infection by viruses or bacteria or to food-poisoning toxins and causes vomiting and diarrhoea. Fluid loss is sometimes severe, especially in infants, and intravenous fluid replacement may be necessary.

General Anaesthesia: See Anaesthesia.

Glaucoma: A group of eye diseases characterized by increased intraocular pressure, resulting in atrophy of the optic nerve and possibly leading to blindness.

Gloss- (glosso-): Prefix denoting the tongue, *e.g.*, glossopharyngeal (relating to the tongue and pharynx); glossoplasty (plastic surgery of).

Glue- (gluco-): Prefix denoting glucose, *e.g.*, glucosuria (urinary excretion of).

Gluteal: Pertaining to the buttock

Glyc- (glyco-): Prefix denoting sugar.

Graafian follicle: A mature follicle in the ovary prior to ovulatiors, containing a large fluid-filed cavity that distends the surface of the ovary.

Graft: Any organ, tissue, or object used for transplantation to replace a faulty part of the body. A skin graft is a piece of skin cut from a healthy part of the body and used to heal a damaged area of skin. A bone graft is healthy bone collected from the patient or from another person and used to fill a defect in a bone or as a stimulus to fracture healing. A healthy kidney removed from one person and transplanted to another individual is described as a kidney for renal) graft. Corneal grafts are taken from a recently dead individual to repair corneal opacity. Diseased coronary arteries may be replaced by a coronary bypass graft. Artificial tubes and valves are used to replace diseased peripheral arteries and heart valves, respectively.

Grey Matter: Neural tissue largely comprising nerve cell bodies and dendrites constituting the cerebral cortex, the brain nuclei and central columns of the spinal cord.

Guarding: A body defence method to prevent movement of an injured part, esp. spasm of abdominal muscles when an examiner attempts to palpate inflamed areas or organs in the abdominal cavity.

Haem-, Haema-, Haemo-, Haemat(o): Prefix denoting blood.

Haemangioma: A benign tumor of dilated blood vessels.

Haemarthrosis: Effusion of blood into cavity of joint.

Haematemesis: The act of vomiting blood. The blood may have been swallowed (*e.g.* following nosebleed or tonsillectomy) but more often arises from bleeding in the oesophagus, stomach, or duodenum. Common causes are gastric and duodenal ulcers and varicose veins in the oesophagus.

Haematoma: An accumulation of blood (usually clotted) within the tissues, organ or space.

Haemodialysis: A technique of removing waste materials or poisons from the blood using the principle of dialysis. It is performed on patients whose kidneys have ceased to function; the process takes place in an artificial kidney, or dialyser. The stream of blood taken from an artery is circulated through the dialyser on one side of a semipermeable membrane, while a solution of similar electrolytic composition to the patient's blood circulates on the other side. Water and waste products from the patient's blood filter through the membrane, whose pores are too small to allow passage of blood cells and proteins. The purified blood is then returned to the patient's body through a vein.

Haemolytie: Causing, associated with, or resulting from destruction of red blood cells, *e.g.*, a haemolytic antibody is one that causes destruction of red cells; a haemolytie anaemia is due to red-cell destruction, *e.g.*, thalassaemia.

Haemolytic Uraemic Syndrome (HUS): A condition in which sudden rapid destruction of red blood cells, causes acute renal failure due partly to obstruction of small arteries in the kidneys. The haemolysis also causes a reduction in the number of platelets, which can lead to severe haemorrhage. The syndrome may occur as a result of septicaemia following a respiratory or gastrointestinal infection (especially by pathogenic) eclamptic fits in pregnancy or as a reaction to certain drugs.

Haemoptysis: Expectoration/spitting of blood derived from the lungs or bronchial tubes.

Haemorrhage: Blood that has escaped from a blood vessel. An abnormal internal or external loss of blood. An extradural haemorrhage becomes an extradural haematoma when the blood begins to clot.

Haemostasis: The arrest of bleeding, involving the physiological processes of blood coagulation and the contraction of damaged blood vessels. The term is also applied to various surgical procedures, (*e.g.*, the application of ligatures or diathermy to cut vessels) used to stop bleeding.

Hemangiohlastoma: A hemangioma of the brain, usually located in the cerebellum.

Hetni-: Prefix denoting (in medicine) the right or left half of the body.

Hemiarthroplasty: Replacement of the end of a bone on one side of a joint with a prosthesis. It is the treatment for some fractures of the hip and shoulder.

Hemiparesis: Unilateral motor weakness, affecting face, arm, and or leg.

Hemiplegia (hemiparesis): Paralysis of one side of the body. Movements of the face and arm are often more severely affected than those of the leg.

Hepat- (hepato-): Prefix denoting the liver, *e.g.*, hepatorenal (relating to the liver and kidney).

Hepaticojejunostomy: Surgically joining the hepatic duct and the jejunum.

Hepatitis: An inflammation of the liver. Most common cause is one of the five hepatitis viruses (A, B, C, D and E) manifested by jaundice and an enlarged liver.

Hernia: Protrusion or projection of an organ or part of an organ through the wall of the cavity that normally contains it, *e.g.*, inguinal hernia in which there is protrusion of the hernial sack containing the intestine at the inguinal opening. Some other forms of hernia are scroial hernia, femoral hernia, diaphragmatic hernia, hiatus hernia, umbilical hernia, etc. The best treatment for hernias is surgical repair.

Hilum, Hilus: 1. Depression or recess at exit or entrance of a duct into a gland or of nerves and vessels into an organ. 2. The root of the lungs at level of 4th and 5th dorsal vertebrae.

Hist- (histio-, histo-): Prefix denoting tissue.

Histology: The study of the structure of tissues by means of special staining techniques combined with light and electron microscopy.

Histopathology: Histology of diseased tissues.

HIV: Human Immuno-deficiency Virus. This is the virus which causes AIDS.

Hodgkin's Disease: A malignant disease of lymphatic tissues—a form of lymphoma—usually characterised by painless enlargement of one or more groups of lymph nodes in the neck, armpits, groin, chest, or abdomen; the spleen, liver, bone marrow, and bones may also be involved. Apart from the enlarging nodes, there may also be weight loss, fever, profuse sweating at night, and itching (known as B symptoms). Hodgkin's disease is distinguished from other forms of lymphoma by the presence of large binucleate cells (Stern berg-Reed cells) in the cancerous lymph nodes.

Homo-: Prefix denoting the same or common.

Homolateral: Pertaining to or on the same side. Opposite of contralateral.

Horner's Syndrome: A syndrome consisting of a constricted pupil, drooping of the upper eyelid (ptosis), and an absence of sweating over the affected side of the face. The symptoms are due to a disorder of the sympathetic nerves in the brain-stem or cervical (neck) region.

Humerus: The bone of the upper arm.

Humoral: Circulating in the blood stream; humoral immunity requires circulating antibodies.

Humour: A body fluid.

Hyaline Membrane Disease (Respiratory distress syndrome): The condition of a newborn infant in which the lungs are imperfectly expanded. Initial inflation and normal expansion of the lungs requires the presence of a substance (surfactant) that reduces the surface tension of the air sacs (alveoli) and prevents collapse of the small airways. Without surfactant the airways collapse, leading to inefficient and 'stiff lungs. The condition is most common and serious among preterm infants, in whom surfactant is liable to be deficient. Breathing is rapid, laboured, and shallow, and microscopic examination of lung tissue in fatal cases has revealed the presence of hyaline material in the collapsed air sacs. The condition is treated by careful nursing, intravenous fluids and oxygen, with or without positive pressure by a respirator.

Hydr- (hydro-): Prefix denoting water or a watery fluid.

Hydrocele: The accumulation of watery liquid in a sac, usually the sac surrounding the testes. It is treated surgically, by drainage of the fluid or removal of the sac.

Hydrocephalus: An abnormal increase in the amount of cerebrospinal fluid within the ventricles of the brain.

Hydro pericardium: Accumulating of a clear serous fluid within the membranous sac surrounding the heart. It occurs in many cases of pericarditis (hydropericarditis). If the heart is compressed the fluid is withdrawn (aspirated) via a needle inserted into the pericardial sac through the chest wall (pericardiocentesis).

Hyp- (hypo-): Prefix denoting: 1. Deficiency, lack, or small size, *e.g.*, hypognathous (having a small lower jaw). 2.'Below (in anatomy); beneath, *e.g.*, hypoglossal (under the tongue).

Hyper-: Prefix denoting 1. Excessive, abnormally increased. 2. Above (in anatomy).

Hyperphagia: Pathological over-eating.

Hypo: Prefix meaning decrease below the normal; anatomical term for below.

Hypoglecemic Coma: Unconsciousness due to a decreased level of glucose in blood caused by a disease of the pancreas, an overdose of insulin or starvation.

Hypoglycaemia: A deficiency of glucose in the blood stream causing muscular weakness and lack of co-ordination, mental confusion and sweating.

Hypomania: A mild degree of mania. Elated mood leads to faulty judgment; behaviour lacks the usual social restraints and the sexual drive is increased; speech is rapid and animated; the individual is energetic but not persistent and tends to be irritable. The abnormality is not so great as in mania and the patient may appear normal and 'a bit of a character' to those who do not know him. Treatment follows the same principles as for mania, and it may be difficult to prevent an individual from damaging his own interests with extravagant behaviour.—Adj. Hypomanic.

Hypoplasia: Underdevelopment of an organ or tissue. Dental hypoplasia is the defective formation of parts of a tooth due to illnesses such as measles or starvation while the tooth is being formed. It is marked by transverse lines of brown defective enamel, which define the date of the illness.

Hypotension: Low blood pressure.

Hypoxia: The condition of the body when it is supplied with insufficient oxygen for its needs.

Hysterectomy: Removal of the uterus.

Hysterosalpingogram: Radiogram of the Fallopian tubes.

Idiopathic: Denoting a disease or condition the cause of which is not known or that arises spontaneously.

Ileum: The lowest of the three portions of the small intestine. It runs from the jejunum to the ileocaecal valve.

Ili-, Ilio-: Prefix denoting the ilium.

Ilizarov Technique: Developed by Dr. Ilizarov of USSR is used to treat a variety of orthopaedic problems, using an innovative modular circular external fixator with tensioned wires. The Ilizarov external fixator permits stabilisation of high-energy fractures with minimal operative trauma to soft tissues, preserving critical blood supply. Early use of the limb, including weight bearing, is permitted and encouraged. This technique often eliminates the need for extensive soft tissue procedures and bone grafting. Tensioned wire fixators are especially useful in treating chronic rnalunion and nonunion, with or without infection. Angulatory, translation, rotational and length deformities can be corrected and union can be obtained in many of these difficult situations. Another application of the Ilizarov device is in salvage arthrodesis of the knee, ankle and hindfoot.

Image Intensifier: An electronic device that provides a TV image from an X-ray source using photomultiplier tubes in place of conventional photographic film. The technique permits discrimination of much smaller objects in the image.

In- (im-): Prefix denoting 1. Not. 2. In; within; into.

Incision: 1. The surgical cutting of soft tissues, such as skin or muscle, with a knife or scalpel. 2. The cut so made.

Incontinence: The inappropriate involuntary passage of urine, resulting in wetting. Stress incontinence is the leak of urine on coughing and straining. It is common in women in whom the muscles of the pelvic floor are weakened after childbirth.

Incubator: A transparent container for keeping premature babies in controlled conditions and protecting them from infection. Other forms of incubator are used for cultivating bacteria in Petri dishes and for hatching eggs.

Inertia: (En physiology) sluggishness or absence of activity in certain smooth muscles.

Infarction: The death of part or the whole of an organ that occurs when the artery carrying its blood supply is obstructed by a blood clot (thrombus) or an embolus, *e.g.*, myocardial infarction, affecting the muscle of the heart, follows coronary thrombosis. A small localised area of dead tissue produced as a result of an inadequate blood supply is known as an infarct.

Informed Consent: A legal requirement that physicians or researchers inform a patient undergoing surgery or invasive tests or a subject involved in a clinical trial of the nature, risks, and probable outcome of the treatment or research. The patient signs an agreement stating that he or she has been informed and accepts the treatment, surgery or research protocol. Without informed consent, the physician or researcher is violating the patient's rights, regardless of whether the treatment is appropriate and successful.

Infusion: 1. The slow injection of a substance, usually into a vein (intravenous infusion). This is a common method for replacing water, electrolytes, and blood products and is also used for the continuous administration of drugs (*e.g.*, antibiotics, painkillers) or nutrition. 2. The process whereby the active principles are extracted from plant material by steeping it in water that has been heated to boiling point (as in the making of tea). 3. The solution produced by this process.

Inguinal: Pertaining to the region of the groin.

Inguinal Canal: Either of a pair of openings that connect the abdominal cavity with the scrotum in the male foetus. The inguinal canals provide a route for the descent of the testes into the scrotum, after which they normally become obliterated.

Insulin: A protein hormone, produced in the pancreas by the beta cells of the islets of Langerhans, that is important for regulating the amount of sugar (glucose) in the blood. Insulin secretion is stimulated by a high concentration of blood sugar. Lack of this hormone gives rise to diabetes mellitus, in which large amounts of sugar are present in the blood and urine. This condition may be treated successfully by insulin injections.

Intelligence: Those aspects of cognitive function which are measured by an intelligence test; may reflect the ability to learn from experience, think in abstract terms and deal effectively with one's environment.

Inter-: Prefix denoting between, *e.g.*, intercostal (between the ribs); intertrochanteric (between the trochanters).

Intercostal: Between the ribs.

Intra-: Prefix denoting inside; within, *e.g.*, intralobular (within a lobule); intrauterine (within the uterus).

Intracranial Hypertension: High tissue pressure inside the skull, not high blood pressure.

Intra-ocular: Of or relating to the area within the eyeball.

Intra-ocular Lens Implant (IOL implant): It is a plastic lens placed inside the eye after cataract extraction to replace the natural lens.

Intravenous Pyelogram (IVP): A succession of X-ray films of the urinary tract following the injection into a vein of a contrast medium. This material is concentrated and excreted by the kidneys, and the IVP reveals details of the kidneys, the ureters, and subsequently the bladder. An IVP tests kidney function and reveals the presence of stones, tumors, or obstruction in the urinary tract.

Intro-: Prefix denoting in; into.

Intubation: The introduction of a tube into part of the body for the purpose of diagnosis or treatment, *e.g.*, endotracheal intubation in which a tube is inserted through the nose or mouth into the trachea to maintain an airway or to facilitate administration of general anesthetics or oxygen.

Intussusception: The telescoping (imagination) of one part of the bowel into another; most common in young children under the age of four. As the contents of the intestine are pushed onwards by muscular contraction more and more intestine is dragged into the invaginating portion, resulting in obstruction. Symptoms include intermittent colic or pain, vomiting and the passing of red jelly with the stools; if the condition does not receive prompt surgical treatment, shock from gangrene of the bowel may result.

In vitro: Describing biological phenomena that are made to occur outside the living body (traditionally in a test tube).

In vitro Fertilisation (IVF): Fertilisation of an ovum outside the body, the resultant zygote being incubated to the blastocyst stage and then implanted in the uterus. The technique, pioneered in Britain, resulted in 1978 in the birth of the first test-tube baby. IVF is employed when a woman has blocked fallopian tubes or some other impediment to the union of sperm and ovum in the reproductive tract. The mother-to-be is given hormone therapy causing a number of ova to mature at the same time. Several of them are then removed from the ovary through a laparoscope. The ova are mixed with spermatozoa from her partner and incubated in a culture medium until the blastocyst is formed. The blastocyst is then implanted in the mother's uterus and the pregnancy allowed to continue normally.

In vivo: Latin: describing biological phenomena that occur or are observed occurring within the bodies of living organisms.

Ipsilateral: On the same side.

IQ (Intelligence Quotient): A statistically derived average of verbal, non-verbal and general ability from one or many test performances which comprise a standardised intelligence test. An individual performance is compared to the average for a particular age group.

Ischaemia: An inadequate flow of blood to a part of the body, caused by constriction or blockage of the blood vessels supplying it. Ischaemia of heart muscle produces angina pectoris. Ischamia of the calf muscles of the legs on exercise (causing intermittent claudication, *i.e.*, a cramping pain) or at rest (producing rest pain) is common in elderly subjects with atherosclerosis of the vessels at or distal to the point where the aorta divides into the iliac arteries.

Isthmus: A constricted or narrowed part of an organ or tissue, such as the band of thyroid tissue connecting the two lobes of the thyroid gland.

-itis: Suffix denoting inflammation of an organ, tissue, etc., *e.g.* arthritis (of a joint); peritonitis (of the peritoneum).

Keloid: Scar formation in the skin following trauma or surgical incision; a raised firm thickened red scar that may grow for a prolonged period of time.

Keratectomy: An operation in which a part of the cornea is removed, usually a superficial layer. This procedure is now frequently done by an excimer laser, as in photorefractive keratectomy, in which the shape of the cornea is altered to correct long- or short-sightedness.

Keratitis: Inflammation of the cornea of the eye. The eye waters and is very painful and vision is blurred. It may be due to physical or chemical agents (abrasions, exposure to dust, chemicals, ultraviolet light, etc.) or result from infection.

Keratotomy: An incision into the comea.

Keratotomy, Radial: Surgical therapy for nearsightedness. Very shallow, bloodless, hairline, radial incisions are made in the outer portion of the cornea where they will not interfere with vision. This allows the cornea to flatten and to help correct the nearsightedness. About two-thirds of patients undergoing this procedure will be able to eliminate the use of glasses or contact lenses.

Kernicterus (bilimbin encephalopathy): Damage to the brain of a neonate by an excess of bilirubin (bile pigment) in the blood.

Keyhole Surgery: See Minimally invasive surgery.

Koch ys Bacillus: The bacillus causing tuberculosis in mammals.

Kyphoscoliosis: Abnormal curvature of the spine both forwards and sideways: kyphosis combined with scoliosis. The deformity may occur during growth for no apparent reason (idiopathic kyphoscoliosis) or may result from any of several diseases, *e.g.*, Pott's disease, involving the vertebrae and spinal muscles.

Kyphosis: Posterior convexity of the spine.

Labour: The sequence of actions by which a baby and the afterbirth (placenta) are expelled from the uterus at childbirth. The process usually starts spontaneously about 280 days after conception, but it may be started by artificial means. The passage of the infant through the vagina is assisted by contractions of the abdominal muscles and conscious pushing by the mother. When the top of the baby's head appears at the vaginal opening the whole infant is eased clear of the vagina, and the umbilical cord is cut. If the emergence of the head is impeded an incision may be made in the surrounding tissue. In the final stage the placenta and membrane are pushed out by the continuing contraction of the uterus, which eventually returns to its unexpanded state. The average duration of labour is about 12 hours in first pregnancies and about 8 hours in subsequent pregnancies

Laceration: A wound or irregular tear of the flesh tissue.

Laminectomy (Rachiotomy): Surgical cutting into the backbone to obtain access to the spinal cord. The operation is performed to remove tumors, to treat injuries to the spine, such as prolapsed intevertebral (slipped) disc (in which the affected disc is removed), or to relieve pressure on the spinal cord or roots.

Laparoscopy: Visual examination of the interior of the peritoneal cavity by means of a laparoscope inserted into it through the abdominal wall or vagina.

Laparotomy: A surgical incision into the abdominal cavity. The operation is done to examine the abdominal organs as a help to diagnosis, *e.g.*, to establish the spread of a growth or as a prelude to major surgery.

LASIK Technology (Laser Assisted in Situ Keratomileusis): A type of eye surgery that is especially useful for correcting severe degrees of myopia (short-sightedness). A thin flap of cornea is raised, the bed (stroma) is reshaped using an excimer laser and the flap is then replaced.

Lateral: Outer side, or external (opposite to medial).

Lavage: Washing out a body cavity, such as the colon or stomach, with water or a medicated solution. In cases of bowel obstruction the washing out can be done during the operation (on-table lavage).

Leptospirosis (Weil's disease): An infectious disease, caused by bacteria of the genus Ieptospira (especially L. ictero haemorrhagiae), that occurs in rodents, dogs and other mammals and may be transmitted to people whose work brings them into contact with these animals. The disease begins with a high fever and headache and may affect the liver (causing jaundice) or kidneys (resulting in renal failure); in some cases patients may go on to develop meningitis.

Lesion: A structural change in a tissue caused by disease or injury; a single infected patch in a skin.

Leucocyte (white blood cell): Any blood cell that contains a nucleus. In health there are three major sub-divisions: granulocytes, lymphocytes and monocytes, which are involved in protecting the body against foreign substances and in antibody production. In disease, a variety of other types may appear in the blood, most notably immature forms of the normal red or white blood cells.

Leukaemia: Any of a group of malignant diseases (cancer) in which the bone marrow and other blood-forming organs produce increased numbers of certain types of white blood cells (leucocytes). Overproduction of these white cells, which are immature or abnormal forms, suppresses the production of normal white cells, red cells and platelets. This leads to increased susceptibility to infection (due to neutropenia), anaemia and bleeding (due to thrombocy-topenia). Other symptoms include enlargement of the spleen, liver and lymph nodes.

Levator: 1. A surgical instrument used for levering up displaced bone fragments in a depressed fracture of the skull. 2. Any muscle that lifts the structure into which it is inserted; for example, the levator scapulis helps to lift the shoulder blade

Ligatwn: The application of a ligature.

Ligature: Any material, *e.g.*, nylon, silk, catgut, or wire, that is tied firmly round a blood vessel to stop it bleeding or around the base of a structure (such as the pedicle of a growth) to constrict it.

Lipo-: Prefix denoting fat, lipid.

Lipolysis: The process by which lipids, particularly triglycerides in fat, are broken down into their constituent fatty acids in the body by the enzyme lipase.

Liposuction: A technique for removing unwanted collections of subscutaneous fat by using a powerful suction tube passed through the skin at different locations.

Lithotripsy: The destruction of calculi (stones) by the application of shock waves.

Local anaesthesia: See Anaesthesia.

Locum tenens: A doctor who stands in temporarily for a colleague who is absent or ill and looks after the patients in his practice.

Lumbar: The 'small' of the back, *i.e.*, situated between the dorsal (thoracic) and sacral levels.

Lumen: The space within a tubular or sac-like part, such as a blood vessel, the intestine, or the stomach.

Lymph: The fluid present within the vessels of the lymphatic system. It consists of the fluid that bathes the tissues, which is derived from the blood and is drained by the lymphatic vessels. Lymph passes through a series of filters (lymph nodes) and is ultimately returned to the bloodstream *via* the thoracic duct. It is similar in composition to plasma, but contains less protein and some cells, mainly lymphocytes.

Lymphangi- (lymphangio-): Prefix denoting a lymphatic vessel.

Lymphocyte: A variety of white blood cell (leucocyte), present also in the lymph nodes, spleen, thymus gland, gut wall, and bone marrow.

Lymphoma: A type of cancer involving the lymphoid tissue.

Lypolysis: The dissolution of fat.

-lysis: 1. Combining form meaning dissolution or decomposition of. 2. Combining form indicating, in medicine, reduction or relief of.

Lysis: 1. The gradual decline of a fever or disease. Opposite of crisis. 2. Destruction of blood cells by a lysine, as when rabbit's red corpuscles are dissolved by dog's serum.

Maceration: The softening of a solid by leaving it immersed in a liquid; (in obstetrics) in natural breakdown of a dead foetus within the uterus.

Magnetic Resonance Imaging (MRI) A diagnostic technique based on analysis of the absorption and transmission of high-frequency radio waves by the water molecules in tissues placed in a strong magnetic field. Using modern high-speed computers, this analysis can be used to 'map out' the variation in tissue signals in any plane and thus produce images of the tissues. It is particularly useful for examining the central nervous system and musculoskeletal system and to a lesser extent the chest and abdomen. MRI can be used for the noninvasive diagnosis and treatment planning of a wide range of disease, including cancer. It has the advantage that it does not use potentially harmful ionizing radiation, such as X-rays.

Malignant: Describing a tumor that invades and destroys the tissue in which it originates and can spread to other sites in the body *via* the blood-stream and lymphatic system. If untreated such tumors cause progressive determination and death. Said of cancerous growths.

Malocclusion: A condition in which there is an abnormal arrangement of the teeth, either within one jaw or in one jaw in relation to the other.

Malunion: Deformity of a bone resulting from union of a fracture in which the bone ends are poorly aligned. Arthritis of adjoining joints may develop as a complication later.

Mammectomy: Removal of the breast. Mammography: X-ray examination of the female breast. Using low-energy X-rays, fine details of breast tissue can be visualised, particularly the presence of classification or soft tissue masses enabling the early diagnosis of breast cancer.

Mammoplasty: Plastic surgery of the breasts, in order to alter their shape or increase or decrease their size. In the case of sagging breasts skin and glandular tissue are removed and the remaining breast tissue is fixed in the normal position.

-mania: Suffix denoting obsession, compulsion, or exaggerated feeling, *e.g.*, pyromania (for starting fires).

Mastectomy: Excision of the breast. Maxilla: The upper jaw and check bones.

Meconium: The first stools of a new born baby, which are sticky and dark green and composed of cellular debris, mucus, and bile pigments. The presence of meconium in the amniotic fluid during labour indicates foetal distress.

Medial: Inner side or internal (opposite to lateral).

Medulla: The inner region of any organ or tissue when it is distinguishable from the outer region (the cortex), particularly the inner part of the kidney, adrenal glands, or lymph nodes.

-megaly: Suffix denoting abnormal enlargement, *e.g.*, splenomegaly (of spleen) hepato megaly (of liver).

Melaena: Black tarry faeces due to the presence of partly digested blood from higher up the digestive tract. It often occurs after vomiting blood, having the same causes, but may be due to disease in the small intestine or upper colon, such as carcinoma or angiodysplasia.

Membrane: 1. A thin layer of tissue surrounding the whole or part of an organ or tissue lining a cavity, or separating adjacent structures or cavities. 2. The lipoprotein envelop surrounding a cell (plasma or cell membrane).—Adj. membranous.

Memory: The mental registration, retention and recall of past experience, knowledge, ideas, sensation and thoughts.

Meninges: The three connective tissue membranes that line the skull and vertebral canal and enclose the brain and spinal cord. The outermost layer, the dura mater (pachymeninx), is inelastic, tough, and thicker than the middle layer (the arachnoid mater) and the innermost layer (thepia mater). The inner two membranes are together called the leptomeninges; between them circulates the cerebrospinalfluid.—Sing. Meninx.

Meningitis: An inflammation of the meninges of the brain or spinal cord due to infection by viruses or bacteria. Meningitis causes an intense headache, fever, loss of appetite, intolerance to light and sound, rigidity of muscles, especially those in the neck, and in severe cases convulsions, vomiting, and delirium leading to death.

Menorrhagia (epimenorrhagia): Abnormally heavy bleeding at menstruation, which may or may not be associated with abnormally long periods. Menorrhagia may be associated with hormonal imbalance (in which case it is described as dysfunctional uterine bleeding), pelvic inflammatory disease, tumors (especially fibroids) in the pelvic cavity, endometriosis, or the presence of an IUCD. In some cases no obvious pathology can be demonstrated.

Mesentery: A peritoneal fold encircling the greater part of the small intestines and connecting the intestines to the posterior abdominal wall.

Metabolism: 1. The sum of all the chemical and physical changes that take place within the body and enable its continued growth and functioning. Metabolism involves the breakdown of complex organic constituents of the body with the liberation of energy, which is required for other processes and the building up of complex substances, which form the material of the tissues and organs, from simple ones. 2. The sum of the biochemical changes undergone by a particular constituent of the body, *e.g.*, protein metabolism.—Adj. Metabolic.

Metastasis: The distant spread of malignant tumor from its site of origin. This occurs by three main routes: (*i*) through the bloodstream; (*ii*) through the lymphatic system; (*iii*) across body cavities, *e.g.*, through the peritoneum. Highly malignant tumors have a greater potential for metastasis. Individual tumors may spread by one or all of the above routes, although carcinoma is said classically to metastasize *via* the lymphatics and sarcoma *via* the bloodstream.—Adj. metastatic.

Micr- (micro-): Prefix denoting: 1. Small size. 2. One millionth part.

Microsurgery: The branch of surgery in which extremely intricate operations are performed through highly refined operating microscopes using miniaturised precision instruments (forceps, scissors, needles, etc.). The technique enables surgery of previously inaccessible parts of the eye, inner ear, spinal cord and brain (*e.g.* for the removal of tumors and repair of cerebral aneurysms), as well as the reattachment of amputated fingers (necessitating the suturing of minute nerves and blood vessels) and the reversal of vasectomies.

Migraine: A familial disorder marked by periodic, usually unilateral, pulsatile headaches that begin in childhood or early adult life and tend to recur with diminishing frequency in later life. Hemicranial headache due to a disturbance in the normal calibre of the cranial blood vessels. May be precipitated by trauma, and has a number of clinical variants.

Minimally Invasive Surgery: Surgical intervention involving the least possible physical trauma to the patient, particularly surgery performed using an operating laparoscope or other endoscope passed through a tiny incision; it is known popularly as keyhole surgery. Several types of abdominal surgery, including gall bladder removal, shock-wave lithotripsy for stones in the urinary or bile drainage system, are commonly performed in this way. Such methods usually allow the patient to resume normal activity much sooner than would be possible after more conventional procedures.

Mitral Incompetence: Failure of the mitral valve to close, allowing a reflux of blood from the left ventricle of the heart to the left atrium. It most often results from scarring of the mitral valve by rheumatic fever, but it can also develop as a complication of myocardial infarction or cardiomyopathies. It may occur as a congenital defect.

Mitral Stenosis: Narrowing of the mitral orifice obstructing free flow of blood from atrium to ventricle of the heart.

Mono- (mon-): Prefix denoting one, single.

Motor: Pertaining to movement (applied particularly to muscle action).

MRI: See Magnetic Resonance Imaging.

Multi-Organ Failure (MOF): The terminal stage of serious illness.

Musculo-: Prefix denoting muscles.

My- (myo-): Prefix denoting muscles.

Myelography: Radiography of the spinal cord and associated nerves after injection of a contrast medium (radio opaque liquid) into the subarachnoid space.

Myelomeningocele: A meningocele is the protrusion of the meninges through the gap in the spine, the skin covering being vestigial. There is a constant risk of damage to the meninges, with resulting infection. Urgent surgical treatment to protect the meninges is therefore required. In a meningomyelocele (myelomeningocele, myelocele) the spinal cord and the nerve roots are exposed, often adhering to the fine membrane that overlies them. There is a constant risk of infection and this condition is accompanied by paralysis and numbness of the legs and urinary incontinence. Hydrocephalus and the Amold-Chiari malformation are usually present. A failure of fusion at the cranial end of the neural tube (cranium bifidum) gives rise to comparable disorders. The bone defect is most often in the occipital region of the skull but it may occur in the frontal or basal regions. A protrusion of the meninges alone is known as a cranial meningocele. The terms meningoencephalocele, encephalocele, and cephalocele are used for the protrusion of brain tissue through the skull defect. This is accompanied by severe mental and physical disorders. See also Neural Tube Defects.

Myocardial Infarction (MI): Death of a segment of a heart muscle which follows partial interruption of its blood supply. It is usually confined to the left ventricle. The patient experiences a 'heart attack'. The symptoms include prolonged heavy pressure or squeezing pain in the centre of the chest behind the stemum. The pain may spread or be localised to the shoulder, neck, arm and fourth and fifth fingers of the left hand; to the back, to the teeth, or to the jaw. These symptoms may be accompanied by nausea and vomiting, sweating and shortness of breath. About 15% to 20% of Mis are painless. It is imperative that medical care be instituted without delay. Many myocardial infarction patients not treated prior to reaching the hospital die. Delaying specific therapy may cause loss of life.

Myomectomy: An operation in which benign tumors (fibroids) are removed from the muscular wall of the uterus.

Myometritis: Inflammation of the muscular wall (myometrium) of the uterus.

Myopathy: Any disease of the muscles. The myopathies are usually subdivided into those that are inherited and those that are acquired. The acquired myopathies include polymyositis and muscular disease complicating endocrine disorders or carcinoma. All are typified by weakness and wasting of the muscles, which may be associated with pain and tenderness.

Necro-: Combing form meaning pertaining to death, dead cells or tissue.

Necrosis: The death of areas of tissue or bone surrounded by healthy parts; end stage of infarction.

Necrosis (mortification): The death of some or all of the cells in an organ or tissue, caused by disease, physical or chemical injury, or interference with the blood supply.—Adj. Necrotic.

Neonate: An infant at any time during the first four weeks of life. The word is particularly applied to infants just born or in the first week of life.

Nephrectomy: Removal of a kidney.

Nephritis (Bright's disease): Inflammation of the kidney. Nephritis is a non-specific term used to describe a condition resulting from a variety of causes.

Nephro-: Prefix denoting the kidney(s).

Nephropathy: Disease of the kidney.

Nephrotic syndrome: A condition in which there is great loss of protein in the urine, reduced levels of albumin in the blood and generalised swelling of the tissues.

Neur- (neuri-, neuro-): Combing form concerning a nerve or the nervous system.

Neural: Pertaining to nerves or connected with the nervous system.

Neural Tube Defects: Defective closures of the neural tube during early embryogenesis. Included are foetal anencephaly, spina bifida, lumbar meningomyelocele and meningocele. The tendency for this condition to be present may be inherited.

Neuritis: A disease of the peripheral nerves showing the pathological change of inflammation. The term is also used in a less precise sense as an alternative to neuropathy.

Neuropathy: Any disease of the peripheral nerves, usually causing weakness and numbness.

Neurosurgery: The surgical or operative treatment of diseases of the brain and spinal cord. This includes the management of head injuries, the relief of raised intracranial pressure and compression of the spinal cord, the eradication of infection, the control of intracranial haemorrhage and the diagnosis and treatment of tumors.

Node: 1. A small swelling or knot of tissue. 2. A small rounded organ or structure.

Nodule: A small swelling or aggregation of cells.

Nucleus: 1. The part of a cell that contains the genetic material, DNA. The DNA, which is combined with protein, is normally dispersed throughout the nucleus as chromatin. During cell division the chromatin becomes visible as chromosomes. The nucleus also contains RNA, most of which is located in the nucleolus. The nucleus is separated from the cytoplasm by a double membrane, the nuclear envelope. 2. An anatomically and functionally distinct mass of nerve cells within the brain or spinal cord. 3. The central part of the lens of the eye, which is harder than the outer cortex.

Occipital (occipito-): Concerning the back part of the head.

Occiput: The back of the head.

Occlusion: 1. The closing or obstruction of a hollow organ or part. 2. (In dentistry) the relation of the upper and lower teeth when they are in contact. Maximum contract between the teeth is known as intercuspal or centric occlusion.

Oculo-: Prefix denoting the eye(s).

Ocular: Concerning the eye or vision.

Oedema: Excessive accumulation of fluid in the body tissues: popularly known as dropsy. The resultant swelling may be local, as with an injury or inflammation or more general, as in heart or kidney failure. In generalised oedema there may be collections of fluid within the chest cavity (pleural effusions), abdomen (ascites), or within the air spaces of the lung (pulmonary oedema). It may result from heart or kidney failure, cirrhosis of the liver, acute nephritis, the nephrotic syndrome, starvation, allergy or drugs (*e.g.* phenylbutazone or cortisone derivatives).—Adj. Oedematous.

Oesophagus: The muscular tube which carries swallowed food from the pharynx to the stomach.

Oliguria: The production of an abnormally small volume of urine. This may be a result of copious sweating associated with intense physical activity and/or hot weather. It can also be due to kidney disease, retention of water in the tissues which may cause oedema, loss of blood, diarrhoea or poisoning.

-oma: Suffix denoting the a tumor, *e.g.*, hepatoma (of the liver): lymphoma (of the lymph nodes).

Onco-: Prefix denoting 1. A tumor. 2. Volume.

Oncology: The study and practice of treating tumors. It is often sub-divided into medical, surgical and radiation oncology.

Oophorectomy (ovariectomy): Surgical removal of an ovary, performed, for example, when the ovary contains tumors or cysts or is otherwise diseased.

Ophthalmitis: The study and practice of treating tumors. It is often sub-divided into medical, surgical and radiation oncology.

Ophthalmo-: Prefix denoting the eye.

Ortho-: Prefix denoting: 1. Straight, *e.g.*, ortfiograde (having straight posture). 2. Normal, *e.g.*, orihocrasia (normal reaction to drugs).

Orthopaedic: Relating to the muscular-skeletal system (bones, joints, cartilage ligaments, etc.)

osis: Suffix denoting 1. A diseased condition, *e.g.*, nephrosis (of the kidney); leptospirosis (caused by Leptospira species). 2. Any condition, *e.g.*, nacrosis (of stupor). 3. An increase or excess, *e.g.*, leucocytosis (of leucocytes).

Ost- (oste-, osteo-): Prefix denoting bone, *e.g.*, ostalgia (pain in), osteocarcinoma (carcinoma of), osteonecrosis (death of), osteoplasty (plastic surgery of), osteitis (inflammation of).

Osteitis: Inflammation of bone, due to infection, damage or metabolic disorder.

Osteomyelitis: Inflammation of bone due to infection. Acute osteomyelitis occurs when bacteria enter the bone *via* the bloodstream and is more common in children. Chronic osteomyelitis may develop from partially treated acute osteomyelitis or after open fractures or surgery during which the bone is contaminated; tuberculosis is an occasional cause. Osteomyelitis can cause fracture and deformity of the bone.

Osteoporosis: Loss of mineral salts from bones, the result of lack of use owing to injury or disease, reducing the mechanical strength of the bone. Ostitis: Inflammation of a bone.

-otomy: Suffix denoting a surgical incision into an organ or part, *e.g.*, gastrotomy (into the stomach).

Ovum: The female reproductive or germ cell. On fertilisation by spermatozoa results in development into a new organism of the same species.

Ovum (egg cell): The mature female sex cell. The term is often applied to the secondary oocyte although this is technically incorrect. The final stage of meiosis occurs only when the oocyte has been activated by fertilization.

Oxytocin: A pituitary harmone that stimulates the uterus to contract, thus inducing birth of baby.

Palate: The roof of the mouth, which separates the mouth from the nasal cavity and consists of two portions. The hard palate, at the front of the mouth, is formed by processes of the maxillae and palatine bones and is covered by mucous membrane. The soft palate, further back, is a movable fold of mucous membrane that tapers at the back of the mouth to form a fleshy hanging flap of tissue.

Palliative: A medicine that gives temporary relief from the symptoms of a disease but does not actually cure the disease. Palliatives are often used in the treatment of such diseases as cancer.

Palpation: The process of examining part of the body by careful feeling with the hands and fingertips. Using palpation it is possible, in many cases, to distinguish between swellings that are solid and those that are cystic. Palpation is also used to discover the presence of a foetus in the uterus.

Palsy: Paralysis. This archaic word is retained in compound terms, such as Bell's palsy, Cerebral palsy, and Todd 's palsy.

Pancreatitis: Inflammation of the pancreas.

Para- (par-): Prefix denoting: 1. Beside or close to. 2. Resembling. 3. Abnormal.

Paramedical personnel: Health care workers who are not physicians. These include medical technicians, emergency medical technicians and physician's assistants.

Paraplegia: Paralysis of both lower limbs. Paresis: Partial or incomplete paralysis.

Patella: The lens-shaped bone that forms the kneecap. It is situated in front of the knee in the tendon of the quadriceps muscle of the thigh.

Patent ductus arteriosis: The ductus arteriosis is a blood vessel adjacent to the heart which allows blood to bypass the lungs while a foetus is in the womb. At birth it should close. If it remains in patent it can require an operation to tie it off.

Paternalism: The policy or practice on the part of people in position of authority of restricting the freedom and responsibility of those subordinate to or otherwise dependent on than in their supposed interest: In relation to medical profession paternalism is an abuse of medical knowledge so as to distort the doctor-patient relationship in such a way that the patient is deprived of his autonomy or of his ability to make arational choice. This is seem in the context of disclosure to the patient.

Path- (Patho-): Prefix denoting disease, *e.g.*, pathophobia (morbid fear of).

-pathy: Suffix denoting 1. Disease, *e.g.* nephropathy (of the kidney). 2. Therapy, *e.g.*, osteopathy (by manipulation).

Peptic ulcer: A breach in the lining (mucosa) of the digestive tract produced by digestion of the mucosa by pepsin and acid. This may occur when pepsin and acid are present in abnormally high concentrations or when some other mechanism reduces the normal protective mechanisms of the mucosa; bile salts may play a part, especially in stomach ulcers. A peptic ulcer may be found in the oesophagus (oesophageal ulcer, which is associated with reflux oeso-phagitis); the stomach (gastric ulcer); duodenum (duodenal ulcer); jejunum (jejunal ulcer), usually in the Zollinger-Eillison syndrome); in a Meckel's diverticulum and close to a gastroenterostomy (stomal ulcer, anastomotic ulcer, marginal ulcer).

Perforation: The creation of a hole in an organ, tissue, or tube. This may occur in the course of a disease (*e.g.*, a duodenal ulcer, colonic diverticulitis, or stomach cancer), allowing the contents of the intestine to enter the peritoneal cavity, which causes acute inflammation (peritonitis) with sudden severe abdominal pain and shock. Perforation may also be caused accidentally by instruments, *e.g.*, a gastroscope may perforate the stomach, a curette may perforate the uterus, or by injury, *e.g.*, to the eardrum.

Peri-: Prefix denoting near, around or enclosing, *e.g.* perianal (around the anus); pericardial (around the heart); perinephric (around the kidney); peritonsillar (around a tonsil).

Perineum: The region of the body between the anus and the urethral opening, including both skin and underlying muscle. In females it is perforated by the vaginal opening.

Peritoneum: The serous membrane of the abdominal cavity. The parietal peritoneum lines the walls of the abdomen and the visceral peritoneum covers the abdominal organs.

Peritonitis: Inflammation of the peritoneum. Primary peritonitis is caused by bacteria spread *via* the bloodstream: examples are pneumococcal peritonitis and tuberculous peritonitis. Symptoms are diffuse abdominal pain and swelling, with fever and weight loss. Fluid may accumulate in the peritoneal cavity or the infection may complicate existing ascites.

Pertussis: Whooping-cough.

Phacoemulsification (Phakoemulsification): The use of a high frequency ultrasound probe to break up a cataract so that it can be removed through a very small incision. This is now a popular method of performing cataract surgery.

Phimosis: Narrowing of the opening of the foreskin, which cannot therefore be drawn back over the underlying glans penis. This predisposes to inflammation, which results in further narrowing. Treatment is by surgical removal of the foreskin.—Adj. Phimotic.

Photorefractive Keratectomy (PRK): See Keratectomy.

Phototherapy: 1. Exposure to sunlight or artificial light for therapeutic purposes. 2. Use of light to treat certain conditions. Hemolytic jaundice of the newborn is treated with either exchange transfusion or phototherapy, or with both. Phototherapy is used by exposing the jaundiced newborn to either natural sunlight or fluorescent light (blue light). Use of phototherapy has decreased the need for exchange transfusion in infants with hemolytic disease of the newborn.

Placenta: An organ within the uterus by means of which the embryo is attached to the wall of the uterus. Its primary function is to provide the embryo with nourishment, eliminate its wastes and exchange respiratory gases. It also functions as a gland, secreting human chorionic gonadotrophin, progesterone and oestrogens, which regulate the maintenance of pregnancy.—Adj. Placental.

Placenta Praevia: A placenta situated wholly or partially in the lower and non-contractile part of the uterus. When this becomes elongated and stretched during the last few weeks of pregnancy and the cervix becomes stretched either before or during labour, placental separation and haemorrhage will occur. In the more severe degrees of placenta praevia, where the placenta is situated entirely before the presenting part of the foetus, delivery must be by caesarean section. In lesser degrees of placenta praevia, vaginal delivery may be undertaken with safety.

Plasma (blood plasma): The straw-coloured fluid in which the blood cells are suspended. It consists of a solution of various inorganic salts of sodium, potassium, calcium, etc., with a high concentration of protein (approximately 70 g/l) and a variety of trace substances.

Plastnapheresis: A method of removing a quantity of plasma from the blood. Blood is withdrawn from the patient and allowed to settle in a container. The plasma is drawn off the top of the blood and the blood cells are then transfused back into the patient.

-plasty: Suffix denoting plastic surgery, *e.g.*, labioplasty (of the lips).

-plegia: Suffix denoting paralysis, *e.g.*, hemiplegia (of one side of the body).

Pleura: The covering of the lungs (visceral pleura) and of the inner surface of the chest wall (parietal pleura). The covering consists of a closed sac of serous membrane, which has a smooth shiny moist surface due to the secretion of small amounts of fluid. This fluid lubricates the opposing visceral and parietal surfaces so that they can slide painlessly over each other during breathing.—Adj. Pleural.

Pleurisy: Inflammation of the pleura, often due to pneumonia in the underlying lung. The normally shiny and slippery pleural surfaces lose their sheen and become slightly sticky, so that there is pain on deep breathing and a characteristic 'rub' can be heard through a stethoscope. Pleurisy is always associated with some other disease in the lung, chest wall, diaphragm, or abdomen.

Pneumonitis: Inflammation of the lung(s).

Pneumothorax: Air in the pleural cavity, *e.g.*, from puncture of the lung by a fractured rib—and causing collapse of the lung.

Poliomyelitis (infantile paralysis, polio): Inflammation of the gray matter of the spinal cord. An acute viral disease characterised by fever, sore throat, headache, vomiting and often stiffness of the neck and back. There may also be subsequent atrophy of groups of muscles ending in contraction and permanent deformity. The virus is excreted in the faeces of an infected person and the disease is therefore most common where sanitation is poor. However, epidemics may occur in more hygienic conditions, where individuals have not acquired immunity to the disease during infancy. Immunization using the oral vaccine is highly effective.

Poly-: Prefix denoting: 1. Many; multiple. 2. Excessive. 3. Generalised; affecting many parts.

Polyradiculitis (Polyradiculopathy): Any disorder of the peripheral nerves in which the brunt of the disease falls on the nerve roots where they emerge from the spinal cord.

Porta: The aperture in an organ through which its associated vessels pass. Such an opening occurs in the liver.

Post-: Prefix denoting: 1. Following; after, *e.g.*, postepileptic (after an epileptic attack). 2. Behind (in anatomy), *e.g.*, pastoral (behind the mouth).

Post-partum: Relating to the period of a few days immediately after birth.

Post-prandial: Occurring after eating.

Post-traumatic stress disorder (PTSD): The development of characteristic symptoms following a psychologically distressing event or situation of an exceptionally threatening or catastrophic nature. The characteristic symptoms include persistent re-experiencing of the traumatic event; persistent avoidance of stimuli associated with the trauma and "psychic numbing"; and persistent symptoms of anxiety or increased arousal.

Pott's Disease (spine): Tuberculosis of the backbone. Untreated, it can lead to a hunchback deformity. Treatment is anti-tuberculous chemotherapy and occasionally surgery.

Prandial: Relating to a meal.

Pre-: Prefix denoting: 1. Before; preceding, *e.g.*, premenstrual (before menstruation); prenatal (before birth). 2. (In anatomy) In front of; anterior to, *e.g.*, precardiac (in front of the heart); prepatellar (in front of the patella).

Prenatal: Before birth.

Probe: 1. A thin rod of pliable metal, such as silver, with a blunt swollen end. The instrument is used for exploring cavities, wounds, fistulae and sinus channels. 2. (Geneprobe) a radioactively labelled cloned section of DNA that is used to detect identical sections of nucleic acid by means of pairing between complementary bases.

Prodromal: Relating to the period of time between the appearance of the first symptoms of an infectious disease and the development of a rash or fever. A prodromal rash is one preceding the full rash of an infectious disease.

Prognosis: An assessment of the future course and outcome of a patient's disease and the estimate of chance for recovery based on knowledge of the course of the disease in other patients together with the general health, age and sex of the patient.

Prolapse: A falling or dropping down of an organ or internal part, such as uterus or rectum.

Prolapsed Intervertebral Disc (PID): A 'slipped disc': protrusion of the pulpy inner material of an intervertebral disc through the fibrous outer coat, causing pressure on adjoining nerve roots, ligaments, etc.

Prosthesis: Any artificial device that is attached to a part of the body as an aid.

Prosthodontics (prosthetic dentistry): Branch of dentistry dealing with the provisions of dentures, bridges and implant-retained prostheses.

Proximal: Nearest the centre (opposite to distal).

Pseud- (pseudo-): Prefix denoting superficial resemblance to; false.

Psoriasis: A chronic skin disease in which scaly pink patches form on the elbows, knees, scalp, and other parts of the body. It sometimes occurs in association with arthritis. Occasionally the disease may be very severe, affecting much of the skin and causing considerable disability in the patient. Drugs, such as lithium or beta blockers, may occasionally be responsible.

Psoriatic Arthritis: Arthritis associated with psoriasis. It occurs in only a small minority of patients with psoriasis but may be painful and disabling. It often affects small joints, such as the terminal joints of the fingers and toes, or the spine (spondylitis) and the sacroiliac joints (sacroilitis).

Ptosis: Drooping or dropping of an organ (*e.g.*, eyelid).

Pubis: A bone forming the lower and anterior part of each side of the hip bone. The two pubes meet at the front of the pelvis at the pubic symphysis.

Puerperal Fever: Infection of the vagina and uterus consequent on childbirth.

Pulmonary: Pertaining to the lung. Purulent: Forming, containing of or containing pus.

Pyrexia (Fever): A rise in body temperature above the normal, *i.e.*, above an oral temperature of 98.6 degrees F (37C) or a rectal temperature of 99 degrees F (37.2C).

Quadriptegia: Paralysis of all four limbs.

Radial Keratotomy: See Keratotomy, radial.

Radical Treatment: Vigorous treatment that aims at the complete cure of a disease rather than the mere relief of symptoms, such as radical surgery. See also Conservative treatment.

Radicle: A structure resembling a rootlet, as a radicle of a nerve or vein.

Radiculitis: Inflammation of the root of a nerve.

Radiculo: Concerning a root or radicle. The tissues on or around a tooth root, *e.g.*, radicular dentin, radicular bone.

Red- (Recto-): Prefix denoting the rectum, *e.g.*, rectouterine (relating to the rectum and uterus); rectovaginal (relating to the rectum and vagina); rectovesical (relating to the rectum and bladder).

Rectus Muscles: 1. Two external abdominal muscles, one on each side, from pubic bone to the ensiform cartilage and 5th, 6th, and 7th ribs. 2. Four short muscles of the eye: exterior, interior, superior and inferior.

Reduction: The restoration of a displaced part of the body to its normal position by manipulation or operation. The fragments of a broken bone are reduced before a splint is applied; a dislocated joint is reduced to its normal seating; or a hernia is reduced when the displaced organ or tissue is returned to its usual anatomical site.

Reflex: An automatic or involuntary activity brought about by relatively simple nervous circuits, without consciousness being necessarily involved. Thus, a painful stimulus such as a pinprick will bring about the reflex of withdrawing the finger before the brain has had time to send a message to the muscles involved.

Regional Anaesthesia: See Anaesthesia

Remission: 1. A lessening in the severity of symptoms or their temporary disappearance during the course of an illness. 2. A reduction in the size of a cancer and the symptoms it is causing.

Renal: In relation to the kidney.

Rent- (Reno-): Prefix denoting the kidney.

Resection: Surgical removal of a portion of any part of the body, *e.g.*, a section of diseased intestine may be removed and the healthy ends sewn together. A submucous resection is removal of part of the cartilage septum (central division) of the nose that has become deviated, usually by injury. Transurethral resection of the prostate (TUR or TURP), an operation performed when the prostate gland becomes enlarged, involves removal of portions of the gland through the urethra using an instrument called a resectoscope.

Respirator: 1. A device used to maintain the breathing movements of paralysed patients. In the positive-pressure respirator air is blown into the patient's lungs *via* a tube passed either through the mouth into the trachea or through a tracheostomy. Air is released from the lungs when the pressure from the respirator is relaxed. The iron lung is a type of respirator in which the patient is enclosed, except for the head, in an airtight container in which the air pressure is decreased and increased mechanically. This draws air into and out of the lungs, through the normal air passages. The cuirass respirator works on a similar principle, but leaves the limbs free. 2. A face mask for administering oxygen or other gas or for filtering harmful fumes, dust, etc.

Resuscitation: The restoration of a person who appears to be dead. It depends upon the revival of cardiac and respiratory function.

Retin- (retino-): Prefix denoting the retina.

Retinal Detachment: Separation of the inner nervous layer of the retina from the outer pigmented layer (retinal pigment epithelium) to which it is attached. It commonly occurs when one or more holes in the retina allow fluid from the vitreous cavity of the eyeball to accumulate under the retina. Vision is lost in the affected part of the retina. The condition can be treated surgically.

Retinopathy: Any disorder of the retina.

Retro-: Prefix denoting at the back or behind.

Retrolental Fibroplasia: It is the abnormal proliferation of fibrous tissue immediately behind the lens of the eye, leading to blindness. It is most commonly seen in newborn preterm infants, in whom it is associated with high concentrations of inhaled oxygen.

Retroperitoneal Fibrosis (RPF): A condition in which a dense plaque of fibrous tissue develops behind the peritoneum adjacent to the abdominal aorta. The ureters become encased and hence obstructed, causing acute anuria and renal failure.

Rhesus Factor (Rh factor): A group of antigens that may or may not be present on the surface of the red blood cells, it forms the basis of the rhesus blood group system. Incompatibility between Rh-positive and Rh-negative blood is an important cause of blood transfusion reactions and haemolytic disease of the newborn.

Rhonchus (pi. Ronchi): An abnormal musical noise produced by air passing through narrowed bronchi. It is heard through a stethoscope, usually when the patient breathes out.

Rigidity: Increased tone (stiffness) in limb or trunk.

Rigor: A sudden paroxysmal chill with high temperature as in malaria, urinary infection, I.V. glucose/blood transfusion reaction; a state of hardness and stiffness.

Rigor Mortis: A stiffness that occurs in a dead body after a certain period.

Salping- (salpingo-): Prefix denoting 1. The Fallopian tube. 2. The auditory tube (meatus).

Salpingectomy The surgical removal of a fallopian tube.

Salpingography: Radiography of one or both Fallopian tubes after a radiopaque substance has been introduced into them *via* an injection into the uterus. Standardised selective salpingography enables occluded tubes, visualised by salpingography, to be restored to patency by means oitubal catheterisation.

Salpingostomy: The operation performed to restore free passage through a blocked Fallopian tube. It is performed in women who have been sterilised previously by tubal occlusion and in others whose Fallopian tubes have become blocked as a result of pelvic infection.

Sarcoma: Any cancer of connective tissue. These tumors may occur in any part of the body, as they arise in the tissues that make up an organ rather than being restricted to a particular organ. They can arise in fibrous tissue, muscle, fat, bone, cartilage, synovium, blood and lymphatic vessels and various other tissues.

Scan: 1. Examination of the body or a part of the body using Ultrasonography, Computerised Tomography (CT), Magnetic Resonance Imaging (MRI), or Scintigraphy. 2. The image obtained from such an examination. 3. To examine the body using any of these techniques.

Schizophrenia: A severe mental disorder (or group of disorders) characterised by a disintegration of the process of thinking, of contact with reality and of emotional responsiveness. Delusions and hallucinations (especially of voices) are usual features, and the patient usually feels that his thoughts, sensations and actions are controlled by, or shared with, others. The main types of schizophrenia are: (*i*) simple, in which increasing social withdrawal and personal ineffectiveness are the major changes: (*ii*) hebephrenic, which starts in adolescence or young adulthood; (*iii*) paranoid, characterised by prominent delusions; and (*iv*) catatonic, with marked motor disturbances. The latter

form is now rare. There are strong genetic factors in the causation and environmental stress can precipitate illness.

Sciatica: Pain felt down the back and outer side of the thigh, leg, and foot. It is usually caused by degeneration of an intervertebral disc, which protrudes laterally to compress a lower lumbar or an upper sacral spinal nerve root. The onset may be sudden, brought on by an awkward lifting or twisting movement. The back is stiff and painful. There may be numbness and weakness in the leg. Bed rest will often relieve the pain but surgical treatment is occasionally necessary.

Scintigraphy: A technique by which a diagram showing the distribution of radioactive tracer in a part of the body is produced by recording the flashes off light given of by a scintillator as it is struck by radiation of different intensities. By scanning the body, section by section, a 'map' of the radioactivity in various regions is built-up, aiding the diagnosis of cancer or other disorders.

Sclera (sclerotic coat): The white fibrous outer layer of the eyeball. At the front of the eye it becomes the cornea.

Sclerosis: Hardening of tissue, usually due to scarring (fibrosis) after inflammation or due to ageing. It can affect the lateral columns of the spinal cord and the medulla of the brain (amyotrophic lateral sclerosis or Lou Gehrig's disease), causing progressive muscular paralysis. It can also occur in scattered patches throughout the brain and spinal cord or in the walls of the arteries.

Sclerotherapy: Treatment of varicose veins by the injection of an irritant solution. This causes thrombophlebitis, which encourages obliteration of the varicose vein by thrombosis and subsequent scarring. Sclerotherapy is also used for treating haemorrhoids and oesophageal varices.

Scoliosis: Lateral (sideways) deviation of the backbone, caused by congenital or acquired abnormalities of the vertebrae, muscles, and nerves. Treatment may require spinal braces and, in cases of severe deformity, surgical correction by fusion or osteotomy.

-scope, -scopy: Suffix denoting an instrument or device for viewing or examining, *e.g.*, gastro-scope (instrument for examining the stomach).

Scrotum: The paired sac that holds the testes and epididymides outside the abdominal cavity. Its function is to allow the production and storage of spermatozoa to occur at a lower temperature than that of the abdomen. Further temperature control is achieved by contraction or relaxation of muscles in the scrotum.

Section: 1. (In surgery) the act of cutting (the cut or division made is also called a section), *e.g.*, an abdominal section is performed for surgical exploration of the abdomen. A transverse section is a cut made at right angles to a structure's long axis. 2. (In microscopy) a thin slice of the specimen to be examined under a microscope.

Sengstaken-Blakemore Tube: A three-lumen tube used to treat bleeding oesophageal varices. One lumen leads to the stomach; another leads to a balloon at the gastric end—it is used to inflate the balloon after the tube is in place; the third lumen leads to an inflatable cuff around a portion of the entire tube. This third lumen allows the cuff to be inflated and provide pressure against the varices. The gastric balloon permits the cuff to resist being inadvertently removed and serves to keep the entire tube in place.

Sensorium: 1. That portion of the brain that functions as a center of sensations. 2. The sensory apparatus of the body taken as a whole. Sensory: Pertaining to sensation.

Septicaemia: Destruction of tissues due to absorption of disease-causing bacteria or their toxins from the blood stream. The presence of pathogenic bacteria in the blood that has become separated from the surrounding tissues. The term is also used loosely for any form of blood poisoning.

Septum: A wall dividing two cavities—pi. septa.

Sequestrum: A fragment of dead bone. Sigmoid colon (sigmoid flexure): The part of the colon that turns medially at the left iliac crest, between the descending colon and the rectum.

Sigmoidoscope: A tubular speculum for examining the lower bowel and for assisting in minor operations therein.

Sinus: (*i*) A track leading from an infected focus, *e.g.*, in a bone to an opening on the surface of the skin; (*ii*) a cavity within a bone. Sinusitis: Inflammation of the para-nasal sinuses. Slipped disc: A colloquial term for a prolapsed intervertebral disc. See Prolapsed Intervertebral disc.

Slough: Dead matter or necrosed tissue separated from living tissue.

Smear: A specimen of tissue or other material taken from part of the body and smeared on a microscope slide for examination.

Sonography: See Ultra-sonography.

Spasm: A sustained involuntary muscular contraction, which may occur either as part of a generalised disorder, such as a spastic paralysis, or as a local response to an otherwise unconnected painful condition. Carpopedal spasm affects the muscles of the hands and feet and is caused by a reduction in the blood calcium level (often transitory, as in hyper ventilation).

Spasmo-: Prefix denoting spasm.

Spasticity: Resistance to the passive movement of a limb that is maximal at the beginning of the movement and gives way as more pressure is applied. It is a symptom of damage to the corticospinal tracts in the brain or spinal cord.

Sphincter: A specialised rim of muscle that surrounds an orifice. Contractions of the sphincter partly or completely close the orifice. Sphincters are found, *e.g.*, around the anus (anal sphincter) and at the opening between the stomach and duodenum (pyloric sphincter).

Spicule: A small splinter of bone.

Spina Bifida: A developmental defect in which the newborn baby has part of the spinal cord and its coverings exposed through a gap in the backbone. The condition can be diagnosed at about the 16th week of pregnancy by a maternal blood test and confirmed by amniocentesis and ultrasound, so making termination of the pregnancy possible.

Spina Bifida Occulta: A defect in the bony arch of the spine that (unlike spina bifida) has a normal skin covering; there may be an overlying hairy patch. The condition is usually an incidental finding on X-ray and it is not associated with neurological involvement.

Spinal: Pertaining to the spine or spinal cord.

Spinal Anaesthesia: See Anaesthesia.

Spinal Cord: The portion of the central nervous system enclosed in the vertebral column, consisting of nerve cells and bundles of nerves connecting all parts of the body with the brain. It contains a core of grey matter surrounded by white matter. It is enveloped in three layers of membrane, the meninges, and extends from the medulla oblongata in the skull to the level of the second lumbar vertebra. From it arise 31 pairs of spinal nerves.

Spino-: Prefix denoting the spine; the spinal cord.

Spondylitis: Inflammation of the synovial joints of the backbone, esp. tuberculous disease of the vertebrae, Pott's disease. See also Ankylosing spondylitis.

Spondylosis: A spinal condition resulting from degeneration of the intervertebral discs in the cervical, thoracic, or lumbar regions.

Status Epilepticus: Epileptic fits, following each other in continuous rapid succession.

Stenosis: The constriction or narrowing of a passage or orifice.

Stent: A splint placed inside a duct or canal, such as the ureter, urethra, oesophagus, or bile duct, or an artery. It may be used at operation to aid healing of an anastomosis, or placed across an obstruction to maintain an open lumen, *e.g.* in a bile duct obstructed by a tumor or stricture or in an artery after angioplasty to prevent restenosis.

Sterile: 1. (Of living organism) barren; unable to reproduce its kind. 2. (Of inanimate objects; completely free from bacteria, fungi, viruses or other micro-organisms that could cause infection.

Sterility: Inability to have children, either due to infertility or (in someone who has been fertile) deliberately induced by surgical procedures as a means of contraception. Sterility may also be an incidental result of an operation or drug treatment undertaken for other reasons, such as removal of the uterus (hysterectomy) because of cancer.

Stevens-Johnson Syndrome (SJS): An illness characterised by a severe wide spread rash and mouth ulcers, often caused by an allergic reaction to a drug. It may also be caused by a viral, bacterial infection, etc.

Stillbirth: Birth of a foetus that shows no evidence of life (heartbeat, respiration, or independent movement) at any time later than 24 weeks after conception. In legal terms, viability is deemed to start at the 24th week of pregnancy and a foetus born dead before this time is known as an abortion or miscarriage. However, some foetuses born alive before the 24th week may now survive as a result of improved perinatal care.

-stomy (-ostomy): Suffix denoting a surgical opening into an organ or part, *e.g.*, colostomy (into the colon).

Stricture: A narrowing or constriction of any tubular structure in the body, such as the oesophagus (gullet), bowel, ureter, or urethra. A stricture may result from inflammation, muscular spasm, growth of a tumor within the affected part, or from pressure on it by neighbouring organs, *e.g.*, a urethral stricture is a fibrous narrowing of the urethra, usually resulting from injury or inflammation,

Stroke (apoplexy): A sudden attack of weakness affecting one side of the body. It is the consequence of an interruption to the flow of blood to the brain. The primary disease is in the heart or blood vessels and the effect on the brain is secondary. An ischaemic stroke occurs when the flow of blood is prevented by clotting or by a detached clot that lodges in an artery. A haemorrhagic stroke results from rupture of an artery wall. Prolonged reduction of blood pressure may result in similar brain damage. A stroke can vary in severity from a passing weakness or tingling in a limb to a profound paralysis, coma and death.

Stupor: A condition of unconsciousness or lethargy with suppression of sense or feeling.

Subphrenic: Below the diaphragm.

Suppuration: The formation of pus.

Supra-: Prefix denoting above; over, *e.g.*, supraclavicular (above the clavicle); suprahyoid (above the hyoid bone); suprarenal (above the kidney).

Surrogate: 1. (In psychology) a person or object in someone's life that functions as a substitute for another person. In the treatment of sexual problems, when the patient does not have a partner to cooperate in treatment, a surrogate provided by the therapist acts as a sexual partner who gives service to the patient up to and including intercourse. 2. (In reproduction). See Surrogate Mother.

Surrogate Mother: A woman who becomes pregnant (by artificial insemination or embryo insertion) following an arrangement made with another party (usually a couple unable themselves to have children) in which she agrees to hand over the child she carries to that party when it is born. Such an arrangement is made on the

understanding that no payment is involved between either parties.

Suture: 1. (In anatomy) a type of immovable joint, found particularly in the skull, that is characterized by a minimal amount of connective tissue between the two bones. The cranial sutures include the coronal suture, between the frontal and parietal bones; the lambodoidal suture, between the parietal and occipital bones; and the sagittal suture, between the two parietal bones. 2. (In surgery) the closure of a wound or incision with material such as silk or catgut, to facilitate the healing process. There is a wide variety of suturing techniques .developed to meet the differing circumstances of injuries to and incisions in the body tissues. 3. The material silk, catgut, nylon, any of various polymers, or wire, used to sew up a wound. 4. To close a wound by suture.

Swab: A pad of absorbent material (such as cotton), sometimes attached to a stick or wire, used for cleaning out or applying medication to wounds, operation sites, or body cavities. In operations, gauze swabs are used to clean blood from the site; such swabs are always carefully counted and contain a radiopaque 'tag' to facilitate identification should it by mischance remain in the body after operation. In surgical procedures swabs are sometimes left behind in the body due to carelessness giving rise to legal action against the surgeon or hospital.

Symphysis: 1. A joint in which the bones are separated by fibrocartilage, which minimizes movement and makes the bony structure rigid. 2. The line that marks the fusion of two bones that were separate at an early stage of development.

Syncope (Fainting): Loss of consciousness induced by a temporarily insufficient flow of blood to the brain. It commonly occurs in otherwise healthy people and may be caused by an emotional shock, by standing for prolonged periods, or by injury and profuse bleeding. An attack comes on gradually, with lightheadedness, sweating, and blurred vision. Recovery is normally prompt and without any persisting ill-effects.

Syndrome: Characteristic collection of signs arid symptoms. A group of symptoms and signs of disordered function related to one another by means of some anatomic, physiologic, or biochemical peculiarity. This definition does not include a precise cause of an illness but does provide a framework of reference for investigating it.

Synechia: An adhesion between the iris and another part of the eye.

Synovitis: Inflammation of the membrane (synovium) that lines a joint capsule, resulting in pain and swelling (arthritis). It is caused by injury, infection or rheumatic disease.

Tachycardia: Increased pulse rate.

Tendon: A tough whitish cord, consisting of numerous parallel bundles of collagen fibres, that serves to attach a muscle to a bone. Tendons are inelastic but flexible; they assist in concentrating the pull of the muscle on a small area of bone. Some tendons are surrounded by tendon sheaths, these are tubular double-layered sacs lined with synovial membrane and containing synovial fluid. Tendon sheaths enclose the flexor tendons at the wrist and ankle, where they minimize friction and facilitate movement.

Teratogenic: Pertaining to teratogenesis — any substance, agent or process that induces the formation of developmental abnormalities in a foetus.

Theca: Outer wall of a Graafian follicle, consisting of an inner vascular layer (theca interna) and outer fibrous layer (theca externa).—Adj. Thecal.

Thorac: Prefix denoting the thorax or chest.—Adj. Thoracic.

Thorax, Thoracic: The chest, pertaining to the chest.

Thromb- (thrombo-): Prefix denoting: 1. A blood clot (thrombus). 2. Thrombosis. 3. Blood platelets.

Thromboangiitis: See Buerger's disease.

Thrombo-embolism: The blocking of a blood vessel by a thrombus (blood clot) that has become detached from its site of formation.

Thrombophlebitis: Inflammation of the wall of a vein with secondary thrombosis occurring within the affected segment of vein.

Thrombosis: A condition in which the blood changes from a liquid to a solid state and produces a blood clot (thrombus). Thrombosis may occur within a blood vessel in diseased states. Thrombosis in an artery obstructs the blood flow to the tissue it supplies: obstruction of an artery to the brain is one of the causes of a stroke and thrombosis in an artery supplying the heart—coronary thrombosis—results in a heart attack.

Thyroidectomy: Surgical removal of the thyroid gland.

Tibia: The shin bone: the inner and larger bone of the lower leg. It articulates with the femur above, with the talus below, and with the fibula to the side (at both ends), at the lower end is a projection, the medial malleolus, forming part of the articulation with the talus. Tinnitus: A subjective ringing or tinkling sound in the ear.

Tissue: A complex of similar cells and fibres forming a structure within an organ of the body.

Tolerance: The reduction or loss of the normal response to a drug or other substance that usually provokes a reaction in the body. Drug tolerance may develop after taking a particular drug over a long period of time. In such cases increased doses are necessary to produce the desired effect. Some drugs that cause tolerance also cause dependence.

-tomy (-otomy): Suffix denoting a surgical incision into an organ or part, *e.g.*, gastrotomy (into the stomach).

Tomo-: Prefix denoting 1. Section or sections- 2. Surgical operation.

Tone: The tension present in a muscle at rest.

Tonometer: An instrument for measuring pressure in a part of the body, *e.g.*, the eye.

Tonsillectomy: Surgical removal of the tonsils.

Topical: Local: used for the route of administration of a drug that is applied directly to the part being treated (*e.g.* to the skin or eye).

Tourniquet: Any constrictor used on an extremity to apply pressure over an artery and thereby control bleeding; also used to distend veins to facilitate venipuncture or intravenous injections.

Toxaemia: Blood poisoning that is caused by toxins formed by bacteria growing in a local site of infection. It produces generalised symptoms, including fever, diarrhoea and vomiting.

Tracheotomy (Trucheostomy): Operative opening into the trachea (windpipe) through the neck to bypass laryngeal or pharyngeal obstruction to the airway. It is usually done to ease breathing. It is also used in conjunction with artificial respiration, when it serves not only to secure the airway but also provides a route for sucking out secretions and protects the airway against the inhalation of pharyngeal contents.

Traction: The application of a pulling force, especially as a means of counteracting the natural tension in the tissues surrounding a broken bone, to produce correct alignment of the fragments. Considerable force, exerted with weights, ropes and pulleys, may be necessary to ensure that a broken femur is kept correctly positioned during the early stages of healing.

Trans-: Prefix denoting through or across, *e.g.*, transwethral (through the urethra), transvaginal (through the vagina).

Transurethral Resection of Prostate (TUR, TURP): Removal of prostatic tissue by use of a device inserted through the urethra.

Triage: A system whereby a group of casualties or other patients is sorted according to the seriousness of their injuries or illnesses so that treatment priorities can be allocated between them. In emergency situations it is designed to maximize the number of survivors.

Trophoblast: The tissue that forms the wall of the blastocyst. At implantation it forms two layers, an inner cellular layer (cytotrophoblast) and an outer syncytial layer (plasmoditrophoblast), which forms the outermost layer of the placenta and attains direct contact with the maternal blood stream.

Trophoblast Sampling: It was the name originally given to the technique now known as chorionic villus sampling. See Chorionic villus sampling.

Tubectomy: Surgical removal of all or part of a tube, especially the fallopian tube.

Tumor (Tumour): 1. Swelling: one of the classical signs of inflammation in a tissue, the other three being calor (heat), rubor (redness), and dolor (pain). The swelling of an inflamed area is due to the leakage from small blood vessels of clear protein-containing fluid, which accumulates between the cells. 2. Any abnormal swelling in or on a part of the body. The term is usually applied to an abnormal growth of tissue, which may be benign or malignant.

Ulcer: A break in the skin extending to all its layers, or a break in the mucous membrane lining the alimentary tract, that fails to heal and is often accompanied by inflammation.—Adj. ulcerative.

Ultrasonography (Sonography): The use of ultrasound, usually in excess of 1 MHz, to produce images of structures of the human body that may be observed on a TV screen and subsequently transferred to photographic film. As far as is known, there are no adverse effects from the use of ultrasound and it has particular value in obstetrics (including the diagnosis of pregnancy, assessment of gestational age, diagnosis of malpresentations and hydatidiform moles, and detection of foetal abnormalities) and in examination of the biliary and urinary tract and the vascular tree. More specialised technique include echocardiography, transvaginalo ultrasonography and intraoperative, transrectal and transoesophageal ultrasound (endoscopic ultrasound) examinations.

Ureter: Either of a pair of tubes, 25-30 cm. long, that conduct urine from the pelvis of kidneys to the bladder.—Adj. ureteral, ureteric.

Urethra: The tube that conducts urine from the bladder to the exterior. The female urethra is quite short and opens just within the vulva, between the clitoris and vagina. The male urethra is longer and runs through the penis. As well as urine, it receives the secretions of the male accessory sex glands (prostate and Cowper's glands and seminal vesicles) and spermatozoa from the vas deferens; thus it also serves as the ejaculatory duct.

Utero-vesical: Relating to the uterus and bladder.

Utero- veslcalfistula (UVF): See Fistula.

Uterus (Womb): The part of the female reproductive tract that is specialised to allow the embryo to become implanted in its inner wall and to nourish the growing foetus from the maternal blood.—Adj. uterine.

Uveities: Inflammation of any part of the uveal tract of the eye, either the iris (iritis), ciliary body (cyclitis), or choroids (choroiditis).

Vagina: The lower part of the female reproductive tract: a muscular tube, lined with mucous membrane, connecting the cervix of the uterus to the exterior. It receives the erect penis during coitus: semen is ejaculated into the upper part of the vagina and from there the sperms must pass through the cervix and uterus in order to fertilise an ovum in the fallopian tube. The wall of the vagina is sufficiently elastic to allow the passage of the newborn child.—:Adj. vaginal.

Vaginitis: Inflammation of the vagina, which may be caused by infection (most commonly with Trichomonas vaginalis), dietary deficiency, or poor hygiene. There is often itching, increased vaginal discharge and pain on passing urine. Vaginitis may indicate the presence of sexually transmitted disease.

Varicose Veins: Veins those are distended, lengthened and tortuous. The superficial veins (saplienous veins) of the legs are most commonly affected; other sites include the oesophagus and testes (varicocele). There is an inherited tendency to varicose veins but obstruction to blood flow is responsible in some cases. Complications including thrombosis, phlebitis and haemorrhage may occur.

Varicosity: Dilatation and twisting of veins.

Vascular: Relating to-or supplied with blood vessels.

Vasectomy: Sterilisation of the male by division of each vas deferens which connects each testis to the urethra; the operation can be carried out under local anaesthesia and on an out-patient basis.

Vegetative: 1. Relating to growth and nutrition rather than to reproduction. 2. Functioning unconsciously; autonomic.

Vegetative State: A condition after severe brain injury, involving a return of wakefulness accompanied by an apparent total lack of cognitive function and awareness of the environment and self.

Vein: A blood vessel conveying blood towards the heart. All veins except the pulmonary vein carry deoxygenated blood from the tissues, via the capillaries, to the vena cava. The walls of veins consist of three tissue layers, but these are much thinner and less elastic than those of arteries. Veins contain valves that assist the flow of blood back to the heart.—Adj. Venous

Venereal Disease (VD): Sexually transmitted disease (STD). STDs include AIDS, syphilis, gonorrhoea, some chlamydia infection, genital herpes and soft sore.

Ventilator: A mechanical device for artificial ventilation of the lungs. The mechanism may be hand-operated or machine-driven and in the latter case may be automatic and very sophisticated with respect to being able to control and monitor flow of air to the lungs.

Ventricle: 1. Either of the two lower chambers of the heart, which have thick muscular walls. The left ventricle, which is thicker than the right, receives blood from the pulmonary vein *via* the left atrium and pumps it into the aorta. The right ventricle pumps blood received from the venae cavae (*via* the right atrium) into the pulmonary artery. 2. One of the four fluid-filled cavities within the brain. The paired first and second ventricles (lateral ventricles), one in each cerebral hemisphere, communicate with the third ventricle in the midline between them. This in turn leads through a narrow channel, the cerebral aqueduct, to the fourth ventricle in the hind brain, which is continuous with the spinal canal in the centre of the spinal cord. Cerebrospinal fluid circulates through all the cavities.

Ventricular Dilatation: An increase in the size of the lateral ventricles of the brain.

Vertebra (pi. vertebrae): One of the 33 bones of which the backbone is composed. Each vertebra typically consists of a body, or centrum, from the back of which arises an arch of bone (the neural arch) enclosing a cavity (the vertebral canal, or foramen) through which the spinal cord passes. The neural arch bears one spinous process and two transverse processes, providing anchorage for muscles and four articular processes, with which adjacent vertebrae articulate. Individual vertebrae are bound together by ligaments and intervertebral discs.

Vertigo: Unpleasant sensation of abnormal rotation; sensation of moving around in space (subjective vertigo) or objects moving around the person (objective or true vertigo).

Vitrectomy: The removal of the whole or part of the vitreous homour of the eye, including vitreous haemorrhage. Vitrectomy is often necessary in surgery to repair a detached retina.

Vitreous Haemorrhage: Haemorrhage into the vitreous body which fills the cavity of the eye ball, behind the lens and in front of the ratina.

Vitreous Humour (Vitreous Body): The transparent jelly-like material that fills the chamber behind the lens of the eye.

Volkmann's Contracture: Fibrosis and shortening of muscles due to inadequate blood supply. It is a complication that arises if the blood supply is interrupted by pressure on the blood vessels from a fracture fragment, or from raised pressure due to compartment syndrome, or by pressure from constricting bandages and plaster casts.

Volvulus: A twisting of the bowel on itself causing obstruction.

Water Bed: A bed with a flexible water-containing mattress. The surface of the bed adapts itself to the patient's posture leading to greater comfort and fewer bed sores.

APPENDIX XIX

Common Ailments Symptoms, Diagnosis & Treatment

ACNE

Definition: Acne vulgaris or just acne is a common skin disease which is caused by changes on the pilosebaceous units (structures of the skin which consist of sebaceous gland and a hair follicle). The severe cases of acne are often inflamed but it can also show up as non-inflamed. Lesions are common and they are called spots, zits or pimples. This condition is common during the stage of puberty (affecting about 85% of teeners) while some cases carry on to adulthood. Most acne cases diminish and then disappear over time and this begins during the early twenties of an individual life. There are no means of predicting when the disease will totally disappear because some cases continue even when the person is already in his thirties or forties. Acne is an altered form of the Greek word akun (or skin eruption). The vernacular name bakne or bacne is used often to specify acne that is found at the back of a person.

Causes: The exact cause of acne is still not known even today. What is certain is that it is hereditary. Some other factors include: family history (the genes can play a great factor in the appearance of the disease); hormonal activities (puberty or menstrual periods); stress (when a person experiences this, the body secretes additional hormones); agitated sebaceous glands; the buildup of dead skin cells; pores that are clogged with bacteria; scratching or skin irritation will enhance inflammation; anabolic steroid usage; using medications which contain halogens (chlorides, iodides, bromides), barbiturates, lithium, or androgens; the patient's exposure to some chemical compounds or drugs which could include narcotics.

Diet: It is important for someone with acne to have a balanced diet. A study that has been made recently showed that dairy products could induce acne. The specific products that were taken by the subjects included skimmed milk, sherbet, instant breakfast drinks, cream and cottage cheese. It is hypothetically proposed that the presence of bovine IGF-I and sex hormones in cow's milk have caused the condition to aggravate. Still, the observations remain hypothetical that is why the association of milk to acne is still not certain. Iodine is the primary content of seafood. This element is known to worsen acne but it should not be sufficient to make an outbreak. Still, people who have acne should avoid the over-consumption of food that are rich in iodine. Vitamins A and E are good supplements to improve the condition of most patients. It has been observed that those who suffer from acne often have very low levels of both these vitamins.

ADDICTION

Definition: Addiction was a term used to describe an attachment, devotion, dedication, inclination, etc. Now-a-days, however, the term addiction is used to describe a recurring compulsion by an individual to engage in some specific activity, despite harmful consequences to the individual's health, social life, or mental state. The term is often reserved for drug addictions but it is sometimes applied to other compulsions, such as compulsive overeating and problem gambling. Factors that have been suggested as causes of addiction include biological/pharmacological, genetic and social factors.

Prevalence: The most frequent drug addictions are to legal substances such as alcohol and nicotine, in the form of tobacco, particularly cigarettes.

Treatment: While addiction or dependency is associated to seemingly uncontrollable urges, and arguably could have roots in genetic predispositions, treatment of dependency is conducted by a wide range of medical and allied professionals, including Addiction Medicine specialists, psychiatrists, and appropriately trained nurses, social workers, and counselors. Early treatment of acute withdrawal often comprises of medical detoxification, which can include doses of anxiolytics or narcotics to reduce symptoms of withdrawal. An experimental drug, ibogaine, is also suggested to treat withdrawal and craving. Other options to medical detoxification include acupuncture detoxification. In chronic opiate addiction, a surrogate drug such as methadone may be sometimes offered as a form of opiate replacement therapy. But treatment approaches universal focus on the individual's ultimate choice to pursue a different course of action. Therapists often categorize patients with chemical dependencies as either interested or not interested in changing. Treatments typically involve planning for specific ways to avoid the addictive stimulus and therapeutic interventions intended to help a client learn healthier ways to find satisfaction. Clinical leaders in recent years have tried to tailor intervention approaches to specific influences that affect addictive behaviour, using therapeutic interviews in an effort to discover factors that led a person to embrace unhealthy, addictive sources of pleasure or relief from pain.

Symptoms and Signs: Some symptoms of a person with an addiction include reclusive behaviour, where the individual spends long periods of time in self-imposed isolation. He may also have a change in friends and start hanging out with a new group. The person may also have long and unexplained absences and lie and steal. He may have involvement with the wrong side of the law, have deteriorating family relationships, possess an obvious intoxication, and may be delirious, incoherent or unconscious. Other signs of addiction are changes in behaviour and attitude and a decrease in school performance.

AIDS

Definition: AIDS means Acquired Immune Deficiency Syndrome which means that the person may get infected by the disease and it will then cause a weakening of his system that resists or fights disease. The disease is caused by the Human Immunodeficiency Virus or HIV. When the person gets infected by the virus, and the body creates its own antibodies to fight off the infection, it is when he is called HIV positive. Thus, the person is called HIV positive when he has these HIV antibodies. However, being HIV positive is different from having AIDS. It is common to find HIV positive person who have lived for many years without getting AIDS although AIDS is generally developed from HIV. A person may get infected with HIV through different ways, such as through blood infection and through semen or vaginal fluids. Thus, having sex with a person with HIV, receiving blood or using the same syringe with the person with HIV may result into getting infected. A child usually gets infected with HIV if the mother has the virus. According to the Center for Disease Control and Prevention (CDC) it is estimated that there are around 1.2 million persons in the US are infected with HIV virus or have AIDS. Despite the number, the death rate due to AIDS has been reduced significantly since the time when it was the leading cause of death in the 90s. This is because of the new treatments available at present. HIV becomes AIDS when the immune system of the person infected with HIV is severely damaged. Thus, a person with no more than 200 CD 4 cells (less than 14% CD4 cells) in his body has AIDS. If the person has AIDS he is more likely to get Pneumocystis pneumonia (PC), a certain lung infection; a Kaposi's sarcoma, a skin cancer; a Cytomegalovirus or infection affecting the eyes and Candida or a fungal infection in the mouth or infections in the throat or vagina. These infections are called opportunistic infections or infections which take advantage of the weak immune system. There is no known cure for AIDS however, at present there are available drugs which slows then development or progress of the HIV virus. At the same time these drugs slows down the effect or the damage done by the HIV to the immune system. There are also other drugs to help the patient treat or prevent the opportunistic infections. The latest drugs available are very effective in reducing the rate of the common opportunistic infections

ALZHEIMER'S DISEASE

Definition: Alzheimer disease, which is named after Alois Alzheimer, is a neurodegenerative disease that occurs in people aged 65 and over. This disease is the most common cause of dementia, affecting over 20 million people worldwide. Once Alzheimer has been diagnosed, the life expectancy of patients is around 7 years. Only 3% of patients live for more than 10 years.

Treatment: There is no available cure for Alzheimer disease. The medications available only offer benefits for patient symptoms, but do not slow down the progression of the disease. However, behavioural and cognitive interventions as well as rehabilitation strategies may be used during the early to moderate stages of Alzheimer disease. Therapies may include reminiscent therapy, counseling, psychotherapy, behavioural reinforcements, reality orientation therapy and cognitive rehabilitation training.

Symptoms and Signs: Alzheimer disease is divided into 4 stages with different symptoms for each stage. In the predementia stage, patients experience only mild cognitive difficulties. Other symptoms include short-term memory loss, semantic memory impairments and subtle executive problems. Depression and apathy may also occur. In the early stage, patients experience impairments in memory and learning. However, older memories are affected only slightly compared to learning new things and making new memories. In terms of language problems, shrinking vocabulary and decreased work frequency may occur. In the moderate dementia stage, patients slowly reduce the possibility of independence. Language difficulties become noticeable and the ability to read and write are forgotten. Complex motor sequences are also affected, making patients lose their ability to perform daily activities. Long-term memory becomes impaired, while behavioural changes occur. Irritability, outbursts, crying, aggression and physical violence also occurs. 30% of Alzheimer patients develop delusional symptoms. In the advanced stage of Alzheimer, patients cannot perform the simplest tasks alone. Apathy, exhaustion and loss of verbal language also occur. Patients will also experience muscle deterioration and inability to feed oneself.

ANOREXIA NERVOSA

Definition: Anorexia nervosa is a psychiatric disorder that describes an eating disorder, which is characterized by body image distortion and low body weight due to an obsessive fear of becoming fat or gaining weight. People with anorexia nervosa usually control their body weight by voluntary vomiting, purging, starving, extreme exercise and other weight control measures, such as taking diuretic drugs and diet pills. It usually affects adolescent females and only 10% of anorexia nervosa patients are male. Anorexia nervosa is an extremely complex disorder, involving neurobiological, sociological and psychological components.

Treatment: Since Anorexia nervosa can be fatal, the first line of treatment is weight gain. In serious cases of Anorexia nervosa, patients can be forced to hospital treatment. However, most cases of Anorexia nervosa can be treated as outpatients with treatments assigned by a physician, a psychiatrist and other mental health professionals.

Clinical Features: There are physical, emotional, psychological, behavioral, interpersonal and social features present in those with anorexia nervosa. Physical symptoms of anorexia nervosa include changes in brain function, muscle weakness, heart failure, immune dysfunction, low phosphate levels and disturbed electrolyte balance, which may all lead to death. Individuals who develop anorexia nervosa before adolescence could suffer from stunted growth and low levels of hormones. Up to 50% of anorexia nervosa patients develop osteoporosis. Anorexia nervosa could cause extreme weight loss, stunted growth, endocrine disorder, decreased libido in both males and females, impotence in males, reduced metabolism, anemia, hypotension, hair thinning and zinc deficiency. Some patients could also develop tooth decay and suffer from dry skin, constipation, chapped lips, creaking bones, sunken eyes, pallid complexion, reduced immune system function, bitter fingernails and headaches. For those with extreme weight loss, anorexia nervosa could cause nerve deterioration, which could result in difficulty to move the feet. Psychological effects of Anorexia nervosa include perfectionism, distorted body imaged, OCD, obsessive thoughts about weight, self-evaluation, poor insight and refusal to accept that the patient's weight is dangerously low. Emotional effects of Anorexia nervosa include self-efficacy, extreme fear of obesity, mood swings and clinical depression. Patients with Anorexia nervosa could develop behavioural changes, such as fainting, excessive exercise, self-harm, suicidal attempts, substance abuse and aggressiveness to eating food.

ARTHRITIS

Definition: Arthritis is a condition that usually involves damage on the joints of the body. For people older than fifty-five years, it is the leading cause of disability. Arthritis is a medicinal term, which mean any kind of joint swelling but the term is usually used to refer to age-related osteoarthritis that is the most usual kind. Though, there are other kinds of arthritis involving rheumatoid arthritis (second-most usual, involving younger adults and juveniles), and different kinds of minor arthritis which are caused by a primary condition: immediate arthritis caused by an infection, psoriatic arthritis from psoriasis, gonococcal arthritis from gonorrhea, and the like. Several probable circumstances with arthritis-like signs involve ankylosing spondylitis and gout.

Treatment: The treatment differs depending on the kind of arthritis and involves physical and occupational therapy, changes in lifestyle which includes weight loss and exercise and medications. To erode appearance of arthritis, arthroplasty may be required. Researches have revealed that physically exercising the affected joint can have evident development in terms of long-term pain relief. Also, work out of the aching joint is encouraged to sustain the healthiness of the particular joint and the general body of the individual.

Subtypes: It has been reported that there are several kinds of arthritis having a different cause. (*a*) Osteoarthritis - is the most common form of arthritis it is caused by a trauma to the joint, joint infection or age. Rising facts recommend that unusual structure may contribute to the premature growth of osteoarthritis. (*b*) Rheumatoid arthritis and psoriatic arthritis - autoimmune ailments in which the body harasses itself. (*c*) Septic arthritis results from a joint infection. (*d*) Gouty arthritis resulted from the deposition of uric acid crystals in the joint, causing irritation. There is in additional unusual type of gout that results from the creation of rhomboid crystals of calcium pyrophosphate. History The earliest well-known traces of human arthritis, traces back as far as 4500 BC while proof of main ankle (kaki) osteoarthritis has been found in dinosaurs. It was eminent in skeletal remnants of Native Americans originate in Tennessee and parts of what is now Olathe, Kansas. Proof of arthritis has been established all throughout history, from Ã–tzi, a mummy (circa 3000 BC) discovered alongside the boundary of contemporary Italy and Austria, to the Egyptian mummies circa 2590 BC.

BACTERIAL FOOD POISONING

Definition: Bacterial food poisoning also generally known as food borne illness it is an illness that it is caused by ingesting a contaminated food.

Symptoms and Signs: The symptoms normally start a few hours to few days following consumption and basing on the agent involved, the symptoms are as follows: Nausea Abdominal pain Vomiting Diarrhea Gastroenteritis Fever Headache or fatigue Permanent health recovery happens in most cases after a period of acute discomfort and illness. However, it can also result to permanent health damage or death to individuals who have poor immune system, like infants, elderly and pregnant women or fetuses. Reactive arthritis results from bacterial food poisoning that occurs one to three weeks afterward. Infections from Vibrio vulnificus that can be found in oysters or crabs can affect individuals who have liver disease susceptibly. Usually food poisoning results from uncooked and unclean food. Symptoms of Creutzfeldt-Jacob disease is acquired typically from eating beef from animals that as bovine spongiform encephalopathy (BSE or most commonly known as mad cow disease) is different from bacterial food poisoning. It appears after a few years and after the symptoms appear the disease becomes deadly. Food poisoning obtained from reef fish or other animals is referred to as Tetrodotoxin poisoning it rapidly displays trouble in breathing and numbness and often deadly.

Causes: Presence of pesticides or medicines in food Improper handling of food Improper storage Improper shipping Improper slaughtering Improper marketing of domestic animals Accidental consumption of naturally toxic substances like mushrooms. Some can also come from the skin or nose such as staphylococcus aureus this can cause death

Incubation period: Incubation period is the delay among the consumption of the infected food and the display of the initial symptoms. The period ranges from hours to days and unusually months or years like for the case of Listeriosis or Creutzfeldt-Jacob disease it depends on the agent and the amount consumed. If the symptoms show in 1-6 hours it indicates that it is caused by a chemical or bacterial toxin rather than a live bacteria. The microbes pass into the stomach to the intestine, connected to the cells lining the intestinal walls, and starts to multiply this happens during the incubation period. Several kinds of microbes live in the intestine or several tissues and the symptoms depend on the kind of microbe.

BIPOLAR DISORDER

Definition: Bipolar disorder is not just a single disorder, but a group of mood disorders defined by the presence of one or more episodes of abnormally elevated mood, clinically referred to as mania. People who experience manic episodes also commonly experience depressive episodes or symptoms, or combined episodes which present with features of both mania and depression. These episodes are normally separated by periods of normal mood, but in some patients, depression and mania may rapidly alternate with each other, known as rapid cycling. The disorder has been sub-divided into bipolar I, bipolar II and cyclothymia and is based on the type and severity of mood episodes experienced.

Diagnosis: Diagnosis is based on the experiences of the patient as reported as well as abnormalities in behaviour reported by family members, friends or co-workers, followed by secondary signs observed by a clinician in a clinical assessment. These depend on both the presence and duration of certain signs and symptoms the patient is displaying. An initial assessment may include a comprehensive history and physical examination by a physician. Although no biological tests can confirm bipolar disorder, tests are carried out to exclude medical illnesses which may rarely present with psychiatric symptoms. These include blood tests measuring TSH for basic electrolytes and serum calcium to rule out a metabolic disturbance, to exclude hypo- or hyperthyroidism, full blood count including ESR to rule out a systemic infection or chronic disease, and serology to exclude syphilis or HIV infection. Two commonly ordered investigations are EEG so as not to include epilepsy, and a CT scan of the head to exclude brain lesions. There are several psychiatric illnesses which may present with similar symptoms, including schizophrenia, brief drug-induced psychosis, drug intoxication, schizophreniform disorder and borderline personality disorder.

Treatment: Bipolar disorder cannot be cured, but instead, the emphasis of treatment is on effective management of acute episodes and prevention of episodes to further develop by use of pharmacological and psychotherapeutic techniques.

Epidemiology: Clinical depression and bipolar disorder are classified as separate and distinct illnesses. Some researchers increasingly see them as part of an overlapping range that also includes anxiety and psychosis. According to Hagop Akiskal, M.D., at the one end of the spectrum is bipolar type schizoaffective disorder, and at the other end is unipolar depression, whether it is recurrent or not. Also included in this view is postpartum depression, premenstrual dysphoric disorder and postpartum psychosis. This view helps explain why many people who have the illness do not have first-degree relatives with clear-cut "bipolar disorder", but who have family members with a history of any of these other disorders.

BRONCHITIS, CHRONIC

Definition: Chronic bronchitis is the inflammation, or irritation, of the airways in the lungs. Airways are the tubes in the lungs where air passes through. They are also known as bronchial tubes. When the airways are irritated, thick mucus forms inside of them. The mucus plugs up the airways and makes it hard for the person to get air into your lungs. Symptoms of chronic bronchitis include a cough that produces mucus (sometimes called sputum), breathing difficulties, and a feeling of tightness in the chest.

Diagnosis: A physical examination will often show decreased intensity of breath sounds, wheeze (rales) and prolonged expiration. Most doctors depend on the presence of a persistent dry or wet cough as evidence of bronchitis. Pulmonary Function Tests (PFT) (or spirometry) must be performed in all patients affected with chronic cough. An FEV1/FVC ratio below 0.7 that is not fully reversible after bronchodilator therapy shows the presence of COPD, which requires more aggressive therapy and brings with it a more severe prognosis than simple chronic bronchitis. A chest X-ray that shows hyperinflation; collapse and consolidation of lung areas would support a diagnosis of pneumonia. Some conditions that look like bronchitis may be indicated by chest radiography. A blood test could indicate some sort of inflammation, as indicated by a raised white blood cell count and elevated C-reactive protein. Further obstruction to the airways is the result of more goblet cells in the small airways. This is generally typical of chronic bronchitis Although infection is not the reason or cause of chronic bronchitis it is seen to help in sustaining the bronchitis.

Treatment: Some treatments for chronic bronchitis include antibiotics, bronchodilators and corticosteroids. For acute worsening of chronic bronchitis, if antibiotics are used a meta-analysis found that "amoxicillin/clavulanic acid, macrolides, second generation or third-generation cephalosporins, and quinolones" may be more effective for treatment. For acute worsening of chronic bronchitis, a clinical practice guideline by the American College of Physicians found that corticosteroids may help.

Symptoms and Signs: The following are the most commonly-found symptoms for chronic bronchitis. However, each individual may undergo symptoms differently. Such symptoms include cough and expectoration (or spitting out) of mucus. Chronic bronchitis may cause frequent and severe respiratory infections, narrowing and plugging of the breathing tubes (bronchi), difficult breathing, and disability. Other symptoms include abnormal lung signs, swelling of the feet, heart failure, and the lips and skin of the patients may appear blue. The symptoms of chronic bronchitis may look like other lung conditions or medical problems.

CANCER

Definition: Cancer is a group of diseases in which cells are hostile, invasive and sometimes metastatic. These three are considered malignant properties of cancers that differentiate them from benign tumors. Although some benign tumor types are capable of being malignant, they are usually self-limited in their growth and don't invade or metastasize. People from all ages, even fetuses, may be affected with cancer but age is a factor that can raise the risks for more common varieties. About 13% of all deaths are caused by cancer and according to the American Cancer Society, 7.6 million people died from cancer in 2007 across the world. Even plants and animals may be affected by cancer. Abnormalities in the genetic material of the transformed cells practically cause all cancers. Carcinogens such as tobacco smoke, chemicals, radiation or infectious agents may have caused said abnormalities. Some however, may be randomly acquired through errors in DNA replication or inherited. DNA methylation and microRNAs are new aspect of the genetics of cancer pathogenesis that are gaining importance. The tissues from which the cancerous cells originate are used as bases in classifying cancer. There are also two general classes of genes affected by cancer namely the oncogenes and tumor suppressor genes.

Diagnosis: Signs or symptoms that appear or found through screening do not lead to definitive diagnosis, which usually require a pathologist opinion. X-rays, blood tests, CT scans and endoscopy are among the medical tests people with suspected cancers undergo. Performing a biopsy or surgery are procedures where a tissue can be obtained for histological examination. Said examination can identify the type of cell that is spreading as well as its histological grade.

Treatment: There are several ways of treating cancer such as chemotherapy, surgery, radiation therapy, immunotherapy, monoclonal antibody therapy and other methods. Several experimental cancer treatments are also under works.

Symptoms and Signs: Cancer symptoms can be divided into three groups: local symptoms, symptoms of metastasis and systemic symptoms. Local symptoms include lumps or swelling, hemorrhage, pain and/or ulceration. Jaundice may also be caused by the compression of surrounding tissues. Enlarged lymph nodes, cough, hemoptysis, hepatomegaly, bone pain, fracture of affected bones and neurological symptoms are among the known symptoms of metastasis. Systemic symptoms meanwhile is comprised of weight loss, fatigue, poor appetite, cacjexia, excessive sweating, specific paraneoplastic phenomena and anemia.

CEREBRAL PALSY

Definition: Cerebral palsy is a group of diseases that are non-progressive and non-contagious. The word cerebral refers to the cerebrum and palsy means disorder of movement. Cerebral palsy is characterized by damaged motor control centers in the brains of young children. The brain damage that occurs does not worsen over time, although orthopedic difficulties may accompany the condition. There are 4 common classifications of cerebral palsy according to the damaged area of the brain. These are spastic, athetoid/dyskinetic, ataxic, and mixed. Spastic cerebral palsy is the most common type, and this type of cerebral palsy affects the motor cortex, corticospinal tract, or pyramidal tract, which leads to neuromuscular conditions. Patients with this type of CP also are hypertonic. Athetoid or dyskinetic type of CP have mixed muscle tone and have either hypertonia or hypotonia. Ataxia, the least most common type of cerebral palsy, is characterized by tremors, hypotonia and possibly some difficulties with motor skills.

Treatment: No treatment is available for cerebral palsy, but there are therapy options that can help patients with cerebral palsy function as best as he can. Early diagnosis is necessary in providing adequate therapy for those with the condition, so that they can learn and adapt to developmental difficulties at a faster pace. Treatment is usually composed of various types of therapy: physical, occupational and speech; medications for seizures, pain, and muscle spasms, surgery for any anatomical deficiencies or correcting muscles, communication aids and walking devices.

Causes: The exact cause of cerebral palsy is still unknown, although there are known contributing factors. The most common contributing factor is premature birth, because the baby organs are not fully developed and this puts them at larger risk for brain injury and asphyxia. Other contributing factors are hypoxia of the brain, birth trauma and asphyxia. Certain conditions in the mother can contribute to her child having cerebral palsy, such as if she has strep infections, trauma, central nervous system infections, consecutive hematoma, multiple birth and placenta abruptio. Developmental milestones and motor skills are taken into account by the physician when diagnosing a child who is suspected of having cerebral palsy. If a child shows a delay in motor skills, accompanied by physical findings such as abnormal muscle tone, other abnormal behavior in movements and reflexes. By the time a child reaches 18 months of age, it would be easier to diagnose and confirm if they do or do not have the disease.

CHICKENPOX

Definition: Chickenpox is a classic infectious disease common among children. It is a rarely fatal illness that is characterized by red spots on the different parts of the body and become itchy over time. Persons that acquire chickenpox as well obtain lifelong immunity from the disease once it heals after a few weeks.

Treatment: Since chickenpox is highly contagious, persons affected by the disease are normally isolated and are not allowed to make outdoor social interactions during while the virus exists. This usually takes two to three weeks. Now-a-days however, chickenpox can now be treated as well as prevented by the use of the varicella vaccine. While the disease is ongoing, drugs such as paracetamol is given to the patient in order to reduce his fever, while baths are mixed with sodium bicarbonate or antihistamine to reduce the itchiness. Aspirin meanwhile is not recommended to be taken as a medication because it can cause complications leading to ReyeSyndrome, which can be fatal. The vaccine however is not available in all countries. In the United Kingdom, using the varicella vaccine is not practiced due to the lack of evidence supporting its lasting benefits. Chickenpox however contributes to serious congenital defects on babies, since pregnant women are not proven to be immune from the virus. These defects may be in form of skin disorders, vision problems and brain damages.

Symptoms and Signs: This disease begins with the appearance of red sores and blisters around the body, starting with the face and arms. Prior to this the virus has already thrived in the body for 10-21 days and once developed, they can be highly contagious especially to those who have not experienced the disease yet. Once the disease has developed, lesions begin to form in the different parts of the body, which are made up of thin-walled vesicles that contain fluid inside. As the vesicles mature the fluid becomes cloudy and cracks open, leaving a crust. The fluid is very contagious until the lesions heal, and the crusts fall off after a week. But new lesions keep on forming during the span of the disease, and will only cease once the virus dies and all the lesions crust over.

Causes: Chickenpox is caused by one of the eight herpes viruses named the varicella-zoster virus. It used to be a fatal illness that threatened children, but now-a-days it can now be cured and prevented through vaccine.

CENANI LENZ SYNDACTYLISM

Definition: Cenani Lenz Syndactylism is a hereditary malformation syndrome that involves both the lower and upper extremity. It an uncommon birth defect that characterized by a variety of bone abnormalities. The syndrome was named after two medical geneticists; Turkish geneticist Asim Cenani, and German geneticist Widukind Lenz.

Diagnosis: Diagnosis of whether the syndrome deformity is due to joint/bone disease or neurologic disease is generally simple; an X-ray of the feet or hands can be useful several congenital and acromegaly disorders. Referral to neurologic or orthopedic specialist is typically specified if neurologic or bone involvement is likely.

Treatment: Treatment options may include therapies and/or surgical procedures to correct the malformation.

Symptoms and Signs: The syndrome is distinguished by almost symmetrical occurrence of spoon-like hand. There is also occasional mesomelic arm shortening, metacarpal and radio-ulnar synostosis, in addition to disorganized phalanges. The feet are mildly affected. Other symptoms include arm bones fusion, metacarpal fusion, brachymesomelia, numeric rays reduction, short radius and short ulna.

Causes: Cenani Lenz Syndactylism shows autosomal recessive heredity as one cause. Some malformations of an individualextremities originate from joint or neurologic diseases; however, there are several exceptions to the rule. Some of these causal diseases include vascular disease, inflammatory disease, neurologic disorders, degenerative diseases, intoxication, congenital disorders, autoimmune diseases, traumatic lesions, and endocrine disorders.

DIABETES MELLITUS

Definition: Diabetes mellitus, popularly known as "diabetes" is a chronic disease. It is associated with very high levels of the glucose sugar present in our blood. There are two mechanisms for diabetes, patients may experience either of the two to suffer from this disease. The first is that there is not enough production of insulin produced by the pancreas as a result, blood glucose level are lowered or type 1. The second is that the cells are not sensitive enough to the action of insulin or type 2.

Diagnosis: Diagnosis of Diabetes is commonly done using the blood and subjecting it to several different laboratory tests like blood glucose testing. Glycosylated hemoglobin levels (glycohemoglobin or hemoglobin A1C) are also subjected to testing and the glucose tolerance test.

Treatment: The mode of treating Diabetes varies, usually depending on what type of diabetes they are dealing with. For type 1 diabetes, the primary treatment is by replacing insulin combined with careful blood sugar level monitoring using monitors for blood testing even at very early stages. Adjusting the lifestyles of the patient is also a step being done and emphasized by physicians. Insulin can be supplied in the body through injections, pump, or through inhaling. Type 2 diabetes, in the other hand, is usually treated by indulging in more physical activities, planning diet and reducing intake of foods with high carbohydrates and therefore losing weight. This method, however doesn't correct the cells' tendency to resist insulin, and so these measures should be continued. Next step, is taking oral anti-diabetic pills.

Symptoms and Signs: The symptoms of type 1 and type 2 diabetes include increase in volume of urine output which are usually sweet and less appetite accompanied with fatigue and stress.

Causes: There is no known direct effect of this disease although it was thought to be a genetic condition which may be passed on to generations.

EXTROPHY OF THE BLADDER

Definition: Extrophy of the Bladder or to use the more appropriate medical term, exstrophy-epispadias complex, which is an extremely rare congenital abnormality. This medical condition involves a number of anomalies affecting the bladder, abdominal walls, external genetalia and anterior bone pelvis.

Diagnosis: Bladder exstrophy is primarily diagnosed usually after birth through ultrasound. It is best to have a prenatal diagnosis to be able to make the necessary preparations for the baby such as scheduling the labor, pre-operative evaluations and surgery and well as preparations for supplementary care.

Treatment: Treatment for bladder extrophy involves a rather complex surgical repair of bladder through a staged procedure. This includes closure of the abdominal and posterior walls, bladder neck reconstruction and urethral closure.

Symptoms and Signs: The symptoms for bladder extrophy includes exposure of the posterior bladder walls, separated pubic rami, wide set ischial bones, ureteral reflux, opening in abdominal wall and dilated ureters.

Causes: The underlying cause of extrophy of the bladder is still unknown. However, among the most popular theory has suggested that it is mainly a result of the overdevelopment of the cloacal membrane. This is the temporary membrane that provides the pathway during the normal development of the fetus.

FOOD ALLERGY

Definition: While there are some people who have bad reactions to certain food, the real food allergy is actually triggered by the body immune system and is known to be a rare condition. The hypersensitivity to food can cause a number of serious problems and can even lead to death.

Diagnosis: A physical examination, blood and skin test are among the primary basis of a diagnosis of food allergy.

Treatment: The only way effective way to avoid an allergic reaction is to diligently avoid the foods that cause all the signs and symptoms of an allergy attack. Antihistamine drugs are also useful.

Symptoms and Signs: The reaction to food allergy can vary from one person to another, ranging from mild to fatal. The reactions and symptoms can be evident after a few minutes after intake of food. This includes the tingling sensation in the mouth, eczema and hives, abdominal pain, nausea and diarrhea, vomiting, nasal congestion and difficulty in breathing, fainting and dizziness and swollen parts of the body.

Causes: The food allergy is primarily cause by the malfunctioning of the immune system, causing it to react as it identifies food as a threat to the body, and produces antibodies. This signals the body to release histamine and other chemicals in to the bloodstream, which are partly the reason for the allergic reactions. Among the identified food that triggers allergies include peanuts, eggs, fish, tree nuts and shellfish.

GINGIVITIS

Definition: Gingivitis, also known as inflammation of the gums, is a group of diseases that affect the gingival, or the gums. Its most common term, inflammation of the gums, is called so due to the occurrence when plaque or bacterial biofilms stick to the surfaces of the tooth.

Diagnosis: Dentists can diagnose gingivitis by examining symptoms as well as the amount of plaque in the mouth.

Treatment: Brushing or flossing alone cannot remove the plaque that causes gingivitis, professional help must be sought. Dentists treat gingivitis by thoroughly cleansing the mouth area especially gums and teeth, and the patient must continue to practice oral hygiene after treatment. Oral hygiene can help prevent gingivitis from occurring again, provided the patient brushes and flosses regularly. Anti-bacterial mouthwashes also help.

Symptoms and Signs: Early stages of gum disease are rarely painful, which is why some people have them yet are not aware of it. The symptoms of gingivitis are soft, swollen gums; gums that have frequently bleed especially after flossing or brushing, mouth sores, itchy gums, receding gumline and color change in the gums from pink to red.

Causes: Plaque is the primary cause for gingivitis; it is a sticky yet invisible film that forms in the areas between the teeth and gums. The plaque results when the sugars and starches in food combine with the normal mouth bacteria. The bacteria in the plaque contain microscopic toxins and foreign chemicals, causing the inflammation in the gum areas around teeth. If plaque stays on teeth for two days or more, they solidify and turn into tartar.

GROWTH HORMONE DEFICIENCY

Definition: Growth hormone deficiency is a disorder affecting the pituitary gland which is responsible for producing the growth hormone, among other hormones. The pituitary gland does not produce enough growth hormones, resulting in slower growth than normal. Both children and adults are affected by the condition.

Diagnosis: For children, pediatric endocrinologists may conduct the diagnosis, while for adults, internist endocrinologists. Several exams and tests are needed to make the diagnosis, this includes auxologic criteria, response to GH treatment, indirect and direct hormonal criteria and corroborative evidence of pituitary dysfunction.

Treatment: The condition may be treated with growth hormone replacement. This type of treatment can restore energy, body composition and metabolism.

Symptoms and Signs: Symptoms of growth hormone deficiency in children include low growth velocity for pubertal stage and age, a child looking younger than others his age, delayed tooth development, short stature and delayed onset of puberty. In adults, the symptoms include weight again especially around the waist area, low energy, decreased strength, low tolerance to exercise, dry and thin skin and feelings of depression and anxiety.

Causes: Causes of growth hormone deficiency includes severe head trauma, mutations of specific genes, damage to the pituitary gland from intracranial diseases, surgery in the area of the pituitary gland, autoimmune inflammation, congenital malformations involving the pituitary, damage in the pituitary due to radiation therapy and hemorrhagic or ischemic infarction due to low blood pressure.

HEPATITIS C

Definition: Hepatitis (plural hepatitides) implies injury to liver marked by presence of inflammatory cells in the liver tissue.

Diagnosis: These viral hepatitis conditions can be diagnosed and followed through the use of readily available blood tests.

Treatment: HCV viral levels can be reduced to undetectable levels by a combination of the antiviral drug ribavirin and interferon.

Symptoms and Signs: Clinically, the course of acute hepatitis varies greatly from mild symptoms requiring no treatment to fulminant hepatic failure needing liver transplantation. Initial features are of non-specific flu-like symptoms, commonly seen in almost all acute viral infections and may include malaise, muscle and joint aches, fever, nausea or vomiting, diarrhea and headache. More specific symptoms, which can be found in acute hepatitis from any cause, are: profound loss of appetite, aversion to smoking among smokers, dark urine, yellowing of the eyes and skin (*i.e.*, jaundice) and abdominal discomfort.

Causes: The Hepatitis C virus (also known as HCV) is spread by direct contact with an infected person's blood. The symptoms of the Hepatitis C virus can mirror those of the Hepatitis A and B viruses. However, infection with the Hepatitis C virus can result to chronic liver disease and is the leading reason for liver transplant in the United States. The Hepatitis C virus can be spread by sharing drug needles, getting a tattoo or body piercing with unsterilized tools, blood transfusions, transmission from mother to newborn and sexual contact, although this is less common. Hepatitis C is also a commonly found threat in kidney dialysis centers. Rarely, people living with an infected individual can contract the disease by sharing items that might contain that person's blood, such as razors or toothbrushes.

HERPES SIMPLEX DISEASE

Definition: Herpes simplex is commonly known as cold sores. It is a viral infection of the skin that arises once or returns again and again. This is because when the virus is cleared from the skin by the immune system it hides in the nerves and is never wholly removed from the body. Herpes infections are very prevalent. Unfortunately, those who carry the herpes virus can spread the disease without even knowing it.

Diagnosis: Isolation of herpes simplex virus (HSV) from brain tissue after biopsy has been known to be the reference standard for the diagnosis of herpes simplex encephalitis (HSE).

Treatment: Unlike other sexually transmitted diseases, herpes cannot be cured because medication that will attack the virus while it lies dormant in the nerve cells will also end up damaging the nerve cells. However, there is treatment available for acute outbreaks that involve the administration of anti-viral drugs such as Acyclovir, Valaclovir or Famcyclovir.

Symptoms and Signs: The initial episode of herpes is worse than outbreaks that come later. The predominant symptom of herpes is the outbreak of painful, itching blisters filled with fluid on and around the external sexual organs or, for oral herpes, on or very near the patient's lip. Symptoms vaguely similar to those of flu may accompany these outbreaks, including fever, headache, fatigue and muscle aches. There may be painful urination and swollen and tender lymph glands in the groin area.

Causes: There are two known types of herpes simplex viruses. HSV type 2 is the one that usually causes genital herpes. One can get HSV type 2 during sexual contact with someone who has a genital HSV-2 infection. One can get HSV-1 by coming into contact with the saliva of an infected person.

HICCUPS

Definition: A hiccup (hiccough) is a spasmodic contraction of the diaphragm that typically repeats several times per minute. In medicine, it is referred to as synchronous diaphramatic flutter (SDF).

Diagnosis: For hiccups lasting longer than 48 hours, the following may be done: blood tests, chest x-ray, ear exam and fluoroscopy.

Treatment: One technique is to increase carbon dioxide levels in the blood, which may reduce the sensitivity of the vagus nerve in the brain. That nerve, one of the longest in the body, sends signals to many muscle groups, including those in the diaphragm. One can increase carbon dioxide levels by holding one's breath, by rebreathing the air exhaled into a paper bag for a few minutes, or by slowly sipping a glass of water without pausing to take a breath.

Symptoms and Signs: Symptoms of hiccups are contraction of diaphragm and a constant chic's sound from the throat.

Causes: The cause of hiccups in children and infants is rarely found. Brief episodes in adults generally are benign and self-limiting. Typical causes include gastric distention (food, alcohol, air), sudden changes in ambient or gastric temperature, and excessive use of alcohol and/or tobacco. Psychogenic causes (excitement, stress) also may result to hiccups. Persistent or intractable episodes are more probable to result from serious pathophysiological processes affecting a component of the hiccup reflex mechanism. More than 100 causes have been described; however, in many cases, the cause remains unknown.

INFLUENZA

Definition: Influenza, more commonly known as "the flu," is an illness caused by viruses that infect the respiratory tract. Compared with most other viral respiratory infections, such as the common cold, influenza infection often leads to a more severe illness with a mortality rate (death rate) of about 0.1% of people who are infected with the virus.

Diagnosis: Secretions from the throat or nose can be used to make a definitive diagnosis of influenza.

Treatment: Much of the illness and death caused by influenza can be prevented by a yearly influenza vaccination. Flu vaccine is specifically recommended for those who are at high risk for developing serious complications as a consequence of influenza infection.

Symptoms and Signs: Common symptoms include: body aches, especially joints and throat; coughing and sneezing; extreme coldness and fever; fatigue; headache; irritated watering eyes; nasal congestion; reddened eyes, skin (especially face), mouth, throat and nose; and abdominal pain (in children with Influenza B). Although nausea, vomiting and diarrhea can sometimes accompany influenza infection, especially in children, gastrointestinal symptoms are rarely seen. The term "stomach flu" is a misnomer that is occasionally used to describe gastrointestinal illnesses caused by other micro-organisms.

Causes: Influenza viruses are grouped into three types, designated A, B, and C. Influenza types A and B are responsible for epidemics of respiratory illness that arise almost every winter and are often associated with increased rates of hospitalization and death.

IRRITABLE BOWEL SYNDROME

Definition: Irritable Bowel Syndrome, also known as Spastic Colon is a functional bowel disorder distinguished with abdominal pain and bowel habit changes. This disorder is relatively common and comprises up to 20% - 50% of consultations to gastroenterologists.

Diagnosis: There is no definite laboratory examination that can aid in diagnosing Irritable Bowel Syndrome, practically because there is still no clear and well-established biochemical cause for Irritable Bowel Syndrome.

Treatment: Knowledge of what caused the disorder is essential in the treatment of Irritable Bowel Syndrome. Treating the underlying symptom is the best way to treat this disorder. However, certain modifications in the diet can also help while in the process of treating the condition. For medications, anti-depressants are sometimes prescribed for relieving pain and anti-diarrhea as remedy for frequent and loose bowel movement. Anti-spasmodics are also given to ease spasm. For constipated patients, laxatives and stool softeners are recommended.

Symptoms and Signs: The most common symptoms of Irritable Bowel Syndrome are abdominal pain, frequent diarrhea, constipation, gas, bloating, distended abdomen, headache, feelings of unfinished bowel movements.

Causes: Underlying conditions and situations that can cause Irritable Bowel Syndrome may include inflammation of the large intestine section of the gastrointestinal tract. Lactose Intolerance or difficulty in properly digesting milk or other lactose containing product like dairy can possibly cause this medical condition. Emotional Stress can also contribute to the development of Irritable Bowel Syndrome; anxiety and depression precisely. Prolonged fever and history of acute gastrointestinal infection can also cause and trigger the condition.

IMPOTENCE

Definition: Impotence is an inability to sustain an erection sufficient for sexual intercourse. Medical professionals commonly use the term erectile dysfunctional to describe this disorder and to differentiate it from other problems that interfere with sexual intercourse, such as lack of sexual desire and problems with ejaculation and orgasm.

Diagnosis: The penis contains two chambers, called the corpora cavernosa, which run the length of the organ. A like spongy tissue fills the chambers. The corpora cavernosa are surrounded by a membrane, also called as the tunica albuginea.

Treatment: Urologists, who are specialties in problems of the urinary tract, have traditionally treated impotence--especially complications of impotence.

Symptoms and Signs: Signs and symptoms mentioned in various sources for impotence are; Inability to attain an erection and inability to sustain an erection. Impotence symptoms usually refers to various symptoms known to a patient, but the phrase Impotence signs may refer to those signs only noticeable by a doctor.

Causes: The physical causes of impotence are; post-surgical side effects, accidental injuries to the penis or testicles, spin or pelvic area, Vascular trauma, birth defects, diseases and conditions like Diabetes, flu, chronic renal failure, liver disease. Another cause is drug abuse— recreational use or regular chronic over use of addictive drug such as cocaine, heroin and amphetamines.

INFERTILITY

Definition: Infertility means not being able to become pregnant after a year of trying. If a woman keeps on having miscarriages, it is also called infertility. Several couples have infertility problems. For the third of the time, infertility can be traced to the woman. In another third case, it is because of the man. While the rest of the time, it is because of either partners or no cause is found.

Diagnosis: A history of genital infections, trauma or environmental exposure to toxins can reduce male fertility. Disorders of the endocrine system (hypothalmus, pituitary), structural dysfunction such as obstruction of the vas deferens, or many other conditions can cause male infertility.

Treatment: Treatment of infertility usually starts with medication. In vitro fertilization (IVF) in addition to different forms and developments of it (ICSI, ZIFT, GIFT) is another solution. They all include that the fertilization at the outside of the body. Moreover, an insemination can make fertilization inside the body. Other techniques are like tuboplasty, assisted hatching and PGD.

Symptoms and Signs: Possible symptoms of androgen excess disorders are: Infertility, Irregular menstrual periods, Excessive hair growth and acne, Obesity and insulin resistance, Polycystic ovaries

Causes: Some women are infertile because their ovaries do not mature and release eggs. During this case synthetic FSH by injection or Clomid (Clomiphene citrate) via a pill can be given to stimulate follicles to mature in the ovaries. While for men the factors that can cause infertility are genetics such as Robertsonian translocation in either partner may cause recurrent spontaneous abortions or complete infertility. However, general factors are like diabetes mellitus, thyroid disorder and adrenal disease.

INSOMNIA

Definition: Insomnia is a sleeping disorder characterized by persistent difficulty falling asleep or staying asleep despite the opportunity. It is typically followed by functional impairment while staying awake. Insomniacs is known to complain about unable to close their eyes or "rest their mind" for more than a few minutes at a time. Both organic and non-organic insomnia results a sleep disorder.

Diagnosis: Patients with delayed sleep phase syndrome are often mis-diagnosed with insomnia. If the patient has trouble getting some sleep, but has normal sleep architecture once asleep, a circadian rhythm disorder is a more likely cause.

Treatment: In several cases, insomnia is caused by another disease or psychological problem.

Symptoms and Signs: Various sources of insomnia are; sleeping problems, difficulty falling asleep, frequent night waking, difficulty returning to sleep, waking very early, racing mind, Daytime tiredness, fatigue, drowsiness, difficulty in concentrating and irritability.

Causes: Probable causes of insomnia are; psychoactive drugs or stimulants, including certain medications, herbs, caffeine, ephedrine, emphetamines, MDMA, methamphetamine and madofinil. Hormone shifts such as those that precede menstruation and those during menopause stage. Emotional problems like fear, stress, anxiety, emotional or mental tension, work problems, financial stress, unsatisfactory sex life. Mental disorders such as clinical depression, schizophrenia, bipolar disorder, primary anxiety disorder.

JOCK ITCH

Definition: Jock itch, also known as tinea cruris, is a fungal infection of the skin in the groin. The warm, moist environment is the best place for the fungus to grow.

Diagnosis: The best way to diagnose tinea cruris is to look for hyphae under the microscope, a KOH test. The skin is scraped with a scalpel or glass slide causing dead skin cells to fall off on a glass slide.

Treatment: Jock itch is best treated with topical creams or ointments since the fungus only affects the top layer of skin. Lots of the antifungal medications require a prescription, but there are three that can be bought over-the-counter (OTC).

Symptoms and Signs: Jock itch is usually less severe other than tinea infections. If it is not treated, though, it can last for weeks or months. Symptoms of jock itch include: a circular, red, raised rash with elevated edges, itching, chafing, or burning in the groin, thigh, or anal area, skin redness in the groin, thigh, or anal area, flaking, peeling or cracking skin.

Causes: The fungus that most commonly causes jock itch is called Trichophyton rubrum. It also cause fungal infections of the toes and body. Under the microscope, the fungus looks like translucent, branching, rod-shaped filaments or hyphae. Therefore, wearing sweaty, wet clothing in the summer season or wearing several layers of clothing in the winter-time causes an increased incidence of jock itch. More often men are prone to this disease than women.

KIDNEY STONES

Definition: Kidney stone also called renal calculi, are solid concretions (crystal aggregations) of dissolved minerals in urine; calculi typically form inside the kidneys or bladder. The terms nephrolithiasis and urolithiasis pertains to the presence of calculi in the kidneys and urinary tract, respectively.

Diagnosis: Clinical diagnosis is usually made on the basis of the location and severity of the pain, which is typically colic in nature (comes and goes in spasmodic waves). Imaging is used to know the diagnosis and a number of other tests can be undertaken to help establish both the possible cause and consequences of the stone. Ultrasound imaging is also helpful as it will give details about the presence of hydronephrosis.

Treatment: There is several treatments for kidney stone disease: Temporizing, Analgesia, Urologic interventions and Ureteral (double-J) stents.

Symptoms and Signs: Symptoms of kidney stones include: Colicky pain: "loin to groin". Commonly described as the "the worst pain ever experienced". Hematuria which is the blood in the urine, due to minor damage to inside wall of kidney, ureter and/or urethra.

Causes: Kidney stones can be due to underlying metabolic conditions, such as renal tubular acidosis, Dent's disease and medullary sponge kidney. Several health facilities will screen for such disorders in patients with recurrent kidney stones. This is commonly done with a 24 hour urine collection that is chemically analyzed for deficiencies and excesses that promote stone formation.

LEUKEMIA, B-CELL, CHRONIC

Definition: Leukemia, B-Cell, chronic, is a cancer of the white blood cells. It attacks a particular lymphocyte called B cell and thrives on the lymph nodes. When the B cell is damaged, it can no longer fight infections and kills other healthy blood cells in the process.

Diagnosis: The disease is easily diagnosed due to the presence of lymphocytosis, or an increased white blood cell count. Abnormal overpopulation of B lymphocytes in the bone marrow, blood and tissues indicate the onset of chronic B cell Leukemia.

Treatment: Leukemia, B-Cell, chronic is treated by chemotherapy, biological therapy, bone marrow transplant and radiotherapy. Other cases of the disease undergo surgery such as splenectomy or by radiation therapy. Medicines such as purine analogues are used in order to prevent relapses. Stem cell transplants meanwhile are also being tested as a good method in treating the disease.

Symptoms and Signs: Persons with Leukemia, B-Cell, chronic feel almost no symptoms unless an abnormally high white blood cell count. Lymph nodes are also enlarged.

LIVER CIRRHOSIS

Definition: Liver cirrhosis is disease characterized by the replacement of the liver tissue with fribrous scar tissue and regenerative lumps that lead to loss of liver functions.

Diagnosis: The best way to determine liver cirrhosis is by liver biopsy. Other laboratory measures are also taken to further learn about other complications of the disease such as imaging and endoscopy.

Treatment: The disease can be treated by taking action on underlying causes as well as preventing complications like those of ascites and esophageal variceal bleeding. For severe cases, there comes a need for liver transplant.

Symptoms and Signs: A lot of symptoms characterize liver cirrhosis, the most common being nail changes, jaundice, hypogonadism, ascites, asterixis and fetor hepaticus.

Causes: Liver cirrhosis is often a result of excessive alcoholism, and other diseases such as Hepatitis C.

MEASLES

Definition: Measles, which is also known as, Rubeola is a viral disease that has had a long history with medical accounts of it going as far back as 600 B.C. It was first clinically described in an Arabic book which significantly distinguished it from small pox. Measles is one of the great childhood killers, claiming the lives of more then 200 million children and adults in the last 150 years. The development of a vaccine has made the effectively checked the disease.

Diagnosis: Diagnosis is normally done from a clinical analysis of the symptoms which are so definitive that adults who have been through the disease can immediately identify it. Reported contact with a person with measles also offers confirmation. Clinical tests include testing for antibodies.

Treatment: There is no specific treatment or any kind of antiviral therapy for uncomplicated measles and patients will normally recover with rest and supportive treatment for the duration of the disease. Complications however can happen like pneumonia and this presents an additional challenge in the treatment.

Symptoms and Signs: The typical symptoms of the disease include a fever that lasts for at least three days, along with coughing, a runny nose and and conjunctivitis. An examination of the mouth may reveal what are called Koplik's spots but these are temporary and may disappear within a day or two of appearing. Then the classic measles rash appears several days after the fever, starting from the head before spreading other parts of the body and are often itchy. The color of the rash changes accordingly.

Causes: Measles is caused by a virus, specifically the paramyxovirus of the genus Morbillivirus and is spread through respiration- it is highly contagious.

MULTIPLE SCLEROSIS

Definition: Multiple sclerosis is a chronic, inflammatory and demyelinating disease affecting the central nervous system. It also known as disseminated sclerosis or encephalomyelitis, which onset, usually occurs in young adults and more common among women. The disease was first described in 1868 by Jean-Martin Charcot.

Diagnosis: MS diagnosis should be based on objective evidence of two or more neurologic signs that are localized to the brain or spinal cord and are disseminated in time and space. During or following a first attack, magnetic resonance imaging with gadolinium contrast can be helpful in providing evidence of lesions in other parts of the brain and spinal cord.

Treatment: There is no specific and known treatment for multiple sclerosis though several therapies have been helpful to patients. Said therapies aim to bring back function after an attack. On the other hand, medications used in the management of MS have several adverse effects and many possible therapies are still under investigation. Some patients are also pursuing alternative treatments.

Symptoms and Signs: A variety of symptoms can be caused by MS including changes in sensation (hypoesthesia), muscle weakness, abnormal muscle spasms, or difficulty in moving. Difficulties with coordination and balance (ataxia), speech problems (dysarthria) or swallowing (dysphagia), visual problems (nystagmus, optic neuritis, or diplopia), fatigue and acute or chronic pain syndromes may also be experienced.

Causes: There is no definitive cause found for MS. It likely occurs as a result of some combination of both environmental and genetic factors and various theories try to integrate the known data into plausible explanations. Autoimmune explanations are accepted but a couple of theories suggest that the disease is an appropriate response to one or several underlying conditions. Poor results of present therapies are therefore supported by the need for alternative theories.

MUSCULAR DYSTROPHY

Definition: Referring to a group of genetic and hereditary muscle disease that cause progressive muscle weakness, muscular dystrophies are characterized by progressive skeletal muscle weakness defects in muscle proteins and the death of muscle cells and tissue. There are nine diseases that are classified as muscular dystrophies namely Duchenne, Becker, limb girdle, congenital, facioscapulohumeral, myotonic, oculopharyngeal, distal and Emery-Dreifuss.

Diagnosis: Results of a muscle biopsy are the basis for the diagnosis of muscular dystrophy. A DNA blood test may be all that is needed in some cases though.

Treatment: The disease has no known cure and inactivity can worsen a patient condition. Orthopedic instruments and physical therapy may be helpful though. The latter can prevent contractures and orthoses. Corrective orthopedic surgery may be considered necessary to improve the quality of life in some cases. For Emery-Dreifuss muscular dystrophy and myotonic muscular dystrophy, a pacemaker may be required.

Symptoms and Signs: Principal symptoms of any form of muscular dystrophy are progressive muscular wasting (weakness), poor balance, frequent falls, walking difficulty, waddling gait, calf pain, respiratory difficulty, muscle contractures, drooping eyelids, gonadal atrophy, scoliosis and inability to walk. There are some types of the disorder that can affect the heart that may cause cardiomyopathy or arrhythmias.

Causes: Muscular dystrophy conditions are genetic and follow various inheritance patterns. Duchenne muscular dystrophy (DMD) for one is inherited in an X-linked recessive pattern, which means that the mutated gene that causes the disorder is located on the X chromosome and is considered sex-linked.

NARCOLEPSY

Definition: Narcolepsy is a neurological condition wherein patients exhibit excessive daytime sleepiness (EDS). The word itself is derived from the French word narcolepsie. It was Jean-Baptiste-Ã‰douard GÃ©lineau, a 19th century French physician, who first coined the term by combining the Greek words narked (meaning numbness) and lepsis (meaning attack or seizure).

Diagnosis: When all the hallmark signs of narcolepsy are present, diagnosis of this disease is relatively easy. However, when sleep attacks and cataplexy are isolated, diagnosis becomes a little more difficult. To screen for narcolepsy, the polysomnogram test and the multiple sleep latency test are often performed by what is known as a sleep specialist. Polysomnogram entails the clinical recording of brain waves while the patient sleeps. Nerve and muscle functions are also closely monitored. Narcoleptic patients usually fall asleep instantly, enter REM sleep earlier than normal and often wake up for no reason during the night. Through polysomnogram, it is possible to identify all other forms of sleep disorders related to the affliction. In the context of multiple sleep latency, patients are allowed to sleep at 2-hour intervals during normal wake periods. The patienttime in reaching various stages of sleep (*i.e.* sleep latency) are closely observed and recorded. The aim of this test is to measure the degree of daytime sleepiness and analyze how soon REM sleep begins. Individuals who rapidly fall asleep and enter REM sleep too early are most likely narcoleptic.

Treatment: The drowsiness of afflicted patients may be treated by stimulants. Examples of these are racemic amphetamine, dextroamphetamine, methylphenidate and methamphetamine or modafinil. Some other forms of medications, such as selegiline and codeine, may also be used. Atomoxetine, which is not a stimulant and Norepinephrine reuptake inhibitor (NRI) may also be recommended.

Symptoms and Signs: Narcoleptic individuals commonly suffer from disturbed nocturnal sleep, which is often wrongly confused with insomnia. Patients also experience abnormalities in rapid eye movement (REM) during sleep. One of the most documented symptoms is the propensity of narcoleptics to fall asleep at any random time (such as in the middle of talking, walking, working, or while performing any normal routine activities). This is because patients suffer from EDS, or excessive daytime sleepiness, even after a full nightrest. As a result, affected people tend to fall asleep without warning, mostly in unexpected times and places. These inappropriate'sœnaps may occur several times a day, but last only briefly.

Causes: To date, the cause of this disorder is yet unknown. However, researches have identified conditions that may increase ones susceptibility to the condition. For example, recent studies have unveiled the correlation between narcoleptics and certain predisposed genetic factors. One possible cause may be rooted in the chromosome 6 of the HLA complex. On the other hand, in spite of experimental proof that narcolepsy may be genetic in nature, the mode of inhèritance has not yet been determined.

NOISE INDUCED DEAFNESS

Definition: Noise Induced Deafness may be a full or partial reduction in the ability to determine and understand sounds. This condition is usually caused by a wide range of environmental factors. Sound waves have varying frequencies and amplitudes. A person who has lost his ability to detect some frequencies and some low-amplitude sounds which should normally be detected is a characteristic of this condition. Whenever humans are exposed to harmful noise and sounds that are too loud and last a long time, the sensitive structures found in the inner ear may be damaged thereby causing noise-induced hearing loss (NIHL) or Noise Induced Deafness. These sensitive structures which are also called hair cells, are small sensory cells found in the inner ear. They convert sound energy into electrical signals which travel towards the brain. Once the hair cells are damaged, they cannot grow back.

Diagnosis: A person with this condition may not even be aware of the loss, but it can be detected with a hearing test.

Symptoms and Signs: A person who is exposed to loud noise for a long time will cause symptoms of Noise Induced Deafness to increase gradually. After some time, the sounds that the person hears can be described as distorted or muffled. Understanding speech may become difficult as well.

Causes: Recent studies proves that exposure to harmful noise can trigger molecular formation inside the ear which can damage or kill hair cells. Noise Induced Deafness may be caused by a single exposure to an intense sound on impulse. This could be in the form of an explosion and other harmful sounds. Another cause may be continuous exposure to loud sounds for a prolonged period of time. This can also cause tinnitus.

NOMA

Definition: Noma came from the Greek term numein which means to devour. This condition is also referred to as Cancrum Oris or Gangrenous Stomatitis. Noma is a form of gangrenous disease which leads to destruction of the tissues of the face. Commonly affected areas are the cheeks and mouth. Noma has significantly high rates of morbidity and mortality. A rough estimate of 80% had been reported. Children under the age of 12 years who are living in the poor countries of Africa have high predisposition to this disease. Asian children as well as several countries within South America also present a certain degree of predisposition. Majority of the children who develop Noma are around the ages 2 to 6 years old. An estimated number of 5,00,000 individuals had developed this disease according to the WHO. 1,00,000 new cases arise every year.

Treatment: Treatment for this condition involves surgical procedures. Plastic surgery needs to be performed in order to restore the facial appearance of children.

Symptoms and Signs: Clinical presentation of Noma includes development of ulcers in the mucous membranes of the mouth. Later on, painless degeneration of tissues follows rapidly. This can also degrade facial bones and tissues. Noma can cause degradation of the children faces usually within days. Noma Pudendi, another condition which is sometimes associated with Noma, can aggravate the disease by causing damages to the tissues of the genitals.

Causes: Noma is usually caused by bacteria. The bacteria responsible for the development of this condition are known as fusospirochetal organisms. Majority of the children afflicted with this condition had other types of illnesses such as scarlet fever, measles, tuberculosis, immunodeficiency and cancer. Although the exact cause is unknown, malnutrition plays a major factor. Noma is not a communicable disease.

NIGHT TERRORS

Definition: Night terror also known as pavor nocturnus, Night terrors are a sleep disorder in which a person quickly awakens from sleep in a terrified state.

Diagnosis: Children from age two to six are most prone to night terrors, and they affect about fifteen percent of all children. Some adult night terror sufferers have a lot of the characteristics of abused and depressed individuals including inhibition of aggression.

Treatment: In several cases, a child who has a night terror only needs comfort and reassurance. Psychotherapy or counseling can be appropriate in some cases. Benzodiazepine medications such as diazepam used at bedtime will often reduce night terrors; but, medication is not usually recommended to treat this disorder.

Symptoms and Signs: Sudden awakening from sleep, Persistent fear or terror that occurs at night, Screaming, Sweating, Confusion, Rapid heart rate, Unable to fully wake up, Difficult to comfort.

Causes: The normal sleep cycle involves distinct stages, from light drowsiness to deep sleep. During rapid eye movement (REM) sleep, the eyes move quickly and vivid dreaming is very common. Each night there are many cycles of non-REM and REM sleep. Night terror (sleep terrors) happens during stage 3 and stage 4 sleep (deep sleep). The cause is still unknown but night terrors are often triggered by fever, lack of sleep, or periods of emotional tension, stress or conflict.

OBESITY

Definition: Obesity is a clinical weight condition in which the body has 20 percent more weight than the recommended weight relative an individual's height, which results in such illness as diabetes and heart disease.

Diagnosis: To diagnose individuals for obesity, doctors evaluate each person's BMI and waist circumference, behaviors like smoking or stressful activities that negatively impacts health and family and medical history. These factors help the doctors' diagnosis and assessment of implications to respective patients and make recommendations on how to treat the condition.

Treatment: Obese patients are presented with various approaches to treat their condition. Depending on an individual's physician, drugs may be prescribed supplemented by weight loss surgery, dietary changes, or exercise programs may be suggested where appropriate. Obese patients must make changes to their lifestyle in order to keep off excess weight. Such changes may include changing your eating habits.

Symptoms and Signs: The patient has more than the required body mass index in reference to his or her height and weight. The patient also has a large body frame and has difficulty even doing daily activities, feels lethargic and often breathless.

Causes: Genetic and environmental factors are two cause of obesity.

OVARIAN CANCER

Definition: Ovarian cancer is one of the most common form of cancer found in women. This is brought about by the abnormal overproduction of ovarian and the development of tumors that may affect one or both of the ovaries. The rate of survival is critically dependent on early detection and expert medical intervention.

Diagnosis: Among the most common basis for diagnosis of ovarian cancer include ultrasound, pelvic examination and blood tests. Other supplementary tests may follow to confirm diagnosis.

Treatment: Treatment of ovarian cancer would typically involve the combination of chemotherapy and surgery. Tumor is usually removed during the early changes and chemotherapy would usually follow surgical procedure.

Symptoms and Signs: The sooner the ovarian cancer is detected and treated, the better the chance for recovery. However, this type of cancer is difficult to detect. Among the common symptoms include vaginal bleeding, pain in lower abdomen, abnormal periods, vomiting, nausea and gas.

Causes: An ovarian tumor is a result of a growth of abnormal cells in the ovary. The tumor may be benign or malignant. However, the primary cause of cancer is still largely unknown. Medical experts believe it has something to do with the tissue repair process of the body.

PANIC ATTACK

Definition: A panic attack is characterized by the sudden episode of an intense fear that would usually develop with real or apparent reason, triggering some severe physical reactions. Panic attacks can usually be frightening since patients often feel loss of control, increased possibility of heart attacks or can even cause death.

Diagnosis: Diagnosis is mainly based on a physical exam, laboratory tests that include CBC and thyroid tests as well as a psychological evaluation. These evaluations would take into consideration the frequency of the panic attacks, the triggering factors and if patients have certain phobias that need to be determined.

Treatment: Treatment for panic attacks known to be highly effective in eliminating the symptoms of the disorder. Many patients that are on medication are able to resume with their usual activities. Some of these treatments include antidepressants, norepinephrine reuptake inhibitors, serotonin, psychotherapy, and tricyclic antidepressants.

Symptoms and Signs: Panic attack symptoms include rapid heart movement, sweating, shortness of breath, hyperventilation, trembling, chills, hot flashes, chest pains, nausea, abdominal cramping, dizziness, headaches and the sense of impending death.

Causes: There are certain factors that are taken into consideration that trigger panic attacks. These mainly include genetic factors, stress, as well as changes in the brain function.

PARKINSON'S DISEASE

Definition: Parkinson's disease is likewise called Parkinson disease which is described as a degenerative disorder involving the central nervous system. Because of this, the sufferer's motor skills and way of speaking are affected. This disorder is classified under the movement disorders group. This disorder is also chronic and progressive in nature.

Diagnosis: The best known way to diagnose Parkinson's disease is through taking down of medical history and employing some neurological tests are run through the patient. Blood samples and laboratory exams are not found to be effective in the diagnosis of such disease.

Treatment: Treatments for Parkinson's disease may have to be based on the underlying cause of its occurrences so it will entail evaluation of the patient. Some drugs may be administered and in some cases also would employ speech therapies and exercises to move the muscles. Surgeries are also done if found out that some abnormal growths are present which may have been causing the problem.

Symptoms and Signs: Most patients with Parkinson's disease suffer from lowered stimulation especially of the motor cortex in the basal ganglia. Other symptoms of this disorder that will manifest in the patients are high level of cognitive dysfunction and slight speech problems. Parkinson's disease is often characterized by tremor, rigidity of the muscle, bradykinesia and in some very extreme cases, patients would loose physical movements or what they call as akinesia.

Causes: There can be various cause of Parkinson's disease. It can be acquired hereditarily or by an accident involving severe injury in the head or head trauma. Other patients may have acquired it as a reaction to certain medications or even toxins.

PEANUT ALLERGY

Definition: Peanut allergy is identified as one of the most common form of food allergy and is often diagnosed during the first years of life. In most cases, children usually outgrow this condition as they grow older, while there are some who tend to develop serious reactions that require emergency medical attention.

Diagnosis: A skin prick test and a blood test are usually conducted to determine the allergen that caused the allergic reaction.

Treatment: General avoidance to peanut is the most effective prevention of an allergy attack. While this allergy may not be a life-threatening condition, it can cause extreme discomfort and difficulty in breathing that often requires immediate medical attention.

Symptoms and Signs: Symptoms for peanut allergy include skin reactions such as redness, swelling and hives. It can also include itching or tingling sensation in as well as around the throat and mouth, digestive problems such as diarrhea and cramps, nasal congestion and shortness of breath.

Causes: Like all other food allergies, peanut allergy is triggered by the malfunction of the immune system. In this case, an allergic reaction may be caused by direct contact to peanut or food products with peanut, cross contact as in the processing and handling of food as well as through inhalation.

PERIODIC FEVER, APHTHOUS STOMATITIS, PHARYNGITIS AND ADENITIS

Definition: Periodic fever, aphthous stomatitis, pharyngitis and adenitis syndrome is a medical condition that usually starts with young children. In this condition children would develop high fever which mostly occurs at a periodic interval of 3-5 weeks. This is often times accompanied with pharyngitis, adenitis, and/or aphthous ulcers.

Diagnosis: Diagnosis of Periodic Fever, Aphthous Stomatitis, Pharyngitis and Adenitis is done through consultation with a doctor and observing the patient for clinical symptoms. Patients manifesting the symptoms are then treated and observed again for initial responses to the treatment given.

Treatment: Physicians have developed a possible treatment for Periodic Fever, Aphthous Stomatitis, Pharyngitis and Adenitis. It is through a single dose of prednisone given at the beginning of the fever episode. Although in some few cases, the dose of prednisone can cause the episodes to become even more frequent.

Symptoms and Signs: The most common symptom of Periodic Fever, Aphthous Stomatitis, Pharyngitis and Adenitis are, as its name implies, periodic high fever, adenitis, aphthous ulcers and pharyngitis.

Causes: Periodic Fever, Aphthous Stomatitis, Pharyngitis and Adenitis is often times discussed with other syndromes of periodic fevers, however it is still unknown if the cause is genetic or because of an initial infection.

PNEUMONIA, EOSINOPHILIC

Definition: Eosinophilic pneumonia is a condition in which certain white blood cells accumulate in the lungs, disrupting normal oxygen intake. The condition has many existing types occurring in any age group.

Diagnosis: Doctors diagnose eosinophilic pneumonia through a patient's symptoms, results of physical examination as well as blood tests and x-rays.

Treatment: Treatment of eosinophilic pneumonia is effective if its cause is treated. Symptoms of acute and chronic eosinophilic pneumonia on the other hand, are rapidly treated with corticosteroids. Patients may have difficulty breathing, thus may need breathing support to live through the use of a bi-level positive airway pressure machine or a breathing tube and ventilator.

Symptoms and Signs: Patients may experience breathing difficulty, cough, fever and nighttime sweating. Acute eosinophilic pneumonia worsens rapidly; the chronic type develops slowly. Patients are usually diagnosed with asthma before their true condition is recognized.

Causes: Eosinophilic pneumonia may result due to allergic reactions of medicines taken by patients, or their exposure to the environment. The disease may be caused parasitic infections or in relation to the diagnosis of certain types of cancer diagnosed in cancer patients. Acute eosinophilic pneumonia is associated with smoking while the chronic type is not. However, most patients with chronic eosinophilic pneumonia are women, which may be associated with breast cancer.

RESTLESS LEGS SYNDROME

Definition: Restless legs syndrome (RLS), also known as Wittmaack-Ekbom's syndrome, is a progressive neurological disease characterized by an irresistible urge to move one body to halt odd or uncomfortable sensations. This condition usually affects the legs, but can also affect the arms and torso.

Diagnosis: To date, there is no single diagnostic test available to confirm restless legs syndrome. However, the condition may be diagnosed clinically based on the patient symptoms and family history. Although recent efforts have been made to standardize the criteria for RLS diagnosis, the disease remains difficult to diagnose and therefore remains largely under-diagnosed or misdiagnosed.

Treatment: While movement provides temporary relief to affected patients, the relief is usually only temporary. Restless legs syndrome can be treated by identifying and treating any underlying disorder. Focusing treatment on the underlying condition or conditions may relieve several symptoms. Other treatment techniques used for patients with idiopathic RLS are mostly focused on alleviating symptoms.

Symptoms and Signs: Restless legs syndrome causes a sensation akin to burning, itching, or tickling in the muscles of the affected body parts. Moving the affected area provides temporary relief. However, the sensations often return immediately after movement is ceased. The sensations associated with restless legs syndrome are odd and unusual and may occur in any body part. While afflicted patients usually have difficulty describing their sensations, the words uncomfortable, creeping, antsy, painful, pins and needles, creepy-crawly, pulling, and the like have been used. On the other hand, there are cases when affected patients have little or no sensation, yet they still experience a strong urge to move. A key factor in restless legs syndrome is the worsening of sensations during relaxation. Any form of inactivity while sitting or lying down can trigger symptoms.

Causes: Restless legs syndrome is believed to be a congenital disease. More than half of documented cases are familiar. RLS is inherited *via* the autosomal recessive trait with variable penetrance. Some medications are also believed to aggravate the condition in those who already have it, or trigger it secondarily.

SCHIZOPHRENIA

Definition: Schizophrenia is a psychiatric term used in reference to a mental disorder characterized by an impaired perception of reality.

Diagnosis: A psychiatric diagnosis of schizophrenia is usually based on the self-described experiences of the patient, as well as his/her behaviour as observed by others. Currently, there is no laboratory test that will confirm the diagnosis.

Treatment: A cure for schizophrenia remains a controversial concept, particularly because there is no consensus regarding the definition of the disease itself. Symptom management seems to be a more realistic treatment mode rather than curing the disease itself. A common medication used in symptom relief today is chlorpromazine. Severe episodes of schizophrenia may require hospitalization of the affected individual. Hospitalization may either be voluntary or involuntary. Currently, long-term inpatient stays are becoming a common supportive treatment option for schizophrenics.

Symptoms and Signs: Schizophrenic patients suffer from an impaired sense of reality, which may take the form of paranoia, auditory hallucinations, delusions, disorganized speech and confusion or muddled thinking. Patients with schizophrenia usually have severe social or occupational dysfunction. Initial symptoms typically manifest in young adulthood and frequently persist throughout the patient lifetime.

Causes: No specific cause of schizophrenia has been identified. However, psychiatric research correlates the disease to genetics, early environmental triggers, neurobiological and psychological factors, as well as a number of social processes. Although current research efforts are focused on the role of neurobiology, no single organic cause of schizophrenia has been identified.

SHINGLES

Definition: Shingles is the common name for Herpes Zoster. It is an infectious viral disease characterized by a painful skin rash positioned in a limited area on one side of the body.

Diagnosis: Diagnosis is easier through visual examination if the skin rash have appeared, without the rash; it would be more difficult to difficult shingles. There are also laboratory tests available to help in diagnosis of Shingles

Treatment: Symptomatic treatment is essential to limit the intensity and interval of pain, condense the length of a shingles episode and reduce at the most prevent further complications.

Symptoms and Signs: The initial symptoms of Shingles are very common and may appear to be non-specific including general feeling of discomfort and uneasiness (malaise), fever and headache. After hours or days, the following symptoms will start to manifest: Itching' Sensations of burning pain's Chills', Sensitive to heat, cold, light or touch (Paresthesia)' Persistent local pain in the affected skin area's¢ Quick stabbing pain's¢ Tingling, numbing, stinging or throbbing sensation. After the initial phase of Shingles, the following symptoms will begin to be obvious. Appearance of the distinguishing skin rash usually on the torso but also may be present on the face, eyes and other parts of the body. Initially the rash will look like the first presentation of hives; subsequently the rash will change appearance forming small blisters that erupts and crust over usually with the combining presence of fever and malaise.

Causes: Shingles is caused by the reactivation of an earlier chicken pox infection.

SHOCK

Definition: Shock is a serious and life-threatening medical condition that happens when the body does not receive sufficient amount of blood causing the cells of the body to receive inadequate supply of oxygen and nutrients. Medical shock is a critical medical emergency and has been reported as one of the leading causes of death for seriously-ill patients. There are four types of shock namely: hypovolemic, cardiogenic, obstructive and distributive shock. The most recent type of shock classified is endocrine shock, which is based on endocrine disruptions.

Diagnosis: Diagnosis of shock is established by means of the patient symptoms in combination with other criteria. There are also laboratory exams aimed to provide diagnosis for shock.

Treatment: On the onset, shock significantly necessitates urgent medical intervention with the main purpose of life preservation. Emergency hospitalization would then require proper management of shock through medical intervention aimed at restoring and maintaining blood circulation volume, achieving effective cardiac function and avoiding further complications. Precise treatment approach to shock depends on the symptoms present and the originating cause of shock.

Symptoms and Signs: Symptoms of shock depend on the type of shock experienced by a person. But the most common and general symptoms include the following Anxiety and restlessness and altered mental state brought about by decreased blood flow in body tissues and consequent hypoxia. Rapid, weak and thready pulse. Cold, clammy skin and usually mottled skin's¢ Rapid and shallow breathing pattern. Excessively low body temperature Feeling of thirst and dry mouth's¢ Dilated pupils Distended jugular veins Fever's¢ Increased cardiac output

Causes: Shock has several causes including low blood volume, inadequate pumping action of the heart or excessive widening of the blood vessels.

THYROID CANCER

Definition: Thyroid cancer refers to one of four kinds of malignant tumors of the thyroid gland: papillary, follicular, medullary and anaplastic.

Diagnosis: After a nodule is detected during a physical examination, a referral to an endocrinologist, or a thyroidologist is the best approach. Most frequently an ultrasound is performed to confirm the presence of a nodule, and assess the status of the whole gland.

Treatment: Thyroid cancer can be treated with the following: surgery, thyroid hormone therapy, radioactive iodine follow-up screening and therapy, external beam radiation and chemotherapy.

Symptoms and Signs: Most often the initial symptom of thyroid cancer is a nodule in the thyroid region of the neck. Many adults, however, have small nodules in their thyroids. But usually under 5% of these nodules are found to be malignant. Sometimes the initlal sign is an enlarged lymph node. Later symptoms that can be found are pain in the anterior region of the neck and changes in voice.

Causes: When DNA is damaged or altered, changes arise in these instructions. One result is that cells may begin to grow out of control and may form a tumor's mass of malignant cells.

TOXIC SHOCK SYNDROME

Definition: Toxic shock syndrome is a rare, life-threatening bacterial infection that has been most often linked with the use of super absorbent tampons and occasionally with the use of contraceptive sponges.

Diagnosis: Recent studies have postulated that early and definitive diagnosis can be made by observing the expansion of TSS-1 reactive V beta2-positive T-cell receptors in peripheral blood mononuclear cells.

Treatment: The severity of this disease requires hospitalization. Treatment consists of aggressive IV fluid administration and antistaphylococcal antibiotics, like cephalosporins, penicillinase-resistant semisynthetic penicillins or vancomycin.

Symptoms and Signs: TSS resultant of infection with the bacteria Staphylococcus aureus typically manifests in otherwise healthy individuals with high fever, together with low blood pressure, malaise and confusion, which can rapidly progress to stupor, coma and multi-organ failure. The characteristic rash, often seen early in the course of illness, is similar to sunburn and can involve any region of the body, including the lips, mouth, eyes, palms and soles.

Causes: Researchers don't know exactly how tampons may lead to toxic shock syndrome. Some believe that when super absorbent tampons are left in place for a long time, the tampons become a breeding ground for the bacteria.

TUBERCULOSIS

Definition: TB or Disseminated tuberculosis is a contagious bacterial infection that has spread from the lungs to other organs of the body through the blood or the lymph system.

Diagnosis: Physical exams usually reveal enlarged lymph nodes, enlarged liver and enlarged spleen. The diagnostic tests conducted to diagnose the disease are biopsies and cultures of affected organs or tissues, bronchoscopy for biopsy or culture, chest x-ray, open lung biopsy, retinal lesions revealed with fundoscopy, sputum cultures and tuberculin skin test.

Treatment: Treatment in the disease is aimed at curing the infection with antitubercular drugs. Among those drugs are Amikacin, Ethambutol, Ethionamide, Isoniazid, Para-aminosalicylic acid, Pyrazinamide, Rifampicin, and Streptomycin. The daily oral doses last 6 months to 1 year. For those suffering from a typical or drug-resistant strains, treatment usually starts with a minimum of three drugs. Admitting the patient to the hospital is also an option to prevent spreading the disease to others until the infectious period is over.

Symptoms and Signs: Disseminated tuberculosis symptoms include cough, fatigue, fever, general discomfort or uneasiness, sweating, shortness of breath and weight loss. Abdominal swelling, chills, joint pain, paleness and swollen glands may also be manifested.

Causes: The infection may develop after inhaling droplets sprayed into the air through coughing or sneezing of an infected person.

ULCERATIVE COLITIS

Definition: Ulcerative colitis or colitis ulcerosa is a type of inflammatory bowel disease that affects the large intestine and rectum. A systemic disease affects many parts of the body outside the intestine; it is often confused with irritable bowel syndrome (IBS).

Diagnosis: A colonoscopy with biopsy, as well as Barium enema is usually performed to diagnose Ulcerative colitis. Doctors may also conduct the following: CBC, sedimentation rate and C-reactive protein.

Treatment: Controlling acute attacks, preventing repeated attacks and helping cure the colon are the goals of treating Ulcerative colitis. For severe attacks, hospitalization may be required and coticosteroids may be prescribed to lessen inflammation. Among the medications used to decrease the frequency of attacks include 5-aminosalicylates such as mesalamine and immunomodulators such as azathioprine and 6-mercaptopurine. Infliximab, an intravenous medicine, has also been found to improve symptoms of the disorder.

Symptoms and Signs: Symptoms of ulcerative colitis include diarrhea, abdominal pain, abdominal sounds, fever, weight loss and tenesmus. Other symptoms associated with Ulcerative colitis are nausea and vomiting, joint pain, and gastrointestinal bleeding.

Causes: The cause of the disorder remains unknown. However, it is known that it may affect any age group though higher incidence have been found among people ages 15-30.

VITAMIN B12 DEFICIENCY

Definition: Vitamin B12 deficiency is the deficiency which usually result from the failure of the digestive tract to absorb Vitamin B12 or Cobalomin which is necessary for making red blood cells and which is responsible for keeping the nervous system functioning. It is said that this deficiency may cause irreversible damage to the person's nerve (Insel, P., Turner, E., Ross, D. (2005). Discovering Nutrition, Jones and Bartlett Publishers, p. 353).

Diagnosis: Diagnosis includes own observation of symptoms and consequently physical examination and medical history evaluation of physician. Medical tests which include blood tests for Vitamin B12 levels to check for antibodies to the intrinsic factors are also used to confirm the condition (Griffith H.W., Moore, S., (2006). Complete Guide to Symptoms, Illness and Surgery, Perigee, p. 148).

Treatment: Treatment includes Vitamin B12 replacement and Vitamin B12 therapy or diet. Administration of Vitamin B12 supplements is also advised.

Symptoms and Signs: Its symptoms usually develop slowly and take time to notice. The most prevalent symptoms are the following: weakness especially in the arms and legs, sore tongue, nausea, loss of appetite and weight loss, numbness or tingling in the hands and feet, difficulty in maintaining proper balance, pale lips, tongue and gums, yellowish eyes and skin, bleeding of the gums, shortness of breathing, depression, confusion, poor memory and dementia, headache and tinnitus or the ringing of the ear.

Causes: Vitamin B12 is due to the lack of intrinsic factor which is a substance made by cells in the stomach that makes it possible to absorb Vitamin B12. The reason for the lack of intrinsic factor is unknown which may be an autoimmune reaction, a genetic factor, or both.

WARTS

Definition: Warts are small, rough tumor that is typically located on the hands and feet and can resemble a cauliflower or a solid blister.

Diagnosis: Diagnosis to confirm the presence of warts includes merely physical examination of the person.

Treatment: There are a lot of medical treatments used in order for warts to vanished among these are: keratolysis or the removal of the dead skin cells by using salicylic acid, immunomodulators and formaldehyde; Cryosurgery where the warts are freezed by liquid nitrogen thereby creating a blister between the ward and the epidermal layer making the dead skin cell fall by itself; surgical curettage of the wart is also used to treat the affected area; laser treatments; administration of Imiquimod which is a topical cream that helps the body's immune system and candida injections on the site of the wart (Horn TD, Johnson SM, Helm RM, Roberson PK (2005) Intralesional immunotherapy of warts with mumps, Candida and Trichophyton skin test antigens. Arch Dermatol 141: 58994) and the use of Catharidin which is a chemical found in Meloidae which causes dermal blistering. There are also over the counter medications available such as those with salicylic acid, silver nitrate in caustic pencil form. Household remedies include various fruits and vegetables such as a bruised garlic, banana skin, unskinned potato or tomato juice, green tea and vinegar. These treatments do not guarantee fast result as it needs re-application of the medication.

Symptoms and Signs: Symptoms includes the presence of the small and rather tough tumor that resembles a cauliflower or a solid blister. There are range of different types of wart which varies in shape, size and place of the body affected and the type of human papillomavirus involved (Mosby's Medical, Nursing & Allied Health Dictionary (5th edn), Anderson KN, Anderson LE, Glanze WD, eds, Mosby). Among these are the common wart or the verruca vulgaris which is a raised rough surface that is most common in hands and feet, flatwart virus or the verruca plana, the filiform or digitate wart the plantar wart, the mosaic wart which is a group of tightly clustered plantar-type warts and the genital warts or the venereal wart.

Causes: Warts are said to be caused by a viral infection particularly the human papillomavirus or the HPV and are usually contagious when in contact with the skin of another person. It is also said that warts may be passed and be acquired from using towels or other objects used to rub the body.

WHOOPING COUGH

Definition: Whooping cough is medically known as pertussis, which is characterized as a highly contagious infection of the respiratory tract. While whooping cough may initially resemble an ordinary cold, it may eventually turn more serious, especially among infants.

Diagnosis: Diagnosing whooping cough during the early stages can be hard since the symptoms are similar to other common respiratory problems. Medical tests used to confirm include a throat or node culture and test as well as blood tests. A chest X-ray may also be conducted to have a supplementary basis for diagnosis.

Treatment: Treatment for whooping cough typically varies, on certain considerations such age as well as the severity of signs and symptoms. Early detection and treatment is important since this condition may develop to other serious complications if lest untreated.

Symptoms and Signs: Whooping cough share the symptoms of an ordinary cold, such as runny nose, sneezing, nasal congestion, red and watery eyes, mild fever, dry cough and general feeling of malaise and lack of appetite. In advanced stages, patients experience severe coughing, that can lead to vomiting as well as fatigue due to exertion during coughing.

Causes: Whooping cough is identified to be a result of a respiratory infection that affects the windpipe and the tubes that branches off from the windpipe. The bacteria are known as the Bordetella pertussis bacterium, typically transmitted through some droplets passed on from coughing or sneezing into the air by an infected person.

YELLOW FEVER

Definition: Yellow fever otherwise known as the yellow jack, the black vomit or the vomito negro, or the American Plague, is a viral and acute disease (Schmaljohn AL, McClain D. (1996 isbn 0-9631172-1-1). Alphaviruses (Togaviridae) and Flaviviruses (Flaviviridae). In: Baron's Medical Microbiology (Baron S et al, eds.), 4th ed., Univ of Texas Medical Branch).

Diagnosis: Diagnosis includes the medical examination especially blood tests.

Treatment: Inasmuch as there is no known cure for the disease Yellow Fever, treatment therefore will focus more on the symptoms as they manifests. Fluid replacement, blood transfusion and dialysis in case of severe conditions.

Symptoms and Signs: Jaundice symptoms appear in patients with this kind of disease, thus the term yellow.

Causes: Yellow Fever is said to be caused by an arbovirus belonging to the family of Flaviviridae which is a gram positive single stranded RNA virus. Depositions of viral particles in the skin by an anthrophod saliva causes the human infection.

ZELLWEGER SYNDROME

Definition: Zellweger syndrome is a congenital disorder caused by reduced or absent peroxisomes in the cells of the liver, kidneys and brain. Peroximes are cell structures that get rid of toxic substances in the body. The syndrome belongs to a group of peroxisomal diseases, which affect brain development and the growth of the myelin sheath on nerve fibers in the brain.

Treatment: Zellweger syndrome neither has a cure nor a standard course of treatment. Infections are monitored to prevent complications such as pneumonia and respiratory distress. Other treatment is based on symptoms and only alleviates the patient's condition. Affected infants usually die at the age of 6 months that may have been caused by respiratory distress, gastrointestinal bleeding or liver failure.

Symptoms and Signs: Individuals with the syndrome usually have an enlarged liver, a blood stream with high levels of iron and copper and vision disturbances. Failure in prenatal growth may show in some affected infants. Congenital symptoms may include an absence of muscle tone, an inability to move and glaucoma. Other affected individuals may have unusual facial features, mental retardation, seizures and an inability to suck or swallow. Others may also have jaundice and gastrointestinal bleeding.

Causes: An abnormality in one of the several genes involved with peroxisome biogenesis causes a person's inability to beta-oxidize very-long chain fatty acids in the peroxisomes of the cell resulting in Zellweger syndrome. PEX1, PEX2, PEX3, PEX5, PEX6, PEX12, PEX14 and PEX26 are some of the peroxins associated with the syndrome.

Disclaimer: The information is for common understanding and research purposes only and can not substitute for the advice of a medical professional. The contents herein is not a medical authority, it is just an understanding tool for one to use in preparation for consulting with a doctor. We can not guarantee our information is accurate or up-to-date. Even if a statement made about a medical condition is accurate, it may not apply to you or your symptoms, so one should always consult a doctor. Nothing should be construed as an attempt to offer or render a medical opinion or otherwise engage in the practice of medicine.

APPENDIX XX
The Oath of Hippocrates

I SWEAR by Apollo the physician and AEsculapius, and Health, and All-heal, and all the gods and goddesses, that, according to my ability and judgment, I will keep this Oath and this stipulation— to reckon him who taught me this Art equally dear to me as my parents, to share my substance with him, and relieve his necessities if required; to look upon his offspring in the same footing as my own brothers, and to teach them this art, if they shall wish to learn it, without fee or stipulation; and that by precept, lecture, and every other mode of instruction, I will impart a knowledge of the Art to my own sons, and those of my teachers, and to disciples bound by a stipulation and oath according to the law of medicine, but to none others. I will follow that system of regimen which, according to my ability and judgment, I consider for the benefit of my patients, and abstain from whatever is deleterious and mischievous. I will give no deadly medicine to any one if asked, nor suggest any such counsel; and in like manner I will not give to a woman a pessary to produce abortion. With purity and with holiness I will pass my life and practice my Art. I will not cut persons labouring under the stone, but will leave this to be done by men who are practitioners of this work. Into whatever houses I enter, I will go into them for the benefit of the sick, and will abstain from every voluntary act of mischief and corruption; and, further, from the seduction of females or males, of freemen and slaves. Whatever, in connection with my professional service, or not in connection with it, I see or hear, in the life of men, which ought not to be spoken of abroad, I will not divulge, as reckoning that all such should be kept secret. While I continue to keep this Oath unviolated, may it be granted to me to enjoy life and the practice of the art, respected by all men, in all times. But should I trespass and violate this Oath, may the reverse be my lot.

APPENDIX XXI
The Modern Oath of Hippocrates

(Please read the "Physicians' Charter," a new Charter on medical professionalism)

One version, approved by the American Medical Association, is as follows:

You do solemnly swear, each by whatever he or she holds most sacred:

That you will be loyal to the Profession of Medicine and just and generous to its members.

That you will lead your lives and practice your art in uprightness and honor.

That into whatsoever house you shall enter, it shall be for the good of the sick to the utmost of your power, your holding yourselves far aloof from wrong, from corruption, from the tempting of others to vice.

That you will exercise your art solely for the cure of your patients, and will give no drug, perform no operation, for a criminal purpose, even if solicited, far less suggest it.

That whatsoever you shall see or hear of the lives of men or women which is not fitting to be spoken, you will keep inviolably secret.

These things do you swear. Let each bow the head in sign of acquiescence. And now, if you will be true to this, your oath, may prosperity and good repute be ever yours; the opposite, if you shall prove yourselves forsworn.

From "Harvard Classics Volume 38"

Copyright 1910 by P.F. Collier and Son.

APPENDIX XXII

Medical Council of India Code of Medical Ethics

This text is placed in the Public Domain, June 1993.

Medword Resources:

The Physicians' Charter

THE PHYSICIANS' CHARTER

Charter on Medical Professionalism

Medical Professionalism in the New Millennium: A Physicians' Charter

Synopsis

Preamble

Fundamental principles

A set of professional responsibilities

Physicians today are experiencing frustration as changes in the health-care delivery systems in virtually all industrialised countries threaten the very nature and values of medical professionalism. Meetings among the European Federation of Internal Medicine, the American College of Physicians and American Society of Internal Medicine (ACP-ASIM) and the American Board of Internal Medicine (ABIM) have confirmed that physicians' views on professionalism are similar in quite diverse systems of health-care delivery. We share the view that medicine's commitment to the patient is being challenged by external forces of change within our societies.

Recently, voices from many countries have begun calling for a renewed sense of professionalism, one that is activist in reforming health-care systems. Responding to this challenge, the European Federation of Internal Medicine, the ACP-ASIM Foundation and the ABIM Foundation combined efforts to launch the Medical Professionalism Project (www.professionalism.org) in late 1999. These three organisations designated members to develop a "charter" to encompass a set of principles to which all medical professionals can and should aspire. The charter supports physicians' efforts to ensure that the health-care systems and the physicians working within them remain committed both to patients' welfare and to the basic tenets of social justice. Moreover, the charter is intended to be applicable to different cultures and political systems.

Preamble

Professionalism is the basis of medicine's contract with society. It demands placing the interests of patients above those of the physician, setting and maintaining standards of competence and integrity, and providing expert advice to society on matters of health. The principles and responsibilities of medical professionalism must be clearly understood by both the profession and society. Essential to this contract is public trust in physicians, which depends on the integrity of both individual physicians and the whole profession.

At present, the medical profession is confronted by an explosion of technology, changing market forces, problems in health-care delivery, bioterrorism and globalisation. As a result, physicians find it increasingly difficult to meet their responsibilities to patients and society. In these circumstances, reaffirming the fundamental and universal principles and values of medical professionalism, which remain ideals to be pursued by all physicians, becomes all the more important.

The medical profession everywhere is embedded in diverse cultures and national traditions, but its members share the role of healer, which has roots extending back to Hippocrates. Indeed, the medical profession must contend with complicated political, legal and market forces. Moreover, there are wide variations in medical delivery and practice through which any general principles may be expressed in both complex and subtle ways. Despite these differences, common themes emerge and form the basis of this charter in the form of three fundamental principles and as a set of definitive professional responsibilities.

FUNDAMENTAL PRINCIPLES

Principle of primacy of patients' welfare

This principle is based on a dedication to serving the interest of the patient. Altruism contributes to the trust that is central to the physician-patient relationship. Market forces, societal pressures and administrative exigencies must not compromise this principle.

Principle of patients' autonomy

Physicians must have respect for patients' autonomy. Physicians must be honest with their patients and empower them to make informed decisions about their treatment. Patients' decisions about their care must be paramount, as long as those decisions are in keeping with ethical practice and do not lead to demands for inappropriate care.

Principle of social justice

The medical profession must promote justice in the health-care system, including the fair distribution of health-care resources. Physicians should work actively to eliminate discrimination in health care, whether based on race, gender, socio-economic status, ethnicity, religion, or any other social category.

A SET OF PROFESSIONAL RESPONSIBILITIES

Commitment to professional competence

Physicians must be committed to lifelong learning and be responsible for maintaining the medical knowledge and clinical and team skills necessary for the provision of quality care. More broadly, the profession as a whole must strive to see that all of its members are competent and must ensure that appropriate mechanisms are available for physicians to accomplish this goal.

Commitment to honesty with patients

Physicians must ensure that patients are completely and honestly informed before the patient has consented to treatment and after treatment has occurred. This expectation does not mean that patients should be involved in every minute decision about medical care; rather, they must be empowered to decide on the course of therapy. Physicians should also acknowledge that, in health care, medical errors that injure patients do sometimes occur. Whenever patients are injured as a consequence of medical care, patients should be informed promptly because failure to do so seriously compromises patients' and societal trust. Reporting and analysing medical mistakes provides the basis for appropriate prevention and improvement strategies and for appropriate compensation to injured parties.

Commitment to patients' confidentiality

Earning the trust and confidence of patients requires that appropriate confidentiality safeguards be applied to disclosure of patients' information. This commitment extends to discussions with people acting on a patient's behalf when obtaining the patient's own consent is not feasible. Fulfilling the commitment to confidentiality is more pressing now than ever before, given the widespread use of electronic information systems for compiling data on patients and an increasing availability of genetic information. Physicians recognise, however, that their commitment to confidentiality must occasionally yield to overriding considerations in the public interest (for example, when patients endanger others).

Commitment to maintaining appropriate relationships with patients

Given the inherent vulnerability and dependency of patients, certain relationships between physicians and patients must be avoided. In particular, physicians should never exploit patients for any sexual advantage, personal financial gain or other private purpose.

Commitment to improving quality of care

Physicians must be dedicated to continuous improvement in the quality of health care. This commitment entails not only maintaining clinical competence but also working collaboratively with other professionals to reduce medical error, increase patients' safety, minimise overuse of health-care resources and optimise the outcomes of care. Physicians must actively participate in the development of better measures of quality of care and the application of quality measures to assess routinely the performance of all individuals, institutions and systems responsible for health-care delivery. Physicians, both individually and through their professional associations, must take responsibility for assisting in the creation and implementation of mechanisms designed to encourage continuous improvement in the quality of care.

Commitment to improving access to care

Medical professionalism demands that the objective of all health-care systems be the availability of a uniform and adequate standard of care. Physicians must individually and collectively strive to reduce barriers to equitable health care. Within each system, the physician should work to eliminate barriers to access based on education, laws, finances, geography and social discrimination. A commitment to equity entails the promotion of public health and preventive medicine, as well as public advocacy on the part of each physician, without concern for the self-interest of the physician or the profession.

Commitment to a just distribution of finite resources

While meeting the needs of individual patients, physicians are required to provide health care that is based on the wise and cost-effective management of limited clinical resources. They should be committed to working with other physicians, hospitals and payers to develop guidelines for cost-effective care. The physician's professional responsibility for appropriate allocation of resources requires scrupulous avoidance of superfluous tests and procedures. The provision of unnecessary services not only exposes patients to avoidable harm and expense but also diminishes the resources available for others.

Commitment to scientific knowledge

Much of medicine's contract with society is based on the integrity and appropriate use of scientific knowledge and technology. Physicians have a duty to uphold scientific standards, to promote research, and to create new knowledge and ensure its appropriate use. The profession is responsible for the integrity of this knowledge, which is based on scientific evidence and physicians' experience.

Commitment to maintaining trust by managing conflicts of interest

Medical professionals and their organisations have many opportunities to compromise their professional responsibilities by pursuing private gain or personal advantage. Such compromises are especially threatening in the pursuit of personal or organisational interactions with for-profit industries, including medical equipment manufacturers, insurance companies and pharmaceutical firms. Physicians have an obligation to recognise, disclose to the general public, and deal with conflicts of interest that arise in the course of their professional duties and activities. Relationships between industry and opinion leaders should be disclosed, especially when the latter determine the criteria for conducting and reporting clinical trials, writing editorials or therapeutic guidelines, or serving as editors of scientific journals.

Commitment to professional responsibilities

As members of a profession, physicians are expected to work collaboratively to maximise patients' care, be respectful of one another, and participate in the processes of self-regulation, including remediation and discipline of members who have failed to meet professional standards. The profession should also define and organise the educational and standard-setting process for current and future members. Physicians have both individual and collective obligations to participate in these processes. These obligations include engaging in internal assessment and accepting external scrutiny of all aspects of their professional performance.

APPENDIX – XXII

MEDICAL COUNCIL OF INDIA CODE OF MEDICAL ETHICS

DECLARATION

At the time of registration, each applicant shall be given a copy of the following declaration by the Registrar concerned and shall read and agree to abide by the same:—

1. I solemnly pledge myself to consecrate my life to the service of humanity.
2. Even under threat, I will not use my medical knowledge contrary, to the laws of humanity.
3. I will maintain the utmost respect for human life from the time of conception.
4. I will not permit consideration of religion, nationality, race, party politics or social standing to intervene between my duty and my patient.
5. I will practise my profession with conscience and dignity.
6. The health of my patient will be my first consideration.
7. I will respect the secrets which are confided in me.
8. I will give to my teachers the respect and gratitude which is their due.
9. I will maintain, by all means in my power, the honour and noble traditions of medical profession.
10. My colleagues will be my brothers.
11. I make these promises solemnly, freely and upon my honour.

CODE OF GENERAL PRINCIPLES

Character of the Physician

The prime object of the medical profession is to render service to humanity; reward of financial gain is a subordinate consideration. Whosoever chooses this profession, assumes the obligation to conduct himself in accord with its ideals. A physician should be an upright man, instructed in the "art of healings." He must keep himself pure in character and be diligent in caring for the sick. He should be modest, sober, patient, prompt to do his whole duty without anxiety; pious without going so far as superstition, conducting himself with propriety in his profession and in all the actions of his life.

The Physician's Responsibility

The principle objective of the medical profession is to render service to humanity with full respect for the dignity of man. Physicians should merit the confidence of patients entrusted to their care, rendering to each a full measure of service and devotion. Physicians should try continuously to improve medical knowledge and skill and should make available to their patients and colleagues the benefits of their professional attainments. The physician should practise methods of healing founded on scientific basis and should not associate professionally with anyone who violates this principle. The honoured ideals of the medical profession imply that the responsibilities of the physician extend not only to individuals but also to society.

Advertising

Solicitation of patients, directly or indirectly, by a physician, by groups of physicians or by institutions or organisations is unethical. A physician shall not make use of or aid or permit others to make use of him (or his name) as subject of any form or manner of advertising or publicity though lay channels, either alone or in conjunction with others which will be of such a character as to invite attention to him or to his professional position, skill, qualification, achievements, attainments, specialities, appointments, associations, affiliations or honours and/or of such character as would ordinarily result in his self aggrandisement, nor shall he give to any person whosoever, whether for compensation or otherwise, any approval, recommendation, endorsement, certificate, report or statement with respect of any drug, medicine, nostrum remedy, surgical or therapeutic article, apparatus or appliance or any commercial product or article with respect of any property, quality or use thereof or any test, demonstration or trial thereof, for use in connection with his name, signature or photograph in any form or manner of advertising though lay channels, nor shall he boast of cases, operations, cures or remedies or permit the publication of report thereof through lay channels. A medical practitioner is permitted a formal announcement in press regarding the following:—

1. On starting practice.
2. On change of type of practice.
3. On changing address.
4. On temporary absence from duty.
5. On resumption of practice.
6. On succeeding to another practice.

Payment of Professional Services

The ethical physician, engaged in the practice of medicine, limits the sources of his income received from professional activities to services rendered to the patient. Remunerations received for such services should be in the form and amount specifically announced to the patient at the time the service is rendered. It is unethical to enter into a contract of "no cure no payment."

Patent and Copyrights

A physician may patent surgical instruments, appliances and medicines or copyright publications, methods and procedures. The use of such patents or copy-right or the receipt of remuneration from them which retards or inhibits research or restrict the benefits derivable therefrom are unethical.

Running an open shop (Dispensing of drugs and appliances by physicians)

A physician should not run an open shop for sale of medicine, for dispensing prescriptions prescribed by doctors other than himself or for sale of medical or surgical appliances. It is not unethical for a physician to prescribe or supply drugs, remedies or appliances so long as there is no exploitation of the patient.

Rebates and Commission

A physician shall not give, solicit, or receive nor shall he offer to give, solicit or receive, any gift, gratuity, commission or bonus in consideration of or in return for the referring, recommending or procuring of any patient for medical, surgical or other treatment. A physician shall not directly or by any subterfuge participate in or be a party to the act of division, transference, assignment, subordination, rebating, splitting or refunding of any fee for medical, surgical or other treatment. The provisions of this para shall apply with equal force to the referring, recommending or procuring by a physician or any person, specimen or material for diagnostic, or other study or work. Nothing in this section, however, shall prohibit payment of salaries by a qualified physician to other duly qualified persons, rendering medical care under his supervision.

Secret Remedies

The prescriptions or dispensing by, a physician of secret medicine or other secret remedial agents of which he does not know the composition, or the manufacture, or promotion of their use is unethical.

Evasion of legal restrictions

The physician will observe the laws of the country in regulating the practice of medicine and will not assist others to evade such laws. He should be co-operative in observance and enforcement of sanitary laws and regulations in the interest of public health. A physician should observe the provisions of the State Acts like Drugs Act, Pharmacy Act, Poisonous and Dangerous Drugs Act and such other Acts, Rules, Regulations made by the Central Government/State Governments or local Administrative Bodies for protection and promotion of public health.

DUTIES OF PHYSICIANS TO THEIR PATIENTS

Obligations to the sick

Though a physician is not bound to treat each and every one asking his services except in emergencies for the sake of humanity and the noble traditions of the profession, he should not only be everready to respond to the calls of the sick and the injured, but should be mindful of the high character of his mission and the responsibility he incurs in the discharge of his professional duties. In his administrations, he should never forget that the health and the lives of those entrusted to his care depend on his skill and attention. A physician should endeavour to add to the comfort of the sick by making his visits at the hour indicated to the patients.

Patience, delicacy and secrecy

Patience and delicacy should characterize the physicians. Confidences concerning individual or domestic life entrusted by patients to a physician and defects in the disposition or character of patients, observed during medical attendance should never be revealed unless their revelation is required by the laws of the State. Sometimes, however, a physician must determine whether his duty to society requires him to employ knowledge, obtained through confidences to him as a physician, to protect a healthy person against a communicable disease to which he is about to be exposed. In such instance, the physician should act as he would desire another to act towards one of his own family in like circumstances.

Prognosis

The physician should neither exaggerate nor minimize the gravity of a patient's condition. He should assure himself that the patient, his relatives or his responsible friends have such knowledge of the patient's condition as will serve the best interests of the patient and the family.

The patient must not be neglected

A physician is free to choose whom he will serve. He should, however, respond to any request for his assistance in an emergency or whenever temperate public opinion expects the service. Once having undertaken a case, the physician should not neglect the patient, nor should he withdraw from the case without giving notice to the patient, his relatives or his responsible friends sufficiently long in advance of his withdraw to allow them to secure another medical attendant. No provisionally or fully registered medical practitioner shall willfully commit an act of negligence that may deprive his patient or patients from necessary medical care.

DUTIES OF THE PHYSICIAN TO THE PROFESSOIN AT LARGE

Upholding the honour of the profession

A physician is expected to uphold the dignity and honour of his profession.

Membership in medical society

For the advancement of his profession, a physician should affiliate with medical societies and contribute his time, energy and means so that these societies may represent the ideals of the profession.

Safeguarding the profession

Every physician should aid in safeguarding the profession against admission to it of those who are deficient in moral character or education. Physician should not employ, in connection with his professional practice, any attendant, who is neither registered nor enlisted under the Medical Act in force, and should not permit such persons to attend, treat or perform operations upon patients in respect of matters regarding professional discretion or skill, as it is dangerous to public health.

Exposure of Unethical Conduct

A physician should expose, without fear or favour, incompetent or corrupt, dishonest or unethical conduct on the part of members of the profession. Questions of such conduct should be considered, first before proper medical tribunals in executive sessions or by special or duly appointed committees on ethical relations, provided such a course is possible, and provided, also that the law is not hampered thereby. If doubt should arise as to the legality of the physician's conduct, the situation under investigation may be placed before officers of the law, and the physician investigators may take the necessary steps to enlist the interest of the proper authority.

PROFESSIONAL SERVICES OF PHYSICIAN TO EACH OTHER

Dependence of physicians on each other

There is no rule that a physician should not charge another physician for his services but a physician should cheerfully and without recompense give his professional service to a physician or his dependents, if they are in his vicinity.

Compensation for expenses

A physician should consider it as a pleasure and privilege to render gratuitous service to all physicians and their immediate family dependents. When a physician is called from a distance to attend or advise another physician or his dependent, reimbursement should however be made for travelling and other incidental expenses.

DUTIES OF PHYSICIAN IN CONSULTATION

Consultation should be encouraged

In case of serious illness, especially in doubtful or difficult conditions, the physician should request consultations.

Consultation for Patient's Benefits

In every consultation, the benefit to the patient is of first importance. All physicians interested in the case should be candid with the patient, a member of his family or responsible friend.

Punctuality in consultation

Utmost punctuality should be observed by a physician in meeting for consultation.

Conduct in consultation

In consultation, no insincerity, rivalry or envy should be indulged in. All due respects should be observed towards the physician incharge of the case, and no statement, or remarks be made which would impair the confidence reposed in him. For this purpose, no discussion should be carried on in the presence of the patient or his representatives.

Statement to patient after consultation

(*a*) All statements of the case to the patient or his representatives should take place in the presence of all the physicians consulting, except as otherwise agreed ; the announcement of the opinion to the patient or his relations or friends shall rest with the medical attendant.

(*b*) Differences of opinion should not be divulged unnecessarily, but when there is an irreconcilable difference of opinion, the circumstances should be frankly and impartially explained to the patient or his friends. It would be open to them to seek further advice should they so desire.

Treatment after consultation

No decision should restrain the attending physician from making such subsequent variations in the treatment as any unexpected change may require, but at the next consultation, reasons for the variations should be stated. The same privilege, with its obligations, belongs to the consultant when sent for in an emergency during the absence of attending physician. The attending physician may prescribe at any time for the patient the consultant only in case of emergency.

Consultant not to take charge of the case

When a physician has been called as a consultant none but the rarest and the most exceptional circumstances would justify that consultant taking charge of the case. He should not do so merely on the solicitation of the patient or friends.

Patients referred to specialists

When a patient is referred to a specialist by the attending physician, a statement of the case should be given to the specialist, who should communicate his opinion in writing in a closed cover direct to the attending physician.

DUTIES OF PHYSICIAN IN CASES OF INTEREFERENCE

Appointment of a substitute

Whenever a physician requests another physician to attend his patient during his temporary absence from his practice, professional courtesy requires the acceptance of such appointment, is consistent with his other duties. The physician acting under such an appointment should give the utmost consideration to the interests and reputation of the absent physician. All such patients should be restored to the care of the latter upon his return.

Visiting another physician's case

A physician called to visit a patient, who has recently been under the care of another physician in the same illness, should not take charge of, nor prescribe for such patient except in a case of emergency when he should communicate to the former explaining the circumstances under which the patient was seen and treatment given, or when the physician has relinquished his case, or when the patient has notified such physician to discontinue his services. When it becomes the duty of a physician occupying an official position to see and report upon an illness or injury, he should communicate to the physician in attendance so as to give him an option of being present. The medical officer should avoid remarks upon the diagnosis or the treatment that has been adopted.

Engagement for an Obstetric case

If a physician agrees to attend a woman during her confinement, he must do so. Inability to do so on an excuse of any other engagement is not tenable, except when he is already engaged on a similar or other serious case. When a physician who has been engaged to attend an obstetric case is absent and another is sent for the delivery accomplished, the acting physician is entitled to his professional fees, but should secure the patient's consent to resign on the arrival of the physician engaged.

DUTIES OF PHYSICIAN TO THE PUBLIC

Physicians as Citizens

Physicians, as good citizens, possessed of special training, should advise concerning the health of the community wherein they dwell. They should bear their part in enforcing the laws of the community and in sustaining the institutions that advance the interests of humanity. They should cooperate especially with the proper authorities in the administration of sanitary laws and regulations.

Public Health

Physicians, especially those engaged in public health work, should enlighten the public concerning quarantine regulations and measures for the prevention of epidemic and communicable diseases. At all times the physician should notify the constituted public health authorities of every case of communicable disease under his care, in accordance with the law, rules and regulations of the health authorities. When an epidemic prevails, a physician must continue his labours without regard to the risk to his own health.

Pharmacists

Physicians should recognise and promote the practice of pharmacy as a profession and should recognise the cooperation of the pharmacist in education of the public concerning the practice of ethical and scientific medicine.

DISCIPLINARY ACTION

The Medical Council of India desires to bring to the notice of the registered medical practitioners the following statement upon offences and forms of professional misconduct which may be brought before the appropriate Medical Council for disciplinary action in view of the authority conferred upon the Medical Council of India and/or State Medical Councils, as provided under Indian Medical Council Act, 1956, or State Medical Council Acts, as may be subsequently amended.

The appropriate Medical Council may award such punishment, as deemed necessary. It may direct the removal altogether (professional death sentence) or for a specified period (penal erasure), from the Register the name of any registered practitioner, who has been convicted of any such offence as implies in the opinion of the Medical Council of India and/or State Medical Councils, a defect of character, or who, after an enquiry, at which opportunity has been given to such registered practitioner to be heard in person or by pleader, has been held by the appropriate Medical Council to have been guilty of serious professional misconduct. The appropriate Medical Council may also direct that any name so removed shall be restored.

It must be clearly understood that the instances of offences of professional misconduct which are given do not constitute and are not intended to constitute, a complete list of the infamous acts, which may be punished by erasure from the Register, and that by issuing this notice the Medical Council of India and/or State Medical Councils are in no way precluded from considering and dealing with any form of professional misconduct on the part of a registered practitioner. Circumstances may and do arise from time to time in relation to which there may occur questions of professional misconduct which do not come within any of these categories. Every care should be taken that the code is not violated in letter or spirit. In such instances, as in all others, the Medical Council of India and/or State Medical Councils have to consider and decide upon the facts brought before the Medical Council of India and/or State Medical Council.

Note: A medical practitioner is entitled to appeal to the Central Health Ministry against the decision of the Medical Councils.

LIST

Adultery or improper Conduct or Association with a patient : Any medical practitioner who abuses his professional position by committing adultery or improper conduct with a patient or by maintaining an improper association with a patient, is liable for disciplinary action, as provided under the Indian Medical Council Act, 1956 and/or State Medical Council Acts, as may be subsequently amended.

Conviction by Court of Law for offences involving moral turpitude.

Professional Certificates, Reports and Other Documents: Registered practitioners are in certain cases bound by law to give, or may from time to time be called upon or requested to give certificates, notifications, reports and other documents, of kindred character, signed by them in their professional capacity for subsequent use in the courts of justice or for administrative purpose, etc.

(*i*) Such documents include, among other certificates, notifications, reports:—

(*a*) Under the Acts relating to birth, death or disposal of the dead.

(*b*) Under the Acts relating to Mental Health and Mental Deficiency and the rules made thereunder.

(*c*) Under the Vaccination Acts and the Regulations made thereunder.

(*d*) Under the Factories Acts and the Regulations made thereunder.

(*e*) Under the Education Act.

(*f*) Under the Public Health Acts and the orders made thereunder.

(*g*) Under the Workmen's Compensation Act

(*h*) Under the Acts and orders relating to the notification of infections diseases.

(*i*) Under the Employees State Insurance Act.

(*j*) In connection with sick benefit insurance and friendly societies.

(*k*) Under the Merchant Shipping Act.

(*l*) For procuring the issuing of passports.

(*m*) For excusing attendance in courts of justice, in public services, in public offices or in ordinary employments.

(*n*) In connection with rural and Military Matters.

(*o*) In connection with matters under the control of Ministry of the pensions.

(*ii*) Any registered practitioner, who shall be shown to have signed or given under his name and authority and such certificate, notification, report or document of a kindred character, which is untrue, misleading or improper, whether relating to the several matters above specified or otherwise, is liable to have his name erased from the Register.

(*iii*) A registered medical practitioner shall maintain a Register of medical certificates, giving full details of the certificates issued. When issuing a medical certificate, always enter the identification marks of the patient and keep a copy of the certificate. Do not omit to note down the signature or thumb mark, address and identification marks of the patient on the medical certificates or reports.

Contravening the provisions of the Drugs Act and Regulations made thereunder.

Selling Schedule Position to the public under cover of his own qualification, except to his patients.

Performing or enabling an unqualified person: to perform an abortion or any illegal operation, for which there is no medical, surgical or psychological indication.

A physician should not issue certificates of efficiency in modern medicine to unqualified or non medical persons.

(*Note*: The foregoing does not apply so as to restrict the proper training and instruction of *bona fide* students, legitimate employees of doctors, midwives, dispensers, surgical attendants, or skilled mechanical and technical assistants under the personal supervision of physicians.)

A physician should not contribute to the lay-press articles and give interviews regarding disease and treatments, which may have the effect of advertising himself or soliciting practice; but it is open to him to write to the lay press under his own name on matter of public health hygienic living or to deliver public lectures, give talks on the radio broadcast for the same purpose and send announcement of the same to the lay press.

An institution run by a physician for a particular purpose such as a maternity home, a sanatorium, a house for the crippled or the blind, etc. may be advertised in the lay press, but such advertisement should not contain anything more than the name of the institution, type of patients admitted, facilities offered and the residential fees. Name of either the superintendent or the doctors attending should not appear in the advertisement.

It is improper for a physician to use an unusually large signboard and write on it anything other than his name, qualifications obtained from a University or a statutory body, titles and name of his speciality. The same should be the contents of his prescription papers. It is improper to affix a board on a chemist's shop or in place where he does not reside or work.

Do not disclose the secrets of a patient that have been learnt in the exercise of your profession. Those may be disclosed only in court of Law under orders of the presiding Judge.

Refusal to give Professional Service on Religious Grounds: Refusing on religious grounds alone, to give assistance in or conduct cases of sterility, birth control, craniotomies on living children and therapeutic abortions, when there is medical indication; unless the medical practitioner feels himself/herself incompetent to do so.

Before performing an operation, obtain in writing the consent from the husband or wife, parent or guardian in the case of a minor, or the patient himself, as the case may be. In an operation which may result in sterility, the consent of both husband and wife is needed.

Do not publish photographs or case reports of your patients in any medical or other journal in a manner, by which their identity could be made out, without their permission. Should the identity be not disclosed, his consent is not needed.

If you are running a nursing home and if you employ assistants to help you, the ultimate responsibility rests on you.

No physician must exhibit publicly the scale of fees. But there is no objection to the same being put in the physician's consulting or waiting rooms. It is not unethical for physician to announce in press, lay or professional, his commencement of practice, interruption or resumption of it after a long interval, or a change of his address, but such announcements containing his address and telephone number shall not appear more than twice.

No physician shall use touts or agents for procuring patients.

Note: This is also known as canvassing.

Do not claim to be a specialist unless you have put in a good few years of study and experience or have a special qualification in that branch. Once you say you are one, do not undertake work outside your speciality even for your friends.

APPENDIX XXIII
Declaration of Geneva

(As amended at Sydney, 1968)

At the time of being admitted as a member of the medical profession:

- I will solemnly pledge myself to consecrate my life to the service of humanity;
- I will give to my teachers the respect and gratitude which is their due;
- I will practise my profession with conscience and dignity;
- The health of my patient will be my first consideration;
- I will respect the secret which are confided in me, even after the patient has died;
- I will maintain by all the means in my power the honour and the noble traditions of the medical profession;
- My colleagues will be my brothers;
- I will not permit considerations of religion, nationality, race, party politics or social standing to intervene between my duty and my patient;
- I will maintain the utmost respect for human life from the time of conception, even under threat. I will not use my medical knowledge contrary to the laws of humanity.
- I make these promises solemnly, freely and upon my honour.

APPENDIX XXIV

Declaration of Helsinki

(Revised 1975)

Recommendations guiding medical doctors in biomedical research involving human subjects

INTRODUCTION

It is the mission of the medical doctor to safeguard the health of the people. His or her knowledge and conscience are dedicated to the fulfillment of this mission.

The Declaration of Geneva of the World Medical Association binds the doctor with the words: 'The health of my patient will be my first consideration' and the International Code of Medical Ethics declares that, 'Any act or advice which could weaken physical or mental resistance of a human being may be used only in his interest.'

The purpose of biomedical research involving human subjects must be to improve diagnostic, therapeutic and prophylactic procedure and the understanding of the aetiology and pathogenesis of disease.

In current medical practice most diagnostic, therapeutic or prophylactic procedures involve hazards. This applies *a fortiori* to biomedical research. Medical progress is based on research which ultimately must rest in part on examination involving human subjects. In the field of biomedical research a fundamental distinction must be recognised between medical research in which the aim is essentially diagnostic or therapeutic for a patient, and medical research the essential object of which is purely scientific and without direct diagnostic or therapeutic value to the person subjected to the research.

Special caution must be exercised in the conduct of research which may affect the environment, and the welfare of animals used for research must be respected.

Because it is essential that the results of laboratory experiments be applied to human beings to further scientific knowledge and to help suffering humanity, the World Medical Association has prepared the following recommendations as a guide to every doctor in biomedical research involving human subjects. They should be kept under review in the future. It must be stressed that the standards as drafted are only a guide to physicians all over the world. Doctors are not relieved from criminal, civil and ethical responsibilities under the laws of their own countries.

I. Basic Principles

1. Biomedical research involving human subjects must conform to generally accepted scientific principles and should be based on adequately accepted scientific principles and should be based on adequately performed laboratory and animal experimentation and on a thorough knowledge of the scientific tradition.

2. The design and performance of each experimental procedure involving human subjects should be clearly formulated in an experimental protocol which should be transmitted to a specially appointed independent committee for consideration, comment and guidance.

3. Biomedical research involving human subjects should be conducted only by scientifically qualified persons and under the supervision of a clinically competent medical person. The responsibility for the human subject must always rest with a medically qualified person and never rest on the subject of the research, even though the subject has given his or her consent.

4. Biomedical research involving human subjects cannot legitimately be carried out unless the importance of the objective is in proportion to the inherent risk to the subject.

5. Every biomedical research project involving human subjects should be preceded by careful assessment of predictable risks in comparison with foreseeable benefits to the subject or to others. Concern for the interests of the subject must always prevail over the interest of science and society.

6. The right of the research subject to safeguard his or her integrity must always be respected. Every precaution should be taken to respect the privacy of the subject and to minimize the impact of the study on the subject's physical and mental integrity and on the personality of the subject.

7. Doctors should abstain from engaging in research projects involving human subjects unless they are satisfied that the hazards involved are believed to be predictable. Doctors should cease any investigation if the hazards are found to outweigh the potential benefits.

8. In publication of the results of his or her research, the doctor is obliged to preserve the accuracy of the results. Reports of experimentation not in accordance with the principles laid down in this Declaration should not be accepted for publication.

9. In any research on human beings, each potential subject must be adequately informed of the aims, methods, anticipated benefits and potential hazards of the study and the discomfort it may entail. He or she should be informed that he or she is at liberty to abstain from participation in the study and that he or she is free to withdraw his or her consent to participation at any time. The doctor should then obtain the subject's freely given informed consent, preferably in writing.

10. When obtaining informed consent for the research project the doctor should be particularly cautious if the subject is in a dependent relationship to him or her or may consent under duress. In that case the informed consent should be obtained by a doctor who is not engaged in the investigation and who is completely independent of this official relationship.

11. In case of legal incompetence, informed consent should be obtained from the legal guardian in accordance with national legislation. Where physical or mental incapacity makes it impossible to obtain informed consent, or when the subject is a minor, permission from the responsible relative replaces that of the subject in accordance with national legislation.

12. The research protocol should always contain a statement of the ethical considerations involved and should indicate that the principles enunciated in the present Declaration are complied with.

II. Medical Research Combined with Professional Care (Clinical Research)

1. In the treatment of the sick person, the doctor must be free to use a new diagnostic and therapeutic measure, if in his or her judgment it offers hope of saving life, re-establishing health or alleviating suffering.

2. The potential benefits, hazards and discomfort of a new method should be weighed against the advantages of the best current diagnostic and therapeutic methods.

3. In any medical study, every patient — including those of a control group, if any — should be assured of the best proven diagnostic and therapeutic method.

4. The refusal of the patient to participate in a study must never interfere with the doctor-patient relationship.

5. If the doctor considers it essential not to obtain informed consent, the specific reasons for this proposal should be stated in the experimental protocol for transmission to the independent committee.

6. The doctor can combine medical research with professional care, the objective being the acquisition of new medical knowledge, only to the extent that medical research is justified by its potential diagnostic of therapeutic value for the patient.

III. Non-therapeutic Biomedical Research involving Human Subjects (Non-Clinical Biomedical Research)

1. In the purely scientific application of medical research carried out on a human being, it is the duty of the doctor to remain the protector of the life and health of that person on whom biomedical research is being carried out.

2. The subjects should be volunteers — either healthy persons or patients for whom the experimental design is not related to the patient's illness.

3. The investigator or the investigating team should discontinue the research if in his/her or their judgment it may, if continued, be harmful to the individual.

4. In research on man, the interest of science and society should never take precedence over considerations related to the wellbeing of the subject.

APPENDIX XXV

Guidelines for Sterilization

(Issued by the Government of India)

Sterilization services are provided free of charge in Government Institutions. Guidelines have been issued from time to time by the Government covering various aspects of sterilization. These are:

(*a*) The age of the husband should not ordinarily be less than 25 years nor should it be over 50 years.

(*b*) The age of the wife should not be less than 20 years or more than 45 years.

(*c*) The motivated couple must have 2 living children at the time of operation.

(*d*) If the couple has 3 or more living children, the lower limit of age of husband or wife may be relaxed at the discretion of the operating surgeon.

(*e*) It is sufficient if the acceptor declares having obtained the consent of his/her spouse to undergo sterilization operation without outside pressure, inducement or coercion, and that he/she knows that for all practical purposes, the operation is irreversible and also that the spouse has not been sterilized earlier.

Personal Notes

Personal Notes